*continued on back inside cover*

# E-commerce

## business. technology. society.

## SEVENTH EDITION

### Kenneth C. Laudon
New York University

### Carol Guercio Traver
Azimuth Interactive, Inc.

**Prentice Hall**

Boston  Columbus  Indianapolis  New York  San Francisco  Upper Saddle River
Amsterdam  Cape Town  Dubai  London  Madrid  Milan  Munich  Paris  Montreal  Toronto
Delhi  Mexico City  Sao Paulo  Sydney  Hong Kong  Seoul  Singapore  Taipei  Tokyo

Editorial Director: Sally Yagan
Editor in Chief: Eric Svendsen
Executive Editor: Bob Horan
Editorial Project Manager: Kelly Loftus
Director of Marketing: Patrice Jones
Senior Marketing Manager: Anne Fahlgren
Marketing Assistant: Melinda Jensen
Senior Managing Editor: Judy Leale
Production Project Manager: Karalyn Holland
Senior Operations Supervisor: Arnold Vila
Operations Specialist: Ilene Kahn
Senior Art Director: Janet Slowik

Art Director: Steve Frim
Cover Designer: Jodi Notowitz
Manager, Rights and Permissions: Megan Miller
Media Editor: Denise Vaughn
Media Project Manager: Lisa Rinaldi
Full Service Project Management: Azimuth Interactive, Inc.
Composition: Azimuth Interactive, Inc.
Printer/Binder: Edwards Brothers, Inc.
Cover Printer: Lehigh-Phoenix Color/Hagarstown
Text Font: ITC Veljovic Std. Book, 9.5pt

Credits and acknowledgements borrowed from other sources and reproduced, with permission, in this textbook appear on page C-1.

Microsoft® and Windows® are registered trademarks of the Microsoft Corporation in the U.S.A. and other countries. Screen shots and icons reprinted with permission from the Microsoft Corporation. This book is not sponsored or endorsed by or affiliated with the Microsoft Corporation.

Library of Congress Cataloging-in-Publication Information is Available

10 9 8 7 6 5 4 3 2

**Prentice Hall**
is an imprint of

www.pearsonhighered.com

ISBN 10: 0-13-609119-9
ISBN 13: 978-0-13-609119-6

# P R E F A C E

## WHAT'S NEW IN THE SEVENTH EDITION

### Currency

The 7th edition features all new or updated opening, closing and "Insight On" cases. The text, as well as all of the data, figures and tables in the book, have been updated through September 2010 with the latest marketing and business intelligence available from eMarketer, Pew Internet & American Life Project, Forrester Research, Jupiter Research, Gartner, comScore and other industry sources.

### New Themes and Content

The 7th edition spotlights the following new themes and content:

### Business

• Impact of the 2010 recession: Despite the recession, e-commerce continues to thrive while traditional retail commerce slowed.
• Emergence of new e-commerce business opportunities for mobile content (the "4th screen"), apps, software applications, location-based services, shopping on the fly, and mobile payment
• Continued explosive growth in Web 2.0 services such as Twitter and Facebook and expansion of social marketing opportunities
• "Social e-commerce" emerges as a powerful new force in online commerce
• E-books finally take off
• New search engines such as Bing challenge Google
• Music labels, Hollywood and TV producers strike deals for Web distribution
• Google's Chrome enters Microsoft's market, threatens to become a new operating system for netbooks

### Technology

• Rapid growth of the mobile digital platform including smartphones, iPads, netbooks, and e-book readers, coupled with 3G and 4G cellular network expansion
• Cloud computing provides the computing infrastructure for a massive increase in digital information and offers a new platform for the distribution of music and videos
• An explosion of apps provides a new model for delivering services and software

• Open source software tools such as Drupal and Hadoop, and declining hardware prices, greatly lower the cost of developing sophisticated Web sites

• Internet security concerns remain high; cyberwarfare incidents increase

• Web 3.0 and the semantic Web continues to inspire technology firms and entpreneurs

• Net neutrality supporters reconsider differential pricing as the costs of expanding mobile platform networks soars

### Society

• Growth of the mobile, "always on" culture in business and family life

• Intellectual property issues remain a source of conflict; movement toward resolution in some areas, such as Google's deal with publishing industry

• Digital piracy remains a problem, despite the shutdown of P2P network The Pirate Bay, but paid content models grow faster than privacy

• Privacy and user control of personal information on social networks conflict with company attempts to monetize investment

• Most new Internet growth occurs in Asia and China; localization of Web increases

• Venture investing in e-commerce drastically falls off, yet entrepreneurial startup firms are as numerous as ever and their stocks soar again.

• Growing government surveillance of Internet users and Web sites

• Growing consumer resistance to behavioral targeting of ads as the practice expands across the Internet

## WELCOME TO THE NEW E-COMMERCE

In the 15 years since it began in 1995, electronic commerce has grown in the United States from a standing start to a $255 billion retail business and a $3.6 trillion business-to-business juggernaut, bringing about enormous change in business firms, markets, and consumer behavior. Economies and business firms around the globe, in Europe, Asia, and Latin America, are being similarly affected. During that short time, e-commerce has itself been transformed from its origin as a mechanism for online retail sales in to something much broader. Today, e-commerce has become the platform for new, unique services and capabilities that are just impossible in the physical world. There is no physical world counterpart to Facebook, or Twittter, or Google search, or a host of other recent online innovations. Welcome to the new e-commerce!

Although e-commerce in 2010 has been impacted by the worldwide economic recession, in the next five years, e-commerce in all of its forms is still projected to continue growing at high single-digit rates, becoming the fastest-growing form of commerce. Just as automobiles, airplanes, and electronics defined the twentieth century, so will e-commerce of all kinds define business and society in the twenty-first century. The rapid movement toward an e-commerce economy and society is being led by both established business firms such as Wal-Mart, Ford, IBM, JCPenney, and General Electric, and newer entrepreneurial firms such as Google, Amazon, Facebook, Yahoo, MySpace, Twitter, YouTube, and Photobucket. Students of business and information technology need a thorough grounding in electronic commerce in order to be effective and successful managers in the next decade. This book is written for tomorrow's managers.

While newer Web 2.0 firms such as Facebook, MySpace, YouTube, Twitter, Photobucket, Flickr, and Blinkx have grown explosively in the last two years and grab our attention, the traditional forms of retail e-commerce and services also remain vital and have proven to be more resilient than traditional retail channels in facing the economic recession that has occurred during the past year. The experience of these firms over the last fifteen years is also a focus of this book. The defining characteristic of these firms is that they are profitable, sustainable, efficient, and innovative firms with powerful brand names. Many of these now-experienced retail and service firms, such as eBay, Amazon, E*Trade, Priceline, and Expedia, are survivors of the first era of e-commerce, from 1995 to spring 2000. These surviving firms have evolved their business models, integrated their online and offline operations, and changed their revenue models to become profitable. Students must understand how to build these kinds of e-commerce businesses in order to help the business firms they manage to succeed in the e-commerce era.

It would be foolish to ignore the lessons learned in the early period of e-commerce. Like so many technology revolutions in the past—automobiles, electricity, telephones, television, and biotechnology—there was an explosion of entrepreneurial efforts, followed by consolidation. By 2005, the survivors of the early period were moving to establish profitable businesses while maintaining rapid growth in revenues. In 2010, e-commerce is entering a new period of explosive entreprenurial activity focusing on social networks, and the mobile digital platform created by smartphones and netbooks. These technologies and social behaviors are bringing about extraordinary changes to markets, industries, individual businesses, and society as a whole. In 2010, the stock values of start-up online firms are being driven to extraordinary heights ominously reminiscent of the early years of e-commerce. E-commerce is generating thousands of new jobs for young managers in all fields from marketing to management, entrepreneurial studies, and information systems. Today, e-commerce has moved into the mainstream life of established businesses that have the market brands and financial muscle required for the long-term deployment of e-commerce technologies and methods. If you are working in an established business, chances are the firm's e-commerce capabilities and Web presence are important factors for its success. If you want to start a new business, chances are very good that the knowledge you learn in this book will be very helpful.

## BUSINESS. TECHNOLOGY. SOCIETY.

We believe that in order for business and technology students to really understand e-commerce, they must understand the relationships among e-commerce business concerns, Internet technology, and the social and legal context of e-commerce. These three themes permeate all aspects of e-commerce, and therefore in each chapter we present material that explores the business, technological, and social aspects of that chapter's main topic.

Given the continued growth and diffusion of e-commerce, all students—regardless of their major discipline—must also understand the basic economic and business forces driving e-commerce. E-commerce has created new electronic markets where prices are more transparent, markets are global, and trading is highly efficient, though not perfect. E-commerce has a direct impact on a firm's relationship with suppliers, customers, competitors, and partners, as well as how firms market products, advertise, and use brands. Whether you are interested in marketing and sales, design, production, finance, information systems, or logistics, you will need to know how e-commerce technologies can be used to reduce supply chain costs, increase production efficiency, and tighten the relationship with customers. This text is written to help you understand the fundamental business issues in e-commerce.

We spend a considerable amount of effort analyzing the business models and strategies of "pure-play" online companies and established businesses now employing "bricks-and-clicks" business models. We explore why many early e-commerce firms failed and the strategic, financial, marketing, and organizational challenges they faced. We also discuss how e-commerce firms learned from the mistakes of early firms, and how established firms are using e-commerce to succeed. Above all, we attempt to bring a strong sense of business realism and sensitivity to the often exaggerated descriptions of e-commerce. As founders of a dot.com company and participants in the e-commerce revolution, we have learned that the "E" in e-commerce does not stand for "easy."

The Web and e-commerce has caused a major revolution in marketing and advertising in the United States. We spend two chapters discussing how marketing and advertising dollars are moving away from traditional media, and towards online media and their huge audiences, creating significant growth in search engine marketing, targeted display advertising, online rich media/video ads, and social marketing techniques.

E-commerce is driven by Internet technology. Internet technology, and information technology in general, is perhaps the star of the show. Without the Internet, e-commerce would be virtually nonexistent. Accordingly, we provide three specific chapters on the Internet and e-commerce technology, and in every chapter we provide continuing coverage by illustrating how the topic of the chapter is being shaped by new information technologies. For instance, Internet technology drives developments in security and payment systems, marketing strategies and advertising, financial applications, business-to-business trade, and retail e-commerce. We discuss the rapid growth of the mobile digital platform, the emergence of cloud computing, new open source software tools and applications that enable Web 2.0, and new types of Internet-based information systems that support electronic business-to-business markets.

E-commerce is not only about business and technology, however. The third part of the equation for understanding e-commerce is society. E-commerce and Internet technologies have important social consequences that business leaders can ignore only at their peril. E-commerce has challenged our concepts of privacy, intellectual property, and even our ideas about national sovereignty and governance. Google, Amazon, and assorted advertising networks maintain profiles on millions of U.S. and foreign online shoppers. The proliferation of illegally copied music and videos on the Internet, and the growth of social networking sites often based on displaying copyrighted materials without permission, are challenging the intellectual property rights of record labels, studios, and artists. And many countries—including the United States—are demanding to control the content of Web sites displayed within their borders for political and social reasons. Tax authorities in the United States and Europe are demanding that e-commerce sites pay sales taxes. As a result of these challenges to existing institutions, e-commerce and the Internet are the subject of increasing investigation, litigation, and legislation. Business leaders need to understand these societal developments, and they cannot afford to assume any longer that the Internet is borderless, beyond social control and regulation, or a place where market efficiency is the only consideration. In addition to an entire chapter devoted to the social and legal implications of e-commerce, each chapter contains material highlighting the social implications of e-commerce.

## FEATURES AND COVERAGE

**Strong Conceptual Foundation** We analyze e-commerce, digital markets, and e-business firms just as we would ordinary businesses and markets using concepts from economics, marketing, finance, philosophy, and information systems. We try to avoid ad hoc theorizing of the sort that sprang breathlessly from the pages of many journals in the early years of e-commerce.

Some of the important concepts from economics and marketing that we use to explore e-commerce are transaction cost, network externalities, social networks, perfect digital markets, segmentation, price dispersion, targeting, and positioning. Important concepts from the study of information systems and technologies play an important role in the book, including Internet standards and protocols, client/server computing, multi-tier server systems, cloud computing, mobile digital platform and wireless technologies, and public key encryption, among many others. From the literature on ethics and society, we use important concepts such as intellectual property, privacy, information rights and rights management, governance, public health, and welfare.

From the literature on business, we use concepts such as business process design, return on investment, strategic advantage, industry competitive environment, oligopoly, and monopoly. One of the witticisms that emerged from the early years of e-commerce and that still seems apt is the notion that e-commerce changes everything except the rules of business. Businesses still need to make a profit in order to survive in the long term.

**Real-World Business Firm Focus** From Akamai Technologies, to Google, Microsoft, Apple, and Amazon, to Facebook, Twitter, and Myspace, to Netflix and VWSupply-Group.com, this book contains well over 100 real-company examples that place coverage in the context of actual dot.com businesses. You'll find these examples in each chapter, as well as in special features such as chapter-opening and chapter-closing cases, and "Insight on" boxes.

**In-depth Coverage of B2B E-commerce** We devote an entire chapter to an examination of B2B e-commerce. In writing this chapter, we developed a unique and easily understood classification schema to help students understand this complex arena of e-commerce. This chapter covers four types of Net marketplaces (e-distributors, e-procurement companies, exchanges, and industry consortia) as well as the development of private industrial networks and collaborative commerce.

**Current and Future Technology Coverage** Internet and related information technologies continue to change rapidly. The most important changes for e-commerce include dramatic price reductions in e-commerce infrastructure (making it much less expensive to develop sophisticated Web sites), the explosive growth in the mobile digital platform such as iPhones, iPads, and netbooks, and expansion in the development of social technologies. What was once a shortage of telecommunications capacity has now turned into a surplus, PC prices have continued to fall, new client-side devices have emerged, Internet high-speed broadband connections are now typical and are continuing to show double-digit growth, and wireless technologies such as Wi-Fi and cellular broadband are playing a larger role in mobile Internet access. While we thoroughly discuss the current Internet environment, we devote considerable attention to describing Web 2.0 and Internet II technologies and applications such as the advanced network infrastructure, fiber optics, wireless Web and 3G and 4G technologies, Wi-Fi, IP multicasting, and future guaranteed service levels.

**Up-to-Date Coverage of the Research Literature** This text is well grounded in the e-commerce research literature. We have sought to include, where appropriate, references and analysis of the latest e-commerce research findings, as well as many classic articles, in all of our chapters. We have drawn especially on the disciplines of economics, marketing, and information systems and technologies, as well as law journals and broader social science research journals including sociology and psychology.

**Special Attention to the Social and Legal Aspects of E-commerce** We have paid special attention throughout the book to the social and legal context of e-commerce. Chapter 8 is devoted to a thorough exploration of four ethical dimensions of e-commerce: information privacy, intellectual property, governance, and protecting public welfare on the Internet. We have included an analysis of the latest Federal Trade Commission and other regulatory and nonprofit research reports, and their likely impact on the e-commerce environment.

## OVERVIEW OF THE BOOK

The book is organized into four parts.

Part 1, "Introduction to E-commerce," provides an introduction to the major themes of the book. Chapter 1 defines e-commerce, distinguishes between e-commerce and e-business, and defines the different types of e-commerce. Chapter 2 introduces and defines the concepts of business model and revenue model, describes the major e-commerce business and revenue models for both B2C and B2B firms, and introduces the basic business concepts required throughout the text for understanding e-commerce firms including industry structure, value chains, and firm strategy.

Part 2, "Technology Infrastructure for E-commerce," focuses on the technology infrastructure that forms the foundation for all e-commerce. Chapter 3 traces the historical development of Internet I—the first Internet—and thoroughly describes how today's Internet works. A major focus of this chapter is Web 2.0 applications, and the emerging Internet II that is now under development and will shape the future of e-commerce. Chapter 4 builds on the Internet chapter by focusing on the steps managers need to follow in order to build a commercial Web site. This e-commerce infrastructure chapter covers the systems analysis and design process that should be followed in building an e-commerce Web site; the major decisions surrounding the decision to outsource site development and/or hosting; and how to choose software, hardware, and other tools that can improve Web site performance. Chapter 5 focuses on Internet security and payments, building on the e-commerce infrastructure discussion of the previous chapter by describing the ways security can be provided over the Internet. This chapter defines digital information security, describes the major threats to security, and then discusses both the technology and policy solutions available to business managers seeking to secure their firm's sites. This chapter concludes with a section on Internet payment systems. We identify the stakeholders in payment systems, the dimensions to consider in creating payment systems, and the various types of online payment systems (credit cards, stored value payment systems such as PayPal, digital wallets such as Google Checkout and others).

Part 3, "Business Concepts and Social Issues," focuses directly on the business concepts and social-legal issues that surround the development of e-commerce. Chapter 6 focuses on e-commerce consumer behavior, the Internet audience, and introduces the student to the basics of online marketing and branding, including online marketing technologies and marketing strategies. Chapter 7 is devoted to online marketing communications, such as online advertising, e-mail marketing, and search-engine marketing. Chapter 8 provides a thorough introduction to the social and legal environment of e-commerce. Here, you will find a description of the ethical and legal dimensions of e-commerce, including a thorough discussion of the latest developments in personal information privacy, intellectual property, Internet governance, jurisdiction, and public health and welfare issues such as pornography, gambling, and health information.

Part 4, "E-commerce in Action," focuses on real-world e-commerce experiences in retail and services, online media, auctions, portals, and social networks, and business-to-business e-commerce. These chapters take a sector approach rather than a conceptual approach as used in the earlier chapters. E-commerce is different in each of these sectors. Chapter 9 takes a close look at the experience of firms in the retail marketplace for both goods and services. Chapter 9 also includes an "E-commerce in Action" case that provides a detailed analysis of the business strategies and financial operating results of Amazon. Additional E-commerce in Action cases will be available online at the authors' Web site for the text, www.azimuth-interactive.com/ecommerce7e. Chapter 10 explores the world of online content and digital media, and examines the enormous changes in online publishing and entertainment industries that have occurred over the last two years. Chapter 11 explores the online world of social networks, auctions, and portals. Chapter 12 explores the world of B2B e-commerce, describing both electronic Net marketplaces and the less-heralded, but very large arena of private industrial networks and the movement toward collaborative commerce.

## CHAPTER OUTLINE

Each chapter contains a number of elements designed to make learning easy as well as interesting.

**Learning Objectives** A list of learning objectives that highlights the key concepts in the chapter guides student study.

**Chapter-Opening Cases** Each chapter opens with a story about a leading e-commerce company that relates the key objectives of the chapter to a real-life e-commerce business venture.

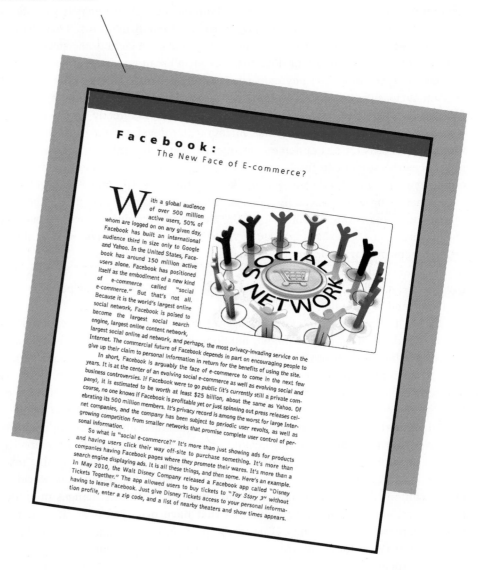

# Facebook:
## The New Face of E-commerce?

With a global audience of over 500 million active users, 50% of whom are logged on on any given day, Facebook has built an international audience third in size only to Google and Yahoo. In the United States, Facebook has around 150 million active users alone. Facebook has positioned itself as the embodiment of a new kind of e-commerce called "social e-commerce." But that's not all. Because it is the world's largest online social network, Facebook is poised to become the largest social search engine, largest online content network, largest social online ad network, and perhaps, the most privacy-invading service on the Internet. The commercial future of Facebook depends in part on encouraging people to give up their claim to personal information in return for the benefits of using the site.

In short, Facebook is arguably the face of e-commerce to come in the next few years. It is at the center of an evolving social e-commerce as well as evolving social and business controversies. If Facebook were to go public (it's currently still a private company), it is estimated to be worth at least $25 billion, about the same as Yahoo. Of course, no one knows if Facebook is profitable yet or just spinning out press releases celebrating its 500 million members. It's privacy record is among the worst for large Internet companies, and the company has been subject to periodic user revolts, as well as growing competition from smaller networks that promise complete user control of personal information.

So what is "social e-commerce?" It's more than just showing ads for products and having users click their way off-site to purchase something. It's more than companies having Facebook pages where they promote their wares. It's more than a search engine displaying ads. It is all these things, and then some. Here's an example. In May 2010, the Walt Disney Company released a Facebook app called "Disney Tickets Together." The app allowed users to buy tickets to *Toy Story 3* without having to leave Facebook. Just give Disney Tickets access to your personal information profile, enter a zip code, and a list of nearby theaters and show times appears.

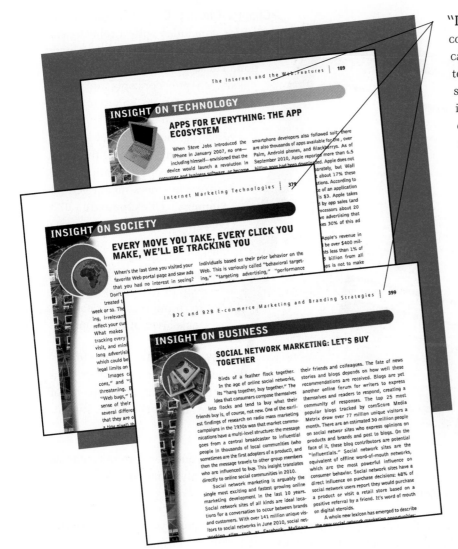

**"Insight on" Cases** Each chapter contains three real-world short cases illustrating the themes of technology, business, and society. These cases create an integrated framework and coverage throughout the book for describing and analyzing the full breadth of the field of e-commerce. The cases probe such issues as the ability of governments to regulate Internet content, how to design Web sites for accessibility, the challenges faced by luxury marketers in online marketing, and the potential anti-competitiveness of Net marketplaces.

**Margin Glossary** Throughout the text, key terms and their definitions appear in the text margin where they are firstintroduced.

Real-Company Examples Drawn from actual e-commerce ventures, well over 100 pertinent examples are used throughout the text to illustrate concepts.

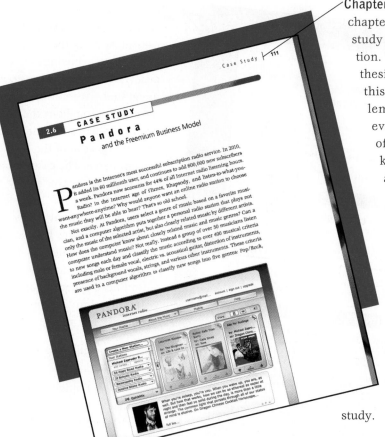

**Chapter-Closing Case Studies** Each chapter concludes with a robust case study based on a real-world organization. These cases help students synthesize chapter concepts and apply this knowledge to concrete problems and scenarios such as evaluating the ethics and legality of advertising spyware, the marketing plans of Liquidation.com, and the business model behind Siemens' Click2procure B2B marketplace.

**Chapter-Ending Pedagogy** Each chapter contains end of chapter materials designed to reinforce the learning objectives of the chapter.

**Key Concepts** Keyed to the learning objectives, Key Concepts present the key points of the chapter to aid student study.

**Review Questions** Thought-provoking questions prompt students to demonstrate their comprehension and apply chapter concepts to management problem solving.

**Projects** At the end of each chapter are a number of projects that encourage students to apply chapter concepts and to use higher level evaluation skills. Many make use of the Internet and require students to present their findings in an oral presentation or written report. For instance, students are asked to evaluate publicly available information about a company's financials at the SEC Web site, assess payment system options for companies across international boundaries, or search for the top ten cookies on their own computer and the sites they are from.

**Web Resources** A section at the end of the chapter directs students to Web resources available at www.azimuth-interactive.com/ecommerce7e that can extend their knowledge of each chapter with projects and exercises and additional content. The Web site contains the following content provided by the authors:

- E-commerce in Action cases analyze the business strategies and financial operating results public e-commerce companies. For each company, we identify the vision of the company, analyze its financial performance, review its current strategy, and assess the near-term future prospects for the firm. These cases are ideal real-world instructional guides for students interested in understanding the financial foundation of e-commerce firms, their strategic visions and customer value propositions, and their changing strategic objectives. They can also be used as projects where students update the case materials using the most current financial and business news, or provide additional analysis.

- Additional projects, exercises, and tutorials.
- Information on how to build a business plan and revenue models.
- Essays on careers in e-commerce.

## SUPPORT PACKAGE

The following supplementary materials are available to qualified instructors through the Online Instructor Resource Center. Contact your Prentice Hall sales representative for information about how to access them.

- **Instructor's Manual with solutions** This comprehensive manual pulls together a wide variety of teaching tools so that instructors can use the text easily and effectively. Each chapter contains an overview of key topics, a recap of the key learning objectives, lecture tips, discussion of the chapter-ending case, and answers to the Case Study Questions, Review Questions, and Student Projects.

- **Test Bank** For quick test preparation, the author-created Test Bank contains multiple-choice, true/false, and short-essay questions that focus both on content and the development of critical/creative thinking about the issues evoked by the chapter. The Test Bank is available in Microsoft Word and TestGen format. The TestGen is also available in WebCT and BlackBoard-ready format. TestGen allows instructors to view, edit, and add questions.

- **PowerPoint lecture presentation slides** These slides illustrate key points, tables, and figures from the text in lecture-note format. The slides can be easily converted to transparencies or viewed electronically in the classroom.

## ACKNOWLEDGMENTS

Pearson Education sought the advice of many excellent reviewers, all of whom strongly influenced the organization and substance of this book. The following individuals provided extremely useful evaluations of this and previous editions of the text:

Carrie Andersen, Madison Area Technical College

Dr. Shirley A. Becker, Northern Arizona University

Prasad Bingi, Indiana-Purdue University, Fort Wayne

Christine Barnes, Lakeland Community College

Cliff Butler, North Seattle Community College

Joanna Broder, University of Arizona

James Buchan, College of the Ozarks

Ashley Bush, Florida State University

Andrew Ciganek, Jacksonville State University

Daniel Connolly, University of Denver

Tom Critzer, Miami University

Dursan Delen, Oklahoma State University

Abhijit Deshmukh, University of Massachusetts

Brian L. Dos Santos, University of Louisville

Robert Drevs, University of Notre Dame

Akram El-Tannir, Hariri Canadian University, Lebanon

Kimberly Furumo, University of Hawaii at Hilo

John H. Gerdes, University of California, Riverside

Philip Gordon, University of California at Berkeley

Allan Greenberg, Brooklyn College

Peter Haried, University of Wisconsin-Milwaukee

Sherri Harms, University of Nebraska at Kearney

Sharon Heckel, St. Charles Community College

David Hite, Virginia Intermont College

Ellen Kraft, Georgian Court University

Gilliean Lee, Lander University

Zoonky Lee, University of Nebraska, Lincoln

Andre Lemaylleux, Boston University, Brussels

Haim Levkowitz, University of Massachusetts, Lowell

Yair Levy, Nova Southeastern University

Richard Lucic, Duke University

John Mendonca, Purdue University

Dr. Abdulrahman Mirza, DePaul University

Kent Palmer, MacMurray College

Karen Palumbo, University of St. Francis

Wayne Pauli, Dakota State University

Jamie Pinchot, Theil College

Barry Quinn, University of Ulster, Northern Ireland

Jay Rhee, San Jose State University

Jorge Romero, Towson University

John Sagi, Anne Arundel Community College

Patricia Sendall, Merrimack College

Dr. Carlos Serrao, ISCTE/DCTI, Portugal

Neerja Sethi, Nanyang Business School, Singapore

Amber Settle, DePaul CTI

Vivek Shah, Texas State University-San Marcos

Seung Jae Shin, Mississippi State University

Sumit Sircar, University of Texas at Arlington

Hongjun Song, University of Memphis

Pamela Specht, University of Nebraska at Omaha

Esther Swilley, Kansas State University

Tony Townsend, Iowa State University

Bill Troy, University of New Hampshire

Susan VandeVen, Southern Polytechnic State University

Hiep Van Dong, Madison Area Technical College

Mary Vitrano, Palm Beach Community College

Andrea Wachter, Point Park University

Catherine Wallace, Massey University, New Zealand

Biao Wang, Boston University

Harry Washington, Lincoln University

Rolf Wigand, University of Arkansas at Little Rock

Erin Wilkinson, Johnson & Wales University

Alice Wilson, Cedar Crest College

Dezhi Wu, Southern Utah University

Gene Yelle, SUNY Institute of Technology

David Zolzer, Northwestern State University

We would like to thank eMarketer, Inc. and David Iankelevich for their permission to include data and figures from their research reports in our text. eMarketer is one of the leading independent sources for statistics, trend data, and original analysis covering many topics related to the Internet, e-business, and emerging technologies. eMarketer aggregates e-business data from multiple sources worldwide.

In addition, we would like to thank all those at Prentice Hall who have worked so hard to make sure that this book is the very best that it can be. We want to thank Bob Horan, Executive Editor of the Prentice Hall MIS list and Kelly Loftus, Editorial Project Manager for their editorial support; Judy Leale and Karalyn Holland for overseeing production of this project; and Steve Frim for the outstanding cover design. Very special thanks to Megan Miller and Will Anderson at Azimuth Interactive, Inc., and Ann Cohen, for all their hard work on the production of, and supplements for, this book.

A special thanks also to Susan Hartman, Executive Editor for the first and second editions and to Frank Ruggirello, Publisher at Addison-Wesley when we began this project, and now Vice Presient and Editorial Director at Benjamin-Cummings.

Finally, last but not least, we would like to thank our family and friends, without whose support this book would not have been possible.

*Kenneth C. Laudon*
*Carol Guercio Traver*

# Brief Contents

xviii Preface

## PART 4  E-commerce in Action

# Contents

| 2 | **E-COMMERCE BUSINESS MODELS AND CONCEPTS** | **62** |
|---|---|---|

# PART 2 Technology Infrastructure for E-commerce

## 5    ONLINE SECURITY AND PAYMENT SYSTEMS    260

# PART 3  Business Concepts and Social Issues

## 6  E-COMMERCE MARKETING CONCEPTS                                    340

## 8 ETHICAL, SOCIAL, AND POLITICAL ISSUES IN E-COMMERCE 492

# PART 4   E-commerce in Action

## 9   ONLINE RETAILING AND SERVICES                                                                                 572

*— Contant — deleted*

*\ updated case*

---

**11 SOCIAL NETWORKS, AUCTIONS, AND PORTALS**    708

**12    B2B E-COMMERCE: SUPPLY CHAIN MANAGEMENT AND COLLABORATIVE COMMERCE        760**

# Introduction to E-commerce

# CHAPTER 1

# The Revolution Is Just Beginning

## LEARNING OBJECTIVES

**After reading this chapter, you will be able to:**

- Define e-commerce and describe how it differs from e-business.
- Identify and describe the unique features of e-commerce technology and discuss their business significance.
- Recognize and describe Web 2.0 applications.
- Describe the major types of e-commerce.
- Discuss the origins and growth of e-commerce.
- Understand the evolution of e-commerce from its early years to today.
- Identify the factors that will define the future of e-commerce.
- Describe the major themes underlying the study of e-commerce.
- Identify the major academic disciplines contributing to e-commerce.

# Facebook:
## The New Face of E-commerce?

**W**ith a global audience of over 500 million active users, 50% of whom are logged on on any given day, Facebook has built an international audience third in size only to Google and Yahoo. In the United States, Facebook has around 150 million active users alone. Facebook has positioned itself as the embodiment of a new kind of e-commerce called "social e-commerce." But that's not all. Because it is the world's largest online social network, Facebook is poised to become the largest social search engine, largest online content network, largest social online ad network, and perhaps, the most privacy-invading service on the Internet. The commercial future of Facebook depends in part on encouraging people to give up their claim to personal information in return for the benefits of using the site.

In short, Facebook is arguably the face of e-commerce to come in the next few years. It is at the center of an evolving social e-commerce as well as evolving social and business controversies. If Facebook were to go public (it's currently still a private company), it is estimated to be worth at least $25 billion, about the same as Yahoo. Of course, no one knows if Facebook is profitable yet or just spinning out press releases celebrating its 500 million members. It's privacy record is among the worst for large Internet companies, and the company has been subject to periodic user revolts, as well as growing competition from smaller networks that promise complete user control of personal information.

So what is "social e-commerce?" It's more than just showing ads for products and having users click their way off-site to purchase something. It's more than companies having Facebook pages where they promote their wares. It's more than a search engine displaying ads. It is all these things, and then some. Here's an example. In May 2010, the Walt Disney Company released a Facebook app called "Disney Tickets Together." The app allowed users to buy tickets to "*Toy Story 3*" without having to leave Facebook. Just give Disney Tickets access to your personal information profile, enter a zip code, and a list of nearby theaters and show times appears.

There was, of course, an option to invite Facebook friends, as well as friends who did not have Facebook accounts. Disney introduced the service on its Toy Story Facebook page, which over 5 million users have indicated that they "like.". Results were encouraging, with many people using the application to buy tickets for large groups of friends.

What was unusual about the Disney application is that the transaction took place on the Facebook site without being redirected to a third-party Web site. In other words, Facebook is turning into an e-commerce platform like Amazon and eBay. Think about how you buy things and, more importantly, how you discover new products. Often, you learn about those products from your friends, relatives, and neighbors--in short, other people in your social networks, some close, some not so close. Television and Internet display ads are important too, but from the beginning of marketing research in the 1930s, social scientists discovered that early adopters and their social networks were critical for introducing other consumers to products and services. We tend to consume the same products our friends consume. For instance, the best predictor of the music you like typically is what your friends like. Increasingly, "natural" face-to-face social networks have migrated to the Web and sites such as Facebook.

Suppose one of your social network friends introduces you to a new product or music track. Then what? You could ask your friend where he or she bought the product, or use a search engine such as Google or Bing to find out. But wouldn't it be easier if your friend could just automatically steer you to the Web site where he or she got the product? That's the future that Facebook envisions. Increasingly, it would like product and service to be available for purchase without leaving Facebook, just like tickets for *Toy Story 3* were. This is ideal for Facebook because it keeps users more involved with Facebook and allows them to show users more ads.

Instead of using Google for search, on Facebook, you can ask your friends if they know the best place to purchase a product. Casting the net further, you might ask all the people in your network, or related networks, for recommendations. In essence, Facebook can operate as a kind of search engine, one that is based on social networks and the members of your network. Search becomes social when it relies on large populations of preferences. . For the most part, people don't use Google to find out "what" to buy, but instead to search for "where" to buy. We all read reviews of products online, but the most powerful influences are close and trusted friends, and beyond them, larger crowds of reviewers. In the future, expect Facebook to develop a trustworthy payment system similar to PayPal. Social e-commerce means that every time you purchase something on participating Web sites, or any time you even explore products on other Web sites, your friends receive a notice. By your actions, you become an important influencer in the online social commerce platform. Google might be a "database of intentions" to buy, but Facebook is a very large database of your name and location, preferences, behaviors, dreams, and aspirations that shape your intention to buy. These elements of consumer behavior are prior to intentions. First things first.

Facebook's ability to achieve these social e-commerce capabilities depend, in part, on how effectively the company can invade its users' privacy. Facebooks' business model is based on selling access to personal information. Facebook needs to persuade its users to give up claims to the privacy of that information. If Facebook users decide not to freely share their profiles and online behavior, the Facebook e-commerce platform will wither away because it is precisely its knowledge of personal information on 500 million people around the globe that it sells to potential advertisers.

In the last three years, Facebook founder and CEO Mark Zuckerberg has done everything in his power to encourage Faceook users to reveal the details of their personal lives, and when persuasion does not work, the company has tried to achieve the same result by catching the many users who do not pay attention to such things. Claiming that privacy is a thing of the past and no longer cool, Facebook changed its initial privacy policy ("only your friends will know about your Facebook profile") to a default "No privacy" policy, in which everyone's basic profile information is posted to the Web and searchable on Google. If you are a Facebook member, do a Google search on your name. Your Facebook profile is likely to be one of the top three results. Facebook started the Beacon program in 2007 to automatically inform participating advertisers about user preferences (the program has since been abandoned due to negative publicity that caused most of the participating advertisers to withdraw). In December 2009, Facebook released new privacy settings encouraging members to share their information with everyone in the world, and make public their name, profile photo, and gender. Privacy, according to Zuckerberg, is an "evolving social norm."

In April 2010, Facebook launched new "social plugins" that could be implemented by outside Websites and apps. For instance, it made the "Like" button that Facebook user had previously been using within Facebook available to outside Web sites and apps. Click the button and all your friends will know what you like -- whether you want them to or not. (In August 2010, a class action lawsuit was filed against Facebook on behalf of minors who clicked the "Like" button and later ended up in ads proclaiming that they "liked" the company or product.)

Bowing to pressure from Congress and privacy groups, facing legislative actions, Facebook has begun reviewing and revising its privacy policies with an eye to simplifying them so users can more readily understand the choices they are making. However, Facebook still flatly refuses to make "no sharing" of personal information the default option. As a a result, much smaller social network start-ups such as Pip.io, OneSocialWeb, Crabgrass, and Elgg are pinning their hopes on attracting Facebook users by promising to keep their personal profiles, friends lists, media preferences, and online behavior totally private and under the user's control.

**SOURCES:** "Statistics," Facebook.com, September 26, 2010; "The Face of Facebook," by Jose Antonio Vargas, *The New Yorker*, September 20, 2010; "Facebook Faces Class Action Over "Like" Buttons," by Jennifer Van Grove, mashable.com, August 27, 2010; "Facebook Makes Headway Around the World," by Miguel Helft, *New York Times*, July 7, 2010; "The Evolution of Privacy on Facebook," by Matt McKeon (mattmckeon.com/facebook-privacy), June 4, 2010; "Facebook's Market Cap On SecondMarket is Now $25 Billion (Bigger Than Yahoo's)," by Erick Schonfeld, techcrunch.com, June 4, 2010; "Disney Puts Tickets on a Facebook Site," by Brooks Barnes, *New York Times*, June 1, 2010; "Rivals Seize on Troubles of Facebook," by Jenna Wortham, *New York Times*, May 23, 2010; "Facebook Wants to Know More Than Just Who Your Friends Are," by Jessica Vascellaro, *Wall Street Journal*, April 22. 2010.

In 1994, e-commerce as we now know it did not exist. In 2010, just 16 years later, around 133 million American consumers are expected to spend about $256 billion, and businesses over $3.6 trillion, purchasing goods and services on the Internet's World Wide Web. And in this short period of time, e-commerce has been reinvented not just once, but twice.

The early years of e-commerce, during the late 1990s, were a period of business vision, inspiration, and experimentation. It soon became apparent, however, that establishing a successful business model based on those visions would not be easy. There followed a period of retrenchment and reevaluation, which led to the stock market crash of 2000–2001, with the value of e-commerce, telecommunications, and other technology stocks plummeting in the space of a year by more than 90%. After the bubble burst, many people were quick to write off e-commerce, predicting that its growth would stagnate, and the Internet audience would plateau. But they were wrong. The surviving firms refined and honed their business models, ultimately leading to models that actually produced profits. Between 2002-2008, retail e-commerce grew at over 25% per year..

Today, we are in the middle of yet another transition: a new and vibrant service/social network-based model of e-commerce growing alongside the more traditional e-commerce retail sales model exemplified by Amazon. Social network sites such as Facebook, Twitter, YouTube, and Photobucket, which enable users to distribute their own content (such as videos, music, photos, personal information, blogs, and software applications), have rocketed to prominence. Spurred by the explosive growth in smartphones such as iPhones and Androids, netbooks, and iPad-like devices for mobile entertainment and reading, a new e-commerce platform is emerging that we call "social e-commerce" because it is so closely intertwined with social networks, mobile computing, and heretofore private social relationships. Never before in the history of media have such large audiences been aggregated and made so accessible. Businesses are grappling with how best to approach this audience from an advertising and marketing perspective. Governments, private groups, and industry players are trying to understand how to protect privacy on this new e-commerce platform. Social networks and user-generated content sites are also examples of technology that is highly disruptive of traditional media firms. The movement of eyeballs towards these sites means fewer viewers of television and Hollywood movies, and fewer readers of newspapers and magazines, and so those industries are also facing a transition. It's probably safe to predict that this will not be the last transition for e-commerce, either.

## 1.1   E-COMMERCE: THE REVOLUTION IS JUST BEGINNING

In fact, the e-commerce revolution is just beginning. For example, in 2010:

- Online consumer sales grew 12.7% compared to traditional retail growth of 2.5% (eMarketer, Inc., 2010a, Reuters, 2010; National Retail Foundation, 2010). This followed the positive results of 2008-2009, when e-commerce sales actually expanded during the recession while traditional retail lost 4.5%.

- The major source of online retail growth in the United States is increased spending by existing online buyers rather than new buyers. As trust and consumer confidence have built, shoppers are now buying expensive, "high-touch" goods online such as consumer electronics, home furnishings, and apparel.

- The number of individuals of all ages online in the United States increased to about 221 million, up from 211 million in 2009 (The total population of the United States is about 308 million.) Of these, about 165 million are adults (over 18) (eMarketer, Inc., 2010b; U.S. Census Bureau, 2009).

- Of the total 116 million households in the United States, the number online increased to 82 million (or about 70% of all households) (U.S. Census Bureau, 2010a; eMarketer, Inc., 2010b).

- On an average day, around 78% of adult U.S. Internet users go online. About 62% send e-mail, 49% use a search engine, and 43% get news. Around 38% use a social network, 26% do online banking, 23% watch an online video, and 17% look for information on Wikipedia (Pew Internet & American Life Project, 2010).

- The number of people who have purchased something online expanded to about 133 million, with an additional 29 million using the Web to gather information on potential product purchases (eMarketer, Inc., 2010a).

- The demographic profile of online shoppers continued to broaden while at the same time significant generational differences in purchase and media consumption patterns have emerged (eMarketer, Inc., 2010a).

- B2B e-commerce—the use of the Internet for business-to-business commerce—will total about $3.6 trillion, comprising about 30% of all business-to-business trade (U.S. Census Bureau, 2010b; authors' estimates).

- The Internet technology base gained greater depth and power, as around 79.5 million households (about 68% of all U.S. households) have broadband cable or DSL access to the Internet and 83 million people access the Internet via mobile devices (eMarketer, Inc., 2010b).

These developments signal many of the themes in the new edition of this book (**see Table 1.1**). Social networks are becoming a new e-commerce platform that will rival traditional e-commerce platforms by providing search, advertising, and payment services to vendors and customers. Who needs Google when you can have a swarm of friends recommend music, clothes, cars, and videos, or see ads on a social site where you spend most of your time online? The mobile digital platform based on smartphones like the iPhone, netbook computers, and devices like the iPad has also finally arrived with a bang, making true mobile e-commerce almost a reality, within grasp. In five years, the majority of Americans will access Internet using mobile devices.

More and more people and businesses are using the Internet to conduct commerce; smaller, local firms are learning how to take advantage of the Internet as Web services and Web site tools become very inexpensive. New e-commerce brands emerge while traditional retail brands such as Sears, JCPenney, and Wal-Mart further extend their multi-channel, bricks-and-clicks strategies and retain their dominant retail positions by strengthening their Internet operations. At the societal level, other

| TABLE 1.1 | MAJOR TRENDS IN E-COMMERCE 2010–2011 |
| --- | --- |

### BUSINESS

- A new "social e-commerce" platform is emerging based on social networks and supported by advertising.
- Retail e-commerce resumes double-digit growth (about 12.5%) annually (six times faster than traditional retail), after slow-growth in 2009 due to the recession.
- Facebook continues to grow, with more than 500 million worldwide users.
- Twitter continues to grow, with over 145 million Tweeple (users) worldwide.
- Consumer packaged goods begin to find their online market.
- Facebook and Google struggle to dominate social interaction on the Internet.
- Search engine marketing continues to challenge traditional marketing and advertising media as more consumers switch their eyes to the Web.
- Social and mobile advertising platforms show strong growth and begin to challenge search engine marketing.
- Online population growth in the United States slows, but the amount of the average purchase expands.
- The online demographics of shoppers continue to broaden with the fastest growth among tweens, teens, and older adults.
- Online businesses continue to strengthen profitability by refining their business models and leveraging the capabilities of the Internet.
- The first wave of e-commerce transformed the business world of music, brokerage, and air travel. Industries facing a similar transformation today include marketing/advertising, telecommunications, entertainment, print media, real estate, hotels, bill payments, and software.
- The breadth of e-commerce offerings grows, especially in entertainment, retail apparel, luxury goods, appliances, and home furnishings.
- Small businesses and entrepreneurs continue to flood into the e-commerce marketplace, often riding on the infrastructures created by industry giants such as Apple, Facebook, Amazon, Google, and eBay.
- Brand extension through the Internet continues to grow as large firms such as Sears, JCPenney, L.L.Bean, and Wal-Mart pursue integrated, multi-channel bricks-and-clicks strategies.
- B2B supply chain transactions and collaborative commerce continue to strengthen and grow beyond the $3.6 trillion mark.

### TECHNOLOGY

- A mobile computing and communications platform based on iPhones, BlackBerries, and other smartphones, netbook computers, and the iPad (the "new client") becomes a reality and begins to rival the PC platform.
- Over 250,000 apps in Apple's App Store create a new model for delivering services and software.
- The Internet broadband foundation becomes stronger in households and businesses. Bandwidth prices fall as telecommunications companies expand their capacities with new technologies.
- Computing and networking component prices continue to fall dramatically.

| TABLE 1.1 | MAJOR TRENDS IN E-COMMERCE 2010–2011 (CONTINUED) |
|-----------|--------------------------------------------------|

- Cloud computing and Web services expand B2B opportunities and radically reduce the cost of infrastructure needed for e-commerce.
- Real-time advertising becomes a reality as firms gain in computing power and database speeds.
- The global population using the Internet continues to expand, with around 25% now online.

### SOCIETY

- Consumer- and user-generated content, and syndication in the form of social networks, tweets, blogs, wikis, and virtual lives, continue to grow and provide an entirely new self-publishing forum that engages millions of consumers.
- The amount of data (34 gigabytes) the average American consumes each day continues to increase.
- Social networks encourage self-revelation, while threatening privacy.
- Traditional media such as television, newspapers, books, and magazines continue to lose subscribers, and adopt online, interactive models and mobile apps that offer new advertising and revenue platforms.
- Conflicts over copyright management and control continue, but there is substantial agreement among Internet distributors and copyright owners that they need one another.
- Explosive growth continues in online viewing of video and television programs.
- Participation by adults in social networks on the Internet increases; Facebook becomes ever more popular in all demographic categories.
- Taxation of Internet sales becomes more widespread and accepted by large online merchants.
- Controversy over content regulation and controls continues.
- Surveillance of Internet communications by repressive regimes and other countries grows.
- Concerns over commercial and governmental privacy invasion increase as firms provide government agencies with access to private personal information.
- Internet security worsens due to botnets, malware, spam, and identity theft occurrences.
- Spam remains a significant problem despite legislation and promised technology fixes.
- Invasion of personal privacy on the Web expands as marketers extend their capabilities to track users.
- China and India Internet populations continue to grow at around 15%–20% annually.
- Google becomes the target of anti-trust claims because of its search engine dominance.

trends are apparent. The Internet has created a platform for millions of people to create and share content, establish new social bonds, and strengthen existing ones through social networks, blogging, and video posting sites. These same social networks have created a massive privacy issue. The major digital copyright owners have increased their pursuit of online file-swapping services with mixed success, while reaching broad agreements with the big technology players like Apple, Amazon, and Google to protect intellectual property rights. States have successfully moved toward taxation of Internet sales, while Internet gaming sites have been severely curtailed through criminal prosecutions in the United States. Sovereign nations have expanded their surveillance of, and control over, Internet communications and content as a part of their anti-terrorist activities and their traditional interest in snooping on citizens. Privacy seems to have lost much of its meaning in an age when millions create public online personal profiles.

## THE FIRST 30 SECONDS

It is important to realize that the rapid growth and change that has occurred in the first 16 years of e-commerce represents just the beginning—what could be called the first 30 seconds of the e-commerce revolution. The same technologies that drove the first decade and a half of e-commerce (described in Chapter 3) continue to evolve at exponential rates. This underlying ferment in the technological ground-work of the Internet and Web presents entrepreneurs with new opportunities to both create new businesses and new business models in traditional industries, and also to destroy old businesses. Business change becomes disruptive, rapid, and even destructive, while offering entrepreneurs new opportunities and resources for investment.

Changes in underlying information technologies and continuing entrepreneurial innovation in business and marketing promise as much change in the next decade as seen in the last decade. The twenty-first century will be the age of a digitally enabled social and commercial life, the outlines of which we can barely perceive at this time. Analysts estimate that by 2014, consumers will be spending about $358 billion and businesses about $5.2 trillion in online transactions. In 2020, industry analysts are calling for e-commerce to be 20% of all retail sales. It appears likely that e-commerce will eventually impact nearly all commerce, and that most commerce will be e-commerce by the year 2050.

Is there a terminal point towards which e-commerce is hurtling? Can e-commerce continue to grow indefinitely? It's possible that at some point, e-commerce growth may slow simply as a result of overload: people may just not have the time to watch yet another online video, open another e-mail, or read another blog, tweet, or Face-book update. However, currently, there is no foreseeable limit to the continued rapid development of Internet and e-commerce technology, or limits on the inventiveness of entrepreneurs to develop new uses for the technology. Therefore, for now at least, it is likely that the disruptive process will continue.

Business fortunes are made—and lost—in periods of extraordinary change such as this. The next five years hold out extraordinary opportunities—as well as risks—for new and traditional businesses to exploit digital technology for market advantage. For society as a whole, the next few decades offer the possibility of extraordinary gains in social wealth as the digital revolution works its way through larger and larger segments of the world's economy, offering the possibility of high rates of productivity and income growth in an inflation-free environment.

As a business or technology student, this book will help you perceive and understand the opportunities and risks that lie ahead. By the time you finish, you will be able to identify the technological, business, and social forces that have shaped the growth of e-commerce and extend that understanding into the years ahead.

## WHAT IS E-COMMERCE?

Our focus in this book is **e-commerce**—the use of the Internet and the World Wide Web (Web) to transact business. (Although the terms Internet and Web are often used interchangeably, they are actually two very different things. The Internet is a worldwide network of computer networks, and the Web is one of the Internet's most popular services, providing access to billions of Web pages. We describe both more fully later in this chapter and in Chapter 3.) More formally, we focus on digitally enabled commercial transactions between and among organizations and individuals. Each of these components of our working definition of e-commerce is important. *Digitally enabled transactions* include all transactions mediated by digital technology. For the most part, this means transactions that occur over the Internet and the Web. *Commercial transactions* involve the exchange of value (e.g., money) across organizational or individual boundaries in return for products and services. Exchange of value is important for understanding the limits of e-commerce. Without an exchange of value, no commerce occurs.

**e-commerce**
the use of the Internet and the Web to transact business. More formally, digitally enabled commercial transactions between and among organizations and individuals

## THE DIFFERENCE BETWEEN E-COMMERCE AND E-BUSINESS

There is a debate among consultants and academics about the meaning and limitations of both e-commerce and e-business. Some argue that e-commerce encompasses the entire world of electronically based organizational activities that support a firm's market exchanges—including a firm's entire information system's infrastructure (Rayport and Jaworski, 2003). Others argue, on the other hand, that e-business encompasses the entire world of internal and external electronically based activities, including e-commerce (Kalakota and Robinson, 2003).

We think that it is important to make a working distinction between e-commerce and e-business because we believe they refer to different phenomena. E-commerce is not "anything digital" that a firm does. For purposes of this text, we will use the term **e-business** to refer primarily to the digital enabling of transactions and processes *within* a firm, involving information systems under the control of the firm. For the most part, in our view, e-business does not include commercial transactions involving an exchange of value across organizational boundaries. For example, a company's online inventory control mechanisms are a component of e-business, but such internal processes do not directly generate revenue for the firm from outside businesses or consumers, as e-commerce, by definition, does. It is true, however, that a firm's e-business infrastructure provides support for online e-commerce exchanges; the same infrastructure and skill sets are involved in both e-business and e-commerce. E-commerce and e-business systems blur together at the business firm boundary, at the point where internal business systems link up with suppliers or customers, for instance (see **Figure 1.1**). E-business applications turn into e-commerce precisely when an exchange of value occurs (see Mesenbourg, U.S. Department of Commerce, 2001, for a similar view). We will examine this intersection further in Chapter 12.

**e-business**
the digital enabling of transactions and processes within a firm, involving information systems under the control of the firm

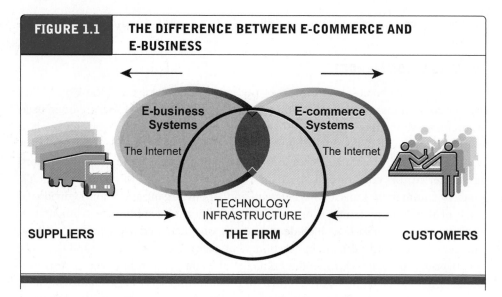

| FIGURE 1.1 | THE DIFFERENCE BETWEEN E-COMMERCE AND E-BUSINESS |

E-commerce primarily involves transactions that cross firm boundaries. E-business primarily involves the application of digital technologies to business processes within the firm.

## WHY STUDY E-COMMERCE?

Why are there college courses and textbooks on e-commerce when there are no courses or textbooks on "TV Commerce," "Radio Commerce," "Direct Mail Commerce," "Railroad Commerce," or "Highway Commerce," even though these technologies had profound impacts on commerce in the twentieth century and account for far more commerce than e-commerce? Many colleges, including Massachusetts Institute of Technology (MIT), University of Michigan, Cornell University, University of California at Berkeley, and INSEAD Business School (France), have also developed courses on social interaction technologies and techniques, online social networks, online community development, and consumer-generated media. At least one college offers a YouTube 101 course called "Learning from YouTube."

The reason for the interest specifically in e-commerce is that e-commerce technology (discussed in detail in Chapters 3 and 4) is different and more powerful than any of the other technologies we have seen in the past century. E-commerce technologies—and the digital markets that result—are bringing about some fundamental, unprecedented shifts in commerce. While these other technologies transformed economic life in the twentieth century, the evolving Internet and other information technologies are shaping the twenty-first century.

Prior to the development of e-commerce, the marketing and sale of goods was a mass-marketing and sales force-driven process. Marketers viewed consumers as passive targets of advertising "campaigns" and branding blitzes intended to influence their long-term product perceptions and immediate purchasing behavior. Companies sold their products via well-insulated "channels." Consumers were trapped by geographical and social boundaries, unable to search widely for the best price and quality. Information about prices, costs, and fees could be hidden from the consumer, creating profitable "information asymmetries" for the selling firm. **Information asymmetry** refers to any disparity in relevant market information among parties in a transaction. It was so expensive to change national or regional prices in traditional retailing (what are called *menu costs*) that "one national price" was the norm, and dynamic pricing to the marketplace—changing prices in real time—was unheard of. In this environment, manufacturers prospered by relying on huge production runs of products that could not be customized or personalized. One of the shifts that e-commerce is bringing about is a reduction in information asymmetry among market participants (consumers and merchants). Preventing consumers from learning about costs, price discrimination strategies, and profits from sales becomes more difficult with e-commerce, and the entire marketplace potentially becomes highly price competitive.

**information asymmetry**
any disparity in relevant market information among parties in a transaction

## EIGHT UNIQUE FEATURES OF E-COMMERCE TECHNOLOGY

**Table 1.2** lists eight unique features of e-commerce technology that both challenge traditional business thinking and explain why we have so much interest in e-commerce. These unique dimensions of e-commerce technologies suggest many new possibilities for marketing and selling—a powerful set of interactive, personalized, and rich messages are available for delivery to segmented, targeted audiences. E-commerce technologies make it possible for merchants to know much more about consumers and to be able to use this information more effectively than was ever true in the past. Potentially, online merchants can use this new information to develop new information asymmetries, enhance their ability to brand products, charge premium prices for high-quality service, and segment the market into an endless number of subgroups, each receiving a different price. To complicate matters further, these same technologies make it possible for merchants to know more about other merchants than was ever true in the past. This presents the possibility that merchants might collude on prices rather than compete and drive overall average prices up. This strategy works especially well when there are just a few suppliers (Varian, 2000a). We examine these different visions of e-commerce further in Section 1.2 and throughout the book.

Each of the dimensions of e-commerce technology and their business significance listed in Table 1.2 deserves a brief exploration, as well as a comparison to both traditional commerce and other forms of technology-enabled commerce.

### Ubiquity

In traditional commerce, a **marketplace** is a physical place you visit in order to transact. For example, television and radio typically motivate the consumer to go some place to make a purchase. E-commerce, in contrast, is characterized by its **ubiquity**: it is available just about everywhere, at all times. It liberates the market from being restricted to a physical space and makes it possible to shop from your desktop, at home, at work, or even from your car, using mobile commerce. The result is called a **marketspace**—a marketplace extended beyond traditional boundaries and removed from a temporal and geographic location. From a consumer point of view, ubiquity reduces *transaction costs*—the costs of participating in a market. To transact,

**marketplace**
physical space you visit in order to transact

**ubiquity**
available just about everywhere, at all times

**marketspace**
marketplace extended beyond traditional boundaries and removed from a temporal and geographic location

| TABLE 1.2 | EIGHT UNIQUE FEATURES OF E-COMMERCE TECHNOLOGY |
|---|---|
| **E-COMMERCE TECHNOLOGY DIMENSION** | **BUSINESS SIGNIFICANCE** |
| **Ubiquity**—Internet/Web technology is available everywhere: at work, at home, and elsewhere via mobile devices, anytime. | The marketplace is extended beyond traditional boundaries and is removed from a temporal and geographic location. "Marketspace" is created; shopping can take place anywhere. Customer convenience is enhanced, and shopping costs are reduced. |
| **Global reach**—The technology reaches across national boundaries, around the Earth. | Commerce is enabled across cultural and national boundaries seamlessly and without modification. "Marketspace" includes potentially billions of consumers and millions of businesses worldwide. |
| **Universal standards**—There is one set of technology standards, namely Internet standards. | There is a common, inexpensive, global, technology foundation for businesses to use. |
| **Richness**—Video, audio, and text messages are possible. | Video, audio, and text marketing messages are integrated into a single marketing message and consuming experience. |
| **Interactivity**—The technology works through interaction with the user. | Consumers are engaged in a dialog that dynamically adjusts the experience to the individual, and makes the consumer a co-participant in the process of delivering goods to the market. |
| **Information density**—The technology reduces information costs and raises quality. | Information processing, storage, and communication costs drop dramatically, while currency, accuracy, and timeliness improve greatly. Information becomes plentiful, cheap, and accurate. |
| **Personalization/Customization**—The technology allows personalized messages to be delivered to individuals as well as groups. | Personalization of marketing messages and customization of products and services are based on individual characteristics. |
| **Social technology**—User content generation and social networks. | New Internet social and business models enable user content creation and distribution, and support social networks. |

it is no longer necessary that you spend time and money traveling to a market. At a broader level, the ubiquity of e-commerce lowers the cognitive energy required to transact in a marketspace. *Cognitive energy* refers to the mental effort required to complete a task. Humans generally seek to reduce cognitive energy outlays. When given a choice, humans will choose the path requiring the least effort—the most convenient path (Shapiro and Varian, 1999; Tversky and Kahneman, 1981).

## Global Reach

E-commerce technology permits commercial transactions to cross cultural and national boundaries far more conveniently and cost-effectively than is true in traditional commerce. As a result, the potential market size for e-commerce merchants is roughly equal to the size of the world's online population (about 1.97 billion) (Internet Worldstats, 2010). The total number of users or customers an e-commerce business can obtain is a measure of its **reach** (Evans and Wurster, 1997).

In contrast, most traditional commerce is local or regional—it involves local merchants or national merchants with local outlets. Television and radio stations, and newspapers, for instance, are primarily local and regional institutions with limited but powerful national networks that can attract a national audience. In contrast to e-commerce technology, these older commerce technologies do not easily cross national boundaries to a global audience.

**reach**
the total number of users or customers an e-commerce business can obtain

## Universal Standards

One strikingly unusual feature of e-commerce technologies is that the technical standards of the Internet, and therefore the technical standards for conducting e-commerce, are **universal standards**—they are shared by all nations around the world. In contrast, most traditional commerce technologies differ from one nation to the next. For instance, television and radio standards differ around the world, as does cell phone technology. The universal technical standards of the Internet and e-commerce greatly lower *market entry costs*—the cost merchants must pay just to bring their goods to market. At the same time, for consumers, universal standards reduce *search costs*—the effort required to find suitable products. And by creating a single, one-world marketspace, where prices and product descriptions can be inexpensively displayed for all to see, *price discovery* becomes simpler, faster, and more accurate (Banerjee, et al., 2005; Bakos, 1997; Kambil, 1997). Users of the Internet, both businesses and individuals, also experience *network externalities*—benefits that arise because everyone uses the same technology. With e-commerce technologies, it is possible for the first time in history to easily find many of the suppliers, prices, and delivery terms of a specific product anywhere in the world, and to view them in a coherent, comparative environment. Although this is not necessarily realistic today for all or even many products, it is a potential that will be exploited in the future.

**universal standards**
standards that are shared by all nations around the world

## Richness

Information **richness** refers to the complexity and content of a message (Evans and Wurster, 1999). Traditional markets, national sales forces, and small retail stores have great richness: they are able to provide personal, face-to-face service using aural and visual cues when making a sale. The richness of traditional markets makes them a powerful selling or commercial environment. Prior to the development of the Web, there was a trade-off between richness and reach: the larger the audience reached, the less rich the message (see **Figure 1.2**). The Internet has the potential for offering considerably more information richness than traditional media such as printing presses, radio, and television because it is interactive and can adjust the message to

**richness**
the complexity and content of a message

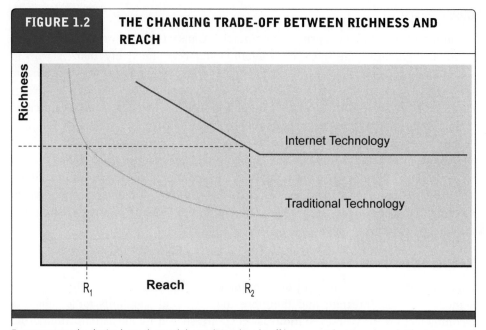

| FIGURE 1.2 | THE CHANGING TRADE-OFF BETWEEN RICHNESS AND REACH |

E-commerce technologies have changed the traditional trade-off between richness and reach. The Internet and Web can deliver, to an audience of millions, "rich" marketing messages with text, video, and audio, in a way not possible with traditional commerce technologies such as radio, television, or magazines.

SOURCE: Evans and Wurster, 2000.

individual users. Chatting with an online sales person, for instance, comes very close to the customer experience in a small retail shop. The richness of the Web allows retail and service merchants to market and sell "complex" goods and services that heretofore really did require a face-to-face presentation by a sales force. Complex goods have multiple attributes, are typically expensive, and cannot be compared easily, such as used cars, non-standard financial instruments, and even diamond rings (Fink, et al., 2004).

### Interactivity

**interactivity**
technology that allows for two-way communication between merchant and consumer

Unlike any of the commercial technologies of the twentieth century, with the possible exception of the telephone, e-commerce technologies allow for interactivity, meaning they enable two-way communication between merchant and consumer. Traditional television, for instance, cannot ask viewers questions or enter into conversations with them, or request that customer information be entered into a form. In contrast, all of these activities are possible on an e-commerce Web site. **Interactivity** allows an online merchant to engage a consumer in ways similar to a face-to-face experience, but on a much more massive, global scale.

### Information Density

**information density**
the total amount and quality of information available to all market participants

The Internet and the Web vastly increase **information density**—the total amount and quality of information available to all market participants, consumers, and merchants alike. E-commerce technologies reduce information collection, storage, processing, and communication costs. At the same time, these technologies increase greatly the currency, accuracy, and timeliness of information—making information more useful and important than ever. As a result, information becomes more plentiful, less expensive, and of higher quality.

A number of business consequences result from the growth in information density. In e-commerce markets, prices and costs become more transparent. *Price transparency* refers to the ease with which consumers can find out the variety of prices in a market; *cost transparency* refers to the ability of consumers to discover the actual costs merchants pay for products (Sinha, 2000). But there are advantages for merchants as well. Online merchants can discover much more about consumers; this allows merchants to segment the market into groups willing to pay different prices and permits them to engage in *price discrimination*—selling the same goods, or nearly the same goods, to different targeted groups at different prices. For instance, an online merchant can discover a consumer's avid interest in expensive exotic vacations, and then pitch expensive exotic vacation plans to that consumer at a premium price, knowing this person is willing to pay extra for such a vacation. At the same time, the online merchant can pitch the same vacation plan at a lower price to more price-sensitive consumers. Merchants also have enhanced abilities to differentiate their products in terms of cost, brand, and quality.

## Personalization/Customization

E-commerce technologies permit **personalization**: merchants can target their marketing messages to specific individuals by adjusting the message to a person's name, interests, and past purchases. The technology also permits **customization**—changing the delivered product or service based on a user's preferences or prior behavior. Given the interactive nature of e-commerce technology, much information about the consumer can be gathered in the marketplace at the moment of purchase. With the increase in information density, a great deal of information about the consumer's past purchases and behavior can be stored and used by online merchants. The result is a level of personalization and customization unthinkable with existing commerce technologies. For instance, you may be able to shape what you see on television by selecting a channel, but you cannot change the contents of the channel you have chosen. In contrast, the online version of *The Wall Street Journal* allows you to select the type of news stories you want to see first, and gives you the opportunity to be alerted when certain events happen. Personalization and customization allow firms to precisely identify market segments and adjust their messages accordingly.

**personalization**
the targeting of marketing messages to specific individuals by adjusting the message to a person's name, interests, and past purchases

**customization**
changing the delivered product or service based on a user's preferences or prior behavior

## Social Technology: User Content Generation and Social Networking

In a way quite different from all previous technologies, the Internet and e-commerce technologies have evolved to be much more social by allowing users to create and share content in the form of Web and Facebook pages, text, videos, music, and photos with a worldwide community. Using these forms of communication, users are able to create new social networks and strengthen existing ones. All previous mass media in modern history, including the printing press, use a broadcast model (one-to-many) where content is created in a central location by experts (professional writers, editors, directors, actors, and producers) and audiences are concentrated in huge aggregates to consume a standardized product. The telephone would appear to be an exception but it is not a "mass communication" technology. Instead the telephone is a one-to-one technology. The new Internet and e-commerce technologies have the potential to invert this standard media model by giving users the power to create and distribute content on a large scale, and permit users to program their own content consumption. The Internet provides a many-to-many model of mass communications that is unique.

## WEB 2.0: PLAY MY VERSION

**Web 2.0**

a set of applications and technologies that allows users to create, edit, and distribute content; share preferences, bookmarks, and online personas; participate in virtual lives; and build online communities

Many of the unique features of e-commerce and the Internet come together in a set of applications and social media technologies referred to as Web 2.0. The Internet started out as a simple network to support e-mail and file transfers among remote computers. Communication among experts was the purpose. The Web started out as a way to use the Internet to display simple pages and allow the user to navigate among the pages by linking them together electronically. You can think of this as Web 1.0—the first Web. By 2007 something else was happening. The Internet and the Web had evolved to the point where users could create, edit, and distribute content to of others; share with one another their preferences, bookmarks, and online personas; participate in virtual lives; and build online communities. This "new" Web is called by many "**Web 2.0**," and while it draws heavily on the "old" Web 1.0, it is nevertheless a clear evolution from the past.

Let's look at some examples of Web 2.0 applications and sites:

- Twitter is a social network/micro-blogging network that encourages users to enter 140-character messages ("tweets") in answer to the question "What are you doing?" Twitter has over 145 million subscribers ("Tweeple"), sending over 2 billion tweets a month. Twitter is growing at over 1,000% a year and has begun to monetize its subscribers by developing an ad platform and providing marketing services to firms that want to stay in instant contact with their customers.

- YouTube, owned by Google after a $1.65 billion purchase, is the world's largest online consumer-generated video posting site. In August 2010, YouTube had around 146 million unique viewers. YouTube reportedly streams more than 2 billion videos per day, and is expected to have its first profitable year in 2010 (comScore, 2010a; Kincaid, 2010).

- Social network sites continue to grow at triple digit rates. Facebook (discussed in the opening case), with over 500 million users worldwide, Twitter (145 million), and MySpace (over 120 million), lead the social network phenomenon. LinkedIn (75 million) is also growing by triple digits. These audience sizes form the foundation for the new social e-commerce platform.

- Photobucket offers users an easy way to post and share photos and videos via e-mail, instant messages, and mobile phone. It also provides convenient "one-click share" links to Facebook, MySpace, Blogger and Live Journal. Photobucket has over almost 100 million registered users worldwide, about 26 million unique visitors a month, stores over 7 billion consumer-generated digital assets, and serves over 4.3 billion images every day (Photobucket, 2010; comScore, 2010b).

- The Apple iPhone (with more than 50 million sold by 2010) supports mobile versions of Web 2.0 applications such as WordPress for the iPhone (which enables users to write posts, post photos, and manage comments to their blog via an iPhone or iPod touch), Mint (a personal financial manager), Borange (an iPhone app for sharing social availability), TagItLikeItsHot (a social bookmarking application), and over 250,000 other apps for business and personal use. Apple's iPad, introduced in 2010, builds on the iPhone foundation for a truly mobile commerce capability.

- Google attracts one of the largest Internet audiences, with around 179 million unique monthly U.S. visitors in August 2010 (comScore, 2010b). Google provides a continual stream of innovations such as Google Apps (a group of Web-based services offering free office productivity tools such as Google Docs, calendar, and other collaborative tools), Google Desktop, Google Maps, Google StreetView (a photo database of U.S. neighborhoods from the street level), Google Chrome (Web browser), Gmail, Google Scholar, and Google Health (Google, 2010). Over 25% of Google search results on the world's top 20 brands provide links to consumer-generated content such as reviews, blogs, and photos.

- Second Life is a 3-D virtual world populated by around 1 million active users ("residents") who have established lives by creating avatars in "The World," spending Linden dollars, owning real estate, and building, sharing, and purchasing "creations," which include custom "skins" for avatars, clothing, buildings, furniture, vehicles, and a host of other items. Residents spend over $500 million real dollars in a year and cash out $55 million to their PayPal accounts) to buy things on the site for their virtual lives, converting the real dollars to Lindens (Second Life, 2010).

- Wikipedia allows contributors around the world to share their knowledge and in the process has become the most successful online encyclopedia, far surpassing "professional" encyclopedias such as Encarta and Britannica. Wikipedia is one of the largest collaboratively edited reference projects in the world, with over 3.4 million articles available in English. In 2010, Wikipedia had over 365 million unique visitors worldwide. Wikipedia relies on volunteers, makes no money, and accepts no advertising. The Wikimedia Foundation, Inc., a not-for-profit organization that relies on fund-raising and donations to survive, owns Wikipedia. Wikipedia is consistently ranked as one of the top 15 most visited sites on the Web (Wikipedia.org, 2010; Wikimedia.org, 2010; comScore, 2010b).

- Digg allows users to "tag" Web pages and share those tags with other users. Users "vote" on what they like best, and those that are most popular are promoted to the front page of the site, where millions can view and comment. In 2010, Digg had around 7-8 million monthly unique visitors (Compete.com, 2010). StumbleUpon, Reddit, Delicious, Kaboodle, Mixx, Newsvine, Diigo, and Tipd offer similar social bookmarking or tagging systems. Twitter is a major competitor of these sites.

- WordPress is software that allows you to easily create and publish a blog or Web site on the Web. WordPress is an open source product built by a community of volunteers and available for use free of charge. According to WordPress, over 27 million people have used the software to create a blog or Web site (WordPress.com, 2010).

What do all these Web 2.0 applications and sites have in common? First, they rely on user- and consumer-generated content. These are all "applications" created by people, especially people in the 18–34 year-old demographic, and in the 7–17 age group as well. "Regular" people (not just experts or professionals) are creating, sharing, modifying, and broadcasting content to huge audiences. Second, easy search capability is a key to their success. Third, they are inherently highly interactive, creating new opportunities for people to socially connect to others. They are "social" sites because they support interactions among users. Fourth, they rely on broadband connectivity to the Web. Fifth, with the exception of Google, they are currently marginally profitable, and their business models unproven despite considerable investment. Nevertheless, the potential monetary rewards for social sites with huge audiences is quite large. Sixth, they attract extremely large audiences when compared to traditional Web 1.0 applications, exceeding in many cases the audience size of national broadcast and cable television programs. These audience relationships are intensive and long-lasting interactions with millions of people. In short, they attract eyeballs in very large numbers. Hence, they present marketers with extraordinary opportunities for targeted marketing and advertising. They also present consumers with the opportunity to rate and review products, and entrepreneurs with ideas for future business ventures. Last, these sites act as application development platforms where users can contribute and use software applications for free. Briefly, it's a whole new world from what has gone before. You'll learn more about Web 2.0 in later chapters.

## TYPES OF E-COMMERCE

There are a variety of different types of e-commerce and many different ways to characterize them. **Table 1.3** lists the five major types of e-commerce discussed in this book.[1] For the most part, we distinguish different types of e-commerce by the nature of the market relationship—who is selling to whom. The exceptions are peer-to-peer (P2P) and m-commerce, which are technology-based distinctions.

### Business-to-Consumer (B2C) E-commerce

**Business-to-Consumer (B2C) e-commerce**
online businesses selling to individual consumers

The most commonly discussed type of e-commerce is **Business-to-Consumer (B2C) e-commerce**, in which online businesses attempt to reach individual consumers. Even though B2C is comparatively small (about $255 billion in 2010), it has grown exponentially since 1995, and is the type of e-commerce that most consumers are likely to encounter. Within the B2C category, there are many different types of business models. Chapter 2 has a detailed discussion of seven different B2C business models: portals, online retailers, content providers, transaction brokers, market creators, service providers, and community providers.

### Business-to-Business (B2B) E-commerce

**Business-to-Business (B2B) e-commerce**
online businesses selling to other businesses

**Business-to-Business (B2B) e-commerce**, in which businesses focus on selling to other businesses, is the largest form of e-commerce, with about $3.6 trillion in

| **TABLE 1.3** | **MAJOR TYPES OF E-COMMERCE** |
| --- | --- |
| TYPE OF E-COMMERCE | EXAMPLE |
| B2C—Business-to-Consumer | Amazon is a general merchandiser that sells consumer products to retail consumers. |
| B2B—Business-to-Business | Go2Paper.com is an independent third-party marketplace that serves the paper industry. |
| C2C—Consumer-to-Consumer | On a large number of Web auction sites such as eBay, and listing sites such as Craigslist, consumers can auction or sell goods directly to other consumers. |
| P2P—Peer-to-Peer | BitTorrent is a software application that permits consumers to share videos and other high-bandwidth content with one another directly, without the intervention of a market maker as in C2C e-commerce. |
| M-commerce—Mobile commerce | Wireless mobile devices such as smartphones and cell phones can be used to conduct commercial transactions. |

transactions in the United States in 2010. There was an estimated $12.2 trillion in business-to-business exchanges of all kinds, online and offline, suggesting that B2B e-commerce has significant growth potential. The ultimate size of B2B e-commerce is potentially huge. There are two primary business models used within the B2B arena: Net marketplaces, which include e-distributors, e-procurement companies, exchanges and industry consortia, and private industrial networks, which include single firm networks and industry-wide networks.

## Consumer-to-Consumer (C2C) E-commerce

**Consumer-to-Consumer (C2C) e-commerce** provides a way for consumers to sell to each other, with the help of an online market maker such as the auction site eBay or the classifieds site Craigslist. Given that in 2010, eBay is expected to generate between $60 to $65 billion in gross merchandise volume around the world, it is probably safe to estimate that the size of the global C2C market in 2010 is over $80 billion (eBay, 2010). In C2C e-commerce, the consumer prepares the product for market, places the product for auction or sale, and relies on the market maker to provide catalog, search engine, and transaction-clearing capabilities so that products can be easily displayed, discovered, and paid for.

**Consumer-to-Consumer (C2C) e-commerce**
consumers selling to other consumers

[1]For the purposes of this text, we subsume Business-to-Government (B2G) e-commerce within B2B e-commerce, viewing the government as simply a form of business when it acts as a procurer of goods and/or services.

### Peer-to-Peer (P2P) E-commerce

Peer-to-peer technology enables Internet users to share files and computer resources directly without having to go through a central Web server. In peer-to-peer's purest form, no intermediary is required, although in fact, most P2P networks make use of intermediary "super servers" to speed operations. Since 1999, entrepreneurs and venture capitalists have attempted to adapt various aspects of peer-to-peer technology into **Peer-to-Peer (P2P) e-commerce**. P2P networks make money by encouraging a very large audience of Internet users to share files, and in the process, expose the audience to advertising messages. P2P networks are in essence advertising networks.

Widely used P2P networks includee BitTorrent (which is used for downloading large video files), eDonkey (used mostly for music files), and The Pirate Bay (see the case study at the end of the chapter). In some countries and regions, P2P network programs account for between 43%–70% of all Internet traffic, but recently P2P file sharing has declined in many countries down to 3% or less as legal streaming services and online music stores gain favor (Naone, 2009).The largest P2P network in the United States is LimeWire, which is facing several law suits over its practices.

### Mobile Commerce (M-commerce)

**Mobile commerce,** or **m-commerce**, refers to the use of wireless digital devices to enable transactions on the Web. Described more fully in Chapter 3, m-commerce involves the use of wireless networks to connect laptops, netbooks, smartphones such the iPhone, Android, and BlackBerry, and iPads to the Web. Once connected, mobile consumers can conduct transactions, including stock trades, in-store price comparisons, banking, travel reservations, and more. M-commerce is expected to grow rapidly in the United States over the next five years.

### GROWTH OF THE INTERNET AND THE WEB

The technology juggernauts behind e-commerce are the Internet and the Web. Without both of these technologies, e-commerce as we know it would be impossible. We describe the Internet and the Web in some detail in Chapter 3. The **Internet** is a worldwide network of computer networks built on common standards. Created in the late 1960s to connect a small number of mainframe computers and their users, the Internet has since grown into the world's largest network. It is impossible to say with certainty exactly how many computers and other wireless access devices such as smartphones are connected to the Internet worldwide at any one time, but the number is clearly over 1 billion. The Internet links businesses, educational institutions, government agencies, and individuals together, and provides users with services such as e-mail, document transfer, shopping, research, instant messaging, music, videos, and news.

**Figure 1.3** illustrates one way to measure the growth of the Internet, by looking at the number of Internet hosts with domain names. (An *Internet host* is defined by the Internet Systems Consortium as any IP address that returns a domain name in the in-addr.arpa domain, which is a special part of the DNS namespace that resolves IP addresses into domain names.) In January 2010, there were over 732 million Internet hosts in over 245 countries, up from just 70 million in 2000 (Internet Systems Consortium, 2010).

---

**Peer-to-Peer (P2P) e-commerce**

use of peer-to-peer technology, which enables Internet users to share files and computer resources directly without having to go through a central Web server, in e-commerce

**mobile commerce (m-commerce)**

use of wireless digital devices to enable transactions on the Web

**Internet**

worldwide network of computer networks built on common standards

The Internet has shown extraordinary growth patterns when compared to other electronic technologies of the past. It took radio 38 years to achieve a 30% share of U.S. households. It took television 17 years to achieve a 30% share. It took only 10 years for the Internet/Web to achieve a 53% share of U.S. households once a graphical user interface was invented for the Web in 1993.

The **World Wide Web (the Web)** is the most popular service that runs on the Internet infrastructure. The Web is the "killer application" that made the Internet

**World Wide Web (the Web)**
the most popular service that runs on the Internet; provides easy access to Web pages

| FIGURE 1.3 | THE GROWTH OF THE INTERNET, MEASURED BY THE NUMBER OF INTERNET HOSTS WITH DOMAIN NAMES |
| --- | --- |

Growth in the size of the Internet 1993–2010 as measured by the number of Internet hosts with domain names.
SOURCE: Internet Systems Consortium, Inc., 2010 (http://www.isc.org).

commercially interesting and extraordinarily popular. The Web was developed in the early 1990s and hence is of much more recent vintage than the Internet. We describe the Web in some detail in Chapter 3. The Web provides access to billions of Web pages indexed by Google and other search engines. These pages are created in a language called *HTML (HyperText Markup Language)*. HTML pages can contain text, graphics, animations, and other objects. You can find an exceptionally wide range of information on Web pages, ranging from the entire catalog of Sears Roebuck, to the entire collection of public records from the Securities and Exchange Commission, to the card catalog of your local library, to millions of music tracks (some of them legal) and videos. The Internet prior to the Web was primarily used for text communications, file transfers, and remote computing. The Web introduced far more powerful and commercially interesting, colorful multimedia capabilities of direct relevance to commerce. In essence, the Web added color, voice, and video to the Internet, creating a communications infrastructure and information storage system that rivals television, radio, magazines, and even libraries.

There is no precise measurement of the number of Web pages in existence, in part because today's search engines index only a portion of the known universe of Web pages, and also because the size of the Web universe is unknown. It is estimated that Google currently indexes between 75–100 billion pages. Google has also reported that its system had, as of July 2008, identified 1 trillion unique URLs, although many of those pages did not necessarily contain unique content. Cuil.com, a rival search engine, claimed in July 2008 to have indexed 120 billion Web pages, "more than 3 times than any other search engine." There are also an estimated 900 billion Web pages in the so-called "deep Web" that are not indexed by ordinary search engines such as Google. What is indisputable, however, is that Web content has grown exponentially since 1993.

Read *Insight on Technology: Spider Webs, Bow Ties, Scale-Free Networks, and the Deep Web* on pages 26–27 for the latest view of researchers on the structure of the Web.

## ORIGINS AND GROWTH OF E-COMMERCE

It is difficult to pinpoint just when e-commerce began. There were several precursors to e-commerce. In the late 1970s, a pharmaceutical firm named Baxter Healthcare initiated a primitive form of B2B e-commerce by using a telephone-based modem that permitted hospitals to reorder supplies from Baxter. This system was later expanded during the 1980s into a PC-based remote order entry system and was widely copied throughout the United States long before the Internet became a commercial environment. The 1980s saw the development of Electronic Data Interchange (EDI) standards that permitted firms to exchange commercial documents and conduct digital commercial transactions across private networks.

In the B2C arena, the first truly large-scale digitally enabled transaction system was deployed in France in 1981. The French Minitel was a videotext system that combined a telephone with an 8-inch screen. By the mid-1980s, more than 3 million Minitels were deployed, and over 13,000 different services were available, including ticket agencies, travel services, retail products, and online banking. The Minitel service continued in existence until December 31, 2006, when it was finally discontinued by its owner, France Telecom.

However, none of these precursor systems had the functionality of the Internet. Generally, when we think of e-commerce today, it is inextricably linked to the Internet. For our purposes, we will say e-commerce begins in 1995, following the appearance of the first banner advertisements placed by AT&T, Volvo, Sprint, and others on Hotwired.com in late October 1994, and the first sales of banner ad space by Netscape and Infoseek in early 1995. Since then, e-commerce has been the fastest growing form of commerce in the United States. **Figure 1.4** and **Figure 1.5** (on page 28) chart the development of B2C e-commerce and B2B e-commerce, respectively, with projections for the next several years. Both graphs show a strong projected growth rate, but the dollar amounts of B2B e-commerce dwarf those of B2C.

## TECHNOLOGY AND E-COMMERCE IN PERSPECTIVE

Although in many respects, e-commerce is new and different, it is also important to keep e-commerce in perspective. First, the Internet and the Web are just two of a long list of technologies that have greatly changed commerce in the United States and

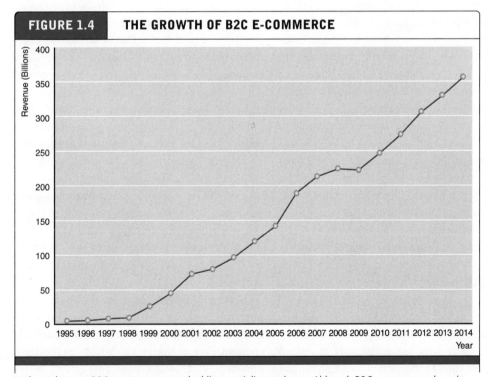

| FIGURE 1.4 | THE GROWTH OF B2C E-COMMERCE |

In the early years, B2C e-commerce was doubling or tripling each year. Although B2C e-commerce slowed to 5% in 2009 due to the economic recession, it has resumed growing at about 12.5% in 2010.

SOURCES: Based on data from eMarketer, Inc., 2010a; authors' estimates.

# INSIGHT ON TECHNOLOGY

## SPIDER WEBS, BOW TIES, SCALE-FREE NETWORKS, AND THE DEEP WEB

In July 2008, Google reported that its system had identified over 1 trillion unique URLs, or Web pages. By 2010 this number has grown to over 2 trillion pages. Although this is a mind-boggling number, consider that it constitutes only a fraction of the entire Web universe. To make matters worse, the number of Web pages is expanding exponentially every year, hindering attempts to catch up, keep up, and truly understand what's out there. Despite this, researchers continue to try.

The World Wide Web conjures up images of a giant spider web where everything is connected to everything else in a random pattern, and you can go from one edge of the Web to another by just following the right links. Theoretically, that's what makes the Web different from a typical index system: you can follow hyperlinks from one page to another. In 1968, sociologist Stanley Milgram put forth the "small-world" theory for social networks by positing that every human was separated from any other human by only six degrees of separation. In the "small world" theory of the Web, every Web page was thought to be separated from any other Web page by an average of about 19 clicks. The theory was supported by early research on a small sampling of Web sites. But subsequent research conducted jointly by scientists at IBM, Compaq, and AltaVista found something entirely different. These scientists used a Web crawler to identify 200 million Web pages and follow 1.5 billion links on those pages.

The researchers discovered that the Web was not like a spider web at all, but rather like a bow tie. The bow-tie Web had a "strongly connected component" (SCC) composed of about 56 million Web pages. On the right side of the bow tie was a set of 44 million OUT pages that you could get to from the center, but could not return to the center from. OUT pages tended to be corporate intranet and other Web site pages that are designed to trap you at the site when you land. On the left side of the bow tie was a set of 44 million IN pages from which you could get to the center, but that you could not travel to from the center. These were recently created pages that had not yet been linked to by many center pages. In addition, 43 million pages were classified as "tendrils," pages that did not link to the center and could not be linked to from the center. Finally, there were 16 million pages totally disconnected from everything.

Further evidence for the non-random and structured nature of the Web is provided in research performed by Albert-Lazlo Barabasi at the University of Notre Dame. Barabasi's team found that far from being a random, exponentially exploding network of billions of Web pages, activity on the Web was actually highly concentrated in "very-connected super nodes" that provided the connectivity to less well-connected nodes. Barabasi dubbed this type of network a "scale-free" network. As its turns out, scale-free networks are highly vulnerable to destruction: destroy their super nodes, and transmission of messages breaks down rapidly. On the upside, if you are a marketer trying to "spread the message" about your products, place your products on one of the super nodes and watch the news spread.

More recently researchers at the University of Michigan found the Web had significantly changed shape in the period 2005-2010. Rapid growth and consolidation of backbone telecommunications providers, a consolidation of applications (video will account for 90% of Web traffic in 2014), and expansion of cloud computing and huge data centers, has created a Web where a significant part

(continued)

of Internet traffic does not flow through the backbone networks of giant Internet companies like AT&T or Level 3. Rather, so-called "hyper-giant" companies such as Google, Yahoo, Comcast, Amazon, and IBM are hooking their networks together in "peering arrangements." A significant part of Web traffic now occurs at the edges in what some call "fat tubes."

Thus, the picture of the Web that emerges from this research is quite different from earlier reports. The notion that most pairs of Web pages are separated by a handful of links, almost always under 20, and that the number of connections would grow exponentially with the size of the Web, is not supported. In fact, there is a 75% chance that there is no path from one randomly chosen page to another. The early notion that Internet traffic moves freely across a network of routers, choosing whatever path happens to work and be available, is replaced by the notion that today's Internet traffic moves along a small number of very big highways, say, from Amazon to IBM cloud computing centers, or Google's YouTube and Akamai's edge network. The big nodes of the past have become the hyper-giants of the present. The rich have become richer.

The problem becomes more severe as the Internet goes global. Google's English language crawler does not crawl Chinese Web sites, and you will rarely see a Chinese language answer to a Google English query. The crawlable Web of about 1 trillion pages is only some unknown part a much larger "deep Web," which arguably could include another 1 trillion pages or more that are not indexed at all. These pages are not easily accessible to Web crawlers that most search engine companies use. Instead, these pages are either proprietary (not available to crawlers and non-subscribers), such as the pages of *The Wall Street Journal*, airline schedule and price information, and medical research findings, or are stuck in databases that themselves are not linked to other pages. The existence of the deep Web means that search engines are often unable to answer common questions like "What's the cheapest fare to Europe from New York this week?" Several groups such as Deeppeep.org are investigating the deep Web.

Given this new understanding of the structure of the Web, the implications for entrepreneurs and marketers are clear. Because e-commerce revenues inherently depend on customers being able to find a Web site using search engines, Web site managers need to take steps to ensure their Web pages are part of the connected central core, or "super nodes," of the Web. One way to do this is to make sure the site has as many links as possible to and from other relevant sites, especially to other sites within the SCC. If your site is part of the deep Web, get out, and make it more accessible to crawlers. If you want to be global, develop foreign language versions of your main site. If you want to optimize your search engine rankings, put a lot of links on your pages to pages on other sites (become a hub). Last, get as many other sites to link to your pages as you possibly can (become an authority). It's called search engine optimization, and the more you know about the structure of the real Internet, the more effective your Web sites will be.

**SOURCES:** "Scientists Strive to Map the Shaper-Shifting Net," by John Markoff; *New York Times*, March 1, 2010; "Atlas Internet Observatory Report," by C. Labovitz , S. Lekel-Johnson, D. McPherson (Arbor Networks), J Oberheide (University of Michigan), and M. Karir (Merit Network, Inc.). Arbornetworks.com, 2010; Deeppeep.org, "About Us," August 2009; Kosmix.com, "About Kosmix," August 2009; "III-COR Discovering and Organizing Hidden-Web Sources," by Juliana Freire, University of Utah. Grant application. National Science Foundation, IIS Division of Information & Intelligent Systems, IIS -0713637. April 2009; "Exploring a 'Deep Web' That Google Can't Grasp," by Alex Wright, *New York Times*, February 23, 2009; "Invisible or Deep Web: What it is, Why it exists, How to find it, and Its inherent ambiguity," www.lib.berkeley.edu, accessed August, 2008; "Accessing the Deep Web," by Bin He, Mitesh Patel, Zhen Zhang, and Kevin Chen-Chuan Chang; *Communications of the ACM (CACM)* 50 (2): 94–101, May 2007; "The Bowtie Theory Explains Link Popularity," by John Heard, Searchengineposition.com, June 1, 2000.

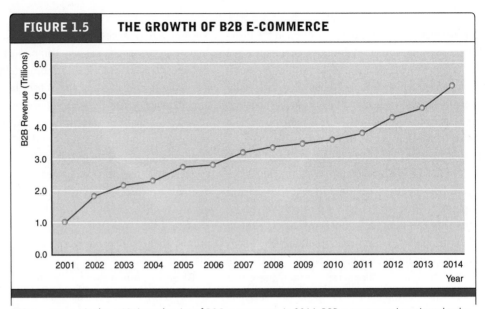

**FIGURE 1.5** | **THE GROWTH OF B2B E-COMMERCE**

B2B e-commerce is about 10 times the size of B2C e-commerce. In 2014, B2B e-commerce is projected to be about $5.2 trillion. (Note: Does not include EDI transactions.)

SOURCES: Based on data from U.S. Census Bureau, 2010b; authors' estimates.

around the world. Each of these other technologies spawned business models and strategies designed to leverage the technology into commercial advantage and profit. They were also accompanied by explosive early growth, which was characterized by the emergence of thousands of entrepreneurial start-up companies, followed by painful retrenchment, and then a long-term successful exploitation of the technology by larger established firms. In the case of automobiles, for instance, in 1915, there were over 250 automobile manufacturers in the United States. By 1940, there were five. In the case of radio, in 1925, there were over 2,000 radio stations across the United States, with most broadcasting to local neighborhoods and run by amateurs. By 1990, there were fewer than 500 independent stations. There is every reason to believe e-commerce will follow the same pattern—with notable differences discussed throughout the text.

Second, although e-commerce has grown explosively, there is no guarantee it will continue to grow forever at these rates and much reason to believe e-commerce growth will cap as it confronts its own fundamental limitations. For instance, B2C e-commerce is still a small part (a little over 6%) of the overall $3.9 trillion retail market. Under current projections, in 2013, all of B2C commerce will still be less than Walmart's 2008 revenue. Wal-Mart is the world's largest and most successful retailer. On the other hand, with only 6% of all retail sales revenue now being generated online, there is tremendous upside potential. At current double digit growth rates, e-commerce will be 20% of all retail commerce by 2020.

## POTENTIAL LIMITATIONS ON THE GROWTH OF B2C E-COMMERCE

The data suggests that, over the next five years, B2C e-commerce will continue to grow by about 10% annually, slower than in earlier years, but much faster than traditional retail sales (about 4%). Nevertheless, there are several reasons to believe that e-commerce revenues from goods and services together will not expand forever at these rates. As online sales become a larger percentage of all sales, which typically grow in the 5%–6% range annually, online sales growth will likely decline to that growth level. This point still appears to be a long way off. Online service sales, everything from music, to video, medical information, games, and entertainment, have an even longer period to grow before they hit any ceiling effects.

There are other limitations on B2C e-commerce that have the potential to cap its growth rate and ultimate size. **Table 1.4** describes some of these limiting factors.

Some limitations may be minimized in the next decade. For instance, the price of an entry-level computer such as a netbook has fallen to $200 to $300, although this still represents a substantial amount of money to many. Other Internet-client devices such as smartphones are within this price range now. This, coupled with enhancements in capabilities such as integration with television, access to entertainment film libraries on a pay-per-view basis, and other software enhancements, will likely raise U.S. Internet household penetration rates to the level of cable television penetration (about 80%) by 2014. The PC operating system will also likely evolve from the current

| TABLE 1.4 | LIMITATIONS ON THE GROWTH OF B2C E-COMMERCE |
|---|---|
| **LIMITING FACTOR** | **COMMENT** |
| Expensive technology | Using the Internet requires an investment of at least $200 to $300 for a computer and a connect charge ranging from about $10 to $50 depending on the speed of service. |
| Sophisticated skill set | The skills required to make effective use of the Internet and e-commerce capabilities are far more sophisticated than, say, for television or newspapers. |
| Persistent cultural attraction of physical markets and traditional shopping experiences | For many, shopping is a cultural and social event where people meet directly with merchants and other consumers. This social experience has not yet been fully duplicated in digital form (although social shopping is a major new development). |
| Persistent global inequality limiting access to telephones and personal computers | Much of the world's population does not have telephone service, PCs, or cell phones. |
| Saturation and ceiling effects | Growth in the Internet population slows as its approaches the size of the total population. |

Windows platform to far simpler interfaces similar to that found on iPhones and Palm OS handheld devices.

The most significant technology that can reduce barriers to Internet access is wireless Web technology (described in more detail in Chapter 3). Today, consumers can access the Internet via a variety of different mobile devices, such as mobile computers (laptops and netbooks), smartphones, and iPads. In 2010, almost 83 million people (around 37% of Internet users in the United States) use a mobile device to access the Internet, and this number is expected to grow to 126 million by 2013 (eMarketer, Inc., 2010b). **Figure 1.6** illustrates the rapid growth projected for mobile Internet access during the period 2008–2013.

On balance, the current technological limits on e-commerce growth, while real, are likely to recede in importance over the next decade. The social and cultural limitations of e-commerce are less likely to change as quickly, but the Web is fast developing virtual social shopping experiences and virtual realities that millions find as entertaining as shopping or seeing their friends face-to-face.

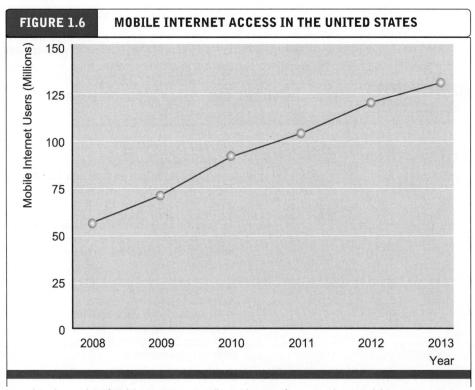

**FIGURE 1.6**  **MOBILE INTERNET ACCESS IN THE UNITED STATES**

Growth in the number of mobile Internet users will provide a significant stimulus to mobile e-commerce.
SOURCES: Based on data from eMarketer, Inc., 2010b.

## 1.2  E-COMMERCE: A BRIEF HISTORY

Although e-commerce is not very old, it already has a tumultuous history. The history of e-commerce can be usefully divided into three periods. The early years of e-commerce were a period of explosive growth and extraordinary innovation, beginning in 1995 with the first widespread use of the Web to advertise products. This period of explosive growth was capped in March 2000 when stock market valuations for dot-com companies reached their peak and thereafter began to collapse. A sobering period of reassessment occurred, followed by strong double-digit growth. In 2006, e-commerce entered a period of redefinition with the appearance of social networks and user-generated content sharing Web sites that have attracted huge audiences.

### E-COMMERCE 1995–2000: INNOVATION

The early years of e-commerce were one of the most euphoric of times in American commercial history. It was also a time when key e-commerce concepts were developed and explored. Thousands of dot-com companies were formed, backed by over $125 billion in financial capital—one of the largest outpourings of venture capital in United States history. **Figure 1.7** (on page 32) depicts the amounts invested by venture capital firms in Internet-related businesses in the period 1995–2009. While venture investment has trended markedly lower since 2000, it is still significantly larger than pre-1996 levels, and investing in dot-com and Internet businesses has begun to increase once again in 2010 after dramatically decreasing in the latter half of 2008 and early 2009 due to the recession (PricewaterhouseCoopers, National Venture Capital Association Moneytree Report, Data: Thomson Financial, 2010).

For computer scientists and information technologists, the early success of e-commerce was a powerful vindication of a set of information technologies that had developed over a period of 40 years—extending from the development of the early Internet to the PC, to local area networks. The vision was of a universal communications and computing environment that everyone on Earth could access with cheap, inexpensive computers—a worldwide universe of knowledge stored on HTML pages created by hundreds of millions of individuals and thousands of libraries, governments, and scientific institutes. Technologists celebrated the fact that the Internet was not controlled by anyone or any nation, but was free to all. They believed the Internet—and the e-commerce that rose on this infrastructure—should remain a self-governed, self-regulated environment.

For economists, the early years of e-commerce raised the realistic prospect of a nearly perfect competitive market: where price, cost, and quality information is equally distributed, a nearly infinite set of suppliers compete against one another, and customers have access to all relevant market information worldwide. The Internet would spawn digital markets where information would be nearly perfect—something that is rarely true in other real-world markets. Merchants in turn would have equal direct access to hundreds of millions of customers. In this near-perfect information marketspace, transaction costs would plummet because search costs—the cost of searching for prices, product descriptions, payment settlement, and

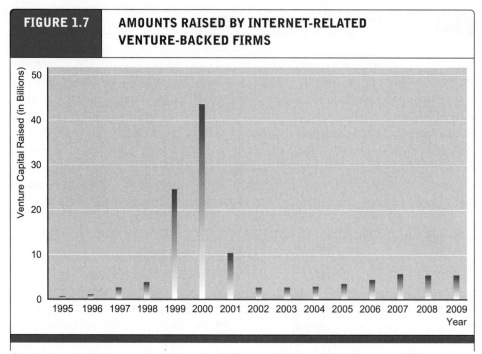

**FIGURE 1.7  AMOUNTS RAISED BY INTERNET-RELATED VENTURE-BACKED FIRMS**

The amounts raised by Internet-related venture-backed firms peaked during the 1999–2001 period, but the amount raised in the 2002–2009 period is still much higher than that raised in the periods prior to 1999.

SOURCES: Based on data from PricewaterhouseCoopers/National Venture Capital Association MoneyTree Report, Data: Thomson Financial, 2010.

**disintermediation**
displacement of market middlemen who traditionally are intermediaries between producers and consumers by a new direct relationship between manufacturers and content originators with their customers

order fulfillment—would all fall drastically (Bakos, 1997). New shopping bot programs would automatically search the entire Web for the best prices and delivery times. For merchants, the cost of searching for customers would also fall, reducing the need for wasteful advertising. At the same time, advertisements could be personalized to the needs of every customer. Prices and even costs would be increasingly transparent to the consumer, who could now know exactly and instantly the worldwide best price, quality, and availability of most products. Information asymmetry would be greatly reduced. Given the instant nature of Internet communications, the availability of powerful sales information systems, and the low cost involved in changing prices on a Web site (low menu costs), producers could dynamically price their products to reflect actual demand, ending the idea of one national price, or one suggested manufacturer's list price. In turn, market middlemen—the distributors, wholesalers, and other factors in the marketplace who are intermediates between producers and consumers, each demanding a payment and raising costs while adding little value—would disappear (**disintermediation**). Manufacturers and content originators would develop direct market relationships with their customers. The resulting intense competition, the decline of intermediaries, and the lower transaction costs would eliminate product brands, and along with it, the possibility of *monopoly profits* based on brands, geography, or special access to factors of production. Prices for products and services would fall to the point where prices covered costs of production plus a fair, "market rate" of return on capital, plus additional small payments for entrepreneurial effort (that would not last long). Unfair competitive advantages (which occur when one competitor has an advantage others cannot purchase) would be eliminated, as would extraordinary returns on invested capital. This vision was called **friction-free commerce** (Smith et al., 2000).

For real-world entrepreneurs, their financial backers, and marketing professionals, the idea of friction-free commerce was far from their own visions. For these players, e-commerce represented an extraordinary opportunity to earn far above normal returns on investment. The e-commerce marketspace represented access to millions of consumers worldwide who used the Internet and a set of marketing communications technologies (e-mail and Web pages) that was universal, inexpensive, and powerful. These new technologies would permit marketers to practice what they always had done—segmenting the market into groups with different needs and price sensitivity, targeting the segments with branding and promotional messages, and positioning the product and pricing for each group—but with even more precision. In this new marketspace, extraordinary profits would go to **first movers**—those firms who were first to market in a particular area and who moved quickly to gather market share. In a "winner take all" market, first movers could establish a large customer base quickly, build brand name recognition early, create an entirely new distribution channel, and then inhibit competitors (new entrants) by building in *switching costs* for their customers through proprietary interface designs and features available only at one site. The idea for entrepreneurs was to create near monopolies online based on size, convenience, selection, and brand. Online businesses using the new technology could create informative, community-like features unavailable to traditional merchants. These "communities of consumption" also would add value and be difficult for traditional merchants to imitate. The thinking was that once customers became accustomed to using a company's unique Web interface and feature set, they could not easily be switched to competitors. In the best case, the entrepreneurial firm would invent proprietary technologies and techniques that almost everyone adopted, creating a network effect. A **network effect** occurs where all participants receive value from the fact that everyone else uses the same tool or product (for example, a common operating system, telephone system, or software application such as a proprietary instant messaging standard or an operating system such as Windows), all of which increase in value as more people adopt them.[2] Successful first movers would become the new intermediaries of e-commerce, displacing traditional retail merchants and suppliers of content, and becoming profitable by charging fees of one sort or another for the value customers perceived in their services and products.

To initiate this process, entrepreneurs argued that prices would have to be very low to attract customers and fend off potential competitors. E-commerce was, after all, a totally new way of shopping that would have to offer some immediate cost benefits to consumers. However, because doing business on the Web was supposedly so much more efficient when compared to traditional "bricks-

**friction-free commerce**
a vision of commerce in which information is equally distributed, transaction costs are low, prices can be dynamically adjusted to reflect actual demand, intermediaries decline, and unfair competitive advantages are eliminated

**first mover**
a firm that is first to market in a particular area and that moves quickly to gather market share

**network effect**
occurs where users receive value from the fact that everyone else uses the same tool or product

---

[2] The network effect is quantified by Metcalfe's Law, which argues that the value of a network grows by the square of the number of participants.

and-mortar" businesses (even when compared to the direct mail catalog business) and because the costs of customer acquisition and retention would supposedly be so much lower, profits would inevitably materialize out of these efficiencies. Given these dynamics, market share, the number of visitors to a site ("eyeballs"), and gross revenue became far more important in the earlier stages of an online firm than earnings or profits. Entrepreneurs and their financial backers in the early years of e-commerce expected that extraordinary profitability would come, but only after several years of losses.

Thus, the early years of e-commerce were driven largely by visions of profiting from new technology, with the emphasis on quickly achieving very high market visibility. The source of financing was venture capital funds. The ideology of the period emphasized the ungoverned "Wild West" character of the Web and the feeling that governments and courts could not possibly limit or regulate the Internet; there was a general belief that traditional corporations were too slow and bureaucratic, too stuck in the old ways of doing business, to "get it"—to be competitive in e-commerce. Young entrepreneurs were therefore the driving force behind e-commerce, backed by huge amounts of money invested by venture capitalists. The emphasis was on *deconstructing* (destroying) traditional distribution channels and disintermediating existing channels, using new pure online companies who aimed to achieve impregnable first-mover advantages. Overall, this period of e-commerce was characterized by experimentation, capitalization, and hypercompetition (Varian, 2000a). Read *Insight on Business: 'Noodlenomics' Guides Internet Investment in 2010* for a further look at the financing of e-commerce ventures.

The crash in stock market values for Internet-related companies throughout 2000 is a convenient marker for ending the early period in the development of e-commerce. Looking back at the first years of e-commerce, it is apparent that e-commerce has been, for the most part, a stunning technological success as the Internet and the Web ramped up from a few thousand to billions of e-commerce transactions per year, generating $256 billion in B2C revenues and around $3.6 trillion in B2B revenues in 2010, with around 133 million online buyers in the United States. With enhancements and strengthening, described in later chapters, it is clear that e-commerce's digital infrastructure is solid enough to sustain significant growth in e-commerce during the next decade. The Internet scales well. The "e" in e-commerce has been an overwhelming success.

From a business perspective, though, the early years of e-commerce were a mixed success, and offered many surprises. Only about 10% of dot-coms formed since 1995 have survived as independent companies in 2010. Only a very tiny percentage of these survivors are profitable. Yet online B2C sales of goods and services are still growing. Consumers have learned to use the Web as a powerful source of information about products they actually purchase through other channels, such as at a traditional "bricks-and-mortar" store. This is especially true of expensive consumer durables such as appliances, automobiles, and electronics. This "Internet-influenced" commerce is very difficult to estimate, but was believed to have been somewhere around $917 billion in 2009 (Forrester Research, 2010). Altogether then, B2C e-commerce (both actual purchases and purchases influenced by Web shopping but actually buying in a store)

# INSIGHT ON BUSINESS

## 'NOODLENOMICS' GUIDES INTERNET INVESTMENT IN 2010

It's reasonable to think that in the midst of the worst global recession since the 1930s, speculative investments in Internet start-ups would come to a complete halt. But this did not happen, even though Internet-related venture capital deals in 2009 fell 39% from 2008 levels, and along with all other industries, experienced the lowest venture capital investment level since 1997. First quarter results for 2010 are more promising, as venture capital flows are down only 14% from 2009. Oddly, from a stock investor's point of view, the tech sector was the place to be in 2009 and 2010: tech stocks advanced 59% in 2009 compared to 23% for the broader S&P 500 index. Tech stocks are hot.

While overall venture investment in Internet companies declined significantly in the recession, some Internet start-ups received impressive investments or were purchased in 2009 and 2010. Intuit bought the online accounting start-up Mint.com for $170 million. Evernote.com, an online application for keeping track of notes and business cards, raised $10 million. OpenTable successfully went public. Bookrenter.com raised $10 million in May 2010 as textbook rentals expanded.

E-commerce was built on Internet technology, but what makes it run is money—or at least did make it run. Between 1998 and 2000, venture capitalists (VCs) poured an estimated $120 billion into approximately 12,450 dot-com start-up ventures. Investment bankers then took 1,262 of these companies public in what is called an initial public offering (IPO) of stock. To prepare for an IPO, investment bankers analyze a company's finances and business plans and attempt to arrive at an estimate of the company's "worth"—how much the investing public might be willing to pay for the shares and how many shares might be purchased by the public and other institutions.

The bankers then underwrite the stock offering and sell the stock on a public stock exchange, making enormous fees for underwriting in the process. The basic process has not changed over time, but the style and fashions have changed since the good old "bad days" of e-commerce.

In the early years of e-commerce, from 1998 to 2000, dot-com IPO shares often skyrocketed within minutes of hitting the trading floor. Some shares tripled and quadrupled in the first day, and a 50% "pump" (or increase in value) was considered just a reasonable showing. Therefore, getting in on the ground floor of an IPO—which meant arranging to purchase a fixed number of shares prior to actual trading on the first day—was a privilege reserved for other large institutions, friends of the investment bankers, or other investment bankers. In what was called "stock spinning," the underwriter would sell IPO shares to entrepreneurs it hoped to obtain business from in the future. The Securities and Exchange Commission made this practice illegal in 1999.

What has happened to the dot-com IPOs of this period? According to a financial services research firm, Thomson Financial, 12% of the companies that went public between 1998 and 2000 were trading at $1 or less a share in April 2001, a fairly shocking development when one considers that just a relatively short time previously, those companies' shares were trading at upwards of 10 to 100 times that price. By 2007, seven years after the peak of the dot-com frenzy, at least 5,000 Internet companies had either been acquired or shut down. On a more positive note, research shows that the attrition rate of these early firms was about 20% a year, on par with what occurred in other industries during their early boom years. More than half the early dot-coms were still in business in 2007.

(continued)

After the big bust of March 2000, the Thermidor period began. Venture capitalists turned away from the "Get Big Fast" and "First-Mover Advantage" religion, and instead focused on companies that demonstrated a profitable prior history. In this second period, investors spent over $200 billion on the purchase of over 4,000 Web companies. Hot properties included Internet retail shopping sites (such as Shopping.com, purchased for $620 million by eBay, and Shopzilla, purchased for $525 million by The E.W. Scripps Company), Internet advertising firms (such as DoubleClick, purchased for $1.1 billion by buyout firm Hellman & Friedman), search engine properties (such as Ask Jeeves [now Ask.com], purchased by IAC/InterActive Corp for $1.85 billion), and community sites (such as About.com, purchased by The New York Times for $410 million). The iconic event of this period, however, was Google's IPO in late 2004. Google had been profitable for three years before going public , and its search-based advertising model was churning out profits. Social networks were just beginning and few thought there was any money in it. Yet in July 2005, Rupert Murdoch's News Corp.'s Fox Interactive Media division purchased MySpace for the unheard of price of $580 million.

By 2006, the period of fiscal discipline began to end, and VCs started once again to make big plays for "get big fast" companies. Tech was "in" again, and once again, audience size became the most important investment criteria. Google's shares soared from its $85 offering price in 2004 to almost $750 in November 2007. About 62% of tech firms going public in 2006-2008 were not profitable companies (still short of the all-time 85% unprofitable in 2000). So far, the king of the Get Big Fast mentality remains YouTube, an unprofitable company with an estimated $200 million in revenue in 2008, for which Google paid $1.65 billion in the belief that YouTube's then 32 million users would be worth something in the future. With a $30 billion cash hoard at the time, this was a small price to pay for a potential gold mine, at least from Google's perspective. Wall Street got the message.

Google's purchase of YouTube put the stamp of approval on what some investors have called the "social networking bubble." Sites such as Facebook, which began in 2004 with a series of small investments from venture capital firms, started receiving huge investments not from VCs but from private equity firms and established giants such as Microsoft. The reasoning behind these investments was the same as Google's: social network sites are "winner take all" markets where, once a firm establishes a lead position, others sites simply cannot compete, and soon a single winner emerges while the rest consolidate or close their doors. In late 2008 and all of 2009, with the decline in the economy, venture capital investments dropped off the table, to levels not seen since 1997. The IPO market virtually shut down for e-commerce and Internet firms. In a hopeful sign, however, angel investors who make investments in early stage start-ups continued to make hundreds of investments in the $500,000 to $1 million range. Helped by the fact that the cost of building new Web sites has fallen drastically from the early days, small investments using today's technology are sufficient to test the viability of an idea on the Internet. The emphasis in 2010 is on LILOs: a little money in, a lot of money out. Investors are looking for "ramen sites" based on "noodlenomics" where firms have enough sales and low costs to make it through the recession. E-commerce start-ups of today tend to be more driven by solid ideas tested on a small scale, rather than big-money investments on totally untried ideas.

**SOURCES:** "Bookrenter Binds Up $10M More As Textbook Rentals Spread," by Tomio Geron, *Wall Street Journal*, June 3, 2010; "Venture Capital Investing Has Modest Start in 2010 Amidst Economic and Market Uncertainty," National Venture Capital Association and PriceWaterhouseCoopers, press release, April 16, 2010; "Mint.com: Nurtured by Super-Angel VCs," by Spencer Ante, *BusinessWeek*, September 15, 2009; "The New Internet Start-Up Boom: Get Rich Slow," by Josh Quittner, *Time Magazine*, April 9, 2009; "OpenTable IPO Lifts Hopes on the Stock Exchange," by Deborah Gage, SFGate.com, May 22, 2009; "Was There Too Little Entry During the Dot Com Era?" by Brent Goldfarb, David Kirsch, and David Miller, Robert H. Smith School Research Paper No. RHS 06-029, April 24, 2006.

amounts to over $1 trillion in 2010, or about 25% of total retail sales. The "commerce" in e-commerce is basically very sound, at least in the sense of attracting a growing number of customers and generating revenues.

## E-COMMERCE 2001–2006: CONSOLIDATION

E-commerce entered a period of consolidation beginning in 2001 and lasting until 2006. Emphasis shifted to a more "business-driven" approach rather than technology driven; large traditional firms learned how to use the Web to strengthen their market positions; brand extension and strengthening became more important than creating new brands; financing shrunk as capital markets shunned start-up firms; and traditional bank financing based on profitability returned.

## E-COMMERCE 2006—PRESENT: REINVENTION

E-commerce entered a third period in 2006 that extends through the present day and into the uncertain future. Google has been one of the driving forces, but so have other large media firms who have quickly bought out very fast-moving entrepreneurial firms, such as MySpace. It is a period of reinvention involving the extension of Internet technologies, and the discovery of new business models based on consumer-generated content and social networks. This period is as much a sociological phenomenon as it is a technological or business phenomenon. Few of the new models have been able to monetize their huge audiences into profitable operations yet, but many eventually will.

**Table 1.5** summarizes e-commerce in each of these three periods.

## ASSESSING E-COMMERCE: SUCCESSES, SURPRISES, AND FAILURES

Although e-commerce has grown at an extremely rapid pace in customers and revenues, it is clear that many of the visions, predictions, and assertions about e-commerce developed in the early years have not have been fulfilled. For instance, economists' visions of "friction-free" commerce have not been entirely realized. Prices are sometimes lower on the Web, but the low prices are sometimes a function of entrepreneurs selling products below their costs. Consumers are less price sensitive than expected; surprisingly, the Web sites with the highest revenue often have the highest prices. There remains considerable persistent and even increasing price dispersion on the Web: the difference between the lowest price and the average price for a basket of goods increased from 8% of the average price in 2000 to 10% in 2010 (Nash-equilibrium.com, 2010). In other words, the standard deviation in Web prices is about 10% of the average price for the same product on the Web. Shop around! The concept of one world, one market, one price has not occurred in reality as entrepreneurs discover new ways to differentiate their products and services. While for the most part Internet prices save consumers about 20% on average when compared to in-store prices, sometimes prices on the Web are higher than for similar products purchased offline, especially if shipping costs are considered. For instance, prices on books and CDs vary by as much as 50%, and prices for airline tickets as much as 20% (Baye, 2004; Baye, et al., 2004; Bailey, 1998a, b; Brynjolfsson and Smith, 2000; Aguiar and Hurst, 2008; Alessandria, 2009). Merchants have adjusted to the competitive Internet environment by engaging in

| TABLE 1.5 | EVOLUTION OF E-COMMERCE | |
|---|---|---|
| 1995–2000 INNOVATION | 2001–2006 CONSOLIDATION | 2006–PRESENT RE-INVENTION |
| Technology driven | Business driven | Audience, customer, and community driven |
| Revenue growth emphasis | Earnings and profits emphasis | Audience and social network growth emphasis |
| Venture capital financing | Traditional financing | Smaller VC investments; early small-firm buyouts by large online players |
| Ungoverned | Stronger regulation and governance | Extensive government surveillance |
| Entrepreneurial | Large traditional firms | Large pure Web-based firms |
| Disintermediation | Strengthening intermediaries | Proliferation of small online intermediaries renting business processes of larger firms |
| Perfect markets | Imperfect markets, brands, and network effects | Continuation of online market imperfections; commodity competition in select markets |
| Pure online strategies | Mixed "bricks-and-clicks" strategies | Return of pure online strategies in new markets; extension of bricks and clicks in traditional retail markets |
| First-mover advantages | Strategic-follower strength; complimentary assets | First-mover advantages return in new markets as traditional Web players catch up |
| Low-complexity retail products | High-complexity retail products | Services |

"hit-and-run pricing" or changing prices every day or hour so competitors never know what they are charging (neither do customers); by making their prices hard to discover and sowing confusion among consumers by "baiting and switching" customers from low-margin products to high-margin products with supposedly "higher quality." Finally, brands remain very important in e-commerce—consumers trust some firms more than others to deliver a high-quality product on time (Slatalla, 2005).

The "perfect competition" model of extreme market efficiency has not come to pass. Merchants and marketers are continually introducing information asymmetries. Search costs have fallen overall, but the overall transaction cost of actually completing a transaction in e-commerce remains high because users have a bewildering number of new questions to consider: Will the merchant actually deliver? What is the time frame of delivery? Does the merchant really stock this item? How do I fill out this form? Many potential e-commerce purchases are terminated in the shopping cart stage because of these consumer uncertainties. For some product areas, it is easier to call a trusted catalog merchant on the telephone than order on a Web site. Finally, intermediaries have not disappeared as predicted. Most manufacturers, for instance, have not adopted the Dell model of online sales (direct sales by the manufacturer to the consumer), and Dell itself has moved towards a mixed model heavily reliant on in-store sales where customers can "kick the tires" by trying the keyboard and viewing the screen. Apple Stores are very successful physical retail locations, and marketing devices. People still like to shop in a physical store.

If anything, e-commerce has created many opportunities for middlemen to aggregate content, products, and services into portals and search engines and thereby introduce themselves as the "new" intermediaries. Yahoo, MSN, and Amazon, along with third-party travel sites such as Travelocity, Orbitz and Expedia, are all examples of this kind of intermediary. As illustrated in **Figure 1.8**, e-commerce did not drive existing retail chains and catalog merchants out of business, although it has created opportunities for entrepreneurial Web-only firms to succeed. In fact, retail chain stores account for more online sales than the pure online companies.

The visions of many entrepreneurs and venture capitalists for e-commerce have not materialized exactly as predicted either. First-mover advantage appears to have succeeded only for a very small group of sites. Historically, first movers have been long-term losers, with the early-to-market innovators usually being displaced by established "fast-follower" firms with the right complement of financial, marketing, legal, and production assets needed to develop mature markets, and this has proved true for e-commerce as well. Many e-commerce first movers, such as eToys, FogDog (sporting goods), WebVan (groceries), and Eve.com (beauty products) are out of business. Customer acquisition and retention costs during the early years of e-commerce were

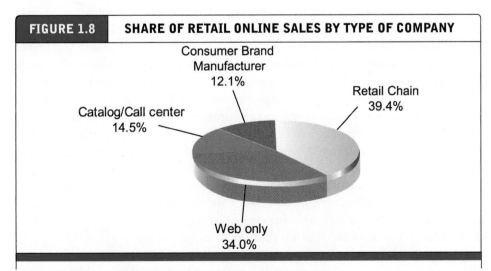

| FIGURE 1.8 | SHARE OF RETAIL ONLINE SALES BY TYPE OF COMPANY |

Consumer Brand Manufacturer 12.1%

Retail Chain 39.4%

Catalog/Call center 14.5%

Web only 34.0%

Web-only firms account for less than one-third of online retail firm revenues.
SOURCES: Based on data from Iternet Retailer, 2010; eMarketer, Inc., 2010c.

extraordinarily high, with some firms, such as E*Trade and other financial service firms, paying up to $400 to acquire a new customer. The overall costs of doing business on the Web—including the costs of technology, site design and maintenance, and warehouses for fulfillment—are no lower than the costs faced by the most efficient bricks-and-mortar stores. A large warehouse costs tens of millions of dollars regardless of a firm's Web presence. The knowledge of how to run the warehouse is priceless, and not easily moved. The start-up costs can be staggering. Attempting to achieve profitability by raising prices has often led to large customer defections. From the e-commerce merchant's perspective, the "e" in e-commerce does not stand for "easy."

## PREDICTIONS FOR THE FUTURE: MORE SURPRISES

Given that e-commerce has changed greatly in the last several years, its future cannot be predicted except to say "Watch for more surprises." There are five main factors that will help define the future of e-commerce. First, there is little doubt that the technology of e-commerce—the Internet, the Web, and the growing number of wireless Internet devices that make up the emerging "mobile digital platform," including smartphones such as the iPhone, Android, and BlackBerry, and iPads, will continue to propagate through all commercial activity. After a flat year in 2009, the overall revenues from e-commerce (goods and services) are expected to continue to rise in 2010 and beyond, most likely in the range of 10%–12% per year through 2014. The number of products and services sold on the Web and the size of the average purchase order will both continue to grow at near double-digit rates. The number of online shoppers in the United States will also continue to grow, although at a more modest rate of less than 5% per year. There has also been a significant broadening of the online product mix compared to the early years when books, computer software, and hardware dominated e-commerce (see **Table 1.6**). This trend will continue as trust in e-commerce transactions grows. (See Chapter 9 for changes in retail products and services.)

Second, e-commerce prices will rise to cover the real costs of doing business on the Web, to price-in the benefits provided to customers shopping online, and to pay investors a reasonable rate of return on their capital. Third, e-commerce *margins* (the difference between the revenues from sales and the cost of goods) and profits will rise to levels more typical of all retailers. Fourth, the cast of players will change radically. Traditional well-endowed, experienced Fortune 500 companies will play a growing and dominant role in e-commerce while at the same time new start-up ventures will quickly gain large online audiences for new products and services not dominated by the large players. There will also be a continuation of audience consolidation on the Internet in general, with the top 25 sites garnering over 90% of the audience share, and nearly one-third of all online sales. **Table 1.7** lists the top 25 online retailers, as ranked by 2009 online sales. The table shows an unmistakable trend toward the appearance of some very well-known, traditional brands from strong traditional businesses, with Staples, Office Depot, OfficeMax, Sears, Best Buy, Sony, Costco, Wal-Mart and Hewlett Packard all in the top 15.

Fifth, the number of successful pure online companies will remain smaller than integrated online/offline stores that combine traditional sales channels such as physical stores and printed catalogs with online efforts. For instance, traditional

| TABLE 1.6 | ONLINE RETAIL SALES BY CATEGORY, 2009 |
|---|---|

| CATEGORY | ANNUAL SALES (IN BILLIONS) |
|---|---|
|  | **2009** |
| Mass merchant/Department store | $43.6 |
| Computers/Electronics | $23.8 |
| Office supplies | $17.6 |
| Apparel/Accessories | $14.9 |
| Books/CDs/DVDs | $4.7 |
| Housewares/Home furnishings | $3.5 |
| Health/Beauty | $3.5 |
| Hardware/Home improvement | $2.8 |
| Specialty/non apparel | $2.7 |
| Food/Drug | $2.7 |
| Flower/Gifts | $2.7 |
| Sporting goods | $1.8 |
| Toys/Hobbies | $1.3 |
| Jewelry | $1.1 |

SOURCES: Based on data from Internet Retailer, 2010; authors' estimates.

catalog sales firms such as L.L.Bean have transformed themselves into integrated online and direct mail firms with more than half of their sales coming from the online channel. Procter & Gamble will continue to develop informative Web sites such as Tide.com; and the major automotive companies will continue to improve the content and value of their Web sites even if they do not enter into direct sales relationships with consumers, but instead use the Web to assist sales through dealers (thereby strengthening traditional intermediaries and channels).

The future of e-commerce will include the growth of regulatory activity both in the United States and worldwide. Governments around the world are challenging the early vision of computer scientists and information technologists that the Internet should be a self-regulating and self-governing phenomenon. The Internet and e-commerce have been so successful and powerful, so all-pervasive, that they directly involve the social, cultural, and political life of entire nations and cultures. Throughout history, whenever technologies have risen to this level of social importance, power, and visibility, they become the target of efforts to regulate and control the technology to ensure that positive social benefits result from their use and to guarantee the public's health and welfare. Radio, television, automobiles, electricity, and railroads are all the subject of regulation and legislation. Likewise,

| TABLE 1.7 | TOP 25 ONLINE RETAILERS RANKED BY ONLINE SALES |
|---|---|
| ONLINE RETAILER | ONLINE SALES (2009) (IN BILLIONS) |
| Amazon | $24.5 |
| Staples | $9.8 |
| Dell | $4.5 |
| Apple | $4.2 |
| Office Depot | $4.1 |
| Wal-Mart | $3.5 |
| OfficeMax | $2.8 |
| Sears | $2.8 |
| CDW | $2.5 |
| Best Buy | $2.5 |
| Libery Media | $2.4 |
| Newegg | $2.3 |
| SonyStyle | $1.8 |
| Netflix | $1.7 |
| Costco. | $1.6 |
| J.C. Penney | $1.5 |
| HP Home and Office | $1.5 |
| Victoria's Secret | $1.4 |
| W.W. Grainger | $1.4 |
| Target | $1.2 |
| Macy's | $1.2 |
| Systemax | $1.2 |
| Gap | $1.1 |
| L.L. Bean | $1.1 |
| HSN | $1.0 |

SOURCES: Based on data from Internet Retailer, 2010; company reports on Form 10-K filed with the Securities and Exchange Commission; eMarketer, Inc., 2010c.

with e-commerce. In the U.S. Congress, there have already been a number of bills passed (as well as hundreds proposed) to control various facets of the Internet and e-commerce, from consumer privacy to pornography, gambling, and encryption. We can expect these efforts at regulation in the United States and around the world to increase as e-commerce extends its reach and importance.

A relatively new factor that will influence the growth of e-commerce is the cost of energy, in particular gasoline and diesel. As fuel costs rise, traveling to shop at physical locations can be a very expensive. Buying online can save customers time and energy costs. There is growing evidence that shoppers are changing their shopping habits and locales because of fuel costs, and pushing the sales of online retailers to higher levels.

In summary, the future of e-commerce will be a fascinating mixture of traditional retail, service, and media firms extending their brands to online markets; early-period e-commerce firms such as Amazon and eBay strengthening their financial results and dominant positions; and a bevy of entirely new entrepreneurial firms with the potential to rocket into prominence by developing huge new audiences in months. Firms that fit this pattern include Facebook, Twitter, MySpace, and PhotoBucket.

## 1.3  UNDERSTANDING E-COMMERCE: ORGANIZING THEMES

Understanding e-commerce in its totality is a difficult task for students and instructors because there are so many facets to the phenomenon. No single academic discipline is prepared to encompass all of e-commerce. After teaching the e-commerce course for several years and writing this book, we have come to realize just how difficult it is to "understand" e-commerce. We have found it useful to think about e-commerce as involving three broad interrelated themes: technology, business, and society. We do not mean to imply any ordering of importance here because this book and our thinking freely range over these themes as appropriate to the problem we are trying to understand and describe. Nevertheless, as in previous technologically driven commercial revolutions, there is an historic progression. Technologies develop first, and then those developments are exploited commercially. Once commercial exploitation of the technology becomes widespread, a host of social, cultural, and political issues arise.

### TECHNOLOGY: INFRASTRUCTURE

The development and mastery of digital computing and communications technology is at the heart of the newly emerging global digital economy we call e-commerce. To understand the likely future of e-commerce, you need a basic understanding of the information technologies upon which it is built. E-commerce is above all else a technologically driven phenomenon that relies on a host of information technologies as well as fundamental concepts from computer science developed over a 50-year period. At the core of e-commerce are the Internet and the World Wide Web, which we describe in detail in Chapter 3. Underlying these technologies are a host of complementary technologies: personal computers, handheld cell phone/computers such as the iPhone, local area networks, relational databases, client/server computing, cloud computing, and fiber-optic switches, to name just a few. These technologies lie at the heart of sophisticated business computing applications such as enterprise-wide computing systems, supply chain management systems, manufacturing resource planning systems, and customer relationship management systems. E-commerce relies on all these basic technologies—not just the Internet. The Internet—while representing a sharp break from prior corporate computing and communications technologies—is nevertheless just the latest development in the evolution of corporate computing and part of the continuing chain of computer-based innovations in business. **Figure 1.9** illustrates the major stages in the development of corporate computing and indicates how the Internet and the Web fit into this development trajectory.

To truly understand e-commerce, then, you will need to know something about packet-switched communications, protocols such as TCP/IP, client/server and cloud computing,mobile digital platforms, Web servers, HTML, and software programming tools such as JavaScript and AJAX. All of these topics are described fully in Part 2 of the book (Chapters 3–5).

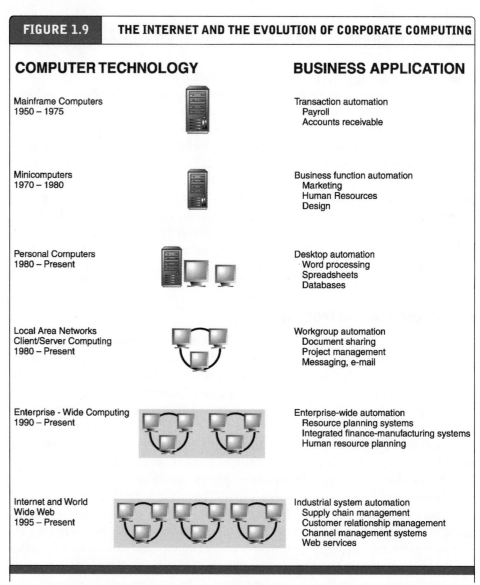

**FIGURE 1.9**    **THE INTERNET AND THE EVOLUTION OF CORPORATE COMPUTING**

**COMPUTER TECHNOLOGY**

Mainframe Computers
1950 – 1975

Minicomputers
1970 – 1980

Personal Computers
1980 – Present

Local Area Networks
Client/Server Computing
1980 – Present

Enterprise - Wide Computing
1990 – Present

Internet and World
Wide Web
1995 – Present

**BUSINESS APPLICATION**

Transaction automation
  Payroll
  Accounts receivable

Business function automation
  Marketing
  Human Resources
  Design

Desktop automation
  Word processing
  Spreadsheets
  Databases

Workgroup automation
  Document sharing
  Project management
  Messaging, e-mail

Enterprise-wide automation
  Resource planning systems
  Integrated finance-manufacturing systems
  Human resource planning

Industrial system automation
  Supply chain management
  Customer relationship management
  Channel management systems
  Web services

The Internet and World Wide Web , and the emergence of a mobile digital platform held together by the Internet cloud, are the latest in a chain of evolving technologies and related business applications, each of which builds on its predecessors.

## BUSINESS: BASIC CONCEPTS

While the technology provides the infrastructure, it is the business applications—the potential for extraordinary returns on investment—that create the interest and excitement in e-commerce. New technologies present businesses and entrepreneurs with new ways of organizing production and transacting business. New technologies change the strategies and plans of existing firms: old strategies are made obsolete and new ones need to be invented. New technologies are the birthing grounds where thousands of new companies spring up with new products and services. New technologies are the graveyard of many traditional businesses, such as record stores. To truly understand e-commerce, you will need to be familiar with some key business concepts, such as the nature of digital electronic markets, digital goods, business models, firm and industry value chains, value webs, industry structure, and consumer behavior in digital markets, as well as basic concepts of financial analysis. We'll examine these concepts further in Chapter 2 , Chapters 6 and 7, and also Chapters 9 through 12.

## SOCIETY: TAMING THE JUGGERNAUT

With over 165 million adult Americans now using the Internet, many for e-commerce purposes, and over 1.8 billion users worldwide, the impact of the Internet and e-commerce on society is significant and global. Increasingly, e-commerce is subject to the laws of nations and global entities. You will need to understand the pressures that global e-commerce places on contemporary society in order to conduct a successful e-commerce business or understand the e-commerce phenomenon. The primary societal issues we discuss in this book are individual privacy, intellectual property, and public welfare policy.

Since the Internet and the Web are exceptionally adept at tracking the identity and behavior of individuals online, e-commerce raises difficulties for preserving privacy—the ability of individuals to place limits on the type and amount of information collected about them, and to control the uses of their personal information. Read *Insight on Society: Who Really Cares About Online Privacy?* to get a view of some of the ways e-commerce sites use personal information.

Because the cost of distributing digital copies of copyrighted intellectual property—tangible works of the mind such as music, books, and videos—is nearly zero on the Internet, e-commerce poses special challenges to the various methods societies have used in the past to protect intellectual property rights.

The global nature of e-commerce also poses public policy issues of equity, equal access, content regulation, and taxation. For instance, in the United States, public telephone utilities are required under public utility and public accommodation laws to make basic service available at affordable rates so everyone can have telephone service. Should these laws be extended to the Internet and the Web? If goods are purchased by a New York State resident from a Web site in California, shipped from a center in Illinois, and delivered to New York, what state has the right to collect a sales tax? Should some heavy Internet users who consume extraordinary amounts of bandwidth be charged extra for service, or should the Internet be neutral with respect to usage? What rights do nation-states and their citizens have with respect to the

## INSIGHT ON SOCIETY

# WHO REALLY CARES ABOUT ONLINE PRIVACY?

In a January 2010 interview, Mark Zuckerburg, the founder of Facebook, declared that the "age of privacy" had to come to an end, due in large part to Facebook and other social network sites. Social norms have changed, he said. Young people using Facebook no longer worry about sharing their personal information and preferences with friends, friends of friends (personal networks), and even the entire public Web population. Older folks might object (the majority of Facebook users are over 35), but they were part of the old privacy culture. Zuckerberg noted, "if he had created Facebook today, as opposed to several years ago, he would have made user information public, not private, by default as it was for years until the company changed dramatically in December 2009." In 2009, Facebook declared it was publishing without subscribers' consent basic personal information (name, profile, and gender) on the Internet where it could be indexed by search engines like Google. In January 2010, it announced new services that would automatically share users' Pandora music selections with friends, and indeed the whole Internet. Supporters of these developments argued that we were entering a new age of "information exhibitionism," heralding a new era of openness and transparency.

With over 500 million users world wide, about 150 million in the United States, Facebook's privacy policies will help shape privacy standards on the Internet for years to come. In May 2010, opposition to Facebook's privacy policies from foreign governments, Congress, members and privacy advocates reached epic proportions. By the end of May 2010, Zuckerberg had apologized, published some new privacy policies, and learned that indeed many powerful institutions along with millions of members do indeed care about privacy.

The economic stakes in the privacy debate are quite large, involving billions of dollars of advertising and transaction dollars. Social network sites such as Facebook, Google's Buzz, and MySpace, along with hundreds of start-ups, use a business model that encourages and sometimes requires users to give up their claim to control personal information and hence their privacy. A "privacy destruction" business model is one based on a database of hundreds of millions of users who volunteer to post personal information, preferences, and behaviors, and who are encouraged, or deceived, into relinquishing control over nearly all their information, which is then sold to advertisers and outside third parties. Privacy destruction is the primary way social network sites can make a profit. It's called politely "monetization of the user base."

The end to the "age of privacy" came as blockbuster news to historians and legal scholars who noted that some of the basic concepts of privacy, such as limiting the power of institutions to intrude on the personal papers and activities of ordinary citizens, originated in the Constitution of the Roman Republic around 542 B.C. Nearly every important founding political document in Western societies, from the Magna Carta (1215) to the Constitution of the United States (1787), provides limitations on the power of government to snoop on private citizens. Privacy—limitations on what personal information government and private institutions can collect and use— is a founding principle of democracies. The age of privacy has a very long history.

Facebook's 2009 privacy policies were quite a flip-flop from its original privacy policy in 2004, whioh promised users near complete con-

(continued)

trol over who could see their profile and personal profile. The default option then was only immediate friends whom you invited to see your personal information and communications were given access. Other users in your network could not get much information about you at all. People outside that network, members of other networks, could find nothing about you. This was the privacy environment that millions of Facebook users signed up for.

Every year since 2004, however, Facebook has extended—most often abruptly and without prior notice—its control over user information and content. In 2007, it made most user private information available to other members on the network. Also in 2007, Facebook announced the Beacon program which was designed to broadcast users' activities on 44 participating Web sites to their friends. In 2009, Facebook published user basic personal information on the Internet, and announced that whatever content users had contributed belonged to Facebook, and that ownership never terminated. In April 2010 Facebook introduced a "Like" button on third party Web sites that alerts friends to browsing and purchases similar to the withdrawn Beacon program. In 2010 Facebook also began sending user profile information to Yelp, Microsoft, and Pandora without user consent. Not to be outdone leading the charge to end the age of privacy, Google's Buzz social network site adopted a policy of putting new subscribers into a ready-made circle of friends based on Google's understanding of subscribers' Gmail and chat contacts!

Facebook and Google have both learned that people do care about the use, control, and ownership of their personal information, which they willingly enter on social network sites, and into various Google sites, from search engine queries to YouTube video viewing histories. At every point in the development of Facebook's self-proclaimed "end of privacy" policies, thousands, sometimes hundreds of thousands, of users

have objected. The Beacon program was resisted initially by a Facebook-based group created by MoveOn.org, demanding that Facebook not publish user activity on other Web sites without explicit permission from the user. In fewer than 10 days, this group gained 50,000 members. Class action suits followed in 2008 and 2009. Facebook tried to mollify members by making the program "opt in" and not the default setting, but even this policy change was discovered to be a sham as personal information continued to flow from Facebook to various Web sites like Fandango, Blockbuster, and HotWire. Facebook apologized to users in 2007 and 2008, finally withdrew the service in 2009, and paid $9.5 million to settle the class action suits.

Facebook's efforts to take permanent control of user information resulted in over 500,000 users joining online resistance groups, and it ultimately withdrew that policy as well. In April 2009 a new Facebook Principles and Statement of Rights and Responsibilities was approved by 75% of its members who voted in an online survey. The new policy explicitly stated that users "own and control their information." Facebook also improved account deletion features, limited sublicenses of information about users, and reduced data exchanges with outside developers. These moves quieted the uproar for a time. Unfortunately, the resulting "new" privacy policy was so complicated that users typically defaulted to "share" rather than work through over 170 information categories that users can choose to make public or private to various groups, the public, the Internet. The result is a choice matrix with several thousand choices that can mystify, confuse and frustrate users.

A year later, in May 2010 Zuckerberg apologized to members one more time, agreeing that the "new" privacy policies were too complex and promising more simplified controls while agreeing with the principal that members of social networks have the right to control the uses of their personal

(continued)

information. User suspicions remained high throughout 2010 as Facebook pushed various new products that resulted in user information passing to third parties without user consent, such as personal choices of music on Pandora passing to advertisers on Facebook. What is needed are simple global privacy controls for users, and changing the default sharing of information from "All" to "No sharing" and then letting users add friends and networks they want to share with.

Public reaction to Facebook's privacy troubles finally have led to Congressional interest. In April 2010, New York Senator Charles Schumer joined other senators asking the Federal Trade Commission (FTC) to investigate whether social network sites are being straight with consumers when it comes to the privacy of their information. He also wants the agency to develop guidelines for the use of private information and require all access to be opt-in. Schumer said Facebook's new policies make opting out of these features "complicated and confusing." The senator said connected profiles are "a gold mine of marketing data that could use by used for spam and potentially scammers, intent on peddling their wares." In June 2010, the FTC announced that it was examining Facebook's efforts to protect user privacy. "We're taking a very close look at Facebook," FTC Chairman Jon Leibowitz said in an interview. "Obviously protecting consumers' privacy and enforcing the law is an enormous part of what we do."

**SOURCES:** "Facebook Redesigns Privacy Controls," by Ben Worthen, *Wall Street Journal*, May 27, 2010; "From Facebook, Answering Privacy Concerns With New Settings," by Mark Zuckerberg, *Washington Post*, May 24, 2010; "How Facebook Pulled a Privacy Bait and Switch," by Dan Tynan, *PC World*, May 2010; "Why No One Cares About Privacy Anymore," by Declan McCullagh, *CNET News*, March 12, 2010; "Technology Coalition Seeks Stronger Privacy Laws," by Miguel Helft, *New York Times*, March 20, 2010. "Redrawing the Route to Online Privacy," by Steve Lohr, *New York Times*, February 28, 2010; "Anger Leads to Apology From Google About Buzz," by Miguel Helft, *New York Times*, February 15 2010; The Constitution of the Roman Republic by Andrew Lintott, Oxford University Press, 1999.

Internet, the Web, and e-commerce? We address issues such as these in Chapter 8, and also throughout the text.

## ACADEMIC DISCIPLINES CONCERNED WITH E-COMMERCE

The phenomenon of e-commerce is so broad that a multidisciplinary perspective is required (see **Figure 1.10**). There are two primary approaches to e-commerce: technical and behavioral.

### Technical Approaches

Computer scientists are interested in e-commerce as an exemplary application of Internet technology. They are concerned with the development of computer hardware, software, and telecommunications systems, as well as standards, encryption, and database design and operation. Management scientists are primarily interested in building mathematical models of business processes and optimizing these processes. They are interested in e-commerce as an opportunity to study how business firms can exploit the Internet to achieve more efficient business operations.

| FIGURE 1.10 | DISCIPLINES CONCERNED WITH E-COMMERCE |
|---|---|

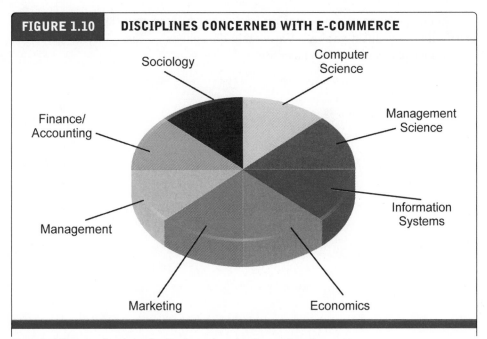

Many disciplines are directly involved in the study and understanding of e-commerce.

## Behavioral Approaches

In the behavioral area, information systems researchers are primarily interested in e-commerce because of its implications for firm and industry value chains, industry structure, and corporate strategy. The information systems discipline spans the technical and behavioral approaches. For instance, technical groups within the information systems specialty also focus on data mining, search engine design, and artificial intelligence. Economists have focused on consumer behavior at Web sites, pricing of digital goods, and on the unique features of digital electronic markets. The marketing profession is interested in marketing, brand development and extension, consumer behavior on Web sites, and the ability of Internet technologies to segment and target consumer groups, and differentiate products. Economists share an interest with marketing scholars who have focused on e-commerce consumer response to marketing and advertising campaigns, and the ability of firms to brand, segment markets, target audiences, and position products to achieve above-normal returns on investment.

Management scholars have focused on entrepreneurial behavior and the challenges faced by young firms who are required to develop organizational structures in short time spans. Finance and accounting scholars have focused on e-commerce firm valuation and accounting practices. Sociologists—and to a lesser extent, psychologists—have focused on general population studies of Internet usage, the role of social inequality in skewing Internet benefits, and the use of the Web as a social network and group communications tool. Legal scholars are interested in issues such as preserving intellectual property, privacy, and content regulation.

No one perspective dominates research about e-commerce. The challenge is to learn enough about a variety of academic disciplines so that you can grasp the significance of e-commerce in its entirety.

## 1.4 CASE STUDY

# The Pirate Bay:
## Stealing Media vs. Streaming Media

Downloading copyrighted music—both legally and illegally—is one of the Internet's most common activities, especially among the under 21. At one point, illegal music file sharing constituted more than half of Internet traffic at some sites like college campuses. However, in 2010, music and video file downloading traffic has fallen dramatically to less than 6% for the Internet as a whole, while streaming of media files has exploded to more than 10% of Internet traffic. Stealing music is just not as popular as it used to be, while streaming music and video has become much more fashionable and convenient. The Internet world has become a tough place for music and video pirates to make a living. The Pirate Bay provides the latest example of the difficulties of sustaining a business model based on theft of intellectual property.

The Pirate Bay (TPB), a Web site located in Sweden (Piratebay.org), has become one of the world's most popular pirated music and content sites, offering free access

to millions of copyrighted songs and thousands of copyrighted Hollywood movies. In June 2010, the site reported that it had 24 million regular users. To put that number in perspective, consider that is more than twice the population of Sweden itself (9 million). It is regularly in the top 100 most popular Web sites in the world, according to Internet analysts in 2010. Despite its popularity, court records indicate The Pirate Bay generates a miserly $1.5 to $3 million in revenue annually.

The Pirate Bay has spearheaded a European social and political movement that opposes copyrighted content and demands that music, videos, TV shows, and other digital content be free and unrestricted. In the words of the Pirate Party, which organized parties and protests outside the Stockholm Court throughout 2009, "The Pirate Bay is a unique platform for distributing culture between regular people and independent artists, and that's something we want to preserve." According to John Kennedy, head of the International Federation of the Phonographic Industry (IFPI), The Pirate Bay has become "The world's No. 1 source of illegal music," following successful court actions against the P2P file-sharing sites Grokster in the United States and Kazaa in Australia.

In a unique twist on prior organized efforts to provide "free" music, The Pirate Bay does not operate a database of copyrighted content. Neither does it operate a network of computers owned by "members" who store the content, nor create, own, or distribute software (like BitTorrent and most other so-called P2P networks) that permit such networks to exist in the first place. These were the old techniques for ripping off music. Instead, The Pirate Bay simply provides a search engine that responds to user queries for free music, or specific movie titles, and generates a list of search results that include P2P networks around the world where the titles can be found. By clicking on a selected link, users gain access to the copyrighted content but only after downloading software and other files from the P2P network.

Voila! "No body, no crime." What could be illegal? The Pirate Bay claims it is merely a search engine providing pointers to existing P2P networks that it does not itself control. It claims that it cannot control what content users ultimately find on those P2P networks, and that it is no different from any other search engine, such as Google or Bing, which are not held responsible for the content found on sites listed in search results. From a broader standpoint, The Pirate Bay's founders also claim that copyright laws in general unjustly interfere with the free flow of information on the Internet, and that in any event, they were not violating Swedish copyright law, which they felt should be the only law that applied. And they further claimed they did not encourage, incite, or enable illegal downloading.

However, in a ruling that puts to rest the notion that the law is always behind the development of technology, on April 2009, the First Swedish Court in Stockholm declared the four founders guilty of violating Swedish copyright law, and sentenced each to one year in prison and payment of $3.5 million in restitution to the plaintiffs, all Swedish divisions of the major record label firms (Warner Music, Sony, and EMI Group among them).

The court said "By providing a website with ... well-developed search functions, easy uploading and storage possibilities, and with a tracker linked to the website, the accused have incited the crimes that the file sharers have committed." The court also said that the four defendants had been aware of the fact that copyrighted material was shared with the help of their site. The prison sentence was justified by "extensive accessibility of others' (copy)rights and the fact that the operation was conducted commercially and in an organized fashion." In other words, the court believed the defendants were engaged in a commercial enterprise, the basis of which was encouraging visitors to violate the copyrights of owners. In fact, the primary purpose of The Pirate Bay was to violate copyrights in order to make money for the owners (commercial intent).

"Enable," "induce," and "encourage" copyright infringement and "intent to sell" are key words in this ruling and the Pirate Bay case. These concepts grounded in Western law are not "disabled" by new technology, but instead can be, and are, extensible to new technologies, and used to shape technology to society's needs and wishes. Indeed, there's a consensus developing among prosecutors and courts worldwide that infringement is not justified simply because it's technically possible to do it on the Internet.

The defendants' initial appeal to Sweden's Supreme Court based on potential bias of the judge who decided the case was dismissed, but a further appeal remains pending and they are unlikely to be settled for many years. The Pirate Bay Web site continues to operate in Sweden much as before, but it has been hounded by law suits initiated by France, Italy, Germany, Denmark, Ireland, the U.K., and Greece. These countries have refused to allow Internet service providers to host The Pirate Bay.

The defendants have never denied theirs was a commercial enterprise. Despite all the talk by the Pirate Party calling for the free, unfettered spread of culture, The Pirate Bay was a money-making operation from the beginning, designed to produce profits for its founders, with advertising as the primary source of revenue. On June 30, 2009, the founders announced that they had entered into an agreement with a Swedish company, Global Gaming Factory X (GGFX), that specializes in Internet café management software, to sell The Pirate Bay for an amount equivalent to about $7.7 million. GGFX claimed that it intended to turn the Web site into a legitimate venture, much to the dismay of many of The Pirate Bay's users. This sale was never consummated.

Meanwhile, the U.S. government pressured the Swedish government to strengthen its copyright laws to discourage rampant downloading. In Sweden, downloading music and videos from illegal sites was very popular, engaged in by 43% of the Swedish Internet population. To strengthen its laws, Sweden adopted the European Union convention on copyrights, which allows content owners to receive from Internet providers the names and addresses of people suspected of sharing pirated files. As a result, Internet traffic in Sweden declined by 40%, and has stayed there.

The Pirate Bay case is just the latest in a saga of court cases involving the record industry, which wants to preserve its monopolies on copyrighted music, and Internet users who want free music. In 2005, after several years of heated court battles, the case of *Metro-Goldwyn-Mayer Studios v. Grokster, et al.* finally reached the U.S. Supreme Court. In June 2005, the Court handed down its unanimous decision: Internet file-sharing services such as Grokster, StreamCast, BitTorrent, and Kazaa could be held liable for copyright infringement because they intentionally sought to induce, enable, and encourage users to share music that was owned by record companies. Indeed, it was their business model: steal the music, gather a huge audience, and monetize the audience by advertising or through subscription fees. Since the court ruling, Kazaa, Morpheus, Grokster, BearShare, iMesh, and many others have either gone out of business or settled with the record firms and converted themselves into legal file-sharing sites by entering into relationships with music industry firms. In May 2010, Mark Gorton, founder of the largest American music pirate site, LimeWire, lost a copyright infringement case and could be forced to pay up to $450 million in damages to the record companies.

These legal victories have not proven to be the magic bullet that miraculously solves all the problems facing the music industry. In addition to the issue of illegal downloads, legitimate digital music sales have so far failed to make up for falling CD sales revenues. These two problems are interrelated: if customers can get the music for free, why should they buy a digital copy or a CD?

Downloading music—legally or illegally—is a major American pastime. About 65 million people downloaded music files in 2009, making the Internet the music box of choice for Americans. Approximately 33 million of these people used illegal P2P networks, while the rest downloaded from legal sites that charge for music. Those who use illegal free sites are predominantly young, tech-savvy males in the 14–21 year age group. People older than 21 tend to use legitimate downloading sites such as iTunes. The presence of so many young people on illegal P2P sites makes selling advertising on these sites very lucrative. Every month, about 1 billion songs are shared on illegal file-sharing P2P networks. In contrast, it took Apple iTunes about two years to achieve that many downloads! Illegal downloads are about 90% of the total music tracks download traffic. In other words, illegal downloaders tend to download a great many songs. How can this be if the Supreme Court declared these networks illegal?

For the record labels, the consequences of downloading music has been significant, although not yet catastrophic. The record industry has historically been based on a few physical products: acetate and vinyl records, and CDs (collections of 12 or more songs in a physical bundle). CD sales have continued to slide, leading to a poor financial performance not just at the record firms but also among their music distributors—the large retail outlets that sell CDs such Wal-Mart, Best Buy, Tower Records and Sam Goody (the latter two both now out of business as retail stores). The big three record labels (EMI, Warner Music, and Sony Music) used to make nearly all their money selling CDs. Sales of CDs started falling in 2004 as the Internet ramped up its broadband connectivity. In 2007, sales of CDs plunged 20% in one year, and continued to plunge at that rate through 2009. In 2010, annual revenue from CD sales is less than half of 2005 levels. Album sales of 12 or more songs, both digital and on CD, are also down 15% annually over the same period. Since 2003, thousands of retail music stores have closed, and Wal-Mart has cut back shelf space devoted to CDs and now carries only the top titles.

The only hope for the music industry is to change its business model and decisively move towards digital distribution platforms. Here they are making striking progress but continue to face revenue declines. In 2010, digital music sales will account for only 20% of industry revenues.

Online music sales of MP3 tracks are growing rapidly led by iTunes. Sales of digital music at iTunes, Rhapsody, and eMusic have been growing at about 50% per year since 2006. Apple dominates the musical download scene and has become the largest retailer of music in the United States, replacing Wal-Mart. By 2010, the iTunes Store has sold over 2.5 billion songs, 50 million TV shows, and over 1.3 million movies, making it the world's most popular online music, TV, and movie store. Its revenues are up 34% in the last year. Firing this performance of course are the sales of its i-devices. Through 2010, Apple has sold over 230 million iPods (all models) and over 51 million iPhones.

Changes in the basic computing platform will also have an impact on illegal downloading and the legitimate sale of music. Apple, Google, and other major players are moving towards a "cloud computing" model where users' music inventory is stored on the Internet, and where for a monthly subscription fee, users can access millions of songs from any digital device they choose—Apple iPhone, Android, or BlackBerry. According to a study by Arbor Networks and the University of Michigan, as peer-to-peer traffic is shrinking dramatically, streaming of video and music from legitimate sites has grown to over 10% of all Internet traffic. Researchers surmise that consumers have just found it a lot easier and more convenient to access videos and music from these sites rather than using P2P sharing sites where a movie can take eight hours to download.

The whole idea of "owning" music in the form of records, tapes, CDs, and MP3 files stored on your hard drive is becoming out of date. While subscription models in the past did not work, they were limited to streaming music to desktop and laptop PCs. In the world of mobile Internet devices, the idea of streaming music all day long to your iPhone or BlackBerry is much more attractive. Apple is preparing for this future. It purchased Lala, an online music service that allows users to store their music online. In 2010, Pandora, the music-streaming service, has over 60 million subscribers, 30% of whom connect with smartphones. Meanwhile, the News Corporation, owner of MySpace, purchased two cloud-based music services, iLike and imeem, in 2010. The U.K. music service Spotify offers subscribers access to 8 million music tracks that can be played instantly by just dragging the song you want to your iPhone app. Users do not need to wait for downloads or clutter their hard drives and flash drives with files, or organize the thousands of songs on their storage devices.

In each of these new media delivery platforms the copyright owners—music labels, artists, and Hollywood studios—have struck licensing deals with the technology platform owners and distributors. These new platforms offer a win-win solution to digital media. Consumers are benefitted by having near instant access to high quality tracks and videos without the hassle of P2P software downloads. Like the pirates of the Carribean, The Pirate Bay and other pirate sites may not be able to compete with new and better ways to listen to music and view videos.

**SOURCES:** "Pirate Bay Keeps Sinking: Another Law Suit Coming," by Stan Schroeder, mashable.com , June 22, 2010; "Idea Man of LineWire at a Crossroads," by Joseph Plambeck, *New York Times*, May 23, 2010; "Pirate Bay Sunk by Hollywood Injunction For Now," by Charles Arthur, *The Guardian*, May 17 2010; "British Put Teeth in Anti-Piracy Proposal," by Eric Pfanner, *New York Times*, March 14, 2010; "How Pandora Slipped Past the Junkyard," by Clain Cain Miller, *New York Times*, March 7, 2010; "Music Business Heads Into a Virtual World," Deal Book, *New York Times*, December 16, 2009; "After Sale, Can Pirate Bay Survive?", by David Kravits, Wired.com, June 30, 2009; "File-Sharing Site Violated Copyright, Court Says," Eric Pfanner, *New York Times*, April 18, 2009; "Four Convicted in Sweden in Internet Piracy Case," by Eric Pfanner, *New York Times*, April 18, 2009; "The Pirate Bay Operators: Heroes or Criminals," Law Blog, *Wall Street Journal*, April 13, 2009.

## Case Study Questions

1. How does The Pirate Bay business make money? What is its business model?

2. How do new "cloud-based" media sites and services make money? What is their business model?

3. Is the record industry justified in attempting to shut down P2P file-sharing sites that make it possible to download copyrighted media? Why or why not?

4. Why might consumers prefer to pay for music from cloud-based sites rather than simply download music from P2P sites?

| 1.5 | **REVIEW** |
|---|---|

## KEY CONCEPTS

■ **Define e-commerce and describe how it differs from e-business.**

- E-commerce involves digitally enabled commercial transactions between and among organizations and individuals. Digitally enabled transactions include all those mediated by digital technology, meaning, for the most part, transactions that occur over the Internet and the Web. Commercial transactions involve the exchange of value (e.g., money) across organizational or individual boundaries in return for products or services.
- E-business refers primarily to the digital enabling of transactions and processes within a firm, involving information systems under the control of the firm. For the most part, e-business does not involve commercial transactions across organizational boundaries where value is exchanged.

■ **Identify and describe the unique features of e-commerce technology and discuss their business significance.**

There are eight features of e-commerce technology that are unique to this medium:
- *Ubiquity*—available just about everywhere, at all times, making it possible to shop from your desktop, at home, at work, or even from your car.
- *Global reach*—permits commercial transactions to cross cultural and national boundaries far more conveniently and cost-effectively than is true in traditional commerce.
- *Universal standards*—shared by all nations around the world. In contrast, most traditional commerce technologies differ from one nation to the next.
- *Richness*—refers to the complexity and content of a message. It enables an online merchant to deliver marketing messages with text, video, and audio to an audience of millions, in a way not possible with traditional commerce technologies such as radio, television, or magazines.
- *Interactivity*—allows for two-way communication between merchant and consumer and enabling the merchant to engage a consumer in ways similar to a face-to-face experience, but on a much more massive, global scale.
- *Information density*—is the total amount and quality of information available to all market participants. The Internet reduces information collection, storage, processing, and communication costs while increasing the currency, accuracy, and timeliness of information.
- *Personalization* and *customization*—merchants can target their marketing messages to specific individuals by adjusting the message to a person's name, interests, and past purchases. Because of the increase in information density, a great deal of information about the consumer's past purchases and behavior can be stored and used by online merchants. The result is a level of personalization and customization unthinkable with existing commerce technologies.
- *Social technology*—provides a many-to-many model of mass communications. Millions of users are able to generate content consumed by millions of other users. The result is the formation of social networks on a wide scale and the aggregation of large audiences on social network platforms.

■ Describe and identify Web 2.0 applications

- A set of applications has emerged on the Internet, loosely referred to as Web 2.0. These applications attract huge audiences and represent significant new opportunities for e-commerce revenues. Web 2.0 applications such as social networks, photo-and video-sharing sites, Wikipedia, and virtual life sites support very high levels of interactivity compared to other traditional media.

■ Describe the major types of e-commerce.

There are five major types of e-commerce:
- B2C involves businesses selling to consumers and is the type of e-commerce that most consumers are likely to encounter. In 2010, consumers will spend about $255 billion in B2C transactions.
- B2B e-commerce involves businesses selling to other businesses and is the largest form of e-commerce, with an estimated $3.6 trillion in transactions in 2010.
- C2C is a means for consumers to sell to each other. In C2C e-commerce, the consumer prepares the product for market, places the product for auction or sale, and relies on the market maker to provide catalog, search engine, and transaction clearing capabilities so that products can be easily displayed, discovered, and paid for.
- P2P technology enables Internet users to share files and computer resources directly without having to go through a central Web server. Music and file-sharing services, such as BitTorrent, Kazaa, and eDonkey, are examples of this type of e-commerce, because consumers can transfer files directly to other consumers without a central server involved.
- M-commerce involves the use of wireless digital devices to enable transactions on the Web.

■ Understand the evolution of e-commerce from its early years to today.

E-commerce has gone through three stages: innovation, consolidation, and reinvention. The early years of e-commerce were a period of explosive growth, beginning in 1995 with the first widespread use of the Web to advertise products and ending in 2000 with the collapse in stock market valuations for dot-com ventures.
- The early years of e-commerce were a technological success, with the digital infrastructure created during the period solid enough to sustain significant growth in e-commerce during the next decade, and a mixed business success, with significant revenue growth and customer usage, but low profit margins.
- E-commerce during its early years did not fulfill economists' visions of perfect friction-free commerce, or fulfill the visions of entrepreneurs and venture capitalists for first-mover advantages, low customer acquisition and retention costs, and low costs of doing business.
- E-commerce entered a period of consolidation beginning in March 2000 and extending through 2005.
- E-commerce entered a period of reinvention in 2006 with the emergence of social networks and Web 2.0 applications that attracted huge audiences in a very short time span.

■ **Identify the factors that will define the future of e-commerce.**

Factors that will define the future of e-commerce include the following:
- E-commerce technology will continue to propagate through all commercial activity, with overall revenues from e-commerce, the number of products and services sold over the Web, and the amount of Web traffic all rising.
- E-commerce prices will rise to cover the real costs of doing business on the Web.
- E-commerce margins and profits will rise to levels more typical of all retailers.
- Traditional well-endowed and experienced Fortune 500 companies will play a growing and more dominant role.
- Entrepreneurs will continue to play an important role in pioneering new social applications which will rival search engines as advertising and e-commerce platforms.
- The number of successful pure online companies will continue to decline and many successful e-commerce firms will adopt an integrated, multi-channel bricks-and-clicks strategy.
- Regulation of e-commerce and the Web by government will grow both in the United States and worldwide.

■ **Describe the major themes underlying the study of e-commerce.**

E-commerce involves three broad interrelated themes:
- *Technology*—To understand e-commerce, you need a basic understanding of the information technologies upon which it is built, including the Internet and the World Wide Web, and a host of complimentary technologies—personal computers, local area networks, client/server computing, packet-switched communications, protocols such as TCP/IP, Web servers, HTML, and relational databases, among others.
- *Business*—While technology provides the infrastructure, it is the business applications—the potential for extraordinary returns on investment—that create the interest and excitement in e-commerce. New technologies present businesses and entrepreneurs with new ways of organizing production and transacting business. Therefore, you also need to understand some key business concepts such as electronic markets, information goods, business models, firm and industry value chains, industry structure, and consumer behavior in electronic markets.
- *Society*—Understanding the pressures that global e-commerce places on contemporary society is critical to being successful in the e-commerce marketplace. The primary societal issues are intellectual property, individual privacy, and public policy.

■ **Identify the major academic disciplines contributing to e-commerce.**

There are two primary approaches to e-commerce: technical and behavioral. Each of these approaches is represented by several academic disciplines. On the technical side:
- Computer scientists are interested in e-commerce as an application of Internet technology.
- Management scientists are primarily interested in building mathematical models of business processes and optimizing them to learn how businesses can exploit the Internet to improve their business operations.

- Information systems professionals are interested in e-commerce because of its implications for firm and industry value chains, industry structure, and corporate strategy.
- Economists have focused on consumer behavior at Web sites, and on the features of digital electronic markets.

On the behavioral side:

- Sociologists have focused on studies of Internet usage, the role of social inequality in skewing Internet benefits, and the use of the Web as a personal and group communications tool.
- Finance and accounting scholars have focused on e-commerce firm valuation and accounting practices.
- Management scholars have focused on entrepreneurial behavior and the challenges faced by young firms who are required to develop organizational structures in short time spans.
- Marketing scholars have focused on consumer response to online marketing and advertising campaigns, and the ability of firms to brand, segment markets, target audiences, and position products to achieve higher returns on investment.

## QUESTIONS

1. What is e-commerce? How does it differ from e-business? Where does it intersect with e-business?
2. What is information asymmetry?
3. What are some of the unique features of e-commerce technology?
4. What is a marketspace?
5. What are three benefits of universal standards?
6. Compare online and traditional transactions in terms of richness.
7. Name three of the business consequences that can result from growth in information density.
8. What is Web 2.0? Give examples of Web 2.0 sites and explain why you included them in your list.
9. Give examples of B2C, B2B, C2C, and P2P Web sites besides those listed in the chapter materials.
10. How are the Internet and the Web similar to or different from other technologies that have changed commerce in the past?
11. Describe the three different stages in the evolution of e-commerce.
12. What are the major limitations on the growth of e-commerce? Which is potentially the toughest to overcome?
13. What are three of the factors that will contribute to greater Internet penetration in U.S. households?
14. Define disintermediation and explain the benefits to Internet users of such a phenomenon. How does disintermediation impact friction-free commerce?
15. What are some of the major advantages and disadvantages of being a first mover?
16. Discuss the ways in which the early years of e-commerce can be considered both a success and a failure.
17. What are five of the major differences between the early years of e-commerce and today's e-commerce?

18. What factors will help define the future of e-commerce over the next five years?
19. Why is a multidisciplinary approach necessary if one hopes to understand e-commerce?

## PROJECTS

1. Define "social e-commerce" and describe why it is a new form of advertising, search, and potentially commerce.

2. Search the Web for an example of each of the five major types of e-commerce described in Section 1.1. Create an electronic slide presentation or written report describing each Web site (take a screenshot of each, if possible), and explain why it fits into one of the five types of e-commerce.

3. Choose an e-commerce Web site and assess it in terms of the eight unique features of e-commerce technology described in Table 1.2. Which of the features does the site implement well, and which features poorly, in your opinion? Prepare a short memo to the president of the company you have chosen detailing your findings and any suggestions for improvement you may have.

4. Given the development and history of e-commerce in the years from 1995–2010, what do you predict we will see during the next five years of e-commerce? Describe some of the technological, business, and societal shifts that may occur as the Internet continues to grow and expand. Prepare a brief electronic slide presentation or written report to explain your vision of what e-commerce looks like today.

5. Follow up on events at Facebook and other social network sites since September 2010 (when the opening case was prepared). Has Facebook continued to challenge Google as an advertising and search platform? Has it launched any new e-commerce initiatives? Prepare a short report on your findings.

# E-commerce Business Models and Concepts

**After reading this chapter, you will be able to:**

- Identify the key components of e-commerce business models.
- Describe the major B2C business models.
- Describe the major B2B business models.
- Recognize business models in other emerging areas of e-commerce.
- Understand key business concepts and strategies applicable to e-commerce.

# Tweet Tweet:
## What's Your Business Model?

Twitter, the social network site based on 140-character text messages, is the latest in a series of unpredicted developments on the Internet. You can think of these as "Black Swan" events that have for the most part had very positive consequences. In fact, most of the wildly successful Internet applications and e-commerce businesses were not predicted by the world's leading experts and technology gurus whom we expect to tell us about the future.

Who could have predicted, for instance, that in 2010, in the United States, 174 million people would use search engines to conduct 15 to 17 billion online searches each month, 150 million would watch 30 billion videos online, and 104 million would read blogs? Who knew that America's population was so starved for communication? No one, least of all the Internet technorati.

In 2010, social network sites continue this long tradition of surprising everyone. Twitter is the buzz social network phenomenon of the year. Like all social network sites, such as Facebook, MySpace, YouTube, Flickr, and others, Twitter provides a platform for users ("Tweeple") to express themselves, by creating content and sharing it with their "friends," in this case "followers" who sign up to receive someone's "tweets." And like most social network sites, Twitter faces the problem of how to make money. As of September 2010, Twitter has produced little revenue and zero profits despite over $160 million in funding. Management is still trying to understand how best to exploit the buzz and user base it has unexpectedly created.

Twitter began in 2006 as a Web-based version of popular text messaging services provided by cell phone carriers. There are around 5 billion cell phones worldwide, and SMS text messaging is the most popular service after voice. The idea originated in March 2006 within a podcasting company called Odeo as executives searched for a new product or service to grow revenues. Jack Dorsey, originator of the idea, along with other executives, bought out other venture investors in Odeo, and eventually split Twitter off from Odeo to become a stand-alone, private company called Twitter.com.

The basic idea was to marry short text messaging on cell phones with the Web and its ability to create social groups. You start by establishing a Twitter account online, and then identify the friends that you would like to receive your messages. By sending a text message called a "tweet" to a short code on your cell phone (40404), you can tell your friends what you are doing, your location, and whatever else you might want to say. You are limited to 140 characters, but there is no installation and no charge. Kaboom: a social network messaging service to keep your buddies informed. Smash success.

Coming up with solid numbers for Twitter is not easy. By September 2010, Twitter had an estimated 145 million registered users, and said it was adding nearly 300,000 new users a day, although it is not clear how many continue to actively use the service after signing up. Industry observers believe Twitter is the third largest social network in the United States behind Facebook and MySpace.

What started out in 2006 with 5,000 tweets has turned into a deluge of 90 million daily tweets worldwide. During the Iran rebellion in June 2009, there were reported to be over 200,000 tweets per hour worldwide; for the 2010 World Cup in the summer of 2010, over 200 million tweets were dispatched (at times over 3,000 a second). On the other hand, experts believe that 80% of tweets are generated by only 10% of users, and that the median number of tweet readers per tweet is 1 (most Tweeple tweet to one follower). In contrast, Lady Gaga routinely generates over 5 million followers to her tweets. On the other hand, Twittter has an estimated 60% churn rate: only 40% of users remain more than one month. Obviously, many users lose interest in learning about their friends' breakfast menu, and many feel "too connected" to their "friends," who in fact may only be distant acquaintances, if that.

The answer to these questions about unique users, numbers of tweets, and churn rate are critical to understanding the business value of Twitter as a firm. To date, Twitter has generated losses and has unknown revenues, but in February 2009, it raised $35 million in a deal that valued the company at $255 million. Investors included Jeff Bezos (Amazon founder), Benchmark Capital, and Spark Capital. Then in September 2009, Twitter announced it had raise $100 million in additional funding, from private equity firms, previous investors, and mutual fund giant T. Rowe Price, based on a company valuation of a staggering $1 billion! Quite a jump in seven short months! But that value is all contingent on making a profit, not just generating fantastic growth curves.

So how can Twitter make money from its users and their tweets? What's its business model and how might it evolve over time? To start, consider the company's assets and customer value proposition. The main asset is user attention and audience size (eyeballs per day). The value proposition is "get it now" or real-time news on just about anything from the mundane to the monumental. An equally important asset is the database of tweets that contains the comments, observations, and opinions of the audience, and the search engine that mines those tweets for patterns. These are real-time and spontaneous observations.

Yet another asset has emerged in the last year: Twitter is a powerful alternative media platform for the distribution of news, videos, and pictures. Once again, no one predicted that Twitter would be the first to report on terrorist attacks in Mumbai, the landing of a passenger jet in the Hudson River, or the Iranian rebellion in June 2009 or the political violence in Bangkok and Kenya in May 2010.

How can these assets be monetized? Advertising, what else! In April 2010, Twitter announced it s first foray into the big-time ad marketplace with Promoted Tweets. Think Twitter search engine: in response to a user's query to Twitter's search function for, say netbooks, a Best Buy ad for netbooks will be displayed. The company claims Promoted Tweets are not really ads because they look like all other tweets, just a part of the tweet stream of messages. These so-called "organic tweets" differ therefore from traditional search engine text ads, or social network ads which are far from organic. So far, Best Buy, Bravo, Red Bull, Sony, Starbucks, and Virgin American have signed up. If this actually works, thousands of companies might sign up to blast messages to millions of subscribers in response to related queries.

A second Twitter monetization effort announced in June 2010 is called "Promoted Trends." "Trends" is a section of the Twitter home page that lets users know what's hot, what a lot of people are talking about. The company claims this is "organic," and a true reflection of what people are tweeting about. Promoted Trends are trends that companies would like to initiate. A company can place a Promoted Trends banner on the bottom of the page and when users click on the banner, they are taken to the follower page for  that movie or product. Disney bought Promoted Trends for its film *Toy Story 3*, according to Twitter.

In July 2010, Twitter announced its third initiative of the year: @earlybird accounts, which users can follow to receive special offers. Walt Disney Pictures has used the service to promote *The Sorcerer's Apprentice* by offering twofers (buy one ticket, get another one free). The service could work nicely with so-called real-time or "flash" marketing campaigns in entertainment, fashion, luxury goods, technology, and beauty products. So far, Twitter has over 50,000 @earlybird followers and hopes to reach "influentials," people who shape the purchasing decisions of many others.

Another monetizing service is temporal real-time search. If there's one thing Twitter has uniquely among all the social network sites, it's real-time information. In 2010, Twitter entered into agreements with Google, Microsoft, and Yahoo to permit these search engines to index tweets and make them available to the entire Internet. This service will give free real-time content to the search engines as opposed to archival content. It is unclear who's doing who a service here, and the financial arrangements are not public.

Other large players are experimenting. Dell created a Twitter outlet account, @DellOutlet, and is using it to sell open-box and discontinued computers. Dell also maintain several customer service accounts. Twitter could charge such accounts a commission on sales because Twitter is acting like an e-commerce sales platform similar to Amazon. Other firms have used their Twitter followers' fan base to market discount air tickets (Jet Blue) and greeting cards (Somecards).

Freemium is another possibility: ask users to pay a subscription fee for premium services such as videos and music downloads. However, it may be too late for this idea because users have come to expect the service to be free. Twitter could charge service providers such as doctors, dentists, lawyers, and hair salons for providing their customers

**SOURCES:** "Twitter Hits 145 Million User Mark, Sees Rise in Mobile Use," by Matthew Shaer, *Christian Science Monitor*, September 3, 2010; "Lady Gaga to Steal Britney Spears' Twitter Crown," by Jason Lipshutz, *Reuters*, August 19, 2010; "Twitter's Early Bird Ad Ploy Takes Flight," by Emir Afrati, *Wall Street Journal*, July 14, 2010; "Twitter Tests New Promoted Trends Feature with 'Toy Story 3' from Disney's Pixar," by Jessica Guynn, *Los Angeles Times*, June 16, 2010; "Will Twitter's Ad Strategy Work," by Erica Naone, *Technology Review*, April 15, 2010; "Twitter Rolls Out Ads," by Jessica Vascellaro and Emily Steel, *Wall Street Journal*, April 14, 2010; "Twitter's Latest Valuation: $1 Billion," *New York Times*, September 24, 2009; "Twitter Makes a Racket. But Revenues?" by Jon Fine, *BusinessWeek*, April 9, 2009.

with unexpected appointment availabilities. But Twitter's most likely steady revenue source might be its database of hundreds of millions of real-time tweets. Major firms such as Starbucks, Amazon, Intuit (QuickBooks and Mint.com), and Dell have used Twitter to understand how their customers are reacting to products, services, and Web sites, and then making corrections or changes in those services and products. Twitter is a fabulous listening post on the Internet frontier.

The possibilities are endless, and just about any of the above scenarios offers some solution to the company's problem, which is a lack of revenue (forget about profits). The company is coy about announcing its business model, what one pundit described as hiding behind a "Silicon Valley Mona Lisa smile." These Wall Street pundits are thought to be party poopers in the Valley. In a nod to Apple's iTunes and Amazon's merchant services, Twitter has turned over its messaging capabilities and software platform to others, one of which is CoTweet.com, a company that organizes multiple Twitter exchanges for customers so they can be tracked more easily. Google is selling ad units based around a company's last five tweets (ads are displayed to users who have created or viewed tweets about a company). Twitter is not charging for this service. In the meantime, observers wonder if Twitter is twittering away its assets and may not ever show a profit for its $160 million investment.

The story of Twitter illustrates the difficulties of turning a good business idea with a huge audience into a successful business model that produces revenues and even profits.

In the early days of e-commerce, thousands of firms discovered they could spend other people's invested capital much faster than they could get customers to pay for their products or services. In most instances of failure, the business model of the firm was faulty from the very beginning. In contrast, successful e-commerce firms have business models that are able to leverage the unique qualities of the Web, provide customers real value, develop highly effective and efficient operations, avoid legal and social entanglements that can harm the firm, and produce profitable business results. In addition, successful business models must scale. The business must be able to achieve efficiencies as it grows in volume. But what is a business model, and how can you tell if a firm's business model is going to produce a profit?

In this chapter, we focus on business models and basic business concepts that you must be familiar with in order to understand e-commerce.

## 2.1  E-COMMERCE BUSINESS MODELS

### INTRODUCTION

A **business model** is a set of planned activities (sometimes referred to as *business processes*) designed to result in a profit in a marketplace. A business model is not always the same as a business strategy although in some cases they are very close insofar as the business model explicitly takes into account the competitive environment (Magretta, 2002). The business model is at the center of the business plan. A **business plan** is a document that describes a firm's business model. A business plan always takes into account the competitive environment. An **e-commerce business model** aims to use and leverage the unique qualities of the Internet and the World Wide Web (Timmers, 1998).

### EIGHT KEY ELEMENTS OF A BUSINESS MODEL

If you hope to develop a successful business model in any arena, not just e-commerce, you must make sure that the model effectively addresses the eight elements listed in **Table 2.1**. These elements are: value proposition, revenue model, market opportunity, competitive environment, competitive advantage, market strategy, organizational development, and management team (Ghosh, 1998). Many writers focus on a firm's value proposition and revenue model. While these may be the most important and most easily identifiable aspects of a company's business model, the other elements are equally important when evaluating business models and plans, or when attempting to understand why a particular company has succeeded or failed (Kim and Mauborgne, 2000). In the following sections, we describe each of the key business model elements more fully.

**business model**
a set of planned activities designed to result in a profit in a marketplace

**business plan**
a document that describes a firm's business model

**e-commerce business model**
a business model that aims to use and leverage the unique qualities of the Internet and the World Wide Web

| TABLE 2.1 | KEY ELEMENTS OF A BUSINESS MODEL |
|-----------|----------------------------------|
| COMPONENTS | KEY QUESTIONS |
| Value proposition | Why should the customer buy from you? |
| Revenue model | How will you earn money? |
| Market opportunity | What marketspace do you intend to serve, and what is its size? |
| Competitive environment | Who else occupies your intended marketspace? |
| Competitive advantage | What special advantages does your firm bring to the marketspace? |
| Market strategy | How do you plan to promote your products or services to attract your target audience? |
| Organizational development | What types of organizational structures within the firm are necessary to carry out the business plan? |
| Management team | What kinds of experiences and background are important for the company's leaders to have? |

## Value Proposition

**value proposition**

defines how a company's product or service fulfills the needs of customers

A company's value proposition is at the very heart of its business model. A **value proposition** defines how a company's product or service fulfills the needs of customers (Kambil, Ginsberg, and Bloch, 1998). To develop and/or analyze a firm's value proposition, you need to understand why customers will choose to do business with the firm instead of another company and what the firm provides that other firms do not and cannot. From the consumer point of view, successful e-commerce value propositions include: personalization and customization of product offerings, reduction of product search costs, reduction of price discovery costs, and facilitation of transactions by managing product delivery (Kambil, 1997; Bakos, 1998).

For instance, before Amazon existed, most customers personally traveled to book retailers to place an order. In some cases, the desired book might not be available and the customer would have to wait several days or weeks, and then return to the bookstore to pick it up. Amazon makes it possible for book lovers to shop for virtually any book in print from the comfort of their home or office, 24 hours a day, and to know immediately whether a book is in stock. Amazon's Kindle takes this one step further by making e-books instantly available with no shipping wait. Amazon's primary value propositions are unparalleled selection and convenience.

## Revenue Model

**revenue model**

describes how the firm will earn revenue, produce profits, and produce a superior return on invested capital

A firm's **revenue model** describes how the firm will earn revenue, generate profits, and produce a superior return on invested capital. We use the terms *revenue model* and *financial model* interchangeably. The function of business organizations is both to generate profits and to produce returns on invested capital that exceed alternative investments. Profits alone are not sufficient to make a company "successful" (Porter, 1985). In order to be considered successful, a firm must produce returns greater than alternative investments. Firms that fail this test go out of existence.

Retailers, for example, sell a product, such as a personal computer, to a customer who pays for the computer using cash or a credit card. This produces revenue. The merchant typically charges more for the computer than it pays out in operating expenses, producing a profit. But in order to go into business, the computer merchant had to invest capital—either by borrowing or by dipping into personal savings. The profits from the business constitute the return on invested capital, and these returns must be greater than the merchant could obtain elsewhere, say, by investing in real estate or just putting the money into a savings account.

Although there are many different e-commerce revenue models that have been developed, most companies rely on one, or some combination, of the following major revenue models: the advertising model, the subscription model, the transaction fee model, the sales model, and the affiliate model.

In the **advertising revenue model**, a Web site that offers its users content, services, and/or products also provides a forum for advertisements and receives fees from advertisers. Those Web sites that are able to attract the greatest viewership or that have a highly specialized, differentiated viewership and are able to retain user attention ("stickiness") are able to charge higher advertising rates. Yahoo, for instance, derives a significant amount of revenue from display and video advertising.

In the **subscription revenue model**, a Web site that offers its users content or services charges a subscription fee for access to some or all of its offerings. For instance, the online version of *Consumer Reports* provides access to premium content, such as detailed ratings, reviews, and recommendations, only to subscribers, who have a choice of paying a $5.95 monthly subscription fee or a $26.00 annual fee. Experience with the subscription revenue model indicates that to successfully overcome the disinclination of users to pay for content on the Web, the content offered must be perceived as a high-value-added, premium offering that is not readily available elsewhere nor easily replicated. Companies successfully offering content or services online on a subscription basis include Match.com and eHarmony (dating services), Ancestry.com (see **Figure 2.1**) and Genealogy.com (genealogy research), Microsoft's Xboxlive.com (video games), Rhapsody.com (music), and Hulu.com.

In the **transaction fee revenue model**, a company receives a fee for enabling or executing a transaction. For example, eBay provides an online auction marketplace and receives a small transaction fee from a seller if the seller is successful in selling the item. E*Trade, an online stockbroker, receives transaction fees each time it executes a stock transaction on behalf of a customer.

In the **sales revenue model**, companies derive revenue by selling goods, information, or services to customers. Companies such as Amazon (which sells books, music, and other products), LLBean.com, and Gap.com, all have sales revenue models.

**advertising revenue model**
a company provides a forum for advertisements and receives fees from advertisers

**subscription revenue model**
a company offers its users content or services and charges a subscription fee for access to some or all of its offerings

**transaction fee revenue model**
a company receives a fee for enabling or executing a transaction

**sales revenue model**
a company derives revenue by selling goods, information, or services

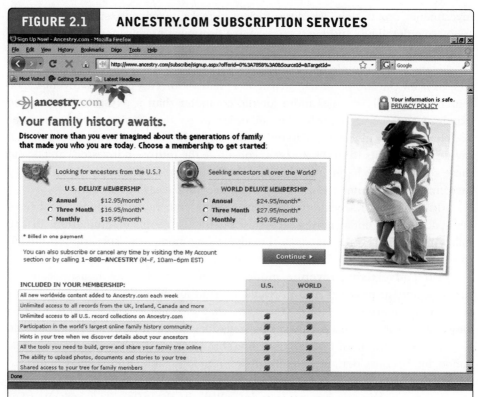

Ancestry.com offers a variety of different membership options for different subscription fees.
SOURCE: Ancestry.com, 2010.

**affiliate revenue model**
a company steers business to an affiliate and receives a referral fee or percentage of the revenue from any resulting sales

In the **affiliate revenue model**, sites that steer business to an "affiliate" receive a referral fee or percentage of the revenue from any resulting sales. For example, MyPoints makes money by connecting companies with potential customers by offering special deals to its members. When they take advantage of an offer and make a purchase, members earn "points" they can redeem for freebies, and MyPoints receives a fee. Community feedback sites such as Epinions receive much of their revenue from steering potential customers to Web sites where they make a purchase.

**Table 2.2** summarizes these major revenue models.

**market opportunity**
refers to the company's intended marketspace and the overall potential financial opportunities available to the firm in that marketspace

## Market Opportunity

The term **market opportunity** refers to the company's intended **marketspace** (i.e., an area of actual or potential commercial value) and the overall potential financial opportunities available to the firm in that marketspace. The market opportunity is usually divided into smaller market niches. The realistic market opportunity is defined by the revenue potential in each of the market niches where you hope to compete.

**marketspace**
the area of actual or potential commercial value in which a company intends to operate

For instance, let's assume you are analyzing a software training company that creates software-learning systems for sale to corporations over the Internet. The overall size of the software training market for all market segments is approximately $70 billion.

| TABLE 2.2 | FIVE PRIMARY REVENUE MODELS | |
|---|---|---|
| REVENUE MODEL | EXAMPLES | REVENUE SOURCE |
| Advertising | Yahoo | Fees from advertisers in exchange for advertisements |
| Subscription | WSJ.com Consumerreports.org | Fees from subscribers in exchange for access to content or services |
| Transaction Fee | eBay E*Trade | Fees (commissions) for enabling or executing a transaction |
| Sales | Amazon L.L.Bean Gap iTunes | Sales of goods, information, or services |
| Affiliate | MyPoints | Fees for business referrals |

The overall market can be broken down, however, into two major market segments: instructor-led training products, which comprise about 70% of the market ($49 billion in revenue), and computer-based training, which accounts for 30% ($21 billion). There are further market niches within each of those major market segments, such as the Fortune 500 computer-based training market and the small business computer-based training market. Because the firm is a start-up firm, it cannot compete effectively in the large business, computer-based training market (about $15 billion). Large brand-name training firms dominate this niche. The start-up firm's real market opportunity is to sell to the thousands of small business firms who spend about $6 billion on computer-based software training and who desperately need a cost-effective training solution. This is the size of the firm's realistic market opportunity (see **Figure 2.2**).

| FIGURE 2.2 | MARKETSPACE AND MARKET OPPORTUNITY IN THE SOFTWARE TRAINING MARKET |
|---|---|

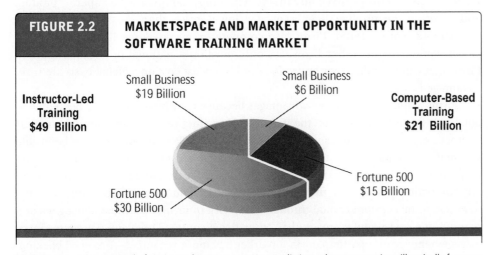

Marketspaces are composed of many market segments. Your realistic market opportunity will typically focus on one or a few market segments.

## Competitive Environment

**competitive environment**
refers to the other companies operating in the same marketspace selling similar products

A firm's **competitive environment** refers to the other companies selling similar products and operating in the same marketspace. It also refers to the presence of substitute products and potential new entrants to the market, as well as the power of customers and suppliers over your business. We discuss the firm's environment later in the chapter. The competitive environment for a company is influenced by several factors: how many competitors are active, how large their operations are, what the market share of each competitor is, how profitable these firms are, and how they price their products.

Firms typically have both direct and indirect competitors. Direct competitors are those companies that sell products and services that are very similar and into the same market segment. For example, Priceline and Travelocity, both of whom sell discount airline tickets online, are direct competitors because both companies sell identical products—cheap tickets. Indirect competitors are companies that may be in different industries but still compete indirectly because their products can substitute for one another. For instance, automobile manufacturers and airline companies operate in different industries, but they still compete indirectly because they offer consumers alternative means of transportation. CNN.com, a news outlet, is an indirect competitor of ESPN.com, not because they sell identical products, but because they both compete for consumers' time online.

The existence of a large number of competitors in any one segment may be a sign that the market is saturated and that it may be difficult to become profitable. On the other hand, a lack of competitors could either signal an untapped market niche ripe for the picking or a market that has already been tried without success because there is no money to be made. Analysis of the competitive environment can help you decide which it is.

## Competitive Advantage

**competitive advantage**
achieved by a firm when it can produce a superior product and/or bring the product to market at a lower price than most, or all, of its competitors

Firms achieve a **competitive advantage** when they can produce a superior product and/or bring the product to market at a lower price than most, or all, of their competitors (Porter, 1985). Firms also compete on scope. Some firms can develop global markets, while other firms can only develop a national or regional market. Firms that can provide superior products at the lowest cost on a global basis are truly advantaged.

Firms achieve competitive advantages because they have somehow been able to obtain differential access to the factors of production that are denied to their competitors—at least in the short term (Barney, 1991). Perhaps the firm has been able to obtain very favorable terms from suppliers, shippers, or sources of labor. Or perhaps the firm has more experienced, knowledgeable, and loyal employees than any competitors. Maybe the firm has a patent on a product that others cannot imitate, or access to investment capital through a network of former business colleagues or a brand name and popular image that other firms cannot duplicate. An **asymmetry** exists whenever one participant in a market has more resources—financial backing, knowledge, information, and/or power—than other participants. Asymmetries lead to

**asymmetry**
exists whenever one participant in a market has more resources than other participants

some firms having an edge over others, permitting them to come to market with better products, faster than competitors, and sometimes at lower cost.

For instance, when Steven Jobs, CEO and founder of Apple Computer, announced iTunes, a new service offering legal, downloadable individual song tracks for 99 cents a tune that would be playable on any PC or digital device with iTunes software, the company was given better-than-average odds of success simply because of Apple's prior success with innovative hardware designs, and the large stable of music labels that Apple had meticulously lined up to support its online music catalog. Few competitors could match the combination of cheap, legal songs and powerful hardware to play them on.

One rather unique competitive advantage derives from being a first mover. A **first-mover advantage** is a competitive market advantage for a firm that results from being the first into a marketplace with a serviceable product or service. If first movers develop a loyal following or a unique interface that is difficult to imitate, they can sustain their first-mover advantage for long periods (Arthur, 1996). Amazon provides a good example. However, in the history of technology-driven business innovation, most first movers often lack the **complementary resources** needed to sustain their advantages, and often follower firms reap the largest rewards (Rigdon, 2000; Teece, 1986). Indeed, many of the success stories we discuss in this book are those of companies that were slow followers—businesses that gained knowledge from failure of pioneering firms and entered into the market late.

Some competitive advantages are called "unfair." An **unfair competitive advantage** occurs when one firm develops an advantage based on a factor that other firms cannot purchase (Barney, 1991). For instance, a brand name cannot be purchased and is in that sense an "unfair" advantage. As we will discuss in Chapter 6, brands are built upon loyalty, trust, reliability, and quality. Once obtained, they are difficult to copy or imitate, and they permit firms to charge premium prices for their products.

In **perfect markets**, there are no competitive advantages or asymmetries because all firms have access to all the factors of production (including information and knowledge) equally. However, real markets are imperfect, and asymmetries leading to competitive advantages do exist, at least in the short term. Most competitive advantages are short term, although some—such as the competitive advantage enjoyed by Coca-Cola because of the Coke brand name—can be sustained for very long periods. But not forever: Coke is increasingly being challenged by fruit, health, and unique flavor drinks. In fact, many respected brands fail every year.

Companies are said to **leverage** their competitive assets when they use their competitive advantages to achieve more advantage in surrounding markets. For instance, Amazon's move into the online grocery business leverages the company's huge customer database and years of e-commerce experience.

## Market Strategy

No matter how tremendous a firm's qualities, its marketing strategy and execution are often just as important. The best business concept, or idea, will fail if it is not properly marketed to potential customers.

**first-mover advantage**
a competitive market advantage for a firm that results from being the first into a marketplace with a serviceable product or service

**complementary resources**
resources and assets not directly involved in the production of the product but required for success, such as marketing, management, financial assets, and reputation

**unfair competitive advantage**
occurs when one firm develops an advantage based on a factor that other firms cannot purchase

**perfect market**
a market in which there are no competitive advantages or asymmetries because all firms have equal access to all the factors of production

**leverage**
when a company uses its competitive advantages to achieve more advantage in surrounding markets

**market strategy**

the plan you put together that details exactly how you intend to enter a new market and attract new customers

Everything you do to promote your company's products and services to potential customers is known as marketing. **Market strategy** is the plan you put together that details exactly how you intend to enter a new market and attract new customers.

For instance, Twitter, YouTube, and Photobucket have a social network marketing strategy that encourages users to post their content on the sites for free, build personal profile pages, contact their friends, and build a community. In these cases, the customer is the marketing staff!

## Organizational Development

Although many entrepreneurial ventures are started by one visionary individual, it is rare that one person alone can grow an idea into a multi-million dollar company. In most cases, fast-growth companies—especially e-commerce businesses—need employees and a set of business procedures. In short, all firms—new ones in particular—need an organization to efficiently implement their business plans and strategies. Many e-commerce firms and many traditional firms who attempt an e-commerce strategy have failed because they lacked the organizational structures and supportive cultural values required to support new forms of commerce (Kanter, 2001).

**organizational development**

plan describes how the company will organize the work that needs to be accomplished

Companies that hope to grow and thrive need to have a plan for **organizational development** that describes how the company will organize the work that needs to be accomplished. Typically, work is divided into functional departments, such as production, shipping, marketing, customer support, and finance. Jobs within these functional areas are defined, and then recruitment begins for specific job titles and responsibilities. Typically, in the beginning, generalists who can perform multiple tasks are hired. As the company grows, recruiting becomes more specialized. For instance, at the outset, a business may have one marketing manager. But after two or three years of steady growth, that one marketing position may be broken down into seven separate jobs done by seven individuals.

For instance, eBay founder Pierre Omidyar started an online auction site, according to some sources, to help his girlfriend trade PEZ dispensers with other collectors, but within a few months the volume of business had far exceeded what he alone could handle. So he began hiring people with more business experience to help out. Soon the company had many employees, departments, and managers who were responsible for overseeing the various aspects of the organization.

## Management Team

**management team**

employees of the company responsible for making the business model work

Arguably, the single most important element of a business model is the **management team** responsible for making the model work. A strong management team gives a model instant credibility to outside investors, immediate market-specific knowledge, and experience in implementing business plans. A strong management team may not be able to salvage a weak business model, but the team should be able to change the model and redefine the business as it becomes necessary.

Eventually, most companies get to the point of having several senior executives or managers. How skilled managers are, however, can be a source of competitive advantage or disadvantage. The challenge is to find people who have both the experience and the ability to apply that experience to new situations.

To be able to identify good managers for a business start-up, first consider the kinds of experiences that would be helpful to a manager joining your company. What kind of technical background is desirable? What kind of supervisory experience is necessary? How many years in a particular function should be required? What job functions should be fulfilled first: marketing, production, finance, or operations? Especially in situations where financing will be needed to get a company off the ground, do prospective senior managers have experience and contacts for raising financing from outside investors?

Read *Insight on Business: Online Grocers: Finding and Executing the Right Model* for a detailed look at how FreshDirect developed a successful business model in an arena—online groceries—in which previous efforts had failed.

## CATEGORIZING E-COMMERCE BUSINESS MODELS: SOME DIFFICULTIES

There are many e-commerce business models, and more are being invented every day. The number of such models is limited only by the human imagination, and our list of different business models is certainly not exhaustive. However, despite the abundance of potential models, it is possible to identify the major generic types (and subtle variations) of business models that have been developed for the e-commerce arena and describe their key features. It is important to realize, however, that there is no one correct way to categorize these business models.

Our approach is to categorize business models according to the different e-commerce sectors—B2C, B2B, C2C, etc.—in which they are utilized. You will note, however, that fundamentally similar business models may appear in more than one sector. For example, the business models of online retailers (often called e-tailers) and e-distributors are quite similar. However, they are distinguished by the market focus of the sector in which they are used. In the case of e-tailers in the B2C sector, the business model focuses on sales to the individual consumer, while in the case of the e-distributor, the business model focuses on sales to another business.

The type of e-commerce technology involved can also affect the classification of a business model. M-commerce, for instance, refers to e-commerce conducted over wireless networks. The e-tail business model, for instance, can also be used in m-commerce, and while the basic business model may remain fundamentally the same as that used in the B2C sector, it will nonetheless have to be adapted to the special challenges posed by the m-commerce environment.

Finally, you will also note that some companies use multiple business models. For instance, eBay can be considered a B2C market maker. At the same time, eBay can also be considered to have a C2C business model and a B2C m-commerce business as well (customers can bid on auctions from their smartphones or wireless Web devices). You can expect many companies will have closely related B2C, B2B, and m-commerce variations on their basic business model. The purpose will be to leverage investments and assets developed with one business model into a new business model.

# INSIGHT ON BUSINESS

## ONLINE GROCERS: FINDING AND EXECUTING THE RIGHT MODEL

What could be easier than ordering all your groceries online and having them delivered to your doorstep at a time you choose? No more driving to the store, wasting gas and time, pushing carts down aisles, jostling with over-anxious shoppers, or waiting in the check-out lines. For those who don't mind giving up the "social experience" of shopping, as well as aspects like thumping melons to test for freshness, tearing off a shock of sweet corn to smell for mold, or sampling a cut of salami before ordering, online grocery shopping provides a compelling value proposition. In 2010, an estimated 4 million online shoppers, who are expected to generate $2.8 billion in online grocery sales in the United States at over 250 online grocers, made that trade-off.

Online grocery sales have grown 75% since 2006, and are expected to grow 10% annually to $13.4 billion by 2014. The United Kingdom has the largest online grocery market at around $10 billion in sales. In fact, online grocery sales are growing at nearly three times the rate of traditional grocery sales offline. In a recession, driven by the high cost of restaurant food, as well as gas for cars, consumers are cooking at home more often, and looking for food deals and convenience online. Online recipe sites are seeing a doubling of traffic. Still, there's a lot of room for future growth: online groceries still account for less than 2% of all grocery sales in the United States.

There are three online grocery business models: start fresh, leverage out, and local build. The history of large-scale online grocery begins with the "start fresh" approach of Webvan, launched in 1999 with $400 million of venture funding, and another $600 million of stock sales to the public. Webvan's business plan was audacious: start a totally new nationwide, online,

grocery distribution system serving 10 cities at first, and expanding to additional major cities in a few years. When Webvan flamed out in July 2001 after having spent almost $1 billion trying to build the Web's largest online grocery store based on huge distribution warehouses in seven U.S. cities, most pundits and investors thought the entire online grocery business model was either a failure or a fraud. Facing the costs of building an entirely new distribution system of warehouses and truck fleets to compete with existing grocery businesses, not to mention the expense of marketing, and a huge IT infrastructure, Webvan compounded its problems by offering below-market prices and free delivery of even small orders at just about any time of the day or night in urban areas often clogged with traffic. Webvan is generally considered to be the largest and most spectacular e-commerce failure in history. That said, it was also ahead of its time: very few customers felt comfortable ordering "high-touch" goods online in 2001. Today, the culture of online purchasing has changed.

Despite Webvan's failure, the pundits have proven to be wrong again. Online grocery is alive, well, growing rapidly, but with different aspirations and business models. Pundits did not count on Manhattan's FreshDirect (and hundreds of other local niche online grocers) or the ability of traditional grocery chains to move into the ashes of the online grocery business to create solid, profitable businesses. These firms are learning how to exploit this potential market with profitable business models.

The largest online players today are traditional firms such as California's huge Safeway Stores, APSupermarket.com, and Shoprite.com in the North East, and Royal Ahold (Dutch owner of the U.S. Stop & Shop and Giant food stores,

(continued)

among others, and the Internet firm Peapod.com). Big-box discount stores such as Costco, BJ's, and Sam's Club also offer online grocery services. Sam's Club, the Wal-Mart-owned big box chain of stores, offers customers a "Click N' Pick" service: order online, pick it up at the nearest Sam's Club store, and you won't even have to stand in line to pay for your groceries. These firms are leveraging their existing nationwide distribution and supply chain systems, as well as their thousands of local stores, to provide shoppers with the opportunity of selecting what they want online, and then picking it up at the local stores or having it delivered by the local stores. These U.S. firms followed the lead of the successful British grocer Tesco. Tesco is the largest chain of supermarkets in Britain and opened an online division in 1990. It is considered to be the largest and most successful online grocery store in the world.

In the United States, Safeway's wholly owned subsidiary GroceryWorks.com provides online shopping and delivery services for Safeway stores in California, Oregon, Washington, Arizona, Maryland, Virginia, and the District of Columbia; and for Vons stores in Southern California and Las Vegas, Nevada. Customers register online, entering their personal information, including their frequent shopper cards. They are shown lists of recently purchased items to speed selection. The prices of goods are the same as those in the stores. Safeway has so-called "pickers" roam the aisles of nearby stores using a computerized picklist that directs them through the store in an efficient pattern, and even specifies the order of packing goods into bags. The orders are put into a van and delivered to the customer within a two-hour window for a fee of $10.

At Royal AHold's Peapod.com, which serves its Stop & Shop and Giant Food store customers in 18 regional markets, shoppers can view both their online ordering history and their offline purchases at nearby stores during the previous four months. Peapod is the largest online grocery in the United States with over $410 million in sales in 2010. Its Web site also features a shopping list that displays items in the order they can be found at the customer's local store. Customers have the option of ordering online and picking it up at the store, or printing the shopping list and taking it to the store. For these traditional supermarket chains, the value being offered to customers is convenience and time savings at prices only marginally higher than self-shopping.

FreshDirect exemplifies the third and most common online grocery business model: local build. Other well-known local niche players include Inland Marine (Houston), Gopher Grocery (St. Paul), and Greenling (Austin), all with revenues greater than $1 million. These local online grocers focus on knowing their local customers, high-quality fresh produce, low costs, and convenient delivery.

In July 2002, Joe Fedele and Jason Ackerman founded FreshDirect as a new kind of high quality and high-tech food preparation and delivery service in Manhattan, and raised $120 million in venture funding. Operating out of a 300,000-square-foot plant in Queens just across the river from Manhattan, FreshDirect trucks deliver groceries to densely populated Manhattan, Brooklyn, and Queens at prices 25% below what most New York grocers charge. It charges a $5.49–$6.79 delivery fee, depending on location and size of order, and requires a minimum order of $30. The value proposition to consumers is convenience and time savings, but also higher quality at lower prices.

How can FreshDirect succeed at these prices? One answer is that FreshDirect concentrates on very fresh perishable foods and stays away from low-margin dry goods. For instance, the FreshDirect Web site features around 3,000 perishables and 3,000 packaged goods com-

(continued)

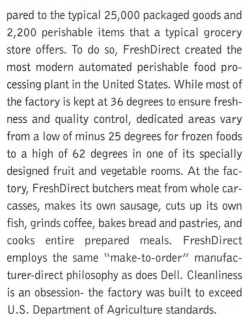

pared to the typical 25,000 packaged goods and 2,200 perishable items that a typical grocery store offers. To do so, FreshDirect created the most modern automated perishable food processing plant in the United States. While most of the factory is kept at 36 degrees to ensure freshness and quality control, dedicated areas vary from a low of minus 25 degrees for frozen foods to a high of 62 degrees in one of its specially designed fruit and vegetable rooms. At the factory, FreshDirect butchers meat from whole carcasses, makes its own sausage, cuts up its own fish, grinds coffee, bakes bread and pastries, and cooks entire prepared meals. FreshDirect employs the same "make-to-order" manufacturer-direct philosophy as does Dell. Cleanliness is an obsession- the factory was built to exceed U.S. Department of Agriculture standards.

Critical to the success of FreshDirect is a powerful IT infrastructure that seamlessly connects online customers to inventory, billing, and then to truck delivery. The firm uses SAP software (an enterprise resource planning system) to track inventory, compile financial reports, tag products to fulfill customers' orders, and precisely control production down to the level of telling bakers how many bagels to cook each day and what temperature to use. It uses automated carousels and conveyors to bring orders to food-prep workers and packers. The FreshDirect Web site is powered by BEA Systems' Weblogic platform, which can track customer preferences, such as the level of fruit ripeness desired, or the preferred weight of a cut of meat. FreshDirect also uses NetTracker, Web site traffic and online behavior analysis software, to help it better understand and market to its online customers. At peak times, the Web site has handled up to 18,000 simultaneous shopping sessions. The final piece in the formula for profit is a supply chain that includes dealing directly with manufacturers and growers, thus cutting out the costs of

middle-level distributors and the huge chains themselves. FreshDirect does not accept slotting fees (payments made by manufacturers for shelf space). Instead, it asks suppliers to help it direct-market to consumers and to lower prices. To further encourage lower prices from suppliers, FreshDirect pays them in four business days after delivery, down from the industry pattern of 35 days.

FreshDirect was profitable for the first time in 2008. The key to profitability has been improving its execution of the initial concept, and a rededication to customer service, just plain listening to customers. In recent years, FreshDirect has introduced the following "customer centric" ideas:

• Produce: Employed experts to rate the freshness of all produce and set prices accordingly. This reduces customer concerns about not being able to feel the product.

• Packaging: Eliminated the use of foam, and reduced the number of cardboard boxes by 1.5 million in response to customer complaints.

• Favorites: Developed a customer relationship management system that tracks each customers' past purchases, and presents them on-screen for re-ordering. Increased order size by 10%.

• Recommender system: Added a YMAL (You-Might-Also-Like) cross-selling tool, which recommends products that other customers purchased. Added 5% to total revenue.

• Rating systems: Developed a rating system for its own produce and seafood that allows grocers to showcase their best goods and customers to decide what "looks" good online.

• Order pattern analysis: Instituted a system to reminds customers of their favorite products and e-mails them when the system thinks they might be running out.

• Computer-driven truck packing: Created to handle over 45,000 deliveries a week in the New York Metro area.

(continued)

- Web apps: In March 2010, FreshDirect introduced an iPhone app that allows mobile shoppers full access to its complete Web offerings. More than 65% of FreshDirect's customers have smartphones, and 50% have iPhones.

With these features and direct mail campaigns, FreshDirect has increased customer loyalty and reduced its churn rate (the number of customers who leave the service). Currently, 65% of its total customer base of around 150,000 active customers are repeat, loyal customers, whose average order size is over $120, and who contribute 80% of FreshDirect revenues. Word among investors is that FreshDirect is planning an IPO in 2011, causing many to roll their eyes as they remember the history of Webvan in early part of the decade. Is this time different? The technology has changed drastically, there's more bandwidth to explore food products online, and the culture has shifted to using smartphones as mobile shopping devices.

▬ **SOURCES:** "US Online Grocery Sales Pack New Punch," by Jonathan Birchall, FT.com, September 14, 2010; "At FreshDirect, Reinvention After a Crisis," by Jessica Bruder, *New York Times*, August 11, 2010; "Inside FreshDirect's Expansion," Ken Bruno, Forbes.com, June 29, 2010; "Online Grocer FreshDirect Enters Mobile Commerce to Drive Sales," by Giselle Tsirulnik, Mobilecommercedaily.com, March 4, 2010; "UK, US Central to Online Grocery Sales Growth," by Chris Brook-Carter, Just-food.com, February 23, 2010; "Top 500 Guide 2010," Internet Retailer.

## 2.2 MAJOR BUSINESS-TO-CONSUMER (B2C) BUSINESS MODELS

Business-to-consumer (B2C) e-commerce, in which online businesses seek to reach individual consumers, is the most well-known and familiar type of e-commerce. **Table 2.3** illustrates the major business models utilized in the B2C arena.

### PORTAL

**Portals** such as Yahoo, MSN, and AOL offer users powerful Web search tools as well as an integrated package of content and services, such as news, e-mail, instant messaging, calendars, shopping, music downloads, video streaming, and more, all in one place. Initially, portals sought to be viewed as "gateways" to the Internet. Today, however, the portal business model is to be a destination site. They are marketed as places where consumers will want to start their Web searching and hopefully stay a long time to read news, find entertainment, and meet other people (think of destination resorts). Portals do not sell anything directly—or so it seems—and in that sense they can present themselves as unbiased. The market opportunity is very large: in 2010, about 220 million people in the United States had access to the Internet at work or home. Portals generate revenue primarily by charging advertisers for ad placement, collecting referral fees for steering customers to other sites, and charging for premium services. AOL, MSN (in conjunction with Verizon), and Yahoo (in conjunction with AT&T)—which in addition to being portals are also Internet Service Providers (ISPs) that provide access to the Internet and the Web—add an additional revenue stream: monthly subscription fees for access.

Although there are numerous portal/search engine sites, the top five sites (Google, Yahoo, MSN/Bing, AOL, and Ask.com) gather more than 95% of the search

**portal**
offers users powerful Web search tools as well as an integrated package of content and services all in one place

| TABLE 2.3 | B2C BUSINESS MODELS | | | |
|---|---|---|---|---|
| **BUSINESS MODEL** | **VARIATIONS** | **EXAMPLES** | **DESCRIPTION** | **REVENUE MODEL** |
| Portal | Horizontal/General | Yahoo<br>AOL<br>MSN<br>Facebook | Offers an integrated package of content, content-search, and social network services: news, e-mail, chat, music downloads, video streaming, calendars, etc. Seeks to be a user's home base | Advertising, subscription fees, transaction fees |
| | Vertical/Specialized (Vortal) | Sailnet | Offers services and products to specialized marketplace | Same |
| | Search | Google<br>Bing<br>Ask.com | Focuses primarily on offering search services | Advertising, affiliate referral |
| E-tailer | Virtual Merchant | Amazon<br>iTunes<br>Bluefly.com | Online version of retail store, where customers can shop at any hour of the day or night without leaving their home or office | Sales of goods |
| | Bricks-and-Clicks | Walmart.com<br>Sears.com | Online distribution channel for a company that also has physical stores | Same |
| | Catalog Merchant | LLBean.com<br>LillianVernon.com | Online version of direct mail catalog | Same |
| | Manufacturer-Direct | Dell.com<br>Mattel.com<br>SonyStyle.com | Manufacturer uses online channel to sell direct to customer | Same |
| Content Provider | | WSJ.com<br>Sportline.com<br>CNN.com<br>ESPN.com<br>Rhapsody.com | Information and entertainment providers such as newspapers, sports sites, and other online sources that offer customers up-to-date news and special interest how-to guidance and tips and/or information sales | Advertising, subscription fees, affiliate referral fees |
| Transaction Broker | | E*Trade<br>Expedia<br>Monster<br>Travelocity<br>Hotels.com<br>Orbitz | Processors of online sales transactions, such as stockbrokers and travel agents, that increase customers' productivity by helping them get things done faster and more cheaply | Transaction fees |
| Market Creator | | eBay<br>Priceline | Web-based businesses that use Internet technology to create markets that bring buyers and sellers together | Transaction fees |
| Service Provider | | VisaNow.com<br>xDrive.com<br>Linklaters BlueFlag | Companies that make money by selling users a service, rather than a product | Sales of services |
| Community Provider | | Facebook<br>MySpace<br>Twitter<br>iVillage | Sites where individuals with particular interests, hobbies, common experiences, or social networks can come together and "meet" online | Advertising, subscription, affiliate referral fees |

engine traffic because of their superior brand recognition (Nielsen, 2010). Many of the top sites were among the first to appear on the Web and therefore had first-mover advantages. Being first confers advantage because customers come to trust a reliable provider and experience switching costs if they change to late arrivals in the market. By garnering a large chunk of the marketplace, first movers—just like a single telephone network—can offer customers access to commonly shared ideas, standards, and experiences (something called *network externalities* that we describe in later chapters).

The traditional portals suddenly have company: Facebook and other social network sites are now the initial start page (portal) for over 60 million Internet users in the United States. In a few years Facebook has created the third largest Web brand with over 148 million unique visitors in August 2010.

Yahoo, AOL, MSN, and others like them are considered to be horizontal portals because they define their marketspace to include all users of the Internet. Vertical portals (sometimes called vortals) attempt to provide similar services as horizontal portals, but are focused around a particular subject matter or market segment. For instance, Sailnet specializes in the consumer sailboat market that contains about 8 million Americans who own or rent sailboats. Although the total number of vortal users may be much lower than the number of portal users, if the market segment is attractive enough, advertisers are willing to pay a premium in order to reach a targeted audience. Also, visitors to specialized niche vortals spend more money than the average Yahoo visitor. Google and Ask.com can also be considered portals of a sort, but focus primarily on offering search and advertising services. They generate revenues primarily from search engine advertising sales and also from affiliate referral fees. For more information, see *Insight on Technology: Can Bing Bong Google?*

## E-TAILER

Online retail stores, often called **e-tailers**, come in all sizes, from giant Amazon to tiny local stores that have Web sites. E-tailers are similar to the typical bricks-and-mortar storefront, except that customers only have to connect to the Internet to check their inventory and place an order. Some e-tailers, which are referred to as "bricks-and-clicks," are subsidiaries or divisions of existing physical stores and carry the same products. REI, JCPenney, Barnes & Noble, Wal-Mart, and Staples are examples of companies with complementary online stores. Others, however, operate only in the virtual world, without any ties to physical locations. Amazon, BlueNile.com, and Drugstore.com are examples of this type of e-tailer. Several other variations of e-tailers—such as online versions of direct mail catalogs, online malls, and manufacturer-direct online sales—also exist.

**e-tailer**
online retail store

Given that the overall retail market in the United States in 2010 is estimated to be around $4.2 trillion, the market opportunity for e-tailers is very large (U.S. Census Bureau, 2010a). Every Internet user is a potential customer. Customers who feel time-starved are even better prospects, since they want shopping solutions that will eliminate the need to drive to the mall or store (Bellman, Lohse, and Johnson, 1999).

# INSIGHT ON TECHNOLOGY

## CAN BING BONG GOOGLE?

Odds are against it so don't hold your breath! But enjoy the competition between the world's largest software company and the world's largest advertising platform. After years of trying to develop a search engine and related search-based advertising platform that would be competitive with Google, in May 2009, Microsoft unveiled its newest effort, called Bing. Why Bing? Allegedly, the name connotes the feeling you get when you discover something (as in "bada bing!"), it's one syllable, and potentially can become a verb (as in "Bing it!") with as much cultural weight as "Google it!" The interface is simple but much richer and more interesting than Google's in part because each day a new full-page nature photo is shown. In fact, Bing is downright elegant according to many observers and users. Google, in contrast, under the influence of computer scientist Marissa Meyer, who controls Google's home page, has not changed its minimalist, stark, white interface since its inception. In contrast, Bing presents a much richer customer experience. In deference to Bing's popular vivid background, Google now allows its users to choose a vivid background if they want (look in the lower left of the Google screen). Already, Bing has had a modest impact on Google.

Microsoft calls Bing a "decision engine" because of its focus on helping users make decisions in four areas: shopping, health, travel, and local business. For instance, a Bing search on "flights from Seattle to San Francisco" will produce a link that shows the lowest extant roundtrip fare, and an icon for calculating the likely future cost of the ticket based on historic trends over the next seven days. There are also links to a Bing travel site from which users can link to airline sites and hotels. In contrast, a sim-

ilar search on Google and Yahoo returns links to airline and other booking sites, but no information on fares or their future price.

In 2010, Microsoft has added some additional bling to Bing:

• Weather searches bring up multiple forecasts, ranking the best forecasters first.

• Left-hand navigational elements put important related searches in the left column.

• Entity cards at top of search results display related relevant information to main search.

• Twitter updates are overlaid, and deep links to Facebook show a picture grid of your friends.

• Search, map and photo technology is integrated where photos change with the zoom level.

• Photos are linked with search terms, e.g. a search for the Metropolitan Museum in New York will return both text results and collections of thousands of amateur and professional photos

• Visual search allows users to search through images rather than text snippets.

While it's unclear if these new features will add markedly to Bing's popularity, they show how seriously Microsoft is taking the competition with Google and how feature innovation will play a key role in the search wars to follow. Score one for Microsoft.

Bing may be just the solution Microsoft needs to break into the big leagues of ad-based search. In August 2010, the industry leader Google commanded the pole position with 65.4% of U.S. searches, Yahoo 17.4%, and Microsoft/Bing 11.1%. Google's search market share has declined by 1.7% since 2009, while Bing has jumped 50% to nearly 13% of online searches, with both Yahoo and Google giving up some market share. Score two for Microsoft.

(continued)

the only "pure" search engine for which search is the major line of business, whereas the other firms are either also content portals (Yahoo and AOL) or, in the case of Microsoft, the provider of 95% of the world's desktop computer operating systems as well as one of the top-visited portal sites in the world (MSN.com)

Google achieved its early and powerful lead in the search business through superior software technology, a highly efficient computer hardware architecture, and excellent Web site design. Google was started in 1998 by two enterprising Stanford grad students, Sergey Brin and Larry Page, who were studying data mining and the process of analyzing data for patterns. Early search engines such as AltaVista (which once had 90% of the search market) merely counted how many times a search term appeared in a given Web site to determine where to rank a particular page. Brin and Page's research reflected the work of Jon Kleinberg, professor of Computer Science at Cornell, who originated an algorithm that rates pages based on the number of links to other pages (hubs) as well as the links they receive from others (authorities). HITS (Hyperlinked Induced Topic Search) is an algorithm for automatically identifying the leading hubs and authorities in a network of hyperlinked pages. In other words, when you search on a topic, the HITS algorithm takes you to those pages that are ranked both high in authority on the topic, and high in the links they have to other sites related to that topic. For instance, if you search for a term such as "measles," the HITS algorithm will often show the Mayo Clinic page

When the Web was first invented, no one envisaged that by 2010, online search would grow to a $12.3 billion dollar advertising business. In fact, early pundits thought that online search would be a commodity business, at best a small niche player in e-commerce. Of course, no one envisaged that search could be married to advertising, and that search was in essence a huge new advertising platform. Today, search ad spending is nearly 50% of all online advertising. The search engine market is booming, along with the larger Internet advertising marketplace, now estimated at about $25 billion for all types of online advertising. It is apparent that search has become a major Web-based industry driven in large part by advances in technology, both hardware and software. What is less apparent is who exactly will dominate this marketspace and what role technology (as opposed to marketing muscle or economics) will play in the ultimate outcome.

Today, five Web sites account for over 95% of all Web searches: Google, Yahoo, Microsoft/Bing, AOL (3.8%), and Ask.com (2.3%), with the rest accounted for by over 100 less popular and specialized search engines such as Kosmix. Of these firms, Google stands out as

(continued)

on this topic in the top results (first page). This is because the Mayo site receives a large number of links for this topic (it is an authority), and also links to a lot of other sites related to measles (it's a hub for information on the topic). Almost all search engines today use some form of the HITS algorithm, which as a set of ideas is not restricted by patent or copyright.

Google's version of the HITS algorithm also uses the popularity of Web pages as the most important criteria for ranking pages, as well as the page content. The more other Web pages link to a particular page, the higher it jumps in Google's ranking structure, called PageRank. This is called "link analysis" and is run independently of the query being made. Once all the Web's indexed pages are ranked, Google also factors in other information, such as the number of links that a site contains to other sites, the text content of a page, its link structure, proximity of search words to one another on the page, fonts, heading, and text of nearby pages. Since the PageRank algorithm was invented by Brin and Page while they were students at Stanford, it is patented and owned by Stanford University, which licenses its use to Google.

However, Google is much more than a page rank algorithm. It's also a hardware superpower. It possesses the largest civilian computing system in the world with an undisclosed number of servers (rumored to be anywhere from 500,000 to 1 million, many of which today have dual- or quad- core processors or "computers") in 16 server "farms" throughout the world. The overall number of computer processors is estimated to be about 3 million.

Google also leads in two related areas: network management software, which permits parallel processing of search queries, and information management software. Google pioneered the concept of using hundreds of thousands of cheap PCs to process huge amounts of data (queries and responses) in microseconds using free Linux software. Searching an index of over 1 billion Web pages requires exceptional software that can coordinate the work of all these PCs. Want to know how many people search on "BMW" on Sundays from 8 a.m. to 8 p.m. in the New York metro area? Where did they come from (prior search), and what was their next search term? Or, maybe you would like to calculate queries and click-through rates for each hour in a 24-hour period in the United States for a single text ad paid for by a customer. To answer these and related marketing-driven questions, Google uses an open source program called HADOOP (named after a toy elephant). HADOOP enables search engines to break large sets of data into smaller chunks stored across thousands of PCs, ask questions of this data, and receive responses in seconds.

However, it is unclear if Google can maintain its technological edge in search given the investments being made by Microsoft, as well as the proliferation of several other smaller but popular search engines. Google only has an exclusive license to the original PageRank patent until 2011. In the competition among search engines, it is clear that search software alone is not the key ingredient, just the foundation for the winning hand. It's a necessary but not sufficient condition for success.

In 2004, Google became a public company, greatly expanding its capital foundation to support further growth. Google's strategy has been to extend its advantages in search into two areas and try to "out-invent" the competition. These areas are advertising and applications: in the words of CEO Eric Schmidt, Google is all about "search, ads, and apps." It has extended search to include images, books,

(continued)

scholars, content, finance, and news. It has extended its advertising services through its AdWords and AdSense programs. AdWords is an auction program that allows advertisers to bid for placement on Google pages. AdSense allows Google to place ads on publisher Web sites (basically any Web site is a "publisher" Web site) based on the content of that site's Web pages. Other services include Google Geo (Maps, Earth, and local content), and Google Checkout (an online wallet). No other online competitor has approached the success of Google's advertising platform.

Bing is arguably the only real competition for Google in the near future. Microsoft is deadly serious about search as the centerpiece of its online revenues. How serious? In May 2008, Microsoft offered to pay $47.5 billion for a 16% share of Yahoo, and outright ownership of Yahoo's search engine, and the banner and search engine ad business built on Yahoo's huge Internet audience of over 150 million in the United States. The deal would have netted Yahoo over $1 billion a year in revenue. Rejected by Yahoo's then president (later fired by its Board for refusing the offer), Microsoft launched Bing with a $120 million marketing effort backed up by another $100 million in "partnership deals" with HP, Dell, and Verizon. Whether you want it or not, Bing will likely appear as the featured search engine on many hardware devices you purchase. Then, in July 2009, Microsoft finally convinced Yahoo to partner with it on search, using Bing as the carrot, and setting the stage for a renewed assault on Google. The 10-year deal gives Microsoft access to the Yahoo's search engine audience. Yahoo will retain 88% of its search engine ad revenue without having to continue investing in search engine technology. While Bing was around 11% of the search market prior to the switch-over, which took at the end of August 2010, Bing's market share, when coupled with Yahoo's, should soar to nearly 30%. Finally, Google will have a credible competitor for search and online advertising. In the process, the rest of us might get a better search experience.

**SOURCES:** "comScore Releases August 2010 U.S. Search Engine Rankings," comScore, Inc., September 16, 2010; "Google Cedes Search Share to Yahoo, Bing Stays Flat," by Clint Boulton, eWeek.com, September 16, 2010; " Bing and Google in Race For Features," by Claire Cain Miller, and Ashlee Vance, *New York Times*, August 1, 2010; "Microsoft Looks to Expand Bing," by Nick Wingfield and Jessica Vascellaro, *Wall Street Journal*, June 10, 2010; "US Ad Spending," by David Hallerman, eMarketer, June 2010; "Bing Adds Visual Search Function," by Miguel Helft, *New York Times*, September 14, 2009; "With Microsoft Deal, Yahoo Tosses in the Search Engine Towel," by Sharon Gaudin, *Computerworld*, July 30, 2009; "Bing Is Off to a Good Start, ComScore Says," by Miguel Helft, *New York Times*, June 9, 2009; "HADOOP ,a Free Software Program, Finds Use Beyond Search," New York Times, March 17, 2009.

The e-tail revenue model is product-based, with customers paying for the purchase of a particular item.

This sector is extremely competitive, however. Since **barriers to entry** (the total cost of entering a new marketplace) into the Web e-tail market are low, tens of thousands of small e-tail shops have sprung up on the Web. Becoming profitable and surviving is very difficult, however, for e-tailers with no prior brand name or experience. The e-tailer's challenge is differentiating its business from existing stores and Web sites.

Companies that try to reach every online consumer are likely to deplete their resources quickly. Those that develop a niche strategy, clearly identifying their target market and its needs, are best prepared to make a profit. Keeping expenses low,

**barriers to entry**
the total cost of entering a new marketplace

selection broad, and inventory controlled are keys to success in e-tailing, with inventory being the most difficult to gauge. Online retail is covered in more depth in Chapter 9.

## CONTENT PROVIDER

**intellectual property**

refers to all forms of human expression that can be put into a tangible medium such as text, CDs or on the Web

**content provider**

distributes information content, such as digital news, music, photos, video, and artwork, over the Web

Although there are many different ways the Internet can be useful, "information content," which can be defined broadly to include all forms of intellectual property, is one of the largest types of Internet usage. **Intellectual property** refers to all forms of human expression that can be put into a tangible medium such as text, CDs, or the Web (Fisher, 1999). **Content providers** distribute information content, such as digital video, music, photos, text, and artwork, over the Web. According to eMarketer, U.S. consumers will spend $10.7 billion for online content such as movies, music, videos, television shows, e-books, and newspapers during 2010.

Content providers make money by charging a subscription fee. For instance, in the case of Rhapsody.com, a monthly subscription fee provides users with access to thousands of song tracks. Other content providers, such as WSJ.com (*The Wall Street Journal's* online newspaper), *Harvard Business Review*, and many others, charge customers for content downloads in addition to or in place of a subscription fee. Micropayment systems technology provides content providers with a cost-effective method for processing high volumes of very small monetary transactions (anywhere from $.25 to $5.00 per transaction). Micropayment systems have greatly enhanced the revenue model prospects of content providers who wish to charge by the download.

Of course, not all online content providers charge for their information: just look at CBSSports.com, CIO.com, CNN.com, and the online versions of many newspapers and magazines. Users can access news and information at these sites without paying a cent. These popular sites make money in other ways, such as through advertising and partner promotions on the site. Increasingly, however, "free content" is limited to headlines and text, whereas premium content—in-depth articles or video delivery— is sold for a fee.

Generally, the key to becoming a successful content provider is owning the content. Traditional owners of copyrighted content—publishers of books and newspapers, broadcasters of radio and television content, music publishers, and movie studios—have powerful advantages over newcomers to the Web who simply offer distribution channels and must pay for content, often at oligopolistic prices.

Some content providers, however, do not own content, but syndicate (aggregate) and then distribute content produced by others. *Syndication* is a major variation of the standard content provider model. Another variation here is Web aggregators, who collect information from a wide variety of sources and then add value to that information through post-aggregation services. For instance, Shopping.com collects information on the prices of thousands of goods online, analyzes the information, and presents users with tables showing the range of prices and Web locations. Shopping.com adds value to content it aggregates, and resells this value to advertisers who advertise on its site.

Any e-commerce start-up that intends to make money by providing content is likely to face difficulties unless it has a unique information source that others cannot access. For the most part, this business category is dominated by traditional content providers.

Online content is discussed in further depth in Chapter 10.

## TRANSACTION BROKER

Sites that process transactions for consumers normally handled in person, by phone, or by mail are **transaction brokers**. The largest industries using this model are financial services, travel services, and job placement services. The online transaction broker's primary value propositions are savings of money and time. In addition, most transaction brokers provide timely information and opinions. Sites such as Monster.com offer job searchers a national marketplace for their talents and employers a national resource for that talent. Both employers and job seekers are attracted by the convenience and currency of information. Online stock brokers charge commissions that are considerably less than traditional brokers, with many offering substantial deals, such as cash and a certain number of free trades, to lure new customers.

**transaction broker**
site that processes transactions for consumers that are normally handled in person, by phone, or by mail

Given rising consumer interest in financial planning and the stock market, the market opportunity for online transaction brokers appears to be large. However, while millions of customers have shifted to online brokers, many have been wary about switching from their traditional broker who provides personal advice and a brand name. Fears of privacy invasion and the loss of control over personal financial information also contribute to market resistance. Consequently, the challenge for online brokers is to overcome consumer fears by emphasizing the security and privacy measures in place, and, like physical banks and brokerage firms, providing a broad range of financial services and not just stock trading. This industry is covered in greater depth in Chapter 9.

Transaction brokers make money each time a transaction occurs. Each stock trade, for example, nets the company a fee, based either on a flat rate or a sliding scale related to the size of the transaction. Attracting new customers and encouraging them to trade frequently are the keys to generating more revenue for these companies. Job sites generate listing fees from employers up front, rather than charging a fee when a position is filled.

Competition among brokers has become more fierce in the past few years, due to new entrants offering ever more appealing offers to consumers to sign on. Those who prospered initially were the first movers such as E*Trade, Ameritrade, Datek, and Schwab. During the early days of e-commerce, many of these firms engaged in expensive marketing campaigns and were willing to pay up to $400 to acquire a single customer. However, online brokerages are now in direct competition with traditional brokerage firms who have joined the online marketspace. Significant consolidation is occurring in this industry. The number of job sites has also multiplied, but the largest sites (those with the largest number of job listings) are pulling ahead of smaller niche companies. In both industries, only a few, very large firms are likely to survive in the long term.

## MARKET CREATOR

**market creator**
builds a digital environment where buyers and sellers can meet, display products, search for products, and establish a price for products

**Market creators** build a digital environment in which buyers and sellers can meet, display products, search for products, and establish prices. Prior to the Internet and the Web, market creators relied on physical places to establish a market. Beginning with the medieval marketplace and extending to today's New York Stock Exchange, a market has meant a physical space for transacting. There were few private digital network marketplaces prior to the Web. The Web changed this by making it possible to separate markets from physical space. A prime example is Priceline, which allows consumers to set the price they are willing to pay for various travel accommodations and other products (sometimes referred to as a reverse auction) and eBay, the online auction site utilized by both businesses and consumers.

For example, eBay's auction business model is to create a digital electronic environment for buyers and sellers to meet, agree on a price, and transact. This is different from transaction brokers who actually carry out the transaction for their customers, acting as agents in larger markets. At eBay, the buyers and sellers are their own agents. Each sale on eBay nets the company a commission based on the percentage of the item's sales price, in addition to a listing fee. eBay is one of the few Web sites that has been profitable virtually from the beginning. Why? One answer is that eBay has no inventory or production costs. It is simply a middleman.

The market opportunity for market creators is potentially vast, but only if the firm has the financial resources and marketing plan to attract sufficient sellers and buyers to the marketplace. At June 30, 2010, eBay had about 87 million active registered users, and this makes for an efficient market (eBay, 2010). There are many sellers and buyers for each type of product, sometimes for the same product, for example, laptop computer models. New firms wishing to create a market require an aggressive branding and awareness program to attract a sufficient critical mass of customers. Some very large Web-based firms such as Amazon have leveraged their large customer base and started auctions. Many other digital auctions have sprung up in smaller, more specialized vertical market segments such as jewelry and automobiles.

In addition to marketing and branding, a company's management team and organization can make a difference in creating new markets, especially if some managers have had experience in similar businesses. Speed is often the key in such situations. The ability to become operational quickly can make the difference between success and failure.

## SERVICE PROVIDER

**service provider**
offers services online

While e-tailers sell products online, **service providers** offer services online. There's been an explosion in online services that is often unrecognized. Web 2.0 applications such as photo sharing, video sharing, and user-generated content (in blogs and social network sites) are all services provided to customers. Google has led the way in developing online applications such as Google Maps, Google Docs, and Gmail. ThinkFree and Adobe Buzzword are online alternatives to Microsoft Word provided as services rather than boxed software (a product). More personal services such as online medical bill management, financial and pension planning, and travel recommender sites are showing strong growth.

Service providers use a variety of revenue models. Some charge a fee, or monthly subscriptions, while others generate revenue from other sources, such as through advertising and by collecting personal information that is useful in direct marketing. Some services are free but are not complete. For instance, Google Apps' basic edition is free, but a "Premier" model with virtual conference rooms and advanced tools costs $50 per employee a year. Much like retailers who trade products for cash, service providers trade knowledge, expertise, and capabilities, for revenue.

Obviously, some services cannot be provided online. For example, dentistry, medical services, plumbing, and car repair cannot be completed via the Internet. However, online arrangements can be made for these services. Online service providers may offer computer services, such as information storage, provide legal services, such as at Linklaters BlueFlag, or offer advice and services to high-net-worth individuals, such as at HarrisMyCFO.com. Grocery shopping sites such as FreshDirect and Peapod are also providing services.[1] To complicate matters a bit, most financial transaction brokers (described previously) provide services such as college tuition and pension planning. Travel brokers also provide vacation-planning services, not just transactions with airlines and hotels. Indeed, mixing services with your products is a powerful business strategy pursued by many hard-goods companies (for example, warranties are services).

The basic value proposition of service providers is that they offer consumers valuable, convenient, time-saving, and low-cost alternatives to traditional service providers or—in the case of search engines and most Web 2.0 applications—they provide services that are truly unique to the Web. Where else can you search 50 billion Web pages, or share photos with as many people instantly? Research has found, for instance, that a major factor in predicting online buying behavior is *time starvation*. Time-starved people tend to be busy professionals who work long hours and simply do not have the time to pick up packages, buy groceries, send photos, or visit with financial planners (Bellman, Lohse, and Johnson, 1999). The market opportunity for service providers is as large as the variety of services that can be provided and potentially is much larger than the market opportunity for physical goods. We live in a service-based economy and society; witness the growth of fast-food restaurants, package delivery services, and wireless cellular phone services. Consumers' increasing demand for convenience products and services bodes well for current and future online service providers.

Marketing of service providers must allay consumer fears about hiring a vendor online, as well as build confidence and familiarity among current and potential customers. Building confidence and trust is critical for service providers just as it is for retail product merchants. Kodak, for instance, has a powerful brand name over a century old, and has translated that brand into a trusted online provider of photo services. In the process, Kodak is transforming itself from a products-only company (cameras and paper) into a more contemporary digital services company.

---

[1]FreshDirect and other e-commerce businesses can also be classified as online retailers insofar as they warehouse commonly purchased items and make a profit based on the spread between their buy and sell prices.

## COMMUNITY PROVIDER

**community provider**

sites that create a digital online environment where people with similar interests can transact (buy and sell goods); share interests, photos, and videos; communicate with like-minded people; and receive interest-related information

Although community providers are not a new entity, the Internet has made such sites for like-minded individuals to meet and converse much easier, without the limitations of geography and time to hinder participation. **Community providers** are sites that create a digital online environment where people with similar interests can transact (buy and sell goods); share interests, photos, videos; communicate with like-minded people; receive interest-related information; and even play out fantasies by adopting online personalities called avatars. The social network sites Facebook, MySpace, LinkedIn, and Twitter, and hundreds of other smaller, niche sites such as Doostang and Sportsvite, all offer users community-building tools and services.

The basic value proposition of community providers is to create a fast, convenient, one-stop site where users can focus on their most important concerns and interests, share the experience with friends, and learn more about their own interests. Community providers typically rely on a hybrid revenue model that includes subscription fees, sales revenues, transaction fees, affiliate fees, and advertising fees from other firms that are attracted by a tightly focused audience.

Community sites such as iVillage make money through affiliate relationships with retailers and from advertising. For instance, a parent might visit Babystyle for tips on diapering a baby and be presented with a link to Huggies.com; if the parent clicks the link and then makes a purchase from Huggies.com, Babystyle gets a commission. Likewise, banner ads also generate revenue. At About.com, visitors can share tips and buy recommended books from Amazon, giving About.com a commission on every purchase. Some of the oldest communities on the Web are Well.com, which provides a forum for technology and Internet-related discussions, and The Motley Fool (Fool.com), which provides financial advice, news, and opinions. The Well offers various membership plans ranging from $10 to $15 a month. Motley Fool supports itself through ads and selling products that start out "free" but turn into annual subscriptions.

Consumers' interest in communities is mushrooming. Community is, arguably, the fastest growing online activity. While many community sites have had a difficult time becoming profitable, over time many have succeeded. Community sites such as Facebook and MySpace are quickly developing advertising revenues as their main source of revenue. Both the very large social network sites such as Facebook, MySpace, and LinkedIn as well as niche sites with smaller dedicated audiences are ideal marketing and advertising territories. Traditional online communities such as the Well, iVillage, and WebMD (which provides medical information to members) find that breadth and depth of knowledge at a site is an important factor. Community members frequently request knowledge, guidance, and advice. Lack of experienced personnel can severely hamper the growth of a community, which needs facilitators and managers to keep discussions on course and relevant. For the newer community social network sites, the most important ingredients of success appear to be ease and flexibility of use, and a strong customer value proposition. For instance, Facebook has leapfrogged over its rival MySpace by encouraging users to build their own revenue-producing applications that run on their profiles, and even take in advertising and affiliate revenues.

Online communities benefit significantly from offline word-of-mouth, viral marketing. Online communities tend to reflect offline relationships. When your friends say they have a profile on Facebook, and ask you to visit, you are encouraged to build your own online profile.

## 2.3 MAJOR BUSINESS-TO-BUSINESS (B2B) BUSINESS MODELS

In Chapter 1, we noted that business-to-business (B2B) e-commerce, in which businesses sell to other businesses, is more than 10 times the size of B2C e-commerce, even though most of the public attention has focused on B2C. For instance, it is estimated that revenues for all types of B2C e-commerce (including spending on online leisure travel and digital content) in 2010 will total around $256 billion, compared to over $3.6 trillion for all types of B2B e-commerce in 2010. Clearly, most of the dollar revenues in e-commerce involve B2B e-commerce. Much of this activity is unseen and unknown to the average consumer.

**Table 2.4** lists the major business models utilized in the B2B arena.

### E-DISTRIBUTOR

Companies that supply products and services directly to individual businesses are **e-distributors**. W.W. Grainger, for example, is the largest distributor of maintenance, repair, and operations (MRO) supplies. MRO supplies are thought of as indirect inputs to the production process—as opposed to direct inputs. In the past, Grainger relied on catalog sales and physical distribution centers in metropolitan areas. Its catalog of equipment went online in 1995 at Grainger.com, giving businesses access to more than 475,000 items. Company purchasing agents can search by type of product, such as motors, HVAC, or fluids, or by specific brand name.

**e-distributor**
a company that supplies products and services directly to individual businesses

E-distributors are owned by one company seeking to serve many customers. However, as with exchanges (described on the next page), critical mass is a factor. With e-distributors, the more products and services a company makes available on its site, the more attractive that site is to potential customers. One-stop shopping is always preferable to having to visit numerous sites to locate a particular part or product.

### E-PROCUREMENT

Just as e-distributors provide products to other companies, **e-procurement firms** create and sell access to digital electronic markets. Firms such as Ariba, for instance, have created software that helps large firms organize their procurement process by creating mini-digital markets for a single firm. Ariba creates custom-integrated online catalogs (where supplier firms can list their offerings) for purchasing firms. On the sell side, Ariba helps vendors sell to large purchasers by providing software to handle catalog creation, shipping, insurance, and finance. Both the buy and sell side software is referred to generically as "value chain management" software.

**e-procurement firm**
creates and sells access to digital electronic markets

| TABLE 2.4 | B2B BUSINESS MODELS | | |
|---|---|---|---|
| BUSINESS MODEL | EXAMPLES | DESCRIPTION | REVENUE MODEL |
| *(1) NET MARKETPLACE* | | | |
| E-distributor | Grainger.com Partstore.com | Single-firm online version of retail and wholesale store; supply maintenance, repair, operation goods; indirect inputs | Sales of goods |
| E-procurement | Ariba Perfect Commerce | Single firm creating digital markets where sellers and buyers transact for indirect inputs | Fees for market-making services; supply chain management, and fulfillment services |
| Exchange | OceanConnect ChemConnect | Independently owned vertical digital marketplace for direct inputs | Fees and commissions on transactions |
| Industry Consortium | Exostar Quadrem Elemica | Industry-owned vertical digital market open to select suppliers | Fees and commissions on transactions |
| *(2) PRIVATE INDUSTRIAL NETWORK* | | | |
| Single Firm | Wal-Mart Procter & Gamble | Company-owned network that coordinates supply chains with a limited set of partners | Cost absorbed by network owner and recovered through production and distribution efficiencies |
| Industry-wide | 1 SYNC Agentrics | Industry-owned network that sets standards, coordinates supply and logistics for the industry | Contributions from industry member firms and recovered through production and distribution efficiencies; fees for transactions and services. |

**B2B service provider** sells business services to other firms

**application service provider (ASP)** a company that sells access to Internet-based software applications to other companies

**scale economies** efficiencies that arise from increasing the size of a business

**B2B service providers** make money through transaction fees, fees based on the number of workstations using the service, or annual licensing fees. They offer purchasing firms a sophisticated set of sourcing and supply chain management tools that permit firms to reduce supply chain costs. In the software world, firms such as Ariba are sometimes also called **application service providers (ASPs)**; they are able to offer firms much lower costs of software by achieving scale economies. **Scale economies** are efficiencies that result from increasing the size of a business, for instance, when large, fixed-cost production systems (such as factories or software systems) can be operated at full capacity with no idle time. In the case of software, the marginal cost of a digital copy of a software program is nearly zero, and finding additional buyers for an expensive software program is exceptionally profitable. This is much more efficient than having every firm build its own supply chain management system, and it permits firms such as Ariba to specialize and offer their software to firms at a cost far less than the cost of developing it.

## EXCHANGES

Exchanges have garnered most of the B2B attention and early funding because of their potential market size even though today they are a small part of the overall B2B picture. An **exchange** is an independent digital electronic marketplace where hundreds of suppliers meet a smaller number of very large commercial purchasers (Kaplan and Sawhney, 2000). Exchanges are owned by independent, usually entrepreneurial start-up firms whose business is making a market, and they generate revenue by charging a commission or fee based on the size of the transactions conducted among trading parties. They usually serve a single vertical industry such as steel, polymers, or aluminum, and focus on the exchange of direct inputs to production and short-term contracts or spot purchasing. For buyers, B2B exchanges make it possible to gather information, check out suppliers, collect prices, and keep up to date on the latest happenings all in one place. Sellers, on the other hand, benefit from expanded access to buyers. The greater the number of sellers and buyers, the lower the sales cost and the higher the chances of making a sale. The ease, speed, and volume of transactions are summarily referred to as *market liquidity*.

In theory, exchanges make it significantly less expensive and time-consuming to identify potential suppliers, customers, and partners, and to do business with each other. As a result, they can lower transaction costs—the cost of making a sale or purchase. Exchanges can also lower product costs and inventory-carrying costs—the cost of keeping a product on hand in a warehouse. In reality, as discussed in Chapter 12, B2B exchanges have had a difficult time convincing thousands of suppliers to move into singular digital markets where they face powerful price competition, and an equally difficult time convincing businesses to change their purchasing behavior away from trusted long-term trading partners. As a result, the number of exchanges has fallen to less than 200, down from over 1,500 in 2002, although the surviving firms have experienced some success

## INDUSTRY CONSORTIA

**Industry consortia** are industry-owned *vertical marketplaces* that serve specific industries, such as the automobile, aerospace, chemical, floral, or logging industries. In contrast, *horizontal marketplaces* sell specific products and services to a wide range of companies. Vertical marketplaces supply a smaller number of companies with products and services of specific interest to their industry, while horizontal marketplaces supply companies in different industries with a particular type of product and service, such as marketing-related, financial, or computing services. For example, Exostar is an online trading exchange for the aerospace and defense industry, founded by BAE Systems, Boeing, Lockheed Martin, Raytheon, and Rolls-Royce in 2000. Exostar connects with over 300 procurement systems and has registered more than 70,000 trading partners in 95 countries around the world.

Industry consortia have tended to be more successful than independent exchanges in part because they are sponsored by powerful, deep-pocketed industry players, and also because they strengthen traditional purchasing behavior rather than seek to transform it.

**exchange**
an independent digital electronic marketplace where suppliers and commercial purchasers can conduct transactions

**industry consortia**
industry-owned vertical marketplaces that serve specific industries

## PRIVATE INDUSTRIAL NETWORKS

**private industrial networks**

digital network designed to coordinate the flow of communications among firms engaged in business together

**Private industrial networks** (sometimes referred to as *private trading exchanges* or *PTXs*) constitute about 75% of all B2B expenditures by large firms and far exceed the expenditures for all forms of Net marketplaces. Private industrial networks are digital networks (often but not always Internet-based networks) designed to coordinate the flow of communications among firms engaged in business together. For instance, Wal-Mart operates one of the largest private industrial networks in the world for its suppliers, who on a daily basis use Wal-Mart's network to monitor the sales of their goods, the status of shipments, and the actual inventory level of their goods. B2B e-commerce relies overwhelmingly on a technology called electronic data interchange (EDI) (U.S. Census Bureau, 2010b). EDI is useful for one-to-one relationships between a single supplier and a single purchaser, and originally was designed for proprietary networks, although it is migrating rapidly to the Internet. Many firms have begun to supplement their EDI systems, however, with more powerful Web technologies that can enable many-to-one, and many-to-many market relationships where there are many suppliers selling to a single or small group of very large purchasers, or, in the case of independent exchanges, there may be many sellers and many buyers simultaneously in the marketplace. EDI is not designed for these types of relationships. There are two types of private industrial networks: single-firm networks and industry-wide networks.

*Single-firm private industrial networks* are the most common form of private industrial network. These single-firm networks are owned by a single large purchasing firm, such as Wal-Mart or Procter & Gamble. Participation is by invitation only to trusted long-term suppliers of direct inputs. Single-firm networks typically evolve out of a firm's own enterprise resource planning (ERP) system, and they are an effort to include key suppliers in the firm's own business decision making.

*Industry-wide private industrial networks* often evolve out of industry associations. These networks are usually owned by a consortium of the large firms in an industry and have the following goals: providing a neutral set of standards for commercial communication over the Internet; having shared and open technology platforms for solving industry problems; and in some cases, providing operating networks that allow members of an entire industry to closely collaborate. To some extent, these industry-wide networks are a response to the success of single-firm private industrial networks. For instance, Wal-Mart has refused to open its very successful network to other members of the retail industry, in effect to become an industry standard, for fear it will be sharing technology secrets with other retailers like Sears.

In response, Sears and other retailers around the world have created their own set of organizations and networks that are open to all in the industry. For instance, Agentrics was formed through the merger of two industry-wide private industrial network for retailers and suppliers that were created to facilitate and simplify trading among retailers, suppliers, partners, and distributors. Agentrics' customers currently include 15 of the the world's top 25 retailers and over 250 suppliers from Africa, Asia, Europe, North America, and South America. Agentrics provides collaborative design tools; planning and management; negotiations and auctions; order execution; demand aggregation; worldwide item management; worldwide logistics; and a global catalog in English, French, German, and Spanish containing trading relationship data for member-sponsored suppliers totaling more than 30,000 items (Agentrics LLC, 2010). From this list of services and capabilities, it is clear that industry-wide private industrial networks offer much more functionality than industry consortia, although the two models appear to be moving closer together. We discuss these developments and other nuances of B2B commerce in Chapter 12.

## 2.4 OTHER E-COMMERCE BUSINESS MODELS

When we think about a business, we typically think of a business firm that produces a product or good, and then sells it to a customer. But the Web has forced us to recognize new forms of business, such as consumer-to-consumer e-commerce, peer-to-peer e-commerce, and mobile commerce. These other business models do not quite fit neatly into the classification schema we have laid out earlier in this chapter. **Table 2.5** lists these three business models and their revenue models.

### CONSUMER-TO-CONSUMER (C2C) BUSINESS MODELS

Consumer-to-consumer (C2C) ventures provide a way for consumers to sell to each other, with the help of an online business. The largest C2C sites are eBay and Craigslist. eBay utilizes an auction market business model while Craigslist offers an online classified service where consumers can find products, or sell products usually for a fixed price. When the sellers get organized and expand into profitable enterprises selling on eBay, they are not so much consumers anymore than they are small businesses selling goods on a marketplace (and hence the business model is that of an e-tailer). Craigslist.com, the largest C2C online classified ads service in the world, is also

| TABLE 2.5 | BUSINESS MODELS IN EMERGING E-COMMERCE AREAS | | |
|---|---|---|---|
| BUSINESS | EXAMPLES | DESCRIPTION | REVENUE MODEL |
| Consumer-to-consumer | eBay<br>Half.com<br>Craigslist.com | Helps consumers connect with other consumers to conduct business | Transaction fees |
| Peer-to-peer | The Pirate Bay<br>Cloudmark | Technology enabling consumers to share files and services via the Web, without a common server | Subscription fees, advertising, transaction fees |
| Mobile commerce | eBay Mobile<br>PayPal Mobile Checkout<br>AOL Mobile-Moviefone | Extending business applications using wireless technology | Sales of goods and services |

a leading example of C2C commerce. There are hundreds of smaller online classified services, many of which are online versions of newspaper classifieds.

Before eBay and Craigslist, individual consumers used garage sales, flea markets, and thrift shops to both dispose of and acquire used merchandise. With the introduction of online auctions, consumers no longer had to venture out of their homes or offices in order to bid on items of interest, and sellers could relinquish expensive retail space that was no longer needed in order to reach buyers. In return for linking like-minded buyers and sellers, eBay takes a small commission. The more auctions, the more money eBay makes. In fact, it is one of the few Web companies that has been profitable from day one—and has stayed so for several years.

Consumers who don't like auctions but still want to find used merchandise can use eBay's fixed-price listings, or visit Half.com (also owned by eBay), which enables consumers to sell unwanted books, movies, music, and games to other consumers at a fixed price. In return for facilitating the transaction, Half.com takes a commission on the sale, ranging from 5%–15%, depending on the sale price, plus a fraction of the shipping fee it charges.

Even small one-person artisanal shops can be seen as C2C efforts. In 2010, Web sites such as Etsy, DaWanda, 1000 Markets, ArtFire, and Silkfair are exemplary models of C2C business on the Internet.

## PEER-TO-PEER (P2P) BUSINESS MODELS

Like the C2C models, P2P business models link users, enabling them to share files and computer resources without a common server. The focus in P2P companies is on helping individuals make information available for anyone's use by connecting users on the Web. Historically, peer-to-peer software technology has been used to allow the sharing of copyrighted music, video, and image files in violation of digital copyright law. The challenge for P2P ventures is to develop viable, legal business models that will enable them to make money. In Chapter 1, we discussed the difficulties faced by The Pirate Bay, one of the most prominent examples of a P2P business model in action. To date, there are few if any examples of successful P2P e-commerce business models outside of the illegal content file—swapping sites. However, one company that has successfully used this model in a legitimate business is Cloudmark, which offers a P2P anti-spam solution called Cloudmark Desktop. In 2010, Cloudmark protects over 1 billion e-mailboxes around the world.

## MOBILE COMMERCE BUSINESS MODELS

Mobile commerce takes traditional e-commerce models and leverages the functionality of mobile devices such as smartphones and netbooks, and broadband wireless technologies—described more fully in Chapter 3—to permit mobile access to the Web. Wireless Web technology is being used to enable the extension of existing Web business models to service the mobile work force and consumer of the future. Wireless networks, both cellular and WiFi, utilize available bandwidth and communication protocols to connect mobile users to the Internet. The major advantage of m-commerce is that it provides Internet access to anyone, anytime, and anywhere, using wireless devices. The key technologies here are cell phone-based 3G and 4G (third and fourth generation cellular wireless), Wi-Fi (wireless local area networks), and Bluetooth (short-range radio frequency Web devices).There are many more cell phone subscribers (an estimated 5 billion worldwide in 2010) than there are Internet users. Cell phone usage is still considerably higher in Asia and Europe than it is in the United States. However, in the United States, the introduction of the iPhone in June 2007 (the first so-called "smartphone"), the 3G version in July 2008, and the 4G version in June 2010 has brought about a resurgence of interest in cell phones and their role in e-commerce. Nearly parallel introductions of BlackBerry and Android-based smartphones have also extended the market for mobile digital devices. The standards implementing Wi-Fi were first introduced in 1997, and since then it has exploded in the United States and elsewhere. Analysts estimate that there are more than 320,000 free and paid wireless hot spots (locations that enable a Wi-Fi-enabled device to connect to a nearby wireless LAN and access the Internet) in 140 countries worldwide in 2010 (JiWire.com, 2010).

Prior to 2009, mobile commerce in the United States had been a disappointment. However, with the introduction of the iPhone and other phones with similar capabilities, as noted above, this has begun to change. For instance, most of the top 100 largest online retailers, such as Amazon, Newegg, 1-800-Flowers.com, and others now have Web sites optimized for mobile commerce or offer shopping applications that can be downloaded onto smartphones, and more are joining them every day. As with all areas of e-commerce, the challenge for businesses will be finding ways to use m-commerce to make money while serving customer needs. Currently, demand is highest for digital content such as ring tones, games, videos, and wallpaper. With the introduction of the iPhone, mobile search applications have become more popular. Consumer applications are also beginning to appear in high-volume personal transaction areas, such as AOL's Moviefone reservation system, eBay's Mobile system, and mobile payment platforms such as PayPal's Mobile Checkout.

What are the unique business functionalities of mobile digital devices and how do they contribute to business model innovation. First, they are mobile and portable, permitting shopping from anywhere, anytime, rather than being confined to a desktop at work or home. This feature greatly expands the time available for shopping online. By June 2010, Amazon Mobile's iPhone app had resulted in over $1 billion in mobile sales. Second, smartphones have cameras that can be used to scan product codes while shopping. This feature allows shoppers in stores to use their smartphones to swipe product codes and do comparison shopping, or receive special offers from the store. Third, smartphones have built-in GPS capabilities that identify where the user is located. This feature makes it possible to sell services to people based on where they are located. For instance, restaurants, museums, and book stores can contact potential customers as they walk down a nearby street. Mobile commerce is the fastest growing form of e-commerce, and the fastest growing advertising platform in the United States. Mobile commerce is discussed in more detail in Chapter 3.

M-commerce business models that rely on location-based advertising, as described in *Insight on Society: Where R U? Not Here!* are becoming increasingly popular, but raise a number of thorny social issues.

# INSIGHT ON SOCIETY

## WHERE R U? NOT HERE!

First, the Internet made the world flat. Location no longer mattered. You could find and purchase products around the world just as easily as ones in your hometown. Now with the advent of GPS chip and software technology that enables your smartphone to track your exact position, where you are located has once again become important to Internet entrepreneurs and marketers. Manufacturers of netbooks and laptops are adding similar location functionality to their products as well. With these new capabilities come new business opportunities, accompanied by some familiar concerns about privacy and security.

For instance, Loopt is a free social network application that allows you to share your status and track the location of friends via smartphones such as the iPhone, BlackBerry, Android, and over 100 other mobile devices. Loopt has more than 4 million users. Loopt describes itself as a mobile "social-mapping service that lets you use the location of your phone to discover the world around you." You can use the Loopt iPhone app to find out where your friends are, discover places nearby to eat or be entertained, and look at advertisements showing you nearby deals and discounts. Loopt's business model, like most location-based services, is advertising. Loopt doesn't sell information to advertisers, but does post ads based on user location: its privacy policy allows it to disclose "some personally identifiable, registration, profile, or location information to subsidiaries, affiliated companies, or other businesses or persons ... in order to serve relevant advertisements." Loopt's target is to deal with advertisers at the walking level (within 200 to 250 meters).

Although the mobile advertising market in 2010 is currently small ($593 million), it is fast-growing (up 50% from last year and expected to grow to over $1.5 billion by 2013), as more and more companies seek ways to exploit new databases of location-specific information and insert ads into mobile messages and search results. For example, Alcatel-Lucent offers a service managed by 1020 Placecast that identifies cell phone users within a specified distance of an advertiser's nearest outlet and notifies them of the outlet's address and phone number, perhaps including a link to a coupon or other promotion. 1020 Placecast's clients include Hyatt, FedEx, and Avis Rent A Car. Burger King and Suburu have run campaigns using Useful Networks' Store Finder application that allows users to click a mobile banner ad to find the nearest store location. The campaignl showed that the location-enabled campaign significantly increased Store Finder conversion rates compared to users who had to manually enter zip codes to find locations. In 2010, Zagats restaurant guide introduced its Go To Zagats app for iPhone and Blackberry, which helps users find just the right restaurant based on their location.

While there's no denying the potential usefulness of such a service, the specter of "Big Brother" location tracking has privacy advocates raising the alarm. Privacy experts such as Lauren Gelman, executive director of Stanford Law School's Center for Internet and Society wonder, "How are we going to get all the benefits that come from doing geo-location without sacrificing people's privacy?" In fact, over 60% of smartphone users fear the geo-location features of these phones will compromise their privacy. As it turns out, location-based services are just great—if you can turn them off easily, or, turn them on momentarily to receive a service. Unfortunately, Google's Lattitude service and Loopt are promotiong the notion of continuously broadcasting your location. You're never "off the grid."

(continued)

To date, wireless location-based services remain largely unregulated. The Wireless Communications and Public Safety Act (often called the "911 Act") added the term "location" to the definition of customer proprietary network information (CPNI) held by telecommunication carriers, to make it eligible for certain privacy protections offered by the Communications Act of 1934. The 911 Act also required that the Federal Communications Commission (FCC) establish rules regarding how telecommunications carriers treat CPNI. The FCC did so in July 2002, adopting an approach that requires an individual's affirmative consent (opt-in) for some circumstances and assuming consent is granted unless an individual indicates otherwise (opt-out) in others.

The 2003 CAN-SPAM Act required the FCC to issue rules to protect wireless subscribers from unwanted mobile service commercial messages, and provides that consumers can list their cell phone numbers in the National Do Not Call Registry. In August 2004, the FCC proposed regulations, most of which went into effect in October 2004, that prohibit sending wireless commercial e-mail messages unless the individual addressee has given the sender express prior authorization. The FCC also created a publicly available list of wireless domain names list used for mobile service messaging so that senders of commercial mail could more easily determine which addresses are directed at mobile services. In 2009, the law was used to force three firms responsible for the infamous "car warranty" scam cell phone calls to cease and pay restitution to consumers.

Congress continues to debate how to protect wireless subscribers further, but thus far no laws have passed since CAN-SPAM in 2003. Europe and Japan, in contrast, have strong government privacy protection policies forbidding the use of location-based data without user consent, and there are strict limitations on selling the information to third parties. The wireless industry, mindful of the privacy issues raised in the online e-commerce context, has issued calls for stringent self-regulation in an attempt to avoid government-imposed regulation. In July 2008, the Mobile Marketing Association (MMA) adopted a global code of conduct for wireless marketing campaigns, broadening the scope of privacy guidelines it had previously issued for the United States. The code focuses on five basic tenets:

- Notice: Users should be informed of the marketer's identity and the purpose for which location information is being captured and used.
- Choice and consent: Opt-in consent should be obtained and a simple opt-out process provided.
- Customization and constraint: Customer data should be handled responsibly and only used for the purpose of providing relevant and valuable services.
- Security: Sufficient security to protect consumer data from unauthorized third-party access and use should be provided.
- Enforcement and accountability: MMA members are expected to comply with the code of conduct, and should self-certify that they are doing so.

In addition, some companies are offering technological solutions. For instance, WaveMarket provides a location aggregation platform called Veriplace that serves as middleware between mobile application developers and wireless carriers. The platform allows developers to access real-time user location data in their application. WaveMarket identifies the platform's "Privacy Engine" as one of its core features. The Privacy Engine allows end users full control over disclosure of their location. For instance, an end user can decide to share or not share location information based on days of the week or hours of the day, or to generalize location information from street-corner level to zip code or city level. End users can also view a history of all location requests, so they can always see who is trying to locate them. Another alternative is provided by

(continued)

Foursquare, a popular mobile social application. After starting up Foursquare on a smartphone, users see a list of local bars and restaurants, select their location, and "check in," which sends a message to their friends. Rather than track people all the time without their consent, the check-in model gives users some control over communicating their locations.

Facebook and Yelp are expected to use check-in models. These and other methods can allow people to proclaim "I'm not here" even though secretly they are. Whether consumers will actually use these capabilities to protect their location and other personal information is a question whose answer remains to be seen.

**SOURCES**: "Apple Isn't the Only Company Making Cool Mobile Ads," *Wall Street Journal*, July 2, 2010; "Apple Could Jump-Start Mobile Advertising, Challenge Old Media," by Nat Worden, *New York Times*, June 7, 2010; "Telling Friends Where You Are (or Not)," by Jenna Wortham, *New York Times*, March 14, 2010; "Always-On Devices and Networks," by Noah Elkin, eMarketer, January 2010. "MetaPlaces 09: Location-based Ads and Privacy," TheWhereBusiness.com, July 16, 2009; "Cellphone Tracking Services: Friend Finder or Big Brother," by Michael B. Farrell, *Christian Science Monitor*, May 1, 2009; "Wireless Communications: Voice and Data Privacy" and "When a Cell Phone Is More Than a Phone: Protecting Your Privacy in the Age of the Smartphone," Privacy Rights Clearinghouse, http://www.privacyrights.org (undated, accessed July 31, 2009).

### E-COMMERCE ENABLERS: THE GOLD RUSH MODEL

Of the nearly 500,000 miners who descended on California in the Gold Rush of 1849, less than 1% ever achieved significant wealth. However, the banking firms, shipping companies, hardware companies, real estate speculators, and clothing companies such as Levi Strauss built long-lasting fortunes. Likewise in e-commerce. No discussion of e-commerce business models would be complete without mention of a group of companies whose business model is focused on providing the infrastructure necessary for e-commerce companies to exist, grow, and prosper. These are the e-commerce enablers: the Internet infrastructure companies. They provide the hardware, operating system software, networks and communications technology, applications software, Web designs, consulting services, and other tools that make e-commerce over the Web possible (see **Table 2.6**). While these firms may not be conducting e-commerce per se (although in many instances, e-commerce in its traditional sense is in fact one of their sales channels), they as a group have perhaps profited the most from the development of e-commerce. We will discuss many of these players in the following chapters.

## 2.5    HOW THE INTERNET AND THE WEB CHANGE BUSINESS: STRATEGY, STRUCTURE, AND PROCESS

Now that you have a clear grasp of the variety of business models used by e-commerce firms, you also need to understand how the Internet and the Web have changed the business environment in the last decade, including industry structures, business strategies, and industry and firm operations (business processes and value chains). We will return to these concepts throughout the book as we explore the e-commerce phenomenon. In general, the Internet is an open standards system available to all players, and this fact inherently makes it easy for new competitors to

| TABLE 2.6 | E-COMMERCE ENABLERS |
|---|---|
| **INFRASTRUCTURE** | **PLAYERS** |
| Hardware: Web Servers | IBM, HP, Dell, Oracle |
| Software: Operating Systems and Server Software | Microsoft, RedHat Linux, Sun/Oracle, Apache Software Foundation |
| Networking: Routers | Cisco, JDS Uniphase, Alcatel-Lucent |
| Security: Encryption Software | VeriSign, Check Point, Entrust, RSA, Thawte |
| E-commerce Software Systems (B2C, B2B) | IBM, Microsoft, Ariba, Broadvision, Oracle (BEA Systems) |
| Streaming and Rich Media Solutions | Real Networks, Microsoft, Apple, Adobe |
| Customer Relationship Management Software | Oracle, SAP, GSI Commerce, Escalate Retail, Salesforce.com |
| Payment Systems | VeriSign, PayPal, Cybersource, Chase Paymentech |
| Performance Enhancement | Akamai, Limelight Networks |
| Databases | Oracle, Microsoft, Sybase, IBM |
| Hosting Services | IBM, WebIntellects, Qwest, Rackspace, Web.com |

enter the marketplace and offer substitute products or channels of delivery. The Internet tends to intensify competition. Because information becomes available to everyone, the Internet inherently shifts power to buyers who can quickly discover the lowest-cost provider on the Web. On the other hand, the Internet presents many new opportunities for creating value, for branding products and charging premium prices, and for enlarging an already powerful offline physical business such as Wal-Mart or Sears.

Recall Table 1.2 in Chapter 1 that describes the truly unique features of e-commerce technology. **Table 2.7** suggests some of the implications of each unique feature for the overall business environment—industry structure, business strategies, and operations.

## INDUSTRY STRUCTURE

E-commerce changes industry structure, in some industries more than others. **Industry structure** refers to the nature of the players in an industry and their relative bargaining power. An industry's structure is characterized by five forces: *rivalry among existing competitors*, the *threat of substitute products, barriers to entry into the industry*, the *bargaining power of suppliers*, and the *bargaining power of buyers* (Porter, 1985). When you describe an industry's structure, you are describing the general business environment in an industry and the overall profitability of doing business in that environment. E-commerce has the potential to change the relative strength of these competitive forces (see **Figure 2.4**).

When you consider a business model and its potential long-term profitability, you should always perform an industry structural analysis. An **industry structural analysis** is an effort to understand and describe the nature of competition in an

**industry structure**
refers to the nature of the players in an industry and their relative bargaining power

**industry structural analysis**
an effort to understand and describe the nature of competition in an industry, the nature of substitute products, the barriers to entry, and the relative strength of consumers and suppliers

| TABLE 2.7 | EIGHT UNIQUE FEATURES OF E-COMMERCE TECHNOLOGY |
|---|---|
| FEATURE | SELECTED IMPACTS ON BUSINESS ENVIRONMENT |
| Ubiquity | Alters industry structure by creating new marketing channels and expanding size of overall market. Creates new efficiencies in industry operations and lowers costs of firms' sales operations. Enables new differentiation strategies. |
| Global reach | Changes industry structure by lowering barriers to entry, but greatly expands market at same time. Lowers cost of industry and firm operations through production and sales efficiencies. Enables competition on global scope. |
| Universal standards | Changes industry structure by lowering barriers to entry and intensifying competition within an industry. Lowers costs of industry and firm operations by lowering computing and communications costs. Enables broad scope strategies. |
| Richness | Alters industry structure by reducing strength of powerful distribution channels. Changes industry and firm operations cost by reducing reliance on sales forces. Enhances post-sales support strategies. |
| Interactivity | Alters industry structure by reducing threat of substitutes through enhanced customization. Reduces industry and firm costs by reducing reliance on sales forces. Enables Web-based differentiation strategies. |
| Personalization/ Customization | Alters industry structure by reducing threats of substitutes, raising barriers to entry. Reduces value chain costs in industry and firms by lessening reliance on sales forces. Enables personalized marketing strategies. |
| Information density | Changes industry structure by weakening powerful sales channels, shifting bargaining power to consumers. Reduces industry and firm operations costs by lowering costs of obtaining, processing, and distributing information about suppliers and consumers. |
| Social network technologies | Changes industry structure by shifting programming and editorial decisions to consumers; creates substitute entertainment products; energizes a large group of new suppliers. |

industry, the nature of substitute products, the barriers to entry, and the relative strength of consumers and suppliers.

E-commerce can affect the structure and dynamics of industries in very different ways. Consider the recorded music industry, an industry that has experienced significant change because of the Internet and e-commerce. Historically, the major record label firms owned the exclusive rights to the recorded music of various artists. With the entrance into the marketplace of substitute providers such as Napster and Kazaa, millions of consumers began to use the Internet to bypass traditional music labels and their distributors entirely. In the travel industry, entirely new middlemen such as Travelocity have entered the market to compete with traditional travel agents. After Travelocity, Expedia, CheapTickets, and other travel services demonstrated the power of e-commerce marketing for airline tickets, the actual owners of the airline seats—the major airlines—banded together to form their own Internet outlet for tickets, Orbitz, for direct sales to consumers (although

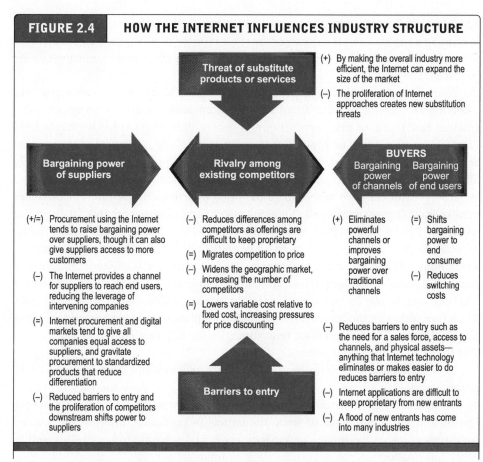

## FIGURE 2.4 — HOW THE INTERNET INFLUENCES INDUSTRY STRUCTURE

**Threat of substitute products or services**

(+) By making the overall industry more efficient, the Internet can expand the size of the market

(–) The proliferation of Internet approaches creates new substitution threats

**Bargaining power of suppliers**

**Rivalry among existing competitors**

**BUYERS**
Bargaining power of channels
Bargaining power of end users

(+/=) Procurement using the Internet tends to raise bargaining power over suppliers, though it can also give suppliers access to more customers

(–) The Internet provides a channel for suppliers to reach end users, reducing the leverage of intervening companies

(=) Internet procurement and digital markets tend to give all companies equal access to suppliers, and gravitate procurement to standardized products that reduce differentiation

(–) Reduced barriers to entry and the proliferation of competitors downstream shifts power to suppliers

(–) Reduces differences among competitors as offerings are difficult to keep proprietary

(=) Migrates competition to price

(–) Widens the geographic market, increasing the number of competitors

(=) Lowers variable cost relative to fixed cost, increasing pressures for price discounting

(+) Eliminates powerful channels or improves bargaining power over traditional channels

(=) Shifts bargaining power to end consumer

(–) Reduces switching costs

(–) Reduces barriers to entry such as the need for a sales force, access to channels, and physical assets—anything that Internet technology eliminates or makes easier to do reduces barriers to entry

(–) Internet applications are difficult to keep proprietary from new entrants

(–) A flood of new entrants has come into many industries

**Barriers to entry**

The Internet and e-commerce have many impacts on industry structure and competitive conditions. From the perspective of a single firm, these changes can have negative or positive implications. In this figure, "+" indicates a positive development for the firm, "–" a negative development, and "=" that neither positive nor negative impacts can be predicted. Each industry will be affected differently and must be analyzed separately. SOURCE: Porter, 2001.

ultimately selling the company to a private investor group). Clearly, e-commerce and the Internet create *new industry dynamics* that can best be described as the give and take of the marketplace, the changing fortunes of competitors.

Yet in other industries, the Internet and e-commerce have strengthened existing players. In the chemical and automobile industries, e-commerce is being used effectively by manufacturers to strengthen their traditional distributors. In these industries, e-commerce technology has not fundamentally altered the competitive forces—bargaining power of suppliers, barriers to entry, bargaining power of buyers, threat of substitutes, or rivalry among competitors—within the industry. Hence, each industry is different and you need to examine each one carefully to understand the impacts of e-commerce on competition and strategy.

New forms of distribution created by new market entrants can completely change the competitive forces in an industry. For instance, when consumers gladly substitute free access to Wikipedia for a $2,500 set of Britannica encyclopedias, or a $50 DVD of Encarta, then the competitive forces in the encyclopedia industry are radically changed. Even if the substitute is an inferior product, consumers are able to satisfy their anxieties about their children's education at a much lower cost (Gerace, 1999).

Inter-firm rivalry (competition) is one area of the business environment where e-commerce technologies have had an impact on most industries. In general, the Internet has increased price competition in nearly all markets. It has been relatively easy for existing firms to adopt e-commerce technology and attempt to use it to achieve competitive advantage vis-à-vis rivals. For instance, the Internet inherently changes the scope of competition from local and regional to national and global. Because consumers have access to global price information, the Internet produces pressures on firms to compete by lowering prices (and lowering profits). On the other hand, the Internet has made it possible for some firms to differentiate their product or services from others. Amazon has patented one-click purchasing, for instance, while eBay has created a unique, easy-to-use interface and a differentiating brand name. REI, Inc.—a specialty mountain climbing-oriented sporting goods company— has been able to use its Web site to maintain its strong niche focus on outdoor gear. Therefore, although the Internet has increased emphasis on price competition, it has also enabled businesses to create new strategies for differentiation and branding so that they can retain higher prices.

It is impossible to determine if e-commerce technologies have had an overall positive or negative impact on firm profitability in general. Each industry is unique, so it is necessary to perform a separate analysis for each one. Clearly, e-commerce has shaken the foundations of some industries, in particular, information product industries (such as the music, newspaper, book, and software industries) as well as other information-intense industries such as financial services. In these industries, the power of consumers has grown relative to providers, prices have fallen, and over-all profitability has been challenged. In other industries, especially manufacturing, the Internet has not greatly changed relationships with buyers, but has changed relationships with suppliers. Increasingly, manufacturing firms in entire industries have banded together to aggregate purchases, create industry digital exchanges or marketplaces, and outsource industrial processes in order to obtain better prices from suppliers. Throughout this book, we will document these changes in industry structure and market dynamics introduced by e-commerce and the Internet.

## INDUSTRY VALUE CHAINS

**value chain**

the set of activities performed in an industry or in a firm that transforms raw inputs into final products and services

While an industry structural analysis helps us understand the impact of e-commerce technology on the overall business environment in an industry, a more detailed industry value chain analysis can help identify more precisely just how e-commerce may change business operations at the industry level (Benjamin and Wigand, 1995). One of the basic tools for understanding the impact of information technology on industry and firm operations is the value chain. The concept is quite simple. A **value chain** is the set of activities performed in an industry or in a firm that transforms raw inputs into final products and services. Each of these activities adds economic value to the final product; hence, the term *value chain* as an interconnected set of value-adding activities.

**Figure 2.5** illustrates the six generic players in an industry value chain: suppliers, manufacturers, transporters, distributors, retailers, and customers.

By reducing the cost of information, the Internet offers each of the key players in an industry value chain new opportunities to maximize their positions by lowering costs and/or raising prices. For instance, manufacturers can reduce the costs they pay for goods by developing Web-based B2B exchanges with their suppliers. Manufacturers can develop direct relationships with their customers through their own Web sites, bypassing the costs of distributors and retailers. Distributors can develop highly efficient inventory management systems to reduce their costs, and retailers can develop highly efficient customer relationship management systems to strengthen their service to customers. Customers in turn can use the Web to search for the best quality, fastest delivery, and lowest prices, thereby lowering their transaction costs and reducing prices they pay for final goods. Finally, the operational efficiency of the entire industry can increase, lowering prices and adding value to consumers, and helping the industry to compete with alternative industries.

## FIRM VALUE CHAINS

The concept of value chain can be used to analyze a single firm's operational efficiency as well. The question here is: How does e-commerce technology potentially affect the value chains of firms within an industry? A **firm value chain** is the set of activities a firm engages in to create final products from raw inputs. Each step in the process of production adds value to the final product. In addition, firms develop support activities that coordinate the production process and contribute to overall operational efficiency. **Figure 2.6** illustrates the key steps and support activities in a firm's value chain.

**firm value chain**
the set of activities a firm engages in to create final products from raw inputs

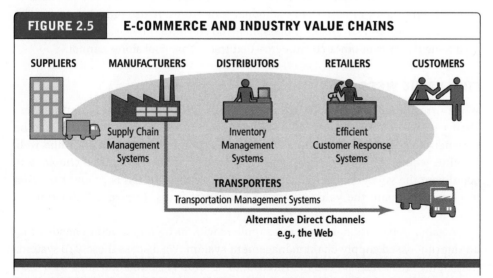

| FIGURE 2.5 | E-COMMERCE AND INDUSTRY VALUE CHAINS |
| --- | --- |

SUPPLIERS    MANUFACTURERS    DISTRIBUTORS    RETAILERS    CUSTOMERS

Supply Chain Management Systems

Inventory Management Systems

Efficient Customer Response Systems

**TRANSPORTERS**
Transportation Management Systems

**Alternative Direct Channels e.g., the Web**

Every industry can be characterized by a set of value-adding activities performed by a variety of actors. E-commerce potentially affects the capabilities of each player as well as the overall operational efficiency of the industry.

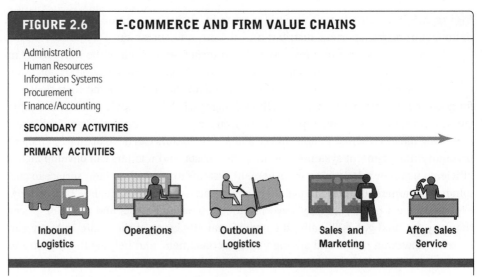

**FIGURE 2.6** | **E-COMMERCE AND FIRM VALUE CHAINS**

Every firm can be characterized by a set of value-adding primary and secondary activities performed by a variety of actors in the firm. A simple firm value chain performs five primary value-adding steps: inbound logistics, operations, outbound logistics, sales and marketing, and after sales service.

The Internet offers firms many opportunities to increase their operational efficiency and differentiate their products. For instance, firms can use the Internet's communications efficiency to outsource some primary and secondary activities to specialized, more efficient providers without such outsourcing being visible to the consumer. In addition, firms can use the Internet to more precisely coordinate the steps in the value chains and reduce their costs. Finally, firms can use the Internet to provide users with more differentiated and high-value products. For instance, Amazon uses the Internet to provide consumers with a much larger inventory of books to choose from, at a lower cost, than traditional book stores. It also provides many services—such as instantly available professional and consumer reviews, and information on buying patterns of other consumers—that traditional bookstores cannot.

## FIRM VALUE WEBS

**value web**
networked trans-business system that coordinates the value chains of several firms

While firms produce value through their value chains, they also rely on the value chains of their partners—their suppliers, distributors, and delivery firms. The Internet creates new opportunities for firms to cooperate and create a value web. A **value web** is a networked business ecosystem that uses Internet technology to coordinate the value chains of business partners within an industry, or at the first level, to coordinate the value chains of a group of firms. **Figure 2.7** illustrates a value web.

A value web coordinates a firm's suppliers with its own production needs using an Internet-based supply chain management system. We discuss these B2B systems in Chapter 12. Firms also use the Internet to develop close relationships with their logistics partners. For instance, Amazon relies on UPS tracking systems to provide its customers with online package tracking, and it relies on the U.S. Postal Service

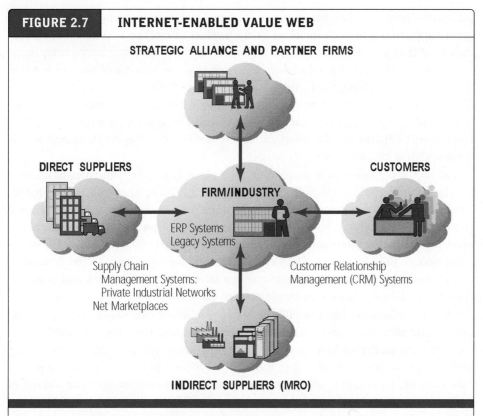

## FIGURE 2.7 INTERNET-ENABLED VALUE WEB

**STRATEGIC ALLIANCE AND PARTNER FIRMS**

**DIRECT SUPPLIERS**

**CUSTOMERS**

**FIRM/INDUSTRY**

ERP Systems
Legacy Systems

Supply Chain
Management Systems:
Private Industrial Networks
Net Marketplaces

Customer Relationship
Management (CRM) Systems

**INDIRECT SUPPLIERS (MRO)**

Internet technology enables firms to create an enhanced value web in cooperation with their strategic alliance and partner firms, customers, and direct and indirect suppliers.

systems to insert packages directly into the mail stream. Amazon has partnership relations with hundreds of firms to generate customers and to manage relationships with customers. (Online customer relationship management systems are discussed in Chapter 6.) In fact, when you examine Amazon closely, you realize that the value it delivers to customers is in large part the result of coordination with other firms and not simply the result of activities internal to Amazon. The value of Amazon is, in large part, the value delivered by its value web partners. This is difficult for other firms to imitate in the short run.

## BUSINESS STRATEGY

A **business strategy** is a set of plans for achieving superior long-term returns on the capital invested in a business firm. A business strategy is therefore a plan for making profits in a competitive environment over the long term. **Profit** is simply the difference between the price a firm is able to charge for its products and the cost of producing and distributing goods. Profit represents economic value. Economic value is created anytime customers are willing to pay more for a product than it costs to produce. Why would anyone pay more for a product than it costs to

**business strategy**
a set of plans for achieving superior long-term returns on the capital invested in a business firm

**profit**
the difference between the price a firm is able to charge for its products and the cost of producing and distributing goods

produce? There are multiple answers. The product may be unique (there are no other suppliers), it may be the least costly product of its type available, consumers may be able to purchase the product anywhere in the world, or it may satisfy some unique needs that other products do not. Each of these sources of economic value defines a firm's strategy for positioning its products in the marketplace. There are four generic strategies for achieving a profitable business: differentiation, cost, scope, and focus. We describe each of these below. The specific strategies that a firm follows will depend on the product, the industry, and the marketplace where competition is encountered.

Although the Internet is a unique marketplace, the same principles of strategy and business apply. As we will see throughout the book, successful e-commerce strategies involve using the Internet to leverage and strengthen existing business (rather than destroy your business), and to use the Internet to provide products and services your competitors cannot copy (in the short term anyway). That means developing unique products, proprietary content, distinguishing processes (such as Amazon's one-click shopping), and personalized or customized services and products (Porter, 2001). Let's examine these ideas more closely.

**Differentiation** refers to all the ways producers can make their products unique and distinguish them from those of competitors. The opposite of differentiation is **commoditization**—a situation where there are no differences among products or services, and the only basis of choosing a product is price. As economists tell us, when price alone becomes the basis of competition and there are many suppliers and many customers, eventually the price of the good falls to the cost to produce it (marginal revenues from the nth unit equal marginal costs). And then profits are zero! This is an unacceptable situation for any business person. The solution is to differentiate your product and to create a monopoly-like situation where you are the only supplier.

There are many ways businesses differentiate their products. A business may start with a core generic product, but then create expectations among users about the "experience" of consuming the product—"Nothing refreshes like a Coke!" or "Nothing equals the experience of driving a BMW." Businesses may also augment products by adding features to make them different from those of competitors. And businesses can differentiate their products further by enhancing the products' abilities to solve related consumer problems. For instance, tax programs such as TurboTax can import data from spreadsheet programs, as well as be used to electronically file tax returns. These capabilities are enhancements to the product that solve a customer's problems. The purpose of marketing is to create these differentiation features and to make the consumer aware of the unique qualities of products, creating in the process a "brand" that stands for these features. We discuss marketing and branding in Chapters 6 and 7.

In their totality, the differentiation features of a product constitute the customer value proposition we described in earlier sections of this chapter. The Internet and the Web offer some unique ways to differentiate products. The ability of the Web to personalize the shopping experience and to customize the product or service to the particular demands of each consumer are perhaps the most

**differentiation**
refers to all the ways producers can make their products unique and different to distinguish them from those of competitors

**commoditization**
a situation where there are no differences among products or services, and the only basis of choosing products is price

significant ways in which the Web can be used to differentiate products. E-commerce businesses can also differentiate products by leveraging the ubiquitous nature of the Web (by making it possible to purchase the product from home, work, or on the road); the global reach of the Web (by making it possible to purchase the product anywhere in the world); richness and interactivity (by creating Web-based experiences for people who use the product, such as unique interactive content, videos, stories about users, and reviews by users); and information density (by storing and processing information for consumers of the product, such as warranty information on all products purchased through a site or income tax information online).

Adopting a *strategy of cost competition* means a business has discovered some unique set of business processes or resources that other firms cannot obtain in the marketplace. Business processes are the atomic units of the value chain. For instance, the set of value-creating activities called Inbound Logistics in Figure 2.6 is in reality composed of many different collections of activities performed by people on the loading docks and in the warehouses. These different collections of activities are called *business processes*—the set of steps or procedures required to perform the various elements of the value chain.

When a firm discovers a new, more efficient set of business processes, it can obtain a cost advantage over competitors. Then it can attract customers by charging a lower price, while still making a handsome profit. Eventually, its competitors go out of business as the market decisively tilts toward the lowest-cost provider. Or, when a business discovers a unique resource, or lower-cost supplier, it can also compete effectively on cost. For instance, switching production to low-wage-cost areas of the world is one way to lower costs.

Competing on cost can be a short-lived affair and very tricky. Competitors can also discover the same or different efficiencies in production. And competitors can also move production to low-cost areas of the world. Also, competitors may decide to lose money for a period as they compete on cost.

The Internet offers some new ways to compete on cost, at least in the short term. Firms can leverage the Internet's ubiquity by lowering the costs of order entry (the customer fills out all the forms, so there is no order entry department); leverage global reach and universal standards by having a single order entry system worldwide; and leverage richness, interactivity, and personalization by creating customer profiles online and treating each individual consumer differently— without the use of an expensive sales force that performed these functions in the past. Finally, firms can leverage the information intensity of the Web by providing consumers with detailed information on products, without maintaining either expensive catalogs or a sales force.

While the Internet offers powerful capabilities for intensifying cost competition, making cost competition appear to be a viable strategy, the danger is that competitors have access to the same technology. The *factor markets*—where producers buy their supplies—are open to all. Assuming they have the skills and organizational will to use the technology, competitors can buy many of the same cost-reducing techniques in the marketplace. Even a skilled labor force can be purchased, ultimately. However, self-knowledge, proprietary tacit knowledge (knowledge that is not published or codified), and a loyal, skilled workforce are in the short term difficult to purchase in factor markets. Therefore, cost competition remains a viable strategy.

Two other generic business strategies are scope and focus. A *scope strategy* is a strategy to compete in all markets around the globe, rather than merely in local, regional, or national markets. The Internet's global reach, universal standards, and ubiquity can certainly be leveraged to assist businesses in becoming global competitors. Yahoo, for instance, along with all of the other top 20 e-commerce sites, has readily attained a global presence using the Internet. A *focus strategy* is a strategy to compete within a narrow market segment or product segment. This is a specialization strategy with the goal of becoming the premier provider in a narrow market. For instance, L.L.Bean uses the Web to continue its historic focus on outdoor sports apparel; and W.W. Grainger—the Web's most frequently visited B2B site—focuses on a narrow market segment called MRO: maintenance, repair, and operations of commercial buildings. The Internet offers some obvious capabilities that enable a focus strategy. Firms can leverage the Web's rich interactive features to create highly focused messages to different market segments; the information intensity of the Web makes it possible to focus e-mail and other marketing campaigns on small market segments; personalization—and related customization—means the same product can be customized and personalized to fulfill the very focused needs of specific market segments and consumers.

Industry structure, industry and firm value chains, value webs, and business strategy are central business concepts used throughout this book to analyze the viability of and prospects for e-commerce sites. In particular, the signature case studies found at the end of each chapter are followed with questions that may ask you to identify the competitive forces in the case, or analyze how the case illustrates changes in industry structure, industry and firm value chains, and business strategy.

**CASE STUDY**

# Pandora
## and the Freemium Business Model

Pandora is the Internet's most successful subscription radio service. In 2010, it added its 60 millionth user, and continues to add 600,000 new subscribers a week. Pandora now accounts for 44% of all Internet radio listening hours. Radio? In the Internet age of iTunes, Rhapsody, and listen-to-what-you-want-anywhere-anytime? Why would anyone want an online radio station to choose the music they will be able to hear? That's so old school.

Not exactly. At Pandora, users select a genre of music based on a favorite musician, and a computer algorithm puts together a personal radio station that plays not only the music of the selected artist, but also closely related music by different artists. How does the computer know about closely related music and music genres? Can a computer understand music? Not really. Instead a group of over 50 musicians listen to new songs each day and classify the music according to over 400 musical criteria including male or female vocal, electric vs. acoustical guitar, distortion of instruments, presence of background vocals, strings, and various other instruments. These criteria are used in a computer algorithm to classify new songs into five genres: Pop/Rock,

Hip-Hop/Electronica, Jazz, World Music, and Classical. Within each of these genres are hundreds of sub-genres. Like Taylor Swift? Create a radio station on Pandora with Taylor Swift as the artist and you can listen all day not only to some Taylor Swift tracks but also to musically related artists such as Carrie Underwood, Rascal Flatts, Anita Nalick, and others.

The algorithm used to identify genres of songs is a result of the Music Genome Project conceived by Will Glaser and Tim Westergren in 1999. Westergren, a jazz musician, and Glaser believed it was possible to identify genres of music, and sub-genres, using their expertise (and that of 50 other musicians) to identify similarities among artists and songs. They have identified over 400 factors to help classify songs, and leave it up to the computer program to select appropriate matches based on a user's,input of a selected artist. To some extent they are mimicking disk jockeys and radio program managers who had no trouble creating jazz radio, classical radio, and pop/electronica stations, and within these general categories, sub-groups of musicians who shared musical characteristics.

In 2005, Glaser and Westergren launched Pandora.com, a music service based on the Music Genome Project. Their biggest challenge was how to make a business out of a totally new kind of online radio station when online competing stations were making music available for free, most without advertising, and online subscription services were streaming music for a monthly fee and finding some advertising support as well. Actually, their biggest challenge was to avoid going broke: over 80% of online music is downloaded from P2P networks for free. iTunes launched in 2001 and by 2005 was a roaring success, charging .99 cents a song with no ad support, and 20 million users at that time. The idea of a "personal" radio station playing your kind of music was very new.

Facing stiff odds, Pandora's first business model was to give away 10 hours of free access to Pandora, and then ask subscribers to pay $36 a month for a year after they used up their free 10 hours. Result: 100,000 people listened to their 10 hours for free and then refused to use their credit cards to pay for the annual service. People loved Pandora but were unwilling to pay for it, or so it seemed in the early years.

Facing financial collapse, in November 2005 Pandora introduced an ad-supported option. Subscribers could listen to a maximum of 40 hours of music in a calendar month for free. After the 40 hours were used up, subscribers had three choices: (a) pay .99 cents for the rest of the month, (b) sign up for a premium service offering unlimited usage, or (c) do nothing. If they chose (c), the music would stop, but users could sign up again the next month. The ad-supported business model was a risky move because Pandora had no ad server or accounting system, but it attracted so many users that in a few weeks they had a sufficient number of advertisers (including Apple) to pay for their infrastructure. In 2006, Pandora added a "Buy" button to each song being played and struck deals with Amazon, iTunes, and other online retail sites. Pandora now gets an affiliate fee for directing listeners to Amazon where users can buy the music. In 2008 , Pandora added an iPhone app to allow users to sign up from their smartphones and listen all day if they wanted. This added 35,000 new users a day. By 2009, this "free" ad-supported model had attracted 20 million users, and by the end of the year Pandora earned $50 million and became a profitable company for the first time. All of Pandora's plans come with restrictions required by the music companies that own the music, including the inability to hear a song on demand, no replay, and a skip limit of six skips per hour per station. Also, the music cannot be used commercially or outside the United States. After struggling for years showing nothing but losses, threatened by the music labels who wanted to raise their Internet radio rates, Pandora finally had some breathing room.

Still not giving up on its premium service, in late 2009, the company launched Pandora One, a premium service that offered no advertising, higher quality streaming music, a desktop app, and fewer usage limits. The service cost $36. By July 2010, Pandora had 600,000 subscribers to its premium service, about 1% of its 60 million users. Do the math: that's revenue of $21.8 million from the premium service alone. At the end of 2009, Pandora reported its first profitable quarter and $50 million in annual revenue, mostly from ads. The remainder of its revenue comes from subscriptions and payments from iTunes and Amazon when people buy music. Wall Street analysts believe revenue will approach $100 million by the end of 2010.

Pandora is an example of the "freemium" business revenue model. The model is based on giving away some services for free to 99% of the customers, and relying on the other 1% of the customers to pay for premium versions of the same service. Chris Anderson, author of *Free: The Future of a Radical Price* in a blog post noted "...you give away 99% of your product to sell 1%. The reason this makes sense is that for digital products, where the marginal cost is close to zero, the 99% costs you little and allows you to reach a huge market. So the 1% you convert, is 1% of a big number." There are many other examples of successful freemium model companies. For many traditional print media like newspapers and magazines the fremium model may be their path to survival. But it won't work for every online business.

There is ongoing debate among e-commerce CEOs and venture capitalists about the effectiveness of the freemium model. The crux of the issue is that while freemium can be an efficient way to gather a large group of potential customers, companies have found that it's a challenge to convert eyeballs into those willing to pay. Absent subscriber revenue, firms need to rely on advertising revenues.

MailChimp's story is both a success and a cautionary tale. The company lets anyone send e-mail newsletters to customers, manage subscriber lists, and track the performance of an e-mail marketing campaign. Despite the powerful tools it gives marketers, and its open applications programming interface, after 10 years in business, the company had only 85,000 paid subscribers.

In 2009, CEO Ben Chestnut decided that it was time to implement new strategies to attract additional customers. MailChimp began giving away its basic tools and charging subscription fees for special features. The concept was that as those customers' e-mail lists grew, they would continue using MailChimp, and be willing to pay for enhanced services. These services included more than just the ability to send e-mails to a greater number of people. Clients would pay to use sophisticated analytics to help them target their e-marketing campaigns more efficiently and effectively.

In seven months, MailChimp saw a 240% growth in the number of users, a 225% increase in e-mail delivery volume (from 200 million to 450 million), and a 200% increase in projected revenue. Sounds good, but it came at a price. The company also saw a 354% increase in abuse, and a 245% increase in legal costs. Much of the abuse was "fuzzy spam," where the spammers successfully disguised their efforts so software such as Spam Assassin couldn't find and block their messages. After studying other corporate Web sites, Chestnut's staff found that almost every site offering freemium had the same issue.

Instead of abandoning the freemium model, MailChimp developed Project Omnivore, an optimization algorithm that could find bad e-mails. Since introducing Omnivore, the company has sent 35,539 warnings, suspended 4,233 accounts, and shut down 1,193 users. Fortunately for MailChimp, the algorithm can add additional value for customers because it can find positive trends, and estimate the odds that users will open a given e-mail in an e-marketing campaign.

For MailChimp, freemium has been worth the price. However, Ning, a company that enables users to create their own social networks, tried freemium and came to a different conclusion. They abandoned it in July 2010.

Mark Andressen, co-author of Mosaic, the first Web browser, and founder of Netscape, launched Ning in 2004. With his assistance, the company has raised $119 million in funding. Despite being the market's leading social network platform with more than 2.3 million user-created networks and 45 million regular users, Ning was having a common problem--converting eyeballs into paying customers. While 13% of customers were paying for some premium services, the revenue was not enough. The more free users Ning acquired, the more it cost the company.

In May 2010, Ning announced the impending end of the freemium model. The company shed staff, going from 167 to 98, and is now using 100% of its resources to capture premium users. It has introduced a three-tiered pricing model, starting at $19.95 per month for the basic service. Ning is giving existing users a 30-day grace period to choose a plan. Its Web site provides detailed information on each option with checklists featuring the number of users, the amount of storage, and the bandwidth available at each price point.

Ning's new business model counts on a variety of revenue streams: premium services, Google ads, partnerships, and sponsorships. Partners include Pearson Publishing, which has committed to sponsor Ning's 8,600 education networks (K-12 and higher education) for the next 3 years, reducing the cost to subscribers to just $19.95 a year. Additional partners include CafePress, which helps customers sell branded merchandise online, and ChipIn, which helps non-profit customers raise money and collect donations.

So when does it make sense to include freemium in a business plan? It makes sense when the product is easy to use and has a very large potential audience, preferably in the millions. A solid customer value proposition is critical. It's helpful if a large user network increases the perceived value of the product (i.e., a dating service). Freemium may work when a company has good long-term customer retention rates, and the product produces more value over time. An extremely important part of the equation is that the variable costs of providing the product or service to additional customers for free must be low.

For example, Evernote, a personal note-taking service, added freemium to its business model and grew its user base to 2.7 million. Around 7,000 new users sign up every day. The company has 50,000 paying users, and has found that over time, inactive users drop out and active users start paying. The number of users is growing 10% per month, while revenue is growing faster, at 18% per month, even with only .5% of those new users choosing to go premium (paid). When the company looked at one year of data, it showed that 2% of users who signed up a year ago are paying now. One of the key metrics for success for Evernote and any other company using freemium, is revenue per active user versus variable expenses. Evernote earns $.25 per user per month, and it spends only $.09 per user per month.

Typically, 2% to 5% of freemium users convert from the free product or service to the paid version, so Evernote's conversion rate of 2% is within the range of what can be expected. When looking at freemium as a strategy, it's important for a company to calculate whether it can make money at the low end of that scale.

Companies also face challenges in terms of what products and/or services to offer for free versus what to charge for (this may change over time), the cost of supporting free customers and how to price premium services. Further it is difficult to predict attrition rates, which are highly variable at companies using freemium. So, while freemium can be a great way to get early users and to provide a company with a built-in pool for upgrades, it's tough to determine how many users will be willing to pay and willing to stay.

A freemium strategy makes sense for companies such as Pandora and Skype, where there is a very low marginal cost, approaching zero, to support free users. It also makes sense for a company where the value to their potential customers depends on a large network, like Facebook. Freemium also works when a business can be run and be supported by the percentage of customers who are willing to pay, like Evernote and Pandora, especially when there are other revenues like affiliate and advertising fees which can make up for shortfalls in subscriber revenues.

**SOURCES:** "How Pandora Grew to Get 60 Million Listeners," by Om Malik, Gigaom.com, July 21, 2010; "Ning Partners with Pearson to Sponsor Free Network Access for Educators," by Leena Rao, Techcrunch.com, June 24, 2010; "How To Avoid The Traps and Make a 'Freemium' Business Model Pay," Anna Johnson, Kikabink.com, June 14th, 2010; "6 Ways for Online Business Directories to Convert More Freemium to Premium," BusinessWeek.com, April 14, 2010; "Case Studies in Freemium: Pandora, Dropbox, Evernote, Automattic and MailChimp," by Liz Gannes, Gigacom.com, Mar. 26, 2010; "Struggling Pandora Earns First Profit, Sets Sights on a Future of Playing Everywhere," by Clair Cain Miller, *New York Times*, March 15, 2010; "Pandora Bringing Web Radio to Cars," by Sarah McBride, *Wall Street Journal*, January 7, 2010; "As Online Music Falters, Pandora Doubled To 40 Million Users This Year," by MG Siegler, Techncrunch.com, December 16, 2009; *Free: The Future of a Radical Price*, by Chris Anderson, Hyperion, 2009.

## Case Study Questions

1. Compare Pandora's original business model with its current business model. What's the difference between "free" and "freemium" revenue models?

2. What is the customer value proposition that Pandora offers?

3. Why did MailChimp ultimately succeed with a freemium model but Ning did not?

4. What's the most important consideration when considering a freemium revenue model?

| 2.7 | **REVIEW** |

## KEY CONCEPTS

■ **Identify the key components of e-commerce business models.**

A successful business model effectively addresses eight key elements:

- *Value proposition*—how a company's product or service fulfills the needs of customers. Typical e-commerce value propositions include personalization, customization, convenience, and reduction of product search and price delivery costs.
- *Revenue model*—how the company plans to make money from its operations. Major e-commerce revenue models include the advertising model, subscription model, transaction fee model, sales model, and affiliate model.
- *Market opportunity*—the revenue potential within a company's intended marketspace.
- *Competitive environment*—the direct and indirect competitors doing business in the same marketspace, including how many there are and how profitable they are.
- *Competitive advantage*—the factors that differentiate the business from its competition, enabling it to provide a superior product at a lower cost.
- *Market strategy*—the plan a company develops that outlines how it will enter a market and attract customers.
- *Organizational development*—the process of defining all the functions within a business and the skills necessary to perform each job, as well as the process of recruiting and hiring strong employees.
- *Management team*—the group of individuals retained to guide the company's growth and expansion.

■ **Describe the major B2C business models.**

There are a number of different business models being used in the B2C e-commerce arena. The major models include the following:

- *Portal*—offers powerful search tools plus an integrated package of content and services; typically utilizes a combined subscription/advertising revenue/transaction fee model; may be general or specialized (vortal).
- *E-tailer*—online version of traditional retailer; includes virtual merchants (online retail store only), bricks-and-clicks e-tailers (online distribution channel for a company that also has physical stores), catalog merchants (online version of direct mail catalog), and manufacturers selling directly over the Web.
- *Content provider*—information and entertainment companies that provide digital content over the Web; typically utilizes an advertising, subscription, or affiliate referral fee revenue model.
- *Transaction broker*—processes online sales transactions; typically utilizes a transaction fee revenue model.
- *Market creator*—uses Internet technology to create markets that bring buyers and sellers together; typically utilizes a transaction fee revenue model.

- *Service provider*—offers services online.
- *Community provider*—provides an online community of like-minded individuals for networking and information sharing; revenue is generated by advertising, referral fees, and subscriptions.

■ **Describe the major B2B business models.**

The major business models used to date in the B2B arena include:
- *E-distributor*—supplies products directly to individual businesses.
- *E-procurement*—single firms create digital markets for thousands of sellers and buyers.
- *Exchange*—independently owned digital marketplace for direct inputs, usually for a vertical industry group.
- *Industry consortium*—industry-owned vertical digital market.
- *Private industrial network*—industry-owned private industrial network that coordinates supply chains with a limited set of partners.

■ **Recognize business models in other emerging areas of e-commerce.**

A variety of business models can be found in the consumer-to-consumer e-commerce, peer-to-peer e-commerce, and m-commerce areas:
- *C2C business models*—connect consumers with other consumers. The most successful has been the market creator business model used by eBay.
- *P2P business models*—enable consumers to share files and services via the Web without common servers. A challenge has been finding a revenue model that works.
- *M-commerce business models*—take traditional e-commerce models and leverage emerging wireless technologies to permit mobile access to the Web.
- *E-commerce enablers*—focus on providing the infrastructure necessary for e-commerce companies to exist, grow, and prosper.

■ **Understand key business concepts and strategies applicable to e-commerce.**

The Internet and the Web have had a major impact on the business environment in the last decade, and have affected:
- *Industry structure*—the nature of players in an industry and their relative bargaining power by changing the basis of competition among rivals, the barriers to entry, the threat of new substitute products, the strength of suppliers, and the bargaining power of buyers.
- *Industry value chains*—the set of activities performed in an industry by suppliers, manufacturers, transporters, distributors, and retailers that transforms raw inputs into final products and services by reducing the cost of information and other transaction costs.
- *Firm value chains*—the set of activities performed within an individual firm to create final products from raw inputs by increasing operational efficiency.
- *Business strategy*—a set of plans for achieving superior long-term returns on the capital invested in a firm by offering unique ways to differentiate products, obtain cost advantages, compete globally, or compete in a narrow market or product segment.

## QUESTIONS

1. What is a business model? How does it differ from a business plan?
2. What are the eight key components of an effective business model?
3. What are Amazon's primary customer value propositions?
4. Describe the five primary revenue models used by e-commerce firms.
5. Why is targeting a market niche generally smarter for a community provider than targeting a large market segment?
6. Besides music, what other forms of information could be shared through peer-to-peer sites? Are there legitimate commercial uses for P2P commerce?
7. Would you say that Amazon and eBay are direct or indirect competitors? (You may have to visit the Web sites to answer.)
8. What are some of the specific ways that a company can obtain a competitive advantage?
9. Besides advertising and product sampling, what are some other market strategies a company might pursue?
10. What elements of FreshDirect's business model may be faulty? Does this business scale up to a regional or national size?
11. Why is it difficult to categorize e-commerce business models?
12. Besides the examples given in the chapter, what are some other examples of vertical and horizontal portals in existence today?
13. What are the major differences between virtual storefronts, such as Drugstore.com, and bricks-and-clicks operations, such as Walmart.com? What are the advantages and disadvantages of each?
14. Besides news and articles, what other forms of information or content do content providers offer?
15. What is a reverse auction? What company is an example of this type of business?
16. What are the key success factors for exchanges? How are they different from portals?
17. What is an application service provider?
18. What are some business models seen in the C2C and P2P e-commerce areas?
19. How have the unique features of e-commerce technology changed industry structure in the travel business?
20. Who are the major players in an industry value chain and how are they impacted by e-commerce technology?
21. What are four generic business strategies for achieving a profitable business?

## PROJECTS

1. Select an e-commerce company. Visit its Web site and describe its business model based on the information you find there. Identify its customer value proposition, its revenue model, the marketspace it operates in, who its main competitors are, any comparative advantages you believe the company possesses, and what its market strategy appears to be. Also try to locate information about the company's management team and organizational structure. (Check for a page labeled "the Company," "About Us," or something similar.)

2.  Examine the experience of shopping on the Web versus shopping in a traditional environment. Imagine that you have decided to purchase a digital camera (or any other item of your choosing). First, shop for the camera in a traditional manner. Describe how you would do so (for example, how you would gather the necessary information you would need to choose a particular item, what stores you would visit, how long it would take, prices, etc.). Next, shop for the item on the Web. Compare and contrast your experiences. What were the advantages and disadvantages of each? Which did you prefer and why?

3.  Visit eBay and look at the many types of auctions available. If you were considering establishing a rival specialized online auction business, what are the top three market opportunities you would pursue, based on the goods and auction community in evidence at eBay? Prepare a report or electronic slide presentation to support your analysis and approach.

4.  During the early days of e-commerce, first-mover advantage was touted as one way to success. On the other hand, some suggest that being a market follower can yield rewards as well. Which approach has proven to be more successful— first mover or follower? Choose two e-commerce companies that prove your point, and prepare a brief presentation to explain your analysis and position.

5.  Prepare a research report (3 to 5 pages) on the current and potential future impacts of e-commerce technology, including mobile devices, on the book publishing industry.

# Technology Infrastructure for E-commerce

## CHAPTER 3

# The Internet and World Wide Web: E-commerce Infrastructure

**After reading this chapter, you will be able to:**

- Discuss the origins of the Internet.
- Identify the key technology concepts behind the Internet.
- Describe the role of Internet protocols and utility programs.
- Explain the current structure of the Internet.
- Understand the limitations of today's Internet.
- Describe the potential capabilities of Internet II.
- Understand how the World Wide Web works.
- Describe how Internet and Web features and services support e-commerce.

# Wikitude.me

Walk down the street in any major metropolitan area and count the number of people pecking away at their iPhones or BlackBerries. Roam your campus—how many of your friends are texting as they speak, using Twitter, or watching a YouTube video on their smartphone? Ride the train, and observe how many fellow travelers are reading an online newspaper on their phone. In a few years, the primary means of accessing the Internet, both in the United States and worldwide, will be through highly portable netbooks and smart phones such as the Apple iPhone, BlackBerry Curve, and others. Traditional desktop and laptop PCs will of course remain important e-commerce and Internet tools, but the action has shifted to the mobile platform. This means that the primary platform for e-commerce products and services will also change to a mobile platform. The number of mobile Internet users is expected grow to 50% of all Internet users by 2013.

Wikitude.me is an example of a online mobile platform "points of interest" location-based service that uses the same kind of wiki tools that power Wikipedia, the online encyclopedia. Wikitude.me focuses on information about where you are currently located. Wikitude provides a special kind of browser for smartphones equipped with a built-in GPS and compass that can identify your precise location and where the phone is pointed. Using information from over 800,000 points of interest available on Wikipedia.com, the browser overlays information about the points of interest you are looking at, and displays that information on your smart phone screen, overlayed on a map or photograph that you just snapped. Mobilizy GmbH, the Austrian firm that invented the browser, refers to these techniques as "augmented reality applications." Wikitude.me also allows users to geo-tag the world around them, and then submit the tags to Wikitude in order to share content with other users around the world. This user-generated database adds thousands of local sites that are not identified on Wikipedia. Users can point their smartphone cameras towards mountains from a tour bus and see the names and heights of the mountains displayed on the screen. Lost in a European medieval city, or downtown Los Angeles? Open up the Wikitude browser, point your camera at a building, and then find the address and other interesting details. At Wimbledon in 2010, Mobilizy worked with

IBM and Ogilvy to develop an application called SEER for Android and iPhone smartphones that displayed real-time information about matches in progress and players, along with dining and transportation information.

Mobilizy and Wikitude are currently in the development stage and have not yet begun to exploit the commercial application of augmented reality. But it's not hard to figure out where the e-commerce might reside in these tools. How would you like your restaurant, or fruit stand, or service company, or movie theater, to show up on the cell phones of users visiting or searching for points of interest in your neighborhood? How much would you pay to have an online travel guide with you all the time for that next trip abroad?

SPRXmobile, a Dutch company, has developed a similar augmented reality, location-based application called Layar. Users can download Layar for free in Amsterdam. Layar is also available as an app on iPhones and Androids. Starting up the Layar application automatically activates the smartphone camera. The embedded GPS automatically knows the location of the phone, and the compass determines in which direction the phone is facing. Commercial partners provide location coordinates with relevant information that forms a digital layer. By tapping the side of the screen, the user easily switches between layers—from a simple picture, to a picture augmented with information, to a map. Local firms, which include restaurants, theaters, financial service firms, and businesses looking for employees, pay a fee to SPRXmobile and can then look through their Android smart phone cameras and see information about ATMs on the street, restaurants, bars, healthcare providers, and job openings displayed in the front of the buildings that house these services and opportunities. The first country in which Layar has been launched is The Netherlands. Partners include local market leaders ING (bank), Funda (real estate firm), Hyves (social network), Tempo-team (temporary employment agency), and Zekur.nl (healthcare provider). Verizon became one of the first commercial users of Layar in May 2010. Verizon is using Layar to promote and market its Android phones.

Mobile digital platform services are also extending to more traditional online activities such as shopping for retail goods and finding the best prices. Slifter is a location-based shopping service that you can use on the Web or download to your BlackBerry or iPhone. Forgot your tie at the hotel on the way to an important business meeting? Or forget the wedding shoes? Not a problem. Slifter will tell you where you can find ties and shoes based on the GPS location of your smartphone. Slifter also tells you the price, whether the product is in stock, provides product information, images, special promotions, and maps. You can save products and promotions into a mobile Shopping List and share finds with friends using Twitter or several social networks. Slifter is based on the premise that most shopping in America takes place in local stores. True: less than 5% of the $3.9 trillion retail goods marketplace in the United States is online, the rest is offline at local stores. Helping consumers find the right store is possibly a much larger market and more solid business model than helping consumers find the right product and lowest price online.

Other players in this space are NearbyNow and Krillion. Related competitors include ShopSavvy, which allows consumers to hold their mobile phone cameras up to a product's UPC code sitting on a retailer's shelf, scan the code, ping the ShopSavvy servers, and receive back information on the best prices both locally and on the Web. Quattro Wireless provides another example of the potential for mobile online location-based services. Quattro Wireless, a mobile advertising network, has combined its service with one of the iPhone's most popular applications called WHERE. WHERE is a mobile app that provides users with information about the people, places, and things around them. Local content available through WHERE includes everything from the weather, news, and restaurant reviews, to the cheapest gas, movie showtimes, and the ability to connect with other users through Buddy Beacon and the WHERE Wall. The combined service sells location-based keyword searches, sponsored widgets, and local search terms. For instance, a consumer pharmacy chain such as Walgreens can purchase mobile keywords such as "headache," "stomach ache," or "back pain" to drive consumers to the nearest Walgreen's pharmacy. A somewhat more aggressive mobile advertising technique is "geo-fencing." These applications use cell phone GPS capabilities to draw fences around their customer's stores. When subscribers walk within the digital fence they are sent ads and discounts. Burger King, Applebee's, and Quizno's are testing this technology in 2010.

Ever get lost in a store looking for a product, or try to buy something only to find out your size is out of stock? Location-based shopping services can solve these problems and be a real boost to local retailers who have for years been directly challenged by online retailers. Manhattan designer Kamali signed up for a service called ScanLife, which allows customers to scan bar codes with their cell phones, and view videos on the items. IBM has developed Presence Zones technology that senses when a shopper enters a store and offers coupons and discounts in real time, and can make product recommendations. The technology is being used in a joint Cisco Systems and IBM service called Mobile Concierge. Enter a product name, and the system tells you where it is located in the store.

Not to be left behind, Facebook introduced its social network, location-based service called Places in August 2010. Like similar services from Foursquare, Yelp, and Gowalla, Places allows users to use their iPhones to check in at places and broadcast their location to friends. Users can also see which of their friends are at locations nearby or at the same location.

Location-based services are in their infancy, producing about $215 million in revenue in 2010, but this is expected to grow to over $700 million by 2013. Other revenue streams generated by the new mobile digital platform in 2010 include software apps sales at stores such as iTunes ($5 billion); entertainment downloads of ringtones, music, video, and TV shows (about $7.2 billion); mobile display advertising ($995 million); direct shopping services such as Slifter ($220 million); and e-book sales ($150 million). While these numbers are still relatively small, mobile e-commerce is the fastest growing form of e-commerce, expanding at the rate of 50% or more a year. By 2013, the mobile platform is expected to generate about 10% of all online B2C e-commerce.

**SOURCES**: "Facebook Unveils a Service to Announce Where Users Are," by Miguel Helf and Jenna Wortham, *New York Times*, August 18, 2010; "Kicking Reality Up a Notch," by Leslie Berlin, *New York Times*, July 12, 2009; "Wikitude Goes Wimbledon 2010," press release, Wikitude.com, June 20, 2010; "IBM Unveils Smart New Mobile Applications to Keep Up to Date With Wimbledon 2009," press release, IBM, June 17, 2009; Mobile Applications," by Noah Elkin, eMarketer, June 2009; "When the Customer is in the Neighborhood," by Diana Ransom, *Wall Street Journal*, May 17, 2010; "Verizon Uses Layar's Augmented Reality to Promote Droid phones," press release, Layar.com, May 14th 2010; "Mobile Location-Based Services Used by US Internet Users, eMarketer, April 20, 2010; "Cell-phones Let Shoppers Point, Click and Purchase," by Stephanie Rosenbloom, *New York Times*, February 27, 2010; "The Emerging Mobile Digital Platform: E-commerce and Business Impacts," by Kenneth Laudon, *Managing the Digital Firm*, 11th edition. Learning Track. January, 2010; "US Mobile Internet Users, 2008–2013," eMarketer, November 1, 2009; "Augmented Reality: Another (Virtual) Brick in the Wall," by Michelle Delio, *MIT Technology Review*, February 15, 2005.

Thischapter examines the Internet and World Wide Web of today and tomorrow, how it evolved, how it works, and how the present and future infrastructure of the Internet and the Web enables new business opportunities.

The opening case illustrates how important it is for business people to understand how the Internet and related technologies work, and to be aware of what's new on the Internet. It could change your business drastically, and open up new opportunities as well. Operating a successful small business on the Web and implementing key Web business strategies such as personalization, customization, market segmentation, and price discrimination, all require that business people understand Web technology and keep track of Web developments.

The Internet and its underlying computer technology is not a static phenomenon in history, but instead is changing very rapidly. The Internet happened, but it is also happening. Computers have merged with cell phone services; broadband access in the home and broadband wireless access to the Internet via smartphones and netbooks is expanding rapidly; self-publishing on the Web via blogging, social networking, and podcasting now engages millions of Internet users; and new software technologies such as Web services, cloud computing, and smartphone apps are revolutionizing the way businesses are using the Internet. Looking forward a few years to the emerging Internet II of 2014, the business strategies of the future will require a firm understanding of these new technologies to deliver products and services to consumers.

## 3.1 THE INTERNET: TECHNOLOGY BACKGROUND

What is the Internet? Where did it come from, and how did it support the growth of the World Wide Web? What are the Internet's most important operating principles? How much do you really need to know about the technology of the Internet?

Let's take the last question first. The answer is: it depends on your career interests. If you are on a marketing career path, or general managerial business path, then you need to know the basics about Internet technology, which you'll learn in this and the following chapter. If you are on a technical career path and hope to become a Web designer, or pursue a technical career in Web infrastructure for businesses, you'll need to start with these basics and then build from there. You'll also need to know about the business side of e-commerce, which you will learn about throughout this book.

**Internet**
an interconnected network of thousands of networks and millions of computers linking businesses, educational institutions, government agencies, and individuals

As noted in Chapter 1, the **Internet** is an interconnected network of thousands of networks and millions of computers (sometimes called *host computers* or just *hosts*) linking businesses, educational institutions, government agencies, and individuals. The Internet provides approximately 1.8 billion people around the world (including about 220 million people in the United States) with services such as e-mail, newsgroups, shopping, research, instant messaging, music, videos, and news (Internetworldstats.com, 2010). No single organization controls the Internet or how it functions, nor is it owned by anybody, yet it has provided the infrastructure for a transformation in commerce, scientific research, and culture. The word Internet is derived from the word *internetwork*, or the connecting together of two or more computer networks. The **World Wide Web**, or **Web** for short, is one of the Internet's most popular services, providing access to billions, perhaps trillions of Web pages, which are documents created in a programming language called HTML that can contain text, graphics, audio, video, and other objects, as well as "hyperlinks" that permit users to jump easily from one page to another.

**World Wide Web (Web)**

one of the Internet's most popular services, providing access to over 100 billion Web pages

## THE EVOLUTION OF THE INTERNET: 1961—THE PRESENT

Today's Internet has evolved over the last 50 or so years. In this sense, the Internet is not "new;" it did not happen yesterday. Although journalists talk glibly about "Internet" time—suggesting a fast-paced, nearly instant, worldwide global change mechanism, in fact, it has taken about 50 years of hard work to arrive at today's Internet.

The history of the Internet can be segmented into three phases (see **Figure 3.1**). In the first phase, the *Innovation Phase,* from 1961 to 1974, the fundamental building blocks of the Internet were conceptualized and then realized in actual hardware and software. The basic building blocks are: packet-switching hardware, client/server computing, and a communications protocol called TCP/IP (all described more fully later in this section). The original purpose of the Internet, when it was conceived in the 1960s, was to link large mainframe computers on different college campuses. This kind of one-to-one communication between campuses was previously only possible through the telephone system or postal mail.

In the second phase, the *Institutionalization Phase*, from 1975 to 1995, large institutions such as the Department of Defense and the National Science Foundation (NSF) provided funding and legitimization for the fledging invention called the

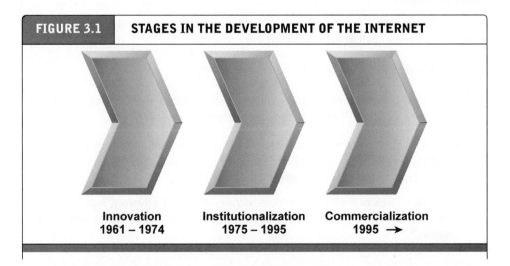

| FIGURE 3.1 | STAGES IN THE DEVELOPMENT OF THE INTERNET |

Innovation
1961 – 1974

Institutionalization
1975 – 1995

Commercialization
1995 →

The Internet developed in three stages over a 40-year period from 1961 to the present. In the Innovation stage, basic ideas and technologies were developed; in the Institutionalization stage, these ideas were brought to life; in the Commercialization stage, once the ideas and technologies had been proven, private companies brought the Internet to millions of people worldwide.

Internet. Once the concepts behind the Internet had been proven in several government-supported demonstration projects, the Department of Defense contributed $1 million to further develop them into a robust military communications system that could withstand nuclear war. This effort created what was then called ARPANET (Advanced Research Projects Agency Network). In 1986, the NSF assumed responsibility for the development of a civilian Internet (then called NSFNET) and began a 10-year-long $200 million expansion program.

In the third phase, the *Commercialization Phase*, from 1995 to the present, government agencies encouraged private corporations to take over and expand both the Internet backbone and local service to ordinary citizens—families and individuals across America and the world who were not students on campuses. By 2000, the Internet's use had expanded well beyond military installations and research universities. See **Table 3.1** for a closer look at the development of the Internet from 1961 on.

## THE INTERNET: KEY TECHNOLOGY CONCEPTS

In 1995, the Federal Networking Council (FNC) took the step of passing a resolution formally defining the term *Internet* (see **Figure 3.2**).

Based on that definition, the Internet means a network that uses the IP addressing scheme, supports the Transmission Control Protocol (TCP), and makes services available to users much like a telephone system makes voice and data services available to the public.

| **FIGURE 3.2** | **RESOLUTION OF THE FEDERAL NETWORKING COUNCIL** |
| --- | --- |

"The Federal Networking Council (FNC) agrees that the following language reflects our definition of the term 'Internet.'

'Internet' refers to the global information system that—

(i) is logically linked together by a globally unique address space based on the Internet Protocol (IP) or its subsequent extensions/follow-ons;

(ii) is able to support communications using the Transmission Control Protocol/Internet Protocol (TCP/IP) suite or its subsequent extensions/follow-ons, and/or other IP-compatible protocols; and

(iii) provides, uses or makes accessible, either publicly or privately, high level services layered on the communications and related infrastructure described herein."

Last modified on October 30, 1995.

SOURCE: Federal Networking Council, 1995.

| TABLE 3.1 | DEVELOPMENT OF THE INTERNET TIMELINE |
|---|---|

| YEAR EVENT | SIGNIFICANCE |
|---|---|
| *INNOVATION PHASE 1961–1974* | |
| 1961 Leonard Kleinrock (MIT) publishes a paper on "packet switching" networks. | The concept of packet switching is born. |
| 1972 E-mail is invented by Ray Tomlinson of BBN. Larry Roberts writes the first e-mail utility program permitting listing, forwarding, and responding to e-mails. | The first "killer app" of the Internet is born. |
| 1973 Bob Metcalfe (XeroxPark Labs) invents Ethernet and local area networks. | **Client/server computing is invented.** Ethernet permitted the development of local area networks and client/server computing in which thousands of fully functional desktop computers could be connected into a short-distance (<1,000 meters) network to share files, run applications, and send messages. Although the Apple and IBM personal computers had not yet been invented, at XeroxPark Labs, the first powerful desktop computers connected into a local network were created in the late 1960s. |
| 1974 "Open architecture" networking and TCP/IP concepts are presented in a paper by Vint Cerf (Stanford) and Bob Kahn (BBN). | **TCP/IP invented.** The conceptual foundation for a single common communications protocol that could potentially connect any of thousands of disparate local area networks and computers, and a common addressing scheme for all computers connected to the network, are born. These developments made possible "peer-to-peer" "open" networking. Prior to this, computers could only communicate if they shared a common proprietary network architecture, e.g., IBM's System Network Architecture. With TCP/IP, computers and networks could work together regardless of their local operating systems or network protocols. |
| *INSTITUTIONAL PHASE 1975–1995* | |
| 1980 TCP/IP is officially adopted as the DoD standard communications protocol. | The single largest computing organization in the world adopts TCP/IP and packet-switched network technology. |
| 1980 Personal computers are invented. | Altair, Apple, and IBM personal desktop computers are invented. These computers become the foundation for today's Internet, affording millions of people access to the Internet and the Web. |
| 1984 Apple Computer releases the HyperCard program as part of its graphical user interface operating system called Macintosh. | The concept of "hyperlinked" documents and records that permit the user to jump from one page or record to another is commercially introduced. |
| 1984 Domain Name System (DNS) introduced. | DNS provides a user-friendly system for translating IP addresses into words that people can easily understand. |

(continued)

| | | |
|---|---|---|
| **TABLE 3.1** | **DEVELOPMENT OF THE INTERNET TIMELINE (CONTINUED)** | |

| YEAR EVENT | | SIGNIFICANCE |
|---|---|---|
| 1989 | Tim Berners-Lee of the physics lab CERN in Switzerland proposes a worldwide network of hyperlinked documents based on a common markup language called HTML—HyperText Markup Language. | **The concept of an Internet-supported service called the World Wide Web based on HTML pages is born.** The Web would be constructed from "pages" created in a common markup language, with "hyperlinks" that permitted easy access among the pages. The idea does not catch on rapidly and most Internet users rely on cumbersome FTP and Gopher protocols to find documents. |
| 1990 | NSF plans and assumes responsibility for a civilian Internet backbone and creates NSFNET.[1] ARPANET is decommissioned. | The concept of a "civilian" Internet open to all is realized through non-military funding by NSF. |
| 1993 | The first graphical Web browser called Mosaic is invented by Mark Andreesen and others at the National Center for Supercomputing at the University of Illinois. | Mosaic makes it very easy for ordinary users to connect to HTML documents anywhere on the Web. The browser-enabled Web takes off. |
| 1994 | Andreesen and Jim Clark form Netscape Corporation. | The first commercial Web browser—Netscape—becomes available. |
| 1994 | The first banner advertisements appear on Hotwired.com in October 1994. | **The beginning of e-commerce.** |

*COMMERCIALIZATION PHASE 1995–PRESENT*

| | | |
|---|---|---|
| 1995 | NSF privatizes the backbone, and commercial carriers take over backbone operation. | **The fully commercial civilian Internet is born.** Major long-haul networks such as AT&T, Sprint, GTE, UUNet, and MCI take over operation of the backbone. Network Solutions (a private firm) is given a monopoly to assign Internet addresses. |
| 1995 | Jeff Bezos founds Amazon; Pierre Omidyar forms AuctionWeb (eBay). | E-commerce begins in earnest with pure online retail stores and auctions. |
| 1998 | The U.S. federal government encourages the founding of Internet Corporation for Assigning Numbers and Names (ICANN). | Governance over domain names and addresses passes to a private nonprofit international organization. |
| 1999 | The first full-service Internet-only bank, First Internet Bank of Indiana, opens for business. | Business on the Web extends into traditional services. |
| 2003 | The Internet2 Abilene high-speed network is upgraded to 10 Gbps. Internet2 now has over 200 university, 60 corporate, and 40 affiliate members. | A major milestone toward the development of ultra-high-speed transcontinental networks several times faster than the existing backbone is achieved. |
| 2005 | NSF proposes the Global Environment for Networking Investigations (GENI) Initiative to develop new core functionality for the Internet, including new naming, addressing, and identity architectures; enhanced capabilities, including additional security architecture and a design that supports high availability; and new Internet services and applications. | Recognition that future Internet security and functionality needs may require the thorough rethinking of existing Internet technology. |

[1] "Backbone" refers to the U.S. domestic trunk lines that carry the heavy traffic across the nation, from one metropolitan area to another. Universities are given responsibility for developing their own campus networks that must be connected to the national backbone.

(continued)

| TABLE 3.1 | DEVELOPMENT OF THE INTERNET TIMELINE (CONTINUED) |
| --- | --- |

| YEAR EVENT | | SIGNIFICANCE |
| --- | --- | --- |
| 2006 | The U.S. Senate Committee on Commerce, Science, and Transportation holds hearings on "Network Neutrality." | The debate grows over differential pricing based on utilization that pits the backbone utility owners against the online content and service providers, and device makers. |
| 2007 | BBN Technologies selected by the NSF to plan and design the next generation Internet (GENI). | Work begins on the new Internet, which can provide differential service levels, guaranteed service levels, and differential pricing. |
| 2008 | The Internet Society (ISOC) identifies Trust and Identity as a primary design element for every layer of the Internet, and launches an initiative in 2008–2010 to address these issues. | The leading Internet policy group recognizes the current Internet is threatened by breaches of security and trust that are built into the existing network. |
| 2008 | National LambdaRail develops the first 40 Gbps network, and the first transcontinental Ethernet network. | Using Cisco optical routers, this leading consortium of universities and businesses provides a nationwide platform for experimentation in very high-speed Internet platforms. |
| 2008 | Internet "cloud computing" becomes a billion-dollar industry. | Internet capacity is sufficient to support on-demand computing resources (processing and storage), as well as software applications, for large corporations and individuals. |
| 2009 | Internet-enabled smartphones become a major new Web access platform. | Smartphones extend the reach and range of the Internet to more closely realize the promise of the Internet anywhere, anytime, anyplace. |
| 2009 | Broadband stimulus package and Broadband Data Improvement Act enacted. | President signs stimulus package containing $7.2 billion for the expansion of broadband access in the United States. |
| 2010 | Cybersecurity Act of 2010, S. 773. | This bill authorizes the president to increase collaboration between the public and private sectors including network operators, utility companies, federal contractors, the financial sector, and other sectors to achieve national cybersecurity goals. |

SOURCES: Based on Leiner, et al., 2000; Zakon, 2005; Gross, 2005; Geni.net, 2007; nlr.net, 2010; ISOC.org, 2010; arstechnica.com, 2010.

Behind this formal definition are three extremely important concepts that are the basis for understanding the Internet: packet switching, the TCP/IP communications protocol, and client/server computing. Although the Internet has evolved and changed dramatically in the last 30 years, these three concepts are at the core of the way the Internet functions today and are the foundation for Internet II.

## Packet Switching

**Packet switching** is a method of slicing digital messages into discrete units called **packets**, sending the packets along different communication paths as they become available, and then reassembling the packets once they arrive at their destination (see **Figure 3.3**). Prior to the development of packet switching, early computer networks used leased, dedicated telephone circuits to communicate with terminals and other computers. In circuit-switched networks such as the telephone system, a complete point-to-point circuit is put together, and then communication can proceed.

**packet switching**
a method of slicing digital messages into packets, sending the packets along different communication paths as they become available, and then reassembling the packets once they arrive at their destination

**packet**
the discrete units into which digital messages are sliced for transmission over the Internet

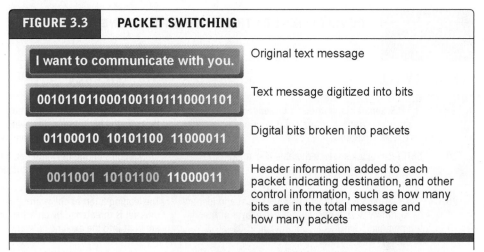

| FIGURE 3.3 | PACKET SWITCHING |
| --- | --- |

| | |
| --- | --- |
| I want to communicate with you. | Original text message |
| 0010110110001001101110001101 | Text message digitized into bits |
| 01100010  10101100  11000011 | Digital bits broken into packets |
| 0011001  10101100  11000011 | Header information added to each packet indicating destination, and other control information, such as how many bits are in the total message and how many packets |

In packet switching, digital messages are divided into fixed-length packets of bits (generally about 1,500 bytes). Header information indicates both the origin and the ultimate destination address of the packet, the size of the message, and the number of packets the receiving node should expect. Because the receipt of each packet is acknowledged by the receiving computer, for a considerable amount of time, the network is not passing information, only acknowledgments, producing a delay called latency.

However, these "dedicated" circuit-switching techniques were expensive and wasted available communications capacity—the circuit would be maintained regardless of whether any data was being sent. For nearly 70% of the time, a dedicated voice circuit is not being fully used because of pauses between words and delays in assembling the circuit segments, both of which increase the length of time required to find and connect circuits. A better technology was needed.

The first book on packet switching was written by Leonard Kleinrock in 1964 (Kleinrock, 1964), and the technique was further developed by others in the defense research labs of both the United States and England. With packet switching, the communications capacity of a network can be increased by a factor of 100 or more. (The communications capacity of a digital network is measured in terms of bits per second.[2]) Imagine if the gas mileage of your car went from 15 miles per gallon to 1,500 miles per gallon—all without changing too much of the car!

In packet-switched networks, messages are first broken down into packets. Appended to each packet are digital codes that indicate a source address (the origination point) and a destination address, as well as sequencing information and error-control information for the packet. Rather than being sent directly to the destination address, in a packet network, the packets travel from computer to computer until they reach their destination. These computers are called routers. A **router** is a special-purpose computer that interconnects the different computer networks that make up the Internet and routes packets along to their ultimate destination as they travel. To ensure that packets take the best available path toward their destination, routers use a computer program called a **routing algorithm**.

**router**
special-purpose computer that interconnects the computer networks that make up the Internet and routes packets to their ultimate destination as they travel the Internet

**routing algorithm**
computer program that ensures that packets take the best available path toward their destination

[2]A bit is a binary digit, 0 or 1. A string of eight bits constitutes a byte. A home telephone dial-up modem connects to the Internet usually at 56 Kbps (56,000 bits per second). Mbps refers to millions of bits per second, whereas Gbps refers to billions of bits per second.

Packet switching does not require a dedicated circuit, but can make use of any spare capacity that is available on any of several hundred circuits. Packet switching makes nearly full use of almost all available communication lines and capacity. Moreover, if some lines are disabled or too busy, the packets can be sent on any available line that eventually leads to the destination point.

## Transmission Control Protocol/Internet Protocol (TCP/IP)

While packet switching was an enormous advance in communications capacity, there was no universally agreed-upon method for breaking up digital messages into packets, routing them to the proper address, and then reassembling them into a coherent message. This was like having a system for producing stamps but no postal system (a series of post offices and a set of addresses). The answer was to develop a **protocol** (a set of rules and standards for data transfer) to govern the formatting, ordering, compressing, and error-checking of messages, as well as specify the speed of transmission and means by which devices on the network will indicate they have stopped sending and/or receiving messages.

In 1974, Vint Cerf and Bob Kahn laid the conceptual foundation for **Transmission Control Protocol/Internet Protocol (TCP/IP)**, which has become the core communications protocol for the Internet (Cerf and Kahn, 1974). **TCP** establishes the connections among sending and receiving Web computers, and makes sure that packets sent by one computer are received in the same sequence by the other, without any packets missing. **IP** provides the Internet's addressing scheme and is responsible for the actual delivery of the packets.

TCP/IP is divided into four separate layers, with each layer handling a different aspect of the communication problem (see **Figure 3.4**). The **Network Interface Layer** is responsible for placing packets on and receiving them from the network medium, which could be a LAN (Ethernet) or Token Ring network, or other network technology. TCP/IP is independent from any local network technology and can adapt to changes at the local level. The **Internet Layer** is responsible for addressing, packaging, and routing messages on the Internet. The **Transport Layer** is responsible for providing communication with the application by acknowledging and sequencing the packets to and from the application. The **Application Layer** provides a wide variety of applications with the ability to access the services of the lower layers. Some of the best-known applications are HyperText Transfer Protocol (HTTP), File Transfer Protocol (FTP), and Simple Mail Transfer Protocol (SMTP), all of which we will discuss later in this chapter.

## IP Addresses

The IP addressing scheme answers the question "How can 500 million computers attached to the Internet communicate with one another?" The answer is that every computer connected to the Internet must be assigned an address—otherwise it cannot send or receive TCP packets. For instance, when you sign onto the Internet using a dial-up, DSL, or cable modem, your computer is assigned a temporary address by your Internet Service Provider. Most corporate and university computers attached to a local area network have a permanent IP address.

**protocol**
a set of rules and standards for data transfer

**Transmission Control Protocol/Internet Protocol (TCP/IP)**
the core communications protocol for the Internet

**TCP**
protocol that establishes the connections among sending and receiving Web compu-ters and handles the assem-bly of packets at the point of transmission, and their re-assembly at the receiving end

**IP**
protocol that provides the Internet's addressing scheme and is responsible for the actual delivery of the packets

**Network Interface Layer**
responsible for placing pac-kets on and receiving them from the network medium

**Internet Layer**
responsible for addressing, packaging, and routing messages on the Internet

**Transport Layer**
responsible for providing communication with the application by acknowledging and sequencing the packets to and from the application

**Application Layer**
provides a wide variety of applications with the ability to access the services of the lower layers

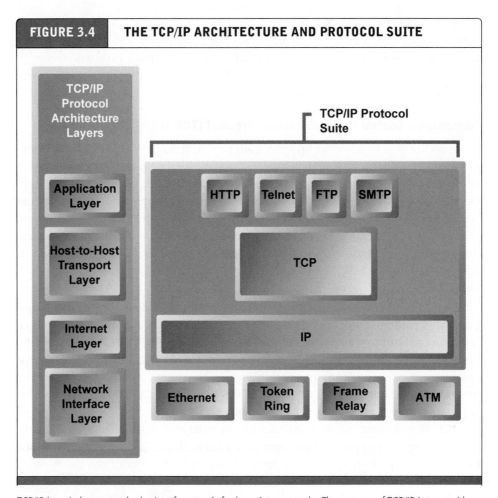

**FIGURE 3.4** THE TCP/IP ARCHITECTURE AND PROTOCOL SUITE

TCP/IP is an industry-standard suite of protocols for large internetworks. The purpose of TCP/IP is to provide high-speed communication network links.

**IPv4 Internet address**
Internet address expressed as a 32-bit number that appears as a series of four separate numbers marked off by periods, such as 64.49.254.91

**IPv6 Internet address**
Internet address expressed as an 128-bit number

There are two versions of IP currently in use. IPv4 (Version 4) is still the most frequently used version. An **IPv4 Internet address** is a 32-bit number that appears as a series of four separate numbers marked off by periods, such as 64.49.254.91. Each of the four numbers can range from 0–255. This "dotted quad" addressing scheme contains up to 4 billion addresses (2 to the $32^{nd}$ power). In a typical Class C network, the first three sets of numbers identify the network (in the preceding example, 64.49.254 is the local area network identification) and the last number (91) identifies a specific computer.

Because many large corporate and government domains have been given millions of IP addresses each (to accommodate their current and future work forces), and with all the new networks and new Internet-enabled devices requiring unique IP addresses being attached to the Internet, a newer version of the IP protocol, called IPv6, has been developed. An **IPv6 Internet address** is 128-bits, so there are about 1 quadrillion (10 to the $15^{th}$ power) addresses available (National Research Council, 2000).

| FIGURE 3.5 | ROUTING INTERNET MESSAGES: TCP/IP AND PACKET SWITCHING |
|---|---|

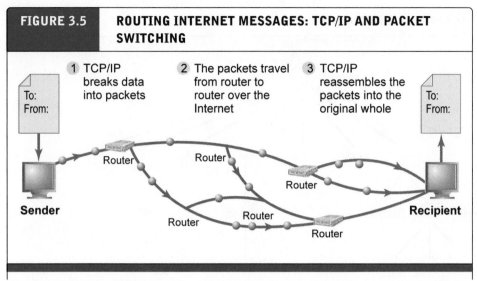

The Internet uses packet-switched networks and the TCP/IP communications protocol to send, route, and assemble messages. Messages are broken into packets, and packets from the same message can travel along different routes.

**Figure 3.5** illustrates how TCP/IP and packet switching work together to send data over the Internet.

## Domain Names, DNS, and URLs

Most people cannot remember 32-bit numbers. An IP address can be represented by a natural language convention called a **domain name**. The **Domain Name System (DNS)** allows expressions such as Cnet.com to stand for a numeric IP address (cnet.com's numeric IP is 216.239.113.101).[2] A **Uniform Resource Locator (URL)**, which is the address used by a Web browser to identify the location of content on the Web, also uses a domain name as part of the URL. A typical URL contains the protocol to be used when accessing the address, followed by its location. For instance, the URL http://www.azimuth-interactive.com/flash_test refers to the IP address 208.148.84.1 with the domain name "azimuth-interactive.com" and the protocol being used to access the address, HTTP. A resource called "flash_test" is located on the server directory path /flash_test. A URL can have from two to four parts; for example, name1.name2.name3.org. We discuss domain names and URLs further in Section 3.4. **Figure 3.6** illustrates the Domain Name System and **Table 3.2** summarizes the important components of the Internet addressing scheme

**domain name**
IP address expressed in natural language

**Domain Name System (DNS)**
system for expressing numeric IP addresses in natural language

**Uniform Resource Locator (URL)**
the address used by a Web browser to identify the location of content on the Web

## Client/Server Computing

While packet switching exploded the available communications capacity and TCP/IP provided the communications rules and regulations, it took a revolution in computing

[2]You can check the IP address of any domain name on the Internet. In Windows, or use Start/Run/cmd to open the DOS prompt. Type "ping < Domain Name >". You will receive the IP address in return.

| FIGURE 3.6 | **THE HIERARCHICAL DOMAIN NAME SYSTEM** |
|---|---|

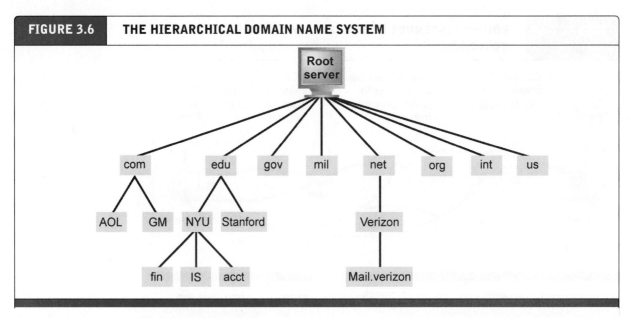

The Domain Name System is a hierarchical namespace with a root server at the top. Top-level domains appear next and identify the organization type (such as .com, .gov, .org, etc.) or geographic location (such as .uk [Great Britain] or .ca [Canada]). Second-level servers for each top-level domain assign and register second-level domain names for organizations and individuals such as IBM.com, Microsoft.com, and Stanford.edu. Finally, third-level domains identify a particular computer or group of computers within an organization, e.g., www.finance.nyu.edu.

**client/server computing**

a model of computing in which powerful personal computers are connected in a network together with one or more servers

**client**

a powerful personal computer that is part of a network

to bring about today's Internet and the Web. That revolution is called client/server computing and without it, the Web—in all its richness—would not exist. **Client/server computing** is a model of computing in which powerful personal computers called **clients** are connected in a network to one or more server computers. These clients are sufficiently powerful to accomplish complex tasks such as displaying rich graphics, storing large files, and processing graphics and sound files, all on a local

| TABLE 3.2 | **PIECES OF THE INTERNET PUZZLE: NAMES AND ADDRESSES** |
|---|---|
| IP addresses | Every device connected to the Internet must have a unique address number called an Internet Protocol (IP) address. |
| Domain names | The Domain Name System allows expressions such as Pearsoned.com (Pearson Education's Web site) to stand for numeric IP locations. |
| DNS servers | DNS servers are databases that keep track of IP addresses and domain names on the Internet. |
| Root servers | Root servers are central directories that list all domain names currently in use for specific domains; for example, the .com root server. DNS servers consult root servers to look up unfamiliar domain names when routing traffic. |

desktop or handheld device. **Servers** are networked computers dedicated to common functions that the client computers on the network need, such as file storage, software applications, utility programs such as Web connections, and printers (see **Figure 3.7**). The Internet is a giant example of client/server computing in which millions of Web servers located around the world can be easily accessed by millions of client computers, also located throughout the world.

To appreciate what client/server computing makes possible, you must understand what preceded it. In the mainframe computing environment of the 1960s and 1970s, computing power was very expensive and limited. For instance, the largest commercial mainframes of the late 1960s had 128k of RAM and 10 megabyte disk drives, and occupied hundreds of square feet. There was insufficient computing capacity to support graphics or color in text documents, let alone sound files or hyperlinked documents and databases.

With the development of personal computers and local area networks during the late 1970s and early 1980s, client/server computing became possible. Client/server computing has many advantages over centralized mainframe computing. For instance, it is easy to expand capacity by adding servers and clients. Also, client/server networks are less vulnerable than centralized computing architectures. If one server goes down, backup or mirror servers can pick up the slack; if a client computer is inoperable, the rest of the network continues operating. Moreover, processing load is balanced over many powerful smaller computers rather than being concentrated in a single huge computer that performs processing for everyone. Both software and hardware in client/server environments can be built more simply and economically.

Today there are over 1.5 billion personal computers in existence worldwide (Gaudin, 2010). Personal computing capabilities are moving to handheld devices such as Apple's iPhones, RIM's BlackBerries, and T-Mobile's Android G1 (much "thinner clients"). In the process, more computer processing will be performed by central servers (reminiscent of mainframe computers of the past).

**server**

networked computer dedicated to common functions that the client computers on the network need

| FIGURE 3.7 | THE CLIENT/SERVER COMPUTING MODEL |

In the client/server model of computing, client computers are connected in a network together with one or more servers.

## THE NEW CLIENT: THE EMERGING MOBILE PLATFORM

There's a new client in town. In a few years, the primary means of accessing the Internet both in the United States and worldwide will be through highly portable netbooks and smartphones, and not traditional desktop or laptop PCs. This means that the primary platform for e-commerce products and services will also change to a mobile platform.

The change in hardware has reached a tipping point. In 2010, although worldwide PC sales shipments overall rebounded from 2009, the most rapidly increasing part of the market are laptops and even smaller netbook computers, rather than desktops. Worldwide, around 60 million netbooks are expected to ship, a figure that is expected to double by 2013 (Shein, 2010). And, while there are an estimated 1.5 billion PCs in the world, the number of cell phones long ago exceeded the population of PCs. In 2010, there are an estimated 5 billion cell phone subscribers, with nearly 300 million in the United States, around 800 million in China, and 600 million in India. The population of cell phone subscribers is at least three times that of PC owners. About 25%, or 1 billion, of the world's cell phones are "smartphones," capable of accessing the Internet using broadband cell networks. In the United States, about 83 million people access the Internet using mobile devices, mostly cell phones. In 2010, there will be more than 1 billion cell phones sold worldwide, and about 156 million of those will be smartphones.

Netbooks are a part of the mobile digital platform because they are designed to connect to the Internet using wireless networks. Netbooks are small computers weighing less than 2 pounds, with 8" displays, no hard drives, solid state memory, often using new energy saving non-Intel chips, and a variety of operating systems from Linux to Windows XP. Netbooks are designed to connect to the wireless Internet (Wi-Fi or cellular) for software applications and data storage, although most can also run scaled-down office applications locally. Netbooks are priced from $200 to $400.

Smartphones are a disruptive technology that radically alters the personal computing and e-commerce landscape. Smartphones involve a major shift in computer processors, and software that is disrupting the 40-year dual monopolies established by Intel and Microsoft, whose chips, operating systems, and software applications have dominated the PC market since 1982. Few cell phones use Intel chips, which power 90% of the world's PCs; only 12% of smartphones use Microsoft's operating system (Windows Mobile) and that's mostly in Asia. Instead smartphone manufacturers either purchase operating systems such as Symbian, the world leader, or build their own, such as Apple's iPhone iOS and BlackBerry's OS, typically based on Linux and Java platforms. Ninety percent of the billion cell phones shipped each year use some version of Advanced RISC Machine (ARM) chips, licensed by ARM Inc. and manufactured by many firms (Hansell, 2009). For instance, Apple's latest 3G iPhone uses an ARM 11 chip with a 600 megahertz (MHz) processor speed, and that uses only .45 milliwatts of power (compared to a typical laptop dual core mobile Intel processor that uses 25 watts—about 500 times more power consumption). Apple's 4G phones and iPads use an Apple-designed ARM chip called A4 with even faster processing speeds and faster graphics. (Apple has not officially released information on the chip or its manufacturer.) Smartphones do not need fans. Cell phones do not use power-hungry hard drives but instead use flash memory chips with storage up to 32 megabytes. While the latest Energy Star 4 laptop disk drives consume 500 milliwatts at idle, and 1 watt writing and reading, flash memory chips consume about 50 milliwatts writing and reading data (20 times less power).

The emerging mobile platform has profound implications for e-commerce because it influences how, where, and when consumers shop and buy.

## THE INTERNET "CLOUD COMPUTING" MODEL: SOFTWARE AND HARDWARE AS A SERVICE

The growing bandwidth power of the Internet has pushed the client/server model one step further, towards what is called the "cloud computing model" (**Figure 3.8**).

**Cloud computing** refers to a model of computing in which firms and individuals obtain computing power and software applications over the Internet, rather than purchasing the hardware and software, and installing it on their own computers. Currently, cloud computing is the fastest growing form of computing, with an estimated market size in 2010 of $68 billion, and a projected size of $148 billion in 2014, according to Gartner research analysts (Gartner, 2010).

Hardware firms such as IBM, HP, and Dell are building very large, scalable cloud computing centers that provide computing power, data storage, and high-speed Internet connections to firms that rely on the Internet for business software applications.

Software firms such as Google, Microsoft, SAP, Oracle, and Salesforce.com sell software applications that are Internet-based. Instead of software as a product, in the cloud computing model, software is a service provided over the Internet. For instance, over

**cloud computing**
model of computing in which firms and individuals obtain computing power and software over the Internet

| FIGURE 3.8 | THE CLOUD COMPUTING MODEL |

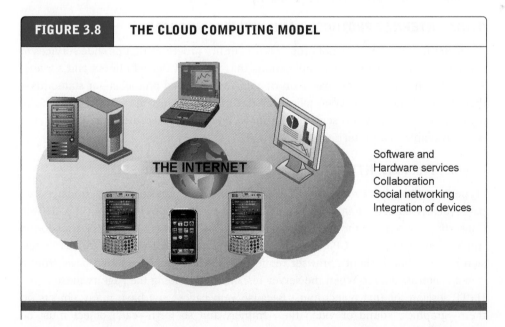

In the cloud computing model, hardware and software services are provided on the Internet by vendors operating very large server farms and data centers.

Google claims there are around 25 million active users of Google Apps, its suite of office software applications such as word processing, spreadsheets, and calendars, that users access over the Internet. In 2010, more than 55,000 firms worldwide will be using Salesforce.com's customer relationship management software, some on their iPhones or Android G1s.

Microsoft, which in the past has depended on selling boxed software to firms and individuals, is adapting to this new marketplace with its own "software plus service" (buy the boxed version and get "free" online services), Windows Live, and Online Technology initiatives.

Cloud computing has many significant implications for e-commerce. For e-commerce firms, cloud computing radically reduces the cost of building and operating Web sites because the necessary hardware infrastructure and software can be licensed as a service from Internet providers at a fraction of the cost of purchasing these services as products. This means firms can adopt "pay-as-you-go" and "pay-as-you-grow" strategies when building out their Web sites. For instance, according to Amazon, hundreds of thousands of customers use Amazon's Web Services arm, which provides storage services, computing services, database services, messaging services, and payment services. For individuals, cloud computing means you no longer need a powerful laptop or desktop computer to engage in e-commerce or other activities. Instead, you can use much less-expensive netbooks or smartphones that cost a few hundred dollars. For corporations, cloud computing means that a significant part of hardware and software costs (infrastructure costs) can be reduced because firms can obtain these services online for a fraction of the cost of owning, and they do not have to hire an IT staff to support the infrastructure. These benefits come with some risks: firms become totally dependent on their cloud service providers.

## OTHER INTERNET PROTOCOLS AND UTILITY PROGRAMS

There are many other Internet protocols and utility programs that provide services to users in the form of Internet applications that run on Internet clients and servers. These Internet services are based on universally accepted protocols—or standards—that are available to everyone who uses the Internet. They are not owned by any organization, but they are services that have been developed over many years and made available to all Internet users.

### Internet Protocols: HTTP, E-mail Protocols, FTP, Telnet, and SSL

**HyperText Transfer Protocol (HTTP)**
the Internet protocol used for transferring Web pages

**HyperText Transfer Protocol (HTTP)** is the Internet protocol used to transfer Web pages (described in the following section). HTTP was developed by the World Wide Web Consortium (W3C) and the Internet Engineering Task Force (IETF). HTTP runs in the Application Layer of the TCP/IP model shown in **Figure 3.4** on page 134. An HTTP session begins when a client's browser requests a resource, such as a Web page, from a remote Internet server. When the server responds by sending the page requested, the HTTP session for that object ends. Because Web pages may have many objects on them—graphics, sound or video files, frames, and so forth—each object must be requested by a separate HTTP message. For more information about HTTP, you can consult RFC 2616, which details the standards for HTTP/1.1, the version of HTTP most commonly used today (Internet Society, 1999). (An RFC is a document published by the Internet Society [ISOC] or one of the other organizations involved in Internet governance that sets forth the standards for various Internet-related technologies. You will learn more about the organizations involved in setting standards for the Internet later in the chapter).

E-mail is one of the oldest, most important, and frequently used Internet services. Like HTTP, the various Internet protocols used to handle e-mail all run in the Application Layer of TCP/IP. **Simple Mail Transfer Protocol (SMTP)** is the Internet protocol used to send e-mail to a server. SMTP is a relatively simple, text-based protocol that was developed in the early 1980s. SMTP handles only the sending of e-mail. To retrieve e-mail from a server, the client computer uses either **Post Office Protocol 3 (POP3)** or **Internet Message Access Protocol (IMAP)**. You can set POP3 to retrieve e-mail messages from the server and then delete the messages on the server, or retain them on the server. IMAP is a more current e-mail protocol supported by all browsers and most servers and ISPs. IMAP allows users to search, organize, and filter their mail prior to downloading it from the server. For more information about SMTP, POP3, and IMAP, you can consult RFCs 2821 (SMTP), 1939 (POP3), and 3501 (IMAP) (Internet Society, 2001, 1996, 2003). You also can see how your browser handles SMTP, and POP or IMAP, by looking in your browser's Preferences or Tools section, where the e-mail settings are defined.

**File Transfer Protocol (FTP)** is one of the original Internet services. FTP runs in TCP/IP's Application Layer and permits users to transfer files from a server to their client computer, and vice versa. The files can be documents, programs, or large database files. FTP is the fastest and most convenient way to transfer files larger than 1 megabyte, which some e-mail servers will not accept. More information about FTP is available in RFC 0959 (Internet Society, 1985).

**Telnet** is a network protocol that also runs in TCP/IP's Application Layer and is used to allow remote login on another computer. The term Telnet also refers to the Telnet program, which provides the client part of the protocol and enables the client to emulate a mainframe computer terminal. (The industry-standard terminals defined in the days of mainframe computing are VT-52, VT-100, and IBM 3250.) You can then attach yourself to a computer on the Internet that supports Telnet and run programs or downloads file from that computer. Telnet was the first "remote work" program that permitted users to work on a computer from a remote location.

**Secure Sockets Layer (SSL)** is a protocol that operates between the Transport and Application Layers of TCP/IP and secures communications between the client and the server. SSL helps secure e-commerce communications and payments through a variety of techniques such as message encryption and digital signatures that we will discuss further in Chapter 5.

## Utility Programs: Ping, Tracert, and Pathping

**Packet InterNet Groper (Ping)** allows you to check the connection between a client computer and a TCP/IP network (see **Figure 3.9**). Ping will also tell you the time it takes for the server to respond, giving you some idea about the speed of the server and the Internet at that moment. You can run Ping from the DOS prompt on a personal

### Simple Mail Transfer Protocol (SMTP)
the Internet protocol used to send mail to a server

### Post Office Protocol 3 (POP3)
a protocol used by the client to retrieve mail from an Internet server

### Internet Message Access Protocol (IMAP)
a more current e-mail protocol that allows users to search, organize, and filter their mail prior to downloading it from the server

### File Transfer Protocol (FTP)
one of the original Internet services. Part of the TCP/IP protocol that permits users to transfer files from the server to their client computer, and vice versa

### Telnet
a terminal emulation program that runs in TCP/IP

### Secure Sockets Layer (SSL)
a protocol that secures communications between the client and the server

### Ping
a program that allows you to check the connection between your client and the server

## FIGURE 3.9   THE RESULT OF A PING

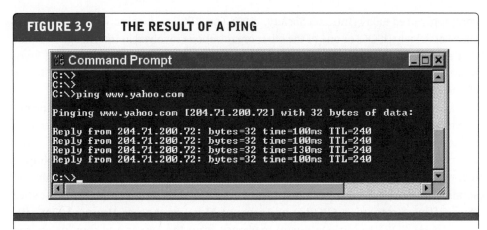

A ping is used to verify an address and test the speed of the round trip from a client computer to a host and back.

computer with a Windows operating system by typing: ping < domain name >. We will discuss Ping further in Chapter 5, because one way to slow down or even crash a domain computer is to send it millions of ping requests.

**Tracert** is one of a several route-tracing utilities that allow you to follow the path of a message you send from your client to a remote computer on the Internet. **Figure 3.10** shows the result of route tracking a message sent to a remote host using a visual route-tracing program called VisualRoute (available from Visualware).

The **Pathping** utility combines the functionality offered by Ping and Tracert. Pathping provides the details of the path between two hosts and statistics for each node in the path based on samples taken over a period of time, depending on the number of nodes between the start and end host.

**Tracert**
one of several route-tracing utilities that allow you to follow the path of a message you send from your client to a remote computer on the Internet

**Pathping**
combines the functionality offered by Ping and Tracert

## FIGURE 3.10   TRACING THE ROUTE A MESSAGE TAKES ON THE INTERNET

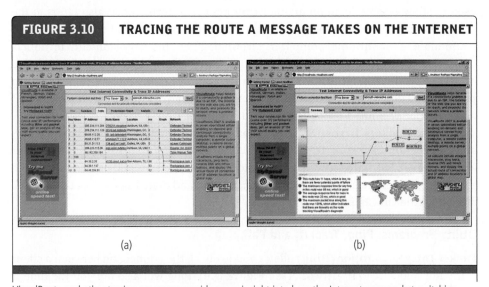

(a)                                    (b)

VisualRoute and other tracing programs provide some insight into how the Internet uses packet switching. This particular message traveled from a computer in Ashburn, Virginia, to San Antonio, Texas.
SOURCE: Visualware, Inc., 2007.

## 3.2 THE INTERNET TODAY

In 2010, there are an estimated 1.96 billion Internet users worldwide, up from 100 million users at year-end 1997. While this is a huge number, it represents only about 23% of the world's population (Internet worldstats.com, 2010). Although Internet user growth has slowed in the United States to about 1% annually, in Asia, Internet growth is about 10% annually, and by 2014, it is expected that there will be over 2 billion Internet users worldwide. One would think that with such incredible growth, the Internet would be overloaded. However, this has not been true for several reasons. First, client/server computing is highly extensible. By simply adding servers and clients, the population of Internet users can grow indefinitely. Second, the Internet architecture is built in layers so that each layer can change without disturbing developments in other layers. For instance, the technology used to move messages through the Internet can go through radical changes to make service faster without being disruptive to your desktop applications running on the Internet.

**Figure 3.11** illustrates the "hourglass" and layered architecture of the Internet. The Internet can be viewed conceptually as having four layers: the Network Technology Substrate, Transport Services and Representation Standards, Middleware Services, and Applications.[3] The **Network Technology Substrate layer** is composed of telecommunications networks and protocols. The **Transport Services and Representation Standards layer** houses the TCP/IP protocol. The **Applications layer** contains client applications such as the World Wide Web, e-mail, and audio or video playback. The **Middleware Services layer** is the glue that ties the applications to the communications networks, and includes such services as security, authentication, addresses, and storage repositories. Users work with applications (such as e-mail) and rarely become aware of middleware that operates in the background. Because all layers use TCP/IP and other common standards linking all four layers, it is possible for there to be significant changes in the network layer without forcing changes in the Applications Layer.

### THE INTERNET BACKBONE

**Figure 3.12** illustrates some of the main physical elements of today's Internet. Originally, the Internet had a single backbone, but today's Internet has several backbones that are physically connected with each other and which transfer information from one private network to another. These private networks are referred to as **Network Service Providers (NSPs)**, which own and control the major backbone networks (see **Table 3.3**). For the sake of clarity we will refer to these networks of backbones as a single "backbone." The **backbone** has been likened to a giant pipeline that transports data around the world in milliseconds. In the United States, the backbone is composed entirely of fiber-optic cable with bandwidths ranging from 155 Mbps to 2.5 Gbps. **Bandwidth** measures how much data can be transferred over a communications medium within a fixed period of time, and is usually expressed in

---

[3]Recall that the TCP/IP communications protocol also has layers, not to be confused with the Internet architecture layers.

---

**Network Technology Substrate layer**
layer of Internet technology that is composed of telecommunications networks and protocols

**Transport Services and Representation Standards layer**
layer of Internet architecture that houses the TCP/IP protocol

**Applications layer**
layer of Internet architecture that contains client applications

**Middleware Services layer**
the "glue" that ties the applications to the communications networks, and includes such services as security, authentication, addresses, and storage repositories

**Network Service Provider (NSP)**
owns and controls one of the major networks comprising the Internet's backbone

**backbone**
high-bandwidth fiber-optic cable that transports data across the Internet

**bandwidth**
measures how much data can be transferred over a communications medium within a fixed period of time; is usually expressed in bits per second (bps), kilobits per second (Kbps), megabits per second (Mbps),or gigabits per second (Gbps)

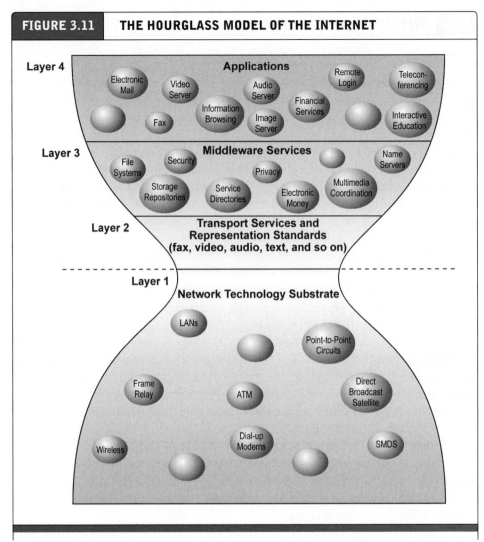

**FIGURE 3.11** | **THE HOURGLASS MODEL OF THE INTERNET**

The Internet can be characterized as an hour-glass modular structure with a lower layer containing the bit-carrying infrastructure (including cables and switches) and an upper layer containing user applications such as e-mail and the Web. In the narrow waist are transportation protocols such as TCP/IP.

SOURCE: Adapted from Computer Science and Telecommunications Board (CSTB), 2000.

bits per second (bps), kilobits (thousands of bits) per second (Kbps), megabits (millions of bits) per second (Mbps), or gigabits (billions of bits) per second (Gbps).

Connections to other continents are made via a combination of undersea fiber-optic cable and satellite links. The backbones in foreign countries typically are operated by a mixture of private and public owners. The U.S. backbone is one of the most developed because the Internet's infrastructure was developed here. The backbone has built-in redundancy so that if one part breaks down, data can be rerouted to another part of the backbone. **Redundancy** refers to multiple duplicate devices and paths in a network.

**redundancy**
multiple duplicate devices and paths in a network

| FIGURE 3.12 | INTERNET I NETWORK ARCHITECTURE |
|---|---|

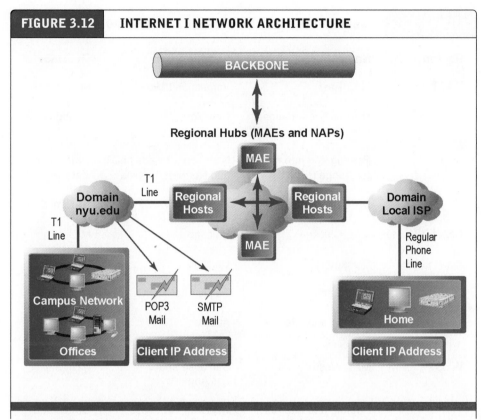

Today's Internet has a multi-tiered open network architecture featuring multiple national backbones, regional hubs, campus area networks, and local client computers.

| TABLE 3.3 | MAJOR U.S INTERNET BACKBONE OWNERS |
|---|---|

| | |
|---|---|
| AT&T | NTT/Verio |
| AOL Transit Data Network (ATDN) | Qwest |
| Cable & Wireless | Sprint |
| Global Crossing | Verizon |
| Level 3 | |

## INTERNET EXCHANGE POINTS

In the United States, there are a number of hubs where the backbone intersects with regional and local networks, and where the backbone owners connect with one another (see **Figure 3.13**). These hubs were originally called Network Access Points (NAPs) or Metropolitan Area Exchanges (MAEs), but now are more commonly referred to as **Internet Exchange Points (IXPs)**. IXPs use high-speed switching computers to connect the backbone to regional and local networks, and exchange messages with one

**Internet Exchange Point (IXP)**

hub where the backbone intersects with local and regional networks and where backbone owners connect with one another

| FIGURE 3.13 | SOME MAJOR U.S. INTERNET EXCHANGE POINTS (IXPs) | | |
| --- | --- | --- | --- |
| **Region** | **Name** | **Location** | **Operator** |
| **EAST** | MAE East | Virginia and Miami | MCI |
| | New York International Internet Exchange (NYIIX) | New York | Telehouse |
| | Peering and Internet Exchange (PAIX) | New York, Philadelphia and Northern Virginia | Switch and Data |
| | NAP of the Americas | Miami | Terramark |
| **CENTRAL** | MAE Chicago | Chicago | MCI |
| | Chicago NAP | Chicago | SBC |
| | MAE Central | Dallas and Atlanta | MCI |
| | Peering and Internet Exchange (PAIX) | Atlanta | Switch and Data |
| **WEST** | MAE West | San Jose and Los Angeles | MCI |
| | Peering and Internet Exchange (PAIX) | Palo Alto, San Jose, and Seattle | Switch and Data |
| | Los Angeles International Internet Exchange (LAIIX) | Los Angeles | Telehouse |

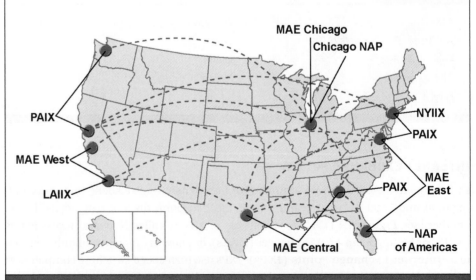

another. The regional and local networks are owned by local Bell operating companies (RBOCs—pronounced "ree-bocks"), and private telecommunications firms; they generally are fiber-optic networks operating at over 100 Mbps. The regional networks lease access to ISPs, private companies, and government institutions.

## CAMPUS AREA NETWORKS

**Campus area networks (CANs)** are generally local area networks operating within a single organization—such as New York University or Microsoft Corporation. In fact, most large organizations have hundreds of such local area networks. These organizations are sufficiently large that they lease access to the Web directly from regional and national carriers. These local area networks generally are running Ethernet (a local area network protocol) and have network operating systems such as Windows Server, or Linux that permit desktop clients to connect to the Internet through a local Internet server attached to their campus networks. Connection speeds in campus area networks are in the range of 10–100 Mbps to the desktop.

**campus area network (CAN)**

generally, a local area network operating within a single organization that leases access to the Web directly from regional and national carriers

## INTERNET SERVICE PROVIDERS

The firms that provide the lowest level of service in the multi-tiered Internet architecture by leasing Internet access to home owners, small businesses, and some large institutions are called **Internet Service Providers (ISPs)**. ISPs are retail providers—they deal with "the last mile of service" to the curb—homes and business offices. ISPs typically connect to IXPs with high-speed telephone or cable lines (45 Mbps and higher).

There are a number of major ISPs, such as AOL, Earthlink, AT&T, Comcast (Optimum Online), Verizon, Sprint, and Qwest, as well as thousands of local ISPs in the United States, ranging from local telephone companies offering dial-up and DSL telephone access to cable companies offering cable modem service, to small "mom-and-pop" Internet shops that service a small town, city, or even county with mostly dial-up phone access. If you have home or small business Internet access, an ISP likely provides the service to you. Satellite firms also offer Internet access, especially in remote areas where broadband service is not available.

**Internet Service Provider (ISP)**

firm that provides the lowest level of service in the multi-tiered Internet architecture by leasing Internet access to home owners, small businesses, and some large institutions

**Table 3.4** summarizes the variety of services, speeds, and costs of ISP Internet connections. There are two types of ISP service: narrowband and broadband. **Narrowband** service is the traditional telephone modem connection now operating at 56.6 Kbps (although the actual throughput hovers around 30 Kbps due to line noise that causes extensive resending of packets). This used to be the most common form of connection worldwide but is quickly being replaced by broadband connections in the United States, Europe, and Asia. Broadband service is based on DSL, cable modem, telephone (T1 and T3 lines), and satellite technologies. **Broadband**—in the context of Internet service—refers to any communication technology that permits clients to play streaming audio and video files at acceptable speeds—generally anything above 100 Kbps. In the United States, broadband users surpassed dial-up users in 2004, and in 2010 there were 79.5 million broadband households and only 2.8 million dial-up households (eMarketer, Inc., 2010a).

**narrowband**

the traditional telephone modem connection, now operating at 56.6 Kbps

**broadband**

refers to any communication technology that permits clients to play streaming audio and video files at acceptable speeds—generally anything above 100 Kbps

| TABLE 3.4 | ISP SERVICE LEVELS AND BANDWIDTH CHOICES | |
|---|---|---|
| SERVICE | COST/MONTH | SPEED TO DESKTOP (KBPS) |
| Telephone modem | $10–$25 | 30–56 Kbps |
| DSL | $15–$50 | 768 Kbps–5 Mbps |
| FiOS | $90-$130 | 15 Mbps–50 Mbps |
| Cable modem | $20–$50 | 1 Mbps–20 Mbps |
| Satellite | $20–$50 | 768 Kbps–5 Mbps |
| T1 | $300–$1,200 | 1.54 Mbps |
| T3 | $2,500–$10,000 | 45 Mbps |

The actual throughput of data will depend on a variety of factors including noise in the line and the number of subscribers requesting service. Service-level speeds quoted are typically only for downloads of Internet content; upload speeds tend to be much slower. T1 lines are publicly regulated utility lines that offer a guaranteed level of service, but the actual throughput of the other forms of Internet service is not guaranteed.

**Digital Subscriber Line (DSL)** service is a telephone technology that provides high-speed access to the Internet through ordinary telephone lines found in a home or business. Service levels range from about 768 Kbps up to 7 Mbps. DSL service requires that customers live within two miles (about 4,000 meters) of a neighborhood telephone switching center.

**Cable modem** refers to a cable television technology that piggybacks digital access to the Internet using the same analog or digital video cable providing television signals to a home. Cable Internet is a major broadband alternative to DSL service, generally providing faster speeds and a "triple play" subscription: telephone, television, and Internet for a single monthly payment. Cable modem services range from 1 Mbps up to 15 Mbps. Comcast, Time Warner Road Runner, and Cox are the largest cable Internet providers.

T1 and T3 are international telephone standards for digital communication. **T1** lines offer guaranteed delivery at 1.54 Mbps, while T3 lines offer delivery at a whopping 45 Mbps. T1 lines cost about $300–$1,200 per month, and **T3** lines between $2,500 and $10,000 per month. These are leased, dedicated, guaranteed lines suitable for corporations, government agencies, and businesses such as ISPs requiring high-speed guaranteed service levels.

Satellite companies provide high-speed broadband Internet access, primarily to homes and offices located in rural areas where DSL or cable access is not available. Access speeds and monthly costs are comparable to DSL and cable, but typically require a higher initial payment for installation of a small (18-inch) satellite dish. Satellite providers typically have policies that limit the total megabytes of data that a single account can download within a set period, usually 24 hours. Accounts that exceed the threshold are penalized by reduced download speeds for a period of time.

**Digital Subscriber Line (DSL)**
delivers high-speed access through ordinary telephone lines found in homes or businesses

**cable modem**
piggybacks digital access to the Internet on top of the analog video cable providing television signals to a home

**T1**
an international telephone standard for digital communication that offers guaranteed delivery at 1.54 Mbps

**T3**
an international telephone standard for digital communication that offers guaranteed delivery at 45 Mbps

The purpose of these policies is to deter heavy users from using excessive amounts of the provider's bandwidth, which has the effect of slowing down data transfer rates overall. The four major satellite providers are HughesNet, WildBlue, Skyway, and StarBand.

Prices are falling drastically to as low as $14.95 per month for DSL service. Cable broadband accounts for around 55% of all broadband users and nearly all large business firms and government agencies have broadband connections to the Internet. Demand for broadband service has grown so rapidly simply because it greatly speeds up the process of downloading Web pages and increasingly large video and audio files located on Web pages (see **Table 3.5**). As the quality of Internet service offerings expands to include Hollywood movies, music, games, and other rich media-streaming content, the demand for broadband access will continue to swell. In order to compete with cable companies, telephone companies have introduced an advanced form of DSL called FiOS (fiber-optic service) that provides up to 50 Mbps speeds for households, which is much faster than cable systems.

## INTRANETS AND EXTRANETS

The very same Internet technologies that make it possible to operate a worldwide public network can also be used by private and government organizations as internal networks. An **intranet** is a TCP/IP network located within a single organization for purposes of communications and information processing. Internet technologies are generally far less expensive than proprietary networks, and there is a global source of new applications that can run on intranets. In fact, all the applications available on the public Internet can be used in private intranets. The largest provider of local area network software is Microsoft, followed by open source Linux, both of which use TCP/IP networking protocols.

**intranet**
a TCP/IP network located within a single organization for purposes of communications and information processing

| TABLE 3.5 | TIME TO DOWNLOAD A 10-MEGABYTE FILE BY TYPE OF INTERNET SERVICE | |
|---|---|---|
| **TYPE OF INTERNET SERVICE** | **TIME TO DOWNLOAD** | |
| *NARROWBAND SERVICES* | | |
| Telephone modem | 25 minutes | |
| *BROADBAND SERVICES* | | |
| DSL @ 1 Mbps | 1.33 minutes | |
| Cable modem @ 10 Mbps | 8 seconds | |
| T1 | 52 seconds | |
| T3 | 2 seconds | |

**extranet**

formed when firms permit outsiders to access their internal TCP/IP networks

**Extranets** are formed when firms permit outsiders to access their internal TCP/IP networks. For instance, General Motors permits parts suppliers to gain access to GM's intranet that contains GM's production schedules. In this way, parts suppliers know exactly when GM needs parts, and where and when to deliver them.

Intranets and extranets generally do not involve commercial transactions in a marketplace, and they are mostly beyond the scope of this text. Extranets will receive some attention as a technology that supports certain types of B2B exchanges (described in Chapter 12).

## WHO GOVERNS THE INTERNET?

Aficionados and promoters of the Internet often claim that the Internet is governed by no one, and indeed cannot be governed, and that it is inherently above and beyond the law. What these people forget is that the Internet runs over private and public telecommunications facilities that are themselves governed by laws, and subject to the same pressures as all telecommunications carriers. In fact, the Internet is tied into a complex web of governing bodies, national legislatures, and international professional societies. There is no one single governing organization that controls activity on the Internet. Instead, there are several organizations that influence the system and monitor its operations. Among the governing bodies of the Internet are:

- The *Internet Architecture Board (IAB)*, which helps define the overall structure of the Internet.
- The *Internet Corporation for Assigned Names and Numbers (ICANN)*, which assigns IP addresses and manages the top-level domain name system. ICANN was created in 1998 by the U.S. Department of Commerce.
- The *Internet Engineering Steering Group (IESG)*, which oversees standard setting with respect to the Internet.
- The *Internet Engineering Task Force (IETF)*, a private-sector group that forecasts the next step in the growth of the Internet, keeping watch over its evolution and operation.
- The *Internet Society (ISOC)*, which is a consortium of corporations, government agencies, and nonprofit organizations that monitors Internet policies and practices.
- The *World Wide Web Consortium (W3C)*, a largely academic group that sets HTML and other programming standards for the Web.
- The *International Telecommunication Union (ITU)*, which helps set technical standards.

While none of these organizations has actual control over the Internet and how it functions, they can and do influence government agencies, major network owners, ISPs, corporations, and software developers with the goal of keeping the Internet operating as efficiently as possible. ICANN comes closest to being a manager of the Internet and reflects the powerful role which the Department of Commerce has played historically in Internet governance.

In addition to these professional bodies, the Internet must also conform to the laws of the sovereign nation-states in which it operates, as well as the technical infrastructures that exist within the nation-state. Although in the early years of the Internet there was very little legislative or executive interference, this situation is changing as the Internet plays a growing role in the distribution of information and knowledge, including content that some find objectionable.

The U.S. Department of Commerce originally created ICANN with the intent that it take over control of the Domain Name System and the 13 root servers that are at the heart of the Internet addressing scheme. However, this is no longer the case. The United States changed its policy in June 2005, when the Department of Commerce announced it would retain oversight over the root servers. There were several reasons for this move, including the use of the Internet for basic communications services by terrorist groups, and the uncertainty that might be caused should an international body take over. In 2008, the Department of Commerce reaffirmed this stance, stating that it "has no plans to transition management of the authoritative root zone file to ICANN" (U.S. Department of Commerce, 2008).

Read *Insight on Society: Government Regulation and Surveillance of the Internet* for a further look at the issue of censorship of Internet content and substance.

## 3.3  INTERNET II: THE FUTURE INFRASTRUCTURE

The Internet is changing as new technologies appear and new applications are developed. We refer to the future infrastructure as Internet II. The second era of the Internet is being built today by private corporations, universities, and government agencies. To appreciate the benefits of Internet II, you must first understand the limitations of the Internet's current infrastructure.

### LIMITATIONS OF THE CURRENT INTERNET

Much of the Internet's current infrastructure is several decades old (equivalent to a century in Internet time). It suffers from a number of limitations, including:

- *Bandwidth limitations.* There is insufficient capacity throughout the backbone, the metropolitan switching centers, and most importantly, the "last mile" to the house and small businesses. The result is slow peak-hour service (congestion) and a limited ability to handle high volumes of video and voice traffic.

- *Quality of service limitations.* Today's information packets take a circuitous route to get to their final destinations. This creates the phenomenon of **latency**—delays in messages caused by the uneven flow of information packets through the network. In the case of e-mail, latency is not noticeable. However, with streaming video and synchronous communication, such as a telephone call, latency is noticeable to the user and perceived as "jerkiness" in movies or delays in voice communication. Today's Internet uses "best-effort" quality of service (QOS), which makes no guarantees about when or whether data will be delivered, and provides each packet with the same level of service, no matter who the user is or what type of data is contained in the packet. A higher level of service quality is required if the Internet is to keep expanding into new services, such as video on demand and telephony.

**latency**
delays in messages caused by the uneven flow of information packets through the network

# INSIGHT ON SOCIETY

## GOVERNMENT REGULATION AND SURVEILLANCE OF THE INTERNET

We like to think of the Internet and the Web as an extraordinary technology unleashing torrents of human creativity, innovation, and expression. On a scale much larger than than the invention of movable type by Gutenberg in 15th century Germany, the Internet allows hundreds of millions of people to e-mail, Facebook, Google and link in (all verbs that are new to our age, the Internet age). How ironic then that the same Internet has spawned an explosion in government control and surveillance of individuals on the Internet! Arguably, totalitarian dictators of the 20th century would have given their eye-teeth for such a marvelous technology that can track what millions of people do, say, think, and search for in billions of e-mails, searches, blogs ,and Facebook posts.

Many people assume that because the Internet is so widely dispersed, it must be difficult to control or monitor. Legions of youthful music and video pirates believe they are anonymous on the Internet and cannot possibly be held accountable for whatever they want to do. "Information," they say, "wants to be free!" Unfortunately, with contemporary surveillance technologies, these statements are either false or misleading.

In reality, state-sponsored surveillance of the Internet and its content turns out to be pretty easy and very widespread. According to the Berkman Center for Internet and Society, and Reporters Without Borders, about three dozen governments, from Iran, China, and Cuba, to Uzbekistan and Russia, control citizen access to the Internet. The United States, various state governments, as well as many European countries and Australia, also exercise Web site access control over Internet users. The number of countries that monitor e-mail and text messages is much larger, and once again, includes the United States, all European nations, and Japan. In fact, just about all governments assert some kind of control and surveillance over Internet content and messages. There's a tug of war going on between young sophisticated users of the Internet, and state-sponsored censors and security police around the world.

Internet traffic in all countries runs through huge fiber-optic trunk lines. In China, there are three such lines, and China requires the companies that own these lines to configure their routers for both internal and external service requests. When a request originates in China for a Web page in Chicago, the Chinese routers examine the request to see if the site is on a blacklist, and then examine words in the requested Web page to see if they contain blacklisted terms. The most famous blacklisted terms are "falun" (a suppressed religious group in China) and "Tiananmen Square massacre" (or any symbols that might lead to such results such as "198964" which signifies June 4, 1989, the date of the massacre). The system is often referred to as "The Great Firewall of China," and is implemented with the assistance of Cisco Systems (the U.S. firm that is the largest manufacturer of routers in the world). Other U.S. Internet firms are also involved in China's censorship and surveillance efforts.

In addition to the Great Firewall of China, the Chinese government relies on a much more effective tactic called "self censorship" (or intimidation). Possibly the leader in Internet censorship in terms of shear scale if not sophistication is the People's Republic of China, and its authoritarian government bent on preventing its people from thinking certain thoughts. When U.S. search engines moved into China in 2002

(Microsoft, Google, and Yahoo), in return for access to the China market, firms agreed to censor the search results of Chinese citizens according to criteria dictated by China's Internet agency.

For instance, in 2002, the Chinese government summarily shut off access from inside China to Google's off shore servers in Hong Kong, which did not exercise self-censorship. Even before this action, Google's results were often slowed by the Great Firewall. After this incident, Google decided in 2006 to locate its servers on Chinese soil (Google.cn), where they became directly subject to China's censorship regime, which bans from the Internet anything that "damages the honor or interests of the state," "disturbs the public order," or "infringes upon national customs and habits."

Flash forward to January 2010: Google announced it was leaving China after a massive cyber assault was launched from Taiwan but that was allegedly instigated by China's regime in an effort to steal user information (such as what Chinese citizens were searching for). Thirty-four other American companies were targeted, all high-tech Internet-related concerns. Google claimed it could no longer abide the regime's growing demands for censorship and surveillance although the attack was also a direct threat to Google's business algorithms and proprietary technology used to operate Google around the world. In other words, this attack was aimed at Google's jugular.

In 2010, Google began automatically re-directing all Chinese mainland traffic to its uncensored Hong Kong servers. China objected. Google, in a minor compromise, stopped the automatic re-direct and instead put a button on the screen that users could click to search the Hong Kong site, otherwise they would default to the censored China site. The regime objected and threatened to withdraw Google's license to

operate in China. By July 2010, Google and China are still uncertain how to resolve their differences. Some call it a lose, lose, lose situation for Google, the government, and Chinese citizens. The other major search firms in China are Baidu (Chinese and Japanese owned), Microsoft, and Yahoo. All voluntarily censor their search queries according to the regime's criteria and think nothing of it under the "when in Rome do as the Romans do" doctrine.

Google's stock has taken a hit because Wall Street investors cannot understand why Google would jeopardize its access to the Chinese market. Google's co-founder Sergei Brin, a Soviet-era survivor of surveillance and repression, said it was vital that the Obama administration address the issue of censorship in China because trade and censorship are inextricably linked in the Internet age. Brin said, "Since services and information are our most successful exports, if regulations in China effectively prevent us from being competitive, then they are a trade barrier."

China is hardly the only government that exercises powerful controls over its citizens' use of the Internet. In June 2009, the video of Neda Adha Soltan, who had been shot by a squad of Iranian riot police and was bleeding to death on the streets of Tehran, quickly raced around the world via the Internet and cell phone networks despite the efforts of the Iranian government, which had completely shut down text messaging in the country; blocked access to selected sites such as YouTube, MySpace, and Facebook; and slowed all Internet traffic in Iran by 90% so it could sift through e-mail messages. In the protests that followed the disputed Iranian election of June 2009, Twitter became the primary organizing tool of the protestors, and an important source of information for the rest of the world, along with YouTube and other social sites to which protestors were able to connect, despite the best efforts of Iranian government censors.

Iran's Internet surveillance of its citizens is considered by security experts to be "one of the world's most sophisticated mechanisms for controlling and censoring the Internet, allowing it to examine the content of individual online communications on a massive scale," far more sophisticated than even China's Internet surveillance activities. The Iranian system goes far beyond preventing access to specific sites such as BBC World News, Google, and Facebook. Because the techniques for getting around government site access censorship are widely known (generally find a proxy server in another country that will allow you access to a forbidden site), governments need to do much more to control access and to figure out what their citizens are really thinking. One technique is deep packet inspection of every e-mail, text, or Twitter tweet. Deep packet inspection allows governments to read messages, alter their contents for disinformation purposes, and identify senders and recipients. It is accomplished by installing computers in the line between users and ISPs, opening up every digitized packet, inspecting for keywords and images, reconstructing the message, and sending it on. This is done for all Internet traffic including Skype, Facebook, e-mail, tweets, and messages sent to proxy servers. These operations can slow down Internet service, but this delay can be avoided by installing additional servers. Iran's Internet Monitoring Center is located in the government telecommunications monopoly, a central choke point for all Internet traffic in the country. Iran has some of the world's finest deep packet monitoring equipment supplied by a joint venture called Nokia Siemens Networks. There are of course reasons why Iran's government did not simply shut down the Internet entirely. Some traffic is required for business purposes, and

keeping the Internet functioning allows the state to identify its enemies and critics.

Not to be outdone, both Europe and the United States have at various times taken steps to control access to Internet sites, censor Web content, and engage in extensive communications, although not to the extent of Iran, China, and many other nations. For instance, Britain has a list of blocked sites, as does Germany and France. The Australian Communications and Media Authority has developed a list of several hundred Web sites that have been refused registration in Australia, mostly violent video game and online pornography sites. The United States and European countries generally ban the sale, distribution, and/or possession of online child pornography. Both France and Germany bar online Nazi memorabilia. The United States has passed laws attempting to restrict ordinary pornographic content, but most of these have been struck down by courts. The United States does ban Internet gambling, and has arrested several European entrepreneurs on U.S. soil for promoting or engaging in Internet gambling sites. In response to terrorism threats, both European governments and the U.S. government have also initiated deep-packet inspection of e-mail and text communications. This surveillance is not limited to cross-border international data flows, and includes large-scale domestic surveillance of "ordinary" e-mail. Although it may seem preposterous that any U.S. government agency could read an estimated 150 billion daily e-mails, this task is, in reality, only slightly more complicated than Google's handling of 10 to 12 billion search queries per month. With the cooperation of the major Internet trunk carriers (AT&T, Verizon, and Sprint), and a dedicated signals intelligence computing capacity equal to Google's, near total e-mail, text, and Twitter surveillance is possible. While the Internet has unleashed an explosion of expression, and even enabled several rebellions and revolutions around the world, at the same time it has become a testing and proving ground for new government surveillance capabilities for both democratic and totalitarian regimes.

**SOURCES**: "Google Co-founder Sergey Brin Urges US to Act Over China Web Censorship," by Bobbie Johnson, The Guardian.co.uk, May 10, 2010; "Journalists' E-mails Hacked in China," by Andrew Jacobs, *New York Times*, March 31, 2010; "Enemies of the Internet. Countries Under Surveillance," Reporters Without Borders,www.rsf.org, March 12, 2010; "Google Hack Smells More and More Like Chinese Government Job," by Katherine Noyes, Technewsworld.com, February 22, 2010; "Google Warns of China Exit Over Hacking," by Jessica Vallero, *Wall Street Journal*, January 13, 2010; "Clash on the Great Firewall," *Wall Street Journal*, January 4, 2010. "Foreign Intelligence Surveillance Act (FISA)," *New York Times*, July 23, 2009; "US and European Countries Jointly Responsible for Internet Censorship," Reporters Without Borders, www.rsf.org, July 23, 2009; "Senate Approves Bill to Broaden Wiretap Powers," by Eric Lichtblau, *New York Times*, July 10, 2009; "In a Death Seen Around the World, a Symbol of Iranian Protests," by Nazila Fathi, *New York Times*, June 23, 2009; "Iran's Web Spying Aided By Western Technology. European Gear Used in Vast Effort to Monitor Communications," by Christopher Rhoads, *Wall Street Journal*, June 22, 2009.

- *Network architecture limitations*. Today, a thousand requests for a single music track from a central server will result in a thousand efforts by the server to download the music to each requesting client. This slows down network performance as the same music track is sent out a thousand times to clients that might be located in the same metropolitan area. This is very different from television, where the program is broadcast once to millions of homes.

- *Language development limitations*. HTML, the language of Web pages, is fine for text and simple graphics, but poor at defining and communicating "rich documents," such as databases, business documents, or graphics. The tags used to define an HTML page are fixed and generic.

- *Wired Internet*. The Internet is based on cables—fiber-optic and coaxial copper cables. Copper cables use a centuries-old technology, and fiber-optic cable is expensive to place underground. The wired nature of the Internet restricts mobility of users although it is changing rapidly as Wi-Fi hotspots proliferate, and cellular phone technology advances. However, cellular systems are often overloaded due to the growth in the number of smartphones.

Now imagine an Internet at least 100 times as powerful as today's Internet, one that is not subjected to the limitations of bandwidth, protocols, architecture, physical connections, and language detailed previously. Welcome to the world of Internet II, and the next generation of e-commerce services and products!

## THE INTERNET2® PROJECT

**Internet2®** is a consortium of more than 200 universities working in partnership with government agencies and private businesses in an effort to make the Internet more efficient.[4] Their work is a continuation of the kind of cooperation among government, private, and educational organizations that created the original Internet.

**Internet2®**
a consortium of more than 200 universities, government agencies, and private businesses that are collaborating to find ways to make the Internet more efficient

[4]The Internet2® project is just one aspect of the larger second generation Internet we call Internet II.

The idea behind Internet2 is to create a "giant test bed" where new technologies can be tested without impacting the existing Internet. The three primary goals of Internet2 are to:

- Create a leading-edge very high-speed network capability for the national research community
- Enable revolutionary Internet applications
- Ensure the rapid transfer of new network services and applications to the broader Internet community

Some of the areas Internet2 participants are focusing on in this pursuit are advanced network infrastructure, new networking capabilities, middleware, and advanced applications. The advanced networks created and in use by Internet2 members provide the environment in which new technologies can be tested and enhanced. Several new networks have been established, including Abilene and vBNS. Abilene and vBNS (short for *very high performance Backbone Network Service*) are high-performance backbone networks with bandwidths ranging from 2.5 Gbps to 10 Gbps that interconnect the GigaPoPs used by Internet2 members to access the network. A **GigaPoP** is a regional Gigabit Point of Presence, or point of access to the Internet2 network that supports data transfers at the rate of 1 Gbps or higher (see **Figure 3.14**). In February 2004, Internet2 upgraded all segments of the Abilene network to 10 Gbps. In 2007, Internet2 deployed a 100 Gbps East-West link. At these

**GigaPoP**

a regional Gigabit Point of Presence, or point of access to the Internet2 network, that supports at least 1 gigabit (1 billion bits) per second information transfer

| FIGURE 3.14 | INTERNET2 GIGAPOP EXCHANGES |
| --- | --- |

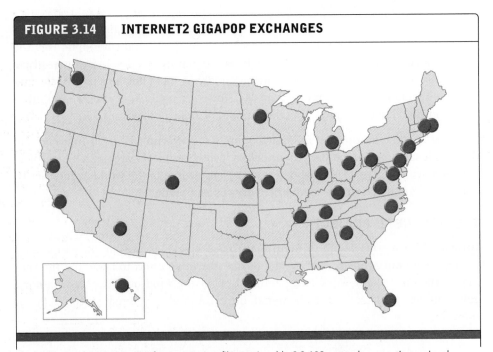

The backbone of the Internet2 infrastructure is a fiber-optic cable OC-192 network connecting regional GigaPoP servers (represented by the blue circles) that operate at billions of bits per second.
SOURCE: Internet2.edu, 2008.

speeds, the ability of the network to process data begins to exceed the speed at which client computers can pull data off their hard drives. With a 100 Gbps Internet, a high-quality version of the movie *The Matrix* could be sent in a few seconds rather than half a minute over the current Internet2 and two days over a typical home broadband line.

## THE LARGER INTERNET II TECHNOLOGY ENVIRONMENT: THE FIRST MILE AND THE LAST MILE

The Internet2 project is just the tip of the iceberg when it comes to near-term future enhancements to the Internet. In 2007, the NSF began work on the Global Environment for Networking Innovations (GENI) Initiative to develop new core functionality for the Internet, including new naming, addressing, and identity architectures; enhanced capabilities, including additional security architecture and a design that supports high availability; and new Internet services and applications (Geni.net, 2008). The most significant privately initiated (but often government-influenced) changes are coming in two areas: fiber-optic trunk line bandwidth and wireless Internet services. Fiber optics is concerned with the first mile or backbone Internet services that carry bulk traffic long distances. Wireless Internet is concerned with the last mile—from the larger Internet to the user's cell phone or laptop.

### Fiber Optics and the Bandwidth Explosion in the First Mile

**Fiber-optic cable** consists of up to hundreds of strands of glass that use light to transmit data. It is frequently replacing existing coaxial and twisted pair cabling because it can transmit much more data at faster speeds, with less interference and better data security. Fiber-optic cable is also thinner and lighter, taking up less space during installation. The hope is to use fiber optics to expand network bandwidth capacity in order to prepare for the expected increases in Web traffic once Internet II services are widely adopted.

**fiber-optic cable**
consists of up to hundreds of strands of glass or plastic that use light to transmit data

The enormous increase in long-haul backbone capacity from 1998 to 2001, coupled with a decline in demand, caused over 60 telecommunications companies including WorldCom and Global Crossing Ltd. to declare bankruptcy and others to struggle with large deficits, leading to painful losses in shareholder value. The cost of a 1.5 Mbps dedicated T1 line between Los Angeles and New York has fallen from over $100,000 per month down to $1,500 per month in 2010. Thousands of miles of fiber-optic cable in the United States are "dark" or "unlit." The decline in the cost of fiber-optic cable is due in part to the continued technical improvement in switching equipment, which allows firms to achieve exponentially higher throughput from the existing fiber-optic cables by improvements in processors and technique. For this reason, the installation of long-haul fiber-optic cable is likely to remain relatively flat for years to come, and the prices companies can charge for long-haul digital transmission will also likely remain flat through 2013.

However, there is a silver lining in this cloudy picture. The fiber-optic cable did not disappear or degrade over time, and it represents a vast digital highway that is currently being exploited by YouTube (Google), Facebook, MySpace, and other high-bandwidth applications; telecommunications companies are re-capitalizing and building new business models based on market prices for digital traffic. The net result is that society ultimately benefited from extraordinarily low-cost, long-haul, very high-bandwidth communication facilities that are already paid for.

Demand for fiber-optic cable is likely to strengthen as consumers demand integrated telephone, broadband access, and video from a single source. Interactive online television, online Hollywood movies, inexpensive Voice over Internet Protocol (VoIP) telephone, and Internet access all from the same company that provides a single cable into the home is the vision driving Verizon, other local Bells, and cable firms. In 2004, Verizon began building its FiOS fiber-optic Internet service, network infrastructure, and since then has spent $23 billion expanding the service. In 2010, there are about 13 million Verizon FiOS broadband customers. FiOS costs consumers from $40 to $200 a month, and provides download speeds of up to 50 Mbps and upload speeds of up to 10 Mbps. This so-called Fiber to the Premises (FTTP) will be the fastest growing form of broadband connection in the next decade. However, FiOS is expensive to install for Verizon, and currently Verizon has halted expansion of the service. **Table 3.6** illustrates several optical bandwidth standards and compares them to traditional T lines.

**Figure 3.15** gives a comparative look at bandwidth demand for various applications.

### The Last Mile: Mobile Wireless Internet Access

Fiber-optic networks carry the long-haul bulk traffic of the Internet—and in the future will play an important role in bringing BigBand to the household and small business. But along with fiber optics and photonics, arguably the most significant development for the Internet and Web in the last five years has been the emergence of mobile wireless Internet access.

Wireless Internet is concerned with the last mile of Internet access to the user's home, office, car, or cell phone anywhere. Up until 2000, the last-mile access to the

| TABLE 3.6 | HIGH-SPEED OPTICAL BANDWIDTH STANDARDS |
|---|---|
| STANDARD | SPEED |
| T1 | 1.544 Mbps |
| T3 | 43.232 Mbps |
| OC3 | 155 Mbps |
| OC12 | 622 Mbps |
| OC48 | 2.5 Gbps |
| OC192 | 9.6 Gbps |

Note: "OC" stands for Optical Carrier and is used to specify the speed of fiber-optic networks conforming to the SONET standard. SONET (Synchronous Optical Networks) includes a set of signal rate multiples for transmitting digital signals on optical fiber. The base rate (OC-1) is 51.84 Mbps.

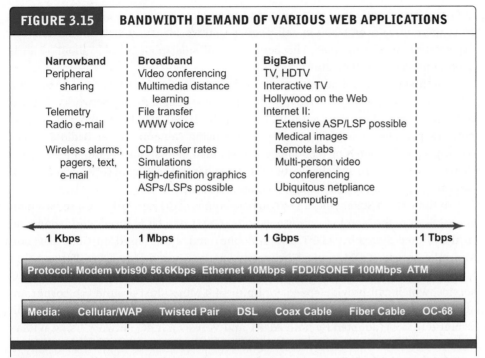

| FIGURE 3.15 | **BANDWIDTH DEMAND OF VARIOUS WEB APPLICATIONS** |

The really exciting e-commerce applications such as high definition television (HDTV) and interactive TV and movies require higher levels of bandwidth to the home than are typically currently available in the United States.

Internet—with the exception of a small satellite Internet connect population—was bound up in land lines of some sort: copper coaxial TV cables or telephone lines or, in some cases, fiber-optic lines to the office. Internet II will increasingly rely on wireless technology to connect users' smartphones and computers to the Web and LANs. In 2010, wireless access to the Internet means either a high-speed cellular phone connection, or a network Wi-Fi connection.

In 2010, more notebook computers (most with wireless networking functionality built in) are expected to be sold in the United States than desktop computers. (Stross, 2009). Smartphones are the fastest growing wireless devices with respect to Internet access. Clearly, a large part of the future Internet will be mobile, access—anywhere, broadband service for the delivery of video, music, and Web search. According to eMarketer, there are already 83 million mobile Internet users in the United States in 2010, and almost 900 million worldwide (eMarketer, Inc.2010a, 2010b).

**Telephone-based versus Computer Network-based Wireless Internet Access** There are two different basic types of wireless Internet connectivity: telephone-based and computer network-based systems.

*Telephone-based wireless Internet access* connects the user to a global telephone system (land, satellite, and microwave) that has a long history of dealing with thousands of users simultaneously and already has in place a large-scale transaction billing system and related infrastructure. Cellular telephones and the telephone industry are currently the largest providers of wireless access to the Internet today. In 2010, there were over 1 billion cell phones sold worldwide, with a similar amount expected to be sold in 2009. The percentage of smartphones sold (about 17%) is continuing to climb (IDC, 2010).

The first generation of cellular networks were analog-based. Second generation (2G) cellular networks are relatively slow circuit-switched digital networks that can transmit data at about 10 Kbps—one fifth of the speed of a home modem. A 2.5G network provides speeds of 60 to 144 Kbps using General Packet Radio Services (GPRS), a packet-switching technology that is much more efficient (and hence faster) than dedicated circuit-switched networks. An enhanced version of GPRS called EDGE can carry data at up from 384 Kbps to around 2 Mbps.

In the United States, there are two basic types of 3G networks—those based on Global System for Mobile Communications (GSM) standards (used worldwide, and in the United States by AT&T and T-Mobile) and those based on Code Division Multiple Access (CDMA, used primarily in the United States, by Verizon and Sprint). Cell phone providers have also begun to offer what they call 3G+ or 3.5G service, which can provide speeds of up to 14.4 Mbps. Just around the corner are 4G networks using Wi-Max technology and a technology known as Long-Term Evolution (LTE) (adopted by both AT&T and Verizon). A 4G network using WiMax can deliver downloads at up to 72 Mbps, while LTE has the potential to provide up to 300 Mbps. **Table 3.7** summarizes the various telephone technologies used for wireless Internet access.

Smart phones, combine the functionality of a cell phone, such as an Apple iPhone, T-Mobile Android G1/G2, or RIM BlackBerry, with that of a mobile laptop computer with Wi-fi capability. This makes it possible to combine in one device music, video, Web access, and telephone service. When these same cellular devices also can provide Wi-Fi connections to the Web, and switch seamlessly from one network to the other, they are referred to as *fully converged devices*. **Table 3.8** describes some of the most popular smartphones available as of August 2010.

Once a connection is established with a user's smartphone, there are a number of different ways to deliver Web pages. The Apple iPhone has such a high resolution and large screen that Web pages are delivered as ordinary HTML pages and the user can scroll around the page to navigate. Likewise with the BlackBerry Storm. Older devices with less-capable screens either use Wireless Application Protocol (WAP) or iMode, a proprietary standard owned by the Japanese company NTT DoCoMo.

*Wireless local area network (WLAN)-based Internet access* derives from a completely different background from telephone-based wireless Internet access. Popularly known as Wi-Fi, WLANs are based on computer local area networks where the task is to connect client computers (generally stationary) to server computers within local areas of, say, a few hundred meters. WLANs function by sending radio signals that are broadcast over the airwaves using certain radio frequency ranges (2.4 GHz to 5.875 GHz, depending on the type of standard involved). The major technologies here are the various versions of the

| TABLE 3.7 | WIRELESS INTERNET ACCESS TELEPHONE TECHNOLOGIES | | |
|---|---|---|---|
| TECHNOLOGY | SPEED | DESCRIPTION | PLAYERS |
| *2G* | | | |
| Global System for Mobile Communications (GSM) | 10 Kbps | European and some American companies' basic cell phone service; text messaging; uses TDMA. | Vodafone (Europe), Cingular, T-Mobile |
| Time Division Multiple Access (TDMA) | 10 Kbps | An early standard for cell phone service. Used by GSM networks worldwide. | GSM networks in Europe and Japan |
| CDMA | 10 Kbps | American standard for basic cell phone service; text messaging. Developed by Qualcomm. | Verizon, Sprint |
| *2.5G* | | | |
| General Packet Radio Services (GPRS) EDGE CDMA2000 1xRTT | 30–170 Kbps | Interim step toward 3G in the United States. Fast enough for Web access. | AT&T, T-Mobile, Vodafone, Verizon, Sprint |
| *3G (THIRD GENERATION)* | | | |
| CDMA2000 EV-DO HSPA (W-CDMA) | 144 Kbps–2 Mbps | High-speed, mobile, always on for e-mail, browsing, instant messaging. Implementing technologies include versions of CDMA2000 EV-DO (used by CDMA providers) and HSPDA (used by GSM providers). Nearly as fast as Wi-Fi. | Verizon, Sprint AT&T, T-Mobile, Vodafone |
| *3.5G (3G+)* | | | |
| CDMA2000 EV-DO, Rev.B | Up to 14.4 Mbps | Enhanced version of CDMA 2000 EV-DO. | Verizon, Sprint |
| HSPA+ | Up to 11 Mbps | Enhanced version of HSPA | AT&T, T-Mobile |
| *4G (FOURTH GENERATION)* | | | |
| Long-Term Evolution (LTE) | Up to 100–300 Mbps | True broadband on cell phone. | AT&T, Verizon |
| WiMax | 72 Mbps | Alternative to LTE wide area network for cities. | Clearwire/Sprint |

Wi-Fi standard and Bluetooth. Emerging WLAN technologies include WiMax, Ultra-Wideband (UWB), and ZigBee (see **Table 3.9**).

In a Wi-Fi network, a *wireless access point* (also known as a "hot spot") connects to the Internet directly via a broadband connection (cable, DSL telephone, or T1 line) and then transmits a radio signal to a transmitter/receiver installed in a laptop computer or PDA, either as a PC card or built-in at manufacture (such as Intel's Cen-

| TABLE 3.8 | POPULAR SMARTPHONES | | | |
|---|---|---|---|---|
| DEVICE | APPLE IPHONE 4G | PALM PRE | ANDROID G2 | BLACKBERRY CURVE |
| Functionality | Phone, Internet access, e-mail, GPS, camera, video recording, voice commands | Phone, Internet access, e-mail, GPS, camera | Phone, Internet access, e-mail, GPS, camera, video recording | Phone, Internet access, e-mail, GPS camera, video recording |
| Applications | iTunes App Store; 250,000 apps | Palm App Catalog, 3,500 apps | Android Marketplace, 100,000 apps | BlackBerry App World, 10,000 apps |
| Hardware | Touch screen, 64 GB storage, Bluetooth | Touch screen, 8 GB storage, Bluetooth, keyboard | Touch screen, 64 GB storage, Bluetooth | Touch screen, Bluetooth |
| Operating System | iOS | Web OS | Google Android | Blackberry OS 6.0 |
| Storage | 64 GB | 64 GB | 64 GB, expandable | 64 GB |
| Provider/Network | AT&T 4G/3G/Wi-Fi | Sprint 4G/3G/Wi-Fi | T-Mobile 4G/3G/Wi-Fi | Verizon 4G/3G/Wi-Fi |

| TABLE 3.9 | WIRELESS INTERNET ACCESS NETWORK TECHNOLOGIES | | |
|---|---|---|---|
| TECHNOLOGY | RANGE/SPEED | DESCRIPTION | PLAYERS |
| Wi-Fi (IEEE 802.11a –802.11n) | 300 feet/11–70 Mbps | Evolving high-speed, fixed broadband wireless local area network for commercial and residential use | Linksys, Cisco, and other Wi-Fi router manufacturers; entrepreneurial network developers |
| WiMax (IEEE 802.16) | 30 miles/50–70 Mbps | High-speed, medium-range, broadband wireless metropolitan area network | Clearwire, Sprint, Fujitsu, Intel, Alcatel, Proxim/Terabeam |
| Bluetooth (wireless personal area network) | 1–30 meters/ 1–3 Mbps | Modest-speed, low-power, short-range connection of digital devices | Ericsson, Nokia, Apple, HP, and other device makers |
| Ultra-Wideband (UWB) (wireless personal area network) | 30 feet/5–10 Mbps | Low-power, short-range, high-bandwidth network technology useful as cabling replacement in home and office networks | Ultrawideband Forum, Intel, Freescale |
| ZigBee (wireless personal area network) | 30 feet/250 Kbps | Short-range, very low-power, wireless network technology useful for remotely controlling industrial, medical, and home automation devices | ZigBee Alliance, Chipcon, Freescale, Mitsubishi, Motorola, MaxStream, San Juan Software |

trino processor, which provides built-in support for Wi-Fi in portable devices). **Figure 3.16** illustrates how a Wi-Fi network works.

Wi-Fi offers high bandwidth capacity from 11 Mbps to 70 Mbps—far greater than any 3G or 4G service even planned—but has a limited range of 300 meters, with the exception of WiMax discussed below. Wi-Fi is also exceptionally inexpensive. The cost of creating a corporate Wi-Fi network in a single 14-story building with an access point for each floor is less than $100 an access point. It would cost well over $500,000 to wire the same building with Ethernet cable. Admittedly, the Ethernet cable would be operating at a theoretical 100 Mbps—10 times as fast as Wi-Fi. However, in some cases, this capacity is not needed and Wi-Fi is an acceptable alternative.

While initially a grass roots, "hippies and hackers" public access technology, billions of dollars have subsequently been poured into private ventures seeking to create for-profit Wi-Fi networks. The most prominent network has been created by Boingo Wireless with over 100,000 hot spots around the globe. Wayport (now owned by AT&) created another large network that provides Wi-Fi service at hotels, airports, McDonalds, IHOPs, and Hertz airport rental offices, with around 20,000 hot spots in the United States. T-Mobile and Sprint have also established nationwide Wi-Fi services at 2,000 Starbuck's coffee shops, and thousands of other public locations. Apple, in turn, has made Wi-Fi automatically available to iPhone and iPad devices as an alternative to the more expensive and much slower 3G and 4G cellular systems.

| **FIGURE 3.16** | **WI-FI NETWORKS** |
| --- | --- |

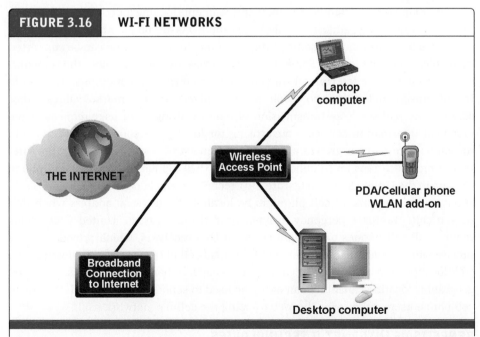

In a Wi-Fi network, wireless access points connect to the Internet using a land-based broadband connection. Clients, which could be laptops, desktops, cell phones, or suitably equipped PDAs, connect to the access point using radio signals.

Will WLAN compete directly against far more expensive telephone 3G services? The answer is "eventually, but not right now." Wi-Fi was originally a local area network technology of limited range, for stationary client computers, but with high capacity suitable for most Web surfing and some corporate uses with modest bandwidth demands. Cellular phone systems are wide area networks of nearly unlimited range, for mobile client computers and handhelds, and with modest but rapidly increasing capacity suitable for e-mail, photos, and Web browsing (on very small screens). However, the rock-bottom price of Wi-Fi coupled with ambitious plans for a 30-mile- range WiMax (802.16) service suggests that Wi-Fi could drain significant business from far more capital-intensive cellular systems.

A second WLAN technology for connecting to the Internet, and for connecting Internet devices to one another, is called Bluetooth. Bluetooth is an industry standard that emanated from Scandinavian telecommunications firms such as Ericsson, Nokia, and Siemens in the 1990s. **Bluetooth** is a personal connectivity technology that enables links between mobile computers, mobile phones, PDAs, and connectivity to the Internet (Bluetooth.com, 2010). Bluetooth is the universal cable cutter, promising to get rid of the tangled mess of wires, cradles, and special attachments that plague the current world of personal computing. With Bluetooth, users wear a cell phone wireless earbud, share files in a hallway or conference room, synchronize their PDA with their laptop without a cradle, send a document to a printer, and even pay a restaurant bill from the table to a Bluetooth-equipped cash register. Bluetooth also is an unregulated media operating in the 2.4 GHz spectrum but with a very limited range of 30 feet or less. It uses a frequency hopping signal with up to 1,600 hops per second over 79 frequencies, giving it good protection from interference. Bluetooth-equipped devices—which could be cell phones or laptops—constantly scan their environments looking for connections to compatible devices. Today, almost all cell phones and PDAs are Bluetooth-enabled.

**Table 3.10** summarizes some of the e-commerce services that can be supported by wireless Internet access. Some of these services are *push services*—the transmission of data at a predetermined time, or under determined conditions. This could include unsolicited information such as news delivery or stock market values. Other services are *pull services*—transmission of data resulting from user requests. Geographical information services—advertising for local pizza shops, restaurants, and museums—are a major growth area for cell phone services in part due to the Wireless Communications and Public Safety Act of 1999, which required all cell phone carriers in the United States to feature E911 technology by 2006. E911 (Enhanced 911) service allows a person's cell phone to be located at a physical address when that person calls the 911 emergency number used throughout the United States. This requires all cell phones to be equipped with GPS receivers, which provide a fairly precise latitude and longitude location. In fact, all cell phone carriers can identify the GPS location of a cell phone regardless of what number is called. This enhanced geographic locating capability can easily be used to send locally based advertising to cell phone users either over the Web or using the cellular network itself.

**Bluetooth**

new technology standard for short-range wireless communication under 10 meters

## BENEFITS OF INTERNET II TECHNOLOGIES

The increased bandwidth and expanded wireless network connectivity of the Internet II era will result in benefits beyond faster access and richer communications.

| TABLE 3.10 | POTENTIAL WIRELESS INTERNET E-COMMERCE SERVICES |
|---|---|
| SERVICE | DESCRIPTION |
| **Horizontal Market Services** | **Services that apply across industries and firms** |
| Personalized information | Stock values, news, quotes based on user profiles and needs |
| Location based local content | Local maps, hotel finders, movie locations and times, and restaurant locations and reviews |
| Media services | Video, photos, news, and music |
| Banking services | Balance checking, money transfer, bill payment, and overdraft alerts |
| Financial services | Trading, stock alerts, and interest rates based on user account information |
| **Vertical Market Services** | **Services that apply within a firm or industry** |
| Sales support | Stock and production information, remote orders, calendars, and planning information |
| Reservation systems | Airline, train, hotel, and event reservations coordinated with inventory |
| Dispatching | Communication of job details, parts information, and repair routines |
| Fleet management | Control of fleet delivery or service staff; monitoring locations and work schedules |
| Parcel delivery | Tracking of packages, queries, and performance monitoring |
| Home automation | Coordinating alarm and other digital services and devices in a home |
| Industrial automation | Coordinating machine controllers in a factory |

First-mile enhancements created by fiber-optic networks will enhance reliability and quality of Internet transmissions and create new business models and opportunities. Some of the major benefits of these technological advancements include IP multicasting, latency solutions, guaranteed service levels, lower error rates, and declining costs. Widespread wireless access to the Internet will also essentially double or even triple the size of the online shopping marketspace because consumers will be able to shop and make purchases just about anywhere. This is equivalent to doubling the physical floor space of all shopping malls in America. We describe some of these benefits in more detail in the following sections.

## IP Multicasting

The future of the Internet is clearly to become the entertainment center of American life, replacing radio, television, and movie theaters. This means Hollywood movies, television shows, and all the music ever digitized will have to routinely move across the Internet from coast to coast on demand from 200 million users. Today, this would cause a near collapse of the Internet. Internet II will potentially solve this problem. One capability of Internet II is IP multicasting.

**IP multicasting**

a set of technologies that enables efficient delivery of data to many locations on a network

**IP multicasting** is a set of technologies that enables efficient delivery of very large files to many locations on a network. Rather than making multiple copies of a message intended to be distributed to multiple recipients at the point of origin of a message, multicasting initially sends just one message and does not copy it to the individual recipients until it reaches the closest common point on the network, thereby minimizing the bandwidth consumed (see **Figure 3.17**). At that point, routers make copies as needed to serve requesting clients, and the sender sends only a single copy over the Internet. Network performance is significantly improved because it isn't bogged down with the processing and transmission of several large data files; each receiving computer doesn't have to query the transmitting server for the file. Multicasting technologies are already making their way into today's Internet through the use of Mbone (a special-purpose backbone for delivering video data). Used in combination with protocols like BitTorrent, IP

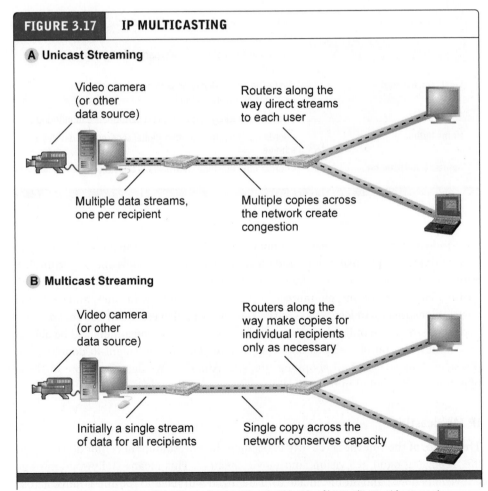

| FIGURE 3.17 | IP MULTICASTING |

**A Unicast Streaming**

Video camera (or other data source)

Routers along the way direct streams to each user

Multiple data streams, one per recipient

Multiple copies across the network create congestion

**B Multicast Streaming**

Video camera (or other data source)

Routers along the way make copies for individual recipients only as necessary

Initially a single stream of data for all recipients

Single copy across the network conserves capacity

IP multicasting is a method for efficiently sending high-bandwidth video files to clients without causing Internet congestion and delay for other traffic.

SOURCES: Adapted from Cisco Systems, 2007; Internet2.edu, 2000.

multicasting has the potential to scale up to serve an entire nation of Internet users.

## Latency Solutions

One of the challenges of packet switching, where data is divided into chunks and then sent separately to meet again at the destination, is that the Internet does not differentiate between high-priority packets, such as video clips, and those of lower priority, such as self-contained e-mail messages. Because the packets cannot yet be simultaneously reassembled, the result can be distorted audio and video streams.

Internet II holds the promise of **diffserv**, or differentiated quality of service—a new technology that assigns levels of priority to packets based on the type of data being transmitted. Video conference packets, for example, which need to reach their destination almost instantaneously, would receive much higher priority than e-mail messages. In the end, the quality of video and audio will skyrocket without undue stress on the network. Live and on-demand television and movies will be possible once Internet II is completed. But differential service is very controversial because it means some users will get more bandwidth than others, and potentially they may have to pay a higher price for more bandwidth.

**differentiated quality of service (diffserv)**
a new technology that assigns levels of priority to packets based on the type of data being transmitted

## Guaranteed Service Levels and Lower Error Rates

In today's Internet, there is no service-level guarantee and no way to purchase the right to move data through the Internet at a fixed pace. Today's Internet promises only "best effort." The Internet is democratic—it speeds or slows everyone's traffic alike. With Internet II, it will be possible to purchase the right to move data through the network at a guaranteed speed in return for higher fees.

Improved capacity and packet switching will also inevitably impact quality of data transmissions, reducing error rates and boosting customer satisfaction.

## Declining Costs

As the Internet pipeline is upgraded, the availability of broadband service will expand beyond major metropolitan areas, significantly reducing the costs of access. More users means lower cost, as products and technology catch on in the mass market. Higher volume usage enables providers to lower the cost of both access devices, or clients, and the service required to use such products. Both broadband and wireless service fees are expected to decline as geographic service areas increase, in part due to competition for that business.

## 3.4 THE WORLD WIDE WEB

Without the Web, there would be no e-commerce. The invention of the Web brought an extraordinary expansion of digital services to millions of amateur computer users, including color text and pages, formatted text, pictures, animations, video, and sound. In short, the Web makes nearly all the rich elements of human expression needed to establish a commercial marketplace available to nontechnical computer users worldwide.

While the Internet was born in the 1960s, the Web was not invented until 1989–1991 by Dr. Tim Berners-Lee of the European Particle Physics Laboratory, better known as CERN (Berners-Lee et al., 1994). Several earlier authors—such as Vannevar Bush (in 1945) and Ted Nelson (in the 1960s)—had suggested the possibility of organizing knowledge as a set of interconnected pages that users could freely browse (Bush, 1945; Ziff Davis Publishing, 1998). Berners-Lee and his associates at CERN built on these ideas and developed the initial versions of HTML, HTTP, a Web server, and a browser, the four essential components of the Web.

First, Berners-Lee wrote a computer program that allowed formatted pages within his own computer to be linked using keywords (hyperlinks). Clicking on a keyword in a document would immediately move him to another document. Berners-Lee created the pages using a modified version of a powerful text markup language called SGML (Standard Generalized Markup Language).

Berners-Lee called this language HyperText Markup Language, or HTML. He then came up with the idea of storing his HTML pages on the Internet. Remote client computers could access these pages by using HTTP (introduced earlier in Section 3.2 and described more fully in the next section). But these early Web pages still appeared as black and white text pages with hyperlinks expressed inside brackets. The early Web was based on text only; the original Web browser only provided a line interface.

Information being shared on the Web remained text-based until 1993, when Marc Andreesen and others at the National Center for Supercomputing Applications (NCSA) at the University of Illinois created a Web browser with a graphical user interface (GUI) called **Mosaic** that made it possible to view documents on the Web graphically—using colored backgrounds, images, and even primitive animations. Mosaic was a software program that could run on any graphically based interface such as Macintosh, Windows, or Unix. The Mosaic browser software read the HTML text on a Web page and displayed it as a graphical interface document within a graphical user interface (GUI) operating system such as Windows or Macintosh. Liberated from simple black and white text pages, HTML pages could now be viewed by anyone in the world who could operate a mouse and use a Macintosh or PC.

Aside from making the content of Web pages colorful and available to the world's population, the graphical Web browser created the possibility of **universal computing**, the sharing of files, information, graphics, sound, video, and other objects across all computer platforms in the world, regardless of operating system. A browser could be made for each of the major operating systems, and the Web pages created for one system, say, Windows, would also be displayed exactly the same, or nearly the same, on computers running the Macintosh or Unix operating systems. As long as each operating system had a Mosaic browser, the same Web pages could be used on all the different types of computers and operating systems. This meant that no matter what kind of computer you used, anywhere in the world, you would see the same Web pages. The browser and the Web have introduced us to a whole new world of computing and information management that was unthinkable prior to 1993.

**Mosaic**
Web browser with a graphical user interface (GUI) that made it possible to view documents on the Web graphically

**universal computing**
the sharing of files, information, graphics, sound, video, and other objects across all computer platforms in the world, regardless of operating system

In 1994, Andreesen and Jim Clark founded Netscape, which created the first commercial browser, **Netscape Navigator**. Although Mosaic had been distributed free of charge, Netscape initially charged for its software. In August 1995, Microsoft Corporation released its own version of a browser, called **Internet Explorer**. In the ensuing years, Netscape has faltered, falling from a 100% market share to less than .5% in 2009. The fate of Netscape illustrates an important e-commerce business lesson. Innovators usually are not long-term winners, whereas smart followers often have the assets needed for long-term survival.

## HYPERTEXT

Web pages can be accessed through the Internet because the Web browser software on your PC can request Web pages stored on an Internet host server using the HTTP protocol. **Hypertext** is a way of formatting pages with embedded links that connect documents to one another, and that also link pages to other objects such as sound, video, or animation files. When you click on a graphic and a video clip plays, you have clicked on a hyperlink. For example, when you type a Web address in your browser such as http://www.sec.gov, your browser sends an HTTP request to the sec.gov server requesting the home page of sec.gov.

HTTP is the first set of letters at the start of every Web address, followed by the domain name. The domain name specifies the organization's server computer that is housing the document. Most companies have a domain name that is the same as or closely related to their official corporate name. The directory path and document name are two more pieces of information within the Web address that help the browser track down the requested page. Together, the address is called a Uniform Resource Locator, or URL. When typed into a browser, a URL tells it exactly where to look for the information. For example, in the following URL:

http://www.megacorp.com/content/features/082602.html

http = the protocol used to display Web pages

www.megacorp.com = domain name

content/features = the directory path that identifies where on the domain Web server the page is stored

082602.html = the document name and its format (an html page)

The most common domain extensions (known as general top-level domains, or gTLDs) currently available and officially sanctioned by ICANN are shown in **Table 3.11**. Countries also have domain names, such as .uk, .au, and .fr (United Kingdom, Australia, and France, respectively). These are sometimes referred to as country-code top-level domains, or ccTLDs. In 2008, ICANN approved a significant expansion of gTLDs, with potential new domains representing cities (such as .berlin), regions (.africa), ethnicity (.eus), industry/activities (such as .health), and even brands (such as .deloitte). In 2009, ICANN began the process of implementing these guidelines.

**Netscape Navigator**
the first commercial Web browser

**Internet Explorer**
Microsoft's Web browser

**Hypertext**
a way of formatting pages with embedded links that connect documents to one another, and that also link pages to other objects such as sound, video, or animation files

| TABLE 3.11 | **TOP-LEVEL DOMAINS** | | |
|---|---|---|---|
| GENERAL TOP-LEVEL DOMAIN (gTLD) | YEAR(S) INTRODUCED | PURPOSE | SPONSOR/ OPERATOR |
| .com | 1980s | Unrestricted (but intended for commercial registrants) | VeriSign |
| .edu | 1980s | U.S. educational institutions | Educause |
| .gov | 1980s | U.S. government | U.S. General Services Administration |
| .mil | 1980s | U.S. military | U.S. Department of Defense Network Information Center |
| .net | 1980s | Unrestricted (but originally intended for network providers, etc.) | VeriSign |
| .org | 1980s | Unrestricted (but intended for organizations that do not fit elsewhere) | Public Interest Registry (was operated by VeriSign until December 31, 2002) |
| .int | 1998 | Organizations established by international treaties between governments | Internet Assigned Numbers Authority (IANA) |
| .aero | 2001 | Air-transport industry | Societe Internationale de Telecommunications Aeronautiques SC (SITA) |
| .biz | 2001 | Businesses | NeuLevel |
| .coop | 2001 | Cooperatives | DotCooperation LLC |
| .info | 2001 | Unrestricted use | Afilias LLC |
| .museum | 2001 | Museums | Museum Domain Name Association (MuseDoma) |
| .name | 2001 | For registration by individuals | Global Name Registry Ltd. |
| .pro | 2002 | Accountants, lawyers, physicians, and other professionals | RegistryPro Ltd |
| .jobs | 2005 | Job search | Employ Media LLC |
| .travel | 2005 | Travel search | Triallance Corporation |
| .mobi | 2005 | Web sites specifically designed for mobile phones | mTLD Top Level Domain, Ltd. |
| .cat | 2005 | Individuals, organizations, and companies that promote the Catalan language and culture | Fundació puntCAT |
| .asia | 2006 | Regional domain for companies, organizations, and individuals based in Asia | DotAsia Organization |
| .tel | 2006 | Telephone numbers and other contact information | ICM Registry |
| .xxx | 2010 | New top level domain for pornographic content. | None yet approved |

SOURCE: Based on data from ICANN, 2010.

## MARKUP LANGUAGES

Although the most common Web page formatting language is HTML, the concept behind document formatting actually had its roots in the 1960s with the development of Generalized Markup Language (GML).

### Standard Generalized Markup Language (SGML)

In 1986, the International Standards Organization adopted a variation of GML called Standard Generalized Markup Language, or SGML. The purpose of SGML was to help very large organizations format and categorize large collections of documents. The advantage of SGML is that it can run independent of any software program but, unfortunately, it is extremely complicated and difficult to learn. Probably for this reason, it has not been widely adopted.

### HyperText Markup Language (HTML)

**HyperText Markup Language (HTML)** is a GML that is relatively easy to use. HTML provides Web page designers with a fixed set of markup "tags" that are used to format a Web page (see **Figure 3.18**). When these tags are inserted into a Web page, they are read by the browser and interpreted into a page display. You can see the source HTML code for any Web page by simply clicking on the "Page Source" command found in all browsers. In Figure 3.18, the HTML code in the first screen produces the display in the second screen.

**HyperText Markup Language (HTML)**
one of the next generation of GMLs that is relatively easy to use in Web page design. HTML provides Web page designers with a fixed set of markup "tags" that are used to format a Web page

| FIGURE 3.18 | EXAMPLE HTML CODE (A) AND WEB PAGE (B) |

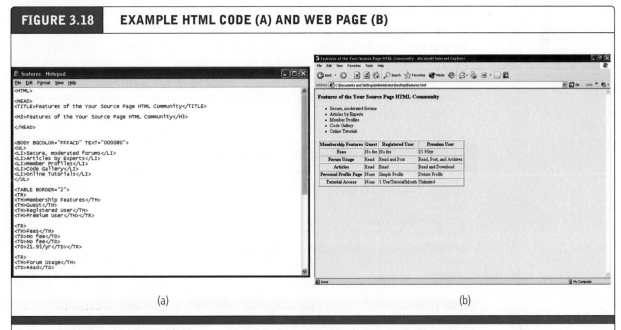

(a)                    (b)

HTML is a text markup language used to create Web pages. It has a fixed set of "tags" that are used to tell the browser software how to present the content on screen. The HTML shown in Figure 3.18 (a) creates the Web page seen in Figure 3.18 (b).

HTML defines the structure and style of a document, including the headings, graphic positioning, tables, and text formatting. Since its introduction, the major browsers have continuously added features to HTML to enable programmers to further refine their page layouts. Unfortunately, some browser enhancements may work only in one company's browser. Whenever you build an e-commerce site, you should take care that the pages can be viewed by the major browsers, even outdated versions of browsers. HTML Web pages can be created with any text editor, such as Notepad or WordPad, using Microsoft Word (simply save the Word document as a Web page) or any one of several Web page development tools such as Microsoft Expression Web or Adobe Dreamweaver.[5]

The current version of HTML is 4.01.HTML 5 is under development. HTML 5 introduce features like video playback and drag-and-drop that in the past were provided by plug-ins like Adobe Flash. YouTube and other video sites are sticking with Flash for 2010, while Apple refuses to use Flash on its i-devices and may build its own playback tools.

### eXtensible Markup Language (XML)

**eXtensible Markup Language (XML)**
a markup language specification developed by the World Wide Web Consortium (W3C) that is designed to describe data and information

**eXtensible Markup Language (XML)** takes Web document formatting a giant leap forward. XML is a markup language specification developed by the World Wide Web Consortium (W3C) that is similar to HTML, but has a very different purpose. Whereas the purpose of HTML is to control the "look and feel" and display of data on the Web page, XML is designed to describe data and information. For example, consider the sample XML document in **Figure 3.19**. The first line in the sample document is the XML declaration, which is always included; it defines the XML version of the document. In this case, the document conforms to the 1.0 specification of XML. The next line defines the first element of the document (the root element): < note >. The next four lines define four child elements of the root (to, from, heading, and body). The last line defines the end of the root element. Notice that XML says nothing about how to display the data, or how the text should look on the screen. HTML is used for information display in combination with XML, which is used for data description.

---

| FIGURE 3.19 | **A SIMPLE XML DOCUMENT** |
|---|---|

```
<?xml version="1.0"?>
<note>
<to>George</to>
<from>Carol</from>
<heading>Just a Reminder</heading>
<body>Don't forget to order the groceries from FreshDirect!</body>
</note>
```

The tags in this simple XML document, such as <note>, <to>, and <from> are used to describe data and information, rather than the look and feel of the document.

[5]A detailed discussion of how to use HTML is beyond the scope of this text.

---

| FIGURE 3.20 | **SAMPLE XML CODE FOR A COMPANY DIRECTORY** |

```
<?xml version="1.0"?>
<Companies>
    <Company>
            <Name>Azimuth Interactive Inc.</Name>
        <Specialties>
                <Specialty>HTML development</Specialty>
                    <Specialty>technical documentation</Specialty>
                <Specialty>ROBO Help</Specialty>
                <Country>United States</Country>
        </Specialties>
        <Location>
                <Country>United States</Country>
            <State />
            <City>Chicago</City>
        </Location>
            <Telephone>301-555-1212</Telephone>
    </Company>
    <Company>
        ...
    </Company>
    ...
</Companies>
```

This XML document uses tags to define a database of company names.

**Figure 3.20** shows how XML can be used to define a database of company names in a company directory. Tags such as < Company >, < Name >, and < Specialty > can be defined for a single firm, or an entire industry. On an elementary level, XML is extraordinarily easy to learn and is very similar to HTML except that you can make up your own tags. At a deeper level, XML has a rich syntax and an enormous set of software tools, which make XML ideal for storing and communicating many types of data on the Web.

XML is "extensible," which means the tags used to describe and display data are defined by the user, whereas in HTML the tags are limited and predefined. XML can also transform information into new formats, such as by importing information from a database and displaying it as a table. With XML, information can be analyzed and displayed selectively, making it a more powerful alternative to HTML. This means that business firms, or entire industries, can describe all of their invoices, accounts payable, payroll records, and financial information using a Web-compatible markup language. Once described, these business documents can be stored on intranet Web servers and shared throughout the corporation.

## WEB SERVERS AND CLIENTS

We have already described client/server computing and the revolution in computing architecture brought about by client/server computing. You already know that a server is a computer attached to a network that stores files, controls peripheral devices, interfaces with the outside world—including the Internet—and does some processing for other computers on the network.

But what is a Web server? **Web server software** refers to the software that enables a computer to deliver Web pages written in HTML to client computers on a network that request this service by sending an HTTP request. The two leading brands of Web server software are Apache, which is free Web server shareware that accounts for about 57% of the market, and Microsoft's Internet Information Services (IIS), which accounts for about 24% of the market (Netcraft, 2010).

Aside from responding to requests for Web pages, all Web servers provide some additional basic capabilities such as the following:

**Web server software**
software that enables a computer to deliver Web pages written in HTML to client computers on a network that request this service by sending an HTTP request

- *Security services*—These consist mainly of authentication services that verify that the person trying to access the site is authorized to do so. For Web sites that process payment transactions, the Web server also supports SSL, the Internet protocol for transmitting and receiving information securely over the Internet. When private information such as names, phone numbers, addresses, and credit card data needs to be provided to a Web site, the Web server uses SSL to ensure that the data passing back and forth from the browser to the server is not compromised.

- *FTP*—This protocol allows users to transfer files to and from the server. Some sites limit file uploads to the Web server, while others restrict downloads, depending on the user's identity.

- *Search engine*—Just as search engine sites enable users to search the entire Web for particular documents, search engine modules within the basic Web server software package enable indexing of the site's Web pages and content, and permit easy keyword searching of the site's content. When conducting a search, a search engine makes use of an index, which is a list of all the documents on the server. The search term is compared to the index to identify likely matches.

- *Data capture*—Web servers are also helpful at monitoring site traffic, capturing information on who has visited a site, how long the user stayed there, the date and time of each visit, and which specific pages on the server were accessed. This information is compiled and saved in a log file, which can then be analyzed. By analyzing a log file, a site manager can find out the total number of visitors, average length of each visit, and the most popular destinations, or Web pages.

The term *Web server* is also used to refer to the physical computer that runs Web server software. Leading manufacturers of Web server computers include IBM, Dell, and Hewlett-Packard. Although any personal computer can run Web server software, it is best to use a computer that has been optimized for this purpose. To be a Web server, a computer must have the Web server software installed and be connected to the Internet. Every public Web server computer has an IP address. For example, if you type http://www.pearsonhighered.com/laudon in your browser, the browser software sends a request for HTTP service to the Web server whose domain name is pearsonhighered.com. The server then locates the page named "laudon" on its hard drive, sends the page back to your browser, and displays it on your screen. Of course, firms also can use Web servers for strictly internal local area networking in intranets.

Aside from the generic Web server software packages, there are actually many types of specialized servers on the Web, from **database servers** that access specific information within a database, to **ad servers** that deliver targeted banner ads, to **mail servers** that provide e-mail messages, and **video servers** that provide video clips. At a small e-commerce site, all of these software packages might be running on a single computer, with a single processor. At a large corporate site, there may be hundreds or thousands of discrete server computers, many with multiple processors, running specialized Web server functions. We discuss the architecture of e-commerce sites in greater detail in Chapter 4.

A **Web client**, on the other hand, is any computing device attached to the Internet that is capable of making HTTP requests and displaying HTML pages. The most common client is a Windows or Macintosh computer, with various flavors of Unix/Linux computers a distant third. However, the fastest growing category of Web clients are not computers at all, but smartphones, netbooks, and iPads outfitted with wireless Web access software. In general, Web clients can be any device—including a printer, refrigerator, stove, home lighting system, or automobile instrument panel—capable of sending and receiving information from Web servers.

**database server**
server designed to access specific information with a database

**ad server**
server designed to deliver targeted banner ads

**mail server**
server that provides e-mail messages

**video server**
server that serves video clips

**Web client**
any computing device attached to the Internet that is capable of making HTTP requests and displaying HTML pages, most commonly a Windows PC or Macintosh

## WEB BROWSERS

A Web browser is a software program whose primary purpose is to display Web pages. Browsers also have added features, such as e-mail and newsgroups (an online discussion group or forum). The leading Web browser is Internet Explorer, with about 60% of the market as of September 2010. Microsoft introduced the beta of the newest version of Internet Explorer, Version 9, in September 2010. Firefox (Mozilla) is currently the second most popular Web browser, with about 23% of the U.S. Web browser market (Marketshare.hitslink.com, 2010). First released in 2004, Firefox is a free, open source Web browser for the Windows, Linux, and Macintosh operating systems, based on Mozilla open source code (which originally provided the code for Netscape). It is small and fast and offers many features such as pop-up blocking and tabbed browsing. The third most popular, with about an 8% market share, is Google's Chrome. First released in beta in September 2008, Chrome is a small, yet technologically advanced open source browser. With the development of Chrome, Google hoped to create a browser that improved upon other browsers' speed, security, and stability, while also serving as a streamlined platform for even the most complex Web pages as well as a wide variety of applications. In the process, the company hoped to make inroads against the market share of Firefox and, more importantly, Internet Explorer. Other browsers include Apple's Safari and Opera, which together make up about 7.5% of the market.

## 3.5 THE INTERNET AND THE WEB: FEATURES

The Internet and the Web have spawned a number of powerful new software applications upon which the foundations of e-commerce are built. You can think of these all as Web services, and it is interesting as you read along to compare these services to other traditional media such as television or print media. If you do, you will quickly realize how rich is the Internet environment.

## E-MAIL

**electronic mail (e-mail)**

the most-used application of the Internet. Uses a series of protocols to enable messages containing text, images, sound, and video clips to be transferred from one Internet user to another

Since its earliest days, **electronic mail**, or **e-mail**, has been the most-used application of the Internet. Worldwide, there are an estimated 2.9 billion e-mail accounts, sending an estimated 9 trillion messages a year! (Radicati Group, 2010). Estimates vary on the amount of spam, ranging from 40% to 90%. E-mail marketing and spam are examined in more depth in Chapter 7.

E-mail uses a series of protocols to enable messages containing text, images, sound, and video clips to be transferred from one Internet user to another. Because of its flexibility and speed, it is now the most popular form of business communication— more popular than the phone, fax, or snail mail (the U.S. Postal Service). In addition to text typed within the message, e-mail also allows **attachments**, which are files inserted within the e-mail message. The files can be documents, images, sounds, or video clips.

**attachment**

a file inserted within an e-mail message

## INSTANT MESSAGING

**instant messaging (IM)**

displays words typed on a computer almost instantaneously. Recipients can then respond immediately to the sender the same way, making the communication more like a live conversation than is possible through e-mail

One of the fastest growing forms of online human communication is **instant messaging (IM)**. An instant messenger is a client software program that signs onto an instant messaging server. IM sends text messages in real time, one line at a time, unlike e-mail. E-mail messages have a time lag of several seconds to minutes between when messages are sent and received. IM displays lines of text entered on a computer almost instantaneously. Recipients can then respond immediately to the sender the same way, making the communication more like a live conversation than is possible through e-mail. To use IM, users create a buddy list they want to communicate with, and then enter short text messages that their buddies will receive instantly (if they are online at the time). And although text remains the primary communication mechanism in IM, users can insert audio clips or photos into their instant messages, and even participate in video conferencing.

The major IM systems are AOL (which first introduced IM as a proprietary consumer service in 1997), Microsoft's Windows Live Messenger, Yahoo Messenger, and Google Talk. Facebook and MySpace also offer instant messaging services. IM systems were initially developed as proprietary systems, with competing firms offering versions that did not work with one another. In 2010 there still is no built-in interoperability among the major IM systems.

## SEARCH ENGINES

No one knows for sure how many Web pages there really are. The surface Web is that part of the Web that search engines visit and record information about. For instance, Google currently searches about 60 to 100 billion Web pages and stores information about those pages in its massive computer network located throughout the United States. But there is also a "deep Web" that could contain over a trillion additional Web pages, many of them proprietary (such as the pages of the online version of *The Wall Street Journal*, which cannot be visited without an access code) or behind corporate firewalls (Zillman, 2005).

But obviously with so many Web pages, finding Web-specific pages that can help you or your business, nearly instantly, is an important problem. The question is: how can you find the one or two Web pages you really want and need out of the 50 billion indexed Web pages?

**Search engines** solve the problem of finding useful information on the Web nearly instantly, and are one of the "killer apps" of the Internet era. Around half of all adult Americans Internet users use a search engine on any given day, generating about 15-18 billion queries a month (Pew Internet & American Life Project, 2010; comScore, 2010a). There are hundreds of different search engines, but the vast majority of the search results are supplied by the top five providers (see **Figure 3.21**).

Web search engines started out in the early 1990s shortly after Netscape released the first commercial Web browser. Early browsers were relatively simple software programs that roamed the nascent Web, visiting pages, and gathering information about the content of each Web page. These early programs were called variously crawlers, spiders, and wanderers; the first full-text crawler that indexed the contents of an entire Web page was called WebCrawler, released in 1994. AltaVista (1995), one of the first widely used search engines, was the first to allow "natural language" queries such as "history of Web search engines" rather than "history + Web search + search engine".

The Google search engine is continuously crawling the Web, indexing the content of each page, calculating its popularity, and caching the pages so that it can respond quickly to your request to see a page. The entire process takes about one-half of a second.

**search engine**
identifies Web pages that appear to match keywords, also called queries, typed by the user and provides a list of the best matches

| FIGURE 3.21 | **TOP FIVE SEARCH ENGINES** |

Google is, by far, the leading search engine based on its percentage share of the number of searches.
SOURCE: Based on data from comScore, 2010a.

The first search engines employed simple keyword indexes of all the Web pages visited. They would count the number of times a word appeared on the Web page, and store this information in an index. These search engines could be easily fooled by Web designers who simply repeated words on their home pages. The real innovations in search engine development occurred through a program funded by the Department of Defense called the Digital Library Initiative, designed to help the Pentagon find research papers in large databases. Stanford, Berkeley, and three other universities became hotbeds of Web search innovations in the mid-1990s. At Stanford in 1994, two computer science students, David Filo and Jerry Yang, created a hand-selected list of their favorite Web pages and called it "Yet Another Hierarchical Officious Oracle," or Yahoo!. Yahoo initially was not a real search engine, but rather an edited selection of Web sites organized by categories the editors found useful. Yahoo has since developed "true" search engine capabilities.

In 1998, Larry Page and Sergey Brin, two Stanford computer science students, released their first version of Google. This search engine was different: not only did it index each Web page's words, but Page had discovered that the AltaVista search engine not only collected keywords from sites but also calculated what other sites linked to each page. By looking at the URLs on each Web page, they could calculate an index of popularity. AltaVista did nothing with this information. Page took this idea and made it a central factor in ranking a Web page's appropriateness to a search query. He patented the idea of a Web page ranking system (PageRank System), which essentially measures the popularity of the Web page. Brin contributed a unique Web crawler program that indexed not just keywords on a Web page, but combinations of words (such as authors and their article titles). These two ideas became the foundation for the Google search engine (Brandt, 2004). **Figure 3.22** illustrates how Google works.

Search engine Web sites have became so popular and easy to use that they also serve as major portals for the Internet (see Chapter 11). The search marketplace has become very competitive despite the dominance of Google. Both Microsoft and Yahoo have invested over a billion dollars each to match Google's search engine. In 2009, Yahoo finally threw in the towel and agreed to adopt Microsoft's Bing search engine instead, in return for 88% of the advertising revenues generated by search on Yahoo's sites.

Initially, few understood how to make money from search engines. That changed in 2000 when Goto.com (later Overture) allowed advertisers to bid for placement on their search engine results, and Google followed suit in 2003 with its AdWords program, which allowed advertisers to bid for placement of short text ads on Google search results. The spectacular increase in Internet advertising revenues (which have been growing over the last few years at around 20%–25% annually), has helped search engines transform themselves into major shopping tools and created an entire new industry called "search engine marketing." Search engine marketing has been the fastest growing form of advertising in the United States, reaching about $12.5 billion in 2010. When users enter a search term at Google, Bing, Yahoo, or any of the other Web sites serviced by these search engines, they receive two types of listings: sponsored links, for which advertisers have paid to be

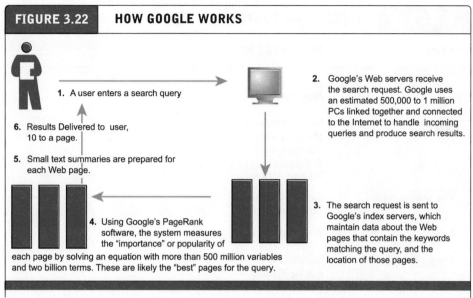

**FIGURE 3.22    HOW GOOGLE WORKS**

1. A user enters a search query

6. Results Delivered to user, 10 to a page.

5. Small text summaries are prepared for each Web page.

4. Using Google's PageRank software, the system measures the "importance" or popularity of each page by solving an equation with more than 500 million variables and two billion terms. These are likely the "best" pages for the query.

2. Google's Web servers receive the search request. Google uses an estimated 500,000 to 1 million PCs linked together and connected to the Internet to handle incoming queries and produce search results.

3. The search request is sent to Google's index servers, which maintain data about the Web pages that contain the keywords matching the query, and the location of those pages.

The Google search engine is continuously crawling the Web, indexing the content of each page, calculating its popularity, and caching the pages so that it can respond quickly to your request to see a page. The entire process takes about one-half of a second.

listed (usually at the top of the search results page), and unsponsored "organic" search results. In addition, advertisers can purchase small text ads on the right side of the search results page. Although the major search engines are used for locating general information of interest to users, search engines have also become a crucial tool within e-commerce sites. Customers can more easily search for the product information they want with the help of an internal search program; the difference is that within Web sites, the search engine is limited to finding matches from that one site. In addition, search engines are extending their services to include maps, satellite images, computer images, e-mail, group calendars, group meeting tools, and indexes of scholarly papers. Outside of e-mail, search engines are the most common online daily activity and produce the largest online audiences.

## INTELLIGENT AGENTS (BOTS)

An **intelligent agent** (also known as a software robot, or bot, for short) is a software program that gathers and/or filters information on a specific topic, and then provides a list of results for the user ranked in a number of ways, such as from lowest price to availability or to delivery terms. Intelligent agents were originally invented by computer scientists interested in the development of artificial intelligence (a family of related technologies that attempt to imbue computers with human-like intelligence). However, with the advent of e-commerce on the Web, interest quickly turned to exploiting intelligent agent technology for commercial purposes. Today, there are a number of different types of bots used in e-commerce on the Web (see **Table 3.12**).

**intelligent agent**
software program that gathers and/or filters information on a specific topic and then provides a list of results for the user

| TABLE 3.12 | TYPES OF WEB BOTS |
| --- | --- |
| **TYPE** | **EXAMPLES** |
| Search Bot | Webcrawler.com<br>Altavista.com |
| Shopping Bot | Shopzilla.com<br>Shopping.com<br>MySimon.com<br>Orbitz.com<br>TripAdvisor.com |
| Web Monitoring Bot | WebSite-Watcher<br>TimelyWeb.com |
| News Bot | WebClipping.com |
| Chatter Bot | Anna (IKEA)<br>Ask Vic (Qantas)<br>Virtual Advisor (Ultralase) |

For instance, as previously noted, many search engines employ Web crawlers or spiders that crawl from server to server, compiling lists of URLs that form the database for the search engine. These Web crawlers and spiders are actually bots, automated programs that search the Web for a variety of reasons.

The shopping bot is another common type of bot. Shopping bots search online retail sites all over the Web and then report back on the availability and pricing of a range of products. For instance, you can use MySimon's shopping bot to search for a Sony digital camera. The bot provides a list of online retailers that carry a particular camera model, as well as report about whether it is in inventory and the price and shipping charges. Orbitz provides bots that find the lowest prices for airfares, hotels, and rental cars. In 2010, popular shoppng sites include NexTag, PriceGrabber, Shopping.com, and Shopzilla/BizRate (eBizMBA, 2010).

Another type of bot, called a Web monitoring bot, allows you to monitor for updated materials on the Web, and will e-mail you when a selected site has new or changed information. News bots create custom newspapers or clip articles for you in newspapers around the world. Really Simple Syndication (RSS), discussed later in this chapter, is also a kind of automated program that sends updates and news to subscribers, and is quickly becoming the most common type of Web content monitoring tool. Chatter bots are intelligent agent online customer support tools.

## ONLINE FORUMS AND CHAT

**online forum**
a Web application that allows Internet users to communicate with each other, although not in real time

An **online forum** (also referred to as a message board, bulletin board, discussion board, discussion group, or simply a board or forum) is a Web application that enables Internet users to communicate with each other, although not in real time. A forum provides a container for various discussions (or "threads") started (or "posted") by members of the forum, and depending on the permissions granted to forum members by the forum's administrator, enables a person to start a thread and reply to other people's threads. Most forum software allows more than one forum to be created. The forum administrator typically can edit, delete, move, or otherwise modify any thread on the forum. Unlike an electronic mailing list (such as a listserv), which automatically sends new messages to a subscriber, an online forum typically requires that the member visit the forum to check for new posts. Some forums offer an "e-mail notification" feature that notifies users that a new post of interest to them has been made.

**Online chat** differs from an online forum in that, like IM, chat enables users to communicate via computer in real time, that is, simultaneously. However, unlike IM, which works only between two people, chat can occur among several users. Typically, users log in to a "chat room" where they can text message others. Some chat rooms offer virtual chat, which enable users to incorporate 2-D and 3-D graphics along with avatars (an icon or representation of the user) into their chat, or offer the ability to communicate via audio and/or video. Chat systems include Internet Relay Chat (IRC), Jabber, Yahoo, and MSN chat, and a number of proprietary systems based on the Microsoft Windows or Java platform. E-commerce firms typically use online forums and online chat to help develop community and as customer service tools. We will discuss the use of online forums as a community-building tool further in Chapter 11.

**online chat**
enables users to communicate via computer in real time, that is, simultaneously. Unlike IM, chat can occur among several users

## STREAMING MEDIA

**Streaming media** enables live Web video, music, video, and other large-bandwidth files to be sent to users in a variety of ways that enable the user to play back the files. In some situations, such as live Web video, the files are broken into chunks and served by specialized video servers to users in chunks. Client software puts the chunks together and plays the video. In other situations, such as YouTube, a single large file is downloaded from a standard Web server to users who can begin playing the video before the entire file is downloaded. Streamed files must be viewed "live"; they cannot be stored on client hard drives without special software. Streamed files are "played" by a software program such as Microsoft Media Player, Apple QuickTime, Flash, and RealMedia Player. There are a number of tools used to create streaming files, but one of the most common is Adobe's Flash program. The Flash player has the advantage of being built into most client browsers; no plug-in is required to play Flash files.

**streaming media**
enables music, video, and other large files to be sent to users in chunks so that when received and played, the file comes through uninterrupted

Sites such as YouTube, Metacafe, and Google Video have popularized user-generated video streaming. Web advertisers increasingly use video to attract viewers. Streaming audio and video segments used in Web ads and news stories are perhaps the most frequently used streaming services. As the capacity of the Internet grows, streaming media will play an even larger role in e-commerce.

## COOKIES

A **cookie** is a tool used by a Web site to store information about a user. When a visitor enters a Web site, the site sends a small text file (the cookie) to the user's computer so that information from the site can be loaded more quickly on future visits. The cookie can contain any information desired by the Web site designers, including

**cookie**
a tool used by Web sites to store information about a user. When a visitor enters a Web site, the site sends a small text file (the cookie) to the user's computer so that information from the site can be loaded more quickly on future visits. The cookie can contain any information desired by the site designers

customer number, pages visited, products examined, and other detailed information about the behavior of the consumer at the site. Cookies are useful to consumers because the Web site will recognize returning patrons and not ask them to register again. Cookies are also used by advertisers to ensure visitors do not receive the same advertisements repeatedly. Cookies can also help personalize a Web site by allowing the site to recognize returning customers and make special offers to them based on their past behavior at the site. Cookies allow Web marketers to customize products and segment markets—the ability to change the product or the price based on prior consumer information (described more fully in later chapters). As we will discuss throughout the book, cookies also can pose a threat to consumer privacy, and at times they are bothersome. Many people clear their cookies at the end of every day. Some disable them entirely using tools built into most browsers.

## WEB 2.0 FEATURES AND SERVICES

Today's broadband Internet infrastructure has greatly expanded the services available to users. These new capabilities have formed the basis for new business models. Digital content and digital communications are the two areas where innovation is most rapid. Web 2.0 applications and services are "social" in nature because they support communication among individuals within groups or social networks.

### Online Social Networks

If there is a "killer app" on the Internet in 2010 and going forward, it is social networks. Online social networks are described throughout this book in many chapters because they have developed very large world-wide audiences, and form the basis for new advertising platforms and for social e-commerce (see chapters 6, 7, and 11). Online social networks are services that support communication within networks of friends, colleagues, and entire professions. The largest social networks are Facebook (500 million world-wide), Twitter (145 million worldwide), MySpace (120 million worldwide) and LinkedIn (75 million worldwide). These networks rely on user generated content (messages, photos and videos) and emphasize sharing of content. All of these features require significant broadband Internet connectivity, and equally large cloud computing facilities to store content.

### Blogs

**blog**
personal Web page that is created by an individual or corporation to communicate with readers

A **blog**, (originally called a weblog), is a personal Web page that typically contains a series of chronological entries (newest to oldest) by its author, and links to related Web pages. The blog may include a blogroll (a collection of links to other blogs) and trackbacks (a list of entries in other blogs that refer to a post on the first blog). Most blogs allow readers to post comments on the blog entries as well. The act of creating a blog is often referred to as "blogging." Blogs are either hosted by a third-party site such as Blogger.com (owned by Google), LiveJournal, TypePad, Xanga, WordPress, or Microsoft's Windows Live Spaces, or prospective bloggers can download software such as Movable Type and bBlog to create a blog that is hosted by the user's ISP. Blog pages are usually variations on templates provided by the blogging service or software and hence require no knowledge of HTML. Therefore, millions of people without HTML skills of any kind can post their own Web pages, and share content with friends and relatives. The totality of blog-related Web sites is often referred to as the "blogoshpere."

Blogs have become hugely popular. While estimates on the number of blogs vary, Technorati, a blog research firm, claims there were over 133 million blogs as of 2009 (Technorati, 2009). According to eMarketer, there are 26 million active U.S. bloggers, and 113 million U.S. blog readers (eMarketer, Inc., 2010c). No one knows how many of these blogs are kept up to date or just yesterday's news. And no one knows how many of these blogs have a readership greater than one (the blog author). In fact, there are so many blogs you need a blog search engine just to find them (such as Google's or Technorati's search engine), or you can just go to a list of the most popular 100 blogs and dig in. We discuss blogs further in Chapters 6 and 7 as a marketing and advertising mechanism, and in Chapter 10 as a part of the significant growth in user-generated content.

## Really Simple Syndication (RSS)

The rise of blogs is correlated with a distribution mechanism for news and information from Web sites that regularly update their content. **Really Simple Syndication (RSS)** is an XML format that allows users to have digital content, including text, articles, blogs, and podcast audio files, automatically sent to their computers over the Internet. An RSS aggregator software application that you install on your computer gathers material from the Web sites and blogs that you tell it to scan and it brings new information from those sites to you. Sometimes this is referred to as "syndicated" content because it is distributed by news organizations and other syndicators (or distributors). Users download an RSS aggregator and then "subscribe" to the RSS "feeds." When you go to your RSS aggregator's page, it will display the most recent updates for each channel to which you have subscribed.

RSS has rocketed from a "techie" pastime to a broad-based movement. No one knows how many people have downloaded RSS client programs, but at the New York Times, the subscriber base for RSS feeds (which include headlines, summaries, and links to full articles) went from 500,000 when first introduced in 2003 to more than 8 million today.

**Really Simple Syndication (RSS)**
program that allows users to have digital content, including text, articles, blogs, and podcast audio files, automatically sent to their computers over the Internet

## Podcasting

A **podcast** is an audio presentation—such as a radio show, audio from a movie, or simply a personal audio presentations—stored as an audio file and posted to the Web. Listeners download the files from the Web and play them on their players or computers. While commonly associated with Apple's iPod portable music player, you can listen to MP3 podcast files with any MP3 player. Podcasting has transitioned from an amateur independent producer media in the "pirate radio" tradition to a professional news and talk content distribution channel. According to eMarketer, about 26 million Americans listen to a podcast at least once a month, and this number is expected to grow to about 38 million by 2013 (eMarketer, 2009).

**podcast**
an audio presentation—such as a radio show, audio from a movie, or simply a personal audio presentation—stored as an audio file and posted to the Web

## Wikis

A **wiki** is a Web application that allows a user to easily add and edit content on a Web page. (The term wiki derives from the "wiki wiki" (quick or fast) shuttle buses at Honolulu Airport.) Wiki software enables documents to be written collectively and collaboratively. Most wiki systems are open source, server-side systems that store content in a relational database. The software typically provides a template that defines layout and elements common to all pages, displays user-editable source code (usually plain text), and then renders the content into an HTML-based page for display in a Web browser. Some wiki software allows only basic text formatting, whereas others allow the use of tables, images, or even interactive elements, such as polls and games. Since wikis by their very nature are very open in allowing anyone to make changes to a page, most wikis provide a means to verify the validity of changes via a "Recent Changes" page, which enables members of the wiki community to monitor and review the work of other users, correct mistakes, and hopefully deter "vandalism."

Wikis are another Web 2.0 killer app. The most well-known wiki is Wikipedia, an online encyclopedia that contains over 3.4 million English-language articles on a variety of topics. The Wikimedia Foundation, which operates Wikipedia, also operates a variety of related projects, including Wikibooks, a collection of collaboratively written free textbooks and manuals; Wikinews, a free content news source; and Wikitionary, a collaborative project to produce a free multilingual dictionary in every language, with definitions, etymologies, pronunciations, quotations, and synonyms. According to comScore, Wikimedia's sites had 73 million unique visitors in August 2010 and are routinely among the top 15 most visited sites on the Web (comScore, 2010b). Wikis are also discussed further in Chapter 10.

## Music and Video Services

With the low-bandwidth connections of the early Internet, audio and video files were difficult to download and share, but with the huge growth in broadband connections, these files are not only commonplace but at major universities and other places where those under 25 years of age log on, they are the majority of Web traffic. Spurred on by the worldwide sales of more than 300 million iPods and iPhones through July 2010, as well as millions of other smartphones and MP3 players, the Internet has become a virtual digital river of music files. Today, the iTunes Store has a catalog with over 11 million tracks, 50,000 television episodes, and over 7,500 movies, including over 2,000 in high definition (Apple, 2010). Online video viewing has also exploded in popularity. In May 2010, around 180 million Americans watched over 33 billion videos online, exceeding 100 videos per person for the first time. (comScore, 2010c).

Companies that want to demonstrate use of their products have found video clips to be extremely effective. And audio reports and discussions have also become commonplace, either as marketing materials or customer reports.

Digital video on demand is considered by many to be the "killer app" for the future Internet. Future digital video networks will be able to deliver better-than-broadcast-quality video over the Internet to computers and other devices in homes and on the road. High-quality interactive video and audio makes sales presentations and demonstrations more effective and lifelike and enable companies to develop new forms of customer support. New video, audio, and presentation approaches are also dramatically changing the nature of the media and news business. One can easily foresee the Internet as a major new distribution channel for Hollywood movies (see Chapter 10).

## Internet Telephony

If the telephone system were to be built from scratch today, it would be an Internet-based packet-switched network using TCP/IP because it would be less expensive and more efficient than the alternative existing system, which involves a mix of circuit-switched legs with a digital backbone. Likewise, if cable television systems were built from scratch today, they most likely would use Internet technologies for the same reasons.

Already, nearly all pre-paid phone cards use the Internet for the long distance portion of calls. About 30% of the international calls from or to the United States use the Internet. Internet telephony is not entirely new. **IP telephony** is a general term for the technologies that use **Voice over Internet Protocol (VoIP)** and the Internet's packet-switched network to transmit voice, fax, and other forms of audio communication over the Internet. VoIP avoids the long distance charges imposed by traditional phone companies.

There are about 21 million residential VoIP subscribers in the United States in 2010, and this number is expanding rapidly as cable systems provide telephone service as part of their "triple play": voice, Internet, and TV as a single package. VoIP's share of international traffic has grown even faster, rising from 0.2% in 1998 to over 20% of the 417 billion minutes of international voice traffic worldwide in 2010. Skype, the most popular VoIP service in the United States, accounts for 8% of all international calling.

VoIP is a disruptive technology. In the past, voice and fax were the exclusive provenance of the regulated telephone networks. With the convergence of the Internet and telephony, however, this dominance is already starting to change, with local and long distance telephone providers and cable companies becoming ISPs, and ISPs getting into the phone market (see **Table 3.13**). Independent service providers such as VoIP pioneers Vonage and Skype accounted for over 60% of VoIP service in the United States in 2004, but this percentage dropped significantly by 2010 as traditional players such as Comcast, Time Warner, Verizon, AT&T, Cox, and other telephone and cable companies moved aggressively into the market.

## Internet Television

There are three ways in which people watch television over the Internet: as a streaming Flash-based video (such as YouTube videos), as download videocasts from a variety of sites such as Apple's iTunes store, or as very high definition streaming files that use the IPTV protocol. By far the most common type of Internet video is provided by YouTube, with more than 4.6 billion video streams a month, some of them short

**IP telephony**
a general term for the technologies that use VoIP and the Internet's packet-switched network to transmit voice and other forms of audio communication over the Internet

**Voice over Internet Protocol (VoIP)**
protocol that allows for transmission of voice and other forms of audio communication over the Internet

| TABLE 3.13 | KEY IP TELEPHONY PLAYERS |
|---|---|
| SPECIALTY | COMPANY |
| **Independent Facilities-based Service Providers** | Vonage<br>Time Warner Digital<br>Comcast Digital Voice<br>Cablevision/Optimum Voice<br>Cox Digital Phone<br>Verizon<br>AT&T<br>SBC |
| **Client-based Service Providers** | Skype (eBay)<br>Net2Phone<br>MSN<br>Yahoo Messenger<br>Google Talk<br>AOL Phoneline |

clips taken from television networks. Television and movie producers use videocasts as a marketing tool, and sites such as Apple's iTunes and independent sites such as videopodcasts.tv distribute millions of television downloads a month. There is very little detailed data on the amount of television content per se (syndicated television shows vs. movies or home-made videos) that is being download. The largest sources of legal, paid television content are the iTunes Store, where you can purchase entire seasons of TV shows, and Hulu, which is owned by major television producers NBC Universal, News Corp., The Walt Disney Company, and Providence Equity Partners.

**IPTV,** the third method of watching television on the Internet, uses high-bandwidth Internet connections to deliver television programming to the home. Standard quality television requires about 3 Mbps Internet connectivity using MPEG2 compression, but high definition TV requires about 19 Mbps. MPEG4 compression requires about half as much bandwidth, but still a substantial connection.

The definition of IPTV is still fluid and many different protocols are used, such as IP multicasting to move compressed digital television streams over the Internet. Quality is an issue, and typical broadband connection speeds can support standard quality television streams, but HDTV requires much more bandwidth. Commercial IPTV is growing in Europe, where it has approximately 11 million subscribers. In North America, there are currently over 5 million subscribers (Point Topic, 2009).

**IPTV**
uses high-bandwidth Internet connections to deliver television programming to the home

### Telepresence and Video Conferencing

Although video conferencing has been available for years, few have used it due to the cost of video equipment and telephone line rental fees. However, in recent years, Internet-based video conferencing has begun to overtake traditional telephone-based systems. Internet video conferencing is accessible to anyone with a broadband

Internet connection and a Web camera (webcam). The most widely used Web conferencing suite of tools is WebEx (now owned by Cisco). VoIP companies such as Skype also provide more limited Web conferencing capabilities.

Telepresence takes video conferencing up several notches. Rather than single persons "meeting" by using Web cams, telepresence creates an environment in a room using multiple cameras, and screens, which surround the users. The experience is uncanny and strange at first because as you look at the people in the screens, they are looking at you directly. Broadcast quality and higher screen resolutions help create the effect. Users have the sensation of "being in the presence of their colleagues" in a way that is not true for traditional webcam meetings. Providers of telepresence software and hardware include Cisco, HP, and Teliris.

## Online Software and Web Services: Web Apps, Widgets, and Gadgets

We are all used to installing software on our PCs. But as the Web and e-commerce moves towards a service model, applications increasingly will be running off Web servers. Instead of buying a "product" in a box, you will be paying for a Web service instead. There are many kinds of Web services now available, many free, all the way from full-function applications, to much smaller chunks of code called "widgets" and "gadgets."

Widgets pull content and functionality from one place on the Web to a place where you want it, such as on your Web page, blog, or Facebook page. You can see Web widget services most clearly in photo sites such as Picnik.com, which offers a free photo-editing application that is powerful and simple to use. Or drag a copy of iLike to your Facebook page and share your favorite musicians, songs, movies, and concert plans with your friends. Over 50 million people use iLike's Music applications on Facebook and other platforms. Wal-Mart, eBay, and Amazon, along with many other retailers, are creating shopping widgets that users can drag to their blogs or profile pages on various social networks so visitors can shop at a full-function online store without having to leave the page. Yahoo, Google, MSN, and Apple all have collections of hundreds of widgets available on their Web sites.

Gadgets are closely related to widgets. They are small chunks of code that usually supply a single limited function such as a clock, calendar, or diary. You can see a collection of gadgets at http://desktop.google.com/plugins.

As bandwidth capabilities of the Internet have increased, major software firms have begun to move away from the boxed model and towards Web distribution of software as a service. The clear leader here is Google, which has online versions of word processing, spreadsheet, and presentation programs, all of which are becoming competitive with Microsoft's Office suite. Microsoft is planning for a future where Microsoft Office is a Web application, but the revenue implications are uncertain.

In the business world, digital libraries of software applications have begun that permit companies and individuals to rent software (or purchase software services) rather than buy it. For instance, SalesForce.com sells customer and sales force management software services to companies over the Internet for a subscription fee instead of a purchase price. Accessing a Web server enables a user to download the desired software. Most enterprise software firms such as SAP and Oracle are moving towards a Web services model for small businesses. This service is especially useful for expensive software packages, such as graphic design or software development tools, that few individuals or small businesses can afford.

Application Service Providers (ASPs) can assist both in processing data and in storing it, dispersing it to multiple servers rather than having it reside on just one. Backing up online has many advantages. You do not need to buy extra hard drives, and your information is backed up entirely offline in a secure environment run by professional staff. Both iBackup.com and Box.net offer backup and data distribution services such as FTP servers for sharing large media and other files.

The case study *Insight on Technology: Apps For Everything: The App Ecosystem* gives you some further background on some new Web applications and services.

### M-commerce Applications: The Next Big Thing

The use of mobile Internet access devices like smartphones, iPads, and netbooks is in its infancy as of 2010 in the United States. From nearly zero mobile commerce prior to 2007, today, mobile e-commerce revenues in the United States from mobile advertising, entertainment, location-based services, e-book sales, and app sales are finally starting to take off, and are expected to reach an estimated $13 billion (about 5% of all e-commerce) in 2010. By 2013, mobile e-commerce revenues are expected to grow to $37 billion (about 10% of all e-commerce) (author estimates and industry sources). There is more complete coverage of these topics in later chapters.

The implications for e-commerce of the "always on" mobile platform are very positive: for the first time consumers will truly be able to shop from anywhere, anytime. The transaction costs and infrastructure costs of shopping will decline significantly, making e-commerce even more comfortable and affordable than fixed-place, physical shopping venues. Mobile e-commerce, talked about for years, is finally poised to take off.

# INSIGHT ON TECHNOLOGY

## APPS FOR EVERYTHING: THE APP ECOSYSTEM

When Steve Jobs introduced the iPhone in January 2007, no one—including himself—envisioned that the device would launch a revolution in consumer and business software, or become a major e-commerce platform, let alone a game platform, advertising platform, and general media platform for television shows, movies, videos, and e-books. In short, it's become the personal computer all over again.

The iPhone's original primary functions, beyond being a cell phone, were to be a camera, text messaging device, and Web browser. What Apple initially lacked for the iPhone were software applications that would take full advantage of the its computing capabilities. The solution was software developed by outside developers, tens of thousands of outside developers, who were attracted to the mission by potential profits and fame from the sale or free distribution of their software applications on a platform approved by the leading innovator in handheld computing and cell devices. Over two-thirds of apps are free. Every month Apple receives over 10,000 new apps from independent developers who may be teenagers in a garage, major video game developers, major publishers, as well as Fortune 500 consumer products firms using apps for marketing and promotion.

In July 2008, Apple introduced the App Store, which provides a platform for the distribution and sales for apps by Apple as well as by independent developers. Following in the footsteps of the iTunes music store, Apple hoped that the software apps—most free—would drive sales of the iPhone device. It was not expecting the App Store itself to become a major source of revenue. Fast forward to 2010: there are now an estimated 250,000 approved Apps in the App Store. Other

smartphone developers also followed suit: there are also thousands of apps available for the , over Palm, Android phones, and Blackberrys. As of September 2010, Apple reported more than 6.5 billion apps had been downloaded. Apple does not report its app revenues separately, but Wall Street analysts estimate that about 17% these downloads are for paid applications. According to this analysis, the average price of an application purchased at the App Store is $3. Apple takes 30% of the revenue generated by app sales (and then pays the credit card processors about 20 cents a sale). Some apps have advertising that users click on, and Apple takes 30% of this ad revenue.

Analysts estimate that Apple's revenue in 2010 from the App Store will be over $400 million. Altogether, this represents less than 1% of Apple's gross profit of $33 billion from all sources. But the point of apps is not to make money, but instead to drive sales of devices—the iPhones, iPads, and iPods that need software to become useful. It's the reverse of printer companies who make cheap printers in order to sell expensive ink. At the same time, apps tie the customer to a hardware platform: as you add more and more apps to your phone, the cost of switching to, say, an Android, rises with each new app installed. It's like Windows all over again, a walled sandbox run by an innovative company that owns 90% of the app marketplace, and all of the iPhone and iPad marketspace.

The app phenomenon, equally virulent on Android and BlackBerry operating system platforms, has spawned a new digital ecosystem composed of tens of thousands of developers, a wildly popular hardware platform, and millions of consumers looking for a computer in their pocket that can replace their now clunky desktop-laptop

(continued)

Microsoft Windows computers, do a pretty good job as a digital media center while on the road., and, by the way, serve as a cell phone.

The range of applications among the 250,000 or so apps on the Apple platform is staggering and defies brief description. The App Store provides the following general categories of apps: Apps for Cooks; Apps for Keeping Current, Apps for the Great Outdoors, Apps for Music, Apps for Work, Apps for Students, Apps for Moms and Dads, Apps for Working Out, Apps for Going Out, and Apps for Managing Money, Apps for Fun and Games, Apps for Traveling, and Apps for Remote Control. You can use the Genius feature to recommends new apps based on ones you already have. There are so many apps that searching for a particular app can be a problem unless you know the name of the app or the developer. Google is probably the best search engine for apps. Enter a search term like "Kraft app" and you'll find that Kraft foods has an app called iFood Assistant that provides recipes using Kraft products.The most commonly downloaded apps are games (65%), followed by music (46%), social networking (54%), news and weather (56%), maps/navigation (55%), and video/movies (25%).

The implications of the app ecosystem for e-commerce are significant. The smartphone in your pocket not only becomes a general purpose computer, but also an always present shopping tool for consumers, as well as an entirely new marketing and advertising platform for vendors. Early e-commerce applications using desktops and laptops were celebrated by pundits as allowing people to shop in their pajamas. Smartphones extend this range from pajamas to office desktops to trains, planes, and cars, all fully clothed. You can shop anywhere, shop everywhere, and shop all the time, in between talking, texting, watching video and listening to music.

The marketing opportunities of the apps platform are just being explored. Here are some typi-cal examples of how firms are using apps to advance and support their brands:

* Bacardi Global Brands Mix Master: Enables users to search for drink recipes

* Benjamin Moore's Ben Color Capture: Enables users to match colors and paints.

* Colgate-Palmolive's Max White Photo App: Enables users to see what they would look like with whiter teeth

* Gap StyleMixer: Enables users to mix and match pieces of clothing from their closets with new items from the store

There are of course dangers in any ecosystem dominated by a single company. The Apple iOS platform is closed and proprietary, a walled garden, a limiting sandbox. The apps you buy there can play nowhere else. Many apps are incredibly single purposed and limited in applicability. While this cannot be said of general purpose readers, it is true of proprietary e-readers like the New York Times and Wall Street Journal e-readers. Do we need two? Do we need a e-reader for every publication? The apps don't come with any warranty. Because Apple controls who can play in the sandbox, there is the possibility, even the likelihood, that Apple acts as a censor of content, or worse, a monopolist that prevents certain applications from entering the marketplace, or more likely, an arbitrary, inscrutable bureaucratic machine that decides which apps will play and which will not. For instance, in early 2010, Apple removed over 5,000 applications because of sexually themed content. One app removed was a game called SlideHer, a puzzle that challenged users to reassemble a photograph of a scantily clad actress. Another, Sexy Scratch Off, depicted a woman whose dress could be whisked away at the swipe of a finger, revealing her undergarments. Such programs often appeared on the store's list of most-downloaded apps. Clearly Apple is con-

(continued)

cerned the App Store will become an adult digital theme park that would turn off parents and families who are the target audience for iPhone and iPad sales. Nevertheless, critics note that a Sports Illustrated swim suit app and a Playboy app survived the purge. Sports Illustrated and Playboy are OK. But apps from some smaller companies did not survive the purge and lost a substantial business as a result.

▬ **SOURCES**: "iPhone Apps Overtaking Songs in Total Downloads," by Sarah Perez, ReadWriteWeb.com, September 8, 2010; "App Store Yields Just One Percent of Apple's Profit" by Adam Dickter, mobiledevice.com, June 23, 2010; "App Watch: Yahoo Reinvents Itself on iPad," *Wall Street Journal*, April 19, 2010; "Looking for a Few More Good Apps on the iPad," by Jennifer Valentino-DeVries, *Wall Street Journal*, April 7, 2010; "Mobile Apps and Consumer Product Brands," by Tobi Elkin, eMarketer, March 2010; "Apple Bans Some Apps for Sex-Tinged Content," by Jenna Wortham, *New York Times*, February 22, 2010; "Apple App Store Has Lost $450 Million To Piracy," by Garrett McIntyre and Phil MacDonald, 247Wallstreet.com, January 13, 2010; "Inside the App Economy," by Douglas MacMillan, *BusinessWeek*, October 22, 2009.

## 3.6 CASE STUDY

# Akamai Technologies:

## When Demand Exceeds Capacity

In 2010, the amount of Internet traffic generated by YouTube is equal to the amount of traffic on the entire Internet in 2000. In the United Kingdom,. BBC introduced a new high definition iPlayer, an application that allows viewers to watch high definition television on their computers. In a few months, the new service consumed 5% of the U.K.'s Internet capacity. Experts call these applications "net bombs" because they threaten the effective operation of the Internet. Several university and industry studies have concluded that Internet traffic in the United States is growing at compound rates of 46% to 60%, with over half of this being video traffic. Mobile platform traffic from smartphones and WiFi devices is growing at 60% and will soon push cell networks and the Internet to their capacities. Cisco Systems, the largest provider of routers in the world, estimates annual traffic on the Internet at over 176 exabytes in 2010, doubling every two years. (That's a 10 with 18 zeros behind it!).

All these numbers translate into a simple fact: the Internet is not growing in capacity anywhere near the growth in demand from consumers and businesses. In the 2010 World Cup games, over 1.1 million people online watched the U.S. soccer team beat Algeria, the largest online sports event in history. Many viewers reported dropped frames, interrupted video, and poor coordination of video and audio. On Jan-

uary 20, 2009, the Internet experienced an unheralded meltdown that generally escaped public notice or concern. It was the inauguration day of Barack Obama in Washington, D.C. More than 10 million people tried to watch the event on the Internet, but many were not able to view the live video feed because the Internet did not have the capacity to handle the traffic. Not only did 3 million users not receive any video, but many of the 7 million who were able to establish a connection were treated to burpy audio, freeze-frame video, and lost backgrounds. Cable and broadcast television viewers had no problem. Hardly the stuff of a bright future for mass audience video over the Web.

Most people love the Web, but hate the wait and the stumble that can occur. Studies have shown that most people won't stay on a Web site if the Web page and its contents take more than a few seconds to load. Other studies show that if a video ad or sports video takes too long to buffer, shows jerky frames, or provides only poor visual quality, over half the customers will seek out a competitor's Web site. For online publishers and retailers, online video is rapidly becoming a serious component of their business strategies. In order for these initiatives to pay off, the viewing experience needs to be nearly flawless. For marketers who increasingly are using video to establish a more intimate relationship with the consumer and the brand, the quality of the Internet video experience is critical. For Web sites such as NBA.com, ESPN, CNN, MySpace, and YouTube, whose entire business model depends on delivery of high-quality video and audio, the need for high speed and quality media is vital to their success.

In today's broadband cable and DSL environment, the threshold of patience is probably much lower than a few seconds. Increased video and audio customer expectations are bad news for anyone seeking to use the Web for delivery of high-quality multimedia content such as CD-quality music and high definition video. YouTube and MySpace have unleashed a torrent of video downloads, causing total Internet traffic to expand yearly at somewhere between 50% and 100%. BitTorrent files used to share videos now account for half of U.S. Internet traffic, and on college campuses more than 80% of campus Internet use. If you are SIRIUS/XM Radio and you want to stream online music to several million users a day, you will definitely need some help. If you are MTV and want to stream music videos to your 6 million customers online, or Apple iTunes and want to download music or video files to your 50 million online customers, you will also need some help. Akamai is one of the Web's major helpers, and each of the preceding companies, along with the Web's top 2,000 domains, use Akamai's services to speed the delivery of content. Akamai serves over 1 million simultaneous media streams on a typical day.

Slow-loading Web pages and Web content—from music to video—sometimes results from poor design, but more often than not, the problem stems from the underlying infrastructure of the Internet. As you have learned in this chapter, the Internet was originally developed to carry text-based e-mail messages among a relatively small group of researchers, not bandwidth-hogging graphics, sound, and video files to tens of millions of people all at once. The Internet is a collection of networks that has to pass information from one network to another. Sometimes the handoff is not smooth. Every 1,500-byte packet of information sent over the Internet must be verified by the receiving server and an acknowledgment sent to the sender. This slows down not only the distribution of content such as music, but also slows down interactive requests, such as purchases, that require the client computer to interact with an online shopping cart. Moreover, each packet may go through many different servers on its way to its final destination, multiplying by several orders of magnitude the number of acknowledgments required to move a packet from New York to San Francisco. The Internet today spends much of its time and capacity verifying packets, contributing to a problem called "latency" or delay. For this reason, a single e-mail with a 1 megabyte attached PDF file can create over 50 megabytes of Internet traffic and data storage on servers, client hard drives, and network back up drives.

In 2014, according to Cisco, Internet video will be nearly 700 times the capacity of the U.S. Internet backbone in 2000. It would take well over half a million years to watch all the online video that will cross the network each month.Cisco expects  Internet video to generate over 18 exabytes per month in 2014. Akamai, and other firms in the CDN (content distribution network) industry are one of the reasons why the Web has not already disintegrated under the load. It is not clear at this time if the entire CDN industry will be able to meet the expected demand in 2014.

Akamai (which means intelligent, clever, or "cool" in Hawaiian) Technologies was founded by Tom Leighton, an MIT professor of applied mathematics, and Daniel Lewin, an MIT grad student, with the idea of expediting Internet traffic to overcome these limitations. When Timothy Berners-Lee, founder of the World Wide Web, realized that congestion on the Internet was becoming an enormous problem, he issued a challenge to Leighton's research group to invent a better way to deliver Internet content. The result was a set of breakthrough algorithms that became the basis for Akamai. Lewin received his masters degree in electrical engineering and computer science in 1998. His master's thesis was the theoretical starting point for the company. It described storing copies of Web content such as pictures or video clips at many different locations around the Internet so that one could always retrieve a nearby copy, making Web pages load faster.

Officially launched in August 1998, Akamai's products include Digital Asset Solutions such as Akamai HD Network, which enables Web sites to deliver an online HD experience, Dynamic Site Solutions, which speed up the delivery of rich interactive content, and Application Performance Solutions, a suite of services that allows corporations to maximize their Web performance. Akamai's products allow customers to move their Web content closer to end users so a user in New York City, for instance, will be served L.L.Bean pages from the New York Metro area Akamai servers, while users of the L.L.Bean site in San Francisco will be served pages from Akamai servers in San Francisco. According to Akamai, 85% of the world's Internet users are withing a single network "hop" of an Akamai server. Akamai has a wide range of large corporate and government clients: 1 out of every 3 global Fortune 500 companies, 90 of the top 100 online U.S. retailers, all branches of the U.S. military, all of the top Internet portals, all the major U.S. sports leagues, and so on. Akamai has over 73,000 servers on nearly 1,000 networks in 70 countries around the world. In 2010 , Akamai delivers between 15% and 30% of all Web traffic, and hundreds of billions of daily Internet interactions. Other competitors in the CDN industry include Blue Coat, LimeLight, SAVVIS, and Mirror Image Internet.

Accomplishing this seemingly simple task requires that Akamai monitor the entire Internet, locating potential sluggish areas and devising faster routes for information to travel. Frequently used portions of a client's Web site, or large video or audio files that would be difficult to send to users quickly, are stored on Akamai's 73,000 servers around the world. When a user requests a song or a video file, his or her request is redirected to an Akamai server nearby and the content served from this local server. Akamai's servers are placed in Tier 1 backbone supplier networks, large ISPs, universities, and other networks. Akamai's software determines which server is optimum for the user and then transmits the "Akamaized" content locally. Web sites that are "Akamaized" can be delivered anywhere from 4 to 10 times as fast as non-Akamaized content. Akamai has developed a number of other business services based on its Internet savvy, including content targeting of advertising based on user location and zip code, content security, business intelligence, disaster recovery, on-demand bandwidth, and computing capacity during spikes in Internet traffic in partnership with IBM, storage, global traffic management, and streaming services.

Akamai also offers a product line called Advertising Decision Solutions, which provides companies with intelligence generated by the Internet's most accurate and comprehensive knowledge base of Internet network activity. Akamai's massive server deployment and relationships with networks throughout the world enable optimal collection of geography and bandwidth-sensing information. As a result, Akamai provides a highly accurate knowledge base with worldwide coverage. Customers integrate a simple program into their Web server or application server. This program communicates with the Akamai database to retrieve the very latest information. The Akamai network of servers is constantly mapping the Internet, and at the same time, each company's software is in continual communication with the Akamai network. The result: data is always current. Advertisers can deliver ads based on country, region, city, market area, area code, county, zip code, connection type, and speed. You can see several interesting visualizations of the Internet that log basic real-time Web activity by visiting the Akamai Web site and clicking on "Data Visualizations."

As impressive as Akamai's operation has become, it is not nearly enough to cope with the next 10 years of Internet growth at over 40% a year. It's unclear that government authorities in the United States or elsewhere are aware of the serious imbalance between demand for Internet services and capacity. The Obama administration has pledged to double broadband wireless Internet capacity in the next 10 years. If successful, the effort would be totally inadequate because Internet mobile traffic is expected to double in four years. Private industry will not be able to meet Internet demands either unless it can obtain permission to charge customers for the bandwidth they use rather than charge a single fee for all users regardless of how much capacity they use. Proponents of "net neutrality" oppose industry demands to charge for usage, and the FTC is unlikely to permit industry to charge for usage. The proponents of net neutrality include some heavy hitters like Google, Microsoft, AOL, and Yahoo, all of whom want their customers to think the Internet is "free" no matter what is clicked on. In an ominous sign of the disconnect between Washington and industry, in May 2010, Verizon halted the $23 billion build-out of its fiber-optic network to homes (FiOS) for fears they would not be able to recover their costs unless they could charge customers for the amount of bandwidth they use.

**SOURCES**: "Facts & Figures," Akamai, September 28, 2010; "Obama Pledges to Increase Internet Capacity," by Stephanie Kirschgassener, FT.com, June 29, 2010; "Web Caught Up in World Cup Mania," by Mark Walsch, mediapost.com, June 25, 2010; "ESPN3.com's World Cup Coverage: A Bit Choppy, But There," Appscout.com, June 11, 2010; "Cisco Visual Networking Index: Forecast and Methodology, 2009-2014," Cisco Systems, Inc., June 2, 2010; "State of the Internet," by Akamai, Inc., June, 2010; "FCC Seeks New Web Plan," by Amy Schatz, *Wall Street Journal*, April 8, 2010; "Neutering the Net," by Holman Jenkins, *Wall Street Journal*, September 23, 2009."

## Case Study Questions

1. Why does Akamai need to geographically disperse its servers to deliver its customers' Web content?

2. If you wanted to deliver software content over the Internet, would you sign up for Akamai's service? What alternatives exist?

3. What advantages does an advertiser derive from using Akamai's EdgeScape service? What kinds of products might benefit from this kind of service?

4. Why don't major business firms distribute their videos using P2P networks like BitTorrent?

5. Do you think Internet users should be charged based on the amount of bandwidth they consume, or a tiered plan where users would pay in rough proportion to their usage?

## 3.7   REVIEW

### KEY CONCEPTS

■ Discuss the origins of the Internet.

The Internet has evolved from a collection of mainframe computers located on a few U.S. college campuses to an interconnected network of thousands of networks and millions of computers worldwide. The history of the Internet can be divided into three phases:

- During the *Innovation Phase* (1961–1974), the Internet's purpose was to link researchers nationwide via computer.
- During the *Institutionalization Phase* (1975–1995), the Department of Defense and National Science Foundation provided funding to expand the fundamental building blocks of the Internet into a complex military communications system and then into a civilian system.
- During the *Commercialization Phase* (1995 to the present), government agencies encouraged corporations to assume responsibility for further expansion of the network, and private business began to exploit the Internet for commercial purposes.

■ Identify the key technology concepts behind the Internet.

The Internet's three key technology components are:

- *Packet switching*, which slices digital messages into packets, routes the packets along different communication paths as they become available, and then reassembles the packets once they arrive at their destination.

- *TCP/IP*, which is the core communications protocol for the Internet. TCP establishes the connections among sending and receiving Web computers and makes sure that packets sent by one computer are received in the sequence by the other, without any packets missing. IP provides the addressing scheme and is responsible for the actual delivery of the packets.
- *Client/server technology*, which makes it possible for large amounts of information to be stored on Web servers and shared with individual users on their client computers (which may be desktop PCs, laptops, netbooks, or smartphones).

■ **Describe the role of Internet protocols and utility programs.**

Internet protocols and utility programs make the following Internet services possible:
- *HTTP* delivers requested Web pages, allowing users to view them.
- *SMTP* and *POP* enable e-mail to be routed to a mail server and then picked up by the recipient's server, while *IMAP* enables e-mail to be sorted before being downloaded by the recipient.
- *SSL* ensures that information transmissions are encrypted.
- *FTP* is used to transfer files from servers to clients and vice versa.
- *Telnet* is a utility program that enables work to be done remotely.
- *Ping* is a utility program that allows users to verify a connection between client and server.
- *Tracert* lets you track the route a message takes from a client to a remote computer.
- *Pathping* combines the functionality offered by Ping and Tracert.

■ **Explain the structure of the Internet today.**

The main structural elements of the Internet are:
- The *backbone*, which is composed primarily of high-bandwidth fiber-optic cable operated by a variety of providers.
- *IXPs*, which are hubs that use high-speed switching computers to connect the backbone with regional and local networks.
- *CANs*, which are local area networks operating within a single organization that connect directly to regional networks.
- *ISPs*, which deal with the "last mile" of service to homes and offices. ISPs offer a variety of types of service, ranging from dial-up service to broadband DSL, cable modem, T1 and T3 lines, and satellite link service.
- *Governing bodies*, such as IAB, ICANN, IESG, IETF, ISOC, W3C, and ITU. Although they do not control the Internet, have influence over it and monitor its operations.

■ **Understand the limitations of today's Internet.**

To envision what the Internet of tomorrow—Internet II—will look like, we must first look at the limitations of today's Internet:
- *Bandwidth limitations*. Today's Internet is slow and incapable of effectively sharing and displaying large files, such as video and voice files.

- *Quality of service limitations*. Data packets don't all arrive in the correct order, at the same moment, causing latency; latency creates jerkiness in video files and voice messages.
- *Network architecture limitations*. Servers can't keep up with demand. Future improvements to Internet infrastructure will improve the way servers process requests for information, thus improving overall speed.
- *Language development limitations*. The nature of HTML restricts the quality of "rich" information that can be shared online. Future languages will enable improved display and viewing of video and graphics.
- *Limitations arising from the "wired" nature of the Internet*. The Internet is based primarily on physical cables, which restricts the mobility of users.

■ Describe the potential capabilities of Internet II.

Internet2 is a consortium working together to develop and test new technologies for potential use on the Internet. Internet2 participants are working in a number of areas, including advanced network infrastructure, new networking capabilities, middleware, and advanced applications that incorporate audio and video to create new services.

In addition to the Internet2 project, other groups are working to expand Internet bandwidth via improvements to fiber optics and photonics. Wireless LAN and 4G telephone technologies will provide users of smartphones with increased access to the Internet and its various services.

The increased bandwidth and expanded connections of the Internet II era will result in a number of benefits, including IP multicasting, which will enable more efficient delivery of data; latency solutions; guaranteed service levels; lower error rates; and declining costs.

■ Understand how the World Wide Web works.

The Web was developed during 1989–1991 by Dr. Tim Berners-Lee, who created a computer program that allowed formatted pages stored on the Internet to be linked using keywords (hyperlinks). In 1993, Marc Andreesen created the first graphical Web browser, which made it possible to view documents on the Web graphically and created the possibility of universal computing. The key concepts you need to be familiar with in order to understand how the Web works are the following:

- *Hypertext*, which is a way of formatting pages with embedded links that connect documents to one another and that also link pages to other objects.
- *HTTP*, which is the protocol used to transmit Web pages over the Internet.
- *URLs*, which are the addresses at which Web pages can be found.
- *HTML*, which is the programming language used to create most Web pages and which provides designers with a fixed set of tags that are used to format a Web page.
- *XML*, which is a newer markup language that allows designers to describe data and information.
- *Web server software*, which is software that enables a computer to deliver Web pages written in HTML to client computers that request this service by sending an HTTP request. Web server software also provides security services, FTP,

search engine, and data capture services. The term Web server also is used to refer to the physical computer that runs the Web server software.

- *Web clients*, which are computing devices attached to the Internet that are capable of making HTTP requests and displaying HTML pages.
- *Web browsers*, which display Web pages and also have added features such as e-mail and newsgroups.

■ Describe how Internet and Web features and services support e-commerce.

Together, the Internet and the Web make e-commerce possible by allowing computer users to access product and service information and to complete purchases online. Some of the specific features that support e-commerce include:

- *E-mail*, which uses a series of protocols to enable messages containing text, images, sound, and video clips to be transferred from one Internet user to another. E-mail is used in e-commerce as a marketing and customer support tool.
- *Instant messaging*, which allows messages to be sent between two users almost instantly, allowing parties to engage in a two-way conversation. In e-commerce, companies are using instant messaging as a customer support tool.
- *Search engines*, which identify Web pages that match a query submitted by a user. Search engines assist users in locating Web pages related to items they may want to buy.
- *Intelligent agents (bots)*, which are software programs that gather and/or filter information on a specific topic and then provide a list of results for the users.
- *Online forums* (message boards), which enable users to communicate with each other, although not in real time, and online chat, which allows users to communicate in real time (simultaneously), are being used in e-commerce as community-building tools.
- *Streaming media*, which enables music, video, and other large files to be sent to users in chunks so that when received and played, the file comes through uninterrupted. Like standard digital files, streaming media may be sold as digital content and used as a marketing tool.
- *Cookies*, which are small text files that allow a Web site to store information about a user, are used by e-commerce as a marketing tool. Cookies allow Web sites to personalize the site to the user and also permit customization and market segmentation.

Web 2.0 featureas and services include:

- *Social networks*, which are online services that support communication within networks of friends, colleagues, and even entire professions.
- *Blogs*, which are personal Web pages that typically contain a series of chronolo-gyical entries (newest to oldest) by the author and links to related Web pages.
- *RSS*, which is an XML format that allows users to have digital content, including text, articles, blogs and podcast audio files, automatically sent to their computers over the Internet.
- *Podcasts*, which are audio presentations—such as a radio show, audio from a movie, or simply personal audio presentations—stored as an audio file and posted to the Web.
- *Wikis*, which are Web applications that allow a user to easily add and edit content on a Web page.
- *Music and video services*, such as iTunes and digital video on demand.

- *Internet telephony*, which uses VoIP to transmit audio communication over the Internet, and *Internet television (IPTV)*.
- *Online software and services*, such as Web apps, widgets, gadgets, and distribution of software applications and distributed storage offered by ASPs.
- *M-commerce applications*, which permit mobile consumers to make payments easily from their cell phones.

## QUESTIONS

1. What are the three basic building blocks of the Internet?
2. What is latency, and how does it interfere with Internet functioning?
3. Explain how packet switching works.
4. How is the TCP/IP protocol related to information transfer on the Internet?
5. What technological innovation made client/server computing possible? What impact has client/server computing had on the Internet?
6. Despite the number of PCs connected to the Internet, rich information sharing is still limited. Why?
7. Why isn't the Internet overloaded? Will it ever be at capacity?
8. What types of companies form the Internet backbone today?
9. What function do the IXPs serve?
10. What is a campus area network, and who uses them?
11. Compare and contrast intranets, extranets, and the Internet as a whole.
12. What are the four major limitations of today's Internet?
13. What are some of the challenges of policing the Internet? Who has the final say when it comes to content?
14. Compare and contrast the capabilities of Wi-Fi and 3G/4G wireless networks.
15. What are some of the new wireless standards, and how are they relevant to Internet II?
16. What are the major technological advancements that are anticipated will accompany Internet II? Define and discuss the importance of each.
17. Why was the development of the browser so significant for the growth of the Web?
18. Name the different Web markup languages and explain the differences among them.
19. Name and describe five services currently available through the Web.
20. What are at least three new services that will be available through the next generation of the Internet?

## PROJECTS

1. Visit the MySimon.com Web site and investigate the following types of purchases: an iPod, a copy of the book *The Girl Who Kicked the Hornet's Nest* (by Stieg Larsson), and a dozen red roses. What did you find as you searched for these items? Describe the process, the search results, and any limitations you encountered. What are the major advantages and disadvantages of such intelligent agents?

2. Locate where cookies are stored on your computer. (They are probably in a folder entitled "cookies" within your browser program.) List the top 10 cookies you find and write a brief report describing the kinds of sites that placed the cookies. What purpose do you think the cookies serve? Also, what do you believe are the major advantages and disadvantages of cookies? In your opinion, do the advantages outweigh the disadvantages, or vice versa?

3. Call a local ISP, cable provider, and DSL provider to request information on their Internet services. Prepare a brief report summarizing the features, benefits, and costs of each. Which is the fastest? What, if any, are the downsides of selecting any of the three for Internet service (such as additional equipment purchases)?

4. Select two countries (excluding the United States) and prepare a short report describing their basic Internet infrastructure. Are they public or commercial? How and where do they connect to backbones within the United States?

5. We have mentioned several high-speed gigabit networks throughout this chapter. Investigate the topic of high-speed networks on the Web and try to find the fastest recorded network (usually used for research purposes). Then try to find the fastest commercial network handling routine Internet traffic.

# CHAPTER 4

# Building an E-commerce Web Site

**After reading this chapter, you will be able to:**

- Explain the process that should be followed in building an e-commerce Web site.
- Describe the major issues surrounding the decision to outsource site development and/or hosting.
- Identify and understand the major considerations involved in choosing Web server and e-commerce merchant server software.
- Understand the issues involved in choosing the most appropriate hardware for an e-commerce site.
- Identify additional tools that can improve Web site performance.

# Tommy Hilfiger
## Right-Sizes Its Web Store

**T**ommy Hilfiger is one of the world's best known premium lifestyle brands in the United States for the 18–35 age demographic. Founded in 1985 by Tommy Hilfiger, a young designer in New York City, the brand expanded its line of casual clothing for men, women, and children through specialty retailers, department stores, and over 1,000 stores and outlets throughout the world. In 2010, the company was purchased by Philips-Van Heusen, owner of the Calvin Klein brand, for $3 billion in 2010. The resulting company is the world's largest clothing companies with $4.6 billion in revenues.

A significant part of the company's growth since 2007 has occurred through its online stores. The company had developed a Web store in 2000 as a simple catalog of products available at retailers, and then expanded into online sales by 2004. By 2006, it was clear that effective online retailing required more than just a storefront with a catalog, and more than a database responding to customer requests for products. The existing Web site did not fit the contemporary needs and expectations of customers or company merchandisers. For instance, it was difficult to change prices, move products around the online catalog depending on demand, change price points, measure results, build promotions, or personalize the offerings based on customer histories and online behavior. There was no recommender system that could suggest clothing to online customers based on their prior behavior. Instead, products were promoted based on what marketing managers wanted or needed to sell regardless of what the customer wanted. If you're buying a pair of jeans, chances are good based on prior customer behavior that you will want to consider a new belt or shoes.

Hilfiger did not want to hire an entire new IT staff to rebuild its Web site, and it did not want to make the investment in hardware and telecommunications that would be required for a new Web site. Instead it turned to Art Technology Group(ATG), a firm specializing in e-commerce software and hardware solutions. The ATG e-commerce platform software provides Hilfiger managers with a state-of-the-art e-commerce platform with automated recommendations that can deliver a personalized experience to each customer, and easy marketing and promotional campaign support to Hilfiger managers through a cutting-edge Business Control Center. Best of all, the ATG platform solution is an on-demand, online software platform. Hilfiger did not have to buy any hardware or software infrastructure, or hire IT staff, to build the new Web site. One way to "right size" a Web's infrastructure site is to shift the risks and costs of infrastructure to external, specialized firms who can operate the infrastructure for you. The result has been a smashing success: online sales for Hilfiger increased 30% in the first year of operation.

Most start-up firms do not outsource the design and infrastructure of their Web sites. Instead they use DIY—do it yourself. It's much less expensive and just the right size for small firms. Let's say you've decided to create a Web site for your successful garden equipment company. You've been in business for five years, have established a regional brand for high-quality gardening tools, and have about 12,000 retail customers and 21 wholesale dealers who purchase from you. Based on a marketing report you commissioned, you expect that in the first year your Web site will have about 1,400 visitors a day. The average visitor will look at eight pages, producing about 4 million page views a year. About 10% will purchase something, and the rest will browse to explore prices and products. However, in peak times (during the months of April, May, June, and December), you expect peak loads of 3,000 customers a day, concentrated during the hours of 9 a.m. to 5 p.m. local time, producing about 375 visitors per hour or 6 per second. During this time, your Web site will have to serve up about 40 screens per second, with most of the content being read from a database of product and price information. Pages must be served up within 2 seconds of a customer click during peak times or customers may lose patience and go elsewhere. You've decided to operate your own on-site Web infrastructure, including hardware and software. You have contracted out the Web site design to a design firm and have made arrangements with the local phone company to provide an Internet connection.

Before you can proceed, there are some questions you will need answered. How many Web servers will your site require? How many CPUs should each server have? How powerful does the site's database server need to be? What kind of connection speed do you need to the Internet? How about power? Is the local utility reliable, and do you need backup diesel-powered generators?

Very large online firms answer these questions using simulation software sold by hardware and software vendors such as IBM, Microsoft, and Hewlett-Packard (HP). IBM's simulator is called the On Demand Performance Advisor (OPERA) (formerly known as the High Volume Web Sites Simulator). OPERA enables users to estimate the performance and capacity of a Web server based on workload patterns, performance objectives, and specific hardware and software. OPERA has a very easy-to-use interface that includes pre-built workload patterns for various e-commerce applications, such as shopping, banking, brokerage, auction, portal, B2B, and reservation systems, that can be modified as necessary based on the user's own data or assumptions. It can provide what-if analyses for various performance parameters such as throughput, response time, resource utilization, number of concurrent users, and page view rate. It also provides special algorithms to address increases in Web traffic during peak usage periods. The simulator includes built-in performance characteristics for various types of hardware (such IBM, Sun, and HP servers), software, and infrastructure models. OPERA uses an analytic model to generate reports that allow users to assess the adequacy of proposed hardware and software configurations, forecast performance, and graphically identify bottlenecks that might develop. IBM also offers Sonoma, a Web service based on OPERA, that can be used to estimate the performance and capacity of service-oriented architecture (SOA) workloads.

But let's say you're not eBay or Fidelity, and are just creating the proverbial "one-person-in-a-garage-just-getting-started" kind of Web site. For instance, Dave Novak created Steamshowers4Less.com using a MacBook Pro computer in a spare bedroom. SteamShowers4Less.com is an eBay success story. Its Web site offers products for luxury bathrooms on a budget, and focuses on DIY market. The company specializes in walk-in and whirlpool computerized steam showers and claims to be the first company to manufacture its own iPod-compatible unit. Luxe bath? Its models have FM stereo, speakers, computer control, LED lighting, foot massagers and much more. Novak now sells over $1 million a year in bath fixtures.

For really small sites, micro-businesses with just one person (the founder) or a few employees or friends, there are many less-costly alternatives to using a sophisticated tool like IBM's OPERA or ATG's sophisticated e-commerce platform. Nevertheless, you still face the same problems as the big Web sites: how many computers, what size, how large a pipe to the Internet, and what kind of database? For a really small company, it generally does not make sense to spend the time and money to DIY. Instead, it makes more sense to let the professionals worry about these problems. For instance, one solution is to build a Web site using pre-built templates offered by Yahoo! Merchant Solutions, Amazon, eBay, Network Solutions, or hundreds of other online sites. Fees range from a few hundred dollars to several thousand. These firms host your Web site and they worry about capacity and scale issues as your firm grows. For instance, Yahoo Merchant Solutions offers three different packages: Starter, Standard, and Professional. As the business grows, you can move up to a more comprehensive package. Amazon will even handle the fulfillment of orders for you and probably do a much better job than you or your limited staff can do.

Another solution is to hire a local professional designer (for about $1,000 to $5,000) and have them build you an e-commerce installation that runs off a single computer and broadband connection to your office. You can grow by trial and error. If your site becomes popular, and you need more computing power, buy a newer PC with multicore processors, greater speed, and a much larger hard drive or hard drive array. You can always upgrade your Web connection to a faster speed if users experience a slow down on your Web site. Still another solution is to do everything yourself (design the Web

**SOURCES:** "ShopTommy.com Dresses For Online Success—On Demand," Case Study, ATG.com, June 2010; "Finding the Right Fit for Multi-Channel Commerce: American Eagle Outfitters," Case Study, ATG.com, June 2010. "Technology for the Solo Entrepreneur," by William Bulkeley, *Wall Street Journal*, May 17, 2010; "Calvin Klein Owner Buys Tommy Hilfiger," BBCnews.co.uk, March 15, 2010; "The Open Source Web Design Toolbox: 100 Web Design Template Sources, Tools and Resources," by Emil ustafa, Designvitality.com, July 28, 2009; "23 Google Tools for Your Website," by Tom Now, StartupNation, July 18th, 2009; "End-to-End Banking Transformation in the Product Domain" by Chin Huang, Nimesh Bhatia, and Steve Chu, IBM High Performance On Demand Solutions (HiPODS), May 2009; "Sonoma: Web Service for Estimating Capacity and Performance of Service-Oriented Architecture (SOA) Workloads," by Eugene Hung, Qi He, Jinzy Zhu, IBM Working Paper, October 9, 2006.

site, procure and build the Web servers, and connect to the Internet) at first until you start attracting customers.

The cost of building Web sites has fallen drastically, not just because of the fall in hardware costs, but also because the cost of software needed to build and operate Web sites has fallen, sometimes to zero. There are thousands of open source software tools available to develop Web sites and associated databases that will cost you nothing. Many of these tools can be used by amateurs, some are as simple to use as blog software tools, while others require a technical background and training. Analysts believe that a Web site costing over $1 million in 2000 could be built for less than $50,000 in 2010. For instance, you can obtain the Linux operating system to run your Web site for next to nothing, along with osCommerce, an open source shopping cart order system. In the past, building your own custom shopping cart could easily cost $250,000 and up to several million dollars. Google provides more than 20 Web site management and operations tools for free. However, in both of these DIY solutions, you will have to worry about how to keep up with growth, about the stability of local power supplies, the ability of your computers to meet peak demands, and the ability of your local Internet connection provider to supply your needs for continuous Internet connectivity. Even if you decide to let an outside vendor host your new Web site, you will still need to address these questions. Remember, the "e" in e-commerce does not stand for easy.

I n Chapter 3, you learned about the infrastructure of the Internet and the Web, e-commerce's technological foundation. Now it's time to focus on the next step: building an e-commerce site. In this chapter, you will examine the important factors that a manager needs to consider when building an e-commerce site. The focus will be on the managerial and business decisions you must make before you begin to build Web pages and Web sites, and which you will continually need to make during the life of your Web site. Although building a sophisticated e-commerce site isn't easy, today's tools for building Web sites are much less expensive and far more powerful than they were during the early days of e-commerce. You do not have to be Amazon or eBay to create a successful Web site. In this chapter, we focus on both small and medium-sized businesses that want to build a Web site, and much larger corporate entities that serve thousands of customers a day, or even an hour. As you will see, although the scale may be very different, the principles and considerations are basically the same.

---

## 4.1    BUILDING AN E-COMMERCE WEB SITE: A SYSTEMATIC APPROACH

Building a successful e-commerce site requires a keen understanding of business, technology, and social issues, as well as a systematic approach. E-commerce is just too important to be left totally to technologists and programmers.

The two most important management challenges in building a successful e-commerce site are (1) developing a clear understanding of your business objectives and (2) knowing how to choose the right technology to achieve those objectives. The first challenge requires you to build a plan for developing your firm's site. The second challenge requires you to understand some of the basic elements of e-commerce infrastructure. Let the business drive the technology.

Even if you decide to outsource the entire e-commerce site development and operation to a service provider, you will still need to have a site development plan and some understanding of the basic e-commerce infrastructure issues such as cost, capability, and constraints. Without a plan and a knowledge base, you will not be able to make sound management decisions about e-commerce within your firm (Laudon and Laudon, 2011).

### PIECES OF THE SITE-BUILDING PUZZLE

Let's assume you are a manager for a medium-sized, industrial parts firm of around 10,000 employees worldwide, operating in 10 countries in Europe, Asia, and North America. Senior management has given you a budget of $1 million to build an e-commerce site within one year. The purpose of this site will be to sell and service the firm's 20,000 customers, who are mostly small machine and metal fabricating shops around the world. Where do you start?

First, you must be aware of the main areas where you will need to make decisions (see **Figure 4.1**). On the organizational and human resources fronts, you will have to bring together a team of individuals who possess the skill sets needed to build and manage a successful e-commerce site. This team will make the key decisions about technology, site design, and the social and information policies that will be applied at your site. The entire site development effort must be closely managed if you hope to avoid the disasters that have occurred at some firms.

You will also need to make decisions about your site's hardware, software, and telecommunications infrastructure. Although you will have technical advisors help you make these decisions, ultimately the operation of the site is your responsibility. The demands of your customers should drive your choices of technology. Your customers will want technology that enables them to find what they want easily, view the product, purchase the product, and then receive the product from your warehouses quickly. You will also have to carefully consider your site's design. Once you have identified the key decision areas, you will need to think about a plan for the project.

### PLANNING: THE SYSTEMS DEVELOPMENT LIFE CYCLE

**systems development life cycle (SDLC)**
a methodology for understanding the business objectives of any system and designing an appropriate solution

Your second step in building an e-commerce site will be creating a plan document. In order to tackle a complex problem such as building an e-commerce site, you will have to proceed systematically through a series of steps. One methodology for developing an e-commerce site plan is the systems development life cycle (see **Figure 4.2**).

The **systems development life cycle (SDLC)** is a methodology for understanding the business objectives of any system and designing an appropriate

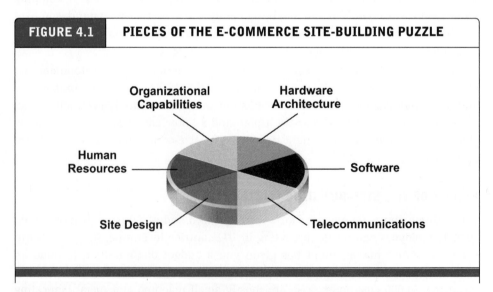

| FIGURE 4.1 | PIECES OF THE E-COMMERCE SITE-BUILDING PUZZLE |

Building an e-commerce Web site requires that you systematically consider the many factors that go into the process.

---

**FIGURE 4.2** | **WEB SITE SYSTEMS DEVELOPMENT LIFE CYCLE**

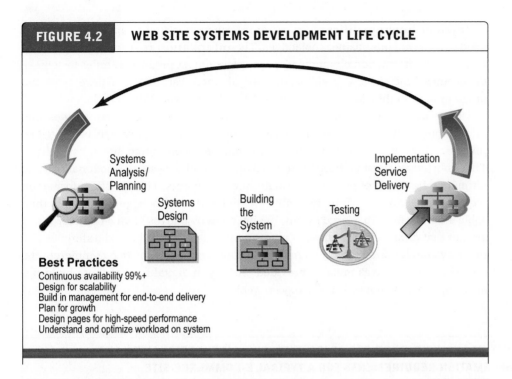

Systems Analysis/ Planning

Systems Design

Building the System

Testing

Implementation Service Delivery

**Best Practices**
Continuous availability 99%+
Design for scalability
Build in management for end-to-end delivery
Plan for growth
Design pages for high-speed performance
Understand and optimize workload on system

---

solution. Adopting a life cycle methodology does not guarantee success, but it is far better than having no plan at all. The SDLC method also helps in creating documents that communicate to senior management the objectives of the site, important milestones, and the uses of resources. The five major steps involved in the systems development life cycle for an e-commerce site are:

- Systems analysis/planning

- Systems design

- Building the system

- Testing

- Implementation

## SYSTEMS ANALYSIS/PLANNING: IDENTIFY BUSINESS OBJECTIVES, SYSTEM FUNCTIONALITY, AND INFORMATION REQUIREMENTS

The systems analysis/planning step of the SDLC tries to answer the question, "What do we want the e-commerce site to do for our business?" The key lesson to be learned here is to let the business decisions drive the technology, not the reverse. This will ensure that your technology platform is aligned with your business. We will assume here that you have identified a business strategy and chosen a business model to achieve your strategic objectives (see Chapter 2). But how do you translate your strategies, business models, and ideas into a working e-commerce site?

One way to start is to identify the specific business objectives for your site, and then develop a list of system functionalities and information requirements. **Business objectives** are simply capabilities you want your site to have.

**business objectives**
capabilities you want your site to have

**system functionalities**
types of information systems capabilities you will need to achieve your business objectives

**System functionalities** are types of information systems capabilities you will need to achieve your business objectives. The **information requirements** for a system are the information elements that the system must produce in order to achieve the business objectives. You will need to provide these lists to system developers and programmers so they know what you as the manager expect them to do.

**information requirements**
the information elements that the system must produce in order to achieve the business objectives

**Table 4.1** describes some basic business objectives, system functionalities, and information requirements for a typical e-commerce site. As shown in the table, there are nine basic business objectives that an e-commerce site must deliver. These objectives must be translated into a description of system functionalities and ultimately into a set of precise information requirements. The specific information requirements for a system typically are defined in much greater detail than Table 4.1 indicates. To a large extent, the business objectives of an e-commerce site are not that different from those of an ordinary retail store. The real difference lies in the system functionalities and information requirements. In an e-commerce site, the business objectives must be provided entirely in digital form without buildings or salespeople, 24 hours a day, 7 days a week.

| TABLE 4.1 | SYSTEM ANALYSIS: BUSINESS OBJECTIVES, SYSTEM FUNCTIONALITY, AND INFORMATION REQUIREMENTS FOR A TYPICAL E-COMMERCE SITE | |
|---|---|---|
| **BUSINESS OBJECTIVE** | **SYSTEM FUNCTIONALITY** | **INFORMATION REQUIREMENTS** |
| Display goods | Digital catalog | Dynamic text and graphics catalog |
| Provide product information (content) | Product database | Product description, stocking numbers, inventory levels |
| Personalize/customize product | Customer on-site tracking | Site log for every customer visit; data mining capability to identify common customer paths and appropriate responses |
| Execute a transaction payment | Shopping cart/payment system | Secure credit card clearing; multiple options |
| Accumulate customer information | Customer database | Name, address, phone, and e-mail for all customers; online customer registration |
| Provide after-sale customer support | Sales database | Customer ID, product, date, payment, shipment date |
| Coordinate marketing/advertising | Ad server, e-mail server, e-mail, campaign manager, ad banner manager | Site behavior log of prospects and customers linked to e-mail and banner ad campaigns |
| Understand marketing effectiveness | Site tracking and reporting system | Number of unique visitors, pages visited, products purchased, identified by marketing campaign |
| Provide production and supplier links | Inventory management system | Product and inventory levels, supplier ID and contact, order quantity data by product |

## SYSTEM DESIGN: HARDWARE AND SOFTWARE PLATFORMS

Once you have identified the business objectives and system functionalities, and have developed a list of precise information requirements, you can begin to consider just how all this functionality will be delivered. You must come up with a **system design specification**—a description of the main components in the system and their relationship to one another. The system design itself can be broken down into two components: a logical design and a physical design. A **logical design** includes a data flow diagram that describes the flow of information at your e-commerce site, the processing functions that must be performed, and the databases that will be used. The logical design also includes a description of the security and emergency backup procedures that will be instituted, and the controls that will be used in the system.

A **physical design** translates the logical design into physical components. For instance, the physical design details the specific model of server to be purchased, the software to be used, the size of the telecommunications link that will be required, the way the system will be backed up and protected from outsiders, and so on.

**Figure 4.3(a)** presents a data flow diagram for a simple high-level logical design for a very basic Web site that delivers catalog pages in HTML in response to HTTP requests from the client's browser, while **Figure 4.3(b)** shows the corresponding physical design. Each of the main processes can be broken down into lower-level designs that are much more precise in identifying exactly how the information flows and what equipment is involved.

## BUILDING THE SYSTEM: IN-HOUSE VERSUS OUTSOURCING

Now that you have a clear idea of both the logical and physical design for your site, you can begin considering how to actually build the site. You have many choices and much depends on the amount of money you are willing to spend. Choices range from outsourcing everything (including the actual systems analysis and design) to building everything yourself (in-house). **Outsourcing** means that you will hire an outside vendor to provide the services involved in building the site that you cannot perform with in-house personnel. You also have a second decision to make: will you host (operate) the site on your firm's own servers or will you outsource the hosting to a Web host provider? These decisions are independent of each other, but they are usually considered at the same time. There are some vendors who will design, build, and host your site, while others will either build or host (but not both). **Figure 4.4** on page 213 illustrates the alternatives.

### Build Your Own versus Outsourcing

Let's take the building decision first. If you elect to build your own site, there are a range of options. Unless you are fairly skilled, you should use a pre-built template to create the Web site. For example, Yahoo Merchant Solutions, Amazon Stores, and eBay all provide templates that merely require you to input text, graphics, and other data, as well as the infrastructure to run the Web site once it has been created. This is the

**system design specification**
description of the main components in a system and their relationship to one another

**logical design**
describes the flow of information at your e-commerce site, the processing functions that must be performed, the databases that will be used, the security and emergency backup procedures that will be instituted, and the controls that will be used in the system

**physical design**
translates the logical design into physical components

**outsourcing**
hiring an outside vendor to provide the services you cannot perform with in-house personnel

## FIGURE 4.3 | A LOGICAL AND PHYSICAL DESIGN FOR A SIMPLE WEB SITE

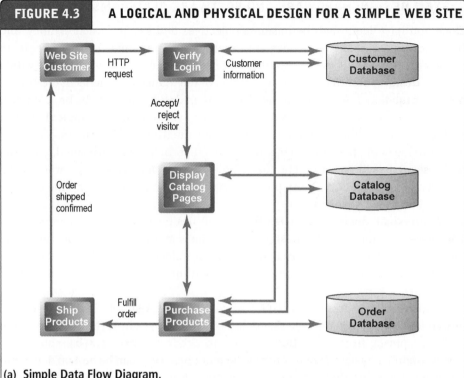

**(a) Simple Data Flow Diagram.**
This data flow diagram describes the flow of information requests and responses for a simple Web site.

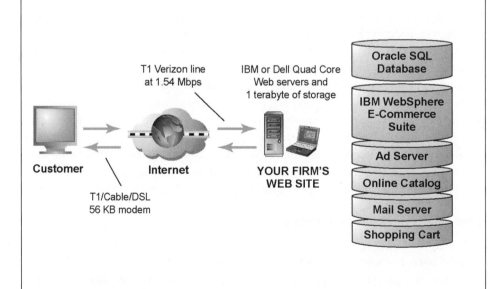

**(b) Simple Physical Design.**
A physical design describes the hardware and software needed to realize the logical design.

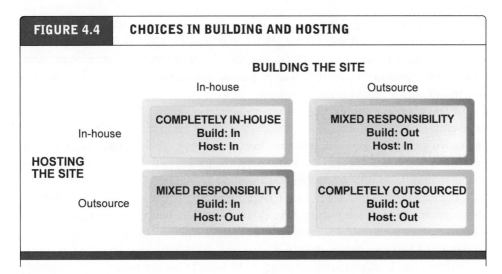

**FIGURE 4.4**  **CHOICES IN BUILDING AND HOSTING**

You have a number of alternatives to consider when building and hosting an e-commerce site.

least costly and simplest solution but you will be limited to the "look and feel" and functionality provided by the template and infrastructure.

If you have some experience with computers, you might decide to build the site yourself "from scratch." There is a broad variety of tools, ranging from those that help you build everything truly "from scratch," such as Adobe Dreamweaver and Microsoft Expression, to top-of-the-line prepackaged site-building tools that can create sophisticated sites customized to your needs. **Figure 4.5** illustrates the spectrum of tools available. We will look more closely at the variety of e-commerce software available in Section 4.2.

The decision to build a Web site on your own has a number of risks. Given the complexity of features such as shopping carts, credit card authentication and processing, inventory management, and order processing, the costs involved are high, as are the risks of doing a poor job. You will be reinventing what other specialized

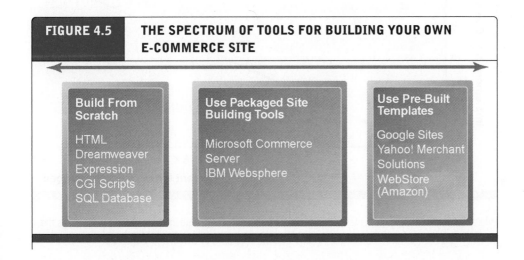

**FIGURE 4.5**  **THE SPECTRUM OF TOOLS FOR BUILDING YOUR OWN E-COMMERCE SITE**

firms have already built, and your staff may face a long, difficult learning curve, delaying your entry to market. Your efforts could fail. On the positive side, you may be better able to build a site that does exactly what you want, and more important, develop the in-house knowledge to allow you to change the site rapidly if necessary due to a changing business environment.

If you choose more expensive site-building packages, you will be purchasing state-of-the art software that is well tested. You could get to market sooner. However, to make a sound decision, you will have to evaluate many different packages and this can take a long time. You may have to modify the packages to fit your business needs and perhaps hire additional outside vendors to do the modifications. Costs rise rapidly as modifications mount. A $4,000 package can easily become a $40,000 to $60,000 development project (see **Figure 4.6**). If you choose the template route, you will be limited to the functionality already built into the templates, and you will not be able to add to the functionality or change it.

In the past, bricks-and-mortar retailers in need of an e-commerce site typically designed the site themselves (because they already had the skilled staff in place and had extensive investments in information technology capital such as databases and telecommunications). However, as Web applications have become more sophisticated, larger retailers today rely heavily on vendors to provide sophisticated Web site capabilities, while also maintaining a substantial internal staff. Small start-ups may build their own sites from scratch using in-house technical personnel in an effort to keep costs low. Medium-size start-ups will often purchase a sophisticated package and then modify it to suit their needs. Very small mom-and-pop firms seeking simple storefronts will use templates. For e-commerce sites, the costs of building has dropped dramatically in the last five years, resulting in lower capital requirements for all

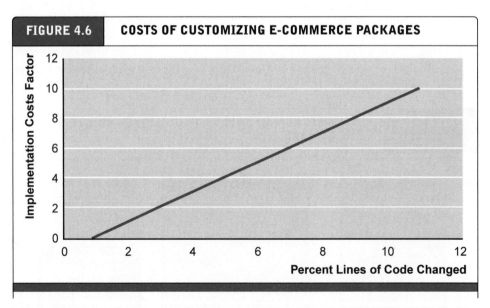

**FIGURE 4.6** | **COSTS OF CUSTOMIZING E-COMMERCE PACKAGES**

While sophisticated site development packages appear to reduce costs and increase speed to market, as the modifications required to fit the package to your business needs rise, costs rise rapidly.

players (see *Insight on Business: Curly Hair and MotorMouths: Getting Started on the Cheap*).

## Host Your Own versus Outsourcing

Now let's look at the hosting decision. Most businesses choose to outsource hosting and pay a company to host their Web site, which means that the hosting company is responsible for ensuring the site is "live," or accessible, 24 hours a day. By agreeing to a monthly fee, the business need not concern itself with many of the technical aspects of setting up a Web server and maintaining it, telecommunications links, nor with staffing needs.

You can also choose to *co-locate*. With a **co-location** agreement, your firm purchases or leases a Web server (and has total control over its operation) but locates the server in a vendor's physical facility. The vendor maintains the facility, communications lines, and the machinery. Co-location has expanded with the spread of virtualization where one server has multiple processors (4–16) and can operate multiple Web sites at once with multiple operating systems. In this case, you do not buy the server but rent its capabilities on a monthly basis, usually at one-quarter of the cost of owning the server itself. See **Table 4.2** for a list of some of the major hosting/co-location providers. There is an extraordinary range of prices for co-hosting, ranging from $4.95 a month, to several hundred thousands of dollars per month depending on the size of the Web site, bandwidth, storage, and support requirements.

Hosting and co-location have become a commodity and a utility: costs are driven by very large providers (such as IBM and Qwest) who can achieve large economies of scale by establishing huge "server farms" located strategically around the country and the globe. What this means is that the cost of pure hosting has fallen as fast as the fall in server prices, dropping about 50% every year! Telecommunications costs have also fallen. As a result, most hosting services seek to differentiate themselves from the commodity hosting business by offering extensive site design, marketing, optimization and other services. Small, local ISPs also can be used as hosts, but service reliability is an issue. Will the small ISP be able to provide uninterrupted service, 24x7x365? Will they have service staff available when you need it?

There are several disadvantages to outsourcing hosting. If you choose a vendor, make sure the vendor has the capability to grow with you. You need to know what kinds of security provisions are in place for backup copies of your site, internal monitoring of activity, and security track record. Is there a public record of a security

**co-location**
when a firm purchases or leases a Web server (and has total control over its operation) but locates the server in a vendor's physical facility. The vendor maintains the facility, communications lines, and the machinery

| TABLE 4.2 | KEY PLAYERS: HOSTING/CO-LOCATION SERVICES |
|---|---|
| GoDaddy.com | Qwest Communications |
| BlueHost | NTT/Verio |
| IBM Global Services | Rackspace |
| GSI Commerce | ServerBeach |

# INSIGHT ON BUSINESS

## CURLY HAIR AND MOTORMOUTHS: GETTING STARTED ON THE CHEAP

With so many big companies with national brand names dominating the e-commerce scene, and with the top 100 retail firms collecting over 90% of the revenues, you may wonder if there's a chance for the little guy anymore, the amateurs. The answer is yes: there's still at least about $23 billion left in potential online retail sales, with additional money to be made from advertising revenues. As it turns out, being big does not necessarily make you nimble. In fact, there's an e-commerce Web site frenzy going on in 2010 that nearly rivals the dot-com era with one exception: the start-ups have much leaner development models made possible in part by much cheaper and available technology, and social networking sites that can bring inex-pensive marketing and sales (no national television marketing budget needed). If your site can create or identify a community of people with shared interests and issues, you'll have a built-in audience.

NaturallyCurly.com is a good example of a low entry cost, niche-oriented portal site that actually created an online community where none existed before. Two reporters, Gretchen Heber and Michelle Breyer, started the site with $500 in 1998. Both had naturally curly hair. "We had long diatribes complaining about our curly hair on very muggy days," says Heber. Or they'd talk about how good it looked on other days. Based on a hunch that other people also needed help coping with curly hair issues, they launched Naturally-Curly.com. They spent $200 on the domain name,

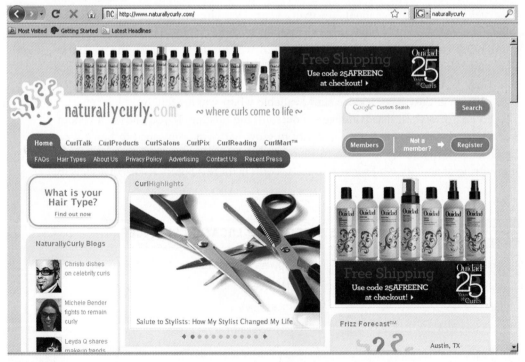

(continued)

and bought some curly hair products to review on the site. The site was built with a simple Web server and the help of a 14-year-old Web page designer. The idea was to act as a content site with community feedback. They added a bulletin board for users to send in their comments.

There were no competitors at first, and even without advertising on Google, they started showing up in Google searches for "curly hair" near or at the top of the search results list. In 2000, after a year of operation, they got an e-mail from Procter & Gamble, the world's largest personal care products company, asking if they would accept advertising for $2,000 a month for two years. From there, the site grew by adding additional advertising from leading hair care products companies such as Aveda, Paul Mitchell, and Redken, among others, and now generates revenue in excess of $1 million from advertising and sales of products on curlmart.com, its online boutique for curly hair products. In May 2007, the firm received an investment of $600,000 from a venture capital firm that was used to hire a marketing person and support staff, improve its Web technology, and expand its shipping and handling operations.

By 2010, NaturallyCurly.com attracts over 450,000 unique visitors a month. The firm has moved aggressively into social marketing by establishing a Facebook site, and a Twitter account, hoping to tap into the "curly hair community", and also operates Curlmart.com, an e-commerce site showcasing 50 different brands and 500 commnunity-vetted products. In September 2010, NaturallyCurly announced that it was acquiring the blog CurlyNikki.com, further expanding its reach and unique visitors.

MotorMouths.com is another good example of a Web site launched on the cheap. Motor-Mouths, a Web site that summarizes car reviews and provides rankings of every model of new car, is the brain child of John Tayman. Tayman began with nothing more than his PowerBook and a $10,000 budget. Researching online, he learned about free open source software such as Ruby on Rails, and RentACoder and Elance, sites that helped him find freelance software programmers that could help him build the site. Within a few months, he had a virtual staff of 20, from five different countries, working on various pieces of his site. MotorMouths.com officially launched in January 2009, for a total cost of $9,800, and about 10 hours a week of "sweat equity" on Tayman's part. Upkeep costs him about $75 a month in server fees.

Growth within the first few months was slow and steady; in 2010, analysts believe the site has about 10,000 visitors a month who find the site primarily through word of- mouth. Revenues are generated selling ads to automotive-related companies like Automotive Magazine, and car manufacturers like BMW Mini. Tayman is optimistic about the future: "If our current growth trends hold and the ad trends hold, MotorMouths could be a $250,000 revenue company in 18 months." Not bad for a $10,000 investment.

The moral of the story: its never been cheaper to start a Web-based company. According to Chris Gill, president of the Silicon Valley Association of Startup Entrepreneurs (SVASE), "What would have cost you a quarter of a million, maybe a million dollars two or three years ago, now costs $25,000." And in fact, the recession may be an entrepreneur's best friend. In a poor economy, failures are not so noticeable, which creates a better environment for risk-taking, which encourages innovation. As one tech investor put it: "The cost of failure is cheap. It's so low, you can swing the bat way more times."

■■■ **SOURCES**: "NaturallyCurly Expands Network and Content Coverage with Acquisition of CurlyNikki.com," NaturallyCurly.com, September16, 2010; "Web Start Up Frenzy 2.0," by Sharon Machlis, Computerworld.com, April 29, 2010; "Splitting Hairs," by Virginia Heffernan, *New York Times*, April 4, 2010; "Launching an E-commerce Site With Social Networking," Marketingsherpa.com, March 3, 2010; "Software and Technology Services NaturallyCurly.com, Inc.," BusinessWeek.com, July 28, 2009; "The New Internet Startup Boom: Get Rich Slow," by Josh Quittner, Time.com, April 9, 2009.

breach at the vendor? Most Fortune 500 firms do their own hosting so they can control the Web environment. On the other hand, there are risks to hosting your own site if you are a small business. Your costs will be higher than if you had used a large outsourcing firm because you don't have the market power to obtain low-cost hardware and telecommunications. You will have to purchase hardware and software, have a physical facility, lease communications lines, hire a staff, and build security and backup capabilities yourself.

## TESTING THE SYSTEM

Once the system has been built and programmed, you will have to engage in a testing process. Depending on the size of the system, this could be fairly difficult and lengthy. Testing is required whether the system is outsourced or built in-house. A complex e-commerce site can have thousands of pathways through the site, each of which must be documented and then tested. **Unit testing** involves testing the site's program modules one at a time. **System testing** involves testing the site as a whole, in the same way a typical user would when using the site. Because there is no truly "typical" user, system testing requires that every conceivable path be tested. Final **acceptance testing** requires that the firm's key personnel and managers in marketing, production, sales, and general management actually use the system as installed on a test Internet or intranet server. This acceptance test verifies that the business objectives of the system as originally conceived are in fact working. It is important to note that testing is generally under-budgeted. As much as 50% of the software effort can be consumed by testing and rebuilding (usually depending on the quality of initial design).

**unit testing**
involves testing the site's program modules one at a time

**system testing**
involves testing the site as a whole, in a way the typical user will use the site

**acceptance testing**
verifies that the business objectives of the system as originally conceived are in fact working

## IMPLEMENTATION AND MAINTENANCE

Most people unfamiliar with systems erroneously think that once an information system is installed, the process is over. In fact, while the beginning of the process is over, the operational life of a system is just beginning. Systems break down for a variety of reasons—most of them unpredictable. Therefore, they need continual checking, testing, and repair. Systems maintenance is vital, but sometimes not budgeted for. In general, the annual system maintenance cost will roughly parallel the development cost. A $40,000 e-commerce site will likely require a $40,000 annual expenditure to maintain. Very large e-commerce sites experience some economies of scale, so that, for example, a $1 million site will likely require a maintenance budget of $500,000 to $700,000.

Why does it cost so much to maintain an e-commerce site? Unlike payroll systems, for example, e-commerce sites are always in a process of change, improvement, and correction. Studies of traditional systems maintenance have found 20% of the time is devoted to debugging code and responding to emergency situations (a new server was installed by your ISP, and all your hypertext links were lost and CGI scripts disabled—the site is down!) (Lientz and Swanson, 1980; Banker and Kemerer, 1989). Another 20% of the time is concerned with changes in reports, data files, and links to backend databases. The remaining 60% of maintenance time is devoted to general administration (making product and price changes in the catalog) and making changes and enhancements to the system. E-commerce sites are never finished: they are always in the process of being built and rebuilt. They are dynamic—much more so than payroll systems.

The long-term success of an e-commerce site will depend on a dedicated team of employees (the Web team) whose sole job is to monitor and adapt the site to changing market conditions. The Web team must be multi-skilled; it will typically include programmers, designers, and business managers drawn from marketing, production, and sales support. One of the first tasks of the Web team is to listen to customers' feedback on the site and respond to that feedback as necessary. A second task is to develop a systematic monitoring and testing plan to be followed weekly to ensure all the links are operating, prices are correct, and pages are updated. A large business may have thousands of Web pages, many of them linked, that require systematic monitoring. Other important tasks of the Web team include **benchmarking** (a process in which the site is compared with those of competitors in terms of response speed, quality of layout, and design) and keeping the site current on pricing and promotions. The Web is a competitive environment where you can very rapidly frustrate and lose customers with a dysfunctional site.

**benchmarking**
a process in which the site is compared with those of competitors in terms of response speed, quality of layout, and design

## FACTORS IN OPTIMIZING WEB SITE PERFORMANCE

The purpose of a Web site is to deliver content to customers and to complete transactions. The faster and more reliably these two objectives are met, the more effective the Web site is from a commerce perspective. If you are a manager or marketing executive, you will want the Web site operating in a way that fulfills customers' expectations. You'll have to make sure the Web site is optimized to achieve this business objective. The optimization of Web site performance is more complicated than it seems and involves at least three factors: page content, page generation, and page delivery (see **Figure 4.7**). In this chapter, we describe the software and hardware choices you will need to make in building an e-commerce site; these are also important factors in Web site optimization.

Using efficient styles and techniques for *page design* and *content* can reduce response times by two to five seconds. Simple steps include reducing unnecessary HTML comments and white space, using more efficient graphics, and avoiding unnecessary links to other pages in the site. *Page generation* speed can be enhanced by segregating computer servers to perform dedicated functions (such as static page generation, application logic, media servers, and database servers), and using various devices from vendors to speed up these servers. Using a single server or multiple servers to perform multiple tasks reduces throughput by over 50%. *Page delivery* can be speeded up by using edge-caching services such as Akamai, or specialized content delivery networks such as RealNetworks, or by increasing local bandwidth. We will discuss some of these factors throughout the chapter, but a full discussion of Web site optimization is beyond the scope of this text.

| FIGURE 4.7 | **FACTORS IN WEB SITE OPTIMIZATION** |
| --- | --- |

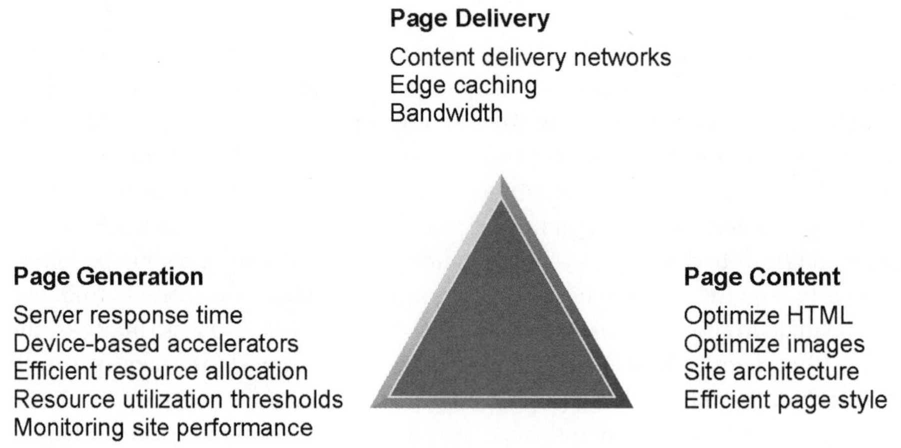

**Page Delivery**
Content delivery networks
Edge caching
Bandwidth

**Page Generation**
Server response time
Device-based accelerators
Efficient resource allocation
Resource utilization thresholds
Monitoring site performance

**Page Content**
Optimize HTML
Optimize images
Site architecture
Efficient page style

Web site optimization requires that you consider three factors: page content, page generation, and page delivery.

## WEB SITE BUDGETS

How much you spend on a Web site depends on what you want it to do. Simple Web sites can be built and hosted with a first-year cost of $5,000 or less. The Web sites of large firms that offer high levels of interactivity and linkage to corporate systems can cost several hundred thousand to millions of dollars a year to create and operate. For instance, in September 2006, Bluefly, which sells women's and men's designer clothes online, embarked on the process of developing an improved version of its Web site based on software from ATG. It launched the new site in August 2008 and capitalized over $5.3 million in connection with its development (Bluefly, Inc., 2009).

While how much you spend to build a Web site depends on how much you can afford, and, of course, the size of the opportunity, **Figure 4.8** provides some idea of the relative size of various Web site costs. In general, the cost of hardware, software, and telecommunications for building and operating a Web site has fallen dramatically (by over 50%) since 2000, making it possible for very small entrepreneurs to build fairly sophisticated sites. At the same time, while technology has lowered the costs of system development, the costs of system maintenance and content creation have risen to make up more than half of typical Web site budgets. Providing content and smooth 24x7 operations are both labor intensive.

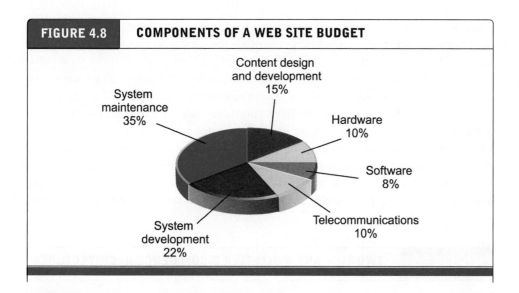

**FIGURE 4.8** | **COMPONENTS OF A WEB SITE BUDGET**

## 4.2 CHOOSING SOFTWARE

Much of what you are able to do at an e-commerce site is a function of the software. As a business manager in charge of building the site, you will need to know some basic information about e-commerce software. The more sophisticated the software and the more ways you can sell goods and services, the more effective your business will be. This section describes the software needed to operate a contemporary e-commerce site. Section 4.3 discusses the hardware you will need to handle the demands of the software.

### SIMPLE VERSUS MULTI-TIERED WEB SITE ARCHITECTURE

Prior to the development of e-commerce, Web sites simply delivered Web pages to users who were making requests through their browsers for HTML pages with content of various sorts. Web site software was appropriately quite simple—it consisted of a server computer running basic Web server software. We might call this arrangement a single-tier system architecture. **System architecture** refers to the arrangement of software, machinery, and tasks in an information system needed to achieve a specific functionality (much like a home's architecture refers to the arrangement of building materials to achieve a particular functionality). The SteamShowers4Less and NaturallyCurly sites both started this way—there were no monetary transactions. Tens of thousands of dot-com sites still perform this way. Orders can always be called in by telephone and not taken online.

However, the development of e-commerce required a great deal more interactive functionality, such as the ability to respond to user input (name and address forms), take customer orders for goods and services, clear credit card transactions on the fly, consult price and product databases, and even adjust advertising on the screen based on user characteristics. This kind of extended functionality required the development of Web application servers and a multi-tiered system architecture to handle the

**system architecture**
the arrangement of software, machinery, and tasks in an information system needed to achieve a specific functionality

processing loads. *Web application servers*, described more fully later in this section, are specialized software programs that perform a wide variety of transaction processing required by e-commerce.

In addition to having specialized application servers, e-commerce sites must be able to pull information from and add information to pre-existing corporate databases. These older databases that predate the e-commerce era are called *backend* or *legacy* databases. Corporations have made massive investments in these systems to store their information on customers, products, employees, and vendors. These backend systems constitute an additional layer in a multi-tiered site.

**Figure 4.9** illustrates a simple two-tier and more complex multi-tier e-commerce system architecture. In **two-tier architecture**, a Web server responds to requests

**two-tier architecture**

e-commerce system architecture in which a Web server responds to requests for Web pages and a database server provides backend data storage

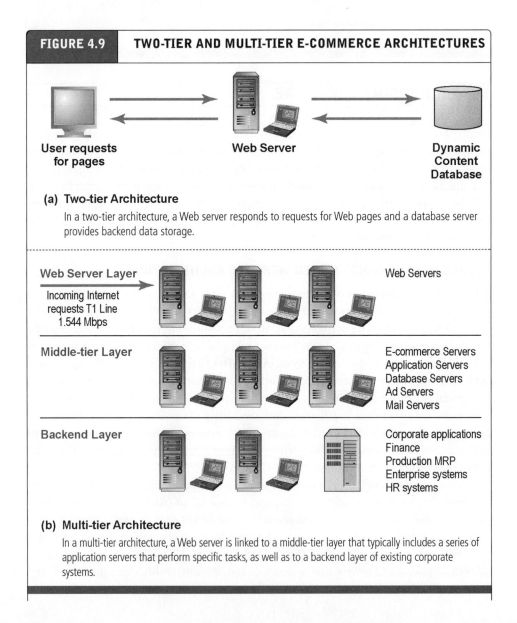

**FIGURE 4.9**   **TWO-TIER AND MULTI-TIER E-COMMERCE ARCHITECTURES**

**User requests for pages** → **Web Server** → **Dynamic Content Database**

**(a) Two-tier Architecture**

In a two-tier architecture, a Web server responds to requests for Web pages and a database server provides backend data storage.

**Web Server Layer** — Incoming Internet requests T1 Line 1.544 Mbps — Web Servers

**Middle-tier Layer** — E-commerce Servers, Application Servers, Database Servers, Ad Servers, Mail Servers

**Backend Layer** — Corporate applications, Finance, Production MRP, Enterprise systems, HR systems

**(b) Multi-tier Architecture**

In a multi-tier architecture, a Web server is linked to a middle-tier layer that typically includes a series of application servers that perform specific tasks, as well as to a backend layer of existing corporate systems.

for Web pages and a database server provides backend data storage. In a **multi-tier architecture**, in contrast, the Web server is linked to a middle-tier layer that typically includes a series of application servers that perform specific tasks, as well as to a backend layer of existing corporate systems containing product, customer, and pricing information. A multi-tiered site typically employs several physical computers, each running some of the software applications and sharing the workload across many physical computers.

The remainder of this section describes basic Web server software functionality and the various types of Web application servers.

## WEB SERVER SOFTWARE

All e-commerce sites require basic Web server software to answer requests from customers for HTML and XML pages.

When you choose Web server software, you will also be choosing an operating system for your site's computers. Looking at all servers on the Web, the leading Web server software, with about 54% of the market, is Apache, which works with Linux and Unix operating systems. Unix is the original programming language of the Internet and Web, and Linux is a derivative of Unix designed for the personal computer. Apache was developed by a worldwide community of Internet innovators. Apache is free and can be downloaded from many sites on the Web; it also comes installed on most IBM Web servers. Literally thousands of programmers have worked on Apache over the years; thus, it is extremely stable. There are thousands of utility software programs written for Apache that can provide all the functionality required for a contemporary e-commerce site. In order to use Apache, you will need staff that is knowledgeable in Unix or Linux.

Microsoft Internet Information Services (IIS) is the second major Web server software available, with about 25% of the market. IIS is based on the Windows operating system and is compatible with a wide selection of Microsoft utility and support programs. These numbers are different among the Fortune 1000 firms, and different again if you include blogs, which are served up by Microsoft and Google at their own proprietary sites.

There are also at least 100 other smaller providers of Web server software, most of them based on the Unix or Sun Solaris operating systems. Note that the choice of Web server has little effect on users of your system. The pages they see will look the same regardless of the development environment. There are many advantages to the Microsoft suite of development tools—they are integrated, powerful, and easy to use. The Unix operating system, on the other hand, is exceptionally reliable and stable, and there is a worldwide open software community that develops and tests Unix-based Web server software.

**Table 4.3** shows the basic functionality provided by all Web servers.

## Site Management Tools

In Chapter 3, we described most of the basic functionality of the Web servers listed in Table 4.3. Another functionality not described previously is site management tools. **Site management tools** are essential if you want to keep your site working, and if

**multi-tier architecture**
e-commerce system architecture in which the Web server is linked to a middle-tier layer that typically includes a series of application servers that perform specific tasks as well as to a backend layer of existing corporate systems

**site management tools**
verify that links on pages are still valid and also identify orphan files

| TABLE 4.3 | BASIC FUNCTIONALITY PROVIDED BY WEB SERVERS |
|---|---|
| FUNCTIONALITY | DESCRIPTION |
| Processing of HTTP requests | Receive and respond to client requests for HTML pages |
| Security services (Secure Sockets Layer) | Verify username and password; process certificates and private/public key information required for credit card processing and other secure information |
| File Transfer Protocol | Permits transfer of very large files from server to server |
| Search engine | Indexing of site content; keyword search capability |
| Data capture | Log file of all visits, time, duration, and referral source |
| E-mail | Ability to send, receive, and store e-mail messages |
| Site management tools | Calculate and display key site statistics, such as unique visitors, page requests, and origin of requests; check links on pages |

you want to understand how well it is working. Site management tools verify that links on pages are still valid and also identify orphan files, or files on the site that are not linked to any pages. By surveying the links on a Web site, a site management tool can quickly report on potential problems and errors that users may encounter. Your customers will not be impressed if they encounter a "404 Error: Page Does Not Exist" on your Web site. Links to URLs that have moved or been deleted are called dead links; these can cause error messages for users trying to access that link. Regularly checking that all links on a site are operational helps prevent irritation and frustration in users who may decide to take their business elsewhere to a better functioning site.

Even more importantly, site management tools can help you understand consumer behavior on your Web site. Site management software and services, such as those provided by Webtrends, can be purchased in order to more effectively monitor customer purchases and marketing campaign effectiveness, as well as keep track of standard hit counts and page visit information. **Figure 4.10** contains two screenshots that illustrate two Web site analytics tools: WebTrends Analytics 9 and Google Analytics.

### Dynamic Page Generation Tools

One of the most important innovations in Web site operation has been the development of dynamic page generation tools. Prior to the development of e-commerce, Web sites primarily delivered unchanging static content in the form of HTML pages. While this capability might be sufficient to display pictures of products, consider all the elements of a typical e-commerce site today by reviewing Table 4.1 (on page 210), or visit what you believe is an excellent e-commerce site. The content of successful e-commerce sites is always changing, often day by day. There are new products and promotions,

| FIGURE 4.10 | WEBTRENDS ANALYTICS; GOOGLE ANALYTICS |
| --- | --- |

Using a sophisticated Web analytics solution such as Webtrends Analytics or Google Analytics, managers can quickly understand the return on investment of their online marketing efforts and determine how to improve conversion by drilling down into abandonment paths, product preferences, and successful campaign elements for different types of customers.

SOURCE: Webtrends, Inc., 2009; Google, 2009.

changing prices, news events, and stories of successful users. E-commerce sites must intensively interact with users who not only request pages but also request product, price, availability, and inventory information. One of the most dynamic sites is eBay—the auction site. There, the content is changing minute by minute. E-commerce sites are just like real markets—they are dynamic. News sites, where stories change constantly, are also dynamic.

The dynamic and complex nature of e-commerce sites requires a number of specialized software applications in addition to static HTML pages. Perhaps one of the most important is dynamic page generation software. With **dynamic page generation**, the contents of a Web page are stored as objects in a database, rather than being hard-coded in HTML. When the user requests a Web page, the contents for that page are then fetched from the database. The objects are retrieved from the database using Common Gateway Interface (CGI), Active Server Pages (ASP), Java Server Pages (JSP), or other server-side programs. CGI, ASP, and JSP are described in the last section of this chapter. This technique is much more efficient than working directly in HTML code. It is much easier to change the contents of a database than it is to change the coding of an HTML page. A standard data access method called *Open Database Connectivity (ODBC)* makes it possible to access any data from any application regardless of what database is used. ODBC is supported by most of the large database suppliers such as Oracle, Sybase, and IBM. ODBC makes it possible for HTML pages to be linked to backend corporate databases regardless of who manufactured the database. Web sites must be able to pull information from, and add information to, these databases. For example, when a customer clicks on a picture of a pair of boots, the site can access the product catalog database stored in a DB2 database, and access the inventory database stored in an Oracle database to confirm that the boots are still in stock and to report the current price.

Dynamic page generation gives e-commerce several significant capabilities that generate cost and profitability advantages over traditional commerce. Dynamic page generation lowers *menu costs* (the costs incurred by merchants for changing product descriptions and prices). Dynamic page generation also permits easy online *market segmentation*—the ability to sell the same product to different markets. For instance, you might want variations on the same banner ad depending on how many times the customer has seen the ad. In the first exposure to a car ad, you might want to emphasize brand identification and unique features. On the second viewing you might want to emphasize superlatives like "most family friendly" to encourage comparison to other brands. The same capability makes possible nearly cost-free *price discrimination*—the ability to sell the same product to different customers at different prices. For instance, you might want to sell the same product to corporations and government agencies but use different marketing themes. Based on a cookie you place on client files, or in response to a question on your site that asks visitors if they are from a government agency or a corporation, you would be able to use different marketing and promotional materials for corporate clients and government clients. You might want to reward loyal customers with lower prices, say on DVDs or musical tracks, and charge full price to first-time buyers. Dynamic page generation allows you to approach different customers with different messages and prices.

**dynamic page generation**

the contents of a Web page are stored as objects in a database, rather than being hard-coded in HTML. When the user requests a Web page, the contents for that page are then fetched from the database

Dynamic page generation also enables the use of Web content management systems. As its name implies, a **Web content management system (WCMS or WebCMS)** is used to create and manage Web content. A WCMS separates the design and presentation of content (such as HTML documents, images, video, audio) from the content creation process. The content is maintained in a database and dynamically linked to the Web site. A WCMS usually includes templates that can be automatically applied to new and existing content, WYSIWIG editing tools that make it easy to edit and describe (tag) content, and collaboration, workflow, and document management tools. Typically, an experienced programmer is needed to install the system, but thereafter, content can be easily created and managed by non-technical staff. There are a wide range of commercial WCMSs available, from top-end enterprise systems offered by Autonomy/Interwoven, EMC/Documentum, Open Text, IBM, and Oracle, to mid-market systems by Ixiasoft, PaperThin, Ektron, and Hot Banana, as well as hosted software as a service (SaaS) versions by Clickability, CrownPeak Technology, and OmniUpdate. There are also several open source content management systems available, such as Joomla, Drupal, OpenCms, and others (RealStoryGroup.com, 2010).

**Web content management system (WCMS, WebCMS)**
used to create and manage Web content

## APPLICATION SERVERS

**Web application servers** are software programs that provide the specific business functionality required of a Web site. The basic idea of application servers is to isolate the business applications from the details of displaying Web pages to users on the front end and the details of connecting to databases on the back end. Application servers are a kind of middleware software that provides the glue connecting traditional corporate systems to the customer as well as all the functionality needed to conduct e-commerce. In the early years, a number of software firms developed specific separate programs for each function, but increasingly, these specific programs are being replaced by integrated software tools that combine all the needed functionality for an e-commerce site into a single development environment, a packaged software approach.

**web application server**
software programs that provide specific business functionality required of a Web site

**Table 4.4** illustrates the wide variety of application servers available in the marketplace. The table focuses on "sell side" servers that are designed to enable selling products on the Web. So-called "buy side" and "link" servers focus on the needs of businesses to connect with partners in their supply chains or find suppliers for specific parts and assemblies. These buy-side and link servers are described more fully in Chapter 12, *B2B E-commerce, Supply Chain Management, and Collaborative Commerce.* There are several thousand software vendors that provide application server software. For Linux and Unix environments, many of these capabilities are available free on the Internet from various sites. Most businesses—faced with this bewildering array of choices—choose to use integrated software tools called merchant server software.

## E-COMMERCE MERCHANT SERVER SOFTWARE FUNCTIONALITY

**E-commerce merchant server software** provides the basic functionality needed for online sales, including an online catalog, order taking via an online shopping cart, and online credit card processing.

**e-commerce merchant server software**
software that provides the basic functionality needed for online sales, including an online catalog, order taking via an online shopping cart, and online credit card processing

| TABLE 4.4 | APPLICATION SERVERS AND THEIR FUNCTION |
|---|---|
| APPLICATION SERVER | FUNCTIONALITY |
| Catalog display | Provides a database for product descriptions and prices |
| Transaction processing (shopping cart) | Accepts orders and clears payments |
| List server | Creates and serves mailing lists and manages e-mail marketing campaigns |
| Proxy server | Monitors and controls access to main Web server; implements firewall protection |
| Mail server | Manages Internet e-mail |
| Audio/video server | Stores and delivers streaming media content |
| Chat server | Creates an environment for online real-time text and audio interactions with customers |
| News server | Provides connectivity and displays Internet news feeds |
| Fax server | Provides fax reception and sending using a Web server |
| Groupware server | Creates workgroup environments for online collaboration |
| Database server | Stores customer, product, and price information |
| Ad server | Maintains Web-enabled database of advertising banners that permits customized and personalized display of advertisements based on consumer behavior and characteristics |
| Auction server | Provides a transaction environment for conducting online auctions |
| B2B server | Implements buy, sell, and link marketplaces for commercial transactions |

## Online Catalog

**online catalog**

list of products available on a Web site

A company that wants to sell products on the Web must have a list, or **online catalog**, of its products, available on its Web site. Merchant server software typically includes a database capability that will allow for construction of a customized online catalog. The complexity and sophistication of the catalog will vary depending on the size of the company and its product lines. Small companies, or companies with small product lines, may post a simple list with text descriptions and perhaps color photos. A larger site might decide to add sound, animations, or videos (useful for product demonstrations) to the catalog, or interactivity, such as customer service representatives available via instant messaging to answer questions. Today, larger firms make extensive use of streaming video.

## Shopping Cart

**shopping cart**

allows shoppers to set aside desired purchases in preparation for checkout, review what they have selected, edit their selections as necessary, and then actually make the purchase by clicking a button

Online **shopping carts** are much like their real-world equivalent; both allow shoppers to set aside desired purchases in preparation for checkout. The difference is that the online variety is part of a merchant server software program residing on the Web server, and allows consumers to select merchandise, review what they have selected, edit their selections as necessary, and then actually make the purchase by clicking a button. The merchant server software automatically stores shopping cart data.

### Credit Card Processing

A site's shopping cart typically works in conjunction with credit card processing software, which verifies the shopper's credit card and then puts through the debit to the card and the credit to the company's account at checkout. Integrated e-commerce software suites typically supply the software for this function. Otherwise, you will have to make arrangements with a variety of credit card processing banks and intermediaries.

## MERCHANT SERVER SOFTWARE PACKAGES (E-COMMERCE SUITES)

Rather than build your site from a collection of disparate software applications, it is easier, faster, and generally more cost-effective to purchase a **merchant server software package** (also called an **e-commerce server suite**). Merchant server software/e-commerce suites offer an integrated environment that promises to provide most or all of the functionality and capabilities you will need to develop a sophisticated, customer-centric site. E-commerce suites come in three general ranges of price and functionality.

Basic packages for elementary e-commerce business applications are provided by Bizland, HyperMart, and Yahoo! Merchant Solutions. FreeWebs.com also offers free Web building tools and hosting services. OSCommerce is a free, open source e-commerce suite used by many small start-up sites. PayPal can be used as a payment system on simple Web sites, and widgets can add interesting capabilities.

Midrange suites include IBM WebSphere Commerce Express Edition and Microsoft's Commerce Server 2009. High-end enterprise solutions for large global firms are provided by IBM WebSphere's Commerce Professional and Enterprise Editions, BroadVision Commerce, and others. There are several hundred software firms that provide e-commerce suites, which raises the costs of making sensible decisions on this matter. Many firms simply choose vendors with the best overall reputation. Quite often this turns out to be an expensive but ultimately workable solution. **Table 4.5** lists some of the most widely adopted midrange and high-end e-commerce suites.

### Choosing an E-commerce Suite

With all of these vendors, how do you choose the right one? Evaluating these tools and making a choice is one of the most important and uncertain decisions you will make in building an e-commerce site. The real costs are hidden—they involve training your staff to use the tools and integrating the tools into your business processes and organizational culture. The following are some of the key factors to consider:

- Functionality
- Support for different business models
- Business process modeling tools
- Visual site management tools and reporting
- Performance and scalability

**merchant server software package (e-commerce server suite)**
offers an integrated environment that provides most or all of the functionality and capabilities needed to develop a sophisticated, customer-centric site

| TABLE 4.5 | WIDELY USED MIDRANGE AND HIGH-END E-COMMERCE SUITES |
|---|---|
| **PRODUCT** | **APPROXIMATE PRICE** |
| Microsoft Commerce Server | $7,075 per processor, Enterprise Edition, $20,218 |
| IBM WebSphere Commerce | Express: $299/PVU; typical configuration about $20, 000 |
| Pricing based on PVU (processor value units) | Professional: $1,130/PVU; typical configuration about $113,000 |
|  | Enterprise: $1,820/PVU; typical configuration about $182,000 |
| Intershop Enfinity Suite 6 Consumer Channel | $125,000–$250,000 |
| ATG (Art Technology Group) | $380,000 for a four-CPU license |

- Connectivity to existing business systems
- Compliance with standards
- Global and multicultural capability
- Local sales tax and shipping rules

For instance, although e-commerce suites promise to do everything, your business may require special functionality—such as streaming audio and video. You will need a list of business functionality requirements. Your business may involve several different business models—such as a retail side and a business-to-business side; you may run auctions for stock excess as well as fixed-price selling. Be sure the package can support all of your business models. You may wish to change your business processes, such as order taking and order fulfillment. Does the suite contain tools for modeling business process and work flows? Understanding how your site works will require visual reporting tools that make its operation transparent to many different people in your business. A poorly designed software package will drop off significantly in performance as visitors and transactions expand into the thousands per hour, or minute. Check for performance and scalability by stress testing a pilot edition or obtaining data from the vendor about performance under load. You will have to connect the e-commerce suite to your traditional business systems. How will this connection to existing systems be made, and is your staff skilled in making the connection? Because of the changing technical environment—in particular, changes in mobile commerce platforms—it is important to document exactly what standards the suite supports now, and what the migration path will be toward the future. Finally, your e-commerce site may have to work both globally and locally. You may need a foreign language edition using foreign currency denominations. And you will have to collect sales taxes across many local, regional, and national tax systems. Does the e-commerce suite support this level of globalization and localization?

## BUILDING YOUR OWN E-COMMERCE SITE: WEB SERVICES AND OPEN SOURCE OPTIONS

While existing firms often have the financial capital to invest in commercial merchant server software suites, many small firms and start-up firms do not. They have to build their own Web sites, at least initially. There are really two options here, the key factor being how much programming experience and time you have. One option is to utilize the e-commerce merchant services provided by hosting sites such as Yahoo's Merchant Solutions. For a $50 setup fee, and a starter plan of $39.95, the service will walk you through setting up your Web site and provide Web hosting, a shopping cart, technical help by phone, and payment processing. Bigstep.com takes users step by step through the process of building an online store. Entrabase.com and Tripod provide easy-to-use site-building tools and e-commerce templates for e-commerce sites. An *e-commerce template* is a pre-designed Web site that allows users to customize the look and feel of the site to fit their business needs and provides a standard set of functionality. Most templates today contain ready-to-go site designs with built-in e-commerce suite functionality like shopping carts, payment clearance, and site management tools.

One of the most popular low-cost tools for creating a Web site without having to have any programming skills is Homestead.com. Building a Web site at Homestead involves three steps: choosing a design from over 2,000 templates, customizing the design with logos and content, and publishing it on the Web on Homestead servers with your own unique IP address, and e-mail. Once you build the Web site, Homestead provides a comprehensive set of services such as PayPal and credit card payment clearing, online catalog, shopping cart, real-time transaction processing, and custom shipping tables. Marketing support is available in the form of search engine optimization for your site, and advertising on Google, Amazon, and MSN. There is a 30-day free trial, and basic service for $4.99 a month, with charges for additional services.

If you have considerable, or at least some, programming background, you can consider open source merchant server software. Open source software, as described in Chapter 3, is software developed by a community of programmers and designers, and is free to use and modify. **Table 4.6** provides a description of some open source options.

The advantage of using open source Web building tools is that you get exactly what you want, a truly customized unique Web site. The disadvantage is that it will take several months for a single programmer to develop the site and get all the tools to work together seamlessly. How many months do you want to wait before you get to market with your ideas?

One alternative to building a Web site first is to create a blog first, and develop your business ideas and a following of potential customers on your blog. Once you have tested your ideas with a blog, and attract a Web audience, you can then move on to developing a simple Web site.

| TABLE 4.6 | OPEN SOURCE SOFTWARE OPTIONS |
|---|---|
| **MERCHANT SERVER FUNCTIONALITY** | **OPEN SOURCE SOFTWARE** |
| Web server | Apache (the leading Web server for small and medium businesses) |
| Shopping cart, online catalog | Many providers: Zen-Cart.com, AgoraCart.com, X-Cart.com, osCommerce.com |
| Credit card processing | Many providers: Echo Internet Gateway; ASPDotNetStorefront. Credit card acceptance is typically provided in shopping cart software but you may need a merchant account from a bank as well. |
| Database | MySQL (the leading open source SQL database for businesses) |
| Programming/scripting language | PHP (a scripting language embedded in HTML documents but executed by the server providing server-side execution with the simplicity of HTML editing). PERL is an alternative language. JavaScript programs are client-side programs that provide user interface components. Ruby on Rails (RoR, Rails) is another popular open source Web application framework. |
| Analytics | Analytics keep track of your site's customer activities and the success of your Web advertising campaign. You can also use Google Analytics if you advertise on Google, which provides good tracking tools; most hosting services will provide these services as well. Other open source analytic tools include Piwik, CrawlTrack, and Open Web Analytics. |

## 4.3 CHOOSING THE HARDWARE FOR AN E-COMMERCE SITE

As the manager in charge of building an e-commerce site, you will be held accountable for its performance. Whether you host your own site or outsource the hosting and operation of your site, you will need to understand certain aspects of the computing hardware platform. The **hardware platform** refers to all the underlying computing equipment that the system uses to achieve its e-commerce functionality. Your objective is to have enough platform capacity to meet peak demand (avoiding an overload condition), but not so much platform that you are wasting money. Failing to meet peak demand can mean your site is slow, or actually crashes. Remember, the Web site may be your only or principal source of cash flow. How much computing and telecommunications capacity is enough to meet peak demand? How many hits per day can your site sustain?

To answer these questions, you will need to understand the various factors that affect the speed, capacity, and scalability of an e-commerce site.

**hardware platform**
refers to all the underlying computing equipment that the system uses to achieve its e-commerce functionality

## RIGHT-SIZING YOUR HARDWARE PLATFORM: THE DEMAND SIDE

The most important factor affecting the speed of your site is the demand that customers put on the site. **Table 4.7** lists the most important factors to consider when estimating the demand on a site.

Demand on a Web site is fairly complex and depends primarily on the type of site you are operating. The number of simultaneous users in peak periods, the nature of customer requests, the type of content, the required security, the number of items in inventory, the number of page requests, and the speed of legacy applications that may be needed to supply data to the Web pages are all important factors in overall demand on a Web site system.

Certainly, one important factor to consider is the number of simultaneous users who will likely visit your site. In general, the load created by an individual customer on a server is typically quite limited and short-lived. A Web session initiated by the

| TABLE 4.7 | FACTORS IN RIGHT-SIZING AN E-COMMERCE PLATFORM | | | | |
|---|---|---|---|---|---|
| SITE TYPE | PUBLISH/ SUBSCRIBE | SHOPPING | CUSTOMER SELF-SERVICE | TRADING | WEB SERVICES/B2B |
| Examples | WSJ.com | Amazon | Travelocity | E*Trade | Ariba e-procurement exchanges |
| Content | Dynamic Multiple authors High volume Not user specific | Catalog Dynamic items User profiles with data mining | Data in legacy applications Multiple data sources | Time sensitive High volatility Multiple suppliers and consumers Complex transactions | Data in legacy applications Multiple data sources Complex transactions |
| Security | Low | Privacy Non-repudiation Integrity Authentication Regulations | Privacy Non-repudiation Integrity Authentication Regulations | Privacy Non-repudiation Integrity Authentication Regulations | Privacy Non-repudiation Integrity Authentication Regulations |
| Percent secure pages | Low | Medium | Medium | High | Medium |
| Cross session information | No | High | High | High | High |
| Searches | Dynamic Low volume | Dynamic High volume | Non dynamic Low volume | Non dynamic Low volume | Non dynamic Moderate volume |
| Unique items (SKUs) | High | Medium to high | Medium | High | Medium to high |
| Transaction volume | Moderate | Moderate to high | Moderate | High to extremely high | Moderate |
| Legacy integration complexity | Low | Medium | High | High | High |
| Page views (hits) | High to very high | Moderate to high | Moderate to low | Moderate to high | Moderate |

**stateless**
refers to the fact that the server does not have to maintain an ongoing, dedicated interaction with the client

typical user is **stateless**, meaning that the server does not have to maintain an ongoing, dedicated interaction with the client. A Web session typically begins with a page request, then a server replies, and the session is ended. The sessions may last from tenths of a second to a minute per user. Nevertheless, system performance does degrade as more and more simultaneous users request service. Fortunately, degradation (measured as "transactions per second" and "latency" or delay in response) is fairly graceful over a wide range, up until a peak load is reached and service quality becomes unacceptable (see **Figure 4.11**).

**I/O intensive**
requires input/output operations rather than heavy-duty processing power

Serving up static Web pages is **I/O intensive**, which means it requires input/output (I/O) operations rather than heavy-duty processing power. As a result, Web site performance is constrained primarily by the server's I/O limitations and the telecommunications connection, rather than speed of the processor.

There are some steps you can take to make sure that you stay within an acceptable service quality. One step is to simply purchase a server with faster CPU processors, multiple CPU processors, or larger hard disk drives. However, the resulting improvement is not linear and at some point becomes cost-ineffective. **Figure 4.12** on page 236 shows the theoretical performance of a Web server as processors are added from a single processor up to eight processors. By increasing processors by a factor of eight, you get only three times more load capacity.

**user profile**
refers to the nature of customer requests and customer behavior at a site

A second factor to consider on the demand side is the **user profile**, which refers to the nature of customer requests and customer behavior on your site (how many pages customers request and the kind of service they want). Web servers can be very efficient at serving static Web pages. However, as customers request more advanced services, such as site searches, registration, order taking via shopping carts, or downloads of large audio and video files, all of which require more processing power, performance can deteriorate rapidly.

The nature of the content your site offers is a third factor to consider. If your site uses dynamic page generation, the load on the processor rises rapidly and performance will degrade. Dynamic page generation and business logic (such as a shopping cart) are **CPU-intensive** operations—they require a great deal of processing power. For instance, a site with only dynamic page content can expect performance of a single processor server to fall to one-tenth the levels described in Figure 4.12. Instead of effectively serving 8,000 users, you can only service 1,000 concurrent users. Any interaction with the user requiring access to a database—filling out forms, adding to carts, purchasing, and completing questionnaires—puts a heavy processing load on the server.

**CPU-intensive**
operations that require a great deal of processing power

A final factor to consider is the telecommunications link that your site has to the Web, and also the changing nature of the client connection to the Web. **Figure 4.13** on page 237 shows that the number of hits per second your site can handle depends on the bandwidth connection between your server and the Web. The larger the bandwidth available, the more customers can simultaneously hit your site. For example, if your connection to the Web is a 1.5 Mbps DSL line, the maximum number of visitors per second for 1 kilobyte files is probably about 100. Most businesses host their sites at an ISP or other provider that contractually is (or should be) obligated to provide enough bandwidth for your site to meet peak demands. However, there are no guarantees and ISPs can blame Web congestion

| FIGURE 4.11 | DEGRADATION IN PERFORMANCE AS NUMBER OF USERS INCREASES |
|---|---|

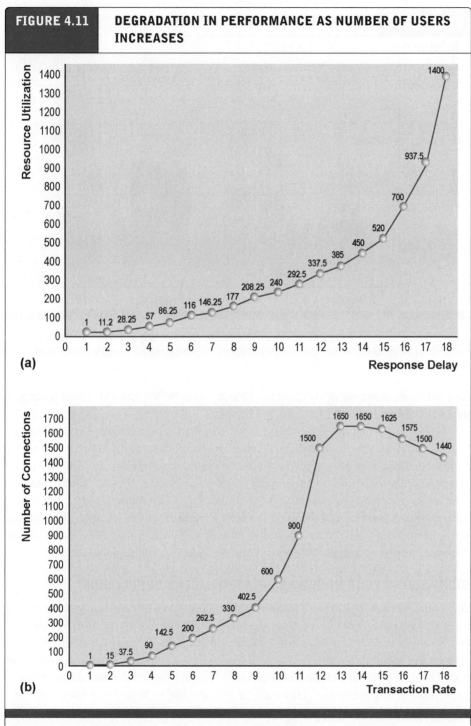

Degradation in Web server performance occurs as the number of users (connections) increases, and as the systems resources (processors, disk drives) become more utilized. In (a), user-experienced delay rises gracefully until an inflection point is reached, and then delay rises exponentially to an unacceptable level. In (b), the transaction rate rises gracefully until the number of users rapidly escalates the transaction rate, and at a certain inflection point, the transaction rate starts declining as the system slows down or crashes.

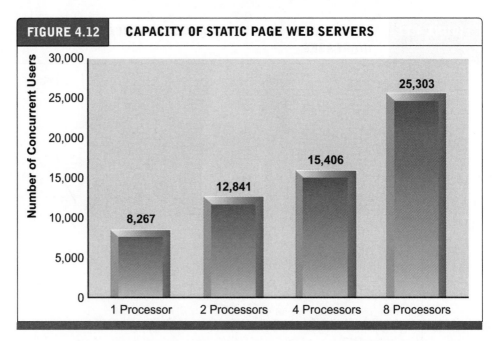

**FIGURE 4.12** **CAPACITY OF STATIC PAGE WEB SERVERS**

A typical Web server with a a single Intel Xeon 3 GHz processor that is serving only static Web pages can handle about 8,000 concurrent users. With eight processors, the same computer could handle about 25,000 concurrent users.

for their own bandwidth limitations. Check your ISP's bandwidth and your site performance daily.

While server bandwidth connections are less a constraint today with the widespread deployment of fiber-optic cable, the connection to the client is improving and this will have implications for your customers' expectations. In 2010, there are approximately 79.5 million broadband households in the United States, and this number is expected to increase to over 91 million by 2014 (eMarketer, Inc., 2010). This means your customers will be able to make far more frequent requests and demand far richer content like videos, games, podcasts, and simulations. This demand will translate quickly into dynamic content and the need for additional capacity.

### RIGHT-SIZING YOUR HARDWARE PLATFORM: THE SUPPLY SIDE

**scalability**
refers to the ability of a site to increase in size as demand warrants

**vertical scaling**
increasing the processing power of individual components

Once you estimate the likely demand on your site, you will need to consider how to scale up your site to meet demand. Once you estimate the likely demand on your site, you will need to consider how to scale up your site to meet demand. We have already discussed one solution that requires very little thought: outsource the hosting of your Web site to a cloud-based service. See Chapter 3 for a discussion of cloud-based computing services. However, if you decide to host your own Web site, scalability is an important consideration. **Scalability** refers to the ability of a site to increase in size as demand warrants. There are three steps you can take to meet the demands for service at your site: scale hardware vertically, scale hardware horizontally, and/or improve the processing architecture of the site (see **Table 4.8**). **Vertical scaling** refers to increasing the processing power of individual components.

| FIGURE 4.13 | THE RELATIONSHIP OF BANDWIDTH TO HITS |
|---|---|

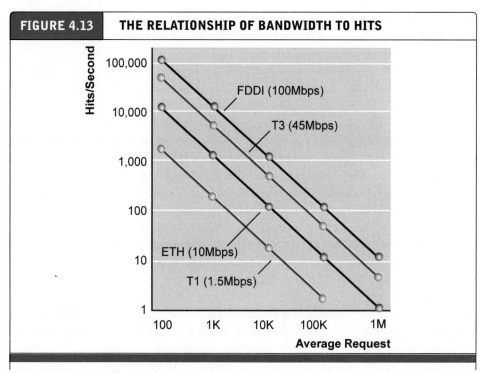

The greater the bandwidth available, the more customers can simultaneously access a Web site without any perceived degradation in performance. SOURCE: IBM, 2003.

**Horizontal scaling** refers to employing multiple computers to share the workload and increase the "footprint" of the installation (IBM, 2002).

**horizontal scaling**
employing multiple computers to share the workload

You can scale your site vertically by upgrading the servers from a single processor to multiple processors (see **Figure 4.14**). You can keep adding processors to a computer depending on the operating system and upgrade to faster chip speeds as well.

There are two drawbacks to vertical scaling. First, it can become expensive to purchase additional processors with every growth cycle, and second, your entire site

| TABLE 4.8 | VERTICAL AND HORIZONTAL SCALING TECHNIQUES |
|---|---|
| TECHNIQUE | APPLICATION |
| Use a faster computer | Applies to edge servers, presentation servers, data servers, etc. |
| Create a cluster of computers | Use computers in parallel to balance loads. |
| Use appliance servers | Special-purpose computers optimized for their task. |
| Segment workload | Segment incoming work to specialized computers. |
| Batch requests | Combine related requests for data into groups, process as group. |
| Manage connections | Reduce connections between processes and computers to a minimum. |
| Aggregate user data | Aggregate user data from legacy applications in single data pools. |
| Cache | Store frequently used data in cache rather than on the disk. |

becomes dependent on a small number of very powerful computers. If you have two such computers and one goes down, half of your site, or perhaps your entire site, may become unavailable.

Horizontal scaling involves adding multiple single-processor servers to your site and balancing the load among the servers. You can also then partition the load so that some servers handle only requests for HTML or ASP pages, while others are dedicated to handling database applications. You will need special load-balancing software (provided by a variety of vendors such as Cisco, Microsoft, and IBM) to direct incoming requests to various servers (see **Figure 4.15**).

There are many advantages to horizontal scaling. It is inexpensive and often can be accomplished using older PCs that otherwise would be disposed of. Horizontal scaling also introduces redundancy—if one computer fails, chances are that another computer can pick up the load dynamically. However, when your site grows from a single computer to perhaps 10 to 20 computers, the size of the physical facility required (the "footprint") increases and there is added management complexity.

A third alternative—improving the processing architecture—is a combination of vertical and horizontal scaling, combined with artful design decisions. **Table 4.9** on page 240 lists some of the more common steps you can take to greatly improve performance of your site. Most of these steps involve splitting the workload into I/O-intensive activities (such as serving Web pages) and CPU-intensive activities (such as taking orders). Once you have this work separated, you can fine-tune the servers for each type of load. One of the least expensive fine-tuning steps is to simply add RAM to a few servers and store all your HTML pages in RAM. This reduces load on your hard drives and increases speed dramatically. RAM is thousands of times faster than hard disks, and RAM is inexpensive. The next most important step is to move your CPU-intensive activities, such as order taking, onto a high-end, multiple processor server that is totally dedicated to handling orders and accessing the necessary databases. Taking these steps can permit you to reduce the number of servers required to service 10,000 concurrent users from 100 down to 20, according to one estimate.

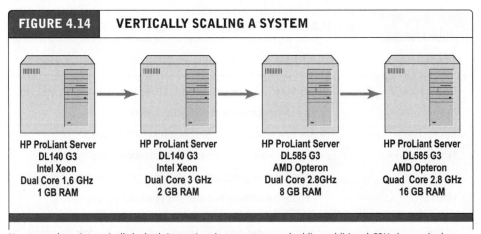

| **FIGURE 4.14** | **VERTICALLY SCALING A SYSTEM** |

HP ProLiant Server
DL140 G3
Intel Xeon
Dual Core 1.6 GHz
1 GB RAM

HP ProLiant Server
DL140 G3
Intel Xeon
Dual Core 3 GHz
2 GB RAM

HP ProLiant Server
DL585 G3
AMD Opteron
Dual Core 2.8GHz
8 GB RAM

HP ProLiant Server
DL585 G3
AMD Opteron
Quad Core 2.8 GHz
16 GB RAM

You can scale a site vertically by both improving the processors and adding additional CPUs into a single physical server.

**FIGURE 4.15** | **HORIZONTALLY SCALING A SYSTEM**

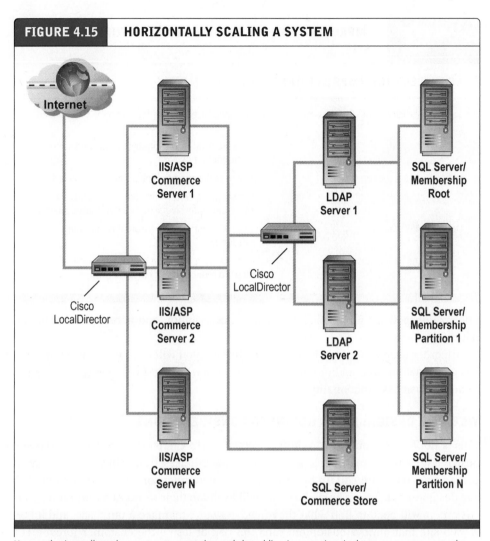

You can horizontally scale a system to meet demands by adding inexpensive single-processor servers to the site and using load-balancing software to allocate incoming customer requests to the correct server, shown in the diagram as a Cisco LocalDirector.

## 4.4 OTHER E-COMMERCE SITE TOOLS

Now that you understand the key factors that affect the speed, capacity, and scalability of your site, we can consider some other important requirements for your Web site. You will need a coherent Web site design effort that makes business sense—not necessarily a site to wow visitors or excite them, but to sell them something. You will also need to know how to build active content and interactivity into your site—not just display static HTML pages. You will definitely want to be able to track customers who come, leave, and return to your site in order to be able to greet return visitors ("Hi Sarah, welcome back!"). You will also want to track customers throughout your site so you can personalize and customize their experience. Finally, you will need to establish a set of

| TABLE 4.9 | IMPROVING THE PROCESSING ARCHITECTURE OF YOUR SITE |
|---|---|
| **ARCHITECTURE IMPROVEMENT** | **DESCRIPTION** |
| Separate static content from dynamic content | Use specialized servers for each type of workload. |
| Cache static content | Increase RAM to the gigabyte range and store static content in RAM. |
| Cache database lookup tables | Cache tables used to look up database records. |
| Consolidate business logic on dedicated servers | Put shopping cart, credit card processing, and other CPU-intensive activity on dedicated servers. |
| Optimize ASP code | Examine your code to ensure it is operating efficiently. |
| Optimize the database schema | Examine your database search times and take steps to reduce access times. |

information policies for your site—privacy, accessibility, and access to information policies.

In order to achieve these business capabilities, you will need to be aware of some design guidelines and additional software tools that can cost-effectively achieve the required business functionality.

## WEB SITE DESIGN: BASIC BUSINESS CONSIDERATIONS

This is not a text about how to design Web sites. (In Chapter 7, we discuss Web site design issues from a marketing perspective.) Nevertheless, from a business manager's perspective, there are certain design objectives you must communicate to your Web site designers to let them know how you will evaluate their work. At a minimum, your customers will need to find what they need at your site, make a purchase, and leave. A Web site that annoys customers runs the risk of losing the customer forever. For instance, a survey by Hostway found that about 75% of respondents said they were extremely or somewhat likely to not visit an offending site again and to unsubscribe from the offending company's promotional messages when they encounter one of their "pet peeves," and around 71% said they might refuse to purchase from the Web site and would view the company in a negative way. About 55% said they would complain about the Web site to friends and associates, and 45% said they might even refuse to make purchases in the company's offline stores (Hostway, 2007). See **Figure 4.16** for a list of the most common consumer complaints about Web sites.

Some critics believe poor design is more common than good design. It appears easier to describe what irritates people about Web sites than to describe how to design a good Web site. The worst e-commerce sites make it difficult to find information about their products and make it complicated to purchase goods; they have missing pages and broken links, a confusing navigation structure, and annoying graphics or sounds that you cannot turn off. **Table 4.10** restates these negative experiences as positive goals for Web site design.

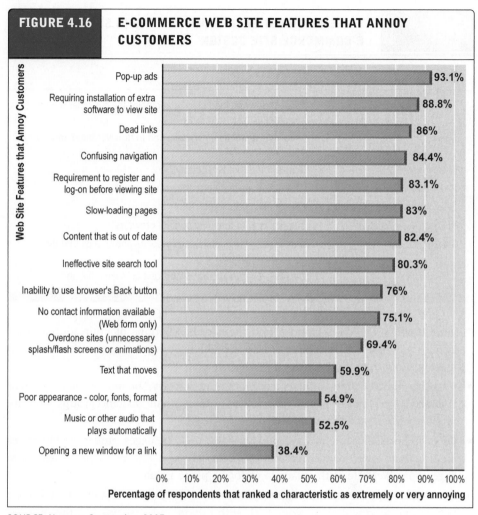

**FIGURE 4.16**    **E-COMMERCE WEB SITE FEATURES THAT ANNOY CUSTOMERS**

SOURCE: Hostway Corporation, 2007.

## TOOLS FOR WEB SITE OPTIMIZATION

A Web site is only as valuable from a business perspective as the number of people who visit. Web site optimization (as we use it here) means how to attract lots of people to your site. One answer, of course, is through search engines such as Google, Bing, Ask, and several hundred others. The first stop for most customers looking for a product or service is to start with a search engine, and follow the listings on the page, usually starting with the top three to five listings, then glancing to the sponsored ads to the right. The higher you are on the search engine pages, the more traffic you will receive. Page 1 is much better than Page 2. So how do you get to Page 1 in the natural (unpaid) search listings? While every search engine is different, and none of them publish their algorithms for ranking pages, there are some basic ideas that work well:

- **Metatags, titles, page contents:** Search engines "crawl" your site and identify keywords as well as title pages and then index them for use in search arguments. Pepper your pages with keywords that accurately describe what you say you do in

| TABLE 4.10 | THE EIGHT MOST IMPORTANT FACTORS IN SUCCESSFUL E-COMMERCE SITE DESIGN |
|---|---|
| **FACTOR** | **DESCRIPTION** |
| Functionality | Pages that work, load quickly, and point the customer toward your product offerings |
| Informational | Links that customers can easily find to discover more about you and your products |
| Ease of use | Simple fool-proof navigation |
| Redundant navigation | Alternative navigation to the same content |
| Ease of purchase | One or two clicks to purchase |
| Multi-browser functionality | Site works with the most popular browsers |
| Simple graphics | Avoids distracting, obnoxious graphics and sounds that the user cannot control |
| Legible text | Avoids backgrounds that distort text or make it illegible |

your metatag site "description" and "keywords" sections of your source code. Experiment: use different keywords to see which work. "Vintage cars" may attract more visitors than "antique cars," or "restored cars."

- **Identify market niches:** Instead of marketing "jewelry," be more specific, such as "Victorian jewelry," or "1950s jewelry" to attract small, specific groups who are intensely interested in period jewelry.

- **Offer expertise:** White papers, industry analyses, FAQ pages, guides, and histories are excellent ways to build confidence on the part of users and to encourage them to see your Web site as the place to go for help and guidance.

- **Get linked up:** Encourage other sites to link to your site; build a blog that attracts people and who will share your URL with others and post links in the process. List your site with Yahoo Directory for $300 a year. Build a Facebook page for your company, and think about using Twitter to develop a following or fan base for your products.

- **Buy ads:** Complement your natural search optimization efforts with paid search engine keywords and ads. Choose your keywords and purchase direct exposure on Web pages. You can set your budget and put a ceiling on it to prevent large losses. See what works, and observe the number of visits to your site produced by each keyword string.

- **Local e-commerce:** Developing a national market can take a long time. If your Web site is particularly attractive to local people, or involves products sold locally, use keywords that connote your location so people can find you nearby. Town, city, and region names in your keywords can be helpful, such as "Vermont cheese" or "San Francisco blues music."

## TOOLS FOR INTERACTIVITY AND ACTIVE CONTENT

As a manager responsible for building a Web site, you will want to ensure that users can interact with your Web site quickly and easily. As we describe in later chapters, the more interactive a Web site is, the more effective it will be in generating sales and encouraging return visitors.

Although functionality and ease of use are the supreme objectives in site design, you will also want to interact with users and present them with a lively "active" experience. You will want to personalize the experience for customers by addressing their individual needs, and customize the content of your offerings based on their behavior or expressed desires. For example, you may want to offer customers free mortgage calculations or free pension advice, based on their interaction with programs available at your site. In order to achieve these business objectives, you will need to consider carefully the tools necessary to build these capabilities. Simple interactions such as a customer submitting a name, along with more complex interactions involving credit cards, user preferences, and user responses to prompts, all require special programs. The following sections provide a brief description of some commonly used software tools for achieving high levels of site interactivity.

## Bling for Your Blog: Web 2.0 Design Elements

One easy way to pump up the energy on your Web site is to include some appropriate widgets (sometimes called gadgets, plug-ins, or snippets). **Widgets** are small chunks of code that execute automatically in your HTML Web page. They are pre-built and many are free. Social networks and blogs use widgets to present users with content drawn from around the Web (news headlines from specific news sources, announcements, press releases, and other routine content), calendars, clocks, weather, live TV, games, and other functionality. You can copy the code to an HTML Web page. A good place to start is Google Gadgets and Yahoo Widgets.

Mashups are a little more complicated, and as explained in Chapter 3, involve pulling functionality and data from one program and including it another. The most common mashup involves using Google Maps data and software and combining it with other data. For instance, if you have a local real estate Web site, you can download Google Maps and satellite images applications to your site so visitors can get a sense of the neighborhood. There are thousands of Google Map mashups, from maps of Myanmar political protests, to maps of the Fortune 500 companies, all with associated news stories and other content. Other mashups involve sports, photos, video, shopping, and news.

The point of these Web 2.0 applications is to enhance user interest and involvement in your site, and to easily include sophisticated functionality and unique data in your Web site.

## Common Gateway Interface (CGI)

**Common Gateway Interface (CGI)** is a set of standards for communication between a browser and a program running on a server that allows for interaction between the user and the server. CGI permits an executable program to access all the information within incoming requests from clients. The program can then generate all the output required to make up the return page (the HTML, script code, text, etc.), and send it back to the client via the Web server. For instance, if a user clicks the My Shopping Cart button, the server receives this request and executes a CGI program. The CGI program retrieves the contents of the shopping cart from the database and returns it to the server. The server sends an HTML page that displays the contents of the shop-

**widget**
a small, pre-built chunk of code that executes automatically in your HTML Web page; capable of performing a wide variety of tasks

**Common Gateway Interface (CGI)**
a set of standards for communication between a browser and a program running on a server that allows for interaction between the user and the server

ping cart on the user's screen. Notice all the computing takes place on the server side (this is why CGI programs and others like it are referred to as "server-side" programs).

CGI programs can be written in nearly any programming language as long as they conform to CGI standards. Currently, Perl is the most popular language for CGI scripting. Generally, CGI programs are used with Unix servers. CGI's primary disadvantage is that it is not highly scalable because a new process must be created for each request, thereby limiting the number of concurrent requests that can be handled. CGI scripts are best used for small to medium-sized applications that do not involve a high volume of user traffic. There are also Web server extensions available, such as FastCGI, that improve CGI's scalability (Doyle and Lopes, 2005).

## Active Server Pages (ASP)

**Active Server Pages (ASP)** a proprietary software development tool that enables programmers using Microsoft's IIS package to build dynamic pages

**Active Server Pages (ASP)** is Microsoft's version of server-side programming for Windows. Invented by Microsoft in late 1996, ASP has grown rapidly to become the major technique for server-side Web programming in the Windows environment. ASP enables developers to easily create and open records from a database and execute programs within an HTML page, as well as handle all the various forms of interactivity found on e-commerce sites. Like CGI, ASP permits an interaction to take place between the browser and the server. ASP uses the same standards as CGI for communication with the browser. ASP programs are restricted to use on Windows 2003/2000/NT Web servers running Microsoft's IIS Web server software.

## Java, Java Server Pages (JSP), and JavaScript

**Java** a programming language that allows programmers to create interactivity and active content on the client computer, thereby saving considerable load on the server

**Java** is a programming language that allows programmers to create interactivity and active content on the client computer, thereby saving considerable load on the server. Java was invented by Sun Microsystems in 1990 as a platform-independent programming language for consumer electronics. The idea was to create a language whose programs (so-called Write Once Run Anywhere [WORA] programs) could operate on any computer regardless of operating system. This would be possible if every operating system at the time (Macintosh, Windows, Unix, DOS, and mainframe MVS systems) had a Java Virtual Machine (VM) installed that would interpret the Java programs for that environment.

By 1995, it had become clear, however, that Java was more applicable to the Web than to consumer electronics. Java programs (known as Java applets) could be downloaded to the client over the Web and executed entirely on the client's computer. Applet tags could be included in an HTML page. To enable this, each browser would have to include a Java VM. Today, the leading browsers do include a VM to play Java programs. When the browser accesses a page with an applet, a request is sent to the server to download and execute the program and allocate page space to display the results of the program. Java can be used to display interesting graphics, create interactive environments (such as a mortgage calculator), and directly access the Web server.

Different vendors, including Microsoft, IBM, HP, and others, have produced several versions of the Java language, and even different VMs. Java applets built using Microsoft Java can play well only on Microsoft's Internet Explorer browser. Therefore, the objective of having Java applets play the same on all Web clients has not succeeded. Many corporations will not allow Java applets through their firewalls for security reasons. Despite the fact that Java applets do not have access to local client system resources (they operate in a "sandbox" for security reasons), information system security managers are extremely reluctant to allow applets served from remote servers to come through the firewall. Many Java applets crash or do not perform well, wasting system resources, and when they do perform, the functions are often trivial (such as flashing logos).

**Java Server Pages (JSP)**, like CGI and ASP, is a Web page coding standard that allows developers to use a combination of HTML, JSP scripts, and Java to dynamically generate Web pages in response to user requests. JSP uses Java "servlets," small Java programs that are specified in the Web page and run on the Web server to modify the Web page before it is sent to the user who requested it. JSP is supported by most of the popular application servers on the market today.

**JavaScript** is a programming language invented by Netscape that is used to control the objects on an HTML page and handle interactions with the browser. It is most commonly used to handle verification and validation of user input, as well as to implement business logic. For instance, JavaScript can be used on customer registration forms to confirm that a valid phone number, zip code, or even e-mail address has been given. Before a user finishes completing a form, the e-mail address given can be tested for validity. JavaScript appears to be much more acceptable to corporations and other environments in large part because it is more stable and also it is restricted to the operation of requested HTML pages.

## ActiveX and VBScript

Microsoft—not to be outdone by Sun Microsystems and Netscape—invented the **ActiveX** programming language to compete with Java and **VBScript** to compete with JavaScript. When a browser receives an HTML page with an ActiveX control (comparable to a Java applet), the browser simply executes the program. Unlike Java, however, ActiveX has full access to all the client's resources—printers, networks, and hard drives. VBScript performs in the same way as JavaScript. Of course, ActiveX and VBScript work only if you are using Internet Explorer. Otherwise, that part of the screen is blank.

In general, given the conflicting standards for Java, ActiveX, and VBScript, and the diversity of user client computers, many e-commerce sites choose to steer clear of these tools. CGI scripts, JSP, and JavaScript are the leading tools for providing active, dynamic content.

## ColdFusion

**ColdFusion** is an integrated server-side environment for developing interactive Web applications. Originally developed by Macromedia and now offered by Adobe, ColdFusion combines an intuitive tag-based scripting language and a tag-based server scripting language (CFML) that lowers the cost of creating interactive features. ColdFusion offers a powerful set of visual design, programming, debugging, and deployment tools.

**Java Server Pages (JSP)**
like CGI and ASP, a Web page coding standard that allows developers to dynamically generate Web pages in response to user requests

**JavaScript**
a programming language invented by Netscape that is used to control the objects on an HTML page and handle interactions with the browser

**ActiveX**
a programming language created by Microsoft to compete with Java

**VBScript**
a programming language invented by Microsoft to compete with JavaScript

**ColdFusion**
an integrated server-side environment for developing interactive Web applications

## PERSONALIZATION TOOLS

You will definitely want to know how to treat each customer on an individual basis and emulate a traditional face-to-face marketplace. *Personalization* (the ability to treat people based on their personal qualities and prior history with your site) and *customization* (the ability to change the product to better fit the needs of the customer) are two key elements of e-commerce that potentially can make it nearly as powerful as a traditional marketplace, and perhaps even more powerful than direct mail or shopping at an anonymous suburban shopping mall. Speaking directly to the customer on a one-to-one basis, and even adjusting the product to the customer is quite difficult in the usual type of mass marketing, one-size-fits-all commercial transaction that characterizes much of contemporary commerce.

There are a number of methods for achieving personalization and customization. For instance, you could personalize Web content if you knew the personal background of the visitor. You could also analyze the pattern of clicks and sites visited for every customer who enters your site. We discuss these methods in later chapters on marketing. The primary method for achieving personalization and customization is through the placement of cookie files on the user's client computer. As we discussed in Chapter 3, a cookie is a small text file placed on the user's client computer that can contain any kind of information about the customer, such as customer ID, campaign ID, or purchases at the site. And then, when the user returns to the site, or indeed goes further into your site, the customer's prior history can be accessed from a database. Information gathered on prior visits can then be used to personalize the visit and customize the product.

For instance, when a user returns to a site, you can read the cookie to find a customer ID, look the ID up in a database of names, and greet the customer ("Hello Mary! Glad to have you return!"). You could also have stored a record of prior purchases, and then recommend a related product ("How about the wrench tool box now that you have purchased the wrenches?"). And you could think about customizing the product ("You've shown an interest in the elementary training programs for Word. We have a special 'How to Study' program for beginners in Office software. Would you like to see a sample copy online?").

We further describe the use of cookies and their effectiveness in achieving a one-to-one relationship with the customer in Chapter 8.

## THE INFORMATION POLICY SET

**privacy policy**
a set of public statements declaring to your customers how you treat their personal information that you gather on the site

**accessibility rules**
a set of design objectives that ensure disabled users can effectively access your site

In developing an e-commerce site, you will also need to focus on the set of information policies that will govern the site. You will need to develop a **privacy policy**—a set of public statements declaring to your customers how you treat their personal information that you gather on the site. You also will need to establish **accessibility rules**—a set of design objectives that ensure disabled users can effectively access your site. There are more than 50 million Americans who are disabled and require special access routes to buildings as well as computer systems (see *Insight on Society: Designing for Accessibility in Web 2.0*). E-commerce information policies are described in greater depth in Chapter 8.

# INSIGHT ON SOCIETY

## DESIGNING FOR ACCESSIBILITY IN WEB 2.0

Ever see a popular YouTube video with captions that can be read by the hearing impaired? Ever roll your mouse over an Amazon product page with your Internet Explorer accessibility features turned on and hear an audio description of the products and prices so sight-impaired people can understand the page? Chances are the answer in both cases is "No." Why not? About 54 million Americans have a disability; 35 million have a severe disability. About 8 million have a hard time reading a newspaper, 8 million cannot hear a conversation, and 16 million have cognitive, mental, or emotional functional disabilities. The prevalence of disabilities in the population will only increase as the population ages.

These and other disabilities can be addressed on the Web with intelligent software and hardware design. For the most part, this is not the case. As a result, the Internet is an unfriendly place for many disabled in America. To begin to remedy these issues, the Federal Communications Commission in April 2010 published a white paper as a part of the expansion of broadband Internet access in the United States, calling for stronger accessibility legislation for broadband service devices, from smartphones to social network sites. This report followed a 2009 effort to legislate changes for Web 2.0 devices and services called the "Twenty-first Century Communications and Video Accessibility Act of 2009."

Disability advocates are also using lawsuits to move the ball forward. In January 2010 Arizona State University (ASU) reached an agreement with blind plaintiffs represented by the National Federation of the Blind and the American Council of the Blind. In July 2009, both had

sued ASU to stop ASU's planned use of Kindle e-book reading devices in a pilot program that would be inaccessible to blind students. Although the Kindle has audio capabilities, and some books would be available in audio form, the menu structure of the Kindle cannot be driven by verbal commands, and most books would not have audio editions. Working with support of Amazon, ASU planned to roll out the Kindle reader campus-wide sometime in 2010 as an experiment and demonstration. For students, Kindle textbooks are available at roughly half the price of a standard book. Four other universities (Princeton, Case Western Reserve, Reed College, Pace University, and University of Virginia) involved in the Amazon trial rollout agreed along with ASU to shelve the Kindle reader experiment until these devices can be used fully by blind students. Amazon is working on changes to the Kindle that make it more friendly for disabled persons.

The lawsuit and settlement raised concerns at the Department of Education and the Justice Department. In June 2010, the Department of Education sent a letter to university presidents and deans requiring colleges that use e-book devices in the classroom to ensure these devices are fully functional for blind students. Otherwise the universities would be in violation of federal law. Similar requirements apply to all K-12 educational institutions in the United States.

In 1998, Congress amended the Rehabilitation Act to require U.S. agencies, government contractors, and others receiving federal money to make electronic and information technology services accessible to people with disabilities. Known as Section 508, this legislation requires Web sites of federally funded organizations to be accessible to users who are blind, deaf, blind and

(continued)

deaf, or unable to use a mouse. However, the legislation applies only to U.S. agencies, government contractors, and others receiving federal money, and not to the broader e-commerce environment of private business firms.

In one of the first lawsuits seeking to enforce Section 508 for Internet services, Access Now Inc., an advocacy group for the disabled, sued Southwest Airlines in 2001 on behalf of more than 50 million disabled Americans for operating a Web site that was inaccessible to the disabled, on the grounds that this violated the 1990 Americans with Disabilities Act (ADA). In November 2002, a Federal District Court in Florida, in one of the first court decisions on the applicability of the ADA to Web sites, ruled that ADA applies only to physical spaces, not virtual spaces. However, the judge noted in a footnote that she was surprised that a customer-oriented firm like Southwest Airlines did not "employ all available technologies to expand accessibility to its Web site for visually impaired customers who would be an added source of revenue."

Since this early decision, however, both the interpretation of the law and public sentiment have resulted in many well-known Web sites attempting to conform to the spirit of Section 508, sometimes voluntarily and sometimes under threat from advocacy groups. For instance, RadioShack, Amazon, Ramada, and Priceline have entered into agreements with the American Council for the Blind, and the American Foundation for the Blind. Meanwhile, the National Federation of the Blind (NFB) brought a class action suit against Target for failing to make its site accessible for the blind. They claimed that blind people could not use Target's shopping cart because it required use of a mouse, used inaccessible image maps and graphics, and lacked compliant alt-text, an invisible code embedded beneath graphics that allows screen reading software to vocalize a description of the image. Target claimed the ADA did not apply to Web sites.

In September 2006, a federal district court ruled that ADA did indeed apply to Web sites. The court held "the 'ordinary meaning' of the ADA's prohibition against discrimination in the enjoyment of goods, services, facilities, or privileges is that whatever goods or services the place provides, it cannot discriminate on the basis of disability in providing enjoyment of those goods and services." The court thus rejected Target's argument that only its physical store locations were covered by the civil rights laws, ruling instead that all services provided by Target, including its Web site, must be accessible to persons with disabilities. In October 2007, the court granted class-action status to the lawsuit.

In August 2008, Target and the NFB settled the suit. Target made no admission or concession that its Web site violated the ADA, but agreed to bring it into compliance with certain online assistive technology guidelines by February 28, 2009, and to have the NFB certify that it is compliant with those guidelines. In addition, Target agreed to pay damages of $6 million. Many accessibility advocates expressed disappointment that the resolution of the case via a settlement failed to provide any clear legal precedent. Nevertheless, a prudent e-commerce firm with a customer orientation will use available technologies to expand accessibility to its Web site for impaired customers both to expand its customer base and avoid costly and embarrassing litigation.

So how does a blind person access the Web, and how should designers build in accessibility for the blind? Most blind persons use the same computers as everyone else. But a blind person's computer uses screen-reader software that translates text information on the screen into synthesized speech or Braille. Internet Explorer is the Web browser most typically used, although other browsers are also available, such as Lynx (a text only browser written originally to run under Unix) and IBM's Home Page Reader, which generate their own speech.

A blind person navigates a Web page by checking the hypertext links on the page, usually by jumping from link to link with the Tab key; the screen-reader software automatically reads the highlighted text as the focus moves from link to link. If the highlighted text is something like "How to Contact Us," a blind user will likely be able to make sense out of the link. If, however, the highlighted text is "Click Here," or "Here," it will be difficult, if not impossible, for a blind user to interpret the meaning of the link without using a different navigation strategy. With the more recent screen-reader software/browser combinations, it is possible for a blind Web surfer to explore the page one line at a time, thus alleviating this problem. However, being forced to examine every detail of a Web page just to learn the meaning of a hypertext link is a time-consuming process that, ideally, should be avoided. The important point to keep in mind is that the screen-reader software is looking for ASCII text, which it can convert to speech or Braille.

Once the desired hypertext link has been located, the blind person presses the Enter key (clicks on the link) to go where the link points. If there is a form to fill out on the page, the blind person will usually tab to the appropriate input field and type the information in the usual way. Other controls such as checkboxes, combo boxes, radio buttons, and the like can all be used if the screen-reader software can detect them. There are several simple strategies Web designers can use to improve accessibility. Embedding text descriptions behind images is one example that allows screen readers to announce those descriptions. So instead of saying "Image," when a screen reader passes over an image, the visually impaired user can hear "Photo of a cruise ship sitting in a harbor." Allowing users to set the color and font schemes can also make a difference for the visually impaired. Adding screen magnification tools and sound labels where hyperlinks appear are two additional ways to increase accessibility.

These are examples of "equivalent alternatives" to visual content that disability advocates suggest should be required, both for visual and auditory content, to ensure individuals with disabilities have equal access information that appears on-screen. Guidelines for creating accessible Web pages include ensuring that text and graphics are understandable when viewed without color, using features that enable activation of page elements via a variety of input devices (such as keyboard, head wand, or Braille reader), and providing clear navigation mechanisms (such as navigation bars or a site map) to aid users.

The World Wide Web Consortium (W3C) issued Web Content Accessibility Guidelines (WCAG) 2.0 in June 2010 (final draft form) that provide all organizations with strategies in Web design for accommodating people with many different kinds of disabilities. Some of the problems encountered by disabled users include so-called "captchas" or distorted text that people are supposed to read and then reenter into a text box to gain access to a site; check-out buttons that are images rather than text and cannot be read by text-reading software; and YouTube videos without captions.

■■■ **SOURCES**: "Federal Government Requiring Colleges to Include Blind-friendly Electronic book Readers," by Dorie Turner, Associated Press, June 29th, 2010; "W3C "Web Accessibility Initiative [Final Draft]," WC3.org, June 2010; "A Giant Leap and a Big Deal:Delivering on the Promise of Equal Access to Broadband for People with Disabilities," Federal Communications Commission, April 23, 2010; "21st Century Communications and Video Accessibility Act of 2009," Hearings, 111th Congress, House of Representatives, H.R. 3101, April 2010; "A Giant Leap & a Big Deal," by Elizabeth Lyle, Federal Communications Commission, Working Paper Series No. 2, April 2010. "Blindness Organizations and Arizona State University Resolve Litigation Over Kindle," National Federation of the Blind, Press Release, January 11, 2010; "Web Accessibility: Making Your Site Accessible to the Blind," by Curtiss Chong, National Federation of the Blind, accessed August 14, 2009.

**CASE STUDY**

# REI

Climbs the Web Mountain

Most stories about Web sites—usually "success stories"—imply that once the site is built it remains pretty much the same over the life of the company, the designers move on to other tasks, and the story ends. In fact, experienced Web site managers and designers know that Web sites are never "built," but instead are tweaked with minor improvements over time, and occasionally re-built completely from the ground up. Successful Web sites evolve over time. If it's a successful company with a long life, its Web sites go through major rebuilds every few years as the technology, consumer expectations, products and services, and managerial experience all change. Recreational Equipment, Inc. (REI) exemplifies this reality.

Washington-based REI is one of the world's largest online retailers of outdoor gear. REI is also one of the e-commerce pioneers in the United States, having launched its first Web site in 1996. In 2010, the company is on its fourth Web site design. REI's story is the story of e-commerce for large national retailers as they adapt both to changing Internet technology and changing consumer taste and culture.

Lloyd and Mary Anderson, mountain climbers from Seattle, Washington, founded REI in 1938. The Andersons imported a special ice axe from Austria for themselves and decided to set up a cooperative to help their friends and other fellow outdoor enthusiasts acquire high-quality climbing and camping gear at reasonable prices. Today, REI is the largest consumer cooperative in the United States, with 3.9 million members who have paid a one-time membership fee of $20 that entitles them to an annual dividend equal to about 10% of their annual purchases. And the business has grown. Today, REI operates 110 retail stores in 27 states, two online stores, an international mail order operation, and REI Adventures, a travel agency. Kiosks in every store allow customers to access products at either of REI's Web sites: REI.com and REI-Outlet.com. REI employs over 9,500 people, and in 2009, generated over $1.45 billion in gross revenues, about $259 million of which comes from its online stores. In 2009, in the midst of recession, REI grew its online sales by 9% while its in-store sales shrunk by 3%.

REI first started exploring the Internet in the summer of 1995. Netscape, the first popular Internet browser, had just gone public, and e-commerce was just getting started. As with many business success stories, REI's online venture began with senior executives who recognized the potentially transformative power of the Web, and the mixture of opportunity and possible threat that it represented to their existing business.

Many traditional bricks-and-mortar retailers at that time feared cannibalization of their retail and/or catalog sales if they introduced an online sales outlet. Their nightmare was that starting an online store would merely "steal" their own customers from their regular sales channels. But REI wasn't deterred. As Dennis Madsen, REI's former president and chief executive officer, said, "We knew that if we could not serve our customers who were looking to shop with us online, they would turn to someone else online. It was never a question for us. Being online meant better serving the customer. Our experience has proven that cannibalization is largely a myth and that our multi-channel customers are our best customers. For instance, dual-channel customers who shopped both online and at stores spent 114% more than single-channel customers. And customers who shop three channels—retail stores, Web, and kiosks—spent 48% more than dual-channel customers."

REI launched its first Web site with a budget of approximately $500,000. At the time, Netscape was the only company offering a complete e-commerce suite, so REI chose Netscape's Merchant 4.5 Server software installed on an IBM RS/6000 server. And although Matt Hyde, the executive in charge of the launch, recognized that REI was a retailer by trade, not a programming shop, he chose to keep design of the site in-house, using off-the-shelf Web authoring tools rather than outsource creation of the Web site. The rationale: "When [we] took the leap of faith that we could launch this compelling value proposition, and that it could be big, [we] realized we needed to make this a core competency. It couldn't be outsourced."

The decision to "build their own" was not without its costs, however: managing REI.com's growth internally, with no outsourcing, strained REI's human resources. REI soon discovered that finding people with the requisite skills could be difficult, and even if they could be found, they were a lot more expensive than salespeople. In September 1996, at a time when few traditional retailers were even looking at online sales, REI.com launched, promoted primarily through direct mail and in-store notices. The Web was in its infancy, and the use of display banner ads and search engine marketing was primitive. The first order arrived 20 minutes later. By February 1997, Hyde and his team knew they were on the right track. Traffic was up by 50% in the two months following Christmas. But that in itself posed a problem. As Hyde remembers, "We chose Netscape early on, and they were clearly the leader [at that time]. But not long after getting the system up, we realized that it was too limited. When you go from a few thousand people checking out your site to a million every month, you need a lot of infrastructure." With thousands of product pages, each one hand-coded in HTML, changing prices or offerings was difficult and expensive.

He also noted, "On the surface, e-commerce sounds relatively easy. It's not until you have experience trying to integrate a high-volume, high-functionality Web site into existing business processes and applications that you realize that it's a lot harder than it seems. It's like an iceberg—the view from the browser is only 10% of what it takes to build a successful and profitable Web site."

In 1998, REI initiated its second Web site design. This time they had more of a choice in the marketplace for Web software and services. They looked at offerings from all the major vendors, including Microsoft, IBM, BroadVision, and Open Market. "When you change commerce packages, there's a huge learning curve. I was going to make this

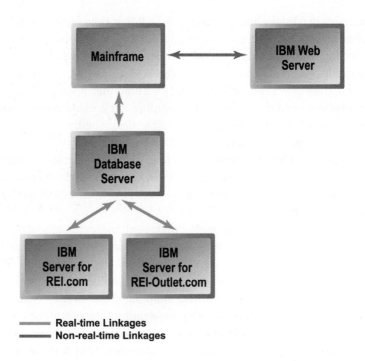

change once, but I wasn't going to do it again, so I wanted to pick the right package... for the next several years." In early 1998, REI decided on IBM's Net.Commerce server software. An important factor in the decision was IBM's ability to preserve all the custom coding REI had done over the past two years to connect its online store to its legacy system. "I had hundreds of thousands, if not millions of dollars tied up in this [system], and we didn't want to throw it away. And since Net.Commerce [would also lessen] the need to do custom coding in the future, it's a two-fold benefit." The new REI.com Web site launched in October 1998.

In 2002, REI began a third rebuilding of its Web site by standardizing on a single platform, IBM's WebSphere, an integrated set of e-commerce site development and operational tools. Prior to that point, REI's e-commerce infrastructure was a mixture of software applications written both in-house and by a variety of different technology vendors. In the period since REI's second re-build in 1998, IBM had developed a suite of tools and functionalities built on standards such as Java and Unix that included WebSphere Application Server and WebSphere Commerce, all running on IBM pSeries Unix-based servers that could be configured with multiple processors as necessary in order to scale the business (see figure above). With its focus on an integrated platform from a single vendor, REI has implemented extensive customer features utilizing the platform's capabilities in personalized service and information, as well as more convenience for both online and in-store shoppers. For instance, REI gained the ability to refer new Web customers to nearby stores that are having sales. It can e-mail coupons for bike helmets redeemable at local stores or online to customers who purchased a bicycle. WebSphere can drop an image of hiking boots featured at REI on to the screen of a customer reading an REI "Learn and Share" article on backpacking.

REI's clicks-and-bricks strategy has paid off handsomely. In addition to improving relationships with existing customers, the online stores have helped create new customers. Over a third of the online customers are not members of the REI cooperative, meaning they are likely new customers, compared to 15% of REI's retail customers. And despite management's early fears, the online stores haven't cannibalized traditional store sales. In fact, the opposite has occurred: the Web site has attracted new customers and strengthened the relationship with existing customers. A service enabled by the WebSphere Commerce platform, REI Store Pickup service, is a case in point. REI Store Pickup service provides in-store pickup as a free shipping option for online orders. To implement the service, REI combined its Web and store fulfillment systems, shipping customer merchandise to the stores on the same trucks that deliver the store's bi-weekly stock orders. The service has proved to be a tremendous success. In its first 12 months, in-store pickups from online sales accounted for $40 million in revenue, and they now account for about a third of online sales. Today, more than 40% of all orders generated on REI.com's Web site are delivered to stores for pickup, and one-third of the customers who pick up orders purchase an additional $90 in merchandise during the visit.

With the ascendancy of Google and search engine marketing, REI realized the importance of appearing on the first page of search engine queries. REI worked with a Web firm called Netconcepts to redesign its Web pages, end the practice of using dynamic URLs for pages, and in general make the catalog Web pages more friendly to search engine Web crawlers so its pages could be properly read. The result was a 200% gain in "natural search" sales produced without making payments to search engines. In 2006, REI began using a software service, Mercent Retail, to help it better manage referrals from comparison shopping portals such as Shopping.com and manufacturer Web sites. The service, which is integrated with REI's backend retail management software systems, helps REI maintain brand and merchandising consistency between its own Web sites and the various third-party sites, and optimizes the product links sent to each of its channel partners. In 2007, REI switched from its proprietary search engine to one from Mercado Software, enabling customers to quickly search for items by brand, price, or best sellers.

In 2008, REI initiated its fourth Web site redesign and completed the re-build in 2010. Today's Internet is more interactive, more personal, more social, and more video-oriented than in the past. REI's 2010 Web site would have been unimaginable in 1996, or even 2006. The emphasis of the new Web site is standardization, personalization, search, and social features (user written product reviews, and lots of on-site opportunities to send messages to friends via various social channels). The focus is on enhancing the shopping experience, resulting in longer average online sessions, and more sales. The average visitor session has increased by 14% to 11 minutes and 23 seconds from 10 minutes in 2007, says Web measurement firm Hitwise.

When you run a Web site with a handful of pages, it's possible to hand-code each page. When you have 40,000 product pages, you need a standardized template in a database that allows you to make one change to the template, and then automatically roll out those changes to the 40,000 product pages. The new site also was built with standard templates on the back end that make it easier for Web developers and programmers to make changes to home and product pages. "It was time to move REI.com into the twenty-first century," says REI vice president of e-commerce and Web strategy Brad Brown. "We can now change the product page template, republish it, and each page that uses that template is updated with the change. One template for 4,000 product pages means one change results in all product pages being changed versus having to change each product page in the pre-template world."

To achieve more personalization, REI is using customer review technology from PowerReviews, Inc. and survey tools from OpinionLab Inc. REI now has 35,000 reviews posted on the site. To keep up with changing technologies and consumer culture, REI has created two free smart phone apps in 2010: Bike Your Drive, a free program that allows bikers to view their progress, save the mileage they've traveled, upload photos tagged by location, and report how much less carbon dioxide there is in the air as a result of their bike trip; and REI Snow Reports, which lets iPhone, BlackBerry, and Windows Mobile users get instant information about conditions at ski resorts and mountains in the United States, Canada, Europe, and elsewhere. Both free apps provide one-touch access to REI's e-commerce site. REI has numerous videos on its site, and plans more videos to augment the expert advice videos customers already can access on topics such as bike maintenance. For example, shoppers can watch a video on how to change a flat bicycle tire. Links for related products appear on the same page. In 2010, REI is implementing even more rich media, videocasts, and other Web 2.0 tools. Rich media applications from HeckYes! Productions enable shoppers to see products in 3-D and from different angles. RSS is another new tool that REI is using. As you learned in Chapter 3, RSS is a data feed that delivers updated information from selected Web sites directly to a subscriber's desktop. REI uses RSS to drive traffic to REI-Outlet.com's "deal of the day."

Continuing to evolve with its customer base, REI has experimented with music and music videos as a marketing tool to attract its young audience and keep them on site for longer periods of time. For instance, the company launched an REI Go Playlist of 10 songs exclusive to REI that customers could download from REIGoPlaylist.com. REI developed the songs in partnership with the bands and its snow sports brands. "All tracks are exclusive to REI Go Playlist and are not on any CDs or other sites," says a spokeswoman. Brand-name manufacturers sponsoring the list included Burton, K2, Marmot, Ride, Rossignol, Smith, Salomon, The North Face, and Völkl. "Through a wide range of music, we hope REI Go Playlist gets new and current customers and members excited about the upcoming skiing and snowboarding season," says Tom Vogl, REI's vice president of marketing. The program ran from October 2008 to March 2009, and was very successful.

REI is also putting the finishing touches on a three-year-long, multi-million dollar project to create a new data warehouse that will combine information collected in stores, on the Web, from call centers, and all other customer contacts into a single database. The data warehouse will allow REI to deliver highly targeted marketing messages and customer service: "People [like you] who like music by Robbers on High Street also like Rossignol skis." Staying atop the Web mountain requires both continuing innovation and investment. The emphasis in 2010 is on developing and enhancing a recommender system using software from Omniture called "Omniture Recommendations."

This software culls the REI data warehouse looking for products that customers often buy together, shopping history of the customer, "most viewed" and "top selling" products, and then presents the online customer with recommend products when shopping. While its too soon to measure the impact on sales, recommender systems can increase purchases by 10 to 20%.

### Case Study Questions

1. Create a simple logical design and physical design for REI.com using information provided in the case study, supplemented as necessary by your own research.

2. After reading the case study, identify the key reasons for REI.com's success thus far. Identify the changes in technology and customer expectations driven the evolution of REI.com?

3. Visit REI.com and rate its performance on the eight factors listed in Table 4.10 on a scale of 1 to 10 (with 1 being the lowest and 10 the highest). Provide reasons for your ratings.

4. Prepare a short industry analysis of the online outdoor sporting goods and apparel industry. Who are REI's primary competitors? How well have they developed multi-channel retailing?

**SOURCES**: "About Us," REI.com, August 2010; "Top 500 Guide, 2010 Edition," Internet Retailer, 2010; "REI Announces 2009 Revenues and Member Dividend; Net Income Recovers in a Challenging Retail Environment," Press Release, REI Inc. , March 22, 2010; "REI Outfits Its E-commerce Site With More Personalization Features," Internet Retailer, January 27, 2010; "REI Peddles Pedaling With a Free Tracking Program for Mobile Phones," Internet Retailer, July 8, 2009; "REI Gives Skiers and Snowboarders Their Own Mobile Application," Internet Retailer, December 18, 2008; "REI's Approach to Online Music: Free and Exclusive," Internet Retailer, October 24, 2008; "REI Makes Standardization the Bedrock of Its New Web Site Design," Internet Retailer, October 1, 2008; "REI Combines 20 Sources of Customer Information into One Data Warehouse," Internet Retailer, March 18, 2008; "Driving Sales," Internet Retailer, March 2008; REI's Online Performance Climbs with Mercent Retail," March 20, 2007,

## 4.6 REVIEW

## KEY CONCEPTS

■ Explain the process that should be followed in building an e-commerce Web site.

Factors you must consider when building an e-commerce site include:
- Hardware architecture
- Software
- Telecommunications capacity
- Site design
- Human resources
- Organizational capabilities

The systems development life cycle (a methodology for understanding the business objectives of a system and designing an appropriate solution) for building an e-commerce Web site involves five major steps:

- Identify the specific business objectives for the site, and then develop a list of system functionalities and information requirements.

- Develop a system design specification (both logical design and physical design).
- Build the site, either by in-house personnel or by outsourcing all or part of the responsibility to outside contractors.
- Test the system (unit testing, system testing, and acceptance testing).
- Implement and maintain the site.

The nine basic business and system functionalities an e-commerce site should contain include:

- *Digital catalog*—allows a site to display goods using text and graphics.
- *Product database*—provides product information, such as a description, stocking number, and inventory level.
- *Customer on-site tracking*—enables a site to create a site log for each customer visit, aiding in personalizing the shopping experience and identifying common customer paths and destinations.
- *Shopping cart/payment system*—provides an ordering system, secure credit-card clearing, and other payment options.
- *Customer database*—includes customer information such as the name, address, phone number, and e-mail address.
- *Sales database*—contains information regarding the customer ID, product purchased, date, payment, and shipment to be able to provide after-sale customer support.
- *Ad server*—tracks the site behavior of prospects and customers that come through e-mail or banner ad campaigns.
- *Site tracking and reporting system*—monitors the number of unique visitors, pages visited, and products purchased.
- *Inventory management system*—provides a link to production and suppliers in order to facilitate order replenishment.

- **Describe the major issues surrounding the decision to outsource site development and/or hosting.**

Advantages of building a site in-house include:
- The ability to change and adapt the site quickly as the market demands
- The ability to build a site that does exactly what the company needs

Disadvantages of building a site in-house include:
- The costs may be higher.
- The risks of failure may be greater, given the complexity of issues such as security, privacy, and inventory management.
- The process may be more time-consuming than if you had hired an outside specialist firm to manage the effort.
- Staff may experience a longer learning curve that delays your entry into the market.

Using design templates cuts development time, but pre-set templates can also limit functionality.

A similar decision is also necessary regarding outsourcing the hosting of the site versus keeping it in-house. Relying on an outside vendor to ensure that the site is live 24 hours a day places the burden of reliability on someone else, in return for a monthly hosting fee. The downside is that if the site requires fast upgrades due to heavy traffic, the chosen hosting company may or may not be capable of keeping up. Reliability versus scalability is the issue in this instance.

- **Identify and understand the major considerations involved in choosing Web server and e-commerce merchant server software.**

Early Web sites used single-tier system architecture and consisted of a single-server computer that delivered static Web pages to users making requests through their browsers. The extended functionality of today's Web sites required the development of a multi-tiered systems architecture, which utilizes a variety of specialized Web servers, as well as links to pre-existing "backend" or "legacy" corporate databases.

All e-commerce sites require basic Web server software to answer requests from customers for HTML and XML pages. When choosing Web server software, companies are also choosing what operating system the site will run on. Apache, which runs on the Unix system, is the market leader.

Web servers provide a host of services, including:

- Processing user HTML requests
- Security services
- File transfer
- Search engine
- Data capture
- E-mail
- Site management tools

Dynamic server software allows sites to deliver dynamic content, rather than static, unchanging information. Web application server programs enable a wide range of e-commerce functionality, including creating a customer database, creating an e-mail promotional program, and accepting and processing orders, as well as many other services.

E-commerce merchant server software is another important software package that provides catalog displays, information storage and customer tracking, order taking (shopping cart), and credit card purchase processing. E-commerce suites can save time and money, but customization can significantly drive up costs. Factors to consider when choosing an e-commerce suite include its functionality, support for different business models, visual site management tools and reporting systems, performance and scalability, connectivity to existing business systems, compliance with standards, and global and multicultural capability.

- **Understand the issues involved in choosing the most appropriate hardware for an e-commerce site.**

Speed, capacity, and scalability are three of the most important considerations when selecting an operating system, and therefore the hardware that it runs on.

To evaluate how fast the site needs to be, companies need to assess the number of simultaneous users the site expects to see, the nature of their requests, the type of information requested, and the bandwidth available to the site. The answers to these questions will provide guidance regarding the processors necessary to meet customer demand. In some cases, adding additional processing power can add capacity, thereby improving system speed.

Scalability is also an important issue. Increasing processing supply by scaling up to meet demand can be done through:

- *Vertical scaling*—improving the processing power of the hardware, but maintaining the same number of servers
- *Horizontal scaling*—adding more of the same processing hardware
- *Improving processing architecture*—identifying operations with similar workloads and using dedicated tuned servers for each type of load

■ **Identify additional tools that can improve Web site performance.**

In addition to providing a speedy Web site, companies must also strive to have a well-designed site that encourages visitors to buy. Building in interactivity improves site effectiveness, as does personalization techniques that provide the ability to track customers while they are visiting the site. Commonly used software tools for achieving high levels of Web site interactivity and customer personalization include:

- *Common Gateway Interface (CGI) scripts*—a set of standards for communication between a browser and a program on a server that allows for interaction between the user and the server
- *Active Server Pages (ASP)*—a Microsoft tool that also permits interaction between the browser and the server
- *Java applets*—programs written in the Java programming language that also provide interactivity
- *JavaScript*—used to validate user input, such as an e-mail address
- *ActiveX and VBScript*—Microsoft's version of Java and JavaScript, respectively
- *Cookies*—text files stored on the user's hard drive that provide information regarding the user and his or her past experience at a Web site

## QUESTIONS

1. Name the six main pieces of the e-commerce site building puzzle.
2. Define the systems development life cycle and discuss the various steps involved in creating an e-commerce site.
3. Discuss the differences between a simple logical and simple physical Web site design.
4. Why is system testing important? Name the three types of testing and their relation to each other.
5. Compare the costs for system development and system maintenance. Which is more expensive, and why?
6. Why is a Web site so costly to maintain? Discuss the main factors that impact cost.
7. What are the main differences between single-tier and multi-tier site architecture?
8. Name five basic functionalities a Web server should provide.
9. What are the three main factors to consider when choosing the best hardware platform for your Web site?
10. Why is Web server bandwidth an important issue for e-commerce sites?

11. Compare and contrast the various scaling methods. Explain why scalability is a key business issue for Web sites.
12. What are the eight most important factors impacting Web site design, and how do they affect a site's operation?
13. What are Java and JavaScript? What role do they play in Web site design?
14. Name and describe three methods used to treat customers individually. Why are they significant to e-commerce?
15. What are some of the policies e-commerce businesses must develop before launching a site, and why must they be developed?

## PROJECTS

1. Go to FreeWebs.com or NetworkSolutions.com. Both sites allow you to create a simple e-tailer Web site for a free trial period. Create a Web site. The site should feature at least four pages, including a home page, product page, shopping cart, and contact page. Extra credit will be given for additional complexity and creativity. Come to class prepared to present your e-tailer concept and Web site.

2. Visit several e-commerce sites, not including those mentioned in this chapter, and evaluate the effectiveness of the sites according to the eight basic criteria/functionalities listed in Table 4.10. Choose one site you feel does an excellent job on all the aspects of an effective site and create an electronic presentation, including screen shots, to support your choice.

3. Imagine that you are the head of information technology for a fast-growth e-commerce start-up. You are in charge of development of the company's Web site. Consider your options for building the site in-house with existing staff, or outsourcing the entire operation. Decide which strategy you believe is in your company's best interest and create a brief presentation outlining your position. Why choose that approach? And what are the estimated associated costs, compared with the alternative? (You'll need to make some educated guesses here—don't worry about being exact.)

4. Choose two of the e-commerce suite software packages listed in Table 4.5 and prepare an evaluation chart that rates the packages on the key factors discussed in the section "Choosing an E-commerce Suite." Which package would you choose if you were developing a Web site of the type described in this chapter, and why?

5. Choose one of the open source Web content management systems such as Joomla or Drupal or another of your own choosing and prepare an evaluation chart similar to that required by Project 4. Which system would you choose and why?

## CHAPTER 5

# Online Security and Payment Systems

**After reading this chapter, you will be able to:**

- Understand the scope of e-commerce crime and security problems.
- Describe the key dimensions of e-commerce security.
- Understand the tension between security and other values.
- Identify the key security threats in the e-commerce environment.
- Describe how technology helps protect the security of messages sent over the Internet.
- Identify the tools used to establish secure Internet communications channels, and protect networks, servers, and clients.
- Appreciate the importance of policies, procedures, and laws in creating security.
- Describe the features of traditional payment systems.
- Understand the major e-commerce payment mechanisms.
- Describe the features and functionality of electronic billing presentment and payment systems.

# Cyberwar:
## Mutually Assured Destruction 2.0

On January 13, 2010, Google announced that it was considering shutting down its Chinese operations because of sophisticated cyberattacks on its computer systems worldwide, which were aimed at the Gmail user accounts of Chinese activists. Google believed the attacks originated from within China. The attacks were part of a larger scale attack against 34 other companies or government agencies worldwide. Google, the world's largest search engine company, the owner of the world's largest collection of personal, private information, and widely regarded as the most sophisticated civilian computing system on earth, sought technical assistance in February from the National Security Agency to learn more about the network of computers that attacked it in January.

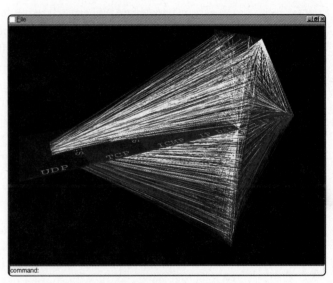

A computer-generated simulation of a DDoS attack.

The attack on Google was aimed not just at individual e-mail accounts, but at the entire password system used by Google to allow users access to its many services. The attack began with a simple instant message sent to a Google employee in China who clicked on a link in the IM. The unsuspecting employee downloaded software that took over his computer, and ultimately gained access to the computers of Google software developers in California responsible for the password system.

Cyberwar is not new, but it has become much more sophisticated in the last decade, and potentially much more devastating as America and other highly developed nations increasingly rely on the Internet for business and government. The Google attack follows a string of fairly sophisticated, yet devastatingly simple, attacks against entire nations and globally important businesses. From 2003 to 2005, government agencies were hit in a series of attacks called "Titan Rain" which were believed to originate in China. In 2007, the nation of Estonia was forced to shut down key government and financial institutions following a coordinated attack by over 1 million computers worldwide that had been organized into a botnet (a network of robot computers under the control of a single person or group). Experts believe the attacks originated in Russia with the backing of the government. In 2008, the financial and government infrastructure of the former Russian state of Georgia was brought to its knees for several days in an attack that

261

originated from Russia. In March 2009, a number of South Korean and U.S. Web sites were similarly attacked. Eleven major government Web sites in South Korea, the daily newspaper Chosun Ilbo, the Internet portal Naver.com, and Korea's Shinhan Bank were hit. Fourteen major U.S. sites were also targeted, including the White House, State Department, Treasury Department, the Secret Service, the Federal Trade Commission, and the New York Stock Exchange. Observers speculated North Korea organized this attack.

The 2010 attack on Google is just one of the more recent large-scale instance of cyberwarfare. Cyberwarfare is a form of war among organizations, states, and societies carried out over the Internet. Cyberwar is not just hacking, or breaking and entering, which are common criminal activities. Cyberwar is a much more serious threat to the infrastructure of entire societies inasmuch as the major financial, health, government, and industrial institutions of modern societies rely on the Internet for daily operations. Cyberwarfare is a state-sponsored activity designed to cripple and defeat an opposing state and nation. The Stuxnet worm is an example. First discovered in June 2010, the Stuxnet worm is one of the first-ever worms designed to attack industrial systems, specifically the Siemens control systems used in nuclear power plants. Over 60% of the infected computers are in Iran, and digital security company Kaspersky Labs speculates that the worm was launched with nation-state support, with the intention of disabling Iran's nuclear power plants.

In the United States, the public Web, air-traffic control systems, healthcare, and telecommunications services have all been attacked. Congressional offices have been told that China has broken into their computers. Both China and Russia have been caught trying to infiltrate the U.S. electric-power grid, leaving behind software code to be used to disrupt the system. The risk of attacks to create massive power outages is so serious that the best option could be unplugging the U.S. power grid from the Internet.

Imagine: about 10% of the world's billion-plus computers connected to the Internet worldwide are captured by stealth malware programs that users unintentionally install by opening e-mail attachments or clicking malicious links that download files, or as a result of using pirated "free" software. RustockB is one common stealth program that adds unwitting users to botnets. These programs then take over the computer without the user knowing and are controlled remotely by a Command and Control server. Once under control, the botnet is used to send spam, as well as useless messages to millions of victim computers. Botnets are responsible for over 80% of the spam sent throughout the world. This is the most profitable use of botnets. They are also used to collect credit card information, personal IDs, and bank information, feeding the underground economy with identity theft candidates. The botnets can be "rented" to run Distributed Denial of Service (DDoS) attacks against any site on the Internet.

Although cyberattacks are reported as discrete incidents, in fact they are on-going activities punctuated by major events. During a three-week period in 2010, CAIDA (Cooperative Association for Internet Data Analysis) observed more than 12,000 attacks against more than 5,000 distinct targets, ranging from well-known e-commerce companies such as Amazon and Hotmail to small foreign ISPs and dial-up connections.

Shadowserver, an organization of volunteer computer security experts, tracks 400,000 known infected botnet slave computers (a small fraction of the total) and about 1,500 active controllers.

While the United States has arguably the largest offensive cyberwar capability, and may have used it already, national defense against cyberwar threats requires a significant investment in additional computing power, as well as management attention. Cyber offensives and counterstrikes by the United States are highly classified. As with nuclear warfare, it's not clear that there is a technological defense. Powerful states are able to launch cyberattacks but not easily defend against them. Offense has the advantage. The Pentagon has created a Cyber Command to lead national security efforts in cyber defense. A national security directive of 2008 formalized efforts to protect the federal government. The Department of Homeland Security conducted a war game called Cyber Storm II also in 2008. In 2010, Secretary of State Hillary Clinton declared the "United States will protect our networks," but failed to indicate what counter-force would be used against state-sponsored cyberwar. The implicit threat is that if the United States' or any of its allies' Internet infrastructure is seriously attacked and damaged, the United States will take cyber offensive actions to destroy the Internet infrastructure of the aggressors. The result would be the destruction of the Internet among a large group of nations. In the cold war nuclear era, this was called "mutually assured destruction," or MAD. In the Internet era it's called MAD 2.0.

The threat of MAD 2.0 may be working. In July 2010, 15 states including the United States and Russia agreed on a set of recommendations after 10 years of debate that will lead to an international computer security treaty. Ultimately, the solution to cyberwar on a large scale may be a political solution based on the dependence of all nations on secure Internet computing facilities, and on the threat of mutually assured Internet destruction for all nations. There's plenty of historical precedents, most notably the International Telecommunications Union (the ITU) founded in 1845 to coordinate telegraph standards across the world. Today the ITU is a United Nations agency coordinating radio, television, and satellite telecommunications services. One of its responsibilities is to ensure that no nation or group of nations interfere with the telecommunications of other nations.

**SOURCES:** "Stuxnet Malware is 'Weapon' Out to Destroy...Iran's Bushehr Nuclear Plant?", by Mark Clayton, *Christian Science Monitor*, September 21, 2010; " Steps Take to End Impasse Over Cybersecurity Talks," by John Markoff, *New York Times*, July 16, 2010; "Obama and Cyber Defense," by L. Gordon Crovitz, *Wall Street Journal*, June 29, 2009; Cyberattack on Google Said to Hit Password System," by John Markoff, *New York Times*, April 10, 2010; *Cyber War: The Next Threat to National Security and What to Do About It* ,by Richard A. Clarke and Robert K. Knake. Ecco/HarperCollins Publishers, March 2010; "Mutually Assured Destruction 2.0," *New York Times*, January 26, 2010; "Cyberwar: In Digital Combat, U.S. Finds No Easy Deterrent," by John Markoff, David Sanger, and Thom Shanker, *New York Times*, January 26, 2010; "Google, Citing Attack, Threatens to Exit China," by Andrew Jacobs, *New York Times*, January 12, 2010; "Security Researchers Zero In On Twitter Hackers," by Gregg Keizer, *Computerworld*, August 7, 2009; "Webs Anonymity Makes Cyberattack Hard to Trace," by John Markoff, *New York Times*, July 17, 2009; "Obama and Cyber Defense," by L. Gordon Crovitz, *Wall Street Journal*, June 29, 2009; "Obama Announces U.S. Cyber Security Plan," by Lolita Baldor, *New York Times*, May 29, 2009; "Vast Spy System Loots Computers in 103 Countries," by John Markoff, *New York Times*, March 29, 2009; "Georgia Takes a Beating in the Cyberwar with Russia," by John Markoff, *New York Times*, August 11, 2008.

As *Cyberwar: Mutually Assured Destruction 2.0* illustrates, the Internet and Web are increasingly vulnerable to large-scale attacks and potentially large-scale failure. Increasingly, these attacks are led by organized gangs of criminals operating globally—an unintended consequence of globalization. Even more worrisome is that a growing number of very large-scale attacks are funded, organized, and led by various nations against the Internet resources of other nations. Currently there are few if any steps that individuals or businesses can take to prevent these kinds of attacks. However, there are several steps you can take to protect your business Web sites and your personal information from routine security attacks. Reading this chapter, you should start thinking about how your business could survive in the event of a large scale "outage" of the Internet.

In this chapter, we will examine e-commerce security and payment issues. First, we will identify the major security risks and their costs, and describe the variety of solutions currently available. Then, we will look at the major payment methods and consider how to achieve a secure payment environment.

## 5.1 THE E-COMMERCE SECURITY ENVIRONMENT

For most law-abiding citizens, the Internet holds the promise of a huge, convenient, global marketplace, providing access to people, goods, services, and businesses worldwide, all at a bargain price. For criminals, the Internet has created entirely new—and lucrative—ways to steal from the more than 1 billion consumers in the world on the Internet. From products and services to cash to information, it's all there for the taking on the Internet.

It's also less risky to steal online. Rather than rob a bank in person, the Internet makes it possible to rob people remotely and almost anonymously. Rather than steal a CD at a local record store, you can download the same music for free and almost without risk from the Internet. The potential for anonymity on the Internet cloaks many criminals in legitimate-looking identities, allowing them to place fraudulent orders with online merchants, steal information by intercepting e-mail, or simply shut down e-commerce sites by using software viruses and swarm attacks. The Internet was never designed to be a global marketplace with a billion users, and lacks many basic security features found in older networks such as the telephone system or broadcast television networks. Who ever heard of the telephone system being hacked and "brought down" by programmers in Eastern Europe? By comparison, the Internet is an open, vulnerable-design network. The actions of cybercriminals are costly for both businesses and consumers, who are then subjected to higher prices and additional security measures. However, the overall security environment is strengthening as business managers and government officials make significant investments in security equipment and business procedures.

## THE SCOPE OF THE PROBLEM

Cybercrime is becoming a more significant problem for both organizations and consumers. Bot networks, DDoS attacks (described in the opening case), Trojans, phishing (fraudulently obtaining financial information from a victim, typically via e-mail and spoofed Web sites), data theft, identity theft, credit card fraud, and spyware are just some of the threats that are making daily headlines. Recently, even social networks such as Twitter and Facebook have had security breaches. For example, an individual hacked into Britney Spears' Twitter account and began sending messages saying the singer had died. But despite the increasing attention being paid to cybercrime, it is difficult to accurately estimate the actual amount of such crime, in part because many companies are hesitant to report crime due to fear of losing the trust of its customers, and because even if crime is reported, it may be difficult to quantify the actual dollar amount of the loss.

One source of information is the Internet Crime Complaint Center ("IC3"), a partnership between the National White Collar Crime Center and the Federal Bureau of Investigation. The IC3 data is useful for gauging the types of e-commerce crimes most likely to be reported by consumers and the typical amount of loss experienced. In 2009, the IC3 processed more than 336,000 Internet crime complaints (up 22% from the previous year) and referred more than 146,000 of them to federal, state, and local law enforcement agencies (a 100% increase from the previous year). The total dollar loss from all referred cases was nearly $559 million, a 100% increase over 2008; and the average dollar loss was about $575, while the highest dollar loss per incident arose from financial fraud where average losses were $3,200. (National White Collar Crime Center and the Federal Bureau of Investigation, 2010). Whatever the specific numbers, there's little doubt the number of complaints, and prosecutions, has grown dramatically in the last year.

The Computer Security Institute's annual *Computer Crime and Security Survey* is another source of information. In 2009, the survey was based on the responses of around 525 security practitioners in U.S. corporations, government agencies, financial institutions, medical institutions, and universities. The survey reported that 49% of responding organizations experienced a computer security incident within the past year. **Figure 5.1** illustrates the various types of attacks against computer systems reported. Not all of these necessarily involve e-commerce, although many of them do. Fewer companies were willing to share numbers. Of those that did, the total loss reported was $41.5 million, with an average annual loss of $288,000. The most expensive security incidents were financial fraud, which averaged $500,000; followed by dealing with bot computers within the organization's network ($345,000) (Computer Security Institute, 2009).

Reports issued by security product providers, such as Symantec, are another source of data. Symantec, for instance, issues a semi-annual *Internet Security Threat Report*, based on 240,000 sensors monitoring Internet activity in over 200 countries, and malicious code reports from over 120 million systems that utilize Symantec's anti-virus products. In 2009, over 1,650,000 new malicious code threats were reported to Symantec, a 165% increase over 2007. It observed an average of about 75,000 active bot-infected computers per day, and there were over 55,000 phishing hosts, up 66% from the prior year (Symantec, 2010). However, Symantec does not attempt to quantify any actual crimes and/or losses related to these threats. Symantec discovered several

| FIGURE 5.1 | TYPES OF ATTACKS AGAINST COMPUTER SYSTEMS (CYBERCRIME) |
|---|---|

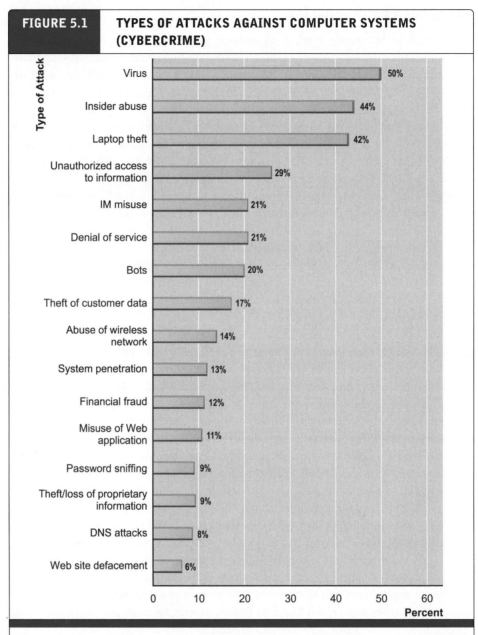

The most common attacks against computer systems are viruses, insider abuse of Internet access, laptop theft, unauthorized access to information, IM misuse, and denial of service. Some of these are specifically related to e-commerce, while others are not.

SOURCE: Based on data from Computer Security Institute, 2009.

crimeware toolkits available on the Web that allow people to customize a piece of malicious code designed to steal data and other personal information. The Zeus21 kit can be purchased for as low as $700. Advances in technology have greatly reduced the entry costs and skills required to enter the cybercrime business.

Online credit card fraud and phishing attacks are perhaps the most high-profile form of e-commerce crimes. Although the average amount of credit card fraud loss experienced by any one individual is typically relatively small, the overall amount is substantial. The research firm CyberSource estimates online credit card fraud in the United States amounted to about $3.3 billion in 2009 (CyberSource, 2010). The overall rate of online credit card fraud is estimated to be about 1.2% of all online card transactions. As a percentage of all e-commerce revenues, credit card fraud is declining as merchants and credit companies expand security systems to prevent the most common types of low-level fraud. But the nature of credit card fraud has changed greatly from the theft of a single credit card number and efforts to purchase goods at a few sites, to the simultaneous theft of millions of credit card numbers and their distributions to thousands of criminals operating as gangs of thieves. The emergence of "identify theft," described in detail later in this chapter, as a major online/offline type of fraud, may well increase markedly the incidence and amount of credit card fraud, since identity theft often includes the use of stolen credit card information and the creation of phony credit card accounts. For instance, the 2010 Identity Fraud Survey by Javelin Strategy & Research found that both overall cost and incidence of identity theft increased. Overall cost of this crime rose to $54 billion, a 12% increase over 2008. Mean fraud amounts remained at $4,871. Around 11 million U.S. adults became victims of identity fraud, up 4.8% from the previous year. Mean costs to consumers declined to $378 from $498 as firms absorbed more of the losses than in previous years (Javelin Research & Strategy, 2010a).

## The Underground Economy Marketplace: The Value of Stolen Information

Criminals who steal information on the Internet do not always use this information themselves, but instead derive value by selling the information to others on so-called "underground economy servers." There are several thousand known underground economy servers around the world that sell stolen information (about half of these are in the United States). **Table 5.1** lists some recently observed prices, which typically vary depending on the quantity being purchased.

| TABLE 5.1 | THE UNDERGROUND ECONOMY MARKETPLACE |
|---|---|
| Credit card | $1–$30 |
| A full identity (U.S. bank account, credit card, date of birth, social security, etc.) | $3–$20 |
| Bank account | $10–$125 |
| E-mail accounts | $5-$12 |
| A single compromised computer | $6–$20 |
| Social security number | $5–$7 |
| Attack toolkits | $120 per month |

SOURCE: Based on data from Symantec, 2010.

Finding these servers is difficult for the average user (and for law enforcement agencies), and you need to be vetted by other criminals before gaining access. This vetting process takes place through e-mail exchanges of information, money, and reputation. Criminals have fairly good, personalized security!

Note that not every cybercriminal is necessarily after money. In some cases, such criminals aim to just deface, vandalize, and/or disrupt a Web site, rather than actually steal goods or services. The cost of such an attack includes not only the time and effort to make repairs to the site but also damage done to the site's reputation and image as well as revenues lost as a result of the attack.

So, what can we can conclude about the overall size of cybercrime? Cybercrime against e-commerce sites is dynamic and changing all the time, with new risks appearing often. The amount of losses to businesses appears to be significant but stable, and may represent a declining percentage of overall sales, because firms have invested in security measures to protect against the simplest crimes. Individuals face new risks of fraud, many of which (unlike credit cards where federal law limits the loss to $50 for individuals) involve substantial uninsured losses involving debit cards and bank accounts. The managers of e-commerce sites must prepare for an ever-changing variety of criminal assaults, and keep current in the latest security techniques.

## WHAT IS GOOD E-COMMERCE SECURITY?

What is a secure commercial transaction? Any time you go into a marketplace, you take risks, including the loss of privacy (information about what you purchased). Your prime risk as a consumer is that you do not get what you paid for. In fact, you might pay and get nothing! Worse, someone steals your money while you are at the market! As a merchant in the market, your risk is that you don't get paid for what you sell. Thieves take merchandise and then either walk off without paying anything, or pay you with a fraudulent instrument, stolen credit card, or forged currency.

E-commerce merchants and consumers face many of the same risks as participants in traditional commerce, albeit in a new digital environment. Theft is theft, regardless of whether it is digital theft or traditional theft. Burglary, breaking and entering, embezzlement, trespass, malicious destruction, vandalism—all crimes in a traditional commercial environment—are also present in e-commerce. However, reducing risks in e-commerce is a complex process that involves new technologies, organizational policies and procedures, and new laws and industry standards that empower law enforcement officials to investigate and prosecute offenders. **Figure 5.2** illustrates the multi-layered nature of e-commerce security.

To achieve the highest degree of security possible, new technologies are available and should be used. But these technologies by themselves do not solve the problem. Organizational policies and procedures are required to ensure the technologies are not subverted. Finally, industry standards and government laws are required to enforce payment mechanisms, as well as investigate and prosecute violators of laws designed to protect the transfer of property in commercial transactions.

The history of security in commercial transactions teaches that any security system can be broken if enough resources are put against it. Security is not absolute.

---

**FIGURE 5.2**    **THE E-COMMERCE SECURITY ENVIRONMENT**

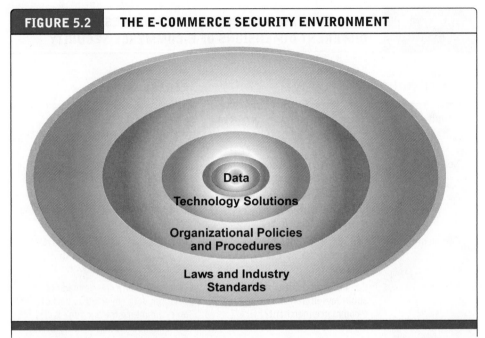

E-commerce security is multi-layered, and must take into account new technology, policies and procedures, and laws and industry standards.

In addition, perfect security forever is not needed, especially in the information age. There is a time value to information—just as there is to money. Sometimes it is sufficient to protect a message for a few hours, days, or years. Also, because security is costly, we always have to weigh the cost against the potential loss. Finally, we have also learned that security is a chain that breaks most often at the weakest link. Our locks are often much stronger than our management of the keys.

We can conclude then that good e-commerce security requires a set of laws, procedures, policies, and technologies that, to the extent feasible, protect individuals and organizations from unexpected behavior in the e-commerce marketplace.

## DIMENSIONS OF E-COMMERCE SECURITY

There are six key dimensions to e-commerce security: integrity, nonrepudiation, authenticity, confidentiality, privacy, and availability (see **Table 5.2**).

**Integrity** refers to the ability to ensure that information being displayed on a Web site, or transmitted or received over the Internet, has not been altered in any way by an unauthorized party. For example, if an unauthorized person intercepts and changes the contents of an online communication, such as by redirecting a bank wire transfer into a different account, the integrity of the message has been compromised because the communication no longer represents what the original sender intended.

**Nonrepudiation** refers to the ability to ensure that e-commerce participants do not deny (i.e., repudiate) their online actions. For instance, the availability of free e-mail accounts with alias names makes it easy for a person to post comments or

**integrity**
the ability to ensure that information being displayed on a Web site or transmitted or received over the Internet has not been altered in any way by an unauthorized party

**nonrepudiation**
the ability to ensure that e-commerce participants do not deny (i.e., repudiate) their online actions

| TABLE 5.2 | CUSTOMER AND MERCHANT PERSPECTIVES ON THE DIFFERENT DIMENSIONS OF E-COMMERCE SECURITY | |
|---|---|---|
| DIMENSIONS | CUSTOMER'S PERSPECTIVE | MERCHANT'S PERSPECTIVE |
| Integrity | Has information I transmit or receive been altered? | Has data on the site been altered without authorization? Is data being received from customers valid? |
| Nonrepudiation | Can a party to an action with me later deny taking the action? | Can a customer deny ordering products? |
| Authenticity | Who am I dealing with? How can I be assured that the person or entity is who they claim to be? | What is the real identity of the customer? |
| Confidentiality | Can someone other than the intended recipient read my messages? | Are messages or confidential data accessible to anyone other than those authorized to view them? |
| Privacy | Can I control the use of information about myself transmitted to an e-commerce merchant? | What use, if any, can be made of personal data collected as part of an e-commerce transaction? Is the personal information of customers being used in an unauthorized manner? |
| Availability | Can I get access to the site? | Is the site operational? |

send a message and perhaps later deny doing so. Even when a customer uses a real name and e-mail address, it is easy for that customer to order merchandise online and then later deny doing so. In most cases, because merchants typically do not obtain a physical copy of a signature, the credit card issuer will side with the customer because the merchant has no legally valid proof that the customer ordered the merchandise.

**Authenticity**
the ability to identify the identity of a person or entity with whom you are dealing on the Internet

**Authenticity** refers to the ability to identify the identity of a person or entity with whom you are dealing on the Internet. How does the customer know that the Web site operator is who it claims to be? How can the merchant be assured that the customer is really who she says she is? Someone who claims to be someone he is not is "spoofing" or misrepresenting himself.

**confidentiality**
the ability to ensure that messages and data are available only to those who are authorized to view them

**Confidentiality** refers to the ability to ensure that messages and data are available only to those who are authorized to view them. Confidentiality is sometimes confused with **privacy**, which refers to the ability to control the use of information a customer provides about himself or herself to an e-commerce merchant.

**privacy**
the ability to control the use of information about oneself

E-commerce merchants have two concerns related to privacy. They must establish internal policies that govern their own use of customer information, and they must protect that information from illegitimate or unauthorized use. For example, if hackers break into an e-commerce site and gain access to credit card or other information, this not only violates the confidentiality of the data, but also the privacy of the individuals who supplied the information.

**Availability** refers to the ability to ensure that an e-commerce site continues to function as intended.

E-commerce security is designed to protect these six dimensions. When any one of them is compromised, it is a security issue.

## THE TENSION BETWEEN SECURITY AND OTHER VALUES

Can there be too much security? The answer is yes. Contrary to what some may believe, security is not an unmitigated good. Computer security adds overhead and expense to business operations, and also gives criminals new opportunities to hide their intentions and their crimes.

### Ease of Use

There are inevitable tensions between security and ease of use. When traditional merchants are so fearful of robbers that they do business in shops locked behind security gates, ordinary customers are discouraged from walking in. The same can be true on the Web. In general, the more security measures added to an e-commerce site, the more difficult it is to use and the slower the site becomes. As you will discover reading this chapter, digital security is purchased at the price of slowing down processors and adding significantly to data storage demands on storage devices. Security is a technological and business overhead that can detract from doing business. Too much security can harm profitability, while not enough security can potentially put you out of business.

### Public Safety and the Criminal Uses of the Internet

There is also an inevitable tension between the desires of individuals to act anonymously (to hide their identity) and the needs of public officials to maintain public safety that can be threatened by criminals or terrorists. This is not a new problem, or even new to the electronic era. The U.S. government began informal tapping of telegraph wires during the Civil War in the mid-1860s in order to trap conspirators and terrorists, and the first police wiretaps of local telephone systems were in place by the 1890s—20 years after the invention of the phone (Schwartz, 2001). No nation-state has ever permitted a technological haven to exist where criminals can plan crimes or threaten the nation-state without fear of official surveillance or investigation. In this sense, the Internet is no different from any other communication system. Drug cartels make extensive use of voice, fax, and data encryption devices; a number of large international organized criminal groups steal information from commercial Web sites and resell it to other criminals who use it for financial fraud. Over the years, the U.S. government has successfully pursued various "carding forums" (Web sites that facilitate the sale of stolen credit card and debit card numbers), such as Shadowcrew.com and Carderplanet.com, resulting in the arrest and prosecution of a number of their members and the shutting down of the sites. However, other criminal organizations have emerged to take their place, including Cardersmarket.com, which reportedly has thousands of members worldwide, and CCpowerForums.com.

Terrorists are also fond users of the Internet and have been for many years. Encrypted files sent via e-mail were used by Ramsey Yousef—a member of the terrorist group responsible for bombing the World Trade Center in 1993—to hide plans for bombing 11 U.S. airliners. The Internet was also used to plan and coordinate the subsequent attacks on the World Trade Center on September 11, 2001. The Aum Shin-rikyo religious cult in Japan that spread poison gas in the Tokyo subway in March 1995 (killing 12 and hospitalizing 6,000 people) stored their records detailing plans for attacks on other countries on computers using a powerful form of encryption called RSA, described later. Fortunately, authorities were lucky to find the encryption key stored on a floppy disk (Denning and Baugh, 1999). In 2010, Pentagon officials say the case of Umar Farouk Abdulmutallab illustrate how terrorists make effective use of the Internet to radicalize, recruit, train, and coordinate youthful terrorists. Abdulmutallab allegedly attempted to blow up an American airliner in Detroit on Christmas Day 2009. He was identified, contacted, recruited, and trained all within six weeks, according to a Pentagon counterterrorism official. That's much faster than the two and a half years it took for Osama bin Laden to hatch the plan to attack the US in 2001.

More recently, Al Qaeda and its offshoots "have understood that both time and space have in many ways been conquered by the Internet," said John Arquilla, a professor at the Naval Postgraduate School who coined the term "netwar" more than a decade ago. Al Qaeda, according to security experts in the United States and Britain, use the Web as a dynamic library of training materials on poison mixing and explosive construction, tactical coordination of imminent attacks, and building a larger terrorist community of like-minded people. The Internet is both anonymous and pervasive, an ideal communication tool for criminal and terrorist groups (Peretti, 2008).

## 5.2 SECURITY THREATS IN THE E-COMMERCE ENVIRONMENT

From a technology perspective, there are three key points of vulnerability when dealing with e-commerce: the client, the server, and the communications pipeline. **Figure 5.3** illustrates a typical e-commerce transaction with a consumer using a credit card to purchase a product. **Figure 5.4** illustrates some of the things that can go wrong at each major vulnerability point in the transaction—over Internet communications channels, at the server level, and at the client level.

In this section, we describe a number of the most common and most damaging forms of security threats to e-commerce consumers and site operators: malicious code, unwanted programs, phishing and identity theft, hacking and cybervandalism, credit card fraud/theft, spoofing (pharming) and spam (junk) Web sites, Denial of Service (DoS) and Distributed Denial of service (DDoS) attacks, sniffing, insider attacks, and finally, poorly designed server and client software.

### MALICIOUS CODE

**malicious code (malware)**

includes a variety of threats such as viruses, worms, Trojan horses, and bots

**Malicious code** (sometimes referred to as "malware") includes a variety of threats such as viruses, worms, Trojan horses, and bots. In 2010, Microsoft reported that its security products had detected a total of nearly 126 million unique malicious files in the second half of 2009 (Microsoft, 2010). Malicious code in the past often was intended simply to impair computers, and was often authored by a lone hacker, but

| FIGURE 5.3 | A TYPICAL E-COMMERCE TRANSACTION |
|---|---|

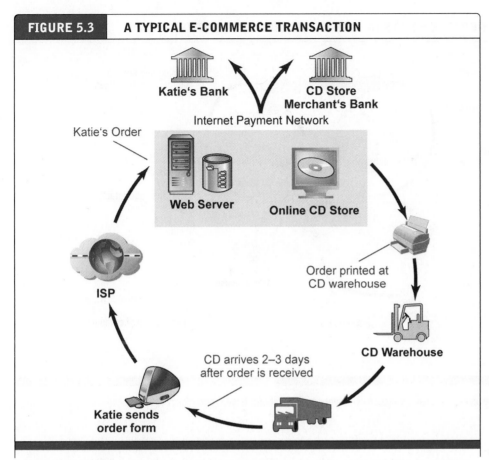

In a typical e-commerce transaction, the customer uses a credit card and the existing credit payment system. The transaction has many vulnerable points.

SOURCE: Boncella, 2000.

increasingly the intent is to steal e-mail addresses, logon credentials, personal data, and financial information. Malicious code is also used to develop integrated malware networks that organize the theft of information and money.

One of the latest innovations in malicious code distribution is to embed it in the online advertising chain, including at Google and other ad networks. As the ad network chain becomes more complicated, it becomes more and more difficult for Web sites to vet ads placed on their sites to ensure they are malware-free. Armorize, a Web security firm, scanned the top 200,000 Web sites in 2010, including the New York Times and the Drudge Report, and found that 1 percent were infected with malware that was used to support so-called "drive by downloads" (downloads of malware that occur when users seek to download files from a site) (Mills, 2010). For instance, Web sites as disparate as eWeek.com (a technology site) to MLB.com (Major League Baseball) to AmericanIdol.com experienced instances where ads placed on their sites either had malicious code embedded or directed clickers to malicious sites. Malicious code embedded in PDF files is also common. Malware

| FIGURE 5.4 | VULNERABLE POINTS IN AN E-COMMERCE TRANSACTION |
|---|---|

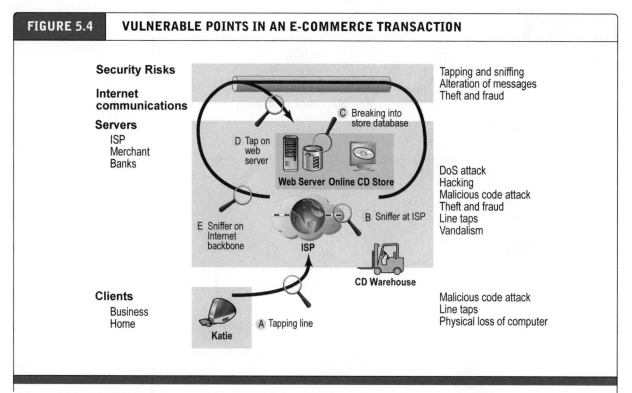

There are three vulnerable points in e-commerce transactions: Internet communications, servers, and clients.
SOURCE: Boncella, 2000.

authors are also increasingly using links embedded within e-mail instead of the more traditional file attachments to infect computers. The links lead directly to a malicious code download or Web sites that include malicious JavaScript code. Equally important, there has been a major shift in the writers of malware from amateur hackers and adventurers to organized criminal efforts to defraud companies and individuals. In other words, it's now more about the money than ever before.

A **virus** is a computer program that has the ability to replicate or make copies of itself, and spread to other files. In addition to the ability to replicate, most computer viruses deliver a "payload." The payload may be relatively benign, such as the display of a message or image, or it may be highly destructive—destroying files, reformatting the computer's hard drive, or causing programs to run improperly. Computer viruses fall into several major categories:

**virus**

a computer program that has the ability to replicate or make copies of itself, and spread to other files

- *Macro viruses* are application-specific, meaning that the virus affects only the application for which it was written, such as Microsoft Word, Excel, or PowerPoint. When a user opens an infected document in the appropriate application, the virus copies itself to the templates in the application, so that when new documents are created, they are infected with the macro virus as well. Macro viruses can easily be spread when sent in an e-mail attachment.

- *File-infecting viruses* usually infect executable files, such as *.com, *.exe, *.drv, and *.dll files. They may activate every time the infected file is executed by copying themselves into other executable files. File-infecting viruses are also easily spread through e-mails and any file transfer system.
- *Script viruses* are written in script programming languages such as VBScript (Visual Basic Script) and JavaScript. The viruses are activated simply by double-clicking an infected *.vbs or *.js file. The ILOVEYOU virus (also known as the Love Bug), which overwrites *.jpg and *.mp3 files, is one of the most famous examples of a script virus.

Viruses are often combined with a worm. Indeed, most researchers agree that classic viruses—the original malicious programs—have become much less common, while the far more dangerous worm has grown exponentially. Some of the reason is simple: viruses infect a single computer, and may destroy data, but produce very little cash. As the nature of the criminal changes from amateur hacker to professional criminal interested in cash, it is much more lucrative to create a worm that can propagate from one computer to another, perhaps to millions.

Instead of just spreading from file to file, a **worm** is designed to spread from computer to computer. A worm does not necessarily need to be activated by a user or program in order for it to replicate itself. For example, the Slammer worm, which targeted a known vulnerability in Microsoft's SQL Server database software, infected more than 90% of vulnerable computers worldwide within 10 minutes of its release on the Internet; crashed Bank of America cash machines, especially in the southwestern part of the United States; affected cash registers at supermarkets such as the Publix chain in Atlanta, where staff could not dispense cash to frustrated buyers; and took down most Internet connections in South Korea, causing a dip in the stock market there. The Conficker worm, which first appeared in November 2008, is the most significant worm since Slammer, and reportedly infected over 9 to 15 million computers worldwide. Other well-known worms include the MyDoom worm, the Sasser worm, the Zotob worm, and the Nymex worm (Symantec, 2010).

**worm**
malware that is designed to spread from computer to computer

A **Trojan horse** appears to be benign, but then does something other than expected. The Trojan horse is not itself a virus because it does not replicate, but is often a way for viruses or other malicious code such as bots or *rootkits* (a program whose aim is to subvert control of the computer's operating system) to be introduced into a computer system. The term *Trojan horse* refers to the huge wooden horse in Homer's *Iliad* that the Greeks gave their opponents, the Trojans—a gift that actually contained hundreds of Greek soldiers. Once the people of Troy let the massive horse within their gates, the soldiers revealed themselves and captured the city. In today's world, a Trojan horse may masquerade as a game, but actually hide a program to steal your passwords and e-mail them to another person. According to Symantec, of the top 10 new malicious code families detected in 2010, six were Trojans. Trojans made up 68% of the volume of the top 50 malicious code reports. (Symantec, 2010). Monster.com, for instance, suffered a highly publicized attack from a Trojan horse called Infostealer.Monstres that stole more than 1.6 million records, such as names, e-mail addresses, home addresses, and phone numbers of job seekers who had filed resumes with Monster (Kreizer, 2007b). In 2010, the most

**Trojan horse**
appears to be benign, but then does something other than expected. Often a way for viruses or other malicious code to be introduced into a computer system

common Trojan horse is Zeus. Zeus steals information from users by keystroke logging. It is distributed through the Zeus botnet, which has millions of slave computers, and utilizes drive-by downloads and phishing tactics to persuade users to download files with the Trojan horse.

**bot**

type of malicious code that can be covertly installed on a computer when attached to the Internet. Once installed, the bot responds to external commands sent by the attacker

**botnet**

collection of captured bot computers

**Bots** (short for robots) are a type of malicious code that can be covertly installed on your computer when attached to the Internet. Ninety percent of the world's spam, and 80% of the world's malware, is delivered by botnets. Once installed, the bot responds to external commands sent by the attacker, and your computer becomes a "zombie," and is able to be controlled by an external third party (the "bot-herder"). **Botnets** are collections of captured computers used for malicious activities such as sending spam, participating in a DDoS attack (described further later), stealing information from computers, and storing network traffic for later analysis. The number of computers which have been "botted" (are a part of a botnet) is variously estimated to be from 6 to 24 million. The number of botnets operating worldwide is not known but is estimated to be in the thousands. Arguably, bots and bot networks are the single most important threat to the Internet and e-commerce in 2010–2011 because they can be used to launch very large-scale attacks using many different techniques. In 2009, the authors of the Conficker worm used it to assemble a massive botnet that is still growing. Thus far, the botnet has not been used for other than installing fake anti-virus software, but security experts caution that it still remains a threat (Kerner, 2009).

The biggest botnet bust in 2010 started in Spain and led across the world, involving Spanish, American, and British authorities. In March 2010, Spanish authorities arrested the leaders of the Mariposa botnet, one of the world's largest. Mariposa had infected and controlled about 12.7 million computers. More than half of the Fortune 1,000, 40 major banks, and numerous government agencies were infected—and did not know it. The primary activity of Mariposa was to steal credit cards and online banking passwords which it then re-sold at various Web sites.

Malicious code is a threat at both the client and the server level, although servers generally engage in much more thorough anti-virus activities than do consumers. At the server level, malicious code can bring down an entire Web site, preventing millions of people from using the site. Such incidents are infrequent. Much more frequent malicious code attacks occur at the client level, and the damage can quickly spread to millions of other computers connected to the Internet. **Table 5.3** lists some well-known examples of malicious code.

## UNWANTED PROGRAMS

In addition to malicious code, the e-commerce security environment is further challenged by unwanted programs such as adware, browser parasites, spyware, and other applications that install themselves on a computer, typically without the user's informed consent. Such programs are increasingly being found on social networking and user-generated content sites where users are fooled into downloading them. Once installed, these applications are usually exceedingly difficult to remove from the computer.

| TABLE 5.3 | | NOTABLE EXAMPLES OF MALICIOUS CODE |
|---|---|---|
| NAME | TYPE | DESCRIPTION |
| Conficker | Worm | First appeared November 2008. Targets Microsoft operating system. Uses advanced malware techniques. Largest worm infection since Slammer in 2003. |
| Sality.AE | Virus/worm | Most common 2010 malware. First appeared in 2009. Removes security applications and services, downloads and installs threats. |
| Netsky.P | Worm/Trojan horse | First appeared in early 2003; still one of the most common computer worms. It spreads by gathering target e-mail addresses from the computers it infects, and sending e-mail to all recipients from the infected computer. It is commonly used by bot networks to launch spam and DoS attacks. |
| Storm (Peacomm, NuWar) | Worm/Trojan horse | First appeared in January 2007. It spreads in a manner similar to the Netsky.P worm. May also download and run other Trojan programs and worms. |
| Nymex | Worm | First discovered in January 2006. Spreads by mass mailing; activates on the 3rd of every month, and attempts to destroy files of certain types. |
| Zotob | Worm | First appeared in August 2005. Well-known worm that infected a number of U.S. media companies. |
| Sasser | Worm | First appeared in 2004. Exploited a vulnerability in LSASS, causing network problems. |
| Mydoom | Worm | First appeared in January 2004. One of the fastest-spreading mass-mailer worms. |
| Slammer | Worm | Launched in January 2003. Caused widespread problems. |
| Klez | Worm | Most prolific virus of 2002. Was distributed via an e-mail with a random subject line and message body. Once launched, the worm sent itself to all addresses in the Windows Address Book, the database of instant-messaging program ICQ, and local files. |
| CodeRed | Worm | Appeared in 2001. It achieved an infection rate of over 20,000 systems within 10 minutes of release and ultimately spread to hundreds of thousands of systems. |
| Melissa | Macro virus/worm | First spotted in March 1999. At the time, Melissa was the fastest-spreading infectious program ever discovered. It attacked Microsoft Word's Normal.dot global template, ensuring infection of all newly created documents. It also mailed an infected Word file to the first 50 entries in each user's Microsoft Outlook Address Book. |
| Chernobyl | File-infecting virus | First appeared in 1998. It wipes out the first megabyte of data on a hard disk (making the rest useless) every April 26, the anniversary of the nuclear disaster at Chernobyl. |

Adware (described further in Chapter 7) is typically used to call for pop-up ads to display when the user visits certain sites. While annoying, adware is not typically used for criminal activities. ZangoSearch and PurityScan are examples of adware programs that open the Web pages or display pop-up ads of partner sites when certain keywords are used in Internet searches. A **browser parasite** is a program that can monitor and change the settings of a user's browser, for instance, changing the browser's home page, or sending information about the sites visited to a remote computer. Browser parasites are often a component of adware. For example, Websearch is an adware component that modifies Internet Explorer's default home page and search settings.

**browser parasite**
a program that can monitor and change the settings of a user's browser

**Spyware**, on the other hand, can be used to obtain information such as a user's keystrokes, copies of e-mail and instant messages, and even take screenshots (and thereby capture passwords or other confidential data). One example of spyware is SpySheriff, which claims to be a spyware removal program but is actually a malicious spyware application. Spyware (along with phishing, described in the next section) is often used for identity theft.

**spyware**
a program used to obtain information such as a user's keystrokes, e-mail, instant messages, and so on

## PHISHING AND IDENTITY THEFT

**Phishing** is any deceptive, online attempt by a third party to obtain confidential information for financial gain. Phishing attacks do not involve malicious code but instead rely on straightforward misrepresentation and fraud, so-called "social engineering" techniques. The most popular phishing attack is the e-mail scam letter. The scam begins with an e-mail: a rich former oil minister of Nigeria is seeking a bank account to stash millions of dollars for a short period of time, and requests your bank account number where the money can be deposited. In return, you will receive a million dollars. This type of e-mail scam is popularly known as a "Nigerian letter" scam (see **Figure 5.5**).

**phishing**
any deceptive, online attempt by a third party to obtain confidential information for financial gain

Thousands of other phishing attacks use other scams, some pretending to be eBay, PayPal, or Citibank writing to you for "account verification" (known as "spear phishing", or targeting a known customer of a specific bank, or other type of business). Click on a link in the e-mail and you will be taken to a Web site controlled by the scammer, and prompted to enter confidential information about your accounts, such as your account number and PIN codes (see **Figure 5.6**). On any given day, millions of these phishing attack e-mails are sent, and, unfortunately, some people are fooled and disclose their personal account information.

Phishers rely on traditional "con man" tactics, but use e-mail to trick recipients into voluntarily giving up financial access codes, bank account numbers, credit card numbers, and other personal information. Often, phishers create ("spoof") a Web site that purports to be a legitimate financial institution and con users into entering financial information, or downloads malware such as a keylogger to the victim's computer. Phishers use the information they gather to commit fraudulent acts such as charging items to your credit cards or withdrawing funds from your bank account, or in other ways "steal your identity" (identity theft). Phishing attacks are one of the fastest-growing forms of e-commerce crime. In 2010, Symantec detected over 2,400 phishing Web site hosts, up 66% over 2009. Financial services are the primary brands

**FIGURE 5.5** **AN EXAMPLE OF A NIGERIAN LETTER E-MAIL SCAM**

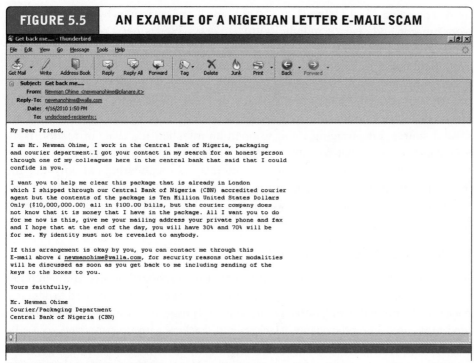

This is an example of a typical Nigerian letter e-mail scam.

**FIGURE 5.6** **AN EXAMPLE OF A PHISHING ATTACK**

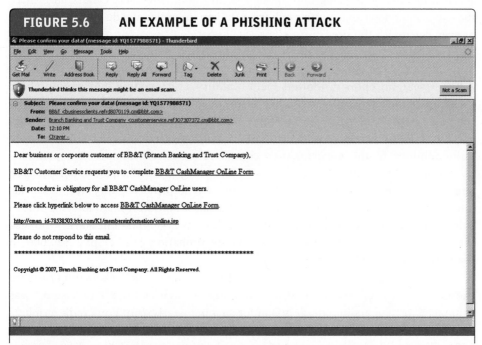

This is an example of a typical phishing e-mail that seeks to obtain personal information from an unwary respondent.

used in phishing attacks (almost 80%). Other top brands exploited by phishing attacks were Amazon and eBay (Symantec, 2010).

Many of the security vulnerabilities described throughout this section use what are called "social engineering" techniques to propagate. These techniques involve fraud or misrepresentation, or in other words, pretending to be something that it is not. For instance, the Netsky.P worm uses an e-mail message that takes the form of an e-mail delivery notification to trick recipients into thinking that the e-mail is from a valid source, encouraging them to open an attached file that, in reality, is an executable program that contains a virus or worm. Once the attachment is opened, the worm begins to execute on the computer. Social engineering not only aids the worm in getting the target recipient to open the infected e-mail, it also allows the worm to evade content filters or scanners, often by masquerading as a compressed zip file.

## HACKING AND CYBERVANDALISM

**hacker**

an individual who intends to gain unauthorized access to a computer system

**cracker**

within the hacking community, a term typically used to denote a hacker with criminal intent

**cybervandalism**

intentionally disrupting, defacing, or even destroying a site

A **hacker** is an individual who intends to gain unauthorized access to a computer system. Within the hacking community, the term **cracker** is typically used to denote a hacker with criminal intent, although in the public press, the terms hacker and cracker tend to be used interchangeably. Hackers and crackers gain unauthorized access by finding weaknesses in the security procedures of Web sites and computer systems, often taking advantage of various features of the Internet that make it an open system that is easy to use. Hackers and crackers typically are computer aficionados excited by the challenge of breaking into corporate and government Web sites. Sometimes they are satisfied merely by breaking into the files of an e-commerce site. Others have more malicious intentions and commit **cybervandalism**, intentionally disrupting, defacing, or even destroying the site.

For instance, Robert Lyttle of San Francisco and Benjamin Stark of St. Petersburg, Florida, were convicted of breaking into and "hacking" a computer at NASA's Ames Research Center in Moffett Field, California. They stole information about members of the agency's Astrobiology Institute and used that information to deface the home page of the NASA Astrobiology Institute. Calling themselves "The Deceptive Duo," Lyttle and Stark stated that their attacks were intended to demonstrate vulnerabilities in the government's computer security systems. The pair also hacked into the Defense Department's Defense Logistics Information Service Web site and the agency's Office of Health Affairs. Lyttle pleaded guilty to the attacks, and the U.S. District Court in Oakland, California, sentenced him to four months in prison, restitution payment of $71,181, and three years probation. Stark, who also pleaded guilty, was sentenced to two years probation and to pay $29,006 in restitution (Butterfield, 2005).

Cyberhacking for fun has gone out of fashion, and today's hackers tend to go for the money. In February 2010, Max Butler, also known as "Max Ray Vision," was sentenced to 13 years in federal prison for stealing nearly 2 million credit numbers from banks, businesses, and other hackers (no honor among thieves). Max ran up $86 million in fraudulent charges. He was ordered to disgorge $27 million in assets as a fine. Max was contrite and said after sentencing: "I have a lot of regrets, but I think my essential failing was that I lost touch with the accountability and responsibility that comes with being a member of society."

The hacker phenomenon has diversified over time. In general, benign hacking and defacement hacking has receded as law enforcement and private agencies learn how to detect perpetrators. Hacker activities have broadened beyond mere system intrusion to include theft of goods and information, as well as vandalism and system damage.

Groups of hackers called *tiger teams* are sometimes used by corporate security departments to test their own security measures. By hiring hackers to break into the system from the outside, the company can identify weaknesses in the computer system's armor. These "good hackers" became known as **white hats** because of their role in helping organizations locate and fix security flaws. White hats do their work under contract, with agreement from clients that they will not be prosecuted for their efforts to break in.

In contrast, **black hats** are hackers who engage in the same kinds of activities but without pay or any buy-in from the targeted organization, and with the intention of causing harm. They break into Web sites and reveal the confidential or proprietary information they find. These hackers believe strongly that information should be free, so sharing previously secret information is part of their mission.

Somewhere in the middle are the **grey hats**, hackers who believe they are pursuing some greater good by breaking in and revealing system flaws. Grey hats discover weaknesses in a system's security, and then publish the weakness without disrupting the site or attempting to profit from their finds. Their only reward is the prestige of discovering the weakness. Grey hat actions are suspect, however, especially when the hackers reveal security flaws that make it easier for other criminals to gain access to a system.

**white hats**
"good" hackers who help organizations locate and fix security flaws

**black hats**
hackers who act with the intention of causing harm

**grey hats**
hackers who believe they are pursuing some greater good by breaking in and revealing system flaws

## CREDIT CARD FRAUD/THEFT

Theft of credit card data is one of the most feared occurrences on the Internet. Fear that credit card information will be stolen frequently prevents users from making online purchases. Interestingly, this fear appears to be largely unfounded. Incidences of stolen credit card information are much lower than users think, around 1.2% of all online card transactions (CyberSource, 2010).

In traditional commerce, there is substantial credit card fraud, but the consumer is largely insured against losses by federal law. In the past, the most common cause of credit card fraud was a lost or stolen card that is used by someone else, followed by employee theft of customer numbers and stolen identities (criminals applying for credit cards using false identities). Federal law limits the liability of individuals to $50 for a stolen credit card. For amounts over $50, the credit card company generally pays the amount, although in some cases, the merchant may be held liable if it failed to verify the account or consult published lists of invalid cards. Banks recoup the cost of credit card fraud by charging higher interest rates on unpaid balances, and by merchants who raise prices to cover the losses.

But today the most frequent cause of stolen cards and card information is the systematic hacking and looting of a corporate server where the information on millions of credit card purchases are stored. For instance, in March 2010, Albert Gonzales was sentenced to 20 years in prison for organizing the largest theft of credit card numbers in American history. Along with two Russian co-conspirators, Gonzalez broke into the central computer systems of TJX, BJs, Barnes & Noble, and other companies, stealing over 160 million card numbers and costing these firms over $200 million in losses.

International orders have been particularly prone to repudiation. If an international customer places an order and then later disputes it, online merchants often have no way to verify that the package was actually delivered and that the credit card holder is the person who placed the order.

The solution for many Web sites is to institute new identity verification mechanisms that are currently in development; these will be discussed in the next section. Until a customer's identity can be guaranteed, online companies are at a much higher risk of loss than traditional offline companies. The federal government has attempted to address this issue through the Electronic Signatures in Global and National Commerce Act (the "E-Sign" law), which gives digital signatures the same authority as hand-written signatures in commerce. This law also intended to make digital signatures more commonplace, and easier to use. Except for large businesses conducting transactions over the Internet, the law has had little impact on B2C commerce, but that may be changing.

### SPOOFING (PHARMING) AND SPAM (JUNK) WEB SITES

**spoof**

to misrepresent oneself by using fake e-mail addresses or masquerading as someone else

Hackers attempting to hide their true identity often **spoof**, or misrepresent themselves by using fake e-mail addresses or masquerading as someone else. Spoofing a Web site is also called "pharming," which involves redirecting a Web link to an address different from the intended one, with the site masquerading as the intended destination. Links that are designed to lead to one site can be reset to send users to a totally unrelated site—one that benefits the hacker.

Although spoofing does not directly damage files or network servers, it threatens the integrity of a site. For example, if hackers redirect customers to a fake Web site that looks almost exactly like the true site, they can then collect and process orders, effectively stealing business from the true site. Or, if the intent is to disrupt rather than steal, hackers can alter orders—inflating them or changing products ordered—and then send them on to the true site for processing and delivery. Customers become dissatisfied with the improper order shipment and the company may have huge inventory fluctuations that impact its operations.

In addition to threatening integrity, spoofing also threatens authenticity by making it difficult to discern the true sender of a message. Clever hackers can make it almost impossible to distinguish between a true and a fake identity or Web address. Spam (junk) Web sites are a little different. These are sites that promise to offer some product or service, but in fact are a collection of advertisements for other sites, some of which contain malicious code. For instance, you may search for "[name of town] weather," and then click on a link that promises your local weather, but then discover that all the site does is display ads for weather-related products or other Web sites.

Junk or spam Web sites typically appear on search results, and do not involve e-mail. These sites cloak their identities by using domain names similar to legitimate firm names, and redirect traffic to known spammer-redirection domains such as topsearch10.com.

## DENIAL OF SERVICE (DOS) AND DISTRIBUTED DENIAL OF SERVICE (DDOS) ATTACKS

In a **Denial of Service (DoS)** attack, hackers flood a Web site with useless page requests that inundate and overwhelm the site's Web servers. Increasingly, DoS attacks involve the use of bot networks and so-called "distributed attacks" built from thousands of compromised client computers. DoS attacks typically cause a Web site to shut down, making it impossible for users to access the site. For busy e-commerce sites, these attacks are costly; while the site is shut down, customers cannot make purchases. And the longer a site is shut down, the more damage is done to a site's reputation. Although such attacks do not destroy information or access restricted areas of the server, they can destroy a firm's online business. Often, DoS attacks are accompanied by attempts at blackmailing site owners to pay tens or hundreds of thousands of dollars to the hackers in return for removing the DoS attack.

> **Denial of Service (DoS) attack**
> flooding a Web site with useless traffic to inundate and overwhelm the network

A **Distributed Denial of Service (DDoS)** attack uses numerous computers to attack the target network from numerous launch points. DoS and DDoS attacks are threats to a system's operation because they can shut it down indefinitely. Major Web sites such as Yahoo and Microsoft have experienced such attacks, making the companies aware of their vulnerability and the need to continually introduce new measures to prevent future attacks. The largest DDoS attack to date occurred in 2007, when a botnet composed of several thousand computers attempted to bring down the part of the Internet domain name system operated by VeriSign. The attack affected 13 domain name servers operated by VeriSign, including the .com and .org domains (Markoff, 2007). The attack impeded but did not bring down any of the servers. Had it succeeded, the Internet itself would have failed for a period of time.

> **Distributed Denial of Service (DDoS) attack**
> using numerous computers to attack the target network from numerous launch points

Hackers continue to use DDoS to attack Web sites, and in 2010, as you learned in the opening case, politically motivated DDoS attacks were launched against a number of South Korean, and U.S. government and commercial Web sites, and also shut down Twitter for almost a day.

## SNIFFING

A **sniffer** is a type of eavesdropping program that monitors information traveling over a network. When used legitimately, sniffers can help identify potential network trouble-spots, but when used for criminal purposes, they can be damaging and very difficult to detect. Sniffers enable hackers to steal proprietary information from anywhere on a network, including e-mail messages, company files, and confidential reports. For instance, in March 2009, hackers inserted code on the servers of Network Solutions (which provides domain registration and hosting services) that sniffed and intercepted credit and debit card and personal identifying information of more than 573,000 customers (Channelinsider.com, 2009). The threat of sniffing is that confidential or personal information will be stolen or made public.

> **sniffer**
> a type of eavesdropping program that monitors information traveling over a network

*E-mail wiretaps* are a variation on the sniffing threat. An e-mail wiretap is hidden code in an e-mail message that allows someone to monitor all succeeding messages forwarded with the original message. E-mail wiretaps can be installed on servers and client computers. For instance, the USA PATRIOT Act permits the FBI to compel ISPs to install a black box on their mail servers that can impound the e-mail of a single person or group of persons for later analysis. In the case of American citizens communicating with other citizens, an FBI agent or government lawyer need only certify to a judge on the secret 11-member U.S. Foreign Intelligence Surveillance Court (FISC) that the information sought is "relevant to an ongoing criminal investigation" to get permission to install the program. Judges have no discretion. They must approve wiretaps based on government agents' unsubstantiated assertions (Associated Press, 2005). Congress adopted a new amendment to the 1978 Foreign Intelligence Surveillance Act, known as FISA, that provides new powers to the National Security Agency to monitor international e-mail and telephone communications where one person is in the United States, and where the purpose of such interception is to collect foreign intelligence (Foreign Intelligence Surveillance Act of 1978; Protect America Act of 2007).

## INSIDER ATTACKS

We tend to think of security threats to a business as originating outside the organization. In fact, the largest financial threats to business institutions come not from robberies but from embezzlement by insiders. Bank employees steal far more money than bank robbers. The same is true for e-commerce sites. Some of the largest disruptions to service, destruction to sites, and diversion of customer credit data and personal information have come from insiders— once trusted employees. Employees have access to privileged information, and in the presence of sloppy internal security procedures, they are often able to roam throughout an organization's systems without leaving a trace. The 2009 CSI survey reports that insider abuse of systems was the second most frequent type of attack during the preceding 12 months, and that around 44% of survey respondents believed that insiders contributed to some portion of the firm's financial losses during the previous year (Computer Security Institute, 2009). A Michigan State University study found that as much as 70% of all identity theft, including credit card theft, is the work of "insiders" (Borden, 2007). In some instances, the insider might not have criminal intent, but inadvertently expose data that can then be exploited by others. For instance, a Ponemon Institute study found that 75% of organizations surveyed in the United States, United Kingdom, France, and Germany had suffered data breaches caused by negligent insiders. (Ponemon Institute, 2009).

## POORLY DESIGNED SERVER AND CLIENT SOFTWARE

Many security threats prey on poorly designed server and client software, sometimes in the operating system and sometimes in the application software, including browsers. The increase in complexity and size of software programs, coupled with demands for timely delivery to markets, has contributed to an increase in software flaws or vulnerabilities that hackers can exploit. Each year, security firms identify thousands of software vulnerabilities in Internet and PC software. For instance, Symantec identified 384 browser vulnerabilities: 169 in Firefox, 94 in Safari, 45 in Internet Explorer, 41 in Chrome, and 25 in Opera in its most recent semi-annual *Internet Security Threat Report*. Some of these vulnerabilities were critical (Symantec, 2010). Six of the top 10 Internet attacks launched in 2009 were attacks against Microsoft Windows server and client software, exploiting various weaknesses. The very design of the personal computer includes many open communication ports that can be used, and indeed are designed to be used, by external computers to send and receive messages. The port typically attacked is TCP port 445. However, given their complexity and design objectives, all operating systems and application software, including Linux and Macintosh, have vulnerabilities. There are also a growing number of "zero-day" vulnerabilities, where the vulnerability is unknown to security experts and is actively exploited before there is a patch available, requiring firms to scurry to develop patches. For instance, for the week of September 20 2010, the U.S. Computer Emergency Readiness Team (US-CERT; Department of Homeland Security) reported on 67 newly discovered vulnerabilities in server and application software, 12 of them rated "high severity" (US-CERT, 2010).

## MOBILE PLATFORM SECURITY

A variety of mobile digital devices from netbooks to iPhones and Blackberrys are becoming common and powerful Internet access devices. Mobile users are filling their phones with personal and financial information, making them excellent targets for hackers. In general, mobile devices face all the same risks as any Internet device as well as some new risks associated with wireless network security. While most PC users are aware their computers and Web sites may be hacked and contain malware, most cell phone users believe their cell phone is as secure as a traditional landline phone.

Mobile cellphone malware was developed as early as 2004 with Cabir, a Bluetooth worm affecting Symbian operating systems (Nokia phones) and causing the phone to continuously seek out other Bluetooth-enabled devices, and quickly draining the battery. More recently Ike4e.B appeared on jailbroken iPhones, turning the phones into botnet controlled devices. An iPhone in Europe could be hacked by an iPhone in the United States, and all its private data sent to a server in Poland. Ike4e.B established the feasibility of cell phone botnets.

Vishing attacks target gullible cell users with verbal messages to call a certain number and, perhaps, donate money to starving children in Haiti. Smishing attacks exploit SMS messages. Compromised text messages can contain e-mail and Web site addresses that can lead the innocent user to a malware site. A very small number of downloaded apps from iTunes and other app stores have also contained malware.

## 5.3 TECHNOLOGY SOLUTIONS

At first glance it might seem like there is not much that can be done about the onslaught of security breaches on the Internet. Reviewing the security threats in the previous section, it is clear that the threats to e-commerce are very real, potentially devastating for individuals, businesses, and entire nations, and likely to be increasing in intensity along with the growth in e-commerce. But in fact a great deal of progress has been made by private security firms, corporate and home users, network administrators, technology firms, and government agencies. There are two lines of defense: technology solutions and policy solutions. In this section, we consider some technology solutions, and in the following section, we look at some policy solutions that work.

The first line of defense against the wide variety of security threats to an e-commerce site is a set of tools that can make it difficult for outsiders to invade or destroy a site. **Figure 5.7** illustrates the major tools available to achieve site security. In the next section, we describe these tools in greater detail.

## PROTECTING INTERNET COMMUNICATIONS

Because e-commerce transactions must flow over the public Internet, and therefore involve thousands of routers and servers through which the transaction packets flow, security experts believe the greatest security threats occur at the level of Internet communications. This is very different from a private network where a dedicated communication line is established between two parties. A number of tools are available to protect the security of Internet communications, the most basic of which is message encryption.

## ENCRYPTION

**Encryption** is the process of transforming plain text or data into **cipher text** that cannot be read by anyone other than the sender and the receiver. The purpose of encryption is (a) to secure stored information and (b) to secure information transmission. Encryption can provide four of the six key dimensions of e-commerce security referred to in Table 5.2 on page 271:

- *Message integrity*—provides assurance that the message has not been altered.
- *Nonrepudiation*—prevents the user from denying he or she sent the message.
- *Authentication*—provides verification of the identity of the person (or computer) sending the message.
- *Confidentiality*—gives assurance that the message was not read by others.

This transformation of plain text to cipher text is accomplished by using a key or cipher. A **key** (or **cipher**) is any method for transforming plain text to cipher text.

Encryption has been practiced since the earliest forms of writing and commercial transactions. Ancient Egyptian and Phoenician commercial records were encrypted using substitution and transposition ciphers. In a **substitution cipher**, every occurrence of a given letter is replaced systematically by another letter. For instance, if we used the cipher "letter plus two"—meaning replace every letter in a word with a new letter two places forward—then the word "Hello" in plain text would be transformed into the following cipher text: "JGNNQ." In a **transposition cipher**, the ordering of the letters in each word is changed in some systematic way. Leonardo Da Vinci recorded his shop notes in reverse order, making them readable only with a mirror. The word "Hello" can be written backwards as "OLLEH." A more complicated cipher would (a) break all words into two words and (b) spell the first word with every other letter beginning with the first letter, and then spell the second word with all the remaining letters. In this cipher, "HELLO" would be written as "HLO EL."

**encryption**

the process of transforming plain text or data into cipher text that cannot be read by anyone other than the sender and the receiver. The purpose of encryption is (a) to secure stored information and (b) to secure information transmission

**cipher text**

text that has been encrypted and thus cannot be read by anyone other than the sender and the receiver

**key (cipher)**

any method for transforming plain text to cipher text

**substitution cipher**

every occurrence of a given letter is replaced systematically by another letter

**transposition cipher**

the ordering of the letters in each word is changed in some systematic way

| FIGURE 5.7 | TOOLS AVAILABLE TO ACHIEVE SITE SECURITY |
| --- | --- |

There are a number of tools available to achieve site security.

## Symmetric Key Encryption

In order to decipher these messages, the receiver would have to know the secret cipher that was used to encrypt the plain text. This is called **symmetric key encryption** or **secret key encryption**. In symmetric key encryption, both the sender and the receiver use the same key to encrypt and decrypt the message. How do the sender and the receiver have the same key? They have to send it over some communication media or exchange the key in person. Symmetric key encryption was used extensively throughout World War II and is still a part of Internet encryption.

The possibilities for simple substitution and transposition ciphers are endless, but they all suffer from common flaws. First, in the digital age, computers are so powerful and fast that these ancient means of encryption can be broken quickly. Second, symmetric key encryption requires that both parties share the same key. In order to share the same key, they must send the key over a presumably *insecure* medium where it could be stolen and used to decipher messages. If the secret key is lost or stolen, the entire encryption system fails. Third, in commercial use, where we are not all part of the same team, you would need a secret key for each of the parties with whom you transacted, that is, one key for the bank, another for the department store, and another for the government. In a large population of users, this could result in as many as n(n–1) keys. In a population of millions of Internet users, thousands of millions of keys would be needed to accommodate all e-commerce customers (estimated at about 133

**symmetric key encryption (secret key encryption)**

both the sender and the receiver use the same key to encrypt and decrypt the message

million in the United States). Potentially, 133 million[2] different keys would be needed. Clearly this situation would be too unwieldy to work in practice.

Modern encryption systems are digital. The ciphers or keys used to transform plain text into cipher text are digital strings. Computers store text or other data as binary strings composed of 0s and 1s. For instance, the binary representation of the capital letter "A" in ASCII computer code is accomplished with eight binary digits (bits): 01000001. One way in which digital strings can be transformed into cipher text is by multiplying each letter by another binary number, say, an eight-bit key number 0101 0101. If we multiplied every digital character in our text messages by this eight-bit key, sent the encrypted message to a friend along with the secret eight-bit key, the friend could decode the message easily.

The strength of modern security protection is measured in terms of the length of the binary key used to encrypt the data. In the preceding example, the eight-bit key is easily deciphered because there are only $2^8$ or 256 possibilities. If the intruder knows you are using an eight-bit key, then he or she could decode the message in a few seconds using a modern desktop PC just by using the brute force method of checking each of the 256 possible keys. For this reason, modern digital encryption systems use keys with 56, 128, 256, or 512 binary digits. With encryption keys of 512 digits, there are $2^{512}$ possibilities to check out. It is estimated that all the computers in the world would need to work for 10 years before stumbling upon the answer.

The **Data Encryption Standard (DES)** was developed by the National Security Agency (NSA) and IBM in the 1950s. DES uses a 56-bit encryption key. To cope with much faster computers, it has been improved by *Triple DES*—essentially encrypting the message three times each with a separate key. Today, the most widely used symmetric key encryption algorithm is **Advanced Encryption Standard (AES)**, which offers key sizes of 128, 192, and 256 bits. There are also many other symmetric key systems with keys up to 2,048 bits.[1]

## Public Key Encryption

In 1976, a new way of encrypting messages called **public key cryptography** was invented by Whitfield Diffie and Martin Hellman. Public key cryptography solves the problem of exchanging keys. In this method, two mathematically related digital keys are used: a public key and a private key. The private key is kept secret by the owner, and the public key is widely disseminated. Both keys can be used to encrypt and decrypt a message. However, once the keys are used to encrypt a message, that same key cannot be used to unencrypt the message. The mathematical algorithms used to produce the keys are *one-way functions*. A one-way irreversible mathematical function is one in which, once the algorithm is applied, the input cannot be subsequently derived from the output. Most food recipes are like this. For instance, it is easy to make scrambled eggs, but impossible to retrieve whole eggs from the scrambled eggs. Public key cryptography is based on the idea of irreversible mathematical functions. The keys are

**Data Encryption Standard (DES)**

developed by the National Security Agency (NSA) and IBM. Uses a 56-bit encryption key

**Advanced Encryption Standard (AES)**

the most widely used symmetric key encryption algorithm. Offers 128-, 192-, and 256-bit keys.

**public key cryptography**

two mathematically related digital keys are used: a public key and a private key. The private key is kept secret by the owner, and the public key is widely disseminated. Both keys can be used to encrypt and decrypt a message. However, once the keys are used to encrypt a message, that same key cannot be used to unencrypt the message

[1]For instance: DESX and RDES with 168-bit keys; the RC Series: RC2, RC4, and RC5 with keys up to 2,048 bits; and the IDEA algorithm, the basis of PGP, e-mail public key encryption software described later in this chapter, which uses 128-bit keys.

sufficiently long (128-, 256-, and 512-bit keys) that it would take enormous computing power to derive one key from the other using the largest and fastest computers available. **Figure 5.8** illustrates a simple use of public key cryptography and takes you through the important steps in using public and private keys.

| FIGURE 5.8 | PUBLIC KEY CRYPTOGRAPHY—A SIMPLE CASE |
|---|---|
| **STEP** | **DESCRIPTION** |
| 1. The sender creates a digital message. | The message could be a document, spreadsheet, or any digital object. |
| 2. The sender obtains the recipient's public key from a public directory and applies it to the message. | Public keys are distributed widely and can be obtained from recipients directly. |
| 3. Application of the recipient's key produces an encrypted ciphertext message. | Once encrypted using the public key, the message cannot be reverse-engineered or unencrypted using the same public key. The process is irreversible. |
| 4. The encrypted message is sent over the Internet. | The encrypted message is broken into packets and sent through several different pathways, making interception of the entire message difficult (but not impossible). |
| 5. The recipient uses his/her private key to decrypt the message. | The only person who can decrypt the message is the person who has possession of the recipient's private key. Hopefully, this is the legitimate recipient. |

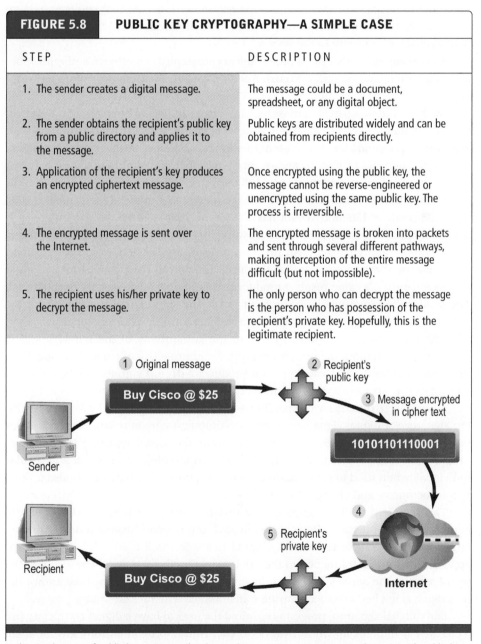

In the simplest use of public key cryptography, the sender encrypts a message using the recipient's public key, and then sends it over the Internet. The only person who can decrypt this message is the recipient, using his or her private key. However, this simple case does not ensure integrity or an authentic message.

### Public Key Encryption Using Digital Signatures and Hash Digests

In public key encryption, some elements of security are missing. Although we can be quite sure the message was not understood or read by a third party (message confidentiality), there is no guarantee the sender really is the sender; that is, there is no authentication of the sender. This means the sender could deny ever sending the message (repudiation). And there is no assurance the message was not altered somehow in transit. For example, the message "Buy Cisco @ $25" could have been accidentally or intentionally altered to read "Sell Cisco @ $25." This suggests a potential lack of integrity in the system.

A more sophisticated use of public key cryptography can achieve authentication, nonrepudiation, and integrity. **Figure 5.9** on page 291 illustrates this more powerful approach.

**hash function**
an algorithm that produces a fixed-length number called a hash or message digest

To check the integrity of a message and ensure it has not been altered in transit, a hash function is used first to create a digest of the message. A **hash function** is an algorithm that produces a fixed-length number called a *hash* or *message digest*. A hash function can be simple, and count the number of digital 1s in a message, or it can be more complex, and produce a 128-bit number that reflects the number of 0s and 1s, the number of 00s, 11s, and so on. Standard hash functions are available (MD4 and MD5 produce 128- and 160-bit hashes) (Stein, 1998). These more complex hash functions produce hashes or hash results that are unique to every message. The results of applying the hash function are sent by the sender to the recipient. Upon receipt, the recipient applies the hash function to the received message and checks to verify the same result is produced. If so, the message has not been altered. The sender then encrypts both the hash result and the original message using the recipient's public key (as in Figure 5.8), producing a single block of cipher text.

One more step is required. To ensure the authenticity of the message and to ensure nonrepudiation, the sender encrypts the entire block of cipher text one more time using the sender's private key. This produces a **digital signature** (also called an *e-signature*) or "signed" cipher text that can be sent over the Internet.

**digital signature (e-signature)**
"signed" cipher text that can be sent over the Internet

A digital signature is a close parallel to a handwritten signature. Like a handwritten signature, a digital signature is unique—only one person presumably possesses the private key. When used with a hash function, the digital signature is even more unique than a handwritten signature. In addition to being exclusive to a particular individual, when used to sign a hashed document, the digital signature is also unique to the document, and changes for every document.

The recipient of this signed cipher text first uses the sender's public key to authenticate the message. Once authenticated, the recipient uses his or her private key to obtain the hash result and original message. As a final step, the recipient applies the same hash function to the original text, and compares the result with the result sent by the sender. If the results are the same, the recipient now knows the message has not been changed during transmission. The message has integrity.

Early digital signature programs required the user to have a digital certificate, and were far too difficult for an individual to use. Newer programs from several small companies are Internet-based and do not require users to install software, or understand digital certificate technology. DocuSign, EchoSign, and Sertifi are companies

## FIGURE 5.9 — PUBLIC KEY CRYPTOGRAPHY WITH DIGITAL SIGNATURES

| STEP | DESCRIPTION |
|---|---|
| 1. The sender creates an original message. | The message could be any digital file. |
| 2. The sender applies a hash function, producing a 128-bit hash result. | Hash functions create a unique digest of the message based on the message contents. |
| 3. The sender encrypts the message and hash result using recipient's public key. | This irreversible process creates a cipher text that can be read only by the recipient using his or her private key. |
| 4. The sender encrypts the result, again using his or her private key. | The sender's private key is a digital signature. There is only one person who could create this digital mark. |
| 5. The result of this double encryption is sent over the Internet. | The message traverses the Internet as a series of independent packets. |
| 6. The receiver uses the sender's public key to authenticate the message. | Only one person could send this message, namely, the sender. |
| 7. The receiver uses his or her private key to decrypt the hash function and the original message. The receiver checks to ensure the original message and the hash function results conform to one another. | The hash function is used here to check the original message. This ensures the message was not changed in transit. |

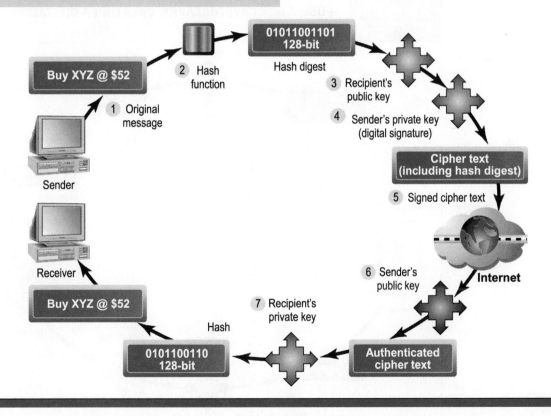

A more realistic use of public key cryptography uses hash functions and digital signatures to both ensure the confidentiality of the message and authenticate the sender. The only person who could have sent the above message is the owner or the sender using his/her private key. This authenticates the message. The hash function ensures the message was not altered in transit. As before, the only person who can decipher the message is the recipient, using his/her private key.

offering online digital signatures. Fidelity National Financial and other insurance, finance, and surety companies are beginning to permit customers to electronically sign documents.

### Digital Envelopes

Public key encryption is computationally slow. If one used 128- or 256-bit keys to encode large documents—such as this chapter or the entire book—significant declines in transmission speeds and increases in processing time would occur. Symmetric key encryption is computationally faster, but as we pointed out previously, it has a weakness—namely, the symmetric key must be sent to the recipient over insecure transmission lines. One solution is to use the more efficient symmetric encryption and decryption for large documents, but public key encryption to encrypt and send the symmetric key. This technique is called using a **digital envelope**. See **Figure 5.10** for an illustration of how a digital envelope works.

**digital envelope**
a technique that uses symmetric encryption for large documents, but public key encryption to encrypt and send the symmetric key

| FIGURE 5.10 | PUBLIC KEY CRYPTOGRAPHY: CREATING A DIGITAL ENVELOPE |
| --- | --- |

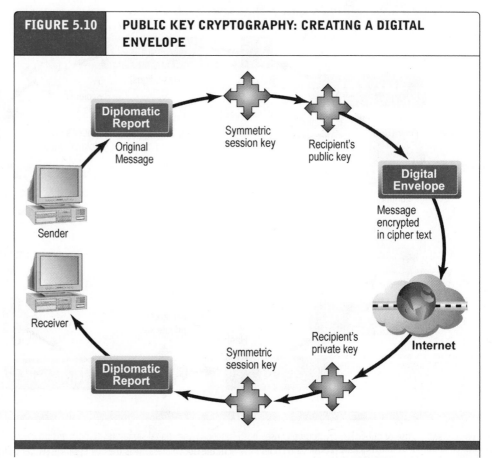

A digital envelope can be created to transmit a symmetric key that will permit the recipient to decrypt the message and be assured the message was not intercepted in transit.

In Figure 5.10, a diplomatic document is encrypted using a symmetric key. The symmetric key—which the recipient will require to decrypt the document—is itself encrypted, using the recipient's public key. So we have a "key within a key" (a *digital envelope*). The encrypted report and the digital envelope are sent across the Web. The recipient first uses his/her private key to decrypt the symmetric key, and then the recipient uses the symmetric key to decrypt the report. This method saves time because both encryption and decryption are faster with symmetric keys.

## Digital Certificates and Public Key Infrastructure (PKI)

There are still some deficiencies in the message security regime described previously. How do we know that people and institutions are who they claim to be? Anyone can make up a private and public key combination and claim to be someone they are not. Before you place an order with an online merchant such as Amazon, you want to be sure it really is Amazon.com you have on the screen and not a spoofer masquerading as Amazon. In the physical world, if someone asks who you are and you show a social security number, they may well ask to see a picture ID or a second form of certifiable or acceptable identification. If they really doubt who you are, they may ask for references to other authorities and actually interview these other authorities. Similarly, in the digital world, we need a way to know who people and institutions really are.

Digital certificates, and the supporting public key infrastructure, are an attempt to solve this problem of digital identity. A **digital certificate** is a digital document issued by a trusted third-party institution known as a **certification authority (CA)** that contains the name of the subject or company, the subject's public key, a digital certificate serial number, an expiration date, an issuance date, the digital signature of the certification authority (the name of the CA encrypted using the CA's private key), and other identifying information (see **Figure 5.11**).

In the United States, private corporations such as VeriSign and government agencies such as the U.S. Postal Service, the Federal Reserve and many private corporations act as CAs. In fact, a hierarchy of CAs is emerging with less well-known CAs being certified by larger and better-known CAs, creating a community of mutually verifying institutions. **Public key infrastructure (PKI)** refers to the CAs and digital certificate procedures that are accepted by all parties.

To create a digital certificate, the user generates a public/private key pair and sends a request for certification to a CA along with the user's public key. The CA verifies the information (how this is accomplished differs from CA to CA). The CA issues a certificate containing the user's public key and other related information. Finally, the CA creates a message digest from the certificate itself (just like a hash digest) and signs it with the CA's private key. This signed digest is called the *signed certificate*. We end up with a totally unique cipher text document—there can be only one signed certificate like this in the world.

There are several ways the certificates are used in commerce. Before initiating a transaction, the customer can request the signed digital certificate of the merchant and decrypt it using the merchant's public key to obtain both the message digest and the certificate as issued. If the message digest matches the certificate, then the

**digital certificate**

a digital document issued by a certification authority that contains the name of the subject or company, the subject's public key, a digital certificate serial number, an expiration date, an issuance date, the digital signature of the certification authority, and other identifying information

**certification authority (CA)**

a trusted third party that issues digital certificates

**public key infrastructure (PKI)**

CAs and digital certificate procedures that are accepted by all parties

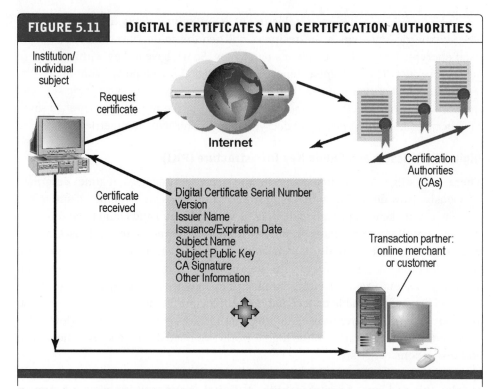

| FIGURE 5.11 | DIGITAL CERTIFICATES AND CERTIFICATION AUTHORITIES |
|---|---|

The PKI includes certification authorities that issue, verify, and guarantee digital certificates that are used in e-commerce to assure the identity of transaction partners.

merchant and the public key are authenticated. The merchant may in return request certification of the user, in which case the user would send the merchant his or her individual certificate. There are many types of certificates: personal, institutional, Web server, software publisher, and CAs themselves.

You can easily obtain a public and private key for personal, noncommercial use at the International PGP Home Page Web site, Pgpi.org. **Pretty Good Privacy (PGP)** was invented in 1991 by Phil Zimmerman, and has become one of the most widely used e-mail public key encryption software tools in the world. Using PGP software installed on your computer, you can compress and encrypt your messages as well as authenticate both yourself and the recipient. The *Insight on Society* story, *Web Dogs and Anonymity*, describes additional efforts to ensure e-mail security.

**Pretty Good Privacy (PGP)**

a widely used e-mail public key encryption software program

### Limitations to Encryption Solutions

PKI is a powerful technological solution to security issues, but it has many limitations. PKI applies mainly to protecting messages in transit on the Internet and is not effective against insiders—employees—who have legitimate access to corporate systems including customer information. Most e-commerce sites do not store customer information in encrypted form. Other limitations are apparent. For one, how is your private key to be protected? Most private keys will be stored on insecure desktop or laptop computers.

# INSIGHT ON SOCIETY

## WEB DOGS AND ANONYMITY

The cartoonist Peter Steiner captured the chaotic security situation on the Internet in an iconic *New Yorker* magazine cartoon illustrating two dogs in front of a computer screen, one entering data. The caption: "On the Internet, no one knows you're a dog." This phrase neatly sums up many of the problems with Internet security: you just don't know who you are dealing with on the Web, you don't know who to trust, and you may not feel comfortable putting your personal information online, either by purchasing, socializing, or communicating. Spammers may even be sending out spam that appears to come from you, potentially destroying your credibility and reputation.

It gets worse. Most Web users have multiple identities across the Web, with large numbers of user accounts, passwords, and personal identifier attributes (for instance, your mother's maiden name) across multiple providers of Web services all of whom have different data sharing and privacy policies. On social sites, many people reveal their unique personal attributes or they can be found with artful searching. As a result, most Web users don't have a clue about who has what information about them, how it is used, or who has access to it. Most computers on the Internet, as well as routers, and smartphones, do not really know who they are communicating with. Routers, the work horse computers that direct traffic on the Internet, send messages to one another about where to route packets of information. Routers trust that the instructions they receive from other routers are valid and legitimate. On numerous occasions in the past three years significant portions of the global Internet traffic were routed to China by mistake, or intentionally, by rogue computer programs.

The federal government, along with private industry, is trying to fix this problem, sometimes called "Identity 2.0." In June 25, 2010, Howard Schmidt, the White House-appointed cyberczar, released a draft policy document describing a "voluntary trusted identity" system that would provide all members of the online community (people, institutions, computers, network routers and other appliances including cell phones) with an incontrovertible digital identity. The document refers to this new environment as an "identify ecosystem," a kind of walled garden where people can safely play. The identity system would rely on a "strong credential" that would work like a combination of a digital key (a private digital key that uniquely identifies your computer), a fingerprint (or some bio marker that uniquely identifies you), and perhaps a digitized photo (or other attribute like your mother's maiden name).

Where would the identity credential be stored? According to the draft, the credential could be stored on a smart card the user carries in his or her pocket like a credit card, or it could be stored on the user's computer. You can think of it as an Internet driver's license, or a credit card on steroids. Internet users would not be required to have a strong credential, but they could not get access to most popular Web sites without a credential.

With this strong credential you would be able to sign in to any Web site requesting your ID, from a bank, or university, to a government agency, either by swiping the smart card or sending a digital ID file. Single sign-in means you have one password and one login across all sites. Google and Microsoft have single sign-on systems to gain access to wide variety of different services. Anonymity, the bane of the Internet because it allows people to abuse the Internet and its users while hiding their identity, would presumably be eliminated or greatly reduced.

(continued)

A computer captured by a botnet theoretically would not be allowed to send spam to any other computer, or a request for service, without first authenticating itself (or the owner of the computer). This would also greatly reduce phishing. A commanding computer controlling a botnet would not be able to launch a million spam e-mails at once across the Internet without identifying itself (IP address), sending its own authentication, and using digital keys to activate all its slave computers. You would not be allowed to post to a blog or Web site without first authenticating who you are. You would not be able to send e-mail to anyone without first authenticating who you are. In this plan, anonymity is not possible.

Who would control this identity system? The federal government proposal calls for a federation of private and public online identity systems. Banks, federal agencies, Google, the U.S. Postal Service, VeriSign, and other trusted institutions would provide the electronic smart ID cards, or digital files, once they have identified who you are. This would be similar to credit cards which are issued by multiple financial institutions and are widely accepted. The other alternative for organizing strong identity regimes is a single federal agency. This alternative is supported primarily by academic and government computer scientists who believe such a solution would be less chaotic and easier to implement. Most privacy advocates and private firms want a mix of public and private entities to control the security ecosystem.

There is considerable doubt among security experts that a new identity ecosystem can be built within the confines of the existing Internet, or if built, would work according to plan. Steven Bellovin, a prominent security researcher notes, "The biggest problem [for Internet security] was and is buggy code. All the authentication in the world won't stop a bad guy who goes around the authentication system, either by finding bugs exploitable before authentication is performed, finding bugs in the authentication system itself, or by hijacking your system and abusing the authenticated connection set up by the legitimate user. All of these attacks have been known for years." A more mundane problem is ensuring that the digital identity granted by the security system matches the real physical identity of the person or institution applying for an online ID. Credit card companies are often fooled into issuing credit cards and credit card clearing services to criminals and imposters who have stolen identities; banks and government agencies often provide services to people with stolen social security numbers. If offline authentication is flawed, then online authentication is hopeless.

Public key encryption has worked well for larger institutions but it never took off among the public. Security is costly: encryption slows down networks and requires additional capacity to cope with all the authentication messages inherent in public key encryption. The American public has never signed up for a "national identity card" system, which privacy advocates believe inevitably follows from the White House proposal. While upwards of 30% of European online banking users swipe Internet ID cards into a personal card reader next to their computers in order to access their accounts, so far this has not been proposed in the United States. Yet many Americans would gladly carry another card in their wallet if it meant a more secure online experience.

**SOURCES:** "White House's Trusted Identities Strategy Doesn't Inspire Trust," by Matthew Harwood, Securitymanagement.com, July 27, 2010, "Real ID Online? New Federal Online Identity Plan Raises Privacy and Free Speech," by Lee Tien and Seth Schoe, Electronic Frontier Foundation, July 20, 2010, "Taking the Mystery Out of Web Anonymity," John Markoff, *New York Times*, July 2, 2010; "White House Strategy For Secure Cyberspace Based on Identify-theft-flawed Meatspace," by Joe Campana, Examiner.com, June 29, 2010; "How Safe Will You Be with Obama's 'trusted' identity solution?," by Kervin McCaney, *Federal Computer Week*, June 29, 2010; "National Strategy for Trusted Identities in Cyberspace Creating Options for Enhanced Online Security and Privacy," Draft, Department of Homeland Security, June 25, 2010.

There is no guarantee the person using your computer—and your private key—is really you. For instance, you may lose your laptop or smartphone, and therefore lose the private key. Likewise, there is no assurance that someone else in the world uses your personal ID papers such as a social security card, to obtain a PKI authenticated online ID in your name. If there's no real world identification system, there can be no Internet identification system. Under many digital signature laws (such as those in Utah and Washington), you are responsible for whatever your private key does even if you were not the person using the key. This is very different from mail-order or telephone order credit card rules, where you have a right to dispute the credit card charge. Second, there is no guarantee the verifying computer of the merchant is secure. Third, CAs are self-selected organizations seeking to gain access to the business of authorization. They may not be authorities on the corporations or individuals they certify. For instance, how can a CA know about all the corporations within an industry to determine who is or is not legitimate? A related question concerns the method used by the CA to identify the certificate holder. Was this an e-mail transaction verified only by claims of applicants who filled out an online form? For instance, VeriSign acknowledged in one case that it had mistakenly issued two digital certificates to someone fraudulently claiming to represent Microsoft. Digital certificates have been hijacked by hackers, tricking consumers into giving up personal information. Last, what are the policies for revoking or renewing certificates? The expected life of a digital certificate or private key is a function of the frequency of use and the vulnerability of systems that use the certificate. Yet most CAs have no policy or just an annual policy for re-issuing certificates.

## SECURING CHANNELS OF COMMUNICATION

The concepts of public key encryption are used routinely for securing channels of communication.

### Secure Sockets Layer (SSL)

The most common form of securing channels is through the *Secure Sockets Layer (SSL)* of TCP/IP (described briefly in Chapter 3). When you receive a message from a server on the Web with which you will be communicating through a secure channel, this means you will be using SSL to establish a secure negotiated session. (Notice that the URL changes from HTTP to HTTPS.) A **secure negotiated session** is a client-server session in which the URL of the requested document, along with the contents, contents of forms, and the cookies exchanged, are encrypted (see **Figure 5.12**). For instance, your credit card number that you entered into a form would be encrypted. Through a series of handshakes and communications, the browser and the server establish one another's identity by exchanging digital certificates, decide on the strongest shared form of encryption, and then proceed to communicate using an agreed-upon session key. A **session key** is a unique symmetric encryption key chosen just for this single secure session. Once used, it is gone forever. Figure 5.12 shows how this works.

**secure negotiated session**
a client-server session in which the URL of the requested document, along with the contents, contents of forms, and the cookies exchanged, are encrypted

**session key**
a unique symmetric encryption key chosen for a single secure session

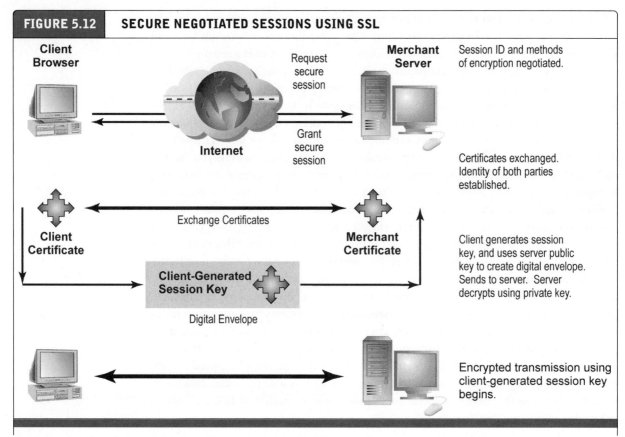

| FIGURE 5.12 | SECURE NEGOTIATED SESSIONS USING SSL |
| --- | --- |

Certificates play a key role in using SSL to establish a secure communications channel.

In practice, most private individuals do not have a digital certificate. In this case, the merchant server will not request a certificate, but the client browser will request the merchant certificate once a secure session is called for by the server.

The SSL protocol provides data encryption, server authentication, optional client authentication, and message integrity for TCP/IP connections. SSL is available in 40-bit and 128-bit levels, depending on what brower version you are using. The strongest shared encryption is always chosen.

SSL was designed to address the threat of authenticity by allowing users to verify another user's identity or the identity of a server. It also protects the integrity of the messages exchanged. However, once the merchant receives the encrypted credit and order information, that information is typically stored in unencrypted format on the merchant's servers.

While the SSL protocol provides secure transactions between merchant and consumer, it only guarantees server-side authentication. Client authentication is optional.

In addition, SSL cannot provide irrefutability—consumers can order goods or download information products, and then claim the transaction never occurred.

Other protocols for protecting financial transactions such as Secure Electronic Transaction Protocol (SET), which requires all parties to a transaction to use digital certificates, have been developed. However, SET has not been widely adopted.

### Secure Hypertext Transfer Protocol (S-HTTP)

A competing method is called **Secure Hypertext Transfer Protocol (S-HTTP)**. S-HTTP is a secure message-oriented communications protocol designed for use in conjunction with HTTP. It is designed to coexist with HTTP and to be easily integrated with HTTP applications. Whereas SSL is designed to establish a secure connection between two computers, S-HTTP is designed to send individual messages securely. Not all browsers and not all Web sites support S-HTTP. You know you are dealing with a supporting site when the URL starts with "SHTTP." The use of this as part of an anchor tag indicates that the target server is S-HTTP capable. Using S-HTTP, any message may be signed, authenticated, encrypted, or any combination of these. Basically, S-HTTP attempts to make HTTP more secure.

**Secure Hypertext Transfer Protocol (S-HTTP)**
a secure message-oriented communications protocol designed for use in conjunction with HTTP. Cannot be used to secure non-HTTP messages

### Virtual Private Networks (VPNs)

A **virtual private network (VPN)** allows remote users to securely access internal networks via the Internet, using the **Point-to-Point Tunneling Protocol (PPTP)**. PPTP is an encoding mechanism that allows one local network to connect to another using the Internet as the conduit. A remote user can dial into a local ISP, and PPTP makes the connection from the ISP to the corporate network as if the user had dialed into the corporate network directly. The process of connecting one protocol (PPTP) through another (IP) is called *tunneling,* because PPTP creates a private connection by adding an invisible wrapper around a message to hide its content. As the message travels through the Internet between the ISP and the corporate network, it is shielded from prying eyes by PPTP's encrypted wrapper.

**virtual private network (VPN)**
allows remote users to securely access internal networks via the Internet, using the Point-to-Point Tunneling Protocol (PPTP)

A VPN is "virtual" in the sense that it appears to users as a dedicated secure line when in fact it is a temporary secure line. The primary use of VPNs is to establish secure communications among business partners—larger suppliers or customers. A dedicated connection to a business partner can be very expensive. Using the Internet and PPTP as the connection method significantly reduces the cost of secure communications.

**Point-to-Point Tunneling Protocol (PPTP)**
an encoding mechanism that allows one local network to connect to another using the Internet as the conduit

## PROTECTING NETWORKS

Once you have protected communications as well as possible, the next set of tools to consider are those that can protect your networks, as well as the servers and clients on those networks.

### Firewalls

Firewalls and proxy servers are intended to build a wall around your network and the attached servers and clients, just like physical-world firewalls protect you from fires for a limited period of time. Firewalls and proxy servers share some similar functions, but they are quite different.

A **firewall** refers to either hardware or software that filters communication packets and prevents some packets from entering the network based on a security policy. The

**firewall**
refers to either hardware or software that filters communication packets and prevents some packets from entering the network based on a security policy

firewall controls traffic to and from servers and clients, forbidding communications from untrustworthy sources, and allowing other communications from trusted sources to proceed. Every message that is to be sent or received from the network is processed by the firewall, which determines if the message meets security guidelines established by the business. If it does, it is permitted to be distributed, and if it doesn't, the message is blocked. Firewalls can filter traffic based on packet attributes such as source IP address, destination port or IP address, type of service (such as WWW or HTTP), the domain name of the source, and many other dimensions. Most hardware firewalls that protect local area networks connected to the Internet have default settings that require little if any administrator intervention and accomplish simple but effective rules that deny incoming packets from a connection that does not originate from an internal request—the firewall only allows connections from servers that you requested service from. A common default setting on hardware firewalls (DSL and cable modem routers) simply ignores efforts to communicate with TCP port 445, the most commonly attacked port. The increasing use of firewalls by home and business Internet users has greatly reduced the effectiveness of attacks, and forced hackers to focus more on e-mail attachments to distribute worms and viruses.

There are two major methods firewalls use to validate traffic: packet filters and application gateways. *Packet filters* examine data packets to determine whether they are destined for a prohibited port or originate from a prohibited IP address (as specified by the security administrator). The filter specifically looks at the source and destination information, as well as the port and packet type, when determining whether the information may be transmitted. One downside of the packet filtering method is that it is susceptible to spoofing, since authentication is not one of its roles.

*Application gateways* are a type of firewall that filters communications based on the application being requested, rather than the source or destination of the message. Such firewalls also process requests at the application level, farther away from the client computer than packet filters. By providing a central filtering point, application gateways provide greater security than packet filters, but can compromise system performance.

**proxy server (proxy)**
software server that handles all communications originating from or being sent to the Internet, acting as a spokesperson or bodyguard for the organization

**Proxy servers (proxies)** are software servers (usually located on a dedicated computer) that handle all communications originating from or being sent to the Internet, acting as a spokesperson or bodyguard for the organization. Proxies act primarily to limit access of internal clients to external Internet servers, although some proxy servers act as firewalls as well. Proxy servers are sometimes called *dual home systems* because they have two network interfaces. To internal computers, a proxy server is known as the *gateway*, while to external computers it is known as a *mail server* or *numeric address*.

When a user on an internal network requests a Web page, the request is routed first to the proxy server. The proxy server validates the user and the nature of the request, and then sends the request onto the Internet. A Web page sent by an external Internet server first passes to the proxy server. If acceptable, the Web page passes onto the internal network Web server and then to the client desktop. By prohibiting users from communicating directly with the Internet, companies can restrict access to certain types of sites, such as pornographic, auction, or stock-trading sites. Proxy servers also improve Web performance by storing frequently requested Web pages locally, reducing upload times, and hiding the internal network's address, thus making it more difficult for hackers to monitor. **Figure 5.13** illustrates how firewalls and proxy servers protect a local area network from Internet intruders and prevent internal clients from reaching prohibited Web servers.

## PROTECTING SERVERS AND CLIENTS

Operating system features and anti-virus software can help further protect servers and clients from certain types of attacks.

### Operating System Security Enhancements

The most obvious way to protect servers and clients is to take advantage of Microsoft's and Apple's automatic computer security upgrades. Windows Server 2008/2003 and the Windows XP, Windows Vista, and Windows 7 client operating systems are continuously being upgraded by Microsoft to patch vulnerabilities discovered by hackers. These patches are autonomic; that is, when using Windows 7, XP, or Vista on the Internet, you are prompted and informed that operating system enhancements are available. Users can easily download these security patches for free. The most common known worms and viruses can be prevented by simply keeping your server and client operating systems and applications up to date. Application vulnerabilities are also fixed in the same manner. For instance, both the Mozilla and Internet Explorer browsers are updated automatically with little user intervention.

| FIGURE 5.13 | FIREWALLS AND PROXY SERVERS |
| --- | --- |

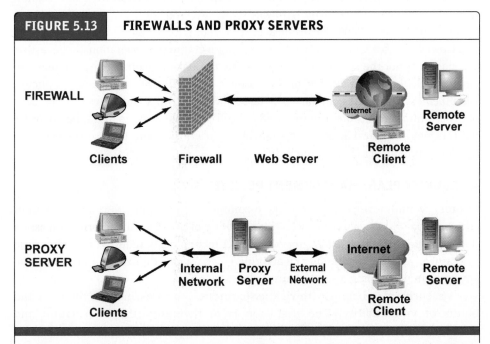

The primary function of a firewall is to deny access by remote client computers to local computers. The primary purpose of a proxy server is to provide controlled access from local computers to remote computers.

### Anti-Virus Software

The easiest and least expensive way to prevent threats to system integrity is to install anti-virus software. Programs by McAfee, Symantec (Norton AntiVirus), and many others provide inexpensive tools to identify and eradicate the most common types of malicious code as they enter a computer, as well as destroy those already lurking on a hard drive. Anti-virus programs can be set up so that e-mail attachments are inspected prior to you clicking on them, and the attachments are eliminated if they contain a known virus or worm. It is not enough, however, to simply install the software once. Since new viruses are developed and released every day, daily routine updates are needed in order to prevent new threats from being loaded. Some premium-level anti-virus software is updated hourly.

Anti-virus suite packages and stand-alone programs are available to eliminate intruders such as bot programs, adware, and other security risks. Such programs work much like anti-virus software in that they look for recognized hacker tools or signature actions of known intruders. Designed to trigger an alarm when such an action is noted, these systems must be monitored by staff members or intrusion detection services in order to work properly.

---

### 5.4   MANAGEMENT POLICIES, BUSINESS PROCEDURES, AND PUBLIC LAWS

U.S. business firms and government agencies spend about 12% of their information technology budgets on security hardware, software, and services. That added up to about $120 billion in 2009 (Forrester Research, 2009).

However, most CEOs and CIOs of existing e-commerce operations believe that technology is not the sole answer to managing the risk of e-commerce. The technology provides a foundation, but in the absence of intelligent management policies, even the best technology can be easily defeated. Public laws and active enforcement of cybercrime statutes are also required to both raise the costs of illegal behavior on the Internet and guard against corporate abuse of information. Let's consider briefly the development of management policy.

### A SECURITY PLAN: MANAGEMENT POLICIES

In order to minimize security threats, e-commerce firms must develop a coherent corporate policy that takes into account the nature of the risks, the information assets that need protecting, and the procedures and technologies required to address the risk, as well as implementation and auditing mechanisms. **Figure 5.14** illustrates the key steps in developing a solid security plan.

**risk assessment**

an assessment of the risks and points of vulnerability

A security plan begins with **risk assessment**—an assessment of the risks and points of vulnerability. The first step is to inventory the information and knowledge assets of the e-commerce site and company. What information is at risk? Is it customer information, proprietary designs, business activities, secret processes, or other internal information, such as price schedules, executive

| FIGURE 5.14 | DEVELOPING AN E-COMMERCE SECURITY PLAN |
| --- | --- |

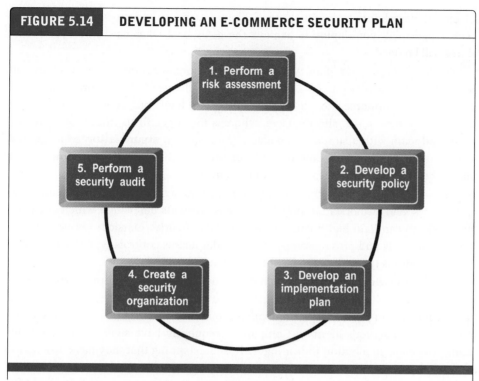

There are five steps involved in building an e-commerce security plan.

compensation, or payroll? For each type of information asset, try to estimate the dollar value to the firm if this information were compromised, and then multiply that amount by the probability of the loss occurring. Once you have done so, rank order the results. You now have a list of information assets prioritized by their value to the firm.

Based on your quantified list of risks, you can start to develop a **security policy**—a set of statements prioritizing the information risks, identifying acceptable risk targets, and identifying the mechanisms for achieving these targets. You will obviously want to start with the information assets that you determined to be the highest priority in your risk assessment. Who generates and controls this information in the firm? What existing security policies are in place to protect the information? What enhancements can you recommend to improve security of these most valuable assets? What level of risk are you willing to accept for each of these assets? Are you willing, for instance, to lose customer credit data once every 10 years? Or will you pursue a 100-year hurricane strategy by building a security edifice for credit card data that can withstand the once-in-100-year disaster? You will need to estimate how much it will cost to achieve this level of acceptable risk. Remember, total and complete security may require extraordinary financial resources. By answering these questions, you will have the beginnings of a security policy.

Next, consider an **implementation plan**—the steps you will take to achieve the security plan goals. Specifically, you must determine how you will translate the levels

**security policy**
a set of statements prioritizing the information risks, identifying acceptable risk targets, and identifying the mechanisms for achieving these targets

**implementation plan**
the action steps you will take to achieve the security plan goals

of acceptable risk into a set of tools, technologies, policies, and procedures. What new technologies will you deploy to achieve the goals, and what new employee procedures will be needed?

To implement your plan, you will need an organizational unit in charge of security, and a security officer—someone who is in charge of security on a daily basis. For a small e-commerce site, the security officer will likely be the person in charge of Internet services or the site manager, whereas for larger firms, there typically is a dedicated team with a supporting budget. The **security organization** educates and trains users, keeps management aware of security threats and breakdowns, and maintains the tools chosen to implement security.

The security organization typically administers access controls, authentication procedures, and authorization policies. **Access controls** determine which outsiders and insiders can gain legitimate access to your networks. Outsider access controls include firewalls and proxy servers, while insider access controls typically consist of login procedures (usernames, passwords, and access codes).

**Authentication procedures** include the use of digital signatures, certificates of authority, and PKI. Now that e-signatures have been given the same legal weight as an original pen-and-ink version, companies are in the process of devising ways to test and confirm a signer's identity. Companies frequently have signers type their full name and click on a button indicating their understanding that they have just signed a contract or document.

Biometric devices are used along with digital signatures to verify physical attributes associated with an individual, such as a fingerprint or retina (eye) scan or speech recognition system. (**Biometrics** is the study of measurable biological, or physical, characteristics.) A company could require, for example, that an individual undergo a fingerprint scan before being allowed access to a Web site, or before being allowed to pay for merchandise with a credit card. Biometric devices make it even more difficult for hackers to break into sites or facilities, significantly reducing the opportunity for spoofing.

**Authorization policies** determine differing levels of access to information assets for differing levels of users. **Authorization management systems** establish where and when a user is permitted to access certain parts of a Web site. Their primary function is to restrict access to private information within a company's Internet infrastructure. Although there are several authorization management products currently available, most operate in the same way: the system encrypts a user session to function like a passkey that follows the user from page to page, allowing access only to those areas that the user is permitted to enter, based on information set at the system database. By establishing entry rules up front for each user, the authorization management system knows who is permitted to go where at all times.

The last step in developing an e-commerce security plan is performing a security audit. A **security audit** involves the routine review of access logs (identifying how outsiders are using the site as well as how insiders are accessing the site's assets). A monthly report should be produced that establishes the routine and non-routine accesses to the systems and identifies unusual patterns of activities. As previously noted, tiger teams are often used by large corporate sites to evaluate the strength of

**security organization**
educates and trains users, keeps management aware of security threats and breakdowns, and maintains the tools chosen to implement security

**access controls**
determine who can gain legitimate access to a network

**authentication procedures**
include the use of digital signatures, certificates of authority, and public key infrastructure

**biometrics**
the study of measurable biological or physical characteristics

**authorization policies**
determine differing levels of access to information assets for differing levels of users

**authorization management system**
establishes where and when a user is permitted to access certain parts of a Web site

**security audit**
involves the routine review of access logs (identifying how outsiders are using the site as well as how insiders are accessing the site's assets)

existing security procedures. Many small firms have sprung up in the last five years to provide these services to large corporate sites.

The *Insight on Technology* story, *Think Your Smartphone is Secure?* discusses a new issue that security policies need to deal with: smartphone security.

## THE ROLE OF LAWS AND PUBLIC POLICY

The public policy environment today is very different from the early days of e-commerce. The net result is that the Internet is no longer an ungoverned, unsupervised, self-controlled technology juggernaut. Just as with financial markets in the last 70 years, there is a growing awareness that e-commerce markets work only when a powerful institutional set of laws and enforcement mechanisms are in place. These laws help ensure orderly, rational, and fair markets. This growing public policy environment is becoming just as global as e-commerce itself. Despite some spectacular internationally based attacks on U.S. e-commerce sites, the sources and persons involved in major harmful attacks have almost always been uncovered and, where possible, prosecuted.

Voluntary and private efforts have played a very large role in identifying criminal hackers and assisting law enforcement. Since 1995, as e-commerce has grown in significance, national and local law enforcement activities have expanded greatly. New laws have been passed that grant local and national authorities new tools and mechanisms for identifying, tracing, and prosecuting cybercriminals. **Table 5.4** lists the most significant federal e-commerce security legislation.

Following passage of the National Information Infrastructure Protection Act of 1996, which makes DoS attacks and virus distribution federal crimes, the FBI and the Department of Justice established the National Infrastructure Protection Center (NIPC). Now subsumed within the National Cyber Security Division of the Department of Homeland Security, this organization's sole mission is to identify and combat threats against the United States' technology and telecommunications infrastructure.

By increasing the punishment for cybercrimes, the U.S. government is attempting to create a deterrent to further hacker actions. And by making such actions federal crimes, the government is able to extradite international hackers and prosecute them within the United States.

After September 11, 2001, Congress passed the USA PATRIOT Act, which broadly expanded law enforcement's investigative and surveillance powers. The act has provisions for monitoring e-mail and Internet use. Currently, this is a temporary act, but there are efforts to make it permanent and to further expand law enforcement's monitoring powers. The Homeland Security Act of 2002 also attempts to fight cyberterrorism and increases the government's ability to compel information disclosure by computer and ISP sources.

### Private and Private-Public Cooperation Efforts

The good news is that e-commerce sites are not alone in their battle to achieve security on the Internet. Several organizations—some public and some private—are devoted to tracking down criminal organizations and individuals engaged in attacks against Internet and e-commerce sites. One of the better-known private

# INSIGHT ON TECHNOLOGY

## THINK YOUR SMARTPHONE IS SECURE?

So far there have been few publicly identified, large-scale, smartphone security breaches. In 2010, the biggest security danger facing smartphone users is that they will lose their phone. All of the personal and corporate data stored on the device, as well as access to corporate data on remote servers, are at risk. In many Wall Street firms, losing your company phone means you lose your job.

Many users believe that their iPhones are unlikely to be hacked into because the iPhone is an Apple product. There are far fewer malware programs attacking Macs than PCs. Why bother attacking a computer system (the Macintosh platform) used by less than 5% of the population when you can attack a computer system used by 95% of the world's population (the PC platform)? Android phone users similarly trust the operating system manufacturer (Google), or the Verizon network service provider, to protect them from viruses and other malware. No one has yet heard of a major smartphone hack resulting in millions of dollars in losses, or the breach of millions of credit cards, or the breach of national security. But with 50 million smartphones in the United States , 83 million people accessing the Internet from mobile devices, business firms increasingly switching their employees to the mobile platform, consumers using their phones for financial transaction and even paying bills, the size and richness of the smartphone target for hackers is growing. The smartphone ecosystem is a very large target today, and rich with potential criminal opportunities.

Users of smartphones download and open files with their browsers, and send and receive financial, personal, and commercial information. In fact, smartphones can be hacked and the security community is expectantly waiting for the roof to come down on smartphone security. Hackers can do to a smartphone just about anything they can do to any Internet device: request malicious files without user intervention, delete files, transmit files, install programs running on the background that can monitor user actions, and potentially convert the smartphone into a robot that can be used in a botnet to send e-mail and text messages to anyone.

Apps are one avenue for potential security breaches. Apple, Google, and RIM (BlackBerry) now offer over 700,000 apps collectively. Apple claims that it examines each and every app to ensure that it plays by Apple's iTunes rules, but risks remain. In April 2008, Apple pulled a popular game from its iTunes Store when it was discovered the program was harvesting users' contact lists (names, telephone numbers, e-mail and postal mail addresses) and sending them to the firm's own servers without the user knowing anything. In 2009, Apple announced it had removed hundreds of other apps because of similar security concerns. Apple iTunes app rules make some user information available to all app programs by default, including the user's GPS position and name. However, a rogue app could easily do much more. A Swiss researcher named Nicolas Seriot built a test app called "SpyPhone" that was capable of tracking users and all their activities, then transmitting this data to remote servers, all without user knowledge. The app harvested geolocation data, passwords, address book entries, and e-mail account information. Apple removed the app once it was identified. The fact that this proof-of-concept app was accepted by the iTunes staff of reviewers suggests that Apple cannot effectively review new apps, which arrive by the thousands each week.

Security on the Android platform is much less under the control of Google because it has an open app model. Google does not review any of the apps for the Android platform, but instead relies on user feedback to identify offending programs.

(continued)

Android apps can use any personal information found on a Droid phone but they must also inform the user what each app is capable of doing, and what personal data it requires. Users are informed (unlike Apple apps which default to a list of personal attributes without user intervention).

Google can perform a remote wipe of offending apps from all Droid phones without user intervention. A wonderful capability, but itself a security threat if hackers gained access to the remote wipe capability at Google. In one incident, Google pulled down dozens of mobile banking apps made by a developer called "09Droid." The apps claimed to give users access to their accounts at many banks in the world. Have an account at an HSBC branch in London? Not a problem. Enter your account information and supposedly you could gain access to your account. The apps in fact were unable to connect users to any bank, and were removed before they could do much harm. Google does take preventive steps to reduce malware apps such as vetting the backgrounds of developers, and requiring developers to register with its Checkout payment service (both to encourage users to pay for apps using their service but also to force developers to reveal their identities and financial information).

Beyond the threat of rogue apps, smartphones of all stripes are susceptible to browser-based malware that takes advantage of vulnerabilities in all browsers. In addition, most smartphones including the iPhone, permit the manufacturers to remotely download configuration files to update operating systems and security protections. Unfortunately, cryptologists in 2010 discovered a flaw in the public key encryption procedures that permit remote server access to iPhones. The result: "There is absolutely no reason for an iPhone/iPod to trust root CAs [Certificate Authorities which are the foundation for public key encryption of files] for over-the-air mobileconfig downloads."

Many commentators dismiss these concerns as more hype than reality. But reality may be catching up with the hype. The FBIs Cyber Division in February 2010 began an investigation of apps that compromise banking on cellphones, and other apps used for espionage by foreign nations. The FBI bars its own employees from downloading apps on FBI-issued phones. In March 2010, the Air Force barred all personnel from downloading apps to service-issued BlackBerrys. The Air Force reported a sharp uptick in attacks against its phones that tried to exploit mobile Web browsers. For security analysts, large-scale smartphone attacks are just disasters waiting to happen. As a precaution, many large corporations have disabled their employees' BlackBerrys so they cannot download any apps.

▬ **SOURCES:** "Experts: Android, iPhone Security Different But Matched," by Elinor Mills, CNET News, July 1, 2010; "Dark Side Arises For Phone Apps," by Spencer Ante, *Wall Street Journal*, June 4, 2010; FBI Probing AT&T iPad Security Breach, Reuters, June 10, 2010; "iPhone Certificate Flaws, iPhone PKI Kandling flaws," by Cryptopath.com, Archive for January 2010, January 2010; "SpyPhone iPhone App Can Harvest Personal Data," by Denis Fisher, Threatpost.com, December 4, 2009.

organizations is the **CERT Coordination Center** (formerly known as the Computer Emergency Response Team) at Carnegie Mellon University. CERT monitors and tracks online criminal activity reported to it by private corporations and government agencies that seek out its help. CERT is composed of full-time and part-time computer experts who can trace the origins of attacks against sites despite the complexity of the Internet. Its staff members also assist organizations in identifying security problems, developing solutions, and communicating with

**CERT Coordination Center**
monitors and tracks online criminal activity reported to it by private corporations and government agencies that seek out its help

| TABLE 5.4 | E-COMMERCE SECURITY LEGISLATION |
|---|---|
| LEGISLATION | SIGNIFICANCE |
| Computer Fraud and Abuse Act (1986) | Primary federal statute used to combat computer crime. |
| Electronic Communications Privacy Act (1986 ) | Imposes fines and imprisonment for individuals who access, intercept, or disclose the private e-mail communications of others. |
| National Information Infrastructure Protection Act (1996) | Makes DoS attacks illegal; creates NIPC in the FBI. |
| Cyberspace Electronic Security Act (2000) | Reduces export restrictions. |
| Computer Security Enhancement Act (2000) | Protects federal government systems from hacking. |
| Electronic Signatures in Global and National Commerce Act (the "E-Sign Law") (2000) | Authorizes the use of electronic signatures in legal documents. |
| USA PATRIOT Act ( 2001) | Authorizes use of computer-based surveillance of suspected terrorists. |
| Homeland Security Act (2002) | Authorized establishment of the Department of Homeland Security, which is assigned responsibility for developing a comprehensive national plan for security of the key resources and critical infrastructures of the United States; DHS becomes the central coordinator for all cyberspace security efforts. |
| CAN-SPAM Act (2003) | Although primarily a mechanism for civil and regulatory lawsuits against spammers, the CAN-SPAM Act also creates several new criminal offenses intended to address situations in which the perpetrator has taken steps to hide his or her identity or the source of the spam from recipients, ISPs, or law enforcement agencies. Also contains criminal sanctions for sending sexually explicit e-mail without designating it as such. |
| U.S. SAFE WEB Act (2006) | Enhances FTC's ability to obtain monetary redress for consumers in cases involving spyware, spam, Internet fraud, and deception; also improves FTC's ability to gather information and coordinate investigations with foreign counterparts. |

**US-CERT**

division of the U.S. Department of Homeland Security that coordinates cyber incident warnings and responses across government and private sectors

the public about widespread hacker threats. The CERT Coordination Center also provides product assessments, reports, and training in order to improve the public's knowledge and understanding of security threats and solutions. The U.S. Department of Homeland Security (DHS) operates the **United States Computer Emergency Readiness Team (US-CERT)**, which coordinates cyber incident warnings and responses across both the government and private sectors.

## Government Policies and Controls on Encryption Software

As noted in the beginning of this chapter, governments have sought to restrict availability and export of encryption systems as a means of detecting and preventing crime and terrorism. In the United States, both Congress and the executive branch have sought to regulate the uses of encryption. At the international level, four organizations have influenced the international traffic in encryption software: the Organization for Economic Cooperation and Development (OECD), G-7/G-8 (the heads of state of the top eight industrialized countries in the world), the Council of Europe, and the Wassnaar Arrangement (law enforcement personnel from the top 33 industrialized counties in the world) (EPIC, 2000). Various governments have proposed schemes for controlling encryption software or at least preventing criminals from obtaining strong encryption tools (see **Table 5.5**).

## OECD Guidelines

In July 2002, the OECD formally released its *Guidelines for the Security of Information Systems and Networks: Towards a Culture of Security*. The guidelines consist of nine principles that aim to increase public awareness, promote education, share information, and provide training that can lead to a better understanding of online security and the adoption of best practices. "A culture of security" represents a new way of thinking—one in which everyone using computers and networks like the Internet has a role to play. The Guidelines represent the consensus views of all 30 OECD member countries and support the OECD's larger goal of promoting economic growth, trade, and development.

| TABLE 5.5 | GOVERNMENT EFFORTS TO REGULATE AND CONTROL ENCRYPTION |
|---|---|
| **REGULATORY EFFORT** | **IMPACT** |
| Restrict export of strong security systems | Supported primarily by the United States. Widespread distribution of encryption schemes weakens this policy. The policy is changing to permit exports except to pariah countries. |
| Key escrow/key recovery schemes | France, the United Kingdom, and the United States supported this effort in the late 1990s, but now have largely abandoned it. There are few trusted third parties. |
| Lawful access and forced disclosure | Growing support in recent U.S. legislation and in OECD countries. |
| Official hacking | All countries are rapidly expanding budgets and training for law enforcement "technical centers" aimed at monitoring and cracking computer-based, encryption activities of suspected criminals. |

| 5.5 | **PAYMENT SYSTEMS** |

## TYPES OF PAYMENT SYSTEMS

In order to understand e-commerce payment systems, you first need to be familiar with the various types of generic payment systems. Then you will be able to clarify the different requirements that e-commerce payments systems must meet and identify the opportunities provided by e-commerce technology for developing new types of payment systems. There are five main types of payment systems: cash, checking transfer, credit cards, stored value, and accumulating balance.

### Cash

**cash**
legal tender defined by a national authority to represent value

**Cash**, which is legal tender defined by a national authority to represent value, is the most common form of payment in terms of number of transactions. The key feature of cash is that it is instantly convertible into other forms of value without the intermediation of any other institution. For instance, free airline miles are not cash because they are not instantly convertible into other forms of value—they require intermediation by a third party (the airline) in order to be exchanged for value (an airline ticket). Private organizations sometimes create a form of private cash called *scrip* that can be instantly redeemed by participating organizations for goods or cash. Examples include trading stamps, "point" programs, and other forms of consumer loyalty currency.

Why is cash still so popular today? Cash is portable, requires no authentication, and provides instant purchasing power for those who possess it. Cash allows for micropayments (payments of small amounts). The use of cash is "free" in that neither merchants nor consumers pay a transaction fee for using it. Using cash does not require any complementary assets, such as special hardware or the existence of an account, and it puts very low cognitive demands on the user. Cash is anonymous and difficult to trace, and in that sense it is "private." Other forms of payment require significant use of third parties and leave an extensive digital or paper trail.

**float**
the period of time between a purchase and actual payment for the purchase

On the other hand, cash is limited to smaller transactions (you can't easily buy a car or house with cash), it is easily stolen, and it does not provide any "**float**" (the period of time between a purchase and actual payment for the purchase); when it is spent, it is gone. With cash, purchases tend to be final and irreversible (i.e., they are irrefutable) unless otherwise agreed by the seller.

### Checking Transfer

**checking transfer**
funds transferred directly via a signed draft or check from a consumer's checking account to a merchant or other individual

A **checking transfer**, which represents funds transferred directly via a signed draft or check from a consumer's checking account to a merchant or other individual, is the second most common form of payment in the United States in terms of number of transactions, and the most common in terms of total amount spent.

Checks can be used for both small and large transactions, although typically they are not used for micropayments (less than $1). Checks have some float (it can take up to 10 days for out-of-state checks to clear), and the unspent balances can earn interest. Checks are not anonymous and require third-party institutions to work. Checks also introduce security risks for merchants: They can be forged more easily than cash, so authentication is required. For merchants, checks also present some additional risk compared to cash because they can be canceled before they clear the account or they may bounce if there is not enough money in the account.

## Credit Card

A **credit card** represents an account that extends credit to consumers, permits consumers to purchase items while deferring payment, and allows consumers to make payments to multiple vendors at one time. **Credit card associations** such as Visa and MasterCard are nonprofit associations that set standards for the **issuing banks**—such as Citibank—that actually issue the credit cards and process transactions. Other third parties (called **processing centers** or **clearinghouses**) usually handle verification of accounts and balances. Credit card issuing banks act as financial intermediaries, minimizing the risk to transacting parties.

Credit cards offer consumers a line of credit and the ability to make small and large purchases instantly. They are widely accepted as a form of payment, reduce the risk of theft associated with carrying cash, and increase consumer convenience. Credit cards also offer consumers considerable float. With a credit card, for instance, a consumer typically need not actually pay for goods purchased until receiving a credit card bill 30 days later. Merchants benefit from increased consumer spending resulting from credit card use, but they pay a hefty transaction fee of 3% to 5% of the purchase price to the issuing banks. In addition, federal Regulation Z places the risks of the transaction (such as credit card fraud, repudiation of the transaction, or nonpayment) largely on the merchant and credit card issuing bank. Regulation Z limits cardholder liability to $50 for unauthorized transactions that occur before the card issuer is notified. Once a card is reported stolen, consumers are not liable for any subsequent charges.

Credit cards have less finality than other payment systems because consumers can refute or repudiate purchases under certain circumstances, and they limit risk for consumers while raising risk for merchants and bankers.

## Stored Value

Accounts created by depositing funds into an account and from which funds are paid out or withdrawn as needed are **stored value payment systems**. Stored value payment systems are similar in some respects to checking transfers—which also store funds—but do not involve writing a check. Examples include debit cards, gift certificates, prepaid cards, and smart cards (described in greater detail later in the chapter). **Debit cards** immediately debit a checking or other demand-deposit account. For many consumers, the use of a debit card eliminates the need to write a paper check. Today, there are over 500 million debit cards in use nationwide. However, because debit cards are dependent on funds being available in a consumer's bank account, larger purchases are still typically paid for by credit card, and their use in the United States still lags behind that of other developed nations, in part because they do not have the protections provided by Regulation Z and they do not provide any float.

Peer-to-peer (P2P) payment systems such as PayPal (discussed further in Section 5.6) are variations on the stored value concept. P2P payment systems do not insist on

**credit card**
represents an account that extends credit to consumers, permits consumers to purchase items while deferring payment, and allows consumers to make payments to multiple vendors at one time

**credit card association**
nonprofit association that sets standards for issuing banks

**issuing bank**
bank that actually issues credit cards and processes transactions

**processing center (clearinghouse)**
institution that handles verification of accounts and balances

**stored value payment system**
account created by depositing funds into an account and from which funds are paid out or withdrawn as needed

**debit card**
immediately debits a checking or other demand-deposit account

prepayment, but do require an account with a stored value, either a checking account with funds available or a credit card with an available credit balance. PayPal is often referred to as a P2P payment system because it allows small merchants and individuals to accept payments without using a merchant bank or processor to clear the transaction.

### Accumulating Balance

**accumulating balance payment system**

account that accumulates expenditures and to which consumers makes periodic payments

Accounts that accumulate expenditures and to which consumers make periodic payments are **accumulating balance payment systems**. Traditional examples include utility, phone, and American Express accounts, all of which accumulate balances, usually over a specified period (typically a month), and then are paid in full at the end of the period.

**Table 5.6** summarizes how payment systems differ on a variety of dimensions and highlights a number of points about payment systems. First, evaluating payment systems is a complex process; there are many dimensions that must be considered. Table 5.6 suggests how difficult it is for entrepreneurs to devise new payment

| TABLE 5.6 | DIMENSIONS OF PAYMENT SYSTEMS | | | | |
|---|---|---|---|---|---|
| DIMENSION | CASH | PERSONAL CHECK | CREDIT CARD | STORED VALUE (DEBIT CARD) | ACCUMULATING BALANCE |
| Instantly convertible without intermediation | yes | no | no | no | no |
| Low transaction cost for small transactions | yes | no | no | no | yes |
| Low transaction cost for large transactions | no | yes | yes | yes | yes |
| Low fixed costs for merchant | yes | yes | no | no | no |
| Refutable (able to be repudiated) | no | yes | yes | no (usually) | yes |
| Financial risk for consumer | yes | no | up to $50 | limited | no |
| Financial risk for merchant | no | yes | yes | no | yes |
| Anonymous for consumer | yes | no | no | no | no |
| Anonymous for merchant | yes | no | no | no | no |
| Immediately respendable | yes | no | no | no | no |
| Security against unauthorized use | no | some | some | some | some |
| Tamper-resistant | yes | no | yes | yes | yes |
| Requires authentication | no | yes | yes | yes | yes |
| Special hardware required | no | no | yes—by merchant | yes—by merchant | yes—by merchant |
| Buyer keeps float | no | yes | yes | no | yes |
| Account required | no | yes | yes | yes | yes |
| Has immediate monetary value | yes | no | no | yes | no |

SOURCE: Adapted from MacKie-Mason and White, 1996.

mechanisms to displace current payment systems (cash, checks, and credit cards). As we will discuss below, consumers in the United States have not, as a general matter, accepted alternative online payment systems and rely primarily on credit cards for online payments.

Table 5.6 also suggests that the various parties that have an interest in payment systems (stakeholders) may have different preferences with respect to the different dimensions. The main stakeholders in payment systems are consumers, merchants, financial intermediaries, and government regulators.

Consumers are interested primarily in low-risk, low-cost, refutable (able to be repudiated or denied), convenient, and reliable payment mechanisms. Consumers have demonstrated they will not use new payment mechanisms unless they are equally or more beneficial to them than existing systems. In general, most consumers use cash, checks, and/or credit cards. The specific payment system chosen will change depending on the transaction situation. For instance, cash may be preferred to keep certain transactions private and anonymous, but the same consumer may want a record of transaction for the purchase of a car.

Merchants are interested primarily in low-risk, low-cost, irrefutable (i.e., final), secure, and reliable payment mechanisms. Merchants currently carry much of the risk of checking and credit card fraud, refutability of charges, and much of the hardware cost of verifying payments. Merchants typically prefer payments made by cash, check, and to a lesser extent credit cards, which usually carry high fees and allow transactions to be repudiated after the fact by consumers.

Financial intermediaries, such as banks and credit card networks, are primarily interested in secure payment systems that transfer risks and costs to consumers and merchants, while maximizing transaction fees payable to themselves. The preferred payment mechanisms for financial intermediaries are checking transfers, debit cards, and credit cards.

Government regulators are interested in maintaining trust in the financial system. Regulators seek to protect against fraud and abuse in the use of payment systems; ensure that the interests of consumers and merchants are balanced against the interests of the financial intermediaries whom they regulate; and enforce information reporting laws. The most important regulations of payment systems in the United States are Regulation Z, Regulation E, and the Electronic Funds Transfer Act (EFTA) of 1978, regulating ATM machines. Regulation Z limits the risk to consumers when using credit cards. In contrast, EFTA and Regulation E place more risk on consumers when using debit or ATM cards. For instance, if you lose an ATM card or debit card, you are potentially liable for any losses to the account. However, in reality, Visa and MasterCard have issued policies that limit consumer risk for loss of debit cards to the same $50 that applies to credit cards.

## 5.6 E-COMMERCE PAYMENT SYSTEMS

The emergence of e-commerce has created new financial needs that in some cases cannot be effectively fulfilled by traditional payment systems. For instance, new types of purchasing relationships—such as auctions between individuals online—have resulted in the need for peer-to-peer payment methods that allow individuals to e-mail payments to other individuals. New types of online information products such as iTunes, video purchases and rentals, newspaper and magazine articles, and other information services require micropayments of less than $5. Yet, for the most part, existing payment mechanisms used in most societies have been able to adapt to the new online environment. E-commerce technology offers a number of possibilities for creating new payment systems that substitute for existing systems, as well as for creating enhancements to existing systems. In this section, we provide an overview of e-commerce payment systems in use today.

In the United States, the primary form of online payment is still the existing credit card system, although the use of alternative payment methods is increasing. In 2009, credit cards are estimated to account for around 55% of online transactions in the United States, with debit cards accounting for about 28%. **Figure 5.15** illustrates the approximate usage of various payment types. PayPal is the most popular alternative to usage of credit and debit cards online. (see the "Online Stored Value Payment Systems" section for more information on PayPal).

In other parts of the world, e-commerce payments can be very different depending on traditions and infrastructure. Credit cards are not nearly as dominant a form of online payment as in the United States. If you plan on operating a Web site in Europe, Asia, or Latin America, you will need to develop different payment systems for each region. Consumers in Europe rely for the most part on bank debit cards (especially in Germany) and some credit cards. Online purchases in China are typically paid for by check or cash when the consumer picks up the goods at a local store. In Japan, consumers use postal and bank transfers and CODs, using local convenience stores (konbini) as the pickup and payment point. Japanese consumers also use accumulated balance accounts with the telephone company for Internet purchases made from their home computers.

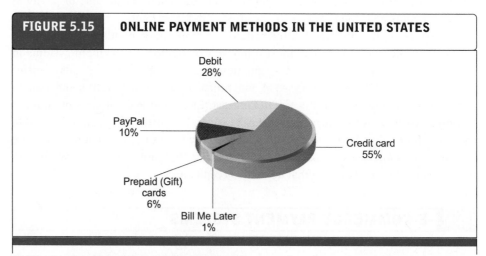

| FIGURE 5.15 | **ONLINE PAYMENT METHODS IN THE UNITED STATES** |

Traditional credit cards are still the dominant method of payment for online purchases, although alternative methods such as PayPal are gaining ground.
SOURCES: Based on data from Javelin Strategy & Research, 2010b; authors' estimates.

## ONLINE CREDIT CARD TRANSACTIONS

Because credit cards are the dominant form of online payment, it is important to understand how they work and to recognize the strengths and weaknesses of this payment system. Online credit card transactions are processed in much the same way that in-store purchases are, with the major differences being that online merchants never see the actual card being used, no card impression is taken, and no signature is available. Online credit card transactions most closely resemble *Mail Order-Telephone Order (MOTO)* transactions. These types of purchases are also called *Cardholder Not Present (CNP)* transactions and are the major reason that charges can be disputed later by consumers. Since the merchant never sees the credit card, nor receives a hand-signed agreement to pay from the customer, when disputes arise, the merchant faces the risk that the transaction may be disallowed and reversed, even though he has already shipped the goods or the user has downloaded a digital product.

**Figure 5.16** illustrates the online credit card purchasing cycle. There are five parties involved in an online credit card purchase: consumer, merchant, clearinghouse, merchant bank (sometimes called the "acquiring bank"), and the consumer's card issuing bank. In order to accept payments by credit card, online merchants must have a merchant account established with a bank or financial institution. A **merchant account** is simply a bank account that allows companies to process credit card payments and receive funds from those transactions.

**merchant account**
a bank account that allows companies to process credit card payments and receive funds from those transactions

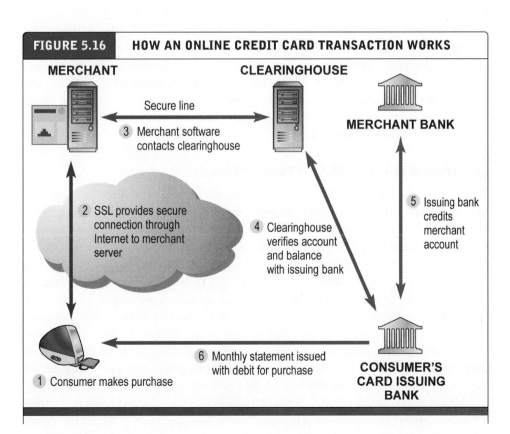

| FIGURE 5.16 | HOW AN ONLINE CREDIT CARD TRANSACTION WORKS |

As shown in Figure 5.16, an online credit card transaction begins with a purchase (1). When a consumer wants to make a purchase, he or she adds the item to the merchant's shopping cart. When the consumer wants to pay for the items in the shopping cart, a secure tunnel through the Internet is created using SSL. Using encryption, SSL secures the session during which credit card information will be sent to the merchant and protects the information from interlopers on the Internet (2). SSL does not authenticate either the merchant or the consumer. The transacting parties have to trust one another.

Once the consumer credit card information is received by the merchant, the merchant software contacts a clearinghouse (3). As previously noted, a clearinghouse is a financial intermediary that authenticates credit cards and verifies account balances. The clearinghouse contacts the issuing bank to verify the account information (4). Once verified, the issuing bank credits the account of the merchant at the merchant's bank (usually this occurs at night in a batch process) (5). The debit to the consumer account is transmitted to the consumer in a monthly statement (6).

### Credit Card E-commerce Enablers

Companies that have a merchant account still need to buy or build a means of handling the online transaction; securing the merchant account is only step one in a two-part process. Today, Internet payment service providers can provide both a merchant account and the software tools needed to process credit card purchases online.

For instance, Authorize.net is an Internet payment service provider. Authorize.net helps a merchant secure an account with one of its merchant account provider partners and then provides payment processing software for installation on the merchant's server. The software collects the transaction information from the merchant's site and then routes it via the Authorize.net "payment gateway" to the appropriate bank, ensuring that customers are authorized to make their purchases. The funds for the transaction are then transferred to the merchant's merchant account.

### Limitations of Online Credit Card Payment Systems

There are a number of limitations to the existing credit card payment system. The most important limitations involve security, merchant risk, cost, and social equity.

The existing system offers poor security. Neither the merchant nor the consumer can be fully authenticated. The merchant could be a criminal organization designed to collect credit card numbers, and the consumer could be a thief using stolen or fraudulent cards. The risk facing merchants is high: consumers can repudiate charges even though the goods have been shipped or the product downloaded. The banking industry attempted to develop a secure electronic transaction protocol (SET) in 2000, but this effort failed because it was too complex for consumers and merchants alike.

Credit costs for merchants are also significant—roughly 3.5% of the purchase plus a transaction fee of 20–30 cents per transaction, plus other setup fees. Stored value systems such as PayPal that rely on the credit card system are even more costly: in addition to paying the credit card fee of 3.5%, PayPal tacks on a variable fee of from 1.5%–3% depending on the size of the transaction. The high costs make it undesirable to sell goods that cost less than $10 on the Web. The sale of individual articles, music tracks, or other small items is not particularly feasible with credit cards. One way around this problem is to aggregate a consumer's purchases over a period of time before actually charging the credit card. This is the tack taken by Apple's iTunes Music Store, which now uses a variable pricing system of 69 cents for older songs, 99 cents for most other songs, and $1.29 for hits and "hot" songs. Instead of charging your credit card for each individual song, Apple aggregates any purchases you make within a 24-hour period so that they're posted to your credit card account as a total for the period, not as individual song purchases. iTunes barely breaks even on a single sale, but can start making money if you purchase several songs. In general, credit companies are opposed to "aggregating" because it reduces their profits.

Credit cards are not very democratic, even though they seem ubiquitous. Millions of young adults do not have credit cards, along with almost 100 million other adult Americans who cannot afford cards or who are considered poor risks because of low incomes.

## DIGITAL WALLETS

Aside from credit cards, there are also a number of new forms of payment that have been attempted, with mixed success. These include digital wallets, digital cash, online stored value payment systems, digital accumulating balance systems, and digital checking systems

A **digital wallet** seeks to emulate the functionality of a regular wallet that you carry on your person. The most important functions of a digital wallet are to (a) authenticate the consumer through the use of digital certificates or other encryption methods, (b) store and transfer value, and (c) secure the payment process from the consumer to the merchant. Early efforts by many companies failed to popularize the idea of a digital wallet. Even Microsoft, which offered a proprietary server-side digital wallet with first Passport and then MSN Wallet, ultimately abandoned the effort in February 2005. The latest effort to develop something like a digital wallet is Google's Checkout, which is a payment processing system designed to make online shopping more convenient and easier. It does not store value like PayPal, but communicates a shopper's credit card and personal information necessary for a transaction to the merchant. Google has yet to match PayPal's strength or popularity, in part due to eBay's refusal to allow merchants to use Checkout. Smartphones are likely to be the saviour of the digital wallet concept. As described in the chapter ending case study, *PayPal Has Company*, smartphones are developing capabilities to pay for goods and services online and offline using digital methods.

**digital wallet**
emulates the functionality of a regular wallet by authenticating the consumer, storing and transferring value, and securing the payment process from consumer to merchant

## DIGITAL CASH

**Digital cash** (sometimes called *e-cash*) was one of the first forms of alternative payment systems developed for e-commerce. The basic idea behind all digital cash systems is payment over the Internet by transmitting unique, authenticated tokens representing cash value from consumers to merchants. In these schemes, users would deposit money in a bank or provide a credit card. Banks would issue digital tokens (unique encrypted numbers) for various denominations of cash, and consumers could "spend" these at merchants' sites. Merchants would in turn deposit these electronic

**digital cash**
an alternative payment system developed for e-commerce in which unique, authenticated tokens representing cash value are tramsmitted from consumers to merchants

tokens in their banks. DigiCash, First Virtual, and Millicent, all early pioneers in digital cash, no longer offer services in the form originally envisioned. In general, the protocols and practices required to make digital cash a reality were far too complex. However, there are still several firms that are continuing to pursue the idea of digital cash. Some firms, such as GoldMoney, have focused on electronic currency backed by gold bullion.

## ONLINE STORED VALUE PAYMENT SYSTEMS

**online stored value payment system**

permits consumers to make instant, online payments to merchants and other individuals based on value stored in an online account

**Online stored value payment systems** permit consumers to make instant, online payments to merchants and other individuals based on value stored in an online account.

PayPal (purchased by eBay in 2002) enables individuals and businesses with e-mail accounts to make and receive payments up to a specified limit. In 2009, PayPal processed $71 billion in payments ($31 billion of which were generated on eBay, and $40 billion elsewhere on the Web), and had 87 million registered users. PayPal builds on the existing financial infrastructure of the countries in which it operates. You establish a PayPal account by specifying a credit, debit, or checking account you wish to have charged or paid when conducting online transactions. When you make a payment using PayPal, you e-mail the payment to the merchant's PayPal account. PayPal transfers the amount from your credit or checking account to the merchant's bank account. The beauty of PayPal is that no personal credit information has to be shared among the users, and the service can be used by individuals to pay one another even in small amounts. Issues with PayPal include its high cost, and lack of consumer protections when a fraud occurs or a charge is repudiated. PayPal is discussed in further depth in the case study at the end of the chapter.

There are also several different categories of online stored value systems in addition to PayPal. Some, such as Valista, are merchant platforms. Others, such as QPass, are primarily aimed at the micropayments market for wireless carriers and publishers selling individual articles.

**smart card**

a credit-card sized plastic cards with an embedded chip that stores personal information; can be used to support mobie wireless e-commerce payments

**Smart cards** are another kind of stored value system based on credit-card-sized plastic cards with embedded chips that store personal information that can be used to support mobile wireless e-commerce payments. They are not used from home PCs to purchase goods, but can be used to pay for generally small ticket items by waving the card at a reader, or passing it through a reader. Whereas credit cards store a single charge account number in the magnetic strip on the back, smart cards can hold 100 times more data, including multiple credit card numbers and information regarding health insurance, transportation, personal identification, bank accounts, and loyalty programs, such as frequent flyer accounts. This capacity makes them an attractive alternative to carrying a dozen or so credit and ID cards in a physical wallet. Smart cards can also require a password, unlike credit cards, adding another layer of security.

There are actually two types of smart cards—*contact and contactless*—depending on the technology embedded. In order for contact cards to be read, they must be physically placed into a card reader, while contactless cards have an antenna built in that enables transmission of data without direct contact using RFID technology. **Radio frequency identification (RFID)** is a method of automatic identification that uses short range radio signals to identify objects and users. A stored-value smart card, such as a retail gift card purchased in a certain dollar value, is an example of a contact card because it must be swiped through a smart card reader in order for payment to be processed. A highway toll payment system such as EZPass is an example of a contactless smart card because the EZPass device in the card is read by a remote sensor, with the appropriate toll automatically deducted from the card at the end of the trip.

Smart cards as payment vehicles are more common in Europe and Asia. The Mondex card is one of the original smart cards, invented in 1990 by NatWest Bank in England. The card allows users to download cash from a bank account to the card via a Mondex-compatible telephone or a card reader attached to a PC, and spend large or small amounts. It can carry five different currencies simultaneously and can be accepted by merchants who have readers installed. Mondex is part of MasterCard's worldwide suite of smart card products.

The Octopus card is a rechargeable contactless stored value smart card used in Hong Kong. The card debuted in 1997 as a fare collection system for Hong Kong's mass transit system. Today, it has become the world's most successful stored value smart card. It can be used to pay not only for public transportation, but also to make payments at convenience stores and fast-food restaurants and for parking, and point-of-sale applications such as gas and vending machines. There are over 17 million Octopus cards in circulation, used to conduct over 10 million transactions a day. The card can be recharged online, over the counter, or via special-purpose "add-value" machines. So far, smart cards have played a limited role in supporting electronic transactions on the fly, where the user is mobile (as in a subway train passenger) and wants to make small payments. However, in the future, smart card technology will be integrated with cell phones, and wireless payment systems to support mobile e-commerce will become more widespread.

## DIGITAL ACCUMULATING BALANCE PAYMENT SYSTEMS

**Digital accumulating balance payment systems** allow users to make micropayments and purchases on the Web, accumulating a balance for which they are billed at the end of the month. Like a utility or phone bill, consumers are expected to pay the entire balance at the end of the month using a checking or credit card account. Digital accumulating balance systems are ideal for purchasing intellectual property on the Web such as single music tracks, chapters of books, or articles from a newspaper. such as ringtones and games. A good example is Valista's PaymentsPlus, a system for accumulating balances for small transactions. PaymentsPlus is used by companies such as AOL, Vodafone, NTT DoCoMo, Tiscali, and T-Online, among others.

Clickshare takes a different approach. Consumers have one account at a Web site of their choice, and then can use that account to purchase digital content from other Web sites without having to reenter credit card or other personal information. Clickshare has found its greatest acceptance with the online newspaper and publishing industry.

**radio frequency identification (RFID)**
a method of automatic identification that uses short range radio signals to identify objects and users

**digital accumulating balance payment system**
allows users to make micropayments and purchases on the Web, accumulating a balance for which they are billed at the end of the month

Bill Me Later offers a variation on the digital accumulating balance system. Bill Me Later, owned by eBay, identifies itself as an open-ended credit account. Users select the Bill Me Later option at checkout and are asked to provide their birthdate and the last four digits of their social security number. They are then billed for the purchase by Bill Me Later within 10-14 days. Bill Me Later appeals to consumers who do not wish to enter their credit card information online. It is currently accepted by over 1,000 online merchants.

## DIGITAL CHECKING PAYMENT SYSTEMS

In December 2004, the Federal Reserve announced that for the first time in history, the number of electronic payment transactions (credit, debit, and other forms of electronic payment) exceeded the number of paper checks. However, the venerable check is not yet moving into retirement. According to the 2007 Federal Reserve Payments Study, over 30 billion checks were written in the United States in 2007. **Digital checking payment systems** seek to extend the functionality of existing checking accounts for use as online shopping payment tools.

**digital checking payment system**

seeks to extend the functionality of existing checking accounts for use as online shopping payment tools

ITI Internet Services's PayByCheck system is based on the consumer's existing checking account. When a consumer wishes to pay by check at a merchant site that offers this service, an online authorization form appears that mimics the appearance of a paper check. The user is prompted to fill in checking account information, including a valid check number, bank routing number, and bank account number. To authorize payment, a user must type his or her full name, and in some instances, if required by the merchant, the last four digits of his or her social security number. The payment information is matched against PayByCheck's various databases containing information on known bad check writers, real-time information from the customer's bank about current bank account status, fraud databases, and an address verification system to verify the customer's name and address. Bio identification in the form of a fingerprint scanner attached to a PC can also be used. PayByCheck then produces a check or electronic debit for the amount of the purchase as indicated on the check, and delivers it to the merchant. The check is deposited by the merchant and routed to the consumer's bank for payment, just like a check written from a checkbook. eBillme is another option. eBillme links to a customer's online banking account. Digital checking has not been successful so far because of the difficulties of verifying the consumer online.

## MOBILE PAYMENT SYSTEMS

There are around 5 billion cell phones in use around the world, and in China, the number of cell phones in 2010 exceeded 1 billion, more than twice the entire population of the United States. The United States' cell phone population is around 300 million. These numbers dwarf the global personal computer population of about 1.5 billion. In Japan, more than 95% of households have cell phones.

Use of mobile handsets as payment devices is already well established in Europe, Japan, and South Korea. Japan is arguably the most advanced in terms of providing non-voice services to consumers, that is, real mobile commerce. Japanese cell phones can act as bar code readers, GPS locators, FM radios, voice recorders, and analog TV tuners, and purchase things such as train tickets, newspapers, restaurant meals, groceries, books, and a host of common retail goods and services. Three kinds of mobile payments systems are used in Japan, and these provide a glimpse of the future of mobile payments in the United States. Japanese cell phones support e-money (stored value systems charged by credit cards or bank accounts), mobile debit cards (tied to personal bank accounts), and mobile credit cards. Japanese cell phones act like mobile wallets, containing a variety of payment mechanisms. Consumers can pay merchants by simply waving the cell phone at a merchant payment device that can accept payments. How do the cell phones communicate with merchants when, say, buying a newspaper at a train station or restaurant meal? Japan's largest phone company, NTT DoCoMo, introduced wireless RFID cell phones and a related payment system (FeliCa) in 2004. Currently, more than 50 million phones equipped with the "Osaifu-Keitai" (literally "wallet phone") system have been sold in Japan (Davies, 2009).

In the United States, the cell phone has not yet evolved into a fully capable mobile commerce and payment system. But with the advent of smartphones, especially the iPhone, mobile payment is starting to grow exponentially. In 2010, mobile digital downloads will generate $7.1 billion in revenue, mobile retail purchasing $350 million, location-based services $215 million, and $3 billion in mobile apps. Payment for these purchases generally involves use of a smartphone. The *Insight on Business* story, *Mobile Payment's Future: WavePayMe, TextPayMe* provides a look at the future of mobile payment in the United States.

## 5.7 ELECTRONIC BILLING PRESENTMENT AND PAYMENT

In 2007, for the first time, the number of bill payments made online exceeded the number of physical checks written (Fiserv, 2007). In the $14.2 trillion U.S. economy with a $10 trillion consumer sector for goods and services, there are a lot of bills to pay. No one knows for sure, but some experts believe the life-cycle cost of a paper bill for a business, from point of issuance to point of payment, ranges from $3 to $7. This calculation does not include the value of time to consumers, who must open bills, read them, write checks, address envelopes, stamp, and then mail remittances. The billing market represents an extraordinary opportunity for using the Internet as an electronic billing and payment system that potentially could greatly reduce both the cost of paying bills and the time consumers spend paying them. Estimates vary, but online payments are believed to cost between only 20 to 30 cents to process.

**Electronic billing presentment and payment (EBPP)** systems are systems that enable the online delivery and payment of monthly bills. EBPP services allow consumers to view bills electronically and pay them through electronic funds transfers from bank or credit card accounts. More and more companies are choosing to issue statements and bills electronically, rather than mailing out paper versions. But even those businesses that do mail paper bills are increasingly offering online bill payment as an option to customers, allowing them to immediately transfer funds from a bank or credit card account to pay a bill somewhere else.

**electronic billing presentment and payment (EBPP) system**
new form of online payment systems for monthly bills

# INSIGHT ON BUSINESS

## MOBILE PAYMENT'S FUTURE: WAVEPAYME, TEXTPAYME

Mobile commerce is finally taking off in the United States. Mobile commerce is a broad term that includes revenues produced by mobile advertising ($313 million), mobile retail purchasing ($1 billion), location-based services ($215 million), media downloads ($7 billion for books, videos, newspapers, television shows), and sales of apps ($3 billion). The combined total of all these revenue streams in 2010 is estimated to be about $13 billion, or about 5% of all e-commerce revenues in 2010. While small compared to the total e-commerce picture, mobile commerce driven by smartphones, netbooks, and cellular networks, is growing at over 20% a year. What has been missing from mobile commerce is mobile payment systems that are fast, convenient, secure, and reliable.

Before the cell phone, smart cards were the primary means of mobile payments in Asian and European countries but not in the United States. Smart cards store value based on a customer's bank balances, and act like electronic debit cards. They can be charged at a variety of locations, and used to pay for services or products without an elaborate online verification system like credit cards use. But cell phones are far more prevalent these days than smart cards, and who needs another card anyway?

Several large-scale experiments around the globe are developing the technology that will make the cell phone the centerpiece of contactless payment. Contactless payment systems do not require the user to swipe a credit card. All that's needed is for the customer to come within several meters of a reader and wave his or her cell phone at the reader to make a payment. In Japan, millions of consumers already use their cell phones to wave-pay for

train tickets, coffee, meals, newspapers, and other small-ticket items purchased on the street. Specially equipped Nokia mobile phones come with built-in RFID chips. RFID is a collection of devices, both readers and tags, which communicate with one another using radio frequencies and help identify people and objects. In payment applications, when you wave the phone at a reader, the RFID chip returns the customers' account information to a reader device. The reader asks for a user verification code (like a PIN). Once the user enters the code, the amount of the purchase is transferred from the customer's account to the merchant's account. It takes just seconds. If someone steals your phone, they cannot use it for payments without the personal verification code.

In the United States in 2009, the number of contactless payment cards issued by banks and credit card companies totaled around 45 million. Industry experts estimate that there are now more than 400,000 contactless readers in place at over 80,000 merchant locations, and that usage is on the rise, especially with consumers in the 25–34 year-old age group, almost 10% of whom report using a contactless payment system at least once a week or more. Smartphones can be turned into contactless systems in at least two ways: embedded RFID chips and SMS texting.

Smartphones are equipped with Near Field Communication (NFC) chips. NFC is a kind of short-range RFID technology that allows the chips to communicate with readers up to about 10 inches away. Nokia is building the chips into some of its cell phones. Motorola is also building handsets. Visa, Cingular, JPMorgan Chase, and Nokia have built a cellular test platform in Atlanta at the Philips Stadium (home to the Atlanta Hawks

(continued)

and the Thrashers hockey team). MasterCard and the 7- Eleven convenience store chain have also launched trial systems based on Nokia's cell phone.

But there is a simpler way to turn a cell phone into a digital wallet using stickers. In 2010, Bling Nation makes sticker tags you can stick to your smartphone. The sticker has a built-in RFID chip, and when you tap the phone on a special sensor (digital cash register), payment is made. PayPal and eBay are equipping their employees with Bling stickers for internal payments. PayPal President Scott Thompson said in a 2010 interview that his company's top priority is to "develop software that transforms mobile phones and other devices into 'digital wallets' that consumers can use to buy merchandise, keep ,coupons and store loyalty program data." Pay-Pal's strategy is to develop software that would allow smartphone users to both buy goods online and at traditional retail stores, whose point-of-sale devices are increasingly connected to the Internet. Another alternative: FaceCash, a start-up in Palo Alto, produces an app that you download to your phone. You pay the cashier at merchant locations by showing a unique bar code displayed on your phone screen. You can also use these phones to do mobile banking and check balances, make payments, and transfer funds. Wave your cell phone at a blouse and it's yours!

PayPal, along with several start-up firms, are also using cell phone text messaging to make P2P payments possible on the fly. PayPal Mobile is built on the PayPal infrastructure that customers use to make purchases on eBay. Users register their phone with PayPal, and open an account if they don't already have one. They enter a PIN code as well, which is used in the authori-zation process. When they want to buy something, they text message PayPal requesting the payment. PayPal calls them back to confirm, and after confirmation, sends the money to the recipient. Other similar services have been developed by Obopay. Citigroup uses Obopay to run its mobile payment service. In 2009, Nokia invested $35 million in Obopay. Previous investors included Citigroup and Qualcomm. In May 2009, MasterCard launched MoneySend, a person-to-person mobile payments platform for its issuers in the United States powered by Obopay. In August 2009, Nokia and Obopay announced a similar mobile payment service called Nokia Money. And let's not forget about Google. In 2007, it applied for a patent for gPay, a platform-independent text-message-based payment system. Google has not yet announced its plans for gPay. The advantage of these texting methods is that you don't need a special NFC-equipped cell phone. New companies are entering this market as well. Boku raised $13 million in venture financing and launched in June 2009. Boku allows users to buy digital goods using text messaging, with billing being handled by the cell phone provider. Zong, another company, offers a similar service.

It is likely that both the RFID cell phone and texting methods of mobile payment will grow exceptionally fast once the cell phone networks in the United States get behind the technology. To date, American carriers have been exceptionally slow in pushing advanced cell phone features in the United States. But this will change once the potential revenue of mobile payments becomes clear to the carriers, and once customers demand a level of service at least equal to that in Europe and Asia.

**SOURCES:** " 'Pay As You Go' Takes on New Meaning," By Spencer Ante and Roger Cheng, *Wall Street Journal*, August 31, 2010; "In Silicon Valley, Forget Your Wallet-But Not Your Phone," *Wall Street Journal*, July 30, 2010; "Cellphone Payments Offer Alternative to Cash," by Claire Cain Miller and Nick Bilton, *Wall Street Journal*, April 28, 2010; "Mobile Payment Systems Are Adapting, Developing," by Brendan Gibbons, *Practical Ecommerce*, January 28, 2010; "Mobile Payments Are Taking Off. But Which One to Use?," by Chris Dannen, *Fast Company*, September 1, 2009; "Nokia, Obopay Launch Mobile Payment Service, by Chris Harnick, MobileMarketer.com, August 27, 2009; "Investors Bet on Payments via Cellphone," by Claire Cain Miller and Matt Richtel, *New York Times*, June 21, 2009; "Nokia Sends $35 Million to Obopay to Develop Mobile Payments," by Claire Cain Miller, *New York Times*, March 25, 2009.

## MARKET SIZE AND GROWTH

There were just 12 million U.S households (11% of all households) using online bill payment in 2001. In 2010, according to Forrester Research, an estimated 52 million U.S. households will use online bill payment, about 65% of all households. Slow but steady growth through 2014 will result in 66 million households using online bill payment (Forrester, 2009).

One major reason for the surge in EBPP usage is that companies are starting to realize how much money they can save through online billing. Not only is there the savings in postage and processing, but payments can be received more quickly (3 to 12 days faster, compared to paper bills sent via regular mail), thereby improving cash flow. In order to realize these savings, many companies are becoming more aggressive in encouraging their customers to move to EBPP by instituting a charge for the privilege of continuing to receive a paper bill.

Financials don't tell the whole story, however. Companies are discovering that a bill is both a sales opportunity and a customer retention opportunity, and that the electronic medium provides many more options when it comes to marketing and promotion. Rebates, savings offers, cross-selling, and upselling are all possible in the digital realm.

Consumers are also becoming more receptive to online bill payment. A survey by research firm Fiserv found that around 80% of those surveyed said they preferred to pay bills online because it was faster than other payment methods. Ease of use, cost savings on stamps, and greater control over timing of payments were also cited by 70% as leading benefits. Environmental concerns were also relevant to about 60% of the respondents.

## EBPP BUSINESS MODELS

There are two main competing business models in the EBPP marketspace: biller-direct and consolidator. The biller-direct system was originally created by utility companies that send millions of bills each month. Their purpose is to make it easier for their customers to pay their utility bills routinely online. Today, telephone and credit card companies also frequently offer this service, as well as a number of individual stores. Companies implementing a biller-direct system can either develop their own system in-house (usually only an option for the very largest companies), install a system acquired from a third-party EBPP software vendor, use a third-party EBPP service bureau (the service bureau hosts a biller-branded Web site that enables consumers to view and pay bills and handles all customer enrollment, bill presentment, and payment processing), or use an application service provider (similar to a service bureau, but runs on the biller's Web site rather than being hosted on the service provider's Web site).

Currently, the biller-direct model is the dominant EBPP model, although Forrester predicts that by 2012, the consolidator model will surpass it. In the consolidator model, a third party, such as a financial institution or portal (either a general portal such as Yahoo! Bill Pay, or a focused portal such as Bills.com or Intuit's Paytrust.com), aggregates all bills for consumers and ideally permits one-stop bill payment (pay anyone). Within this model are two submodels—"thick" consolidation and "thin" consolidation. In thick consolidation, both the bill summary and bill detail are stored at the consolidator's site, while in thin consolidation, only the summary bill information is available, and the consumer must click on a link to access a detailed bill that is stored at another location, such as the biller's site or elsewhere. Currently, financial institutions have been more successful than portals in attracting online bill payers. The consolidator model faces several challenges. For billers, using the consolidator model means an increased time lag between billing and payment, and also inserts an intermediary between the company and its customer. For consumers, security continues to be a major issue. Most consumers are unwilling to pay any kind of fee to pay bills online, and many are concerned about sharing personal financial information with non-financial institutions. Today, more and more banks are offering online bill payment free to some or all of their customers as an enticement.

Supporting these two primary business models are infrastructure providers such as Harbor Payments, Online Resources (which acquired Princeton eCom in 2006), Yodlee, Fiserv (which also offers its own bill payment portal, MyCheckFree.com), Metavante, MasterCard RPPS (Remote Payment and Presentment Service), Corillian, and others that provide the software to create the EBPP system or handle billing and payment collection for the biller. **Figure 5.17** categorizes the major players in the EBPP marketspace.

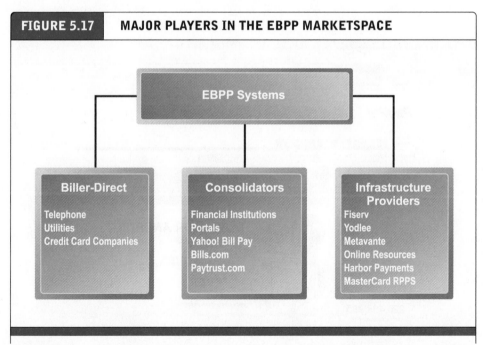

**FIGURE 5.17**     **MAJOR PLAYERS IN THE EBPP MARKETSPACE**

The main business models in the EBPP marketspace are biller-direct and consolidator. Infrastructure providers support both of these competing models.

## 5.8 CASE STUDY

# Paypal
## Has Company

PayPal—the online payment processor now owned by eBay—was the first truly successful Internet-based e-commerce payment system. Its origins were quite simple. On November 16, 1999, Peter Theil sat with friends at a restaurant. When the bill arrived, Theil used his Palm Pilot to "beam" his share to a friend sitting across the table. Theil and fellow co-founder Max Levchin had built a system that would allow them to send money to one another via a Palm Pilot's infrared links. From this idea sprang one of the first "peer-to-peer" payment systems: a system that allows individuals to send money to one another via e-mail.

PayPal emphasizes ease of use for both senders and receivers of cash. Here's a brief synopsis of how it works. First, you create a PayPal account at the PayPal Web site by filling out a one-page application form and providing credit or debit card or bank account information. Only PayPal is privy to this information, not the receiving party. Then, when you use PayPal to pay for a purchase, money is drawn from the credit card or bank account and transmitted to the Automated Clearing House (ACH) Network, a privately operated financial intermediary that tracks and transfers funds

between financial institutions. The party who is to receive the payment is notified via e-mail that money is waiting. If the receiving party has a PayPal account, the funds are automatically deposited into the account; if the person does not have a PayPal account, he or she must set one up, and then the money is credited to his or her account. Once the funds are in the PayPal account, the recipient can then transfer them electronically to a checking account, request a paper check, or use PayPal to send the funds to someone else.

Levchin and Theil originally conceived of PayPal as a method for "beaming" money to users of handheld PDAs. When this idea did not pan out, they changed their target to arranging payments between individuals who knew one another. However, they quickly realized that it would also work for a company such as eBay, providing purchasers and sellers with a way to short-cut the time-consuming and cumbersome process of mailing checks and money orders and waiting for checks to clear before shipping items. Moreover, for small merchants selling items on the Web, it is difficult and expensive to obtain the capability to accept credit cards. Credit companies extend these merchant services only to bona fide businesses, usually requiring a physical place of business.

Today, PayPal is the largest and most popular online payment service, growing from a handful of users when it launched in late 1999 to around 87 million active accounts in 2010 in 190 nations. In 2009, PayPal processed $71 billion in payments ($31 billion of which were generated on eBay, and $40 billion elsewhere on the Web). PayPal operates in 190 markets, 17 local languages, transacts in 19 currencies, and works with 27 global financial networks and 15,000 local banks around the world. PayPal has a 15% share of the U.S. consumer e-commerce payments market and a 6% share of the global market for merchant payments. The company's objective is to dominate e-commerce payments throughout the world. There's plenty of room for PayPal to grow.

One reason PayPal has grown so fast is because it experiences the benefits of network economics or the "viral effect": the more people who accept and use PayPal, the greater the benefit to the consumer. If I send you a PayPal payment via e-mail, then you are incentivized to open a PayPal account to receive the funds.

PayPal earns money in many different ways. First, online sellers (who may be individuals or small businesses that do not want the difficulties associated with obtaining a merchant credit card account) pay a transaction fee for the service (30 cents plus 1.9%–2.9% of the proceeds of the transaction). This generally works out to 3.3% of the transaction on a $100 transaction. Credit card firms generally charge about the same or 0.3% more due to their higher customer acquisition costs. PayPal, in other words, can be slightly less costly than credit cards for merchants. PayPal earns transaction fees when a Business or Premier account receives a payment or, in certain qualified transactions, when a sender elects to pay the fee in lieu of the recipient, and a foreign exchange fee when users convert currencies.

One advantage for merchants on eBay is that they are not required to have a merchant bank account, which is required by credit card issuers. Merchant banks clear credit card transactions and charge fees. Consumers are not charged directly for the use of their PayPal account although they do pay ultimately because retailers need to recover the costs of the transaction by raising the prices on goods sold using PayPal. Second, PayPal earns revenue by collecting the interest earned on consumer funds not yet transferred out of the PayPal system. PayPal has charges for transferring funds to foreign banks, converting currencies, and new financial products such as a PayPal credit card.

Part of the strength of PayPal lies in its simplicity: it piggybacks on existing credit card and checking payment systems. This is also one of its weaknesses, however. PayPal reportedly suffers relatively high levels of fraud related to the credit card system on which it relies. To protect against fraud, PayPal requires special authorization for payments over $200.

In 2002, PayPal went public and issued shares in an initial public offering. One of the main reasons PayPal grew so rapidly was because of its popularity on eBay. In an effort not to lose this lucrative transaction business to PayPal, eBay spent over $100 million promoting its own similar system called Billpoint—but to no avail. In October 2002, eBay purchased PayPal for $1.5 billion—about $20 a share. At the time, analysts felt the price was too high, but eBay has had the last laugh. Today, PayPal accounts for an increasing share of eBay's revenue (around 30% in 2009), a trend that is expected to continue. For the first time, in the second half of 2008, the payment volume generated by PayPal's merchant services business exceeded its volume from eBay, and this trend continued in 2009 as well, with PayPal generated around $41 billion of its net total payment volume from outside (non-eBay) transactions, representing approximately 56% of PayPal's total volume for the year.. PayPal's revenue increased by about 13%, from $2.3 billion in 2008 to $2.6 billion in 2009. This is a lower growth rate than the prior year, mostly due to a decrease in overall consumer purchases, particularly in the second half of the year. But even this lower growth rate is impressive when one considers that, in contrast, eBay's auction revenue declined by 6% in the recession of 2009.

For a brief period, PayPal enjoyed its position as the only widely adopted online platform (aside from the credit card companies). But this is changing rapidly. Already present in the exploding market for merchant payment services are Google Checkout and Amazon Payments, as well as Apple's iTunes Store where millions of micro transactions (.99 cent songs) are processed using Apple accounts and credit cards. However, these merchant payment systems used to pay for goods on retail Web sites are not so easily converted into P2P payment systems. In the P2P payment market, Facebook, Apple, and Twitter are planning new services. eBay executives are concerned that PayPal may lose market share to these other technologies and services.

Google has already made its foray into the merchant payment market with Google Checkout and is working on P2P payment systems for its mobile Android platform. Google Checkout stores a user's financial information, including credit card information, and then presents this information to merchants when the user checks out. The customer does not have to fill out forms or reveal credit information to online merchants. Checkout does not support P2P payments, at least not yet. Google has been careful not to directly challenge PayPal in the P2P market, if only because eBay (the owner of PayPal) is the largest single advertiser on Google, and Google directs a significant traffic volume to eBay. They need one another. Google also uses

Checkout to support its advertising network. Ads for online stores that accept Checkout are highlighted with an icon, increasing the chances that users will click on those sites. Once users click on an ad, they are more likely to purchase. Merchants who accept Checkout on their sites receive more traffic simply for offering the convenience of the service. Translating Google Checkout to a mobile peer-to-peer market place is difficult, and Google is discussing with PayPal how to integrate the PayPal system into the Android marketplace. PayPal would bring to Android a sizable user base of 87 million registered accounts.

Apple, which already has developed an extremely successful merchant micropayment processing system with its iTunes Stores, may be entering the fray. Some analysts believe Apple is considering the idea of extending its existing iTunes payment system to third-party vendors selling digital goods on the Internet. iPhone users can already use their iTunes account to buy some third-party virtual and subscription goods. In August 2010, Apple applied for a patent on a peer-to-peer financial transaction device and methods. The device is clearly an iPhone or iPad. The method uses a near field communication interface (NFC), which is an RFID chip that transmits over short ranges. This patent is the foundation for an Apple mobile P2P payment system that consumers could use to pay for everything from movie tickets to a cup of Starbucks. Other P2P options include Square, a very small square plastic credit card reader that plugs into iPhones and iPads (squareup.com). Square was invented by Jack Dorsey, one of the founders of Twitter. The product can be used for P2P credit card payments, such as for purchases on Craigslist.

During the summer of 2009, Facebook began to gradually expand the scope of a virtual currency called "Pay with Facebook" credits (purchased with a credit card) that allow users to buy items from merchants in Facebook's Gift Shop. In May 2009, the service was extended to include a few third-party game developers and virtual gift makers. Facebook began accepting 14 new currencies, in addition to the U.S. dollar. In August 2009, Facebook revealed that it was testing a system that would allow users to buy physical merchandise via its payment system. It also launched a test to let some users buy Facebook Credits by billing their mobile phones. Analysts believe that Facebook will try to establish its payment system as an on-site "wallet" and then leverage Facebook Connect (Facebook's API platform) to deliver one-click purchasing across the Web. However, for international audiences (about 350 million users), Facebook is teaming up with PayPal, which already is widely accepted outside the United States.

Twitter is also considering a P2P payment system based on its text messaging service. There are already two Twitter payment systems in 2010: Twippr and Twitpay. Payments are made in both by simply entering messages into their Twitter stream. When the message is downloaded by Twippr or Twitpay, the recipient, amount, and currency are identified, and the recipient is notified of the transaction. However, both of these services rely on PayPal in the backend to clear the transactions. Twippr charges .05 cents for each transaction, while TwitPay charges 4% of the funds transferred.

An even more direct challenge is coming from another source: cell phone carriers such as AT&T and Verizon, especially in P2P payments. PayPal is built upon the existing credit card system. What if you could eliminate the credit card intermediaries? Mobile payment company Obopay allows subscribers to transfer money and make purchases through their cell phones. Users can send money to anyone with a cell phone on any wireless network. Obopay has deals with Verizon, Nokia, BlackBerry, Citigroup, and MasterCard. Currently, Obopay customers have to load their Obopay accounts at the Obopay Web site with a credit or debit card, or a bank account. But in the future, Obopay hopes to integrate its service with the cell phone providers' monthly billing service, thereby eliminating credit card companies altogether from the payment loop, reducing transaction costs for merchants and customers, and making it easier to use the service. That's what start-ups Boku and Zong hope to do.

To compete with these new services, in June 2009, PayPal announced that it would open up its API to software developers in order to allow them to integrate PayPal functionality into programs created for mobile phones and social networks like Facebook. PayPal is also pursuing a number of other growth initiatives. PayPal signed up both Napster and Apple's iTunes Music Store as merchants in its first foray into the micropayments market. The experience proved so successful that PayPal introduced a micropayments pricing plan designed to increase and encourage the purchase of low-priced digital goods. PayPal is also pursuing an overseas expansion strategy. It has added localized Web sites in 18 different markets. Currently, businesses and consumers with e-mail can use PayPal to send online payments in 190 countries, and receive payments in 65 of those countries. Payments can be made or accepted in any one of 19 different currencies. PayPal is expanding beyond eBay sales by setting up preferred merchant relationships with other large Internet retailers such as Yahoo and Amazon, with mixed success. Amazon has its own credit card and preferred methods of payment, but Yahoo uses PayPal as a recommended payment method. PayPal also expanded its presence to e-commerce sites such as American Airlines, Omaha Steaks, Walmart.com, Zappos, and Ferrari. PayPal continues to enhance its mobile text message payment system, which allows cell phone users to pay for goods and services by texting PayPal payments to merchants.

PayPal's protections for consumers are also still weaker than what credit card companies are required to offer. For instance, you can deny a credit card charge and have a $50 maximum liability if your credit card information is stolen and used in commerce. With PayPal, you may or may not receive your money back, depending on whether PayPal can receive its money back, and a host of other conditions. PayPal has developed a consumer protection program, but it also settled in 2006 with 28 state attorneys general involving concerns about certain business practices. Chief among these practices was encouraging users to allow PayPal to directly debit consumer bank accounts, because PayPal can avoid paying credit companies a 2% funds transfer fee, making the direct deduction option more profitable for PayPal. If you have given PayPal both your credit card information and bank account information, the default payment method used by PayPal is your bank account. Once funds are withdrawn from your bank account, they cannot be recovered, unlike credit card transactions. Hence, the risk to consumers is substantially greater. Credit card companies can retrieve funds from misbehaving merchants more quickly by simply reverse-crediting their merchant bank accounts. In its latest attempt to address these issues, eBay paid $169 million to buy a company called Fraud

Services, to accelerate the next generation of fraud detection and enhance PayPal's risk management.

Despite the challenges, however, the future for PayPal appears bright. In fact, some analysts believe that PayPal may someday become an even bigger phenomenon than its acquirer, eBay.

## Case Study Questions

1. What is the value proposition that PayPal offers consumers? How about merchants?

2. What are some of the risks of using PayPal when compared to credit cards and debit cards?

3. Are P2P payments systems developed by Apple or Google for use on their mobile devices a threat to PayPal? Can PayPal develop its own P2P app for the iPhone?

4. What strategies would you recommend that PayPal pursue in order to maintain its growth over the next five years?

**SOURCES**: "Making Online Payments Using Twitter," Squidoo.com, August 27, 2010; "Apple Hires Expert on Mobile Payments," by Nick Bilton, *New York Times*, August 16, 2010; "eBay's PayPal Looks to Social Media," *Wall Street Journal*, February 24, 2010; "Facebook Integrates PayPal, Targets International," *Wall Street Journal*, February 18, 2010; eBay Inc. Report on 10-K For the Fiscal Year Ended December 31, 2009; filed with the Securities and Exchange Commission, February 17, 2010; "Mobile Payments are Taking Off. But Which One to Use?" by Chris Dannen, *Fast Company*, September 1, 2009; "Facebook Sets Sights on Online Payments Business, cnnmoney.com, August 31, 2009; "eBay's PayPal Faces Increasing Competition in Payments Space," by Ina Steiner, Auctionbytes.com, August 27, 2009; "Apple Wants to Build a PayPal Killer, Say Wall Street Gossips," by Nicholas Carlson, *Silicon Alley Insider*, August 4, 2009.

## 5.9 REVIEW

## KEY CONCEPTS

■ Understand the scope of e-commerce crime and security problems.

While the overall size of cybercrime is unclear at this time, cybercrime against e-commerce sites is growing rapidly, the amount of losses is growing, and the management of e-commerce sites must prepare for a variety of criminal assaults.

■ Describe the key dimensions of e-commerce security.

There are six key dimensions to e-commerce security:
- *Integrity*—ensures that information displayed on a Web site or sent or received via the Internet has not been altered in any way by an unauthorized party.
- *Nonrepudiation*—ensures that e-commerce participants do not deny (repudiate) their online actions.
- *Authenticity*—verifies an individual's or business's identity.
- *Confidentiality*—determines whether information shared online, such as through e-mail communication or an order process, can be viewed by anyone other than the intended recipient.
- *Privacy*—deals with the use of information shared during an online transaction. Consumers want to limit the extent to which their personal information can be divulged to other organizations, while merchants want to protect such information from falling into the wrong hands.

- *Availability*—determines whether a Web site is accessible and operational at any given moment.

■ **Understand the tension between security and other values.**

Although computer security is considered necessary to protect e-commerce activities, it is not without a downside. Two major areas where there are tensions between security and Web site operations include:

- *Ease of use*—The more security measures that are added to an e-commerce site, the more difficult it is to use and the slower the site becomes, hampering ease of use. Security is purchased at the price of slowing down processors and adding significantly to data storage demands. Too much security can harm profitability, while not enough can potentially put a company out of business.
- *Public safety*—There is a tension between the claims of individuals to act anonymously and the needs of public officials to maintain public safety that can be threatened by criminals or terrorists.

■ **Identify the key security threats in the e-commerce environment.**

The nine most common and most damaging forms of security threats to e-commerce sites include:

- *Malicious code*—viruses, worms, Trojan horses, and bot networks are a threat to a system's integrity and continued operation, often changing how a system functions or altering documents created on the system.
- *Unwanted programs (adware, spyware, etc.)*—a kind of security threat that arises when programs are surreptitiously installed on your computer or computer network without your consent.
- *Phishing*—any deceptive, online attempt by a third party to obtain confidential information for financial gain.
- *Hacking and cybervandalism*—intentionally disrupting, defacing, or even destroying a site.
- *Credit card fraud/theft*—one of the most-feared occurrences and one of the main reasons more consumers do not participate in e-commerce. The most common cause of credit card fraud is a lost or stolen card that is used by someone else, followed by employee theft of customer numbers and stolen identities (criminals applying for credit cards using false identities).
- *Spoofing*—occurs when hackers attempt to hide their true identities or misrepresent themselves by using fake e-mail addresses or masquerading as someone else. Spoofing also can involve redirecting a Web link to an address different from the intended one, with the site masquerading as the intended destination.
- *Denial of Service (DoS) attacks*—hackers flood a Web site with useless traffic to inundate and overwhelm the network, frequently causing it to shut down and damaging a site's reputation and customer relationships.
- *Sniffing*—a type of eavesdropping program that monitors information traveling over a network, enabling hackers to steal proprietary information from anywhere on a network, including e-mail messages, company files, and confidential reports. The threat of sniffing is that confidential or personal information will be made public.

- *Insider jobs*—although the bulk of Internet security efforts are focused on keeping outsiders out, the biggest threat is from employees who have access to sensitive information and procedures.
- *Poorly designed server and client software*—the increase in complexity and size of software programs has contributed to an increase in software flaws or vulnerabilities that hackers can exploit weaknesses.

■ **Describe how technology helps protect the security of messages sent over the Internet.**

Encryption is the process of transforming plain text or data into cipher text that cannot be read by anyone other than the sender and the receiver. Encryption can provide four of the six key dimensions of e-commerce security:

- *Message integrity*—provides assurance that the sent message has not been altered.
- *Nonrepudiation*—prevents the user from denying that he or she sent a message.
- *Authentication*—provides verification of the identity of the person (or computer) sending the message.
- *Confidentiality*—gives assurance that the message was not read by others.

There are a variety of different forms of encryption technology currently in use. They include:

- *Symmetric key encryption*—Both the sender and the receiver use the same key to encrypt and decrypt a message. Advanced Encryption Standard (AES) is the most widely used symmetric key encryption system on the Internet today.
- *Public key cryptography*—Two mathematically related digital keys are used: a public key and a private key. The private key is kept secret by the owner, and the public key is widely disseminated. Both keys can be used to encrypt and decrypt a message. Once the keys are used to encrypt a message, the same keys cannot be used to unencrypt the message.
- *Public key encryption using digital signatures and hash digests*—This method uses a mathematical algorithm called a hash function to produce a fixed-length number called a hash digest. The results of applying the hash function are sent by the sender to the recipient. Upon receipt, the recipient applies the hash function to the received message and checks to verify that the same result is produced. The sender then encrypts both the hash result and the original message using the recipient's public key, producing a single block of cipher text. To ensure both the authenticity of the message and nonrepudiation, the sender encrypts the entire block of cipher text one more time using the sender's private key. This produces a digital signature or "signed" cipher text that can be sent over the Internet to ensure the confidentiality of the message and authenticate the sender.
- *Digital envelope*—This method uses symmetric encryption to encrypt and decrypt the document, but public key encryption to encrypt and send the symmetric key.
- *Digital certificates and public key infrastructure*—This method relies on certification authorities who issue, verify, and guarantee digital certificates (a digital document that contains the name of the subject or company, the subject's public key, a digital certificate serial number, an expiration date, an issuance date, the digital signature of the certification authority, and other identifying information).

■ Identify the tools used to establish secure Internet communications channels and protect networks, servers, and clients.

In addition to encryption, there are several other tools that are used to secure Internet channels of communication, including:

- *Secure Sockets Layer (SSL)*—This is the most common form of securing channels. The SSL protocol provides data encryption, server authentication, client authentication, and message integrity for TCP/IP connections.
- *Secure Hypertext Transfer Protocol (S-HTTP)*—S-HTTP secures only Web protocols and cannot be used to secure non-HTTP messages.
- *Virtual private networks (VPNs)*—These allow remote users to securely access internal networks via the Internet, using the Point-to-Point Tunneling Protocol (PPTP), an encoding mechanism that allows one local network to connect to another using the Internet as the conduit.

After communications channels are secured, tools to protect networks, the servers, and clients should be implemented. These include:

- *Firewalls*—software applications that act as filters between a company's private network and the Internet itself, denying unauthorized remote client computers from attaching to your internal network.
- *Proxies*—software servers that act primarily to limit access of internal clients to external Internet servers and are frequently referred to as the gateway.
- *Operating system controls*—built-in username and password requirements that provide a level of authentication. Some operating systems also have an access control function that controls user access to various areas of a network.
- *Anti-virus software*—a cheap and easy way to identify and eradicate the most common types of viruses as they enter a computer, as well as to destroy those already lurking on a hard drive.

■ Appreciate the importance of policies, procedures, and laws in creating security.

In order to minimize security threats:

- E-commerce firms must develop a coherent corporate policy that takes into account the nature of the risks, the information assets that need protecting, and the procedures and technologies required to address the risk, as well as implementation and auditing mechanisms.
- Public laws and active enforcement of cybercrime statutes are also required to both raise the costs of illegal behavior on the Internet and guard against corporate abuse of information.

The key steps in developing a security plan are:

- *Perform a risk assessment*—an assessment of the risks and points of vulnerability.
- *Develop a security policy*—a set of statements prioritizing the information risks, identifying acceptable risk targets, and identifying the mechanisms for achieving these targets.
- *Create an implementation plan*—a plan that determines how you will translate the levels of acceptable risk into a set of tools, technologies, policies, and procedures.
- *Create a security team*—the individuals who will be responsible for ongoing maintenance, audits, and improvements.

- *Perform periodic security audits*—routine reviews of access logs and any unusual patterns of activity.

■ **Describe the features of traditional payment systems.**

Traditional payment systems include:
- *Cash*, whose key feature is that it is instantly convertible into other forms of value without the intermediation of any other institution.
- *Checking transfers*, which are funds transferred directly through a signed draft or check from a consumer's checking account to a merchant or other individual; these are the second most common forms of payment.
- *Credit card accounts*, which are accounts that extend credit to a consumer and allow consumers to make payments to multiple vendors at one time.
- *Stored value systems*, which are created by depositing funds into an account and from which funds are paid out or are withdrawn as needed. Stored value payments systems include debit cards, phone cards, and smart cards.
- *Accumulating balance systems*, which accumulate expenditures and to which consumers make periodic payments.

■ **Understand the major e-commerce payment mechanisms.**

The major types of digital payment systems include:
- *Online credit card transactions,* which are the primary form of online payment system. There are five parties involved in an online credit card purchase: consumer, merchant, clearinghouse, merchant bank (sometimes called the "acquiring bank"), and the consumer's card issuing bank. However, the online credit card system has a number of limitations involving security, merchant risk, cost, and social equity.
- *Digital wallets*, which emulate the functionality of a traditional wallet containing personal identifying information and store value in some form.
- *Digital cash*, which are online numeric tokens based on bank deposits or credit card accounts.
- *Online stored value systems*, which permit consumers to make instant, online payments to merchants and other individuals based on value stored in an online account. Some stored value systems require the user to download a digital wallet, while others require users to simply sign up and transfer money from an existing account into an online stored value account.
- *Digital accumulating balance systems*, which allow users to make purchases on the Web, accumulating a debit balance for which they are billed at the end of the cycle (such as at the end of a day or month); consumers are then expected to pay the entire balance using a checking or credit card account. Accumulating balance systems are ideal for purchasing digital content such as music tracks, chapters of books, or articles from a newspaper.
- *Digital checking payment systems*, which are extensions to the existing checking and banking infrastructure.
- *Wireless payment systems*, which are cell phone-based payment systems that enable mobile payments.

■ **Describe the features and functionality of electronic billing presentment and payment systems.**

EBPP systems are a form of online payment systems for monthly bills. EBPP services allow consumers to view bills electronically and pay them through electronic funds transfers from bank or credit card accounts. Major players in the EBPP marketspace include:

- *Biller-direct systems*, which were originally created by large utilities to facilitate routine payment of utility bills, but which are increasingly being used by other billers.
- *Consolidators*, which attempt to aggregate all bills for consumers in one place and ideally permit one-stop bill payment.
- *Infrastructure providers* which support the biller-direct and consolidator business models.

## QUESTIONS

1. Why is it less risky to steal online? Explain some of the ways criminals deceive consumers and merchants.
2. Explain why an e-commerce site might not want to report being the target of cybercriminals.
3. Give an example of security breaches as they relate to each of the six dimensions of e-commerce security. For instance, what would be a privacy incident?
4. How would you protect your firm against a Denial of Service attack?
5. Explain why the U.S. government wants to restrict the export of strong encryption systems. And why would other countries be against it?
6. Name the major points of vulnerability in a typical online transaction.
7. How does spoofing threaten a Web site's operations?
8. Why is adware or spyware considered to be a security threat?
9. What are some of the steps a company can take to curtail cybercriminal activity from within a business?
10. Explain some of the modern-day flaws associated with encryption. Why is encryption not as secure today as it was earlier in the century?
11. Briefly explain how public key cryptography works.
12. Compare and contrast firewalls and proxy servers and their security functions.
13. Is a computer with anti-virus software protected from viruses? Why or why not?
14. Identify and discuss the five steps in developing an e-commerce security plan.
15. How do biometric devices help improve security? What particular type of security breach do they particularly reduce?
16. What are tiger teams, who uses them, and what are some of the tactics they use in their work?
17. How do the interests of the four major payment systems stakeholders impact each other?
18. Compare and contrast stored value payment systems and checking transfers.
19. Why is a credit card not considered an accumulating balance payment system?
20. Name six advantages and six disadvantages of using cash as a form of payment.
21. Describe the relationship between credit card associations and issuing banks.
22. What is Regulation Z, and how does it protect the consumer?
23. Briefly discuss the disadvantages of credit cards as the standard for online payments. How does requiring a credit card for payment discriminate against some consumers?

24. Describe the major steps involved in an online credit card transaction.
25. Compare and contrast smart cards and traditional credit cards.
26. How is money transferred in transactions using wireless devices?
27. Discuss why EBPP systems are becoming increasingly popular.
28. How are the two main types of EBPP systems both alike and different from each other?

## PROJECTS

1. Imagine you are the owner of an e-commerce Web site. What are some of the signs that your site has been hacked? Discuss the major types of attacks you could expect to experience and the resulting damage to your site. Prepare a brief summary presentation.

2. Given the shift toward mobile commerce, do a search on mobile commerce crime. Identify and discuss the new security threats this type of technology creates. Prepare a presentation outlining your vision of the new opportunities for cybercrime.

3. Find three certification authorities and compare the features of each company's digital certificates. Provide a brief description of each company as well, including number of clients. Prepare a brief presentation of your findings.

4. Research the challenges associated with payments across international borders and prepare a brief presentation of your findings. Do most e-commerce companies conduct business internationally? How do they protect themselves from repudiation? How do exchange rates impact online purchases? What about shipping charges? Summarize by describing the differences between a U.S. customer and an international customer who each make a purchase from a U.S. e-commerce merchant.

# Business Concepts and Social Issues

## CHAPTER 6

# E-commerce Marketing Concepts

**After reading this chapter, you will be able to:**

- Identify the key features of the Internet audience.
- Discuss the basic concepts of consumer behavior and purchasing decisions.
- Understand how consumers behave online.
- Describe the basic marketing concepts needed to understand Internet marketing.
- Identify and describe the main technologies that support online marketing.
- Identify and describe basic e-commerce marketing and branding strategies.

# Netflix

## Strengthens and Defends Its Brand

I n a recession, Americans go to the movies. If you're looking for a success story in 2010, Netflix is a good candidate. Its 2009 annual revenues hit $1.6 billion, 22% higher than 2008. In 2010, second quarter results were even better: revenue and profits up 25% over the previous year. Netflix is adding about 300,000 subscribers a month in 2010. It recently delivered its 2 billionth movie. If you ever wondered how many of its 100,000 DVD titles are rented at least once on a typical day, the answer is an astounding 51,000. Most people guess about 1,000, and they seriously underestimate the breadth of American tastes in movies, and the overall demand for Hollywood fare. But, in 2010, Netflix is also preparing for its own destruction: DVD rentals delivered by the postal service are declining 25% a year. But, at the same time its subscriber base is growing 50% a year. How is this anomaly explained? The answer is that 60% of the new subscribers stream movies rather than rent DVDs.

Netflix is the largest online entertainment subscription service in the United States, providing more than 15 million customers in 2010 with access to over 100,000 DVD titles (and more than 55 million DVDs in stock). Netflix's basic business is renting DVD titles on a subscription basis and streaming movies to a wide variety of devices from televisions, to computers, game machines, iPhones, and iPads. Netflix offers different plans ranging from $4.99 a month to $16.99 a month. The more you pay, the larger the number of DVDs you can possess simultaneously, and the more movies you can stream to your PC or TV. Since 1999, Netflix subscribers have grown at an annual rate of 79%, and its revenues have grown at 113%.

Netflix is recognized as an "iconic" brand: it's a symbol of how a powerful Web-based service backed up by superior customer experience can differentiate itself from competitors. When people think DVD they often think of Netflix first, and competitors are far down the list. Over 90% of subscribers have recommended Netflix to their friends. Netflix believes its primary competitive advantages are its brand recognition and personalization—the ability to provide customers with videos they want, or may want even before they knew themselves.

Despite its obvious strengths, Netflix is in for the fight of its brief life. Just as Netflix destroyed the business model of Blockbuster, so are new competitors threatening Netflix's business model and market. Heavy weight Wal-Mart bought Vudu in 2010, a Silicon Valley start-up whose movie service is being built into televisions and Blu-ray players. Amazon has started a service streaming movies to Tivo DVRs in the home. In June 2010, Hulu, owned by the major television networks, announced a subscription streaming service allowing users to watch television shows on their TVs and other devices. Even YouTube (think Google) is pressing to get into the high quality movie distribution business. At the lower end of the market, Redbox, the start-up with over 15,000 vending machines renting DVDs for $1 a day in supermarkets and stores, is chipping away at the DVD rental market. Under this kind of sustained attack from multiple quarters, even a company with a strong brand cannot rest on its past successes or brand history. In fact, Netflix needs to reinvent itself.

Let's start first with some background. How did Netflix build up a nationally recognized successful brand in a marketplace filled with established brand names such as behemoth Blockbuster, which had over 50 million customers and 90,000 rental DVD titles distributed by over 7,000 local neighborhood stores and 500 kiosks?

Netflix started out in Los Gatos, California (in the heart of Silicon Valley and the San Francisco Bay Area) as a regionally based online movie store. It offered Bay Area customers a simple list of videos arranged by title and lead actor. Rentals were mailed out, and renters were charged the usual late fees for failure to return within a week. Despite the simplicity of its business model and regional character, Netflix had gross revenues of over $1 million in 1998, but lost over $11 million. It was hardly an auspicious beginning, even though these first years demonstrated a market for online video rentals. Many doubted the U.S. Postal Service was up to the task of delivering DVDs in the region, let alone hundreds of thousands daily on a national scale.

In 2000, Netflix changed its business model to that of a nationally based subscription model, entered into a number of relationships with Hollywood producers to speed up access to recent titles, expanded the functionality of its Web site, and changed its strategic marketing objectives toward becoming a nationally recognized online brand name. Unlike most neighborhood video rental stores at the time, Netflix changed from charging a fee for each video rental to assessing a monthly service charge for unlimited video rentals. Customers can rent as many videos as they want (with its most popular plan allowing a limit of three videos signed out at any given time) every month. For hardcore video fans, Netflix has developed a $16.99 a month plan that allows eight movies to be checked out at once. Moreover, Netflix eliminated late fees—the single largest complaint of video store customers around the country. To fulfill orders on a national basis, Netflix established video warehouse operations in various metropolitan areas around the United States (now totaling 58) and entered into a long-term relationship with the U.S. Postal Service to ensure delivery within one or two days for 95% of its subscribers in most parts of the country at very low cost for high-volume deliveries. Netflix provides a pre-stamped mailer for postal returns, absorbing the cost by using revenues from sales of DVDs to some renters.

To build national brand awareness, Netflix used every method in the e-commerce playbook. Netflix marketed its service by purchasing pay-for-performance banner advertising from Yahoo, MSN, and AOL. The familiar Netflix red banner ad is one of the most frequently seen leave-behind ads on the Web. It used search engine marketing and pay-for-placement ads on major search engines and permission-based e-mail.

On its own Web site, Netflix offered free trial periods and experienced high conversion rates. Hollywood studios typically distribute their filmed entertainment to the home video market six months after the theater release, to the pay-per-view (PPV) market seven months after theater release, to premium satellite and cable systems one year after release, and to general broadcast television and basic cable about two to three years after release. Rather than invest heavily in the purchase of DVDs from Hollywood, Netflix entered into a revenue-sharing arrangement with several studios, which allowed Netflix to purchase the DVDs below cost but to share the revenues from rentals with the studios. In this way, Netflix was able to build a bigger inventory faster and with less investment.

But building a brand also involves building a trusted high-value relationship with the customer, a unique value proposition that the customer cannot obtain elsewhere and might even pay a premium to receive. To build this relationship, Netflix enlarged its titles library from a few thousand to over 100,000 titles, providing customers 10 times more titles than can be found in the typical large Blockbuster store (and adding customer value through the "library effect" described later in the chapter).

Ever get confused at Blockbuster trying to find a movie for the night? A major focus of Netflix is "the customer experience" on-site. In an effort to provide personalized video rental advice, Netflix added a recommender system to its Web site, which reduces customer confusion. Using its own customers as a knowledge base, it asked customers to submit online reviews, comments, and recommendations on videos they rented. So far, Netflix has gathered over 3 billion movie ratings, which it then makes available to the entire online customer base—a valuable and inimitable resource. Sixty percent of Netflix subscribers use the recommender system to select their movies.

In 2006, the company started a contest offering $1 million to any person or group who could improve Netflix's recommendations by 10%. In 2009, a team from AT&T Research called BelKor Pragmatic Chaos was one of two teams to pass the 10% improvement mark. Using data mining techniques and a collaborative filtering tool similar to Amazon's, Netflix is able to recommend to its customers new videos based on each customer's personal profile of previous rentals and the rentals of other similar customers. Netflix sends e-mail to its customer base offering recently released videos that, given the customer's previous rental history, might be of special interest to that customer.

Aside from improving the online customer experience by providing plenty of inventory and recommendations to reduce customer confusion, Netflix is taking a number of steps to defend its brand. In 2010, it entered into a deal with Warner Brothers to obtain greater access to Warner's huge backlist of titles and agreed to delay release of Warner movies by at least one month after the movie appears in theaters. In July 2010, Netflix cut a deal with Relativity Media to stream Hollywood-quality films on the same schedule as PPV cable channels like the Starz movie channel. In August 201, Netflix paid $1 billion to add films from Paramount, Lions Gate, and MGM to its online subscription service. Netflix is slowly entering a new emergent market in which Web providers can compete with PPV cable channels and eventually movie theaters on a nearly equal footing.

**SOURCES:** "Netflix to Pay Nearly $1 Billion to Add Films to On-Demand Service," *New York Times*, August 10, 2010; "Always Pushing Beyond the Envelope," by Damon Darlin, *New York Times*, August 7, 2010; "Analysts' Views: What Hulu's New Service Means For Netflix," by Jennifer Valentino-DeVries, *Wall Street Journal*, June 30, 2010; "Redbox's Vending Machines Are Giving Netflix Competition," Associated Press, *New York Times*, June 22, 2009; Netflix Inc Form 10-Q for the quarter ended March 31, 2010, filed with the Securities and Exchange Commission on April 28, 2010; "Blockbuster Shares Fall on Chapter 11 Warning," by Associated Press, *New York Times*, March 17, 2010; Netflix Inc Form 10- K for the fiscal year ended December 31, 2009, filed with the Securities and Exchange Commission on March 15, 2010; "Netflix Deal With Warner," by Brad Stone, *New York Times*, January 11, 2010; "Adding Wal-Mart's Clout to Streamed Shows," by Brad Stone, *New York Times*, February 23, 2010; "Netflix Awards $1M Price to Improve Movie Picks," by Barbara Ortutay, AP Technology, Monday September 21, 2009; "Netflix Announces Agreement with Disney-ABC Television Group to Stream Several Hit ABC Series," Netflix, August 3, 2009."

Netflix provides an example of how the Internet has changed the nature of entire industries and how it enables new types of businesses to thrive even in highly competitive environments. But perhaps no area has been more affected than marketing and marketing communications. As a communications tool, the Internet affords marketers new ways of contacting millions of potential customers at costs far lower than traditional media. The Internet also provides new ways—often instantaneous and spontaneous—to gather information from customers, adjust product offerings, and increase customer value. In the case of Netflix, and in the other cases in this and the following chapter, the Internet has spawned entirely new ways to identify and communicate with customers, including search engine marketing, data mining, recommender systems, and targeted e-mail.

In the Web 2.0 environment of 2010-2011, advertisers are following huge shifts in audience away from traditional media and towards social networking, user-generated content, and online content destinations. For instance, according to Internet Retailer, almost 75% of its Top 500 e-retailers have a presence on Facebook, over 50% had posted commercials, product demos, or other types of videos on YouTube, or had a Twitter feed (Internet Retailer, 2010). In this chapter and Chapter 7, we discuss avenues for marketing and advertising on the Internet. This chapter focuses on the basic marketing concepts you need to understand to evaluate e-commerce marketing programs. Here, we examine consumer behavior on the Web, brands, the unique features of electronic markets, and special technologies that support new kinds of branding activities. For some of you, this will be a useful review of material you first learned in marketing classes, while for others this will be a first-time exposure to basic marketing concepts. Chapter 7 discusses e-commerce marketing communications, including advertising and other tools.

## 6.1  CONSUMERS ONLINE: THE INTERNET AUDIENCE AND CONSUMER BEHAVIOR

Before firms can begin to sell their products online, they must first understand what kinds of people they will find online and how those people behave in the online marketplace. In this section, we focus primarily on individual consumers in the B2C arena. However, many of the factors discussed apply to the B2B arena as well, insofar as purchasing decisions by firms are made by individuals.

### THE INTERNET AUDIENCE

We will start with an analysis of some basic background demographics of Web consumers in the United States. The first principle of marketing and sales is "know thy customer." Who uses the Web, who shops on the Web and why, and what do they buy?

## INTERNET TRAFFIC PATTERNS: THE ONLINE CONSUMER PROFILE

In 2010, around 221 million people of all ages and over 82 million U.S. households (about 70% of all U.S. households) will have access to the Internet (eMarketer, Inc., 2010a). By comparison, 98% of all U.S. households currently have televisions and 94% have telephones.

Although the number of new online users increased at a rate of 30% a year or higher in the late 1990s, over the last several years, this growth rate has slowed to about 2%–3% a year. Because of the cost and complexity of computer use required for Internet access, it is unlikely that Internet use will equal that of television or radio use in the near future, although this may change as computers become less expensive and complex. E-commerce businesses can no longer count on an annual 30% growth rate in the online population to fuel their revenues. The days of extremely rapid growth in the U.S. Internet population are over.

### Intensity and Scope of Usage

The slowing rate of growth in the U.S. Internet population is compensated for in part by an increasing intensity and scope of use. Several studies show that a greater amount of time is being spent online by Internet users. Overall, users are going online more frequently, with 78% of adult users in the United States (128 million people) logging on in a typical day (Pew Internet & American Life Project, 2010a). The more time users spend online, becoming more comfortable and familiar with Internet features and services, the more services they are likely to explore, according to the Pew Internet & American Life Project.

People who go online are engaging in a wider range of activities than in the past. While e-mail remains the most-used Internet service, other popular activities include using search engines, researching products and services, catching up on news, gathering hobby-related information, seeking health information, conducting work-related research, and reviewing financial information. **Table 6.1** identifies the range of online activities for the typical adult U.S. Internet user. Each percent translates into about 1.68 million people.

### Demographics and Access

The demographic profile of the Internet—and e-commerce—has changed greatly since 1995. Up until 2000, single, white, young, college-educated males with high incomes dominated the Internet. This inequality in access and usage led to concerns about a possible "digital divide." However, in recent years, there has been a marked increase in Internet usage by females, minorities, and families with modest incomes, resulting in a notable decrease—but not elimination—in the earlier inequality of access and usage. The following discussion is based on data collected in surveyed conducted by the Pew Internet & American Life Project.

**Gender** An equal percentage of both men (79%) and women (79%) use the Internet. Women are also almost as likely to use the Internet on a daily basis as men, although somewhat less likely to purchase online.

| TABLE 6.1 | A GROWING RANGE OF ONLINE ACTIVITIES: AN AVERAGE DAY IN THE LIFE OF AN INTERNET USER |
|---|---|
| **ACTIVITY** | **PERCENT OF INTERNET USERS WHO REPORTED ENGAGING IN ACTIVITY "YESTERDAY"** |
| | 2010 |
| Use the Internet | 78% |
| Send or read e-mail | 62% |
| Use a search engine to find information | 49% |
| Get news | 43% |
| Go online just for fun or to pass time | 38% |
| Use an online social networking site | 38% |
| Check the weather | 34% |
| Do banking online | 26% |
| Watch a video on a video-sharing site | 23% |
| Look online for news or information about politics | 19% |
| Look for information on Wikipedia | 17% |
| Send instant messages | 15% |
| Get financial information online | 12% |
| Visit a government Web site | 12% |
| Use online classified ads or sites | 11% |
| Read an online journal or blog | 10% |
| Look for health/medical information | 10% |
| Look online for job information | 10% |
| Use Twitter or other status update service | 10% |
| Post comments to an online news group, Web site, blog, or photo site | 8% |
| Search for information about someone you know or might meet | 8% |
| Buy a product | 8% |
| Look for "how-to," "do-it-yourself" information | 7% |
| Look for religious/spiritual information | 5% |
| Rate a product, service, or person using an online rating system | 4% |
| Create or work on own online journal or blog | 4% |
| Buy or make a reservation for travel | 3% |
| Download a podcast | 3% |
| Download or share files using P2P file sharing networks | 3% |
| Participate in an online auction | 3% |
| Use an online dating Web site | 2% |
| Participate in an online discussion group | 1% |

SOURCE: Pew Internet & American Life Project, 2010a.

**Age** Teens (12–17) and young adults (18-29) form the age groups with the highest percentage of Internet use at 95%. Adults in the 30–49 group (87%) are also strongly represented and growing their Internet presence. The percentage of the very young (about 19% of children) going online is also growing dramatically, in part due to increased access to computers and the Internet both at school and at home and the use of the Internet as an entertainment platform. Another fast growing group online is the 65 and over segment, 42% of whom now use the Internet, more than double the level of 2002.

**Ethnicity** Variation across ethnic groups is not as wide as across age groups. In 2002, there were significant differences among ethnic groups, but this has receded. White user participation is 80% in 2010, Hispanic 82%, and African-American 71%. The growth rates for both Hispanics and African-Americans over the period from 2002 to 2010 is higher than those for whites, which has helped close the gap.

**Community Type** Historically, Internet access rates have been significantly lower in rural areas than other kinds of communities although this is slowly changing. Still, in 2010, only about 67% of rural households had any kind of Internet connection with wide variations from state-to-state.

**Income Level** About 95% of households with income levels above $75,000 have Internet access, compared to only 63% of households earning less than $30,000. However, those households with lower earnings are gaining Internet access at faster rates than households with incomes of $75,000 and above. Over time, income differences have declined, but they remain significant. Income is not significantly related to exposure or hours using the Internet.

**Education** Amount of education also makes a significant difference when it comes to online access. Of those individuals with less than a high school education, 52% were online in 2010, compared to 96% of individuals with a college degree or more. Even a high school education boosted Internet usage, with that segment reaching 67% accessing the Web. In general, educational disparities far exceed other disparities in Internet access and usage.

Overall, there remains a strong relationship between age, income, ethnicity, and education on one hand and Internet usage on the other. The so-called "digital divide" has indeed moderated, but it still persists along the income, education, age, regional, and ethnic dimensions. **Table 6.2** summarizes some of the major intergroup differences discussed above and their pace of change.

## Type of Internet Connection: Broadband Impacts

In 2010, around 79.5 million households had broadband service in their homes—68.5% of all households (eMarketer, Inc., 2010a). Research suggests the broadband audience is different from the dial-up audience (see **Table 6.3**) and marketers need to take this into account when devising marketing plans. The broadband audience is more educated, wealthier, and more middle-aged. The broadband audience is much more intensely involved with the Internet and much more capable of using the Internet. For marketers, this audience offers unique opportunities for the use of multime-

| TABLE 6.2 | CHANGING DEMOGRAPHIC DIFFERENCES IN INTERNET ACCESS | |
|---|---|---|
| GROUP | THE PERCENT OF EACH GROUP ONLINE | |
| | 2010 | 2002 |
| Total Adults | 79% | 50% |
| Women | 79% | 56% |
| Men | 79% | 60% |
| *AGE* | | |
| 18–29 | 95% | 74% |
| 30–49 | 87% | 67% |
| 50–64 | 78% | 52% |
| 65+ | 42% | 18% |
| *RACE/ETHNICITY* | | |
| White, Non-Hispanic | 80% | 60% |
| Black, Non-Hispanic | 71% | 45% |
| Hispanic (English-speaking) | 82% | 54% |
| *COMMUNITY TYPE* | | |
| Urban | 81% | 67% |
| Suburban | 82% | 66% |
| Rural | 67% | 52% |
| *HOUSEHOLD INCOME* | | |
| Less than $30,000/yr | 63% | 38% |
| $30,000–$50,000 | 84% | 65% |
| $50,000–$75,000 | 89% | 74% |
| More than $75,000 | 95% | 86% |
| *EDUCATIONAL ATTAINMENT* | | |
| Less than High School | 52% | N/A |
| High School | 67% | 45% |
| Some College | 90% | 72% |
| College + | 96% | 82% |

SOURCE: Based on data from Pew Internet & American Life Project, 2010b, 2005a, 2005b.

| TABLE 6.3 | ONLINE ACTIVITIES OF U.S. INTERNET USERS BY ACCESS TECHNOLOGY, NOVEMBER 2009 (% OF RESPONDENTS IN EACH GROUP) | |
|---|---|---|
| **ACTIVITY** | **DIAL-UP USERS** | **BROADBAND USERS** |
| Buy a product online | 56% | 83% |
| Get local or community news | 55% | 80% |
| Visit local, state, or federal government Web site | 53% | 79% |
| Get international or national news | 54% | 77% |
| Bank online | 43% | 69% |
| Get information about or apply for a job | 39% | 60% |
| Use a social networking site | 41% | 55% |
| Submit a review for a product or service | 36% | 55% |
| Get advice from a government agency about a health or safety issue | 39% | 54% |
| Download or stream music | 22% | 52% |
| Play games online | 38% | 48% |
| Upload or share content | 26% | 48% |
| Download or stream video | 18% | 42% |
| Post to own blog or group blog | 7% | 26% |
| Take a class online | 8% | 24% |
| Play complicated role-playing games online | 9% | 14% |

SOURCE: Based on data from Federal Communications Commission, 2010

dia advertising and marketing campaigns, and for the positioning of products especially suited for this audience. On the other hand, the 2.8 million dial-up households buy products online, visit news sites, and use social networking sites—just not as frequently or intensely as broadband households.

## Community Effects: Social Contagion

For a physical retail store, the most important factor in shaping sales is location, location, and location. If you are located where thousands of people pass by every day, you will tend to do well. But for Internet retailers, physical location has almost no consequence as long as customers can be served by shipping services such as UPS or the post office or their services downloaded to anywhere. What does make a difference for consumer purchases on the Internet is whether or not the consumer is located in "neighborhoods" where others purchase on the Internet. These so-called neighborhood effects, and the role of social emulation in consumption decisions, are well-known for other goods such as personal computers. Research on an Internet grocery found that being located near other users of the online grocery increased the likelihood of purchasing at the site by 50% (Bell and Song, 2004). Online marketers are beginning to realize the importance of online and offline social ties, and communities, for branding and sales. Social networking sites, blogs, and social tagging sites are increasingly influential in consumer behavior as you will see throughout this chapter. People tend to go to those Web sites where their friends go.

### Lifestyle and Sociological Impacts

There are some worrisome potential impacts to intensive Internet use. Ask many parents of young teenagers, and they will often complain their children are spending too much time instant messaging and playing games online. Early research suggested that the Internet might be causing a decline in traditional social activities, such as talking face-to-face with neighbors and family members, encouraging users to spend less time with family and friends, and more time working, whether at home or at the office. According to an early study performed at Stanford University by a group of political scientists, Internet users lose touch with those around them; individuals spending just two to five hours a week online spend far less time talking with friends and family face-to-face and on the phone. Users who spend up to five hours a week online frequently experience an increase in time spent working while at home, while those who spend more than five hours a week online find themselves working more at work as well; the Internet is taking up a larger portion of what used to be free time for some workers. On the other hand, e-mail, instant messaging, and chat groups, all decidedly social activities, albeit not face-to-face ones, are among the most popular uses of the Internet.

More recent research has found that the use of the Internet strengthens and complements traditional face-to-face relationships. While Internet use involves a single user sitting in front of a screen—much like television—it is very different from television because of the high levels of social interaction possible on the Internet. Insofar as Internet use deters children from face-to-face interaction or from undirected "play" out of doors, undesirable effects on child social development may result (Nie and Erbring, 2000). On the other hand, a recent study demonstrated that the Internet has strengthened ties among cousins (the "clicking cousins effect"), children, and parents through the use of e-mail to stay in touch on a daily basis. A meta-analysis of multiple studies on the impact of the Internet on social interaction from 1995–2003 found mixed results, with offline and online interaction stimulating one another, but online communication did not translate into more visiting face-to-face (Saunders and Chester, 2008; Shklovski, et al., 2004).

The contemporary "always on" Internet culture driven by smartphones and mobile Internet access has raised concerns among scientists that focused search engines are truncating scientific research efforts, narrowing their focus; that addiction to smartphones causes a decline in intra-family communication, weakening family ties, and merging work and family. Researchers are finding that multi-taskers, and students distracted in class with digital devices, perform poorly when compared to people who turn of their computers and focus (Carr, 2010; Greenfield, 2009). Other research points to declines in productivity due to e-mail, IM, and texting interruptions during the day, coupled with mindless wandering on the Internet while at work. Research on use of computers in middle schools and at home suggests that both lower school achievement tests in English and math but raise computer skills (Malamud and Pop-Echeles, 2010).

### Media Choices and Multitasking: The Internet versus Other Media Channels

What may be of even more interest to marketers, however, is that the more time individuals spend using the Internet, "the more they turn their back on traditional media," according to the Stanford study. For every additional hour users spend online, they reduce their corresponding time spent with traditional media, such as television, newspapers, and radio. Traditional media are competing with the Internet for consumer attention, and so far, the Internet appears to be gaining on print media (newspapers and magazines) but not television. Media multitasking is rising: over 100 million U.S. adult Internet users watch television while going online. Others listen to the radio, read magazines, or newspapers. A USC study found that more than 80% of Internet users multitasked at least some of the time they spent online (Annenberg Center, 2010). Multitasking makes measurement of media exposure difficult because people can "expand" their media time by using multiple media at once. We discuss media consumption in greater depth in Chapter 10.

### CONSUMER BEHAVIOR MODELS

Once firms have an understanding of who is online, they need to focus on how consumers behave online. The study of **consumer behavior** is a social science discipline that attempts to model and understand the behavior of humans in a marketplace. Several social science disciplines play roles in this study, including sociology, psychology, and economics. Models of consumer behavior attempt to predict or "explain" what consumers purchase and where, when, how much, and why they buy. The expectation is that if the consumer decision-making process can be understood, firms will have a much better idea how to market and sell their products. **Figure 6.1** illustrates a general consumer behavior model that takes into account a wide range of factors that influence a consumer's marketplace decisions.

**consumer behavior**
a social science discipline that attempts to model and understand the behavior of humans in a marketplace

Consumer behavior models seek to predict the wide range of decisions that consumers make on the basis of background demographic factors, and on a set of intervening, more immediate variables that shape the consumer's ultimate decisions.

Background factors are cultural, social, and psychological in nature. Firms must recognize and understand the behavioral significance of these background factors and adjust their marketing efforts accordingly. **Culture** is the broadest factor in consumer behavior because it shapes basic human values, wants, perceptions, and behaviors. Culture creates basic expectations that consumers bring to the marketplace, such as what should be bought in different markets, how things should be bought, and how things should be paid for. Generally, culture affects an entire nation, and takes on major significance in international marketing. For instance, an American-style e-commerce site that sells cooking spices might have difficulty in an Asian culture such as China or Japan, where food and spice shopping takes place at local neighborhood markets, large food stores do not exist, and shoppers tend to pick out and smell each spice before purchasing it.

**culture**
shapes basic human values, wants, perceptions, and behaviors

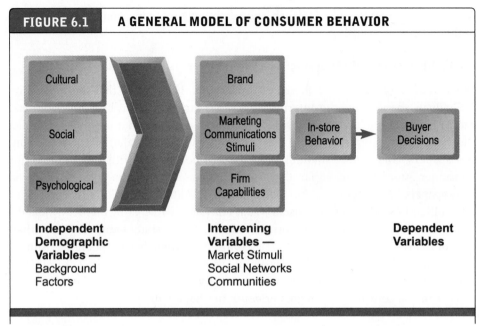

Consumer behavior models try to predict the decisions that consumers make in the marketplace.
SOURCE: Adapted from Kotler and Armstrong, 2009.

**subculture**

subset of cultures that form around major social differences

Within nations, subcultures are extremely important in consumer behavior. **Subcultures** are subsets of cultures that form around major social differences such as ethnicity, age, lifestyle, and geography. In the United States, ethnicity plays a very large role in consumer behavior. There are an estimated 40 million African-Americans with an annual purchasing power of around $1 trillion, about 47 million Hispanics with a total annual purchasing power of also about $1 trillion, and almost 15.5 million Asian-Americans with a total purchasing power of over $500 billion (Catalyst, 2010). Each of these ethnic groups represents a significant market segment that firms can target. For instance, Toyota was one of the first automotive manufacturers to use the Internet to target Hispanic customers. Toyota places Web advertisements on Spanish-language portals such as MSN Latino, Yahoo en Espanol, AOL Latino, Univision, and Terra to direct Hispanic customers to its Toyota.com Spanish-language Web site. As a result, Toyota now ranks 1st in the new vehicle sales registered by Latinos. Best Buy also has a Spanish-language Web site. Among the important social factors that shape consumer behavior are the many reference groups to which all consumers "belong," either as direct participating members, or as indirect members by affiliation, association, or aspiration. Among the more powerful intervening variables are the social networks and communities to which a person belongs and which invariably send market stimuli. In the offline face-to-face world, these groups are referred to as **direct reference groups** and include one's family, profession or occupation, religion, neighborhood, and schools. In the online world, these groups are simply referred to as online social and professional networks and communities to which consumers belong. **Indirect reference groups** include one's life-cycle stage, social class, and lifestyle group (discussed later). In the online world an analog would be celebrity blog and

**direct reference groups**

one's family, profession or occupation, religion, neighborhood, and schools

**indirect reference groups**

one's life-cycle stage, social class, and lifestyle group

news sites, commentary sites of all sorts, fashion sites, and fan sites where consumers tend to be consumers of content and identify with the content and activities at the site. Online social networks are important for understanding how viral marketing works on the Internet.

Within each of these reference groups, there are **opinion leaders** (or **viral influencers**, as they are termed by online marketers), who because of their personality, skills, or other factors, influence the behavior of others. Marketers seek out opinion leaders (so-called influentials) in their communications and promotional efforts because of their presumed influence over other people. Some have argued that these "influentials" are about 10% of any population and directly influence the other 90% in the population (Barry and Keller, 2003). For instance, many Web sites include testimonials submitted by successful adopters of a product or service. Generally, those giving the testimonials are portrayed as opinion leaders—"smart people in the know." At Procter & Gamble's Web site, for example, testimonials come from "P&G Advisors," who are consumers who take an active interest in Procter & Gamble products.

The concept of "influentials" while intuitively attractive may not in fact describe how or why viral messages spread across the Web (Barrry and Keller, 2003). A counter view is that the 90% of non-influentials need to be receptive to any messages from influentials (Watts, 2004). In this view, the "Like" buttons on Web sites spread messages from one person to another regardless of their social position in a network.

A unique kind of reference group is a **lifestyle group**, which can be defined as an integrated pattern of activities (hobbies, sports, shopping likes and dislikes, social events typically attended), interests (food, fashion, family, recreation), and opinions (social issues, business, government).

Lifestyle group classification systems—of which there are several—attempt to create a classification scheme that captures a person's whole pattern of living, consuming, and acting. The theory is that once you understand a consumer's lifestyle, or the lifestyles typical of a group of people—such as college students, for instance—then you can design products and marketing messages that appeal specifically to that lifestyle group. Lifestyle classification then becomes another method of segmenting the market.

In addition to lifestyle classification, marketers are interested in a consumer's psychological profile. A **psychological profile** is a set of needs, drives, motivations, perceptions, and learned behaviors—including attitudes and beliefs. Marketers attempt to appeal to psychological profiles through product design, product positioning, and marketing communications. For instance, many health e-commerce sites emphasize that they help consumers achieve a sense of control over their health destiny by providing them with information about diseases and treatments. This message is a powerful appeal to the needs of a wealthy, educated, professional, and technically advanced set of Web users for self-control and mastery over what might be a complex, health-threatening situation.

Marketers cannot influence demographic background factors, but they can adjust their branding, communications, and firm capabilities to appeal to demographic realities. For instance, the National Basketball Association's Web site, NBA.com, appeals to a variety of basketball fan subgroups from avid fans interested in specific

**opinion leaders (viral influencers)**
influence the behavior of others through their personality, skills, or other factors

**lifestyle group**
an integrated pattern of activities, interests, and opinions

**psychological profile**
set of needs, drives, motivations, perceptions, and learned behaviors

team statistics, to fashion-conscious fans who can purchase clothing for specific NBA teams, to fans who want to auction memorabilia.

## PROFILES OF ONLINE CONSUMERS

Online consumer behavior parallels that of offline consumer behavior with some obvious differences. It is important to first understand why people choose the Internet channel to conduct transactions. **Table 6.4** illustrates the main reasons consumers choose the online channel.

While price appears on this list, overwhelmingly, consumers shop on the Web because of convenience, which in turn is produced largely by saving them time. Overall transaction cost reduction appears to be the major motivator for choosing the online channel, followed by other cost reductions in the product or service.

## THE ONLINE PURCHASING DECISION

Once online, why do consumers actually purchase a product or service at a specific site? There are many models and several research studies that attempt to provide answers to this question. **Psychographic research** (research that combines both demographic and psychological data and divides a market into different groups based on social class, lifestyle, and/or personality characteristics) on the profile of active e-commerce shoppers attempts to understand the characteristics of users—in particular their various lifestyles—that lead to online buying behavior. For instance, in a study by the Wharton Forum on Electronic Commerce, a panel of 2,500 people was surveyed to understand the factors that predict e-commerce purchases (Lohse, Bellman, and Johnson, 2000). The survey found that the most important factors in predicting buying behavior were (1) looking for product information online, (2) leading a "wired lifestyle" (one where consumers spend a considerable amount of their working and home lives online), and (3) recently ordering from a catalog. **Figure 6.2** also lists factors that influence consumers' decisions to purchase online.

**psychographic research**

divides a market into different groups based on social class, lifestyle, and/or personality characteristics

| TABLE 6.4 | WHY CONSUMERS CHOOSE THE ONLINE CHANNEL |
|---|---|
| REASON | PERCENTAGE OF RESPONDENTS |
| Can shop at any time of day | 88% |
| Can research many products at the same time | 66% |
| Can find products that are not available in stores | 54% |
| Do not need to deal with salespeople | 53% |
| Can get better information on products online | 45% |
| Easier to find information on Web sites than it is to find in-store employees to help | 44% |
| Prices are better online | 40% |
| Products are usually in stock | 40% |

SOURCES: Based on data from eMarketer, Inc., 2007a; Sterling Commerce and Deloitte Consulting, 2007.

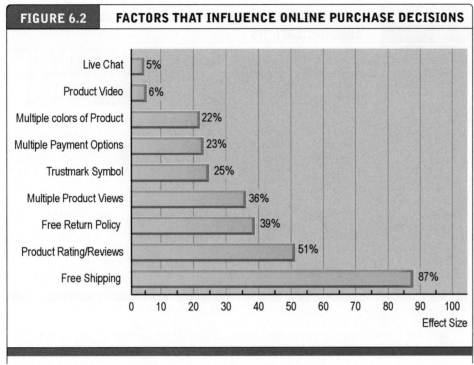

**FIGURE 6.2**   **FACTORS THAT INFLUENCE ONLINE PURCHASE DECISIONS**

The availability of free shipping, product rating/reviews, free return policies, multiple product views, trustmark symbols, and multiple payment options are all factors that influence the online purchase decision (variables are listed from lowest to highest effect).

SOURCE: Channel Advisor, 2009.

But aside from individual characteristics, you need to consider the process that buyers follow when making a purchase decision, and how the Internet environment affects consumers' decisions. There are five stages in the consumer decision process: awareness of need, search for more information, evaluation of alternatives, the actual purchase decision, and post-purchase contact with the firm (Kotler and Armstrong, 2009). **Figure 6.3** shows the consumer decision process and the types of offline and online marketing communications that support this process and seek to influence the consumer before, during, and after the purchase decision.

As shown in Figure 6.3, traditional mass media, along with catalogs and direct mail campaigns, are used to drive potential buyers to Web sites. What's new about online purchasing is the new media marketing communications capabilities afforded by the Web: search engines, social media such as blogs, social networks and social shopping sites, online product reviews, video ads, targeted banner ads and permission e-mail, bulletin boards, chat rooms, and the like. Simply put, the Web offers marketers an extraordinary increase in marketing communications tools and power, and the ability to envelop the consumer in a very rich information and purchasing environment (Awad, et al., 2007). In Chapter 7, we describe these new communications techniques and gauge their effectiveness in greater detail.

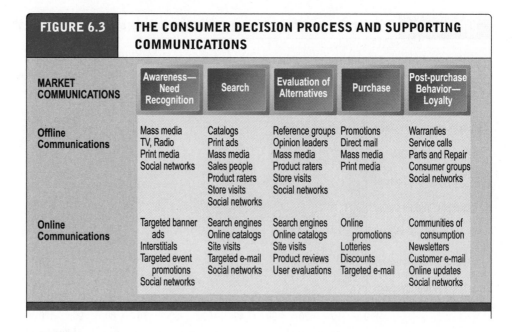

**FIGURE 6.3** THE CONSUMER DECISION PROCESS AND SUPPORTING COMMUNICATIONS

| MARKET COMMUNICATIONS | Awareness—Need Recognition | Search | Evaluation of Alternatives | Purchase | Post-purchase Behavior—Loyalty |
|---|---|---|---|---|---|
| **Offline Communications** | Mass media TV, Radio Print media Social networks | Catalogs Print ads Mass media Sales people Product raters Store visits Social networks | Reference groups Opinion leaders Mass media Product raters Store visits Social networks | Promotions Direct mail Mass media Print media | Warranties Service calls Parts and Repair Consumer groups Social networks |
| **Online Communications** | Targeted banner ads Interstitials Targeted event promotions Social networks | Search engines Online catalogs Site visits Targeted e-mail Social networks | Search engines Online catalogs Site visits Product reviews User evaluations | Online promotions Lotteries Discounts Targeted e-mail | Communities of consumption Newsletters Customer e-mail Online updates Social networks |

Both offline and online communications tools can be used to support the online consumer decision process at each of the five stages of the process.

## A MODEL OF ONLINE CONSUMER BEHAVIOR

Is offline consumer behavior fundamentally different from online consumer behavior? Arguably not. Consumer behavior offline and online has both similarities and differences. The e-commerce world is not quite so revolutionary as some would have us believe. For instance, the stages of the consumer decision process are basically the same whether the consumer is offline or online. On the other hand, the general model of consumer behavior requires modification to take into account new factors. In **Figure 6.4**, we have modified the general model of consumer behavior to focus on user characteristics, product characteristics, and Web site features, along with traditional factors such as brand strength and specific market communications (advertising) and the influence of both online and offline social networks (Watts, 2004; Lohse, et al. 2000; Pavlou and Fygenson, 2005; Pavlou and Dimoka, 2006). Figure 6.4 attempts to summarize and simplify current research.

In the online model, Web site features, along with consumer skills, product characteristics, attitudes towards online purchasing, and perceptions about control over the Web environment come to the fore. Web site features include latency (delay in downloads), navigability, and confidence in a Web site's security. (We examine Web site design issues as they relate to marketing more fully in Chapter 7.) There are parallels in the analog world. For instance, it is well known that consumer behavior can be influenced by store design, and that understanding the precise movements of consumers through a physical store can enhance sales if goods and promotions are arranged along the most likely consumer tracks. For instance, because consumers almost invariably enter a store and move to the right, high-margin items—jewelry and cosmetics—tend to be located there. And because it is known that consumers purchase fresh dairy products

| FIGURE 6.4 | A MODEL OF ONLINE CONSUMER BEHAVIOR |
| --- | --- |

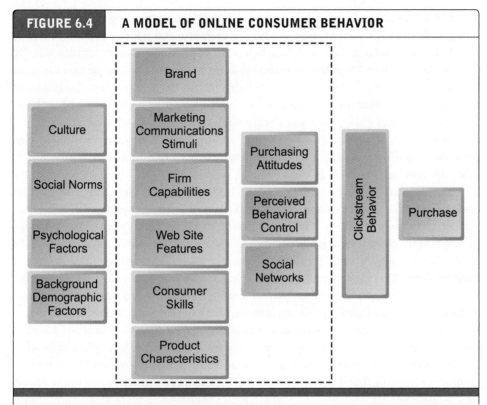

In this general model of online consumer behavior, the decision to purchase is shaped by background demographic factors, several intervening factors, and finally influenced greatly by clickstream behavior very near to the precise moment of purchase.

frequently, they are put at the back of grocery stores. Wal-Mart uses consumer-tracking databases within its stores to optimize the convenience to consumers—putting clothing nearest the entry, and electronics and cameras toward the back. Proper store design and precision tracking of consumers is not new—but its technical implementation on the Web, its lowered cost, its ubiquity, and its comprehensiveness on the Web are new.

*Consumer skills* refers to the knowledge that consumers have about how to conduct online transactions (which increases with experience). *Product characteristics* refers to the fact that some products can be easily described, packaged, and shipped over the Internet (such as books, software, and DVDs), whereas others cannot. Combined with traditional factors, such as brand, advertising, and firm capabilities, these factors lead to specific attitudes about purchasing at a Web site (trust in the Web site and favorable customer experience) and a sense that the consumer can control his or her environment on the Web site.

**Clickstream behavior** refers to the transaction log that consumers establish as they move about the Web, from search engine, to a variety of sites, then to a single site, then to a single page, and then, finally, to a decision to purchase. These precious moments are similar to "point-of-purchase" moments in traditional retail.

**clickstream behavior**
the transaction log that consumers establish as they move about the Web

A number of researchers have argued that understanding the background demographics of Internet users is no longer necessary, and not that predictive in any event. In most studies of consumer behavior, background demographics usually account for less than 5% of the observed behavior. Many believe instead that the most important predictors of online consumer behavior are the session characteristics and the clickstream behavior of people online very close to the moment of purchase. The theory is that this information will enable marketers to understand what the consumer was looking for at each moment, and how much they were willing to pay, thus allowing the marketers to precisely target their communications in an effort to sway the purchase decision in their favor.

For instance, a study by Booz Allen & Hamilton and NetRatings found that background demographics alone, and even background demographics with attitudinal and lifestyle factors, fail to take into account the different types of user sessions and different clickstream patterns. Analyzing the clickstream behavior of 2,466 individuals engaged in 186,797 user sessions, the study identified seven categories of user sessions: "Quickies," "Just the Facts," "Single Mission," "Do It Again," "Loitering," "Information Please," and "Surfing." Researchers called these segments "occasions," and suggested "occasion-based" marketing is more effective than static market segmentation based on demographics and/or consumer attitudes. Segmenting the market in this way, they found that in some types of sessions, users are more likely to buy, whereas in other sessions, they appear to be immune to online advertising. A study of over 10,000 visits to an online wine store found that detailed and general clickstream behavior were as important as customer demographics and prior purchase behavior in predicting a current purchase (Van den Poel and Buckinx, 2005). The most important clickstream factors were:

- Number of days since last visit
- Speed of clickstream behavior
- Number of products viewed during last visit
- Number of pages viewed
- Number of products viewed
- Supplying personal information (trust)
- Number of days since last purchase
- Number of past purchases

Clickstream marketing takes maximum advantage of the Internet environment. It presupposes no prior knowledge of the customer (and in that sense is "privacy-regarding"), and can be developed dynamically as customers use the Internet. For instance, the success of search engine marketing (the display of paid advertisements on Web search pages) is based in large part on what the consumer is looking for at the moment and how they go about looking (detailed clickstream data). After examining the detailed data, general clickstream data is used (days since last visit, past purchases). If available, demographic data is used (region, city, and gender).

## SHOPPERS: BROWSERS AND BUYERS

The picture of Internet use sketched in the previous section emphasizes the complexity of behavior online. Although the Internet audience still tends to be concentrated among the well educated, affluent, and youthful, increasingly the audience is becoming more diverse. Clickstream analysis shows us that people go online for many different reasons. Online shopping is similarly complex. Beneath the surface of the $255 billion B2C e-commerce market in 2010 are substantial differences in how users shop online.

For instance, as shown in **Figure 6.5**, about 72% of online users are "buyers" who actually purchase something entirely online. Another 16% of online users research products on the Web ("browsers"), but purchase them offline. This combined group, referred to as "shoppers," constitutes approximately 87.5% of the online Internet audience. With the teen and adult U.S. Internet audience (14 years or older) esti- mated at about 185 million in 2010, online shoppers (the combination of buyers and browsers) add up to a market size of around 162 million consumers. Most marketers find this number exciting.

The significance of online browsing for offline purchasing should not be underestimated. Although it is difficult to precisely measure the amount of offline sales that occur because of online product research, several different studies have found that about one-third of all offline retail purchasing is influenced by online product research, blogs, banner ads, and other Internet exposure. The offline influence varies by product. This amounts to about $1 trillion in annual retail sales, a truly extraordinary number (Forrester Research, 2010a).

E-commerce is a major conduit and generator of offline commerce. The reverse is also true: online traffic is driven by offline brands and shopping. While online research influences offline purchase, it is also the case that offline marketing media heavily influence online behavior including sales. Traditional print media (magazines and newspapers) and television are by far the most powerful media for reaching and engaging consumers with information about new products and directing them to the Web (see **Table 6.5**). Online communities and blogging are also very influential but not yet as powerful as traditional media. This may be surprising to many given the

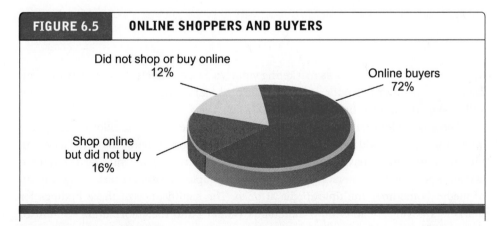

**FIGURE 6.5** | **ONLINE SHOPPERS AND BUYERS**

Did not shop or buy online
12%

Online buyers
72%

Shop online
but did not buy
16%

About 88% of the online audience shops online, either by researching products or by purchasing products online. The percentage of the online audience actually purchasing has increased by 11% since 2005 to 72%. Only 12% of the online audience does not buy or shop online.

SOURCE: Based on data from eMarketer, Inc., 2010b.

| TABLE 6.5 | MEDIA THAT INFLUENCE CONSUMERS TO START SEARCH FOR MERCHANDISE ONLINE |
|---|---|
| MEDIA | PERCENTAGE OF RESPONDENTS |
| Magazines | 47% |
| Reading an article | 43% |
| Broadcast TV | 43% |
| Newspapers | 41% |
| Face-to-face communication | 39% |
| Cable TV | 36% |
| Coupons | 36% |
| Direct mail | 30% |
| Radio | 29% |
| In-store promotions | 27% |
| Online advertising | 26% |
| Internet advertising | 26% |
| E-mail advertising | 25% |
| Online communities | 19% |
| Outdoor billboards | 12% |
| Blogs | 10% |
| Instant messaging | 8% |
| Mobile phone | 7% |
| Yellow pages | 7% |
| Text messaging | 6% |
| Other | 6% |
| Mobile pictures/video | 4% |

SOURCES: Based on data from Retail Advertising & Marketing Association (RAMA), 2010; industry sources, authors' estimates.

attention to social networks as marketing vehicles, but it reflects the diversity of influences on consumer behavior and the real-world marketing budgets of firms that are still heavily dominated by traditional media.

These considerations strongly suggest that e-commerce and traditional commerce are coupled and should be viewed by merchants (and researchers) as part of a continuum of consuming behavior and not as radical alternatives to one another. Commerce is commerce; the customers are often the same people. Customers use a wide variety of media, sometimes multiple media at once. The significance of these findings for marketers is very clear. Online merchants should build the information content of their sites to attract browsers looking for information, build content to rank high in search engines, put less attention on selling per se, and promote services and products (especially new products) in offline media settings in order to support their online stores.

## WHAT CONSUMERS SHOP FOR AND BUY ONLINE

You can look at online sales as divided roughly into two groups: small-ticket and big-ticket items. Big-ticket items include computer equipment and consumer electronics, where orders can easily be over $500. Small-ticket items include apparel, books, health and beauty supplies, office supplies, music, software, videos, and toys, where the average purchase is typically less than $100. In the early days of e-commerce, sales of small-ticket items vastly outnumbered those of large-ticket items for a variety of reasons. First movers on the Web sold these products early on; the purchase price was low (reduced consumer risk); the items were physically small (shipping costs were low); margins were high (at least on CDs and software); and there was a broad selection of products (e-commerce vendors could compete on scope when compared to traditional offline stores). But the recent growth of big-ticket items such as computer hardware, consumer electronics, furniture, and jewelry has changed the overall sales mix. Consumers are now much more confident spending online for big-ticket items. Although furniture and large appliances were initially perceived as too bulky to sell online, these categories have rapidly expanded in the last few years. The types of purchases made also depend on levels of experience with the Web (U.S.C. Annenberg School Center for the Digital Future, 2004). New Web users tend primarily to buy small-ticket items, while experienced Web users are more willing to buy large-ticket items in addition to small-ticket items. **Figure 6.6** illustrates how much consumers spent online for various categories of goods at the top 500 Internet retailers in 2009.

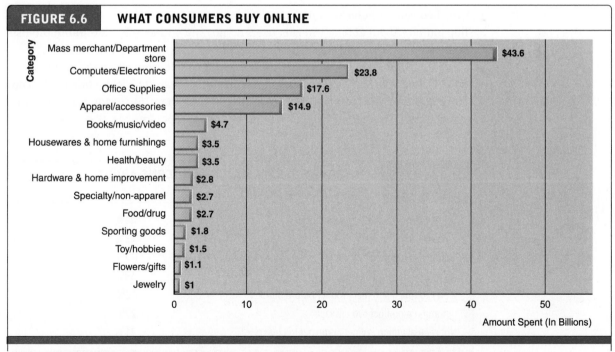

**FIGURE 6.6**    **WHAT CONSUMERS BUY ONLINE**

This figure illustrates how much consumers spent online for various categories of goods at the top 500 Internet retailers in 2009.

SOURCES: Based on data from eMarketer, Inc., 2010b; Internet Retailer, 2010,

## INTENTIONAL ACTS: HOW SHOPPERS FIND VENDORS ONLINE

Given the prevalence of "click here" banner ads, one might think customers are "driven" to online vendors by spur-of-the-moment decisions. In fact, only a tiny percentage of shoppers click on banners to find vendors. Once they are online, 59% of consumers use a search engine as their preferred method of research or purchasing a product, 29% go to coupon Web sites with a specific product in mind, 27% go to price comparison sites, and 25% rely on e-mail newsletters. Social networks are far down the list for targeted search, around 5% (eMarketer, Inc., 2009a).E-commerce shoppers are highly intentional. Typically, they are focused browsers looking for specific products, companies, and services. Merchants can convert these "goal-oriented," intentional shoppers into buyers if the merchants can target their communications to the shoppers and design their sites in such a way as to provide easy-to-access and useful product information, full selection, and customer service and do this at the very moment the customer is searching for the product (Wolfinbarger and Gilly, 2001). No small task. There are, of course, exceptions. Some people go on the Web and are not quite clear what they are looking for. StumbleUpon.com is a site for these unintentional searchers who, for the most part, are subject and community searchers rather than product searchers. StumbleUpon identifies the general topic of interest for the user, and then relies on collaborative filtering tools to direct visitors to other sites on the Web that similarly interested people have visited and found interesting.

## WHY MORE PEOPLE DON'T SHOP ONLINE

A final consumer behavior question to address is: Why don't more online Web users shop online? About 28% of Internet users do not buy online. Why not? **Table 6.6** lists the major online buying concerns among Internet users in the United States.

Arguably, the largest factor preventing more people from shopping online is the "trust factor," the fear that online merchants will cheat you, lose your credit card information, or use personal information you give them to invade your personal privacy, bombarding you with unwanted e-mail, and pop-up ads. Secondary factors

| TABLE 6.6 | INTERNET USERS' MAJOR CONCERNS ABOUT PURCHASING ONLINE | |
|---|---|---|
| Uneasy about online credit card use | | 44% |
| Concerns about privacy of data | | 42% |
| Shipping charges | | 37% |
| No need to purchase online | | 33% |
| Prefer to touch and feel product before purchase | | 32% |
| Returning a product too difficult | | 27% |
| Not seen anything online interested in buying | | 21% |

SOURCES: Based on data from eMarketer, Inc., 2010c.

can be summarized as "hassle factors," like shipping costs, returns, and inability to touch and feel the product (Doolin, et al., 2007).

## TRUST, UTILITY, AND OPPORTUNISM IN ONLINE MARKETS

Recent research shows that the two most important factors shaping the decision to purchase online are utility and trust (Ba and Pavlou, 2002). The decision to purchase anything on the Web is strongly affected by these two factors. Consumers want good deals, bargains, convenience, and speed of delivery. In short, consumers are looking for utility. On the other hand, in any seller-buyer relationship, there is an asymmetry of information. The seller usually knows a lot more than the consumer about the quality of goods and terms of sale. This can lead to opportunistic behavior by sellers (Akerlof, 1970; Williamson, 1985; Mishra, 1998). Consumers need to trust a merchant before they make a purchase. Sellers can develop trust among online consumers by building strong reputations of honesty, fairness, and delivery of quality products—the basic elements of a brand. Feedback forums such as Epinions.com (now part of Shopping.com), Amazon's book reviews from reviewers, and eBay's feedback forum are examples of trust-building online mechanisms (Opinion Research Corporation, 2009). Online sellers who develop trust among consumers are able to charge a premium price for their online products and services (Kim and Benbaset, 2006; Kim and Benbasat, 2007; Pavlou, 2002). A review of the literature suggests that the most important factors leading to a trusting online relationship are perception of Web site credibility, ease of use, and risk (Corritore, et al., 2006).

## 6.2  BASIC MARKETING CONCEPTS

In Section 6.1, we discussed who's on the Web and online behavior as it relates to purchase decisions. In this section, we expand our focus to look at the broader topic of **marketing**—the strategies and actions firms take to establish a relationship with a consumer and encourage purchases of its products or services. The key objective of **Internet marketing** is to use the Web—as well as traditional channels—to develop a positive, long-term relationship with customers (who may be online or offline) and thereby create a competitive advantage for the firm by allowing it to charge a higher price for products or services than its competitors can charge.

To begin, you must first be familiar with some basic marketing concepts. Recall from Chapter 2 (Section 2.5) that the profitability of an industry depends on (1) the ease with which substitute products or services can enter the market, (2) the ease with which new entrants can enter the industry, (3) the power of customers and suppliers to influence pricing, and (4) the nature of competition within the industry. Competitive markets are ones that have lots of substitutes, easy entry, and customers and suppliers who possess strong bargaining power.

Marketing directly addresses the competitive situation of industries and firms. Marketing seeks to create unique, highly differentiated products or services that are produced or supplied by one trusted firm ("little monopolies"). There are few, if any, substitutes for an effectively marketed product or service, and new entrants have a difficult time matching the product or service's **feature set** (the bundle of capabilities

**marketing**
the strategies and actions firms take to establish a relationship with a consumer and encourage purchases of its products or services

**Internet marketing**
using the Web—as well as traditional channels—to develop a positive, long-term relationship with customers, thereby creating a competitive advantage for the firm by allowing it to charge a higher price for products or services than its competitors can charge

**feature set**
the bundle of capabilities and services offered by the product or service

and services offered by the product or service). When successful, these little monopolies reduce the bargaining power of consumers because they are the sole sources of supply; they also enable firms to exercise significant power over their suppliers.

Marketing is designed to avoid pure price competition and to create markets where returns on investment are above average, competition is limited, and consumers are willing to pay premium prices for products that have no substitute because they are perceived as unique. Marketing encourages customers to buy on the basis of nonmarket (i.e., nonprice) qualities of a product. Firms use marketing to prevent their products and services from becoming commodities. A **commodity** is a good or service for which there are many dealers supplying the same product and all products in the segment are essentially identical. Price and delivery terms are the only basis for consumer choice. Examples of commodities include wheat, corn, and steel.

**commodity**

a good or service for which there are many dealers supplying the same product, and all products in the segment are essentially identical

## FEATURE SETS

A central task of marketing is to identify and then communicate to the customer the unique, differentiated capabilities and services of a product or service's feature set. **Figure 6.7** illustrates the three levels of a product or service: core, actual, and augmented. Although the example given is for a physical product, the concept applies equally to a digital product or service.

The core product is at the center of the feature set. The **core product** is the core benefit the customer receives from the product. Let's say, for example, that the core product is a cell phone. The **actual product** is the set of characteristics designed to deliver the product's core benefits. Marketers must identify the features of the cell

**core product**

the core benefit the customer receives from the product

**actual product**

the set of characteristics designed to deliver the product's core benefits

| FIGURE 6.7 | FEATURE SET |
| --- | --- |

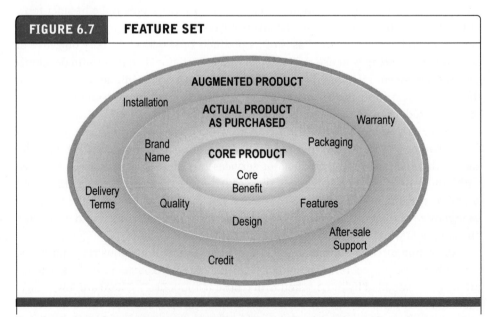

Each element in the feature set can be used to differentiate a product from others in the market.

phone that differentiate it from those of other manufacturers. In the case of a "cell phone" like Apple's iPhone, the actual product is a cell phone and music player with a wide screen that connects through wireless networks to the Internet. It comes with the Apple name and with certain features and capabilities, such as high-speed network connectivity, a large screen for Web browsing, design elegance, extraordinary packaging, and selected utility programs. The **augmented product** is a product with additional benefits to customers beyond the core benefits embodied in the actual product. In the case of the iPhone, the augmented product includes a standard one-year warranty, an available AppleCare Protection Plan that extends the warranty and support for an additional year, iPhone support Web pages, and other after-sale support. The augmented product forms the basis for building the iPhone brand (a process known as *branding*) described next. The augmented product is the foundation for the product brand.

**augmented product**
a product with additional benefits to customers beyond the core benefits embodied in the actual product

## PRODUCTS, BRANDS, AND THE BRANDING PROCESS

What makes products truly unique and differentiable in the minds of consumers is the product's brand. A **brand** is a set of expectations that a consumer has when consuming, or thinking about consuming, a product or service from a specific company. These expectations are based in part on past experiences the consumer has had actually using the product, on the experiences of trusted others who have consumed the product, and on the promises of marketers who extol the unique features of the product in a variety of different channels and media.

**brand**
a set of expectations that consumers have when consuming, or thinking about consuming, a product or service from a specific company

The most important expectations created by brands are quality, reliability, consistency, trust, affection, loyalty, and ultimately, reputation. Marketers create promises, and these promises engender consumer expectations. As Charles Revson, the founder of Revlon noted, "In the factory we make cosmetics; in the store we sell hope" (Kotler and Armstrong, 2009). The promise made by cosmetic manufacturers to consumers is: "If you use this product, you will perceive yourself to be more beautiful." In the case of Apple's iPhone, marketers (including Steve Jobs himself) have artfully created expectations among users for superb industrial design, quality construction, and unique products. The Apple iPhone brand connotes to iPhone owners a cool, hip, technologically advanced style of life. Consumers are willing to pay a premium price for Apple iPhones not only because of the augmented product features, but also because of these brand expectations. **Figure 6.8** illustrates the process of brand creation or **branding**.

**branding**
process of brand creation

Marketers identify the differentiating features of the actual and augmented product. They engage in a variety of marketing communications activities to transmit the feature set to the consumer. Based on the consumers' experiences and the promises made by marketers in their communications, consumers develop expectations about a product. For instance, when a consumer purchases an Apple iPhone, he or she expects to receive a unique, high-quality, very easy-to-use cell phone. Consumers are willing to pay a premium price in order to obtain these qualities. If iPhones do not in fact perform according to these expectations, the brand will be weakened and consumers will be less willing to pay a premium price. In other words, a strong brand requires a strong product. But if iPhones do perform according to

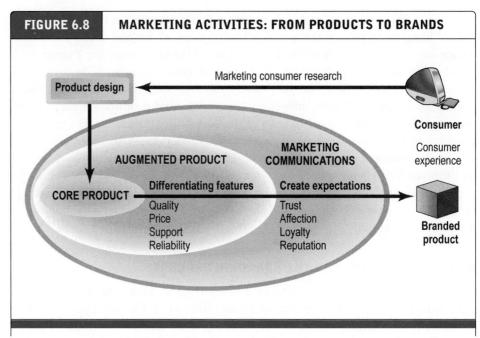

| FIGURE 6.8 | MARKETING ACTIVITIES: FROM PRODUCTS TO BRANDS |

Marketers aim to create a "brand identity" for a product, based on consumer perceptions of trust, affection, loyalty, and reputation.

expectations, then customers will feel loyal to the product; they will purchase again or recommend it to others; and they will trust, feel affection for, and ascribe a good reputation to both the product and the company that makes it.

Ideally, marketers directly influence the design of products to ensure the products have desirable features, high quality, correct pricing, product support, and reliability. When marketers are able to directly influence the design of a core product based on market research and feedback, this is called **closed loop marketing**. While ideal, it is more often the case that marketers are hired to "sell" a product that has already been designed. E-commerce—as we see next—offers some unique opportunities to achieve closed loop marketing.

Marketers devise and implement brand strategies. A **brand strategy** is a set of plans for differentiating a product from its competitor, and communicating these differences effectively to the marketplace. In developing new e-commerce brands, the ability to devise and develop a brand strategy has been crucial in the success and failure of many companies, as described throughout this book.

What kinds of products can be branded? According to many marketing specialists, there is no limit. Every product can potentially be branded. Sneakers that make you soar from Nike, cars from Volvo that make you feel safe on dark rainy nights, shirts from Polo that make you appear as if you were on the way to a country club—these are all examples of products with extraordinary brand names for which consumers pay premium prices.

How much is a brand worth? Brands differ in their power and value in the marketplace. A brand can represent corporate value as an asset, it can also represent

**closed loop marketing**
when marketers are able to directly influence the design of the core product based on market research and feedback from the market

**brand strategy**
a set of plans for differentiating a product from its competitors, and communicating these differences effectively to the marketplace

customer loyalty or attachment, and it can be seen as a set of associations that consumers have about products. **Brand equity** is the estimated value of the premium customers are willing to pay for using a branded product when compared to unbranded competitors (Feldwick, 1996). According to Interbrand's 2010 World's Most Valuable Brands survey, the top five brands and their estimated equity value are Coca-Cola ($70.4 billion), IBM ($64.7 billion), Microsoft ($60.9 billion), Google ($43.5 billion), and General Electric ($42.8 billion). Brand equity also affects stock prices insofar as brands strengthen future revenue streams, and insofar as brands are intangible assets that have a market value. There are several methodologies used to calculate brand value, but this discussion is beyond the scope of this book (Berg, et al., 2007; Ailawadi, 2003).

**brand equity**
the estimated value of the premium customers are willing to pay for using a branded product when compared to unbranded competitors

## SEGMENTING, TARGETING, AND POSITIONING

Markets are not unitary, but in fact are composed of many different kinds of customers with different needs. Firms seek to segment markets into distinct groups of customers who differ from one another in terms of product needs. Once the segments are established, each segment can be *targeted* with differentiated products. Within each segment, the product is *positioned* and branded as a unique, high-value product, especially suited to the needs of segment customers.

There are six major ways in which marketers segment and target markets (**Table 6.7**). By segmenting markets, firms can differentiate their products to more closely fit the needs of customers in each segment. Rather than charge one price for the same product, firms can maximize revenues by creating several different variations on the same product and charging different prices in each market segment. While segmenting and targeting are not new, the Internet offers an unusual opportunity for very fine-grained segmenting down to the level of the individual. Potentially, with enough personal information, marketers on the Internet can personalize market messages to precisely fit an individual's needs and wants. In the physical world of marketing using other technologies like newspapers, radio, and television, it is more difficult to personalize messages.

Once markets are segmented, the branding process proceeds within each segment by appealing to the segment members. For instance, automobile manufacturers segment their markets on many dimensions: demographics (age, sex, income, and occupation), geographic (region), benefits (special performance features), and psychographics (self-image and emotional needs). For each market segment, they offer a uniquely branded product.

## ARE BRANDS RATIONAL?

Coca-Cola is one of the most enduring, powerful brands in U.S. commercial history. The core product is colored, flavored, carbonated sugar water. The augmented branded product is a delightful, refreshing, reputable, unique-tasting drink available worldwide, based on a secret formula that consumers are willing to pay up to twice as much for when compared to unbranded grocery store cola. Coca-Cola is a marketing-created micro-monopoly. There is only one Coke and only one supplier. Why would consumers pay twice as much for Coke compared to unbranded cola drinks? Is this rational?

| TABLE 6.7 | MAJOR TYPES OF ONLINE MARKET SEGMENTATION AND TARGETING |
|---|---|
| Behavioral | Segmenting on the basis of behavior in the marketplace. In traditional stores, this involves observing how customers walk through stores. On the Internet, Web site owners and members of advertising networks can dynamically assign users to groups, and merge their behavioral information with other data. Using preferences and mentions on social networks to assign ads to individuals and network groups of friends. |
| Demographic | Using age, ethnicity, religion, and other demographic factors to segment. On the Internet, using registration data or other self-revelations. Sites visited also serves as proxy measures of age, e.g., music sites are visited by young persons. |
| Psychographic | Using common interests, values, and opinions along with personality, attitude, and lifestyle preferences to segment consumers into groups. On the Internet, Web sites visited can substitute for direct measurement, e.g., the fashion Web sites visited by consumers reflect a self-chosen lifestyle and values. |
| Technical | Using information gathered by a shopping technology as a basis for segmentation. Nearly everyone who shops at malls owns a car. On the Internet, each consumer visit generates a record of the user's domain, IP address, browser, computer platform, and connection type, as well as what URL the user linked to the site from and the date and time. People who connect using broadband media, for instance, are much more likely to download music from the Internet. |
| Contextual | Using the context of an event, or the content of an event, as a basis for segmentation. People who attend rock concerts tend to purchase music CDs as well. On the Internet, people who read the online *Wall Street Journal* are very good targets for financial service advertising. |
| Search | Using consumers' explicitly expressed interest at this moment to segment and target. Perhaps the simplest of all segmenting, search direct response follows the ageless maxim "sell them what they want." |

The answer is a qualified yes. Brands introduce market efficiency by reducing the search costs and decision-making costs of consumers. Strong brands signal strong products that work. Brands carry information. Confronted with many different drinks, the choice of Coke can be made quickly, without much thought, and with the assurance that you will have the drinking experience you expect based on prior use of the product. Brands reduce consumer risk and uncertainty in a crowded marketplace. Brands are like an insurance policy against nasty surprises in the marketplace for which consumers willingly pay a premium—better safe than sorry.

The ability of brands to become a corporate asset (to attain brand equity) based on future anticipated premiums paid by consumers also provides an incentive for firms to build products that serve customer needs better than other products. Therefore, although brands create micro-monopolies, increase market costs, and lead to above-average returns on investment (monopoly rents), they also introduce market efficiencies for the consumer.

For business firms, brands are a major source of revenue and are obviously rational. Brands lower customer acquisition costs and increase customer retention.

The stronger the brand reputation, the easier it is to attract new customers. **Customer acquisition costs** refer to the overall costs of converting a prospect into a consumer, and include all marketing and advertising costs. **Customer retention costs** are those costs incurred in convincing an existing customer to purchase again. In general, it is much more expensive to acquire a new customer than to retain an existing customer. For instance, Reichheld and Schefter calculated that e-commerce sites lose from $20 to $80 on each customer in the first year because of the high cost of acquiring a customer, but potentially can make up for this loss in later years by retaining loyal customers (Reichheld and Schefter, 2000). In some instances, however, e-commerce companies have gone out of business before they ever reached that point.

A successful brand can constitute a long-lasting, impregnable unfair competitive advantage. As we discussed in Chapter 2, a competitive advantage is considered "fair" when it is based on innovation, efficient production processes, or other factors that theoretically can be imitated and/or purchased in the marketplace by competitors. An "unfair competitive advantage" cannot be purchased in the factor markets and includes such things as patents, copyrights, secret processes, unusually skilled or dedicated employees and managers, and, of course, brand names. Brands cannot be purchased (unless one buys the entire company).

**customer acquisition costs**
the overall costs of converting a prospect into a consumer

**customer retention costs**
costs incurred in convincing an existing customer to purchase again

## DO BRANDS LAST FOREVER?

Brands, however, do not necessarily last forever, and the micro-monopolies they create may not be stable over the long term. In a study of brand endurance, Golder found that between 1923 and 1997, only 23% of the firms that ranked first in market share in 1923 were still in the market-leading position in 1997, while 28% of the leaders failed altogether (Golder, 2000). Less than 10% of the Fortune 500 companies of 1917 still exists (Starbuck and Nystrom, 1997). Some brands that may disappear in 2010 include Reader's Digest, Blockbuster, Dollar Thrift, T-Mobile, and RadioShack (McIntyre, 2010). Life at the top is sweet, but often short, and market efficiency is restored long-term as entrepreneurs exploit new technologies and new public tastes at a faster rate than the incumbent market leaders.

## CAN BRANDS SURVIVE THE INTERNET? BRANDS AND PRICE DISPERSION ON THE INTERNET

As we noted in Chapter 1, during the early days of e-commerce, many academics and business consultants postulated that the Web would lead to a new world of information symmetry and "frictionless" commerce. In this world, newly empowered customers, using intelligent shopping agents and the nearly infinite product and price information available on the Internet, would shop around the world (and around the clock) with minimal effort, driving prices down to their marginal cost and driving intermediaries out of the market as customers began to deal directly with producers (Wigand and Benjamin, 1995; Rayport and Sviolka, 1995; Evans and Wurster, 1999; Sinha 2000).[1] The result was supposed to be an instance of the "**Law of One Price**":

**Law of One Price**
with complete price transparency in a perfect information marketplace, there will be one world price for every product

[1]The theory of frictionless commerce is not unique to the Internet. Computerized stock and options markets over the last 20 years have also attempted to achieve low-friction transactions.

with complete price transparency in a perfect information marketplace, one world price for every product would emerge. "Frictionless commerce" would, of course, mean the end of marketing based on brands.

But it didn't work out this way. Price has not proven to be the only determinant of online consumer behavior. E-commerce firms continue to rely heavily on brands to attract customers and charge premium prices. For instance, online retailers use "flash pricing," where some popular products are marked down significantly for a day or even a few hours to create market buzz, and then are increased significantly the next day. Internet technologies can be used to infinitely differentiate products by using personalization, customization, and community marketing techniques (described in the next section), thereby overcoming the price-lowering effects of lower search costs and a large number of worldwide suppliers for goods. By introducing information asymmetries into the marketplace, merchants can avoid direct price competition.

Whether or not prices are lower online than offline is still a point of debate. For instance, Bailey and Brynjolfsson (1997) found that prices for books, music CDs, and software were not substantially lower at e-commerce sites than in traditional stores or catalogs (see also Clay, et al., 1999 for similar results). Later studies found that prices at e-commerce sites were 9%–16% lower than at conventional retail outlets for musical CDs (depending on whether taxes and shipping costs were included in the price), but also found substantial price dispersion—nearly as much as in traditional markets for the same goods (Brynjolfsson and Smith, 2000). Other research finds that online prices vary with season: during the holiday season of October-December, online prices rise, and then fall in the spring. This phenomenon is not dissimilar from traditional retail stores.

**price dispersion**

the difference between the highest and lowest prices in a market

**Price dispersion** refers to the difference between the highest and lowest prices in a market. In a perfect market, with perfect information, there is not supposed to be any price dispersion. Other evidence suggests that many suppliers and price comparisons can overwhelm consumers, and that consumers achieve efficiencies by quickly purchasing from a trusted, high-price provider. In general, the most frequently visited and used e-commerce sites are not the lowest-price sites (Smith, et al., 1999).

Research on brands and price dispersion illustrates the complexities of Internet marketing as well as the continuing power of brands, customer loyalty, and information symmetries. Some found that online prices were higher relative to offline prices (Baye, et al., 2002a; Scholten and Smith, 2002). Others found that, in general, online prices were less than offline prices depending on the product category and other variables. Price dispersion, a measure of competitiveness, typically is less for commodities (memory chips) than for books or other differentiated products. Moreover, Internet-savvy users systematically seek out the lowest prices by visiting shopping comparison sites, while other Internet users choose not to inform themselves and just purchase from a well-known online brand like Amazon. Sellers invest heavily in ways to differentiate their product or service—they create online brands that permit charging a premium for many products. The result is large differences in price sensitivity for the same products. For instance, researchers estimate that a 1% increase in prices at Amazon decreases sales by about 0.5%, while at Barnes & Noble, a 1% increase in prices results in a decrease in sales of about 4% (Baye, et al., 2002b). Price dispersion is also heavily influ-

enced by "market thickness," the number of competitors selling the same undifferentiated goods. The more sellers in an online market (like photography), the less the price
dispersion (Leiter and Warin, 2007). Nash-equilibrium.com, a site run by economists
Michael Bay, John Morgan, and Patrick Sholten, charts market thickness, relative price
dispersion, and other economic indicators on the Web (see **Figure 6.9**).

Another tactic used by online sellers is the "**library effect**" (or "catalog effect").
How much is it worth to you to shop at a store that has everything? Just one stop, and
chances are that you can get what you want. Would you rather visit a library with 10
million volumes, or one with a few hundred thousand? The number of books on sale
at Amazon is 23 times larger than the number of books found at a typical Barnes &
Noble superstore, and 57 times larger than the number of books typically found at a
large independent bookstore. One analysis puts the gain in economic value (or "consumer welfare") produced by online bookstores at about $1 billion annually, five times
larger than the gain in economic value produced by lower prices on the Internet
(Brynjolfsson, Smith, and Hu, 2003). Stores such as Amazon make the size of their
product offerings a part of their brand image and marketing communications in order
to charge premium prices. Obviously, library effects apply only where there is a large

**library effect**
an attempt to appeal to
consumers on the basis of
the total number of
products offered

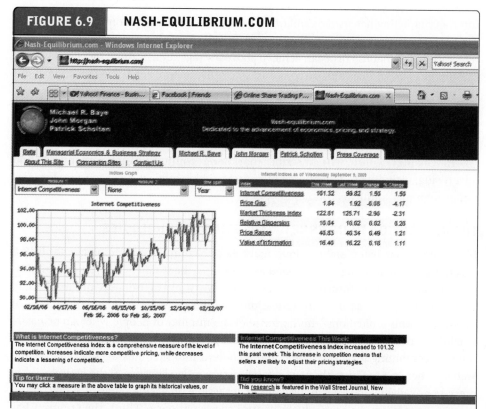

| FIGURE 6.9 | NASH-EQUILIBRIUM.COM |

Nash-equilibrium.com is a Web site run by economists Michael Baye, John Morgan, and Patrick Scholten that
provides a variety of economic indices related to the Internet, including Internet competitiveness, price gaps,
price ranges, and relative dispersion statistics.
SOURCE: Nash-equilibrium.com, 2008.

number of SKUs or products available to sell—like music, DVDs, CDs, books, travel arrangements, airline tickets, and many of the products available on the Web—but not for unique collector items.

We can conclude from the research evidence that brands are alive and well on the Web, that consumers are willing to pay premium prices for products and services they perceive as differentiated, that consumers are willing to shop online as opposed to offline at stores where product variety is high, and that in many instances Web prices may be higher than those available in retail stores because of the premium consumers will pay for convenience. The evidence also suggests some solid reasons for the adage popular during the early days of e-commerce: "Get Big Fast." Selection, not price, may be your e-commerce site's biggest advantage and largest contributor to consumer welfare. Another strategic way to look at these data is to expect growing ownership concentration among Internet merchants as they pursue scale economies and library effects that derive from size.

Now that you have covered these basic concepts, the next section describes what makes Internet marketing different from ordinary marketing.

## 6.3 INTERNET MARKETING TECHNOLOGIES

Internet marketing has many similarities to and differences from ordinary marketing. The objective of Internet marketing—as in all marketing—is to build customer relationships so that the firm can achieve above-average returns (both by offering superior products or services and by communicating the feature set to the consumer). But Internet marketing is also very different from ordinary marketing because the nature of the medium and its capabilities are so different from anything that has come before. In order to understand just how different Internet marketing can be and in what ways, you first need to become familiar with some basic Internet marketing technologies.

In Chapter 7, we will describe marketing communications channels, and advertising, including search engine marketing, which tends to be used more for sales rather than marketing and branding.

### THE REVOLUTION IN INTERNET MARKETING TECHNOLOGIES

In Chapter 1, we listed eight unique features of e-commerce technology. **Table 6.8** describes how marketing has changed as a result of these new technical capabilities.

On balance, the Internet has had three very broad impacts on marketing. First, the Internet, as a communications medium, has broadened the scope of marketing communications—in the sense of the number of people who can be easily reached. Second, the Internet has increased the richness of marketing communications by combining text, video, and audio content into rich messages. Arguably, the Web is richer as a medium than even television or video because of the complexity of messages available, the enormous content accessible on a wide range of subjects, and the ability of users to interactively control the experience. Third, the Internet has greatly expanded the information intensity of the marketplace by providing marketers (and customers) with unparalleled fine-grained, detailed, real-time information about consumers as they transact in the marketplace.

| TABLE 6.8 | IMPACT OF UNIQUE FEATURES OF E-COMMERCE TECHNOLOGY ON MARKETING |
|---|---|
| **E-COMMERCE TECHNOLOGY DIMENSION** | **SIGNIFICANCE FOR MARKETING** |
| Ubiquity | Marketing communications have been extended to the home, work, and mobile platforms; geographic limits on marketing have been reduced. The marketplace has been replaced by "marketspace" and is removed from a temporal and geographic location. Customer convenience has been enhanced, and shopping costs have been reduced. |
| Global reach | Worldwide customer service and marketing communications have been enabled. Potentially hundreds of millions of consumers can be reached with marketing messages. |
| Universal standards | The cost of delivering marketing messages and receiving feedback from users is reduced because of shared, global standards of the Internet. |
| Richness | Video, audio, and text marketing messages can be integrated into a single marketing message and consuming experience. |
| Interactivity | Consumers can be engaged in a dialog, dynamically adjusting the experience to the consumer, and making the consumer a co-producer of the goods and services being sold. |
| Information density | Fine-grained, highly detailed information on consumers' real-time behavior can be gathered and analyzed for the first time. "Data mining" Internet technology permits the analysis of terabytes of consumer data everyday for marketing purposes |
| Personalization/Customization | This feature potentially enables product and service differentiation down to the level of the individual, thus strengthening the ability of marketers to create brands. |
| Social technology | User-generated content and social networking sites, along with blogs, have created new, large, online audiences where the content is provided by users. These audiences have greatly expanded the opportunity for marketers to reach new potential customers in a nontraditional media format. Entirely new kinds of marketing techniques are evolving. These same technologies expose marketers to the risk of falling afoul of popular opinion by providing more market power to users who now can "talk back." |

## WEB TRANSACTION LOGS

How can e-commerce sites know more than a department store does about consumer behavior? A primary source of consumer information on the Web is the transaction log maintained by all Web servers. A **transaction log** records user activity at a Web

**transaction log**
records user activity at a
Web site

site. The transaction log is built into Web server software. **Figure 6.10** shows one second from the Web transaction log for Azimuth-interactive.com, a Web-based software training site. The log has been edited to eliminate the names of real persons and show only a few entries for each visitor. In fact, visitors usually create tens or hundreds of entries in the log, one entry for each page or object they request.

**Table 6.9** lists the data elements contained in a Web transaction log and shows how these elements can be used in marketing, using the first entry in the transaction log in Figure 6.10 as an example.

Webtrends, discussed in Chapter 4, is a leading log file analysis tool. Transaction log data becomes even more useful when combined with two other visitor-generated data trails: registration forms and the shopping cart database. Users are enticed through various means (such as free gifts or special services) to fill out registration forms. **Registration forms** gather personal data on name, address, phone, zip code, e-mail address (usually required), and other optional self-confessed information on interests and tastes. When users make a purchase, they also enter additional information into the shopping cart database. The **shopping cart database** captures all the item selection, purchase, and payment data. Other potential additional sources of data are information users submit on product forms, contribute to chat groups, or send via e-mail messages using the "Contact Us" option on most sites.

For a Web site that has a million visitors per month, and where, on average, a visitor makes 15 page requests per visit, there will be 15 million entries in the log each month. These transaction logs, coupled with data from the registration forms and shopping cart database, represent a treasure trove of marketing information for both individual sites and the online industry as a whole. Nearly all the new Internet marketing capabilities are based on these data-gathering tools. For instance, here are just a few of the interesting marketing questions that can be answered by examining a site's Web transaction logs, registration forms, and shopping cart database:

- What are the major patterns of interest and purchase for groups and individuals?
- After the home page, where do most users go first, and then second and third?
- What are the interests of specific individuals (those we can identify)?
- How can we make it easier for people to use our site so they can find what they want?
- How can we change the design of the site to encourage visitors to purchase our high-margin products?
- Where are visitors coming from (and how can we optimize our presence on these referral sites)?
- How can we personalize our messages, offerings, and products to individual users?

Answering these questions requires some additional technologies. As noted by Jupiter Research, businesses can choke on the massive quantity of information found in a typical site's log file. We describe some technologies that help firms more effectively utilize this information below.

## SUPPLEMENTING THE LOGS: COOKIES AND WEB BUGS

While transaction logs create the foundation of online data collection, they are supplemented by two other data collection techniques: cookies and Web bugs.

**registration forms**

gather personal data on name, address, phone, zip code, e-mail address, and other optional self-confessed information on interests and tastes

**shopping cart database**

captures all the item selection, purchase, and payment data

## FIGURE 6.10 — ONE SECOND FROM THE WEB TRANSACTION LOG OF AZIMUTH-INTERACTIVE.COM

dsl254-068-173.nyc1.dsl.speakeasy.net - - [22/Oct/2010:11:29:32 -0400] "GET /masthead.cgi?page=hompage&ad=1 HTTP/1.1" 200 3646 "http://www.azimuth-interactive.com/" "Mozilla/5.0 (Windows; U; Windows NT 5.0; en-US; rv:1.6) Gecko/20040113"

dsl254-068-173.nyc1.dsl.speakeasy.net - - [22/Oct/2010:11:29:32 -0400] "GET /images/newredspacer.gif HTTP/1.1" 200 35 "http://www.azimuth-interactive.com/homepage2.php" "Mozilla/5.0 (Windows; U; Windows NT 5.0; en-US; rv:1.6) Gecko/20040113"

dsl254-068-173.nyc1.dsl.speakeasy.net - - [22/Oct/2010:11:29:32 -0400] "GET /images/azimuthweblogo2.gif HTTP/1.1" 200 1494 "http://www.azimuth-interactive.com/masthead.cgi?page=hompage&ad=1" "Mozilla/5.0 (Windows; U; Windows NT 5.0; en-US; rv:1.6) Gecko/20040113"

dsl254-068-173.nyc1.dsl.speakeasy.net - - [22/Oct/2010:11:29:32 -0400] "GET /images/newmastheadart.gif HTTP/1.1" 200 26349 "http://www.azimuth-interactive.com/masthead.cgi?page=hompage&ad=1" "Mozilla/5.0 (Windows; U; Windows NT 5.0; en-US; rv:1.6) Gecko/20040113"

dsl254-068-173.nyc1.dsl.speakeasy.net - - [22/Oct/2010:11:29:32 -0400] "GET /images/whitespacer.gif HTTP/1.1" 200 45 "http://www.azimuth-interactive.com/masthead.cgi?page=hompage&ad=1" "Mozilla/5.0 (Windows; U; Windows NT 5.0; en-US; rv:1.6) Gecko/20040113"

dsl254-068-173.nyc1.dsl.speakeasy.net - - [22/Oct/2010:11:29:32 -0400] "GET /images/corpsolutionsnav.gif HTTP/1.1" 200 206 "http://www.azimuth-interactive.com/masthead.cgi?page=hompage&ad=1" "Mozilla/5.0 (Windows; U; Windows NT 5.0; en-US; rv:1.6) Gecko/20040113"

dsl254-068-173.nyc1.dsl.speakeasy.net - - [22/Oct/2010:11:29:32 -0400] "GET /images/softcoursesnav.gif HTTP/1.1" 200 239 "http://www.azimuth-interactive.com/masthead.cgi?page=hompage&ad=1" "Mozilla/5.0 (Windows; U; Windows NT 5.0; en-US; rv:1.6) Gecko/20040113"

dsl254-068-173.nyc1.dsl.speakeasy.net - - [22/Oct/2010:11:29:32 -0400] "GET /images/coursebooksnav.gif HTTP/1.1" 200 165 "http://www.azimuth-interactive.com/masthead.cgi?page=hompage&ad=1" "Mozilla/5.0 (Windows; U; Windows NT 5.0; en-US; rv:1.6) Gecko/20040113"

dsl254-068-173.nyc1.dsl.speakeasy.net - - [22/Oct/2010:11:29:32 -0400] "GET /images/onlinecoursesnav.gif HTTP/1.1" 200 174 "http://www.azimuth-interactive.com/masthead.cgi?page=hompage&ad=1" "Mozilla/5.0 (Windows; U; Windows NT 5.0; en-US; rv:1.6) Gecko/20040113"

dsl254-068-173.nyc1.dsl.speakeasy.net - - [22/Oct/2010:11:29:32 -0400] "GET /images/onlinetestingnav.gif HTTP/1.1" 200 175 "http://www.azimuth-interactive.com/masthead.cgi?page=hompage&ad=1" "Mozilla/5.0 (Windows; U; Windows NT 5.0; en-US; rv:1.6) Gecko/20040113"

| TABLE 6.9 | MARKETING USES OF DATA FROM WEB TRANSACTION LOGS |
|---|---|
| **DATA ELEMENT** | **MARKETING USE** |
| IP address of the visitor: dsl254-068-173.nyc1.dsl.speakeasy.net | Can be used to send return e-mails for marketing when the visitor is using a dedicated URL as opposed to a dial-in modem. Dial-in modems use temporary IPs and cannot be used for return mail. |
| Date and time stamp: [22/Oct/2009:11:29:32 -0400] | Used to understand patterns in the time of day and year of consumer activity. |
| Pages and objects requested and visited ("Get" statements): "GET /masthead.cgi?page=hompage& ad=1 HTTP/1.1" | Used to understand what this specific consumer was interested in finding (the clickstream). Can be used later to send "personalized"messages, "customized products," or simply return mail regarding related products. |
| Response of site server: 200 | Used to monitor for broken links, pages not returned. |
| Size of pages sent (bytes of information): 3646 | Used to understand capacity demands on servers and communications links. |
| Name of page or site from which the consumer came to this site: "http://www.azimuth-interactive.com/" | Used to understand how consumers come to a site, and once there, their patterns of behavior. |
| Name and version of the browser used: "Mozilla/5.0 (Windows; U; Windows NT 5.0; en-US; rv:1.6) Gecko/20040113" | Useful for understanding target browsers, ensuring your site is compatible with browsers being used. |
| Name and version of the operating system of the consumer's client computer: (Windows; U; Windows NT 5.0; en-US; rv:1.6) | Useful for understanding the capabilities of target client computers; more recent operating systems indicates new computer, or technically savvy user. |
| History of all the pages and objects visited during a session at the site. | Used to establish personal profiles of individuals, analyze site activity, and understand the most popular pages and resources. |

As described in Chapter 3, a cookie is small text file that Web sites place on the hard disk of visitors' client computers every time they visit, and during the visit, as specific pages are visited. Cookies allow a Web site to store data on a user's computer and then later retrieve it. The Mozilla Firefox Cookies dialog box in **Figure 6.11** shows the components in a typical cookie file on a client computer (in this case, a cookie from the *New York Times* Web site). The cookie typically includes a name, a unique ID number for each visitor that is stored on the user's computer, the domain (which specifies the Web server/domain that can access the cookie), a path (if a cookie comes from a particular part of a Web site instead of the main page, a path will be given), a security setting that provides whether the cookie can only be transmitted by a secure server, and an expiration date (not required). First-party cookies come from the same domain name as the page the user is visiting, while third-party cookies come from

| FIGURE 6.11 | **FIREFOX COOKIES DIALOG BOX** |
| --- | --- |

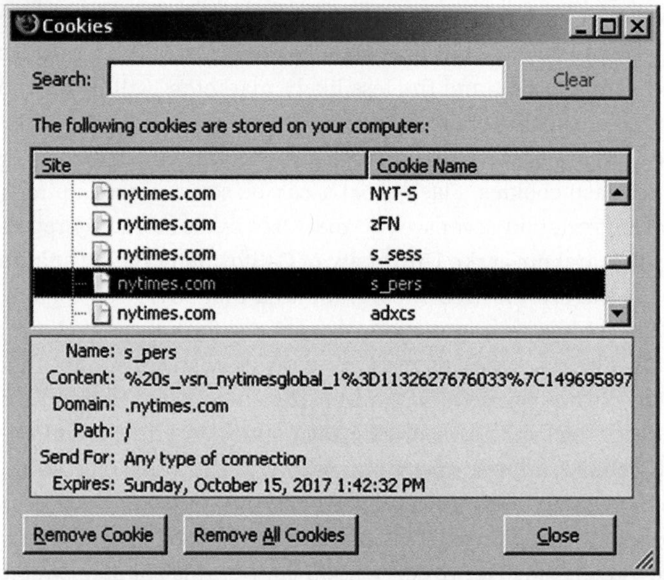

Firefox's Cookies dialog box identifies the various components of a typical cookie file on your computer.

another domain, such as ad serving or adware companies, affiliate marketers, or spyware servers.

A cookie provides Web marketers with a very quick means of identifying the customer and understanding his or her prior behavior at the site. Web sites use cookies to determine how many people are visiting the site, whether they are new or repeat visitors, and how often they have visited, although this data may be somewhat inaccurate because people share computers, they often use more than one computer, and cookies may have been inadvertently or intentionally erased. Cookies make shopping carts and "quick checkout" options possible by allowing a site to keep track of a user as he or she adds to the shopping cart. Each item added to the shopping cart is stored in the site's database along with the visitor's unique ID value.

The location of cookie files on a computer depends on the browser version being used. Cookie files can be accessed on a computer using Firefox 3.6 or higher by opening the Tools menu, clicking Options, selecting the Privacy tab, and clicking the Remove Individual Cookies link (earlier versions have a Show Cookies button), which opens the Cookies dialog box. In Internet Explorer 7 or 8, users have a bit more control over the level of privacy. You can set the level of privacy you desire all the way from rejecting all cookies (Block All Cookies) or accepting some cookies from third and first parties if they have a privacy policy in place (Medium) or accepting all cookies (Accept All Cookies ). Select Tools, Internet Options, and then the Privacy tab. You adjust the level of privacy you want by using the slider. In the latest browsers, users can opt for a privacy mode that extinguishes all records of browsing activity on the client computer.

With growing privacy concerns, over time the percentage of people deleting cookies has risen (Truste, 2009). The more cookies are deleted, the less accurate are Web page and ad server metrics, and the less likely marketers will be able to understand who is visiting their sites or where they came from. As a result, advertiser have sought other methods. One way is using Adobe Flash software, which creates its own cookie files, known as Flash cookies. Flash cookies can be set to never expire, and can store about 5 MB of information compared to the 1,024 bytes stored by regular cookies. A 2009 study by researchers at the University of California-Berkeley analyzed the use of Flash cookies at the top 100 Web sites, and found that 98% used regular cookies and 54% used Flash cookies, many to store the same information at the regular cookie. Some used the Flash cookies to recreate cookies that consumers had previously deleted. Private Browsing mode in Internet Explorer 8 and Firefox 3 do not delete Flash cookies, nor does the Clear Private Data option in Firefox (Soltani, et al., 2009)

Although cookies are site-specific (a Web site can only receive the data it has stored on a client computer and cannot look at any other cookie), when combined with Web bugs, they can be used to create cross-site profiles. We discuss this practice further in the "Advertising Networks" section later in this chapter.. Web bugs are tiny (1-pixel) graphic files embedded in e-mail messages and on Web sites. Web bugs are used to automatically transmit information about the user and the page being viewed to a monitoring server. For instance, when a recipient opens an e-mail in HTML format or opens a Web page, a message is sent to a server calling for graphic information. This tells the marketer that the e-mail was opened, indicating that the recipient was at least interested in the subject header. Web bugs are often clear or colored white so they are not visible to the recipient. You may be able to determine if a Web page is using Web bugs by using the View Source option of your browser and examining the IMG (image) tags on the page. As noted above, Web bugs are typically 1 pixel in size and contain the URL of a server that differs from the one that served the page itself (see w2.eff.org/Privacy/Marketing/web_bug.html). *Insight on Society: Every Move You Take, Every Click You Make, We'll Be Tracking You* examines the use of Web bugs.

## DATABASES, DATA WAREHOUSES, AND DATA MINING: DEVELOPING PROFILES

Databases, data warehouses, data mining, and the variety of marketing decision-making techniques loosely called *profiling* are at the heart of the revolution in Internet marketing. Together, these techniques attempt to identify precisely who the online customer is and what they want, and then, to fulfill the customer's criteria exactly. These techniques are more powerful and far more precise and fine-grained than the gross levels of demographic and market segmentation techniques used in mass marketing media or by telemarketing.

In order to understand the data in transaction logs, registration forms, shopping carts, cookies, Web bugs, and other sources, Internet marketers need massively powerful and capacious databases, database management systems, and data modeling

## INSIGHT ON SOCIETY

# EVERY MOVE YOU TAKE, EVERY CLICK YOU MAKE, WE'LL BE TRACKING YOU

When's the last time you visited your favorite Web portal page and saw ads that you had no interest in seeing? Don't think long! Most people online are treated to thousands of irrelevant ads in a week or so. The solution to the problem of annoying, irrelevant ads is "targeted ads," which reflect your current or even longer term interests What makes targeted advertising possible is tracking every click you make and every site you visit, and mining that information for however long advertising platforms like Google want, which could be forever. There are no statutory or legal limits on this process, yet.

Images called "clear GIFs," "Web beacons," and "invisible GIFs" don't sound too threatening. But when they're referred to as "Web bugs," Internet users begin to get a better sense of their true purpose. Web bugs come in several different varieties, but the basic idea is that they are objects (in the form of an image or a tiny pixel) that are embedded invisibly on Web pages and in an e-mail that cause a part of the Web page (usually that image or pixel) to be retrieved by a completely different third-party Web site by sending a signal to that third-party site. As a result, the third-party Web site knows that you visited the original Web site, and they can know much more if they want to, such as where you've been and what you've bought.

Marketers using Web bugs claim they have two purposes. One is to improve the efficiency of display ads by aiding in collecting detailed information about Web usage, including how many visitors a particular site has had, which pages on a site are most popular, and which banner ads are providing the best results. A second purpose involves improving the efficiency of marketing and advertising by targeting ads to

individuals based on their prior behavior on the Web. This is variously called "behavioral targeting," "targeting advertising," "performance driven advertising," or what Yahoo calls and sells as SmartAds. The idea is to display banner ads to individuals no matter where they browse on the Web based on their personal preferences revealed in prior Web visits, searches, and purchases. In general, banner ads have very poor response rates, less than .1%, much less than search engine ads (varies from 1% to 6%). A Microsoft-sponsored study found that targeted ads increased click-through rates six fold.

Search engine marketing and portal companies such as Google, Microsoft, and AOL use them, as do advertising networks such as DoubleClick. Canadian Web security firm Security Space periodically samples over 20 million Web pages from 2 million Web domains to identify the top 100 bug-using sites. The leading Web bugger is Google Analytics, followed by Google Syndication, Google, Yahoo, Amazon, and your favorite Web 2.0 sites, YouTube, Photobucket, and Flickr. All Google sites account for about 20% of Web bugging. Anytime you use these sites, your every move is bugged. Collectively, these sites capture a significant portion of the Web behavior of 221 million Internet users in the United States. The activities of these Web buggers is largely beyond current federal or state regulations or law.

In 2009, Google announced the launch of "interest-based advertising," which targets banner ads on its DoubleClick ad network based not just on context but on the Web pages you previously viewed. How do Google and DoubleClick know what pages you have visited? Simple: thousands of the most popular Web sites belong to the DoubleClick network and partici-

(continued)

pate in the rewards of using the collected data. When you land on these sites DoubleClick is notified immediately. The system is driven by Web bugs and cookies placed on your browser, and you may end up receiving ads based on another user's behavior (e.g., your children) using that browser. Privacy advocates fear that interest-based advertising is just the first step toward more highly targeted advertising that draws upon everything Google knows about your behavior on Google sites, including YouTube, Picassa, and other applications. Mike Zaneis, vice president of public policy at the Internet Advertising Bureau, acknowledges that highly targeted advertising can be creepy. But, he says, "creepiness is not in and of itself a consumer harm."

Google does allow users to opt out of the DoubleClick targeted advertising program at the Google Privacy Center. But to find the Center, you would need to read this book or other sources. Google's Chief Privacy Officer claims its personal information policy is based on three bedrock principles: "We don't sell it. We don't collect it without permission. We don't use it to serve ads without permission." He failed to note the difficulties you will have denying permission: you must go to the Privacy Center to opt out, otherwise you're in. Google does not publish how many people opt out and deny permission.

If Web bugs are so harmless, why go to the trouble of hiding them? Why not just let people know the site is bugged, perhaps using a yellow caution sign on each bug? That's what privacy advocates are asking. And what they've learned is that although Web bugs may have been designed to simply provide traffic counts, when combined with information from third-party sources, bugs can give marketers an all too complete picture of an individual consumer—right down to home address, online account balances, account numbers, and whatever else the user has entered

into his or her computer. This is very valuable marketing information.

Bugs enable marketers to know who's online, which Web sites they've visited, where they've spent money, what their address is, and more. When the technology is used by a network of sites linked to a third party, such as DoubleClick, consumer profiling becomes even more detailed, leading to a potentially significant loss of privacy. Use of Web bug technology is rising sharply as marketers seek to gain a foothold in Web 2.0 communities such as Facebook, MySpace, YouTube, and Photobucket. Personal pages and user-generated content are favorite locations for buggers to place their works. The Privacy Foundation has issued guidelines for Web bug usage. The guidelines suggest that Web bugs should be visible as an icon on the screen, the icon should be labeled to indicate its function, and it should identify the name of the company that placed the Web bug on the page. In addition, if a user clicks on the Web bug, it should display a disclosure statement indicating what data is being collected, how the data is used after it is collected, what companies receive the data, what other data the Web bug is combined with, and whether or not a cookie is associated with the Web bug. Users should be able to opt out of any data collection done by the Web bug, and the Web bug should not be used to collect information from Web pages of a sensitive nature, such as medical, financial, job-related, or sexual matters.

In an effort to address growing congressional concerns about privacy, and build consumer trust online, an industry advertising group, the Network Advertising Initiative (NAI), released self-regulatory guidelines for the industry. Major advertising industry groups have adopted the Self Regulatory Principles for Online Behavioral Advertising, which emphasize transparency (tell consumers how you use their information) and choice (opt-in and opt-out). The NAI renamed Web bugs as "Web beacons" and

(continued)

requires online firms to notify customers of Web bug usage whether in e-mail or on Web sites, state the purpose of their use, and disclose any data that could be released to third parties. The NAI also called for users to be given a choice (whether opt-in or opt-out) of any release of personally identifiable information (PII) to third parties, and to provide an opt-in choice for any release of information related to PII. These restrictions do not apply to the Web site itself (agents). In addition, the NAI provides a capability open to all Web users to opt out of online advertising networks collecting non-personal information on them. However, for this to work, users need to have a cookie downloaded to their browser that will inform the networks not to collect information on this user.

Currently, Internet users are not protected by government regulation against Web bugs or other forms of behavioral targeting. Fearing the public outcry against Web tracking, Google, Microsoft, Yahoo, and AT&T have been lobbying Congress to come up with legislation that would legitimate and regulate online tracking which some see as essential to the growth of the Internet and continued innovation. Others, social and computer scientists, are dreaming up ways to protect consumers. One idea: "privacy nudges" based on software that provides you with real-time reminders that what you are entering into the computer has real privacy implications. "When we go online, there are a lot of ways we can inadvertently give up our privacy," notes Lorrie Cranor, a computer scientist at Carnegie Mellon. As an attorney with Consumers Union said, "You shouldn't have to give up your privacy to shop online. The technology is outpacing the existing consumer protections." Meanwhile, tracking technology is significantly expanding in 2010 to include your cell phone location.

**SOURCES:** "Web Bug Report," SecuritySpace, July 2010; "Technology Coalition Seeks Stronger Privacy Laws," by Miguel Helft, *New York Times*, March 30, 2010; "Study Finds Behaviorally-Targeted Ads More Than Twice As Valuable, Twice as Effective As Non-targerted Online Ads," Network Advertising Initiative, March 24, 2010; "Redrawing the Route to Online Privacy," by Steve Lohr, *New York Times*, February 28, 2010; "The Collection and Use of Location Information for Commercial Purposes Hearings," U.S. House of Representatives, Committee on Energy and Commerce, Subcommittee on Commerce, Trade and Consumer Protection, February 24, 2010; "Groups Call for New Checks on Behvioral Ad Data," by Tom Krazit, CNET News, September 1, 2009; "What Google Knows About You," by Richard Mitchell, Computerworld, May 11, 2009; "A Push to Limit the Tracking of Web Surfers' Clicks," by Louise Story, *New York Times*, March 20, 2008.

tools. Just examine the transaction log in Figure 6.10 again, and then imagine trying to find the patterns in millions of entries each day!

## Databases

The first step in interpreting huge transaction streams is to store the information systematically. A **database** is a software application that stores records and attributes. A telephone book is a physical database that stores records of individuals and their attributes such as names, addresses, and phone numbers. A **database management system (DBMS)** is a software application used by organizations to create, maintain, and access databases. The most common DBMS are DB2 from IBM and a variety of SQL databases from Oracle, Sybase, and other providers. **Structured query language (SQL)** is an industry-standard database query and manipulation language used in relational databases. **Relational databases** such as DB2 and SQL represent data as two-dimensional tables with records organized in rows, and attributes in columns, much like a spreadsheet. The tables—and all the data in them—can be flexibly related to one another as long as the tables share a common data element.

**database**
a software application that stores records and attributes

**database management system (DBMS)**
a software application used by organizations to create, maintain, and access databases

**structured query language (SQL)**
an industry-standard database query and manipulation language used in relational databases

**relational databases**

represent data as two-dimensional tables with records organized in rows and attributes in columns; data within different tables can be flexibly related as long as the tables share a common data element

**data warehouse**

a database that collects a firm's transactional and customer data in a single location for offline analysis

Relational databases are extraordinarily flexible and allow marketers and other managers to view and analyze data from different perspectives very quickly. **Figure 6.12** illustrates a relational database view of customers. The data are organized into four tables: customer, order, product, and supplier. The tables all share at least one data element. Using this model, it would be possible to query the database for a list of all customers who bought a certain product, or to message a supplier when the inventory falls below a certain level (and message a customer automatically via e-mail that the product is temporarily out of stock).

### Data Warehouses and Data Mining

A **data warehouse** is a database that collects a firm's transactional and customer data in a single location for offline analysis by marketers and site managers. The data originate in many core operational areas of the firm, such as Web site transaction logs, shopping carts, point-of-sale terminals (product scanners) in stores, warehouse inventory levels, field sales reports, external scanner data supplied by third parties, and financial payment data. The purpose of a data warehouse is to gather all the firm's transaction and customer data into one logical repository where it can be

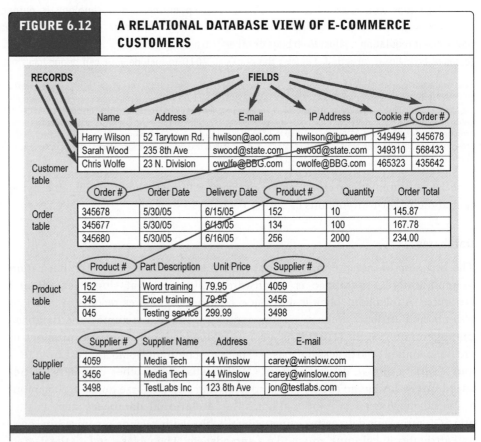

| **FIGURE 6.12** | **A RELATIONAL DATABASE VIEW OF E-COMMERCE CUSTOMERS** |

**RECORDS**    **FIELDS**

Customer table

| Name | Address | E-mail | IP Address | Cookie # | Order # |
|---|---|---|---|---|---|
| Harry Wilson | 52 Tarytown Rd. | hwilson@aol.com | hwilson@ibm.com | 349494 | 345678 |
| Sarah Wood | 235 8th Ave | swood@state.com | swood@state.com | 349310 | 568433 |
| Chris Wolfe | 23 N. Division | cwolfe@BBG.com | cwolfe@BBG.com | 465323 | 435642 |

Order table

| Order # | Order Date | Delivery Date | Product # | Quantity | Order Total |
|---|---|---|---|---|---|
| 345678 | 5/30/05 | 6/15/05 | 152 | 10 | 145.87 |
| 345677 | 5/30/05 | 6/15/05 | 134 | 100 | 167.78 |
| 345680 | 5/30/05 | 6/16/05 | 256 | 2000 | 234.00 |

Product table

| Product # | Part Description | Unit Price | Supplier # |
|---|---|---|---|
| 152 | Word training | 79.95 | 4059 |
| 345 | Excel training | 79.95 | 3456 |
| 045 | Testing service | 299.99 | 3498 |

Supplier table

| Supplier # | Supplier Name | Address | E-mail |
|---|---|---|---|
| 4059 | Media Tech | 44 Winslow | carey@winslow.com |
| 3456 | Media Tech | 44 Winslow | carey@winslow.com |
| 3498 | TestLabs Inc | 123 8th Ave | jon@testlabs.com |

In a relational database, data gathered from an e-commerce site is stored on hard drives and presented to managers of sites in the form of interrelated tables.

analyzed and modeled by managers without disrupting or taxing the firm's primary transactional systems and databases. Data warehouses grow quickly into storage repositories containing terabytes of data (trillions of bytes) on consumer behavior at a firm's stores and Web sites. With a data warehouse, firms can answer such questions as: What products are the most profitable by region and city? What regional marketing campaigns are working? How effective is store promotion of the firm's Web site? Data warehouses can provide business managers with a more complete awareness of customers through data that can be accessed quickly.

**Data mining** is a set of different analytical techniques that look for patterns in the data of a database or data warehouse, or seek to model the behavior of customers. Web site data can be "mined" to develop profiles of visitors and customers (see **Figure 6.13**). A **customer profile** is simply a set of rules that describe the typical behavior of a customer or a group of customers at a Web site. Customer profiles help to identify the patterns in group and individual behavior that occur online as millions of visitors use a firm's Web site. For example, almost every financial transaction you engage in is processed by a data mining application to detect fraud. Phone companies closely monitor your cell phone use as well to detect stolen phones and unusual calling patterns. Financial institutions and cell phone firms use data mining to develop fraud profiles. When a user's behavior conforms to a fraud profile, the transaction is not allowed or terminated (Mobasher, 2007).

There are many different types of data mining. The simplest type is **query-driven data mining**, which is based on specific queries. For instance, based on hunches of marketers who suspect a relationship in the database or who need to

**data mining**
a set of analytical techniques that look for patterns in the data of a database or data warehouse, or seek to model the behavior of customers

**customer profile**
a description of the typical behavior of a customer or a group of customers at a Web site

**query-driven data mining**
data mining based on specific queries

**FIGURE 6.13**     **DATA MINING AND PERSONALIZATION**

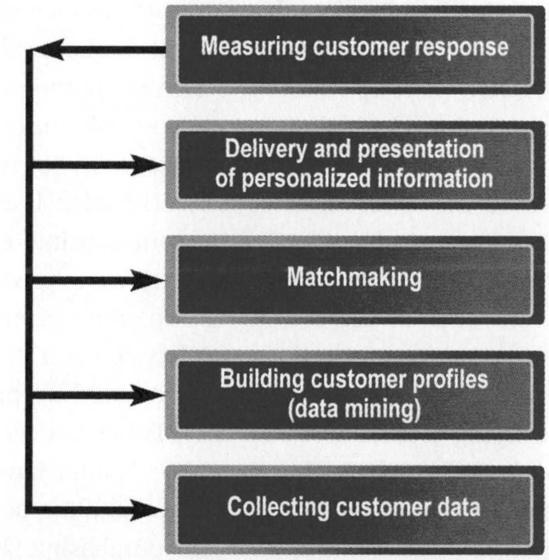

Personalization of content and marketing is based on data mining techniques that can produce reliable profiles of individual consumer behavior.
SOURCE: Adomavicius and Tuzhilin, 2001b. ©2001 IEEE.

answer a specific question, such as "What is the relationship between time of day and purchases of various products at the Web site?", marketers can easily query the data warehouse and produce a database table that rank-orders the top 10 products sold at a Web site by each hour of the day. Marketers can then change the content of the Web site to stimulate more sales by highlighting different products over time or placing particular products on the home page at certain times of day or night.

**model-driven data mining**

involves the use of a model that analyzes the key variables of interest to decision makers

Another form of data mining is model-driven. **Model-driven data mining** involves the use of a model that analyzes the key variables of interest to decision makers. For example, marketers may want to reduce the inventory carried on the Web site by removing unprofitable items that do not sell well. A financial model can be built showing the profitability of each product on the site so that an informed decision can be made.

**rule-based data mining**

examines demographic and transactional data of groups and individuals at a Web site and attempts to derive general rules of behavior for visitors

A more interesting kind of data mining is rule-based. **Rule-based data mining** examines demographic and transactional data of groups and individuals at a Web site and attempts to derive general rules of behavior for visitors. There are factual and behavioral approaches as well as different levels of granularity, from market segments down to individuals. In the *factual approach*, factual demographic and transactional data (purchase price, products purchased) and material viewed at the site are analyzed and stored in a customer profile table in order to segment the marketplace into well-defined groups. For instance, female customers who purchased items worth more than $50 in an average visit and who viewed travel articles might be shown a vacation travel advertisement. The rules are specified by marketing managers as a set of *filters* based on their expert opinions, as well as trial and error, and are applied to aggregate groups of visitors or market segments. There can be thousands of different types of visitors, and hence thousands of marketing decisions or filters that marketers have to make.

**collaborative filtering**

site visitors classify themselves into affinity groups characterized by common interests; products are then recommended based on what other people in the group have recently purchased

A different *behavioral approach* to data mining is **collaborative filtering** (see *Insight on Technology: The Long Tail: Big Hits and Big Misses*). Behavioral approaches try to "let the data speak for itself" rather than impose rules set by expert marketers. Collaborative filtering was first developed at the MIT Media Lab and commercialized by an MIT Media Lab–backed start-up company, Firefly. Rather than having expert marketers make decisions based on their own "rules of thumb," experience, and corporate needs (a need to move old inventory, for instance), site visitors collaboratively classify themselves based on common selections. The idea is that people classify themselves into "affinity groups" characterized by common interests. A query to the database can isolate the individuals who all purchased the same products. Later, based on purchases by other members of the affinity group, the system can recommend purchases based on what other people in the group have bought recently. For example, visitors who all purchased books on amateur flying could be pitched a video that illustrates small-plane flying techniques. And then later, if several members of this "amateur flying interest group" purchased books on parachuting, then all members of the group would be pitched a recommendation to buy parachuting books, based on what other people collaboratively "like themselves" were purchasing. This pitch would be made regardless of the demographic background of the individuals.

A more fine-grained behavioral approach that seeks to deal with individuals as opposed to market segments or affinity groups derives rules from individual consumer behavior (along with some demographic information) (Adomavicius and Tuzhilin, 2001a; Chan, 1999; Fawcett and Provost, 1996, 1997). Here, the pages actually visited by specific users are stored as a set of conjunctive rules. For example, if an individual visits a site and typically ("as a rule") moves from the home page to the financial news section to the Asian report section, and then often purchases articles from the "Recent Developments in Banking" section, then this person—based on purely past behavioral patterns—might be shown an advertisement for a book on Asian money markets. These rules can be constructed to follow an individual across many different Web sites.

There are many drawbacks to all these techniques, not least of which is that there may be millions of rules, many of them nonsensical, and many others of short-term duration. Hence, the rules need extensive validation and culling (Adomavicius and Tuzhilin, 2001a). Also, there can be millions of affinity groups and other patterns in the data that are temporal or meaningless. The difficulty is isolating the valid, powerful (profitable) patterns in the data and then acting on the observed pattern fast enough to make a sale you would otherwise not have made. As we see later, there are practical difficulties and trade-offs involved in achieving these levels of granularity, precision, and speed.

## CUSTOMER RELATIONSHIP MANAGEMENT (CRM) SYSTEMS

Customer relationship management systems are another important Internet marketing technology. A **customer relationship management (CRM) system** is a repository of customer information that records all of the contacts that a customer has with a firm (including Web sites) and generates a customer profile available to everyone in the firm with a need to "know the customer." CRM systems also supply the analytical software required to analyze and use customer information. Customers come to firms not just over the Web but also through telephone call centers, customer service representatives, sales representatives, automated voice response systems, ATMs and kiosks, in-store point-of-sale terminals, and mobile devices (m-commerce). In the past, firms generally did not maintain a single repository of customer information, but instead were organized along product lines, with each product line maintaining a customer list (and often not sharing it with others in the same firm).

In general, firms did not know who their customers were, how profitable they were, or how they responded to marketing campaigns. For instance, a bank customer might see a television advertisement for a low-cost auto loan that included an 800-number to call. However, if the customer came to the bank's Web site instead, rather than calling the 800-number, marketers would have no idea how effective the television campaign was because this Web customer contact data was not related to the 800-number call center data. **Figure 6.14** (on page 388) illustrates how a CRM system integrates customer contact data into a single system.

CRMs are part of the evolution of firms toward a customer-centric and marketing-segment-based business, and away from a product-line-centered business. CRMs are essentially a database technology with extraordinary capabilities for addressing the needs of each customer and differentiating the product or service on the basis of

**customer relationship management (CRM) system**

a repository of customer information that records all of the contacts that a customer has with a firm and generates a customer profile available to everyone in the firm with a need to "know the customer"

# INSIGHT ON TECHNOLOGY

## THE LONG TAIL: BIG HITS AND BIG MISSES

The "Long Tail" is a colloquial name given to various statistical distributions characterized by a small group of events of high amplitude and a very large group of events with low amplitude. Coined by *Wired Magazine* writer Chris Anderson in 2004, the Web's Long Tail has since gone on to fascinate academics and challenge online marketers. The concept is straightforward. Think Hollywood movies: there are big hits that really hit big, and thousands of films that no one ever hears about and only a few people ever see. In economics, it's the Pareto principle: 20% of anything produces 80% of the effects. That means 20% of the hits produce 80% of the revenue, and by extension, 80% of the product line only returns 20% of the revenue. It's these non-hit misses that make up the Long Tail. Anderson claims to have discovered a new 98% rule: no matter how much content you put online, someone, somewhere will show up to buy it. Rather than 20:80, Anderson suggests the Internet changes the Pareto principle by making it easier for consumers to find more obscure products that are very satisfying. Likewise, demand for very popular products declines according to Anderson. eBay would seem to be a perfect example. The online tag sale contains millions of items drawn from every Aunt Tilly's closet in the world and still seems to find a buyer somewhere for just about anything, revenue that would not be realized without an online marketplace.

On the Internet, where search costs are tiny, and storage and distribution costs are near zero, Amazon is able to offer millions of books for sale compared to a typical large bookstore with 40,000-100,000 titles. The same is true of CDs, DVDs, digital cameras, and MP3 players.

Wherever you look on the Web, you find huge inventories, and a great many items that few people are interested in buying. But someone is almost always searching for something. With a billion people online, even a one-in-a-million product will find 1,000 buyers. According to Anderson, online music sites sell access to 98% of their titles once a quarter, and 15% of Netflix's revenue comes from titles ranked 3,000 or below. According to Netflix, over 50% of its 100,000 titles are rented at least once a day by someone. Unlike physical stores such as Wal-Mart and Sears, online merchants have much lower overhead costs because they do not have physical stores and have lower labor costs. Therefore they can load up on inventory, including items that rarely sell. Researchers argue that one impact of the Internet is to alter the 20:80 rule to something more like 30:70, where the niche products make up a larger share of the revenues than in traditional catalogs or stores.

There are several implications of the Long Tail phenomenon for Web marketing. Some writers such as Anderson claim that the Internet revolutionizes digital content by making even niche products highly profitable, and that the revenues produced by small niche products will ultimately outweigh the revenues of hit movies, songs, and books. For Hollywood, and all content producers, this means less focus on the blockbusters that bust the budget, and more emphasis on the steady base-hit titles that have smaller audiences but make up for it in numbers of titles. The Long Tail is a democratizing phenomenon: even less well-known movies, songs, and books can now find a market on the Web. There's hope for your blog and garage band! For economists, the Long Tail represents a net gain

(continued)

for social welfare because now customers can find exactly the niche content they really want rather than accept the "big hits" on the shelf. The Web's Long Tail makes more customers happy, and the possibility of making money on niche products should encourage more production of "indie" music and film.

The problem with all these misses in the Long Tail is that few people can find them because they are—by definition—largely unknown. Search engines help but return so much information that choice is difficult. Faced with hundreds of titles the user never heard of is perplexing, delays decision, raises consumer anxiety levels, and potentially wastes consumer time. Hence, in their native state, the revenue value of low-demand products is locked up in collective ignorance. Here's where recommender systems come into play: they can guide consumers to obscure but wonderful works based on the recommendations of others. Netflix just spent a million dollars in 2010 on improving its recommender system by 10%.

Recommender systems use historical data on user preferences or behavior to predict how new users will behave. Using a similarity metric, which is a means of segmenting the user base, a sub segment of users are selected whose behavior or preferences are similar to the user seeking recommendations. An average purchase propensity for a specific product by members of that subsegment is calculated, with a recommendation made based on that average. Recommendations are made based on past purchasing behavior of the user, which may or may not reflect the needs or preferences of the user today. The ability to narrow down the list of potential options, however, makes the information-gathering process more efficient and, for many users, very helpful. It's also possible that social networks make the Long Tail phenomenon even stronger. One online person discovers an unheard-of niche product and shares his or her feelings with others.

But recent research casts some doubt on the revenue potential in the Long Tail. In an odd twist, the number of DVD titles online that never get played is increasing rapidly, while at the same time the big blockbuster "winner-take-all" titles are increasing. Solid "best sellers" have expanded and produce the vast part of online DVD revenues. Over time, the number of titles in the Long Tail has exploded, and the "no play" rate has expanded at music sites from 2% to 12%. A massive study of millions of digital downloads in England found that 75% of the digital titles were not downloaded even once. The Long Tail is a very lonely, quiet place. In reality there seems to be more selling of less (the hits) than less selling of more (the misses). A U.S. study similarly found that 10% of the music titles at Rhapsody, a music site, produced 78% of the revenues. Researchers at Wharton examined over 17,000 movies at Netflix viewed by 480,000 users between 2000 and 2005. They found Long Tail effects missing: demand for the top 20% of movies actually expanded from 86% to 90%. They also point out that Long Tail effects may not apply forcefully to Internet retailers who have physical inventory like Netflix and Amazon, or where users have high search costs to find niche content. While recommender systems are helpful, they aren't very smart, and you still need several people to discover the niche product before alerting their friends. Long Tail effects might be stronger for pure digital content businesses like Rhapsody or online newspapers.

Both the Long Tail and the winner-take-all approaches have implications for marketers and product designers. In the Long Tail approach, online merchants, especially those selling digital goods such as content, should build up huge libraries of content because they can make signifi-

(continued)

cant revenues from niche products that have small audiences. In the winner-take-all approach, the niche products produce little revenue, and firms should concentrate on hugely popular titles and services. Surprisingly, contrary to what Anderson originally theorized, the evidence for online digital content increasingly supports a winner-take-all perspective. Tom Cruise: do not worry.

**SOURCES:** "Keyword Strategies—The Long Tail," by Matt Daily Searchengineguide.com, July 2010; "Anatomy of the Long Tail: Ordinary People with Extraordinary Tastes," by Sharad Goel, et. al., (Yahoo Research). Proceedings of the Third ACM International Conference on Web Search and Data Mining, New York, New York. 2010; "Rethinking the Long Tail Theory: How to Define Hits and Misses, by Serguel Netessine and Tom Tan, Knowledge@Wharton, October 7, 2009; "The Long Tail of P2P," by Will Page and Eric Garland, *Economic Insight*, August 14, 2009; "Should You Invest in the Long Tail?," by Anita Elberse, *Harvard Business Review*, July-August 2008; "Superstars and Underdogs: An Examination of the Long Tail Phenomenon in Video Sales," by Anita Elberse and Felix Oberholzer-Gee, Harvard Business School Working Paper Series, No. 07-015, December, 2006; "From Niches to Riches: Anatomy of the Long Tail," by Eric Brynjolfsson, Yu Hu, and Michael Smith, *MIT Sloan Management Review*, Summer 2006; "The Long Tail," by Chris Anderson, *Wired Magazine*, October 2004.

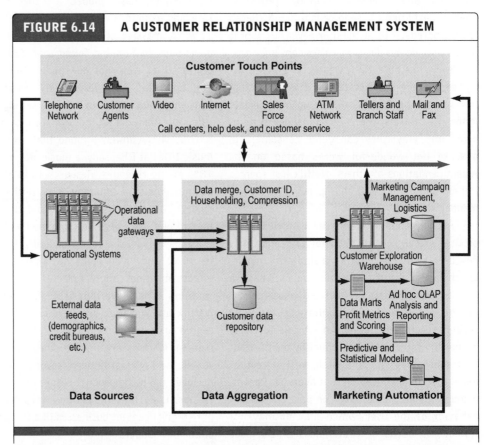

**FIGURE 6.14**  **A CUSTOMER RELATIONSHIP MANAGEMENT SYSTEM**

This is an example of a CRM system for a financial services institution. The system captures customer information from all customer "touch" points as well as other data sources, merges the data, and aggregates it into a single customer data repository or data warehouse where it can be used to provide better service, as well as to construct customer profiles for marketing purposes. Online Analytical Processing (OLAP) allows managers to dynamically analyze customer activities to spot trends or problems involving customers. Other analytical software programs analyze aggregate customer behavior to identify profitable and unprofitable customers as well as customer activities.

SOURCE: Compaq, 1998.

treating each customer as a unique person. Customer profiles can contain the following information:

- A map of the customer's relationship with the institution
- Product and usage summary data
- Demographic and psychographic data
- Profitability measures
- Contact history summarizing the customer's contacts with the institution across most delivery channels
- Marketing and sales information containing programs received by the customer and the customer's responses
- E-mail campaign responses

With these profiles, CRMs can be used to sell additional products and services, develop new products, increase product utilization, reduce marketing costs, identify and retain profitable customers, optimize service delivery costs, retain high lifetime value customers, enable personal communications, improve customer loyalty, and increase product profitability.

For instance, Home Depot saw increased competition from online hardware stores and decided to emphasize e-commerce as part of its business strategy. The company sought a comprehensive CRM solution that could organize and analyze information from both clicks and mortar. They used a CRM software package called Epiphany Insight to gain a better understanding of which Home Depot products were selling on the Web and enabled their customer service focus from their stores to exist on the Web as well. Epiphany has since been acquired by Infor. Other leading CRM vendors include SAP, SalesForce.com, Oracle, Kana, and eGain.

## 6.4 B2C AND B2B E-COMMERCE MARKETING AND BRANDING STRATEGIES

The new marketing technologies described previously have spawned a new generation of marketing techniques and added power to some traditional techniques (such as direct mail campaigns with Web site addresses displayed). In this section, we describe a variety of Internet marketing strategies for market entry, customer acquisition, customer retention, pricing, and dealing with channel conflict. It is important to note that although B2C and B2B e-commerce do have differentiating features (for instance, in B2C e-commerce, marketing is aimed at individual consumers, whereas in B2B e-commerce, typically more than just one individual is involved with the purchase decision), the strategies discussed in this section in most instances can be, and are, applied in both the B2C and B2B arenas.

### MARKET ENTRY STRATEGIES

Both new firms and traditional existing firms have choices about how to enter the market, and ways to establish the objectives of their online presence. **Figure 6.15** illustrates four basic market entry strategies.

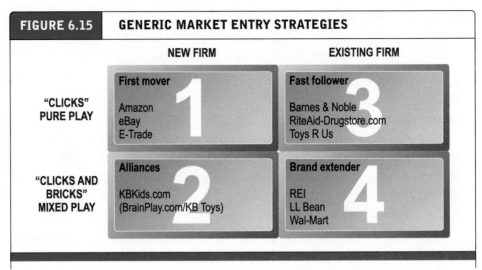

Both new and traditional firms face a basic choice—"clicks" or "bricks and clicks"—when entering the e-commerce marketplace.

Let's examine the situation facing new firms—quadrants 1 and 2 in Figure 6.15. In the early days of e-commerce, the typical entry strategy was pure clicks/first-mover advantage, utilized by such companies as Amazon, eBay, and E*Trade (quadrant 1). Indeed, this strategy was at the heart of the so-called new economy movement, and provided the capital catch basin into which billions of investment dollars flowed. The ideas are beguiling and simplistic: enter the market first and experience "first-mover" advantages—heightened user awareness, followed rapidly by successful consumer transactions and experiences—and grow brand strength. According to leading consultants of this era, first movers would experience a short-lived mini-monopoly. They would be the only providers for a few months, and then other copycats would enter the market because entry costs were so low. To prevent new competitors from entering the market, growing audience size very rapidly became the most important corporate goal rather than profits and revenue.

Firms following this strategy typically spent the majority of their marketing budget (which, in and of itself, may have constituted a large part of their available capital) on building brand (site) awareness by purchasing high-visibility advertising in traditional mass media such as television (Super Bowl game ads), radio, newspapers, and magazines. If the first mover gathered most of the customers in a particular category (pets, wine, gardening supplies, and so forth), the belief was that new entrants would not be able to enter because customers would not be willing to pay the switching costs. Customers would be "locked in" to the first-mover's interface. Moreover, the strength of the brand would inhibit switching, even though competitors were just a click away.

In retrospect, it is now clear that pursuing first-mover advantage as a marketing strategy was not particularly successful for most firms. Although first movers may have interesting advantages, they also have significant liabilities. The history of first movers in most areas of business is that statistically, they are losers for the most part because they lack the complementary assets and resources required to compete over the long term. While innovative, first movers usually lack financial depth, marketing and sales resources, loyal customers, strong brands, and production or fulfillment facilities needed to meet customer demands once the product succeeds (Teece, 1986). Research on Internet advertising indicates that while expensive ad campaigns may have increased brand awareness, the other components of a brand such as trust, loyalty, and reputation did not automatically follow, and more important, site visits did not necessarily translate into purchases (Ellison, 2000).

Another possibility for new firms is to pursue a mixed bricks-and-clicks strategy, coupling an online presence with other sales channels (quadrant 2). However, few new firms can afford the "bricks" part of this strategy. Therefore, firms following this entrance strategy often ally themselves with established firms that have already developed brand names, production and distribution facilities, and the financial resources needed to launch a successful Internet business. For instance, BrainPlay, Inc., an e-tailer of children's goods, entered into an alliance with the established Consolidated Stores Corporation KB Toys unit to form a new online presence called KBkids.com. KBkids was later closed, but KBToys.com survives today.

Now let's look at traditional firms. Traditional firms face some similar choices, with of course one difference: they have significant amounts of cash flow and capital to fund their e-commerce ventures over a long period of time. For example, Barnes & Noble, the world's largest book retailer, formed Barnesandnoble.com (quadrant 3), a follower site, when faced with the success of upstart Amazon.com (quadrant 1). The Web site was established as an independent firm, a Web pure-play, although obviously making use of the Barnes & Noble brand name. Likewise, Rite Aid followed the success of online pharmacies by establishing its own Web site (Riteaid.com) and then forming an alliance with Drugstore.com to fulfill and service prescriptions ordered online at Drugstore.com (and perform backend processing of insurance payments).

The most common strategy for existing firms is to extend their businesses and brands by using a mixed bricks-and-clicks strategy in which online marketing is closely integrated with offline physical stores (quadrant 4). These "brand-extension" strategies characterize REI, L.L.Bean, Wal-Mart, and many other established retail firms. Like fast followers, they have the advantage of existing brands and relation-ships. However, even more than fast followers, the brand extenders do not set up separate pure-play online stores, but instead typically integrate the online firm with the traditional firm from the very beginning. L.L.Bean and Wal-Mart both saw the Web as an extension of their existing order processing and fulfillment, marketing, and branding efforts.

Each of the market entry strategies discussed above has seen its share of successes and failures. While the ultimate choice of strategy depends on a firm's existing brands, management strengths, operational strengths, and capital resources (Gulati and Garino, 2000), today most firms are opting for a mixed bricks-and-clicks strategy in the hope that it will enable them to reach profitability more quickly.

## ESTABLISHING THE CUSTOMER RELATIONSHIP

Once a firm chooses a market entry strategy, the next task is establishing a relationship with the customer. Traditional public relations and advertising media (newsprint, direct mail, magazines, television, and even radio) remain vital for establishing awareness of the firm. However, a number of unique Internet marketing techniques have emerged that have proven to be very powerful drivers of Web site traffic and purchases. Here we discuss several of these new techniques, including advertising networks, permission marketing, affiliate marketing, viral marketing, blog marketing, and social network marketing. The use of keyword purchases and pay-for-placement and rank on search engines (so-called "search engine marketing") is discussed in some detail in Chapter 8 as a special type of advertising or marketing communications.

### Advertising Networks

In the early years of e-commerce, firms placed ads on the few popular Web sites in existence, but by early 2000, there were hundreds of thousands of sites where ads could be displayed. Most firms by themselves, even very large firms, did not have the capabilities to place banner ads and marketing messages on thousands of Web sites, and monitor the results. Specialized marketing firms called **advertising networks** appeared to help firms take advantage of the powerful tracking and marketing potential of the Internet.

**advertising networks**
present users with banner advertisements based on a database of user behavioral data

Advertising networks represent the most sophisticated application of Internet database capabilities to date, and illustrate just how different Internet marketing is from traditional marketing. These networks sell advertising and marketing opportunities (slots) to companies who wish to buy exposure to an online audience. Advertising networks obtain their inventory of ad opportunities from a network of participating sites that want to display ads on their sites in return for receiving a payment from advertisers. These sites are usually referred to as Web publishers. The advertising network shares the revenue with the publisher. Advertising networks have developed software that tracks customer movements among the network members, say, from Amazon, to Travelocity, to Google, Yahoo, and eBay. At each visit the ad network software decides which banner ads, videos, and other ads to show the customer based in part on the customer's behavior at various sites on the network. For instance, at Travelocity, the customer may research a vacation to England. On Google, the customer may search for English cities. When the customer goes to Yahoo, he or she may be shown ads for raincoats. The advertiser works with the network to determine the rules for showing ads. If you wonder, for instance, why you see so many ads for home mortgages despite the fact you have never looked at an apartment or house for sale, it is because the advertising mortgage company and the ad network have determined your age demographic and geographic location, and on that basis, show mortgage ads to everyone meeting those criteria regardless of previous network behavior. Ad networks are not always very discriminating in their behavior.

Perhaps the best-known advertising network is DoubleClick, which released its first-generation tracking system, DART, in 1996. Google purchased DoubleClick for $3.1 billion in April 2007. Other advertising networks include 24/7 Real Media's Open AdStream (purchased by WPP, the world's largest advertising firm, for $649 million in June 2007), and aQuantive (purchased by Microsoft for $6.1 billion in May 2007).

Why are billions of dollars being invested in these companies? For technology firms such as Google and Microsoft, purchasing these companies allows them to buy large chunks of the online display advertising business, which amounts to about $3 billion a year in revenue. For marketing firms such as WPP, the purchase of 24/7 Real Media allows it to extend its traditional business of creating and placing ads, and develop a third line of business in the Internet display ad market.

DoubleClick serves about 60 billion ads per month (in round numbers, about 24,000 ads per second) and maintains over 100 million user profiles on individual Web consumers. Specialized ad servers are used to store and send to users the appropriate banner ads. All these systems rely on cookies, Web bugs, and massive backend user profile databases to pitch banner ads to users and record the results, including sales. This process allows feedback from the market to be entered into the database. For instance, DoubleClick's Intelligent Targeting service allows advertisers to send ads to consumers who have indicated a specific interest area, either through recent or frequent visits to particular types of Web sites, while its Boomerang service allows a Web site to target visitors to that site by advertising to those anonymous visitors when they visit other DoubleClick client sites.

**Figure 6.16** illustrates how these systems work. Advertising networks begin with a consumer requesting a page from a member of the advertising network (1). A connection is established with the third-party ad server (2). The ad server identifies

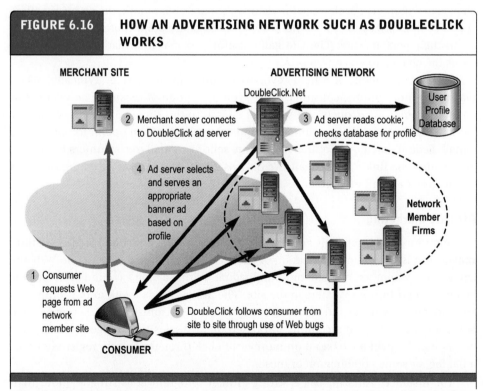

**FIGURE 6.16**  **HOW AN ADVERTISING NETWORK SUCH AS DOUBLECLICK WORKS**

Advertising networks have become controversial among privacy advocates because of their ability to track individual consumers across the Internet. We discuss privacy issues further in Chapter 8.

the user by reading the cookie file on the user's hard drive and checks its user profile database for the user's profile (3). The ad server selects an appropriate banner ad based on the user's previous purchases, interests, demographics, or other data in the profile (4). Whenever the user later goes online and visits any of the network member sites, the ad server recognizes the user and serves up the same or different ads regardless of the site content. The advertising network follows users from site to site through the use of Web bugs (5).

### Permission Marketing

**permission marketing**

marketing strategy in which companies obtain permission from consumers before sending them information or promotional messages

The phrase "**permission marketing**" was coined by author and consultant Seth Godin to describe the strategy of obtaining permission from consumers before sending them information or promotional messages (Godin, 1999). Godin's premise was that by obtaining permission to send information to consumers up front, companies are much more likely to be able to develop a customer relationship. When consumers agree to receive promotional messages, they are *opting in*; when they decide they do not want to receive such messages, they *opt out*.

Most consumers need an incentive to spend time reading promotional material, or to provide personal information companies can use to improve their own marketing. Godin's former company, Yoyodyne, pioneered the creation of online sweepstakes and games that gathered information from participants in return for the chance to win money and prizes. Another company, portal Iwon.com, gives users the chance to win money each week for visiting the site; each month, the company offers special bonus prizes to users who are willing to complete a more in-depth survey about their personal life. The site gains useful personal information, and the user earns the chance to win a free prize.

A key component of e-mail involves permission marketing. Typically, when placing an order online, consumers are given the option of receiving newsletters or announcements of products and sales via e-mail. In the United States, the default is usually "opt-in," and the consumer is required to check off an option to not receive e-mail. Federal law now requires merchants sending e-mail to consumers to provide an Unsubscribe link for all e-mail. We discuss e-mail as a marketing communication tool in greater detail in Chapter 7.

### Affiliate Marketing

**affiliate marketing**

one Web site agrees to pay another Web site a commission for new business opportunities it refers to the site

In the offline world, referrals are one of the best sources of qualified leads. **Affiliate marketing** is the online application of this marketing method, where one Web site agrees to pay another Web site or an individual writing a blog a commission for new business opportunities it refers to the site. The affiliate adds a link to the company's Web site on its own site and encourages its visitors to patronize its marketing partner. Some affiliates are paid a commission based on any sales that are generated, while others may be paid a fee based on number of click-throughs or new registrations, or a flat fee, or some combination of these.

For instance, Amazon has a strong affiliate program consisting of more than 1 million participant sites, called Associates, which receive up to 15% on sales their referrals generate. Members of eBay's Affiliates Program can earn between $20 and

$35 for each active registered user sent to eBay. Amazon, eBay, and other large e-commerce companies with affiliate programs typically administer such programs themselves. Smaller e-commerce firms who wish to use affiliate marketing often decide to join an *affiliate network* (sometimes called an *affiliate broker*), which acts as an intermediary. The affiliate network brings would-be affiliates and merchants seeking affiliates together, helps affiliates set up the necessary links on their Web site, tracks all activity, and arranges all payments. Leading affiliate networks include Commission Junction and LinkShare. In return for their services, affiliate networks typically take about 20% of any fee that would be payable to the affiliate. The total size of the affiliate market is not known, but industry experts estimate that around 10% of all retail online sales are generated through affiliate programs (as compared, say, to search engine ads which account for over 30% of online sales).

A key benefit of affiliate marketing is the fact that it typically operates on a "pay-for-performance" basis. Affiliates provide qualified sales leads in return for pre-agreed upon compensation. Another advantage is the existence of an established user base that a marketer can immediately tap into through an affiliate. For affiliates, the appeal is a steady income—potentially large—that can result from such relationships. In addition, the presence of another company's logo or brand name can provide a measure of prestige and credibility.

Affiliate marketing can have some drawbacks, however, if not managed carefully. Too many links that are not relevant to a firm's primary focus can lead to brand confusion, for instance. Affiliate marketing works best when affiliates choose products and services that match and supplement the content of their own Web site. Web sites with affiliate links also risk "losing" those customers who click on a link and then never return, unless the Web site takes action to prevent this, such as by having the link open a new window that when closed returns the customer to the original site.

## Viral Marketing in the Web 2.0 Milieu

Just as affiliate marketing involves using a trusted Web site to encourage users to visit other sites, **viral marketing** is the process of getting customers to pass along a company's marketing message to friends, family, and colleagues. It's the online version of word-of-mouth advertising, which spreads even faster than in the real world. In the offline world, next to television, word of mouth is the second most important means by which consumers find out about new products. Millions of online adults in the United States are "influencers" who share their opinions about products in a variety of online settings. In addition to increasing the size of a company's customer base, customer referrals also have other advantages: they are less expensive to acquire since existing customers do all the acquisition work, and they tend to use online support services less, preferring to turn back to the person who referred them for advice. Also, because they cost so little to acquire and keep, referred customers begin to generate profits for a company much earlier than customers acquired through other marketing methods. There are a number of online venues where viral marketing appears in the Web 2.0 era. E-mail used to be the primary online venue for e-mail marketing ("please forward this e-mail to your friends"), but Web 2.0 venues such as blogs and social networking sites are beginning to play a major role as described below.

**viral marketing**
the process of getting customers to pass along a company's marketing message to friends, family, and colleagues

Half.com's Take Five! program is an example of viral marketing, where registered users at the site selling used books, music, movies, and games are given an incentive (coupons) to tell their friends about the site. When a user submits a friend's name and e-mail address on Half.com's Take Five page, Half.com sends the friend a coupon valid for $5 off the friend's first order of $10 or more. Then, when the friend uses the Take Five coupon, Half.com gives the referring user a $5 coupon that also can be used on a $10 order. The process of viral marketing can also involve users who do not know each other. When a consumer decides to make a major purchase, such as a new mountain bike, getting advice and opinions from people who own such bikes is usually the first step. And with the Internet, it is fairly easy to find and read reviews of various bike models written by knowledge-able consumers. Sites such as Epinions.com and ConsumerReports.org provide objective product reviews by people who have bought and used a long list of products and services. Armed with feedback and input from online aficionados, consumers can then click through to an e-commerce site and make a purchase. Epinions has links to a number of affiliate online retailers who pay a fee back to the site for each purchase that originates there.

### Blog Marketing

Blogs have become a part of mainstream online culture (see Chapter 3 for a description of blogs and RSS). Around 113 million Americans read a blog at least once a month in 2010, and around 26 million have created blogs. The number of blog readers is expected to grow to about 150 million, and blog creators to 33 million by 2014 (eMarketer, 2010d). Thousands of high-ranking corporate officials, politicians, journalists, academics, and government officials have created blogs, along, of course, with the rest of us. Blog creators tend to be young, broadband users, Internet veter-ans, wealthy, and educated. It did not take long for marketers to discover this large number of "eyeballs" and seek out ways to market and advertise to them. Because blogs are based on the personal opinions of the writers, they are ideal locations to start a viral marketing campaign.

Blogs, like ordinary Web sites, can be used to display both branding ads not geared towards sales, as well as advertising aimed at making sales. But because blogs are usually created by private individuals wishing to make a public statement, bloggers do not have the Web marketing and advertising resources of large corporations, and the number of eyeballs viewing any one site is miniscule compared to portal Web sites such as Yahoo. The problem is how to efficiently aggregate these tiny audiences into a significant block of eyeballs worthy of an advertiser's attention.

One solution is to build an advertising network of bloggers and allow bloggers to subscribe to this network, agreeing to display ads on their blogs, and then paying them a fee for each visitor who clicks on the ad. Within the last two years, two major players in the blogging industry, Technorati and Six Apart, have launched blog advertising networks designed to connect blog sites with advertisers. Blogads.com provides a similar service.

Google's AdSense is also a major blog marketer. The AdSense service "reads" a blog and identifies the subject of the blog's postings. Then AdSense places appropriate ads on the blog, adjusted to the blog's content. For instance, BoingBoing.net, a very popular technology blog known for its love of gadgets, displays ads from major advertisers like HP, Verizon, and Rackspace.

Given the growth of this phenomenon—well over 50% a year in the past few years—and the novelty, blog marketing will likely show substantial gains over the next several years. In 2009, blog advertising revenue was estimated to be about $530 million, growing to about $746 million by 2012, although this estimate does not take into account the impact of the recession (eMarketer, 2008a). There may also be limits on this phenomenon just as with e-mail marketing. The *blogosphere* (the Internet's aggregate blogging community) is already buzzing about blogs set up merely for personal financial gain. The founder of one site on asbestos litigation, for instance, freely admits he set up the site in order to tap into the revenues flowing to individuals and law firms in connection with asbestos litigation (Rodgers, 2005). Firms are tempted to hire bloggers to report favorably on their products, leading to what one wag called "blogola." This behavior reduces the credibility and effectiveness of blog marketing, and makes larger advertisers fearful of advertising on blogs when they cannot control the content of the blog.

We cannot leave a discussion of blog marketing without mentioning Twitter. As you learned in Chapter 2, Twitter is an example of microblogging—mini-blog postings (tweets) of 140 characters or less. Twitter has attracted enormous attention in the popular press in 2010, and marketers (and Twitter) are still figuring out how best to exploit the service. Marketers use Twitter to gather and share information from and with consumers, and deliver special offers. Some marketers are also experimenting with applications that aggregate or segment Twitter feeds, such as Federated Media's ExecTweets.

## Social Network Marketing and Social Shopping

Social networks in the offline world are collections of people who voluntarily communicate with one another over an extended period of time. Online social networks, such as Facebook, MySpace, LinkedIn, Ning, Tagged, Xanga, Orkut, Friendster, Buzznet, and Bebo, are Web sites that enable users to communicate with one another, form close group and individual relationships, and share interests, values, and ideas. Individuals establish online profiles, which may include pictures, and then invite their friends to create their own profiles and link to their profile. The network grows by word of mouth and through e-mail links. According to Nielsen, nearly 25% of the total time spent online in June 2010 was spent on social network sites, up from around 15% a year ago (Nielsen Company, 2010). The fastest growing smartphone applications are social network apps: about 30% of smartphone users use their phones to visit social sites (comScore, 2010). Marketers will spend over $1.6 billion on social network marketing in 2010, about 5% of all online marketing. It is estimated that Facebook, the most popular social network, will generate about $835 million in online ad revenues in 2010, and MySpace, about $320 million. These two sites together account for around 70% of all online social networking ad revenues (eMarketer Inc., 2010e).

Firms are beginning to harness the spectacular popularity and growth of social networking sites by marketing to participants. The idea is that consumers will tend to buy what their friends buy and recommend. All of the top 50 online retailers have Facebook profiles. At Yub.com, which has several patents on **social shopping**, users can view their friends' purchases and interests, click an image of the products, and link to a Web site where they can buy the products. Yub.com keeps the referral fees of 10%–15%. Friendster uses similar techniques to send customers to Amazon, keeping a referral fee. Other online retail sites are attempting to create their own user communities. At Overstock.com, users of that site's auction service are invited to create free online profiles, and share news of their recent purchases with friends at the site. Social marketing is expanding rapidly in B2B applications such as lead generation, customer service, and podcasts (thought leadership papers) (eMarketer, Inc., 2010f). *Insight on Business* story, *Social Network Marketing: Let's Buy Together*, further examines the emergence of social network marketing.

**social shopping**
sharing product choices with friends online

## Mobile Platform Marketing

With more than 83 million mobile device users in the United States accessing the Internet, mobile marketing is the fastest growing marketing platform. Although still in its infancy, mobile marketing includes the use of display banner ads, games, e-mail, text messaging, in-store messaging, and location-based services. Over 90% of retail marketing professionals have plans for mobile marketing campaigns in 2010. Estimating the size of this market is difficult, but most estimates place mobile platform marketing revenues at about $600 million in 2010, composed mostly of display ads and location-based services. By 2013, these revenues are expected to rise to about $1.3 billion (eMarketer, 2009b).

## Marketing Based on the Wisdom of Crowds

So far we have described Web 2.0 social marketing techniques in which firms push the message to the customer by purchasing advertising, sending e-mails, and promoting events, and contests. This certainly is one way of establishing a relationship with the customer. But in the Web 2.0 era, there are a number of techniques where the customer speaks to the firm, and the firm adjusts its products and services accordingly. In this new relationship, the customers are in charge of the message, and this is not always a very comfortable position for a firm if the message is negative.

**The Wisdom of the Crowds** Is it possible that decisions, predictions, or estimates made by a large group of people are better and more accurate than decisions made by any individual, or small group of experts, in the group? In 2004, James Surowiecki wrote a book titled *The Wisdom of Crowds* exploring this thesis. There are plenty of precedents for the notion that large aggregates produce better estimates and judgments than individuals or small groups of experts. For instance, one premise of democracy is that a very large number of diverse and independent voters, will over the long run, produce superior political decisions than a single dictator, king, bureaucrat, or committee. Economists have studied the problem of how to find the best restaurant in a strange town. Answer: the restaurant with the largest crowds (surely the locals know where there's good food). In financial theory, the best estimate of the current value of a firm

# INSIGHT ON BUSINESS

## SOCIAL NETWORK MARKETING: LET'S BUY TOGETHER

Birds of a feather flock together. In the age of online social networks, its "hang together, buy together." The idea that consumers compose themselves into flocks and tend to buy what their friends buy is, of course, not new. One of the earliest findings of research on radio mass marketing campaigns in the 1930s was that market communications have a multi-level structure: the message goes from a central broadcaster to influential people in thousands of local communities (who sometimes are the first adopters of a product), and then the message travels to other group members who are influenced to buy. This insight translates directly to online social communities in 2010.

Social network marketing is arguably the single most exciting and fastest growing online marketing development in the last 10 years. Social network sites of all kinds are ideal locations for a conversation to occur between brands and customers. With over 141 million unique visitors to social networks in June 2010, social networking sites such as Facebook, MySpace, Twitter, Flickr, YouTube, and scores of niche sites are natural targets for marketers who want to be where their customers, and their customers friends are. Facebook alone has 500 million users worldwide. In April 2010, Twitter announced its new ad platform called "Promoted Tweets" where firms can post marketing messages that blend into users' streams of tweets.

Alongside these social network and microblogging sites are social news/social bookmarking sites such as Digg, Reddit, Delicious (formerly Newsvine), and StumbleUpon, which attract additional millions of viewers. At social news/bookmarking sites, visitors send links to stories or their favorite bookmarked sites to their friends and colleagues. The fate of news stories and blogs depends on how well these recommendations are received. Blogs are yet another online forum for writers to express themselves and readers to respond, creating a community of responses. The top 25 most popular blogs tracked by comScore Media Metrix draw over 77 million unique visitors a month. There are an estimated 30 million people on social networ sites who express opinions on products and brands and post to blogs. On the face of it, these blog contributors are potential "influentials." Social network sites are the equivalent of offline word-of-mouth networks, which are the most powerful influence on consumer behavior. Social network sites have a direct influence on purchase decisions: 68% of social network users report they would purchase a product or visit a retail store based on a positive referral by a friend. It's word of mouth on digital steroids.

A whole new lexicon has emerged to describe the new social network marketing opportunities:

- Online word-of-mouth-marketing: Giving people a reason to talk about your products online
- Buzz marketing: Using high-profile entertainment, games, or news to get people talking about your products online
- Online viral marketing: Creating messages designed to be passed along by e-mail, blogging, or networking with others
- Online community marketing: Forming online niche communities to share interests about your brand
- Online grassroots marketing: Organizing volunteers or paying people to reach out to their friends online

(continued)

- Influencer marketing: Finding people in online communities who are opinion leaders or key influencers
- Conversation marketing: Interesting or fun online advertising to start word-of-mouth campaigns via e-mail, blogs, and networking profiles
- Brand blogging: Creating blogs, or participating on blogs, or hiring bloggers to share and promote the value of your brands

Marketers are starting to follow the opportunity: it is estimated that social network marketing will hit $1.3 billion in 2010, still less than 5% of all online marketing, but growing at 13% a year. This makes social marketing the fastest growing form of online marketing just at a time when search engine marketing growth is slowing. There are risks, however. For instance, you cannot control what bloggers, tweeters, chatters, and networkers say about your brand or products, and while they may provide valuable feedback that is useful for product design and improvement, unfair characterizations of your products, intentions, or policies can kill sales. You will not want your brand name associated with some raunchy content found at YouTube and Facebook. How do you know what the chattering masses are saying about your brand, and what can you do about it? One possibility: listen and respond.

Levi's was one of the first national brands to use Facebook and Twitter and allow consumers to socialize and share their purchases with friends. The Levi's Facebook page has posted 500,000 "Like" messages posted by friends sharing their favorite jeans. Within the first week of its share campaign, Levis received 4,000 "Likes". The company began using Twitter in 2010 by creating a "Levi's Guy," 23-year-old USC graduate Gareth, to interest customers. He has over 6,000 followers and is responsible for responding to and engaging in conversations about the Levi's brand on Twitter. Geo-targeted event ads are next on the agenda: if you're at a SXSW concert next year

expect to receive tweets from Levi's. Levi's director of digital marketing, Megan O'Connor, said "The engagement with both Twitter and Facebook is about creating and informing brand ambassadors that will help drive sales through their own actions and word of mouth."

Social network marketing is very different from traditional media marketing where the firm can control the message and the medium. Social network marketing is a no-holds-barred dialogue between the customer and the company. A number of firms have sprung up to help solve this problem with "social media analytics." For instance, Nielsen BuzzMetrics is a company formed by the media ratings firm A.C. Nielsen that uses search engines to sweep the Internet for phrases, opinions, keywords, sentences, and images that impact one of its customers' brands. It then analyzes the vocabulary, language patterns, and phrasing to determine if the comments are positive or negative, and the demographics of the people making the comments wherever possible. In a sense, it is using the Internet as an online focus group. BuzzMetrics warns "Every day, millions of consumers converse in online communities, discussion boards, blogs, and social networks. They turn to the Internet to share opinions, advice, grievances, and recommendations. Are you listening, connecting, and responding in a way that protects and promotes your brand?" Other firms performing similar services are Umbria, Cymfony, and Biz360. Coke has used BuzzMetrics to gauge responses to a video it posted on YouTube; ConAgra has used these techniques to anticipate lifestyle and food trends; Sony has used these firms to track interest in its computer games.

The online brand intelligence field is also moving towards real-time monitoring of the social network ecosystem. VML, based in Kansas City, a unit of WPP Group, tracks the blogosphere in real time with its SEER™ brand management

(continued)

tool and produces visual maps of the blogosphere that pinpoint the originators of comments about a firm, the subscribers, and the links among them (see screenshot below). They can tell a customer such as Adidas that the blogosphere is complaining about fading colors on the Predator, a new soccer cleat. As a result, Adidas began telling customers at the point of purchase to treat the leather before wearing the cleats, and then changed the formulation of dyes used in the color process.

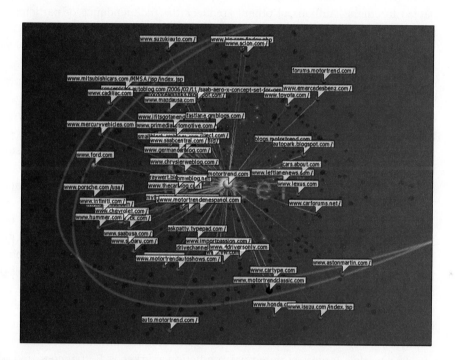

**SOURCES:** '"The Blogosphere:--Colliding with Social and Mainstream Media," by Paul Verna, eMarketer, September 2010, "Social Media Draws a Crowd: Start-Ups and Established Agencies Look to Carve a Niche in Online Action," by Suzanne Vranica, *Wall Street Journal*, July 18, 2010; "How Social Media Drives New Business: Six Case Studies," by Leena Rao, TechCrunch.com, July 17, 2010; "Linking Customer Loyalty With Social Networking," by Stephanie Clifford, *New York Times*, April 28, 2010; "Marketers Watch as Friends Interact Online," by Emily Steel, *New York Times*, April 15, 2010; "Twitter Rolls Out Ads," by Jessica Vascellaro and Emily Steel, *Wall Street Journal*, April 14, 2010; "Social Media Analytics," by Rick Lawrence, et. al., OR-MS Today, February 2010; "Social Network Ad Spending: 2010 Outlook," by Debra Aho Williamson, eMarketer, December 2009.

can be found in free, open markets where millions of participants vote with their pocketbooks. In statistics, the best estimate of the value of a parameter is the mean or average arrived at by taking thousands of independent samples of the population.

In general, crowds are wise when there are many decision makers who make decisions independent of one another, come from diverse backgrounds, and where there is a mechanism (like a market or an election process) that can aggregate opinions to produce a single outcome or choice. However, there are many crowds which do not fit these conditions, and the result can be a failure of collective judgment.

Mobs, herds, and runaway stock market bubbles are examples of where crowds can produce very bad estimates and decisions. In these cases, the lack of diversity and independence among participants can lead to an "information cascade," which prevents independent judgments. If you recall standing around a luggage carousel at an airport after a flight, you already know that crowds behave in strange ways that are not rational at all!

Nevertheless, when the four conditions of wise crowds are met, Surowiecki argues, crowds produce superior judgments, forecasts, and estimates. In the eyes of many, the conditions for crowds to be "wise" are quite rare, especially so in a "connected" Internet world where millions of people are blogging, networking, and e-mailing. Being connected to others—millions of others—reduces the independence of participants and makes them more susceptible to manipulation and hysteria (Surowiecki, 2004).

The idea of the social basis of wisdom and knowledge is reflected in many Web 2.0 applications. For instance, Wikipedia is based on the idea that millions of diverse contributors can produce an encyclopedia of knowledge that is superior to those produced by small groups of experts. In marketing, the "wisdom of crowds" concept suggests that firms should consult with thousands of customers first as a way of establishing a relationship with them, and second, to better understand how their products and services are used and appreciated by their customers (or why they are rejected by customers). Actively soliciting the comments of your customers builds trust and sends the message to your customers that you care what they are thinking, and that you need their advice. There are new forums where firms can apply these techniques.

**Prediction Markets** While all markets make predictions or estimates of value based on buy-sell transactions among a group of participants, or bets among a group of bettors with a "gambling house" clearing the bets, prediction markets are established as peer-to-peer betting markets where participants make bets on specific outcomes of, say, quarterly sales of a new product, designs for new products, or outcomes of political elections. Participants make bets with their own funds that a certain outcome will occur. Others bet against that outcome. The result is that an asset is created (a contract, for example), which reflects the market's aggregate value for that outcome.

The world's largest commercial prediction market is Betfair.com, founded in 2000, where you bet for or against specific outcomes on football games, horse races, and whether or not the Dow Jones will go up or down in a single day. The Iowa Electronic Markets (IEM) is an academic market focused on elections. You can place bets on the outcome of local and national elections. The IEM allows traders to buy and sell contracts based on political election results and economic indicators. The contract is the asset with a value determined by long buyers and short sellers. Positions are limited to $500.

Let's say you trying to decide which of two Web site designs works best for your firm. Rather than have a small internal committee make the decision, or a few senior executives, why not let thousands of your customers bet which Web site is most effective by placing bets on a contest Web site. You will of course have to hand out $100 worth of script money (not legal tender) to each customer, and offer them a chance to buy and sell shares in a market based on their opinion of which would be the most successful with your customers. After a week of buying and selling, the market closes and the winning Web site will have the highest share price. The reward for participating and having chosen the winning site can be anything from $100 in cash to a year's supply of your services.

**Folksonomies and Social Tagging** Another application of the "wisdom of crowds" to marketing is the use of a large number of people to classify objects, which could be movies, photos, books, PowerPoint slides, or consumer products. Folksonomy is a play on the term "taxonomy," which refers to any classification schema for organizing a collection of objects. Generally, taxonomies are created by individuals or a group of experts. Folksonomies are created by groups of people looking at a set of objects, and then tagging them (or bookmarking them) using their own criteria. Folksonomies are a bottom-up, self-organizing activity in which thousands of people classify objects.

A related phenomenon that relies on large numbers of online users to identify and classify products, services, events, and content is social tagging. Social tagging sites allow millions of people to post their bookmarks or "favorite" content to a single site where others can review the links. If your Diggs become popular as other people Digg them, they will bounce to the top of the list of Diggs where millions more people can see and review them.

As an online marketer, how can you use social tagging and folksonomies to your advantage? One way to influence social tagging sites is to organize the placement of social tags by customers who love your products. Alternatively, ask your customers on your Web site to tag your site, and send it to their friends. Setting aside the ethics of such moves, to a large extent these phenomena are inherently difficult to manipulate, and the act of attempted manipulation can bring aspersion down on a firm.

## Leveraging Brands

Brand leveraging is one of the most successful online customer acquisition strategies (Carpenter, 2000). **Brand leveraging** refers to the process of using the power of an existing brand to acquire new customers for a new product or service. For instance, while Tab was the first to discover a huge market for diet cola drinks, Coca-Cola ultimately succeeded in dominating the market by leveraging the Coke brand to a new product called Diet Coke.

In the online world, some researchers predicted that offline brands would not be able to make the transition to the Web because customers would soon learn who was offering products at the cheapest prices and brand premiums would disappear (price transparency). But this has not occurred. In retail, firms such as Wal-Mart and JCPenney have leaped into the top 10 online retail firms in a very short period in large part because of the strength of their offline brand, which gave them the ability to attract millions of their offline customers to their Web sites. In the financial service industry sector, firms such as Wells Fargo, Citibank, Fidelity, and Merrill Lynch have all succeeded in acquiring millions of online customers based on their large offline customer bases and brands. In the content provider industry, the *Wall Street Journal* and *Consumer Reports* have become among the most successful subscription-based content providers. A major advantage of brand leveraging—when compared to a start-up venture with no brand recognition—is that it significantly reduces the costs of acquiring new customers (Kotler and Armstrong, 2009).

**brand leveraging**
using the power of an existing brand to acquire new customers for a new product or service

## CUSTOMER RETENTION: STRENGTHENING THE CUSTOMER RELATIONSHIP

The Internet offers several extraordinary marketing techniques for building a strong relationship with customers and for differentiating products and services.

### Personalization and One-to-One Marketing

**one-to-one marketing**

segmenting the market based on a precise and timely understanding of an individual's needs, targeting specific marketing messages to these individuals, and then positioning the product vis-à-vis competitors to be truly unique

No Internet-based marketing technique has received more popular and academic comment than "one-to-one" or "personalized marketing." **One-to-one marketing** segments the market on the basis of individuals (not groups), based on a precise and timely understanding of their needs, targeting specific marketing messages to these individuals, and then positioning the product vis-à-vis competitors to be truly unique (Peppers and Rogers, 1997). One-to-one marketing is the ultimate form of market segmentation, targeting, and positioning—where the segments are individuals.

The movement toward market segmentation has been ongoing since the development of systematic market research and mass media in the 1930s. However, e-commerce and the Internet are different in that they enable personalized one-to-one marketing to occur on a mass scale. **Figure 6.17** depicts the continuum of marketing: from mass marketing of undifferentiated products, where one size and one price fits all, to personalized one-to-one marketing.

| FIGURE 6.17 | THE MASS MARKET-PERSONALIZATION CONTINUUM | | |
|---|---|---|---|
| **MARKETING STRATEGIES** | **MARKETING ATTRIBUTES** | | |
| | **Product** | **Target** | **Pricing** | **Techniques** |
| Mass Marketing | Simple | All consumers | One nation, one price | Mass media |
| Direct Marketing | Stratified | Segments | One price | Targeted communications, e.g., mail and phone |
| Micromarketing | Complex | Micro-segments | Variable pricing | Segment profiles |
| Personalized, One-to-one Marketing | Highly complex | Individual | Unique pricing | Individual and social network profiles |

Personalized one-to-one marketing is part of a continuum of marketing strategies. The choice of strategy depends on the nature of the product as well as the technologies that are available to enable various strategies.

*Mass marketing*, based on national media messages aimed at a single national audience and with a single national price, is appropriate for products that are relatively simple and attractive to all consumers in a single form. Think of Coke, Tide, and McDonalds. *Direct marketing*, which is based on direct mail or phone messages and aimed at segments of the market likely to purchase and which has little variation in price (but special offers to loyal customers), is most often used for products that can be stratified into different categories. *Micromarketing*, which is aimed at geographical units (neighborhoods, cities) or specialized market segments (technology buffs), is the first form of true database marketing. Frito-Lay, for instance, maintains a national sales database for each of 10,000 route sales personnel and over 50,000 store outlets. Frito-Lay marketers know precisely at the end of every day how many small bags of Salsa Chips sell in Los Angeles, and how many bags of Ranch Chips sell in Cambridge, Massachusetts, store by store. Although seemingly simple, the corn chip can take on fairly complex and nuanced taste experiences that attract different customers in different neighborhoods. Using its database, Frito-Lay dynamically adjusts prices to market conditions and competitor product and pricing, every day.

Personalized one-to-one marketing is suitable for products (1) that can be produced in very complex forms, depending on individual tastes, (2) whose price can be adjusted to the level of personalization, and (3) where the individual's tastes and preferences can be effectively gauged.

A good example of personalization at work is Amazon or Barnesandnoble.com. Both sites greet registered visitors (based on cookie files), recommend recent books based on user preferences (based on a user profile in their database), and expedite checkout procedures based on prior purchases.

Several U.S. firms such as the New York Times and Orbitz have adopted a form of permission-based, personalized "direct-messaging" banner advertising in which customers are shown ads addressed to them by name, mentioning some of their past purchases. For instance, Dotomi Direct Messages (dotomi.com) is a marketing company that develops personalized banner ads for publisher Web sites. Consumers agree to receive messages from various companies, and the ads are personal in the sense of being based on the consumer's prior purchases and behavior. Invented by Yair Goldfinger, who created instant messaging while working for AOL, the system uses cookies to identify returning visitors to a network of sites. In a sense, the ads are specially built for each unique user. The response rate to traditional banner ads is currently about 0.1% in 2010, whereas the response rate to personalized banner ads is about 34% (Giuliani, 2009). Unfortunately, consumers who sign up for this service do not receive fewer of the old-style, mass market, banner ads.

Is Web-based personalization as good as the personal attention you would receive from a local, independent bookstore owner? Probably not. Nevertheless, these Web-based techniques use more individual knowledge and personalization than traditional mass media, and more than a direct mail post card.

Personalization is not necessarily an unmitigated good, however. Research indicates that most consumers appreciate personalization when it increases their sense of control and freedom, such as through personalized order tracking, purchase histories, databases of personalized information to ensure quicker transactions during future sessions, and opt-in e-mail notification of new products and special deals. The online buyers participating in Wolfinbarger and Gilly's focus groups saw personalization as negative, however, when it resulted in unsolicited offers or reduced anonymity; such features are perceived to take away user control and freedom (Wolfinbarger and Gilly, 2001). Furthermore, although personalization technologies have made significant advances over the past several years, it is still difficult for a computer to accurately understand and anticipate the interests and needs of a customer. "Personalized" offers that miss the mark can lead to more customer disdain than satisfaction (Waltner, 2001). How often do you open up a Web site such as Yahoo and find ads that are totally irrelevant to your interests?

### Customization and Customer Co-Production

**customization**

changing the product, not just the marketing message, according to user preferences

**customer co-production**

in the Web environment, takes customization one step further by allowing the customer to interactively create the product

Customization is an extension of personalization. **Customization** means changing the product—not just the marketing message—according to user preferences. **Customer co-production** means the users actually think up the innovation and help create the new product. For instance, studies of new and improved products find that many come directly from intensive users. The operating system Linux is built by users, and innovations in mountain bikes, sail boards, sailboats and gear, ski equipment, and thousands of other industrial products often came from "lead users" (von Hippel, 2005, 1994). Customer co-production in the Web environment takes customization one step further by allowing the customer to interactively create the product.

Many leading companies now offer "build-to-order" customized products on the Internet on a large scale, creating product differentiation and, hopefully, customer loyalty. Customers appear to be willing to pay a little more for a unique product. The key to making the process affordable is to build a standardized architecture that lets consumers combine a variety of options. For example, Nike has been offering customized sneakers through its Nike iD program on its Web site since 1999. Consumers can choose the type of shoe, colors, material, and even a logo of up to eight characters. Nike transmits the orders via computers to specially equipped plants in China and Korea. The sneakers cost only $10 extra and take about three weeks to reach the customer. At the Shop M&M's Web site, customers can get their own message printed on custom-made M&Ms; Timberland.com also offers online customization of its boots.

*Information goods*—goods whose value is based on information content—are also ideal for this level of differentiation. For instance, the New York Times—and many other content distributors—allows customers to select the news they want to see on a daily basis. Many Web sites, particularly portal sites such as Yahoo, MSN, and AOL, allow customers to create their own customized version of the Web site. Such pages frequently require security measures such as usernames and passwords to ensure privacy and confidentiality.

### Transactive Content

According to several studies, the most common reasons people go online are to communicate (e-mail) and to find information. As we noted in Section 6.1, shopping is not the primary Internet consumer activity.

Marketers have adjusted their Web marketing strategies accordingly. The result is "transactive content," a term originally coined by Forrester Research (Forrester Research, 1997, 1998). **Transactive content** results from the combination of traditional content, such as articles and product descriptions, with dynamic information—such as new product announcements—culled from product databases, tailored to each user's profile. Such applications dynamically respond to user needs and preferences, for instance, by featuring a product within a price range typically preferred by the customer on the order page. You might be reading an article on travel to Africa at Iexplore.com, a travel company with an extensive Web site for adventure-travel advice, products, and services. Based on data drawn from your user profile as well as real-time clickstream behavior (for instance, you had previously expressed an interest in water sports), you might be served a link to information on kayaking safaris in Africa. Transactions, content, and interactivity are combined into a seamless experience.

**transactive content**
results from the combination of traditional content, such as articles and product descriptions, with dynamic information culled from product databases, tailored to each user's profile

## Customer Service

A Web site's approach to customer service can significantly help or hurt its marketing efforts. Online customer service is more than simply following through on order fulfillment; it has to do with users' ability to communicate with a company and obtain desired information in a timely manner. Customer service can help reduce consumer frustration, cut the number of abandoned shopping carts, and increase sales.

According to Wolfinbarger and Gilly, most consumers want to, and will, serve themselves as long as the information they need to do so is relatively easy to find. Online buyers largely do not expect or desire "high-touch" service unless they have questions or problems, in which case they want relatively speedy answers that are responsive to their individual issue. Wolfinbarger and Gilly noted that participants in their study said that the first opportunity to cement them to an online brand came when they had a problem with the order; customer loyalty increased substantially when online buyers learned that customer service representatives were available online or at an 800-number and were willing and able to resolve the situation quickly. Conversely, online buyers who did not receive satisfaction at these critical incidents terminated their relationship and became willing to do business with a site that might charge more, but offered better customer service (Wolfinbarger and Gilly, 2001).

There are a number of tools that companies can use to encourage interaction with prospects and customers and provide customer service—FAQs, customer service chat systems, intelligent agents, and automated response systems—in addition to the customer relationship management systems described in the preceding section.

**Frequently asked questions (FAQs)**, a text-based listing of common questions and answers, provide an inexpensive way to anticipate and address customer concerns. Adding an FAQ page on a Web site linked to a search engine helps users track down needed information more quickly, enabling them to help themselves resolve questions and concerns. By directing customers to the FAQs page first, Web sites can give customers answers to common questions. If a question and answer do not appear, it is important for sites to make contact with a live person simple and easy. Offering an e-mail link to customer service at the bottom of the FAQs page is one solution.

**frequently asked questions (FAQs)**
a text-based listing of common questions and answers

**real-time customer service chat systems**
a company's customer service representatives interactively exchange text-based messages with one or more customers on a real-time basis

**Real-time customer service chat systems** (in which a company's customer service representatives interactively exchange text-based messages with one or more customers on a real-time basis) are an increasingly popular way for companies to assist online shoppers during a purchase. Chats with online customer service representatives can provide direction, answer questions, and troubleshoot technical glitches that can kill a sale. Leading vendors of customer service chat systems include LivePerson and InstantService. Vendors claim that chat is significantly less expensive than telephone-based customer service. However, critics point out this conclusion may be based on optimistic assumptions that chat representatives can assist three or four customers at once, and that chat sessions are shorter than phone sessions. Also, chat sessions are text sessions, and not as rich as talking with a human being over the phone. On the plus side, chat has been reported to raise per-order sales figures, providing sales assistance by allowing companies to "touch" customers during the decision-making process. According to comScore, anecdotal evidence suggests that chat can lower shopping cart abandonment rates, increase the number of items purchased per transaction, and increase the dollar value of transactions. In 2010, about 5% of online retailers offered live chat, while another 5% offered automated virtual chat. However, 37% of online retailers plan to adopt these services in the next year because they significantly increase sales (Forrester Research, 2010b; Internet Retailer, 2010). "Click to call" or "live call" is another version of a real-time online customer service system, in which the customer clicks a link or accepts an invitation to have a customer service representative call them on the telephone.

*Intelligent agent technology*, described in Chapter 3, is another way customers are providing assistance to online shoppers. Intelligent agents are part of an effort to reduce costly contact with customer service representatives. **Automated response systems** send e-mail order confirmations and acknowledgments of e-mailed inquiries, in some cases letting the customer know that it may take a day or two to actually research an answer to their question. Automating shipping confirmations and order status reports are also common. Although the upfront expenditure to install and implement automated systems may be costly, the potential reduction in calls to live telephone operators and online help centers is an incentive for companies to increasingly automate as many aspects of the online shopping experience as possible. Firms must use and monitor automated response systems carefully, however, or they may backfire. Many customers still resent automated communications, even if they appear personalized. If automated replies are not useful, they may drive consumers to use live support even more.

**automated response system**
sends e-mail order confirmations and acknowledgments of e-mailed inquiries

## NET PRICING STRATEGIES

In a competitive market, firms compete for customers through price as well as product features, scope of operations, and focus. **Pricing** (putting a value on goods and services) is an integral part of marketing strategy. Together, price and quality determine customer value. Pricing of e-commerce goods has proved very difficult for both entrepreneurs and investors to understand.

In traditional firms, the prices of traditional goods—such as books, drugs, and automobiles—are usually based on their fixed and variable costs as well as the market's

**pricing**
putting a value on goods and services

**demand curve** (the quantity of goods that can be sold at various prices). Fixed costs are the costs of building the production facility. *Variable costs* are costs involved in running the production facility—mostly labor. In a competitive market, with undifferentiated goods, prices tend toward their *marginal costs* (the incremental cost of producing the next unit) once manufacturers have paid the fixed costs to enter the business.

Firms usually "discover" their demand curves by testing out various price and volume bundles, closely watching their cost structure. Normally, prices are set to maximize profits. A profit-maximizing company sets its prices so that the *marginal revenue* (the revenue a company receives from the next unit sold) from a product just equals its marginal costs. If a firm's marginal revenue is higher than its marginal costs, it would want to lower prices a bit and sell more product (why leave money on the table when you can sell a few more units?). If its marginal revenue for selling a product is lower than its marginal costs, then the company would want to reduce volume a bit and charge a higher price (why lose money on each additional sale?).

During the early days of e-commerce, something unusual happened. Sellers were pricing their products far below their marginal costs. Some sites were losing money on every sale. How could this be? New economics? New technology? The Internet Age? No. Internet merchants could sell below their marginal costs (even giving away products for free) simply because a large number of entrepreneurs and their venture capitalist backers thought this was a worthwhile activity, at least in the short term. The idea was to attract "eyeballs" with free goods and services, and then later, once the consumer was part of a large, committed audience, charge advertisers enough money to make a profit, and (maybe) charge customers subscription fees for value-added services (the so-called *"piggy-back" strategy* in which a small number of users can be convinced to pay for premium services that are piggy-backed upon a larger audience that receives standard or reduced value services). To a large extent, social networking sites and user-generated content sites have resurrected this revenue model with a focus on the growth in audience size and not short-term profits. To understand the behavior of entrepreneurial firms, it is helpful to examine a traditional demand curve (see **Figure 6.18**).

A small number of customers are willing to pay a great deal for the product—far above $P_1$. A larger number of customers would happily pay $P_1$, and an even larger number of customers would pay less than $P_1$. If the price were zero, the demand might approach infinity! Ideally, in order to maximize sales and profits, a firm would like to pick up all the money in the market by selling the product at the price each customer is willing to pay. This is called **price discrimination**—selling products to different people and groups based on their willingness to pay. If some people really want the product, sell it to them at a high price. But sell it to indifferent people at a much lower price; otherwise, they will not buy. This only works if the firm can (a) identify the price each individual would be willing to pay, and (b) segregate the customers from one another so they cannot find out what the others are paying. Therefore, most firms adopt a fixed price for their goods ($P_1$), or a small number of prices for different versions of their products.

During the early days of e-commerce, and even today in the case of Web 2.0 firms, e-commerce firms were willing to charge far below their costs, sometimes giving away valuable services, in order to attract huge audiences.

**demand curve**
the quantity of goods that can be sold at various prices

**price discrimination**
selling products to different people and groups based on their willingness to pay

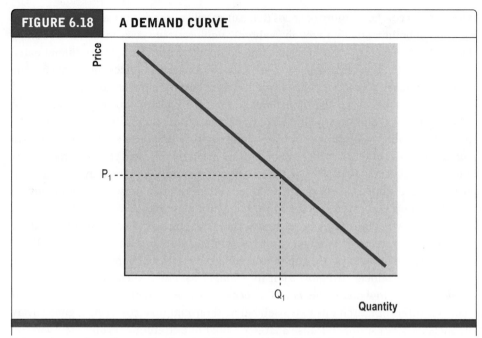

**FIGURE 6.18** **A DEMAND CURVE**

A demand curve shows the quantity of product (Q) that could be sold at various prices (P).

What if the marginal cost of producing a good is zero? What should the price be for these goods? It would be impossible then to set prices based on equalizing marginal revenue and marginal cost—because marginal cost is zero. The Internet is primarily filled with information goods—from music to research reports, to stock quotes, stories, weather reports, articles, pictures, and opinions—whose marginal cost of production is zero when distributed over the Internet. Thus, another reason certain goods, such as information goods, may be free on the Internet is that they are "selling" for what it costs to produce them—next to nothing. Content that is stolen from television, CDs, and Hollywood movies has zero production costs. Content that is contributed by users also has zero production costs for the Web sites themselves.

Over 90 million Internet users have uploaded user-generated content to social sites including profiles, photos, videos, blogs, and reviews, usually in return for free storage and display. Social sites generally rely on this "free" (to them) content to attract users and sell ads (eMarketer, Inc., 2010g; Trendstream, 2009). These firms, however, face substantial network and computing costs to store all this "free" content.

### Free and Freemium

Let's examine free pricing of Internet services. Everyone likes a bargain, and the best bargain is something for free. Businesses give away free PCs, free data storage, free music, free Web sites, free photo storage, and free Internet connections. Free is not new: banks used to give away "free" toasters to depositors in the 1950s. Google offers free office apps, free e-mail, and free collaboration sites. There can be a sensible economic logic to giving things away. Free content can help build market awareness (such as the free online *New York Times* that contains only the daily stories—not the archived stories) and can lead to sales of other follow-on products. Finally, free products and services knock out potential and actual competitors (the free browser Internet Explorer from Microsoft spoiled the market for Netscape's browser) (Shapiro and Varian, 1999).

Today, online "free" is increasingly being implemented as "freemium" to borrow a phrase from Chris Anderson's book *Free: The Future of a Radical Price.* The freemium pricing model is a cross-subsidy online marketing strategy where users are offered a basic service for free, but must pay for premium or add-on services. The people who pay for the premium services hopefully will pay for all the free riders on the service. Skype uses a freemium model: millions of users can call other Skype users on the Internet for free, but there's a charge for calling a landline or cell phone. Flickr, Google Sites, Yahoo, and a host of others offer premium services at a price in order to support "free" services. Even YouTube is launching a premium movie service where Hollywood movies are streamed for a price. Evernote.com offers online users a "universal memory drawer" that allows you to store any digital information (photos, videos, and documents) on the Evernote site, and then coordinate all of your digital devices from laptops, desktops, and smartphones. The basic service is free, but additional storage and special services cost $5 a month (Takahashi, 2010).

"Free" and "freemium" as pricing strategies do have limits. In the past, many e-commerce businesses found it difficult to convert the eyeballs into paying customers. YouTube is still not profitable. Free sites attract hundreds of millions of price-sensitive "free loaders" who have no intention of ever paying for anything, and who switch from one free service to another at the very mention of charges. The piggyback strategy has not been a universal success. "Free" eliminates a rich price discrimination strategy. Clearly some of the free loaders would indeed pay a small amount each month, and this revenue is lost to the firms who offer significant services for free. Some argue that everything digital will one day be free in part because Internet users expect it to be so. But the history of "free" includes broadcast television, which used to be "free" (it was advertising-supported) but the public eventually had no problem moving to cable television and DVDs as paid services. The exceptions to "free" are really valuable streams of information that are exclusive, not widely distributed, unique, and have immediate consumption or investment value. Even in the age of the Internet, these digital streams will sell for a price greater than zero. There probably is no free lunch after all, at least not one that's worth eating.

## Versioning

One solution to the problem of free information goods is **versioning**—creating multiple versions of the goods and selling essentially the same product to different market segments at different prices. In this situation, the price depends on the value to the consumer. Consumers will segment themselves into groups that are willing to pay different amounts for various versions (Shapiro and Varian, 1998). Versioning fits well with a modified "free" strategy. A reduced value version can be offered for free, while premium versions can be offered at higher prices. What makes a "reduced-value version?" Low-priced—or in the case of information goods, even "free"—versions might be less convenient to use, less comprehensive, slower, less powerful, and offer less support than the high-priced versions. Just as there are different General Motors car brands appealing to different market segments (Cadillac, Buick, Chevrolet, and Pontiac), and within

**versioning**

creating multiple versions of information goods and selling essentially the same product to different market segments at different prices

these divisions, hundreds of models from the most basic to the more powerful and functional, so can information goods be "versioned" in order to segment and target the market and position the products. In the realm of information goods, online magazines, music companies, and book publishers offer sample content for free, but charge for more powerful content. The *New York Times*, for instance, offers free daily content for several days after publication, but then charges per article for access to the more powerful archive of past issues. Writers, editors, and analysts are more than willing to pay for access to archived, organized content. Some Web sites offer "free services" with annoying advertising, but turn off the ads for a monthly fee.

### Bundling

"Ziggy" Ziegfeld, a vaudeville entrepreneur at the turn of the twentieth century in New York, noticed that nearly one-third of his theater seats were empty on some Friday nights, and during the week, matinee shows were often half empty. He came up with an idea for bundling tickets into "twofers": pay for one full-price ticket and get the next ticket free. Twofers are still a Broadway theater tradition in New York. They are based on the idea that (a) the marginal cost of seating another patron is zero, and (b) a great many people who would not otherwise buy a single ticket would buy a "bundle" of tickets for the same or even a slightly higher price.

**bundling**

offers consumers two or more goods for one price

Bundling of information goods online extends the concept of a twofer. **Bundling** offers consumers two or more goods for one price. The key idea behind the concept of bundling is that although consumers typically have very diverse ideas about the value of a single product, they tend to agree much more on the value of a bundle of products offered at a fixed price. In fact, the per-product price people are willing to pay for the bundle is often higher than when the products are sold separately. Bundling reduces the variance (dispersion) in market demand for goods. **Figure 6.19** illustrates how the demand curve changes when information goods are offered in a bundle.

Examples of bundling abound in the information goods marketplace. Microsoft bundles its separate Office tools (Word, Excel, PowerPoint, and Access) into a single Microsoft Office package. Even though many people want to use Word and Excel, far fewer want Access or PowerPoint. However, when all products are put into a single bundle, a very large number of people will agree that about $399 (or around $100 per tool) is a "fair" price for so many products. Likewise, the more software applications that Microsoft bundles with its basic operating system, the more the marketplace agrees that as a package of functionality, it is reasonably priced. On the Web, many content sites bundle as opposed to charge individual prices. Electronic libraries such as NetLibrary.com offer access to thousands of publications for a fixed annual fee. Theoretically, bundlers have distinct competitive advantages over those who do not or cannot bundle. Specifically, on the supply side, bundler firms can pay higher prices for content, and on the demand side, bundlers can charge higher prices for their bundles than can single-good firms (Bakos and Brynjolfsson, 2000).

However, bundling of digital goods does not always work. It depends on the bundle and the price. For instance, Reed Elsevier, the world's largest publisher of scientific journals, created a bundle of 1,500 digital scientific journals for American universities, and priced the bundle at a substantial markup to what universities were paying for a much smaller number of journals. It then raised the price to universities that did not want the

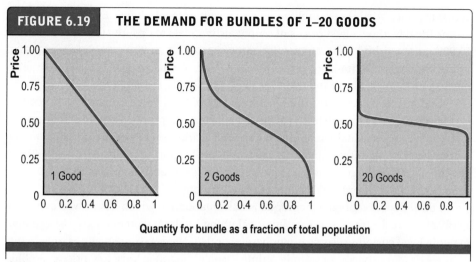

**FIGURE 6.19  THE DEMAND FOR BUNDLES OF 1–20 GOODS**

Quantity for bundle as a fraction of total population

The larger the number of goods bundled in a package, the higher the per-product price consumers are willing to pay.
SOURCE: Bakos and Brynjolfsson, 1999.

bundle. The result was a marketplace rebellion shaped in part by the fact that much of the research in these journals was paid for by taxpayers through government grants.

## Dynamic Pricing and Flash Marketing

The pricing strategies we have discussed so far are all fixed-price strategies. Versions and bundles are sold for fixed prices based on the firm's best effort at maximizing its profits. But what if there is product still left on the shelf along with the knowledge that someone, somewhere, would be willing to pay something for it? It might be better to obtain at least some revenue from the product, rather than let it sit on the shelf, or even perish. Imagine also that there are some people in every market who would pay a hefty premium for a product if they could have it right away. In other situations, such as for an antique, the value of the product has to be discovered in the marketplace (usually because there is a belief that the marketplace would value the product at a much higher price than its owner paid as a cost). In other cases, the value of a good is equal to what the market is willing to pay (and has nothing to do with its cost). Or let's say you want to build frequent visits to your site and offer some really great bargains for a few minutes each day, or the whole day with a set time limit. Here is where dynamic pricing mechanisms come to the fore, and where the strengths of the Internet can be seen.

Two prevalent kinds of *dynamic pricing mechanisms* are auctions and yield management. Auctions have been used for centuries to establish the instant market price for goods. Auctions are flexible and efficient market mechanisms for pricing unique or unusual goods, as well as commonplace goods such as computers, flower bundles, and cameras.

Yield management is quite different from auctions. In *auctions*, thousands of consumers establish a price by bidding against one another. In *yield management*, managers set prices in different markets, appealing to different segments, in order to sell excess capacity. Airlines exemplify yield management techniques. Every few minutes during the day, they adjust prices of empty airline seats to ensure at least some of the 50,000 empty airline seats are sold at some reasonable price—even below marginal cost of production. Frito-Lay, as mentioned earlier, also uses yield management techniques to ensure products move off the shelf in a timely fashion.

Yield management works under a limited set of conditions. Generally, the product is perishable (an empty airline seat perishes when the plane takes off without a full load); there are seasonal variations in demand; market segments are clearly defined; markets are competitive; and market conditions change rapidly (Cross, 1997). In general, only very large firms with extensive monitoring and database systems in place have been able to afford yield management techniques.

A third dynamic pricing technique is flash marketing, which has proved extraordinarily effective for travel services, luxury clothing goods, and other goods. Using e-mail to notify loyal customers (repeat purchasers) or dedicated Web site features, merchants offer goods and services for a limited time (usually hours) at very low prices. JetBlue has offered $14 flights between New York and Los Angeles. Deluxe hotel rooms are flash marketed at $1 a night. Companies like HauteLook and Gilt Groupe are based on flash marketing techniques. Blink and you can easily miss these great prices. Gilt.com purchases overstocked items from major fashion brands and then offers them to their subscribers at discounted prices via daily e-mail flash messages. Typically, the sale of an item lasts for two hours or until the inventory is depleted. On many occasions, Gilt.com rises to the top of most frequently visited Web sites when it conducts a sale. (Sweeney, 2010; Higgins, 2009). Critics point out that these sites take advantage of compulsive shoppers and leads to over-shopping for unneeded goods.

The Internet has truly revolutionized the possibilities to engage in dynamic, and even misleading pricing strategies. With millions of consumers using a site every hour, and access to powerful databases, merchants can raise prices one minute, and drop them another minute when a competitor threatens. Bait-and-switch tactics become more common: a really low-price on one product is used to attract people to a site where in fact the product is not available.

We discuss dynamic pricing, auctions, and yield management techniques in greater detail in Chapter 11.

## CHANNEL STRATEGIES: MANAGING CHANNEL CONFLICT

**channel**
refers to different methods by which goods can be distributed and sold

**channel conflict**
occurs when a new venue for selling products or services threatens to destroy existing venues for selling goods

In the context of commerce, the term **channel** refers to different methods by which goods can be distributed and sold. Traditional channels include sales by manufacturers, both directly and through intermediaries such as manufacturer representatives, distributors, and retailers. The emergence of e-commerce on the Web has created a new channel and has led to channel conflict. **Channel conflict** occurs when a new venue for selling products or services threatens to destroy existing venues for selling goods. Channel conflict is not new, but the Web creates incentives for producers of goods and services to establish direct relationships with consumers and thereby eliminate "middle persons" such as distributors and retailers.

For instance, Levi Strauss & Co. decided to begin selling Levi's jeans and Dockers on its Levi.com and Dockers.com sites. Initially, it forbade retailers (such as Macy's—

one of Levi's largest retailers) from selling Levi's products on the Web. However, the storm of protest from retailers, falling sales, and drooping profits forced Levi's to allow retailers to sell through their Web channels.

Rather than engage in direct confrontation with alternative channels, some manufacturers have turned toward a partnership model. For instance, Ethan Allen developed its own Web site for direct sales of its entire line of furniture. At the same time, Ethan Allen recognizes the importance of its independent retail stores for delivery, service, and support, and pays dealers in a local area 25% of the Internet sale for delivery and service, and 10% of the Internet sale even if the dealer does not participate in any way.

At the other end of the spectrum, some manufacturers use the Web solely as a marketing and branding mechanism in order to prevent channel conflict. For instance, Ford, General Motors, and most automobile manufacturers continue to rely on sales made by their dealerships rather than attempt to sell their cars directly online.

## 6.5 CASE STUDY

# Building a Brand:

ExchangeHunterJumper.com

The Internet and Web have enabled thousands of business ideas to become online realities. The Internet has reduced the costs of starting a small business, and allowed small players to effectively use the same marketing and selling tools as major corporations. Small businesses usually occupy a market niche not occupied by big players or corporations. One market niche in America is the high-end horse show circuit. These are people who are willing to drop $200,000 on a horse that can jump a 5' foot fence with ease. This is a very small market for sure, but its members are highly motivated to both buy and sell horses, and they are willing to spend in the process. ExchangeHunterJumper.com is one example of how a small business focusing on a tiny niche market was able to successfully build an online brand.

According to Dagny Amber Aslin, founder and owner of ExchangeHunter-Jumper.com (The Exchange), a Web site created to help owners and professional trainers sell high-end competition horses, it's hard to "get rich" or even make money on the

Internet. She adds, "There are a lot of preconceived notions... I beat down a path previously unplowed. It cost us a lot of money and we suffered many setbacks from our mistakes."

Yet the site is still growing and has succeeded where others failed. How did Amber Aslin break through and develop a site that works for professionals selling and buying alike? How did she build trust? How did she market her services?

Experience helps. Aslin started with applicable experience—in the horse world and in the world of Internet marketing. In addition to riding and competing as a child, Ms. Aslin spent several years working as a professional trainer. Working six-day weeks, including weekends, and spending most of her time outdoors riding, teaching, and competing, she saw first hand the challenges facing professional horsemen, and she gained valuable credibility with those who would become her audience.

While working in the horse business, and learning how difficult it was to make a living, she took a part-time job as assistant to a top California real estate agent, helping him market and sell high-end real estate in the Santa Barbara area. Among other activities, she helped him develop and expand his Web site. Through that experience, she realized that "selling six-figure horses and seven-figure houses are ridiculously similar—both tend to be overpriced, have emotional strings attached, require vettings and exhaustive negotiations, involve agents, and the list goes on."

In 2005, when she moved from California back to the Midwest, where she had spent her childhood, The Exchange was born. Five years later, the equine marketing model she has built is "a customized carbon copy" of the real estate program she assisted with in Santa Barbara.

Ms. Aslin knew busy horse professionals needed a high quality, reliable source of suitable mounts for their clients, but their day-to-day business lives left them little time to thoroughly search the market, and they often lacked a good grasph of modern media technology. The same dilemma applied with it came to selling high-end horses.

In response, she created an organized, professional process for preparing online horse sale advertisements. It included detailed forms for sellers to fill out, and she insisted that quality photos and video be provided for each horse advertised, enabling her to turn the descriptions into accurate portrayals of each animal and its capabilities. She created a fee structure that was reasonable and affordable, and she developed a multi-channel marketing program.

Ms. Aslin understood that her business plan needed to be a living document, evolving over time based on what the market was telling her. This helped her make inroads in a traditional industry that is very resistant to change. Most horse professionals spend their days outside, tend to do business only with those they know personally, the level of trust is very low, and most existing horse sale Web sites are no more than online classifieds with information that is often unreliable and not given much credence. Although professional horsemen have been slow to use computers and the Intenet, the rise of smartphones has helped increase their comfort level with e-mail and Web technology.

The Exchange took all of these things into account, and Ms. Aslin went further. In order to remain true to her business goal of providing a *reliable* service to professionals in the horse industry that would become a source of good horses that were as described,

Ms. Aslin personally reviewed all potential advertisers. In some cases she went back to sellers and insisted on higher quality photographs and video, and in other cases where she determined the horse was not as represented, she turned down their business.

Here's how it works. The Exchange handles advertising for sellers and trainers across the country. In 2010, show horses are typically priced from $15,000 well into the six figures, and the average asking price is $75,000. The recession has caused prices to fall about 10%-15%. The players in this market tend to be recession-resistant. The Exchange specializes strictly in hunter-jumper show horses, and specifically those suited for high-level competition. Revenue comes from seller ads and banner advertising. Buyer services are free of charge.

Trainers/sellers pay a flat fee for the initial advertisement, which includes photos, a written description, video, show record, and a monthly fee for ongoing maintenance, updating, and additional marketing. Sellers currently fill out two separate forms, a quick stats form and a fact sheet for each horse. The forms include a combination of fields with a list of pre-determined choices to check off as well as text fields to help standardize language so buyers can differentiate among horses for sale. Going forward, the two forms will be replaced by one comprehensive form.

The Exchange develops a specific marketing strategy for each horse listed. This includes reviewing information submitted, combing through a horse's official show record, considering impartial impressions, and identifying the most likely buyers. Advertising copy is professionally written and carefully targeted to buyers. If The Exchange thinks that the photos or videos don't help to sell the horse, they advise the seller on how to improve them. This advice stems from experience in marketing all types of horses from coast to coast, and an understanding of varied buyer profiles and geographic trends that exist in the market.

In addition, the Exchange works to personalize marketing for potential buyers, who are encouraged to fill out a form about their needs and budget so that Ms. Aslin can comb the listings and make recommendations to match buyers with horses that are for sale on the site.

Web site advertisements submitted by sellers are the core of the Exchange's marketing efforts. In an average month, the site has 50,000 sessions, 20,000 videos are downloaded, and new listings receive about 1,000-2,000 views. Sellers report inquiries are frequent and legitimate. With horses described honestly and partnered with appropriate pictures and quality video, success remains impressive even in slow markets.

Other elements of The Exchange's marketing strategy include a National Sales list distributed at "A" rated horse shows around the country, e-mail campaigns and RSS feeds that reach approximately 1,200 people a month, magazine advertising that reaches about 20,000 per month, the use of social media, and word of mouth.

The national sales list is one of the Exchange's latest marketing innovations. In addition to print distribution, it's available on YUDU.com, an award-winning online publishing website. By searching the site for The Exchange, a user can browse the catalog and link directly to full advertisements for all horses listed. This replaces DVD video catalogs that were prepared at great expense by the Exchange and mailed directly to professionals and distributed at horse shows.

Starting in 2009, the Exchange began experimenting with viral marketing and social media including Facebook, Twitter, a YouTube account, RSS feeds, and an experimental iPhone application. These efforts helped account for a 33% increase in site traffic for the year. Today, more than 2,000 people receive updates that promote new media, upcoming show appearances, show results, changes to listings, and more.

Ms. Aslin has concluded that for The Exchange, Facebook is the most effective way to reach her target audience and boost sales. While posting sale horse videos on YouTube does boost traffic to the site, it has not had a direct impact on sales. The longer term impact of YouTube exposure cannot be measured, and it is difficult to determine if a sale was the result of a YouTube initial contact, or a confirming experience for the customer. Customers may originate from multiple sources. Because every business is different, Ms. Aslin's experience suggests that it's important for e-commerce sites to experiment with social media to determine which outlets are most effective in reaching their specific target audiences.

For the Exchange, combined social media efforts in 2010 directed 15,000 visitors to ExchangeHunterJumper.com (with over 11,000 of those coming from Facebook). This resulted in 44,000 additional page views, which suggests visitors viewed several horses in addition to the one that originally grabbed their attention..

Another point of differentiation from competitors is that the Exchange has an in-house production studio for media preparation, strategy development, and campaign management that requires professional expertise, technological expertise, and labor. The level of professional attention to detail throughout the marketing process is far more extensive than other horse sale Web sites.

Ms. Aslin is directly involved in review of all media, and she travels to shows and conducts photo shoots to help promote horses listed on the site. Editing and formatting of videos is done in-house to ensure proper reproduction in online video and print marketing platforms.

Statistics show that a horse's first month online is most successful in terms of the number of Web page visits. With the addition of monthly campaign management, The Exchange helps keep each horse's marketing fresh and up-to-date. Updates can immediately escalate a horse's popularity as much as 30% and attract new potential buyers. Sellers are encouraged to provide updates as frequently as possible. Useful updates include upcoming competition appearances, recent competition results with impressive results, changes to listing details (such as a price adjustment), new photos, and video. Online videos add to the brand of the horse for sale, and are especially important for young horses or those "growing into" their price tags. Updates are added to the Web site and promoted through various media outlets including Facebook and e-mail campaigns,

Web traffic to the site has grown every month since January 2009. For 2009, there was a 33% increase in traffic and a 220% increase in page views. In the second half of the year there were $1.5 million in horse sales. In January 2010, there were 52,000 sessions, 210,000 page views, 16,500 video views, $.5 million in sales with an average price of $86,000 and a median price of $74,000.

Revenue comes from payment for running advertisements: a $250 loading fee for each horse, plus $35 per month as long as needed. Banner advertisements bring in additional revenue, and are priced between $150–$250 per 50,000 impressions. The audience is a wealthy and desirable demographic, but its size is relatively small for major advertisers, so the ads are not a tremendous source of revenue.

The value of an Exchange Equine Marketing Campaign lies behind the scenes. The tasks performed in the in-house production studio, such as media preparation, strategy development, and campaign management, require hours of labor and a wealth of technological expertise. Therein lies the difference between the average equine sale site and The Exchange: professional attention to detail at every step of the marketing process.

In discussing some of the obstacles she faced in getting The Exchange up and running, Ms. Aslin starts with education–her own or lack thereof, specifically in the areas of graphic design and Web technology. While she knew what professional horsemen needed, she did not how to translate that into graphic design or onto the Web. She says that looking back on the original logo and print designs is "a painful exercise," but she is happy with the current direction.

The budget was also an initial obstacle, as there wasn't a lot of money to spend up front. However, in hindsight, she believes that gave her an advantage because she had to learn what her market wanted and was able to do so without breaking the bank. Conversely, her main competitor took an opposite track, spent big up front, missed the mark with customers, and is now defunct.

In addition, she faced the negative perception among industry professionals and prospective buyers that equine Internet advertising was "worthless." Further, much of her target audience barely knew how to use a computer, didn't have e-mail addresses, and had been doing business in the same old-school manner for decades. For a few key players this worked very well, but it left a void for those outside of that inner circle to move horses. Through a combination of knowledge of the marketplace, on-the-job training, perseverance, and listening to what the market was telling her, the Exchange has successfully begun to fill that void.

Every iteration of the Web site and overall multi-channel marketing strategy has been focused on meeting this group's needs and showing that the Exchange is much more than a classified Web site. With each iteration, site views have grown, the number of listings has increased, and sales have increased. The initial business plan process involved strict screening, and it meant turning away money and valuing quality over quantity in every area - horses, buyers, traffic, and ads. It was a hard and expensive premise to adhere to when building a reputation from scratch, but through persistence and dedication it's worked.

Today the Web site is undergoing a redesign to update the backend technology, which is left over from 2005. It will enable much faster updating, which will allow more effective use of staff time, and thus the ability to market more horses. Ms. Aslin built the original site herself, and this time she is using coding professionals to do the backend build. It will cost her significant money, but she is willing to pay the price to get the database and CMS platform necessary to manage and update a site with this much content.

Finally, the biggest challenge, one that is ongoing, is pricing structure. People perceive that posting a horse to the Internet is easy, but The Exchange does far more than that. According to Ms. Aslin, "Unfortunately, many don't see the full value of the product until they've listed and paid the money. We are still mistaken as an 'online horse sale site' and in a cost comparison to this type of site we seem ridiculously expensive. The good news is that most of our clients give us repeat business after they see how much we do to help them make the sale."

Her next challenge is making the site cost-effective for professionals who run sale barns. To help do that, The Exchange is currently exploring new pricing structures that involve incentives for multiple horses, and strip some of the most expensive and time-consuming products of out of the campaigns.

**SOURCES**: "About The Exchange and Eohippus, LLC,," .exchange-hunterjumper.com/about.htm, August 2010; Interview with Amber Aslin, founder of Exchange-HunterJumper, August 2010.

### Case Study Questions

1. Find a site on the Web that offers classified ads for horses. Compare this site to Exchangehunterjumper.com in terms of the services offered (the customer value proposition). What does the Exchange offer that other sites do not?

2. In what ways were social media effective in promoting the Exchange brand? Which media led to the most increase in sales and inquiries? Why?

3. Make a list of all the ways Exchange attempts to personalize its services to both sellers and buyers.

## 6.6 | REVIEW

## KEY CONCEPTS

■ Identify the key features of the Internet audience.

Key features of the Internet audience include:
- *The number of users online in the United States.* In 2010, around 221 million. However, the rate of growth in the U.S. Internet population has begun to slow.
- *Intensity and scope of use.* Both are increasing, with around 78% of adult users in the United States logging on in a typical day and engaging in a wider set of activities, including sending and reading e-mail, gathering hobby-related information, catching up on news, browsing for fun, buying products, seeking health information, conducting work-related research, and reviewing financial information.
- *Demographics and access.* Although the Internet population is growing increasingly diverse, some demographic groups have much higher percentages of online usage than other groups, and different patterns of usage exist across various groups.

- *Lifestyle impacts.* Intensive Internet use may cause a decline in traditional social activities. The social development of children who use the Internet intensively instead of engaging in face-to-face interactions or undirected play out of doors may also be negatively impacted.
- *Media choices.* The more time individuals spend using the Internet, the less time they spend using traditional media.

■ **Discuss the basic concepts of consumer behavior and purchasing decisions.**

Models of consumer behavior attempt to predict or explain what consumers purchase, and where, when, how much, and why they buy. Factors that impact buying behavior include:
- Cultural factors
- Social factors
- Psychological factors

There are five stages in the consumer decision process:
- Awareness of need
- Search for more information
- Evaluation of alternatives
- The actual purchase decision
- Post-purchase contact with the firm

The online consumer decision process is basically the same, with the addition of two new factors:
- *Web site capabilities*—the content, design, and functionality of a site.
- *Consumer clickstream behavior*—the transaction log that consumers establish as they move about the Web and through specific sites. Analysts believe the most important predictors of online consumer behavior are the session characteristics and the clickstream behavior of people online, rather than demographic data.

■ **Understand how consumers behave online.**

Clickstream analysis shows us that people go online for many different reasons, at different times, and for numerous purposes.
- About 70% of online users are "buyers" who actually purchase something entirely online. Another 16% of online users research products on the Web, but purchase them offline. This combined group, referred to as "shoppers," constitutes approximately 86% of the online Internet audience.
- Online sales are divided roughly into two groups: small-ticket and big-ticket items. In the early days of e-commerce, sales of small-ticket items vastly out-numbered those of large-ticket items. However, the recent growth of big-ticket items such as computer hardware and consumer electronics has changed the overall sales mix.
- There are a number of actions that e-commerce vendors could take to increase the likelihood that shoppers and non-shoppers would purchase online more frequently. These include better security of credit card information and privacy of personal information, lower shipping costs, and easier returns.

■ **Describe the basic marketing concepts needed to understand Internet marketing.**

The key objective of Internet marketing is to use the Web—as well as traditional channels—to develop a positive, long-term relationship with customers (who may be online or offline) and thereby create a competitive advantage for the firm by allowing it to charge a higher price for products or services than its competitors can charge.

- Firms within an industry compete with one another on four dimensions: differentiation, cost, focus, and scope. "Competitive markets" are ones with lots of substitute products, easy entry, low differentiation among suppliers, and strong bargaining power of customers and suppliers.

- Marketing is an activity designed to avoid pure price competition, and to create imperfect markets where returns on investment are above average, competition is limited, and consumers are convinced to pay premium prices for products that have no substitute because they are unique. Marketing encourages customers to buy on the basis of perceived and actual nonmarket, that is, non-price, qualities of products.

- A product's brand is what makes products truly unique and differentiable in the minds of consumers. A brand is a set of expectations, such as quality, reliability, consistency, trust, affection, and loyalty, that consumers have when consuming, or thinking about consuming, a product or service from a specific company.

- Marketers devise and implement brand strategies—a set of plans for differentiating a product from its competitors and communicating these differences effectively to the marketplace. Segmenting the market, targeting different market segments with differentiated products, and positioning products to appeal to the needs of segment customers are key parts of brand strategy.

- Brand equity is the estimated value of the premium customers are willing to pay for using a branded product when compared to unbranded competitors. Consumers are willing to pay more for branded products in part because they reduce consumers' search and decision-making costs. The ability of brands to attain brand equity also provides incentive for firms to build products that serve customer needs better than other products. Brands also lower customer acquisition cost and increase customer retention.

- Although some predicted that the Web would lead to "frictionless commerce" and the end of marketing based on brands, recent research has shown that brands are alive and well on the Web and that consumers are still willing to pay price premiums for products and services they perceive and differentiate.

■ **Identify and describe the main technologies that support online marketing.**

- *Web transaction logs*—records that document user activity at a Web site. Coupled with data from the registration forms and shopping cart database, these represent a treasure trove of marketing information for both individual sites and the online industry as a whole.

- *Cookies*—small text files that Web sites place on visitors' client computers every time they visit, and during the visit, as specific pages are visited. Cookies provide Web marketers with a very quick means of identifying the customer and understanding his or her prior behavior at the site.

- *Web bugs*—tiny (1 pixel) graphic files hidden in marketing e-mail messages and on Web sites. Web bugs are used to automatically transmit information about the user and the page being viewed to a monitoring server.
- *Databases, data warehouses, data mining, and "profiling"*—technologies that allow marketers to identify exactly who the online customer is and what they want, and then to present the customer with exactly what they want, when they want it, for the right price.
- *CRM systems*—a repository of customer information that records all of the contacts that a customer has with a firm and generates a customer profile available to everyone in the firm who has a need to "know the customer."

■ **Identify and describe basic e-commerce marketing and branding strategies.**

The marketing technologies described above have spawned a new generation of marketing techniques and added power to some traditional techniques.

- Internet marketing strategies for market entry for new firms include pure clicks/first-mover and mixed bricks-and-clicks/alliances; and for existing firms include pure clicks/fast-follower and mixed bricks-and-clicks/brand extender.
- Online marketing techniques to online customers include the use of advertising networks, permission marketing, affiliate marketing, viral marketing, blog marketing, social network marketing, and brand leveraging.
- Online techniques for strengthening customer relationships include one-to-one marketing, customization and customer co-production, transactive content, and customer service (such as CRMs, FAQs, live chat, intelligent agents, and automated response systems).
- Online pricing strategies include offering products and services for free, versioning, bundling, and dynamic pricing.
- Companies operating in the e-commerce environment must also have marketing strategies in place to handle the possibility of channel conflict.

## QUESTIONS

1. Is growth of the Internet, in terms of users, expected to continue indefinitely? What will cause it to slow, if anything?
2. Other than search engines, what are some of the most popular uses of the Internet?
3. Would you say that the Internet fosters or impedes social activity? Explain your position.
4. Why would the amount of experience someone has using the Internet likely increase future Internet usage?
5. Research has shown that many consumers use the Internet to investigate purchases before actually buying, which is often done in a physical storefront. What implication does this have for online merchants? What can they do to entice more online buying, rather than pure research?
6. Name four improvements Web merchants could make to encourage more browsers to become buyers.
7. Name the five stages in the buyer decision process and briefly describe the online and offline marketing activities used to influence each.
8. Why are "little monopolies" desirable from a marketer's point of view?

9. Describe a perfect market from the supplier's and customer's perspective.
10. Explain why an imperfect market is more advantageous for businesses.
11. What are the components of the core product, actual product, and augmented product in a feature set?
12. List some of the major advantages of having a strong brand. How does a strong brand positively influence consumer purchasing?
13. How are product positioning and branding related? How are they different?
14. List the differences among databases, data warehouses, and data mining.
15. Name some of the drawbacks to the four data mining techniques used in Internet marketing.
16. Why have advertising networks become controversial? What, if anything, can be done to overcome any resistance to this technique?
17. Which of the four market entry strategies is most lucrative?
18. Compare and contrast four marketing strategies used in mass marketing, direct marketing, micromarketing, and one-to-one marketing.
19. What pricing strategy turned out to be deadly for many e-commerce ventures during the early days of e-commerce? Why?
20. Is price discrimination different from versioning? If so, how?
21. What are some of the reasons that freebies, such as free Internet service and giveaways, don't work to generate sales at a Web site?
22. Explain how versioning works. How is this different from dynamic pricing?
23. Why do companies that bundle products and services have an advantage over those that don't or can't offer this option?

# PROJECTS

1. Go to the SRI Web site at www.strategicbusinessinsights.com/vals/presur-vey.shtml. Take the survey to determine which lifestyle category you fit into. Then write a brief two-page paper describing how your lifestyle and values impact your use of the Web for e-commerce. How is your online consumer behavior affected by your lifestyle?

2. Find an example of a Web site that you feel does a good job appealing to both goal-directed and experiential consumers. Explain your choice.

3. Choose a digital content product available on the Web and describe its feature set.

4. Visit Eluxury.com and create an Internet marketing plan for it that includes each of the following:

   - One-to-one marketing
   - Affiliate marketing
   - Viral marketing
   - Blog marketing
   - Social network marketing

   Describe how each plays a role in growing the business, and create an electronic slide presentation of your marketing plan.

## CHAPTER 7

# E-commerce Marketing Communications

**After reading this chapter, you will be able to:**

- Identify the major forms of online marketing communications.
- Understand the costs and benefits of online marketing communications.
- Discuss the ways in which a Web site can be used as a marketing communications tool.

# Video Ads:
## Shoot, Click, Buy

The age of online video ads is upon us, just in case you haven't noticed. Improvements in video production tools, bigger bandwidth, and better streaming quality have fueled an online video surge. Video production is no longer the exclusive province of just a few major players in New York and Hollywood, but instead has expanded to a much larger group of potential creators. In addition, the ways online video can be viewed has also expanded, from desktop PCs and laptops to smartphones, netbooks, and Web-enabled television sets. The front pages of online news and newspaper sites display their video offerings on the top of the page, and the online version of the *Wall Street Journal* now offers two live, twice-a-day newscasts.

The online audience for videos is huge. In August 2010, 178 million U.S. Internet users watched online video content during the month, with each viewer spending an average of 14.3 hours! Because this is where the eyeballs are, video is an obvious advertising medium. And just in time: Internet users have learned how to avoid traditional banner ads by instinctively moving their eyes to a different part of the screen. Click-throughs on banner ads are miniscule but videos are another story: next to search engine marketing, and focused e-mail campaigns, videos have the highest click-through rate. Zappos, the shoe retailer, found a 6% to 30% increase in click-through rates in products that have videos. Advertisers are jumping on the bandwagon. Seventy percent of the top 50 online retailers feature video. Americans viewed nearly 3.8 billion video ads in August 2010!

Firms are using online video for marketing in two primary ways. Many companies produce their own videos to promote their brands and sell products. Other companies seek to attach their ads to videos created by others to support their brand or make sales.

Evan Sofron's company, Actiontuners, is an example of the first type of online video promotion where the retailer makes their own videos. String Master is a robotic guitar tuner that uses a computer-based listening device and a geared motor to tune a guitar to a perfect pitch. Evan initially used Google AdWords and text ads in both keyword and site-targeted campaigns. He saw a 15% increase in sales, but felt it was difficult to convey the features of his product, or what it looked like, with just text ads. Evan was also disappointed that the click-through rates for the ads were only 0.5%. Several years ago, Google began developing the capability to distribute video ads on its AdSense network. Evan created a 30-second video that demonstrated how String Master actually worked. Then, working with the Google Content Network, he chose various guitar, music, and musician sites on which the video ad would be displayed. Evan focused on optimizing the number of plays for his video and the time viewers spent watching his ads on the various sites. In a few weeks, he could tell which sites were most productive and focused his ads on those sites while removing them from the other sites. In a few months, Evan increased sales of String Master by 40%. Click-through rates averaged 8.5% across all sites, and went as high as 30% on some sites.

Major Fortune 500 companies have learned a similar lesson: people are far more likely to watch a video, and pay attention to the content, than look at a banner ad or remember a text ad on Google. Many large firms are moving into the online video advertising marketplace with sophisticated campaigns and big budgets. For instance, Rite Aid was searching for ways to boost sales in a recessionary period. One idea was to use its Web site to drive sales at its 4,800 retails stores. In 2010, introduced its Video Values program. Online visitors who watch videos about Rite Aid products receive a coupon they can redeem at the store. Watch 20 videos and they receive a $5 bonus coupon in addition to product coupons. Currently Rite Aid is streaming 500,000 videos a month, which are generating a 20% coupon redemption rate. The coupons are personalized, and participants have to register. Rite-Aid generates extensive demographic data on its most engaged customers who can later be contacted in e-mail campaigns. In turn, bargain hunting sites and blogs add a social component to the effort by driving bargain hunters to Rite Aid's site.

Other big-name firms using online video include The Gap and Allstate. The Gap, struggling to get back into the high fashion jeans market, is promoting its 1969 Premium Jeans line at borntofit.com with a video interview featuring Patrick Robinson, the jeans' designer. Allstate has an entire YouTube channel devoted to explaining storm risks to its potential customers and building its brand name. Many Fortune 500 firms have YouTube channels where they control the video content and ad environment.

Smaller firms are also using video. Online fashion retailer KarmaLoop offers KarmaLoopTV, which places all its videos under a single tab on its Web site, with the objective of creating an online fashion community. The videos feature exclusive interviews with fashion designers, brands, artists, and musicians. KarmaLoopTV streams over 100,000 videos a week.

People care and get excited about videos far more than banner ads and e-mail. This makes them an ideal advertising medium. Several changes in the underlying technology of video advertising are helping to increase the effectiveness of these ads. For instance, it is now possible to make video ads interactive so viewers can click on a product and add it to their shopping cart as the video is playing. It's sort of like "streaming e-commerce." These "interactive video ads" are appearing throughout the Web especially at newspaper sites in 2010 as an alternative to display ads that are increasingly ignored. Video ads can also be optimized, allowing retailers to change elements of the videos and measure the impacts in near real time. The introduction of the iPad in 2010 made viewing videos much more pleasant and mobile. Interaction rates with videos displayed on iPads are six times higher than desktop PCs. The challenge is figuring out how to package advertising messages more directly with the videos, and how to piggyback advertising onto millions of user-generated videos, and measure the impact on sales. Google, Yahoo, AOL, and literally hundreds of smaller firms, are hard at work trying to attach the right ads to the right videos, a tricky process since computers cannot "understand" the content of videos (although they can "understand" the audio script—sort of). One start-up firm, YuMe.com, specializes in matching ads to popular online videos. One risk: your ad is attached to a perfectly inappropriate video. No one wants their product ads attached to stolen, pornographic, or inappropriate videos.

Another challenge is to figure out how to show the ad while the video plays without destroying the viewing experience. The final challenge is to avoid turning the viewer off, and causing a kind of video blindness on a mass scale, which is the fate of display ads today. One solution: YouTube is testing "skippable" ads that allow users to skip the pre-roll ad embedded in videos and don't charge the advertiser for skipped ads. Skippable ads offer the prospect that the video ad marketplace will be self-cleansing with really unpopular, annoying, frequently skipped ads disappearing.

**SOURCES:** "comScore Releases August 2010 U.S. Online Video Rankings, comScore, September 30, 2010; "YouTube to Introduce 'Skippable" Ads," *Wall Street Journal*, June 29, 2010; "2010 Promises Massive Digital Video Adoption—and Advertising Potential," by Meghan Keane, eConsultancy.com, June 15, 2010; "Video E-Commerce: Innovative Models Drive Sales," by Jeffrey Grant, eMarketer, May, 2010; "Video Ad Start-Up YuMe Raises $25 Million," by Brad Stone, *New York Times*, February 17, 2010; "Online Ads Are Booming, if They're Attached to a Video," by Brian Stelter, *New York Times*, November 11, 2009; "YouTube Wedding Spurs Music Sales," by Brad Stone, *New York Times*, July 30, 2009.

The opening case provides an interesting glimpse into how the increasing broadband video capacity of homes and businesses, coupled with new Internet technologies and widespread distribution of digital video cameras, is being used to influence consumer choice and build brand awareness. It also illustrates some of the challenges that marketers should be aware of when using these new forms of advertising.

In the last few years, Internet advertising has been on a tear. While the recession in 2008 and 2009 caused a drop of 3% in online advertising, in 2010, online ad growth picked up again to 11% while ad spending in all other media shrank 2%. (Newspapers were off 11%, for instance.) In the meantime, the advertising industry as a whole—both offline and online—is going through a period of tumultuous change. The Internet and online advertising are disrupting the traditional advertising business, which was dominated by television and print media. Advertising budgets are following customer eyeballs and moving onto the Web, while expenditures for print and television are static or declining. **Table 7.1** summarizes the significant changes in the advertising industry for 2010–2011.

After taking a steep plunge in 2001 following the dot-com bust, aggressive forms of "push" advertising such as animated banners, and pop-ups that greet you on entering and leaving Web sites, have exploded, along with unsolicited e-mail or "spam," which now consumes about 80%–90% of all e-mail traffic on the Internet. Paid search advertising (also called "pull" advertising)—where consumers search for and find information and advertisers pay for text ads, such as that offered by Google, Yahoo, Microsoft, and many others—has skyrocketed in popularity to become the single largest online ad form. Video advertising is still a small part of the overall Internet ad pie, but it is the fastest growing form of advertising. Internet advertising has become more costly as demand has exploded but still costs far less than traditional media advertising.

In Chapter 6, we described brands as a set of expectations that consumers have about products offered for sale. We discussed some of the marketing activities that companies engage in to create those expectations. In this chapter, we focus on understanding **online marketing communications**—all the major methods that online firms use to communicate to the consumer, create strong brand expectations, and drive sales. What are the best methods for attracting people to a Web site and converting them into customers? We also examine the Web site as a marketing communications tool. How does the design of a Web site affect sales? How can you optimize a Web site for search engines?

**online marketing communications**

methods used by online firms to communicate to the consumer and create strong brand expectations

## 7.1 MARKETING COMMUNICATIONS

Marketing communications have a dual purpose: branding and sales. One purpose of marketing communications is to develop and strengthen a firm's brands by informing consumers about the differentiating features of the firm's products and services. In addition, marketing communications are used to promote sales directly by encouraging the consumer to buy products (the sooner, the better).

| TABLE 7.1 | WHAT'S NEW IN INTERNET ADVERTISING 2010–2011 |
|---|---|
| **TREND** | **IMPACT** |
| Internet advertising grows as a share of the total advertising budget at the expense of traditional media. | Online advertising in the United States will grow in 2010–2011 to around 15% of the total spending for all forms of advertising. |
| Online ad spending increases, even as the total ad budget declines. | Despite the recession, online advertising grows in 2010 by 11% to $25 billion and will keep growing, by 9% in 2011, while total ad spending slips. |
| Search engine advertising spending continues to be the dominant form of spending on online advertising, accounting for about 50% of all online spending. | Search engine advertising grows in 2010 by 15.7% to almost $12 billion, and will keep growing, to $13.5 billion in 2011, over twice the size of the display banner ad format ($5.4 billion). However, the rate of growth is slowing. |
| Industry giants embrace Internet advertising. | Major packaged goods companies from Procter & Gamble to Budweiser move additional ad spending to the Web with an emphasis on interactive branding formats like video, brand sites (BudTV), Twitter, and social network sites. |
| New ad formats emerge | The banner display ad, in all its forms, gives way to an explosion in video ads, in-game ads, ads in widgets, and ads on virtual sites. |
| Behavioral advertising and personalized Web experiences increase | Behavioral marketing technologies come closer to the ideal of showing ads at the right time, to the right person, as well as personalizing the Web experience. Privacy protests grow. |
| Social network sites seek to monetize their audience through display and interactive ad formats. | Social network site ad revenues grow over $1.6 billion (5% of total ad spending) as ads follow the eyeballs. |
| Google, AOL, Microsoft, and Yahoo compete for the display ad industry. | Declining growth rate in search advertising causes search and portal companies to leverage their online positions in search advertising into the display ad industry by purchasing online ad networks. |
| Metrics: challenges and solutions | Lack of industry standards complicate the problem of measuring the impact of online ads, and understanding how much these ads are worth. |

The distinction between the branding and sales purposes of marketing communications is subtle but important because branding communications differ from promotional communications. **Promotional sales communications** almost always suggest that the consumer "buy now," and they make offers to encourage immediate purchase. **Branding communications** rarely encourage consumers to buy now, but instead emphasize the differentiable benefits of consuming the product or service.

There are many different forms of online marketing communications, including online advertising, e-mail marketing, and public relations. Even the Web site itself can be viewed as a marketing communications tool.

**promotional sales communications**
suggest the consumer "buy now" and make offers to encourage immediate purchase

**branding communications**
focus on extolling the differentiable benefits of consuming the product or service

## ONLINE ADVERTISING

**online advertising**

a paid message on a Web site, online service, or other interactive medium

Advertising is the most common and familiar marketing communications tool. Companies will spend an estimated $166 billion on advertising in 2010, and an estimated $25 billion of that amount on **online advertising** (defined as a paid message on a Web site, paid search listing, video, widget, game, or other online medium, such as instant messaging) (see **Figure 7.1**) (eMarketer, Inc., 2010a).

In the last five years, advertisers have aggressively increased online spending and cut outlays on traditional channels such as radio, television, and newspapers. However, although online advertising is the fastest growing form of advertising, it will still remain a small part of total advertising for some time to come, reaching only 20% of all advertising by 2014.

Spending on online advertising among different industries is somewhat skewed. Retail accounts for the highest percentage (20%), followed by telecommunications (16%), financial services (12%), automotive (11%) and computers (10%) (Interactive Advertising Bureau/PricewaterhouseCoopers, 2010). Travel and consumer packaged goods/food products each account for 6%. Online advertising has both advantages and disadvantages when compared to advertising in traditional media, such as television, radio, and print (magazines and newspapers). One big advantage

| FIGURE 7.1 | ONLINE ADVERTISING FROM 2002–2014 |

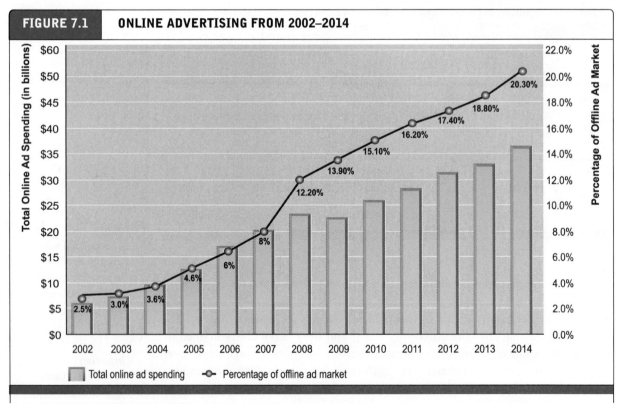

Online advertising is expected to grow about 10% a year to 2014, and to comprise an increasing percentage of total advertising expenditures.
SOURCES: Based on data from eMarketer, Inc., 2010a.

for online advertising is that the Internet is where the audience is moving, especially the very desirable 18–34 year olds, as well as the ballooning baby boomers who are over 65 years of age. A second large advantage for online advertising is the ability to target ads to narrow segments and track performance of advertisements in almost real time. **Ad targeting**, the sending of market messages to specific subgroups in the population in an effort to increase the likelihood of a purchase, is as old as advertising itself. Ad targeting is also the foundation of price discrimination: the ability to charge different types of consumers different prices for the same product or service. The six major online segmentation and targeting methods (behaviorial, demographic, pyschographic, technical, contextual, and search) were described in Table 6.7 in Chapter 6. We further discuss ad targeting later in this section.

> **ad targeting**
> the sending of market messages to specific subgroups in the population

Theoretically, online advertising can personalize every ad message to precisely fit the needs, interests, and values of each consumer. In practice, as we all know from spam and constant exposure to pop-up ads that are of little interest, the reality is very different. Online advertisements also provide greater opportunities for interactivity— two-way communication between advertisers and potential customers. The primary disadvantages of online advertising are concerns about its cost versus its benefits, how to adequately measure its results, and the supply of good venues to display ads. For instance, the owners of Web sites who sell advertising space ("publishers") do not have agreed-upon standards or routine audits to verify their claimed numbers as do traditional media outlets. We examine the costs and benefits of online advertising as well as research on its effectiveness in Section 7.2.

There are a number of different forms of online advertisement:

- Display ads (banners and pop-ups)
- Rich media ads
- Video ads
- Search engine advertising
- Social network, blog, and game advertising
- Sponsorships
- Referrals (affiliate relationship marketing)
- E-mail marketing
- Online catalogs

**Table 7.2** provides some comparative data on the amount of spending for certain advertising formats. The online advertising format that currently produces the highest revenue is paid search, followed by display ads, but the fastest growing online ad format is rich media/video ads. We discuss the various online ad formats in more depth next.

## Display Ads: Banners and Pop-Ups

Display ads were the first Internet advertisements. A **banner ad** displays a promotional message in a rectangular box at the top or bottom of a computer screen. A banner ad is similar to a traditional ad in a printed publication but has some added advantages. If clicked on, it can bring a potential customer directly to the advertiser's Web site. It also is much more dynamic than a printed ad: it can present multiple images or otherwise

> **banner ad**
> displays a promotional message in a rectangular box at the top or bottom of a computer screen

| TABLE 7.2 | ONLINE ADVERTISING SPENDING FOR SELECTED FORMATS (IN BILLIONS) | | |
|---|---|---|---|
| FORMAT | 2010 | 2014 | %CHANGE |
| Search | $12,374 | $16,771 | 36% |
| Banner ads | $5,477 | $7,373 | 35% |
| Classifieds | $1,958 | $1,960 | 0% |
| Rich media | $1,576 | $1,815 | 15% |
| Lead generation | $1,531 | $2,033 | 33% |
| Video | $1,506 | $5,518 | 266% |
| Sponsorships | $402 | $501 | 25% |
| E-mail | $276 | $330 | 20% |
| Total | $25,100 | $36,300 | 45% |

SOURCES: Based on data from eMarketer, Inc., 2010a.

change its appearance.

Banner ads sometimes feature Flash video and animations or animated GIFs, which display different images in relatively quick succession, creating an animated effect. The Interactive Advertising Bureau (IAB), an industry organization, has established voluntary industry guidelines for banner ads. A full banner, the most common, is 468 pixels wide by 60 pixels high with a resolution of 72 dpi (dots per inch) and a maximum file size of 13 KB.

The IAB guidelines include specifications for virtually all types of ads and buttons, including skyscrapers (a tall, narrow banner ad almost three times the height of the traditional vertical banner ad), rectangles of various sizes, and a square pop-up (which opens in a separate window), to allow marketers to develop ads featuring enhanced interactivity as well as expanded creativity. The various types of ads (including the rich media/video ads discussed in the next section) are designed to help advertisers break through the "noise" and clutter created by the high number of display ad impressions that a typical user is exposed to within a given day. Advertising networks such as DoubleClick serve over 500 billion impressions of various types in a single year, and research firms estimate that Internet users are exposed to over 1,000 display ads per day. **Figure 7.2** shows examples of some of the different types of display ads, as specified by the IAB.

**Pop-up ads** are those banners and buttons that appear on the screen without the user calling for them. Generally, these ads conform to the size specifications of the IAB banner and button specifications. One type of pop-up ad is the **pop-under ad**, which opens underneath a user's active browser window and does not appear until the user closes the active window. The ad remains visible until the user takes action

**pop-up ad**
banners and buttons that appear on the screen without the user calling for them

**pop-under ad**
opens underneath a user's active browser window and does not appear until the user closes the active window

| FIGURE 7.2 | TYPES OF DISPLAY ADS |
|---|---|

**Full Banner:**
468 x 60 pixels

**Skyscraper:**
120 ´ 600 pixels

**Half Banner:**
234 x 60 pixels

**Micro Bar:**
88 x 31 pixels

**Vertical Banner:**
120 x 240 pixels

**Button-1:**
120 x 90 pixels

**Button-2:**
120 x 60 pixels

**Square Button:**
125 x 125 pixels

**Rectangle:**
180 x 150 pixels

In addition to the various display ads shown above, IAB also provides standards for a medium, large, and vertical rectangle, a square pop-up, a wide skyscraper, a half-page ad, and an ad it calls a "leaderboard" (728 x 90 pixels).

SOURCE: Interactive Advertising Bureau, 2008.

to close it. Pop-ups can appear prior to display of the consumer's target page, during, or after the display on leaving.

Multiple surveys have found that pop-up ads that appear over a user's Web page cause negative consumer sentiment. Online consumers rate pop-ups right next to telemarketing as the most annoying form of marketing communication. A number of ISPs and search engine/portal sites, such as Yahoo, Google, AOL, and Earthlink, now offer consumers pop-up blocking toolbars, as do Web browsers such as Mozilla Firefox and Internet Explorer 7 and 8. Unfortunately, studies have found that pop-up ads are twice as effective in terms of click-through rates than normal banner ads (although this may occur because people get confused about how to close the ads and end up unintentionally clicking to the advertised site). As a result, despite the backlash, although the number of pop-ups and pop-unders are likely to decline, they will not disappear entirely.

## Rich Media Ads

**rich media ads**

ad employing animation, sound, and interactivity, using Flash, DHTML, Java, and JavaScript

**Rich media ads** are ads that employ animation, sound, and interactivity, using Flash, dynamic HTML (DHTML), Java, and JavaScript. Rich media ads will account for about $1.5 billion in online advertising expenditures (about 7% of total online advertising) in 2010 and are expected to grow to about $1.8 billion by 2014. Rich media ads tend to be more about branding than driving sales per se and have been found to be more effective than display ads. For instance, one research report found that exposure to rich media ads boosted brand awareness by 10% over a control group. The same methodology applied to normal banner ads found that it took 3 exposures to a large rectangle ad to produce a similar increase, 6 exposures to a skyscraper unit to get an 8% increase, and 10 exposures to a regular banner ad to get a 6% increase (Dynamic Logic, 2004).

**interstitial ad**

a way of placing a full-page message between the current and destination pages of a user

Interstitial ads are typically considered a kind of "rich media" ad. An **interstitial ad** (interstitial means "in between") is a way of placing a full-page message between the current and destination pages of a user. Interstitials are usually inserted within a single Web site, and displayed as the user moves from one page to the next. The interstitial typically moves automatically to the page the user requested after allowing enough time for the ad to be read. Interstitials can also be deployed over an advertising network and appear as users move among Web sites.

Since the Web is such a busy place, people have to find ways to cope with overstimulation. One means of coping is known as *sensory input filtering*. This means that people learn to filter out the vast majority of the messages coming at them. Internet users quickly learn at some level to recognize banner ads or anything that looks like a banner ad and to filter out most of the ads that are not exceptionally relevant. Interstitial messages, like TV commercials, attempt to make viewers a captive of the message. Typical interstitials last 10 seconds or less and force the user to look at the ad for that time period. IAB standards for pre-roll ads also limit their length. To avoid boring users, ads typically use animated graphics and music to entertain and inform them. A good interstitial will also have a "skip through" or "stop" option for users who have no interest in the message.

**superstitial**

a rich media ad that is pre-loaded into a browser's cache and does not play until fully loaded and the user clicks to another page

A **superstitial** (now offered by a firm by the name of Enliven and sometimes referred to as a Unicast Transitional with Flash) is a rich media ad that can be any screen display size up to full screen 900 x 500 (the full-screen superstitial), and with a file size of up to 600 KB. Superstitials differ from interstitials in that they are pre-loaded into a browser's cache and do not play until fully loaded. When the file is finished downloading, like an interstitial, it waits until the user clicks to another page before popping up in a separate window.

### Video Ads

**Video ads** are TV-like advertisements that appear as in-page video commercials or before, during, or after a variety of content. **Table 7.3** describes some of the IAB standards for video ads.

**video ad**
TV-like advertisement that appears as an in-page video commercial or before, during, or after, content

Video ads are the fastest growing form of online advertisement, accounting for about $1.5 billion in online advertising spending, which is expected to almost triple to $5.5 billion by 2014 (a five-fold increase). However, from a total revenue standpoint, online video ads are still very small when compared to the amount spent on search engine advertising, and of course, are dwarfed by the amount spent on television advertising.

The explosion of online video content across major news and entertainment sites, Web portals, and humor and user-generated sites has created huge opportunities for brand marketers to better reach their target audiences. About 80% of the 221 million U.S. Internet users watched 33 billion online videos a month in 2010. YouTube.com achieved record levels of viewing activity in May 2010 with an all-time high of 14.6 billion videos viewed, surpassing the threshold of 100 videos per viewer for the first time. Despite its explosive growth, video advertising in 2014 will only account for 5% of all online advertising (comScore, 2010a). Online video has become the audience aggregator of the 21st century, displacing television broadcast networks and Hollywood film producers .

Exactly how to take advantage of this opportunity is still a puzzle. Internet users are willing to listen to advertising in order to see short video clips as long as the ads

| TABLE 7.3 | TYPES OF VIDEO ADS | | |
|---|---|---|---|
| FORMAT | DESCRIPTION | WHEN USED | USED WITH |
| Linear video ad | Pre-roll; takeover; ad takes over video for a certain period of time | Before, between, after video | Text, banners, rich media video player skins |
| Non-linear video ad | Overlay; Web bugs; ad runs at same time as video content and does not take over full screen | During, over, or within video | |
| In-banner video ad | Rich media; ad is triggered within banner, may expand outside banner | Within Web page, generally surrounded by content | None |
| In-text video ad | Rich media; ad is delivered when user mouses over relevant text | Within Web page, identified as a highlighted word within relevant content | None |

don't interfere, and the ads are not too long. There are many formats for displaying ads with videos. Currently, the most widely used format is the "pre-roll" (followed by the mid-roll and the post-roll) where users are forced to watch an ad, often another video, either before, in the middle of, or at the end of the video they originally clicked on. While advertising firms have been successful in selling the video ad format to firms, the major video sites such as YouTube and MySpace have had a difficult time selling their ad space and monetizing their huge audiences.

There are many specialized video advertising networks such as VideoEgg, Advertsing.com, Broadband, Roo, and others who run video advertising campaigns for national advertisers and place these videos on their respective network of Web sites. Firms can also establish their own video and television sites to promote their products. For instance Anheuser Busch created Bud.tv, where "beer drinkers to kick back and take a break with original comedy, sports, and web video entertainment.".

Regardless of the type of advertising, most large advertisers work through intermediaries such as advertising networks (e.g., DoubleClick), or advertising agencies that have an ad placement and creative staff. Other options include swapping ad space with other sites, and dealing directly with the publisher (the Web site that will post the advertisement). **Banner swapping** arrangements among firms allow each firm to have its banners displayed on other affiliate sites for no cost. **Advertising exchanges** arrange for banner swapping among firms, usually small firms that cannot afford expensive ad networks such as DoubleClick. By displaying the banners of other firms, the firm can earn credits toward the display of its banner on other Web sites. Smaller firms have many more opportunities than in the past to place banner ads inexpensively using Yahoo Advertising, Google Ads, and Microsoft's Advertising. Each of these firms provides targeting, segmentation, cross-selling techniques, and ad customization.

**banner swapping**
an arrangement among firms that allows each firm to have its banners displayed on other affiliate sites for no cost

**advertising exchanges**
arrange for banner swapping among firm

### Search Engine Advertising: Paid Search Engine Inclusion and Placement

Arguably, one of the most significant changes in online marketing in the past five years has been the explosive growth in search engine marketing. More than any other form of online advertising, search engine marketing has altered the entire marketing communications industry. This form of marketing communications has been one of the fastest growing: revenues generated by search engine marketing have grown from 1% of total online advertising spending in 2000 to almost 50% in 2010 (see **Figure 7.3**), although the rate of growth is slowing to around 10%–13% a year (eMarketer, Inc., 2010a). The search engine audience is huge—almost as big as the e-mail user population. On an average day in the United States, around 83 million American adults (around 50% of the adult online population) will use a search engine (Pew Internet & American Life Project, 2010). Collectively, they generate around 15–17 billion searches a month. Briefly, this is where the eyeballs are (at least for a few moments) and this is where advertising can be very effective by responding with ads that match the interests and intentions of the user. The click-through rate for search marketing generally is 1%–5% and has been fairly steady over the years.

**FIGURE 7.3** **SEARCH ENGINE MARKETING REVENUES**

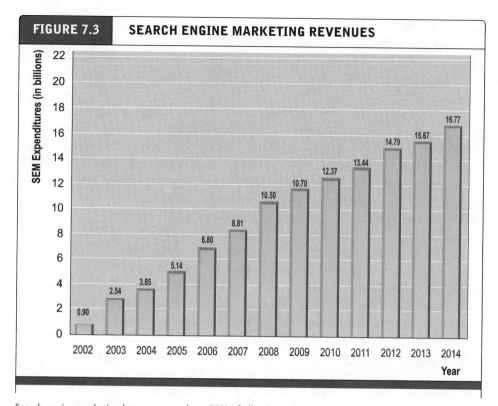

Search engine marketing has grown to about 50% of all online advertising. However, its growth rate has slowed considerably to the low double digits.

SOURCES: Based on data from eMarketer, Inc., 2010a, 2007, 2005.

Today there are hundreds of search engines on the Internet, with about 25 "major" search sites that generate most of the search traffic. Search engine marketing is highly concentrated. The top three search engine providers (Google, Yahoo, and Microsoft) supply over 92% of all the searches to the top 20 sites (see Figure 3.21).

Types of Search Engine Marketing There are at least three different types of search engine marketing: keyword paid inclusion or rank, advertising keywords, and search engine-based advertising networks. Search engine sites originally performed unbiased searches of the Web's huge collection of Web pages and derived most of their revenue from banner advertisements. This form of search engine results is often called **organic search** because the inclusion and ranking of Web sites depends on a more or less "unbiased" application of a set of rules (an algorithm) imposed by the search engine. Since 1998, search engine sites have slowly been transforming themselves into digital yellow pages, where firms pay for inclusion in the search engine index and/or pay for specific locational placement or rank in the results of searches—so-called paid placement or paid rank.

Most search engines offer **paid inclusion** programs which, for a fee, guarantee a Web site's inclusion in its list of search results, more frequent visits by its Web crawler, and suggestions for improving the results of organic searching. Search engines claim

**organic search**
inclusion and ranking of sites depends on a more or less unbiased application of a set of rules imposed by the search engine

**paid inclusion**
for a fee, guarantees a Web site's inclusion in its list of sites, more frequent visits by its Web crawler, and suggestions for improving the results of organic searching

that these payments—costing some merchants hundreds of thousands a year—do not influence the organic ranking of a Web site in search results, just inclusion in the results. However, it is the case that page inclusion ads get more hits, and the rank of the page appreciates, causing the organic search algorithm to rank it higher in the organic results.

Some search engines do not have a paid inclusion program, but do charge for placing small text ads in either sponsored link areas of the results pages or sometimes mixed with organic results (unbeknownst to the user). Google claims it does not permit firms to pay for their rank in the organic results, although it does allocate two to three sponsored links at the very top of their pages, albeit labeling them as "Sponsored Links." Some search engines make it very difficult for the user to know if the top-listed results of a search are paid inclusions or the result of objective search criteria. Merchants who refuse to pay for inclusion typically fall far down on the list and off the first page of results, which is akin to commercial death.

Research demonstrates the significance of rank in both organic and paid placements, and equally important, the greater power that users attach to organic search results (see **Figure 7.4**). Researchers used an eye-tracking tool to gauge Web users' behavior at search engines. They discovered an "F" shaped pattern in which viewers scan search result pages from top to bottom, with greater attention to the left side of the page looking for clues. They spend less time on the right side of the page looking at paid text advertisements, and usually only at the top three advertisements. Users always viewed the first three organic listings, but were much less likely to view

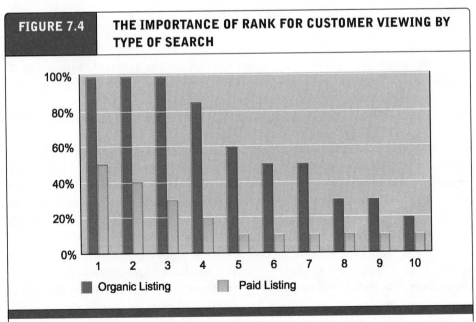

**FIGURE 7.4**   **THE IMPORTANCE OF RANK FOR CUSTOMER VIEWING BY TYPE OF SEARCH**

■ Organic Listing   ■ Paid Listing

Nearly everyone reads the top three-ranked results in organic search results, but readership drops off rather dramatically for the 4th through 10th-ranked results. Sponsored links are heavily discounted by readers—only 50% read the top-ranked sponsored results listed, and readership drops off sharply after that.

SOURCE: Based on data from Hotchkiss, et al., 2007.

the sponsored listings. These results have been replicated several times using eye heat maps (Google, 2009; Shrestha and Lenz, 2007; Nielsen, 2006).

The two other types of search engine marketing rely on selling keywords in online auctions.

In **keyword advertising**, merchants purchase keywords through a bidding process at search sites, and whenever a consumer searches for that word, their advertisement shows up somewhere on the page, usually as a small text-based advertisement on the right, but also as a listing on the very top of the page. The more merchants pay, the higher the rank and greater the visibility of their ads on the page. Generally, the search engines do not exercise editorial judgment about quality or content of the ads although they do monitor the use of language. In addition, some search engines rank the ads in terms of their popularity rather than merely the money paid by the advertiser so that the rank of the ad depends both on the amount paid and the number of clicks per unit time. Google's keyword advertising program is called AdWords, Yahoo's is called Sponsored Search, and Microsoft's is called adCenter.

**Network keyword advertising** (**context advertising**), introduced by Google in 2002, differs from ordinary keyword advertising described previously. Here's how these search engine networks operate. Publishers (Web site owners) join the network, and allow the search engine to place "relevant" ads on their sites. The ads are paid for by advertisers who want their messages to appear across the Web. Google-like text messages are the most common. The revenue from the resulting clicks is split between the search engine and the site publisher although in some cases the publisher gets much more than half. The publisher has no direct control over what ads are shown on his/her site. The advertiser has no control over where their ads appear either. But the search engines use a variety of tools (keyword analysis and propinquity of keywords) to ensure only "relevant" and "appropriate" ads appear. For this reason, network keyword advertising is often called "context marketing" because an effort is made to understand the context where the ad will be shown. Google calls this "AdSense," knowing where to place ads based on the surrounding context. Yahoo's program is called Content Match. Together, keyword and network keyword advertising account for most of the revenue growth in search engine marketing. About half of Google's revenue comes from AdWords and the rest comes from AdSense.

In this manner, search engines have greatly extended their keyword advertising beyond their own sites (where users do not linger) to tens of thousands of other sites on the Web. Unfortunately, these programs have also led to the creation of "junk AdSense" sites composed of re-hashed links from the Web, and an entire industry of illegitimate poachers who nevertheless are paid when their Web site visitors click an AdSense link.

Keywords for both types of keyword advertising range in price from a few pennies per click to $25 or above for high-priced popular items (see **Figure 7.5**). The highest keyword prices are paid for potential litigation customers by law firms. The family of "mesothelioma" keywords sell for up to $800 a click. How much would you pay (or should you pay) to place your company's listing in front of the consumer just at the precise moment the consumer is looking for products provided by your company? This depends, of course, on how much customers are likely to spend at your site. And it depends on how much your competitors are willing to pay for the same keyword. In an auction environment, it is easy to overpay or under pay.

**keyword advertising**
merchants purchase keywords through a bidding process at search sites, and whenever a consumer searches for that word, their advertisement shows up somewhere on the page

**network keyword advertising (context advertising)**
network of publishers accepts ads placed by Google on their Web sites, and receive a fee for any click-throughs from those ads

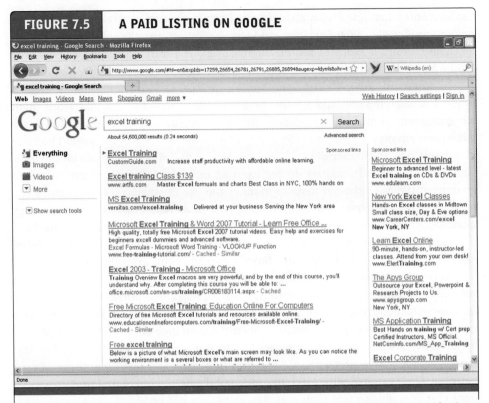

A search on "Excel training" on Google's search engine brings up a list of companies that have paid for their inclusion and placement on the search results list.
SOURCE: Google.com . Reproduced with permission of Google Inc. © 2010 Google.

Search engine marketing is nearly an ideal targeted marketing technique: at precisely the moment that a consumer is looking for a product, an advertisement for that product is presented. While originally this was the idea behind advertising networks such as DoubleClick and Real Media 24/7, their database techniques cannot deliver the advertisement with as much accuracy or speed at the moment of interest. Unlike traditional online and offline targeted marketing approaches, which are based on searching large databases for customer profiles and information, search engine marketing is based on the much more efficient idea of responding to keyword searches at that moment (although prior searches from the IP address, or keywords gleaned from other sources such as Google's Gmail, can also influence the results). No databases on clickstream behavior or background demographics are generally used. The most important fact for search engine marketers is that the customer is looking for a product like the one sold by the merchant.

In some cases, search engines do not inform the user that the results of a query have been paid for by participating firms, or they make it difficult to tell what is paid and what is the result of unbiased search. Some analysts argue that users don't care if merchants pay for listings—just as they don't care when they use the yellow pages—

as long as the searches produce relevant results. Some have even argued that informing the user about the commercial nature of placement and listings would harm e-commerce because users have been trained by the industry to "avoid anything that looks commercial." Users might actually not pursue appropriate and relevant links if they thought the listing was commercially influenced. A number of complaints had been filed with the Federal Trade Commission (FTC) that search engines that fail to clearly indicate they accept payments for higher search ranking are engaging in deceptive practices. In July 2002, the FTC recommended to the search engine industry that it should improve the disclosure of paid content within search results (Sullivan, 2003). A follow-up study by Consumer Reports WebWatch found that paid inclusion was not satisfactorily disclosed or explained by any of the search engines tested; meta-engines, which present results from several search engines simultaneously, repeatedly failed to adequately disclose the presence of paid placement and paid inclusion within search results; and disclosures when made are generally hard to find, making them easy for consumers to overlook. The report also found that information disclosed by Web sites about business practices with advertisers—and how these practices may affect search results—was often confusing and jargon-laden. Some search engines, such as Google (one of the few major search engines not named in the original FTC complaint) took pains to visually segregate paid results from non-paid results (Consumer Reports WebWatch, 2004, 2005). The search engine industry has the online population pretty confused about where the results come from. A Pew Internet & American Life Project study found that 62% of search engine users were not aware of the difference between paid and unpaid results, and 70% accepted the concept of sponsored results. Half said they would stop using a search engine if they felt it was not being honest about how the results are produced (Pew Internet & American Life Project, 2005).

Why does search engine marketing work so well and why is it so popular with both merchants and consumers? For merchants, search engine marketing is close to ideal for sales promotion. Paid search engine inclusion and placement is one of the most effective marketing communications tools on the Web, given that on any given day about 83 million American adults use a search engine to find products and information.

The major search engines have been very helpful to small businesses that cannot afford large marketing campaigns. Because shoppers are looking for a specific product or service when they use search engines, they are what marketers call "hot prospects"—people who are looking for information and often intending to buy. Moreover, search engines charge only for click-throughs to a site. Merchants do not have to pay for ads that don't work. Last, merchants do not have to be at the mercy of search engine ranking and listing rules that they—and most others—cannot understand. No one really knows, for instance, exactly how or why Google decides to organically rank one company over another, or to refuse a company a listing in the front pages. No one really knows how to improve their rankings (although there are hundreds of firms who claim otherwise). In fact, according to Google's own self-description of its search engine, listings are biased toward already popular Web sites to whom many consumers connect, and ignore new startup companies or put them on back pages. Google editors intervene in unknown ways to punish certain Web sites and reward others. Search engines such as Google maintain a stranglehold over small companies trying to get national market exposure. Paid listings change much of this. A company simply pays Google or another search engine and has the certain knowledge that its ad will appear on the page and with a rank that reflects its bid. For many merchants who can afford this, the reduction in uncertainty is worth the price.

What about consumers? Consumers benefit from search engine marketing because ads for merchants appear only when consumers are looking for a specific product. There are no pop-ups, Flash animations, videos, interstitials, e-mails, or other irrelevant communications to deal with. Thus, search engine marketing saves consumers cognitive energy. Search engine marketing works because it is primarily pull-oriented: consumers pull the information they are looking for.

**Search Engine Click Fraud and Ad Nonsense** The Achilles' heel of search engine marketing is "click fraud." Just as spam has greatly reduced the utility of e-mail marketing, so has click fraud raised the costs and reduced the attractiveness of search engine marketing to merchants. Much of the Internet depends on openness, trust, and ethical behavior by participants. Click fraud strikes at the heart of these assumptions.

Anyone, including competitors, can click on search engine ads, driving up a merchant's costs, without ever purchasing anything. If you are a Web site publisher, you can increase your revenue by having friends and relatives click on the ads Google or Microsoft place on your site. **Click fraud** occurs when (a) a competitor fraudulently clicks on another competitor's ads in order to drive up their marketing costs, or (b) a Web site publisher fraudulently clicks on ads posted on their sites in order to increase ad revenue. Some fraudsters have developed "click bots" that automatically click on ads from hundreds of different IP addresses, and utilize zombie computers (unprotected clients on the Web that have been captured by adware programs) to generate the clicks, which are untraceable. A related type of click fraud involves fraudsters who call up a search results page where their competitors' ads appear, and then fail to click on competitor ads. This results in a low ad popularity rank for these Google AdWords and AdSense ads, which in turn can result in their being pushed down the rank order of ads onto the lower part of the page.

Search engines attempt to monitor and prevent this behavior by observing traffic patterns, but find it difficult to trace fraudulent clicks because defrauders can hide their offshore IP addresses. Current research suggests the click fraud rate in the United States is around 18% of all clicks (Click Forensics, 2010). The amount of publisher-originated click fraud is not known. SEMPO, the Search Engine Marketing Professional Organization (a trade association of marketers in part sponsored by search engine firms), reports that 40% of large advertisers felt click fraud was a problem, 19% of advertisers attempt to track click fraud, and about 50% of advertisers have reduced their keyword search budgets because of click fraud (Fair Isaac Corporation, 2007). Click fraud can be difficult but not impossible to detect. The typical click fraud pattern is one where clicks increase and sales remain the same or decline. Large departures from historical click rates (such as one standard deviation or more) are suspect. Search engine firms such as Google and Yahoo do refund

**click fraud**

occurs when a competitor hires third parties (typically from low-wage countries) to fraudulently click on another competitor's ads

charges in suspicious situations. A somewhat less severe issue is the appearance of "ad nonsense," which occurs because Google's AdSense program places ads on thousands of Web sites using a computer program that attempts to understand the content of the Web page. Sometimes, the computer program makes mistakes, such as when a search on the term "lost dogs" produces ads on Google offering "great deals" on lost dogs, and ads for "disease," "sewage," and "rot." Even more disturbing to advertisers, sometimes ads for products show up on Web sites totally unrelated to that product. For instance, Kraft Foods ads for cheese appeared on a Web site of a "White Nationalist" hate group that used the words "Thanksgiving" on its Web site.

## Mobile Advertising: iAd and AdMob

Mobile devices such as smartphones, iPhones, and iPads are increasingly the tools of choice for consumers to access the Internet. Roughly half the American Internet user population, about 83 million people, use mobile devices to access the Internet in 2010. Smartphone users spend on average about 30 minutes every day accessing apps and the Internet. Both Apple and Google are in a race to develop a new mobile advertising platform based on their respective operating systems and the software apps that are the foundation of their popularity and functionality. In 2010, this is a nascent and tiny market of about $500 million in advertising revenue, but it is arguably the fastest growing platform at 35% in the last year. The mobile ad market comes along at a time when growth in search and display advertising is slowing to the low double digits (Kane and Steel, 2010).

In November 2009, Google beat out Apple for the purchase of AdMob, a company that had developed software to display ads within apps, paying $750 million. In January 2010, Apple bought Quattro Wireless, which had also developed software for displaying ads within apps, for $275 million. Both Apple and Google are folding these capabilities into their operating systems. Unlike traditional Web advertising (and most mobile advertising), the new mobile ad platforms do not take users to external Web sites, but instead display ads within the application. This has certain benefits for the app developers because it keeps consumers in the app rather than having them drift off to another Web site.

Application developers make money both charging for their apps, as well as showing ads. Large media companies like ESPN, CBS, CNN and others offer free apps largely to extend their brands, leverage their content, and find new venues to show their ads. Advertisers currently are in an experimental mode developing iAd and AdMob formats and seeking to ensure they have a presence on the new platform (LeClaire, 2010; Clifford, 2009).

## Sponsorships

A **sponsorship** is a paid effort to tie an advertiser's name to particular information, an event, or a venue in a way that reinforces its brand in a positive yet not overtly commercial manner. Sponsorships typically are more about branding than immediate sales. A common form of sponsorship is targeted content (or advertorials), in which editorial content is combined with an ad message to make the message more valuable

**sponsorship**
a paid effort to tie an advertiser's name to information, an event, or a venue in a way that reinforces its brand in a positive yet not overtly commercial manner

and attractive to its intended audience. For instance, WebMD.com, the leading medical information Web site in the United States, offers "sponsorship sites" on the WebMD Web site to companies such as Phillips to describe their home defibrillators, and Lilly to describe their pharmaceutical solutions for attention deficit disorders among children. According to eMarketer, sponsorships accounted for around $402 million in online advertising revenues in 2008 (eMarketer, Inc., 2010a).

### Referrals (Affiliate Relationship Marketing)

**affiliate relationships**
permit a firm to put its logo or banner ad on another firm's Web site from which users of that site can click through to the affiliate's site

An **affiliate relationship** permits a firm (the originating Web site) to place its logo, banner ad, or text link on another firm's Web site (called the affiliate) from which users of that site can click through to the originating site. Millions of personal Web sites have Amazon and other logos that when clicked will take the visitor to Amazon, and generate revenue for the Web site. Among large firms, affiliate relationships are sometimes called "tenancy deals" because they allow a firm to become a long-term "tenant" on another site. Amazon has tenancy relationships with a number of retailers. In some cases, the firms share a single corporate parent or investor group that is seeking to optimize the performance of all its Web sites by creating links among its "children" sites. In other cases, two Web sites may sell complementary products and the firms may strike an affiliate relationship to make it easier for their customers to find the products they are looking for.

### E-MAIL MARKETING AND THE SPAM EXPLOSION

**direct e-mail marketing**
e-mail marketing messages sent directly to interested users

In the early days of e-commerce, **direct e-mail marketing** (e-mail marketing messages sent directly to interested users) was one of the most effective forms of marketing communications. Direct e-mail marketing messages were sent to an "opt-in" audience of Internet users who, at one time or another, had expressed an interest in receiving messages from the advertiser. Unsolicited e-mail was not common. By sending e-mail to an opt-in audience, advertisers were targeting interested consumers. Response rates to legitimate, opt-in e-mail campaigns average just over 6%, depending on the targeting and freshness of the list. By far, in-house e-mail lists are more effective than purchased e-mail lists. Because of the comparatively high response rates and low cost, direct e-mail marketing remains a common form of online marketing communications. In 2010, the total amount U.S. companies spent on e-mail marketing was about $276 million (eMarketer, Inc., 2010a). Click-through rates for legitimate e-mails depend on the promotion (the offer), the product, and the amount of targeting, but average 6% for an in-house list, higher than postal mail response rates (3.5%) (Direct Marketing Association, 2010). Despite the deluge of spam mail, e-mail remains a highly cost-effective way of communicating with existing customers, and to a lesser extent, finding new customers.

E-mail marketing and advertising is inexpensive and somewhat invariant to the number of mails sent. The cost of sending 1,000 mails is about the same as the cost to send 1 million. The primary cost of e-mail marketing is for the purchase of the list of names to which the e-mail will be sent. This generally costs anywhere from 5 to 20 cents a name, depending on how targeted the list is. Sending the e-mail is virtually cost-free. In contrast, a direct mail 5 x 7-inch post card mailing costs about 15 cents per name, but printing and mailing costs raise the overall cost to around 75 to 80 cents a name. While the cost of legitimate e-mail messages based on high-quality commercial opt-in e-mail lists is $5 to $10 per thousand, the direct mail cost is $500 to $700 per thousand when all costs are added up.

In 2010, however, e-mail no longer commands quite as much respect as it once did because of three factors: spam, software tools used to control spam that eliminate much e-mail from user in-boxes, and poorly targeted purchased e-mail lists. **Spam** is "junk e-mail," and *spammers* are people who send unsolicited e-mail to a mass audience that has not expressed any interest in the product. Spammers tend to market pornography, fraudulent deals and services, scams, and other products not widely approved in most civilized societies. Legitimate direct opt-in e-mail marketing is not growing as fast as behaviorally targeted banners, pop-ups, and search engine marketing because of the explosion in spam. Consumer response to even legitimate e-mail campaigns has become more sophisticated. Almost three-quarters of Internet users say they see value in e-mail from companies they do business with, while only 17% saw value when the e-mail came from companies they do not do business with. As Internet users become more experienced with spam filters, more and more (currently around 70%) delete spam before opening based on the "From" line or the "Subject" line. Over 60% of users find commercial spam unpleasant and 20% report reducing their use of e-mail due to spam. In general, e-mail works well for maintaining customer relationships, but poorly for acquiring new customers.

While click fraud may be the Achilles' heel of search engine marketing, spam is the nemesis of effective e-mail marketing and advertising. The percentage of all e-mail that is spam is estimated at around 90% in 2010 (Symantec MessageLabs, 2010) (see **Figure 7.6**). The largest spamming nation is the United States, which has the largest number of botnets and accounts for about 10% of all spam in the world.

The cost of entry to the spam business or "mass bulk e-mailing business" is small. Hundreds of programs that can be purchased on the Web allow spammers to harvest e-mail addresses across the Web from message boards and chat rooms; downloads of millions of names are available. Spammers do not generally pay anything for the cost of distributing their spam because they send the messages using captured client and server computers. About 85% of all spam originates with botnets. The explosion in spam has led to many unsuccessful efforts to control the deluge. There are four solutions to spam: technology, government legislation, voluntary self-regulation, and volunteer efforts to identify spammers and either shut them down or inform authorities. Obviously, none of these approaches has been successful to date, each approach has many advocates and entrepreneurs, and all approaches combined just might make a difference.

Legislative attempts to control spam have also largely not succeeded. Thirty-seven states in the United States have laws regulating or prohibiting spam (National Conference of State Legislatures, 2010). State legislation typically requires that unsolicited mail (spam) contain a label in the subject line ("ADV") indicating the message is an advertisement, require a clear opt-out choice for consumers, and prohibit e-mail that contains false routing and domain name information (nearly all

**spam**
unsolicited commercial e-mail

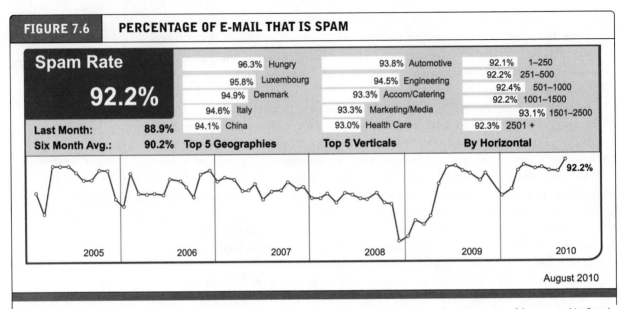

**FIGURE 7.6** | **PERCENTAGE OF E-MAIL THAT IS SPAM**

After a period of decline, spam volume has resumed growth largely because of the greater number and sophistication of "spam zombies" and "bot networks," which consist of thousands of captured PCs that can initiate and relay spam messages. Spam is seasonally cyclical, and varies monthly due to the impact of new technologies (both supportive and discouraging of spammers), new prosecutions, and seasonal demand for products and services. Spam seems to peak in June.

SOURCE: Symantec MessageLabs, 2010.

spammers hide their own domain, ISP, and IP address). Some states, such as California and Delaware, are much stricter and prohibit all unsolicited e-mail to or from state citizens and require a specific "opt-in" choice before consumers can be sent e-mail. In Virginia, sending spam is a criminal felony offense.

Congress passed the first national anti-spam law ("Controlling the Assault of Non-Solicited Pornography and Marketing" or CAN-SPAM Act) in 2003, and it went into effect in January 2004. The act does not prohibit unsolicited e-mail (spam) but instead requires unsolicited commercial e-mail messages to be labeled (though not by a standard method) and to include opt-out instructions and the sender's physical address. It prohibits the use of deceptive subject lines and false headers in such messages. The FTC is authorized (but not required) to establish a "do-not-e-mail" registry. State laws that require labels on unsolicited commercial e-mail or prohibit such messages entirely are pre-empted, although provisions merely addressing falsity and deception may remain in place. The act imposes fines of $10 for each unsolicited pornographic e-mail and authorizes state attorneys general to bring lawsuits against spammers. The act obviously makes lawful legitimate bulk mailing of unsolicited e-mail messages (what most people call spam), yet seeks to prohibit certain deceptive practices and provide a small measure of consumer control by requiring opt-out notices. In this sense, critics point out, CAN-SPAM ironically legalizes spam as long as spammers follow the rules. For this reason, large spammers have been among the bill's biggest supporters, and consumer groups have been the

Act's most vociferous critics. Major business interest groups also lobbied against the CAN-SPAM bill. Citicorp, Schwab, Procter & Gamble, the National Retail Foundation, the Securities Industry Association, and the American Insurance Association all argued that the act would harm legitimate e-mail marketing and put e-commerce at a disadvantage.

There have been a number of state and federal prosecutions of spammers, and private civil suits by large ISPs such as Microsoft. For instance, in May 2007, Robert Soloway, a 27-year-old Seattle man also known as the "Spam King," was arrested after being indicted by a federal grand jury on 16 counts of mail fraud, e-mail fraud, wire fraud, and aggravated identity theft. According to the indictment, Soloway, operating under the name "Newport Internet Marketing," claimed to have a list of 158 million e-mail addresses, and charged $495 for a typical blast of 20 million e-mails sent over 15 days. Soloway obtained the e-mail addresses from "harvesting" programs and spyware programs that read lists from infected computers. He sold the lists to businesses claiming they contained only the addresses of "opt-in" prospects. Then, using remote botnets, he sent out blast e-mails of 20 to 100 million spam messages at a time. In 2007, prosecutors won a $7.8 million judgment against the Spam King, and in March 2008 he pleaded guilty to federal criminal charges that he failed to pay income taxes on his spam income. Soloway faces 26 years in prison. Currently, the FBI and Justice Department have over 100 spam and phishing investigations under way. The largest prosecution to date occurred in June 2009 when five spammers from Detroit were sentenced to six years in prision. They were charged with masterminding a systematic campaign to deceive consumers with messages containing "materially false and misleading information or omissions" promoting junk stocks for U.S. companies owned and controlled by individuals in Hong Kong and China.

Volunteer efforts by industry are another potential control point. Notably, the Direct Marketing Association (DMA), an industry trade group that represents companies that use the postal mail system as well as e-mail for solicitations, is now strongly supporting legislative controls over spam, in addition to its voluntary guidelines. The DMA would like to preserve the legitimate use of e-mail as a marketing technique. The DMA has formed a 15-person anti-spam group and spends $500,000 a year trying to identify spammers. The DMA also is a supporter of the National Cyber-Forensics & Training Alliance (NCFTA), a purportedly non-profit organization with "close ties" to the FBI. NCFTA operates a program called Operation Slam Spam, which seeks to identify the IP addresses of the largest spammers, and has a database of over 400 known spam addresses.

## ONLINE CATALOGS

Online catalogs are the equivalent of a paper-based catalog. Online catalogs were popular in the early years of e-commerce but quickly went out of favor among advertisers because the pages took so long to load. But with about 96% of the online households using broadband high-speed connections in 2010, graphic-intense pages load quickly, and the possibilities for advertisers to re-use their paper catalog photos increase. Web publishers such as Catalogs.com have made it far easier for even small merchants to find an audience and re-purpose their expensive four-color offline catalogs. The result is a resurgence in online catalogs. The number of online catalogs in 2010 has more than doubled since 2005. E-catalog sales in 2009 were over $14 billion, down from $18 billion due to the recession. Future growth is estimated to be 10% annually as before the recession (Internet Retailer, 2010a; eMarketer, Inc., 2010b).

The basic function of a catalog is to display the merchant's wares (see **Figure 7.7**). The electronic version typically contains a color image of each available product and a description of the item, as well as size, color, material composition, and pricing information. There are two different types of online catalogs: full-page spreads and grid displays. Most online retailers use a grid display in which multiple products are shown in very small postage-stamp photos. This is typical of Amazon, LLBean.com, and Gap.com. The other alternative is to use larger page spreads using large photos to display one or two products; Hammacher.com, Landsend.com, and Restorationhardware.com use this approach, among others. The cost of building an online catalog ranges from $30,000–$50,000 for smaller Web sites, to several million for an online catalog with thousands of products and images.

How do companies integrate online catalogs with physical catalogs? Most direct mail catalog companies continue to use physical direct mail catalogs, and pure online

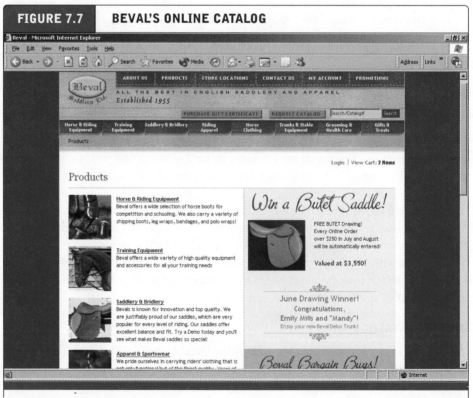

**FIGURE 7.7**   **BEVAL'S ONLINE CATALOG**

Beval Saddlery Ltd.'s Web site offers a variety of riding apparel and equipment. Customers can click on one of the product categories listed on the left side of the screen and are taken to a page listing products within that category. Clicking on a particular product takes the customer to a page with a description and photo of the product and an order button.

SOURCE: Beval Saddlery, Ltd., 2010.

companies have begun to supplement their online advertising with physical catalogs. Direct mail companies can increase their operational efficiency by sending electronic catalogs to customers before sending out the physical catalogs. This evens out the flow of orders. In general, merchants find that online and offline catalogs are complementary and do not cannibalize or substitute for one another. The flow of orders increases as the overall awareness of the company brand increases when both channels are used simultaneously. On the other hand, research suggests that the effects are subtle, and that much depends on the type of customer ("good" versus "best" customers) and their prior Internet experience (Anderson, et al., 2005).

## SOCIAL MARKETING: BLOGS, SOCIAL NETWORKS, AND GAMES

The two key elements of Web 2.0 are the rapid growth of user-generated content and the use of the Internet for socializing and sharing. In 2010, there are an estimated 500 millions Facebook members worldwide,145 million Twitter users, and 75 million who have joined LinkedIn. In the United States, in August 2010, Facebook had around 150 million unique visitors, while Fox Interactive (MySpace) had around 80 million (comScore, 2010b). It's little wonder that marketers and advertisers are joyous at the prospect of connecting with this large audience. Microsoft's purchase of an interest in Facebook, and Google's purchase of YouTube, suggest the excitement in the marketing community for the advertising potential of social networks. Although in the past, major brands have been reluctant to risk advertising on sites whose content they cannot control, they are beginning to experiment with a number of new formats. In 2010, social site advertising and marketing are expected to exceed $1.6 billion (eMarketer Inc., 2010e).

It is difficult to define "social marketing" precisely. At one level it's simply placing display ads on social sites. But a more complete working definition might be that it is advertising that adopts a many-to-many model as opposed to a one-to-many model of traditional advertising, where a central broadcaster sends the same message to millions of people. For instance, when Disney released its *Toy Story 3* video trailer on YouTube in June 2010, it quickly generated 13 million views. Over 1 million viewers shared it with friends, and another 800,000 clicked "Like" to share it with their friends on Facebook or other social sites. So an existing social network composed of many people and their friends distributes the Disney message to a great many other people.

This kind of marketing is "social" because, like traditional word-of-mouth and viral marketing, it relies on pre-existing social networks to spread the message. However, in this case, the social networks exist on the Internet, and they are digitally enabled networks whose members have extraordinary tools to spread the message far, wide, and very quickly. The vast majority of online social network members are also friends offline, or friends of friends offline (Ellison, et. al., 2006). Hence the offline world and the online world are intimately connected.

The three main areas of social marketing are blog, social network, and game advertising.

## Blog Advertising

Blogs are high on the list of advertising tactics that marketing executives consider. In 2010, blog advertising revenue will be about $500 million (out of a total online ad spend of $25 billion) during that year, and is expected to grow to $746 million by 2012 (eMarketer, Inc., 2008). Blogs have proved difficult to monetize because few blogs attract large audiences, and the subject matter of most blogs is highly personal and idiosyncratic. Search engines have a difficult time "reading" blogs, understanding their content, and making a judgment about the appropriateness of their ad inventory. Advertising dollars are therefore concentrated in the top 100 blogs, which have a coherent theme that consistently attracts larger audiences. Because blog readers and creators tend to be more educated, have higher incomes, and be opinion leaders, they are ideal recipients of ads for many products and services that cater to this kind of an audience. Advertising networks that specialize in blogs provide some efficiency in placing ads, as do blog networks, which are collections of a small number of popular blogs, coordinated by a central management team, and which can deliver a larger audience to advertisers. Nevertheless, outside of the established top 100 blogs, blog advertising will be a small part of online advertising.

## Social Network Advertising

Social marketing on all sites is growing at 34% a year, faster than any other online format as advertisers chase the social network population. Although still in its infancy, social network advertising is the largest and fastest growing form of social marketing, generating over $1.6 billion in revenue for 2010. There are a number of different types of social networks, from general purpose (Facebook), to niche networks of professionals and hobbyists, to sponsored networks created by firms. However, most of the social advertising action is at Facebook ($835 million), MySpace ($330 million), and YouTube (estimated to be somewhere between $500 and $800 million) (eMarketer, Inc., 2010e). Twitter and LinkedIn ad revenues are still quite small at this point, but growing.

Social networks offer advertisers all the formats found on portal and search sites including banner ads (the most common), short pre-roll and post-roll ads before a video, and sponsorship of content. For instance, Adidas, Burger King, General Electric, Toyota Yaris, and Verizon have profile pages on MySpace and Facebook. Other national brand names have posted videos on YouTube. Chevrolet, Geico, and Mars have encouraged users to create their own ads, and sponsored contests to choose the best ads.

There are several dangers to social network advertising. User-generated ads can obviously generate negative messages that are widely distributed. The content of many YouTube videos and MySpace profiles is repugnant to many American consumers and could taint brands associated with sites that permit this kind of content although entertainment firms may benefit from this milieu. While Google and YouTube have developed ways to display text and background ads alongside playing videos, many advertisers do not yet trust the software used to select the appropriate videos for an ad.

For instance, a 2010 study found that 79 percent of regular social networkers say they would be likely to watch a television show based on a recommendation from a friend via a social network site. Thirty-three percent of regular social networkers said they learned about a new television show because of something they saw on a social network site. Clearly, social networks are influential in shaping consumer viewing habits (Cable & Telecommunications Association for Marketing (CTAM), 2010).

It is easy to overstate the growth in social marketing, and it is risky to ignore it. Currently, the three major search engines/portals have a much higher Internet audience share of the U.S. online population visiting their sites on a daily and weekly basis than even the largest social network sites, or even all of the social sites combined. Google and Yahoo each have more than around 180 million unique visitors a month, Microsoft about 165 million, and AOL, 107 million. Still, the social media sites have substantial audiences. Therefore, marketers should continue investing in search engine and portal display advertising, while experimenting in social marketing. In the longer term of the next five years, with current trends, it is likely that social network sites will equal the audience share of major portals and search engines, challenging these "older" venues for dominance in advertising platforms.

## Game Advertising

According to a report published by CTAM, there is a video game console in around 40% of American households (50 million) (Cable & Telecommunications Association for Marketing (CTAM), 2009).The game advertising platform is expanding rapidly in part because of smartphone mobile gaming: 64 million people every month will play games on their smartphones this year. Today most games are played in social environments with multiple players in the same room, or over the Internet. We include them in a discussion of social marketing because of the mutually influential social environment in which most digital video games are played today. There are, of course, many kinds of games that are broadcast by a game sponsor—over 800 million sponsored games were downloaded in 2009 to millions of users. So-called "advergames" are sponsored games to promote brands. Coca-Cola, Burger King, and Taco Bell, along with many other national brands, have used advergames. These kinds of games could be considered a unique kind of display ad that is highly interactive, but not necessarily social.

U.S. video in-game advertising will generate about $1.1 billion in 2010, and it is estimated that it will increase to over $1.4 billion by 2013. While we tend to think of online gamers as mostly male, in fact over 40% of gamers are female, a percentage that increased significantly with the introduction of the Nintendo Wii. One quarter of gamers are over 50, and half of gamers are 18–49.

The limitations of game advertising are due in part to game content, which tends to be attractive to young males and females, but not to a much larger audience. Many advertisers do not want their brands to be associated with violence, mayhem, and war-like scenarios, or sexual content that is often present in video games. *Insight on Society: Marketing to Children of the Web in the Age of Social Networks* considers some of the social issues that marketing to children on the Web present.

# INSIGHT ON SOCIETY

## MARKETING TO CHILDREN OF THE WEB IN THE AGE OF SOCIAL NETWORKS

Children grow up today in an Internet world where 70% of all American households are online. There are around 42 million kids under the age of 18 online, with tens of millions of them visiting Web sites such as Wrigley's Candystand.com ("the sweetest games online"), Postopia.com ("a fun site for kids"), and Millsberry.com ("a town full of millions of kids just like you and me"). Millsberry is a General Mills-sponsored site with games encouraging kids to watch Lucky Charms webisodes and play games to hunt for Reese's Puffs online. Kids spend more time on these sites than they do watching TV commercials. Industry self-regulation requires firms not to advertise to children younger than 12, but sites such as Kraft's NabiscoWorld.com includes games that appeal to younger audiences, such as Oreos Race for the Stuf, whereby a player-controlled character can twist, lick, and dunk oversize Oreo cookies. An FTC report concluded that U.S. food firms were spending $1.6 billion on advertising to children, about half of that to children under 12. Critics argue, and the FTC expresses concern, that most of this advertising is for foods that make children obese and pose a health threat.

Children as young as three or four years old can often recognize brands and status items before they can even read, and almost 75% of four-year olds generally ask their parents for specific brands. These findings are cause for celebration for some marketers. In the United States, 56 million school-age children spend approximately $100 billion annually of their own and their family's money on food, drinks, video and electronic products, toys, and clothing, and they influence family spending decisions valued at another $165 billion.

In order to capture a portion of this spending and position themselves for future purchases as the child ages, marketers are becoming increasingly interested in advertising aimed at children. In addition to investing in television advertising, which accounts for around 70% of the total amount spent on advertising to children in the United States, marketers focus on children have who have migrated to the Web. Over 20% of all Internet users are children, totaling more than 43 million users under the age of 18, split fairly evenly between the 2–11 year age group (20 million) and the 12–17 year old age group (23 million).

The Web provides marketers an entirely new arsenal to influence really young children. What's in the arsenal? Here are some of the most common child-advertiser tools: mobile phone marketing; behavioral profiling; digital "360 buzz" campaigns; commercialized online "communities," viral videos; game advertising; and avatar advertising. Using online custom banner ads, product characters, games, virtual worlds, and surveys, marketers are both influencing behaviors and gathering valuable data about purchasing preferences and family members. Coupled with in-bedroom televisions, video games, cell phones, and other digital paraphernalia, a children's "digital culture" has been created with built-in avenues to the psyche of very young minds—minds that are so young they are unlikely to know when they are being marketed to and when they are given misleading or even harmful information.

And as if this wasn't enough—then came social network sites, virtual worlds aimed at kids, and social bookmarking sites. In 2010, there are an estimated 200 virtual worlds aimed at children

(continued)

under 18 in the United States. Over 16 million children in the United States visit virtual worlds on a regular basis, and 17 million visit social network sites. A study funded by Microsoft, News Corp. (MySpace), and Verizon found that 70% of children visit social network sites weekly and over 50% had participated in some kind of advertiser-branded activity such as visiting a company profile page in the past month. Marketers are moving aggressively to use online social networks and viral marketing to get kids hooked on brands early in life. For instance, Red Bull does little traditional TV advertising in the 100 countries where it sells energy drinks. Instead it has been using Web-based contests and games such as the Red Bull Art of Can, where people create sculptures out of Red Bull cans and submit photos of their handiwork. The prize: a trip for two to Switzerland.

You may not have heard of AXE (a product of Unilever), a deodorant for young men that apparently drives girls crazy for them. AXE Vice President Russell Taylor's goal is for the brand to become truly global. The sales pitch is simple: "Hey, dude, spray AXE deodorant all over your body, and you will become irresistible to beautiful young women." The branding message: a female wolf whistle and the phrase "Bom Chicka Wah Wah," expressed in a woman's sexy voice. Armed with this powerful message to the world's teenagers, AXE launched the product in the United States by posting online videos that supposedly show the "AXE effect" of women chasing men who used the spray. The response was sensational: millions of people forwarded the videos to friends by e-mail in a massive viral outpouring. Marketers also created an online game wherein guys indicated the kind of young woman they were interested in and got recommendations on which AXE fragrance to buy. You can bet that many of these postings and shared experiences were by children under the age of 13. Using social networks, blogs, and YouTube, in a way much more powerful than earlier Web marketing to children, marketers are able to circumvent what few restrictions on marketing to children exist.

While such moves may be savvy marketing, are they ethical? Some people say no. Research conducted in 1996 by the Center for Media Education (CME), showed that young children cannot understand the potential effects of revealing their personal information; neither can they distinguish between substantive material on Web sites and the advertisements surrounding it. While some parents tried to monitor their children's use of the Internet services, many of them failed due to lack of time, computer skills, or awareness of risk. Targeting of children by marketing techniques resulted in the release of a large amount of private information into the market and triggered the need for regulation.

Experts argue that since children don't understand persuasive intent until they are eight or nine years old, it is unethical to advertise to them before they can distinguish between advertising and the real world. Others believe that fair advertising is an important, and necessary, part of the maturation process for future adults in today's society. But does that argument hold when children are gaining increased access to information about unhealthy activities, such as beer drinking through Web sites geared to a younger audience? Although brewers admit they are targeting a younger market segment—twenty-somethings—they have set up warning screens and registration pages that require users to enter a birth date proving they are of legal drinking age. Of course, there is no process to verify such data, making it easy for underage consumers to gain access to, and be influenced by, entertaining content at drinking-oriented Web sites.

In 1998, Congress passed the Children's Online Privacy Protection Act (COPPA) after the FTC discovered that 80% of Web sites were collecting personal information from children, but only 1% required their parents' permission.

(continued)

Under COPPA, companies must post a privacy policy on their Web sites, detailing exactly how they collect information from consumers, how they'll use it, and the degrees to which they'll protect consumer privacy. Companies are not permitted to use personal information collected from children under 13 years of age without the prior, verifiable consent of parents. But the problem is that the FTC and others have been unable to specify exactly what "verifiable consent" means. Until technologies such as digital signatures are widely available, there appears to be no reliable way to provide verifiable consent online. The FTC recognized this fact by issuing a temporary ruling (now permanent) requiring a "sliding scale of verifiable parental consent." If firms want to use the personal information of children for internal uses only, the FTC requires an e-mail from the parent plus one other form of verification (such as a credit card or phone number). A stricter standard is required of firms who want to sell personal information about children: these Web sites are required to use one of the following means of verification in addition to an e-mail: a print-and send consent form, credit card transaction, a toll free number staffed by trained personnel, or an e-mail with a password or PIN.

Since the law took effect, the FTC has obtained a number of settlements and issued fines as high as $1 million. For instance, in December 2008, Sony BMG Music Entertainment (Sony Music) got clipped for $1 million as part of a settlement to resolve FTC charges that it violated COPPA. The Commission's complaint alleged that, through its music fan Web sites, Sony Music improperly collected, maintained, and disclosed personal information from thousands of children under the age of 13, without their parents' consent. The civil penalty paid by Sony Music matches the largest penalty ever in a COPPA case. Previously, the operators of imbee.com, a social network site specifically targeting kids and "tweens," agreed to settle FTC

charges that their data-collection practices violated federal law. Their fine: $130,000, a mere pittance in comparison. Industrious Kid, Inc., and owner Jeanette Symons, promoted the imbee.com Web site as a "free, secure, social networking and blogging destination specifically designed for kids ages 8 to 14." In addition, the Web site was promoted as "purposely designed to ensure the greatest level of safety and satisfaction for young members," and as "safer than other social networking sites." According to the FTC, imbee.com collected and maintained personal information from children under the age of 13 without first notifying parents and obtaining their consent. In an earlier enforcement action, Xanga paid up $1 million in part because it collected, used, and disclosed personal information from children under the age of 13 without first notifying parents and obtaining their consent. The complaint charged that the defendants had actual knowledge they were collecting and disclosing personal information from children. The Xanga site stated that children under 13 could not join, but then allowed visitors to create Xanga accounts even if they provided a birth date indicating they were under 13. Further, they failed to notify the children's parents of their information practices or provide the parents with access to and control over their children's information. The defendants created 1.7 million Xanga accounts for users who submitted age information indicating they were under 13. Previous FTC COPPA cases included Mrs. Fields' Original Cookies, Hershey Foods, UMG recordings, and Bonzi Software. These cases involved no actual intent or knowledge, just lack of attention.

In 2010, Iconix Brand Group agreed to pay $250,000 for violations of COPPA. Iconix owns, licenses, and markets—both offline and online— several popular apparel brands that appeal to children and teens, including Mudd, Candie's, Bongo, and OP. Iconix required consumers on

(continued)

many of its brand-specific Web sites to provide personal information, such as full name, e-mail address, zip code, and in some cases mailing address, gender, and phone number—as well as date of birth—in order to receive brand updates, enter sweepstakes contests, and participate in interactive brand-awareness campaigns and other Web site features. According to the FTC, since 2006, Iconix knowingly collected and stored personal information from approximately 1,000 children without first notifying their parents or obtaining parental consent, according to the FTC's complaint. On one Web site, MyMuddWorld.com, Iconix also enabled girls to publicly share personal stories and photos online, according to the FTC complaint.

While in general, voluntary compliance with COPPA has been good, and most Web sites are careful to avoid gathering personal information on children as a part of their marketing effort, Web sites are directly aimed at very young children. Sites such as ClubPenguin, Webkinz (the most popular children's site), and NeoPets provide online tools and play environments that enable young users to interact, adopt pets, play sponsored advergames, and reveal personal information. In the process of playing the games, children produce marketing information for product designers. While each of these Web sites' privacy policies claim strict adherence to the restrictions of COPPA, it is unclear how they ascertain who is over 13 and who is under 13, or if those under 13 have parental consent.

In 2010, the rapid growth of social network sites aimed at children has heightened concerns about what information is being collected by Web sites, and how it is being used. The Senate Commerce Committee held hearings in April 2010 to consider how social networks aimed at children are observing the restrictions of COPPA. Social networks provide new environments for children to share information, and for advertisers to collect information. Privacy groups argued that the age restrictions in COPPA be advanced from 13 to 18 years of age before personal information could be collected, and no location information be collected. Marketing industry and Facebook representatives argued against both proposals.

▬ **SOURCES:** "Watchdog Group Calls For Stronger Online Child Privacy Law, by Mike Sachoff, Webpronews.com, April 29, 2010; "Virtual Worlds and Kids: Mapping the Risks. A Report to Congress," Federal Trade Commission, December 2009; "Iconix Brand Group Settles Charges Its Apparel Web Sites Violated Children's Online Privacy Protection Act," Federal Trade Commission, Press Release, October 20, 2009; "The Maine Act: Preventing Predatory Marketing Practices Against Minors," by Eric Sinrod, Blog.findlaw.com/technologist, August 11, 2009; "Ad It Up: Kids in a Commercial World," Federal Trade Commission, March 12, 2009; "Sony Music Settles Charges Its Music Fan Websites Violated the Children's Online Privacy Protection Act," Federal Trade Commission, December 11, 2008; "Online Age Verification for Children Brings Privacy Worries," by Brad Stone, *New York Times*, November 16, 2008; "No Escape: Marketing to Kids in the Digital Age," by Jeff Chester and Kathryn Montgomery, Multinational Monitor, July/August 2008.

## BEHAVIORAL TARGETING: GETTING PERSONAL

In Chapter 6, you learned about the six major ways that marketers target markets (refer to Table 6.7)—through behavioral, demographic, psychographic, technical, contextual, and search data collected online. Behavioral targeting of ads involves using the online and offline behavior of consumers to adjust the advertising message delivered online, often in real time (milliseconds from the consumers first URL entry). The intent is to increase the efficiency of marketing and advertising, and to increase the revenue streams of firms who are in a position to behaviorally target visitors. Because "behavioral targeting" as a label has somewhat unfavorable connotations, the online advertising industry, led by Google, has introduced a new name for behavioral targeting. They call it "interest-based advertising."

One of the original promises of the Web has been that it can deliver a marketing message tailored to each consumer based on this data, and then measure the results in terms of click-throughs and purchases. In the past, Yahoo, Google, and other Web sites would show you ads based on the content of the page you were visiting. If you are visiting a jewelry site, you would be shown jewelry ads. If you entered a search query like "diamonds," you would be shown text ads for diamonds and other jewelry. This was taken one step further by advertising networks composed of several thousand sites. An advertising network could follow you across thousands of Web sites and come up with an idea of what you are interested in as you browse, and then display ads related to those interests. For instance, if you visit a few men's clothing sites in the course of a few hours, you will be shown ads for men's clothing on most other sites you visit subsequently regardless of their subject content. Behavioral targeting takes this all another step further by combining nearly all of your online behavioral data into a collection of interest areas, and then showing you ads based on those interests, as well as the interests of your friends. What's new about today's behavioral targeting is the breadth of data collected: your e-mail content, social network page content, purchases online, books read or purchased, newspaper sites visited, and many other behaviors. And finally, **ad exchanges** take the marketing of all this information one step further. Most popular Web sites have over 100 tracking programs owned by third-party data collector firms who then sell this information in real-time to the highest bidding advertiser in real-time online auctions.

There are three methods that online advertisers use to behaviorally target ads: search engine queries, and the collection of data on individual browsing history online (in the past, generally not personally identifiable data), and increasingly, the integration of this online data with offline data like income, education, address, purchase patterns, credit records, driving records, and hundreds of other personal descriptors tied to specific, identifiable persons. This level of integration, involving both online "anonymous" personal data and offline personal data, is not engaged in by Google or most other direct players. Rather, it is carried out by less well-known data aggregators and then sold to third-party advertisers. On average, offline information bureaus maintain 1,500 data elements on each adult person, and online information repositories maintain an equally detailed profile of Internet users.

Earlier in the chapter we described search engine marketing in some detail. Search engine advertising has turned out to be the most effective online advertising format by several orders of magnitude, and provides over 90% of the revenue of Google, the world's largest online advertising agency. Why is search engine advertising so effective? Most agree that when users enter a query into a search engine, it reveals a very specific intention to shop, compare, and possibly purchase. When ads are shown at these very moments on customer behavior, they are 4 to 10 times as effective as other formats. In 2003, the author John Battelle coined the phrase and the notion that the Web is a database of intentions:

"The Database of Intentions is simply this: The aggregate results of every search ever entered, every result list ever tendered, and every path taken as a

**ad exchange**
An online, real-time auction where data aggregators sell personal tracking information to to advertisers

result. It lives in many places, but three or four places in particular hold a massive amount of this data (i.e., MSN, Google, and Yahoo). This information represents, in aggregate form, a place holder for the intentions of humankind—a massive database of desires, needs, wants, and likes that can be discovered, subpoenaed, archived, tracked, and exploited to all sorts of ends. Such a beast has never before existed in the history of culture, but is almost guaranteed to grow exponentially from this day forward. This artifact can tell us extraordinary things about who we are and what we want as a culture. And it has the potential to be abused in equally extraordinary fashion." (Battelle, 2003.)

The decline in the growth rate of search engine advertising, from the early days of double-digit growth to today's growth of high single digits, has caused the major search engine firms to seek out alternative forms of future growth. Likewise with banner display portals like Yahoo and AOL: the effectiveness of banner ads has fallen, and so have their prices. Portal firms are turning to behavioral targeting in the effort to secure their future growth in Internet advertising. Advertising agencies are willing to pay a great deal more for targeted ads than non-targeted ads.

Behavioral targeting seeks to optimize consumer response by using information that Web visitors reveal about themselves online, and if possible, combine this with offline identity and consumption information gathered by companies such as Acxiom. Behavioral targeting is based on real-time information about visitors use' of Web sites, including pages visited, content viewed, search queries, ads clicked, videos watched, content shared, and products they purchase. Once this information is collected and analyzed on the fly, behavioral targeting programs attempt to develop profiles of individual users, and then show advertisements most likely to be of interest to the user. In 2010, U.S. firms will spend more than an estimated $2 billion on behavioral targeting, and this is expected to double by 2014, growing at the rate of 50% a year, the fastest growing form of online marketing techniques (eMarketer, 2008b). Twenty-three percent of online display advertising will be behaviorally targeted in 2014. Interest in this area has spurred four recent acquisitions: Google-DoubleClick, Yahoo-Right Media, WPP Group-24/7 Media, and Microsoft-aQuantive. You cannot target consumers on the Internet without a very large-scale advertising network than can follow people's movements closely and display ads. Many of these techniques are not new, just extensions of offline techniques. The difference is obtaining this information online, unobtrusively, without the user knowing, dynamically analyzing the information on the fly, and taking the appropriate action within a tolerable 5 to 10 milliseconds of response time. The advertising industry's own studies find that targeted ads are twice as effective as non-targeted ads (NAI, 2010). As one industry enthusiast claimed, "...Internet ad exchanges are basically markets for eyeballs on the Web. Advertisers bid against each other in real time for the ability to direct a message at a single Web surfer. The trades take 50 milliseconds to complete."

For a variety of technical and other reasons, this vision has, thus far, not been widely achieved. The quality of the data, largely owned by the online advertising networks, is quite good, but the ability to understand and respond—the business intelligence and analytics—are weak, preventing companies from being able to respond quickly in meaningful ways when the consumer is online. Although in general targeted ads are 4 to 10 times more effective than non-targeted ads, this is not always the case and depends on the product, and nearness of a consumer decision. And marketing companies are not yet prepared to accept the idea that there needs to be several hundred or a thousand variations on the same display ad depending on the customer's profile. Such a move would raise costs. Last, consumer resistance to targeting is allowing more consumers to escape the tracking net. Reflecting consumer polls in previous years, an independent study conducted at the University of Pennsylvania and the University of California, Berkeley, found that 67% of U.S. Internet users did not approve of behavioral tracking, and the percentage rose as respondents learned of the various tracking mechanisms. Even 18–24 year olds opposed targeting ads despite the claims of many industry leaders who argue that young people don't care about their privacy. It turns out that they do, although not quite as much as older people (Turow et al, 2009).

As a result, just about everyone using the major Web portals is exposed to advertising that has nothing to do with their personal interests. Consumers are increasingly turning off tracking options when they understand how to do this. Second, search-engine marketing is still the only technique that reliably comes close to revealing consumers' intentions.

Nevertheless, firms are experimenting with more precise targeting methods. Snapple used behavioral targeting methods (with the help of an online ad firm Tacoda) to identify the types of people attracted to Snapple Green Tea. Answer: people who like the arts and literature, travel internationally, and visit health sites. Microsoft offers MSN advertisers access to personal data derived from 270 million worldwide Windows Live users. Some advertisers have reported over 50% increases in click-through rates. General Motors uses Digitas (a Boston-based online ad firm) to create several hundred versions of a single ad for its Acadia crossover vehicle. Viewers are initially shown ads that emphasize brand, features, and communities. On subsequent viewing, they are shown different ads based on demographics, lifestyle, and behavioral considerations. Men are shown versions of the ads emphasizing engines, specifications, and performance, while women are shown versions that emphasize comfort, accessibility, and families (Story, 2007).

The growth in the power, reach, and scope of behavioral targeting has drawn the attention of privacy groups and the FTC. In November 2007, the FTC opened hearings to consider proposals from privacy advocates to develop a "do not track list," develop visual online cues for people to alert them to tracking, and allow people to opt out. In June 2008, the Senate held hearings on behavioral marketing and privacy. While Google, Microsoft, and Yahoo pleaded for legislation to protect them from consumer lawsuits, the FTC refused to consider new legislation to protect the privacy of Internet users. Instead, the FTC proposed industry self-regulation. In 2009, a consortium of advertising firms (Network Advertising Initiative) responded positively to FTC proposed principles to regulate online behavioral advertising. In the Senate, hearings on behavioral targeting are ongoing throughout 2009. In 2010, privacy advocates and consumer groups petitioned the FTC to regulate behavioral targeting by forcing firms to adopt an opt in strategy, recognize that personal information is being traded, and ensure consumers are fairly compensated for their information (Center for Digital Democracy, 2010). All of these regulatory efforts emphasize transparency, user control over their information, security, and the temporal stability of privacy promises (unannounced and sudden changes in information privacy may not be allowed). Currently there are few, if any, industry or government regulations on behavioral targeting.

Perhaps the central question is understanding what rights individuals have in their own personally identifiable Internet profiles. Are these "ownership" rights, or merely an "interest" in an underlying asset? Do consumers have viewing and editing rights for their profiles? Why not? Can consumers opt out using a federal "Do Not Track" list? Who can possibly "own" the intentions of an entire culture? We consider these issues further in Chapter 8.

## MIXING OFFLINE AND ONLINE MARKETING COMMUNICATIONS

Many early proponents of e-commerce believed that the traditional world of marketing based on mass media was no longer relevant to the exploding online commercial world and that in the "new Internet economy," nearly all marketing communications would be online. As it turned out, this did not happen. What did happen is that offline marketing powerhouses in consumer-oriented industries learned how to use the Web to extend their brand images and sales campaigns to an educated, wealthy, and computer-literate, online audience. The large advertising agencies that specialized in mass media opened up Internet practices, and learned quickly how to integrate online and offline campaigns. Pure online companies learned how to use traditional print and television advertising as a means for driving sales to their Web sites. As it turns out, physical catalogs are excellent drivers of Web sales.

The marketing communications campaigns most successful at driving traffic to a Web site have incorporated both online and offline tactics, rather than relying solely on one or the other. The objective is to draw the attention of people who are already online and persuade them to visit a new Web site, as well as attract the attention of people who will be going online in the near future in order to suggest that they, too, visit the Web site. Several research studies have shown that the most effective online advertisements are those that use consistent imagery with campaigns running in other media at the same time (Briggs, 1999). Offline mass media such as television and radio have nearly a 100% market penetration into the 116 million households in the United States. U.S. daily newspapers have a total circulation of around 48 million. It would be foolish for pure online companies not to use these popular media to drive traffic to the online world of commerce. In the early days of e-commerce, the Internet audience was quite different from the general population, and perhaps was best reached by using online marketing alone. This is no longer true as the Internet population becomes much more like the general population.

Many online ventures have used offline marketing techniques to drive traffic to their Web sites, increase awareness, and build brand equity. For instance, LendingTree.com has used television advertising to direct people to its Web site to look for mortgages. Barnes & Noble, as well as JCPenney and REI Inc., use print media to inform customers of their in-store Web kiosks. Such "tie-ins" between a print product and a firm's Web site have proven to be very successful in driving Web traffic.

Another example of the online/offline marketing connection is the use of print catalogs by heretofore entirely online ventures. Some online ventures have created paper catalogs and mailed them to their customers to improve their relationship with that group.

The development of multi-channel marketing and communications reflects the fact that the behavior of consumers is increasingly multi-channel (see Chapter 9). Around 60% of all consumers research products online before buying in a store, 48% of total U.S. retail sales are influenced by online research, and 35% of the online retail sales generated by Internet Retailer's Top 500 Web sites were made by mass merchant, multi-channel retailers—retailers who had physical stores and catalogs in addition to Web sites (eMarketer, Inc., 2010c).

*Insight on Business: Are The Very Rich Are Different from You and Me?* examines how luxury goods providers use online marketing in conjunction with their offline marketing efforts.

---

## 7.2 UNDERSTANDING THE COST AND BENEFITS OF ONLINE MARKETING COMMUNICATIONS

As we saw in Section 7.1, online marketing communications still comprise only a very small part of the total marketing communications universe. While there are several reasons why this is the case, two of the main ones are concerns about whether online advertising really works and about how to adequately measure the costs and benefits of online advertising. We will address both of these topics in this section. But first, we will define some important terms used when examining the effectiveness of online marketing.

### ONLINE MARKETING METRICS: LEXICON

**impressions**
number of times an ad is served

**click-through rate (CTR)**
the percentage of people exposed to an online advertisement who actually click on the banner

**view-through rate (VTR)**
measures the 30-day response rate to an ad

**hits**
number of http requests received by a firm's server

In order to understand the process of attracting prospects to your firm's Web site via marketing communications and converting them into customers, you will need to be familiar with Web marketing terminology. **Table 7.4** lists some terms commonly used to describe the impacts and results of online marketing.

The first nine metrics focus primarily on the success of a Web site in achieving audience or market share by "driving" shoppers to the site. These measures often substitute for solid information on sales revenue as e-commerce entrepreneurs seek to have investors and the public focus on the success of the Web site in "attracting eyeballs" (viewers).

**Impressions** are the number of times an ad is served. **Click-through rate (CTR)** measures the percentage of people exposed to an online advertisement who actually click on the advertisement. Because not all ads lead to an immediate click, the industry has invented a new term for a long-term hit called **view-through rate** (VTR), which measures the 30-day response rate to an ad. **Hits** are the number of HTTP requests received by a firm's server. Hits can be misleading as a measure of Web site activity because a "hit" does not equal a page. A single page may account for several hits if the page contains multiple images or graphics. A single Web site visitor

| TABLE 7.4 | MARKETING METRICS LEXICON |
|---|---|
| **COMMON MARKETING E-METRICS** | **DESCRIPTION** |
| Impressions | Number of times an ad is served |
| Click-through rate (CTR) | Percentage of times an ad is clicked |
| View-through rate (VTR) | Percentage of times an ad is not clicked immediately but the Web site is visited within 30 days |
| Hits | Number of HTTP requests |
| Page views | Number of pages viewed |
| Stickiness (duration) | Average length of stay at a Web site |
| Unique visitors | Number of unique visitors in a period |
| Loyalty | Measured variously as the number of page views, frequency of single-user visits to the Web site, or percentage of customers who return to the site in a year to make additional purchases |
| Reach | Percentage of Web site visitors who are potential buyers; or the percentage of total market buyers who buy at a site |
| Recency | Time elapsed since the last action taken by a buyer, such as a Web site visit or purchase |
| Acquisition rate | Percentage of visitors who indicate an interest in the Web site's products by registering or visiting product pages |
| Conversion rate | Percentage of visitors who become customers |
| Browse to buy ratio | Ratio of items purchased to product views |
| View to cart ratio | Ratio of "Add to cart" clicks to product views |
| Cart conversion rate | Ratio of actual orders to "Add to cart" clicks |
| Checkout conversion rate | Ratio of actual orders to checkouts started |
| Abandonment rate | Percentage of shoppers who begin a shopping cart purchase but then leave the Web site without completing a purchase (similar to above) |
| Retention rate | Percentage of existing customers who continue to buy on a regular basis (similar to loyalty) |
| Attrition rate | Percentage of customers who do not return during the next year after an initial purchase |
| *E-MAIL METRICS* | |
| Open rate | Percentage of e-mail recipients who open the e-mail and are exposed to the message |
| Delivery rate | Percentage of e-mail recipients who received the e-mail |
| Click-through rate (e-mail) | Percentage of recipients who clicked through to offers |
| Bounce-back rate | Percentage of e-mails that could not be delivered |
| Unsubscribe rate | Percentage of recipients who click unsubscribe |
| Conversion rate (e-mail) | Percentage of recipients who actually buy |

## INSIGHT ON BUSINESS

# ARE THE VERY RICH DIFFERENT FROM YOU AND ME?

The very rich are different from you and me," Nick Carroway observed, in a memorable line from *The Great Gatsby*, a novel by F. Scott Fitzgerald about life among the very wealthy in the 1920s. Palm Beach has its Worth Avenue, New York has its Fifth Avenue, Los Angeles has its Rodeo Drive, and Chicago has the Magnificent Mile. So where do the rich go on the Web to get that $5,000 cocktail dress, or that $3,000 Italian suit? How about a Jimmy Choo handbag? Something Armani? Well, today, it turns out they may not be so different from the rest of us: they look for online deals, say, the $5,000 cocktail dress for only $3,500. Or they might try eBay for the white-studded leather tote bag for only $510. Who could resist?

There are 16 million affluent households in the United States with a net worth of more than $500,000. Over 50 million people in households with incomes of $100,000 or more are online. Those with incomes of greater than $100,000 account for 40% of all online spending. Retail consumption in general is highly skewed: the wealthiest top 10% of households account for 35% of all consumption. Around 80% of U.S. consumers with a net worth greater than $5 million use the Web, and shop on the Web for clothes and jewelry, as well as more common items such as music and videos. Around 60% of rich Internet users hobnob on social sites. Households with more than $100,000 in income increased their online spending by 17% in 2009, and maintained that level going into 2010. Nevertheless, the rich have cut back a bit on consumption.

Yes, the recession has hit even the really rich. Let's say you have a "mere" $5 million in net worth (placing you in the "minor rich"), including the house, the second house, three cars (all still with money owed on them), and stocks and bonds, and then all this booty sinks in value by 30% to 40% in the Big Recession. What to do? You have a job, so you cut back on spending, sell one of the cars, engage in a little "cheap chic" by shopping at Wal-Mart, and look for incredible sales at luxe spending stores such as Tiffany, Nieman Marcus, and Marni. Online, you learn to pay attention to your e-mail because that's where luxe retailers will flash-market their wares to you, a preferred customer.

The problem is the real luxe online stores typically don't have sales, at least not in public. Luxe retailers are loathe to offer sales because they believe sales detract from their reputations for timeless quality. As a vice president at the world-renowned jeweler Tiffany's noted, "We certainly don't engage in price promotion. We say, 'Here's the product, and here's the price, and the price is justified."

Change is in the air (or online as it were). Times are changing when Lacoste (the polo shirts with the crocodile logo) pulls the plug on print advertising and puts all its U.S. marketing dollars on the Internet in 2010. You know something is different when Faberge introduces its first new line of luxe jewelery in 90 years with a Web-only marketing effort on a single Web site. The site offers 100 pieces of jewelry ranging in price from $48,000 to $10 million. A Faberge marketing report found the rich like to buy online if they have plenty of personal attention. Shopping carts? Please [are you kidding?]! "No, thank you." A personal sales rep to "walk you through"

(continued)

the Web site? "Yes of course." "How about a visit to the office or club?"

It used to be that luxe brands either avoided the Web entirely or just put up sites with flashy Flash videos and high-end photography. But in the recession, when ordinary department stores are discounting even luxe branded goods, the high-end brands are getting down and dirty on the Web, re-building their sites for active competition with the department stores.

Luxe retailers are in fact offering more discounts—but they're secret. How can a sale be secret? Whispered discounts at the physical stores ("Shhhh! There's a special sale in the dress department!") have their online counterpart in flash e-mail campaigns and "private online sales" in which selected online customers are e-mailed alerts such as "A $3,000 handbag on sale for the next two hours for $800." Neiman Marcus calls them "midday dash" sales. Two-hour online-only sales promise 50% off on luxe goods that can be purchased only by clicking on a link in the e-mail. One week's "dash sale" featured a $697 Burberry handbag, marked down from $1,395. A Carmen Marc Valvo chiffon gown, just right for that special charity party, was offered at $575, down from $1,150. Cole Haan flats only $82, down from $165.

With in-store sales suffering as a result of the recession, the action has moved to the Internet where luxe retailers can offer discrete sales to a select group of customers without tarnishing the brand, preserving exclusivity, and creating a sense of urgency by limiting the time to purchase. At the same time, they can deny they discount their items. If prices were public, customers would know that the $800 Marni skirt they bought today was sold the next day on sale for $400. They might conclude that none of these goods are worth the price charged, certainly not the retail price, no matter what it is. Online dash sales are sort of like impulse buying at Wal-Mart, but instead of 20 batteries for $5, it's more like one Burberry bag for a $1,000. Rich people can indulge bigger impulses. But like the rest of us, the rich just can't seem to get enough of a good thing, especially if its half price.

Overall, times are not great for online luxe retailers, but they are not so bad either. While the physical store retail world struggles with 20%-30% declines in revenues, online retail has been flat or slightly down. The bright spot is luxe online sales have only declined 8% during the recession. Through rapid cost cutting, and inventory control, luxe retailers have managed to remain profitable throughout the period. Tiffany, the quintessential luxe firm, experienced lower profits in the 2009 second quarter, but they were still positive. Sales of $50,000+ items are off, while increased sales of silver and gold fashion jewelry is making up most of the difference. Tiffany's strategy, echoed by Hermes, is not to lower prices but to add more lowered-price items to the marketing mix. For instance, pendants are going for $150 to "only" $15,000 (those are the ones with the big shiny things). Neiman Marcus, Saks Inc. and Hermes International reported similar results despite the recession.

U.S. luxury online sales in 2010 are expected to be around $3.8 billion, up about 20% from the previous year according to Bain, a consulting firm, compared to an 8% decline in the luxe industry overall. Conspicuous consumption is still with us but a little less flashy: online jewelry sales were down 7% in 2009. Other categories like expensive clothing are way up. Yoox, Saks.com, Zagliani, and Marni all report their online sales are now approaching the sales of their flagship stores. Many luxe consumers who lost 30% of their net worth apparently still have a lot left over.

Yet luxury retailers such as Neiman Marcus, Tiffany, Armani, and Christian Dior have had a difficult time developing an online presence for

(continued)

their wealthy customers. Critics argue they have had a difficult time understanding their wealthy online customers. A recent report from the Luxury Institute found that online luxe goods retailers fall short in community building. Most sites do not track online customer comments on rating and review sites, or blogs (let alone Twitter), although most use search engine optimization. When you're really good and charging accordingly, why ask customers what they think?

Luxury brands and retailers do face a difficult market where they must try to please not only their wealthy older customers, but also those customers' children and grandchildren who are used to shopping online. And they have had a hard time coming up with a credible online image that supports their brand, but is still an online site that appeals to the online customer.

For instance, when Neiman Marcus introduced its first Web site with two virtual boutiques, featuring tours of Kate Spade handbags and John Hardy silver cuff links, Web designers were awed by the display of graphics and motion. But most customers were turned off because they could not find enough goods for sale, and could not easily navigate the site. Pretty snazzy stuff, but today it's all gone. Neimanmarcus.com no longer features any animations or Flash graphics, but instead has much more merchandise neatly arranged by category and designer: in short, an online catalog much like JCPenney's. The current Neiman Marcus Web site gets generally high marks for the simplicity of design and efficiency of navigation, although critics point out that it's still somewhat difficult to find the online version of Neiman Marcus' most popular offline marketing tool: its Christmas catalog that features "beyond the pale" luxury items such as a "his and hers" double portrait in chocolate for $100,000 and an underwater personal submarine for $1.4 million.

Developing an online marketing approach that increases a company's access to consumers while retaining an image of exclusivity was the challenge faced by Tiffany & Co. when it redesigned its Web site in 1999. The company was in the enviable position of being perhaps the most famous jewelry company in the United States. Tiffany's offline marketing communications sought to engender feelings of beauty, quality, and timeless style—all hallmarks of the Tiffany brand. How could Tiffany maintain its approach on the Web, a medium that often emphasizes speed and flashy graphics over grace and elegance, and low-cost bargains over high-priced exclusive fashion? The Web, at least in its early days, was all about low prices and great deals—concepts that are anathema to the high-fashion merchant.

Tiffany's first effort on the Web was designed by Oven Digital Inc., who built a Web site that used soft, neutral colors throughout, sparse wording, and pictures that faded slowly onto the screen. The shopping portion of the Web site showed just one large item, with some smaller photos that could be enlarged by clicking at the bottom of the screen. But that same "reserved" quality made it difficult for consumers to find out what was for sale. Critics complained that the Tiffany Web site had too few products online, the Flash graphics were slow, there were too many animations, and the product line available was poorly organized. While Tiffany claimed there were 2,000 products online, finding them and buying them was an arduous process. The site was redesigned by an in-house team with a view toward making it more focused. Today, Tiffany has shifted more of its direct marketing effort from the offline catalog to the online catalog. The results improved dramatically. It has opened new sites in Canada, the United Kingdom, and Japan. Tiffany sites carry over 2,800 products in 5 categories of goods: diamonds, jewelry, watches, table

(continued)

settings, gifts, and accessories. In 2009, Tiffany's online sales were over $140 million, 5% of their $2.8 billion worldwide sales, placing it in second place in the online jewelry industry. (Blue Nile is first with over $300 million in sales.)

Other cutting-edge fashion houses such as Christian Dior, Armani, and Bottega Veneta insisted on managing their own Web sites initially. The results were not impressive. The Web sites were typically a collection of photos with directions to the nearest store. Embracing the Internet ran counter to their strategies to keep tight control over their images and customers. As a result of the difficulties they encountered, some luxury sites began reluctantly to outsource their Web sites. For instance, Louis Vuitton, DKNY, and Armani have all outsourced their online boutiques to Web operations outfits such as Yoox, a fashion retailer with a long experience on the Web. In the case of Armani, Emporio Armani personally directed the online effort. To avoid the cheaper catalog look, he had his store design team hand over architectural plans to the flagship store in Milan so that Yoox could use it as a metaphor and model for the Web site. Now visitors can turn left or right as they would at the Milan store, and take a virtual tour of the goods on display. Armani wanted a three-dimensional look, and the ability to shine bright lights on the products being examined, a trick used in his stores to impart the sense of elegance. The cost of opening the site has been a fraction of the cost of launching a new store, and less risky. "At least we don't have to worry about the location, or opening a store on the wrong corner." A trip to the Armani Web site is a trip all unto itself: stunning video images of the latest seasonal collections, Armani Jeans, and the Armani Exchange, where you can actually buy something from the Emporio Armani retail collection.

**SOURCES:** "High Fashion Relents to Web's Pull," by Stephanie Clifford, *New York Times*, July 11, 2010; Luxury Brands Warming to the Web, Reuters, June 3, 2010; "The New Must-Have Accessory," by Vanessa O'Connell, *New York Times*, October 31, 2009; "From the Runway to Your Laptop," by Christina Binkley, *Wall Street Journal*, October 1, 2009; "Online Luxury Retail Remains Elusive," by Lauren Sherman, *BusinessWeek*, November 19, 2009; "Faberge Takes New Jewels Online," by Vidya Ram, Forbes.com, September 10, 2009; "Lacoste Shoots Its Wad Online," by Laurie Burkitt, Forbes.com, October 29, 2009; "CEO Helps Jimmy Choo Diversify," Jimmychoo.com, September 2, 2009; "High End Retailers Offering More Discounts," by Stephanie Rosenblum, New York Times, August 1, 2009; "In Luxury Sector, Discounting Can Be Dangerous," by Brian Burnsaid, *BusinessWeek*, July 23, 2009; "Luxury Goods Retailers Fall Short in Online Community Building," *Internet Retailer*, July 3, 2009; "Affluents Online: Living the Life in Private," by Lisa Phillips, eMarketer, May 2009.

can generate hundreds of hits. For this reason, hits are not an accurate representation of Web traffic or visits, even though they are generally easy to measure; the sheer volume of hits can be huge—and sound impressive—but not be a true measure of activity. **Page views** are the number of pages requested by visitors. However, with increased usage of Web frames that divide pages into separate sections, a single page that has three frames will generate three page views. Hence, page views per se are also not a very useful metric.

**Stickiness** (sometimes called *duration*) is the average length of time visitors remain at a Web site. Stickiness is important to marketers because the longer the amount of time a visitor spends at a Web site, the greater the probability of a purchase. In 2010, for instance, Google's 179 million unique visitors stayed on-site an average of 2 hours and 5 minutes during a month's time; Yahoo's 178 million visitors stayed an average of 2 hours and 28 minutes; Facebook's 148 million visitors stayed on-site an average of 7 hours and 1 minute! While Facebook generates a great deal of stickiness,

**page views**
number of pages requested by visitors

**stickiness (duration)**
average length of time visitors remain at a site

**unique visitors**
the number of distinct, unique visitors to a site

**loyalty**
percentage of purchasers who return in a year

**reach**
percentage of the total number of consumers in a market who will visit a site

**recency**
average number of days elapsed between visits

**acquisition rate**
percentage of visitors who register or visit product pages

**conversion rate**
percentage of visitors who purchase something

**browse-to-buy ratio**
ratio of items purchased to product views

**view-to-cart ratio**
ratio of "Add to cart" clicks to product view

**cart conversion rate**
average number of days elapsed between visits

**checkout conversion ratio**
ratio of actual orders to checkouts started

**abandonment rate**
percentage of shoppers who begin a shopping cart, but then fails to complete a form

**retention rate**
percentage of existing customers who continue to buy on a regular basis

**attrition rate**
percentage of customers who purchase once, but do not return within a year

it's not the case that this translates directly into more advertisements, more sales, and more revenue. Equally important is what people do when they visit a Web site and not just how much time they spend there. People don't go to Facebook to buy or research goods, whereas Google visitors are more likely to visit because they are searching for something to buy (Nielsen, 2010; comScore, 2010b).

The number of unique visitors is perhaps the most widely used measure of a Web site's popularity. The measurement of **unique visitors** counts the number of distinct, unique visitors to a Web site, regardless of how many pages they view. **Loyalty** measures the percentage of visitors who return in a year. This can be a good indicator of a site's Web following, and perhaps the trust shoppers place in a site. **Reach** is typically a percentage of the total number of consumers in a market who visit a Web site; for example, 10% of all book purchasers in a year will visit Amazon at least once to shop for a book. This provides an idea of the power of a Web site to attract market share. **Recency**—like loyalty—measures the power of a Web site to produce repeat visits and is generally measured as the average number of days elapsed between shopper or customer visits. For example, a recency value of 25 days means the average customer will return once every 25 days.

The metrics described so far do not say much about commercial activity or help understand the conversion from visitor to customer. Several other measures are more helpful in this regard. **Acquisition rate** measures the percentage of visitors who register or visit product pages (indicating interest in the product). **Conversion rate** measures the percentage of visitors who actually purchase something. Conversion rates can vary widely, depending on the success of the site. E-tailing Group's 9th Annual Merchant Survey found that 56% of the respondents reported conversion rates in the 1%–3% range, 21% in the 3%–5% range, and 17% in the 5%–8% range (e-Tailing Group, 2010). The **browse-to-buy ratio** measures the ratio of items purchased to product views. The **view-to-cart ratio** calculates the ratio of "Add to cart" clicks to product views. **Cart conversion rate** measures the ratio of actual orders to "Add to cart" clicks. **Checkout conversion rate** calculates the ratio of actual orders to checkouts started. **Abandonment rate** measures the percentage of shoppers who begin a shopping cart form but then fail to complete the form and leave the Web site. Abandonment rates can signal a number of potential problems—poor form design, lack of consumer trust, or consumer purchase uncertainty caused by other factors. A study by PayPal and comScore found that 45% of U.S. online shoppers had abandoned shopping carts multiple times in the three weeks prior to being surveyed. The average cost of the abandoned goods was over $100. Among the reasons for abandonment were security concerns (21%), couldn't find customer support (22%), couldn't find preferred payment option (24%), and the item being unavailable at checkout (23%) (eMarketer, Inc.,2009b). Given that more than 80% of online shoppers generally have a purchase in mind when they visit a Web site, a high abandonment rate signals many lost sales. **Retention rate** indicates the percentage of existing customers who continue to buy on a regular basis. **Attrition rate** measures the percentage of customers who purchase once but never return within a year (the opposite of loyalty and retention rates).

E-mail campaigns have their own set of metrics. **Open rate** measures the percentage of customers who open the e-mail and are exposed to the message. Generally, open rates are quite high, in the area of 50% or greater. However, some browsers open mail as soon as the mouse cursor moves over the subject line, and therefore this measure can be difficult to interpret. **Delivery rate** measures the percentage of e-mail recipients who received the e-mail. **Click-through rate (e-mail)** measures the percentage of e-mail recipients who clicked through to the offer. Finally, **bounce-back rate** measures the percentage of e-mails that could not be delivered.

There is a lengthy path from simple online ad impressions, Web site visits, and page views to the purchase of a product and the company making a profit (see **Figure 7.8**). You first need to make customers aware of their needs for your product and somehow drive them to your Web site. Once there, you need to convince them you have the best value—quality and price—when compared to alternative providers. You then must persuade them to trust your firm to handle the transaction (by providing a secure environment and fast fulfillment). Based on your success, a percentage of customers will remain loyal and purchase again or recommend your Web site to others.

**open rate**
percentage of customers who open the e-mail and are exposed to the message

**delivery rate**
percentage of e-mail recipients who received the e-mail

**click-through rate (e-mail)**
percentage of e-mail recipients who clicked through to the offer

**bounce-back rate**
percentage of e-mails that could not be delivered

**FIGURE 7.8 — AN ONLINE CONSUMER PURCHASING MODEL**

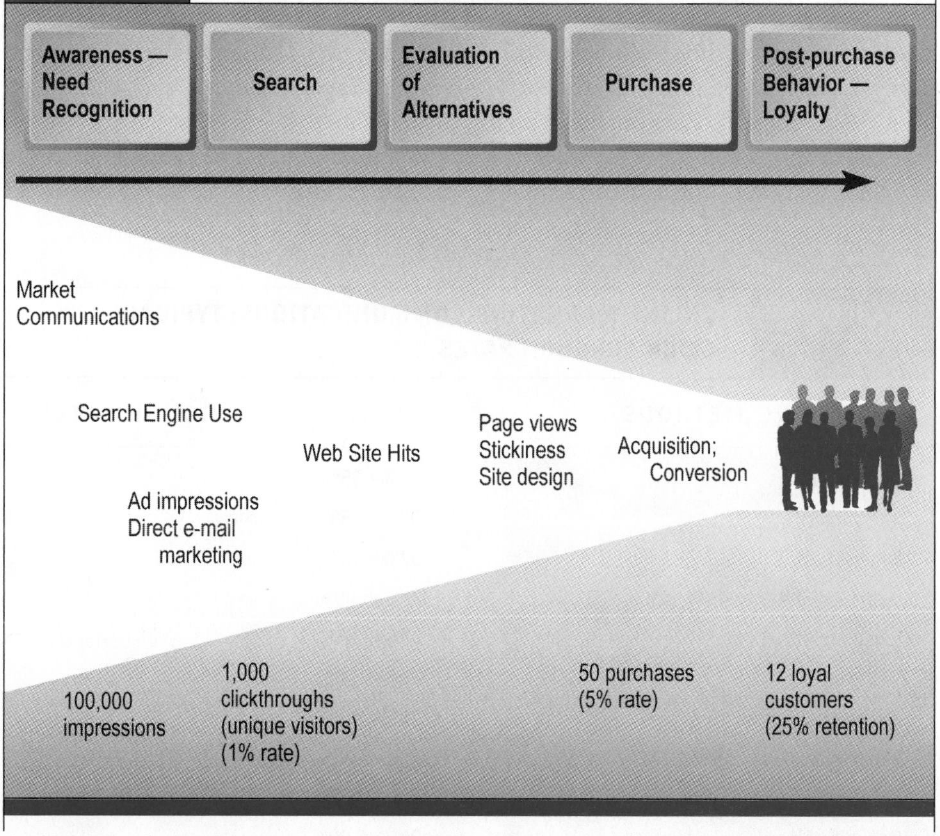

The conversion of visitors into customers, and then loyal customers, is a complex and long-term process that may take several months.

## HOW WELL DOES ONLINE ADVERTISING WORK?

What is the most effective kind of online advertising? How does online advertising compare to offline advertising? The answers depend on the goals of the campaign, the nature of the product, and the quality of the Web site you direct customers toward. The answers also depend on what you measure. Click-through rates are interesting, but ultimately it's the return on the investment in the ad campaign that counts. A broader understanding of the matter requires that you consider the cost of purchasing the promotional materials and mailing lists, and the studio production costs for radio and TV ads. Also, each media has a different revenue-per-contact potential because the products advertised differ. For instance, online purchases tend to be for smaller items when compared to newspaper, magazine, and television ads (although this too seems to be changing).

**Table 7.5** lists the click-through rates for various types of online marketing communications tools. There is a great deal of variability within any of these types, so the figures in Table 7.5 should be viewed as general estimates. Click-through rates on all these formats are a function of personalization, and other targeting techniques. For instance, several studies have found that e-mail response rates can be increased 20% or more by adding social sharing links. And while the average Google click through rate is 2%, some merchants can hit 10% or more by making their ads more specific and attracting only the most interested people. Permission e-mail click-through rates have been fairly consistent over the last five years, in the 5%–6% range. Putting the recipient's name in the subject line can double the click-through rate. (For unsolicited e-mail and outright spam, response rates are much lower, even though about 20% of U.S. e-mail users report clicking occasionally on an unsolicited e-mail.)

The click-through rates for video ads may seem low, but it is twice as high as the rate for display ads. The "interaction rate" (sometimes referred to as "dwell rate") with

| TABLE 7.5 | ONLINE MARKETING COMMUNICATIONS: TYPICAL CLICK-THROUGH RATES |
| --- | --- |
| **MARKETING METHODS** | **TYPICAL CLICK-THROUGH RATES** |
| Display ads | .06%–.35% |
| Interstitials | .02%–.16% |
| Superstitials | .02%–.16% |
| Search engine keyword purchase | 1.00%–5.00% |
| Video and rich media | .50%–2.65% |
| Sponsorships | 1.50%–3.00% |
| Affiliate relationships | .20%–.40% |
| E-mail marketing in-house list | 5.00%–6.00% |
| E-mail marketing purchased list | .01%–1.50% |
| Online catalogs | 3.00%–6.00% |

SOURCES: Based on data from eMarketer, Inc., 2010d, 2010e; industry sources; author estimates

rich media ads and video ads videos is quite high, about 7%–8%. "Interaction" means the user clicks on the video, plays it, stops it, or takes some other action (possibly skips the ad altogether) (eMarketer, 2009c, Eyeblaster, 2009).

As consumers become more accustomed to new online advertising formats, click-through rates tend to fall. Response rates to banner ads have fallen about 50% over the last four years, and e-mail response has also fallen from its initial high rates. This is not true of video and rich media where response rates have remained steady, perhaps due to the growing quality and novelty of online video.

How effective is online advertising when compared to offline advertising? **Figure 7.9** provides some insight into this question. In general, the online channels (e-mail, banner ads, and video) compare favorably with traditional channels. Search engine marketing over the last five years has grown to be one of the most cost-effective forms of marketing communications and accounts for, in large part, the growth of

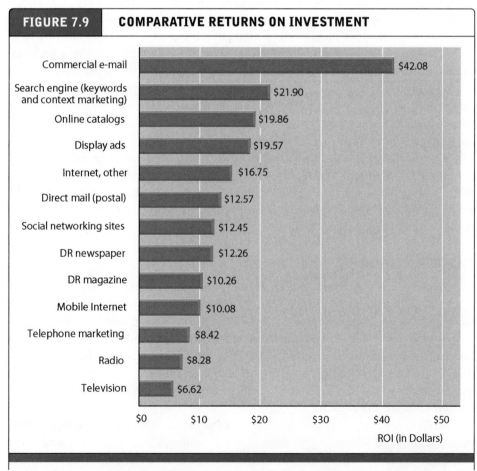

**FIGURE 7.9** | **COMPARATIVE RETURNS ON INVESTMENT**

| Channel | ROI (in Dollars) |
| --- | --- |
| Commercial e-mail | $42.08 |
| Search engine (keywords and context marketing) | $21.90 |
| Online catalogs | $19.86 |
| Display ads | $19.57 |
| Internet, other | $16.75 |
| Direct mail (postal) | $12.57 |
| Social networking sites | $12.45 |
| DR newspaper | $12.26 |
| DR magazine | $10.26 |
| Mobile Internet | $10.08 |
| Telephone marketing | $8.42 |
| Radio | $8.28 |
| Television | $6.62 |

This figure shows the average returns in dollars for every dollar spent using different types of advertising techniques. Search engine placement has replaced e-mail as the most cost-effective form of online advertising. These amounts are estimates and will vary by product, ad effectives, page placement, and degree of targeting.

SOURCES: Based on data from eMarketer, Inc., 2010.b; Direct Marketing Association (DMA), 2009.

Google, as well as other search engines. Surprisingly, direct opt-in e-mail is nearly twice as cost-effective as search engine advertising. This is in part because email lists are so inexpensive compared to keywords.

There is growing evidence that the cost-effectiveness of search engine marketing has peaked, and may actually be declining because the cost of keywords has grown significantly, and the number of keywords being purchased has also expanded as retailers branch out from their core keywords into more peripheral words. The result is a rising cost per click and a declining efficacy of keywords that are peripheral to the brand. Growth in search engine advertising revenues are likely to slow in the near future, and search engine firms such as Google and Microsoft are seeking other opportunities for growth by purchasing advertising networks, display ad firms, and mobile ad firms.

A study of the comparative impacts of offline and online marketing concluded that the most powerful marketing campaigns used multiple forms of marketing, including online, catalog, television, radio, newspapers, and retail store. Traditional media like television and print media remain the primary means for consumers to find out about new products even though advertisers have reduced their budgets for print media ads. The consensus conclusion is that consumers who shop multiple channels are spending more than consumers who shop only with a single channel, in part because they have more discretionary income but also because of the combined number of "touch points" that marketers are making with the consumers. The fastest growing channel in consumer marketing is the multi-channel shopper.

Banner ads can be made far more effective if they are targeted to specific occasions (occasion-based marketing), particular keyword search arguments, or users who have an identified user profile and can be pitched the ad at just the right moment. Usually, this kind of precision ad pitching requires the services of an advertising network firm such as DoubleClick or 24/7 Real Media.

## THE COSTS OF ONLINE ADVERTISING

**cost per thousand (CPM)**
advertiser pays for impressions in 1,000-unit lots

Effectiveness cannot be considered without an analysis of costs. Initially, most online ads were sold on a barter or **cost per thousand (CPM)** impressions basis, with advertisers purchasing impressions in 1,000-unit lots. Today, other pricing models have developed, including **cost per click (CPC)**, where the advertiser pays a prenegotiated fee for each click an ad receives, **cost per action (CPA)**, where the advertiser pays a prenegotiated amount only when a user performs a specific action, such

**cost per click (CPC)**
advertiser pays prenegotiated fee for each click an ad receives

as a registration or a purchase, and hybrid arrangements, combining two or more of these models (see **Table 7.6**).

While in the early days of e-commerce, a few online sites spent as much as $400 on marketing and advertising to acquire one customer, the average cost was never that high. **Table 7.7** shows the estimated average cost per acquisition for various different types of media.

**cost per action (CPA)**
advertiser pays only for those users who perform a specific action

While the costs for offline customer acquisition are higher than online, typically the offline items are far more expensive. If you advertise in the *Wall Street Journal,* you are tapping into a wealthy demographic interested in buying islands, jets, other

| TABLE 7.6 | DIFFERENT PRICING MODELS FOR ONLINE ADVERTISEMENTS |
|---|---|
| **PRICING MODEL** | **DESCRIPTION** |
| Barter | Exchange of ad space for something of equal value |
| Cost per thousand (CPM) | Advertiser pays for impressions in 1,000-unit lots |
| Cost per click (CPC) | Advertiser pays prenegotiated fee for each click ad receives |
| Cost per action (CPA) | Advertiser pays only for those users who perform a specific action, such as registering, purchasing, etc. |
| Hybrid | Two or more of the above models used together |
| Sponsorship | Term-based; advertiser pays fixed fee for a slot on a Web site |

corporations, and expensive homes in France. A full-page black and white ad in the *Wall Street Journal* National Edition costs about $350,000, whereas other papers are in the $10,000 to $100,000 range. For these kinds of prices you will need to either sell quite a few apples, or a small number of corporate jet lease agreements.

One of the advantages of online marketing is that online sales can generally be directly correlated with online marketing efforts. The online merchant can measure precisely just how much revenue is generated by specific banners or e-mail messages sent to prospective customers. One way to measure the effectiveness of online marketing is by looking at the ratio of additional revenue received divided by the cost of the campaign (Revenue/Cost). Any positive whole number means the campaign was worthwhile.

A more complex situation arises when both online and offline sales revenues are affected by an online marketing effort. A large percentage of the online

| TABLE 7.7 | AVERAGE COST PER CUSTOMER ACQUISITION FOR SELECT MEDIA IN THE UNITED STATES, 2010 |
|---|---|
| Internet search engine | $8.50 |
| E-mail (opt-in) | $10.00 |
| Television | $11.00 |
| Magazine | $19.00 |
| Yellow pages | $20.00 |
| Newspaper | $25.00 |
| Online display ads | $50.00 |
| Direct mail | $50.00 |

SOURCES: Industry sources; authors' estimates

audience uses the Web to "shop" but not buy. These shoppers buy at physical stores. Merchants such as Sears and Wal-Mart will use e-mail to inform their registered customers of special offers available for purchase either online or at stores. Unfortunately, purchases at physical stores cannot be tied precisely with the online e-mail campaign. In these cases, merchants have to rely on less precise measures such as customer surveys at store locations to determine the effectiveness of online campaigns.

In either case, measuring the effectiveness of online marketing communications—and specifying precisely the objective (branding versus sales)—is critical to profitability. To measure marketing effectiveness, you need to understand the costs of various marketing media and the process of converting online prospects into online customers.

In general, online marketing communications are more costly on a CPM basis than traditional mass media marketing, but are more efficient in producing sales. **Table 7.8** shows costs for typical online and offline marketing communications. For instance, a local television spot (30 seconds) can cost $4,000–$40,000 to run the ad and an additional $40,000 to produce the ad, for a total cost of $44,000–$80,000. The ad may be seen by a population of, say, 2 million persons (impressions) in a local area for a CPM ranging from 2 to 4 cents, which makes television very inexpensive for reaching large audiences quickly. A Web site banner ad costs virtually nothing to produce and can be purchased at Web sites for a cost of from $2–$15 per thousand impressions. Direct postal mail can cost 80 cents to $1 per household drop for a post card, but e-mail can be sent for virtually nothing and costs only $5–$15 per thousand targeted names. Hence, e-mail is far less expensive than postal mail on a CPM basis.

## SOFTWARE FOR MEASURING ONLINE MARKETING RESULTS

A number of software programs are available to automatically calculate activities at a Web site. **Figure 7.10** illustrates the information that a Web site activity analysis might provide.

Other software programs and services assist marketing managers in identifying exactly which marketing initiatives are paying off and which are not. See *Insight on Technology: It's 10 P.M. Do You Know Who Is On Your Web Site?* on pages 477–479 for a description of one such program.

## 7.3 THE WEB SITE AS A MARKETING COMMUNICATIONS TOOL

One of the strongest online marketing communications tools is a functional Web site that customers can find easily, and once there, locate what they are looking for quickly. In some ways, a Web site can be viewed as an extended online advertisement. An appropriate domain name, search engine optimization, and proper Web site design are integral parts of a coordinated marketing communications strategy, and ultimately, necessary conditions for e-commerce success.

| TABLE 7.8 | TRADITIONAL AND ONLINE ADVERTISING COSTS COMPARED |
|---|---|
| **TRADITIONAL ADVERTISING** | |
| Local television | $4,000 for a 30-second commercial during a movie; $45,000 for a highly rated show |
| Network television | $80,000–$600,000 for a 30-second spot during prime time; the average is $120,000 to $140,000 |
| Cable television | $5,000–$8,000 for a 30-second ad during prime time |
| Radio | $200–$1,000 for a 60-second spot, depending on the time of day and program ratings |
| Newspaper | $120 per 1,000 circulation for a full-page ad |
| Magazine | $50 per 1,000 circulation for an ad in a regional edition of a national magazine, versus $120 per 1,000 for a local magazine |
| Direct mail | $15–$20 per 1,000 delivered for coupon mailings; $25–$40 per 1,000 for simple newspaper inserts |
| Billboard | $5,000–$25,000 for a 1–3 month rental of a freeway sign |
| **ONLINE ADVERTISING** | |
| Banner ads | $2–$15 per 1,000 impressions on a Web site, depending on how targeted the ad is (the more targeted, the higher the price) |
| Video and rich media | $20–$25 per 1,000 ads, depending on the Web site's demographics |
| E-mail | $5–$15 per 1,000 targeted e-mail addresses |
| Sponsorships | $30–$75 per 1,000 viewers, depending on the exclusivity of the sponsorship (the more exclusive, the higher the price) |

## DOMAIN NAMES

One of the first communications an e-commerce Web site has with a prospective customer is via its URL. Domain names play an important role in reinforcing an existing brand and/or developing a new brand. There are a number of considerations to take into account in choosing a domain name. Ideally, a domain name should be short, memorable, not easily confused with others, and difficult to misspell. The name of a Web site may or may not reflect the nature of the company's business. The name of most major brands do not. Companies that choose a name unrelated to the nature of their business must be willing to spend extra time, effort, and money to establish the name as a brand. Dot-com domain names (as opposed to .net or .org) are still considered the most preferable, especially in the United States.

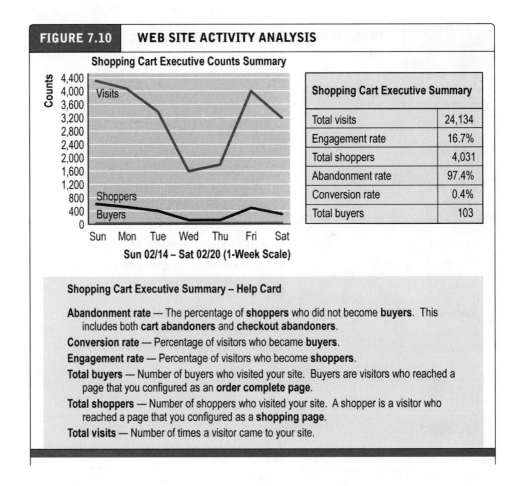

**FIGURE 7.10** **WEB SITE ACTIVITY ANALYSIS**

**Shopping Cart Executive Counts Summary**

| Shopping Cart Executive Summary | |
|---|---|
| Total visits | 24,134 |
| Engagement rate | 16.7% |
| Total shoppers | 4,031 |
| Abandonment rate | 97.4% |
| Conversion rate | 0.4% |
| Total buyers | 103 |

Sun 02/14 – Sat 02/20 (1-Week Scale)

**Shopping Cart Executive Summary – Help Card**

**Abandonment rate** — The percentage of **shoppers** who did not become **buyers**. This includes both **cart abandoners** and **checkout abandoners**.

**Conversion rate** — Percentage of visitors who became **buyers**.

**Engagement rate** — Percentage of visitors who become **shoppers**.

**Total buyers** — Number of buyers who visited your site. Buyers are visitors who reached a page that you configured as an **order complete page**.

**Total shoppers** — Number of shoppers who visited your site. A shopper is a visitor who reached a page that you configured as a **shopping page**.

**Total visits** — Number of times a visitor came to your site.

Today, however, it may be difficult to find a domain name that satisfies all of the above criteria. Many of the "good" .com domain names have already been taken. A number of companies exist that list domain names for sale (such as Great-Domains.com and BuyDomains.com). Most of the online domain registration sites such as Networksolutions.com, Godaddy.com, and Register.com have tools that can help you find appropriate names.

## SEARCH ENGINE OPTIMIZATION

Given that over 100 million Americans use search engines daily, it makes sense for a company to optimize its Web site for search engine recognition. Despite the fact that most major search engines allow Web sites to pay for inclusion in their search results listing (but not the organic ranking), and most major search engines have also adopted a paid search engine advertising model, it is still advisable to take the steps needed to objectively improve a Web site's visibility to search engines. Even if you use paid search engine marketing, by optimizing your Web site to improve its rank in the organic listings, you increase the chances of being noticed by consumers on the all important first page of search results, and reduce your customer acquisition costs. For small firms, organic ranking is the primary tool for driving sales.

# INSIGHT ON TECHNOLOGY

## IT'S 10 P..M. DO YOU KNOW WHO IS ON YOUR WEB SITE?

Chances are you don't, but if you used a Web site analytics software suite such as Adobe SiteCatalyst you would. And if you did pay attention to these matters, you most surely would be making more money from your Web site, increasing your conversion rates by about 5% and your receive vs. payment (RVP) by up to 8%. Why? Because if you knew in real time what types of people were on your Web site hour by hour, minute by minute, you would be able to adjust your Web site marketing and advertising messages in real time, adjust your product mix, change product placement, and greatly improve the conversion process from mere visitors to actual purchasers.

In an industry where the players cannot seem to agree on standards for measuring Web site performance, and where webmasters are overwhelmed with literally millions of bits of information about the behavior of consumers on their Web sites, SiteCatalyst is working to help Web managers make sense out of their click-stream traffic. SiteCatalyst is software as a service (SaaS) provided over the Internet to customers rather than installed on their firms' servers. In 2009, SiteCatalyst generated over $300 million in revenue, double its revenue of 2007! In 2010, its first revenues jumped 134% in an odd sign of consumer enthusiasm in the midst of a recession.

The company that created SiteCatalyst, Omniture, was purchased by Adobe Systems in 2009, which had its own suite of Web monitoring products. SiteCatalyst is used by approximately 5,100 customers in the United States and Europe, including Newsweek, Delta, Macy's, TV Guide, Kohl's, and Scotts. The software suite is a collection of tools that allow managers to see in real time who is on their site, how customers flow through their site, and which are the most popular and profitable pages. In addition, it allows marketers to make real-time changes in Web site content and measure results immediately.

Other competitors in the same business include Coremetrics and Nedstat; network management software and business intelligence vendors such as NetIQ and SPSS, which offer Web analytics as part of their larger product offerings; and digital marketing and e-commerce services providers such as Microsoft Advertising (formerly aQuantive) and Digital River, which incorporate Web analytics in their services. Google markets its Google Analytics program to users of its search engine marketing tools AdSense and AdWord.

SiteCatalyst allows webmasters to monitor and analyze their Web traffic in real time, collect visitor intelligence, and enable faster adjustments to underperforming pages. It also provides most, if not all, of the answers to questions about performance and return on investment (ROI) that Web site marketing managers want. SiteCatalyst collects, processes, stores, and reports on Internet user behavior based on browser activity. Reports allow customers to measure which marketing initiatives visitors responded to, what search engines they used, what keywords they entered, how much time they spent on pages, what they bought online, when they abandoned shopping carts, and where they live. The available reports and features include Web site navigation analysis, conversion rate analysis including calculating the long-term value of customers, marketing campaign measurement, and executive dashboards.

SiteCatalyst can evaluate a page-by-page navigation path a visitor has taken through a

(continued)

Web site. The service works by embedding a small piece of code into each HTML page a client wants to track and analyze. One benefit to clients is that SiteCatalyst eliminates the need to capture, store, and process log files, which are expensive to run and maintain and consume a good bit of a company's time and resources. SiteCatalyst does not need to be installed on a customer's own computers and infrastructure, but instead operates as a Web service (SaaS, software as a service) model. There is no "installation" involved. Hence, maintenance and operational costs are borne by SiteCatalyst.

SiteCatalyst is able to segment customers live, in real time, as they poke around a Web site. For instance, some visitors come for replacement parts and can be cross-sold to other products from your firm in the process. Looking for a printer cartridge? Why not consider buying a whole new printer on sale today? Most visitors come to Web sites (especially brand-name Web sites like Microsoft, HP, or Macy's) looking for specific products. But as long as they are on your site, why not entice them to consider related products or services? If an L.L.Bean customer comes to LLBean.com looking for pajamas, Site-Catalyst is able to determine which ads and prompts lead to additional sales. In general, people looking for pajamas can be sold sleep- and warmth-related products like underwear, blankets, and pillows.

Not to be left behind by Web 2.0, SiteCatalyst also provides "Social Networking Optimization" tools. If you have social network elements on your Web site like user comments, user-generated content, video with sharing possibilities, or bookmarking, SiteCatalyst's networking optimization can help you understand the consumption and creation habits of visitors, identify how much the social network elements add to sales, engage users with content that is motivational, and help create emotional links to your products and brand.

The National Geographic Society, one of the world's largest non-profit organizations devoted to exploration and geographic knowledge, reported in 2009 that SiteCatalyst and SearchCenter services had increased its Web site visits by 150%. Ted McDonald, Web analytics manager at National Geographic, said "Prior to using SiteCatalyst, we didn't have the data needed to understand the value of different parts of our site to our visitors or how our keyword advertising was translating into subscriptions. Using SiteCatalyst and SearchCenter together has given us insight into our paid search spend and return on every part of our site, which has been invaluable to our business." National Geographic deployed Search Center to optimize its paid search initiatives with the goal of realizing a specific return on ad spend. Its primary goal from paid search was to drive subscriptions, and using Search-Center, it discovered that 90% of the company's keywords were losing money. As a result, the National Geographic team identified which keyword variations were ineffective and reallocated spend to the remaining profitable 10%, turning all of the company's paid search ads profitable, it reports. "With SearchCenter, we've optimized our ads to a point where we don't need to change them often, which increases the productivity of the team and allows us to focus on more valuable tasks," says McDonald. "When the profitability changes, I have dashboards set up that show the return on investment for each search campaign and I can make changes accordingly."

SteveMadden.com adopted SiteCatalyst in order to remove guessing from their marketing and Web site designs and replace it with hard data on consumer behavior. Steve Madden is the founder of the footwear company Steve Madden Ltd., and his shoes are among the hottest fashion

(continued)

items available on the Internet and in stores throughout the United States. Steven Madden, Ltd. designs, sources, and sells footwear, handbags, and accessories. It has only 84 retail stores in America, and generates 52% of its revenue from wholesale sales to department stores , specialty stores, catalog sites, and independent boutiques. It's biggest customers are Macy's, DSW, Nordstrom, Famous Footwear, Dillard's, Lord & Taylor, and Victoria's Secret. It's own Web site SteveMadden.com made up about 18% of revenue in 2009, and it plays an important part in the overall profit picture at the firm.

Prior to using SiteCatalyst, marketers at the firm's Web site did not know why shoppers converted to shoppers, and had to guess which products and which promotional messages worked best. Marketers lacked real-time, actionable data on visitors to their site. What they wanted was the ability to make changes to the Web site and see immediately how visitor behavior changed. Using SiteCatalyst, they are able to change offers, content, page functions and other features, and measure results. In on,e test, for instance, marketers sought to reduce shopping cart abandonment by testing different version of the shopping cart banner. A new version of the banner was shown to visitors from states where Steve Madden had retail stores: "Shop With Confidence." A second version was shown to visitors from states without Steve Madden stores: "Enjoy no sales tax." Both uses of what had been blank screen real estate boosted conversion ratios by 5%. In a second promotional test of e-mail messages to shoppers who signed up for Steve Madden marketing e-mails, customers were shown different banners involve countdown ("flash") sales, free shipping banners, and personalized messages based on prior purchases. These micro-level changes in marketing messages resulted in an average 7% increase in conversion.

**SOURCES:** "SteveMadden.com Increases Sales and Continuously Optimizes E-commerce Site," Case Study, SteveMadden.com, August 2010; "Steve Madden's Online Sales Jump After Site Redesign," by Rose Gordon, DMNews.com, June 11, 2010; "RE/MAX launched a new Internet strategy using Google Analytics," Google.com/analytics/case_study, June 29, 2010; "Buying Your Brand On Search—Up To 23% Revenue Lift!," SiteCatalyst Articles, September 1, 2009; "National Geographic Increases Site Visits, Page Views and Return on Ad Spend With SiteCatalyst SearchCenter and SiteCatalyst SiteCatalyst," Case Study, SiteCatalyst, August 26, 2009.

Search engines today operate primarily with the use of Web crawlers, software programs that search the Web for pages, index their content, identify the number of sites linking to the page, and report the content to very large databases where it can be searched.

The method of indexing and ranking Web pages varies across search engines and is proprietary. There are many consulting firms, books, and online sources that provide guidance on how to enhance the visibility of a Web site to crawler programs. Most of this advice is quite commonsensical and none of it is guaranteed to work despite the promises.

The first step in improving a firm's search engine ranking is to register with as many search engines as possible, so that a user looking for similar Web sites has a chance of coming across the firm's site. Nearly all search engines have registration pages.

The second step to improve a firm's ranking is to ensure that keywords used in the Web site description match keywords likely to be used as search terms by prospective customers. Using the keyword "lamps," for example, will not help your search engine ranking if most prospective customers are searching for "lights." Search engines differ, but most search engines read home page title tags, metatags, and other text on the home page in order to understand and index the content of the page.

Third, place keywords in a Web site's metatag and page title. A *metatag* is an HTML tag containing a list of words describing the Web site. Metatags are heavily used by search engines to determine the relevance of Web sites to search terms used frequently by users. The title tag provides a brief description of the Web site's content. The words in both the metatags and the title tags should match words on the home page. In addition, it is wise to include many references on the home page to the subject matter of likely consumer searches. Most crawlers will index the text content of the home page and may not go deeper into the Web site's secondary pages.

Fourth, link the Web site to as many other Web sites as possible, both in-coming links and out-going links. Search engines evaluate both kinds of links, and their quality to identify how popular a page is and how linked it is to other content on the Web. Search engines such as Google are guessing that when you enter a query for a product, chances are good that the product is located at one of the highly connected Web sites. The assumption is that the more links there are to a Web site, the more useful the Web site must be. How can a firm increase links to its Web site? Placing advertising is one way: banner ads, buttons, interstitials, and superstitials are all links to a firm's Web site. You can also create Web sites, even hundreds of Web sites, whose only function is to link to your main Web site, although search engines can discover this and place you on the last page of search returns. Entering into affiliate relationships with other Web sites is another method. Search engines attempt to cancel out all efforts to mislead their search engines with varying and unknown success.

While the steps listed above are a beginning, increasing a firm's ranking is still a bit of an art form and usually requires a full-time professional effort to tweak metatags, keywords, and network links before solid results are obtained. The task often requires several months and is complicated by the fact that each search engine uses slightly different indexing methods, and changes their indexing methods in order to fool search engine optimizers.

## WEB SITE FUNCTIONALITY

Attracting users to a company's Web site is the objective of marketing, but once a consumer is at a Web site, the sales process begins. This means that whatever brought the individuals to the Web site becomes much less relevant, and what they find at the Web site will ultimately determine whether they will make a purchase or return. Recall that a Web page and Web site are, first and foremost, a software interface. The question is: What makes for an effective software interface? In general, people use software interfaces that they perceive to be useful and easy to use (a literature that is referred to as the "technology acceptance model"). Utility and ease of use are, therefore, the main factors to focus on when designing a site. Other factors involved in the credibility and trust that users place in a Web site—both are very important for making decisions—are described in a growing literature on Web site design (Fogg, et al., 2003). In an exploratory study of Web site credibility based on 2,600 participants, the top three factors in Web site credibility were design look, information design/structure, and information focus (Fogg, et al., 2003) (see **Figure 7.11**). Similar results were reported by Flanigan and Metzger in a 2007 study (Flanigan and Metzger, 2007). The message is: design counts.

The authors of this study were disappointed that users were most impressed by the design look of a Web site rather than its utility or ease of use.

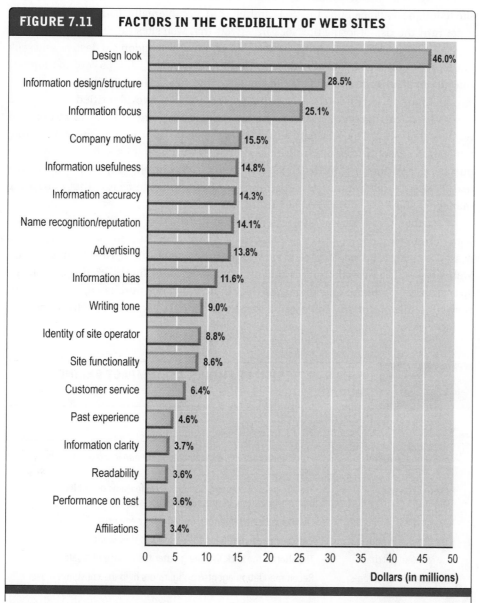

**FIGURE 7.11 FACTORS IN THE CREDIBILITY OF WEB SITES**

When evaluating the credibility of a Web site, survey participants commented on the design look of the Web site more than any other Web site feature.

SOURCE: Based on data from Fogg, et al., 2003.

Research on Web site utilization has found that the way information is organized on a Web site, while important for first-time users, declines in importance over time. Gradually, information content becomes the major factor attracting further visits (Davern, et al., 2001). In this research, frequency of Web site use is a function of four independent variables: content quality, Web site organization, perceived usefulness of the Web site, and perceived ease of use. Over time, people get used to the organization of a Web site and learn how to use it effectively to gather information. This suggests that improving content and usefulness ought to be the first priority of a firm, and that Web site redesign should be implemented carefully and incrementally. Radically redesigning a site runs the risk of losing the "lock-in" effects that Web sites can induce (Davern, et al., 2001). Most firms risk user discomfort and eventually abandon old designs and seek out more useful and interesting designs that produce more sales: 65% of the top 500 Internet retailers redesigned their sites in 2010 (Internet Retailer, 2010b).

In Chapter 4 (Section 4.4, especially Table 4.10), we identified eight basic design features that were necessary, from a business point of view, to attract and retain customers. The Web site must be functional, informative, employ simple navigation (ease of use), use redundant navigation, make it easy for customers to purchase, and feature multi-browser functionality, simple graphics, and legible text. Researchers have also found a number of other design factors that marketing managers should be aware of (see **Table 7.9**).

Sites that offer a "compelling experience" in the sense of providing entertainment with commerce or interactivity, or that are perceived as "fun" to use, are more successful in attracting and keeping visitors (Internet Retailer, 2010b; Novak, et al., 2000). Web sites with editorial content that informs users also increases the time users spend on the Web site and increases the chance of them purchasing a product or service. While simplicity of design is hard to define, Lohse et al. (2000) found that

| TABLE 7.9 | WEB SITE DESIGN FEATURES THAT IMPACT ONLINE PURCHASING |
|---|---|
| **DESIGN FEATURE** | **DESCRIPTION** |
| Compelling experience | Provide interactivity, entertainment, human interest; site is fun to use. |
| Editorial content | Provide helpful content, opinions, and features on subjects of interest to visitors in order to increase stickiness. |
| Fast download times | Quicker is better; if longer, provide amusement. |
| Easy product list navigation | Consumers can easily find the products they want. |
| Few clicks to purchase | The shorter the click list, the greater the chance of a sale. |
| Customer choice agents | Recommendation agents/configurators help the consumer make quick, correct choices. |
| Responsiveness | Personal e-mail response; 1-800 phone capability shown on Web site. |

the most important factor in predicting monthly sales was product list navigation and choice features that save consumers time. Thus, Amazon's "one-click" purchase capability is a powerful tool for increasing sales.

More and more Web sites are using interactive consumer-decision aids to help the shopper make choices. Recommendation agents are programs that can suggest a product based on either consumer surveys or a review of a consumer's profile. Dell uses an online configurator to help consumers decide what computer to order.

Responsiveness of Web sites is also important to credibility. Firms are improving but have a long way to go. An eGain survey found that 70% of leading North American enterprise businesses were rated "below average" or "poor" in multi-channel customer service experience, although the online retail sector was a bright spot, with better scores than previous year (eGain, 2010). In general, large companies with Web sites receive favorable respect ratings for "simplicity of design and use" but weak ratings on responding to customers. Other researchers have found that consumers purchase more at sites where there are strong privacy policies and these are known to visitors (Tsai, et al., 2007).

No matter how successful the offline and online marketing campaign, a Web site that fails to deliver information, customer convenience, and responsiveness spells disaster. Attention to these Web site design features will help ensure success.

# Instant Ads:
## Real-Time Marketing on Exchanges

The holy grail of advertising and marketing is to deliver the right message to the right person at the right time. If this were possible, no one would receive ads they did not want to see, and then no advertising dollars would be wasted, reducing the costs to end users and increasing the efficiency of each ad dollar. In the physical world, only a very rough approximation of this ideal is possible. Advertisers can buy television and radio spots, newspaper ads, and billboards based on broad demographics and interests of likely potential customers. The Internet promised to change this. On the Internet, ads supposedly could be targeted to individual consumers based on their personal characteristics, interests, and recent clickstream behavior. One early vision of e-commerce was a trade-off between privacy and efficiency: let us know a little more about you, and we will show you only the advertising and products you are interested in seeing, and even offer free content. E-commerce was supposed to end the mass advertising that exploded in the television era.

But contrary to popular impressions and the fears of privacy advocates, most of the display ads shown to site visitors are marvelously irrelevant to visitors' interests, both short term and long term. For this reason, the click-through rate for banner advertising is a stunningly low 0.5%, and the price of display ads given their poor performance has fallen to a few cents. Check this out: point your browser at Yahoo (the largest display advertiser on earth), look at the prominent ads shown on the right, and ask yourself if you are really interested in the ad content at this moment in time? How about ever? Chances are slim you are interested at this moment even if the ad is somewhat appropriate to your demographics. Often it's an ad for something you are totally not interested in and never have been!

A part of the problem is that online display ad publishers like Yahoo, and the advertising networks they ended up owning, until recently did not know very much about you, and what they did know was quite general: female, zip code, age, and perhaps some prior purchases. They could build a "profile" of you but it was very imprecise. The resulting ads displayed were frequently far off the mark of what you were interested in at the moment. And even if they knew everything about you, the advertising networks did not have the mechanism to sell that information instantly to a potential advertiser. For this reason, banner ads displayed on the Web sites you visited rarely had anything to do with your interests at the time. Rather than achieve the holy grail of advertising, much of Web-based display advertising was extraordinarily ignorant of who you were or what you were looking for. Search engine advertising was typically better, since it would be responding to search terms you yourself had entered.

In the last two years, behavioral targeting and tracking of online behavior have begun to improve the situation for display advertisers by expanding the scope, breadth, and depth of personal information, making it possible for advertisers to fine-tune their display ads and to develop a much finer-grained, digital image of individual customers, real people not just profiles. Using beacons, Web bugs, cookies, and Flash cookies, almost all the top Web sites now install tracking software onto visitor computers. A *Wall Street Journal* study of the 50 top Web sites in the United States, accounting for 40% of U.S. page views, found these sites installed 3,180 tracking files on a test computer that visited each site. Only one top-50 site installed no tracking files: Wikipedia. Over two-thirds of the tracking files were installed by 131 companies. Guess who the biggest trackers were? Google, Microsoft, and Yahoo. The vast majority of these tracking files are third-party cookies and beacons (they are not installed by the Web site you are visiting, but through a commercial arrangement with the Web site you are visiting, tracking firms are allowed to place cookies and beacons).

Today, when a user visits a site, a tracking number or cookie is assigned to the user. Often a "beacon" or Web bug is installed, which captures what people are typing on a Web site. For instance, a beacon will record comments on automobiles or illness; favorite movies; the fact you like *American Idol*; do crossword puzzles; bought a Kindle; purchased romantic titles; have an iPad; and installed the *New York Times* reader. When the user visits other sites where the tracking firm has installed its software, the user is recognized, more behavior is observed, and this information is added to the original cookie file on the user's computer, or sent to the firm's tracking server using the installed beacon. The file keeps growing the more the user visits Web sites. These tracking files monitor all the keystrokes and sites visited by an Internet user. It is unclear how long this information is held by tracking firms although the largest have voluntarily set some restrictions: some retain data forever, Google anonymizes after 9 months; Bing deletes everything after 6 months; Yahoo deletes data in 90 days. Smaller firms operating under the radar have not announced their policies.

So what happens to all this information about you and others? The cookie and beacon owners collect all this information and sell it to advertisers. On the basis of all this personal and click stream information, a profile of the individual user is developed by data exchange firms such as BlueKai Inc. and eXelate Media as well as the three big players. The information and the profile are sold to advertisers usually for 10 cents a piece. Advertisers specify the profiles they are looking for: male, 24-35, urban, drives a sports sedan, sports fan, high income, and likes books (think possible BMW customer). Once individuals fitting this profile appear at a Web site, the advertiser pays to have a pre-fabricated ad displayed to that person. Voila! Targeting, personalization! A more efficient market communications process, happier Internet users who see what they are interested in looking at, and users who click more often.

Not quite yet. One thing is missing from this heady mix of behavioral tracking and targeting: immediacy. When you click on a search engine result it's because you are interested in that product or service right now, this moment, this instant. Google, which is currently used by 75% of global Internet users, or approximately 943 million people, is believed to be the largest and best repository of immediate user interests. For display ads, even targeted ones, this is not quite possible yet. Advertisers reserved slots (available pages, location on page, time of day/week) based on their best guesstimates of the types of people (i.e., profiles) who would show up to see those pages and be exposed to the ad. They really are clueless when it comes to who you are, and what you are interested in at the moment of opening a Web page. Advertisers could not make on-the-fly, instant decisions about ads to show Web site visitors based on what they were doing just before this instant, and just before they landed on a page.

In 2010, this situation is changing ,and for the first time display advertisers--portals and ad networks they own--are building the capability to display banner ads that are based on the granular behavior of individuals just prior to displaying the ad. There are two players here. The often small-fry data collection firms (the third-party owners of cookies and beacons), as well as the large players, are developing data exchanges where advertisers can purchase all the individual-level data available. There's a lot of data looking for a use and a market. The second part of the change is the really large Web advertisers like Google, Microsoft, and Yahoo who have each developed advertising exchanges that permit advertisers to buy ads in the few milliseconds between a user entering a Web address (or clicking on a search query) and the page appearing based on the data purchased from data exchanges.

For instance, Google has developed a real-time bidding system or exchange for selling and buying display ads. Ad sellers (Web publishers) provide the inventory of slots available on the Internet. Ad buyers bid on these slots based on the likelihood their ads will be seen by the kinds of people they are targeting. Google calls this the DoubleClick Ad Exchange; Yahoo calls its exchange Right Media. Currently, over 50 advertising networks buy display ads through Google's network. With ad exchanges, advertisers buy ads in milliseconds between the time you enter a URL on your keyboard and the time the Web page loads. In that interval, advertisers can decide based on your cookies and beacon data they have acquired, what ad to show you.

These ad exchanges have moved closer to the ideal Web advertising environment by allowing advertisers to decide where to place their ads on the fly, and based on fairly solid data on the people most likely to see the ad. This is far different from the traditional ad placement process which placed ads weeks and months in advance of the ad being displayed.

Taking it a step further, start-up firms like AppNexus have fine-tuned the tracking process to individual-level behavior, and then display ads to individuals based not on their profile membership but on what they clicked on somewhere on the Web just seconds ago. For instance, eBay has been working with AppNexus to develop "instant ads" based on immediate prior behavior. Suppose a man searched for running shoes on eBay. eBay can follow this person across the Web in real time and display ads which are highly personalized to his interest in exercise, including socks, shorts, and shirts. Exercise-related vacations can be offered, along with muscle-building pills, and exercise machines. How about a heart monitor? These new capabilities allow advertisers to evaluate each individual on a granular, personal basis, in real time. Matthew

Ackley, eBay Vice President of Internet Marketing and Advertising, commented, "We have found that we can get 'search quality' results from display advertising and that's a new world for us."

What's next? Currently, the individual information located in private data exchanges is not shared to a single large data exchange, and the future will likely involve industry consolidation and the large players like Google, Yahoo, and Microsoft purchasing the smaller data exchanges and combining their in-house data with newly purchased data. Some, but not all, of the large players have held back merging data from their separate services for fear of alienating their customers. For instance, Google has chosen not to merge its Google Checkout data with Gmail, or its location services. It is unclear if Yahoo merges the contents of user mail with display advertising, but they certainly could. Google's stance will change as Google is pressured by competitors to develop larger tracking databases. Google, through its ad exchange, is seeking to become the clearinghouse for as many ad transactions on the Internet as possible, even if these transactions are using data from other sources. Yahoo and Microsoft are close behind, hoping to develop their own encompassing ad and data exchanges. Self-restraint and self-regulation is unlikely to work in this market place, and many of the firms involved are working with Congress to develop guidelines for protecting consumer privacy, and protecting their future revenues from Congressional meddling. One question faced by all parties to these debates: what is the meaning of privacy in a commercial world where advertisers know more about you than your family members and friends?

**SOURCES**: "Google Agonizes on Privacy as Ad World Vaults Ahead," by Jessica Vascellaro, *Wall Street Journal*, August 10, 2010; "Sites Feed Personal Details to New Tracking Industry," by Julia Angwin and Tom McGinty, *Wall Street Journal*, July 30, 2010; "Yahoo Finally Allows Real-Time Bidding on Network and Exchange," Kate Kaye, ClickZ.com, March 15, 2010; "Google Gains Traction in Display-Ad Push," by Jessica Vascellaro and Emily Steel, *Wall Street Journal*, March 11, 2010; "Instant Ads Set the Pace on the Web," by Stephanie Clifford, *New York Times*, March 10, 2010; "Online Ad Auctions," by Hal Varian, Draft, University of California and Google, February 16, 2009.

## Case Study Questions

1. Pay a visit to your favorite portal and count the total ads on the opening page. Count how many of these ads are (a) immediately of interest and relevant to you, (b) sort of interesting or relevant but not now, and (c) not interesting or relevant. Do this 10 times and calculate the percentage of the three kinds of situations. Describe what you find and explain the results using this case.

2. Advertisers use different kinds of 'profiles' in the decision to display ads to customers. Identify the different kinds of profiles described in this case, and explain why they are relevant to online display advertising.

3. How can display ads achieve search engine-like results?

4. Do you think instant display ads based on your immediately prior clickstream will be as effective as search engine marketing techniques? Why or why not?

## 7.5 REVIEW

### KEY CONCEPTS

■ Identify the major forms of online marketing communications.

Marketing communications include promotional sales communications that encourage immediate purchases and branding communications that focus on extolling the differentiable benefits of consuming a product or service. There are a number of different forms of marketing communications:

- *Banner and rich media/video ads* are promotional messages that users can respond to by clicking on the banner and following the link to a product description or offering. Variations include different size banners, buttons, skyscrapers, pop-ups, and pop-unders. Rich media ads use Flash, DHTML, Java, JavaScript, and streaming audio and/or video, and typically seek to involve users more deeply than static banner ads.
- *Interstitial ads* are a way of placing full-page messages between the current and destination pages of a user. They are usually inserted within a single site, and are displayed as the user moves from one page to the next; they can also be made to appear as users move among sites.
- *Superstitials* are rich media ads that pre-load into a browser's cache and do not play until fully loaded and the user clicks to another page.
- *Paid search engine inclusion and placement* is a relatively recent phenomenon. Firms now pay search engines for inclusion in the search engine index (formerly free and based on "objective" criteria), receiving a guarantee that their firm will appear in the results of relevant searches.
- *Sponsorships* are paid efforts to tie an advertiser's name to particular information, an event, or a venue in a way that reinforces its brand in a positive yet not overtly commercial manner. Advertorials are a common form of online sponsorship.
- *Affiliate relationships* permit a firm to put its logo or banner ad on another firm's Web site from which users of that site can click through to the affiliate's site.
- *Direct e-mail marketing* sends e-mail directly to interested users, and has proven to be one of the most effective forms of marketing communications. The key to effective direct e-mail marketing is "interested users"—Internet users who, at one time or another, have expressed an interest in receiving messages from the advertiser (people who have "opted in").
- *Online catalogs* are the online equivalent of paper-based catalogs. Their basic function is to display an e-commerce merchant's wares.
- Offline marketing combined with online marketing communications is typically the most effective. Although many e-commerce ventures want to rely heavily on online communications, marketing communications campaigns most successful at driving traffic to a Web site have incorporated both online and offline tactics.

■ Understand the costs and benefits of online marketing communications.

Key terms that one must know in order to understand evaluations of online marketing communications' effectiveness and its costs and benefits include:

- *Impressions*—the number of times an ad is served.
- *Click-through rate*—the number of times an ad is clicked.
- *Hits*—the number of http requests received by a firm's server.
- *Page views*—the number of pages viewed by visitors.
- *Stickiness (duration)*—the average length of time visitors remain at a site.
- *Unique visitors*—the number of distinct, unique visitors to a site.
- *Loyalty*—the percentage of purchasers who return in a year.
- *Reach*—the percentage of total consumers in a market who will visit a site.
- *Recency*—the average number of days elapsed between visits.
- *Acquisition rate*—the percentage of visitors who indicate an interest in the site's product, by registering or visiting product pages.
- *Conversion rate*—the percentage of visitors who purchase something.
- *Browse-to-buy ratio*—the ratio of items purchased to product views.
- *View-to-cart ratio*—the ratio of "Add to cart" clicks to product views.
- *Cart conversion rate*—the ratio of actual orders to "Add to cart" clicks.
- *Checkout conversion rate*—the ratio of actual orders to checkouts started.
- *Abandonment rate*—the percentage of shoppers who begin a shopping cart form, but then fail to complete the form.
- *Retention rate*—the percentage of existing customers who continue to buy on a regular basis.
- *Attrition rate*—the percentage of customers who purchase once, but do not return within a year.
- *Open rate*—the percentage of customers who open the mail and are exposed to the message.
- *Delivery rate*—the percentage of e-mail recipients who received the e-mail.
- *Click-through rate (e-mail)*—the percentage of e-mail recipients who clicked through to the offer.
- *Bounce-back rate*—the percentage of e-mails that could not be delivered

Studies have shown that low click-through rates are not indicative of a lack of commercial impact of online advertising, and that advertising communication does occur even when users do not directly respond by clicking. Online advertising in its various forms has been shown to boost brand awareness and brand recall, create positive brand perceptions, and increase intent to purchase.

Effectiveness cannot be considered without analysis of cost. Typical pricing models for online marketing communications include:

- *Barter*—the exchange of ad space for something of equal value.
- *Cost per thousand (CPM)*—the advertiser pays for impressions in 1,000-unit lots.
- *Cost per click (CPC)*—the advertiser pays a prenegotiated fee for each click an ad receives.
- *Cost per action (CPA)*—the advertiser pays only for those users who perform a specific action.
- *Hybrid models*—combines two or more other models.
- *Sponsorships*—the advertiser pays a fixed fee for a particular term.

Online marketing communications are typically less costly than traditional mass media marketing. Also, online sales can generally be directly correlated with online marketing efforts, unlike traditional marketing communications tactics.

The online merchant can measure precisely just how much revenue is generated by specific banners or specific e-mail messages sent to prospective customers.

- Discuss the ways in which a Web site can be used as a marketing communications tool.

A functional Web site that customers can find is one of the strongest online communications tools. The following are all integral parts of a coordinated marketing communications strategy:

- *Appropriate domain name*—Companies should choose a domain name that is short, memorable, hard to confuse or misspell, and indicative of a firm's business functions, and that preferably uses .com as its top-level domain.
- *Search engine optimization*—Companies should register with all the major search engines so that a user looking for similar sites has a better chance of finding that particular site, ensure that keywords used in the Web site description match keywords likely to be used as search terms by prospective customers, and link the site to as many other sites as possible.
- *Web site functionality*—Once at a Web site, visitors need to be enticed to stay and to buy. Web site design features that impact online purchasing include how compelling the experience of using the Web site is, download time, product list navigation, the number of clicks required to purchase, the existence of customer choice agents, and the Web site's responsiveness to customer needs.

## QUESTIONS

1. Explain the difference between marketing and marketing communications.
2. Explain the difference between branding communications and sales/promotional communications.
3. What are some reasons why online advertising constitutes only about 15% of the total advertising market?
4. What kinds of products are most suited to being advertised online?
5. What is the difference between an interstitial ad and a superstitial ad?
6. What are some of the reasons for the decline in click-through rates on banner ads today? How can banner ads be made more effective?
7. Why are some affiliate relationships called "tenancy" deals? How do they differ from pure affiliate arrangements?
8. There is some controversy surrounding paid placements on search engines. What are the issues surrounding paid-placement search engines? Why might consumers object to this practice?
9. What are some of the advantages of direct e-mail marketing?
10. Why is offline advertising still important?
11. What is the difference between hits and page views? Why are these not the best measurements of Web traffic? Which is the preferred metric for traffic counts?
12. Define CTR, CPM, CPC, CPA, and VTR.
13. What are the key attributes of a good domain name?
14. What are some of the steps a firm can take to optimize its search engine rankings?
15. List and describe some Web site design features that impact online purchasing.

## PROJECTS

1. Use the Online Consumer Purchasing Model (Figure 7.8) to assess the effectiveness of an e-mail campaign at a small Web site devoted to the sales of apparel to the ages 18–26 young adult market in the United States. Assume a marketing campaign of 100,000 e-mails (at 25 cents per e-mail address). The expected click-through rate is 5%, the conversion to customer rate is 10%, and the loyal customer retention rate is 25%. The average sale is $60, and the profit margin is 50% (the cost of the goods is $30). Does the campaign produce a profit? What would you advise doing to increase the number of purchases and loyal customers? What Web design factors? What communications messages?

2. Surf the Web for at least 15 minutes. Visit at least two different e-commerce sites. Make a list describing in detail all the different marketing communication tools you see being used. Which do you believe is the most effective and why?

3. Do a search for a product of your choice on at least three search engines. Examine the results page carefully. Can you discern which results, if any, are a result of a paid placement? If so, how did you determine this? What other marketing communications related to your search appear on the page?

4. Examine the use of rich media and video in advertising. Find and describe at least two examples of advertising using streaming video, sound, or other rich media technologies. (Hint: Check the sites of Internet advertising agencies for case studies or examples of their work.) What are the advantages and/or disadvantages of this kind of advertising? Prepare a short 3-to 5-page report on your findings.

5. Visit your Facebook page and examine the ads shown in the right margin. What is being advertised and how do you believe it is relevant to your interests or online behavior? You could also search on a retail product on Google several times, and related products, then visit Yahoo or another popular site to see if your past behavior is helping advertisers track you.

# CHAPTER 8

# Ethical, Social, and Political Issues in E-commerce

## LEARNING OBJECTIVES

**After reading this chapter, you will be able to:**

- Understand why e-commerce raises ethical, social, and political issues.
- Recognize the main ethical, social, and political issues raised by e-commerce.
- Identify a process for analyzing ethical dilemmas.
- Understand basic concepts related to privacy.
- Identify the practices of e-commerce companies that threaten privacy.
- Describe the different methods used to protect online privacy.
- Understand the various forms of intellectual property and the challenges involved in protecting it.
- Understand how governance of the Internet has evolved over time.
- Explain why taxation of e-commerce raises governance and jurisdiction issues.
- Identify major public safety and welfare issues raised by e-commerce.

# Discovering Law and Ethics
## in a Virtual World

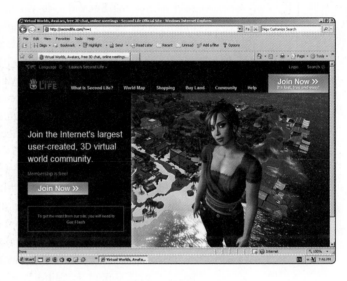

econd Life is a massively multiplayer online role playing game (MMORPG) experience where around 1 million active monthly users engage in online "virtual life." For the most part, players come not to compete with one another but to escape the real world and have some fun. Many come to make money. Linden dollars, which can be purchased with real dollars (currently $1 = 250–270 Linden dollars), provide liquidity, and avatars that users create can buy and sell virtual assets—goods and services—from handbags and cars, to furniture, buildings, real estate, avatar design, clothing, and accessories. The global market for virtual goods is estimated to be approximately $1.5 billion a year, and Second Life plays a significant role in this market. In 2009, residents of Second Life purchased or sold around USD $500 million of virtual goods and services, and that number is expected to continue growing, with the value of user-to-user transactions reaching record highs in 2010. Shopping for virtual goods has become one of the most compelling and popular aspects of the Second Life experience, with nearly a million different items typically listed for sale.

Others come to create mischief. Mischief, so much a part of the real world where law and custom aim to hold it in check, poses an interesting challenge for virtual worlds where there are no laws, and yet where actions taken online can injure people and corporations offline. It's like the Old West, where law and order were not quite established and people sought solutions, looking at times for a strong High Noon sheriff to bring order. Every now and then, the Sheriff sets down the law in Second Life, when its owners declare certain activities illegal and attempt to set up a system of self-regulation (if not quite law).

For instance, many of the assets, goods, and services sold on Second Life do not "belong" to the people who are selling them. You can buy virtual Gucci bags, Ferrari cars (L$1,995—what a deal!), Rolex watches, Rayban sunglasses, Prada and Oakley clothes for your avatars, Nike shoes, and Apple iPods. In a small study conducted by several lawyers, of 10 randomly selected virtual stores on Second Life, 7 sold knockoff goods that exhibited obvious trademark infringements. Some stores sold nothing but brand-name goods. But because this is all virtual, none of the mentioned trademark owners have thus far brought a lawsuit against residents. As lawyers point out, if and when companies seek to develop their trademarks on virtual sites, they will not want to compete with hundreds or thousands of residents selling knockoffs. And unless companies actively enforce their trademarks in the face of infringement, they can lose the trademark altogether. In 2009, one company finally did. Taser, the maker of real world stun guns, filed a lawsuit in the U.S. District Court, District of Arizona, charging that Linden Lab had damaged its reputation and hurt sales by allowing virtual Tasers to be sold within the Second Life world. The case was later dropped after Linden Lab's management removed the offending products from the Web site. Linden Lab does indeed have an intellectual property rights policy as a part of its terms of service, which tells users "You should not use copyrighted, trademarked, or celebrity material in Second Life, unless of course you are the intellectual property owner or have permission from the intellectual property owner." However, its enforcement of these terms is haphazard and is triggered largely from complaints by trademark owners.

In a further sign of emerging legal and ethical issues, six major content creators on Second Life filed a real-world copyright and trademark infringement lawsuit against Thomas Simon, a Queens, New York, resident. Simon allegedly found a flaw in the Second Life program, and used a third-party copy program to make thousands of copies of the creators' products. Included in the alleged theft were avatar clothing, skins, and shapes, scripted objects, furniture, and other objects. To complicate matters, the plaintiffs "broke into" his skybox to find the evidence of infringement. In the real world, the evidence obtained by unlawful means would be disallowed. The plaintiffs settled the lawsuit, with Simon agreeing to pay $525 in damages for profits made as a result of unauthorized copying of the plaintiff's intellectual property. Linden Lab takes the position that it is an ISP under the Digital Millennium Copyright Act and thus is not itself responsible for any copyright infringement by its users.

Linden Lab has been forced to confront other issues of governance and ethics on Second Life. It has banned six behaviors: intolerance (including slurs against groups), harassment, assault (including use of software tools to attack people's avatars), disclosure of information about other people's real-world lives, indecency (sexual behavior outside areas rated as mature), and disturbing the peace. Violations prompt warnings, suspension or banishment, enforced by Linden managers. There is no appeal process or due process. In an effort to shield kids from many of these behaviors, Linden Lab launched Teen Second Life for kids aged 13 to 17, which enforces even stricter behavioral standards.

The large-scale trademark and copyright infringements on Second Life raise concerns about virtual life and real-life law and statutes. Stealing in virtual life would seem to parallel stealing in real life. Gambling is another matter. Linden Lab's terms of service ban any illegal activity, but the company itself was not sure whether in-world gambling crossed the line. The FBI and federal prosecutors were invited to visit Second Life gambling operations in 2007, but issued no opinion on the legality of the operation. According to Ginsu Yoon, Vice President of Business Affairs, "It's not always clear to us whether a 3-D simulation of a casino is the same thing as a casino, legally speaking—and it's not clear to the law enforcement authorities we have asked." Even if the law were clear, he said the company would have no way to monitor or prevent in-world gambling, much as law enforcement cannot police every neighborhood poker game or office basketball pool. "There are millions of registered accounts and tens of millions of different objects in Second Life; there is simply no way for us to monitor content prospectively even if we wanted to," Yoon said. "That would be a harder task than pre-monitoring all e-mail sent through Yahoo Mail or Gmail, and no one expects those services to prevent all possible use of e-mail for illegal activity." This sounds like no one is in control, and real-world laws just don't apply, an argument that used to be made by P2P music sites. Ultimately, the Supreme Court in the real world shut down those music sites because they intentionally established a mechanism to violate copyright laws. Later in 2007, Linden Lab decided to outlaw all forms of gambling.

In 2010, Second Life's users filed a class action lawsuit against Linden Lab regarding virtual property rights. Originally, according to Linden Lab's policy, Second Life users owned the combined $100 million in virtual property and items they purchased in Second Life. But the company began removing references to users' property rights from the site and adjusted the terms of use to state that users have "a license to computing resources" that can be redistributed "at Linden Lab's discretion." Linden Lab has since confiscated the property of some of its users without compensation, which prompted the suit. The Second Life users who are plaintiffs in the lawsuit hope to recover at least $5 million in damages for alleged violations of consumer protection laws.

Linden Lab and Second Life have a strong libertarian history. Its founders fashioned Second Life as a self-regulating community where good people could amuse themselves in a fantasy world. But in 2009, Linden Lab launched several efforts to integrate Second Life into the real world. At the beginning of the year, it purchased OnRez and xStreet SL, two Web-based marketplaces for virtual goods to aid in its effort to build an internal Amazon-like market where citizens can buy and sell virtual goods (and Linden can earn transaction fees). It also launched AvaLine, a service that allows its residents to receive cell, landline, or VoIP calls in-world from people outside Second Life. Linden Lab has also focused on enticing real-world companies such as IBM, Northrop, Nike, and Coca-Cola to increase their use of Second Life for business meetings, product introductions, product training, marketing events, and conferences.

These efforts haven't produced the desired results for Linden Lab. The future they envisioned for of Second Life as a support system for real-world corporations, and an economically viable platform for e-commerce, has been difficult to realize. Although Second Life entrepreneurs can make over $1 million (USD) per year, such profitable virtual businesses are the exception, not the norm, and the economic downturn and the growth of Facebook as a gaming platform have hampered the virtual world's growth. In 2010, Linden Lab announced that it would cut 30% of its workforce in an effort to remain profitable. Second Life is still doing well, but unless its managers continue to innovate while closely integrating their ethics and legal practices with those of the real world, the real-world businesses that are so important to Second Life's future may continue to abandon it.

**SOURCES:** "Second Life's Linden Lab to Cut 30% of Staff," by Steven E.F. Brown, *San Francisco Business Times,* June 9, 2010; "A Real-World Battle over Virtual-Property Rights," by David Lazarus, *Los Angeles Times,* April 30, 2010; "Second Life Economy At Record High," by Curt Hopkins, www.readwriteweb.com, April 28, 2010; "Trademarked, Copyrighted, and Celebrity Material in Second Life," wiki.secondlife.com/wiki/Intellectual_Property, accessed September 7, 2009; "Linden Lab Hires VP of Web Development to Help Users More Closely Integrate Second Life with their Online Lives," press release, Linden Lab, August 31, 2009; "Taser Sues 'Second Life' for Trademark Infringement," by Ian Rowan,Switched.com, April 24, 2009; "Linden Goes Shopping, Buys Virtual Goods Marketplace to Integrate Web Shopping With Second Life," press pelease, Linden Lab, January 20, 2009; "Ethics of Practice in Virtual Worlds," by Benjamin Duranske, Virtuallyblind.com, November 2, 2008; "Rapid Trademark Infringement in Second Life Costs Millions, Undermines Future Enforcement," by Benjamin Duranske, Virtuallyblind. com, October 30, 2007.

D etermining how to regulate virtual behavior that may have a real-world impact is just one of many ethical, social, and political issues raised by the rapid evolution of the Internet and e-commerce. These questions are not just ethical questions that we as individuals have to answer; they also involve social institutions such as family, schools, and business firms. And these questions have obvious political dimensions because they involve collective choices about how we should live and what laws we would like to live under.

In this chapter, we discuss the ethical, social, and political issues raised in e-commerce, provide a framework for organizing the issues, and make recommendations for managers who are given the responsibility of operating e-commerce companies within commonly accepted standards of appropriateness.

## 8.1 UNDERSTANDING ETHICAL, SOCIAL, AND POLITICAL ISSUES IN E-COMMERCE

The Internet and its use in e-commerce have raised pervasive ethical, social, and political issues on a scale unprecedented for computer technology. Entire sections of daily newspapers and weekly magazines are devoted to the social impact of the Internet. But why is this so? Why is the Internet at the root of so many contemporary controversies? Part of the answer lies in the underlying features of Internet technology itself, and the ways in which it has been exploited by business firms. Internet technology and its use in e-commerce disrupt existing social and business relationships and understandings.

Consider for instance Table 1.2 (in Chapter 1), which lists the unique features of Internet technology. Instead of considering the business consequences of each unique feature, **Table 8.1** examines the actual or potential ethical, social, and/or political consequences of the technology.

We live in an "information society," where power and wealth increasingly depend on information and knowledge as central assets. Controversies over information are often disagreements over power, wealth, influence, and other things thought to be valuable. Like other technologies, such as steam, electricity, telephones, and television, the Internet and e-commerce can be used to achieve social progress, and for the most part, this has occurred. However, the same technologies can be used to commit crimes, despoil the environment, and threaten cherished social values. Before automobiles, there was very little interstate crime and very little federal jurisdiction over crime. Likewise with the Internet: before the Internet, there was very little "cybercrime."

Many business firms and individuals are benefiting from the commercial development of the Internet, but this development also exacts a price from individuals, organizations, and societies. These costs and benefits must be carefully considered by those seeking to make ethical and socially responsible decisions in this new environment. The question is: How can you as a manager make reasoned

| TABLE 8.1 | UNIQUE FEATURES OF E-COMMERCE TECHNOLOGY AND THEIR POTENTIAL ETHICAL, SOCIAL, AND/OR POLITICAL IMPLICATIONS |
|---|---|
| **E-COMMERCE TECHNOLOGY DIMENSION** | **POTENTIAL ETHICAL, SOCIAL, AND POLITICAL SIGNIFICANCE** |
| **Ubiquity**—Internet/Web technology is available everywhere: at work, at home, and elsewhere via mobile devices, anytime. | Work and shopping can invade family life; shopping can distract workers at work, lowering productivity; use of mobile devices can lead to automobile and industrial accidents. Presents confusing issues of "nexus" to taxation authorities. |
| **Global reach**—The technology reaches across national boundaries, around the Earth. | Reduces cultural diversity in products; weakens local small firms while strengthening large global firms; moves manufacturing production to low-wage areas of the world; weakens the ability of all nations—large and small—to control their information destiny. |
| **Universal standards**—There is one set of technology standards, namely Internet standards. | Increases vulnerability to viruses and hacking attacks worldwide affecting millions of people at once. Increases the likelihood of "information" crime, crimes against systems, and deception. |
| **Richness**—Video, audio, and text messages are possible. | A "screen technology" that reduces use of text and potentially the ability to read by focusing instead on video and audio messages. Potentially very persuasive messages that may reduce reliance on multiple independent sources of information. |
| **Interactivity**—The technology works through interaction with the user. | The nature of interactivity at commercial sites can be shallow and meaningless. Customer e-mails are frequently not read by human beings. Customers do not really "co-produce" the product as much as they "co-produce" the sale. The amount of "customization" of products that occurs is minimal, occurring within predefined platforms and plug-in options. |
| **Information density**—The technology reduces information costs, raises quality. | While the total amount of information available to all parties increases, so does the possibility of false and misleading information, unwanted information, and invasion of solitude. Trust, authenticity, accuracy, completeness, and other quality features of information can be degraded. The ability of individuals and organizations to make sense of out of this plethora of information is limited. |
| **Personalization/Customization**—The technology allows personalized messages to be delivered to individuals as well as groups. | Opens up the possibility of intensive invasion of privacy for commercial and governmental purposes that is unprecedented. |
| **Social technology**—The technology enables user content generation and social networking. | Creates opportunities for cyberbullying, abusive language, and predation; challenges concepts of privacy, fair use, and consent to use posted information; creates new opportunities for surveillance by authorities and corporations into private lives. |

judgments about what your firm should do in a number of e-commerce areas—from securing the privacy of your customer's clickstream to ensuring the integrity of your company's domain name?

## A MODEL FOR ORGANIZING THE ISSUES

E-commerce—and the Internet—have raised so many ethical, social, and political issues that it is difficult to classify them all, and hence complicated to see their relationship to one another. Clearly, ethical, social, and political issues are interrelated. One way to organize the ethical, social, and political dimensions surrounding e-commerce is shown in **Figure 8.1**. At the individual level, what appears as an ethical issue—"What should I do?"—is reflected at the social and political levels—"What should we as a society and government do?" The ethical dilemmas you face as a manager of a business using the Web reverberate and are reflected in social and political debates. The major ethical, social, and political issues that have developed around e-commerce over the past 10 years can be loosely categorized into four major dimensions: information rights, property rights, governance, and public safety and welfare.

Some of the ethical, social, and political issues raised in each of these areas include the following:

- **Information rights:** What rights to their own personal information do individuals have in a public marketplace, or in their private homes, when Internet technologies make information collection so pervasive and efficient? What rights do individuals have to access information about business firms and other organizations?

- **Property rights:** How can traditional intellectual property rights be enforced in an Internet world where perfect copies of protected works can be made and easily distributed worldwide in seconds?

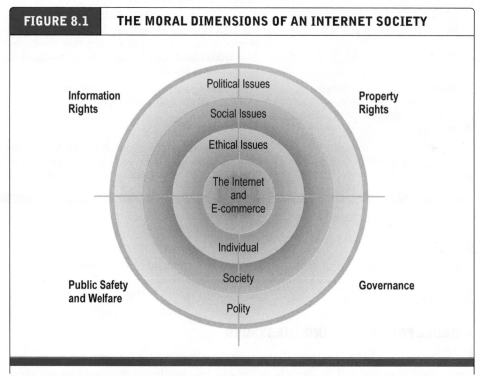

| FIGURE 8.1 | THE MORAL DIMENSIONS OF AN INTERNET SOCIETY |

The introduction of the Internet and e-commerce impacts individuals, societies, and political institutions. These impacts can be classified into four moral dimensions: property rights, information rights, governance, and public safety and welfare.

- **Governance:** Should the Internet and e-commerce be subject to public laws? And if so, what law-making bodies have jurisdiction—state, federal, and/or international?

- **Public safety and welfare:** What efforts should be undertaken to ensure equitable access to the Internet and e-commerce channels? Should governments be responsible for ensuring that schools and colleges have access to the Internet? Are certain online content and activities—such as pornography and gambling—a threat to public safety and welfare? Should mobile commerce be allowed from moving vehicles?

To illustrate, imagine that at any given moment, society and individuals are more or less in an ethical equilibrium brought about by a delicate balancing of individuals, social organizations, and political institutions. Individuals know what is expected of them, social organizations such as business firms know their limits, capabilities, and roles, and political institutions provide a supportive framework of market regulation, banking, and commercial law that provides sanctions against violators.

Now, imagine we drop into the middle of this calm setting a powerful new technology such as the Internet and e-commerce. Suddenly, individuals, business firms, and political institutions are confronted by new possibilities of behavior. For instance, individuals discover that they can download perfect digital copies of music tracks from Web sites without paying anyone, something that, under the old technology of CDs, would have been impossible. This can be done, despite the fact that these music tracks still "belong" as a legal matter to the owners of the copyright—musicians and record label companies. Then, business firms discover that they can make a business out of aggregating these digital musical tracks—or creating a mechanism for sharing musical tracks—even though they do not "own" them in the traditional sense. The record companies, courts, and Congress were not prepared at first to cope with the onslaught of online digital copying. Courts and legislative bodies will have to make new laws and reach new judgments about who owns digital copies of copyrighted works and under what conditions such works can be "shared." It may take years to develop new understandings, laws, and acceptable behavior in just this one area of social impact. In the meantime, as an individual and a manager, you will have to decide what you and your firm should do in legal "gray" areas, where there is conflict between ethical principles but no clear-cut legal or cultural guidelines. How can you make good decisions in this type of situation?

Before examining the four moral dimensions of e-commerce in greater depth, we will briefly review some basic concepts of ethical reasoning that you can use as a guide to ethical decision making, and provide general reasoning principles about the social and political issues of the Internet that you will face in the future.

## BASIC ETHICAL CONCEPTS: RESPONSIBILITY, ACCOUNTABILITY, AND LIABILITY

Ethics is at the heart of social and political debates about the Internet. **Ethics** is the study of principles that individuals and organizations can use to determine right and wrong courses of action. It is assumed in ethics that individuals are free moral agents who are in a position to make choices. When faced with alternative courses of action,

**ethics**
the study of principles that individuals and organizations can use to determine right and wrong courses of action

what is the correct moral choice? Extending ethics from individuals to business firms and even entire societies can be difficult, but it is not impossible. As long as there is a decision-making body or individual (such as a Board of Directors or CEO in a business firm, or a governmental body in a society), their decisions can be judged against a variety of ethical principles.

If you understand some basic ethical principles, your ability to reason about larger social and political debates will be improved. In western culture, there are three basic principles that all ethical schools of thought share: responsibility, accountability, and liability. **Responsibility** means that as free moral agents, individuals, organizations, and societies are responsible for the actions they take. **Accountability** means that individuals, organizations, and societies should be held accountable to others for the consequences of their actions. The third principle—liability—extends the concepts of responsibility and accountability to the area of law. **Liability** is a feature of political systems in which a body of law is in place that permits individuals to recover the damages done to them by other actors, systems, or organizations. **Due process** is a feature of law-governed societies and refers to a process in which laws are known and understood and there is an ability to appeal to higher authorities to ensure that the laws have been applied correctly.

You can use these concepts immediately to understand some contemporary Internet debates. For instance, consider the 2005 U.S. Supreme Court decision in the case of *Metro-Goldwyn-Mayer Studios v. Grokster, et al.* MGM had sued Grokster and other P2P networks for copyright infringement. The court decided that because the primary and intended use of Internet P2P file-sharing services such as Grokster, StreamCast, and Kazaa was the swapping of copyright-protected music and video files, the file-sharing services should be held accountable, and shut down. Although Grokster and the other networks acknowledged that the most common use of the software was for illegal digital music file-swapping, they argued that there were substantial, nontrivial uses of the same networks for legally sharing files. They also argued they should not be held accountable for what individuals do with their software, any more than Sony could be held accountable for how people use VCRs, or Xerox for how people use copying machines. Ultimately, the Supreme Court ruled that Grokster and other P2P networks could be held accountable for the illegal actions of their users if it could be shown that they intended their software to be used for illegal downloading and sharing, and had marketed the software for that purpose. The court relied on copyright laws to arrive at its decisions, but these laws reflect some basic underlying ethical principles of responsibility, accountability, and liability.

Underlying the *Grokster* Supreme Court decision is a fundamental rejection of the notion that the Internet is an ungoverned "Wild West" environment that cannot be controlled. Under certain defined circumstances, the courts will intervene into the uses of the Internet. No organized civilized society has ever accepted the proposition that technology can flaunt basic underlying social and cultural values. Through all of the industrial and technological developments that have taken place, societies have intervened by means of legal and political decisions to ensure that the technology serves socially acceptable ends without stifling the positive consequences of innovation and wealth creation. The Internet in this sense is no different, and we can expect societies around the world to exercise more regulatory control over the

**responsibility**

as free moral agents, individuals, organizations, and societies are responsible for the actions they take

**accountability**

individuals, organizations, and societies should be held accountable to others for the consequences of their actions

**liability**

a feature of political systems in which a body of law is in place that permits individuals to recover the damages done to them by other actors, systems, or organizations

**due process**

a process in which laws are known and understood and there is an ability to appeal to higher authorities to ensure that the laws have been applied correctly

Internet and e-commerce in an effort to arrive at a new balance between innovation and wealth creation, on the one hand, and other socially desirable objectives on the other. This is a difficult balancing act, and reasonable people will arrive at different conclusions.

## ANALYZING ETHICAL DILEMMAS

Ethical, social, and political controversies usually present themselves as dilemmas. A **dilemma** is a situation in which there are at least two diametrically opposed actions, each of which supports a desirable outcome. When confronted with a situation that seems to present an ethical dilemma, how can you analyze and reason about the situation? The following is a five-step process that should help:

**dilemma**
a situation in which there are at least two diametrically opposed actions, each of which supports a desirable outcome

1. **Identify and clearly describe the facts.** Find out who did what to whom, and where, when, and how. In many instances, you will be surprised at the errors in the initially reported facts, and often you will find that simply getting the facts straight helps define the solution. It also helps to get the opposing parties involved in an ethical dilemma to agree on the facts.

2. **Define the conflict or dilemma and identify the higher-order values involved.** Ethical, social, and political issues always reference higher values. Otherwise, there would be no debate. The parties to a dispute all claim to be pursuing higher values (e.g., freedom, privacy, protection of property, and the free enterprise system). For example, supporters of the use of advertising networks such as DoubleClick argue that the tracking of consumer movements on the Web increases market efficiency and the wealth of the entire society. Opponents argue this claimed efficiency comes at the expense of individual privacy, and advertising networks should cease their activities or offer Web users the option of not participating in such tracking.

3. **Identify the stakeholders.** Every ethical, social, and political issue has stakeholders: players in the game who have an interest in the outcome, who have invested in the situation, and usually who have vocal opinions. Find out the identity of these groups and what they want. This will be useful later when designing a solution.

4. **Identify the options that you can reasonably take.** You may find that none of the options satisfies all the interests involved, but that some options do a better job than others. Sometimes, arriving at a "good" or ethical solution may not always be a balancing of consequences to stakeholders.

5. **Identify the potential consequences of your options.** Some options may be ethically correct, but disastrous from other points of view. Other options may work in this one instance, but not in other similar instances. Always ask yourself, "What if I choose this option consistently over time?"

Once your analysis is complete, you can refer to the following well-established ethical principles to help decide the matter.

## CANDIDATE ETHICAL PRINCIPLES

Although you are the only one who can decide which ethical principles you will follow and how you will prioritize them, it is helpful to consider some ethical principles with deep roots in many cultures that have survived throughout recorded history:

- **The Golden Rule:** Do unto others as you would have them do unto you. Putting yourself into the place of others and thinking of yourself as the object of the decision can help you think about fairness in decision making.
- **Universalism:** If an action is not right for all situations, then it is not right for any specific situation (Immanuel Kant's categorical imperative). Ask yourself, "If we adopted this rule in every case, could the organization, or society, survive?"
- **Slippery Slope:** If an action cannot be taken repeatedly, then it is not right to take at all (Descartes' rule of change). An action may appear to work in one instance to solve a problem, but if repeated, would result in a negative outcome. In plain English, this rule might be stated as "once started down a slippery path, you may not be able to stop."
- **Collective Utilitarian Principle:** Take the action that achieves the greater value for all of society. This rule assumes you can prioritize values in a rank order and understand the consequences of various courses of action.
- **Risk Aversion:** Take the action that produces the least harm, or the least potential cost. Some actions have extremely high failure costs of very low probability (e.g., building a nuclear generating facility in an urban area) or extremely high failure costs of moderate probability (speeding and automobile accidents). Avoid the high-failure cost actions and choose those actions whose consequences would not be catastrophic, even if there were a failure.
- **No Free Lunch:** Assume that virtually all tangible and intangible objects are owned by someone else unless there is a specific declaration otherwise. (This is the ethical "no free lunch" rule.) If something someone else has created is useful to you, it has value and you should assume the creator wants compensation for this work.
- **The *New York Times* Test (Perfect Information Rule):** Assume that the results of your decision on a matter will be the subject of the lead article in the *New York Times* the next day. Will the reaction of readers be positive or negative? Would your parents, friends, and children be proud of your decision? Most criminals and unethical actors assume imperfect information, and therefore they assume their decisions and actions will never be revealed. When making decisions involving ethical dilemmas, it is wise to assume perfect information markets.
- **The Social Contract Rule:** Would you like to live in a society where the principle you are supporting would become an organizing principle of the entire society?

For instance, you might think it is wonderful to download illegal copies of music tracks, but you might not want to live in a society that did not respect property rights, such as your property rights to the car in your driveway, or your rights to a term paper or original art.

None of these rules is an absolute guide, and there are exceptions and logical difficulties with all of them. Nevertheless, actions that do not easily pass these guidelines deserve some very close attention and a great deal of caution because the appearance of unethical behavior may do as much harm to you and your company as the actual behavior.

Now that you have an understanding of some basic ethical reasoning concepts, let's take a closer look at each of the major types of ethical, social, and political debates that have arisen in e-commerce.

## 8.2 PRIVACY AND INFORMATION RIGHTS

**Privacy** is the moral right of individuals to be left alone, free from surveillance or interference from other individuals or organizations, including the state. Privacy is a girder supporting freedom: Without the privacy required to think, write, plan, and associate independently and without fear, social and political freedom is weakened, and perhaps destroyed. **Information privacy** is a subset of privacy. The right to information privacy includes both the claim that certain information should not be collected at all by governments or business firms, and the claim of individuals to control the use of whatever information that is collected about them. Individual control over personal information is at the core of the privacy concept.

Due process also plays an important role in defining privacy. The best statement of due process in record keeping is given by the Fair Information Practices doctrine developed in the early 1970s and extended to the online privacy debate in the late 1990s (described later in this section).

There are two kinds of threats to individual privacy posed by the Internet. One threat originates in the private sector and concerns how much personal information is collected by commercial Web sites and how it will be used. A second threat originates in the public sector and concerns how much personal information federal, state, and local government authorities collect, and how they use it. While these threats are conceptually distinct, in practice they are related as the federal government increasingly relies on Internet companies to provide intelligence on specific individuals and groups, and as Internet records held by search engine companies and others (like Amazon) are sought by legal authorities and attorney's.

Privacy claims—and thinking about privacy—mushroomed in the United States at the end of the nineteenth century as the technology of photography and tabloid journalism enabled the invasion of the heretofore private lives of wealthy industrialists. For most of the twentieth century, however, privacy thinking and legislation focused on restraining the government from collecting and using personal information. With the explosion in the collection of private personal information by Web-based marketing firms since 1995, privacy concerns are increasingly directed toward restraining the activities of private firms in the collection and use of information on the Web. Claims to privacy are also involved at the workplace. Millions of employees are subject to various forms of electronic surveillance that in many

**privacy**
the moral right of individuals to be left alone, free from surveillance or interference from other individuals or organizations, including the state

**information privacy**
includes both the claim that certain information should not be collected at all by governments or business firms, and the claim of individuals to control the use of whatever information that is collected about them

cases is enhanced by firm intranets and Web technologies. For instance, the majority of U.S. companies monitor which Web sites their workers visit, as well as employee e-mail and instant messages. Employee posts on message boards and blogs are also coming under scrutiny.

In general, the Internet and the Web provide an ideal environment for both business and government to invade the personal privacy of millions of users on a scale unprecedented in history. Perhaps no other recent issue has raised as much widespread social and political concern as protecting the privacy of 200 million Web users in the United States alone. The major ethical issues related to e-commerce and privacy include the following: Under what conditions should we invade the privacy of others? What legitimates intruding into others' lives through unobtrusive surveillance, market research, or other means? The major social issues related to e-commerce and privacy concern the development of "expectations of privacy" or privacy norms, as well as public attitudes. In what areas of life should we as a society encourage people to think they are in "private territory" as opposed to public view? The major political issues related to e-commerce and privacy concern the development of statutes that govern the relations between record keepers and individuals. How should both public and private organizations—which may be reluctant to remit the advantages that come from the unfettered flow of information on individuals—be restrained, if at all? In the following section, we look first at the various practices of e-commerce companies that pose a threat to privacy.

## INFORMATION COLLECTED AT E-COMMERCE SITES

As you have learned in previous chapters, e-commerce sites routinely collect a variety of information from or about consumers who visit their site and/or make purchases. Some of this data constitutes **personally identifiable information (PII)**, which is defined as any data that can be used to identify, locate, or contact an individual (Federal Trade Commission, 2000a). Other data is **anonymous information**, composed of demographic and behavioral information, such as age, occupation, income, zip code, ethnicity, and other data that characterizes your life without identifying who you are. **Table 8.2** lists some of the personal identifiers routinely collected by online e-commerce sites. This is not an exhaustive list.

**personally identifiable information (PII)**
any data that can be used to identify, locate, or contact an individual

**anonymous information**
demographic and behavioral information that does not include any personal identifiers

| TABLE 8.2 | PERSONAL INFORMATION COLLECTED BY E-COMMERCE SITES | |
|---|---|---|
| Name | Bank accounts | Education |
| Address | Credit card accounts | Preference data |
| Phone number | Gender | Transaction data |
| E-mail address | Age | Clickstream data |
| Social security number | Occupation | Browser type |

Advertising networks and search engines also track the behavior of consumers across thousands of popular sites, not just at one site, via cookies, Web beacons, tracking software, spyware, and other techniques

**Table 8.3** illustrates some of the major ways online firms gather information about consumers.

| TABLE 8.3 | THE INTERNET'S MAJOR INFORMATION GATHERING TOOLS AND THEIR IMPACT ON PRIVACY |
|---|---|
| **INTERNET CAPABILITY** | **IMPACT ON PRIVACY** |
| Advertising networks | Used to track individuals as they move among thousands of Web sites. |
| Social networks | Used to gather information on user-provided content such as books, music, and other interests, preferences, and life styles. |
| Cookies | Used to track individuals at a single site. |
| Third-party cookies | Cookies placed by outside third-party advertising networks. Used to monitor and track online behavior, searches, and sites visited across thousands of sites that belong to the advertising network for the purpose of displaying "relevant" advertising. |
| Spyware | Can be used to record all the keyboard activity of a user, including Web sites visited and security codes used; also used to display advertisements to users based on their searches or other behavior. |
| Search engine behavioral targeting (Google, and other search engines) | Uses prior search history, demographic, expressed interests, geographic, or other user-entered data to target advertising. |
| Deep packet inspection | Uses software installed at the ISP level to track all user clickstream behavior, sells this information to advertisers, and then attempts to show users "relevant ads." |
| Shopping carts | Can be used to collect detailed payment and purchase information. |
| Forms | Online forms that users voluntarily fill out in return for a promised benefit or reward that are linked with clickstream or other behavioral data to create a personal profile. |
| Site transaction logs | Can be used to collect and analyze detailed information on page content viewed by users. |
| Search engines | Can be used to trace user statements and views on newsgroups, chat groups, and other public forums on the Web, and profile users' social and political views. Google returns name, address, and links to a map with directions to the address when a phone number is entered. |
| Digital wallets (single sign-on services) | Client-side wallets and software that reveal personal information to Web sites verifying the identity of the consumer. |
| Digital Rights Management (DRM) | Software (Windows Media Player) that requires users of online media to identify themselves before viewing copyrighted content. |
| Trusted Computing Environments | Hardware and software that controls the viewing of copyrighted content and requires users identification. |

## SOCIAL NETWORKS AND PRIVACY

Social networks pose a unique challenge for the maintenance of personal privacy because they encourage people to reveal details about their personal lives (passions, loves, favorites, photos, videos and personal interests), and to share them with their friends. Some social networkers share these personal details with everyone on the social network! On the face of it, this would seem to indicate that people who participate in social networks voluntarily give up their rights to personal privacy. How could they claim an expectation of privacy? When everything is shared, what's private?

But the reality is that many adult (18 or over) participants in social networks have a very keen sense of their personal privacy. Every time a leading social network has sought to use the personal information provided by participants as a method of monetizing social networks by displaying ads and targeting individuals, it has been vociferously rejected by members of the networks. Facebook is a prime example of a senior management that just didn't get it when it comes to members' sense of their privacy. In December 2007, Facebook CEO Mark Zuckerberg announced the Beacon Program, sponsored by over 40 large firms, that would track what Facebook members purchased at their corporate sites, send the information to Facebook, who would then share that information with their friends without asking permission. In a few days, hundreds of thousands of members had organized a fierce resistance to the program. Management then declared that members could opt-out of the program and turn it off completely. Coca-Cola withdrew from sponsorship because it thought the program was an opt-in program only. Other corporate sponsors started pulling out from the program, as member resistance mounted. Open source programs were created  to block Beacon, and Mozilla added a Beacon Blocker add-on for FireFox to prevent corporate sites from sending any information to Facebook. Due to all this resistance, Facebook ultimately decided to terminate Beacon.

In a similar gaffe, in February 2009, Facebook sought to change its information retention and collection policy (Terms of Service) which had the effect of granting Facebook nearly unlimited data collection and control over user-generated information forever, without redress. Management acted without warning, provided no opportunity for public comment, and applied the new policy to personal information that had been collected under the old policy. Over 100,000 people joined various blog sites and privacy groups to protest, based on the belief that their information belonged to them, not Facebook. Within days the firm retreated to the old policy, and set up user forums to discuss the Terms of Service and user attitudes about personal information. In the meantime, though, millions of people on Facebook continue to use third-party quiz applications (such as "Which Cocktail Best Suits Your Personality?") without realizing the extent to which developers of the quizzes and other applications have access to personal information. Facebook's default privacy settings allow nearly unfettered access to a user's profile information. Only "sensitive information" such as contact information is not available. By 2010, Facebook had greatly increased the amount of personal information that would be made available not just to close friends, but the entire Internet. Its privacy controls had become so complex they were seldom used. In May 2010, facing pressure from American and European governments responding to citizen complaints, Facebook announced a new privacy policy that simplified privacy controls (Helft, 2010).

The result of these conflicts suggests that social network participants do indeed have a strong expectation of privacy in the sense that they want to control how "their" information is used. People who contribute user-generated content have a strong sense of ownership over that content that is not diminished by posting the information on a social network for one's friends. What's involved are some basic tenets of privacy thinking: personal control over the uses of personal information, choice, informed consent, participation in formulation of information policies, and due process. Some of these ideas are foreign to managers and owners seeking to monetize huge social network audiences. As for members who post information to everyone, not just friends, these should be seen as "public performances" where the contributors voluntarily publish their performances, just as writers or other artists do. This does not mean they want the entirety of their personal lives thrown open to every Web-tracking automaton on the Internet

## PROFILING AND BEHAVIORAL TARGETING

On an average day, around 128 million adult Americans go online (Pew Internet & American Life Project, 2010). Marketers would like to know who these people are, what they are interested in, and what they buy. The more precise the information, the more complete the information, and the more valuable it is as a predictive and marketing tool. Armed with this information, marketers can make their ad campaigns more efficient by targeting specific ads at specific groups or individuals, and they can even adjust the ads for specific groups.

Many Web sites allow third parties—including online advertising networks such as Microsoft Advertising (formerly aQuantive), DoubleClick, and others—to place "third-party" cookies and Web tracking software on a visitor's computer in order to engage in profiling the user's behavior across thousands of Web sites. A third-party cookie is used to track users across hundreds or thousands of other Web sites who are members of the advertising network. **Profiling** is the creation of digital images that characterize online individual and group behavior. **Anonymous profiles** identify people as belonging to highly specific and targeted groups, for example, 20-to 30-year-old males, with college degrees and incomes greater than $30,000 a year, and interested in high-fashion clothing (based on recent search engine use). **Personal profiles** add a personal e-mail address, postal address, and/or phone number to behavioral data. Increasingly, online firms are linking their online profiles to personal offline consumer data collected by database firms tracking credit card purchases, as well as established retail and catalog firms. In the past, individual stores collected data on customer movement through a single store in order to understand consumer behavior and alter the design of stores accordingly. Also, purchase and expenditure data was gathered on consumers purchasing from multiple stores—usually long after the purchases were made—and the data was used to target direct mail and in-store campaigns, in addition to mass-media advertising.

The online advertising networks such as DoubleClick and 24/7 Real Media have added several new dimensions to established offline marketing techniques. First, they have the ability to precisely track not just consumer purchases, but all browsing behavior on the Web at thousands of the most popular member sites, including brows-

**profiling**
the creation of digital images that characterize online individual and group behavior

**anonymous profiles**
identify people as belonging to highly specific and targeted groups

**personal profiles**
add a personal e-mail address, postal address, and/or phone number to behavioral data

ing book lists, filling out preference forms, and viewing content pages. Second, they can dynamically adjust what the shopper sees on screen—including prices. Third, they can build and continually refresh high-resolution data images or behavioral profiles of consumers (Laudon, 1996). Other advertising firms have created spyware software that, when placed on a consumer's computer, can report back to the advertiser's server on all consumer Internet use, and is also used to display advertising on the consumer's computer.

A different kind of profiling and a more recent form of behavioral targeting is Google's results-based personalization of advertising. Google has a patent on a program that allows advertisers using Google's AdWord program to target ads to users based on their prior search histories and profiles, which Google constructs based on user searches, along with any other information the user submits to Google or that Google can obtain, such as age, demographics, region, and other Web activities (such as blogging). Google also applied for a second patent on a program that allows Google to help advertisers select keywords and design ads for various market segments based on search histories, such as helping a clothing Web site create and test ads targeted at teenage females. In August 2007, Google began to put some of those ideas into practice, using behavioral targeting to help it display more relevant ads based on keywords. According to Google, the feature is aimed at capturing a more robust understanding of user intent, and thereby delivering a better ad. Google's Gmail, a free e-mail service, offers a powerful interface, and as of September 2009, 7.3 gigabytes of free storage. In return, Google computers read all incoming and outgoing e-mail and place "relevant" advertising in the margins of the mail. Profiles are developed on individual users based on the content in their e-mail. Google's Chrome browser has a Suggest feature that automatically suggests related queries and Web sites when the user enters a search. Critics pointed out this was a "keylogger" device that would record every keystroke of users forever. Google has since announced it will anonymize the data within 24 hours. In 2010, Google began "personalizing" search results without asking users. Opt-in is the default option. Google uses your past personal search history to influence the ads you see on the page. It also can track the pages you subsequently visit if you have the Google toolbar turned on.

**deep packet inspection**

a technology for recording every key stroke at the ISP level

**Deep packet inspection** is another technology for recording every keystroke at the ISP level of everyone (no matter where they ultimately go on the Web), and then using that information to make suggestions, and target ads. While advertising networks are limited, and even Google does not constitute the universe of search, deep packet inspection at the ISP level really does capture the universe of all Internet users. The leading firm in this technology is NebuAd. After testing the hardware and software with several ISPs in 2008, the outcry from privacy advocates and Congress caused these ISPs to withdraw from the experiment, and NebuAd withdrew the product from the market (Nakashima, 2008).

What is different about these efforts at online profiling and behavioral targeting (when compared to offline methods used in the past) is the scope and intensity of the data dragnet, and the ability to manipulate the shopping environment to the advantage of the merchant. Most of this activity occurs in the background without the knowledge of the shopper, and it takes place dynamically online in less than a second. Arguably, no other Web-based technique comes so close to being a real-world implementation of George Orwell's novel *1984* and its lead character, Big Brother. Here's an illustration of online profiling from "Online Profiling: A Report to Congress," an FTC report:

> Online consumer Joe Smith goes to a Web site that sells sporting goods. He clicks on the pages for golf bags. While there, he sees a banner ad, which he ignores as it does not interest him. The ad was placed by USAad Network. He then goes to a travel site and enters a search on "Hawaii." The USAad Network also serves ads on this site, and Joe sees an ad for rental cars there. Joe then visits an online bookstore and browses through books about the world's best golf courses. USAad Network serves ads there as well. A week later, Joe visits his favorite online news site, and notices an ad for golf vacation packages in Hawaii. Delighted, he clicks on the ad, which was served by USAad Network. Later, Joe begins to wonder whether it was a coincidence that this particular ad appeared and, if not, how it happened (Federal Trade Commission, 2000b).

The sample online profile illustrates several features of such profiles. First, the profile created for Joe Smith was completely anonymous and did not require any personal information, such as a name, e-mail address, or social security number. Obviously, this profile would be more valuable if the system did have personal information because then Joe could be sent e-mail marketing. Second, ad networks do not know who is operating the browser. If other members of Joe's family used the same computer to shop the Web, they would be exposed to golf vacation ads, and Joe could be exposed to ads more appropriate to his wife or children. Third, profiles are usually very imprecise, the result of "best guesses" and just plain guesses. Profiles are built using a product/service scoring system that is not very detailed, and as a result, the profiles tend to be very crude.

In the preceding example, Joe is obviously interested in golf and travel because he intentionally expressed these interests. However, he may have wanted to scuba dive in Hawaii, or visit old friends, not play golf. The profiling system in the example took a leap of faith that a golf vacation in Hawaii is what Joe really wants. Sometimes these guesses work, but there is considerable evidence to suggest that simply knowing Joe made an inquiry about Hawaii would be sufficient to sell him a trip to Hawaii for any of several activities and the USAad Network provided little additional value.

Network advertising firms argue that Web profiling benefits both consumers and businesses. Profiling permits targeting of ads, ensuring that consumers see advertisements mostly for products and services in which they are actually interested. Businesses benefit by not paying for wasted advertising sent to consumers who have no interest in their product or service. The industry argues that by increasing the effectiveness of advertising, more advertising revenues go to the Internet, which in turn subsidizes free content on the Internet. Last, product designers and entrepreneurs benefit by sensing demand for new products and services by examining user searches and profiles.

Critics argue that profiling undermines the expectation of anonymity and privacy that most people have when using the Internet, and change what should be a private experience into one where an individual's every move is recorded. As people become aware that their every move is being watched, they will be far less likely to explore sensitive topics, browse pages, or read about controversial issues. In most cases, the profiling is invisible to users, and even hidden. Consumers are not notified that

**weblining**

charging some customers more money for products and services based on their profiles

profiling is occurring. Profiling permits data aggregation on hundreds or even thousands of unrelated sites on the Web. The cookies placed by ad networks are persistent, and they can be set to last days, months, years, or even forever. Their tracking occurs over an extended period of time and resumes each time the individual logs on to the Internet. This clickstream data is used to create profiles that can include hundreds of distinct data fields for each consumer. Associating so-called anonymous profiles with personal information is fairly easy, and companies can change policies quickly without informing the consumer. Some critics believe profiling permits **weblining**—charging some customers more money for products and services based on their profiles. Although the information gathered by network advertisers is often anonymous (non-PII data), in many cases, the profiles derived from tracking consumers' activities on the Web are linked or merged with personally identifiable information. DoubleClick and other advertising network firms have attempted to purchase offline marketing firms that collect offline consumer data for the purpose of matching offline and online behavioral data at the individual level. However, public reaction was so negative that no network advertising firm publicly admits to matching offline PII with online profile data. Nevertheless, client Web sites encourage visitors to register for prizes, benefits, or content access in order to capture personal information such as e-mail addresses and physical addresses. Anonymous behavioral data is far more valuable if it can be linked with offline consumer behavior, e-mail addresses, and postal addresses.

This consumer data can also be combined with data on the consumers' offline purchases, or information collected directly from consumers through surveys and registration forms. As the technology of connection to the Internet for consumers moves away from telephone modems where IP addresses are assigned dynamically, and toward static assigned IP addresses used by DSL and cable modems, then connecting anonymous profiles to personal names and e-mail addresses will become easier and more prevalent.

From a privacy protection perspective, the advertising network raises issues about who will see and use the information held by private companies, whether the user profiles will be linked to actual personally identifying information (such as name, Social Security number, and bank and credit accounts), the absence of consumer control over the use of the information, the lack of consumer choice, the absence of consumer notice, and the lack of review and amendment procedures.

The pervasive and largely unregulated collection of personal information online has raised significant fears and opposition among consumers. According to a 2010 survey of 2,111 respondents, 81% said they were "somewhat" or "very" concerned about companies tracking their Web surfing habits and using that information for advertising, while 88% said it was "unfair" for companies to do such tracking without an user's permission  An independent survey in 2009 found that two-thirds of American Internet users object to online tracking. About 80% said they would favor implementation of a "do not track" list (Gruenwald, 2010). One result of the lack of trust toward online firms and specific fears of privacy invasion is a reduction in online purchases. For instance, one survey found that over 70% of respondents had decided against registering or making a purchase online because those actions required them to provide information that they did not want to divulge. A Gartner survey found that nearly half of online U.S. adults said that concerns about theft of information, data breaches, or Internet-based attacks affected their purchasing, payment, online transaction, or e-mail behavior. The actual amount of lost sales is unknown, but if 25% of consumers stopped purchasing online, that would add up to a hefty $57 billion in lost sales. If even just 10% of this number turned out to be accurate, that would still be a $22.8 billion loss in sales. (eMarketer, Inc., 2009).

The Internet and e-commerce—as we have seen in previous chapters— strengthen the ability of private firms to collect, store, and analyze personal information at a level never envisioned by privacy thinkers and legislators. With Web technologies, the invasion of individual privacy is low-cost, profitable, and effective.

## THE INTERNET AND GOVERNMENT INVASIONS OF PRIVACY: E-COMMERCE SURVEILLANCE

Today, the e-commerce behavior, profiles, and transactions of consumers are routinely available to a wide range of government agencies and law enforcement authorities, contributing to rising fears among online consumers, and in many cases, their withdrawal from the online marketplace. While the Internet used to be thought of as impossible for governments to control or monitor, nothing could be actually further from the truth. Law enforcement authorities have long claimed the right under numerous statutes to monitor any form of electronic communication pursuant to a court order and judicial review and based on the reasonable belief that a crime is being committed. This includes the surveillance of consumers engaged in e-commerce. In the case of the Internet, this is accomplished by placing sniffer software and servers at the ISP being used by the target suspect, in a manner similar to pen registers and trap-and-trace devices used for telephone surveillance. The Communications Assistance for Law Enforcement Act (CALEA), the USA PATRIOT Act, the Cyber Security Enhancement Act, and the Homeland Security Act all strengthen the ability of law enforcement agencies to monitor Internet users without their knowledge and, under certain circumstances when life is purportedly at stake, without judicial oversight. In addition, government agencies are among the largest users of private sector commercial data brokers, such as ChoicePoint, Acxiom, Experian, and TransUnion Corporation, that collect a vast amount of information about consumers from various offline and online public sources, such as public records and the telephone directory, and non-public sources, such as "credit header" information from credit bureaus (which typically contains name, aliases, birth date, social security number, current and prior addresses, and phone numbers). Information contained in individual reference services' databases ranges from purely identifying information (e.g., name and phone number) to much more extensive data (e.g., driving records, criminal and civil court records, property records, and licensing records). This information can be linked to online behavior information collected from other commercial sources to compile an extensive profile of individual's online and offline behavior (Frackman, Ray, and Martin, 2002; Federal Trade Commission, 1997).

In June 2006, the Justice Department appointed a task force to investigate a proposal that Internet companies retain records that would allow the government to identify which individuals visited certain Web sites and conducted searches using certain terms, and also records about whom users exchange e-mail with, for as long two years. The European Parliament had passed similar legislation in December 2005. In 2007, the four major search engines (Google, Yahoo, Microsoft, and Ask.com) all announced new policies on how long they would retain search information, ranging from 18 months (Google and Microsoft) to 13 months (Yahoo), while Ask.com announced a new tool, Ask Eraser, that would allow users to block any retention of specific search terms and the user's IP address. In April 2008, the European Parliament's Data Protection Working Party called for search engines to set their data retention at six months. In September 2008, under pressure from European regulators, Google announced that it would reduce the amount of time it stores IP addresses on its server logs to nine months in both the United States and Europe. In December 2008, Yahoo went a step better, and announced that going forward, it would delete a users' personally identifiable information (the last 8 bits in the users' IP address) from its records within three months. Yahoo also said it would hide cookie data related to each log, and strip out any personally identifiable information, such as a name, phone, address, or social security number, from queries. The policy also extends to other types of data it collects, such as page view, page clicks, ad views, and ad clicks. In 2010, the European Union (EU) requires search engines to set their data retention limit at 18 months.

## LEGAL PROTECTIONS

In the United States, Canada, and Germany, rights to privacy are explicitly granted in, or can be derived from, founding documents such as constitutions, as well as in specific statutes. In England and the United States, there is also protection of privacy in the common law, a body of court decisions involving torts or personal injuries. For instance, in the United States, four privacy-related torts have been defined in court decisions involving claims of injury to individuals caused by other private parties: intrusion on solitude, public disclosure of private facts, publicity placing a person in a false light, and appropriation of a person's name or likeness (mostly concerning celebrities) for a commercial purpose (Laudon, 1996). In the United States, the claim to privacy against government intrusion is protected primarily by the First Amendment guarantees of freedom of speech and association, the Fourth Amendment protections against unreasonable search and seizure of one's personal documents or home, and the Fourteenth Amendment's guarantee of due process.

In addition to common law and the Constitution, there are both federal laws and state laws that protect individuals against government intrusion and in some cases define privacy rights vis-à-vis private organizations such as financial, educational, and media institutions (cable television and video rentals) (see **Table 8.4**).

| TABLE 8.4 | FEDERAL AND STATE PRIVACY LAWS |
| --- | --- |

| NAME | DESCRIPTION |
| --- | --- |
| *GENERAL FEDERAL PRIVACY LAWS* | |
| Freedom of Information Act of 1966 | Gives people the right to inspect information about themselves held in government files; also allows other individuals and organizations the right to request disclosure of government records based on the public's right to know. |
| Privacy Act of 1974, as amended | Regulates the federal government's collection, use, and disclosure of data collected by federal agencies. Gives individuals a right to inspect and correct records. |
| Electronic Communications Privacy Act of 1986 | Makes conduct that would infringe on the security of electronic communications illegal. |
| Computer Matching and Privacy Protection Act of 1988 | Regulates computerized matching of files held by different government agencies. |
| Computer Security Act of 1987 | Makes conduct that would infringe on the security of computer-based files illegal. |
| Driver's Privacy Protection Act of 1994 | Limits access to personal information maintained by state motor vehicle departments to those with legitimate business purposes. Also gives drivers the option to prevent disclosure of driver's license information to marketers and the general public. |
| E-Government Act of 2002 | Regulates the collection and use of personal information by federal agencies. |
| *FEDERAL PRIVACY LAWS AFFECTING PRIVATE INSTITUTIONS* | |
| Fair Credit Reporting Act of 1970 | Regulates the credit investigating and reporting industry. Gives people the right to inspect credit records if they have been denied credit and provides procedures for correcting information. |
| Family Educational Rights and Privacy Act of 1974 | Requires schools and colleges to give students and their parents access to student records and to allow them to challenge and correct information; limits disclosure of such records to third parties. |
| Right to Financial Privacy Act of 1978 | Regulates the financial industry's use of personal financial records; establishes procedures that federal agencies must follow to gain access to such records. |
| Privacy Protection Act of 1980 | Prohibits government agents from conducting unannounced searches of press offices and files if no one in the office is suspected of committing a crime. |
| Cable Communications Policy Act of 1984 | Regulates the cable industry's collection and disclosure of information concerning subscribers. |
| Video Privacy Protection Act of 1988 | Prevents disclosure of a person's video rental records without court order or consent. |
| Child Online Privacy Protection Act (1998) | Prohibits deceptive practices in connection with the collection, use, and/or disclosure of personal information from and about children on the Internet. |
| Financial Modernization Act (Gramm-Leach-Bliley Act) (1999) | Requires financial institutions to inform consumers of their privacy policies and permits consumers some control over their records. |
| Health Insurance Portability and Accountability Act of 1996 (HIPAA) | Requires health care providers and insurers and other third parties to promulgate privacy policies to consumers and establishes due process procedures. |

| TABLE 8.4 | FEDERAL AND STATE PRIVACY LAWS (CONT'D) |
|---|---|
| NAME | DESCRIPTION |
| *SELECTED STATE PRIVACY LAWS* | |
| Online privacy policies | The California Online Privacy Protection Act of 2003 was the first state law in the United States requiring owners of commercial Web sites or online services to post a privacy policy. The policy must, among other things, identify the categories of PII collected about site visitors and categories of third parties with whom the information may be shared. Failure to comply can result in a civil suit for unfair business practices. Nebraska and Pennsylvania prohibit false and misleading statements in online privacy policies. At least 16 states require government Web sites to establish privacy policies or procedures or incorporate machine-readable privacy policies into their Web sites. |
| Spyware legislation | A number of states, including California, Utah, Arizona, Arkansas, and Virginia, among others, have passed laws that make the installation of spyware on a user's computer without consent, illegal. |
| Disclosure of security breaches | In 2002, California enacted legislation that requires state agencies or businesses that own or license computer data with personal information to notify state residents if they experience a security breach involving that information; today, nearly every state has enacted similar legislation |
| Privacy of personal information | Two states, Nevada and Minnesota, require ISPs to keep their customers' PII private unless the customer consents to disclose the information. Minnesota also requires ISPs to get permission from subscribers before disclosing information about subscribers' online surfing habits. |
| Data encryption | In October 2007, Nevada passed the first law that requires encryption for the transmission of customer personal information. The law took October 1, 2008. |

## Informed Consent

**informed consent**
consent given with knowledge of all material facts needed to make a rational decision

The concept of **informed consent** (defined as consent given with knowledge of all material facts needed to make a rational decision) also plays an important role in protecting privacy. In the United States, business firms (and government agencies) can gather transaction information generated in the marketplace and then use that information for other marketing purposes, without obtaining the informed consent of the individual. For instance, in the United States, if a Web shopper purchases books about baseball at a site that belongs to an advertising network such as DoubleClick, a cookie can be placed on the consumer's hard drive and used by other member sites to sell the shopper sports clothing without the explicit permission or even knowledge of the user. This online preference information may also be linked with personally identifying information. In Europe, this would be illegal. A business in Europe cannot use marketplace transaction information for any purpose other than supporting the current transaction, unless of course it obtains the individual's consent in writing or by filling out an on-screen form.

There are traditionally two models for informed consent: opt-in and opt-out. The **opt-in** model requires an affirmative action by the consumer to allow collection and use of information. For instance, using opt-in, consumers would first be asked if they approved of the collection and use of information, and then directed to check a selection box if they agreed. Otherwise, the default is not to approve the collection of data. In the **opt-out** model, the default is to collect information unless the consumer takes an affirmative action to prevent the collection of data by checking a box, or by filling out a form.

Until recently, many U.S e-commerce companies rejected the concept of informed consent and instead simply published their information use policy on their site. U.S. businesses argue that informing consumers about how the information will be used is sufficient to obtain the users' informed consent. Most U.S. sites that offer informed consent make opting in the default option, and require users to go to special pages to request to opt-out of promotional campaigns. Some sites have an opt-out selection box at the very bottom of their information policy statements where the consumer is unlikely to see it. Privacy advocates argue that many information/privacy policy statements on U.S. Web sites are obscure, difficult to read, and legitimate just about any use of personal information. For instance, Yahoo's privacy policy begins with the statement that "Yahoo! takes your privacy seriously." It then states that it "does not rent, sell, or share personal information about you with other people or non-affiliated companies." However, there are a number of exceptions that significantly weaken this statement. For instance, Yahoo may share the information with "trusted partners," which could be anyone that Yahoo does business with, although perhaps not a company that the user might choose to do business with.

**opt-in**

requires an affirmative action by the consumer to allow collection and use of consumer information

**opt-out**

the default is to collect information unless the consumer takes an affirmative action to prevent the collection of data

## The FTC's Fair Information Practices Principles

In the United States, the FTC has taken the lead in conducting research on online privacy and recommending legislation to Congress. The FTC is a cabinet-level agency charged with promoting the efficient functioning of the marketplace by protecting consumers from unfair or deceptive practices and increasing consumer choice by promoting competition. In addition to reports and recommendations, the FTC enforces existing legislation by suing corporations it believes are in violation of federal fair trade laws.

In 1995, the FTC began a series of investigations of online privacy based on its belief that online invasion of privacy potentially involved deceit and unfair behavior. In 1998, the FTC issued its Fair Information Practice (FIP) principles, on which it has based its assessments and recommendations for online privacy. **Table 8.5** describes these principles. Two of the five are designated as basic, "core" principles that must be present to protect privacy, whereas the other practices are less central. The FTC's FIP principles restate and strengthen in a form suitable to deal with online privacy the Fair Information Practices doctrine developed in 1973 by a government study group (U.S. Department of Health, Education and Welfare, 1973).

The FTC's FIP principles set the ground rules for what constitutes due process privacy protection procedures at e-commerce and all other Web sites—including government and nonprofit Web sites—in the United States.

| TABLE 8.5 | FEDERAL TRADE COMMISSION'S FAIR INFORMATION PRACTICE PRINCIPLES |
|---|---|
| Notice/Awareness (core principle) | Sites must disclose their information practices before collecting data. Includes identification of collector, uses of data, other recipients of data, nature of collection (active/inactive), voluntary or required, consequences of refusal, and steps taken to protect confidentiality, integrity, and quality of the data |
| Choice/Consent (core principle) | There must be a choice regime in place allowing consumers to choose how their information will be used for secondary purposes other than supporting the transaction, including internal use and transfer to third parties. Opt-in/opt-out must be available. |
| Access/Participation | Consumers should be able to review and contest the accuracy and completeness of data collected about them in a timely, inexpensive process. |
| Security | Data collectors must take reasonable steps to assure that consumer information is accurate and secure from unauthorized use. |
| Enforcement | There must be in place a mechanism to enforce FIP principles. This can involve self-regulation, legislation giving consumers legal remedies for violations, or federal statutes and regulation. |

SOURCE: Based on data from Federal Trade Commission, 1998, 2000a.

At this point, the FTC's FIP principles are guidelines, not laws. They have stimulated private firms and industry associations to develop their own private guidelines (discussed next). However, the FTC's FIP guidelines are being used as the basis of new legislation. The most important online privacy legislation to date that was directly influenced by the FTC's FIP principles is the Children's Online Privacy Protection Act (COPPA) (1998), which requires Web sites to obtain parental permission before collecting information on children under 13 years of age.

In July 2000, the FTC recommended legislation to Congress to protect online consumer privacy from the threat posed by advertising networks. **Table 8.6** summarizes the Commission's recommendations. The FTC profiling recommendations significantly strengthen the FIP principles of notification and choice, while also including restrictions on information that may be collected.[1] Although the FTC supports industry efforts at self-regulation, it nevertheless recommended legislation to ensure that all Web sites using network advertising and all network advertisers comply. To date, however, Congress has not passed such legislation.

[1]Much general privacy legislation affecting government, e.g., the Privacy Act of 1974, precludes the government from collecting information on political and social behavior of citizens. The FTC restrictions are significant because they are the FTC's first effort at limiting the collection of certain information.

| TABLE 8.6 | FTC RECOMMENDATIONS REGARDING ONLINE PROFILING |
|---|---|
| **PRINCIPLE** | **DESCRIPTION OF RECOMMENDATION** |
| Notice | Complete transparency to user by providing disclosure and choice options on the host Web site. "Robust" notice for PII (time/place of collection; before collection begins). Clear and conspicuous notice for non-PII. |
| Choice | Opt-in for PII, opt-out for non-PII. No conversion of non-PII to PII without consent. Opt-out from any or all network advertisers from a single page provided by the host Web site. |
| Access | Reasonable provisions to allow inspection and correction. |
| Security | Reasonable efforts to secure information from loss, misuse, or improper access. |
| Enforcement | Done by independent third parties, such as seal programs and accounting firms. |
| Restricted collection | Advertising networks will not collect information about sensitive financial or medical topics, sexual behavior or sexual orientation, or use social security numbers for profiling. |

In November 2007, the FTC held a two-day workshop on online advertising, behavioral targeting, and online privacy. Consumer privacy groups have asked for the institution of a "Do Not Track" list similar to the FTC's "Do Not Call" telemarketing list, which would permit people to more easily opt out of behavioral tracking programs, as well as disclosure notices that tracking is occurring, and the ability for consumers to view and edit any profiles about themselves that ad networks build. The online advertising industry, not surprisingly, believes that FTC regulation would stifle innovation in the industry. At least one FTC member suggested at the conference that rules about privacy policies might need to be established, and that the FTC needed to increase its scrutiny of the online targeting (Story, 2007).

In 2008, the growing fear of widespread behavioral targeting, strengthened by the buyouts of the largest advertising networks by search engines (e.g., Google's purchase of DoubleClick), led to a Congressional hearings in June. Industry leaders such as Google and Microsoft called for new privacy legislation that would legitimate their behavioral targeting programs. In August 2008, four legislators sent a letter to 33 Internet companies, including the top search engines, requesting detailed explanations of their privacy policies (Clifford, 2008).

In February 2009, the FTC held hearings to discuss its program for voluntary industry principles for regulating behavioral targeting. The online advertising trade group Network Advertising Initiative (discussed later in this section), published its own self-regulatory principles that largely agreed with the FTC. Nevertheless, the government, privacy groups, and the online ad industry are still at loggerheads over two issues. Privacy advocates want both an opt-in policy at all sites and a national Do Not Track list. The industry opposes these moves and continues to insist on an opt-out capability as being the only way to avoid tracking (Federal Trade Commission, 2009). In 2010, the FTC and U.S. Senate continue to hold hearings and seminars on the protection of personal privacy on the Internet.

### The European Data Protection Directive

In Europe, privacy protection is much stronger than it is in the United States. In the United States, private organizations and businesses are permitted to use PII gathered in commercial transactions for other business purposes without the prior consent of the consumer (so-called secondary uses of PII). In the United States, there is no federal agency charged with enforcing privacy laws. Instead, privacy laws are enforced largely through self-regulation by businesses, and by individuals who must sue agencies or companies in court to recover damages. This is expensive and rarely done. The European approach to privacy protection is more comprehensive and regulatory in nature. European countries do not allow business firms to use PII without the prior consent of consumers. They enforce their privacy laws by creating data protection agencies to pursue complaints brought by citizens and to actively enforce privacy laws.

On October 25, 1998, the European Commission's Data Protection Directive went into effect, standardizing and broadening privacy protection in the EU nations. The Directive is based on the Fair Information Practices doctrine, but extends the control individuals can exercise over their personal information. The Directive requires companies to inform people when they collect information about them and to disclose how it will be stored and used. Customers must provide their informed consent before any company can legally use data about them, and they have the right to access that information, correct it, and request that no further data be collected. Further, the directive prohibits the transfer of PII to organizations or countries that do not have similarly strong privacy protection policies. This means that data collected in Europe by American business firms cannot be transferred or processed in the United States (which has weaker privacy protection laws). This would potentially interfere with a $350 billion annual trade flow between the United States and Europe.

**safe harbor**
a private self-regulating policy and enforcement mechanism that meets the objectives of government regulators and legislation but does not involve government regulation or enforcement

The Department of Commerce, working with the European Commission, developed a safe harbor framework for U.S. firms. A **safe harbor** is a private self-regulating policy and enforcement mechanism that meets the objectives of government regulators and legislation, but does not involve government regulation or enforcement. The government plays a role in certifying safe harbors, however. Organizations that decide to participate in the safe harbor program must develop policies that meet European standards, and they must publicly sign on to a Web-based register maintained by the Department of Commerce. Enforcement occurs in the United States and relies to a large extent on self-policing and regulation, backed up by government enforcement of fair trade statutes. For more information on the safe harbor procedures and the EU Data Directive, see www.export.gov/safeharbor.

### PRIVATE INDUSTRY SELF-REGULATION

The online industry in the United States has historically opposed privacy legislation, arguing that industry can do a better job of protecting privacy than government. However, individual firms such as AOL, Yahoo, and Google have adopted policies on their own in an effort to address the concerns of the public about personal privacy on the Internet. The online industry formed the Online Privacy Alliance (OPA) in 1998 to encourage self-regulation in part as a reaction to growing public concerns and the threat of legislation being proposed by FTC and privacy advocacy groups.

Private industry in the United States has created the idea of safe harbors from government regulation. For instance, COPPA includes a provision enabling industry groups or others to submit for the FTC's approval self-regulatory guidelines that implement the protections of the FIP principles and FTC rules. In May 2001, the FTC approved the TRUSTe Internet privacy protection program under the terms of COPPA as a safe harbor.[2]

OPA has developed a set of privacy guidelines that members are required to implement. The primary focus of industry efforts has been the development of online "seals" that attest to the privacy policies on a site. The Better Business Bureau (BBB), TRUSTe, WebTrust, and major accounting firms—among them PricewaterhouseCoopers' BetterWeb—have established seals for Web sites. To display a seal, Web site operators must conform to certain privacy principles, a complaint resolution process, and monitoring by the seal originator. Around 2,500 sites now display the TRUSTe seal, and over 57,000 display the BBB's Reliability seal. Nevertheless, online privacy seal programs have had a limited impact on Web privacy practices. Critics argue that the seal programs are not particularly effective in safeguarding privacy. For these reasons, the FTC has not deemed the seal programs as "safe harbors" yet (with the exception of TRUSTe's children's privacy seal under COPPA), and the agency continues to push for legislation to enforce privacy protection principles.

The advertising network industry has also formed an industry association, the Network Advertising Initiative (NAI), to develop privacy policies. The NAI has developed a set of privacy principles in conjunction with the FTC. The NAI policies have two objectives: to offer consumers a chance to opt out of advertising network programs (including e-mail campaigns), and to provide consumers redress from abuses. In order to opt out, the NAI has created a Web site—Networkadvertising.org—where consumers can use a global opt-out feature to prevent network advertising agencies from placing their cookies on a user's computer. If a consumer has a complaint, the NAI has a link to the Truste.org Web site where the complaints can be filed. Consumers still receive Internet advertising just as before, but the ads will not be targeted to their browsing behavior (Network Advertising Initiative, 2009a).

In 2009, the NAI published its version of behavioral tracking self-regulation guidelines, which emphasize their agreement with the FTC's set of principles. The self-regulatory principles are: transparency, choice, security and data retention, and changes to privacy policies. In April 2010, NAI released the Control Links for Education and Advertising Responsibly (CLEAR) Ad Notice Technical Specifications. NAI is recommending that advertisers and ad networks offer a clickable icon in or near online ads that directs users to additional information about online behavioral advertising and choices about such ads. The idea is to increase transparency and user control over their personal information (Network Advertising Initiative, 2009b, 2010).

In general, industry efforts at self-regulation in online privacy have not succeeded in reducing American fears of privacy invasion during online transactions, or in reducing the level of privacy invasion. At best, self-regulation has offered consumers notice about whether a privacy policy exists, but usually says little about

---

[2]Another longstanding industry group with a safe harbor program for children online is the Children's Advertising Review Unit (CARU), founded in 1974 as the advertising industry's self-regulation program for the protection of children.

the actual use of the information, does not offer consumers a chance to see and correct the information or control its use in any significant way, offers no promises for the security of that information, and offers no enforcement mechanism (Hoofnagle, 2005). At the same time, the FTC and Congress point to efforts at self-regulation as a reason for not legislating in this area. Read *Insight on Business: Chief Privacy Officers* to see a different approach to industry self-regulation.

## PRIVACY ADVOCACY GROUPS

There are a number of privacy advocacy groups on the Web that monitor developments in privacy. Some of these sites are industry-supported, while others rely on private foundations and contributions. Some of the better-known sites are listed in **Table 8.7**.

## THE EMERGING PRIVACY PROTECTION BUSINESS

As Web sites become more invasive and aggressive in their use of personal information, and as public concern grows, a number of firms have sprung up to sell products that they claim will help people protect their privacy. Venture capital firms have picked up the scent in 2010 and invested millions in small start-up companies based on the premise that people will pay for their privacy protection. ReputationDefender received $15 million in financing in June 2010. Other firms raising money in the business of privacy protection are SocialShield, Abine, SaveWeb, and TRUSTe. For as little as $14.95 a month, you can monitor what people are saying about you on social Web sites, or about your children. It's too early to tell if these firms will succeed. Previous efforts failed to attract enough customers although the threats to personal and business reputations were far less threatening (Tam and Worthen, 2010).

## TECHNOLOGICAL SOLUTIONS

There are a number of privacy-enhancing technologies for protecting user privacy during interactions with Web sites that have been developed (see **Table 8.8** on page 523). Most of these tools emphasize security—the ability of individuals to protect their communications and files from illegitimate snoopers. This is just one element of privacy. The other

| TABLE 8.7 | PRIVACY ADVOCACY GROUPS |
| --- | --- |
| ADVOCACY GROUP | FOCUS |
| Epic.org (Electronic Privacy Information Center) | Washington-based watch-dog group |
| Privacyinternational.org | Tracks international privacy developments |
| Cdt.org (Center for Democracy and Technology) | Foundation- and business-supported group with a legislative focus |
| Privacy.org | Clearinghouse sponsored by EPIC and Privacy International |
| Privacyrights.org | Educational clearinghouse |
| Privacyalliance.org | Industry-supported clearinghouse |

# INSIGHT ON BUSINESS

# CHIEF PRIVACY OFFICERS

How can you tell if your own corporate practices actually conform to the privacy policy stated on your Web site? How can your business keep track of all the new privacy legislation and changes in European policies? How can you avoid taking some embarrassing action that insults your customers' sense of what's an acceptable use of their personal information?

The answer for many corporations is to create an executive position—chief privacy officer (CPO). The position is one that firms first started to create about 10 years ago, but today is one of fastest growing in corporate management. The use of personal information on commercial Web sites in the United States is largely unregulated, and a potential minefield for companies whose business relies on using the personal information of their customers for financial gain. Industries that have added CPOs include health care, financial services, technology, and consumer goods, in part due to growing regulatory requirements with respect to data privacy. Examples include Facebook, Google, IBM, AT&T, Verizon, DoubleClick (owned by Google), New York Life, Intel, Loopt, ChoicePoint, and Microsoft. The International Association of Privacy Professionals (IAPP), a professional group composed of chief privacy officers, now has 7,000 members across the globe in 2010, 85% of whom are located in the United States, more than double the number from 2007. In a recent survey, privacy leaders rank high in their organizations, with 61% one or two reporting levels away from the CEO; around 60% of privacy leaders reported two or more full-time employees; 36% indicated their privacy program was at the mature stage.

What does a CPO do? The job has several aspects. Often, a CPO's first job is to plan and then implement a privacy plan for the firm to follow. Once a plan is in place, it needs to be enforced, and monitored, and the company's business units and employees may need to be educated about the plan and the importance of privacy. For instance, at Marriott International, Chris Zoladz, vice president of information protection and privacy, notes that "Good privacy is good business." When Marriott marketing executives proposed personalizing the information that appears on the hotel chain's Web site so that it was customized based on personal information collected from guests as part of the reservation process, Zoladz got involved to make sure the information was used properly.

Another job is helping the company avoid privacy "land mines," which are avoidable mistakes in policy or technology that would obviously be embarrassing to the company because of the potential for a storm of protest from privacy protection groups. It seems that at least once a year, a major firm makes a mistake and issues a policy or takes an action that communicates to customers that they have lost control over their personal private information.

In recent years, the company committing the most privacy gaffes has been Facebook. In February 2009, the social networking site released a new terms of service agreement that gave Facebook new powers of information shared by its users. Facebook CEO Mark Zuckerberg initially defended the new policy, but reversed course to placate a horde of angry users. In 2010, the privacy gaffes continued. The site introduced a new set of changes intended to expand Facebook's presence to other sites and to "make the Web more social and personalized." But once again, users lacked sufficient ability to control the information that Facebook shared with other sites and users. Zuckerberg again publicly apologized and adjusted the new features to include more control, but after yet another privacy-related gaffe,

(continued)

many Facebook users have become suspicious of any new features. For example, Facebook rolled out its Places feature in August 2010, which lets your friends know where you are and when you get there. The problem was that your friends could tag you as having checked into a location without your permission, and that opting out of the feature was difficult or impossible.

Social network sites make money ("monetize their audience" in Wall Street argot) by selling information about their members to advertisers who can use this information to target their ads. The more information Facebook can sell to advertisers, the more money it makes. Privacy invasion is very profitable. Facebook's Chief Privacy Officer Chris Kelly has been a voice within the firm advocating for user controls and opt-in functionality for personal information. While Kelly has stated that the privacy policy at Facebook is that "Facebook users own all their data," the seemingly endless string of privacy slipups suggests that he is fighting an uphill battle to cultivate a responsible attitude toward user privacy at Facebook.

In other cases, in the absence of a CPO, disaster is possible. U.S. Bancorp decided to sell personal financial data to a direct-marketing company in violation of its own stated policies. This cost Bancorp $3 million in a legal settlement in Minnesota. Real Networks had to apologize to users and change its data collection policies after a disclosure that the company's RealJukebox Internet music software captured data about users' preferences. A string of data losses, criminal intrusions, and accidents at data brokerage firms such as ChoicePoint and Reed Elsevier's LexisNexis unit resulted in the diversion and theft of hundreds of thousands of complete personal profiles. This in turn has led to Congressional investigations, fines, and the threat of restrictive legislation for the entire data brokerage industry.

The new corporate emphasis on privacy has also created a new business for the big accounting firm PricewaterhouseCoopers. PWC has conducted hundreds of privacy audits. Companies are taking this issue very seriously because data theft or loss and invasions of privacy directly threaten the brand names of firms. Privacy audits identify the risks that firms face and prescribe corrective actions that may help them avoiding class action suits, Internet-based protests, and shareholder enmity. And what do the auditors find? About 80% of the companies audited by PWC do not follow their own stated privacy policies. Most of the time this is the result of poor training and human error. After Expedia completed a privacy audit led by PWC, it changed its information collection policy from opt-out to opt-in. Now Expedia's customers have to actively click a button and ask to be informed of new offers from the travel site. The result is that far fewer customers ask to unsubscribe from mailing solicitations. Expedia executives believe trust and privacy are major concerns of their customers, and anything they can do to enhance trust is good for their business.

What do CPOs worry about? They often have a hard time with their own employees taking privacy seriously and changing policies to cope with the risks. After ChoicePoint lost 145,000 personal dossiers to criminals posing as real companies, ChoicePoint decided to hire a CPO to report directly to the Board of Directors and the CEO. The CPO discovered that ChoicePoint did not verify the authenticity or legitimacy of people claiming a business need to access their databases.

Another challenge facing CPOs is federal legislation that requires companies to inform consumers of their privacy policies, and the trend towards a narrow legalistic emphasis on compliance. The Gramm-Leach-Bliley Act of 1999 requires all financial service firms to inform consumers of their privacy policies. This results in tens of millions of pamphlets being sent to consumers, often written in confusing legal jargon that few can understand. HIPAA, designed to make the transfer of records among health care

(continued)

agencies more efficient as well as to safeguard the privacy of those records, has also unleashed a flood of privacy pamphlets that few can understand. HIPAA requires that all health care providers and insurers have a privacy officer, even in small medical practices with seven doctors. Professional associations such as the International Association of Privacy Professionals openly worry that legalistic compliance with federal laws fails to take into account the real interests of consumers and the strategic implications for the firm.

Currently the Obama administration is faced with demands that the executive branch and Congress develop a legal framework for the uses of personal information on the Internet. It is likely that CPOs will continue to be much in demand and have much work to do in the near future.

▬ **SOURCES:** "About the IAPP," Privacyassociation.org, accessed September 30, 2010; "Microsoft's Chief Privacy Officer Opens Up," by Wendy M. Grossman, TheInquirer.net, September 8, 2010; " Facebook's Chief Privacy Officer: Balancing Needs of Users with the Business of Social Networks," by C.G. Lynch, *CIO Magazine*, April 1, 2009; "Facebook's Chief Privacy Officer: Users Own All Their Data," Insidefacebook.com, February 22nd, 2009; "Facebook's About-Face on Data," by Jessica Vascellaro, *Wall Street Journal*, February 10, 2009; "Online Privacy Decisions Confront Obama," by Kim Hart, *Washington Post*, January 13, 2009.

| TABLE 8.8 | TECHNOLOGICAL PROTECTIONS FOR ONLINE PRIVACY | |
|---|---|---|
| **TECHNOLOGY** | **PRODUCTS** | **PROTECTION** |
| Spyware blockers | Spyware Doctor, ZoneAlarm, Ad-Aware and Spybot—Search & Destroy (Spybot-S&D) (freeware) | Detects and removes spyware and adware, keyloggers, and other malware |
| Pop-up blockers | Browsers: Firefox, IE 6 SP2, 7/8 Safari,Opera Toolbars: Google, Yahoo, MSN Add-on programs: STOPzilla, Adbock, NoAds | Prevents calls to ad servers that push pop-up, pop-under, and leave-behind ads; restricts downloading of images at user request |
| Secure e-mail | ZL Technologies; SafeMessage.com, Hushmail.com, Pretty Good Privacy (PGP) | E-mail and document encryption |
| Anonymous remailers | W3-Anonymous Remailer, Jack B Nymble, Java Anonymous Proxy | Send e-mail without trace |
| Anonymous surfing | Freedom Websecure, Anonymizer.com, Tor, GhostSurf, IE 8 InPrivate Browing | Surf without a trace |
| Cookie managers | CookieCrusher, and most browsers | Prevents client computer from accepting cookies |
| Disk/file erasing programs | Mutilate File Wiper, Eraser, DiskVac 2.0 | Completely erases hard drive and floppy files |
| Policy generators | OECD Privacy Policy Generator | Automates the development of an OECD privacy compliance policy |
| Privacy Policy Reader | P3P | Software for automating the communication of privacy policies to users |
| Public Key Encryption | PGP Desktop | Program that encrypts your mail and documents |

is the development of private and public policies that enable consumers to control the collection and use of information that is gathered in the course of market transactions.

The growth in consumer use of spyware blockers, cookie blockers, and pop-up controls on browsers threatens the online advertising industry that relies on cookies, placed mostly by advertising networks, although thus far, it has not appreciably reduced reliance on these techniques by advertisers.

Perhaps the most comprehensive technological privacy protection effort is **P3P**, the **Platform for Privacy Preferences** sponsored by W3C (the World Wide Web Consortium—an international, nonprofit, industry-supported Web standards group). P3P is a standard designed to communicate a Web site's privacy policy to Internet users, and to compare that policy to the user's own preferences, or to other standards such as the FTC's FIP principles or the EU Data Protection Directive. P3P does not establish privacy standards and relies on government and industry to develop them. The basic idea behind P3P and subsequent efforts like TAMI (MIT) and PRIME (Europe) is to allow individuals to express their privacy preferences in a machine readable form that all Web sites can universally understand.

P3P works through a user's Web browser. On the server side, P3P enables sites to translate their privacy policies into a standardized machine-readable XML format that can be read either by the browser or by installed software plug-ins. On the user client side, the browser automatically fetches a Web site's privacy policy and informs the user. **Figure 8.2(A)** illustrates how this could work.

**Platform for Privacy Preferences (P3P)**

a standard designed to communicate to Internet users a Web site's privacy policy, and to compare that policy to the user's own preferences, or to other standards such as the FTC's FIP guidelines or the EU Data Protection Directive

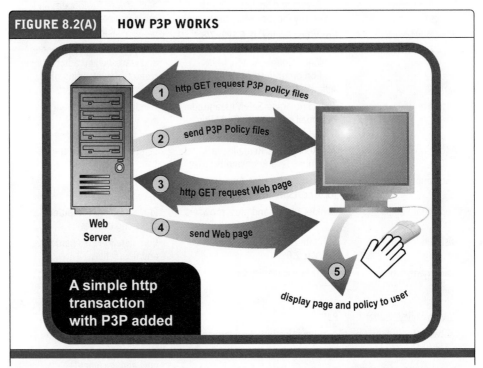

**FIGURE 8.2(A)    HOW P3P WORKS**

1. http GET request P3P policy files
2. send P3P Policy files
3. http GET request Web page
4. send Web page
5. display page and policy to user

Web Server

A simple http transaction with P3P added

The Platform for Privacy Preferences enables the automatic communication of privacy policies between e-commerce sites and consumers.

SOURCE: W3C Platform for Privacy Preferences Initiative, 2003.

P3P is now built into browsers such as Firefox and Internet Explorer 6.0/8.0. By using a slider, users can set the privacy policy they desire; their browser will automatically read the privacy policy of sites they visit and warn them when a site does not match their preferences (see **Figure 8.2 (B)**).

While P3P is one step in the direction of increasing consumer awareness and understanding of Web site privacy, it fails to achieve other goals of fair information policies such as limits on what information is collected, the use of personal information, user control of personal information, security, and enforcement of privacy rights. In this sense, it has failed to increase the consumer's sense of trust when shopping online. Most users simply leave the default settings for P3P at "medium," not knowing exactly what this means (Van Kirk, 2005). There are also issues with the implementation of P3P. A recent Carnegie-Mellon study analyzed 33,000 Web sites, and detected P3P errors in over 11,000 of them, resulting in misrepresenation of the Web site's privacy practices (Leon et al., 2010).

*Insight on Technology: The Privacy Tug of War: Advertisers vs. Consumers* describes some other new technologies being used to both invade and protect privacy.

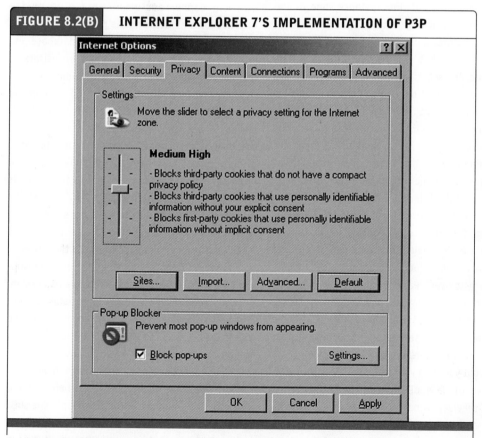

| FIGURE 8.2(B) | INTERNET EXPLORER 7'S IMPLEMENTATION OF P3P |
| --- | --- |

To implement your P3P personal privacy settings in Internet Explorer 7, click the Tools command, then Internet Options. Then click the Privacy tab in the Internet Options dialog box.

# INSIGHT ON TECHNOLOGY

## THE PRIVACY TUG OF WAR: ADVERTISERS VS. CONSUMERS

On today's Internet, online marketers and data companies can find out more about you than you might realize, such as your income, credit score, home ownership, the car you drive, what car you're interested in buying, and whether or not you have any traffic offenses, as well as your online behavior, such as the music you listen to, the books you've ordered from Amazon, the frequency of your purchases, and your use of Twitter and iPhone apps. In the past, offline marketers and data companies knew much more personal information about you than online companies did. For instance, one of the biggest offline tracking firms is Acxiom. Acxiom estimates it stores more than 1,500 data items on each American adult. But the separation of offline and online, the separation of data bases, and the isolation of information in unconnected "pools" is changing as offline market information firms merge their data with online marketers. It's the total coordination of the technological means of tracking individuals that is new. The result is that all of us leave a huge digital footprint (total Web activities) on the Internet. You can check the size of your digital footprint at emc.com. Ken Laudon's footprint, for instance, is over 427 gigabytes.

We are all engaged in a technological tug of war between technologies that make invading customer privacy very easy versus technologies and policies that make protecting privacy easier for us, the consumer. On the privacy invasion side, Google has become the largest tracker on the Internet, and as one commentator put it, "Google knows more about you than your mother." With its treasure trove of data developed from users of its search service, Gmail, Google Sites, Google Health, and a host of other applications, Google has entered a new phase of behavioral targeting.

In the past, Google engaged in "context advertising": enter a search argument, and Google would display "relevant" ads. Google has since shifted some of its focus to what it calls "interest-based" advertising, what people on the sell side of ads call "performance-based advertising" and what everyone else calls behavioral targeting. For instance, mention in a Gmail to your doctor that you're having acid stomach problems, and you'll be shown ads for stomach acid products. Now that Google owns the largest online advertising network, DoubleClick, it's quite likely you will be shown stomach acid banner ads wherever you go on the Internet for an indeterminate period of time.

Experian links Web sites to its database and provides the names and addresses of visitors to the sites in real time. Other companies such as Acxiom combine offline and online purchasing and behavioral data into one central database. Acxiom's service, Relevance-X, draws on that database to determine which online ads to show. MySpace has developed its HyperTargeting ad program, which scours user profiles for interests and then delivers related ads. In 2007, Facebook introduced Beacon, an advertising system that broadcast members' activities on other Web sites (such as what you had purchased) to their friends on Facebook. Beacon was launched with the support of 40 other firms from Coca-Cola to Verizon. Beacon created a fire storm of resistance from Facebook members and privacy groups. By the end of 2007, Facebook CEO, Mark Zuckerberg, apologized to Facebook members and changed the Beacon program so that users needed to explicitly approve of their activities being shared with others. In August 2008, Facebook was sued in a class action suit for violating several federal and state laws that prohibit the unauthorized

(continued)

release of personal information. In September 2009, Beacon was shut down, but Facebook has since launched other features and services that serve targeted ads or share information.

Advertisers justify their intrusions into our private lives and our private use of the Internet with two arguments. They point out that the Internet is not really free. According to senior executives at advertising networks such as DoubleClick: the implicit bargain underlying the "free" Internet is that consumers get content because they are looking at ads. Never mind that you paid around $1,000 for your computer system, and $50-$100 monthly for Internet service. Take away the ads, and some other way will have to be found to pay for what you get on the Internet. Take away the targeted ads, Web sites make less money, and they will provide less service. No more "free" Google Apps. Expect charges for even minimal service. The second rationale behind all these intrusive behaviors is marketing efficiency and effectiveness: the more advertisers know about you, the more they can customize and personalize the advertising to exactly what you are looking for at the right time, and, of course, the more they can charge their customers, the firms that pay for the advertising. Online advertisers believe that consumers are saying, "Take my privacy, but please send the content and the services for free." But is this really what consumers are saying?

In one of the more insightful studies of consumer attitudes towards Internet privacy, a group of Berkeley students conducted surveys of online users, and of complaints filed with the FTC involving privacy issues. Here are some of their results. User concerns: people feel they have no control over the information collected about them, and they don't know who to complain to. Web site practices: Web sites collect all this information, but do not let users have access; the policies are unclear; they share data with "affiliates" but never identify who the affiliates are and how many there are. (MySpace, owned by News Corp, has over 1,500 affiliates with whom it shares online information.) Web bug trackers: they are ubiquitous and we are not informed they are on the pages we visit. The results of this study and others suggest that consumers are not saying "Take my privacy, I don't care, send me the service for free." They are saying "We want access to the information, we want some controls on what can be collected, what is done with the information, the ability to opt out of the entire tracking enterprise, and some clarity on what the policies really are, and we don't want those policies changed without our participation and permission." (The full report is available at knowprivacy.org.)

Confirming these views, an industry-backed survey of over 1,000 Web users found that only 14% said they liked giving information to Web sites in order to receive customized content, and 71% said they disliked it but did so only if necessary to obtain content or information. Another survey found that 41% said that, in the past six months, they had provided inaccurate information to Web sites that required personal information, which respondents did not want to share. They seem to be saying, "Send the content, but let me keep my privacy!" While some studies suggest that many teenagers and young adults do not care as much about privacy as older adults, privacy experts believe that this is because they do not understand how much information is being gathered about them. Other independent studies find young people nearly as concerned as older people. Mark Zuckerberg, CEO of Facebook, has argued that young people of this generation really don't care that much about privacy.

On the privacy protection side, there are some tools available to consumers. Admittedly, P3P, an

(continued)

industry-sponsored effort to provide users some choice in privacy by making them aware of Web site privacy policies, has not been too successful. But ISPs and independent software companies now provide a host of tools that work wonders and are easy to use. AOL offers a "Do Not Track" service that links consumers directly to opt-out lists offered by the large advertising networks. Google has followed: anyone may opt out of the DoubleClick cookie (for AdSense partner sites, DoubleClick ad serving, and certain Google services using the DoubleClick cookie) at any time by clicking a button on the Google Privacy Center page (assuming you know enough to go to that page). Using a tool created by the Network Advertising Initiative, you can opt out of several third-party ad servers' and networks' cookies simultaneously. Web browsers have effective pop-up and image blockers. Adoption rates of cookie blockers and anti-spyware software are increasing as software makers such as Symantec make them available as a part of their software suites that install automatically. For instance, a recent survey found that anti-virus, anti-spyware, and firewall software are used by over 80% of U.S. adult Internet users, and that over two-thirds had configured their browser or operating system to block pop-ups, reject cookies, or block specific Web sites.

The most important spur to industry initiatives protecting privacy is the growing public pressure to do something to protect privacy that gets reflected in congressional hearings, and ultimately legislation. As public concern over behavioral targeting has grown, with calls for greater transparency and accountability, the pressure from Washington on the industry also grows, and attitudes have changed. Gone are the days when Silicon Valley leaders who profit from the invasion of Internet users' privacy could announce to the American public: "Privacy is dead. Get over it!" Instead, a broad consensus between industry, privacy advocates, and Congress has emerged that users want transparency, control, choice, security, and data retention rules, and no changes in privacy promises. Facebook users don't want to wake up some morning and discover that Mark Zuckerberg has decided to sell all their personal information to "affiliates." The leading advertising industry associations have adopted "Self Regulatory Principles for Online Behavioral Advertising," which address many but not all concerns described above. Disagreement persists on questions of user access to the data collected, opt-out vs. opt-in, how "transparency" will be implemented, and the sharing of information with so-called affiliates. The Center for Democracy and Technology supports the idea of a Web-based Do Not Track List where users could sign up at one government site, and all Web advertisers would have to consult that database before targeting ads at users. The industry believes this would be too easy for consumers, and thereby too successful, preventing them from effectively exploiting consumers' personal information.

**SOURCES:** "On the Web's Cutting Edge, Anonymity in Name Only," by Emily Steel and Julia Angwin, *Wall Street Journal*, August 4, 2010; "Microsoft Quashed Effort to Boost Online Privacy," by Nick Wingfield, *Wall Street Journal*, August 2, 2010; "What They Know About You," by Jennifer Valentino-Devries, *Wall Street Journal*, July 31, 2010; "Sites Feed Personal Details to New Tracking Industry," by Julia Angwin and Tom McGinty, *Wall Street Journal*, July 30, 2010; "The Web's New Goldmine: Your Secrets," by Julia Angwin, *Wall Street Journal*, July 30, 2010; "Know Privacy. The Current State of Web Privacy, Data Collection, and Information Sharing," Knowprivacy.org, accessed September 8, 2009; "Ads Follow Web Users, and Get More Personal," by Stephanie Clifford, *New York Times*, July 31, 2009; "The Paradox of Privacy," by Eric Pfanner, *New York Times*, July 13, 2009; "Web Privacy Efforts Targeted. Facing Rules, Ad Firms Give Consumers More Control," by Emily Steel, *Wall Street Journal*, June 25, 2009; "Social Networking Sites Could Be Embroiled in Privacy Crackdown," Telegraph, June 18, 2009; "Google to Offcer Ads Based on Interests," by Miguel Helft, *New York Times*, March 11, 2009; "When Everyone's a Friend, Is Anything Private," by Randall Stross, *New York Times*, March 8, 2009; "Link by Link. As Data Collecting Grows, Privacy Erodes," by Noam Cohen, *New York Times*, February 16, 2009; "Self-Regulatory Principles For Online Behavioral Advertising. Behavioral Advertising, Tracking, Targeting, and Technology," Federal Trade Commission Staff Report, Washington D.C., February 2009; "Many See Privacy on Web as Big Issue, Survey Says," by Stephanie Clifford, *New York Times*, March 16, 2009; "A Call to Legislate Internet Privacy," by Saul Hansell, *New York Times*, March 13, 2009; "Facebook Rules," *New York Times*, February 18, 2009; "Agency Skeptical of Internet Privacy Policies," by Saul Hansell, *New York Times*, February 13, 2009.

## 8.3 INTELLECTUAL PROPERTY RIGHTS

Congress shall have the power to "promote the progress of science and useful arts, by securing for limited times to authors and inventors the exclusive right to their respective writings and discoveries."

—Article I, Section 8, Constitution of the United States, 1788.

Next to privacy, the most controversial ethical, social, and political issue related to e-commerce is the fate of intellectual property rights. Intellectual property encompasses all the tangible and intangible products of the human mind. As a general rule, in the United States, the creator of intellectual property owns it. For instance, if you personally create an e-commerce site, it belongs entirely to you, and you have exclusive rights to use this "property" in any lawful way you see fit. But the Internet potentially changes things. Once intellectual works become digital, it becomes difficult to control access, use, distribution, and copying. These are precisely the areas that intellectual property seeks to control.

Digital media differ from books, periodicals, and other media in terms of ease of replication, transmission, and alteration; difficulty in classifying a software work as a program, book, or even music; compactness—making theft easy; and difficulty in establishing uniqueness. Before widespread use of the Internet, copies of software, books, magazine articles, or films had to be stored on physical media, such as paper, computer disks, or videotape, creating some hurdles to distribution.

The Internet technically permits millions of people to make perfect digital copies of various works—from music to plays, poems, and journal articles—and then to distribute them nearly cost-free to hundreds of millions of Web users. The proliferation of innovation has occurred so rapidly that few entrepreneurs have stopped to consider who owns the patent on a business technique or method their site is using. The spirit of the Web has been so free-wheeling that many entrepreneurs ignored trademark law and registered domain names that can easily be confused with another company's registered trademarks. In short, the Internet has demonstrated the potential for destroying traditional conceptions and implementations of intellectual property law developed over the last two centuries.

The major ethical issue related to e-commerce and intellectual property concerns how we (both as individuals and as business professionals) should treat property that belongs to others. From a social point of view, the main questions are: Is there continued value in protecting intellectual property in the Internet age? In what ways is society better off, or worse off, for having the concept of property apply to intangible ideas? Should society make certain technology illegal just because it has an adverse impact on some intellectual property owners? From a political perspective, we need to ask how the Internet and e-commerce can be regulated or governed to protect the institution of intellectual property while at the same time encouraging the growth of e-commerce and the Internet.

## TYPES OF INTELLECTUAL PROPERTY PROTECTION

There are three main types of intellectual property protection: copyright, patent, and trademark law. In the United States, the development of intellectual property law begins in the U.S. Constitution in 1788, which mandated Congress to devise a system of laws to promote "the progress of science and the useful arts." Congress passed the first copyright law in 1790 to protect original written works for a period of 14 years, with a 14-year renewal if the author was still alive. Since then, the idea of copyright has been extended to include music, films, translations, photographs, and most recently (1998), the designs of vessels under 200 feet (Fisher, 1999). The copyright law has been amended (mostly extended) 11 times in the last 40 years.

The goal of intellectual property law is to balance two competing interests—the public and the private. The public interest is served by the creation and distribution of inventions, works of art, music, literature, and other forms of intellectual expression. The private interest is served by rewarding people for creating these works through the creation of a time-limited monopoly granting exclusive use to the creator.

Maintaining this balance of interests is always challenged by the invention of new technologies. In general, the information technologies of the last century—from radio and television to CD-ROMs, DVDs, and the Internet—have at first tended to weaken the protections afforded by intellectual property law. Owners of intellectual property have often but not always been successful in pressuring Congress and the courts to strengthen the intellectual property laws to compensate for any technological threat, and even to extend protection for longer periods of time and to entirely new areas of expression. In the case of the Internet and e-commerce technologies, once again, intellectual property rights are severely challenged. In the next few sections, we discuss the significant developments in each area: copyright, patent, and trademark.

## COPYRIGHT: THE PROBLEM OF PERFECT COPIES AND ENCRYPTION

**copyright law**

protects original forms of expression such as writings, art, drawings, photographs, music, motion pictures, performances, and computer programs from being copied by others for a minimum of 70 years

In the United States, **copyright law** protects original forms of expression such as writings (books, periodicals, lecture notes), art, drawings, photographs, music, motion pictures, performances, and computer programs from being copied by others for a period of time. Up until 1998, the copyright law protected works of individuals for their lifetime plus 50 years beyond their life, and for works created for hire and owned by corporations such as Mickey Mouse of the Disney Corporation, 75 years after initial creation. Copyright does not protect ideas—just their expression in a tangible medium such as paper, cassette tape, or handwritten notes.

In 1998, Congress extended the period of copyright protection for an additional 20 years, for a total of 95 years for corporate-owned works, and life plus 70 years of protection for works created by individuals (the Copyright Term Extension Act, also known as CTEA). In *Eldred v. Ashcroft*, the Supreme Court ruled on January 16, 2003, that CTEA was constitutional, over the objections of groups arguing that Congress had given copyright holders a permanent monopoly over the expression of ideas, which ultimately would work to inhibit the flow of ideas and creation of new works by making existing works too expensive (Greenhouse, 2003a). Librarians, academics, and others who depend on inexpensive access to copyrighted material opposed the legislation.

Since the first federal Copyright Act of 1790, the congressional intent behind copyright laws has been to encourage creativity and authorship by ensuring that creative people receive the financial and other benefits of their work. Most industrial nations have their own copyright laws, and there are several international conventions and bilateral agreements through which nations coordinate and enforce their laws.

In the mid-1960s, the Copyright Office began registering software programs, and in 1980, Congress passed the Computer Software Copyright Act, which clearly provides protection for source and object code and for copies of the original sold in commerce, and sets forth the rights of the purchaser to use the software while the creator retains legal title. For instance, the HTML code for a Web page—even though easily available to every browser—cannot be lawfully copied and used for a commercial purpose, say, to create a new Web site that looks identical.

Copyright protection is clear-cut: it protects against copying of entire programs or their parts. Damages and relief are readily obtained for infringement. The drawback to copyright protection is that the underlying ideas behind a work are not protected, only their expression in a work. A competitor can view the source code on your Web site to see how various effects were created and then reuse those techniques to create a different Web site without infringing on your copyright.

## Look and Feel

"Look and feel" copyright infringement lawsuits are precisely about the distinction between an idea and its expression. For instance, in 1988, Apple Computer sued Microsoft Corporation and Hewlett-Packard Inc. for infringing Apple's copyright on the Macintosh interface. Among other claims, Apple claimed that the defendants copied the expression of overlapping windows. Apple failed to patent the idea of overlapping windows when it invented this method of presenting information on a computer screen in the late 1960s. The defendants counterclaimed that the idea of overlapping windows could only be expressed in a single way and, therefore, was not protectable under the "merger" doctrine of copyright law. When ideas and their expression merge (i.e., if there is only one way to express an idea), the expression cannot be copyrighted, although the method of producing the expression might be patentable (*Apple Computer, Inc. v. Microsoft*, 1989). In general, courts appear to be following the reasoning of a 1992 case—*Brown Bag Software vs. Symantec Corp.*—in which the court dissected the elements of software alleged to be infringing. There, the Federal Circuit Court of Appeals found that neither similar concept, function, general functional features (e.g., drop-down menus), nor colors were protectable by copyright law (*Brown Bag vs. Symantec Corp.*, 1992).

## Fair Use Doctrine

Copyrights, like all rights, are not absolute. There are situations where strict copyright observance could be harmful to society, potentially inhibiting other rights such as the right to freedom of expression and thought. As a result, the doctrine of fair use has been created. The **doctrine of fair use** permits teachers and writers to use copyrighted materials without permission under certain circumstances.

**doctrine of fair use**
under certain circumstances, permits use of copyrighted material without permission

**Table 8.9** describes the five factors that courts consider when assessing what constitutes fair use.

The fair use doctrine draws upon the First Amendment's protection of freedom of speech (and writing). Journalists, writers, and academics must be able to refer to, and cite from, copyrighted works in order to criticize or even discuss copyrighted works. Professors are allowed to clip a contemporary article just before class, copy it, and hand it out to students as an example of a topic under discussion. However, they are not permitted to add this article to the class syllabus for the next semester without compensating the copyright holder.

What constitutes fair use has been at issue in a number of recent cases, including the Google Book Search Project described in the case study at the end of the chapter, and in several recent lawsuits. In *Kelly v. ArribaSoft* (2003) and *Perfect 10, Inc. v. Amazon.com, Inc.* (2007), the Federal Circuit Court of Appeals for the 10th Circuit held that the display of thumbnail images in response to search requests constituted fair use. A similar result was reached by the district court for the District of Nevada with respect to Google's storage and display of Web sites from cache memory, in *Field v. Google, Inc.* (2006). In all of these cases, the courts accepted the argument that caching the material and displaying it in response to a search request was not only a public benefit, but also a form of marketing of the material on behalf of its copyright owner, thereby enhancing the material's commercial value. Fair use is also at issue in the lawsuit filed by Viacom against Google and YouTube in March 2007, described further in the next section.

### The Digital Millennium Copyright Act of 1998

**Digital Millennium Copyright Act (DMCA)**

the first major effort to adjust the copyright laws to the Internet age

**The Digital Millennium Copyright Act (DMCA)** of 1998 is the first major effort to adjust the copyright laws to the Internet age. This legislation was the result of a confrontation between the major copyright holders in the United States (publishing, sheet music, record label, and commercial film industries), ISPs, and users of copyrighted materials such as libraries, universities, and consumers. While social and

| TABLE 8.9 | FAIR USE CONSIDERATIONS TO COPYRIGHT PROTECTIONS |
|---|---|
| FAIR USE FACTOR | INTERPRETATION |
| Character of use | Nonprofit or educational use versus for-profit use. |
| Nature of the work | Creative works such as plays or novels receive greater protection than factual accounts, e.g., newspaper accounts. |
| Amount of work used | A stanza from a poem or a single page from a book would be allowed, but not the entire poem or a book chapter. |
| Market effect of use | Will the use harm the marketability of the original product? Has it already harmed the product in the marketplace? |
| Context of use | A last-minute, unplanned use in a classroom versus a planned infringement. |

political institutions are sometimes thought of as "slow" and the Internet as "fast," in this instance, powerful groups of copyright owners anticipated Web music services such as Napster by several years. Napster was formed in 1999, but work by the World Intellectual Property Organization (WIPO)—a worldwide body formed by the major copyright-holding nations of North America, Europe, and Japan—began in 1995. **Table 8.10** summarizes the major provisions of the DMCA.

The penalties for willfully violating the DMCA include restitution to the injured parties of any losses due to infringement. Criminal remedies are available to federal prosecutors that include fines up to $500,000 or five years imprisonment for a first offense, and up to $1 million in fines and 10 years in prison for repeat offenders. These are serious remedies.

The DMCA attempts to answer two vexing questions in the Internet age. First, how can society protect copyrights online when any practical encryption scheme imaginable can be broken by hackers and the results distributed worldwide? Second, how can society control the behavior of thousands of ISPs, who often host infringing Web sites, or who provide Internet service to individuals who are routine infringers? ISPs claim to be like telephone utilities—just carrying messages—and they do not want to put their users under surveillance or invade the privacy of users. The DMCA recognizes that ISPs have some control over how their customers use their facilities.

The DMCA implements the WIPO Copyright treaty of 1996, which declares it illegal to make, distribute, or use devices that circumvent technology-based protections of copyrighted materials, and attaches stiff fines and prison sentences for violations. WIPO is an organization within the United Nations. Recognizing that these provisions alone cannot stop hackers from devising circumventions, the DMCA makes it difficult

| TABLE 8.10 | THE DIGITAL MILLENNIUM COPYRIGHT ACT |
| --- | --- |
| **SECTION** | **IMPORTANCE** |
| Title I, WIPO Copyright and Performances and Phonograms Treaties Implementation | Makes it illegal to circumvent technological measures to protect works for either access or copying or to circumvent any electronic rights management information. |
| Title II, Online Copyright Infringement Liability Limitation | Requires ISPs to "take down" sites they host if they are infringing copyrights, and requires search engines to block access to infringing sites. Limits liability of ISPs and search engines. |
| Title III, Computer Maintenance Competition Assurance | Permits users to make a copy of a computer program for maintenance or repair of the computer. |
| Title IV, Miscellaneous Provisions | Requires the Copyright Office to report to Congress on the use of copyright materials for distance education; allows libraries to make digital copies of works for internal use only; extends musical copyrights to include "webcasting." |

SOURCE: Based on data from United States Copyright Office, 1998.

for such inventors to reap the fruits of their labors by making the ISPs (including universities) responsible and accountable for hosting Web sites or providing services to infringers once the ISP has been notified. ISPs are not required to intrude on their users. However, when copyright holders inform the ISP that a hosted site or individual users are infringing, they must "take down" the site immediately to avoid liability and potential fines. ISPs must also inform their subscribers of the ISP's copyright management policies. Copyright owners can subpoena the personal identities of any infringers using an ISP. There are important limitations on these ISP prohibitions that are mostly concerned with the transitory caching of materials for short periods without the knowledge of the ISP. However, should the ISP be deriving revenues from the infringement, it is as liable as the infringer, and is subject to the same penalties.

Title I of the DMCA provides a partial answer to the dilemma of hacking. It is probably true that skilled hackers can easily break any usable encryption scheme, and the means to do so on a large scale through distribution of decryption programs already exists. The WIPO provisions accept this possibility and simply make it illegal to do so, or to disseminate or to enable such dissemination, or even store and transmit decrypted products or tools. These provisions put large ISPs on legal notice.

There are a number of exceptions to the strong prohibitions against defeating a copyright protection scheme outlined above. There are exceptions for libraries to examine works for adoption, for reverse engineering to achieve interoperability with other software, for encryption research, for privacy protection purposes, and for security testing. Many companies, such as YouTube, Google, and MySpace have latched on to the provision of the DMCA that relates to removing infringing material upon request of the copyright owner as a "safe harbor" that precludes them from being held responsible for copyright infringement. This position is currently being tested in a $1 billion lawsuit brought by Viacom against Google and YouTube for willful copyright infringement.

In the Viacom case, Viacom alleges that YouTube and Google engaged in massive copyright infringement by deliberately building up a library of infringing works to draw traffic to the YouTube site and enhance its commercial value. In response, Google and YouTube claim that they are protected by the DMCA's safe harbor and fair use, and that it is often impossible to know whether a video is infringing or not. YouTube also does not display ads on pages where consumers can view videos unless it has an agreement with the content owner. In October 2007, Google announced a filtering system aimed at addressing the problem. It requires content owners to give Google a copy of their content so Google can load it into an auto-identification system. The copyright owner can specify whether it will allow others to post the material. Then after a video is uploaded to YouTube, the system attempts to match it with its database of copyrighted material, and removes any unauthorized material. Whether content owners will be satisfied with this system is unknown, particularly since guidelines issued by a coalition of major media and Internet companies with respect to the handling of copyrighted videos on user-generated Web sites calls for the use of filtering technology that can block infringing material before it is posted online. In June 2010, the federal district court ruled against Viacom, on the grounds that YouTube had taken down over 100,000 videos requested by Viacom, as required by the DMCA, and that YouTube was protected by the safe harbor provisions of DMCA. Viacom is appealing the case.

The disturbing truth facing YouTube and its owner Google is that amateur videos attract few viewers, and cannot be easily monetized because advertisers are loath to have their products displayed against cats-on-skateboard amateur videos. And the only videos that routinely draw huge audiences on YouTube are copyrighted music videos, Hollywood trailers, and parts of feature movies. These videos can indeed be monetized. As a result, YouTube has dramatically changed its attitude towards copyright owners and the concept of copyright. Whereas in the initial years YouTube encouraged users to post whatever videos they wanted, since 2008, YouTube has begun to work closely with content owners to either take down copyrighted material or to place ads next to the material and share the revenues with the owners. Hollywood and New York production studios have changed their attitudes towards YouTube as well from that of an adversary to that of a new, lucrative distribution network. In 2010, it appears the world's largest media producers are learning how to do business with world's largest content distributor.

While courts may allow YouTube to post copyrighted material without the owner's consent until otherwise notified, the same is not true of college campus networks, or Web sites that stream first-run Hollywood movies. In June 2010, a federal task force shut down nine Web sites that illegally streamed first-run movies, confiscated cash and computers, and sought to arrest the owners. The National Intellectual Property Rights Coordination Center is a combined effort of ICE (Immigration and Customs Enforcement), the FBI, and the FDA. College campuses, which historically were hotbeds of illegal file-sharing, are now subject to requirements that universities take serious steps to eliminate on-campus network piracy, or give up their federal funding. As of July 2010, universities have initiated new rules of expulsion for violation of the network rules, and implemented new surveillance technologies to observe individual network usage.

## PATENTS: BUSINESS METHODS AND PROCESSES

"Whoever invents or discovers any new and useful process, machine, manufacture, or composition of matter, or any new and useful improvement thereof, may obtain a patent therefore, subject to the conditions and requirements of this title."

—Section 101, U.S. Patent Act

A **patent** grants the owner a 20-year exclusive monopoly on the ideas behind an invention. The congressional intent behind patent law was to ensure that inventors of new machines, devices, or industrial methods would receive the full financial and other rewards of their labor and still make widespread use of the invention possible by providing detailed diagrams for those wishing to use the idea under license from the patent's owner. Patents are obtained from the United States Patent and Trademark Office (USPTO), created in 1812. Obtaining a patent is much more difficult and time-consuming than obtaining copyright protection (which is automatic with the creation of the work). Patents must be formally applied for, and the granting of a patent is determined by Patent Office examiners who follow a set of rigorous rules. Ultimately, federal courts decide when patents are valid and when infringement occurs.

**patent**
grants the owner an exclusive monopoly on the ideas behind an invention for 20 years

Patents are very different from copyrights because patents protect the ideas themselves and not merely the expression of ideas. There are four types of inventions for which patents are granted under patent law: machines, man-made products, compositions of matter, and processing methods. The Supreme Court has determined that patents extend to "anything under the sun that is made by man" (*Diamond v. Chakrabarty*, 1980) as long as the other requirements of the Patent Act are met. There are three things that cannot be patented: laws of nature, natural phenomena, and abstract ideas. For instance, a mathematical algorithm cannot be patented unless it is realized in a tangible machine or process that has a "useful" result (the mathematical algorithm exception).

In order to be granted a patent, the applicant must show that the invention is new, original, novel, nonobvious, and not evident in prior arts and practice. As with copyrights, the granting of patents has moved far beyond the original intent of Congress's first patent statute that sought to protect industrial designs and machines. Patent protection has been extended to articles of manufacture (1842), plants (1930), surgical and medical procedures (1950), and software (1981). The Patent Office did not accept applications for software patents until a 1981 Supreme Court decision that held that computer programs could be a part of a patentable process. Since that time, thousands of software patents have been granted. Virtually any software program can be patented as long as it is novel and not obvious.

Essentially, as technology and industrial arts progress, patents have been extended to both encourage entrepreneurs to invent useful devices and promote widespread dissemination of the new techniques through licensing and artful imitation of the published patents (the creation of devices that provide the same functionality as the invention but use different methods) (Winston, 1998). Patents encourage inventors to come up with unique ways of achieving the same functionality as existing patents. For instance, Amazon's patent on one-click purchasing caused Barnesandnoble.com to invent a simplified two-click method of purchasing.

The danger of patents is that they stifle competition by raising barriers to entry into an industry. Patents force new entrants to pay licensing fees to incumbents, and thus slow down the development of technical applications of new ideas by creating lengthy licensing applications and delays.

### E-commerce Patents

Much of the Internet's infrastructure and software was developed under the auspices of publicly funded scientific and military programs in the United States and Europe. Unlike Samuel F. B. Morse, who patented the idea of Morse code and made the telegraph useful, most of the inventions that make the Internet and e-commerce possible were not patented by their inventors. The early Internet was characterized by a spirit of worldwide community development and sharing of ideas without consideration of personal wealth (Winston, 1998). This early Internet spirit changed in the mid-1990s with the commercial development of the World Wide Web.

In 1998, a landmark legal decision, *State Street Bank & Trust v. Signature Financial Group, Inc.*, paved the way for business firms to begin applying for "business methods" patents. In this case, a Federal Circuit Court of Appeals upheld the claims of Signature

Financial to a valid patent for a business method that allows managers to monitor and record financial information flows generated by a partner fund. Previously, it was thought business methods could not be patented. However, the court ruled there was no reason to disallow business methods from patent protection, or any "step by step process, be it electronic or chemical or mechanical, [that] involves an algorithm in the broad sense of the term" (*State Street Bank & Trust Co. v. Signature Financial Group*, 1998). The State Street decision led to an explosion in applications for e-commerce "business methods" patents, with over 15,000 in 2009 (see **Figure 8.3**). Note that the overall number of patent applications filed has also increased dramatically, from about 237,000 in 1995 to over 482,000 in 2009.

**Table 8.11** lists some of the better-known, controversial e-commerce patents. Reviewing these, you can understand the concerns of commentators and corporations. Some of the patent claims are very broad (for example, "name your price" sales methods), have historical precedents in the pre-Internet era (shopping carts), and seem "obvious" (one-click purchasing). Critics of online business methods patents argue that the Patent Office has been too lenient in granting such patents and that in most instances, the supposed inventions merely copy pre-Internet business

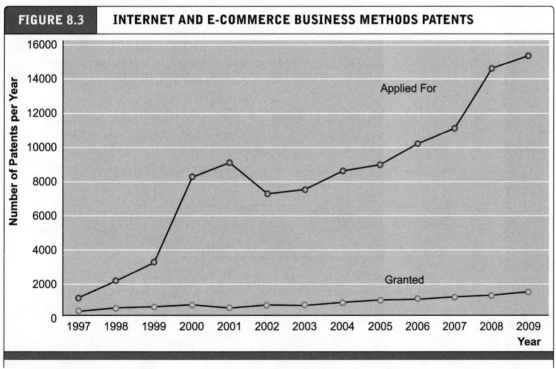

**FIGURE 8.3** | **INTERNET AND E-COMMERCE BUSINESS METHODS PATENTS**

Bolstered by the 1998 *State Street Bank* decision, patents on computer-related business methods increased exponentially from 1998 when 1,337 applications were filed, to 2001, when 9,288 applications were submitted. During the period 2002–2005, applications dropped off somewhat and remained relatively steady at around 7,500–8,500 per year, but in beginning in 2006, they began to increase significantly again, rising to over 15,000 applications in 2009.
SOURCE: Based on data from U.S. Patent and Trademark Office, 2010.

| TABLE 8.11 | SELECTED E-COMMERCE PATENTS |
|---|---|

| COMPANY | SUBJECT | UPDATE |
|---|---|---|
| Leon Stambler | Secure communications | Private inventor with seven patents (1992–1998) covering creation of an authentication code to be used in electronic communications. In 2003, a Delaware jury found that RSA Security and VeriSign did not infringe on the patents. Stambler's appeal to the U.S. Court of Appeals for the Federal Circuit was rejected in February 2005. |
| Amazon | One-click purchasing | Amazon attempted to use patent originally granted to it in 1999 to force changes to Barnes & Noble's Web site, but a federal court overturned a previously issued injunction. Eventually settled out of court. In September 2007, a USPTO panel rejected most of the patent because of evidence another patent predated it, sending it back to the patent examiner for reconsideration. |
| Eolas Technologies | Embedding interactive content in a Web site | Eolas Technologies, a spin-off of the University of California, obtained patent in 1998. Eolas filed suit against Microsoft in 1999 for infringing the patent in Internet Explorer and was awarded a $520 million judgment in 2003. |
| Priceline | Buyer-driven "name your price" sales | Originally invented by Walker Digital, an intellectual property laboratory, and then assigned to Priceline. Granted by the USPTO in 1999. Shortly thereafter, Priceline sued Microsoft and Expedia for copying its patented business method. |
| Sightsound | Music downloads | Sightsound won a settlement in 2004 against Bertelsmann subsidiaries CDNow and N2K music sites for infringing its patent. |
| Akamai | Internet content delivery global hosting system | A broad patent granted in 2000 covering techniques for expediting the flow of information over the Internet. Akamai sued Digital Island (subsequently acquired by Cable & Wireless) for violating the patent and, in 2001, a jury found in its favor. |
| DoubleClick | Dynamic delivery of online advertising | The patent underlying DoubleClick's business of online banner ad delivery, originally granted in 2000. DoubleClick sued competitors 24/7 Real Media and L90 for violating the patent and ultimately reached a settlement with them. |
| Overture | Pay for performance search | System and method for influencing position on search result list generated by computer search engine, granted in 2001. Competitor FindWhat.com sued Overture, charging that patent was obtained illegally; Overture countered by suing both FindWhat and Google for violating patent. Google agreed to pay a license fee to Overture in 2004 to settle. |
| Acacia Technologies | Streaming video media transmission | Patents for the receipt and transmission of streaming digital audio and or video content originally granted to founders of Greenwich Information Technologies in 1990s. Patents were purchased by Acacia, a firm founded solely to enforce the patents, in 2001. |
| Soverain Software | Purchase technology | The so-called "shopping cart" patent for network-based systems, which involves any transaction over a network involving a seller, buyer, and payment system. In other words, e-commerce! Originally owned by Open Markets, then Divine Inc., and now Soverain. Soverain filed suit against Amazon for patent infringement. |
| MercExchange (Thomas Woolston) | Auction technology | Patents on person-to-person auctions and database search, originally granted in 1995. eBay ordered to pay $25 million in 2003 for infringing on patent. In July 2007, the U.S. district court denied a motion for permanent patent injunction against eBay using the "Buy It Now" feature, and moved to the final stages of allowing the damages award to be paid. |
| Google | Search technology | Google PageRank patent was filed in 1998 and granted in 2001. |
| Google | Location technology | Google issued a patent in 2010 for a method of using location information in an advertising system. |
| Apple | Social technology | Apple applied for a patent in 2010 that allows groups of friends attending events to stay in communication with each other and share reactions to live events as they are occurring. |

methods and thus do not constitute "inventions" (Harmon, 2003; Thurm, 2000; Chiappetta, 2001). The Patent Office argues, on the contrary, that its Internet inventions staff is composed of engineers, lawyers, and specialists with many years of experience with Internet and network technologies, and that it consults with outside technology experts before granting patents. To complicate matters, the European Patent Convention and the patent laws of most European countries do not recognize business methods per se unless the method is implemented through some technology (Takenaka, 2001).

In June 2010, the U.S. Supreme Court issued a divided opinion on business method patents in the *Bilski et al. v. Kappos* case (*Bilski et al. v. Kappos*, 2010). The majority argued that business method patents were allowable even though they did not meet the traditional "machine or transformation test" in which patents are granted to devices that are tied to a particular machine, are a machine, or transform articles from one state to another. The minority wanted to flatly declare business methods are not patentable in part because any series of steps could be considered a business method (Schwartz, 2010).

## Patent Reform

Issues related to business method patents, patent "trolls" (companies such as Acacia Technologies that buy up broadly-worded patents on a speculative basis and then use them to threaten companies that are purportedly violating the patent), and confusing legal decisions have led to increasing calls for patent reform over the last few years, particularly by companies in the technology sector. One target of such legislation are firms that produce nothing but simply collect patents and then seek to enforce them. In 2000, Nathan Myhrvold formed a new kind of patent investment firm called Intellectual Ventures. A former Microsoft Chief Technology Officer, Myhrvold has amassed a collection of over 20,000 patents in the digital technology field, including e-commerce, by purchasing them from small companies and entrepreneurs. He discovers large firms that may be violating those patents and threatens to sue. Sony, Google, Verizon, and many other large firms have paid up, and in addition, have invested in the company so they can participate in future revenues (Sharma and Clark, 2008). In 2010, Microsoft co-founder Paul Allen, one of the world's richest men, sued most of Silicon Valley including Google, Facebook, and eBay, claiming that he had invented many elements of their operations years before. Allen claims his former company Interval Research invented pop-up stock quotes, suggestions for related reading, and videos alongside a screen, among other common elements of today's Web sites. In another patent troll case, NTP sued Microsoft in 2010 and others over patents related to the wireless delivery of e-mail to cell phones (Searcy, 2010).

In September 2007, the House of Representatives passed its version of a patent reform bill that includes provisions that change the patent system from a "first to invent" system to a "first to file" system, change the way damages for patent infringement are calculated, provide a new way to challenge patents out of court, limit where patent suits can be filed (to prevent suits from being filed in districts that have a reputation for being more favorable), and impose heightened standards for a finding of willful infringement. The Senate Judiciary Committee is currently considering the Patent Reform Act of 2010.

## TRADEMARKS: ONLINE INFRINGEMENT AND DILUTION

> Trademark is "any word, name, symbol, or device, or any combination thereof ... used in commerce ... to identify and distinguish ... goods . . . from those manufactured or sold by others and to indicate the source of the goods."
>
> —The Trademark Act, 1946

**trademark**

a mark used to identify and distinguish goods and indicate their source

Trademark law is a form of intellectual property protection for **trademarks**—a mark used to identify and distinguish goods and indicate their source. Trademark protections exist at both the federal and state levels in the United States. The purpose of trademark law is twofold. First, the trademark law protects the public in the marketplace by ensuring that it gets what it pays for and wants to receive. Second, trademark law protects the owner—who has spent time, money, and energy bringing the product to the marketplace—against piracy and misappropriation. Trademarks have been extended from single words to pictures, shapes, packaging, and colors. Some things may not be trademarked: common words that are merely descriptive ("clock"), flags of states and nations, immoral or deceptive marks, or marks belonging to others. Federal trademarks are obtained, first, by use in interstate commerce, and second, by registration with the USPTO. Trademarks are granted for a period of 10 years, and can be renewed indefinitely.

Disputes over federal trademarks involve establishing infringement. The test for infringement is twofold: market confusion and bad faith. Use of a trademark that creates confusion with existing trademarks causes consumers to make market mistakes, or misrepresents the origins of goods is an infringement. In addition, the intentional misuse of words and symbols in the marketplace to extort revenue from legitimate trademark owners ("bad faith") is proscribed.

In 1995, Congress passed the Federal Trademark Dilution Act, which created a federal cause of action for dilution of famous marks. This legislation dispenses with the test of market confusion (although that is still required to claim infringement), and extends protection to owners of famous trademarks against **dilution**, which is defined as any behavior that would weaken the connection between the trademark and the product. Dilution occurs through blurring (weakening the connection between the trademark and the goods) and tarnishment (using the trademark in a way that makes the underlying products appear unsavory or unwholesome).

**dilution**

any behavior that would weaken the connection between the trademark and the product

### Trademarks and the Internet

The rapid growth and commercialization of the Internet have provided unusual opportunities for existing firms with distinctive and famous trademarks to extend their brands to the Internet. These same developments have provided malicious individuals and firms the opportunity to squat on Internet domain names built upon famous marks, as well as attempt to confuse consumers and dilute famous or distinctive marks (including your personal name or a movie star's name). The conflict between legitimate trademark owners and malicious firms was allowed to fester and grow because Network Solutions Inc. (NSI), originally the

Internet's sole agency for domain name registration for many years, had a policy of "first come, first served." This meant anyone could register any domain name that had not already been registered, regardless of the trademark status of the domain name. NSI was not authorized to decide trademark issues (Nash, 1997).

In response to a growing number of complaints from owners of famous trademarks who found their trademark names being appropriated by Web entrepreneurs, Congress passed the **Anticybersquatting Consumer Protection Act (ACPA)** in November 1999. The ACPA creates civil liabilities for anyone who attempts in bad faith to profit from an existing famous or distinctive trademark by registering an Internet domain name that is identical, confusingly similar, or "dilutive" of that trademark. The act does not establish criminal sanctions. The act proscribes using "bad-faith" domain names to extort money from the owners of the existing trademark (**cybersquatting**), or using the bad-faith domain to divert Web traffic to the bad-faith domain that could harm the good will represented by the trademark, create market confusion, tarnish, or disparage the mark (**cyberpiracy**). The Act also proscribes the use of a domain name that consists of the name of a living person, or a name confusingly similar to an existing personal name, without that person's consent, if the registrant is registering the name with the intent to profit by selling the domain dame to that person.

Trademark abuse can take many forms on the Web. **Table 8.12** lists the major behaviors on the Internet that have run afoul of trademark law, and the some of the court cases that resulted.

## Cybersquatting and Brandjacking

In one of the first cases involving the ACPA, E. & J. Gallo Winery, owner of the registered mark "Ernest and Julio Gallo" for alcoholic beverages, sued Spider Webs Ltd. for using the domain name Ernestandjuliogallo.com. Spider Webs Ltd. was a domain name speculator that owned numerous domain names consisting of famous company names. The Ernestandjuliogallo.com Web site contained information on the risks of alcohol use, anti-corporate articles about E. & J. Gallo Winery, and was poorly constructed. The court concluded that Spider Webs Ltd. was in violation of the ACPA and that its actions constituted dilution by blurring because the Ernestandjuliogallo.com domain name appeared on every page printed off the Web site accessed by that name, and that Spider Webs Ltd. was not free to use this particular mark as a domain name (*E. & J. Gallo Winery v. Spider Webs Ltd.*, 2001). In 2009, incidents of cybersquatting increased by 8% to 565,000 according to MarkMonitor's Brandjacking Index, with a total of over 260,000 instances identified in the 4th quarter of 2009 alone (MarkMonitor, 2010). In August 2009, a court upheld the largest cybersquatting judgment to date: a $33 million verdict in favor of Verizon against OnlineNIC, an Internet domain registration company that had used over 660 names that could easily be confused with legitimate Verizon domain names.

## Cyberpiracy

Cyberpiracy involves the same behavior as cybersquatting, but with the intent of diverting traffic from the legitimate site to an infringing site. In *Ford Motor Co. v.*

**Anticybersquatting Consumer Protection Act (ACPA)**
creates civil liabilities for anyone who attempts in bad faith to profit from an existing famous or distinctive trademark by registering an Internet domain name that is identical, or confusingly similar, or "dilutive" of that trademark

**cybersquatting**
involves the registration of an infringing domain name, or other Internet use of an existing trademark, for the purpose of extorting payments from the legitimate owners

**cyberpiracy**
involves the same behavior as cybersquatting, but with the intent of diverting traffic from the legitimate site to an infringing site

| TABLE 8.12 | INTERNET AND TRADEMARK LAW EXAMPLES | |
|---|---|---|
| ACTIVITY | DESCRIPTION | EXAMPLE CASE |
| Cybersquatting | Registering domain names similar or identical to trademarks of others to extort profits from legitimate holders | *E. & J. Gallo Winery v. Spider Webs Ltd.*, 129 F. Supp. 2d 1033 (S.D. Tex., 2001) aff'd 286 F. 3d 270 (5th Cir.,2002) |
| Cyberpiracy | Registering domain names similar or identical to trademarks of others to divert Web traffic to their own sites | *Ford Motor Co. v. Lapertosa*, 2001 U.S. Dist. LEXIS 253 (E.D. Mich., 2001); *PaineWebber Inc. v. Fortuny*, Civ. A. No. 99-0456-A (E.D. Va., 1999); *Playboy Enterprises, Inc. v. Global Site Designs, Inc.*, 1999 WL 311707 (S.D. Fla., 1999), *Audi AG and Volkswagen of America Inc. v. Bob D'Amato* (No. 05-2359; 6th Cir., November 27, 2006). |
| Metatagging | Using trademark words in a site's metatags | *Bernina of America, Inc. v. Fashion Fabrics Int'l, Inc.*, 2001 U.S. Dist. LEXIS 1211 (N.D. Ill., 2001); *Nissan Motor Co., Ltd. v. Nissan Computer Corp.*, 289 F. Supp. 2d 1154 (C.D. Cal., 2000), aff'd, 246 F. 3rd 675 (9th Cir., 2000). |
| Keywords | Placing trademarked keywords on Web pages, either visible or invisible | *Playboy Enterprises, Inc. v. Netscape Communications, Inc.*, 354 F. 3rd 1020 (9th Cir., 2004); *Nettis Environment Ltd. v. IWI, Inc.*, 46 F. Supp. 2d 722 (N.D. Ohio, 1999); *Government Employees Insurance Company v. Google, Inc.*, Civ. Action No. 1:04cv507 (E.D. VA, 2004); *Google, Inc. v. American Blind & Wallpaper Factory, Inc.*, Case No. 03-5340 JF (RS) (N.D. Cal., April 18, 2007) |
| Linking | Linking to content pages on other sites, bypassing the home page | *Ticketmaster Corp. v. Tickets.com*, 2000 U.S. Dist. Lexis 4553 (C.D. Cal., 2000) |
| Framing | Placing the content of other sites in a frame on the infringer's site | *The Washington Post, et al. v. TotalNews, Inc., et al.*, (S.D.N.Y., Civil Action Number 97-1190) |

*Lapertosa*, Lapertosa had registered and used a Web site called Fordrecalls.com as an adult entertainment Web site. The court ruled that Fordrecalls.com was in violation of the ACPA in that it was a bad-faith attempt to divert traffic to the Lapertosa site and diluted Ford's wholesome trademark (*Ford Motor Co. v. Lapertosa*, 2001).

The Ford decision reflects two other famous cases of cyberpiracy. In the *Paine Webber Inc. v. Fortuny* case, the court enjoined Fortuny from using the domain name Wwwpainewebber.com—a site that specialized in pornographic materials—because it diluted and tarnished Paine Webber's trademark and diverted Web traffic from Paine Webber's legitimate site—Painewebber.com (*Paine Webber Inc. v. Fortuny*, 1999). In the *Playboy Enterprises, Inc. v. Global Site Designs, Inc.* case, the court enjoined the defendants from using the Playboy and Playmate marks in their domain names Playboyonline.net and Playmatesearch.net and from including the Playboy trademark in their metatags. In these cases, the defendants' intention was diversion for financial gain (*Playboy Enterprises, Inc. v. Global Site Designs, Inc.*, 1999).

In a more recent case, *Audi AG and Volkswagen of America Inc. v. Bob D'Amato*, the Federal Circuit Court of Appeals for the Sixth Circuit affirmed the district court's ruling that the defendant Bob D'Amato infringed and diluted the plaintiffs' Audi, Quattro, and Audi Four Rings logo marks, and violated the ACPA by operating the Audisport.com Web site (*Audi AG and Volkswagen of America Inc. v. Bob D'Amato*, 2006).

*Typosquatting* is a form of cyberpiracy in which a domain name contains a common misspelling of another site's name. Often the user ends up at a site very different from one they intended to visit. For instance, John Zuccarini is an infamous typosquatter who was jailed in 2002 for setting up pornographic Web sites with URLs based on misspellings of popular children's brands, such as Bob the Builder and Teletubbies. The FTC fined him again in October 2007 for engaging in similar practices (McMillan, 2007).

## Metatagging

The legal status of using famous or distinctive marks as metatags is more complex and subtle. The use of trademarks in metatags is permitted if the use does not mislead or confuse consumers. Usually this depends on the content of the site. A car dealer would be permitted to use a famous automobile trademark in its metatags if the dealer sold this brand of automobiles, but a pornography site could not use the same trademark, nor a dealer for a rival manufacturer. A Ford dealer would most likely be infringing if it used "Honda" in its metatags, but would not be infringing if it used "Ford" in its metatags. (Ford Motor Company would be unlikely to seek an injunction against one of its dealers.)

In the *Bernina of America, Inc. v. Fashion Fabrics Int'l, Inc.* case, the court enjoined Fashion Fabrics, an independent dealer of sewing machines, from using the trademarks "Bernina" and "Bernette," which belonged to the manufacturer Bernina, as metatags. The court found the defendant's site contained misleading claims about Fashion Fabrics' knowledge of Bernina products that were likely to confuse customers. The use of the Bernina trademarks as metatags per se was not a violation of ACPA, according to the court, but in combination with the misleading claims on the site would cause confusion and hence infringement (*Bernina of America, Inc. v. Fashion Fabrics Int'l, Inc.*, 2001).

In the *Nissan Motor Co. Ltd. v. Nissan Computer Corp.* case, Uzi Nissan had used his surname "Nissan" as a trade name for various businesses since 1980, including Nissan Computer Corp. He registered Nissan.com in 1994 and Nissan.net in 1996. Nissan.com had no relationship with Nissan Motor, but over the years began selling auto parts that competed with Nissan Motor. Nissan Motor Company objected to the use of the domain name Nissan.com and the use of "Nissan" in the metatags for both sites on grounds it would confuse customers and infringe on Nissan Motor's trademarks. Uzi Nissan offered to sell his sites to Nissan Motor for several million dollars. Nissan Motor refused. The court ruled that Nissan Computer's behavior did indeed infringe on Nissan Motor's trademarks, but it refused to shut the site down. Instead, the court ruled Nissan Computer could continue to use the Nissan name, and metatags, but must post notices on its site that it was not affiliated with Nissan Motor (*Nissan Motor Co. Ltd. v. Nissan Computer Corp.*, 2000).

### Keywording

The permissibility of using trademarks as keywords on search engines is also subtle and depends on the extent to which such use is considered to be a "use in commerce," causes "initial customer confusion" and on the content of the search results.

In *Playboy Enterprises, Inc. v. Netscape Communications, Inc.*, Playboy objected to the practice of Netscape's and Excite's search engines displaying banner ads unrelated to Playboy Magazine when users entered search arguments such as "playboy," "playmate," and "playgirl." The Ninth Circuit Court of Appeals denied the defendant's motion for a summary judgment and held that when an advertiser's banner ad is not labeled so as to identify its source, the practice could result in trademark infringement due to consumer confusion (*Playboy Enterprises, Inc. v. Netscape Communications, Inc.*, 2004).

In the *Nettis Environment Ltd. v. IWI, Inc.* case, Nettis and IWI Inc. were competitors in the ventilation business. IWI had registered the trademarks "nettis" and "nettis environmental" on over 400 search engines, and in addition, used these marks as metatags on its site. The court required IWI to remove the metatags and de-register the keywords with all search engines because consumers would be con fused—searching for Nettis products would lead them to an IWI Web site (*Nettis Environment Ltd. v. IWI, Inc.*, 1999).

Google has also faced lawsuits alleging that its advertising network illegally exploits others' trademarks. For instance, insurance company GEICO challenged Google's practice of allowing competitors' ads to appear when a searcher types "Geico" as the search query. In December 2004, a U.S. district court ruled that this practice did not violate federal trademark laws as long as the word "Geico" was not used in the ads' text (*Government Employees Insurance Company v. Google, Inc.*, 2004). Google quickly discontinued allowing the latter, and settled the case (Associated Press, 2005). However, these settlements have not prevented other companies from also suing Google. For instance, in July 2009, Rosetta Stone, the language-learning software firm, filed a lawsuit against Google for trademark infringement, alleging its AdWords program allowed other companies to use Rosetta Stone's trademarks for online advertisements without permission. The suit is one of nine similar lawsuits against Google instituted since May 2009, when Google expanded to more than 190 new countries its policy of allowing anyone to buy someone else's trademark as a keyword trigger for ads. Google also announced in May 2009 that it would allow the limited use of other companies' trademarks in the text of some search ads, even if the trademark owner objected. In 2009, the European Court of Justice handed Google a victory against luxury brand behemoth LVMH by allowing Google to continue selling advertisements based on keyword searches for luxury goods makers. Even competitor firms can bid on LVMH brand names (Ram, 2009). Currently anyone can buy anyone else's trademark as a keyword.

### Linking

**linking**
building hypertext links from one site to another site

**deep linking**
involves bypassing the target site's home page, and going directly to a content page

**Linking** refers to building hypertext links from one site to another site. This is obviously a major design feature and benefit of the Web. **Deep linking** involves bypassing the target site's home page and going directly to a content page. In *Ticketmaster Corp. v. Tickets.com*, Tickets.com—owned by Microsoft—competed directly against Ticketmaster in the events ticket market. When Tickets.com did not have tickets for an event, it would direct users to Ticketmaster's internal pages, bypassing the Ticketmaster home page. Even though its logo was displayed on the internal pages, Ticketmaster objected on the grounds that such "deep linking" violated the terms and conditions of use for its site (stated on a separate page altogether and construed by Ticketmaster as equivalent to a shrink-wrap license), and constituted false advertising, as well as the violation of copyright. The court found, however, that deep linking per se is not illegal, no violation of copyright occurred because no copies were made, the terms and conditions of use were not obvious to users, and users were not required to read the page on which the terms and conditions of use appeared in any event. The court refused to rule in favor of Ticketmaster, but left open further argument on the licensing issue. In an out-of-court settlement, Tickets.com nevertheless agreed to stop the practice of deep linking (*Ticketmaster v. Tickets.com*, 2000).

## Framing

**Framing** involves displaying the content of another Web site inside your own Web site within a frame or window. The user never leaves the framer's site and can be exposed to advertising while the target site's advertising is distorted or eliminated. Framers may or may not acknowledge the source of the content. In *The Washington Post, et al. v. TotalNews, Inc.* case, The Washington Post, CNN, Reuters, and several other news organizations filed suit against TotalNews Inc., claiming that TotalNews's use of frames on its Web site, TotalNews.com, infringed upon the respective plaintiffs' copyrights and trademarks, and diluted the content of their individual Web sites. The plaintiffs claimed additionally that TotalNews's framing practice effectively deprived the plaintiffs' Web sites of advertising revenue.

TotalNews's Web site employed four frames. The TotalNews logo appeared in the lower left frame, various links were located on a vertical frame on the left side of the screen, TotalNews's advertising was framed across the screen bottom, and the "news frame," the largest frame, appeared in the center and right. Clicking on a specific news organization's link allowed the reader to view the content of that particular organization's Web site, including any related advertising, within the context of the "news frame." In some instances, the framing distorted or modified the appearance of the linked Web site, including the advertisements, while the appearance of TotalNews's advertisements, in a separate frame, remained unchanged. In addition, the URL remained fixed on the TotalNews address, even though the content in the largest frame on the Web site was from the linked Web site. The "news frame" did not, however, eliminate the linked Web site's identifying features.

The case was settled out of court. The news organizations allowed TotalNews to link to their Web sites, but prohibited framing and any attempt to imply affiliation with the news organizations (*The Washington Post, et al. v. TotalNews, Inc.*, 1997).

**framing**
involves displaying the content of another Web site inside your own Web site within a frame or window

### CHALLENGE: BALANCING THE PROTECTION OF PROPERTY WITH OTHER VALUES

In the areas of copyright, patent law, and trademark law, societies have moved quickly to protect intellectual property from challenges posed by the Internet. In each of these areas, traditional concepts of intellectual property have not only been upheld, but often strengthened. The DMCA seems to restrict journalists and academics from even accessing copyrighted materials if they are encrypted, a protection not true of traditional documents (which are rarely encrypted anyway). Patents have been extended to Internet business methods, and trademarks are more strongly protected than ever because of fears of cybersquatting. In the early years of e-commerce, many commentators believed that Internet technology would sweep away the powers of corporations to protect their property (Dueker, 1996). The experience of the music industry in the past decade is a powerful example of how a new technology can disrupt an entrenched business model and an entire industry. The music industry has not hesitated to use the legal system and in many instances has been victorious. However, despite these legal victories, the software for file sharing itself is now widely distributed. (BitTorrent, for instance, is in the public domain and can be used by anyone with a computer.) Because shared music files can be split up across thousands of user computers on these networks, there is no one in charge, no corporate entity to sue. On the other hand, industry associations can identify and sue not only the operators of computing systems on the networks who act as primary repositories and distributors of stolen music, but also individuals.

For instance, in 2009 and 2010, the Recording Industry Association of America (RIAA) successfully pursued a number of civil suits against individuals storing even modest numbers of music tracks on their computers and making them available to others for downloading, as well as against universities who permit their servers to download stolen files. (By 2009, the RIAA had filed over 30,000 separate lawsuits.) In September 2008, the Federal Bureau of Investigation arrested a Los Angeles man on copyright-infringement charges for posting on his Web site nine songs from a yet-to-be-released album by the rock band Guns N' Roses. This was only the second criminal prosecution for piracy in U.S. history, but it may signal a growing belief among copyright owners that the reality of going to jail can stop illegal file sharing.

It is apparent that corporations have some very powerful legal tools for protecting their digital properties. The difficulty now may be in going too far to protect the property interests of the powerful and the rich, preventing parody sites or parody content from receiving wide distribution and recognition, and in this sense interfering with the exercise of First Amendment guarantees of freedom of expression.

**governance**

has to do with social control: who will control e-commerce, what elements will be controlled, and how the controls will be implemented

### 8.4    GOVERNANCE

**Governance** has to do with social control: Who will control the Internet? Who will control the processes of e-commerce, the content, and the activities? What elements will be controlled, and how will the controls be implemented? A natural question arises and needs to be answered: Why do we as a society need to "control" e-commerce? Because e-commerce and the Internet are so closely intertwined (though not identical), controlling e-commerce also involves regulating the Internet.

## WHO GOVERNS E-COMMERCE AND THE INTERNET?

Governance of both the Internet and e-commerce has gone through four stages. **Table 8.13** summarizes these stages in the evolution of e-commerce governance.

Prior to 1995, the Internet was a government program. Beginning in 1995, private corporations were given control of the technical infrastructure as well as the process of granting IP addresses and domain names. However, the NSI monopoly created in this period did not represent international users of the Internet, and was unable to cope with emerging public policy issues such as trademark and intellectual property protection, fair policies for allocating domains, and growing concerns that a small group of firms were benefiting from growth in the Internet.

In 1995, President Clinton, using funds from the Department of Commerce, encouraged the establishment of an international body called the Internet Corporation for Assigned Names and Numbers (ICANN) that hopefully could better represent a wider range of countries and a broad range of interests, and begin to address emerging public policy issues. ICANN was intended to be an Internet/e-commerce industry self-governing body, not another government agency.

| TABLE 8.13 | THE EVOLUTION OF GOVERNANCE OF E-COMMERCE |
| --- | --- |
| **INTERNET GOVERNANCE PERIOD** | **DESCRIPTION** |
| Government Control 1970–1994 | DARPA and the National Science Foundation control the Internet as a fully government-funded program. |
| Privatization 1995–1998 | Network Solutions Inc. is given a monopoly to assign and track high-level Internet domains. Backbone is sold to private telecommunications companies. Policy issues are not decided. |
| Self-Regulation 1995–present | President Clinton and the Department of Commerce encourage the creation of a semiprivate body, ICANN, to deal with emerging conflicts and establish policies. ICANN currently holds a contract with the Department of Congress to govern some aspects of the Internet. |
| Governmental Regulation 1998–present | Executive, legislative, and judicial bodies worldwide begin to implement direct controls over the Internet and e-commerce. |

The explosive growth of the Web and e-commerce created a number of issues over which ICANN had no authority. Content issues such as pornography, gambling, and offensive written expressions and graphics, along with commercial issue of intellectual property protection, ushered in the current era of growing governmental regulation of the Internet and e-commerce throughout the world. Currently, we are in a mixed-mode policy environment where self-regulation through a variety of Internet policy and technical bodies co-exists with limited government regulation.

Today, ICANN remains in charge of the domain name system that translates domain names (such as www.company.com) into IP addresses. It has subcontracted the work of maintaining the databases of the domain registries to several private corporations. The U.S. government controls the "A-root" server. However, these arrangements are increasingly challenged by other countries, including China, Russia, Saudi Arabia, and most of the European Union, all of whom want the United States to give up control over the Internet to an international body such as the International Telecommunication Union (ITU) (a UN agency). In November 2005, an Internet Summit sponsored by the ITU agreed to leave control over the Internet domain servers with the United States and instead called for an international forum to meet in future years to discuss Internet policy issues (Miller and Rhoads, 2005). The position of the United States with respect to international governance of the Internet changed significantly after the terrorist attacks of September 11, 2001. Currently, the United States has no intention of diminishing its role in control over the global or domestic Internet.

## Can the Internet Be Controlled?

Early Internet advocates argued that the Internet was different from all previous technologies. They contended that the Internet could not be controlled, given its inherent decentralized design, its ability to cross borders, and its underlying packet switching technology that made monitoring and controlling message content impossible. Many still believe this to be true today. The slogans are "Information wants to be free," and "The Net is everywhere" (but not in any central location). The implication of these slogans is that the content and behavior of e-commerce sites—indeed Internet sites of any kind—cannot be "controlled" in the same way as traditional media such as radio and television. However, attitudes have changed as many governments and corporations extend their control over the Internet and the World Wide Web (Stone, 2010).

In fact, the Internet is technically very easily controlled, monitored, and regulated from central locations (such as network access points, as well as servers and routers throughout the network). For instance, in China, Saudi Arabia, Iran, North Korea, Thailand, Singapore, and many other countries, access to the Web is controlled from government-owned centralized routers that direct traffic across their borders and within the country (such as China's "Great Firewall of China," which permits the government to block access to certain U.S. or European Web sites), or via tightly regulated ISPs operating within the countries. In China, for instance, all ISPs need a license from the Ministry of Information Industry (MII), and are prohibited from disseminating any information that may harm the state or permit pornography, gambling, or the advocacy of cults. In addition, ISPs and search engines such as Google, Yahoo, and MSN typically self-censor their Asian content by using only government-approved news sources. MySpace also self-censors content it believes might upset the Chinese government. Despite this, in October 2007, it was reported that China was redirecting traffic from search engines operated by Google, Microsoft, and Yahoo to Chinese-operated Baidu.com (Ho, 2007; Elgin and Einhorn, 2006). In the 2008 Olympics, China routinely censored access by Western media to common Internet sites, including BBC.com.

In some instances, the firms have also cooperated with the Chinese government's pursuit of bloggers and journalists as a condition of its continuing business in China. For instance, Yahoo has been roundly denounced for helping the Chinese government convict and sentence a man to 10 years in jail for posting information to a U.S. Web site.

Following the outbreak of street demonstrations in June 2009 protesting a rigged election, the Iranian government unleashed one of the world's most sophisticated mechanisms for controlling and censoring the Web. Built with the assistance of Western companies like Siemens and Nokia, the system uses deep packet inspection to open every packet, look for keywords, re-seal it, and send it on the network.

In the United States, as we have seen in our discussion of intellectual property, e-commerce sites can be put out of business for violating existing laws, and ISPs can be forced to "take down" offending or stolen content. Government security agencies such as the FBI can obtain court orders to monitor ISP traffic and engage in widespread monitoring of millions of e-mail messages. Under the USA PATRIOT Act, passed after the World Trade Center attack on September 11, 2001, American intelligence authorities are permitted to tap into whatever Internet traffic they believe is relevant to the campaign against terrorism, in some circumstances without judicial review. Working with the large ISP firms such as AT&T, Verizon, and others, U.S. security agencies have access to nearly all Internet communications through the country. And many American corporations are developing restrictions on their employees' at-work use of the Web to prevent gambling, shopping, and other activities not related to a business purpose.

In the United States, efforts to control media content on the Web have run up against equally powerful social and political values that protect freedom of expression, including several rulings by the Supreme Court that have struck down laws attempting to limit Web content in the United States. The U.S. Constitution's First Amendment says "Congress shall make no law … abridging the freedom of speech, or of the press." As it turns out, the 200-year-old Bill of Rights has been a powerful brake on efforts to control twenty-first-century e-commerce content.

## PUBLIC GOVERNMENT AND LAW

The reason we have governments is ostensibly to regulate and control activities within the borders of the nation. What happens in other nations, for the most part, we generally ignore, although clearly environmental and international trade issues require multinational cooperation. E-commerce and the Internet pose some unique problems to public government that center on the ability of the nation-state to govern activities within its borders. Nations have considerable powers to shape the Internet.

## TAXATION

Few questions illustrate the complexity of governance and jurisdiction more potently than taxation of e-commerce sales. In both Europe and the United States, governments rely on sales taxes based on the type and value of goods sold. In Europe, these taxes are collected along the entire value chain, including the final sale to the consumer, and are called "value-added taxes" (VAT), whereas in the United States, taxes are collected by states and localities on final sales to consumers and are called consumption and use taxes. In the United States, there are 50 states, 3,000 counties, and 12,000 municipalities, each with unique tax rates and policies. Cheese may be taxable in one state as a "snack food" but not taxable in another state (such as Wisconsin), where it is considered a basic food. Consumption taxes are generally recognized to be regressive because they disproportionately tax poorer people, for whom consumption is a larger part of total income.

Sales taxes were first implemented in the United States in the late 1930s as a Depression-era method of raising money for localities. Ostensibly, the money was to be used to build infrastructure such as roads, schools, and utilities to support business development, but over the years the funds have been used for general government purposes of the states and localities. In most states, there is a state-based sales tax, and a smaller local sales tax. The total sales tax ranges from zero in some states (North Dakota) to as much as 13% in New York City.

The development of "remote sales" such as mail order/telephone order (MOTO) retail in the United States in the 1970s broke the relationship between physical presence and commerce, complicating the plans of state and local tax authorities to tax all retail commerce. States sought to force MOTO retailers to collect sales taxes for them based on the address of the recipient, but Supreme Court decisions in 1967 and 1992 established that states had no authority to force MOTO retailers to collect state taxes unless the businesses had a "nexus" of operations (physical presence) in the state. Congress could, however, create legislation giving states this authority. But every congressional effort to tax catalog merchants has been beaten back by a torrent of opposition from catalog merchants and consumers, leaving intact an effective tax subsidy for MOTO merchants.

The explosive growth of e-commerce, the latest type of "remote sales," has once again raised the issue of how—and if—to tax remote sales. Since its inception, e-commerce has benefited from a tax subsidy of up to 13% for goods shipped to high sales tax areas. Local retail merchants have complained bitterly about the e-commerce tax subsidy. E-commerce merchants have argued that this new form of commerce needs to be nurtured and encouraged in its early years, and that in any event, the crazy quilt of sales and use tax regimes would be difficult to administer for Internet merchants. Online giants like Amazon claim they should not have to pay taxes in states where they have no operations because they do not benefit from local schools, police, fire and other governmental services. State and local governments meanwhile see billions of tax dollars slipping from their reach. In 2010, thousands of online retailers, including Amazon, BlueNile, eBay, and Overstock, pay no taxes in states where they do not have a presence.

In 1998, Congress passed the Internet Tax Freedom Act, which placed a moratorium on "multiple or discriminatory taxes on electronic commerce" as well as on taxes on Internet access, for three years until October 2001, and in November 2001, extended the moratorium to November 2003. In November 2002, delegates from 32 states approved model legislation designed to create a system to tax Web sales. Spearheaded by the National Governor's Association (NGA), the Streamlined Sales Tax Project (SSTP) requires participating states to have only one tax rate for personal property or services effective by the end of 2005. By 2007, 15 states had agreed to support the SSTP. The governors are trying to get Congress to override judicial opinions and force online merchants to start collecting taxes. Nevertheless, in December 2004, Congress enacted the Internet Tax Nondiscrimination Act (Public Law 108–435), which extended the moratorium on states and local governments imposing taxes on Internet access and taxes on electronic commerce through November 1, 2007. In October 2007, Congress extended the moratorium once again, this time for an additional seven years to 2014 (Gross, 2007). As it turns out, taxing online commerce is a very unpopular idea in the United States.

The merger of online e-commerce with offline commerce further complicates the taxation question. Currently, almost all of the top 100 online retailers collect taxes when orders ship to states where these firms have a physical presence. But others, like eBay, still refuse to collect and pay local taxes, arguing that the so-called tax simplification project ended up with taxes for each of 49,000 zip codes, hardly a simplification. The taxation situation is also very complex in services. For instance, none of the major online travel sites collect the full amount of state and local hotel occupancy taxes, or state and local airline taxes. Instead of remitting sales tax on the full amount of the consumer's purchase, these sites instead collect taxes on the basis of the wholesale price they pay for the hotel rooms or tickets.

The states have not given up on collecting hundreds of millions of dollars from Internet merchants. In 2010, they are using two strategies. One is to define "nexus" to include having affiliates in a state, which they argue is the equivalent of a store. Amazon, Blue Nile, and Overstock have eliminated their affiliate programs in states adopting this tactic. A second tactic is to agree to a tax simplification plan. Congress and the courts have at least considered taxing e-commerce if the states have a simplified and uniform state tax system. To date, 20 states have adopted the simplified system although none of them are large states.

The taxation situation in Europe, and trade between Europe and the United States, is similarly complex. The Organization for Economic Cooperation and Development (OECD), the economic policy coordinating body of European, American, and Japanese governments, is currently investigating different schemes for applying consumption and business profit taxes for e-commerce digitally downloaded goods. The EU began collecting a VAT on digital goods such as music and software delivered to consumers by foreign companies in 2003. Previously, European Union companies were required to collect the VAT on sales to EU customers, but U.S. companies were not. This gave American companies a huge tax edge.

Thus, there is no integrated rational approach to taxation of domestic or international e-commerce (Varian, 2001). In the United States, the national and international character of Internet sales is wreaking havoc on taxation schemes that were built in the 1930s and based on local commerce and local jurisdictions. Although there appears to be acquiescence among large Internet retailers such as Amazon to the idea of some kind of sales tax on e-commerce sales, their insistence on uniformity will probably delay taxation for many years, and any proposal to tax e-commerce will likely incur the wrath of around 133 million U.S. e-commerce consumers. Congress is not likely to ignore their voices.

## NET NEUTRALITY

"Net neutrality" is more a political slogan than a concept. It means different things to different people. Currently, all Internet traffic is treated equally (or "neutrally") by Internet backbone owners in the sense that all activities—word processing, e-mailing, video downloading, etc.—are charged the same flat rate regardless of how much bandwidth is used. However, the telephone and cable companies that provide the Internet backbone would like to be able to charge differentiated prices based on the amount of bandwidth consumed by content being delivered over the Internet, much like a utility company charges according to how much electricity consumers use. Utility companies do this because electricity is a scarce resource, costs money to produce, and can be easily metered. Telephone and cable companies would also like to ration bandwidth so that in times of excessive demand they would slow down some traffic ("bandwidth hogs") so that other traffic such as e-mail can proceed more quickly. There are two ways to achieve this rationing: pricing or speed (bandwidth controls). Heavy bandwidth users can be charged higher usage fees if they overstep a limit. This is referred to as "congestion pricing" or "Web metering."

Heavy bandwidth users can also have their applications slowed down based on metering of their usage. In addition, high bandwidth vendors such as YouTube could be charged additional fees. The content of companies that pay an additional fee would be given preferential treatment in terms of delivery speed. The content of companies that refused to pay would be delivered at a slower rate.

Likewise, individual home users who downloaded enormous movie files would be charged a higher monthly fee for Internet service compared to neighbors who use the Internet only for e-mail and surfing. For instance, in 2008, Comcast, the largest ISP in the U.S., began to slow down traffic using the BitTorrent protocol not because the content was pirated but because these video users were consuming huge chunks of the Comcast network capacity during peak load times. Comcast claims its policy was a legitimate effort to manage capacity. The FCC disagreed, and ruled in August 2008 that Comcast illegally inhibited users of its high-speed network from using file-sharing software cast has appealed and filed suit against the FCC in the U.S. Court of Appeals for the District of Columbia. In April 2010, a U.S. appeals court ruled that the FCC had no authority to regulate Internet providers, or to prevent Comcast from charging some users more for bandwidth, or slowing their service. Currently, Time Warner Cable is experimenting with Web metering in Beaumont, Texas, charging $1 for every gigabyte over a 5-gigabyte base service. This kind of differential pricing is typical of the cable television industry.

Those who oppose the idea of "net metering" and charging more for heavy users of bandwidth have been lobbying Congress to create a new layer of Internet regulation that would require network providers to manage their networks in a nondiscriminatory manner. In general, the very heavy users of bandwidth including Google, YouTube, Facebook, Microsoft, and others do not want their customers to pay extra for premium services, fearing customers might think twice about using their services if they had to pay more. Other advocates of so-called net neutrality argue that the future of innovation on the Internet requires no premium pricing. In 2009, the FCC began developing a national broadband strategy in connection with the enactment of the government stimulus package. As part of the plan, the FCC is expected to issue regulations as to what sort of rules, if any, should be applied to guarantee delivery of Internet traffic. The plan is currently under wraps given the FCC's questionable authority in the area. Meanwhile, telecommunications providers such as Verizon and Internet distributors such as Google have reached a market-based compromise: maintain existing rules for landlines, but implement differential pricing for mobile wireless networks . Both the content distributors and the network providers are starting to realize they need one another. In the end, net neutrality is about generating revenue for content distributors and Internet network owners. Keep your eyes on the money.

## 8.5 PUBLIC SAFETY AND WELFARE

Governments everywhere claim to pursue public safety, health, and welfare. This effort produces laws governing everything from weights and measures to national highways, to the content of radio and television programs. Electronic media of all kinds (telegraph, telephone, radio, and television) have historically been regulated by governments seeking to develop a rational commercial telecommunications environment and to control the content of the media—which may be critical of government or offensive to powerful groups in a society. Historically, in the United States, newspapers and print media have been beyond government controls because of constitutional guarantees of freedom of speech. Electronic media such as radio and television have, on the other hand, always been subject to content regulation because they use the publicly owned frequency spectrum. Telephones have also been regulated as public utilities and "common carriers," with special social burdens to provide service and access, but with no limitations on content.

In the United States, critical issues in e-commerce center around the protection of children, strong sentiments against pornography in any public media, efforts to control gambling, and the protection of public health through restricting sales of drugs and cigarettes.

### PROTECTING CHILDREN

Pornography is an immensely successful Internet business. The most recent statistics with respect to revenues generated by online pornography are now several years old, and range widely. However, it is probably safe to estimate that the online pornography industry in 2010 generates over $3 billion in revenue. Adult Web sites reportedly attract over 75 million unique visitors a month and make up 12% of the Internet. (New York Times, 2009; Worthen, 2009; Wondracek et al., 2010).

To control the Web as a distribution medium for pornography, in 1996, Congress passed the Communications Decency Act (CDA). This act made it a felony criminal offense to use any telecommunications device to transmit "any comment, request, suggestion, proposal, image, or other communications which is obscene, lewd, lascivious, filthy, or indecent" to anyone, and in particular, to persons under 18 years of age (Section 502, Communications Decency Act of 1996). In 1997, the Supreme Court struck down the CDA as an unconstitutional abridgement of freedom of speech protected by the First Amendment. While the government argued the CDA was like a zoning ordinance designed to allow "adult" Web sites for people 18 years of age or over, the Court found the CDA was a blanket proscription on content and rejected the "cyberzoning" argument as impossible to administer. In 2002, the Supreme Court struck down another law, the Child Pornography Prevention Act of 1996, which made it a crime to create, distribute, or posses "virtual" child pornography that uses computer-generated images or young adults rather than real children, as overly broad (*Ashcroft v. Free Speech Coalition*).

In 1998, Congress passed the Children's Online Protection Act (COPA). This act made it a felony criminal offense to communicate for "commercial purposes" "any material harmful to minors." Harmful material was defined as prurient, depicting sexual acts, and lacking value for minors. The act differed from the CDA by focusing on "commercial speech" and minors exclusively. In February 1999, a federal district court in Pennsylvania struck down COPA as an unconstitutional restriction on Web content that was protected under the First Amendment. The court nevertheless recognized the interest of Congress and society to protect children on the Internet and in e-commerce. In May 2002, the U.S. Supreme Court returned the case to the court of appeals for a decision, leaving in place an injunction barring enforcement of the law. In March 2003, the Third Circuit Court of Appeals ruled for the second time that COPA was unconstitutional, finding that the law violated the First Amendment because it improperly restricted access to a substantial amount of online speech that is lawful for adults. In 2004, the Supreme Court blocked enforcement of the law again, saying that it likely violated the First Amendment, but remanded it to the district court for a further trial examining Internet filtering technologies that might be used to achieve the law's goals. In January 2006, it was revealed that in preparation for this trial, the Department of Justice had issued subpoenas to Google, AOL, Yahoo, and Microsoft seeking a week's worth of search queries and a random sampling of 1 million Web addresses in the effort to understand the prevalence of material that could be deemed harmful to minors and the effectiveness of filtering technology, raising a storm of additional controversy. AOL, Microsoft, and Yahoo all agreed to supply the requested data, but Google refused on a variety of grounds, including protection of its trade secrets, privacy, and public relations (Hafner and Richtel, 2006). In response, the court limited the subpoena to just a sample of URLs in Google's database. In March 2007, the district court struck down COPA, ruling once again that the law violated the First and Fifth Amendments, and issued an order permanently prohibiting the government from enforcing COPA. The government once again appealed, and in July 2008, the Third Circuit Court of Appeals upheld the district court opinion that COPA violated the First amendment. On January 21, 2009, the Supreme Court refused an appeal of the circuit court decision, putting an end to the saga of litigation over the act.

The 2003 Protect Act is an omnibus bill intended to prevent child abuse that includes prohibitions against computer-generated child pornography. Part of that statute was previously held to be unconstitutional by the Eleventh Circuit Court of Appeals, but in May

2008, the Supreme Court reversed the circuit court and upheld the provision (Greenhouse, 2008).

Although Congress has had a difficult time framing constitutionally acceptable legislation to protect children and other consumers from pornography, in the Children's Online Privacy Protection Act (COPPA) (1998) (described in Section 8.2), it appears to have been successful in preventing e-commerce sites from collecting information on minors without parental consent. Pornographers who collect information on children without parental consent are potential felons. Because COPPA does not regulate e-commerce content per se, to date it has not been challenged in the courts.

In 2001, Congress passed the Children's Internet Protection Act (CIPA), which required schools and libraries in the United States to install "technology protection measures" (filtering software) in an effort to shield children from pornography. In June 2003, the Supreme Court upheld CIPA, overturning a federal district court that found the law interfered with the First Amendment guarantee of freedom of expression. The Supreme Court, in a 6–3 opinion, held that the law's limitations on access to the Internet posed no more a threat to freedom of expression than limitations on access to books that librarians choose for whatever reason not to acquire. The dissenting justices found this analogy inappropriate and instead argued the proper analogy was if librarians were to purchase encyclopedias and then rip out pages they thought were or might be offensive to patrons. All the justices agreed that existing blocking software was overly blunt, unable to distinguish child pornography from sexually explicit material (which is protected by the First Amendment), and generally unreliable (Greenhouse, 2003b). Other legislation such as the 2002 Domain Names Act seeks to prevent unscrupulous Web site operators from luring children to pornography using misleading domain names or characters known to children, while the 2002 Dot Kids Act authorizes the creation of a second-level domain on the Internet where all Web sites would have to declare they contain no material harmful to children. An alternative plan, to create an .xxx domain for adult Web site content, was finally approved by ICANN in June 2010, but has not yet been implemented.

In addition to government regulation, pressure from organized groups has also been successful in forcing some Web sites to eliminate the display of pornographic materials. In June 2008, in response to pressure from Andrew Cuomo, New York's attorney general, Verizon, Time Warner Cable, and Sprint, agreed to limit access to some or all Usenet groups in an effort to block access to child pornography. AT&T, AOL, and Comcast followed suit in July 2008. In September 2010, in response to pressure from 17 states attorney general, Craigslist removed its sexual services listings and replaced them with a "Censored" screen logo. .

## CIGARETTES, GAMBLING, AND DRUGS: IS THE WEB REALLY BORDERLESS?

In the United States, both the states and the federal government have adopted legislation to control certain activities and products in order to protect public health and welfare. Cigarettes, gambling, medical drugs, and of course addictive recreational drugs, are either banned or tightly regulated by federal and state laws (see *Insight on Society: The Internet Drug Bazaar*). Yet these products and services are ideal for distribution over the Internet through e-commerce sites. Because the sites can be

# INSIGHT ON SOCIETY

## THE INTERNET DRUG BAZAAR

In July 2010, a federal court jury in Beaumont, Texas, found David Allen Vogel guilty of distribution of controlled substances and money laundering. Vogel was the ringleader of a Web-based pharmacy that earned millions per year. He was ordered to repay $24 million to the government on top of the $4.3 million that state investigative agencies seized from six separate bank accounts, and faces up to 45 years in prison. His pharmacy, the Madison Pain Clinic in Dallas, illegally solicited and filled Internet orders for prescription drugs from 2000 to 2007, primarily high dosage forms of the narcotic hydrocodone and the anxiety-reliever Xanax. The operation had a doctor purportedly review customer's online questionnaires, but according to authorities, none of the patient information was ever verified before the order was filled.

One year earlier, a U.S. District Judge in Orlando sentenced Jude Lacour to eight years in federal prison for drug trafficking and money laundering. Lacour and his associates were convicted of operating an Internet drug operation referred to as Jive Network that distributed controlled substances and prescription drugs to customers who did not have prescriptions, who were never examined by a doctor, and without performing a proper health history. Jive Network generated in excess of $85 million in revenue during the three years of its operation. Lacour was required to make a cash payment to the government in the amount of $9.8 million. These are just two examples of an increasingly common trend of illegal Internet pharmacies distributing drugs such as Ritalin, Xanax, Vicodin, and other highly addictive drugs.

According to a study done by the Treatment Research Institute at the University of Pennsylvania, addictive and potentially lethal medications are available without prescription from more than 2 million Web sites around the world, with many sites based in countries that impose little if any regulation on pharmaceuticals. MarkMonitor, a company specializing in online brand protection, studied 2,968 online pharmacies and found questionable business practices were more the norm than the exception. A Google search on "drugs" "no prescription" returns over 16 million results. The study scoured the paid search ads delivered when queries for prescription-based pain medications and erectile dysfunction drugs were submitted. Most of the top advertisers proved to be bogus, offshore pharmacies that don't ask for prescriptions or perform age verification checks.

The International Narcotics Control Board, a U.N. narcotics watchdog agency, issued guidelines in March 2009 that provide guidelines and a framework for governments struggling to contain growing abuse of prescription drugs on the Internet. According to the report, a U.S. study found that only 2 of 365 so-called Internet pharmacies it surveyed were legitimate. In many countries, the report said, trafficking in illegal prescription drugs now equals or exceeds the sale of heroin, cocaine, and amphetamines. According to the World Health Organization, 8 percent of the bulk drugs imported into the United States in 2010 are counterfeit or substandard, and illegal pharmacies will earn $21 billion in counterfeit drugs in 2010, accounting for 10 percent of the worldwide pharmaceutical trade. While properly reg-

(continued)

ulated Internet pharmacies offer a valuable service by increasing competition and access to treatments in underserved regions, Web pharmacies are a long way from proper regulation.

The sale of drugs without a prescription is not the only danger posed by the Internet drug bazaar. Rogue online pharmacy sites may be selling counterfeit drugs, or unapproved drugs. For instance, in the past, the FDA has issued warnings that a number of consumers who had purchased Ambien, Xanax, and Lexapro online from several different Web sites had instead received a product containing haloperial, a powerful anti-psychotic drug. Drug pushers on the Internet also include legitimate U.S. pharmaceutical firms who have discovered search engine advertising. Enter a search for ''high cholesterol'' on Bing or Google and you will be faced with multiple ads extolling the benefits of Lipitor (Pfizer's leading statin drug). In 2009, the FDA issued a warning to these firms that their search engine ads violated laws that required them to clearly state the risks of drugs they are marketing.

But despite these dangers, online pharmacies remain alluring and are one of the fastest growing business models, with, oddly, senior citizens—usually some of the most law-abiding citizens—leading the charge for cheaper drugs. The top 1,000 Internet pharmacies are estimated to generate about $4 billion in revenue. The main attraction of online drug sites is price. Typically, online pharmacies are located in countries where prescription drugs are price-controlled, or where the price structure is much lower, such as Canada, the United Kingdom, and European countries, as well as India and Mexico. U.S. citizens can often save 50%-75% by purchasing from online pharmacies located in other countries.

Currently, a patchwork regulatory structure governs the sale of drugs online. At the federal level, the 1938 Food, Drug, and Cosmetic Act (FDCA) requires that certain drugs may only be purchased with a valid doctor's prescription and must be dispensed by a state-licensed pharmacy. To get around this requirement, some online pharmacies use questionnaires to diagnose disease and have these questionnaires reviewed by doctors who write the prescription. This practice has not been allowed by U.S. courts. Congress has considered legislation to establish a federal definition of what constitutes a valid prescription, but to date such legislation has not passed. Complicating matters is the fact that many online pharmacies operate offshore, making it difficult for federal and state authorities to exercise jurisdiction over them. Older legislation requires online pharmacies to comply with pharmacy licensing laws in every state where they do business, and to register with the FDA before beginning to sell drugs online. This requirement is virtually unenforceable because foreign online pharmacies can easily develop their Web sites offshore. The act does not prohibit online pharmacies anywhere in the world from providing drugs based on a legitimate doctor's prescription. In September 2010, Congress planned to meet with ICANN, the manager of the Internet's domain name system, to discuss ways to identify and crack down on online pharmacies.

In the meantime, the Food and Drug Administration recommends that consumers look for the National Association of Boards of Pharmacy (NABP) Verified Internet Pharmacy Practices Sites (VIPPS) seal, which verifies that the site is legitimate with respect to conformance with state laws, and requires a prescription for controlled drugs. So far, 23 major Internet pharmacies have signed on, including Drugstore.com, Caremark.com, CVS.com, Walgreens.com, and many other U.S. online pharmacies. Unfortunately, as an American trade association, the NABP never consid-

(continued)

ers Canadian or European pharmacies, and locks the American consumer into high-priced drugs. That leaves thousands of sites that con-

sumers should approach with a "buyer beware" attitude.

■■■ **SOURCES:** "White House Calls Meeting on Rogue Online Pharmacies," Krebsonsecurity.com, August 26, 2010; "Drug Scam May Lead to a View that Has Bars, " by Cindy Horswell, *Houston Chronicle*, July 5,, 2010; "Jury Finds New Yorker Guilty In Internet Drug Conspiracy," U.S. Department of Justice, July 1, 2010. "Rogue Pharmacies Still a Problem For Search Engines," by Lance Whitney, CNET News, August 19, 2009; "Eleven Members of Internet Drug Organization Sentenced," United States Attorney's Office, Middle District of Florida, July 29, 2009; "Microsoft's Bing Hit With Illegal Pharmacy Ads," by Rick Aristotle Munarriz, Fool.com, August 19, 2009; "Report on Yahoo! Rogue Internet Pharmacy Ads," LegitScript.com, August 18, 2009; "FDA Warns Drug Firms Over Internet Ads," by Jerod Favole, *Wall Street Journal*, April 4, 2009; "U.N. Issues Guidelines on Illegal Web Pharmacies," by Reuters, *PC Magazine*, March 17, 2009; "Don't Put Your Health in the Hands of Crooks," Federal Bureau of Investigation, Headline Archives, March 3, 2009; "Owner of Hi-Tech Pharmaceuticals and Co-conspirators Sentenced in Prescription Drug Importation Ring," U.S. Department of Justice, February 3, 2009; "Ryan Haight Online Pharmacy Consumer Protection Act," H.R. 6353, 110th Congress, 2008.

located offshore, they can operate beyond the jurisdiction of state and federal prosecutors. Or so it seemed until recently. In the case of cigarettes, state and federal authorities have been quite successful in shutting down tax-free cigarette Web sites within the United States by pressuring PayPal and credit card firms to drop cigarette merchants from their systems. The major shipping companies—UPS, FedEx, and DHL—have been pressured into refusing shipment of untaxed cigarettes. Phillip Morris has also agreed not to ship cigarettes to any resellers that have been found to be engaging in illegal Internet and mail order sales. However, East European sites and Web sites located on American Indian reservations continue to operate using checks and money orders as payments and the postal system as a logistics partner, but their level of business has plummeted as consumers fear state tax authorities will present them with huge tax bills if they are discovered using these sites. In 2010, President Obama signed the Prevent All Cigarette Trafficking Act. The law restricts the sale of untaxed cigarettes and other tobacco products over the Internet and bans the delivery of tobacco products through the U.S. mail.

Gambling also provides an interesting example of the clash between traditional jurisdictional boundaries and claims to a borderless, uncontrollable Web. The online gambling market, based almost entirely offshore—primarily in the United Kingdom and various Caribbean Islands—grew by leaps and bounds between 2000 and 2006, generating as much as $50 billion to $60 billion a year, and with much of the action (some estimate up to 50%) coming from customers based in the United States. Although the federal government contended online gambling was illegal under U.S. federal law, they were initially unable to stop it, with various federal courts offering mixed opinions. However, in the summer of 2006, federal officials turned up the heat and arrested two executive officers of offshore gambling operations as they passed through the United States, leading their companies to cease U.S. operations. Then in October 2006, Congress passed the Unlawful Internet Gambling Enforcement Act, which makes it a crime to use credit cards or online payment systems for Internet betting. This effectively bars online gambling companies from operating legally in the United States, and shortly thereafter a number of the leading, publicly traded companies suspended their business in the United States. However, the bill has not eliminated all online gambling in the United States, with some smaller companies still offering offshore gambling. An association of online gambling groups challenged the law as unconstitutional, claiming that Internet gambling is protected by First Amendment privacy rights and that filtering technology exists to make sure that children and compulsive gamblers cannot access offshore betting sites. These arguments were rejected by the Third Circuit Court of Appeals in September 2009. Several countries are also seeking compensation from the United States on the basis of a World Trade Organization ruling that American Internet gambling restrictions are illegal. In 2010, legislation was introduced in the House of Representatives calling for legalization of online gambling and taxation of gambling revenues by both states and the federal government. Proponents argue Internet gambling goes on anyway, so why not regulate and tax the activity?

# The Google Book Settlement:
## Is It Fair?

In the Internet age, books are supposed to die off and go away. Who wants to read books when YouTube streams over 33 billion videos a month in 2010, covering most topics known to man, and Google can provide online access to the world's information? Steve Jobs noted in an interview about the Kindle e-book reader, "It doesn't matter how good or bad the product [e-book reader] is, the fact is that people don't read anymore. Forty percent of the people in the U.S. read one book or less last year. The whole conception is flawed at the top because people don't read anymore."

Actually, in 2010, over 600,000 new titles will be published, and 3 billion books will be sold, generating around $25 billion in revenue, down 1% from 2009. According to the American Association of Publishers, e-book sales exploded in 2010, growing from 1.5% of book sales in the U.S. to 5%. Amazon reports annual e-book growth at around 400% in the last year. Americans in fact read 10 books per year per person on average, and people over 17 tend to read many more than that. In a recession when "not down much" is actually "up," the book industry is holding very steady, much better than industrials, con-

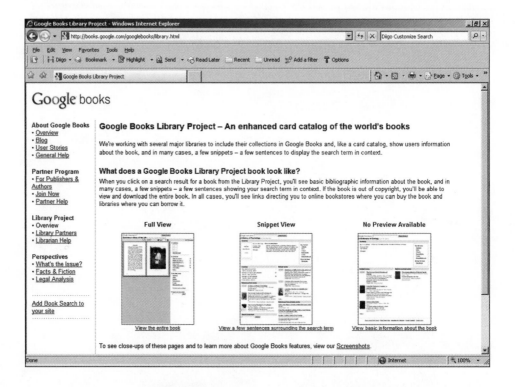

sumer products, and of course financial services, which tanked. Only high-tech Silicon Valley firms did better in 2009 and 2010. Books are surprisingly a very hot topic in 2010 as e-readers and the iPad are exploding in popularity and Google battles the major heavy-hitter tech companies, authors, publishing firms, the United States Congress, the Department of Justice, and the European Commission over the future of online digital books.

Google is on a tear to put everything digital on its servers and then, as the founders promise in ceaseless self-congratulatory announcements, provide access to "all the world's information" through its efforts. And make a buck, as it turns out, by selling ads aimed at you that are "relevant" to your searches. A problem arises, however, when what Google wants to put on its servers does not belong to them. We're all familiar with the copyrighted music and video situation, where firms often operating offshore, beyond the law (or so they think) and enable, induce, and encourage Internet users to illegally download copyrighted material without paying a dime for it, while in the meantime raking in millions of advertising dollars from companies willing to advertise on their networks.

But Google is no criminal organization. For a firm who's motto is "Don't be evil," it seems out of character for it to initiate a program of scanning millions of copyrighted books it does not own and then, without permission, providing its search engine users with access to those books without charge, while selling ad space and pocketing millions for its own account without sharing that revenue with publishers or authors. One major difference between Google and most file-sharing firms is that Google has very deep pockets filled with cash, and they are based in the United States, making it an excellent legal target.

It all started with Google's secret 2002 project to scan all the books in libraries and make parts ("snippets") available online, and of course, display ads next to the results of book searches, even on the pages of snippets. In 2004, Google announced a program it first called Google Print and now just calls Google Books. There are two parts to the project. Under the Partner Program (previously called the Publisher Program), publishers give permission to Google to scan their books, or make scans available, and then make parts of the work, or simply bibliographic information (title, author, and publisher), available on Google's search engine. No problem there: publishers and authors get a chance to find a wider market, and Google sells more ads. Publishers may even choose to sell online editions of their books. And publishers were promised a hefty 70% of the display ad revenues and book sales (far better than Amazon's cut of book sales which is about 50%).

It's the second part of the project that became controversial. Under the Library Project, Google proposed to scan millions of books in university and public libraries and then allow users to search for key phrases, and display "relevant" portions of the text (what it calls "snippets"), all without contacting the publisher or seeking permission or paying a royalty fee. Google said it would "never show a full page without the right from the copyright holder," just the "relevant" portion. Google gave the publishing industry until November 2005 to opt out by providing Google with a list of books they did not want to be included. In addition, Google proposed to scan millions of books for which the copyright has lapsed and make those available on its servers for free. In these early days, Google's public stance towards authors and publishers was "Stop us if you can."

Google has the backing of a number of prestigious libraries, such as the University of Michigan, Harvard University, Stanford University, the New York Public Library, and Oxford University. But not all librarians agree. Some believe this is a marvelous extension of public access to library collections, while other librarians fear it is harmful to book authors and publishers. A number of well-known libraries, such as the Smithsonian Institution, and the Boston Public Library, as well as a consortium of 19 research and academic libraries in the Northeast, have refused to participate, in part because of restrictions that Google wants to place on the collection. Libraries that work with Google must agree to make the material unavailable to other commercial search services. Google claims it is performing a public service by making an index of books, and relevant portions, available to millions on the Internet, and perhaps even helping publishers sell new copies of books that currently sit on dusty library shelves.

In 2005, the publishing industry struck back at Google's book-scanning program and two lawsuits were filed in federal court in New York, one a class-action suit by the Authors Guild and the second by five major publishing companies (McGraw Hill, Pearson Education, Penguin Group, Simon & Schuster, and John Wiley & Sons), claiming copyright infringement. The publishers' consortium, the American Association of Publishers (AAP), alleged that Google was claiming the right to "unilaterally change copyright law and copy anything unless somebody tells [them] "No" [making it] impossible for people in the intellectual property community to operate. They [Google] keep talking about doing this because it is good for the world. That has never been a principle in law. They 'do no evil' except they are stealing people's property." Or, as one commentator put it, it's like having a thief break into your house and clean the kitchen—it's still breaking and entering.

Google, on the other hand, claimed its use was "fair" under the "fair use" doctrine that has emerged from a number of court decisions issued over the years, and which is codified in the Copyright Act in 1976. The copying and lending of books by libraries has been considered a fair use since the late 1930s under a "gentleman's agreement" between libraries and publishers, and a library exemption was codified as Section 108 of the Copyright Act of 1976. Libraries loan books to patrons for a limited period, and they must purchase at least one copy. Many people read books borrowed from libraries and recommend them to friends, who often buy the books rather than take the time and effort to go to a library. Libraries are also considered by many in the publishing industry as helping to market a book to a larger public, and libraries are believed to be performing a public service by increasing literacy and education.

In 2008, Google agreed to a settlement of the lawsuit with the authors and publishers. Google decided to cut a deal for cash and other considerations. In return for the nonexclusive right to sell books scanned into its database, place advertisements on those pages, display snippets, and make other commercial uses of its database of scanned books, Google agreed to pay about $125 million to the parties. Of this amount, $15 million will be used to reimburse legal expenses and establish a fund to aid authors and publishers in pursuing their rights; $45 million will be put into the settlement fund for books digitized prior to an opt-out deadline (September 1, 2009); $34.5 million will be used to fund the launch of a central registry of books involved in the program; and the remaining $31 million will be used to pay for administrative and operating expenses of the registry. In addition, Google agreed to pay the registry 70% of Google's revenues from the project, less 10% for operating expenses. No provision is made in the agreement for (a) public domain books (government and out-of-copyright books) and (b) "orphaned books" where the copyright holders cannot be identified. All books that Google digitizes will be listed in the central registry available to the public on the Internet.

In 2009, a flurry of companies such as Microsoft, Yahoo, and Amazon; university groups; private organizations such as the American Association of Publishers; members of the Author's guild; and publishers in the European Union all filed briefs with the court disputing the settlement. The technology companies formed the Open Book Alliance to oppose the settlement. They were joined by privacy protection groups who claimed (not without merit) that Google would be able to track whatever e-books people accessed and read. Sony is the only technology company supporting Google. European publishers, authors, and copyright holders have also objected to the proposed settlement in the American courts. In September 2009, representatives of those groups spoke out at a hearing sponsored by the European Commission against the proposed deal. They said it would give Google too much power, including exclusive rights to sell out-of-print works that remain under copyright, a category that includes millions of books.

The Justice Department is also nvestigating the antitrust implications of the settlement. Critics argue the settlement will create a de facto monopoly position for Google, make it difficult for competitors to enter the field, and give Google broad copyright immunity. The settlement provides that Google's access to publishers' books is "non exclusive," but competitors would have to scan all the same books over again in order to establish a competitive position, something that experts believe is financially prohibitive. Google, and settlement parties, including the AAP and Author's Guild, argue the settlement will expand digital access to millions of books that are gathering dust on library shelves. Critics retort that Google's database of books will be exclusive, not available to other firms or non-profit groups, and the costs of developing an open source, competing database of scanned books would be prohibitive. Google, they argue, would end up owning the digital book, which is like owning the libraries of the future.

In 2010, Google announced its intentions of launching Google Editions, an online store intended to compete with Amazon, Apple, Barnes & Noble, and other e-book retailers. Just as Google Apps competes with Microsoft Office by offering the same functionality online, Google Editions will be a fully online service and will not require a dedicated e-reader to use. If Google has its way, any Internet-enabled device will become an e-reader. As of September 2010, the service has not yet been launched, but it may pose an eventual threat to the players in the e-book market.

**SOURCES:** "What is Google Editions?" by Peter Osnos, Theatlantic.com, July 10, 2010. "AAP Reports Book Sales Estimated at \$23.9 Billion in 2009", Publishers.org, April 7, 2010. "11th Hour Filings Oppose Google's Book Settlement," by Miguel Helft, *New York Times*, September 9, 2009; "Congress to Weigh Google Books Settlement," *New York Times*, September 9, 2009; "Tech Heavyweightgs Put Google's Books Deal in Crosshairs," by Jessica Vascellaro and Geoffrey Fowler, *Wall Street Journal*, August 21,2009; "Probe of Google Book Deal Heats Up," by Elizabeth Williamson, J. Trachtenberg, and J. Vascellaro, *Wall Street Journal*, June 10, 2009; "Preparing to Sell E-books, Google Takes on Amazon," by Motoko Rich, *New York Times*, June 1, 2009; "Justice Department Opens Antitrust Inquiry Into Google Books Deal," by Miguel Helft, *New York Times*, April 29, 2009; *The Authors Guild, Inc., Association of American Publishers, Inc., et al., v. Google Inc.,* Preliminary Settlement, Case 1:05-cv-08136-JES Document 56, Filed 10/28/2008; *The McGraw Hill Companies, et. al., v. Google Inc.,* United States Southern District Court, Southern District of New York, October 19, 2005.

## Case Study Questions

1. Who is harmed by Google's Library Project? Make a list of harmed groups, and for each group, try to devise a solution that would eliminate or lessen the harm.

2. Why is Google pursuing the Library Project program? What is in it for Google? Make a list of benefits to Google.

3. If you were a librarian, would you support Google's Library Project? Why or why not?

4. Why do firms like Amazon, Yahoo, and Microsoft opposed the Google book project? Why would a firm like Sony support Google?

5. Do you think Google's book project will result in a de facto monopoly in e-books, or will there be other competitors?

## 8.7   REVIEW

### KEY CONCEPTS

■ **Understand why e-commerce raises ethical, social, and political issues.**

Internet technology and its use in e-commerce disrupts existing social and business relationships and understandings. Suddenly, individuals, business firms, and political institutions are confronted by new possibilities of behavior for which understandings, laws, and rules of acceptable behavior have not yet been developed. Many business firms and individuals are benefiting from the commercial development of the Internet, but this development also has costs for individuals, organizations, and societies. These costs and benefits must be carefully considered by those seeking to make ethical and socially responsible decisions in this new environment, particularly where there are as yet no clear-cut legal or cultural guidelines.

■ **Recognize the main ethical, social, and political issues raised by e-commerce.**

The major issues raised by e-commerce can be loosely categorized into four major dimensions:
- *Information rights*—What rights do individuals have to control their own personal information when Internet technologies make information collection so pervasive and efficient?
- *Property rights*—How can traditional intellectual property rights be enforced when perfect copies of protected works can be made and easily distributed worldwide via the Internet?
- *Governance*—Should the Internet and e-commerce be subject to public laws? If so, what law-making bodies have jurisdiction—state, federal, and/or international?
- *Public safety and welfare*—What efforts should be undertaken to ensure equitable access to the Internet and e-commerce channels? Do certain online content and activities pose a threat to public safety and welfare?

■ **Identify a process for analyzing ethical dilemmas.**

Ethical, social, and political controversies usually present themselves as dilemmas. Ethical dilemmas can be analyzed via the following process:
- Identify and clearly describe the facts.
- Define the conflict or dilemma and identify the higher-order values involved.
- Identify the stakeholders.
- Identify the options that you can reasonably take.
- Identify the potential consequences of your options.

- Refer to well-established ethical principles, such as the Golden Rule, Universalism, Descartes' Rule of Change, the Collective Utilitarian Principle, Risk Aversion, the No Free Lunch Rule, the *New York Times* Test, and the Social Contract Rule to help you decide the matter.

■ **Understand basic concepts related to privacy.**

To understand the issues concerning online privacy, you must first understand some basic concepts:
- *Privacy* is the moral right of individuals to be left alone, free from surveillance or interference from others.
- *Information privacy* includes both the claim that certain information should not be collected at all by governments or business firms, and the claim of individuals to control the use of information about themselves.
- *Due process* as embodied by the Fair Information Practices doctrine, informed consent, and opt-in/opt-out policies also play an important role in privacy.

■ **Identify the practices of e-commerce companies that threaten privacy.**

Almost all e-commerce companies collect some personally identifiable information in addition to anonymous information and use cookies to track clickstream behavior of visitors. Advertising networks and search engines also track the behavior of consumers across thousands of popular sites, not just at one site, via cookies, spyware, search engine behavioral targeting, and other techniques

■ **Describe the different methods used to protect online privacy.**

There are a number of different methods used to protect online privacy. They include:
- Legal protections deriving from constitutions, common law, federal law, state laws, and government regulations. In the United States, rights to online privacy may be derived from the U.S. Constitution, tort law, federal laws such as the Children's Online Privacy Protection Act (COPPA), the Federal Trade Commission's Fair Information Practice principles, and a variety of state laws. In Europe, the European Commission's Data Protection Directive has standardized and broadened privacy protection in the European Union nations.
- Industry self-regulation via industry alliances, such as the Online Privacy Alliance and the Network Advertising Initiative, that seek to gain voluntary adherence to industry privacy guidelines and safe harbors. Some firms also hire chief privacy officers.
- Privacy-enhancing technological solutions include secure e-mail, anonymous remailers, anonymous surfing, cookie managers, disk file-erasing programs, policy generators, and privacy policy readers.

■ **Understand the various forms of intellectual property and the challenge of protecting it.**

There are three main types of intellectual property protection: copyright, patent, and trademark law.
- *Copyright law* protects original forms of expression such as writings, drawings, and computer programs from being copied by others for a minimum of 70 years. It does not protect ideas—just their expression in a tangible medium. "Look and feel" copyright infringement lawsuits are precisely about the distinction between an idea and its expression. If there is only one way to express an idea,

then the expression cannot be copyrighted. Copyrights, like all rights, are not absolute. The doctrine of fair use permits certain parties under certain circumstances to use copyrighted material without permission. The Digital Millennium Copyright Act (DMCA) is the first major effort to adjust the copyright laws to the Internet age. The DMCA implements a World Intellectual Property Organization treaty, which declares it illegal to make, distribute, or use devices that circumvent technology-based protections of copyrighted materials, and attaches stiff fines and prison sentences for violations.

- *Patent law* grants the owner of a patent an exclusive monopoly to the ideas behind an invention for 20 years. Patents are very different from copyrights in that they protect the ideas themselves and not merely the expression of ideas. There are four types of inventions for which patents are granted under patent law: machines, man-made products, compositions of matter, and processing methods. In order to be granted a patent, the applicant must show that the invention is new, original, novel, non-obvious, and not evident in prior arts and practice. Most of the inventions that make the Internet and e-commerce possible were not patented by their inventors. This changed in the mid-1990s with the commercial development of the World Wide Web. Business firms began applying for "business methods" and software patents.

- *Trademark protections* exist at both the federal and state levels in the United States. The purpose of trademark law is twofold. First, trademark law protects the public in the marketplace by ensuring that it gets what it pays for and wants to receive. Second, trademark law protects the owner who has spent time, money, and energy bringing the product to market against piracy and misappropriation. Federal trademarks are obtained, first, by use in interstate commerce, and second, by registration with the U.S. Patent and Trademark Office (USPTO). Trademarks are granted for a period of 10 years and can be renewed indefinitely. Use of a trademark that creates confusion with existing trademarks, causes consumers to make market mistakes, or misrepresents the origins of goods is an infringement. In addition, the intentional misuse of words and symbols in the marketplace to extort revenue from legitimate trademark owners ("bad faith") is proscribed. The Anticybersquatting Consumer Protection Act (ACPA) creates civil liabilities for anyone who attempts in bad faith to profit from an existing famous or distinctive trademark by registering an Internet domain name that is identical, confusingly similar, or "dilutive" of that trademark. Trademark abuse can take many forms on the Web. The major behaviors on the Internet that have run afoul of trademark law include cybersquatting, cyberpiracy, metatagging, keywording, linking, and framing.

■ **Understand how governance of the Internet has evolved over time.**

Governance has to do with social control: who will control e-commerce, what elements will be controlled, and how the controls will be implemented. Governance of both the Internet and e-commerce has gone through four stages:

- *Government control (1970–1994).* During this period, DARPA and the National Science Foundation controlled the Internet as a fully government funded program.
- *Privatization (1995–1998).* Network Solutions was given a monopoly to assign and track high-level Internet domain names. The backbone was sold to private telecommunications companies and policy issues remained undecided.

- *Self-regulation (1995–present).* President Clinton and the Department of Commerce encouraged creation of ICANN, a semi-private body, to deal with emerging conflicts and to establish policies.
- *Governmental regulation (1998–present).* Executive, legislative, and judicial bodies worldwide began to implement direct controls over the Internet and e-commerce.

We are currently in a mixed-mode policy environment where self-regulation, through a variety of Internet policy and technical bodies, co-exists with limited government regulation.

■ Explain why taxation of e-commerce raises governance and jurisdiction issues.

E-commerce raises the issue of how—and if—to tax remote sales. The national and international character of Internet sales is wreaking havoc on taxation schemes in the United States that were built in the 1930s and based on local commerce and local jurisdictions. E-commerce has benefited from a tax subsidy since its inception. E-commerce merchants have argued that this new form of commerce needs to be nurtured and encouraged, and that in any event, the crazy quilt of sales and use tax regimes would be difficult to administer for Internet merchants. In 1998, Congress passed the Internet Tax Freedom Act, which placed a moratorium on multiple or discriminatory taxes on electronic commerce, and any taxation of Internet access, and since that time has extended the moratorium three times, most recently until November 2014. In November 2002, delegates from 32 states approved model legislation designed to create a system to tax Web sales, and by 2007, 15 states had agreed to support the program. Although there appears to be acquiescence among large Internet retailers to the idea of some kind of sales tax on e-commerce sales, insistence on uniformity will delay taxation for many years, and any proposal to tax e-commerce will likely incur the wrath of U.S. e-commerce consumers.

■ Identify major public safety and welfare issues raised by e-commerce.

Critical public safety and welfare issues in e-commerce include:
- The protection of children and strong sentiments against pornography. The Children's Online Protection Act (COPA) of 1998 made it a felony criminal offense to communicate for commercial purposes any material harmful to minors. This law has thus far been struck down as an unconstitutional restriction on Web content that is protected under the First Amendment. The Children's Internet Protection Act (CIPA), which requires schools and libraries in the United States to install "technology protection measures" (filtering software) in an effort to shield children from pornography, has however, been upheld by the Supreme Court. In addition to government regulation, private pressure from organized groups has also been successful in forcing some Web sites to eliminate the display of pornographic materials.
- Efforts to control gambling and restrict sales of cigarettes and drugs. In the United States, cigarettes, gambling, medical drugs, and addictive recreational drugs are either banned or tightly regulated by federal and state laws. Yet these products and services are often distributed via offshore e-commerce sites operating beyond the jurisdiction of federal and state prosecutors. At this point, it is not clear that the Web will remain borderless or that e-commerce can continue to flaunt national, state, and local laws with impunity.

## QUESTIONS

1. What basic assumption does the study of ethics make about individuals?
2. What are the three basic principles of ethics? How does due process factor in?
3. Explain Google's position that YouTube does not violate the intellectual property rights of copyright owners.
4. Define universalism, slippery slope, the *New York Times* test, and the social contract rule as they apply to ethics.
5. Explain why someone with a serious medical condition might be concerned about researching his or her condition online, through medical search engines or pharmaceutical sites, for example. What is one technology that could prevent one's identity from being revealed?
6. Name some of the personal information collected by Web sites about their visitors.
7. How does information collected through online forms differ from site transaction logs? Which potentially provides a more complete consumer profile?
8. How is the opt-in model of informed consent different from opt-out? In which type of model does the consumer retain more control?
9. What are the two core principles of the FTC's Fair Information Practice principles?
10. How do safe harbors work? What is the government's role in them?
11. Name three ways online advertising networks have improved on, or added to, traditional offline marketing techniques.
12. Explain how Web profiling is supposed to benefit both consumers and businesses.
13. What are some of the challenges that chief privacy officers (CPOs) face in their jobs?
14. How could the Internet potentially change protection given to intellectual property? What capabilities make it more difficult to enforce intellectual property law?
15. What does the Digital Millennium Copyright Act attempt to do? Why was it enacted? What types of violations does it try to prevent?
16. Define cybersquatting. How is it different from cyberpiracy? What type of intellectual property violation does cybersquatting entail?
17. What is deep linking and why is it a trademark issue? Compare it to framing—how is it similar and different?
18. What are some of the tactics illegal businesses, such as betting parlors and casinos, successfully use to operate outside the law on the Internet?

## PROJECTS

1. Go to Google and click on Search > Search Settings (at the upper-right corner of the home page). Examine its SafeSearch filtering options available on the Preferences page. Surf the Web in search of content that could be considered objectionable for children using each of the options. What are the pros and cons of such restrictions? Are there terms that could be considered inappropriate to the filtering software but be approved by parents? Name five questionable terms. Prepare a brief presentation to report on your experiences and to explain the positive and negative aspects of such filtering software.

2. Develop a list a privacy protection features that should be present if a Web site is serious about protecting privacy. Then, visit at least four well-known Web sites and examine their privacy policies. Write a report that rates each of the Web sites on the criteria you have developed.

3. Review the provisions of the Digital Millennium Copyright Act of 1998. Examine each of the major sections of the legislation and make a list of the protections afforded property owners and users of copyrighted materials. Do you believe this legislation balances the interests of owners and users appropriately? Do you have suggestions for strengthening "fair use" provisions in this legislation?

4. Visit at least four Web sites that take a position on e-commerce taxation, beginning with the National Conference of State Legislatures (Ncsl.org) and the National Governor's Association (Nga.org). You might also include national associations of local businesses or citizen groups opposed to e-commerce taxation. Develop a reasoned argument for, or against, taxation of e-commerce.

5. Consider the issue of the Department of Justice's subpoena of search query records discussed on page 556. Prepare a list of reasons why the firms subpoenaed should or should not have complied with this request. What moral dilemmas are presented? What higher-order values, and what kind of value conflicts, are revealed in this list? How do you propose that we as a society resolve these dilemmas? You might conclude by applying each of the Candidate Ethical Principles described in Section 8.1.

6. The opening case describes the virtual world created by Second Life. Find another virtual world on the Web and compare and contrast it to the features offered by Second Life. Prepare a brief presentation or report on your findings.

# E-commerce in Action

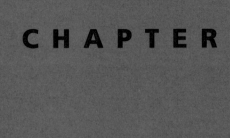

# CHAPTER 9

# Online Retail and Services

**After reading this chapter, you will be able to:**

- Understand the environment in which the online retail sector operates today.
- Explain how to analyze the economic viability of an online firm.
- Identify the challenges faced by the different types of online retailers.
- Describe the major features of the online service sector.
- Discuss the trends taking place in the online financial services industry.
- Describe the major trends in the online travel services industry today.
- Identify current trends in the online career services industry.

# Blue Nile Sparkles
## for Your Cleopatra

**M**en: looking for that special gift for your Cleopatra, but don't want to spend a lot of time shopping? Want to give the "Big Rock" certified by the independent Gemological Institute of America (GIA) or the American Gem Society Laboratories (AGSL) without spending a mountain of cash for the engagement experience? How about 35% less than retail prices? Not sure about the future value of diamonds? Then how about pearls, gold, or platinum?

Your answer has arrived: BlueNile.com offers you an online selection of about 60,000 diamonds for that special someone. You can buy them cut and polished, or put them into settings like rings, bracelets, earrings, necklaces, pendants, watches, and broaches that you can choose online. All the diamonds are graded by the 4Cs: carats (size), cut, color, and clarity, and a report for each diamond prepared by the GIA is available online. To make it easier, fellas, the carats are translated into milligrams, and one carat is exactly 200 milligrams of mass (if that helps). Just ask her what size she wants, and then look in your wallet. Although the majority of visitors to the site are women, about 85% of Blue Niles customers are men.

In June 2007, Blue Nile sold the biggest item in Internet history, a $1.5 million single diamond of around 10 carats, a size that would cover your finger with a penny-size rock. That's about 2,000 milligrams, the biggest mouse click ever. The mouse that roared?

BlueNile.com started out as RockShop.com in March 1999 in Seattle, Washington. In May 1999, the company purchased Williams and Son, a Seattle jeweler with a Web site, and changed its name to Internet Diamonds, Inc. In November 1999, the company launched the Blue Nile brand and changed its name to Blue Nile Inc., opening up its Web site, BlueNile.com, in December 1999. In May 2004, Blue Nile went public at $20, and jumped to $28 (a 38% pop) in the first day of trading. The received wisdom of Web gurus in 1999 was that the Internet would never be a place where fine jewelry could be sold. Why? CDs and books are what everyone thought the Web was good at back then.

Purchasing jewelry, especially high-cost diamonds, is what marketers call a "significant event." Typically, gifts of diamonds are associated with a significant emotional event, such as an engagement, marriage, or an anniversary. Generally, the event is shared with a significant other and often involves shopping together for the gem. Shopping on the Web (alone or together) hardly matches the emotional impact of walking into Tiffany's or another established retail store, with marvelous clear glass cases filled with brilliantly shining baubles, attended by a small army of unctuous perfumed sales clerks that make you feel so special. Diamonds represent a significant cost, and there is significant uncertainty about their value and pricing. Surveys show that most shoppers believe jewelry is highly overpriced, but they lack the knowledge and information to negotiate a better price or even judge the quality of what they are buying. Consumers generally have no rational way to compare diamonds, and face a limited selection at a single store, often in a high-pressured environment where sales employees are helping several customers at the same time. Most experts thought that, given the emotional significance and uncertainty of purchasing diamonds, few consumers would heighten the built-in anxiety by going to a strange Web site and plunking down $5,000 or more for a diamond they could not see or touch for several days.

But jewelry and high fashion retailers are leading the second act of online retailing, bursting on the scene in 2004 with high growth rates and spectacular average sales transaction levels. As it turns out, the retail jewelry industry is an ideal candidate for Web sales. Here's why.

The $60 billion traditional jewelry industry is a byzantine, fragmented collection of over 50,000 physical stores in the United States. About 95% of all retail jewelry firms operate only a single store. To supply this fragmented market, several layers of wholesalers and middlemen intervene, from rough diamond brokers to diamond cutters, diamond wholesalers, jewelry manufacturers, jewelry wholesalers, and finally, regional distributors. Oddly, the source of raw mined diamonds is monopolized by a single company, De Beers, which controls over two-thirds of the world market. The fragmented supply and distribution chains add to huge markups based on monopoly-set prices for the raw diamonds. Currently, the typical retail store markup for diamonds is between 50% and 100%. Blue Nile's markup is around 30%.

Although in 2008 and early 2009, the entire jewelry industry was hit hard by the recession as wealthy buyers and young lovers cut back their purchases, by the second half of 2009, sales had begun to rebound. For fiscal 2009, Blue Nile's revenues were $302 million, up 2.3% from $295 million in 2008. Net income also increased, to $12.8 million in 2009 from $11.6 million in 2008. International sales (in more than 40 countries worldwide) continued to be a bright spot, growing almost 20%, and accounting for almost 11% of total sales. In the first half of 2010, sales continued to increase by over 14% compared to the prior year, and international sales continued at record pace, up by almost 50%.

Blue Nile's main competitor is Bidz.com, a Web jewelry discount site. Other competitors include Tiffany.com and Ice.com, and even Amazon. Together, these companies are transforming the byzantine jewelry business. Blue Nile, for instance, has simplified the supply-side of diamonds by only ordering and paying for a diamond after the customer has ordered it. Blue Nile has cut out several supply-side layers of middlemen and instead deals directly with wholesale diamond owners and jewelry manufacturers.

Blue Nile minimizes its inventory costs and limits its risk of inventory markdowns. On the sell side of distribution, Blue Nile has eliminated the expensive stores, sales clerks, and beautiful but expensive glass cases. Instead, Blue Nile offers a single Web site at which it can aggregate the demand of thousands of unique visitors for diamonds and present them with a more attractive shopping experience than a typical retail store. The result of rationalizing the supply and distribution chain is much lower markups. For example, Blue Nile will purchase a pair of oval emerald and diamond earrings from a supplier for $850 and charge the consumer $1,020. A traditional retailer would charge the consumer $1,258.

Blue Nile has improved the shopping experience primarily by creating a trust- and knowledge-based environment that reduces consumer anxiety about the value of diamonds. In essence, Blue Nile and the other online retailers give the consumer as much information as a professional gemologist would give them. The Web site contains educational guides to diamonds and diamond grading systems, and provides independent quality ratings for each diamond provided by non-profit industry associations, such as the GIA. There's a 30-day, money-back, no-questions-asked guarantee. According to CEO Diane Irvine, the company's focus is "empowering the customer with information." And empower they do. The average customer visits the Web site repeatedly over a several week period, views at least 200 pages, and typically calls Blue Nile's live customer service line at least once.

In 2009, for the first time in a decade, Blue Nile rebuilt its Web site, strengthening its appeal to its mostly male customer base while at the same time attempting to draw more women to the site. The new site removed the left menu so common to older Web designs, enlarged the pictures, added visualization software so visitors can see the jewelry with shadows and sparkles, expanded the product detail, and improved the search engine. The site's "Build Your Own Ring" feature has a new layout that's easier to use and to see more precisely what you're building. Blue Nile also added functionality to the Web site that allows customers to transact in their local currency, and now supports 24 different currencies in addition to the U.S. dollar.

Despite its lower gross margins due to its low prices, Blue Nile has higher net operating margins than its chief offline physical store competitor, Zales Inc., the country's largest jewelry chain. To get an idea of Blue Nile's efficiency, in order to sell $300 million in jewelry, a traditional physical store chain such as Zales would need around 300 stores. Blue Nile achieves $300 million in sales with three Web sites, two warehouses, and 180 workers.

So far the "Blue Nile" effect of lower margins and Internet efficiency has mainly impacted the small mom and pop jewelry stores. About 3,000 small retailers have disappeared in the last few years for a variety of reasons. The big retailers, such as Tiffany, Zales, and others, sell more than Blue Nile, and continue to benefit from consumer interest in diamond engagement and wedding rings. Both Tiffany and Zales have online Web sites. Tiffany's site is primarily a branding site, but it has greatly improved its online graphics and online sales capabilities. The Zales site is a much more effective sales site than Tiffany's, with a marvelous build-a-ring capability, but still not quite up to the level of Blue Nile with respect to certification. Still, the success of Blue Nile, and the size of its competitors, mean that Blue Nile will have to keep a keen watch on its competitors who are not far behind. But for now, the future of Blue Nile looks, well, sparkling.

**SOURCES:** "Selling Information, Not Diamonds," by Kaihan Krippendorf, Fastcompany.com, September 1, 2010; "Blue Nile Sparkles," by Kaihan Krippendorf, Fastcompany.com, August 30, 2010; Blue Nile Inc. Report on Form 10-Q for the fiscal quarter ended July 4, 2010, filed with the Securities and Exchange Commission on August 11, 2010; Blue Nile Inc. Report on Form 10-K for the fiscal year ended January 3, 2010, filed with the Securities and Exchange Commission on February 25, 2010; "Digital Bling: Diamonds For Sale Online," by Wendy Kaufman, NPR.org, February 14, 2010; "Blue Nile Gets Makover to Please Ladies," by Geoffrey Fowler, *Wall Street Journal*, September 1, 2009; "New Blue Site Hits Web," *New York Times*, September 1, 2009; "Blue Niles Aims to Sparkle With Re-designed Web Site," *Internet Retailer*, September 1, 2009; "Blue Nile: A Guy's Best Friend," by Jay Greene, *Business Week*, May 29, 2008.

The Blue Nile case illustrates some of the advantages that a pure-play, start-up retail company has over traditional offline retailers, and some of the disadvantages. A pure-play consumer service company can radically simplify the existing industry supply chain and develop an entirely new Web-based distribution system that is far more efficient than traditional retail outlets. At the same time, an online pure-play retailer can create a better value proposition for the customer, improving customer service and satisfaction in the process. On the other hand, pure-play start-up companies often have razor-thin profit margins, lack a physical store network to bolster sales to the non-Internet audience, and are often based on unproven business assumptions that, in the long term may not prove out. In contrast, large offline retailers, such as Wal-Mart, JCPenney, Sears, and Target, have established brand names, a huge real estate investment, a loyal customer base, and extraordinarily efficient inventory control and fulfillment systems. As we shall see in this chapter, traditional offline catalog merchants are even more advantaged. We will also see that, in order to leverage their assets and core competencies, established offline retailers need to cultivate new competencies and a carefully developed business plan to succeed on the Web.

As with retail goods, the promise of pure-online service providers is that they can deliver superior-quality service and greater convenience to millions of consumers at a lower cost than established bricks-and-mortar service providers, and still make a respectable return on invested capital. The service sector is one of the most natural avenues for e-commerce because so much of the value in services is based on collecting, storing, and exchanging information—something for which the Web is ideally suited. And, in fact, online services have been extraordinarily successful in attracting banking, brokerage, travel, and job-hunting customers. The quality and amount of information online to support consumer decisions in finance, travel, and career placement is extraordinary, especially when compared to what was available to consumers before e-commerce.

The online service sector—like online retail—has shown both explosive growth and some recent impressive failures. Despite the failures, online services have established a significant beachhead and are coming to play a large role in consumer time on the Internet. In areas such as brokerage, banking, and travel, online services are an extraordinary success story, and are transforming their industries. As with the retail sector, many of the early innovators—delivery services such as Kozmo and WebVan and consulting firms such as BizConsult.com—are gone. However, some early innovators, such as E*Trade, Schwab, Expedia, and Monster, have been successful, while many established service providers, such as Citigroup, JPMorgan Chase, Wells Fargo, Bank of America, and the large airlines, have developed successful online e-commerce service delivery sites. In Sections 9.5–9.7 of this chapter, we take a close at three of these most successful online services: financial services (including insurance and real estate), travel services, and career services.

## 9.1 THE ONLINE RETAIL SECTOR

**Table 9.1** summarizes some of these leading trends in online retailing for 2010–2011. Perhaps the most important theme in online retailing is the effort by retailers—both offline and online—to integrate their operations so they can serve customers in the various ways they want to be served.

By any measure, the size of the U.S. retail market is huge. In a $14.2 trillion economy, personal consumption of retail goods and services accounts for $10 trillion (about 70%) of the total gross domestic product (GDP)—or over two-thirds of all economic activity (U.S. Census Bureau, 2010).

---

**TABLE 9.1    WHAT'S NEW IN ONLINE RETAIL, 2010–2011**

- Continued rapid growth in social networks and user-generated content sites encourages "social shopping," where users pass on their opinions and recommendations to others in several online viral networks.

- Despite the recession in 2010, the number of online buyers increased by 6% to 133 million, and the average annual purchase is up 5% to $1,139. Amazon's sales grew by 28% in the year.

- Online retailers remain generally profitable, despite the recession, by focusing on revenue growth, increasing the size of average purchase amounts, and improving efficiency of operations.

- Online retail remains the fastest growing retail channel, and in 2010 surpassed the mail order/telephone order (MOTO) catalog sales channel.

- Buying online has become a normal, mainstream, everyday experience. Around 87% of Internet users in the United States are now online shoppers.

- The selection of goods for purchase online continues to increase to include luxury goods, such as jewelry, gourmet groceries, furniture, and wine, as customer trust and experience increase.

- Informational shopping for big-ticket items such as cars and appliances continues to expand rapidly to include nearly all retail goods (both durables and non-durables).

- Specialty retail sites show the most rapid growth in online retail as they develop customized retail goods and customer online configuration of goods.

- Online retailers place an increased emphasis on providing an improved "shopping experience," including ease of navigation and use, online inventory updates, interactive tools, customer feedback and ratings and social shopping opportunities.

- Online retailers increase the use of interactive multimedia marketing technologies and Web 2.0 techniques such as blogs, user-generated content, and video that exploit the dominance of broadband connections and offer features such as zoom, color switch, product configuration, and virtual simulations of households and businesses.

- Retail intermediaries strengthen in many areas, including groceries, automobiles, appliance, and furniture dealers.

- Retailers become increasingly efficient in integrating multiple retailing channels, beyond "bricks-and-clicks" to "click-and-drive" and in-store Web kiosk ordering.

- More than half of online shopping and nearly a third of online purchases occur at work. However, growth of at-home broadband connections increases, making evening purchases from home the fastest growing time segment for retail purchases online, relieving some pressure on workplace purchasing.

If we examine the personal consumption sector more closely, we find that about 61% of personal consumption is for services, 10% is for durable goods, and 29% is for nondurable goods. Services include medical, educational, financial, and food services. **Durable goods** are those that are consumed over a longer period of time (generally more than a year), such as automobiles, appliances, and furniture. **Nondurable goods** are consumed quickly and have shorter life spans, and include general merchandise, clothing, music, drugs, and groceries.

**durable goods**
goods that are consumed over a longer period of time (generally more than a year)

**nondurable goods**
goods that are consumed quickly and have shorter life spans

The distinction between a "good" and a "service" is not always clear-cut, and is becoming more ambiguous over time. Increasingly, manufacturers and retailers of physical goods sell support services that add value to the physical product. It is difficult to think of a sophisticated physical good that does not include significant services in the purchase price. The movement toward "product-based services" can be seen in the packaged software market. Microsoft offers purchasers of its Windows and Office suite products additional value-added services from a variety of Microsoft Web sites. Charging for services, particularly on a monthly subscription basis, can be highly profitable. For instance, warranties, insurance policies, after-sale repairs, and purchase loans are increasingly a large source of revenue for manufacturers and retailers. Nevertheless, in this chapter, retail goods refer to physical products, and retailers refer to firms that sell physical goods to consumers, recognizing that retail goods include many services.

## THE RETAIL INDUSTRY

The retail industry is composed of many different types of firms. **Figure 9.1** divides the retail industry into 8 segments: durable goods, general merchandise, food and beverage, specialty stores, gasoline and fuel, eating and drinking, MOTO, and online retail firms.

Each of these segments offers opportunities for online retail, and yet in each segment, the uses of the Internet may differ. Some eating and drinking establishments use the Web to inform people of their physical locations and menus, while others offer delivery via Web orders (although this has not been a successful model). Retailers of durable goods typically use the Web as an informational tool rather than as a direct purchasing tool, although this is beginning to change as consumers have begun to purchase furniture and building supplies over the Internet. For instance, automobile manufacturers still do not sell cars over the Web, but they do provide information to assist customers in choosing among competing models. In fact, almost 90% of the respondents in a 2009 survey said that they viewed products, services, and rates on company or dealership Web sites when comparison shopping for a car (Microsoft, 2009).

The largest segment of the U.S. retail market is consumer durables, followed by general merchandise. These segments, particularly general merchandise, are highly concentrated, with large firms dominating sales. These very large firms have developed highly automated real-time inventory control systems (systems that collect point-of-sale data from cash registers, update inventory records, and inform vendors of stock levels), large national customer bases, and customer databases containing detailed purchasing information.

| FIGURE 9.1 | COMPOSITION OF THE U.S. RETAIL INDUSTRY |
| --- | --- |

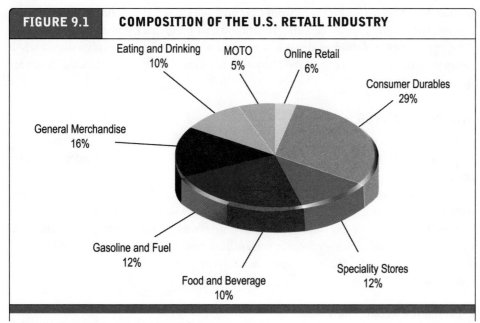

The retail industry can be grouped into eight major segments.

SOURCE: Based on data from U.S. Census Bureau, 2010.

General merchandisers have always competed against a more traditional form of retail commerce called specialty retailers. In fact, modern retail trade began as a collection of small retail shops in a concentrated location that customers visited in serial order. Shopping used to mean a visit to a shoemaker, dressmaker, pharmacy, butcher, and dry goods store. While mass-market general department stores were the fastest growing form of retail commerce for most of the twentieth century, in the 1960s, boutique and specialty stores catering to much smaller market segments with higher priced goods became the fastest growing form of physical retail stores. Stores such as The Gap, Banana Republic, Athlete's Foot, Sports Authority, Victoria's Secret, Staples, and many others developed national and international chain store strategies based on upscale youth market segments. The success of specialty retailing depends on building unique products for a market segment, offering strong customer service, and providing a persuasive shopping experience to support the brand image.

The MOTO sector is the most similar to the online retail sales sector. In the absence of physical stores, MOTO retailers distribute millions of physical catalogs (their largest expense) and operate large telephone call centers to accept orders. They have developed extraordinarily efficient order fulfillment centers that generally ship customer orders within 24 hours of receipt. MOTO was the fastest growing retail segment throughout the 1970s and 1980s. It grew as a direct result of improvements in the national toll-free call system, the implementation of digital switching in telephone systems, falling long distance telecommunications prices, and of course, the expansion of the credit card industry and associated technologies, without which neither MOTO nor e-commerce would be possible on a large national scale. MOTO was the last "technological" retailing revolution that preceded e-commerce. Because of their experience in fulfilling small orders rapidly, MOTO firms are advantaged when competing in e-commerce, and the transition to e-commerce has not been difficult for these firms.

## ONLINE RETAILING

Online retail is perhaps the most high-profile sector of e-commerce on the Web. Over the past decade, this sector has experienced both explosive growth and spectacular failures.

Many of the early pure-play online-only firms that pioneered the retail marketspace failed. Entrepreneurs and their investors seriously misjudged the factors needed to succeed in this market. But the survivors of this early period emerged much stronger, and along with traditional offline general and specialty merchants, as well as new start-ups, the e-tail space is growing very rapidly and is increasing its reach and size.

### E-commerce Retail: The Vision

In the early years of e-commerce, literally thousands of entrepreneurial Web-based retailers were drawn to the marketplace for retail goods, simply because it was one of the largest market opportunities in the U.S. economy. Many entrepreneurs initially believed it was easy to enter the retail market. Early writers predicted that the retail industry would be revolutionized, literally "blown to bits"—as prophesized by two consultants in a famous Harvard Business School book (Evans and Wurster, 2000). The basis of this revolution would be fourfold. First, because the Internet greatly reduced both search costs and transaction costs, consumers would use the Web to find the lowest-cost products. Several results would follow. Consumers would increasingly drift to the Web for shopping and purchasing, and only low-cost, high-service, quality online retail merchants would survive. Economists assumed that the Web consumer was rational and cost-driven—not driven by perceived value or brand, both of which are nonrational factors.

Second, it was assumed that the entry costs to the online retail market were much less than those needed to establish physical storefronts, and that online merchants were inherently more efficient at marketing and order fulfillment than offline stores. The costs of establishing a powerful Web site were thought to be minuscule compared to the costs of warehouses, fulfillment centers, and physical stores. There would be no difficulty building sophisticated order entry, shopping cart, and fulfillment systems because this technology was well known, and the cost of technology was falling by 50% each year. Even the cost of acquiring consumers was thought to be much lower on the Web because of search engines that could almost instantly connect customers to online vendors.

Third, as prices fell, traditional offline physical store merchants would be forced out of business. New entrepreneurial companies—such as Amazon—would replace the traditional stores. It was thought that if online merchants grew very quickly, they would have first-mover advantages and lock out the older traditional firms that were too slow to enter the online market.

Fourth, in some industries—such as electronics, apparel, and digital content—the market would be disintermediated as manufacturers or their distributors entered to build a direct relationship with the consumer, destroying the retail intermediaries or middlemen. In this scenario, traditional retail channels—such as physical stores, sales clerks, and sales forces—would be replaced by a single dominant channel: the Web.

Many predicted, on the other hand, a kind of hypermediation based on the concept of a virtual firm in which online retailers would gain advantage over established offline merchants by building an online brand name that attracted millions of customers, and outsourcing the expensive warehousing and order fulfillment functions—the original concept of Amazon and Drugstore.com.

As it turned out, few of these assumptions and visions were correct, and the structure of the retail marketplace in the United States, with some notable exceptions, has not been blown to bits, disintermediated, or revolutionized in the traditional meaning of the word revolution. With several notable exceptions, online retail has often not been successful as an independent platform on which to build a successful "pure-play" Web-only business. As it turns out, the consumer is not primarily price-driven when shopping on the Internet but instead considers brand name, trust, reliability, and delivery time as at least as important as price (Brynjolfsson, Dick, and Smith, 2004).

However, the Internet has created an entirely new venue for multi-channel firms that have a strong offline brand, and in some cases, the Internet has supported the development of pure-play online-only merchants, both general merchandisers as well as specialty retailers. As predicted, online retail has indeed become the fastest growing and most dynamic retail channel in the sense of channel innovation. The Web has created a new marketplace for millions of consumers to conveniently shop. The Internet and Web have continued to provide new opportunities for entirely new firms using new business models and new online products—such as Blue Nile, as previously described. The new online channel can conflict with a merchant's other channels, such as direct sales forces, physical stores, and mail order, but this multi-channel conflict can be managed and turned into a strength.

## The Online Retail Sector Today

Although online retailing is one of the smallest segments of the retail industry, constituting about 6% of the total retail market today, it is growing at a faster rate than its offline counterparts, with new functionality and product lines being added every day (see **Figure 9.2**). Due to the recession, online retail revenues were basically flat in 2009 compared to 2008, but they are expected to resume their upward trajectory at the rate of 10%–15% a year during the period between 2010 and 2014. When we refer to online retail, we will not be including online services revenues such as travel, job-hunting, or the purchase of digital downloads such as software applications and music. Instead, for the purposes of this chapter, online retail refers solely to sales of physical goods over the Internet. The Internet provides a number of

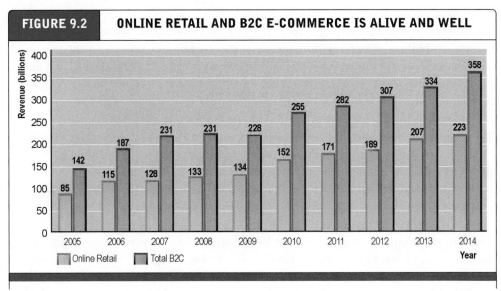

**FIGURE 9.2    ONLINE RETAIL AND B2C E-COMMERCE IS ALIVE AND WELL**

Online retail revenues were flat in 2008–2009, but are expected to reach $152 billion by 2010 and $223 billion by 2014. Total B2C e-commerce revenues (including travel, other services and digital downloads) are projected to reach around $358 billion by 2014.

SOURCES: Based on data from eMarketer, 2010a; author estimates.

unique advantages and challenges to online retailers. **Table 9.2** summarizes these advantages and challenges.

Despite the high failure rate of online retailers in the early years, more consumers than ever are shopping online. For most consumers, the advantages of shopping on the Web overcome the disadvantages. In 2010, it is estimated that around 72% of Internet users over the age of 14 (around 133.5 million people) will buy at an online retail store, generating about $152 billion in online retail sales. While the number of new Internet users in the United States is not growing as rapidly at it was, with around 71% of the U.S. population already on the Internet, this slowdown will not necessarily slow the growth in online retail e-commerce because the average shopper is spending more on the Internet each year, and finding many new categories of items to buy. For instance, in 2003, the average annual amount spent online by users was $675, but by 2010, it had jumped to $1,139 (eMarketer, Inc., 2010a, 2005). Also, as noted in Chapter 6, millions of additional consumers research products on the Web and are influenced in their purchase decisions at offline stores.

The primary beneficiaries of this growing consumer support are not only the pure online companies, but also the established offline retailers who have the brand-name recognition, supportive infrastructure, and financial resources to enter the online marketplace successfully. Table 1.7 on page 42 lists the top online retail firms ranked by online sales. The list contains pure-play online retailers for whom the Internet is the only sales channel, such as Amazon (in first place) and Newegg (in 11th); multi-channel firms that have established brand names and for whom e-commerce plays a relatively small role when compared to their offline physical store channels, such as Staples (2nd), Office Depot (5th), Wal-Mart (6th), OfficeMax (7th), Sears (8th), Best Buy (10th),

| TABLE 9.2 | ADVANTAGES AND CHALLENGES TO ONLINE RETAIL |
|---|---|
| **ADVANTAGES** | **CHALLENGES** |
| Lower supply chain costs by aggregating demand at a single site and increasing purchasing power | Consumer concerns about the security of transactions |
| Lower cost of distribution using Web sites rather than physical stores | Consumer concerns about the privacy of personal information given to Web sites |
| Ability to reach and serve a much larger geographically distributed group of customers | Delays in delivery of goods when compared to store shopping |
| Ability to react quickly to customer tastes and demand | Inconvenience associated with return damaged or exchange goods |
| Ability to change prices nearly instantly | Overcoming lack of consumer trust in online brand names |
| Ability to rapidly change visual presentation of goods | Added expenses for online photography, video and animated presentations |
| Avoidance of direct marketing costs of catalogs and physical mail | Online marketing costs for search, e-mail, and displays |
| Increased opportunities for personalization, customization | Added complexity to product offerings and customer service |
| Ability to greatly improve information and knowledge delivered to consumer | Greater customer information can translate into price competition and lower profits |
| Ability to lower consumers' overall market transaction costs | |

JCPenney (17th), and manufacturers of computer and electronic equipment, such as Dell (3rd), Apple (4th), and Sony (14th). The top 15 retailers account for over 40% of all online retail. For pure-play firms heavily dependent on Web sales, the challenge is to turn visitors into customers, and to develop efficient operations that permit them to achieve long-term profitability. For traditional firms that are much less dependent on e-commerce sales, their challenge is to integrate the offline and online channels so customers can move seamlessly from one environment to another.

## Multi-Channel Integration

Clearly one of the most important e-commerce retail themes of 2010–2011 and into the future, is the ability of offline traditional firms such as Wal-Mart, Target, JCPenney, Staples, and others to continue to integrate their Web operations with their physical store operations in order to provide an "integrated shopping customer experience," and leverage the value of their physical stores. **Table 9.3** illustrates some of the various ways in which traditional retailers have integrated the Web and store operations to develop nearly seamless multi-channel shopping. This list is not exclusive, and retailers continue to develop new links between channels.

Another important part of the multi-channel strategy is the growing importance of mobile commerce. In 2010, mobile commerce finally became a significant factor in

| TABLE 9.3 | RETAIL E-COMMERCE: MULTI-CHANNEL INTEGRATION METHODS |
|---|---|
| **INTEGRATION TYPE** | **DESCRIPTION** |
| Online order, in-store pickup | Probably one of the first types of integration. |
| Online order, store directory and inventory | When items are out of stock online, customer is directed to physical store network inventory and store location. |
| In-store kiosk Web order, home delivery | When retail store is out of stock, customer orders in store and receives at home. Presumes customer is Web familiar. |
| In-store retail clerk Web order, home delivery | Similar to above, but the retail clerk searches Web inventory if local store is out of stock as a normal part of the in-store check out process. |
| Web order, in-store returns and adjustments | Defective or rejected products ordered on the Web can be returned to any store location. |
| Online Web catalog | Online Web catalog supplements offline physical catalog and often the online catalog has substantially more product on display. |
| Manufacturers use online Web site promotions to drive customers to their distributors' retail stores | Consumer product manufacturers such as Colgate-Palmolive and Procter & Gamble use their Web channels to design new products and promote existing product retail sales. |
| Gift card, loyalty program points can be used in any channel | Recipient of gift card, loyalty program points can use it to purchase in-store, online, or via catalog, if offered by merchant. |

the online retail landscape. Consumers have begun to move beyond browsing and comparing prices, and are now buying. For instance, eBay reported $600 million in sales via its iPhone app and m-commerce site in 2009, and estimates that sales will reach $1.5 billion in 2010 (Internet Retailer, 2010). Retailers are anticipating significant continued growth into 2011 and beyond.

Rather than demonstrate disintermediation, online retailing provides an example of the powerful role that intermediaries continue to play in retail trade. Established offline retailers have rapidly gained online market share. Increasingly, consumers are attracted to stable, well-known, trusted retail brands and retailers. The online audience is very sensitive to brand names (as described in Chapter 6) and is not primarily cost-driven. Other factors such as reliability, trust, fulfillment, and customer service are equally important.

## 9.2 ANALYZING THE VIABILITY OF ONLINE FIRMS

In this and the following chapters, we analyze the viability of a number of online companies that exemplify specific e-commerce models. We are primarily interested in understanding the near-to-medium term (1–3 years) economic viability of these firms and their business models. **Economic viability** refers to the ability of firms to survive as profitable business firms during the specified period. To answer the question of economic viability, we take two business analysis approaches: strategic analysis and financial analysis.

**economic viability**
refers to the ability of firms to survive as profitable business firms during a specified period

## STRATEGIC ANALYSIS

Strategic approaches to economic viability focus on both the industry in which a firm operates and the firm itself (see Chapter 2, Sections 2.2 and 2.5). The key industry strategic factors are:

- *Barriers to entry*: Can new entrants be barred from entering the industry through high capital costs or intellectual property barriers (such as patents and copyrights)?

- *Power of suppliers*: Can suppliers dictate high prices to the industry or can vendors choose from among many suppliers? Have firms achieved sufficient scale to bargain effectively for lower prices from suppliers?

- *Power of customers*: Can customers choose from many competing suppliers and hence challenge high prices and high margins?

- *Existence of substitute products*: Can the functionality of the product or service be obtained from alternative channels or competing products in different industries? Are substitute products and services likely to emerge in the near future?

- *Industry value chain*: Is the chain of production and distribution in the industry changing in ways that benefit or harm the firm?

- *Nature of intra-industry competition*: Is the basis of competition within the industry based on differentiated products and services, price, scope of offerings, or focus of offerings? How is the nature of competition changing? Will these changes benefit the firm?

The strategic factors that pertain specifically to the firm and its related businesses include:

- *Firm value chain*: Has the firm adopted business processes and methods of operation that allow it to achieve the most efficient operations in its industry? Will changes in technology force the firm to realign its business processes?

- *Core competencies*: Does the firm have unique competencies and skills that cannot be easily duplicated by other firms? Will changes in technology invalidate the firm's competencies or strengthen them?

- *Synergies*: Does the firm have access to the competencies and assets of related firms either owned outright or through strategic partnerships and alliances?

- *Technology*: Has the firm developed proprietary technologies that allow it to scale with demand? Has the firm developed the operational technologies (e.g., customer relationship management, fulfillment, supply chain management, inventory control, and human resource systems) to survive?

- *Social and legal challenges*: Has the firm put in place policies to address consumer trust issues (privacy and security of personal information)? Is the firm the subject of lawsuits challenging its business model, such as intellectual property ownership issues? Will the firm be affected by changes in Internet taxation laws or other foreseeable statutory developments?

## FINANCIAL ANALYSIS

Strategic analysis helps us comprehend the competitive situation of the firm. Financial analysis helps us understand how in fact the firm is performing. There are two parts to a financial analysis: the statement of operations and the balance sheet. The statement of operations tells us how much money (or loss) the firm is achieving based on current sales and costs. The balance sheet tells us how many assets the firm has to support its current and future operations.

Here are some of the key factors to look for in a firm's Statement of Operations:

- *Revenues*: Are revenues growing and at what rate? Many e-commerce companies have experienced impressive, even explosive revenue growth, as an entirely new channel is created.

- *Cost of sales*: What is the cost of sales compared to revenues? Cost of sales typically includes the cost of the products sold and related costs. The lower the cost of sales compared to revenue, the higher the gross profit.

- *Gross margin*: What is the firm's gross margin, and is it increasing or decreasing? **Gross margin** is calculated by dividing gross profit by net sales revenues. Gross margin can tell you if the firm is gaining or losing market power vis á vis its key suppliers.

**gross margin**
gross profit divided by net sales

- *Operating expenses*: What are the firm's operating expenses, and are they increasing or decreasing? Operating expenses typically include the cost of marketing, technology, and administrative overhead. They also include, in accordance with professional accounting standards (see below), stock-based compensation to employees and executives, amortization of goodwill and other intangibles, and impairment of investments. In e-commerce companies, these turn out to be very important expenses. Many e-commerce firms compensated their employees with stock shares (or options), and many e-commerce firms purchased other e-commerce firms as a part of their growth strategy. Many of the companies were purchased at extremely high values using company stock rather than cash; in numerous instances, the purchased companies fell dramatically in market value. All these items are counted as normal operating expenses.

**operating margin**
calculated by dividing operating income or loss by net sales revenue

- *Operating margin*: What did the firm earn from its current operations? **Operating margin** is calculated by dividing operating income or loss by net sales revenue. Operating margin is an indication of a company's ability to turn sales into pre-tax profit after operating expenses have been deducted. Operating margin tells us if the firm's current operations are covering its operating expenses, not including interest expenses and other non-operating expenses.

**net margin**
the percentage of its gross sales revenue the firm is able to retain after all expenses are deducted; calculated by dividing net income or loss by net sales revenue

- *Net margin*: **Net margin** tells us the percentage of its gross sales revenue the firm was able to retain after all expenses are deducted. Net margin is calculated by dividing net income or loss by net sales revenue. Net margin sums up in one number how successful a company has been at the business of making a profit on each dollar of sales revenues. Net margin also tells us something about the efficiency of the firm by measuring the percentage of sales revenue it is able to retain after all expenses are deducted from gross revenues, and within a single industry can be used to measure the relative efficiency of competing firms. Net margin takes into account many non-operating expenses such as interest and stock compensation plans.

When examining the financial announcements of e-commerce companies, it is important to realize that online firms often choose not to announce their net income according to generally accepted accounting principles (GAAP). These principles have been promulgated by the Financial Accounting Standards Board (FASB), a board of professional accountants that establishes accounting rules for the profession, and which has played a vital role since the 1934 Securities Act, which sought to improve financial accounting during the Great Depression. Many e-commerce firms in the early years instead reported an entirely new calculation called *pro forma earnings* (also called EBITDA—earnings before income taxes, depreciation, and amortization). Pro forma earnings generally do not deduct stock-based compensation, depreciation, or amortization. The result is that pro forma earnings are always better than GAAP earnings. The firms that report in this manner typically claim these expenses are non-recurring and special and "unusual." In 2002 and 2003, the SEC issued new guidelines (Regulation G) that prohibit firms from reporting pro forma earnings in official reports to the SEC, but still allow firms to announce pro forma earnings in public statements (Weil, 2003). Throughout this book, we consider a firm's income or loss based on GAAP accounting standards only.

A **balance sheet** provides a financial snapshot of a company's assets and liabilities (debts) on a given date. **Assets** refer to stored value. **Current assets** are those assets such as cash, securities, accounts receivable, inventory, or other investments that are likely to be able to be converted to cash within one year. **Liabilities** are outstanding obligations of the firm. **Current liabilities** are debts of the firm that will be due within one year. Liabilities that are not due until the passage of a year or more are characterized as **long-term debt**. For a quick check of a firm's short-term financial health, examine its **working capital** (the firm's current assets minus current liabilities). If working capital is only marginally positive, or negative, the firm will likely have trouble meeting its short-term obligations. Alternatively, if a firm has a large amount of current assets, it can sustain operational losses for a period of time.

## 9.3 E-COMMERCE IN ACTION: E-TAILING BUSINESS MODELS

So far, we have been discussing online retail as if it were a single entity. In fact, as we briefly discussed in Chapter 2, there are four main types of online retail business models: virtual merchants, multi-channel merchandisers (sometimes referred to as bricks-and-clicks or clicks-and-bricks), catalog merchants, and manufacturer-direct

**balance sheet**
provides a financial snapshot of a company on a given date and shows its financial assets and liabilities

**assets**
refers to stored value

**current assets**
assets such as cash, securities, accounts receivable, inventory, or other investments that are likely to be able to be converted to cash within one year

**liabilities**
outstanding obligations of the firm

**current liabilities**
debts of the firm that will be due within one year

**long-term debt**
liabilities that are not due until the passage of a year or more

**working capital**
firm's current assets minus current liabilities

firms. In addition, there are small "mom and pop" retailers that use eBay, Amazon, and Yahoo Stores sales platforms, as well as affiliate merchants whose primary revenue derives from sending traffic to their "mother" sites. Each of these different types of online retailers faces a different strategic environment, as well as different industry and firm economics.

### VIRTUAL MERCHANTS

**virtual merchant**

single-channel Web firms that generate almost all of their revenue from online sales

**Virtual merchants** are single-channel Web firms that generate almost all their revenue from online sales. Virtual merchants face extraordinary strategic challenges. They must build a business and brand name from scratch, quickly, in an entirely new channel and confront many virtual merchant competitors (especially in smaller niche areas). Because these firms are totally online stores, they do not have to bear the costs associated with building and maintaining physical stores, but they face large costs in building and maintaining a Web site, building an order fulfillment infrastructure, and developing a brand name. Customer acquisition costs are high, and the learning curve is steep. Like all retail firms, their gross margins (the difference between the retail price of goods sold and the cost of goods to the retailer) are low. Therefore, virtual merchants must achieve highly efficient operations in order to preserve a profit, while building a brand name as quickly as possible in order to attract sufficient customers to cover their costs of operations. Most merchants in this category adopt low-cost and convenience strategies, coupled with extremely effective and efficient fulfillment processes to ensure customers receive what they ordered as fast as possible. In the following *E-commerce in Action* section, we take an in-depth look at the strategic and financial situation of Amazon, the leading online virtual merchant. In addition to Amazon, other successful virtual merchants include Newegg, Netflix, Zappos (now part of Amazon), Drugstore.com, Buy.com, Blue Nile (profiled in the opening case), Bluefly, Bidz.com, and eBags.com.

## E-COMMERCE IN ACTION

### AMAZON.COM

Amazon, the Seattle-based pure-online merchant is one of the most best-known names on the Web. Never suffering from modesty, Amazon's founder, Jeff Bezos, has proclaimed in its annual report that the objective of Amazon is to "offer the Earth's Biggest Selection and to be Earth's most customer-centric company where customers can find and discover anything they may want to buy." Just exactly what these claims mean, and how it might be possible to achieve them, is still a matter of speculation for both customers and investors. Yet this has not stopped Bezos and his team from becoming the Web's most successful and innovative pure-play, online retailer.

Few business enterprises have experienced a similar roller-coaster ride from explosive early growth, to huge losses, and then on to profitability. No Internet business has been both so hotly reviled and so hotly praised. Its stock reflects these changing fortunes, fluctuating over the past 10 years, from an early high of $106 in 1999, to a low of $6 a share in 2001, and then bouncing back and forth between 2003–2009 between $50–$90, then climbing toward its current high of $140 in September 2010. The story for now is that Amazon is an Internet survivor, one that is likely to succeed in the long term. It had its first profitable quarter in fall 2002, and its first profitable year in 2003. While controversial, Amazon has also been one of the most innovative online retailing stories in the history of e-commerce. From the earliest days of e-commerce, Amazon has continuously adapted its business model based both on its market experience and its insight into the online consumer.

## The Vision

The original vision of founder Jeff Bezos and his friends was that the Internet was a revolutionary new form of commerce and that only companies that became really big early on (ignoring profitability) would survive. The path to success, according to founder Bezos, was to offer consumers three things: the lowest prices, the best selection, and convenience (which translates into feature-rich content, user-generated reviews of books and products, fast and reliable fulfillment, and ease of use). Currently, Amazon offers consumers millions of unique new, used, and collectible items in 13 major categories: books; movies, music and games; digital downloads; Kindle e-book reader products; computers and office; electronics; home, garden, and pets; grocery, health, and beauty; toys, kids, and baby; clothing, shoes, and jewelry; sports and outdoors; tools and home improvement, and auto and industrial. And if Amazon does not carry it, they have created systems for helping you find it at online merchants who rent space from Amazon, or even at other places on the Web. In short, Amazon has come close to becoming the largest, single one-stop merchant on the Web, a kind of combined "shopping portal" and "product search portal" that puts it in direct competition with other large online general merchants, eBay, and general portals such as Yahoo, MSN, and even Google. As Amazon has succeeded in becoming the world's largest online store, it expanded its original vision to become one of the Web's largest suppliers of merchant and search services.

## Business Model

Amazon's business is currently organized into two basic segments, North American and International. Within those segments, it serves not only retail customers but also merchants and developers. The retail component of the business sells goods that Amazon has purchased and then resells to consumers just like a traditional retailer. It also manufactures and sells the Kindle.

Another major component of Amazon's business is its third-party merchant segment. Amazon Services' enables third parties to integrate their products into Amazon's Web site, and use Amazon's customer technologies. In the early years of its business, Amazon entered into partnerships with large merchants such as Toys "R" Us, Borders, and Target, and created storefronts for these companies within the larger Amazon site. Today, Amazon has increasingly left the enterprise-level business to competitors (Target announced it will be ending its partnership with Amazon in 2011) although it still runs Web sites for Bebe (a youth retailer), OshKosh B'Gosh (children's clothing), Timex, and Marks & Spencer (an English department store). Instead it has been focusing its efforts on small and medium-sized retail merchants.

Thousands of these types of merchants have signed on with Amazon, offering products that in some instances even compete with those that Amazon itself sells. For instance, a single product on the Amazon Web site may be listed for sale simultaneously by Amazon, by a large branded merchant participant such as Target, and by a business or individual selling a new, used, or collectible version of the product through Amazon Marketplace or an Amazon WebStore created by the merchant. For these types of merchants, Amazon is not the seller of record, does not own these products, and the shipping of products is usually handled by the third party (although in some instances, Amazon provides fulfillment services as well). Amazon collects a monthly fixed fee, sales commission (generally estimated to be between 10% and 20% of the sale), per-unit activity fee, or some combination thereof from the third party. In this segment, Amazon acts as an online shopping mall, collecting "rents" from other merchants and providing "site" services such as order entry and payment.

In many respects, Amazon's third-party seller segment is an effort to compete directly with eBay, the Web's most successful third-party merchant sales platform, which has, at any given time, a registered trading community of active buyers and sellers of over 90 million people. Amazon has even developed its own version of PayPal: Checkout by Amazon. At the same time, eBay itself has moved closer to Amazon's business model by encouraging merchants to sell rather than auction goods on its sites. ("Buy It Now", eBay stores, and other fixed-price trading features now account for more than half [53%] of all products sold by eBay.)

Another major part of Amazon's business is Amazon Web Services (AWS). Through this segment, Amazon offers a variety of Web services that provide developers with direct access to Amazon's technology platform, and allow them to build their own applications based on that platform. The company launched the program in 2002, and five years later, Amazon had over 200,000 volunteers building applications and services, strengthening the business. Bezos, however, was not satisfied with only a slew of cool new applications for his company's Web site. In 2006, Amazon introduced the first of several services that Bezos hoped would transform the future of Amazon as a business. With Simple Storage Service (S3) and, later, Elastic Compute Cloud (EC2), Amazon entered the utility computing market. The company realized that the benefits of its $2 billion investment in technology could also be valuable to other companies. Amazon has tremendous computing capacity, but like most companies, only uses a small portion of it at any one time. Moreover, the Amazon infrastructure is considered by many to be among the most robust in the world. Amazon began to sell its computing power on a per-usage basis, just like a power company sells electricity.

S3, for example, is a data storage service that is designed to make Web-scale computing easier and more affordable for developers. United States customers pay 15 cents per gigabyte of data for up to the first 50 terabytes stored per month on Amazon's network of disk drives, and a declining amount for additional storage. There is also a charge of 10 cents per gigabyte for data transferred in and 15 cents per giga-byte for the first 10 terabytes of data transferred out, again with a declining amount for additional transfers over that amount. Customers pay for exactly what they use and no more. Working in conjunction with S3, EC2 enables businesses to utilize Amazon's servers for computing tasks, such as testing software. Using EC2 incurs charges of 8.5 cents per standard (small instance) hour consumed for Linux/Unix usage and 12 cents per hour for Windows usage.. A standard "small instance" supplies the user with the equivalent of 1.7 GB of RAM, 1.0–1.2 GHz Opteron or Xeon processor, a 160 GB hard drive, a 32-bit platform, and 250 MB of bandwidth on the network. Other "infrastructure" Web services offered by Amazon include Simple Queue Service (SQS), which offers a hosted queue for storing messages as they travel between computers; SimpleDB, a database Web service; CloudFront, a content delivery Web service; and Elastic MapReduce, a Web service that enables users to perform data-intensive tasks.

In addition to these Web services, Amazon also offers Virtual Private Cloud, which can be used to create a VPN between the Amazon cloud and a company's existing IT infrastructure. Flexible Payments Service (FPS) provides a payments service for developers. DevPay is an online billing and account management service for developers who create Amazon cloud applications. Amazon Mechanical Turk provides a marketplace for work that requires human intelligence. Alexa Web Information Services provides Web traffic data and information for developers. Fulfillment Web Services (FWS) allows merchants to access Amazon's fulfillment capabilities through a simple Web services interface.

Although Amazon does not provide a breakout of its revenues in its financial reports, analysts estimate that AWS will earn Amazon approximately $500–$650 million in 2010, and grow to $1 billion within the next three years. If accurate, that figure would place Amazon at the forefront of the "infrastructure-as-service market." Even with the success of AWS, Amazon still continues to generate revenue primarily by selling products. While Amazon started out as an online merchant of books, CDs, and DVDs, since 2002 it has diversified into becoming a general merchandiser of millions of other products. In 2009, around 52% of its revenue came from media sales such as books, CDs, DVDs, and music, while 45% came from electronics and other general merchandise.

In addition to Amazon.com in the United States, Amazon also operates localized sites in Japan, Germany, the United Kingdom, France, and Canada. The success of its international business often does not attract much attention. For instance, in 2009, Amazon derived almost $11.7 billion, or over 47%, of its $24.5 billion of gross revenues offshore, and international sales grew by 31% for the year. In 2009–2010, Amazon opened several new Web stores and continued to develop new technology offerings from AWS and new versions of the Kindle, its electronic reader. It also expanded its international Kindle offerings, and added Kindle applications for the iPad, BlackBerry, and Android. According to Amazon, the Kindle has been its best selling product for the previous two years.

## Financial Analysis

Amazon's revenues have increased from about $600 million in 1998 to $24.5 billion in 2009. In the last three years, Amazon's revenues have grown an incredible 65% (see

**Table 9.4**). This is very impressive, explosive revenue growth. In an effort to attract sales, Amazon has offered free shipping on orders over $25, and this has increased its operating costs and lowered net margins. However, Amazon has been able to compensate for the cost of its low price strategy and free shipping policies by focusing on operating expenses and by eliminating marketing in offline magazines and television. Marketing costs have remained steady at a little over 2% of revenues despite a 28% increase in sales in 2009. General and administrative costs as a percentage of sales have also remained nearly constant, at around 1%. This means that Amazon's increase in sales did not come about by increases in marketing, head count, or administrative overhead. Amazon instead relies heavily on affiliates and third-party merchants to drive sales. In addition, it has demonstrated an ability to scale its operations without rapidly increasing its administrative expenditures. As a result of its cost-saving measures, Amazon was able to grow its net income by a factor of more than 25 from 2003 ($35 million) to 2009 ($902 million). Net margin has fluctuated from a low of .7% in 2003, to a high of 8.5% in 2004, and was 3.7% in 2009. For every dollar in net sales in 2008, Amazon was earning a profit of about 4 cents—positive but not wonderful and not any better than a lot of bricks-and-mortar retailers. The reason for this fall off in net margin is clearly related to its free shipping policy and low cost policies. Nevertheless, the prospect for Amazon based on this financial analysis looks much improved from earlier years when it was showing negative margins and losing money on every sale.

Amazon's balance sheet has improved significantly over the last three years. At the end of December 2009, it had about $6.3 billion in cash and marketable securities. The cash and securities were obtained from sales, sales of stock and notes to the public, venture capital investors, and institutional investors in return for equity (shares) in the company or debt securities. Total assets are listed at $13.8 billion. The company emphasizes the strength of its "free cash flow" as a sign of financial strength, suggesting it has more than enough cash available to cover short-term liabilities (such as financing holiday season purchasing). In 2009, Amazon continued to decrease its long-term debt, ending the year with just $109 million in long term debt on its books. Amazon's cash assets should certainly be enough to cover future short-term deficits should they occur.

### Strategic Analysis—Business Strategy

Amazon engages in a number of business strategies that seek to maximize growth in sales volume, while cutting prices to the bare bones. Its revenue growth strategies include driving the growth of e-book sales by offering continuing enhancements of its Kindle e-reader, both in the United States and internationally, expanding its Amazon Web Services offerings and extending their geographic reach, moving towards a broader trading platform by expanding the third-party seller segment, and moving towards greater product focus by grouping its offerings into major categories called stores. In the past three years, Amazon has created numerous new online stores that group together sellers and products: such as an outdoor recreation store; an AmazonWireless store offering cell phones and service plans; others focused on beauty, gourmet food, sporting goods, jewelry and watches, health and personal care,

| TABLE 9.4 | **AMAZON'S CONSOLIDATED STATEMENTS OF OPERATIONS AND SUMMARY BALANCE SHEET DATA 2007–2009** |
|---|---|

**CONSOLIDATED STATEMENTS OF OPERATIONS (in thousands)**

| For the fiscal year ended December 31, | 2009 | 2008 | 2007 |
|---|---|---|---|
| **Revenue** | | | |
| Net sales | $ 24,509,000 | $ 19,166,000 | $ 14,835,000 |
| Cost of sales | $ 18,978,000 | 14,896,00 | $11,482,000 |
| | | | |
| **Gross profit** | **5,531,000** | **4,270,000** | **3,353,000** |
| **Gross margin** | **22.5** | **22%** | **23%** |
| **Operating expenses** | | | |
| Marketing | 680,000 | 482,000 | 344,000 |
| Fulfillment | 2,052,000 | 1,658,000 | 1,292,000 |
| Technology and content | 1,240,000 | 1,033,000 | 818,000 |
| General and administrative | 328,000 | 279,000 | 235,000 |
| Other operating expense (income), net | 102,000 | 24,000 | 9,000 |
| Total operating expenses | 4,402,000 | 3,428,000 | 2,698,000 |
| | | | |
| **Income from operations** | **1,129,000** | **842,000** | **655,000** |
| **Operating margin** | **4.6%** | **4.4%** | **4.4%** |
| Total non-operating income | 32,000 | 59,000 | 5,000 |
| | | | |
| Income before income taxes | | 901,000 | 660,000 |
| Provision for income taxes | (253,000) | (247,000) | (184,000) |
| Equity-method investment activity, net of tax | (6,000) | (9,000) | — |
| Income before change in accounting principle | | — | 476,000 |
| **Net income (loss)** | — | **645,000** | **476,000** |
| | | | |
| **Net margin** | **3.7%** | **3.4%** | **3.2%** |

**SUMMARY BALANCE SHEET DATA (in thousands)**

| At December 31, | 2009 | 2008 | 2007 |
|---|---|---|---|
| **Assets** | | | |
| Cash, cash equivalents and marketable securities | 6,366,000 | 3,727,000 | 3,112,000 |
| Total current assets | 9,797,000 | 6,157,000 | 5,164,000 |
| Total assets | 13,813,000 | 8,314,000 | 6,485,000 |
| **Liabilities** | | | |
| Total current liabilities | 7,364,000 | 4,746,000 | 3,714,000 |
| Long-term debt and other | 1,192,000 | 896,000 | 1,574,000 |
| Working capital | 2,433,000 | 1,411,000 | 1,450,000 |
| Stockholders' Equity (Deficit) | 5,257,000 | 2,672,000 | 1,197,000 |

SOURCE: Amazon.com ,Inc., 2010.

and office supplies; a Software en Espanol store for Spanish-language and bilingual software products; and a motorcycle and ATV store. Early results suggest these stores are growing faster than Amazon as a whole, particularly jewelry and watches. Amazon is still following Wal-Mart's and eBay's examples by attempting to be a mass-market, low-price, high-volume online supermarket where you can get just about anything. To achieve profitability in this environment, Amazon has invested heavily in supply chain management and fulfillment strategies to reduce its costs to the bare minimum while still providing excellent customer service and even free shipping.

Specific programs to increase retail revenues are the continuation of free shipping from Amazon Retail (a strategy that has increased order sizes by 25%), Amazon Prime (which for $79 a year provides free two-day shipping and one-day delivery upgrades for $3.99), greater product selection, and shorter order fulfillment times. In October 2009, Amazon announced it would offer customers same-day shipping in seven major cities while not charging additional fees. Internet customers have long been frustrated both by high shipping and handling charges as well as long delays in receiving goods. A ticking clock can be seen next to some Amazon sale items indicating the hours remaining for an order to make it to the customer by the next day.

Amazon also made several strategic acquisitions in 2009 and 2010, including Zappos.com, a popular online shoe shopping destination, and Woot.com, a retailer that had made a name for itself selling just one item a day.

Amazon is increasingly moving into the mobile shopping space as well, launching a shopping app for the iPhone in December 2008, the BlackBerry in April 2009, and the Android in August 2009, and the iPad in May 2010. In July 2010, Jeff Bezos noted that in the previous 12 months, customers had ordered more than $1 billion of products from Amazon using a mobile device. In 2009–2010, Amazon also introduced significant enhancements to its wireless Kindle e-book reader, with several new versions, including the Kindle 2; the Kindle DX, a large-screen version more appropriate for newspapers, magazines, and textbooks; and the Kindle 3G/Kindle Wi-Fi, a smaller, lighter version with better contrast and increased book storage. By the end of August 2010, its Kindle Store was offering more than 630,000 books.

On the cost side, Amazon has taken significant steps to lower costs in the past three years. Important initiatives included the hiring of mathematicians and operations specialists to optimize the location of storing goods in Amazon's six warehouses, optimizing the size of shipments, and consolidating orders into larger batches prior to shipping. The company increasingly uses "postal injection" for shipping, in which Amazon trucks deliver pre-posted packages to U.S. Postal System centers.

### Strategic Analysis—Competition

Amazon's competitors are general merchandisers who are both offline and online, and increasingly both. This includes the largest online competitor, eBay, and multi-channel retailers such as Wal-Mart, Sears, and JCPenney. Amazon also competes with catalog merchants such as L.L.Bean and Lands' End in a number of product areas. As the Web's largest bookseller, Amazon is in competition with bookstores such as Barnesandnoble.com. Insofar as other portal sites such as MSN and Yahoo are involved in operating online stores or auctions, or selling their own products, Amazon also competes with these portals. In addition, Amazon competes with other firms who sell Web services such as hosting, shopping cart, and fulfillment services. Amazon has also engaged iTunes, Netflix, and Blockbuster in competition by offering video and audio downloads. In 2007, Amazon started selling MP3 music files without the Digital Rights Management (DRM) shackles that prevent iTunes users from playing their downloaded music on anything but an iPod, and by September 2010, was offering over 13 million DRM-free MP3 songs from all four major music labels and thousands of independent labels that can be played on virtually any hardware device and managed with any music software. In September 2008, Amazon also introduced Amazon Video On Demand Service, which offers over 75,000 movies and television shows that can be viewed instantly on a PC or Mac, as well as downloaded onto a computer or Tivo box. In April 2009, Amazon added high definition movies and television episodes to the service.

## Strategic Analysis—Technology

The person who said that "IT doesn't make a difference" clearly does not know much about Amazon. Amazon arguably has the largest and most sophisticated collection of online retailing technologies available at any single site on the Web. Amazon has implemented numerous Web site management, search, customer interaction, recommendation, transaction processing, and fulfillment services and systems using a combination of its own proprietary technologies and commercially available, licensed technologies. Amazon's transaction-processing systems handle millions of items, a number of different status inquiries, gift-wrapping requests, and multiple shipment methods. These systems allow customers to choose whether to receive single or several shipments based on availability and to track the progress of each order. Amazon's technology extends to its employees as well. Every warehouse worker carries a shoehorn-size device that combines a bar code scanner, a display screen, and a two-way data transmitter. In 2009, Amazon spent over $1.2 billion on technology and new content, and is on track to spend a similar amount in 2010.

## Strategic Analysis—Social and Legal Challenges

In 2009, Amazon finally settled a long-standing lawsuit with its previous partner Toys "R"Us. Toys"R"Us had sued Amazon over what it claimed was its exclusive right to sell toys on Amazon. After an initial ruling in favor of Toys"R"Us, Amazon appealed, but ultimately agreed to pay Toys"R"Us $51 million in full settlement for all its claims. Amazon still faces a number of lawsuits concerning various aspects of its business. One series of lawsuits alleges that Amazon wrongfully failed to collect and remit sales and use taxes for sales of personal property and knowingly created records and statements falsely stating it was not required to collect or remit such taxes. Amazon historically has also been faced with a number of patent infringement suits, which it typically settles out of court. Currently, there are several pending patent suits, including some involving Amazon's Kindle.

In May 2008, Amazon filed a lawsuit against the State of New York, which in April 2008 amended its sales tax law to specifically cover sales by out-of-state online retailers who get customers through New York-based affiliate Web sites. Amazon has charged that the statute is unconstitutional and overly broad and vague. The New York State Supreme Court rejected Amazon's position in January 2009, but Amazon has appealed, and the case remains pending as of September 2010.

### Future Prospects

Amazon clearly has improved its financial performance through consistent gains in operational efficiency and extraordinary growth in sales. In 2009, net sales grew 28% to $24.5 billion, and net income rose by almost 40% to $902 million. Through the second quarter of 2010, Amazon showed significant gains over the previous year in net sales, operating income, and net income. For the first six months of the year, the company registered over $13.7 billion in sales, as opposed to $9.5 billion for the same period in 2009, paced by increases in Kindle, Amazon Web Services, third-party sales, retail, and mobile sales. Net income for the period was $505 million compared to $319 million. Projections for the third quarter indicated a growth in net sales of between 27%–40%. Although many worry about its ability to maintain high levels of customer service, Amazon routinely ranks among the top five online e-commerce sites for customer service, accuracy of delivery, and speed of fulfillment.

However, when compared to Wal-Mart, a very profitable retailing giant, Amazon still comes up short because its net margins are paper thin. Although it has turned the corner and achieved several years of consecutive profitability, when compared to Wal-Mart's return on invested capital and consistent growth rate in sales and profits, Amazon still has a long way to go.

## MULTI-CHANNEL MERCHANTS: BRICKS-AND-CLICKS

**bricks-and-clicks**

companies that have a network of physical stores as their primary retail channel, but also have introduced online offerings

Also called multi-channel merchants, **bricks-and-clicks** companies have a network of physical stores as their primary retail channel, but also have introduced online offerings. These are multi-channel firms such as Wal-Mart, Sears, JCPenney, Staples, Office Max, Costco, Macys, Target, and other brand-name merchants. While bricks-and-clicks merchants face high costs of physical buildings and large sales staffs, they also have many advantages such as a brand name, a national customer base, warehouses, large scale (giving them leverage with suppliers), and a trained staff. Acquiring customers is less expensive because of their brand names, but these firms face challenges in coordinating prices across channels and handling returns of Web purchases at their retail outlets. However, these retail players are used to operating on very thin margins and have invested heavily in purchasing and inventory control systems to control costs, and in coordinating returns from multiple locations. Bricks-and-clicks companies face the challenge of leveraging their strengths and assets to the Web, building a credible Web site, hiring new skilled staff, and building rapid-response order entry and fulfillment systems. According to Internet Retailer, in 2009, the chain retailers accounted for around $50 billion (almost 40%) of all online retail sales. However, there remains much room for growth (Internet Retailer, 2010).

JCPenney.com is a prime example of a traditional merchant based on physical stores and a catalog operation moving successfully to a multi-channel online store. In 2009, JCPenney.com ranked 16th on Internet Retailer's list of the top 500 retail Web sites ranked by annual sales.

James Cash Penney founded JCPenney in 1902. Penney's original vision was to create a nationwide chain of stores based on the newly emerging business model called a "department store," which aggregated a wide variety of general merchandise at a central location, usually near local transportation hubs formed by streets, highways, and street car lines. In addition, Penney envisioned a national catalog mail-order business to rival the successful Sears model. Today, JCPenney is one of the largest national department store chains, with more than 1,100 department stores in the United States and Puerto Rico. In addition to its department stores, JCPenney had one of the largest catalog operations in the United States, but in December 2009, it announced that its twice-yearly "big-book" catalog was being phased out, because "big-book catalogs have become less relevant as customers have embraced shopping online." and in September 2010, decided to stop publishing its remaining dozen specialty catalogs as well (Internet Retailer, 2010; Halkias, 2010).

Like many traditional retailers, however, JCPenney has had to change its business model to accommodate the Internet and consumer demands for low cost and unparalleled product depth and selection, which could only be achieved by enhancing its Web operations. JCPenney opened its Web site for business in 1998 and placed its full catalog inventory online. Its department stores and Internet channels primarily serve the same target market: "modern spenders" and "starting-outers," or two-income families with median annual incomes of $50,000.

At JCPenney.com, customers can buy family clothing, jewelry, shoes, accessories, and home furnishings. And whether they buy merchandise in a bricks-and-mortar store, through the catalog, or on the Internet, customers can return items either at a store or through the mail. Indeed, the current essence of multi-channel retailing is the nearly complete integration of offline and online sales and operations while presenting a single branded experience to the customer. A second feature of successful multi-channel retailing is understanding customer preferences so that each channel sells products appropriate to that channel. For instance, not only can customers pick up and return at a local store what they order from JCPenney.com, but they can also order from the store's counters items not in the store but available online. The in-store point-of-sale system is integrated with Penney's Web catalog, and they both share a common inventory system. Many items are too expensive to hold in physical store inventory, but they can be offered economically on the Web site. The company has also invested in state-of-the-art interactivity and imaging tools for the Web site, such as a tool that lets shoppers mix and match 142,000 combinations of window treatments, and fitting guides that enable shoppers to zoom in on products such as jeans and create more custom-fitted orders. It has also embraced social media, with a presence on Facebook, YouTube, and Twitter.

The company has achieved online success through some savvy decisions: putting approximately 250,000 products online, from lingerie to home furnishings, surpassing the competition in terms of selection, targeting women as the primary consumer, and making it easy to move from one category to the next on the site. JCPenney is able to directly compete against Amazon given its large selection, especially in apparel lines. In doing so, online sales are attracting new, younger JCPenney shoppers, 25% of whom have never bought anything in a JCPenney store. According to Internet Retailer, in 2009, 90% of JCPenney Web customers also shopped in their stores. Online sales are complementing, rather than cannibalizing, store and catalog sales. Shoppers who buy through all three channels spend four times more—$1,000—than the shopper who makes purchases only at the retail store.

As a result, JCPenney appears to have successfully made the transition from department store/catalog merchant to store/Web merchant. Web sales in 2009 were $1.5 billion, about the same as in 2008, but a bright light when compared to 5% overall decline in sales from its other operations. Continued improvement in this segment, coupled with a strong focus on high-margin apparel products for families, an area where Amazon and eBay are weak, offers a chance for continuing improved long-term performance (JCPenney, 2010; Internet Retailer, 2010).

## CATALOG MERCHANTS

**catalog merchants**

established companies that have a national offline catalog operation that is their largest retail channel, but who have recently developed online capabilities

**Catalog merchants** such as Lands' End, L.L.Bean, Eddie Bauer, Victoria's Secret, and Lillian Vernon are established companies that have a national offline catalog operation that is their largest retail channel, but who have also developed online capabilities. JCPenney could also be included here, given the large scale of its catalog operation. Catalog merchants face very high costs for printing and mailing millions of catalogs each year—many of which have a half-life of 30 seconds after the customer receives them. Nevertheless, catalog merchants have the highest margins in the retail sector because they have achieved very efficient operations. They generally have few, if any, physical stores. They also typically have developed centralized fulfillment and call centers, extraordinary service, and excellent fulfillment in partnership with package delivery firms such as FedEx and UPS. Catalog firms have suffered in recent years as catalog sales growth rates have fallen to levels that are still far above general retail but much slower than the early years of the 1980s, when annual revenues were growing at 30% a year. As a result, catalog merchants have had to diversify their channels either by building stores (L.L.Bean), being bought by store-based firms (Sears purchased Lands' End), or by building a strong Web presence.

Catalog merchants face many of the same challenges as bricks-and-mortar stores—they must leverage their existing assets and competencies to a new technology environment, build a credible Web presence, and hire new staff. Catalog firms are uniquely advantaged, however, because they already possess very efficient order entry and fulfillment systems. In 2009, according to Internet Retailer, catalog merchants generated combined Web sales of about $18.3 billion (Internet Retailer, 2010)..

Arguably one of the most successful online catalog merchants is LandsEnd.com. Lands' End started out in 1963 in a basement of Chicago's tannery district selling sailboat equipment and clothing, handling 15 orders on a good day. Since then it expanded into a direct catalog merchant, distributing over 200 million catalogs annually and selling a much expanded line of "traditionally" styled sport clothing, soft luggage, and products for the home. Lands' End launched its Web site in 1995 with 100 products and travelogue essays. Located in Racine, Wisconsin, it has since grown into one of the Web's most successful apparel sites.

Lands' End has always been on the leading edge of online retailing technologies, most of which emphasize personal marketing and customized products. Lands' End was the first e-commerce Web site to allow customers to create a 3-D model of themselves to "try on" clothing. Lands' End "Get Live Help" enables customers to chat online with customer service representatives; Lands' End Custom allows customers to create custom-crafted clothing built for their personal measurements. While customized clothing built online was thought to be a gimmick in the early years of online retailing, today 40% of Lands' End clothing sold online is customized. In 2003, Lands' End was purchased by Sears (which itself was purchased by Kmart in 2004) but retains an independent online presence and catalog operation. In 2009, Lands' End was named a service winner in the E-tailing Group's 11th annual Mystery Shopping Study of the top 100 online retailers. Lands' End was one of only nine online retailers that passed the study's nine main criteria, such as customer service adequately and correctly answering an e-mail question within 24 hours; requiring six or fewer clicks to checkout; and sending an e-mail shipping confirmation and order confirmation. Sears has incorporated many of Lands' End's online techniques into its own Web site, Sears.com (Landsend.com, 2010).

## MANUFACTURER-DIRECT

**Manufacturer-direct** firms are either single- or multi-channel manufacturers that sell directly online to consumers without the intervention of retailers. Manufacturer-direct firms were predicted to play a very large role in e-commerce, but this has generally not happened. The primary exception is computer hardware, where firms such as Dell, Apple, Sony, and Hewlett-Packard, account for over 70% of computer retail sales online. Some of these firms had retail experience prior to the Web (Dell was built on the direct sales model), while others, such as Hewlett-Packard, had no prior direct sales experience. Overall, according to Internet Retailer, consumer brand manufacturers account for about 12% of online retail sales (about $15 billion) (Internet Retailer, 2010).

> **manufacturer-direct**
> single- or multi-channel manufacturers who sell directly online to consumers without the intervention of retailers

As discussed in Chapter 6, manufacturer-direct firms face channel conflict challenges. Channel conflict occurs when physical retailers of products must compete on price and currency of inventory directly against the manufacturer, who does not face the cost of maintaining inventory, physical stores, or sales staffs. Firms with no prior direct marketing experience face the additional challenges of developing a fast-response online order and fulfillment system, acquiring customers, and coordinating their supply chains with market demand. Switching from a **supply-push model** (where products are made prior to orders received based on estimated demand and then stored in warehouses awaiting sale) to a **demand-pull model** (where products are not built until an order is received) has proved extremely difficult for traditional manufacturers. Yet for many products, manufacturer-direct firms have the advantage of an established national brand name, an existing large customer base, and a lower cost structure than even catalog merchants because they are the manufacturer of the goods and thus do not pay profits to anyone else. Therefore, manufacturer-direct firms should have higher margins.

> **supply-push model**
> products are made prior to orders received based on estimated demand
>
> **demand-pull model**
> products are not built until an order is received

The most frequently cited manufacturer-direct retailer is Dell Inc., the world's largest direct computer systems supplier, providing corporations, government agencies, small-to-medium businesses, and individuals with computer products and services ordered straight from the manufacturer's headquarters in Austin, Texas. Although sales representatives support corporate customers, individuals and smaller businesses buy direct from Dell by phone, fax, and via the Internet, with about $4.5 billion in sales generated online in 2009 (ranking 3rd on Internet Retailer's list of top 500 online retailers).

When Michael Dell started the company in 1984 in his college dorm room, his idea was to custom-build computers for customers, to eliminate the middleman, and more effectively meet the technology needs of his customers. Today, the company sells much more than individual computer systems; it also offers enterprise systems, desktop, and laptop computers, as well as installation, financing, repair, and management services. By relying on a build-to-order manufacturing process, the company achieves faster inventory turnover (five days), and reduced component and finished goods inventory levels; this strategy virtually eliminates the chance of product obsolescence.

The direct model simplifies the company's operations, eliminating the need to support a wholesale and retail sales network, as well as cutting out the costly associated markup, and gives Dell complete control over its customer database. In addition, Dell can build and ship custom computers nearly as fast as a mail-order supplier can pull a computer out of inventory and ship it to the customer.

To extend the benefits of its direct sales model, Dell has aggressively moved sales, service, and support online. Each month, the company typically has about 13–14 million unique visitors at Dell.com, where it maintains an estimated 80 country-specific Web sites. The Premier.Dell.com service enables companies to investigate product offerings, complete order forms and purchase orders, track orders in real time, and review order histories all online. For its small business customers, it has created an online virtual account executive, as well as a spare-parts ordering system and virtual help desk with direct access to technical support data. Dell has also continued to broaden its offerings beyond pure hardware product sales, adding warranty services, product integration and installation services, Internet access, software, and technology consulting, referring to them as "beyond the box" offerings. These include nearly 30,000 software and peripheral products from leading manufacturers that can be bundled with Dell products. In 2009, Dell opened a download store in the United States, the United Kingdom, France, and Germany, that enables customers to download software purchases rather than wait to receive them on a CD. Dell has also embraced social media, adding Web site features such as instructions on how to create and maintain a blog, edit and post online vidoes, and build and share online photo scrapbooks. Dell Lounge allows visitors to create video and audio mashups, while StudioDell shows how to work with digital photo and videos and allows visitors to upload videos they've created showing how they use Dell technology. Dell has a presence on Facebook, MySpace, and Twitter, and posts Twitter-exclusive sales for those who follow Dell Outlet. It also emphasizes customer reviews, posting both positive and negative reviews from 67 countries and in 15 languages (Dell, Inc., 2010; Internet Retailer, 2010).

## COMMON THEMES IN ONLINE RETAILING

We have looked at some very different companies in the preceding section, from entrepreneurial Web-only merchants to established offline giants. Online retail e-commerce is indeed alive and well for some retailers, particularly for established offline retailers with existing brands. Online retail is the fastest growing channel in retail on a revenue basis, has the fastest growing consumer base, and has growing penetration across many categories of nonessential goods. On the other hand, profits for new start-up ventures have been difficult to achieve, and it took even Amazon eight years to show its first profit.

The reasons for the difficulties experienced by online retailers in achieving profits are also now clear. The path to success in any form of retail involves having a central location in order to attract a larger number of shoppers, charging high enough prices to cover the costs of goods as well as marketing, and developing highly efficient inventory and fulfillment systems so that the company can offer goods at lower costs than competitors and still make a profit. In the early years, many online merchants failed to follow these fundamental ideas, and lowered prices below the total costs of goods and operations, failed to develop efficient business processes, or spent far too much on customer acquisition and marketing. In recent years, however, online retail firms have begun to raise prices, often matching the prices of offline stores in some categories. Consumers have been willing to accept higher prices in return for the convenience of shopping online, and avoiding the inconvenience of shopping at stores and malls.

For the most part, disintermediation did not occur and the retail middleman did not disappear. Indeed, virtual merchants, along with powerful offline merchants who moved online, maintained their powerful grip on the retail customer, with some notable exceptions in electronics and software. Manufacturers—with the exception of electronic goods—have used the Web primarily as an informational resource, driving consumers to the traditional retail channels for transactions.

Leaving Amazon aside, the most significant online growth has been that of offline general merchandiser giants such as Wal-Mart, Sears, Costco, JCPenney, Macy's, Target, and Nordstrom's. Many of the first-mover, Web pure-play merchants failed to achieve profitability and closed their doors en masse in 2000 and 2001 as their venture capital funds were depleted. Traditional retailers have been the fast followers (although many of them cannot be characterized as particularly "fast") most likely to succeed on the Web by extending their traditional competencies and assets. In this sense, e-commerce technological innovation is following the historical pattern of other technology-driven commercial changes, from automobiles to radio and television.

To succeed online, established merchants need to create an integrated shopping environment that combines their catalog, store, and online experiences into one. Established retailers have significant fulfillment, inventory management, supply chain management, and other competencies that apply directly to the online channel. And although established merchants have moved online, their e-commerce operations are not always profitable. To succeed online, established retailers need to extend their brands, provide incentives to consumers to use the online channel, avoid channel conflict, and build partnerships with online portals such as Yahoo, MSN, and AOL.

A second area of very rapid online growth is a new crop of specialty merchants selling high-end, fashionable and luxury goods, such as Blue Nile, the online diamond merchant, or selling discounted electronics, such as BestBuy.com (electronics), apparel (Gap.com), or office products (OfficeDepot.com). These firms are demonstrating the vitality and openness of the Internet for innovation and extending the range of products available on the Web. Many virtual merchants have developed large, online customer bases, as well as the online tools required to market to their customer base. These online brands can be strengthened further through alliances and partnerships that add the required competencies in inventory management and fulfillment services. Virtual merchants need to build operational strength and efficiency before they can become profitable.

Both Web-only and established offline retailers wishing to strengthen their e-commerce revenues will be favorably affected in the future by new retailing technologies—from extending high-speed Internet access to the majority of potential consumers, to mobile commerce using cell phones, to new services such as enhanced comparison shopping sites, as described in *Insight on Technology: Using the Web to Shop 'Till You Drop*.

## 9.4  THE SERVICE SECTOR: OFFLINE AND ONLINE

The service sector is typically the largest and most rapidly expanding part of the economies in advanced industrial nations such as the United States, and in European and some Asian countries. In the United States, services (broadly defined) employ about 112 million people (77% of the labor force) and account for about $8.6 trillion (about 60%) of the U.S. gross domestic product (GDP) (U.S. Census Bureau, 2010). Only 12% of the U.S. workforce is involved in the production of physical goods.

On the other hand, productivity in the service sector has lagged far behind productivity in factories and on farms. Productivity in the service sector over the last decade has averaged about 1%, while farm and factory productivity has averaged about 5% (U.S. Census Bureau, 2010). While the explosion in information technology capital investment since 1995 has certainly added to overall productivity, "white collar" service sector employees did not benefit from this as much as factory employees. In part, this is because the very nature of services—performing activities for others in a highly personalized and customized manner—is somewhat immune to the beneficial aspects of computerization. The productivity of doctors, lawyers, accountants, and business consultants—all service occupations—has not been markedly affected in terms of unit output per unit time by the explosion in information technology, although the quality of their work has undoubtedly improved. Unfortunately, increases in quality of service are not measured by productivity statistics. Being able to find the lowest price in the United States for a flight from New York to Los Angeles in a matter of minutes (as opposed to many hours in the past) will never be measured in productivity statistics. What this means for e-commerce is that the service sector offers extraordinary opportunities insofar as e-commerce sites can deliver information, knowledge, and transaction efficiencies.

# INSIGHT ON TECHNOLOGY

## USING THE WEB TO SHOP 'TILL YOU DROP

The original idea was simple and leveraged many of the unique features of e-commerce technology: Create a Web site listing thousands of products where consumers can compare prices, features, consumer reviews of the actual product performance, and reputations of merchants. Then, when visitors click on a product and price they like, they are taken to the merchant's Web site where they can make the purchase. The merchant pays the Web site a fee or commission for sending the customer, as well as a listing fee usually determined by bidding on key words. The idea: Shoppers would not have to shop till they dropped, but instead could conveniently compare prices at one site, and then buy from the lowest-price merchant on the Web. Merchants would support this service because they would obtain additional customers and sales. Merchants join the shopping services and provide a digital feed to the comparison sites providing information on both products and prices.

The idea first appeared in the mid-1990s in academic papers on potential uses of the Web and Internet, and was referred to as "shopping robots." Shopping robots are essentially search engines that scour the Web for prices on specific products. Now referred to much more descriptively as comparison shopping sites, they have become big business, with products tracked numbering in the millions. No one knows for sure, but observers believe there are over 100 price comparison sites on the Web in 2010. The top sites include NexTag, PriceGrabber, Shopping.com (which also includes Epinions.com, and is owned by eBay), Shopzilla/BizRate (owned by Scripps), Pronto, TheFind, Become, and Smarter. NexTag says more than 30 million people a month use its site to research and compare products and services online. According to Channel Advisor, a leading e-commerce software and services provider, comparison shopping sites drive about 15% of e-commerce, making them an important channel for retailers. Shopping.com, PriceGrabber, and Pronto, among others, are used by over 50% of Internet Retailer's top 500 online merchants.

General merchandisers such as Amazon and search engines such as Google and Bing have also developed their own comparison shopping capabilities. Shopping sites make money by charging participating merchants on a per-click basis regardless of whether a sale is made. A twist on shopping search engines is comparison shopping coupon systems. Sites like Wow-Coupons, CurrentCodes, and FatWallet search the Web for deals and coupons.

Comparison shopping sites focused originally on tracking online prices for electronic consumer goods and computers. Consumer electronics are fairly commoditized products by a few branded manufacturers, with standard features, making it relatively easy to compare one product to another. Type in "digital camera," select the number of megapixels you want, enter the zoom range and price, press the Enter key on your keyboard, and you will receive a long list of cameras and dealers. You can refine your search as you move along the purchase process, and explore the reputations of dealers before you decide to purchase.

However, although Shopping.com tracks over 60 million products and about 2,700 different brands, very few of these items are so-called "soft goods" purchased by women, who have risen to equal the purchasing power of men on the Web. In 1998, 65% of Web purchases were made by men, while today, over 60% are made by women who are much more likely to be looking for soft goods, such as apparel, jewelry, accessories, luggage, and

(continued)

gifts. In fact, these are among the fastest growing consumer product categories on the Web. For this reason, the shopping comparison sites are currently adding soft goods to their services.

But the process of comparison shopping for soft goods is not as simple as for hard goods such as digital TVs or digital cameras. The strength of a comparison shopping site is to present highly similar or identical items from different merchants at varying prices and reputation levels. Generally, these kinds of electronic goods have a limited number of suppliers (mostly solid brand names) and limited features. But in more complex product areas, such as apparel or jewelry, such standards do not exist. In fact, manufacturers of these products emphasize their uniqueness, not their similarity. One solution is to focus on the brands of soft goods and not the price: bags from Gucci, sweaters from Benetton, and mountain climbing gear from REI. Yahoo and search engines such as Bing and Google are moving closer to the brand model of comparison shopping as price becomes a less powerful factor in consumer purchases of soft goods.

As more attention focuses on comparison shopping sites, the sites themselves continue to innovate and add features, and they attempt to go beyond simply finding customers the lowest-price products. Shopping.com tracks its visitors to help consumers decide what to buy, and where to buy. It does this by showing visitors the most popular sites for each category of product selected. It is also moving into the mobile arena, and in March 2010 launched an iPhone app that allows consumers to research products and compare prices while they are in a store. Shopzilla has developed a data categorization technology that it calls Robozilla, designed to help expedite the shopping process. In 2009, Shopzilla redesigned its Web site seeking to enhance the customer experience by adding speed, a better search engine, and more product detail. Shopzilla was able to reduce the search time for products from 6 to 9 seconds, down to 1.2 seconds on average. PriceGrabber is focused on adding product tours and more content, such as user and third-party reviews, and discussion boards. NexTag offers consumers e-mail price alerts and product price history charting, and for merchants, a new data feed auto-import option. Most of the larger sites are adding user-generated reviews and opinions of products.

Companies are also continuing to enter the market every day. HealthPricer lists over 360,000 health products. StylePath focuses on soft goods from jewelry, to clothing, and bed linens, and finds consumers products based on their tastes and interests that they reveal to the shopping engine. StylePath features 200,000 products. Discount-More relaunched its search engine to include a search of all the Web's shopping sites. The site enables consumers to get results from the top 26 shopping sites all on one page. Why not shop all shopping sites at once from a single site?

Despite these innovations, visitors to shopping comparison sites continue to be primarily price motivated: 85% of visitors press the "sort by price" button despite the search engines' efforts to provide more qualitative assessments of quality and reliability. The comparison sites are obviously in competition with search engines, such as Google and Bing (which have their own comparison service). As keyword prices have risen on search engines, shopping comparison sites have become an excellent bargain. But in 2009, some merchants began to complain the comparison sites are getting greedy, and charging excessively high commissions for steering traffic their way. Google Product Search is the most popular comparison shopping engine for merchants in 2010 (73% of the top 500 Internet retailers list with Google Product Search) in large part

(continued)

because it is free. Merchants do not have to bid for keywords or listings, are not charged a commission, and can use Google Analytics to understand their Web performance. Google makes money on this service by placing ads next to the merchant's offering using its AdSense system.

Google's efforts have not yet paid off in terms of visitors, but its user base is growing at greater than 10% a year, and may put downward pressure on the keyword listing fees and commissions charged by other comparison shopping sites.

■■■ **SOURCES:** "Comparison Shopping Engines: Strategies for Smaller Merchants," *Practical eCommerce*, August 25, 2010; "Amazon Moves Up in a Ranking of Comparison Shopping Sites," by Don Davis, *Internet Retailer*, July 20, 2010; "Beyond Compare," by Don Davis, *Internet Retailer*, May 27, 2010; "8 Top Sites for Online Shopping Deals," by Jennifer Mulrean, moneycentral.msn.com, September 14, 2009; "Shopzilla Site Redo—You Get What You Measure," by Philip Dixon, en.oreilly.com, June 24, 2009.

## WHAT ARE SERVICES?

Just what are services? The U.S. Department of Labor defines **service occupations** as "concerned with performing tasks" in and around households, business firms, and institutions (U.S. Department of Labor, 1991). The U.S. Census Bureau defines **service industries** as those "domestic establishments providing services to consumers, businesses, governments, and other organizations" (U.S. Census Bureau, 2001). The major service industry groups are finance, insurance, real estate, travel, professional services such as legal and accounting, business services, health services, and educational services. Business services include activities such as consulting, advertising and marketing, and information processing.

## CATEGORIZING SERVICE INDUSTRIES

Within these service industry groups, companies can be further categorized into those that involve **transaction brokering** (acting as an intermediary to facilitate a transaction) and those that involve providing a "hands-on" service. For instance, one type of financial service involves stockbrokers who act as the middle person in a transaction between buyers and sellers. Online mortgage companies such as LendingTree.com refer customers to mortgage companies that actually issue the mortgage. Employment agencies put a seller of labor in contact with a buyer of labor. The service involved in all these examples is brokering a transaction.

In contrast, legal, medical, accounting, and other such industries perform specific hands-on activities for consumers. In order to provide their service, these professionals need to interact directly and personally with the "client." For these service industries, the opportunities for e-commerce are somewhat different. Currently, doctors and dentists cannot treat patients over the Internet. However, the Internet can assist their services by providing consumers with information, knowledge, and communication.

**service occupations**
occupations concerned with performing tasks in and around households, business firms, and institutions

**service industries**
establishments providing services to consumers, businesses, governments, and other organizations

**transaction brokering**
acting as an intermediary to facilitate a transaction

## KNOWLEDGE AND INFORMATION INTENSITY

With some exceptions (for example, providers of physical services, such as cleaning, gardening, and so on), perhaps the most important feature of service industries (and occupations) is that they are knowledge- and information-intense. In order to provide value, service industries process a great deal of information and employ a highly skilled, educated work force. For instance, to provide legal services, you need lawyers with law degrees. Law firms are required to process enormous amounts of textual information. Likewise with medical services. Financial services are not so knowledge-intensive, but require much larger investments in information processing just to keep track of transactions and investments. In fact, the financial services sector is the largest investor in information technology, with over 80% of invested capital going to information technology equipment and services (Laudon and Laudon, 2011).

For these reasons, many services are uniquely suited to e-commerce applications and the strengths of the Internet, which are to collect, store, and disseminate high-value information and to provide reliable, fast communication.

## PERSONALIZATION AND CUSTOMIZATION

Services differ in the amount of personalization and customization required, although just about all services entail some personalization or customization. Some services, such as legal, medical, and accounting services, require extensive personalization—the adjustment of a service to the precise needs of a single individual or object. Others, such as financial services, benefit from customization by allowing individuals to choose from a restricted menu. The ability of Internet and e-commerce technology to personalize and customize service, or components of service, is a major factor undergirding the extremely rapid growth of e-commerce services. Future expansion of e-services will depend in part on the ability of e-commerce firms to transform their customized services—choosing from a list—into truly personalized services, such as providing unique advice and consultation based on a digital yet intimate understanding of the client (at least as intimate as professional service providers).

## 9.5   ONLINE FINANCIAL SERVICES

Financial services (finance, insurance, and real estate) contribute over $2.8 trillion to the U.S. GDP or about 20% of the total GDP. The online financial services sector is a shining example of an e-commerce success story, but one with many twists and turns. While the innovative, pure-online firms such as E*Trade have been instrumental in transforming the brokerage industry, the impacts of e-commerce on the large, powerful banking, insurance, and real estate firms have been delayed by consumer resistance and the lack of industry innovation. For instance, online-only banks have not displaced or transformed the large national banks or even regional and local banks. But e-commerce has nevertheless transformed the banking and financial industries, as the major institutions have deployed their own online applications to service an increasingly connected online customer base. Four out of five online households now use online banking. Over 20% of mobile Internet users (about 16 million people) are now using mobile banking applications on iPhones and BlackBerries. Insurance has become more standardized and easier to purchase on the Web. In the meltdown of financial institutions in 2008–2009, consumers turned to online financial advice and tracking services as they lost confidence in banks. Consumers are much more willing to trust online sites with their financial information than in the past. Entrepreneurial start-up firms such as Mint.com, SmartyPig, Cake Financial, Wesabe, and Credit Karma showed double-digit growth in 2008 and 2009, but slowed to the upper single digits during 2010. Multi-channel, established financial services firms—the slow followers—also continue to show modest gains in online transactions of about 2%–4% annually.

## FINANCIAL SERVICES INDUSTRY TRENDS

The financial services industry provides four generic kinds of services: storage of and access to funds, protection of assets, means to grow assets, and movement of funds. Historically, in the United States and elsewhere, separate institutions provided these financial services (see **Table 9.5**).

However, two important global trends in the financial services industry that have direct consequences for online financial services firms are changing the institutional structure of financial services. The first trend is industry consolidation (see **Figure 9.3**).

In the United States, the banking, finance, brokerage, and insurance industries were legally separated by the Glass-Steagall Act of 1934, which prohibited banks, insurance firms, and brokerages from having significant financial interests in one another in order to prevent a repetition of the calamitous financial institution failures that followed the stock market crash of 1929 and the ensuing Depression. The Glass-Steagall Act also prevented large banks from owning banks in other states. This legal separation meant that financial institutions in the United States could not provide customers with integrated financial services, and could not operate nationwide. One result was the proliferation of small, inefficient, local banks in the United States, arguably the most "over-banked" country in the world. West European and Japanese financial institutions did not face similar restrictions, putting the

| TABLE 9.5 | TRADITIONAL PROVIDERS OF FINANCIAL SERVICES |
| --- | --- |
| FINANCIAL SERVICE | INSTITUTIONAL PROVIDER |
| Storage of and access to funds | Banking, lending |
| Protection of assets | Insurance |
| Growth | Investment and brokerage firms |
| Movement of funds (payment) | Banks, credit card firms |

| FIGURE 9.3 | INDUSTRY CONSOLIDATION AND INTEGRATED FINANCIAL SERVICES |
|---|---|

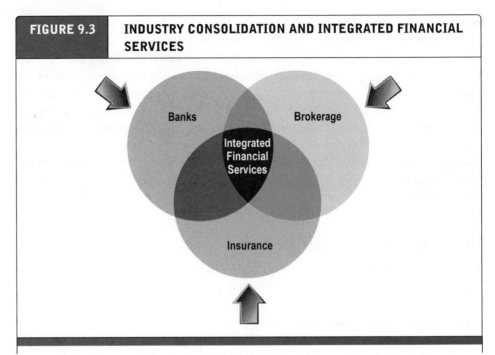

The major trends in financial services are industry consolidation and the provision of integrated financial services to consumers.

American industry at a disadvantage. The Financial Reform Act of 1998 amended Glass-Steagall and permitted banks, brokerages, and insurance firms to merge and to develop nationwide banks. This new law touched off an avalanche of financial service sector consolidations.

The financial meltdown of 2008–2009 demonstrated the risks of permitting financial institution consolidation. The rapid growth of risk-transfer instruments (credit default swaps), and collateralized debt obligations, which began in the late 1990s, greatly expanded the pools of capital available for investment, allowing banks to greatly expand their leverage, and to make loans to subprime customers. The merger of commercial banks with insurance and investment banking meant that they now shared risks: if investment banks failed, so would commercial banks, and the insurance companies that guaranteed all these new instruments. When the U.S. housing and credit markets collapsed in 2007 and 2008, so did the foundation of banking and investment institutions worldwide. Suddenly, what looked like solid assets were worth very little, sometimes nothing. One result is that large money center banks are buying up failed regional and local commercial banks, as well as investment banks and brokerage firms. Consolidation in the banking and investment sphere continues on an accelerated schedule.

A second related trend is the movement toward integrated financial services. Once banks, brokerages, and insurance companies are permitted to own one another, it becomes possible to provide consumers with what countless surveys have documented they really want: trust, service, and convenience. The movement toward financial service integration began in the 1980s when Merrill Lynch developed the first "cash management account" that integrated the brokerage and cash management services provided to Merrill Lynch's customers into a single account. Spare cash in each customer account was invested at the close of business each day into a money market fund. In the 1990s, Citibank and other large money center banks developed the concept of a financial supermarket, where consumers can find any financial product or service at a single physical center or branch bank. Nearly all large national banks now provide some form of financial planning and investment service. As a result of the financial meltdown in 2008, Bank of America took over a failed Merrill Lynch (brokerage and investment banking). Citibank, largely owned by the federal government, continues its former integrated business model of banking, investment banking, insurance, and brokerage.

The Internet has created the technical foundations for an online financial supermarket to operate, but, for the most part, it has still not arrived. It is not yet possible to arrange for a car loan, obtain a mortgage, receive investment planning advice, and establish a pension fund at any single financial institution with one account. Nevertheless, this is the direction in which large banking institutions are attempting to move.

The promise of the Internet in the long term is to take the financial supermarket model one step further by providing a truly personalized, customized, and integrated offering to consumers based on a complete understanding of the consumer and his or her financial behavior, life cycle status, and unique needs. It will take many years to develop the technical infrastructure, as well as change consumer behavior toward a much deeper relationship with online financial services institutions.

## ONLINE FINANCIAL CONSUMER BEHAVIOR

Surveys show that consumers are attracted to financial sites because of their desire to save time and access information rather than save money, although saving money is an important goal among the most sophisticated online financial households. About 67% of generation Xer's and 57% of generation Y users go online to obtain financial information or use online banking or other financial services (Pew Internet & American Life Report, 2009b; USC Annenberg School Center for the Digital Future, 2009). In addition, 69.7 million households use online banking and 64.4 million pay at least one bill online (Fiserv, 2009). Most online consumers use financial services sites for mundane financial management, such as checking balances of existing accounts, and paying bills most of which were established offline. Once accustomed to performing mundane financial management activities, consumers move on to more sophisticated capabilities such as using personal financial management tools, making loan payments, and considering offers from online institutions. **Table 9.6** shows the results of a survey of consumer interest in a wide variety of personal financial services, indicating that consumers are expanding their expectations of online banking.

## ONLINE BANKING AND BROKERAGE

NetBank and Wingspan Bank pioneered online banking in the United States in 1996 and 1997, respectively. Traditional banks had developed earlier versions of telephone bank-

| TABLE 9.6 | INTEREST IN ONLINE PERSONAL FINANCIAL SERVICES |
|---|---|
| ONLINE BANKING SERVICES | PERCENTAGE OF RESPONDENTS INTERESTED |
| Free identity theft services | 63% |
| Free credit score monitoring | 52% |
| Personal financial management | 37% |
| Chat/Instant messaging service | 30% |
| Widget | 27% |
| Blog | 20% |

SOURCES: Based on data from comScore, 2009; Reuters, 2009.

banking, but did not use online services until 1998. Although late by a year or two, the established brand-name national banks have taken a substantial lead in market share as the percentage of their customers who bank online has grown rapidly. **Table 9.7** lists the top five online banks in 2010, ranked by the percentage of all Web visits to online banks. The top banks are all large, national and international banks. Pure online banks such as ING Direct and VirtualBank continue to offer higher returns to consumers, but have not grown at the rates initially expected. NetBank, one of the original pioneers, declared bankruptcy in 2007, primarily as a result of the subprime mortgage loan crisis.

According to eMarketer, around 99 million U.S. consumers are expected to conduct some online banking activity in 2010, and this number is expected to show slow but steady growth of 4-5% a year, growing to around 116 million by 2014 (eMarketer, Inc., 2010b; comScore, 2010a) (see **Figure 9.4**).

The history of online brokerage has been similar to that of online banking. Early innovators such as E*Trade have been displaced from their leadership positions in

| TABLE 9.7 | TOP ONLINE BANKS: SEPTEMBER 2010 |
|---|---|
| BANK (RANKED BY VISITORS) | PERCENTAGE OF TOTAL WEB BANK VISITS |
| Bank of America Online Banking | 7.33% |
| Chase Online | 6.93% |
| Wells Fargo-Online Banking | 4.16% |
| Wachovia Online Services | 3.23% |
| Capital One Online Banking | 1.82% |

SOURCES: Based on data from Hitwise, 2010.

| FIGURE 9.4 | THE GROWTH OF ONLINE BANKING |

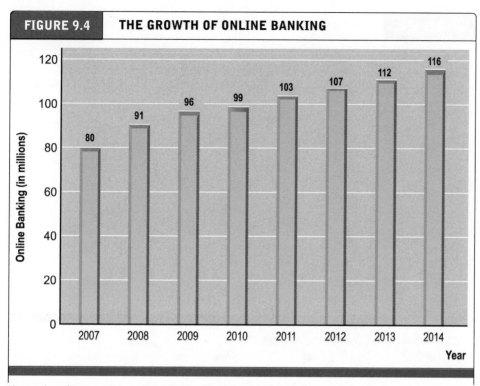

The number of Internet users using online banking is expected to grow to around 116 million by 2014. About 60% of the U.S. Internet population visits at least one of the top 20 online banks. Increases in mobile banking may impact these numbers over the next three years.

SOURCES: Based on data from comScore, 2010; eMarketer, 2010b; authors' estimates.

terms of numbers of online accounts by discount broker pioneer Charles Schwab and financial industry giant Fidelity (which has more mutual fund customers and more funds under management than any other U.S. firm).

Today, according to Nielsen Net Ratings, 20 million U.S. investors trade online, a number expected to increase to approximately 29 million by 2013. According to a survey of online financial activities over the previous 12 months among U.S. adult Internet users, 20% traded stocks (eMarketer, Inc., 2009). According to Nielsen, in terms of unique visitors, the top trading Web site among U.S. Internet users in 2010 was Fidelity Investments, with around 4.5 million (see **Table 9.8**).

## Multi-channel vs. Pure Online Financial Services Firms

Online consumers prefer to visit financial services sites that have physical outlets or branches. In general, multi-channel financial services firms that have both physical branches or offices and solid online offerings are growing faster than pure-online firms that have no physical presence, and they are assuming market leadership as well. Traditional banking firms have literally thousands of branches where customers can open accounts, deposit money, take out loans, find home mortgages, and rent a safety deposit box. Top online brokerage firms do not have

| TABLE 9.8 | TOP ONLINE BROKERAGES, 2010 |
|---|---|
| FIRM | NUMBER OF UNIQUE VISITORS (IN MILLIONS) |
| Fidelity.com | 4.5 |
| ShareBuilder | 3.7 |
| Scottrade | 2.2 |
| Ameritrade | 1.8 |
| E*Trade | 1.8 |
| Vanguard | 1.7 |
| Charles Schwab | 1.5 |
| Merrill Lynch | 0.8 |
| SaneBull | 0.7 |
| Troweprice.coml | 0.7 |

SOURCES: Based on data from Marketingcharts.com, 2010.

the same physical footprint as the banks do, but each has a strong physical presence or telephone presence to strengthen its online presence. Fidelity has urban walk-in service center branches, but it primarily relies on the telephone for interacting with investors. Charles Schwab has decided to open investment centers around the country as an integral part of its online strategy. Pure-online banks and brokerages cannot provide customers with some services that still require a hands-on interaction.

### Financial Portals and Account Aggregators

**financial portals**
sites that provide consumers with comparison shopping services, independent financial advice, and financial planning

**Financial portals** are sites that provide consumers with comparison shopping services, independent financial advice, and financial planning. Independent portals do not themselves offer financial services, but act as steering mechanisms to online providers. They generate revenue from advertising, referral fees, and subscription fees. For example, Yahoo's financial portal, Yahoo Finance, offers consumers credit card purchase tracking, market overviews, real-time stock quotes, news, financial advice, streaming-video interviews with financial leaders, and Yahoo Bill Pay, an EBPP system. Other independent financial portals include Intuit's Quicken.com, MSN's MSN Money, CNN Money, and America Online's Money & Finance channel. A host of new, smaller financial portal sites have sprung up to help consumers with financial management and planning such as Mint.com, SmartPiggy, Wesabe, and Credit Karma.

In general, the financial portals do not offer financial services (they make their money from advertising); instead, they add to the online price competition in the industry and run counter to the strategy of large banking institutions to ensnare consumers into a single branded, financial institutional system, with a single account and high switching costs.

**Account aggregation** is the process of pulling together all of a customer's financial (and even nonfinancial) data at a single personalized Web site, including brokerage, banking, insurance, loans, frequent flyer miles, personalized news, and much more. For example, a consumer can see his or her TD Ameritrade brokerage account, Fidelity 401(k) account, Travelers Insurance annuity account, and American Airlines frequent flyer miles all displayed on a single site. The idea is to provide consumers with a holistic view of their entire portfolio of assets, no matter what financial institution actually holds those assets.

**account aggregation**
the process of pulling together all of a customer's financial (and even nonfinancial) data at a single personalized Web site

The leading provider of account aggregation technology is Yodlee. It uses screen-scraping and other techniques to pull information from over 12,000 different data sources. A smart-mapping technology is also used so that if the underlying Web sites change, the scraping software can adapt and still find the relevant information. Today, Yodlee has more than 25 million personal financial management (PFM) users worldwide and is used by 200 leading financial institutions (Yodlee, 2010).

## ONLINE MORTGAGE AND LENDING SERVICES

During the early days of e-commerce, hundreds of firms launched pure-play online mortgage sites to capture the U.S. home mortgage market. Early entrants hoped to radically simplify and transform the traditional mortgage value chain process, dramatically speed up the loan closing process, and share the economies with consumers by offering lower rates.

By 2003, over half of these early-entry, pure-online firms had failed. Early pure-play online mortgage institutions had difficulties developing a brand name at an affordable price and failed to simplify the mortgage generation process. They ended up suffering from high start-up and administrative costs, high customer acquisition costs, rising interest rates, and poor execution of their strategies.

Despite this rocky start, the online mortgage market is slowly growing; it is dominated by established online banks and other online financial services firms, traditional mortgage vendors, and a few successful online mortgage firms.

About $2 trillion worth of mortgages were originated in 2009, down from over $2.8 trillion in 2008 due to the collapse of the housing market and weakness in the banking sector (MBA, 2010). More than half of all mortgage shoppers research mortgages online, but few actually apply online because of the complexity of mortgages. Most mortgages today are written by intermediary mortgage brokers, with banks still playing an important origination role but generally not servicing mortgages they originate.

Although online mortgage originations currently represent a small percentage of all mortgages, their number is expected to continue to grow slowly but surely over the next several years, although in 2010 the number of mortgages being originated in all forms has been negatively impacted by the subprime mortgage crisis.

There are three kinds of online mortgage vendors:

- Established banks, brokerages, and lending organizations such as Chase, Bank of America/Countrywide Credit Industries, Wells Fargo, Ameriquest Mortgage, and Citigroup (which operates Mortgage.com).

- Pure online mortgage bankers/brokers such as E-Loan, Quicken Loans, and E*Trade Mortgage. These companies aim to expedite the mortgage shopping and initiation process, but still require extensive paperwork to complete a mortgage.

- Mortgage brokers such as LendingTree.com, owned by IAC/InterActiveCorp. These companies offer visitors access to hundreds of mortgage vendors who bid for their business.

Consumer benefits from online mortgages include reduced application times, market interest rate intelligence, and process simplification that occurs when participants in the mortgage process (title, insurance, and lending companies) share a common information base. Mortgage lenders benefit from the cost reduction involved in online processing of applications, while charging rates marginally lower than traditional bricks-and-mortar institutions.

Nevertheless, the online mortgage industry has not transformed the process of obtaining a mortgage. A significant brake on market expansion is the complexity of the mortgage process, which requires physical signatures and documents, multiple institutions, and complex financing details—such as closing costs and points—that are difficult for shoppers to compare across vendors. Nevertheless, as in other areas, the ability of shoppers to find low mortgage rates on the Web has helped reduce the fees and interest rates charged by traditional mortgage lenders.

## ONLINE INSURANCE SERVICES

In 1995, the price of a $500,000 20-year term life policy for a healthy 40-year-old male was $995 a year. In 2010, the same policy could be had for around $400—a decline of about 60%—while other prices have risen 15% in the same period. In a study of the term life insurance business, Brown and Goolsbee discovered that Internet usage led to an 8%–15% decline in term life insurance prices industry-wide (both offline and online), and increased consumer surplus by about $115 million per year (and hence reduced industry profits by the same amount) (Brown and Goolsbee, 2000). Price dispersion for term life policies initially increased, but then fell as more and more people began using the Internet to obtain insurance quotes.

Unlike books and CDs, where online price dispersion is higher than offline, and in many cases online prices are higher than offline, term life insurance stands out as one product group supporting the conventional wisdom that the Internet will lower search costs, increase price comparison, and lower prices to consumers. Term life insurance is a commodity product, however, and in other insurance product lines, the Web offers insurance companies new opportunities for product and service differentiation and price discrimination.

The insurance industry forms a major part of the $2.8 trillion financial services sector. It has four major segments: automobile, life, health, and property and casualty. Insurance products can be very complex. For example, there are many different types of non-automotive property and casualty insurance: liability, fire, homeowners, commercial, workers' compensation, marine, accident, and other lines such as vacation insurance. Writing an insurance policy in any of these areas is very information-intense, often necessitating personal inspection of the properties, and it requires considerable actuarial experience and data. The life insurance industry has also developed life insurance policies that defy easy comparison and can only be explained and sold by an experienced sales agent. Historically, the insurance industry has relied on thousands of local insurance offices and agents to sell complex products uniquely suited to the circumstances of the insured person and the property. Complicating the insurance marketplace is the fact that the insurance industry is not federally regulated, but rather is regulated by 50 different state insurance commissions that are strongly influenced by local insurance agents. Before a Web site can offer quotations on insurance, it must obtain a license to enter the insurance business in all the states where it provides quotation services or sells insurance.

Like the online mortgage industry, the online insurance industry has been very successful in attracting visitors who are looking to obtain prices and terms of insurance policies. While many national insurance underwriting companies initially did not offer competitive products directly on the Web because it might injure the business operations of their traditional local agents, the Web sites of almost all of the major firms now provide the ability to obtain an online quote. Even if consumers do not actually purchase insurance policies online, the Internet has proven to have a powerful influence on consumer insurance decisions by dramatically reducing search costs and changing the price discovery process. Some of the leading online insurance services companies are InsWeb, Insure.com, Insurance.com, QuickQuote, and NetQuote.

## ONLINE REAL ESTATE SERVICES

Real estate is a $1.7 trillion industry. Commercial real estate involves around 4.9 million commercial buildings with around 64 billion square feet of floor space. During 2009, there were approximately 129 million housing units in the United States, of which approximately 18.7 million were available for sale or rent. Finally, about $46 billion changed hands in real estate commissions for real estate transactions of all kinds. All together, despite the economic downturn, these metrics still make real estate a very attractive market (U.S. Census Bureau, 2010).

During the early days of e-commerce, real estate seemed ripe for an Internet revolution that would rationalize this historically local, complex, and local agent-driven industry that monopolized the flow of consumer information. Potentially, the Internet and e-commerce might have disintermediated this huge marketspace, allowing buyers and sellers, renters, and owners to transact directly; lower search costs to near zero; and dramatically reduce prices. However, this did not happen. What did happen is extremely beneficial to buyers and sellers, as well as to real estate agents. At one point, there was an estimated 100,000 real estate sites on the Internet worldwide. Many of these sites have disappeared. However, the remaining online sites have started to make headway toward transforming the industry. In addition, most local real estate brokers in the United States have their own agency Web sites to deal with clients, in addition to participating with thousands of other agencies in multiple listing services that list homes online. Some of the major online real estate sites are Realtor.com, HomeGain, RealEstate.com, ZipRealty, Move.com, Craigslist.com, and Zillow.

Real estate differs from other types of online financial services because it is impossible to complete a property transaction online. Clearly, the major impact of Internet real estate sites is in influencing offline decisions. The Internet has become a compelling method for real estate professionals, homebuilders, property managers and owners, and ancillary service providers to communicate with and provide information to consumers. According to a survey conducted by the National Association of Realtors, the percentage of respondents receiving leads from the Internet grew to 50% in recent years, and 93% of those who received Internet leads indicated that the leads ultimately resulted in a sale (Center for Realtor Technology, National Association of Realtors, 2007). Another survey, the California Association of Realtors "2008 Survey of California Home Buyers," found that over 78% of all first-time homebuyers used the Internet for a significant part of the home-buying process, compared to only 28% in 2000. In general, Internet buyers were younger, wealthier, better educated, and more likely to be married than traditional buyers. According to the survey, more than nine out of 10 indicated that the Internet helped them better understand the process of buying a home. Most indicated that they preferred the dynamic online experience offered by the Internet compared to the static experience provided by newspaper advertisements. In particular, multiple pictures/slide shows, and maps showing the location of homes, were among the highest-rated online features (California Association of Realtors, 2008).

The primary service offered by real estate sites is a listing of houses available. For example, Realtor.com, the official site of the National Association of Realtors, listed over 4 million homes, and had over 10 million unique visitors in August 2010. The offerings have become sophisticated and integrated. Listings typically feature detailed property descriptions, multiple photographs, and virtual 360-degree tours. Consumers can link to mortgage lenders, credit reporting agencies, house inspectors, and surveyors. There are also online loan calculators, appraisal reports, sales price histories by neighborhood, school district data, crime reports, and social and historical information on neighborhoods. Some online real estate brokers now charge substantially less than traditional offline brokers who typically charge 6% of the sale price. They can do this because the buyers (and in some cases, the seller) do much of the work of traditional real estate agents, such as prospecting, choosing neighborhoods, and identifying houses of interest prior to contacting an online agent. For instance, Move.com also offers a "Find a Neighborhood" feature that allows users to choose the type of neighborhood they want to live in by weighing factors such as the quality (and tax costs) of schools, age of the population, number of families with children nearby, and available social and recreational services.

Despite the revolution in available information, there has not been a revolution in the industry value chain. The listings available on Web sites are provided by local multiple listing services supported by local real estate agents. Sometimes, addresses of the houses are not available, and online users are directed to the local listing agent who is hired by the seller of house. Traditional hands-on real estate brokers will show the house and handle all transactions with the owner to preserve their fees, typically ranging from 5% to 6% of the transaction.

## 9.6 ONLINE TRAVEL SERVICES

Travel and tourism in the United States contribute over $748 billion to the U.S. GDP, with online travel services becoming an ever larger part of the picture. Online travel is one of the most successful B2C e-commerce segments. The Internet is becoming the most common channel used by consumers to research travel options, seek the best possible prices, and book reservations for airline tickets, hotel rooms, rental cars, cruises, and tours. According to eMarketer, 2007 was the first year in which more travel (51%) was booked online than offline. Online booking revenues declined slightly to $88 billion in 2009 from $94 billion in 2008 due to the recession, but have begun to growing again in 2010, increasing to around $119 billion by 2014. (see **Figure 9.5**) (eMarketer, Inc., 2010c). For more on some of the issues facing online travel services, see *Insight on Society: Hotel Tax Battle: The Online Travel Industry vs. Local Government*.

### WHY ARE ONLINE TRAVEL SERVICES SO POPULAR?

Online travel sites offer consumers a one-stop, convenient, leisure and business travel experience where travelers can find content (descriptions of vacations and facilities), community (chat groups and bulletin boards), commerce (purchase of all travel elements), and customer service (usually through call centers). Online sites offer much more information and many more travel options than traditional travel agents.

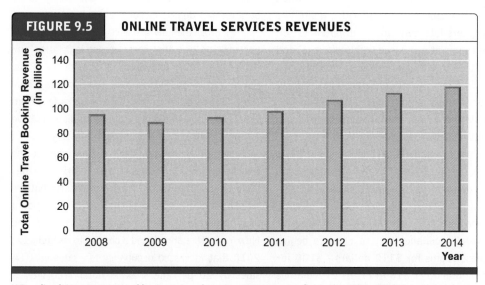

**FIGURE 9.5** | **ONLINE TRAVEL SERVICES REVENUES**

U.S. online leisure/unmanaged business travel service revenues were flat in the 2008–2009 time period, but began growing in 2010.

SOURCE: Based on data from eMarketer, 2010c.

# INSIGHT ON SOCIETY

## HOTEL TAX BATTLE: THE ONLINE TRAVEL INDUSTRY VS. LOCAL GOVERNMENT

Online travel agencies (OTAs) are one of the staples of e-commerce, with over 47 million unique Internet users visiting an online travel site in July 2010. Sites like Expedia, Orbitz, Priceline, and Travelocity are all successful and have remained profitable despite the ongoing economic downturn. Part of the reason these sites have been so successful is their strong relationship with hotels, which provide rooms in bulk to OTAs. The OTA then resells the rooms to its customers at a slight markup. This partnership has been a lucrative one for both parties, since online travel agencies make money on each sale, and hotels often sell many more rooms than they could on their own.

However, cash-strapped local governments have their sights set on OTAs for a taxation practice that they believe is unfair and possibly illegal, straining the relationship between hotels and online agencies in the process. Online travel sites most often use the wholesale booking model when dealing with hotels. Under this model, a site like Expedia enters into contracts with hotels to sell blocks of rooms at a reduced wholesale rate, and then sells the room at the regular price. But when it comes time for Expedia to remit taxes to local governments, it uses the reduced wholesale rate to calculate the money owed, instead of the price at which it resold the room.

Let's use an example to illustrate what OTAs are doing. Suppose that Expedia purchased a block of rooms for $70 apiece. The rooms normally cost $100 for customers paying directly through the hotel. The hotel is in a state with a 10 percent hotel occupancy tax, so Expedia begins selling these rooms for $110 dollars - $100 for the room and another $10 in taxes. Expedia has made a profit on the transaction, and must pay a tax of its own to local authorities. But Expedia will use the $70 base price of the room to calculate the taxes it owes, rather than the $100 base price at which it sold the room. In this example, that means local governments would collect only $7 instead of $10. Where do those extra three dollars go? Into Expedia's pockets, of course.

Three dollars might not seem like much, but for sites like Expedia, which is the top U.S. online travel site with nearly 32 million unique online visitors in 2010, it adds up quickly. But the Interactive Travel Services Association (ITSA), which represents Expedia and other online travel agencies, has argued that this practice is far from illegal. Because the OTAs classify their markup from the wholesale rate as a 'service fee', they believe that it's not a taxable service and therefore not subject to the same taxation regulations. Andrew Weinstein, an ITSA spokesman, stated the following in defense of the policy: "We believe there's a very clear emerging standard of law in this area, that online companies are not covered by occupancy taxes because they do not own or operate hotels."

In fact, the law's stance on the practice is unclear. It's true that some recent legislation and court cases have come down in favor of the OTAs. For example, Missouri recently passed a law barring all of its cities from collecting extra fees from the OTAs. Other individual cities and districts have followed suit. But there are just as many rulings and drafts of legislation that plan to increase the taxes that OTAs must pay. New York City has already rewritten its ordinances to ensure that the amount that travelers get charged is the amount used to determine the tax that must be paid, and New York state announced a change to its budget in 2010 that increased occupancy tax rates on OTA sales by 20 percent, making hotel Web sites a cheaper alternative. In May 2009, a court in Washington state ruled that Expedia had to pay $184.5

(continued)

million in damages due to hidden charges and misleading their customers regarding fees. More than 40 other cities have lawsuits pending with OTAs, and that number is steadily growing.

Because booking hotels has been one of the most profitable streams of revenue for online travel sites, they don't plan to accept these changes quietly. Expedia, Orbitz, Travelocity, and a host of their affiliates as well as other travel sites have been promoting a piece of legislation called the Internet Travel Tax Fairness Act (ITTFA). The ITTFA is a draft of a bill created by ITSA that the organization claims "will protect online travelers from being taxed twice on each hotel visit they book online - once on the cost of the hotel room and a second time on the service fees for booking the room." The Senate has already begun considering the prospective bill (you can read the draft bill at TravelersFirst.org). Each of the major online travel sites have sent out e-mails and created links to TravelersFirst on their own site to sway their customers in favor of the bill. Users can log on and send a form letter supporting the bill to their state's senators. By describing the change as an extra tax, the OTAs hope to galvanize their customers in favor of the status quo, even though not much will change for customers either way.

Rival organizations like the American Hotel and Lodging Association (AHLA) and the National Association of Counties (NACO) have both blasted the prospective ITTFA, claiming that it would give preferential treatment to online travel companies at the expense of their constituents: hotel companies and local governments. Hotel companies would be forced to pull some of their rooms back from online travel sites to minimize their disadvantage, and local governments would be forced to raise taxes on hotel companies to replace the revenues lost by making the OTAs' tax status official.

Lost in the squabble is the fact that during tough times, the two groups need each other more than ever, and that the friction between them is only hurting consumers and an already weakened travel industry. For example, in Georgia, where court rulings in Columbus and Atlanta specified that online travel sales must pay taxes on the final sale price for rooms they sell, many OTAs have taken down all of the hotels affiliated with those cities from their sites, limiting consumers' options. The travel industry has been hampered by the recession, unemployment, terrorism, and general uncertainty. A protracted legal battle between online travel agencies and local government and businesses isn't likely to make things any better.

**SOURCES:** "Leading US Online Travel Sites, Ranked by Number of Unique Visitors, July 2009-July 2010," eMarketer, August 19, 2010; "New York Eyes Special Hotel Occupancy Tax on Online Travel Intermediaries," Dennis Schaal, tnooz.com, August 2, 2010; "Cities, Websites and Hotels At Odds Over Taxes", Alan Greenblatt, npr.org, July 30, 2010; "Online giants take their hotel-tax battle to consumers," Jeri Clausing, *Travel Weekly*, July 14, 2010; "Hotel-Tax Debate Widens," *Wall Street Journal*, July 8, 2010; "TravelersFirst.org Debuts to Fight Taxes on Online Travel", www.travelpulse.com; "It May Be 'Bon Voyage' for a Travel Site's Fee," Gretchen Morgenson, *New York Times*, June 6, 2009.

For suppliers—the owners of hotels, rental cars, and airlines—the online sites aggregate millions of consumers into singular, focused customer pools that can be efficiently reached through onsite advertising and promotions. Online sites create a much more efficient marketplace, bringing consumers and suppliers together in a low transaction cost environment.

Travel services appear to be an ideal service for the Internet, and therefore e-commerce business models should work well for this product. Travel is an information-intensive product requiring significant consumer research. It is an electronic product in the sense that travel requirements—planning, researching, comparison shopping, reserving, and payment—can be accomplished for the most part online in a digital environment. On the travel reservation side, travel does not require any "inventory": there are no physical assets. And the suppliers of the product—owners of hotels, airlines, rental cars, vacation rooms, and tour guides—are highly fragmented and often have excess capacity. Always looking for customers to fill vacant rooms and rent idle cars, suppliers will be anxious to lower prices and willing to advertise on Web sites that can attract millions of consumers. The online agencies—such as Travelocity, Expedia, and others—do not have to deploy thousands of travel agents in physical offices across the country but can instead concentrate on a single interface with a national consumer audience. Travel services may not require the kind of expensive multi-channel "physical presence" strategy required of financial services (although they generally operate centralized call centers to provide personal customer service). Therefore, travel services might "scale" better, permitting earnings to grow faster than costs. But these efficiencies also make it hard for reservation sites to make a profit.

## THE ONLINE TRAVEL MARKET

There are four major sectors in the travel market: airline tickets, hotel reservations, car rentals, and cruises/tours. Airline tickets are the source of the greatest amount of revenue in online travel, accounting for an estimated $54 billion in 2010, and projected to grow at a rate of about 5%–6% a year to $69 billion in 2014. Hotels and car rentals, although not as large from a dollar standpoint as airline reservations, are also expected to grow at about the same rate (see **Figure 9.6** on page 623).

The huge size and continued growth in online airline reservations reflects several factors. Airline reservations are largely a commodity. They can be easily described over the Web. The same is true with car rentals; most people can reliably rent a car over the phone or the Web and expect to obtain what they ordered (see *Insight on Business: Zipcars* for a different kind of car rental business model). Although hotels are somewhat more difficult to describe, hotel branding, supplemented by Web sites that include descriptions, photographs, and virtual tours, typically provide enough information to most consumers to allow them to feel as if they know what they are purchasing, making them more comfortable making hotel reservations online.

Increasingly, corporations are outsourcing their travel offices entirely to vendors who can provide Web-based solutions, high-quality service, and lower costs. Online vendors to corporations provide **corporate online booking solutions (COBS)** that provide integrated airline, hotel, conference center, and auto rental services at a single site.

**corporate online-booking solutions (COBS)**

provide integrated airline, hotel, conference center, and auto rental services at a single site

## ONLINE TRAVEL INDUSTRY DYNAMICS

Because much of what travel agency sites offer is a commodity, and thus they face the same costs, competition among online providers is intense. Price competition is difficult because shoppers, as well as online site managers, can comparison shop easily. Therefore, competition among sites tends to focus on scope of offerings, ease

# INSIGHT ON BUSINESS

## ZIPCARS

How would you like to have all the functionality of a car but not have to deal with any of the headaches typically associated with ownership of a car, such as maintenance and insurance, garaging, or even with the rental of a car from a traditional car rental agency that requires that you go to an office, stand in line, and fill out papers in order to rent, and that mandates a minimum rental period of at least one day?

This might sound like an impossible dream, but it's not. In the late 1990s, a new business model for renting cars was imported from Europe by a group of environmentally conscious entrepreneurs that leverages the power of the Web to make the dream a reality. Today, Zipcar, along with a number of other smaller companies, are using this model on their way towards sustained growth.

Zipcar began in 1999 with a single lime-green Volkswagen Bug in Cambridge, Massachusetts, and slowly grew within the city. Members ("Zipsters") could pick up cars at any one of several parking spots around Cambridge, use them for as long as they wanted, and then return them to the same parking spot. Today, the combined company has 9,000 cars and 400,000 members, who pay $25 to enroll and $50 a year for membership and as low as $7 per hour to use a car depending on the city. The company operates in 13 metropolitan areas in the U.S. cities, more than 150 college campuses, and in London, Toronto and Vancouver.

Zipcar brings the Web 2.0 culture of sharing online videos and tweets to the car transportation market. An online application costs $25 and takes minutes to complete, and 94% of applicants are accepted. Zipcars are parked mostly in small clusters—between 2 and 20—in neighborhood garages, shoulder to shoulder with the owned and leased cars of the unenlightened. There over 1,000 Zipcars in the New York area, where 4.5 million people live within a 10-minute walk of one. In Manhattan, a mix of Honda Civics, Toyotas, Volkswagens, Volvos, and BMW Mini Coopers are available. As one commentator noted: "It's such a brazen conceit that it would seem positively communist if Zipcar weren't run by a bunch of fervent free marketers." Zipcar's predicate is that sharing is big business too—bigger, potentially, than anyone can fathom. Its claim is that the winners in the new economy will be those who crack the puzzle posed by scarce resources. In other words, in certain circles, sharing a Zipcar is cooler than owning a BMW!

In order to make the business work, Zipcar uses a lot of technology and tries to reduce the human-customer contact as much as possible to keep expenses low. Here's how it works. Customers pay an annual subscription fee and are issued a Zipcard, a card subscribers use to lock and unlock Zipcars that they've reserved. Customers go online or call an automated central number to reserve a car. Rates start at $7 per hour and vary depending on the vehicle, or $77 for a full day. Once a customer rents a car, a central computer activates the car's key card entry system to permit that customer to enter the car and start the engine. Customers return cars to the same locations and their credit cards are billed. Using wireless technology, the Internet, and automated voice recognition software at each city's central office, Zipcar is able to keep costs very low.

Zipcar is supported by universities as well as city governments looking for ways to discourage car ownership, and encourage car sharing, to reduce pollution and congestion. Zipcar has exclu-

(continued)

sive arrangements with Johns Hopkins, University of Michigan, University of North Carolina, Ohio State, Notre Dame, Yale, and many others. In these deals, the universities promise the car will make a certain revenue level per year (usually about $100,000) and make up the difference if they do not hit that revenue target. In September 2009, Los Angeles Zipcar expanded its fleet to 40 cars and partnered with city officials, UCLA, and USC by moving vehicles into their neighborhoods. In San Francisco, when the Bay Bridge closed for repairs in September 2009, over 350 Zipcars were located near BART rapid transit terminals in the Bay Area so residents could take trains to stations, and hop into Zipcars to drive to their final destinations. In an emergency, Zipcars can act as a reserve mini-mass transportation system.

Zipcar's customers are not Middle America, the people who own 200 million cars. Instead, most of Zipcar's customers are young urban professionals or college students, a market shunned by traditional car rental companies who typically will not rent to drivers under 21. The attraction for college students is that they save money compared to owning cars that sit idle while they are in classes. In urban areas, Zipcar users report they are saving over $500 a month on car operational and parking costs alone. Consider that in Manhattan, where studio apartments rent for $2,500 a month, garage parking for your personal four-wheeler will run another $300.

Car sharing is also green: national studies show that each shared car replaces up to 20 privately owned vehicles. Some corporations in major cities are thinking about eliminating their urban fleets and using car-sharing services.

However, it's unclear that Zipcar can expand beyond large cities and universities. The idea might not work as well in the suburbs, because customers would have to drive a car to pick up a Zipcar rental. On the other hand, Zipcar executives see a fleet of about 1 million cars in the future just in urban areas. This fleet would replace 20 million privately owned vehicles, one-tenth of the U.S. private fleet. Who needs the burbs? Traditional car rental companies have begun to respond to Zipcar by opening small neighborhood rental shops that make it much more convenient to rent cars. But these firms are not Web-enabled like Zipcar, and lack the technology infrastructure to compete effectively. Zipcar, for instance, spent over $500,000 on a fleet reservation system that connects users, their Web site, and the cars themselves. Avis, Budget, National? Call the 800-number. But the majors are not standing still now that Zipcar has pioneered the marketplace. In 2009, Hertz started its own car-sharing service Connect by Hertz in New York, London, and Paris, with a fleet of Mini Coopers in each city. Hertz charges a flat hourly fee and its rates are lower than Zipcar's. In the New York area, Hertz has over 40,000 vehicles, many of which could ultimately be put into the program.

So far, Zipcar is not worrying about the competition. In June 2010, Zipcar filed for an IPO, and though it hasn't set a date or a price as of September 2010, the company expects to raise about $75 million. Zipcar hasn't yet turned a profit, but it has steadily increased its revenue throughout the economic recession. As the dominant leader in the car-sharing market with over 75% market share, the company is also encouraged by analysts' predictions that the industry could grow from $253 million today to $3.3 billion by 2016. That's a lot of reasons to be optimistic about Zipcar's future.

**▬    SOURCES:** "Car Sharing: Ownership by the Hour," by Ken Belson, *New York Times*, September 10, 2010; "Zipcar Files for an IPO," by Lynn Cowan and Brendan Conway, *Wall Street Journal*, June 2, 2010; "The IPO Class of 2010," by Steve Schaefer, Forbes.com, September 2, 2009; "Share My Ride," by Mark Levine, New York Times, March 8, 2009.

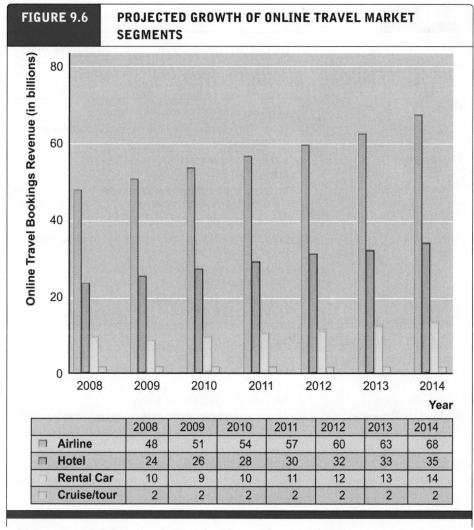

| FIGURE 9.6 | PROJECTED GROWTH OF ONLINE TRAVEL MARKET SEGMENTS |
|---|---|

|  | 2008 | 2009 | 2010 | 2011 | 2012 | 2013 | 2014 |
|---|---|---|---|---|---|---|---|
| Airline | 48 | 51 | 54 | 57 | 60 | 63 | 68 |
| Hotel | 24 | 26 | 28 | 30 | 32 | 33 | 35 |
| Rental Car | 10 | 9 | 10 | 11 | 12 | 13 | 14 |
| Cruise/tour | 2 | 2 | 2 | 2 | 2 | 2 | 2 |

Airline reservations will continue to dominate the online travel market, although hotel reservations and car reservations are growing at a faster rate.

SOURCE: Based on data from eMarketer, Inc., 2010c.

of use, payment options, and personalization. Some well-known travel sites are listed in **Table 9.9**.

The online travel services industry has gone through a period of consolidation with stronger offline, established firms such as Sabre Holdings (which now owns Travelocity, Lastminute, and Site59, among others) purchasing weaker and relatively inexpensive online travel agencies in order to build stronger multi-channel travel sites. Orbitz and Expedia have also been involved in the industry consolidation. Orbitz was initially an industry consortium, then went public, then was purchased by Cendant (along with other travel firms such as CheapTickets and Trip.com), then sold by Cendant to Blackstone Group, and finally went public again in 2007. Expedia,

| TABLE 9.9 | MAJOR ONLINE TRAVEL SITES |
|---|---|
| NAME | DESCRIPTION |
| *LEISURE/UNMANAGED BUSINESS TRAVEL* | |
| Expedia | Largest online travel service; leisure focus. |
| Travelocity | Second-largest online travel service; leisure focus. Owned by Sabre Holdings. |
| TripAdvisor | Travel shopping bot that searches for the lowest fares across all other sites. |
| Orbitz | Began as supplier-owned reservation system; now part of Orbitz Worldwide, a public company. |
| Priceline | "Name your price" model; leisure focus. |
| CheapTickets | Discount airline tickets, hotel reservations, and auto rentals. Part of Orbitz Worldwide. |
| Hotels.com | Largest hotel reservation network; leisure and corporate focus. Owned by Expedia. |
| Hotwire | Seeks out discount fares based on airline excess inventory. Owned by Expedia. |
| *MANAGED BUSINESS TRAVEL* | |
| GetThere.com | Corporate online booking solution (COBS). Owned by Sabre Holdings. |
| Travelocity Business | Full-service corporate travel agency. |

originally begun by Microsoft, was purchased by Barry Diller's conglomerate IAC/InterActiveCorp, but has now been spun off as an independent company once again, picking up IAC's Hotels.com, Hotwire, TripAdvisor, and TravelNow in the process.

In addition to industry consolidation, the online travel industry is also being roiled by new technologies in the form of meta-search engines that scour the Web for the best prices on travel and lodging, and then collect finder or affiliate fees for sending consumers to the lowest-price sites. For instance, TripAdvisor has created a one-stop Web site where consumers can find the lowest price airfares and hotels by searching over 100 other Web travel sites and presenting the fares in rank order. Similar "travel aggregator" sites are SideStep and Mobissimo. These sites, in the eyes of many industry leaders, commoditize the online travel industry even further, cause excessive price competition, and divert revenues from the leading, branded firms who have made extensive investments in inventory and systems.

## 9.7 ONLINE CAREER SERVICES

Next to travel services, one of the Internet's most successful online services has been job services (recruitment sites) that provide a free posting of individual resumes, plus many other related career services; for a fee, they also list job openings posted by companies. Career services sites collect revenue from other sources as well, by providing value-added services to users and collecting fees from related service providers.

The online job market is dominated by two large players: CareerBuilder (which provides job listings for AOL and MSN). and Monster. (Yahoo Hot Jobs, which had been the third large player, as acquired by Monster for $225 million in 2010.). Other popular sites include Job.com, Indeed.com, SimplyHired, and USAJobs. These top sites generate more than $1 billion annually in revenue from employers' fees and consumer fees. Rising unemployment during late 2008 to 2010 has led to an increasing number of Americans seeking jobs and career opportunities online, according to comScore Media Metrix, with career services and development Web sites among the top 10 fastest growing site categories, with a total of over 51 million visitors in January 2010. (comScore, 2010b). The professional social networking site LinkedIn experienced a 20% increase in traffic in 2010 compared to 2009.

Traditionally, companies have relied on five employee recruitment tools: classified and print advertising, career expos (or trade shows), on-campus recruiting, private employment agencies (now called "staffing firms"), and internal referral programs. In comparison to online recruiting, these tools have severe limitations. Print advertising usually includes a per-word charge that limits the amount of detail employers provide about a job opening, as well as a limited time period within which the job is posted. Career expos do not allow for pre-screening of attendees and are limited by the amount of time a recruiter can spend with each candidate. Staffing firms charge high fees and have a limited, usually local, selection of job hunters. On-campus recruiting also restricts the number of candidates a recruiter can speak with during a normal visit and requires that employers visit numerous campuses. And internal referral programs may encourage employees to propose unqualified candidates for openings in order to qualify for rewards or incentives offered.

Online recruiting overcomes these limitations, providing a more efficient and cost-effective means of linking employers and potential employees, while reducing the total time-to-hire. Online recruiting enables job hunters to more easily build, update, and distribute their resumes while gathering information about prospective employers and conducting job searches.

## IT'S JUST INFORMATION: THE IDEAL WEB BUSINESS?

Online recruitment is ideally suited for the Web. The hiring process is an information-intense business process that involves discovering the skills and salary requirements of individuals and matching them with available jobs. In order to accomplish this match up, there does not initially need to be face-to-face interaction, or a great deal of personalization. Prior to the Internet, this information sharing was accomplished locally by human networks of friends, acquaintances, former employers, and relatives, in addition to employment agencies that developed paper files on job hunters. The Internet can clearly automate this flow of information, reducing search time and costs for all parties.

**Table 9.10** lists some of the most popular recruitment sites.

| TABLE 9.10 | POPULAR ONLINE RECRUITMENT SITES |
|---|---|
| **RECRUITMENT SITE** | **BRIEF DESCRIPTION** |
| **General Recruitment Sites** | |
| CareerBuilder | Owned by Gannett, Tribune, McClatchy (all newspaper companies), and Microsoft. Provides job search centers for more than 9,000 Web sites, including AOL and MSN, and 140 newspapers; 1.6 million jobs listed. |
| Monster | One of the first commercial sites on the Web in 1994. Today, a public company offering general job searches in 50 countries, generating revenue of over $905 million a year. |
| Yahoo HotJobs | General job searches. Partners with consortium of newspapers, including Hearst, Cox, MediaNews General, Scripps, and others for cross-listing of job postings. Purchased by Monster in 2010 for $225 million. |
| Kenexa (formerly Brassring) | Management recruitment and job searches |
| Craigslist | Popular classified listing service focused on local recruiting |
| Indeed.com | Job site aggregator |
| SimplyHired | Job site aggregator |
| **Executive Search Sites** | |
| Futurestep | Korn/Ferry site, low-end executive recruiting |
| Spencerstuart.com | Middle-level executive recruiting |
| ExecuNet | Executive search firm |
| **Niche Job Sites** | |
| USAJobs | Federal government jobs |
| HigherEdJobs | Education industry |
| EngineerJobs | Engineering jobs |
| Medzilla | Medical industry |
| Showbizjobs | Entertainment industry |
| Salesjobs | Sales and marketing |
| Dice | Information technology jobs |
| MBAGlobalNet | MBA-oriented community site |

Why are so many job hunters and employers using Internet job sites? Recruitment sites are popular largely because they save time and money for both job hunters and employers seeking recruits. For employers, the job boards expand the geographical reach of their searches, lower costs, and result in faster hiring decisions.

For job seekers, online sites are popular not only because their resumes can be made widely available to recruiters but also because of a variety of other related job-hunting services. The services delivered by online recruitment sites have greatly expanded since their emergence in 1996. Originally, online recruitment sites just provided a digital version of newspaper classified ads. Today's sites offer many other services, including skills assessment, personality assessment questionnaires, personalized account management for job hunters, organizational culture assessments, job search tools, employer blocking (prevents your employer from seeing your posting), employee blocking (prevents your employees from seeing your listings if you are their employer), and e-mail notification. Online sites also provide a number of educational services such as resume writing advice, software skills preparation, and interview tips.

For the most part, online recruitment sites work, in the sense of linking job hunters with jobs, but they are just one of many ways people actually find jobs. A survey by The Conference Board found that the majority (70%) of job seekers rely equally on both the Internet and newspapers to look for jobs, with about half relying on word-of-mouth leads, and about a quarter on employment agencies. Given that the cost of posting a resume online is zero, the marginal returns are very high.

The ease with which resumes can be posted online has also raised new issues for both job recruiters and job seekers. If you are an employer, how do you sort through the thousands of resumes you may receive when posting an open job? If you are a job seeker, how do you stand out among the thousands or even millions of others? Perhaps one way is to post a video resume. In a survey by Vault, nearly nine in 10 employers said they would watch a video resume if it were submitted to them, in part because it would help them better assess a candidate's professional presentation and demeanor, and over half said they believed video would become a common addition to future job applications. CareerBuilder became the first major online job site to implement a video resume tool for job candidates, following a previous launch for an online video brand-building tool for employers.

Perhaps the most important function of online recruitment sites is not so much their capacity to actually match employees with job hunters but their ability to establish market prices and terms, as well as trends in the labor market. Online recruitment sites identify salary levels for both employers and job hunters, and categorize the skill sets required to achieve those salary levels. In this sense, online recruitment sites are online national marketplaces that establish the terms of trade in the labor markets. For instance, Monster.com offers its U.S. Monster Employment Index. This index monitors over 1,500 online job sites and calculates employment demand for the nation, regions, and specific occupations. The existence of these online national job sites should lead to a rationalization of wages, greater labor mobility, and higher efficiency in recruitment and operations because employers will be able to quickly find the people they need.

## ONLINE RECRUITMENT INDUSTRY TRENDS

Trends for 2010–2011 in the online recruitment services industry include the following:

- **Consolidation**: The two major job services are CareerBuilder (owned by newspapers and Microsoft) and Monster (which now owns Yahoo HotJobs). In 2010, these two sites dominate the market, and are expected to do so for some time to come.

- **Diversification**: While the national online market is becoming larger and consolidating into a few general sites, there is an explosion in specialty niche employment sites that focus on specific occupations. This is creating greater online job market diversity and choice.

- **Localization**: While local classified ads in newspapers remain a significant source of jobs, the large national online sites are also developing local boards in large metropolitan areas that compete more directly against local newspapers. The local newspapers themselves have responded by building local Web sites that focus on local job markets, especially hourly and contract jobs that often do not appear on the large national job boards. Craigslist is another source of local job listings. Hence there is a growing focus on local job markets by all participants in the marketplace because this is where so many new jobs first appear.

- **Job search engines/aggregators**: As with travel services, search engines that focus specifically on jobs are posing a new threat to established online career sites. For instance, Indeed.com, SimplyHired, and JobCentral "scrape" listings from thousands of online job sites such as Monster, CareerBuilder, specialty recruiting services, and the sites of individual employers, to provide a free, searchable index of thousands of job listings in one spot. Because these firms do not charge employers a listing fee, they are currently using a pay-per-click or other advertising revenue model.

- **Social networking**: LinkedIn, probably the most well-known business-oriented social network, has grown significantly to over 75 million members representing over 150 different industries in 2,000 countries as of September 2010. Consumers are using sites such as LinkedIn to establish business contacts and networks, while employers use them to conduct searches to find potential job candidates that may not be actively job hunting. For instance, LinkedIn offers companies a tool called LinkedIn Talent Advantage that includes tools that help corporate recruiters find "passive talent" (people who are not actively looking for a new job), as well as custom company profiles that are specifically designed for recruitment (LinkedIn.com, 2009). CareerBuilder offers a job and internship matching application on Facebook that allows users to receive continuously updated listings based on the information found in their profiles. Social network sites are also being used by employers to "check up" on the background of job candidates. A study by Harris Interactive of 2,667 managers and human resource employees found that 45% are using social networks to screen job candidates, and 35% have rejected candidates because of content on a social site. Employers search Facebook, MySpace, and LinkedIn. Seven percent follow candidates on Twitter. Provocative photos were the biggest negative factor followed by drinking and drug references (Careerbuilder.com, 2009).

## 9.8 CASE STUDY

# OpenTable:
## Your Reservation Is Waiting

OpenTable is the leading supplier of reservation, table management, and guest management software for restaurants. In addition, the company operates, OpenTable.com, the world's most popular Web site for making restaurant reservations online. In 12 years, OpenTable has gone from a start-up to a successful and growing public company that counts one-third of the nation's reservation-taking restaurants as clients. And, in the second quarter of 2010, an average of 5 million diners per month made reservations using OpenTable.

Today, more than 12,000 restaurants in the United States, Canada, Mexico, the United Kingdom, Germany, France, Spain, and Japan use the OpenTable hardware and software system. This system automates the reservation-taking and table management process, while allowing restaurants to build diner databases for improved guest recognition and targeted e-mail marketing. The Web site provides a fast, efficient way for diners to find available tables in real time. The Web site connects directly to the thousands of computerized reservation systems at OpenTable restaurants, and reservations are immediately recorded in a restaurant's electronic reservation book.

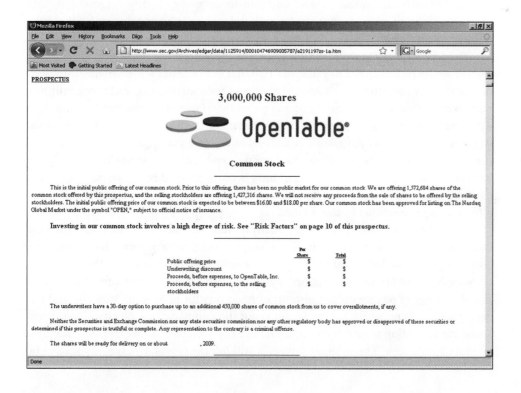

Restaurants subscribe to the OpenTable Electronic Reservation Book (ERB), the company's proprietary software, which is installed on a touch-screen computer system and supported by asset-protection and security tools. The ERB software provides a real-time map of the restaurant floor and enables the restaurant to retain meal patterns of all parties, serving as a customer relationship management (CRM) system for restaurants. The software is upgraded periodically, and the latest version, introduced in August 2010, was designed to provide increased ease of use and a more thorough view of table availability to help turn more tables, enhance guest service, personalize responses to diners, coordinate the seating process and maximize guest seating. The ERBs at OpenTable's customer restaurants connect via the Internet to form an online network of restaurant reservation books.

OpenTable's revenue comes from two sources. Restaurants pay a one-time fee for onsite installation and training, a monthly subscription fee of $199 for software and hardware, and a $1 transaction fee for each restaurant guest seated through online reservations. The online reservation service is free to diners. The business model encourages diners to assist in viral marketing. When an individual makes a reservation, the site "suggests" that they send e-vites to their dinner companions directly from OpenTable.com. The e-vites include a link back to the OpenTable site.

OpenTable is a service-based (software as service, or SaaS) e-commerce company. In other words, customers don't buy software and install it on their computers, but instead go online and get the software functionality through subscriptions. OpenTable is also an online service that does not sell goods, but instead enables diners to make reservations, like social networking sites provide services.

The restaurant industry was slow to leverage the power of the Internet. This was in part because the industry was, and continues to be, highly fragmented, and local—made up of more than 30,000 small, independent businesses or local restaurant-owning groups.

The founders of OpenTable knew that dealing with these restaurants as a single market would be difficult. They also realized that the Internet was changing things for diners by providing them with instant access to reviews, menus, and other information about dining options. And there was no method for making reservations online— we all know reserving by phone is time-consuming, inefficient, and prone to errors. In order to make the system work, reach and scale were very important. For diners to use an online reservation system, they would need real-time access to a number of local restaurants, and the ability to instantly book confirmed reservations around the clock. If customers were planning a trip to another city, OpenTable would need participating restaurants in those cities.

The company was originally incorporated in San Francisco in 1998 as Easyeats.com. In 1999, its name was changed to OpenTable.com, Inc. When the company was founded, most restaurants did not have computers, let alone systems that would allow online reservations made through a central Web site. OpenTable's initial strategy of paying online restaurant reviewers for links to its Web site and targeting national chains for fast expansions got the company into 50 cities, but it was spending $1 million a month and bringing in only $100,000 in revenue. Not exactly a formula for success. The original investors still felt there was a viable business to be built, and they made a number of management changes, including installing investor and board member Thomas Layton, founder of CitySearch.com, as OpenTable's CEO. Mr. Layton cut staff, shut down marketing efforts, and got the company out of all but four cities: Chicago, New York, San Francisco, and Washington, D.C.

The company retooled its hardware and software to create the user-friendly ERB system, and deployed a door-to-door sales force to solicit subscriptions from high-end restaurants. The combination of e-commerce, useful, user-friendly technology, and the personal touch, worked. The four markets Open Table targeted initially developed into active, local networks of restaurants and diners that continue to grow. OpenTable has implemented the same strategy across the country, and now includes approximately 12,250 OpenTable restaurant customers spanning all 50 states as well as over 1,800 in select markets outside of the United States. In 12 years, the company has seated approximately 160 million diners through OpenTable.com.

As the company grew, investors began making plans for it to go public. Mr. Layton stepped down from his position as CEO in 2007, though he remains a board member. He was replaced by Jeffrey Jordan, former president of PayPal. Mr. Jordan had some experience with public companies from working with eBay on their acquisition of PayPal. In 2009, he chose an aggressive strategy—going ahead with an initial public offering (IPO) despite a terrible economy and worse financial markets. So far, his gamble has paid off. On its first day of trading, OpenTable's shares climbed 59%. The share price at the end of September 2010 was $66.33, more than triple the $20 IPO price.

Despite the challenging economy, OpenTable's numbers at the time of the IPO were strong. For the 12 months ended December 31, 2007 and 2008, revenues were $41.1 million and $55.8 million, respectively. During the three-year period from January 2006 through December 2008, OpenTable's revenue grew at an annualized rate of 43%. Despite the severe recession, results from the first quarter of 2009 showed growth as well—revenues in the second quarter of 2010 were $21.2 million, up 36% over the previous year's numbers.

The company benefited tremendously from having e-commerce revenue streams from subscription fees and per-transaction charges, instead of from advertising at a time when advertising expenditures—by companies large and small—have dropped precipitously. Further, more than 50% of OpenTable's revenue comes from B2B subscriptions, which are typically part of long-term contracts. Restaurants that have invested in OpenTable's software package are less likely to want to incur the switching costs associated with changing to a different reservation management package.

Another reason for its success is that OpenTable has a large number of satisfied customers. Restaurant owners report that they and their staff members find the software easy to use, and it helps them manage their business better. Specifically, it streamlines operations, helps fill additional seats, and improves quality of service, providing a concrete return on investment. This has led to both high customer satisfaction and high retention rates.

OpenTable has also taken advantage of the interconnected needs of restaurants and diners. Restaurants want cost-effective ways to attract guests and manage their reservations, while diners want convenient ways to find available restaurants, choose among them, and make reservations. By creating an online network of restaurants and diners that transact with each other through real-time reservations, OpenTable has figured out how to successfully address the needs of both.

OpenTable's market is susceptible to network effects: the more people use it, the more utility the system delivers. OpenTable's growth continually provides diners with expanded choices. More diners discover the benefits of using the online reservation system, which in turn delivers value to restaurant customers, and helps attract more restaurants to the network. Diners serve as a source of viral marketing, as the OpenTable Web site encourages them to e-vite their dinner companions to the meal. When they do so, the e-mail provides links back to the OpenTable Web site. And the OpenTable link appears on the restaurant's Web site, linking directly to the reservation page. OpenTable has been able to improve its efficiency even as diners are staying home more often.

While OpenTable is the biggest, most successful online player in the restaurant reservations market, it does have competitors. MenuPages.com offers access to restaurant menus and reviews, but visitors to the site can't make reservations, and the site covers only eight U.S. cities. UrbanSpoon.com offers a reservation service, but its technology is not compatible with OpenTable, so those reservations must be entered manually into the OpenTable system. Like OpenTable, UrbanSpoon charges $1 for each diner. DinnerBroker.com offers the ability to make online reservations, and offers dining discounts for those willing to eat at off-peak hours. In 2009, they are working with 1,500 restaurants nationwide, far fewer than OpenTable's 14,000-plus. Foodline.com and SavvyDiner.com offer similar services; however, only OpenTable and Foodline provide the option for restaurants to track customer behavior.

While some may argue that there are better ways to make reservations that don't take visitors away from restaurant's Web sites (once someone clicks on the OpenTable link, they navigate away), restaurant owners like the OpenTable software, and diners have an enormous range of dining choices. Those two factors make this argument a relatively weak one. In the past six months, OpenTable's bookings have tripled; a good sign for the future.

The company is committed to innovation when it makes sense, for example, it recently introduced OpenTable applications for PDAs—the Palm Pre, the BlackBerry, and the iPhone. These applications help users find restaurants with the use of GPS, and make reservations. OpenTable also launched Facebook Connect, allowing users to share their reservations on Facebook, as well as a Facebook application called Reservations which allows partner restaurants to offer reservations directly on Facebook.

Along with innovation, OpenTable continues to use its tried and true business model that combines technology with old-fashioned door-to-door sales. Using this model, OpenTable's new North American markets have grown predictably over time, and this growth is projected to continue. OpenTable plans a selective international expansion into countries where there are large numbers of online consumer transactions and reservation-taking restaurants. The company currently has operations in Germany, Japan, and the United Kingdom, each supported with a direct sales force, and has signed on approximately 1,000 restaurant customers in these markets.

The company's international strategy is to replicate the successful U.S. model by focusing initially on building a restaurant customer base. OpenTable believes the localized versions of its software will compete favorably against competitive software offerings, enabling them to expand across a broad selection of local restaurants.

The company is well-positioned for future growth. Its size, track record of growth, and high customer satisfaction rates should continue to work in its favor.

### Case Study Questions

1. Why will OpenTable competitors have a difficult time competing against OpenTable?

2. What characteristics of the restaurant market make it difficult for a reservation system to work?

3. How did OpenTable change its marketing strategy to succeed?

4. Why would restaurants find the SaaS model very attractive?

## 9.9 REVIEW

## KEY CONCEPTS

■ **Understand the environment in which the online retail sector operates today.**

Personal consumption of retail goods and services comprise about 70% and account for about $10 trillion of total GDP. The retail sector can be broken down into three main categories:
- Services, which account for 60% of total retail sales
- Durable goods, which account for 11% of total retail sales
- Nondurable goods, which account for 29% of total retail sales

Although the distinction between a good and a service is not always clear-cut and "product-based services" are becoming the norm, we use the term retail goods to refer to physical products and retailers to refer to firms that sell physical goods to consumers. The retail industry can be further divided into nine major firm types:
- Clothing
- General merchandise
- Groceries
- Durable goods
- Specialty stores
- Eating and drinking
- Gasoline and fuel
- MOTO
- Online retail firms

**SOURCES:** "Behind OpenTable's Success," Kevin Kelleher, CNNMoney.com, September 23, 2010; "OpenTable Introduces the Next Generation of Its Electronic Reservation Book Software," RestaurantNews.com, August 17, 2010; "OpenTable, Inc., Announces Second Quarter Financial Results," OpenTable.com, August 3, 2010; "Open Table: the Hottest Spot in Town," by Maha Atal, CNNMoney.con, August 14, 2009; "OpenTable Unveils Version 2.0 of its iPhone App," AppScout.com, August 14, 2009; Open Table,. Form10-Q for quarter ended June 30, 2009, filed with the Securities and Exchange Commission, August 11, 2008; "Gadgetell: Fight for Your Dinner: Urbanspoon vs. Open Table," NewsFactor.com, August 8, 2009; "Urbanspoon is Now Taking Online Reservations: Takes on OpenTable," by Federic Lardinois, ReadWriteWeb.com, August 7, 2009; "OpenTable Launches BlackBerry App," by Jamie Lendino, PCMag.com, August 5, 2009; "OpenTable App Hits the Palm Pre," AppScout.com, July 29, 2009; "Yelp vs. OpenTable—Where Should Restaurants Spend Their Marketing Dollars," Dinner Rush Blog, reservationdc.wordpress.com, July 19, 2009; May 22, 2009; "What Media Companies Could Learn from Open Table," The Media Wonk, May 20, 2009; Open Table S-1/A Amendment #6, filed with the Securities and Exchange Commission, May 19, 2009.

Each type offers opportunities for online retail. The biggest opportunities for direct online sales are within those segments that sell small-ticket items (less than $100). This includes specialty stores, general merchandisers, mail-order catalogers, and grocery stores. The MOTO sector is the most similar to the online retail sales sector, and MOTO retailers are among the fastest growing online retail firms.

During the early days of e-commerce, some predicted that the retail industry would be revolutionized, based on the following beliefs:

- Greatly reduced search costs on the Internet would encourage consumers to abandon traditional marketplaces in order to find the lowest prices for goods. First movers who provided low-cost goods and high-quality service would succeed.
- Market entry costs would be much lower than those for physical storefront merchants, and online merchants would be more efficient at marketing and order fulfillment than their offline competitors because they had command of the technology (technology prices were falling sharply).
- Online companies would replace traditional stores as physical store merchants were forced out of business. Older traditional firms that were too slow to enter the online market would be locked out of the marketplace.
- In certain industries, the "middleman" would be eliminated (disintermediation) as manufacturers or their distributors entered the market and built a direct relationship with the consumer. This cost savings would ensure the emergence of the Web as the dominant marketing channel.
- In other industries, online retailers would gain the advantage over traditional merchants by outsourcing functions such as warehousing and order fulfillment, resulting in a kind of hypermediation, in which the online retailer gained the upper hand by eliminating inventory purchasing and storage costs.

Today, it has become clear that few of the initial assumptions about the future of online retail were correct. Also, the structure of the retail marketplace in the United States has not been revolutionized. The reality is that:

- Online consumers are not primarily cost-driven—instead, they are as brand-driven and influenced by perceived value as their offline counterparts.
- Online market entry costs were underestimated, as was the cost of acquiring new customers.
- Older traditional firms, such as the general merchandising giants and the established catalog-based retailers, are taking over as the top online retail sites.
- Disintermediation did not occur. On the contrary, online retailing has become an example of the powerful role that intermediaries play in retail trade.

■   **Explain how to analyze the economic viability of an online firm.**

The economic viability, or ability of a firm to survive during a specified time period, can be analyzed by examining the key industry strategic factors, the strategic factors that pertain specifically to the firm, and the financial statements for the firm. The key industry strategic factors include:

- *Barriers to entry*, which are expenses that will make it difficult for new entrants to join the industry.
- *Power of suppliers*, which refers to the ability of firms in the industry to bargain effectively for lower prices from suppliers.
- *Power of customers*, which refers to the ability of the customers for a particular product to shop among the firm's competitors, thus keeping prices down.

- *Existence of substitute products*, which refers to the present or future availability of products with a similar function.
- The *industry value chain*, which must be evaluated to determine if the chain of production and distribution for the industry is changing in ways that will benefit or harm the firm.
- The *nature of intra-industry competition*, which must be evaluated to determine if the competition within the industry is based on differentiated products and services, price, the scope of the offerings, or the focus of the offerings and whether any imminent changes in the nature of the competition will benefit or harm the firm.

The key firm strategic factors include:

- The *firm value chain*, which must be evaluated to determine if the firm has adopted business systems that will enable it to operate at peak efficiency and whether there are any looming technological changes that might force the firm to change its processes or methods.
- *Core competencies*, which refer to unique skills that a firm has that cannot be easily duplicated. When analyzing the economic viability of a firm, it is important to consider whether technological changes might invalidate these competencies.
- *Synergies*, which refer to the availability to the firm of the competencies and assets of related firms that it owns or with which it has formed strategic partnerships.
- The firm's current *technology*, which must be evaluated to determine if it has proprietary technologies that will allow it to scale with demand and if it has developed the customer relationship, fulfillment, supply chain management, and human resources systems that it will need in order to be viable.
- The *social and legal challenges facing the firm*, which should be examined to determine if the firm has taken into account consumer trust issues such as the privacy and security of personal information and if the firm may be vulnerable to legal challenges.

The key financial factors include:

- *Revenues*, which must be examined to determine if they are growing and at what rate.
- *Cost of sales*, which is the cost of the products sold, including all related costs. The lower the cost of sales compared to revenue, the higher the gross profit.
- *Gross margin*, which is calculated by dividing gross profit by net sales revenue. If the gross margin is improving consistently, the economic outlook for the firm is enhanced.
- *Operating expenses*, which should be evaluated to determine if the firm's needs in the near interim will necessitate increased outlays. Large increases in operating expenses may result in net losses for the firm.
- *Operating margin*, which is calculated by dividing operating income or loss by net sales revenue, and is an indication of a company's ability to turn sales into pre-tax profit after operating expenses are deducted.
- *Net margin*, which is calculated by dividing net income or net loss by net sales revenue. It evaluates the net profit or loss for each dollar of net sales. For example, a net margin of -24% indicates that a firm is losing 24 cents on each dollar of net sales revenue.
- The firm's *balance sheet,* which is a financial snapshot of a company on a given date that displays its financial assets and liabilities. If current assets are less than or not much more than current liabilities, the firm will likely have trouble meeting its short-term obligations.

■ **Identify the challenges faced by the different types of online retailers.**

There are four major types of online retail business models, and each faces its own particular challenges:

- *Virtual merchants* are single-channel Web firms that generate all of their revenues from online sales. Their challenges include building a business and a brand name quickly, many competitors in the virtual marketplace, substantial costs to build and maintain a Web site, considerable marketing expenses, large customer acquisition costs, a steep learning curve, and the need to quickly achieve operating efficiencies in order to preserve a profit. Amazon is the most well-known example of a virtual merchant.

- *Multi-channel merchants* (bricks-and-clicks) have a network of physical stores as their primary retail channel, but have also begun online operations. Their challenges include high cost of physical buildings, high cost of large sales staffs, the need to coordinate prices across channels, the need to develop methods of handling cross-channel returns from multiple locations, building a credible Web site, hiring new skilled staff, and building rapid-response order entry and fulfillment systems. JCP.com is an example of a bricks-and-clicks company.

- *Catalog merchants* are established companies that have a national offline catalog operation as their largest retail channel, but who have recently developed online capabilities. Their challenges include high costs for printing and mailing, the need to leverage their existing assets and competencies to the new technology environment, the need to develop methods of handling cross-channel returns, building a credible Web site, and hiring new skilled staff. Lands' End is an example of a catalog merchant.

- *Manufacturer-direct merchants* are either single- or multi-channel manufacturers who sell to consumers directly online without the intervention of retailers. They were predicted to play a very large role in e-commerce, but this has not generally happened. Their challenges include channel conflict, which occurs when physical retailers of a manufacturer's products must compete on price and currency of inventory with the manufacturer who does not face the cost of maintaining inventory, physical stores, and a sales staff; quickly developing a rapid-response online order and fulfillment system; switching from a supply-push (products are made prior to orders being received based on estimated demand) to a demand-pull model (products are not built until an order is received); and creating sales, service, and support operations online. Dell.com is an example of a manufacturer-direct merchant.

■ **Describe the major features of the online service sector.**

The service sector is the largest and most rapidly expanding part of the economy of advanced industrial nations. Service industries are companies that provide services (i.e., perform tasks for) consumers, businesses, governments, and other organizations. The major service industry groups are financial services, insurance, real estate, business services, and health services. Within these service industry groups, companies can be further categorized into those that involve transaction brokering and those that involve providing a "hands-on" service. With some exceptions, the service sector is by and large a knowledge- and information-intense industry. For this reason, many services are uniquely suited to e-commerce and the strengths of the Internet.

The rapid expansion of e-commerce services in the areas of finance, including insurance and real estate, travel, and job placement, can be explained by the ability of these firms to:

- collect, store, and disseminate high value information
- provide reliable, fast communication
- personalize and customize service or components of service

E-commerce offers extraordinary opportunities to improve transaction efficiencies and thus productivity in a sector where productivity has so far not been markedly affected by the explosion in information technology.

- **Discuss the trends taking place in the online financial services industry.**

The online financial services sector is a good example of an e-commerce success story, but the success is somewhat different than what had been predicted in the early days of e-commerce. Today it is the multi-channel established financial firms that are growing the most rapidly and that have the best prospects for long-term viability. Other significant trends include the following:

- Management of financial assets online is growing rapidly.
- In the insurance and real estate industries, consumers still generally utilize the Internet just for research and use a conventional transaction broker to complete the purchase.
- Historically, separate institutions have provided the four generic types of services provided by financial institutions. Today, as a result of the Financial Reform Act of 1998, which permitted banks, brokerage firms, and insurance companies to merge, this is no longer true. This has resulted in two important and related global trends in the financial services industry that have direct consequences for online financial services firms: the move toward industry consolidation and the provision of integrated financial services.

Key features of the online banking and brokerage industries include the following:

- Multi-channel firms that have both physical branches and solid online offerings have assumed market leadership over the pure-online firms that cannot provide customers with many services that still require hands-on interaction.
- Customer acquisition costs are significantly higher for Internet-only banks and brokerages that must invest heavily in marketing versus their established brand-name bricks-and-mortar competitors, which can simply convert existing branch customers to online customers at a much lower cost.
- Financial portals provide comparison shopping services and steer consumers to online providers for independent financial advice and financial planning.
- Account aggregation is another rapidly growing online financial service, which pulls together all of a customer's financial data on a single personalized Web site.
- During the early days of e-commerce, a radically altered online mortgage and lending services market was envisioned in which the mortgage value chain would be simplified and the loan closing process speeded up, with the resulting cost savings passed on to consumers. Affordably building a brand name, the resulting high customer acquisition costs, and instituting these value chain changes proved to be too difficult. Today it is the established banks and lenders who are reaping the benefits of a relatively small but growing market.

- There are three basic types of online mortgage lenders, including established banks, brokerages, and lending organizations; pure-online bankers/brokers; and mortgage brokers.

Key features of the online insurance industry include the following:

- Term life insurance stands out as one product group supporting the early visions of lower search costs, increased price transparency, and the resulting consumer savings. However, in other insurance product lines, the Web offers insurance companies new opportunities for product and service differentiation and price discrimination.
- The insurance industry has several other distinguishing characteristics that make it difficult for it to be completely transferred to the new online channel, such as policies that defy easy comparison and that can only be explained by an experienced sales agent, a traditional reliance on local insurance offices and agents to sell complex products uniquely suited to the circumstances of the insured person and/or property, and a marketplace that is coordinated by state insurance commissions in each state with differing regulations. Although search costs have been dramatically reduced and price comparison shopping is done in an entirely new way, the industry value chain has so far not been significantly impacted.

Key features of the online real estate services industry include the following:

- The early vision that the historically local, complex, and agent-driven real estate industry would be transformed into a disintermediated marketplace where buyers and sellers could transact directly has not been realized. What has happened has been beneficial to buyers, sellers, and real estate agents alike.
- Since it is not possible to complete a property transaction online, the major impact of the online real estate industry is in influencing offline purchases.
- The primary service is a listing of available houses, with secondary links to mortgage lenders, credit reporting agencies, neighborhood information, loan calculators, appraisal reports, sales price histories by neighborhood, school district data, and crime reports.
- The industry value chain, however, has remained unchanged. Home addresses are not available online and users are directed back to the local listing agent for further information about the house.
- Buyers benefit because they can quickly and easily access a wealth of valuable information; sellers benefit because they receive free online advertising for their property; and real estate agents have reported that Internet-informed customers ask to see fewer properties.

■ **Discuss the major trends in the online travel services industry today.**

Online travel services attract the largest single e-commerce audience and the largest slice of B2C revenues. The Internet has become the most common channel used by consumers to research travel options. It is also the most common way for people to search for the best possible prices and book reservations for airline tickets, rental cars, hotel rooms, cruises, and tours. Some of the reasons why online travel services have been so successful include the following:

- Online travel sites offer consumers a one-stop, convenient, leisure and business travel experience where travelers can find content, community, commerce, and customer service. Online sites offer more information and travel options than traditional travel agents, with such services as descriptions of vacations and facilities, chat groups and bulletin boards, and the convenience of purchasing all travel elements at one stop. They also bring consumers and suppliers together in a low transaction cost environment.

- Travel is an information-intensive product as well as an electronic product in the sense that travel requirements can be accomplished for the most part online. Since travel does not require any inventory, suppliers (which are highly fragmented) are always looking for customers to fill excess capacity. Also, travel services do not require an expensive multi-channel physical presence. For these reasons, travel services appear to be particularly well suited for the online marketplace.
- It is important to note that various segments of the travel industry fit this description better than others—for instance, airline reservations, auto rentals, and to a lesser extent, hotels. Cruises and tours are more differentiated with varying quality and a more complex level of information required for the decision-making process..
- Corporations are increasingly outsourcing their travel offices entirely to vendors who can provide  Web-based solutions, high-quality service, and lower costs.

The major trends in online travel services include the following:

- The online travel services industry is going through a period of consolidation as stronger offline, established firms purchase weaker and relatively inexpensive online travel agencies in order to build stronger multi-channel travel sites that combine physical presence, television sales outlets, and online sites.
- Suppliers—such as airlines, hotels, and auto rental firms—are attempting to eliminate intermediaries such as GDSs and travel agencies, and develop a direct relationship with consumers. At the same time, successful online travel agencies are attempting to turn themselves into merchants by purchasing large blocks of travel inventory and then reselling it to the public, eliminating the global distributors and earning much higher returns.

■ Identify current trends in the online career services industry.

Next to travel services, job-hunting services have been one of the Internet's most successful online services because they save money for both job hunters and employers. In comparison to online recruiting, traditional recruitment tools have severe limitations:

- Online recruiting provides a more efficient and cost-effective means of linking employers and job hunters and reduces the total time-to-hire.
- Job hunters can easily build, update, and distribute their resumes, conduct job searches, and gather information on employers at their convenience and leisure.
- It is an information-intense business process that the Internet can automate, and thus reduce search time and costs for all parties.

Online recruiting can also serve to establish market prices and terms, thereby identifying both the salary levels for specific jobs and the skill sets required to achieve those salary levels. This should lead to a rationalization of wages, greater labor mobility, and higher efficiency in recruitment and operations as employers are able to more quickly fill positions.

The major trends in the online career services industry are:

- *Consolidation*: The online recruitment industry is going through a period of rapid consolidation led by Monster.

- *Diversification*: There is an explosion of specialty niche employment sites that focus on specific occupations.
- *Localization*: There is a growing focus on local job markets.
- *Job search engines*: New online job search engines that scrape listings from thousands of online job sites pose a threat to established career sites.
- *Social networking*: Many Internet users are beginning to use social networking sites to establish business contacts and find jobs; employers are also using them to identify and find out further information about job candidates.

## QUESTIONS

1. Why were so many entrepreneurs drawn to start businesses in the online retail sector initially?
2. What frequently makes the difference between profitable and unprofitable online businesses today?
3. Which segment of the offline retail business is most like online retailing? Why?
4. Name the largest segment of U.S. retail sales. Explain why businesses in this segment have achieved and continue to dominate online retailing.
5. Describe the technological retail revolution that preceded the growth of e-commerce. What were some of the innovations that made later online retailing possible?
6. Name two assumptions e-commerce analysts made early on about consumers and their buying behavior that turned out to be false.
7. Why were customer acquisition costs assumed early on to be lower on the Web? What was supposed to reduce those costs?
8. Explain the distinction between disintermediation and hypermediation as it relates to online retailing.
9. How would you describe the top 10 online retailers as a group? Do they account for a small or a large percentage of online business, for example?
10. Compare and contrast virtual merchants and bricks-and-clicks firms. What other type of online retailer is most like the virtual merchant?
11. What is the difference between a supply-push and a demand-pull sales model? Why do most manufacturer-direct firms have difficulty switching to one of these?
12. What are five strategic issues specifically related to a firm's capabilities? How are they different from industry-related strategic issues?
13. Which is a better measure of a firm's financial health: revenues, gross margin, or net margin? Why?
14. What are some of the difficulties in providing services in an online environment? What factors differentiate the services sector from the retail sector, for example?
15. Compare and contrast the two major types of online services industries. What two major features differentiate services from other industries?
16. Name and describe the types of online mortgage vendors. What are the major advantages of using an online mortgage site? What factors are slowing the growth of such service businesses?
17. What is the biggest deterrent to growth of the online insurance industry nationally?

18. Define channel conflict and explain how it currently applies to the mortgage and insurance industries. Name two online insurance companies or brokers.

19. What is the most common use of real estate Web sites? What do most consumers do when they go there?

20. Name and describe the four types of services provided by financial services firms on the Web.

21. Who are the major players in the financial industry consolidation currently occurring worldwide?

22. Explain the two global trends impacting the structure of the financial services industry and their impact on online operations.

23. How have travel services suppliers benefited from consumer use of travel Web sites?

24. Name and describe five traditional recruitment tools companies have used to identify and attract employees. What are the disadvantages of such tools compared to online career sites?

25. In addition to matching job applicants with available positions, what larger function do online job sites fill? Explain how such sites can affect salaries and going rates.


# PROJECTS

1. Find the Securities and Exchange Commission Web site at Sec.gov, and access the EDGAR archives, where you can review 10-K filings for all public companies. Search for the 10-K report for the most recent completed fiscal year for two online retail companies of your choice (preferably ones operating in the same industry, such as Staples Inc. and Office Depot Inc.). Prepare a presentation that compares the financial stability and prospects of the two businesses, focusing specifically on the performance of their respective Internet operations.

2. Examine the financial statements for Amazon and Best Buy Co. Inc. What observations can you make about the two businesses? Which one is stronger financially and why? Which one's business model appears to be weaker and why? If you could identify two major problem areas for each, what would they be? Prepare a presentation that makes your case.

3. Conduct a thorough analysis—strategic and financial—of one of the following companies or another of your own choosing: Bluefly Inc., Drugstore.com, Inc. or 1-800-Flowers.com, Inc. Prepare a presentation that summarizes your observations about the company's Internet operations and future prospects.

4. Find an example not mentioned in the text of each of the four types of online retailing business models. Prepare a short report describing each firm and why it is an example of the particular business model.

5. Drawing on material in the chapter and your own research, prepare a short paper describing your views on the major social and legal issues facing online retailers.

6.  Conduct a thorough analysis—strategic and financial—of one of the following Web sites: Progressive.com, Insure.com, or Insweb.com. Prepare a presentation that summarizes your observations about the company's operations and future prospects.

7.  Choose a services industry not discussed in the chapter (such as legal services, medical services, accounting services, or another of your choosing). Prepare a 3- to 5-page report discussing recent trends affecting online provision of these services.

8.  Together with a teammate, investigate the use of wireless applications (including iPhone apps) in the financial services industries. Prepare a short joint presentation on your findings.

9.  Find at least two examples of companies not mentioned in the text that act as transaction brokers and at least two examples of companies that provide a hands-on service. Prepare a short memo describing the services each company offers and explaining why the company should be categorized as a transaction broker or a hands-on service provider.

## CHAPTER 10

# Online Content and Media

**After reading this chapter, you will be able to:**

- Identify the major trends in the consumption of media and online content.
- Discuss the concept of media convergence and the challenges it faces.
- Describe the five basic content revenue models.
- Discuss the key challenges facing content producers and owners.
- Understand the key factors affecting the online publishing industry.
- Understand the key factors affecting the online entertainment industry.

# Information Wants to Be Expensive

The age of "free news" may be over, victim of a failed online business model. The old Web adage that "information wants to be free" is being replaced by a new realization that "information wants to be expensive," especially if that information is high value and exclusive.

In 2007, upon purchasing the Dow Jones Corporation, News Corp CEO Rupert Murdoch announced that he would shortly eliminate fees for subscriptions to the online edition of the *Wall Street Journal* and grow the paper's online audience to 50 million readers. But just two years later, in August 2009, Murdoch announced that visitors to Web sites of newspapers owned by News Corp, including the *Wall Street Journal*, will have to start paying fees to read the news online.

What changed in those two years for Murdoch and owners of newspapers around the world was a rapid decline in advertising revenues (both display and classifieds) of newspapers, in some cases down 50% over two years. News Corp itself posted a loss of $230 million in the second quarter of 2009, as revenues fell 11%. Though the company returned to profitability in 2010, the outlook is still mixed. While newspaper readership is falling and advertising is moving to the Web, readers of online newspapers are booming, especially among the young, as more and more people turn to the Internet as their source of news. Nearly three out of five Internet users read newspapers online each month; in May 2010, 123 million Americans visited an online newspaper. Anyone who thinks newspaper organizations (highly skilled reporters, editors, and managers) are dead just isn't paying attention to the data. Unfortunately, the online ad revenue from display ads has failed to replace the lost revenues from physical newspaper ads. The problem is not getting people to read the paper online. The problem is making money from what newspapers publish online. Declining newspaper revenues pose a strong challenge to the notion that newspapers can survive the Internet by giving away for free their news and editorial content in order to build audience size, page views, and sufficient revenue from display ads to post a profit.

While the news is filled with now passé articles asking the question "Can newspapers survive the Web?", a small group of analysts believe this is the wrong question. A better question is "Can newspapers create valuable online content that people are willing to pay for?" This latter question raises other questions, such as how to define "valuable content." Two newspapers in the world stand out as examples of successful online subscription newspapers that are profitable: the *Wall Street Journal* and the *Financial Times* (owned by Pearson Ltd.). Let's look at the *Wall Street Journal* to see how it has succeeded online and how it may be a online model for other newspapers to follow.

The Dow Jones News Service began publishing the *Wall Street Journal* in 1889 as a blend of general international and national news, along with in-depth financial reporting. It has a worldwide paid print and online readership of around 2.7 million. In April 1996, the *Journal* launched WSJ.com. In 2010, the *Journal* had 414,000 subscribers to its online editions and attracted more than 11 million non-subscribing monthly visitors, and it is the most successful online newspaper in terms of revenue and profits. The *Journal* is one of the very few online newspapers to successfully employ a subscription revenue model. Nearly all other news and magazine publishers have adopted an advertiser supported "free content" model. Currently, subscribers to the *Wall Street Journal* print edition pay $49 a year for access to the online edition; non-subscribers pay $99. Print subscribers pay $119 for the physical newspaper delivered to their door.

But the *Wall Street Journal* is different from most newspapers. Most of the 10,000 online newspapers in the world offer free content. The common view among newspaper publishers is that most online consumers expect information to be free. For instance, when the online magazine Salon switched to a subscription fee model, it lost 90% of its readers. Since then, Salon's readership has stabilized and grown, and it has adopted a mixture of free content and premium paid subscriptions, but remains only barely profitable. Online newspapers typically are supported by advertising and sales of classified ads—just as traditional print newspapers have been for centuries—rather than monthly subscription fees. Newspaper publishers seem unable to unlearn the Salon experience, and learn a new experience being delivered by content providers such as iTunes.

Why has the *Wall Street Journal* succeeded with a subscription model where others have failed? Brand is certainly one reason. *The Wall Street Journal* has strong brand recognition among American investors. It is well known for its stock quotation services and in-depth reporting on business and general news issues. However, many newspapers such as the *Los Angeles Times,* and *Washington Post* also have strong national brands, but are fearful of charging subscription fees.

Perhaps one key to the *Wall Street Journal's* success is that a subscription gives users access to premium content in the form of 25,000 in-depth background reports on companies, an archive of news articles going back to 1996, and access to the Dow Jones Publication Library, which features current and past articles from 7,000 newspapers, magazines, and business-news sources. If you are a stock analyst or an individual investor looking for information on a specific company, this archive of material may be well worth the relatively small annual subscription fee. Coupled with a fine-grained search engine, the *Wall Street Journal's* archives are unique and differentiated from most other online newspaper offerings. The Journal sells access to this premium archival content on a per-article basis. The experience of the Journal is that you can successfully charge for high-value information that is exclusive to your newspaper, and differentiated. In contrast, no one wants to pay for information that is widely shared.

Readers of the *Journal* are also attracted to its timeliness and Web suitability. Using a structured markup technology provided by OmniMark's Content Engineering system, writers and editors are able to simultaneously author articles for both print and online editions, and then automatically generate Web pages that conform to the *Journal's* unique print style. This system also permits them to make dynamic changes in news story content, shortening or lengthening stories as needed, without costly page redesign. Writers and editors can post hundreds of up-to-date articles around the clock, and the key page elements—such as size of headlines, space between articles, positioning of navigation buttons, and placement of advertisements—are all generated by the OmniMark system. The same system creates a consistent content archive of news and opinion that can be searched by subscribers. In this sense, Internet distribution technology has led to a convergence in content creation and delivery: news is news, whether it is printed on paper or on a Web page.

The new technology has transformed the online newspaper experience. Instead of having content trapped on static print pages that are updated daily, the online edition can offer timely breaking news much like a television or radio news show, and like television, provide video access to important news events and newsmakers. WSJ.com uses personalization features to make its content even more compelling. Subscribers can create a personalized WSJ.com home page with user-selected columnists, stock portfolio updates, and company news. In addition, along with other online publishers, users can have news stories on topics and subjects they choose pushed to them using a *Wall Street Journal* RSS feed. The Journal also has added major sections available only online: interactive features walk readers through complex stories, and in-depth reports explore topics such as retirement, mutual fund returns, and pension planning. The *Journal* has multiple free Web sites from MarketWatch to the Real Estate and College journals. The *Journal* has been able to leverage this new functionality into higher subscription fees.

The *Wall Street Journal's* online edition reflects the capabilities of the Internet and Web 2.0. There are reporter blogs, user comments on all articles, and videos, all updated in real time. The most radical change is the addition of a social network capability: the online *Journal* allows its half a million subscribers to comment on any article, pose discussion questions, e-mail one another, and set up profiles that will allow other subscribers to see what they are doing on the site. The goal is to increase reader loyalty, expand the amount of time users spend on the site, and of course increase ad revenues. In April 2009, the *Journal* developed an iPhone app, which makes some of its content available for free, but in the near future a subscription model or advertising model is planned for the iTunes version of the *Journal*. While the *Journal* and the *Financial Times* are successfully charging for their content, whether other newspapers can succeed will depend in part on their ability to produce high-value content available nowhere else, but also, on the culture of the Internet.

**SOURCES:** "USA Today to Remake Itself to Stress Digital Operations," by Jeremy W Peters, *New York Times*, August 27, 2010; "*The New York Times* Ranks as Top Online Newspaper According to May 2010 U.S. comScore Media Metrix Data," comScore, June 16, 2010; "Newspaper Circulation Falls Nearly 9%," by Joseph Plambeck, *New York Times*, April 26, 2010; "The Times to Charge for Frequent Access to Its Web Site," by Richard Perez-Pena, *New York Times*, January 21, 2010; "NAA/Nielsen Stats Show Newspapers Own Less Than One Percent of the U.S. Online Audience Page Views, Time Spent," Nieman Journalism Lab, Niemanlab. org, August 10, 2009; "Is Free News a Thing of the Past?" by Clare Davidson, BBC News, August 7, 2009; "News Corp. Plans Fees for Newspaper Sites," by Associated Press, *New York Times*, August 6, 2009; "Looking to Big Screen E-Readers to Help Save the Daily Press," by Brad Stone, *New York Times*, May 4, 2009; "Newspapers' Essential Strengths," by David Carr, New York Times, May 4, 2009; "Annual Internet Survey by the Center for the Digital Future Finds Large Increases in Use of Online Newspapers," Center for the Digital Future, USC Annenberg School of Communication, April 28, 2009; "*Wall Street Journal* iPhone App Sets Content Free," by John Abell, Wall Street Journal, April 15, 2009; "Media Executives Plan Online Service to Charge for Content," by Richard Perez-Pena, *New York Times*, April 15, 2009; "They Pay for Cable, Music, and Extra Bags. How About News?," by Richard Perez- Pena, *New York Times*, April 8, 2009; "Information Wants to Be Expensive," by L. Gordon Crovitz, *Wall Street Journal*, February 23, 2009.

*The New York Times*, whose 32 million unique monthly visitors make it the most frequently visited online newspaper, will soon switch to a subscription-based model for its Web site as well. Starting January 2011, visitors to the *Times* Web site will only be allowed to view a fixed number of articles for free each month until they are prompted to pay a flat fee for continued access. The *Times* is hoping to develop a system which monetizes the loyalty of its most devoted readers while imposing no new fees for its current print subscribers, who will pay no extra fees for online access. Because the majority of the *Times'* online visitors view only a small number of articles, most of their online viewers won't notice the change. The *Times'* switch was prompted by dropping advertising revenues, despite the fact that they are also the leaders in online advertising revenue. The *Times* hopes that they will gain more revenue from subscriptions than they will lose in advertising. Other prominent newspapers, including *USA Today*, are also revamping their business models to focus on their Web sites and digital operations, including Kindle and iPad versions of their papers.

Up until iTunes, the prevailing wisdom of the Web glitterati was that Web users expected all information to be free, and users would never pay for content. But the culture of the Internet is changing faster than the experts can change their predictions. iTunes shows us that 50 million Web users are willing to pay for music tracks. Amazon's Kindle is showing us that millions of book readers are willing to pay 9.99 for an e-book. In this new culture of the Web, people are willing to pay for high quality, high-value, differentiated content served up in a customer friendly experience where it's "cool" to pay.

The opening case illustrates how traditional media companies are attempting to adapt to the new opportunities of the Web by developing content experiences for online consumers that would be impossible offline, including mobile apps, video, blogs, interactive features such as games and online crossword puzzles, and more recently, social network opportunities. It is clear that the future of content—news, music, and video—is online. In the past, online companies had a difficult time becoming profitable. Today, the print industry, including newspapers and magazines, is having a difficult time coping with the movement of their readership to the Web. Broadcast and cable television, along with Hollywood and the music labels, are also wrestling with outdated business models based on physical media. Established media giants are continuing to make extraordinary investments in unique online content, new technology, new digital distribution channels, and entirely new business models. In this chapter, we focus primarily on the publishing and entertainment industries as they attempt to transform their traditional media into Web-deliverable forms and experiences for consumers.

## 10.1 ONLINE CONTENT

No other sector of the American economy has been so challenged by the Internet and the Web than the content industries. The content industries involve all those businesses that use print, television, and film to communicate, as well as the distribution businesses such as cable, broadcast television, satellite, printers, and retail content stores (like music and video rental stores). As a communications medium, the Web is, by definition, a source of online content. In this chapter, we will look closely at publishing (newspapers, books, and magazines) and entertainment (music, film, games, and television). These industries make up the largest share of the commercial content marketplace, both offline and online. In each of these industries, there are powerful offline brands, significant new pure-play online providers, consumer constraints and opportunities, a variety of legal issues, and new technology platforms that offer an entirely new content distribution system.

**Table 10.1** describes the most recent trends in online content for 2010–2011.

### CONTENT AUDIENCE AND MARKET: WHERE ARE THE EYEBALLS AND THE MONEY?

The average American adult spends over 3,900 hours each year consuming various media, almost twice the amount of time spent at work (2,000 hours/year) (see **Figure 10.1**). Media revenues in 2010 are estimated to be $973 billion, and they are expected to grow at a compound rate of 8% (U.S. Census Bureau, 2010).

#### Media Utilization

The most popular medium is television, followed by radio and the Internet. Together, these three media account for over 80% of the hours spent consuming various media.

| **TABLE 10.1** | **TRENDS IN ONLINE CONTENT, 2010–2011** |
|---|---|

- **Media consumption**: Americans spend over 3,900 hours a year consuming various types of media, nearly twice as many hours as they work. Internet time exposure grows rapidly, surpassing newspapers, and music, but far behind traditional television and radio.

- **Revenue**: Revenues from Internet media are the fastest-growing media revenues.

- **Eyeballs**: Traditional content audience moves to the Internet, and the annual growth in the Internet audience outpaces all other media.

- **User-generated content**: The Internet inverts the traditional production and business model by having users create much content. Social network sites, video sites like YouTube, personal blogs, and photo sites show extraordinary growth, threaten traditional entertainment firms, and challenge traditional media for user attention, total audience size, and even legitimacy. User-generated video and TV shows engage more and more users.

- **Technology**: Mobile smartphones and netbooks make Web-based music, news, and entertainment available anytime and anywhere.

- **Advertising**: The growing Internet audience causes a rapid expansion in Internet advertising revenues as advertisers move to where the eyeballs are focused.

- **Business models**: Content owners adopt a mixture of business models from advertising-supported content to subscription to a la carte payment for unbundled products like individual songs, television shows, and movies.

- **Paid content and free content coexist**: The common notion of "Internet means free information" is being replaced by consumer acceptance of paying for premium content, which is growing far faster than other media or than the Internet itself in the United States. At the same time, music, television, and Hollywood studios are making some content free and supporting other content through advertising revenues.

- **Convergence**: Traditional media—newspapers, magazines, and studios—are moving closer to a convergent model based on new technologies and new industry alignments among major media conglomerates. Hollywood and television studios begin video streaming of movies and shows. Internet television divisions of traditional TV studios are formed. Newspapers and magazines add video to their online sites. Yahoo, Google, AOL, Microsoft, and Apple move into traditional media spaces such as television, telephone, and movie distribution by offering a variety of new online services.

- **Print media**: Newspapers and magazines are in the middle of a painful transition to online models buoyed by the growth in online advertising, which is not sufficient to replace lost advertising revenues. Online newspaper readership grows at 12% on average with the top 10 growing at over 16% annually.

- **Entertainment content**: Led by music, an explosion in online video, and the growing interest in online television and feature-length films, the Web emerges as an entertainment powerhouse rivaling broadcast networks, cable, and satellite distribution systems.

- **Consumer taste**: Consumers want to control their own programming. Consumers increasingly support time-shifting and space-shifting in media consumption by demanding to see or hear just about any media wherever and whenever they want using any of several devices like PCs, cell phones, PDAs, or conventional devices.

While the Internet is currently third, Internet utilization has been growing rapidly. (U.S. Census Bureau, 2010). In another survey, the Online Publishers Association found that the amount of time people spent online per month had increased from an

## FIGURE 10.1 MEDIA CONSUMPTION

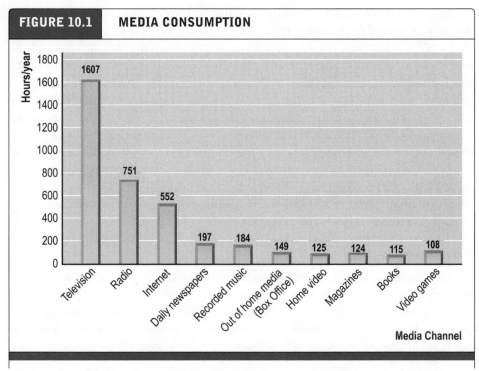

Each American spends around 3,900 hours annually, on average, consuming various media, mostly television, radio, and recorded music. However, time spent on the Internet is growing rapidly—it has doubled since 2000 and has overtaken newspapers, music, and magazine.

SOURCES: Based on data from U.S. Census Bureau, 2010; authors' estimates.

average of about 11 hours a month (132 hours a year) in 2003 to over 44 hours a month in 2010, about the same as television (eMarketer, Inc., 2010a). Although television rating services like Nielsen do not report a fall in hours of television watching, consumer surveys find that 20% to 30% of media users report using traditional media such as television, radio, and newspapers less, and substituting online entertainment. Over half of television viewers go online using their computers while watching TV (Frank N. Magid Associates, 2009; Emigh, 2008).

### Internet and Traditional Media: Cannibalization versus Complementarity

Most studies reveal that time spent on the Internet reduces consumer time available for other media (Pew Internet & American Life Project, 2010a). There has been a massive shift of the general audience to the Web, and once there, a large percentage of time is spent on viewing content. In 2010, consumers are spending about 38% of their time online (an average of about 17 hours a month) at content sites (news, information, and entertainment), 25% (around 11 hours) at community sites, 21% (about 9 hours a month) at communications sites (e-mail and instant messaging), 11% (about 5 hours) at commerce sites, and 5% (about 2 hours) at search sites (Online Publishers Association, 2010). In general, Internet users spend 15%–20% less time reading books, newspapers, and magazines, watching television and box office movies, talking on the phone, or listening to the radio. On the other hand, Internet users consume more media of all types than non-Internet users. This reflects the demographics of the Internet user as more literate, wealthier, more technically savvy, and more media aware. In addition, Internet users multitask when using the Internet, frequently listening to music, watching television, and using instant messaging while working on other tasks. Multimedia use reduces the cannibalization impact of the Internet for some visual and aural media, but obviously not for reading physical books or newspapers. And even for these print media, the Internet is simply an alternative source; Internet users are increasing the time they spend online reading newspapers, magazines, and even books. Ironically, the new mobile media platform of smartphones and table computers has led to an explosion in reading of both newspapers and books–but digital versions, not the printed versions.

## Media Revenues

An examination of media revenues reveals a somewhat similar pattern when compared to media consumption (see **Figure 10.2**). Television—broadcast, cable, and satellite—remains a major producer of media revenues (41%). Other forms of entertainment (box office events, home video, video games, recorded music, and radio) garnered about 28% of revenues, while newspapers generated 4% of revenues, down from 10% in previous years.

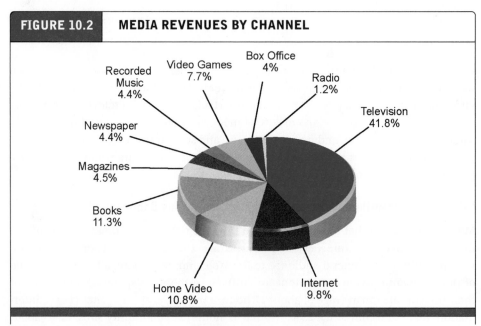

| **FIGURE 10.2** | **MEDIA REVENUES BY CHANNEL** |

Television, home video, and Internet dominate media revenues with 66% of the revenues.
The revenue share for traditional media such as newspapers and magazines has shrunk, while book publishing revenues have remained fairly constant over many years.
SOURCE: Based on data from U.S. Census Bureau, 2010; authors' estimates.

The Internet constitutes 9.8% of total media revenues in 2010, but this is substantially higher than the 5% of media channel revenues it produced in 2004. Once again, the Internet has grown in a few short years from a zero base to a substantial share of media revenues today. In the next section, we describe the current and emerging online content marketplace.

**Figure 10.3** gives some idea of the relative size of the content market, based on per-person spending. Television and home video combined are more than three times the size of online (Internet) content, but online content expenditures are rising at twice the rate of home video or TV. At some point in the near future, online revenues will exceed those of broadcast and cable television.

## Two Models For Digital Content Delivery: Paid and User-Generated Content

There are three commercial models for delivering content on the Internet: paid, "free" with advertiser support, and freemium, where some content is free but more complete content requires paid subscriptions. There is also completely free user-generated content, which we will discuss later. Contrary to early analysts' projections that "free" would drive "paid" out of business ("information wants to be free"), it turns out that both models are viable now and in the near future. Consumers increasingly choose to pay for high-quality, convenient, and unique content, and they have gladly accepted "free" advertiser-supported content when that content is deemed not worth paying for but entertaining nevertheless. There's nothing contradictory about all three models working in tandem, and cooperatively: free content can drive customers to paid content, as the recorded music firms have discovered with services like Pandora.

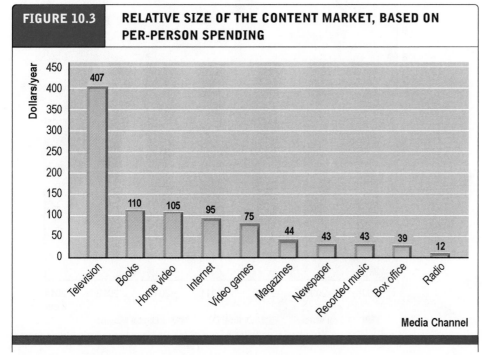

**FIGURE 10.3** **RELATIVE SIZE OF THE CONTENT MARKET, BASED ON PER-PERSON SPENDING**

SOURCES: Based on data from U.S. Census Bureau, 2010; authors' estimates.

Now let's look at what consumers are buying on the Internet in terms of paid digital content. About 37% of Internet users (81 million users) have downloaded music, and 62 million have actually paid for music downloads. Around 80% (177 million users) have watched a video online and about 22% (48 million users) have paid for video content at sites such as Hulu and Viacom (comScore, 2010a; eMarketer, Inc. 2009a; Pew Internet & American Life Project, 2010b).The online paid ontent audience, however, is growing at about 20% a year, faster than the Internet itself. Increasingly, the Internet is changing from primarily a communication medium to an entertainment medium. The growth in the audience size is largely attributable to the growth in the entertainment segment of music, news, television, and high quality professional videos, Hollywood movies, and production television shows.

**Figure 10.4** shows the estimated revenues from digital music, online TV, and digital movies. For instance, in 2010, total paid digital music, TV, and movie content is $6.3 billion, and will grow to $12.2 billion in 2014.

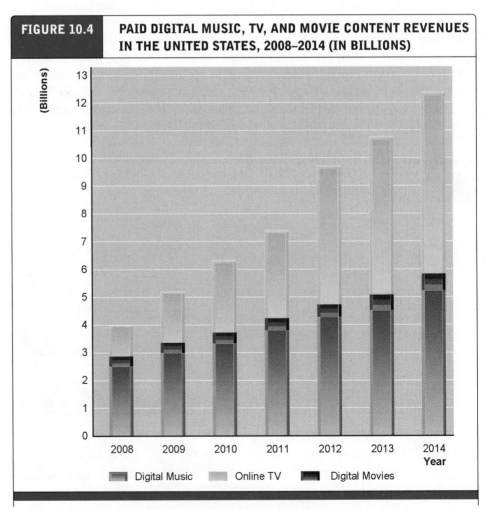

| FIGURE 10.4 | PAID DIGITAL MUSIC, TV, AND MOVIE CONTENT REVENUES IN THE UNITED STATES, 2008–2014 (IN BILLIONS) |

Legend: Digital Music, Online TV, Digital Movies

SOURCES: Based on data from eMarketer, 2010b, 2009a; industry sources; authors' estimates.

| TABLE 10.2 | TOP 10 U.S. ONLINE VIDEO SITES (JULY 2010 VS JULY 2009) | | | |
|---|---|---|---|---|
| SITE | UNIQUE VIEWERS MAY 2010 (in millions) | AVG. VIDEOS PER VIEWER | PERCENT INCREASE/DECREASE IN UNIQUE VIEWERS FROM JULY 2009 | UNIQUE VIEWERS JULY 2009 |
| Google sites | 144.6 | 101.2 | +20% | 121 |
| Yahoo! sites | 46.0 | 7.3 | − 2% (decrease) | 47 |
| Vevo | 45.6 | 9.4 | NA | NA |
| Facebook | 45.5 | 5.4 | +128% | 20 |
| Fox Interactive Media | 44.3 | 7.4 | −15% (decrease) | 52 |
| Hulu | 43.5 | 27.0 | +14% | 38 |
| CBS Interactive | 41.0 | 8.1 | +32% | 31 |
| Microsoft sites | 39.4 | 16.3 | −39% (decrease) | 65 |
| Turner Network | 35.3 | 9.4 | − 2% (decrease) | 36 |
| Viacom Digital | 34.6 | 10.0 | −18% (decrease) | 42 |

SOURCE: Based on data from comScore, 2010b; eMarketer, Inc., 2010c; authors' estimates.

Now let's look at the user-generated digital content audience. This audience is huge and growing very rapidly. User-generated content—music, videos, and text in the form of blogs—is free and typically advertiser-supported. In 2010, about 89 million Internet users have created user-generated content, and about 124 million have viewed it (eMarketer, Inc., 2009b). Revenue is generated by advertisers who by 2014 are expected to be spending between $615 million and $870 million advertising around user-generated content. **Table 10.2** shows the top video and user-generated content sites. User-generated content falls into seven primary categories: video, audio, photos, information (news), personal data, reviews, and recommendations (favorites, social bookmarking). By far the largest and potentially most valuable to marketers is the online video audience.

It will come as no surprise that YouTube is the leading advertiser-supported video site, and that the overall size of the online video audience (with over 400 million monthly unique viewers worldwide) is much larger than traditional television audiences, which number in the 10 million range for exceptionally popular shows (Google, 2010). During peak loads, YouTube has to deliver 30 million megabits per second, and spends around $360 million annually just for bandwidth. The social network sites are just now learning how to monetize this audience through advertising revenues, but so far they have only achieved break-even results.

The simultaneous growth of both paid and free advertiser-supported content on the Internet suggests that these phenomena are complementary in some cases, and can grow together. This may not be true of newspapers and magazines where online content has lessened their readership, and substitution is taking place. But music offers an example of complementarity. Illegal P2P file sharing is just as prevalent as before, involving millions of songs. Yet the parallel growth of paid content sites such as iTunes suggest both models can exist and prosper. "Free" legal music streaming sites like Pandora, one of the most popular Internet music sites, work with record label firms to drive customers toward purchase sites.

One question remains: Can the commercial content industries of movies, music, and text that depend on payments or subscriptions make enough money using the advertiser-supported model to make up for losses caused by the decline of their traditional models? In music, the answer is not so far. In high-quality video, the answer is probably yes.

### Free or Fee: Attitudes About Paying For Content and the Tolerance for Advertising

In the early years of online content, multiple surveys found that large majorities of the Internet audience expected to pay nothing for online content although equally large majorities were willing to accept advertising as a way to pay for free content. In reality, on the early Web, there wasn't much high-quality content. Until Internet services such as iTunes arrived, few thought the "fee" model could compete with the "free" model, and most Internet aficionados and "experts" just felt that "information [on the Internet] wants to be free." Cable TV systems offer a totally different history: they always charged for service and content, and cable TV "experts" never thought information wanted to be free. Neither did the Hollywood and New York media companies that provided the content to television and movie theaters. Like cable TV, Apple iTunes charges for service and content as well. In a demonstration of just how much quality online content is worth paying for, by 2010, Apple had sold 10 billion songs, 100 million TV shows, and over 2 million movies. While 33 million Internet users in the United States still download songs from illegal P2P sites, 29 million buy music from legal sites in 2010. Most experts thought free would drive out fee models. As you learned in the opening case, newspapers are now considering charging fees for "premium" content, while offering "free" ad-supported but limited content. These developments were totally unexpected. The culture of the Internet is beginning to change when firms such as YouTube (and its parent Google), which started out with a business model based on amateur videos, and illegally uploaded music videos, begin cooperating closely with Hollywood and New York production studios for premium content. As it turns out, "free" content isn't worth very much and should be free, especially if producers give it away. Premium content is worth a great deal, and should be priced accordingly. As one wag put it, "information wants to be expensive." This witticism was written by Stuart Brand in 1984, the same person who said "information wants to be free." Brand wrote, "On the one hand information wants to be expensive, because it's so valuable. The right information in the right place just changes your life. On the other hand, information wants to be free, because the cost of getting it out is getting lower and lower all the time. So you have these two fighting against each other." (Brand, 1984).

### MEDIA INDUSTRY STRUCTURE

The media content industry prior to 1990 was composed of many smaller independent corporations specializing in content creation and distribution in the separate industries of film, television, book and magazine publishing, and newspaper publishing. During the 1990s and into this century, after an extensive period of consolidation, huge entertainment and publishing media conglomerates emerged.

The media industry is still organized largely into three separate vertical stovepipes, with each segment dominated by a few key players. We do not include the delivery platform firms here, such as AT&T, Verizon, Sprint, Dish Network, or Comcast, because in general they do not create content; they just move content across cable, satellite, and telephone lines. Generally, there is very little crossover from one segment to another. Newspapers do not also produce Hollywood films, and publishing firms do not own newspapers or film production studios. Even within media conglomerates that span several different media segments, separate divisions control each media segment. The competition between corporate divisions in mega-sized corporations is often more severe than with marketplace competitors. On the other hand, as the audience moves increasingly to the Internet, even large conglomerates will be forced to follow.

While the commercial media industry is highly concentrated, yet fragmented across media firms, the much larger media ecosystem includes literally millions of individuals and independent entrepreneurs creating content in the form of blogs, videos on YouTube and VeVo, and music on MySpace. At times, the viewership (or readership) of these much smaller but numerous players exceeds that of the media titans.

## MEDIA CONVERGENCE: TECHNOLOGY, CONTENT, AND INDUSTRY STRUCTURE

Media convergence is a much used but poorly defined term. There are at least three dimensions of media where the term convergence has been applied: technology, content (artistic design, production, and distribution), and to the industry's structure as a whole. Ultimately for the consumer, convergence means being able to get any content you want, when you want it, on whatever platform you want it—from an iPod to a wireless PC to a handheld computer.

### Technological Convergence

Convergence from a technology perspective (**technological convergence**) has to do with the development of hybrid devices that can combine the functionality of two or more existing media platforms, such as books, newspapers, television, radio, and stereo equipment, into a single device. Examples of technological convergence include the iPad, iPhone, BlackBerry, and Palm Pre ("smartphones") that combine voice, Internet, Wi-Fi, and media services; iPod, which can combine in a handheld computing device music, video, photos, and text; digital interactive television sets that can surf the Web; video game machines that can also surf the Internet; and PCs that play and record music and videos.

> **technological convergence**
> development of hybrid devices that can combine the functionality of two or more existing media platforms into a single device

### Content Convergence

A second dimension of convergence is **content convergence**. There are three aspects to content convergence: design, production, and distribution.

> **content convergence**
> convergence in the design, production, and distribution of content

There is a historical pattern in which content created in an older media technology migrates to the new technology largely intact, with little artistic change. Slowly, the different media are integrated so that consumers can move seamlessly back and forth among them, and artists (and producers) learn more about how to deliver content in the new media. Later, the content itself is transformed by the new media as artists learn how to fully exploit the capabilities in the creation process. At this point, content convergence and transformation has occurred—the art is different because of the new capabilities inherent to new tools. For instance, European master painters of the fifteenth century in Italy, France, and the Netherlands (such as van Eyck, Caravaggio, Lotto, and Vermeer) quickly adopted new optical devices such as lenses, mirrors, and early projectors called *camera obscura* that could cast near-photographic quality images on canvases, and in the process they developed new theories of perspective and new techniques of painting landscapes and portraits. Suddenly, paintings took on the qualities of precision, detail, and realism found only in photographs (Boxer, 2001). A similar process is occurring today as artists and writers assimilate new digital and Internet tools into their toolkits. For instance, GarageBand from Apple enables low-budget independent bands (literally working in garages) to mix and control eight different digital music tracks to produce professional sounding recordings on a shoestring budget.

On the production side, new tools for digital editing and processing (for film and television) are driving content convergence. Given that the most significant cost of content is its creation, if there is a wide diversity of target delivery platforms, then it is wise to develop and produce only once using technology that can deliver to multiple platforms. Generally, this means creating content on digital devices (hardware and software) so that it can be delivered on multiple digital platforms. Once captured on digital devices, the same content can be archived, sliced into atomistic units, and repurposed for a wide variety of other platforms and distribution channels.

On the distribution side, it is important that distributors and ultimate consumers have the devices needed to receive, store, and experience the product. While for the most part technology companies have succeeded in giving consumers portable devices to receive online content, it has been more difficult for the content owners to come up with new, profitable distribution platforms. The music industry has seen its music store model collapse. The feature-length film industry struggles with online digital distribution. The book industry is challenged by the appearance of e-books. In the past, the only way Hollywood studios could deliver copies of new films to theaters across the country was in trucks. A feature-length film may have required six large, heavy canisters containing reels of 35mm film. In 2010, about 16,000 movie screens in the United States use digital projectors, and the movies are delivered via satellite or fiber optic cable (MPAA, 2010).

**Figure 10.5** depicts the process of media convergence and transformation using the example of books. For example, consider this book. The book was designed from the beginning as content to be delivered using both traditional text and the Internet. In that sense, this book is in the media transformation stage.

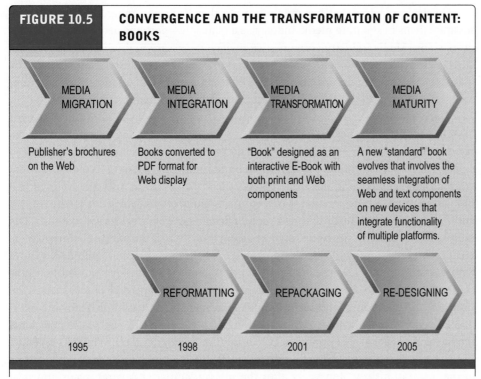

| FIGURE 10.5 | CONVERGENCE AND THE TRANSFORMATION OF CONTENT: BOOKS |
|---|---|

The Internet is making it possible for publishers and writers to transform the standard "book" into a new form that integrates features of both text and the Internet, and also transforms the content of the book itself.

In subsequent years, this same book will be available both as a purely digital work and as a mixed book + Web product. Eventually, it is likely that this book will be available mostly as a purely digital product with substantial visual and aural content that can be displayed on many different digital devices including e-book readers. By that time, the "learning experience" will be transformed. Traditional bound books will probably still be available (books have many advantages), but most likely, print editions will be printed on demand by customers using their own print facilities.

## Industry Convergence

A third dimension of convergence is the structure of the various media industries. **Industry convergence** refers to the merger of media enterprises into powerful, synergistic combinations that can cross-market content on many different platforms and create new works that use multiple platforms. This can take place either through purchases or through strategic alliances. Traditionally, each type of media—film, text, music, television—had its own separate industry, typically composed of very large players. For instance, the entertainment film industry has been dominated by a few large Hollywood-based production studios, book publication is dominated by a few large book publishers, and music production is dominated by five global record label firms.

**industry convergence**
merger of media enterprises into synergistic combinations that create and cross-market content on different platforms

However, the Internet has created forces that make the merger of traditionally separate firms in separate media industries a plausible—perhaps necessary—business proposition. Media industry convergence may be necessary to finance the substantial changes in both the technology platform and the content. Traditional media firms by themselves generally do not possess the core competencies, financial heft, content ownership, or channel ownership to bring about Internet media convergence.

The best-known example of media industry convergence is the $100 billion merger of AOL and Time Warner in January 2001. Time Warner was the largest multimedia conglomerate in the United States, but had no Web content per se, and had experienced an early failure in attempting to build a Web presence. AOL brought to the merger the largest online audience in the United States (nearly 40% of U.S. Internet users at that time), a substantial ISP operation with a monthly billing relationship with the consumer, and a successful track record in providing Internet and Web services and content. The merger plans called for the two companies to provide a single corporate platform for the creation and distribution of high-value content. AOL/Time Warner combined content with distribution. Senior executives at both AOL and Time Warner believed that new content would be created for distribution on both traditional and new media such as the Internet, and the process of transforming media and content to optimize the new Internet technology would begin in earnest with financing provided by successful traditional media such as cable subscriptions and feature film and television production revenue. In this case, convergence did not work well at all, and the merger became known as one of the worst in history. Ten years after the merger, and after several major efforts at revival, Time Warner sold AOL, which in 2009 produced $3.2 billion in revenue, down 38% in the last two years. In 2010, AOL will generate about $2.4 billion in revenue.

Rupert Murdoch's News Corporation provides a more successful example of convergence. In 2005, News Corp (now a conglomerate with both newspaper and satellite distribution) purchased the Web's most dynamic and fast-growing social network, MySpace. The acquisition has been successful, and MySpace is reportedly operating profitably although it has lost ground to Facebook in the social network space. If traditional media companies have not done well in purchases of Internet platform companies, the technology owners such as Apple, Microsoft, Google, and others have done a bit better in developing content and content distribution channels. Apple created its own online music store and now sells more labeled music than any other retailer; Microsoft created its Xbox 360, and owns other content sources; Google has purchased a social network site, an online video repository, and has created software applications that include entertainment content. Other online pure-play firms like Amazon have also had a significant impact on digital content distribution. In 2010, Amazon generated more revenue from e-books than printed books.

In the end, consumers' demands for content anywhere, anytime, and on any device is pushing all the technology and content companies towards cooperation and convergent behavior.

## ONLINE CONTENT REVENUE MODELS AND BUSINESS PROCESSES

We have already discussed the "free" (with ad support) versus paid content models for delivering online content. But the situation is more complex: there are several different "free" revenue models. The basic content revenue models include: marketing, advertising, pay-per-view, subscription, and mixed, which combines several of the other types (see **Table 10.3**).

In the *marketing revenue model*, media companies give away content for free in the hope that visitors to the site will purchase the product offline or view a show offline. The Web site is intended to generate interest, develop word-of-mouth viral marketing, and deepen the emotional experience for offline product users. Consumer products companies like Procter & Gamble use this model. The revenues produced by this model are difficult to measure directly. Costs of operating the site can be hidden in larger marketing budgets and to some extent recovered through the sale of product-related paraphernalia, such as T-shirts, caps, and toys. This model appears to be effective in deepening the emotional involvement of consumers with the product, thereby engendering loyalty. It has been effective in the marketing of automobiles, personal care and health brands, new films, and media events in general.

In the *advertising revenue model*, content is free to the consumer; advertisers are expected to pay for the cost of the site through placement of ads. In general, the advertising model works exceptionally well for portals, search engines, social networks, and solid niche community sites that can attract either huge general audiences, or committed niche audiences. YouTube, Facebook, and Photobucket rely on this model although each of these "free" sites are adding premium services and content for which users will be charged. Newspapers historically have used this model in combination with premium subscriptions (paid); and as up to half their audience moves to their Internet editions, they will increasingly rely on the same ad model online as they do offline and bring back the concept of subscriptions for Internet

| TABLE 10.3 | ONLINE CONTENT REVENUE MODELS | |
|---|---|---|
| TYPE OF REVENUE MODEL | DESCRIPTION | COMMENTS |
| Marketing: Tide.com | Free content drives offline revenues | May work for strong brands or niche products; used to deepen customer experience |
| Advertising: Yahoo | Free content is paid for by online advertising | Depends on growth in online ad volume and rates, as well as audience size |
| Pay-per-view/Pay-for-download: Apple's iTunes Store | Charge for premium content is either a la carte (single tune) or for entire works (e-books) | Opportunities for unbundling digital products; works best with an integrated platform like iTunes Store and iPhones/iPods/iPads. |
| Subscription: Rhapsody | Monthly charges for service | The leading paid content model (more than 80% of online paid content); works for high-value products |
| Mixed: MSN | Combination of above models | Market segmentation opportunities make this an attractive model, charging for premium service |

reading of their premium content. Small players, like Salon.com, and most blogs, may not have sufficient audience size to make this model work.

In the *pay-per-view/pay-for-download revenue model* (sometimes called "a la carte"), content providers charge for each viewing of premium content such as a video, book, archived newspaper article, or consulting report. Apple's iTunes Music Store, which charges 99 cents to a $1.99 per song download, depending how much music owners believe the market will bear, is the most common example. In general, the online pay-per-view/download model works only for high-perceived-value content that is unique and targeted. Pay-per-view is currently hindered by the difficulty of using the Internet to view sporting events, feature films, and video content, all of which require substantial download times and resources. In other words, if there is little to view, there is no reason to pay for anything. However, in the future, if the Internet can deliver television-quality video or live coverage of sports events, new films, or music concerts, then the pay-per-view revenue model might work for these high-bandwidth media as effectively as it works for cable television.

In the *subscription revenue model*, content providers such as the *Wall Street Journal* and *Consumer Reports* charge a monthly or annual fee for bulk access to online content. Rhapsody and the new Napster music sites use a subscription model of $9.95 to $14.95 (mobile service) per month for access to digital music archives. Both the pay-per-view and subscription models run up against the "free" model offered by P2P networks. Nevertheless, the subscription and pay-per-view models have begun growing at double-digit rates because consumers trust the legitimate firms and are willing to pay for brand-name quality.

The subscription model works very well for valuable, niche content. Hoover's business information services (Hoovers.com) are provided on a subscription basis to company and stock analysts willing to pay the monthly and annual subscription fee. Perhaps one of the most successful "new media" online content firms is RealNetworks. RealNetworks is known mainly for its online media player RealPlayer. But it also operates an online subscription service for streaming video. RealNetworks is a content aggregator bringing together video from CNN, NASCAR auto racing, professional sports teams, and ABC news, and allows the viewer to select content sources. To make things only slightly more complex, most content providers use a variety of revenue models in combination (**Table 10.4**) to maximize revenues, often by offering "premium" services.

This appears to be the model that most online content publishers have adopted. For instance, the online magazine *Salon* receives 40% of its revenue from subscriptions ($29 a year) and 60% from advertising. *Salon* also charges for discussion areas. The company says its Web site has more than 3 million readers a month, of which 74,000 are paying subscribers. Most portals and other Web sites that used to offer free content in the past are now segueing into mixed models to generate revenues and profits. Free content still abounds, but it is mixed judiciously with pay-for-view, or premium subscription, content options.

### Making a Profit with Online Content: From Free to Fee

Despite the resistance of users in the early years of e-commerce, there is broad consensus that many online consumers, perhaps 25%, are increasingly willing to pay

| TABLE 10.4 | EXAMPLES OF THE GROWING USE OF MIXED REVENUE MODELS FOR ONLINE CONTENT |
|---|---|
| **COMPANY** | **CONTENT** |
| Salon Media Group | Premium subscription: $29 a year, no banner or pop-up ads, Table Talk login, annual subscribers receive free or discounted additional magazine subscriptions, download Salon to PDA or cell phone |
| Yahoo | Real-time quotes: $10.95 a month (annual rate), $13.95 a month (monthly rate) |
| | Yahoo Web Hosting: $12.95 for one month, 26.88 for three months, or $111.93 annually |
| | Yahoo Mail: MailPlus—$19.95/year for no graphical ads and SpamGuard Plus |
| | Yahoo Games: Allstar—$7.95/month, $59.95/year, no advertisements, special tournaments, access to special games |
| RealNetworks | Real SuperPass—free 14-day trial, $14.99/month |
| | Rhapsody Unlimited: $12.99/month, stream unlimited music on PC |
| | Rhapsody ToGo: $14.99/month, stream unlimited music, transfer a limited number of songs to a portable device |
| MSN | Windows Live Hotmail: Free; Hotmail Plus $19.95 a year |
| New York Times | Crossword puzzles: $39.95/annually, $6.95/monthly |
| Financial Times | Standard online subscription: $181/year, Premium: $299/year |
| Wall Street Journal | Print and online subscription: $155/year. |

for high quality content, at their discretion, and that sites offering a mix of free and fee content will optimize their revenues.

There appear to be four factors required to charge for online content: focused market, specialized content, sole-source monopoly, and high perceived net value (see **Figure 10.6**). **Net value** refers to that portion of perceived customer value that can be attributed to the fact that content is available on the Internet. Net value derives from the ability of consumers to instantaneously access the information on the Web, search large and deep historical archives, and move the online information to other documents easily. For instance, Hoover's Online, a source of detailed information on businesses and executives worldwide, provides four different subscriptions ranging from $75 a month to $2,995 for a professional subscription. Hoover's content addresses a focused market (business analysts and executive search firms); it has specialized content (data gathered by its own reporters and other sources); it is the sole source for some of this information; and it has high perceived value because it can be quickly accessed, searched, and downloaded into other documents and made a part of business decision making. And the consumers are in a hurry to get the information. In general, the opportunity for paid content varies by the nature of the content and the audience.

**net value**
that portion of perceived customer value that can be attributed to the fact that content is available on the Internet

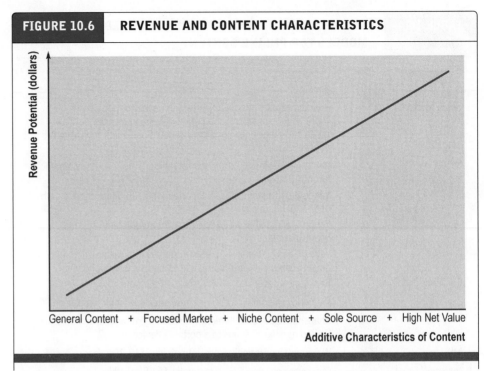

| FIGURE 10.6 | **REVENUE AND CONTENT CHARACTERISTICS** |

As content becomes more focused and more specialized, is controlled by a single source, and provides real value to consumers for an Internet delivery (i.e., speed, searchability, and portability), the prospects for charging fees for access increases.

## KEY CHALLENGES FACING CONTENT PRODUCERS AND OWNERS

While finding a revenue model that works has been the primary business challenge facing online content companies, there are other challenges as well.

### Technology

In the past, technology issues (including low bandwidth, poor and unstable desktop and laptop operating systems, low-bandwidth mobile networks offering Internet access, and poor digital production platforms) were the major inhibiting factor in the growth of online content. This is no longer true. The technology platforms to deliver acceptable online content are now available. The only exception is lack of bandwidth for high definition full-screen video, full-screen standard quality television, and CD-quality music (as opposed to MP3 quality). Yet the streaming quality of video is acceptable and far better than in the past.

### Cost

Internet distribution is far more costly than anticipated. Media companies face substantial costs of migrating, repackaging, and ultimately redesigning content for online delivery. The simplest and least-expensive first-step approach is to migrate existing content to the Web. Even this step requires new staff with new skills, a delivery mechanism, Web designers, and technicians. The costs of migrating can only be justified by increasing sales of offline units. Repackaging content requires substantial creative input and management. The most cost and effort occurs in the third level of media transformation—the redesign of content. There, creative costs can explode as artists, writers, producers, directors, and editors spend thousands of hours designing a "new" content product that optimizes Internet technology while still using many traditional writing and video techniques. For instance, the transformation of traditional film-based movie-making into computer-animated graphical experiences such as *X-Men Origins: Wolverine* requires tens of millions of dollars, and many creative individuals. Other rising costs include paying content writers, actors, and musicians for downloaded content at an acceptable rate.

## Distribution Channels and Cannibalization

Many traditional media companies stumble when they try to repurpose their content to the Web. Short of merging with companies that have large Web audiences—as in the AOL/Time Warner merger—media companies are often tempted to strike alliances with intermediaries such as portals or redistributors. Such alliances carry the risk that the media company's brand name might be displaced by the portal's or aggregator's brand name; in addition, whatever revenues are generated must be shared with the intermediary. Hollywood studios and most television broadcasters want to own their customers and prefer to handle distribution from their own portals For instance, Disney, distributes television and video through Apple's iTunes Store as do most television and movie content owners. But why should movie and television studios be dependent on YouTube or Apple iTunes for distribution? Why not own the Internet distribution channels as well? For instance, Hulu.com (one of the most successful online movie sites) was established by NBC Universal (GE), Fox Entertainment Group (News Corp),and ABC Inc. (The Walt Disney Company) in 2008 to control the distribution of movies and television shows. In 2010, Hulu.com has turned into one of the top 10 online video and movie distributors.

A related and perhaps more vexing challenge is cannibalization of existing channels. What happens to bookstore or music store sales when books and music are available online for half the price—or even lower? What happens to movie theaters when feature films can be downloaded or streamed off the Internet? Here, content producers must be very careful about pricing and value so as to avoid destroying their existing distribution channels.

## Digital Rights Management (DRM)

The uncertainties of content protection are clearly one of the reasons why more high-quality content is not available online. This is especially true of commercial video content. **Digital rights management (DRM)** refers to a combination of technical (both hardware and software) and legal means for protecting digital content from unlimited reproduction without permission. For instance, in 2003, Apple and the music industry attempted to control the distribution of songs downloaded from its iTunes Music Store (now known as the "iTunes Store") by using technology to limit the number of times the songs can be copied to five times, prevent play on uncontrolled

**digital rights management (DRM)**
refers to the combination of technical and legal means for protecting digital content from unlimited reproduction without permission

MP3 players by using a proprietary file format named Advanced Audio Coding (AAC), and prevent more than seven CD burns of the songs. These actions shored up Apple's position in the music download market, where it has a 90% market share. Finally, it relied on the Digital Millennium Copyright Act to discourage hackers from publishing code to break the encryption scheme. In 2009, Apple abandoned the DRM software because of user objections, and because Amazon opened an online music store in 2007 without any DRM protections, with the support of music label firms.

Some firms with subscription services use technologies that limit the time period that a song can be played without re-subscribing. For instance, songs downloaded from Napster and RealOne will simply not play after 30 days unless the user pays the monthly subscription fee. And if you don't pay, you will lose access to all your songs.

While the issue of DRM is often cast as a contest between content owners and hackers bent on distributing and using "free music," the industry titans themselves are divided on digital rights management. Many industries benefit from the illegal and unfettered downloading of music. For instance, Apple Computer, Intel, Sony, and Microsoft all benefit from the explosion in what Apple CEO Steve Jobs calls computers that can "rip, mix, and burn." In other words, sales of computers (and CD burners from Sony) depend heavily on killer applications like P2P networks and the theft of musical rights. Likewise, Verizon, SBC Communications, and Time Warner Cable (and the major Internet trunk line owners) also depend on their networks being kept as busy as possible. Oddly, many of these companies themselves are significant owners of content—like AOL Time Warner and Sony. Typically, it is the technology companies, such as Apple, Microsoft, Google, Yahoo, and others who are delivery pipes for content, that argue for the elimination of DRM techniques. These companies make very little on content per se, but a great deal on the devices and software that carry the content. And it is the content creators and owners who insist on DRM: they make nothing on the delivery devices, and all their revenue comes from the content. Generally, the telecommunications pipeline companies also favor the elimination of DRM because their revenues come from carrying content. To understand all this, you need to keep your eye on the money.

*Insight on Business: Who Owns Your Files* takes a further look at these issues.

## 10.2 THE ONLINE PUBLISHING INDUSTRY

Nothing is quite so fundamental to a civilized society as reading text. Text is the way we record our history, current events, thoughts, and aspirations, and transmit them to all others in the civilization who can read. Even videos require scripts. Today, the publishing industry is a $200 billion media sector based originally on print, and now moving rapidly to the Internet (U.S. Census Bureau, 2010). The Internet offers the text publishing industry an opportunity to move toward a new generation of newspapers, magazines, and books that are produced, processed, stored, distributed, and sold over the Web, available anytime, anywhere, and on any device. The same Internet offers the possibility of destroying many existing print-based businesses that may not be able to make this transition and remain profitable.

# INSIGHT ON BUSINESS

## WHO OWNS YOUR FILES?

In George Orwell's novel, *1984*, the fictional dictator called "Big Brother" directs a pervasive surveillance network of telescreens that monitor what citizens of Oceania read, listen to, and say. In a "life imitates art" management action, on July 17, 2009, Amazon reached into the Kindles of many of their customers to delete digital copies of both *1984* and another Orwell novel, *Animal Farm*, from their e-readers. Amazon also deleted all the notes that students may have taken on the book using Kindle's note function. Amazon had discovered that a vendor of books to its Kindle operation had uploaded the two Orwell books using an automated self-service facility but did not actually own the copyrights to the two novels. The rights are held by the Orwell estate and other firms. The Kindle operates on a cellular network where users can download digital e-books from Amazon's servers for play exclusively on the Kindle device. Apparently, the network can operate in reverse as well, something Kindle owners never realized. Amazon can reach down into every Kindle user's device and delete or add files without obtaining permission of the Kindle's owner.

After thousands of Kindle users protested and one filed a lawsuit, Amazon apologized to its customers, promised never to delete downloaded files again, and admitted they had made a mistake. But the Amazon affair brought to the forefront of national attention the question: "Who owns digital entertainment files once they are downloaded to your computers, including smartphones?" The answer is changing and also unclear.

It used to be that when you bought a CD, or a book, you owned it and you could pretty much do what you wanted with it. "Ownership" from a legal perspective means that you have the exclusive right to control and dispose of property (both tangible and intangible goods). If you create and/or own content, you have exclusive rights to that content. From a customer perspective, this also applies. Under the "first sale doctrine," consumers who purchase a product can resell it without infringing on the copyright. In the pre-digital world, copyrighted material was fairly safe from rampant, uncontrolled copying and distribution. Not so in the new digital world: uncontrolled copying and distribution is very easy. From the copyright owners' business perspective, the ease of duplication and distribution threatens the future revenue stream from the copyrighted products.

Creators and publishers of content, from musicians and writers to music label firms and book publishers, have sought to deal with the threat of losing control (and therefore revenues) of the content they own in two ways: software called Digital Rights Management (DRM), and hardware-based walled environments where digital content can be read or played but not used or copied to any other hardware device. Let's take a brief look at these two strategies.

DRM software is intended to stop uncontrolled copying and distribution. DRM software ensures you can't do pretty much anything you want, but instead only things the owner of the content wants. As a matter of fact, you don't really own the music but just "license" it under terms and conditions specified somewhere (usually in the fine print or on a back page on a Web site). It's called a EULA: End User License Agreement, and when you open the package and break the seal, you are agreeing to the terms of this license. DRM software is computer code embedded in songs, movies, or e-books that dictate how these files can be used. DRM software is both hated and loved—by different groups of course.

(continued)

For consumers, DRM is generally hated but tolerated in most instances if the bargain is right. DRM places restrictions on how a music track, for instance, can be used, copied, and distributed.

The best known DRM was Apple's FairPlay. FairPlay rigged each song you "bought" for 99 cents so that you could play it on only five computers, and so that you could burn only seven CDs. And just to add a little salt to these wounds, the songs could only be downloaded in the default iPod Apple AAC format and played only on Apple iPod devices and not on competing MP3 devices, which use a marginally inferior sound-compression protocol called MP3. Users could not edit or sample the song, and Apple reserved the right to change the DRM restrictions any time it wanted. Apple didn't "voluntarily" arrive at this arrangement but instead negotiated it with the real owners of the content, the record label companies. Without these restrictions, the record labels refused to license Apple any content.

Apple was very successful with this business model despite user complaints. But in January 2009, Apple abandoned its DRM software, and removed all anti-copying restrictions from all songs on the iTunes site. Purchasers of earlier DRM-protected songs could convert their originals for new Premium songs for 30 cents a song (hardly a bargain when you have 16 gigabytes of songs). The three major labels (Sony, Universal, and Time Warner) and Apple reached a compromise: no anti-copying restrictions in return for pricing power to the record labels which raised the price on newly release popular songs to $1.29, keeping most songs at 99 cents, and less popular songs at 69 cents. It's called price discrimination, a basic marketing strategy, and the music labels found it in their business interest to allow copying in return for price discrimination. Apple found it in its business interest to allow variable pricing in the hope that more customers would buy more songs, and more iPods and iPhone devices.

Apple was also responding to competition from Amazon. While iTunes commands 80% of the music download business, Amazon has risen from zero to 20% in a single year. At launch in 2007, Amazon offered over 2 million songs from more than 180,000 artists and over 20,000 labels. In 2010, Amazon's library contains over 8 million songs. All of its songs are available as MP3 tracks without any digital rights protection, and at variable prices determined by the record labels, from 89 cents to $1.29, with albums going for $5.99 to $9.99. A year before Apple launched its DRM-free music, the record labels had cut a deal with Amazon reportedly as a means of reducing Apple's market dominance in the music download business where it was a near monopoly for a short period of time. The strategy worked.

In this sense, DRM is dead in the music world although it survives in the Hollywood movie world and is reappearing in the newspaper content world. The Associated Press (AP), an organization owned by major newspapers to share news stories, announced in July 2009 that it will "envelope" its articles, photos, videos, and headlines in a "protective wrapper" to track the use of its information through a news database that keeps track of Internet content. AP chief executive Tom Curley told the *New York Times* "If someone [Google] can build a multibillion-dollar business out of keywords, we can build a multi-hundred-billion business out of headlines, and we're going to do that." DRM is also alive and well on cable TV where pay-per-view movies cannot be recorded, stored, or copied because of encoding software.

Paid music downloads are growing rapidly, much more rapidly than illegal downloads. But competition for both Apple and Amazon is coming from subscription services and social networks, challenging the entire download-a-tune business model. While everyone has heard of iTunes and Amazon, consumers are turning to streaming sites such as Last.FM, Spotify, and

(continued)

most prominently Pandora, which doubled in size since 2008, and now attracts 18% of all Internet users! Pandora's online streaming service is free to users and is supported by advertisements for iTunes and Amazon, among others, where listeners can purchase the music being played. Social networks, especially MySpace, YouTube, and Facebook, are growing huge music audiences—20% of online consumers (and 50% of teenagers) listen to music social networks in 2010. While illegal sites still attract a significant number of Internet consumers who are under the age of 25, by the time people are 30 and older, only 4% are still downloading music from illegal sites. Strengthened by the Supreme Court ruling against file-sharing sites, the last commercially viable U.S.-based file-sharing service, Bear-Share, collapsed under legal assault from the record label industry. However, pirate and offshore sites in 2010 continue to fuel the P2P downloading phenomenon mostly among the under-20 crowd.

In the near future, many major music providers, including Apple and Google, are poised to make all of their music available only through the cloud. "The cloud" refers to cloud computing in which very large data centers located around the country provide computer services, including music and video file storage, over the Internet. It's conceivable that a cloud-based music service could offer constant access to a selection of music bigger than anything offered using traditional music ownership models. Users could listen to music anytime, anywhere, on any Internet device. To this end, Apple bought music-streaming service provider Lala, whose flagship product scans hard drives for music files and replicates them in the cloud. Google followed suit, purchasing Simplify Media, which developed a product that allows users to access all of their files, including music, from the cloud across multiple devices and systems. Problems with the

system includes working out a system of royalties that is satisfactory both to the music streaming services, record labels, and artists, as well as perfecting the technique of streaming music, mainly to increase download speeds. In early 2010, Apple shut down Lala as an independent service, and absorbed its technology as the foundation for a new, cloud-based business model for iTunes. The cloud model does not solve the ownership issue: you paid for the music, but do you own it, especially if it's not on your hard drive?

Up until 2009, it looked as if the ownership interests of consumers and the ownership interests of copyright owners were diametrically opposed. Consumers either expected to download free content and not pay the owners of content, or they expected to pay for and download a book or music track, and just like the traditional physical products, do whatever they wanted to do with the product. Copyright owners expected consumers to pay for every copy of the book or music that was downloaded, just like the physical products. The situation was complicated by the presence of Internet channel owners: companies such as Verizon and AT&T, which own the cellular and Internet networks, and Apple, Microsoft, and Google, all of whom made money by attracting customers to view free content. The more free content, the larger the audience. They have no business interest in protecting the rights of music, movie, writers, artists, musicians, and content owners. The ensuing debate has raged since MP3 music files first became popular on the Internet in 1997. Sloganeering such as "information wants to be free" and lawsuits by record companies against file-sharers spurred the debate to new heights of frenzy. A deal seemed impossible.

But a new reality is slowly taking hold in which content owners and Internet distributors are recognizing they need one another. Digital

(continued)

device firms such as Apple, which also runs the world's largest download music service, now recognize that they need the quality content of record labels and Hollywood studios. They can't dictate terms to the music industry. Online content servers such as Google (especially YouTube) also recognize that without the major newspapers, studios, and music firms, they would have little high-quality popular content to sell. What would Google news be without news reporting organizations and newspapers? YouTube without Hollywood music videos? Along with the players' various business interests, there's been a change in consumer culture as well. Largely as the result of Apple's iTunes Store, it's become acceptable, even cool, to pay for content such as music online.

**SOURCES:** "Tech Heavyweights Set to Move Music into the Cloud,", by MacGregor Campbell, *New Scientist* , September 6, 2010; "Apple Kills Lala Music Service," by Eliot van Buskirk, Wired.com, April 30, 2010; "Blood on the Tracks: DRM Debate Heats Up," by Pat Pilcher, *New Zealand Herald*, August 5, 2009; "Associated Press to Protect News with Digital Rights Management," Out-law.com, July 27, 2009; "Amazon Faces a Fight Over Its E-Books," by Brad Stone, *New York Times*, July 27, 2009; "A.P. Cracks Down on Unpaid Use of Articles on Web," by Richard Perez-Pena, *New York Times*, July 24, 2009; "Sony Agrees to Provide Its Older Songs to eMusic," by Brad Stone, *New York Times*, June 1, 2009; "Music Labels Cut Friendlier Deals with Start-Ups," by Brad Stone, *New York Times*, May 28, 2009; "Music Consumption Habits Continue to Shift: NPD," by Joseph Palenchar, Twice.com, March 17, 2009; "Want to Copy iTunes Music? Go Ahead, Apple Says," by Brad Stone, *New York Times*, January 7, 2009.

## ONLINE NEWSPAPERS

Newspapers in 2010 are the most troubled segment of the publishing industry, troubles that result almost exclusively from the availability of alternatives to the printed newspaper, as well as a sluggish response by management to the opportunities on the Internet for news, if not newspapers. Also important is the failure of newspaper management to protect its valuable content from being distributed for free by aggregators such as Yahoo, MSN, and Google. As it turns out, there wouldn't be a Google or Yahoo news functionality without traditional reporters and editors who work for newspapers and create the content.

Over 60% of newspapers have reduced news staff in the last three years, and 61% report shrinking the size of the newspaper. Readership has been declining for 10 years, advertising is down 15% a year, subscriptions are down, and old readers are not being replaced by young readers, who instead get their news online. To make matters worse, in the recession of 2009, online ads declined another 28%, and the amount spent on Internet advertising in general now equals that spent on newspaper advertising. Alternative online sources of news such as Yahoo, Google, and even blogs, have became major sources of news for many Americans. Much of this "news" is redistributed content generated by newspapers! Alternatives to newspaper classified ads like Craigslist have decimated newspaper classified revenues.

But there is some good news too. Online readership of newspapers is growing at 16% a year. New reading devices from smartphones to e-readers, iPads and tablet PCs connected to wireless networks offer opportunities for online newspapers to be read everywhere. A new Internet culture is supportive of paying for quality content. Newspaper owners, faced with extinction, are exploring ways to protect their content, and introduce paid "premium" news and views. Pure Internet aggregators of news such as Google and Yahoo are beginning to recognize that if the newspaper industry disappears, there will be little news to aggregate, distribute, and place ads against. Amateur blogs and tweets may be wonderful for expressing opinions, or making instant reports on events as they occur, but they are no substitute for professional reporters and editors, and not a place for brand-conscious advertisers. Therefore, the Internet distributors are recognizing they have a vested interest in keeping the newspaper content industry in working order.

According to the Newspaper Association of America, in 2010, print newspapers have around 49 million paid subscribers, down from 62 million in 1990. On an average day, 95 million people read a newspaper, and on Sunday there are more than 105 million readers. Even when compared to YouTube (18–20 million unique visitors a day), these are impressive audience sizes. Offline newspaper readership of physical papers has declined at about 2% a year for several years, while online readership is at an all-time high of about 72 million in 2010, growing at 17% a year. One-third of all Web users on a typical day visit an online newspaper. The online audience increases the overall footprint of the newspaper media. Total advertising at newspapers in 2010 is $26 billion, and declining at 5% a year. However, online newspaper ad revenues in 2010 are $4 billion and are growing by 14% annually. In a nutshell, this is the problem confronting newspapers: how to grow online revenues fast enough so as to offset the losses from print advertising (eMarketer, 2010c; Newspaper Association of America, 2010).

### Audience Size and Growth

There are more than 10,000 online newspapers in the world. Online newspaper readership is growing at 17% a year. According to Nielsen Online, the total Web audience for online newspapers in the United States during the first seven months of 2010 was typically between 70 and 75 million (Newspaper Association of America, 2010) (see **Figure 10.7** for a list of the top 10). The average online visitor stayed on the site for 35 to 45 minutes. Online newspapers are the dominant local Web site: 62% of Internet users look for local news on a local newspaper Web site. Given this huge online newspaper audience, it is clear that the future of newspapers lies in the online market even as readership and subscriptions to the traditional print newspapers continues to decline at a steady pace.

Next to social networks, newspapers produce the largest online audiences of any media, and in that sense, contrary to popular opinion, are one of the most successful forms of online content to date. The Internet provides existing branded newspapers the opportunity to extend their brands to a new online audience, and also gives entrepreneurial firms the opportunity to offer services—such as classified job listings—on the Web that were previously delivered by newspapers. Online newspapers are the top choice for local news and information for Internet users in the United States.

While newspapers have done an excellent job at increasing their Web presence and audience, few have reached break-even operations, although some are close. Instead, online classified and advertising revenues have not kept pace with the fall in revenues from their traditional print editions. There are several reasons for this: increased competition from general portal sites moving into the content aggregation

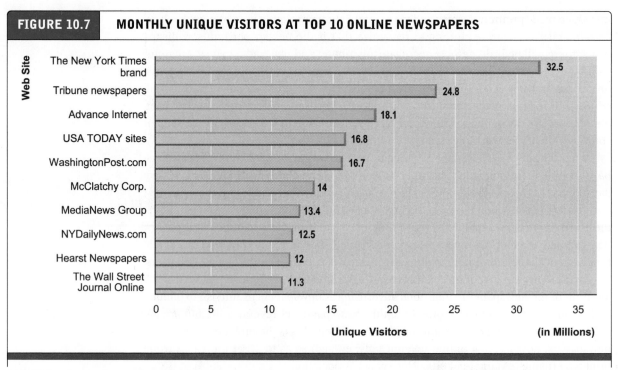

| FIGURE 10.7 | MONTHLY UNIQUE VISITORS AT TOP 10 ONLINE NEWSPAPERS |

SOURCES: Based on data from comScore, 2010c; eMarketer, Inc. 2010d.

business, loss of classified ads to online portals, job sites, and free listing services such as Craigslist. Craigslist is reported to have wiped out $50 million in classified ads for the *San Francisco Chronicle* alone.

The Web has provided an opportunity for newspapers to extend their offline brands, but at the same time it has given entrepreneurs the opportunity to take part of the newspapers' content—such as weather, classified ads, or current national and international news (but not local news).

Internet firms have emerged that threaten to take much of the classified ads business away from newspapers. Sites such as Monster, Craigslist, Autobytel, and CNET have moved aggressively to develop online classified ads for jobs, automobiles, and real estate, while others have developed deep and rich content in specialized areas such as automobiles, computers, cameras, and other hobbyist topics. Many of these firms have drained significant readership from newspapers for specialized, deep content; created nationwide marketplaces that did not exist before; and put a significant dent in local newspaper classified revenues. Classified revenues account for approximately 40% of newspaper revenue.

## Newspaper Business Models

The online newspaper industry has gone through several business models, from fee, to free, and most recently, struggling to return to a fee-based business model. In the past, a few online newspapers such as the *New York Times*, *Wall Street Journal*, and *Financial Times* (U.K.) charged for some or all online content, especially premium content. In the case of the *Times*, access to the *Times* archives was a paid service. Most newspapers did not charge for online content, and even the *Times* abandoned its Times Select subscription service for archived content. The result was that content generated by newspapers became freely available across the Web, where it could be indexed by search engines that redistributed the headlines and content. Newspaper headlines became the primary content on Google News and Yahoo News. Newspapers benefitted from this because a Google listing brought readers to the newspaper, where readers could be exposed to advertising. In 2010, the threatened destruction of the newspaper industry is causing newspaper management to rethink free content supported by online ads placed at the newspapers' sites. The Associated Press has started negotiations with Google to consider payment schemes for the use of its head-lines, and exploring ways to use DRM software to protect its headlines. The *Wall Street Journal* was prepared to abandon the fee model in 2008, but in 2009, the parent News Corp, the largest owner of newspapers in the world, announced plans to begin charg-ing for all its online content across the world.

In response to declining or stagnant revenue growth, newspapers have sought alliances with one another and with online technology power houses such as Yahoo and Google in response to the challenge posed by pure-play online classified job sites, and the newspaper industry has sought industry-wide alliances to develop competing sites and to move toward a value-added revenue model for this segment. To compete against Monster.com, the *New York Times*, Times-Mirror Company, the *Tribune*, and the *Washington Post* created a territorial model called CareerBuilder, a job-listing site with more than 1 million jobs and 23 million monthly visitors. Gannett, McClatchy, and Tribune Co., which collectively own hundreds of local newspapers, formed an alliance called Open Network to offer advertisers one-stop shopping for national (as opposed to local) newspaper advertising. Yahoo and a consortium of seven newspaper chains representing 176 daily papers around the country have a partnership to share content, technology, and advertising. Consortium members are ablet to offer local businesses targeted advertising for both their own sites as well as Yahoo sites. Google has a system for auctioning ads for many of the largest newspaper companies, including Gannett, Tribune, the *New York Times*, Hearst, and others.

Many, but not all, efforts by newspapers to adapt to the Internet involve making alliances with Internet titans such as Google and Yahoo, which have huge online audiences. These efforts involve sharing revenue with Internet partners. A different strategy is emerging based on the proliferation of e-reader devices such as smartphones like the iPhone, netbooks and tablets like the iPad, and dedicated devices like the Kindle, Sony e-reader, and Barnes & Noble's Nook. Sales of the new e-readers are expected to reach well over 3 million dedicated readers in 2010, and more than 7 million iPads. Each of these devices has, or will have, reader apps that present newspaper content in a way that closely matches the offline editions and is familiar to readers.

These new reader devices offer newspapers an opportunity to connect directly with their readers anytime and anywhere. What's missing is a newspaper version of the iTunes Store, a single online store where you can find newspaper content from any newspaper in the U.S. or the world. But not for long. NewspaperDirect is an online store that has same-day online editions of more than 1,600 newspapers from 92 countries in 48 languages. Unlimited subscriptions are $29.00 a month, economy editions are $9.95 for 31 articles, and most individual articles cost 99 cents. Along with other traditional providers of text products such as Barnes & Noble, sites like News-paperDirect offer the newspaper industry a way to deliver their content on a contemporary digital platform.

## Convergence

In terms of our schema of convergence—technology, content, and industry structure—the newspaper industry is rushing pell mell to a convergent model of news, content, and services. Soon newspapers will be offering social network sites for local groups.

**Technology** The movement of published text to the Web was the first step toward technology platform convergence, but obviously this did not take advantage of the interactive features of the Web. The newspaper industry has been slow to invest in Internet technology, although this is changing as video, RSS feeds, blogs, and user feedback forums grow.

**Content** Online newspapers have transformed themselves into multimedia platforms with a variety of digital content. Four content changes are apparent: premium archived content, fine-grained search, videos reporting, and RSS feeds. **Figure 10.8** summarizes the transformation of online newspapers as digital outlets.

The online environment permits considerable extension to traditional newspaper content. For instance, newspapers can offer access to premium archive content by permitting users to search back issues. The inherent fine-grained search capability of the Internet platform increases ease of access to news and archival information for consumers. The most significant change in content is timeliness. The Internet frees newspapers from the time-bound character of paper and printing presses and allows for instant updates to breaking stories. In this sense, online newspapers can, for the first time, compete directly with television and radio for reporting breaking stories. Visit the online *New York Times* or *Wall Street Journal*, or a local online newspaper today, and you will see breaking news that is just a few minutes old. This is a sea change from traditional newspapers.

**Industry Structure** The newspaper industry is a mature industry that is ripe for further consolidation and expansion onto the Web. Historically, hundreds of local newspapers have been combined into larger national chains. Now the chains themselves need to be consolidated in order to create truly national advertising markets, and leverage their local readership (something Google, Microsoft, and Yahoo do not have). The problem has been finding deep-pocket media titans to purchase the papers and make hefty technology investments. Generally, the returns on newspaper investments do not meet the hurdle rates for most media titan firms. Instead, newspaper companies tend to buy one another, or are bought as play things for the idle rich. The McClatchy Company purchased the second largest newspaper chain,

| FIGURE 10.8 | INTERACTIVE FEATURES OFFERED ON THE WEB SITES OF THE TOP 100 U.S. NEWSPAPERS (% OF TOTAL) |
|---|---|

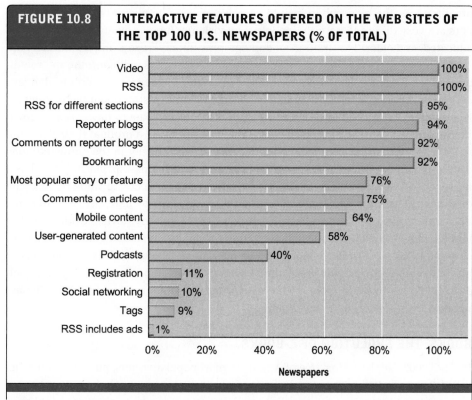

| | |
|---|---|
| Video | 100% |
| RSS | 100% |
| RSS for different sections | 95% |
| Reporter blogs | 94% |
| Comments on reporter blogs | 92% |
| Bookmarking | 92% |
| Most popular story or feature | 76% |
| Comments on articles | 75% |
| Mobile content | 64% |
| User-generated content | 58% |
| Podcasts | 40% |
| Registration | 11% |
| Social networking | 10% |
| Tags | 9% |
| RSS includes ads | 1% |

**Newspapers**

This graph illustrates the adoption of interactive features on the Web sites of the top 100 newspapers.
SOURCES: Based on data from the Bivings Group, 2008; eMarketer, 2009c.

Knight Ridder, in June 2006. In April 2007, Sam Zell, Chicago real estate magnate, purchased the Tribune Company in an $8.2 billion deal, but only put up $315 million of his own money. The new company took on $8 billion in debt, most of it owned by the employee pension plan. In 2008, the company declared bankruptcy, and in 2010 is still struggling with creditors. The only exception to this pattern has been the News Corp.'s purchase of Dow Jones, publisher of the *Wall Street Journal*.

## Challenges: Disruptive Technologies

The online newspaper industry would appear at first glance to be a classic case of disruptive technology destroying a traditional business model based on physical products and physical distribution. This may turn out to be the case, but it cannot be the final assessment just yet. The industry is changing rapidly. There are significant assets that newspapers have—excellent content and writing, strong local readership, strong local advertising, and a fragmented but huge audience of nearly 100 million readers that rivals Yahoo, Google, and Microsoft's audience. Content is still king: the thousands of blogs in the blogospheres depend on traditional reporting media like television and newspapers to create the content that the blog writers can react to. Without the original content creators in the form of professional reporters and news organizations, the blogosphere would be a dull place. The people who read newspapers are very different from the people who visit YouTube: they are wealthier, more educated, and older. This is an ideal demographic for advertisers and a potential gold mine for newspapers. The online audience for newspapers will continue to grow in both sheer numbers and sophistication, demanding higher-quality online delivery and more services. The industry has made significant investments in technology for Web content creation and delivery. Many national newspapers have slowed down investment in online operations because they did not make a profit at first. The challenge is for newspaper owners and managers to invest heavily in the online editions even if they do not meet investment criteria at first. If the newspaper industry has a future, it will be online. The challenge for newspapers is to create value by focusing on differentiated, timely, and exclusive content available nowhere else. And to make this content available anywhere, anytime, any place, on any device. Oddly, Apple's iTunes may have shown newspapers the future by developing micro-payment systems to sell individual music content files for .99 cents, and to sell bundles of music (albums) for a reasonable price. There's no reason newspapers cannot sell articles, stories, and editorials online for .99 cents or $10 for a monthly bundle. Today, none do.

## BOOKS: THE EVOLUTION OF E-BOOKS

In April 2000, Stephen King, one of America's most popular writers, published a novella called *Riding the Bullet*. This novella was only available as an e-book. King was the first major fiction writer to create an e-book-only volume of a new work. King's publisher, Simon & Schuster, arranged for sales online through online retailers such as Amazon. In the first day, there were 400,000 downloads, so many that Amazon's servers nearly crashed several times. More than 500,000 downloads occurred in the first week, for a price of $2.50 for a 66-page novella—about the same price per page as a standard King hardcover novel. While Amazon gave the book away for free in the first two weeks, when it began charging for the book, sales continued to be brisk.

In 2010, Amazon's e-book store contains an estimated 650,000 titles (many titles are classic out-of-print and public domain books, but there are many popular copyrighted books as well). There are an estimated 600,000 Kindles being used today, and Amazon is racking up 600,000 e-book sales a week (Kindle users are avid readers and typically purchase a book a week.) In 2010, Amazon's unit sales of e-books exceeded its unit sales of hard cover books for the first time.

E-books are surprisingly a very hot topic in 2010 as Google battles the major tech companies, authors, publishing firms, the United States Congress, the Department of Justice, and the European Commission over the future of online digital books. Meanwhile, device makers such as Apple (iPad and iPod Touch), Amazon, Sony, IREX, and Barnes & Noble (Nook) are delivering new readers to the market seemingly every month.

In the Internet age, books are supposed to die off and go away. Who wants to read books when YouTube has billions of video streams covering most topics known to man, and Google can provide access to the world's information? Steve Jobs noted in an interview about the Kindle e-book reader, "It doesn't matter how good or bad the product [e-book reader] is, the fact is that people don't read anymore. Forty percent of the people in the U.S. read one book or less last year. The whole conception is flawed at the top because people don't read anymore." Actually, in 2010, over 3 billion books will be sold in the United States, generating around $24 billion in revenue. Americans in fact read 10 books per year per person.

The essential questions facing the book publishing industry are: If people are willing to buy physical books, would they also be willing to buy electronic versions of books? What kind of device would readers like to use when reading digital books? The next question is, "How much would they be willing to pay for an e-book?" And finally, "What changes to the concept of the book itself might be necessary to encourage people to buy e-books online?" The preliminary answer to these questions is suggested by e-book sales results in 2010. To date, 3 million dedicated readers have been sold, 7 million iPads (not to mention millions of iPhones and iPod Touch units), and an estimated total e-book sales of 22 million. These results are preliminary because the e-book revolution is just beginning.

The Internet already has brought about significant changes in book sales and distribution, and is beginning to have an impact on the design, creation, and production of books. The book itself, and the reading experience, is starting to slowly morph into a truly different product. The concept of the traditional book is beginning to change from a passive form of entertainment to a more interactive form of engagement.

The modern book is not really very different from the first two-facing page, bound books that began to appear in 17th-century Europe. The traditional book has a very simple, non-digital operating system: text appears left to right, pages are numbered, there is a hard front and back cover, and text pages are bound together by stitching or glue. In educational and reference books, there is an alphabetical index in the back of the book that permits direct access to the book's content. While these traditional books will be with us for many years given their portability, ease of use, and flexibility, a parallel new world of e-books is expected to emerge in the next five years.

## E-books

E-books have had a glorious history of birth, death, and rebirth. In 2010, e-books are back, this time with powerful backers such as Amazon, Sony, Yahoo, Google, and Microsoft, along with start-ups like IREX. The Google Books Library Project is scanning millions of books in large university libraries. When you click on a search result for a book from the Library Project, you will see basic bibliographic information about the book and, in many cases, a few sentences (called "snippets") showing your search term in context. If the book is out of copyright, you will be able to view and download the entire book. In all cases, you'll see links directing you to online bookstores where you can buy the book and libraries where you can borrow it. Google books, of course, are only searchable with the Google search engine, and none of the scanned books are compatible with similar efforts by Microsoft or members of the Open Book Alliance (see the case study at the end of Chapter 8).

Electronic books were around for many years before the Internet. In 1971, Michael Hart began Project Gutenberg at the Materials Research Lab at the University of Illinois. Hart began by typing in the Declaration of Independence, and proceeded to put more than 2,000 classic books online at the University's Computer Center. The books are all in ASCII plain text without traditional book fonts or formatting. While not a joy to read, they are free. In 1990, Voyager Company, a New York-based media company, began putting books such as *Jurassic Park* and *Alice in Wonderland* on CDs. However, with the exception of encyclopedias and large reference texts, popular books on CDs never were a commercial success. They were expensive to produce and distribute, and appeared in the marketplace before most PC users had CD-ROM drives.

The development of the Internet and the Web, along with small, powerful handheld devices, have greatly changed the possibilities for e-books. The Web offers publishers much lower distribution costs (each "copy" on the Web can be downloaded for almost no cost), and unlike the early computer-based e-books, all the formatting, fonts, and colors used by publishers in high-quality books are preserved when Adobe's Portable Document Format (PDF) is used to create the text.

There are many different types of commercial e-books (see **Table 10.5**). The two most common e-books are Web-accessed or Web-downloadable. **Web-accessed e-books** are stored on the publisher's servers and purchasers pay a fee for reading the book on-screen; in some cases these e-books can also be printed by the individual user. The most successful Web-accessed e-books are online encyclopedias such as the abridged edition of the *Encyclopedia Britannica*, and open source encyclopedias like Wikipedia.com. CourseSmart is an e-textbook service formed by the six largest publishers of textbooks in the world. With CourseSmart, college students can subscribe to online textbooks for half the price of purchasing a physical textbook (including this book!). The book can be accessed from any Internet connected computer, anywhere, anytime. Students can also print chapters.

**Web-accessed e-book**

an e-book stored on a publisher's server that consumers access and read on the Web

| TABLE 10.5 | TYPES OF E-BOOKS |
|---|---|
| **E-BOOK TYPE** | **DESCRIPTION** |
| Web-accessed e-books | E-book remains on publisher's Web site and is read only on the site. Purchasers pay a subscription fee for access. |
| Web-downloadable e-books | Contents of e-book can be downloaded to client PC for reading. Printing may or may not be possible. Purchaser pays for initial download and reading, or content is paid for by advertising, such as Google e-books. Subsequent use may be metered or free. |
| Dedicated e-book reader | Contents of e-book can be downloaded only to dedicated hardware device either directly connected to the Web or through a PC connection. Kindle, Sony, and Nook readers. |
| General-purpose PDA reader | Contents of e-book can be downloaded from the Web to a general-purpose handheld smartphone such as an iPhone , Palm Pre, or BlackBerrry. |
| Print-on-demand books | Contents of a book are stored on a Web server; they can be downloaded on demand for local printing and even binding. |

**Web-downloadable e-books** are a more user-friendly e-book that can be downloaded from the Web, stored as a file on the client PC, and in many cases printed, although some e-books have security locks that prevent printing. The largest collections of downloadable e-books are held by Google (Google Books Project, and Google Books Library Project). The Google Books Project involves scanning millions of entire physical books, many of them out of copyright, or "orphaned" by authors and publishers. Google refuses to say how many books it has scanned, but estimates suggest somewhere between 1 and 2 million titles are in the book database. The Google Books Library Project works with many large research and public libraries to scan all their holdings, and make them available to the public as a library resource. Google's plan is to monetize these databases by posting advertisements next to book pages. These plans are currently held in check because of a lawsuit brought by authors and publishers against Google. Other large downloadable e-book collections are held by NetLibrary and Questia.

**Dedicated e-book readers** are single-purpose devices that have proprietary operating systems that can download from the Web and read proprietary formatted files created for those devices. Each dedicated reader makes available to customers several thousand generally popular titles. Franklin Electronic Publisher's eBook-Man was one of the first dedicated e-book readers. Prices ranged from a low of $129 to a high of $199 retail. The product was discontinued in 2001 after sales failed to reach expectations. Other players have since stepped up to the plate. Amazon, Sony, and IREX have brought back the dedicated e-book reader device from what most considered certain death. The Amazon Kindle is now in its third generation, comes in both a Wi-Fi and 3G + Wi-Fi version and can hold 3,500 books. The Kindle DX provides a larger screen. Dedicated readers rely on electronic ink technology, which comes close to the clarity of print, and are continuously connected to 3G or WiFi networks so new books can be purchased and downloaded.

General-purpose Internet device readers like iPhones, iPads, and BlackBerrys, and their associated reader apps, are a major comptetitor of dedicated readers. iPhone has an estimated 3.5 million e-book app users, and after games (20% of apps), e-book apps are the second largest category of apps (14%). There are about 10,000 e-book apps in the iTunes Store, over 90% of which are free.

**Print-on-demand books** are less well known, but arguably are one of the largest forms of electronic publishing. Sometimes called "custom publishing," print-on-demand books are usually professional or educational titles that are stored on mainframe storage devices ready for printing in small print runs on demand. For instance, most college publishers have a "custom book" program that allows professors to put together digitally stored chapters from many different books, along with articles from scholarly journals, and to publish a small print run of, say, 400 books for a single class. Generally, these books are no less costly to produce or purchase, but they have the advantage of flexible content that can be changed to meet the specific needs of users. "Print on demand" books is also a euphemism for vanity press books, or self-published books on the Internet. There is a lively market for self-published books on the Internet, although it is difficult to identify the precise size of this market, or who is paying the money for publishing—the writer or the reader.

**Web-downloadable e-book**
an e-book that can be downloaded from the Web, stored as a file on the client PC, and perhaps even printed

**dedicated e-book reader**
a single-purpose device with a proprietary operating system that can download from the Web and read proprietary formatted files created for that device

**print-on-demand book**
custom-published book

### Book Audience Size and Growth

In 2010, consumers will spend about $25 billion for the purchase of 3.2 billion books: $13 billion on consumer trade books, and $12 billion for professional, scholarly, and higher education textbooks (AAP, 2010). Americans in fact read 10 books per year per person, and many more for people over 17. In a recession when not down much is actually up, the book industry is holding very steady, much better than industrials, consumer products, and of course financials, which tanked, and a little better than the high-tech Silicon Valley firms. However, book readership is flat, with young people reading fewer books than in the past while an expanding elderly population reads more than in the past.

Publishing the same number of titles and raising prices, publishers have kept revenues about even with inflation. Unlike newspapers, the number of book readers has been constant and is anchored in the large, over-40-years-of-age demographic. Per capita spending for trade books was about $106 in 2009, higher than video games ($44), and in-theater movies and other box office events ($44). In other words, books are a substantial element in the consumer's time and revenue content budgets, and for professional and educational titles, book publishing is growing more than twice as fast as the general U.S. economy (U.S. Census Bureau, 2009).

While total e-book sales on all digital platforms is only about 2% of all book sales, this is expected to grow to about $2 billion in 2014 or nearly 10% of all book sales. E-book sales are nevertheless the fastest growing delivery platform for text content: 45% annual growth in revenues since 2004, and 50% annual increases going forward to 2013.

**Figure 10.9** describes the current and estimated future growth of e-book sales on the Web. There is no single catalog of e-books, and therefore it is difficult to estimate

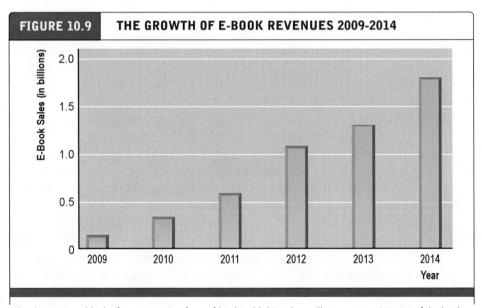

**FIGURE 10.9    THE GROWTH OF E-BOOK REVENUES 2009-2014**

E-books are arguably the fastest growing form of book publishing, but still represent a tiny part of the book publishing industry.

SOURCES: Based on data from Assocation of American Publishers, 2010; authors' estimates.

the total number of new e-books each year. However, it is likely that between 3,000 to 4,000 new e-books will be published in 2010, not counting several thousand self-published e-books, and not counting titles created by the Google Library project.

## E-book Industry Revenue Models

The e-book industry is composed of intermediary retailers, traditional publishers, technology developers, and vanity presses. Some of the key players in the new e-book industry are listed in **Table 10.6**. Together, these players have pursued a wide variety of business models and developed many alliances in a collective effort to move text onto the computer screen.

In the traditional commercial book business model, publishers pay authors advances against earnings to write books. Publishers provide editorial, marketing, and sales expertise, and then sell these works to national distributors or directly to large retail book chains. In the case of noncommercial books, authors pay so-called vanity presses to publish and sell their books, receiving very little if any editorial or marketing assistance. The development of e-books has brought about several changes in this traditional model.

The primary consumer e-book revenue model is pay-for-download, a model that involves traditional publishers and authors creating electronic editions of books, and publishers and distributors selling these works in their entirety through new online bookstore intermediaries such as Barnesandnoble.com and Amazon. E-books have not changed the traditional revenue model significantly. In general, publishers have not begun to sell e-books directly to the online audience simply because they do not have the experience or expertise to do so, although in the future they could. Barnesandnoble.com is a special case. It occasionally acts as a publisher by commissioning new e-works; at the same time, it is a retailer of those e-works.

A second e-book revenue model involves the licensing of entire e-libraries of content. This market involves major institutional customers like public and academic libraries, and corporate libraries. Licensing is similar to a subscription model; users pay either a monthly subscription fee or a flat fee for annual access to hundreds of titles. The licensing model is exemplified by NetLibrary. NetLibrary was the first large-scale experiment that involved the licensing of entire electronic libraries to universities and colleges. Many public libraries have begun to reach out to their Internet-enabled users, and greatly expand their local reach by offering e-books. For instance, New York City Public Library has over 3,000 electronic titles; the King County Library in Washington has over 8,500 online titles.

A third business model exemplified by Google is an advertising-supported model where the distributor (Google) arranges with publishers for the rights to display a book, and then shares revenue with the publishers (about 70%) generated by ads placed on book pages.

## Convergence

The publishing industry is making very uneven progress toward media convergence in terms of technology platform, content, and industry structure. In the past, progress was slowed by poor business models and lack of financial resources. Today, it is

| TABLE 10.6 | EXAMPLE E-BOOK INDUSTRY FIRMS |
|---|---|
| COMPANY | E-BOOK ACTIVITIES |
| ***Distributors*** | |
| Amazon | Largest online general retailer of physical and e-books; creator of the Kindle e-book reader |
| Google | Largest collection of downloadable e-books in the world |
| Barnesandnoble.com | General audience online retailer of books and publisher of e-books. |
| NetLibrary | Second largest online e-library, now owned by EBSCO) |
| Questia | Largest online research library and e-book site by subscription (over 70,000 books and 2 million articles) |
| ebrary | Online research library by subscription using proprietary reader for PCs. |
| Fictionwise | Distributor of multi-platform e-books; owned by Barnes and Noble |
| Adobe eBookstore | Online sales of e-books demonstrating the Acrobat platform |
| ***Technology Developers*** | |
| Adobe Systems Inc. | Owners of Acrobat and PDF file format for e-book display on PC screens |
| Intertrust Technologies | DRM software tools |
| Microsoft | Microsoft Reader software for e-book display on cell phones and PCs; supporter of Open eBook standard |
| Palm | Smartphone hardware and operating system; can be used for e-books |
| Sony | Manufacturer of e-book readers |
| MobiPocket | French company; creator of universal reader for cell phones and PCs, with DRM software for publishers; secure and encrypted books based on serial number of handheld devices |
| Amazon | Creator of the most popular e-book reader, the Kindle. |
| Apple | Creator of the most popular smartphone platform also used as a reader device. |
| ***Traditional Publishers*** | |
| Pearson PLC | Developing new models of online educational e-books |
| Cengage Learning | Educational publisher that offers a variety of e-book and e-chapter options |
| Random House | Largest trade book publisher; has developed a separate division to develop e-book titles |
| CourseSmart | Consortium of the six largest textbook publishers offering thousands of e-textbooks to college students at half price |
| ***Vanity e-Presses (on-demand publishers)*** | |
| Xlibris (Random House) | Self-publishing online |
| Ebooks.com | Online sales and publishing |
| AuthorHouse | Self-publishing online |

slowed by greed and competition among technology firms, each of which is seeking to develop a proprietary solution to the problem of getting books online with a viable business model.

**Technology** One would think that it would be a simple matter to merge the world of text and books with that of the Internet and the Web, which originally were both text-based media. However, four technology-based difficulties have slowed this aspect of convergence: poor computer screen resolution, the lack of portable reader devices that can compete with the portability of the traditional book, the absence of a powerful DRM technology that can protect the copyrights of digital works, and the lack of standards to define cross-platform e-books. Some of these issues have been addressed by the new mobile platforms, but the open PC platform continues to raise problems for the e-book industry. The new dedicated readers using e-ink technology, and the iPhone and iPad screens using very high resolution LCD technology, can now display books with enough resolutuion for easy reading. The mobile readers now offer platform security: book files cannot be played outside the walled gardens of the device. This is not true for PCs, however, where files can be copied and distributed easily.

Competing standards and platforms pose a problem: buy a book for the Kindle and it does not work on your PC, and works on an iPad only with the Kindle app. Buy a Kindle book and you cannot play it on a Nook. **Table 10.7** describes the current leading standards for e-books. The most widely adopted standard is the Adobe Acrobat PDF file format. Tens of millions of computer users use Adobe Acrobat Reader to access Acrobat PDFs. Acrobat preserves fonts, formatting, and graphics information and can be used on almost any computer including Macintosh, Unix-based, and PCs. Open eBook (OEB) is an emerging industry-formatting standard that is supported by publishers and software firms such as Microsoft. OEB provides a specification for representing the content of e-books, and is based on HTML and XML, making it universal across all platforms and types of screens. Currently, OEB supports only minimal formatting and is best for simple text, not complex graphics combined with text.

Online Information Exchange (ONIX) is an industry standard for transmitting information about books, or "meta data." For instance, a book jacket may contain review comments, a description of contents, a picture of the author, and an author biography. Currently, there is no way to communicate this information electronically from the publisher to the online bookstore that wants to display this meta data on a Web page. ONIX is an XML-based set of approximately 200 tags (e.g., < PublisherName > Scribner's < /PublisherName >) that can easily be read and communicated to book distributors and retailers (Editeur.org, 2009; Book Industry Study Group, 2009).

**Content** E-books today have made little progress toward content convergence. Most e-books contain only text and graphics, and often are simply PDF versions of files sent to the printers to run the physical presses. E-books can be placed along a continuum of transformation (and cost). E-books currently are in the media integration stage where text is being reformatted for electronic display. This is a low-cost beginning, allowing publishers to focus their attention and budgets on building their online distribution networks. However, some firms are beginning to experiment with more interactive experiences that will transform e-books into

| TABLE 10.7 | STANDARDS FOR E-BOOKS |
|---|---|
| **E-BOOK STANDARD/SOFTWARE** | **DESCRIPTION** |
| ***Screen Display*** | |
| Microsoft Reader Clear-Type | Free software for improving LCD text display through sub-pixel rendering on Microsoft CE PDA devices |
| Adobe CoolType | Free software for improving LCD text display through sub-pixel rendering on PDAs |
| E-Ink | Electronic ink display for LCDs |
| ***Formats*** | |
| Open eBook (OEB and OEB.LIT) | Microsoft-supported industry group to define e-book formatting. OEB.LIT adds DRM capabilities |
| Adobe Portable Document Format (PDF) | Adobe's software for PC and PDA screen display of rich text, complex fonts, and formatting; works best on PC screens; new versions contain DRM capabilities |
| MobiPocket | Proprietary format that plays on all handheld devices |
| AZW | Amazon Kindle DRM format |
| ***Book Industry Product Description*** | |
| ONIX | Universal, international industry standard for describing book products and contents based on XML |

multimedia events containing lectures, speeches, interviews with the authors, online polls and quizzes, online updates of content, and videos to support the experience (see *Insight on Society: The Future of Books*).

**Industry Structure** Unlike the recorded music industry, the book industry has not been transformed by the Internet. However, it is being challenged by Google and Microsoft, both of which want to index copyrighted books and make portions ("snippets" determined by Google) available online; by college students, their parents, and Congress, who want lower prices for textbooks; by very large distributors like Barnes & Noble, who want to move into actual publishing with very low-cost books; to a lesser extent by user-generated content in the form of blogs and self-published books; and by slow growth in physical book sales. The book publishing industry and the creation, production, and distribution of e-books is still dominated by a few titans, with the level of industry concentration increasing as large media companies such as Bertelsmann (Random House), and large text publishing companies, such as Pearson, Thomson, and McGraw-Hill, absorb smaller presses. Nevertheless, the Internet has created many new opportunities for authors, publishers, distributors, and specialized book retailers. Entrepreneurial start-up firms such as NetLibrary demonstrated that a

# INSIGHT ON SOCIETY

# THE FUTURE OF BOOKS

What do you think of when you think about what a "book" is, or looks like? Chances are you still think of the traditional "book," printed on paper, and bound with a hard or soft cover, with a finite beginning, middle, and end. When most people think of an e-book, they think of a traditional book converted into a page-turner. All e-book readers today are based on the metaphor of "the page." However, in the near future, traditional notions about what constitutes a "book" will change, and "books" will assume a variety of different forms that integrate audio and video with text. The result will not be a "book" in the traditional sense. Perhaps it will be called a "learning experience" or just an "experience." Instead of asking your friends if they've read a book, you'll ask instead "Have you experienced this?".

For instance, you've read in this chapter about different types of e-books, readable on Kindles, iPads, or other e-reader devices. However, these are often traditional books just being delivered on a new format. Taking e-books one step further, say out to 2014, they most likely will evolve into much richer learning environments with substantial audio, video, and community participation than is true of today's text-only e-books. You can see the potential future of the e-book by visiting the *Wall Street Journal* Web site. There you will find one of the world's most successful business publications integrating text with video, reporter blogs, user commentary, up-to-the-minute reporting, interviews, and podcasts. Social networks have also been added to enable the creation of financial communities. If newspapers can look like this, why can't e-books?

But what about the form of the book itself? Why, for instance, should a book have just a single author or a few authors? Why should books be read alone? Sagas—the ancient lengthy stories of an entire people shared through an oral tradition—had multiple authors. Sagas were read and repeated in groups. It is possible on the Internet to have a community of readers contribute to both the authorship of the online e-book and the experience of reading the book. You can call it "social publishing" or "social writing." Wikipedia, for instance, is a constantly updated online "e-book" encyclopedia written by thousands of contributors. Wikibooks, its less well-known cousin, brings the wiki movement to the creation of textbooks. David Carr, a journalist for the *New York Times*, and Simon and Schuster have collaborated to create NightoftheGun.com, a Web site that is part and parcel of Carr's memoir, *The Night of the Gun*. When Carr created his work, he developed a database of content, including hundreds of hours of recorded interviews, documents, reports, letters, legal communications, photos, and keepsakes. The Web site offers a fully immersive multimedia experience where the story is in the hands of the reader.

To provide this multimedia experience to their customers, electronic booksellers like Apple and Amazon are adding unique new features to some of their latest releases. For example, English actor and comedian Stephen Fry's 2010 autobiography, *The Fry Chronicles*, was released in hardcover, paperback, and Kindle e-book versions, but was also released as an "enhanced book" available at Apple's iBook store as well as an interactive iPad and iPhone app titled myFry. myFry allows users to navigate through the book's table of contents, displayed as an interactive wheel, and sort through various tags to find the content that interests them in each chapter. In the future, as online booksellers develop different forms of media like myFry, customers may come to prefer some forms of books over others. It's possible that bundling multiple forms of media together, say a hardback, an interactive e-book, and an iPhone application, will

(continued)

be an attractive option for booksellers to convince their customers to spend more.

Unigo offers another take on the future of "books" by creating online experiences that involve text and media. If you're like most college students, when you began to think about applying to college, probably one of the first places you turned to for information was a traditional college guidebook, like those published by The Princeton Review, Peterson's, or U.S. News and World Report, or perhaps *The Insider's Guide to Colleges* by the staff of the Yale Daily News. But even books hundreds of pages long are limited in terms of the volume and type of information they can provide about the thousands of different colleges across the country. For Jordan Goldman, a 26-year-old recent Wesleyan graduate, this was a problem looking for a solution; and his solution is one that may threaten the publishing industry's stranglehold on the delivery of college information via traditionally published books.

What Goldman envisioned, and launched in September 2008, with the backing of Frank Sica, a former president of Soros Private Funds Management, is Unigo.com, a free, advertising-supported site that offers a student-generated guide to North American colleges. The site features brief editorial overviews of each of the colleges featured, but the real meat is furnished by students in the form of responses to essay-based questionnaires, photos, videos, and uploaded writing samples. When launched, over 30,000 individual bits of content had been submitted. Today, 15,000 students have contributed profiles for 250 colleges, which include text and video. Fifteen editors monitor the quality of the content submitted. At Davidson College, for example, about 230 current students (1/8th of the student body) submitted photos, reviews, and video. As one person noted, its one thing to read in a guidebook that a school sits on a lake, and another to look at a video and see students hanging out in beautiful surroundings.

Every student who joins Unigo has a user profile, and users can search the site for material submitted by those who they believe might be similar to themselves. For instance, a user can search for reviews of Harvard by English majors, and contact students who submitted material with follow-up questions. Users can also search for schools by size, setting, region, selectivity, and tuition. And branching into the social network space, the My Unigo section of the site allows users to organize all of the site's content according to their personal interests, and also add their own content.

As Goldman notes: "That the best resource for a four-year, $200,000 decision are these books—with no photos, no videos, no interactivity, only three-to-five pages per school on average, fully updated usually once every several years—just doesn't make the grade." For many students and parents, spending a few hours on Unigo's site can be just as valuable as spending $3,000 to $5,000 dollars on a college counselor who provides advice on what colleges would be good for you. Goldman and Unigo's financial backers think their "grassroots" movement to wrest control over the dissemination of information about colleges from traditional publishers will revolutionize the way students decide which school to attend.

As we see throughout this chapter, the Internet is changing the consumer's sense of entertainment and even education. Heightened expectations for participation, involvement, engagement, and self-control are driving consumers toward Web sites and content providers that can provide these kinds of experiences, creating new opportunities for innovative publishers. The future of books is only just beginning to take shape.

**SOURCES:** "MyFry iPhone App Presents Stephen Fry's Autobiography in Easy-to-Read Format," Gizmodo.com, September 13, 2010; " The Conversation: College Rankings that Make Parents Blush," ABCnews.com, August 25, 2010; "Unigo.com Gives Everyone a Say About College Picks," by Walter Mossberg, *Wall Street Journal*, February 19, 2009; "About This Site," Nightofthegun.com, September 24, 2008; "Envisioning the Next Chapter for Electronic Books," by Brad Stone, *New York Times*, September 7, 2007.

market existed for inexpensive digital libraries. Entrepreneurial online book distributors, from Amazon and Barnesandnoble.com to much smaller, specialized-topic, boutique online distributors, have demonstrated a huge marketplace for online distribution of traditional books. Online book distributors such as Barnesandnoble.com have commissioned new e-book titles and moved into publishing. Authors have published works directly to the public without the intervention of publishers in the blogosphere, as well as through online vanity presses that charge authors for the privilege of publishing their works. The open source movement has created online encyclopedias like Wikipedia that offer incredible depth (but also occasional erroneous and misleading entries). Publishers such as Random House have simultaneously moved into direct distribution to the public of selected works, while continuing to utilize online distributors such as Amazon. In this sense, the industry has become much more diverse than in the past, including hardware and software makers who have an interest in the success of e-books.

## 10.3 THE ONLINE ENTERTAINMENT INDUSTRY

The entertainment industry is generally considered to be composed of four traditional, commercial players and one new arrival: television, radio broadcasting, Hollywood films, music, and video games (the new arrival). **Figure 10.10** illustrates the estimated relative sizes of these commercial entertainment markets as of 2010. By far, the largest entertainment producer is motion pictures (full-length Hollywood movies), and then television (broadcast, satellite, and cable), followed by video games,

| FIGURE 10.10 | THE FIVE MAJOR PLAYERS IN THE ENTERTAINMENT INDUSTRY: 2010 ESTIMATED REVENUES (in billions) |

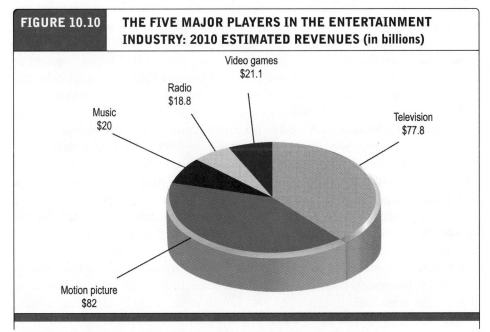

Video games
$21.1

Radio
$18.8

Music
$20

Television
$77.8

Motion picture
$82

SOURCES: Based on data from U.S. Census Bureau, 2010; NPD Group, 2010; authors' estimates.

music, and radio. While PC and console games have grown to be larger than film box office revenues, total Hollywood film revenues dwarf the game industry when DVD sales and rentals, licensing, and ancillary products are added.

Along with the other content industries, the entertainment segment is undergoing a transformation brought about by the Internet. Several forces are at work. Accelerated platform development such as the iPhone/iPad video and music platform, and digital cellular networks, have changed consumer preferences and increased demand for video, television, and game entertainment delivered over Internet devices whether in subscription or a la carte pay-per-view forms. Other social network platforms are also spurring the delivery of entertainment content to desktop and laptop PCs and smartphones. iTunes and other legitimate music subscription services like Rhapsody have also demonstrated a viable business model where millions of consumers are willing to pay reasonable prices for high-quality content, portability, and convenience. The growth in broadband has obviously made possible both wired and wireless delivery of all forms of entertainment over the Internet, potentially displacing cable and broadcast television networks. The development of high-quality customer experiences at online entertainment sites has in many cases eliminated the need for digital rights management restrictions. Closed platforms, like the Kindle, also work to obviate the need for DRM. Subscription services for music and video are inherently copyright-protected because the content is never downloaded to a PC (similar to cable TV). All of these forces have combined in 2010 to bring about a transformation in the entertainment industries.

The ideal Internet content e-commerce world would allow consumers to watch any movie, listen to any music, watch any TV show, and play any game, when they want, where they want, and using whatever Internet device is convenient. Consumers would be billed monthly for these services by a single provider of Internet service. This idealized version of a convergent media world is many years away, but clearly this is the direction of the Internet-enabled entertainment industry.

When we think of the producers of entertainment in the offline world, we tend to think about television networks such as ABC, NBC, or CBS; Hollywood film studios such as MGM, Disney, Paramount, and Twentieth Century Fox; and music labels such as Sony BMG, Atlantic Records, Columbia Records, and Warner Records. Interestingly, none of these international brand names have a significant entertainment presence on the Internet. Although traditional forms of entertainment such as television shows and Hollywood movies are just now appearing on the Web, neither the television nor film industries have built an industry-wide delivery system. Instead, they are building alliances with portals like Yahoo, Google, and MSN, and Apple, which has become a very significant player in media distribution.

While industry titans waver, online consumers are redefining and considerably broadening the concept of entertainment. We refer to this development as "non-traditional" entertainment or what most refer to as user-generated content, which also has entertainment value including user videos uploaded to YouTube, photos uploaded to Photobucket and shared, as well as blogs. User-generated content reflects some of the same shifts in consumer preferences experienced by traditional media: people want to participate in the creation and distribution of content.

## ONLINE ENTERTAINMENT AUDIENCE SIZE AND GROWTH

Measuring the size and growth of the Internet content audience is far less precise than measuring a television audience simply because there is no reliable audience measurement service for the Internet. Estimates of audience size are typically based on responses to surveys rather than actual consumer behavior.

### Online Traditional Entertainment

Recognizing the difficulties of measuring an Internet audience, let's first examine the use of "traditional" entertainment content, such as films, music, sports, and games; then we will look at non-traditional online entertainment. **Figure 10.11** shows the

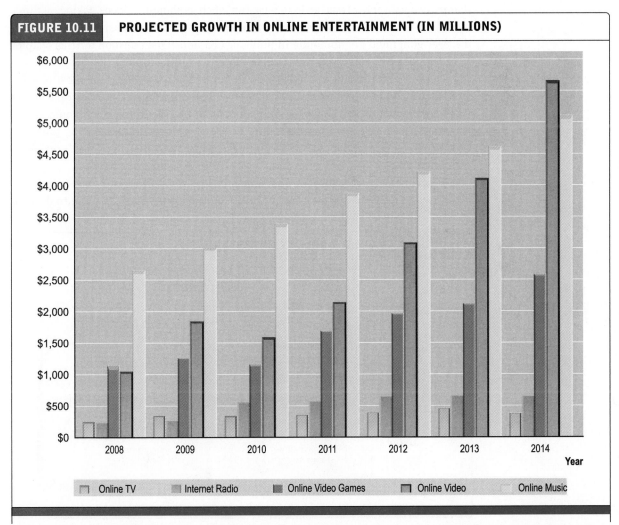

**FIGURE 10.11**  **PROJECTED GROWTH IN ONLINE ENTERTAINMENT (IN MILLIONS)**

Among commercial forms of mass entertainment, online music downloads engages the largest number of people and generates the largest revenues on the Web in 2010. However, online video and games will grow dramatically in the next four years, with video approaching music in revenues.

SOURCES: Based on data from eMarketer, 2010a, b, c; Veronis Suhler Stevenson, 2010; authors' estimates.

current and projected growth for commercial online entertainment revenues for the major players: music, Internet radio, online TV, online games, and online video. Music leads the list of commercial entertainment revenues in 2010, followed by online games, TV, radio, and online video.

There are some interesting changes by 2014. Video surpasses music as the largest form of online entertainment, and online games expands very rapidly from its small base. Online TV and radio remain relatively smaller generators of revenue, declining in significance when compared to music and video.

### User-Generated Content: Where Does It Fit?

Whereas traditional commercial entertainment is produced by professional entertainers and producers, user-generated entertainment involves all those other activities that people voluntarily engage in to have fun, such as shooting videos, taking pictures, recording music and sharing it, and writing blogs. We have extensively documented the user-generated phenomenon in previous chapters. One question for this chapter is, "How does this content fit into the overall entertainment picture?"

The answer appears to be that user-generated content is both a substitute for as well as a complement to traditional commercial entertainment. As people spend more time consuming user-generated content, one might think they would spend less time consuming commercial content. But this does not seem to be the case. Consumer-generated content seems to increase the acceptance of the Internet as a content channel, and consumption of all content seems to expand.

**Figure 10.12** characterizes different types of Web entertainment experiences along two dimensions: user focus and user control. Sites that offer nontraditional

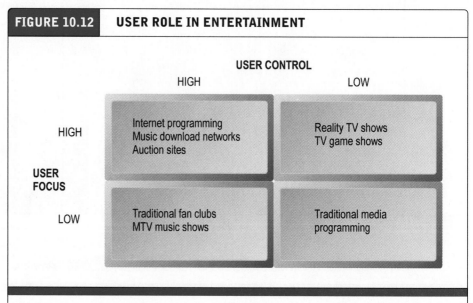

**FIGURE 10.12    USER ROLE IN ENTERTAINMENT**

USER CONTROL

| | HIGH | LOW |
|---|---|---|
| **HIGH** | Internet programming<br>Music download networks<br>Auction sites | Reality TV shows<br>TV game shows |
| **USER FOCUS** | | |
| **LOW** | Traditional fan clubs<br>MTV music shows | Traditional media<br>programming |

Popular Internet entertainment sites offer users high levels of control and user focus. Traditional media programming content is determined by programmers and has a celebrity focus. Traditional media has moved to become more participatory and more user-focused, but cannot match Internet levels of interactivity and user contribution to content.

user-generated forms of entertainment are unique not only because they afford access to large digital archives, promote fine-grained searching, and enable users to create their own archives, but also because they permit users high levels of control over both the program content and the program focus. For example, a social network site like MySpace offers user-generated content that is viewed by others as "entertaining." The hypothesis is that sites that offer both high user focus and high user control will have the fastest rates of growth. MySpace is illustrative of this hypothesis. MySpace started out as a independent, music-oriented social network site where new bands not signed by major record labels could find new listeners, and where people could form networks of friends by creating their own home pages and displaying personal comments, text, photos, and music. By giving users control over their environment and focusing the site on users, the site routinely attracts around 95 million visitors a month worldwide in 2010 (Efrati, 2010).

## CONTENT

The Internet has greatly changed the packaging, distribution, marketing, and sale of traditional entertainment content, with the largest impacts on music. Music may be a precursor to similar changes in the film and television segments. In the case of music, the package is being transformed from a traditional CD album containing 12 to 15 songs, to the download of single songs a la carte. In other words, the impact of the Internet has been to unbundle the traditional music package, permitting customers to buy what they want. The distribution is changing from retail stores selling physical product, to Internet delivery and playback on a wide variety of digital devices from iPods to PCs to PDAs. Finally, the marketing and sales have changed as well. New groups have their own Web sites, and can find their own niche audiences on MySpace and other sites, to some extent democratizing the process of establishing a music brand. Established groups can bypass traditional marketing and sales organizations by creating their own Web distribution network. Not many established groups have gone this route entirely, but most such groups use the Web to market themselves.

## ONLINE ENTERTAINMENT INDUSTRY REVENUE MODELS

Online entertainment sites have adopted many of the same revenue models as depicted previously in Table 10.3: marketing, advertising, pay-per-view, subscription, value-added, and mixed. Television networks and Hollywood studios are beginning to sell episodes on a pay-per-view basis on iTunes, and entire series online on their own corporate sites.

## CONVERGENCE

While there is clearly a movement toward convergence in technology platform, content, and industry structure, this movement has been slow because of both technological and market institutional forces.

**Technology** In musical entertainment, the technology platform has converged as PCs and handheld devices such as Apple's iPad and iPhone become music listening stations playing music tracks, and general-purpose computing and communication devices. The PC has also become a game station, capable of playing highly interactive rich media games with the same responsiveness as dedicated game stations. In turn, many dedicated game stations such as Microsoft's Xbox 360, Nintendo's Wii and Sony's PlayStation can be connected to the Web for interactive play, downloading new game software, and to watch streaming video..

For movies and television, technology convergence had previously been hampered by the unwillingness of the movie industry to make its products available on a wide range of Internet-enabled devices, in large part because of concerns over piracy. Illegal downloading of movies has grown almost as fast as illegal music downloads, although because of the size of movie downloads, and the movie industry's efforts to close down illegal movie-sharing sites, illegal video downloads do not approach the volume of illegal musical downloads. The industry estimates it is losing around $5 billion in sales a year from Internet piracy, and $4 billion a year from counterfeit DVDs (out of a total industry revenue of $55 billion in 2010).

While Hollywood and New York film and television network producers are obviously concerned about increasing piracy and the lack of Internet security, they have made several important moves towards legitimate Internet distribution through alliances with platform owners like Apple (iTunes Store/Apple TV) , Google (with the forthcoming Google TV), Amazon ( which has announced plans to move beyond its current video-on-demand service into a new streaming subscription service), NetFlix, CinemaNow, and Hulu.

As of September 2010, NetFlix has movie streaming rights that cover almost 50% of all new releases in the United States. Over 60% of Netflix's subscribers streamed at least 15 minutes of video in the April to June 2010 period, up from 36% at the end of 2009 (Liedtke and Nakashima, 2010).

CinemaNow holds the Internet distribution rights to the most extensive and comprehensive library of content available on demand via the public Internet and private broadband networks. The CinemaNow library contains approximately 12,000 feature-length films, shorts, music concerts, and television programs from more than 250 film production studios.

Perhaps the largest movie industry-sponsored, Internet success story is Hulu.com. Hulu is a joint venture of NBC Universal Films, Disney, News Corp, and private investors. Hulu offers streaming TV shows, trailers, and older movies for free using an advertiser-supported model. In July 2010, Hulu announced Hulu Plus, an ad-supported subscription service Hulu is often among the top 10 destination sites on the Internet.

While these industry consortia have developed significant delivery capabilities, it is also the case that if millions of Americans decide to download movies over the Internet on a Saturday night, more than 50% of the Internet's capacity could be consumed, leading to significant brownouts and server outages in local areas.

**Content** In a convergent world, the creation, production, and distribution of entertainment content would be entirely digital, with few, if any, analog devices or physical products and their physical distribution channels. The Internet increasingly will come into direct competition with cable and satellite distribution channels. However, these physical and analog distribution channels are under increasing challenge from digital and Internet-based distribution. Hence, the content is moving off physical delivery platforms and toward Internet delivery platforms under user control.

In the areas of content creation and production, there has been significant progress for digital tools. Hollywood filmmakers are increasingly using digital cameras for selected movie scenes, and digital effects have come to play a larger role in many movies. Much of the editing of film is currently performed on digital editing computer workstations before the images are returned to analog 35mm film for distribution to theaters. Independent and low-budget filmmakers are creating feature-length films on digital cameras, editing in digital environments, and distributing directly on the Web to niche audiences at independent film sites. In television, digital cameras are now typical while editing and production is almost entirely digital. Likewise, in music, recording is performed on digital devices and mixed using digital mixers before production of digital CDs. Independent bands move their music directly from digital mixers to the Internet, skipping the CD production stage entirely. Composers, arrangers, and music educators have widely adopted two digital notation programs, Finale and Sibelius, to create music scores.

**Industry Structure** The existing industry value chain is highly inefficient and fractured. For the entertainment industry to move aggressively onto the Web there needs to be a reorganization of the value chain either through corporate mergers, or strategic alliances, or both. In the process of reorganization, traditional distributors (like cable TV and broadcast television) most likely will experience severe disruptions to their business models as the Internet replaces them as a distribution media.

**Figure 10.13** illustrates the existing players and industry value chain and three alternative arrangements. The entertainment industry has never been a neat and tidy industry to describe. There are many players and forces—including government regulators and courts—that shape the industry. In the existing model, creators of entertainment such as music labels or television producers sell to distributors, who in turn sell to local retail stores or local television stations, who then sell or rent to consumers. In the film industry, court decisions in the 1930s and 1940s forced production studios to give up ownership of local theaters on antitrust grounds, fearing the large Hollywood production studios would monopolize the film industry. One possible alternative to this fractionated industry is the *content owner direct model*. The Internet offers entertainment content producers (the music labels, Hollywood studios, and television content producers) the opportunity to dominate the industry value chain by eliminating the distributors and retailers and selling directly to the consumer. This has not yet been a successful model to date because the content producers know so little about the Internet and have not been successful on the Internet. A second possibility is the *Internet aggregator model*. In this model, Web-based intermediaries such as Yahoo, Google, Amazon, and MSN that aggregate large audiences enter into strategic alliances with content owners to provide content to the aggregators. Yahoo fits into this model because it has begun hiring its own news reporters, and funding production of independent films that it can distribute on its portal.

A third possible model is the *Internet innovator model* in which successful Internet technology companies that develop the technology platforms (such as

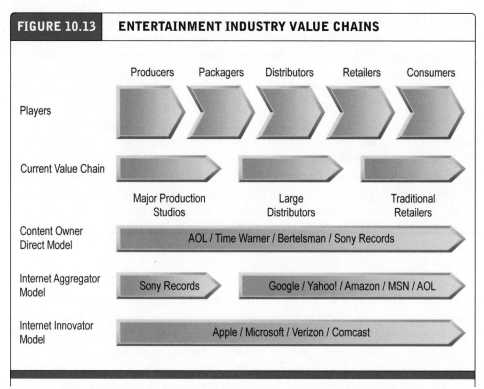

There are a variety of possible entertainment industry value chains in the near-term future.

Apple and Microsoft, as well as Internet communications platform providers like Verizon and Comcast Cable) move back into the value chain and begin creating their own content for exclusive distribution on their proprietary platform or channels. Good examples are Microsoft's Xbox video game platform, Yahoo's move into content creation in 2009, Apple's iTunes Store, and Verizon's premium service package for DSL broadband.

*Insight on Technology: Hollywood Meets the Internet: Round 3* describes how Hollywood studios are struggling with the issues presented by the Internet.

## INSIGHT ON TECHNOLOGY

# HOLLYWOOD MEETS THE INTERNET, ROUND 3

In tough times, real people go to the movies. All things considered, 2009 was an acceptable year for the movie industry. Despite the worst recession since the 1930s, box office receipts in the United States reached $10.4 billion, and ticket sales were up about 5% from the previous year. Overall, there are around 40,000 movie screens in the United States, of which about 16,000 have switched to digital (they receive and display movies as digital files as opposed to multiple 35mm cans). The year 2009 also boasted the premiere of the highest-grossing movie of all time, *Avatar*, which grossed $2.7 billion in global box office. *Avatar*'s budget was estimated at $300 million. If only all movies could produce results like that, Hollywood would be golden again.

Sales of DVDs, on the other hand, have been on a continued downward spiral since 2006. In 2010, DVD sales dropped to $28.6 billion from $32 billion a year ago, and in 2013, DVD sales are predicted to reach just $16.2 billion. This is important because Hollywood makes a huge profit on DVD sales, about $12 to $17 per DVD. While some of these losses will be offset by gains in sales of Blu-ray versions of movies, overall, movie industry total revenues are starting to decline, dropping to $55 billion from $60 billion just two years ago. In addition to the recession, the costs of producing the average Hollywood film have skyrocketed to about $120 million per title on average, while costs for DVDs and Blu-ray discs have remained stable.

There are several reasons for the falloff in DVD sales, but chief among them are piracy of DVD products, declining prices in other distribution channels (pay-per-view and cable televi-

sion), and alternative forms of movie entertainment available on the Internet. Pirates often steal production-quality DVDs before the movies are introduced to the box office, and then put them on file sharing networks. For example, *X-Men Origins: Wolverine*, the Marvel Comics-based American superhero film was released worldwide on May 1, 2009. Unfortunately, pirates obtained an unfinished production-quality DVD copy of the movie. By March 31, 2009, the movie had been downloaded more than a million times according to TorrentFreak, a blog devoted to BitTorrent file sharing. At least 1 million fewer people paid at the box office. All told, the last survey of movie piracy claimed the loss to Hollywood of piracy worldwide is about $5 billion annually.

Unlike the music industry, which until recently focused primarily on an aggressive legal assault on pirates with some success, the movie industry has taken both defensive and offensive measures. Hollywood continues to support DRM and other strategies to prevent piracy. The Motion Picture Association of America (MPAA) has won several cases against providers of software that strips DRM from DVDs, such as RealNetwork's RealDVD, arguing that the software violates the Digital Millennium Copyright Act (DMCA). The DMCA made circumventing DRM protections illegal.

But the motion picture industry has also taken a number of steps to develop online delivery mechanisms and new innovative products that customers hopefully will want to buy. The industry introduced BluRay technology, which drastically improved picture quality and disc capacity. Other innovations include permitting iTunes to download movies to customers'

(continued)

iPhones, in-store kiosks that offer a dozen titles on physical DVDs, and other kiosks offering thousands of titles that are burned to a disc while you wait and are stored digitally in the kiosks. Hollywood is also planning for "cloud movies," movies that you purchase or subscribe to and which are stored on the Internet where you can access them from any device of your choice, at any time.

Perhaps the most forward-thinking move on the part of Hollywood has been its determination to take control of the Internet digital distribution channel by setting up its own Web sites such as Hulu and CinemaNow. Rather than have YouTube (Google) distribute their movies, Hollywood uses these and other sites to deliver movies to the customer, controlling the price, the form of distribution (download versus streaming) selection, and total revenue stream. YouTube, Amazon, and Apple have come around to making deals with Hollywood on all these matters in order to gain access to legitimate, high-quality content that their customers want. In 2009, YouTube, seeking high-quality videos that advertisers would not feel embarrassed about, cut a deal with MGM to distribute MGM's backlist (old films) and full-length episodes of *Star Trek*.

Movie studios have continued to adapt to their viewers' format preferences. Movie viewers increasingly want to stream movies online and watch movies on their mobile devices. In August 2010, several movie studios, including Paramount, Lions Gate, and MGM, struck deals with Netflix that will allow their movies to be streamed online much earlier than in the past. Netflix is likely to pay in the neighborhood of $1 billion in licensing fees over the five years of the deal for the ability to stream movies over the Internet. This represented both a win for Netflix, which has struggled to compete with TV movie operators like HBO and Showtime for the ability to show new releases, as well as the movie industry, which stands to gain from the increased competition between Netflix and TV companies.

Mobile phone users are also increasingly interested in watching TV shows and movies on their mobile devices, and both content providers and mobile device manufacturers are scrambling to meet this demand. Approximately 17.6 million Americans watched a video on their phones in the fourth quarter of 2009, a sizable increase from 11.2 million in 2008. Qualcomm has devoted $1 billion to its mobile video distribution unit, called Flo TV, which sends ESPN, MTV, and Fox News to phones. Other services, such as News Corp's Bitbop, rent movies to smartphone users, charging less than $5 for a 24-hour viewing period.

The result is that Hollywood is getting its products to the public, including using the Internet, at a "reasonable" price and in a customer-friendly environment, which demands movies that can be played anytime, on a variety of devices, on demand. Moreover, the Internet culture is changing, becoming more mature about paying for content. Maybe it's a result of the "graying" of America, or an acceptance by all demographic groups on the Web that paying a reasonable fee for a high-quality content experience is worth it. Hollywood is banking on this willingness to pay for content across a variety of platforms as a way to recapture some of the revenue that DVDs provided just a few years ago.

**— SOURCES:** "Movie Industry Slouches Toward Digital Future," by Paul Verna, eMarketer, Inc., August 30, 2010; "Netflix to Stream Films From Paramount, Lions Gate, MGM," by Brian Stelter, *New York Times*, August 10, 2010; "Theatrical Market Statistics," Motion Picture Association of America, MPAA.org, 2009; "Hollywood Wins Key Round Against RealNetworks' RealDVD," by Stephen Wildstrom, BusinessWeek.com, August 11, 2009; "Warner Brothers Launches On Demand DVD Sales," by Thomas Arnold, *USAToday*, July 17, 2009; "In Digital Age Can Movie Piracy Be Stopped?" by Lisa France, CNN.com, May 2, 2009; "Fox's New Plan to Spur DVD Sales: Rip Out the Extras from Rentals," by M.G. Siegler, Digitalventurebeat.com, March 5, 2009.

**CASE STUDY**

# Google and YouTube Together:
## Pass the Popcorn While This Ad Plays

Ever since Google bought YouTube in November 2006, some have wondered just exactly how Google was going to make the $1.65 billion purchase price worthwhile. Wall Street, on the other hand, had no doubts that Google would make a killing, and Google's stock price quickly shot up from the unprecedented $500 level for most of 2007 to the utterly absurd level of $700 in November 2007. This gave Google a price-to-earnings ratio of 49, just shy of the moon, and a market capitalization of $200 billion, which was over 10 times the market capitalization of General Motors at the time, the largest car company on earth. In 2008, with the world in a recession, advertising in general stalling, and Internet advertising growing more slowly, Google's stock dropped 70% to the $250 range. In 2010, as economic conditions slowly brighten, Google's stock has made a comeback, and is selling at about $500 with a price-to-earnings ratio of 22.5, up considerably from its lowest levels on the strength of search engine advertising. YouTube has not helped Google's stock price, but analysts expect that YouTube may finally become profitable in late 2010 after losing money for years. Why did the stock market value Google's YouTube purchase so fondly at first, and then have second thoughts? What are the skeptics saying? Are they just jealous of Google's evident success in purchasing the largest group of eyeballs on the Web, namely, YouTube's audience of over 400 million unique monthly visitors worldwide?

The answer from Google is that it plans to turn the Web's largest repository of video, and the largest video audience share, into the next big, killer app for advertising, namely, the largest advertising platform in history. Bigger than search, and bigger than television. What it tells investors is that this huge audience can be "monetized" by displaying ads alongside the videos, and displaying banners on opening screens.

Just how much video does YouTube have? This has turned into an amateur sport and estimates vary, but the most recent estimates are that YouTube has somewhere between 84 million and 142 million videos stored on up to or about 1 petabyte of hard drives around the world, representing about 1,700 *years* worth of video. In 2010, YouTube is serving over 2 billion video streams a day, and 33 billion a month. If only each of these streams would pay a penny! YouTube itself is secretive about the number of videos in part because it raises the question of "Why does it have so many videos if it can't make enough money to pay the rent?" And "How can YouTube/Google continue to pay the infrastructure costs of so many videos?"

How many people are attracted to these videos and for how long? comScore estimates that in August 2010, YouTube drew over 146 million unique visitors in the United States, with the average time spent of about 15 minutes a day. in 2010. However, only 2% of these monthly viewers view daily, compared to Yahoo, for instance, where 40% of visitors visit every day. Yahoo's network of sites has around

179 million unique visitors, who stay on average about one hour a visit to view all types of content (not just video). Google (just the search site itself) has about 145 million unique monthly visitors, who stay less than 24 minutes, on their way to their destination Web site. Over 30% of Google visitors visit daily. So while YouTube has grown explosively, it still has a way to go to catch Yahoo or Google and lacks the retention time and frequency of visits found at the major portals.

What YouTube needs is not just more content but quality content, content that is really interesting, keeps people on the sites, and draws millions of viewers back every day. Chances are this does not mean user-generated videos, which typically have an average audience of around 10 people, are top listed for one day, then fall into oblivion. Really popular user-generated videos or music videos launched by record label companies that get passed around the Web in a viral network may top off with 2 million viewers, but this is a rare event and usually reserved for celebrities caught in compromising situations, already popular musicians, or popular copyrighted videos illegally posted.

No, what YouTube needs is expertly crafted video that accounts for the lion's share of their visitors' attention. Where can this video be obtained? In the early years, the answer was to have unique visitors upload snippets of Hollywood movies and television shows such as *The Sopranos*, *The Colbert Report*, and Jon Stewart's *The Daily Show*. As you learned in Chapter 8, this situation caused heartburn among copyright owners such as Viacom (a media conglomerate that owns Paramount Pictures, MTV, and BET cable networks), which sued Google in 2007 for $1 billion, a fair chunk of change. The complaint alleged that "YouTube deliberately built up a library of infringing works to draw traffic to the YouTube site, enabling it to gain a commanding market share, earn significant revenues and increase its enterprise value." Google responded that copyright law shields it from liability for clips posted by its users. In June 2010, Google ended up winning the lawsuit, with the ruling stating that Google and YouTube qualify for "safe harbor" and are therefore protected against Viacom's allegations, but YouTube has long since abandoned the strategy of relying on users to upload pirated high quality content.

In order to deal with the complaints of the big Hollywood studios and New York television producers, YouTube restricted advertising to only those pages where the permission of copy right holders has been obtained. Google also developed copyright management technology called Content ID that scans all of YouTube's videos periodically to root out copyright infringements. Copyright owners have two choices: they can ask YouTube to take the material down, or they can place advertisements for their products right next to the illegal postings! Brilliant. In this manner, Google has reversed the opposition among copyright holders and changed them into rank opportunists. In September 2010, more than one-third of the views of YouTube advertisements are within clips of this sort: uploaded without the copyright owner's permission, located using Content ID, but left up by choice. While most large-scale advertisers do not want their ads showing up next to an amateur home video, they are more than willing to place their ads next to high-quality, copyrighted material that they happen to own. Universal Pictures and other studios are now using YouTube to plant clips from their movies and seek to take advantage of YouTube's viral marketing platform. Now the copyright owners are saying, "Watch this content, pass it around, and come to our movies!"

In the last two years, under the threat of endless lawsuits for copyright infringement, and the rise of alternative video sources that have the backing of the movie and television industries such as Hulu, Epix, CinemaNow, Movielink, and Apple's iTunes Store, YouTube and Google have radically changed their business approach to quality video content. While still taking in millions of videos a day from amateurs, they have begun courting the likes of Hollywood and New York film and television producers. In 2008, YouTube struck deals with CBS, ESPN, HBO, Showtime, C-Span, and MGM, to obtain copyrighted content against which ads can be displayed. YouTube now emphasizes that it's a "great place for premium content." YouTube allows these heavy hitters to establish their own exclusive "channel" on YouTube where they can control the content, and then display ads against that content, sharing the revenue with YouTube. The concept of "channels," where content is reliable, supplied by the advertiser, and under their control, has greatly increased the attractiveness of YouTube as an advertising venue.

In 2010, YouTube continued to broaden its premium content offerings. The company has cut deals with Sony, Lions Gate, the BBC, Starz, Discovery, and National Geographic to provide full-length movies and TV shows for free on YouTube. Other partners include Anime Network, Cinetic Rights Management, Current TV, Documentary Channel, FirstLook Studios, and IndieFlix. These full-length movies will all be "back list" or older movies that have gone through the traditional movie and television maturation process. For YouTube, these deals provide an opportunity to display ads during commercial breaks, and to provide visitors with a coherent, reliable entertainment menu. Insiders report that YouTube is considering charging for "premium video." In 2010, YouTube also announced plans to offer live streaming on the site for the first time, as broadband speeds continue to improve and sports leagues become more comfortable with the idea.

Sony is participating in part because it wants to drive traffic to its own movie site, Crackle.com. Crackle.com offers free films and TV shows and makes money from selling ads before, during, and after the video. Crackle currently has about 60 movies on its site, and will provide only 12 of these movies to YouTube. "It's all about driving traffic to Crackle," said a source close to the deal. Similarly, the other studios in the deals will send viewers to their owners' proprietary video services or split ad revenue with YouTube. In the process of striking deals with the major content owners, Google has finally come to the realization that YouTube will not be the Internet's single source for all the world's video. Google now recognizes it's a pluralistic and diverse world with lots of powerful players that it needs to survive and make a profit. Gone is the in-your-face attitude of earlier years when YouTube claimed that in Silicon Valley, copyrights didn't matter.

YouTube has also developed a "sponsored videos" program (also called "promoted videos") in which it selects amateur videos with unusual appeal, and offers advertisers text ads displayed on the lower portion of the video screen. In this program, advertisers bid for keywords (just like Google's AdSense) and Google uses its search algorithms to match a proper video with the keywords. The sponsored videos have a Flash animation overlaid on the bottom of the video window, starting 10 seconds after the real video rolls, and disappearing in 10 seconds unless the user clicks on the animation, in which case they are taken to the advertiser's site. Google research claims that 10 times more people click on these overlays than standard banner ads (no great achievement given the low rate of banner ad clicks), suggesting a 1% click-through rate, and that fewer than 10% close the banner window. The video is paused while the ad runs its 10 seconds. How annoying is that? On a recent day, for instance, clicking on "Nora the Piano Playing Cat" brought up a video of the cat Nora "playing" the piano, with an ad for pet care products displayed in the lower quarter of the screen. With so many people searching on YouTube each day, it's a wonder they did not think of this sooner. However, advertisers are still wary of the program simply because their ads may show up on an embarrassing video. What Fortune 1000 company would want to place ads next to amateur videos? Analysts estimate that only 4% of YouTube's videos are of sufficient quality and sanity to support advertising.

Setting aside where the page views are coming from, what is Google's formula for making a profit from this investment? The thinking on the Street is that the purchase price of $1.65 billion indicates that Google expected to generate profits of over $150 million a year (assuming a 10% discount rate, an unending stream of revenue, and that people don't get tired of videos and turn elsewhere). The formula Google has come up with is advertising to the 146 million unique visitors. One problem with this is that most users on the Internet expect video to be free and without ads. In fact, the response rate to videos used in display advertising is still nothing to write home about—just .4%, although four times as good as a regular banner ad. The standard preroll video that you get every time you want to watch something interesting has turned out to be a big audience killer. Half the viewers just hit the return button and skip the video they wanted to see rather than sit through the video ad, or hit the "Skip this" button if one is offered.

Up to this point, all of Google's efforts have not made YouTube profitable, but that may soon be changing. In September 2010, Google CEO Eric Schmidt stated that "YouTube is nearing profitability and its revenue is doing quite well." Although several Google executives have predicted YouTube's profitability before and it has not yet come to pass, Google's strategy of embracing high quality content providers and monetizing a larger portion of their videos looks be paying off. YouTube reports that its ad-enabled videos are garnering over 2 billion views per week in 2010, which is likely to be enough to make the company profitable. The YouTube audience and Google have both matured, and the site has become more legitimate as major Fortune 500 companies establish channels (even universities have channels), and visitors become accustomed to advertiser-supported videos and paying for quality content if necessary. It's increasingly looking like Google may not have paid too much for YouTube, but it will still need its viewers to pass the popcorn while this ad plays.

**SOURCES:** "YouTube Ads Turn Videos Into Revenue," by Claire Cain Miller, *New York Times*, September 2, 2010; "Judge Sides with Google in Viacom Video Suit," by Miguel Helft, *New York Times*, June 23, 2010; "YouTube Surpasses Two Billion Video Views Daily," by Ben Parr, Mashable.com, May 17, 2010; "Google to Host Time Warner Content on YouTube," by John Kell, *Wall Street Journal*, August 19, 2009; "Google to Buy On2 as It Looks To Boost Video," by Jerry Dicolo, *Wall Street Journal*, August 6, 2009; "Google Still Loves YouTube," by Jessi Hempel, Brainstormtech.net, July 31, 2009; "YouTube Logs Film, TV Deals," by Marc Graser, *Variety*, April 16, 2009; "YouTube May Lose $470 Million in 2009: Analysts," by Todd Spangler, Multichannel.com, April 3, 2009; "YouTube is Missing a Golden Opportunity," by Liz Gannes, *Business Week*, March 16, 2009.

**Case Study Questions**

1. In your view, and experience on YouTube, will typical YouTube viewers accept advertising while watching the videos?

2. What responsibility does YouTube have in removing copyrighted material from its site? YouTube claims it is in compliance with the Digital Millenium Copyright Act, which requires owners of content to notify Web sites when their copyrights are infringed. Why is this a good solution for YouTube but a poor solution for copyright owners?

3. Assume you were a manufacturer of sporting goods, and wanted to use YouTube videos as a marketing tool to establish your brand. What concerns would you have about using YouTube? How would you use YouTube's various innovations to promote your firm?

4. When you think of YouTube, what perceptions come to mind? Do you think YouTube can become an outlet for feature-length Hollywood movies?

## 10.5 REVIEW

### KEY CONCEPTS

- Identify the major trends in the consumption of media and online content.

Major trends in the consumption of media and online content include the following:

- The average American adult spends over 3,900 hours per year consuming various media. The most hours are spent viewing television, followed by listening to the radio, and then the Internet.
- Recent studies have suggested that television viewing among Internet users is lower than among non-users and that Internet users spend less time reading books, newspapers, and magazines, and less time on the phone and listening to the radio, supporting the view that Internet usage cannibalizes other media distribution channels. However, Internet users also consume more media of all types than non-Internet users, in large part because they often multitask using multiple media.
- In terms of revenue, television garners the largest share of revenue, followed by home video, and then consumer Internet.
- Total direct paid online content revenues for digital music, television, and movies in the United States in 2007 is over $6 billion.

- Discuss the concept of media convergence and the challenges it faces.

The concept of media convergence has three dimensions:

- *Technological convergence,* which refers to the development of hybrid devices that can combine the functionality of two or more media platforms, such as books, newspapers, television, radio. and stereo equipment, into a single device.
- *Content convergence*, with respect to content design, production, and distribution.
- *Media industry convergence,* which refers to the merger of media enterprises into powerful, synergistic combinations that can cross-market content on many different platforms and create works that use multiple platforms.

In the early years of e-commerce, many believed that media convergence would occur quickly. However, many early efforts failed, and new efforts are just now appearing.

■ **Describe the basic content revenue models.**

In general, most content on the Web is free and most users expect it to remain free. Overcoming this expectation is the major challenge for the online content industry. Thus far, five basic revenue models have been employed in the online content arena:

- *The marketing revenue model.* Content is given away for free in the hope that site visitors will purchase the product or view a show offline. This model is thought to increase brand loyalty while the costs of the site are at least partially recouped through the sales of product-related paraphernalia.
- *The advertising revenue model.* Content is given away for free, and advertisers are expected to pay for the cost of the site through the placement of banner and rich-media ads. This model has become successful and supports sites like Yahoo.
- *The pay-per-view/pay-for-download revenue model.* Each viewing of premium content or downloading is charged to the user. This model—sometimes called "a la carte"—has been successful for music audiences. It works for targeted audiences who are looking for deep, rich, niche content. Pay-per-view is expected to be a more prevalent and successful business model when the bandwidth capability to view sporting events, feature films, and other video content is perfected and becomes more widespread.
- *The subscription revenue model.* A monthly or annual access fee is charged to users for access to content. So far, this model has worked for music sites like Rhapsody and some newspapers. It may work for high-value niche content that is not available anywhere else, such as music tracks that are released to these users before they are released to the general population.
- *The mixed revenue model.* A model that combines several of the other types of revenue models.

For the most part, content firms have decided that there is more to be gained from the advertising model, offering free content to users and in return exposing them to graphical display ads. In order to generate meaningful revenues, firms must do four things:

- Target a focused audience.
- Provide specialized content.
- Be the sole source monopoly for the content.
- Engender high perceived net value so consumers believe that there is value in obtaining the information instantaneously on the Web.

■ **Discuss the key challenges facing content producers and owners.**

The key challenges facing content producers and owners are as follows:

- *Bandwidth challenges.* Although there is plenty of long-haul fiber-optic bandwidth available, there are critical bottlenecks in home bandwidth. These limitations restrict both the ability for pay-per-view revenue models to develop for films and video and the development of advanced e-books using video and audio.
- *Platform challenges.* These include the current unsuitability of the PC screen for viewing DVDs and e-books, the unsuitability of PDAs for text display, and the lack of acceptance of wireless cell phones as Web devices in the United States.
- *Cost challenges.* Internet distribution is far more costly than was originally anticipated, and substantial costs are faced by media companies in migrating, repackaging, and redesigning content for online delivery.
- *Consumer attitudes.* Consumers have strongly resisted paying for Web content, although this is changing as media companies learn how to use the Web to deliver high-value, focused, and deep information and content.
- *Cannibalization of existing distribution channels.* Media companies are often tempted to strike alliances with successful portals or redistributors. The risk is that the media firm's brand name will become diluted or displaced and that any revenues generated will have to be shared with the intermediary. There is the risk that existing traditional distribution channels will be destroyed because they are no longer profitable.
- *Pricing and value when redesigning content for the Web.* If the price is set too low, higher-priced and profitable distribution channels could be choked off.
- *Rights management challenges.* These include the ability to protect content from being stolen, duplicated, and distributed for free and the issue of royalties paid to artists and writers.

- ■ Understand the key factors affecting the online publishing industry.

Key factors affecting online newspapers include:
- *Audience size and growth.* There are more than 10,000 online newspapers worldwide, with about 70-75 million readers in the United States. In terms of sheer audience size, this makes online newspapers the most successful online content providers to date.
- *Content.* Online newspapers offer premium archived content, fine-grained searching ability, timeliness, and content with reach and depth.
- *Competition.* New online classified ad firms have challenged newspapers by developing deep, rich content in specialized areas.
- *Revenue models and results.* Online newspapers predominantly rely upon an advertising model. Some also supplement revenues by using a pay-per-view model for premium or archival content. This has not for the most part been a successful business model. The *Wall Street Journal* is one of the few standouts that has successfully used the subscription business model for newspapers.
- *Convergence.* Technology convergence is in its infancy, with only the first step accomplished: the movement of published text to the Web. Wireless mobile news delivery is the next step, and this is currently being invested in by the top 10 newspapers despite overall losses. Content convergence has occurred in a limited way in the areas of production and distribution. Industry structure has seen no movement toward cross-media convergence, although consolidation of the industry has occurred.
- *Challenges.* Technology challenges include developing wireless mobile delivery platforms and micropayment systems to provide a low-cost mechanism for

selling single articles. Consumer attitudes have remained intransigent on the issue of paying for news content, and some online newspapers have experienced cannibalization of their main distribution channel. Another challenge is digital leakage, which occurs when a paid for and downloaded article is redistributed via e-mail or posted for free viewing on a Web site.

Key factors affecting e-books include:

- *Audience size and growth.* In 2010, online e-book sales are expected to generate around $340 million in revenue, compared with $25 billion overall for all books. E-book sales are the fastest-growing type of book sale. Reading books online is not a popular activity, but buying books online is one of the most popular activities of Internet users. This huge online audience for published books has had a significant impact on book distribution and sales, and represents an extraordinary opportunity to introduce new electronic editions of books. The future market for e-books is going to depend largely on how rapidly traditional trade and academic book publishers move existing and new works to the e-book format, and on new technology.

- *Content.* E-books have advantages over published books. Instant downloading can reduce transaction costs, and text is searchable and can be easily integrated with new text via cutting and pasting. They can be modularized down to the sentence and word level, and thus can be much more easily updated or changed, resulting in lower production and distribution costs and a longer-lasting work. However, they also have disadvantages. E-books require expensive and complex electronic devices to use, are difficult to read on-screen, have multiple competing standards and uncertain business models, and raise copyright and royalty issues with authors. Although the prices for dedicated e-book readers are falling and the sizes of libraries are increasing, these challenges are formidable.

- *Revenue models and results.* The e-book industry is composed of intermediary retailers, traditional publishers, technology developers, and vanity presses. The primary e-book revenue model is pay-for-download, in which traditional publishers and authors create e-books and publishers sell these works in their entirety through online bookstore intermediaries. The traditional revenue model for the commercial book industry has not been changed much by the introduction of e-books, mainly because most publishers have chosen not to develop online capabilities. A second revenue model involves the licensing of entire e-libraries. This model is similar to the subscription model in that users pay either a monthly or an annual fee for access to hundreds of titles. Neither business model is yet profitable, but a five-year development period is expected.

- *Convergence.* The publishing industry is making steady progress toward media convergence. Technological convergence has been slowed by the poor resolution of computer screens, the lack of portable reader devices that can compete with the portability of a published book, the absence of DRM technology, and the lack of standards to define cross-platform e-books so that they can be viewed on many different devices. A likely solution to the portability problem is the use of PDAs, but the current PDAs are too small for comfortable reading. Several screen enhancement solutions have been developed using sub-pixel display technologies, and the development of electronic ink and electronic paper displays. Several technology firms have also developed DRM software to control printing and copying of downloaded materials; however, hackers have been able to break most DRM technologies, so the hesitancy of publishing firms to publish works on the Web has yet to be overcome. Some cross-platform standards are already available and new ones are beginning to emerge. Adobe Acrobat PDF files are the most commonly used standard to date; other standards include OEB and ONIX. Not much content design convergence has yet occurred. So far, text is simply being integrated into electronic display forms, and experimentations with more interactive formats are just beginning. Content production and distribution convergence have seen more progress. The development of XML and large-scale online text/graphic storage systems have transformed the book production process and made it more efficient. In distribution of book content, the Web has opened up an entirely new distribution channel. Industry structure has not changed much.

Huge publishing behemoths have long dominated the publishing industry, and the 1990s saw even further consolidation of power. Nevertheless, the Internet has created new opportunities for authors, publishers, and distributors. Authors have published works directly to the public; publishers have moved into direct distribution to the public of selected works; large online book distributors have commissioned new e-book titles and moved into publishing; technology providers have begun limited distribution of e-books; and NetLibrary demonstrated that a market exists for inexpensive digital libraries that can be distributed to colleges, universities, and traditional libraries.

■  **Understand the key factors affecting the online entertainment industry.**

There are five main players in the entertainment sector: television, film, music, video games, and radio broadcasting. The entertainment segment is currently undergoing great change, brought about the Internet. Consumers have begun to accept paying for content, and working with DRM restrictions.

Key factors include the following:
*   *Audience size and growth.* Music downloads are the most popular form of entertainment, with online games second, followed by film, and sports. However, the amount of time users spend at music sites is not high because they typically download and store a track for future use. The sites with the highest usage levels are those that allow high levels of user control and participation. In the absence of film and TV on the Web, users are defining new forms of non-traditional entertainment that do not involve the traditional media titans, including blogs and user-generated content on social network sites.
*   *Content.* Packaging, distribution, marketing, and sales of music tracks have greatly changed in the Internet age. Huge online digital searchable music archives with millions of songs now exist from which users can mix and match to create their own personalized library. One main reason for the popularity of these services is that they enable users to become their own music packagers and distributors. This is the unique feature of online entertainment as compared to traditional entertainment. It offers users high levels of control over both program content and program focus.
*   *Revenue models and results.* Television and movie sites typically use a marketing model, attempting to extend their brand influence and the audience for their offline product. Apple's a la carte model where users pay for a single music track download has been exceptionally successful. Many film sites use a pay-

per-view rental model, or pay-for-download model. Many music entertainment sites are now successful with a monthly subscription model as well.

- *Convergence.* Convergence has been slow due to both technological and market forces. The technology platform for music has converged PCs and handheld devices such as Apple's iPod to become digital music listening systems. A new platform has arrived. The PC has also become a game station, with capabilities rivaling dedicated game stations. In turn, many dedicated game stations can now be connected to the Web for interactive play and streaming video. Technology convergence for movies and television was initially been stalled by the lack of standards, the slow acceptance of high-bandwidth connections in the United States, and inadequate Internet backbone capacity, but that has changed as the film industry is finally moving to make content available ove the Internet through sites such as NetFlix, Hulu, CinemaNow and others. Content creation and production convergence is occurring, with filmmakers and television studios increasingly using digital cameras and film editing done at digital computer workstations. Music is recorded on digital devices using digital mixers before it is digitally imprinted on CDs. Industry structure convergence in the entertainment industry, as in all content industries, is moving toward the merger of content and distribution. Content owners and producers are largely seeking to own their own distribution channels, cutting out the profits of distributors, resellers, and retailers. The belief appears to be widespread that successful media companies will need to own their entire value chain from content creation to consumer use.

## QUESTIONS

1. What are the three dimensions in which the term "convergence" has been applied? What does each of these areas of convergence entail?
2. Why has media industry convergence not occurred as rapidly as predicted?
3. What are the five basic revenue models for online content, and what is their major challenge? What will have to be done in order to overcome this obstacle to profitability?
4. What is the pay-per-view/pay-per-download revenue model, what type of content is it suitable for, and when is it expected to be successful?
5. What four things must content provider firms do in order to generate meaningful revenues?
6. What are the technological challenges facing content producers and owners?
7. Identify and explain the four other challenges facing content producers and owners.
8. How has the Internet impacted the content that newspapers can offer?
9. What changes have occurred for newspapers in the classified ads department?
10. What are the key challenges facing the online newspaper industry?
11. What are the advantages and disadvantages of e-book content?
12. How has the Internet changed the packaging, distribution, marketing, and sale of traditional music tracks?
13. What are the factors that make nontraditional, distinctly Web entertainment sites so popular with users?
14. What would complete content convergence in the entertainment industry look like? Has it occurred?

## PROJECTS

1. Research the issue of media convergence in the newspaper industry. Do you believe that convergence will be good for the practice of journalism? Develop a reasoned argument on either side of the issue and write a 3- to 5-page report on the topic. Include in your discussion the barriers to convergence and whether these restrictions should be eased.

2. Go to Amazon and explore the different digital products that are available. Prepare a presentation to convey your findings to the class. For example, are there Web-accessed, Web-downloadable, dedicated e-books, or books for smart-phones offered? Which are in greater abundance?

3. Go to TBO.com (Tampa Bay Online). Surf the site and sample the offerings. Prepare a presentation to describe and display the efforts you see at technology, content, and industry structure convergence as well as the revenue model being used. Who owns this site?

4. Examine and report on the progress made with respect to the delivery of movies on demand over the Internet.

5. Has technology platform, content design, or industry structure convergence occurred in the online magazine industry? Prepare a short report discussing this issue.

CHAPTER 11

# Social Networks, Auctions, and Portals

## LEARNING OBJECTIVES

**After reading this chapter, you will be able to:**

- Explain the difference between a traditional social network and an online social network.
- Understand how a social network differs from a portal.
- Describe the different types of social networks and online communities and their business models.
- Describe the major types of auctions, their benefits and costs, and how they operate.
- Understand when to use auctions in a business.
- Recognize the potential for auction abuse and fraud.
- Describe the major types of Internet portals.
- Understand the business models of portals.

# Social Network Fever
## Spreads to the Professions

**W**hen social networks first appeared a few years ago, it was widely believed this phenomenon would be limited to crazed teenagers already incapacitated by excessive time spent on video game machines. Most of the technorati in Silicon Valley, and Wall Street, felt this was a blip on the horizon, and their full attention was occupied primarily by search engines, search engine marketing, and ad placement. But when the population of social network participants pushed past 50 million, then 75 million, even the technical elite woke up to the fact that these huge audiences were not just a bunch of teenagers, but that instead a wide slice of American society was also participating. Steve Ballmer, CEO of Microsoft, said in September 2007 that "I think these things [social networks] are going to have some legs, and yet there's a faddishness, a faddish nature about anything that basically appeals to younger people." This was a month before Microsoft paid $250 million for a small stake in Facebook, which valued the company at $15 billion. Trying to sound convincing, Eric Schmidt, CEO of Google, declared that "I know a lot of people think this [social networking] is a blip, but it's real, it's serious." He said this just before spending $1.65 billion for YouTube. By 2010, Facebook has grown to 500 million subscribers worldwide, challenging Google and Yahoo for facetime with the Internet audience.

The social network craze obviously has awakened the technology giants, but they focus mostly on the really huge audiences attracted to general social network sites such as Facebook, MySpace, and YouTube. However, in the background there are a fast-growing collection of social networks that are aimed at communities of practitioners or specific interest groups.

Take LinkedIn, for example, probably the best-known and most popular business network site. LinkedIn is an online network with more than 75 million worldwide members in over 200 countries, representing 170 different industries. A new member joins LinkedIn approximately every second. LinkedIn allows a member to create a profile, including a photo, that summarizes his or her professional accomplishments. Members' networks include their connections, their connections' connections, as well as people they know, potentially linking you to thousands of others. LinkedIn has been valued by its investors at $1 billion and reportedly has annual revenue over $100 million. Many analysts expected LinkedIn to go public sometime in 2010, but chairman Reid Hoffman has stated that while the company plans to go public, it has no plans to do so in the near future.

Those with a particular interest in the stock market can choose from a whole crop of Web sites aimed at stock investors who want to share their ideas with other investors. These social networks are not just bulletin boards with anonymous comments, but active communities where users are identified and their performance ranked according to the performance of their stock picks. One network is StockTickr, which has about 2,500 members. The first page on the screen is a list of stocks that his friends are investing in, along with their stock picking scores. Like the larger social network sites, the financial sites allow users to connect with other investors, discuss issues focused on the stock market, and sometimes just show off users' investing prowess. Some of the new sites include Duedee, where users are rated against other members on the performance of their "virtual" portfolios, and TradeKing, where users can search for others with similar trading styles and view recent trades. While most of these sites have fewer than 5,000 members, they are relatively new. The Motley Fool, one of the best-known online stock investment services, started its CAPS stock-rating social network in 2006 and has around 170,000 members.

You can find similar social network sites for a variety of specific professional groups such as health care (DailyStrength.org), law (LawLink), physicians (Sermo), wireless industry executives (INmobile.org), and advertising professionals (AdGabber). These social networks encourage members to discuss the realities of their professions and practices, sharing successes and failures. There are also general business social networks designed more to develop a network for career advancement, such as Ecademy and Ryze. The rapid growth of professional social networks linked to industry and careers shows how widespread and nearly universal the appeal of social networks are. While e-mail remains the Web's most popular activity, it is about to be eclipsed by social networks. What explains the very broad attraction to social networks? E-mail is excellent for communicating with other individuals, or even a small group. But e-mail is not very good at getting a sense of what others in the group are thinking, especially if the group numbers more than a dozen people. The strength of social networks lies in their ability to reveal group attitudes and opinions, values, and practices.

Professionals who join social networks need to be careful about the content they provide, and the distribution of this content. As business social networks have grown, and as the number of participants expands, employers are finding them a great place to discover the "inner" person who applies for a job. A recent survey commissioned by Microsoft found that 79% of employers use social networks to screen job candidates, and 70% have decided not to offer a job to a candidate based on the content discovered on social network sites. Provocative photos and references to drinking and drugs are the most common factors in deciding not to offer a job. For this reason, it is a very wise move to use Facebook's and other sites' maximum privacy settings, and release to the public only the most innocuous content. Likewise, be cautious of social network sites that do not provide "take down" policies, which allow users to remove embarrassing materials from their pages.

**SOURCES:** "The Social Network That Gets Down to Business," by Miguel Helft, *New York Times*, September 29, 2010; "LinkedIn IPO Hopes Face Global Challenge," by Brad Stone, *Bloomberg Businessweek*, September 6, 2010; "About LinkedIn," Linkedin.com, September 2010; "LinkedIn Now 60 Million Strong," by Leena Rao, Techcrunch, February 11, 2010; "Online Reputation in a Connected World," Cross-Tab Marketing, January 2010; "Influence Marketing With Social Networks," by Lee Oden, Toprankblog.com, September 16, 2009; "Online Social Networks Go to Work," by Xeni Jardan, Msnbc.com, September 16, 2009.

I n this chapter, we discuss social networks, auctions, and portals. One might ask, "What do social networks, auctions, and portals have in common?" They are all based on feelings of shared interest and self-identification—in short, a sense of community. Social networks and online communities explicitly attract people with shared affinities, such as ethnicity, gender, religion, and political views, or shared interests, such as hobbies, sports, and vacations. The auction site eBay started as a community of people interested in trading unwanted but functional items for which there was no ready commercial market. That community turned out to be huge—much larger than anyone expected. Portals also contain strong elements of community by providing access to community-fostering technologies such as e-mail, chat groups, bulletin boards, and discussion forums.

## 11.1  SOCIAL NETWORKS AND ONLINE COMMUNITIES

The Internet was designed originally as a communications medium to connect scientists in computer science departments around the continental United States. From the beginning, the Internet was intended, in part, as a community building technology that would allow scientists to share data, knowledge, and opinions in a real-time online environment (see Chapter 3) (Hiltzik, 1999). The result of this early Internet was the first "virtual communities" (Rheingold, 1993). As the Internet grew in the late 1980s to include scientists from many disciplines and thousands of university campuses, thousands of virtual communities sprang up among small groups of scientists in very different disciplines that communicated regularly using Internet e-mail, listservs, and bulletin boards. The first articles and books on the new electronic communities began appearing in the mid- to late 1980s (Kiesler et al. 1984; Kiesler, 1986). One of the earliest online communities, The Well, was formed in San Francisco in 1985 by a small group of people who once shared an 1,800-acre commune in Tennessee. The Well is a online community that now has thousands of members devoted to discussion, debate, advice, and help (Hafner, 1997; Rheingold, 1998). With the development of the Web in the early 1990s, millions of people began obtaining Internet accounts and Web e-mail, and the community-building impact of the Internet strengthened. By the late 1990s, the commercial value of online communities was recognized as a potential new business model (Hagel and Armstrong, 1997).

The early online communities involved a relatively small number of Web aficionados, and users with intense interests in technology, politics, literature, and ideas. The technology was largely limited to posting text messages on bulletin boards sponsored by the community, and one-to-one, or one-to-many e-mails. In addition to The Well, early networks included GeoCities, a Web site hosting service based on neighborhoods. By 2002, however, the nature of online communities had begun to change. Cell phones and mobile Internet devices provided widespread access, making it possible to communicate nearly instantly with friends and relatives, and keep track of one another in a way not possible before. User-created Web sites called blogs became inexpensive and easy to set up without any technical expertise. These technologies also enabled sharing of rich media such as photos and videos made possible by the spreading use of digital cameras, digital video cameras, cell phones with cameras, and portable digital music players. Suddenly there was a much wider audience for sharing interests and activities, and much more to share.

A new culture emerged as well. The broad democratization of the technology and its spread to the larger population meant that online social networks were no longer limited to a small group but instead broadened to include a much wider set of people and tastes, especially pre-teens, teens, and college students who were the fastest to adopt many of these new technologies. The new social network culture is very personal and "me" centered, displaying photos and broadcasting personal activities, interests, hobbies, and relationships on social network profiles. Today's social networks are as much a sociological phenomenon as they are a technology phenomenon.

Currently, social network participation is one of the most common usages of the Internet. About 80% of all Internet users in the United States—about 175 million Americans—have at one time or another gone online to a social network site. Facebook has 500 million active users worldwide (about 150 million in the United States), and is now much larger than MySpace, which reports 130 million active users worldwide and 70 million in the United States. Twitter, a newer entrant in the social network arena, is growing exponentially, with an estimated 145 million unique visitors worldwide as of September 2010 (eMarketer, Inc., 2010a; comScore, 2010).

Worldwide, the social network phenomena is even stronger. According to a Universal McCann survey, seven other countries (Russia, India, China, Brazil, the United Kingdom, South Korea, and Spain) had even higher percentages of social network participation than the United States. Worldwide, over 60% of active Internet users ages 16–54 had a social network profile in 2010, and over 70% had visited a friend's profile. Users spend an average of 5.5 hours per month on social networks, with Russian users leading the pack at 6.6 hours (Nielsen Company, 2010). Although Facebook and MySpace dominate the global social network marketspace, in some countries, more localized social networks are signficant, such as Orkut (owned by Google) in Brazil, Mixi in Japan, 51 in China, and Werkentwenn in Germany. There is an online social network for you to join almost anywhere you go! Unfortunately, there's very little communication across social networks.

## WHAT IS AN ONLINE SOCIAL NETWORK?

So exactly how do we define an online social network, and how is it any different from, say, an offline social network? Sociologists, who frequently criticize modern society for having destroyed traditional communities, unfortunately have not given us very good definitions of social networks and community. One study examined 94 different sociological definitions of community and found four areas of agreement. **Social networks** involve (a) a group of people, (b) shared social interaction, (c) common ties among members, and (d) people who share an area for some period of time (Hillery, 1955). This will be our working definition of a social network. Social networks do not necessarily have shared goals, purposes, or intentions. Indeed, social networks can be places where people just "hang out," share space, and communicate.

**social network**

involves a group of people, shared social interaction, common ties among members, and people who share an area for some period of time

It's a short step to defining an **online social network** as an area online where people who share common ties can interact with one another. This definition is very close to that of Howard Rheingold's—one of The Well's early participants—who coined the term *virtual communities* as "cultural aggregations that emerge when enough people bump into each other often enough in cyberspace." It is a group of people who may or may not meet one another face to face, and who exchange words and ideas through the mediation of an online social meeting space. The Internet removes the geographic and time limitations of offline social networks. To be in an online network, you don't need to meet face to face, in a common room, at a common time.

**online social network**
an area online, where people who share common ties can interact with one another

## THE DIFFERENCE BETWEEN SOCIAL NETWORKS AND PORTALS

We describe portals in the last section of this chapter. Portals began as search engines and then added content, Internet, and e-commerce services. In order to survive, portals have added many community-building and social network features including chat groups, bulletin boards, free Web site design and hosting, and other features that encourage visitors to stay on the site and interact with others who share their interests. Yahoo, for instance, uses deep vertical content features to retain its audience on-site and maximize revenue opportunities. Portals have begun to measure their success in terms of their social network features. For instance, Yahoo has purchased several Web properties, such as Flickr (a photo-sharing site), which has social network features. Portals have moved toward becoming general community meeting places in an effort to enlarge and retain audience share and increase revenues. User-generated content on portals is one way to entice visitors to stay online at the site (and of course view more commercials).

Similarly, sites that began as narrowly focused content or affinity group community sites, such as iVillage, a site devoted to women's issues, have added more general portal-like services including general Web searching, general news, weather, travel information, and a wide variety of e-commerce services, often provided by portals seeking alliances. Browsers such as Mozilla's Firefox and Microsoft's Internet Explorer 7 and 8 have added social network features as well. There is no reason why social networks have to be limited to self-proclaimed social network sites such as Facebook. Social networking is a functionality, not a Web site. As a result, social networks and portals have moved closer together and at times are indistinguishable from one another.

## THE GROWTH OF SOCIAL NETWORKS AND ONLINE COMMUNITIES

Facebook, MySpace, Twitter, and Classmates.com are all examples of popular online communities. **Figure 11.1** shows the top 10 social network sites , which together account for well over 90% of the Internet's social network activity.

In 2009, Facebook passed MySpace as the largest social network in terms of total members. MySpace has been relegated to second place, with about 130 million members worldwide and around 70 million unique visitors per month in the United States. While social networks originally attracted mostly young Internet users, today social networks are not just about teens and college students, but a much larger social phenomenon. 54% of Facebook's users are over 35.

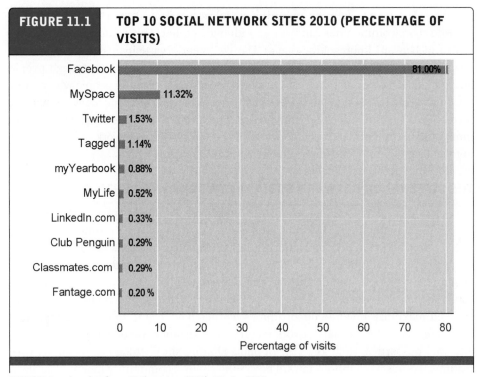

**FIGURE 11.1** TOP 10 SOCIAL NETWORK SITES 2010 (PERCENTAGE OF VISITS)

SOURCES: Based on data from eMarketer, Inc., 2010b; Hitwise, 2010.

It is easy to both overestimate and underestimate the significance of social networks. According to comScore, the social network category has a total unique audience in the United States of about 175 million. In contrast, the top four portal/search engine sites (Google, Yahoo, MSN, and AOL) together have a total monthly unique audience of over 510 million. (Obviously, with 221 million people on the Internet in the United States, users are unique to more than one site.) Although Facebook's 150 million unique U.S. visitors seems high, consider that Yahoo's various sites have around 180 million. Still, in four years, Facebook has grown from a very small Internet audience of less than 20 million, to an Internet behemoth among the top three Web sites on the Internet.

The number of unique visitors is just one way to measure the influence of a site. Time on site is another important metric. The more time people spend on a site, the more time to display ads and generate revenue. In this sense, Facebook is three times more addictive and immersive than the other top sites on the Web. The average time a user spends on Facebook is over six hours, and on Yahoo, two hours, and less than two hours on Google and Microsoft sites.

The amount of advertising revenue generated by sites is perhaps the ultimate metric. The top four portal/search engines (Google, Yahoo, MSN, and AOL) will generate about $14 billion in U.S. advertising revenue in 2010. In contrast, social network sites in the United States in 2010 are expected to generate about $1.6 billion in advertising revenue. Social network sites are the fastest growing form of Internet usage, but they are not yet as powerful as traditional search engines/portals in terms of unique visitors, overall reach, and ad dollars generated. A part of the problem is that subscribers do not go to social network sites to seek ads for relevant products, or pay attention to the ads that are flashed before their eyes.

## TURNING SOCIAL NETWORKS INTO BUSINESSES

While the early social networks had a difficult time raising capital and revenues, today's top social network sites are now learning how to monetize their huge audiences. Early social network sites relied on subscriptions, but today, social networks rely on advertising. Users of portals and search engines have come to accept advertising as the preferred means of supporting Web experiences rather than paying for it. **Figure 11.2** shows the amount of ad spending on social networks.

The techniques for marketing on social networks are still being worked out. Unlike portals where banner ads are an accepted phenomenon, this is not true on some social network sites such as LinkedIn.

## TYPES OF SOCIAL NETWORKS AND THEIR BUSINESS MODELS

There are many types and many ways of classifying social networks and online communities. While the most popular general social networks have adopted an advertising model, other kinds of networks have different revenue sources. Social networks have different types of sponsors, and different kinds of members. For instance, some are created by firms such as IBM for the exclusive use of their sales force or other employees (intra-firm communities or B2E [business-to-employee] communities); others are built for suppliers and resellers (inter-organizational or B2B communities); and others are built by dedicated individuals for other similar persons

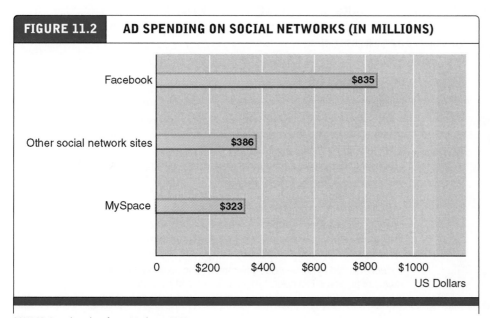

**FIGURE 11.2** — **AD SPENDING ON SOCIAL NETWORKS (IN MILLIONS)**

- Facebook: $835
- Other social network sites: $386
- MySpace: $323

US Dollars

SOURCE: Based on data from eMarketer, 2010c.

with shared interests (P2P [people-to-people] communities). In this chapter, we will discuss B2C communities for the most part, although we also discuss briefly P2P communities of practice.

**Table 11.1** describes in greater detail the five generic types of social networks and online communities: general, practice, interest, affinity, and sponsored. Each type of community can have a commercial intent or commercial consequence. We use this schema to explore the business models of commercial communities.

**General communities** offer members opportunities to interact with a general audience organized into general topics. Within the topics, members can find hundreds of specific discussion groups attended by thousands of like-minded members who share an interest in that topic. The purpose of the general community is to attract enough members to populate a wide range of topics and discussion groups. The business model of general communities is typically advertising supported by selling ad space on pages and videos.

**Practice networks** offer members focused discussion groups, help, information, and knowledge relating to an area of shared practice. For instance, Linux.org is a non-profit community for the open source movement, a worldwide global effort involving thousands of programmers who develop computer code for the Linux operating system and share the results freely with all. Other online communities involve artists, educators, art dealers, photographers, and nurses. Practice networks can be either profit-based or nonprofit, and support themselves by advertising or user donations.

**Interest-based social networks** offer members focused discussion groups based on a shared interest in some specific subject, such as business careers, boats, horses,

**general communities**
offer members opportunities to interact with a general audience organized into general topics

**practice networks**
offer members focused discussion groups, help, information, and knowledge relating to an area of shared practice

**interest-based social networks**
offer members focused discussion groups based on a shared interest in some specific topic

| TABLE 11.1 | TYPES OF SOCIAL NETWORKS AND ONLINE COMMUNITIES |
|---|---|
| **TYPE OF SOCIAL NETWORK/ ONLINE COMMUNITY** | **DESCRIPTION** |
| General | Online social gathering place to meet and socialize with friends, share content, schedules, and interests. Examples: Facebook and MySpace |
| Practice | Social network of professionals and practitioners, creators of artifacts such as computer code or music. Examples: Just Plain Folks (musicians community) and LinkedIn (business) |
| Interest | Community built around a common interest, such as games, sports, music, stock markets, politics, health, finance, foreign affairs, or lifestyle. Examples: E-democracy.org (political discussion group) and SocialPicks (stock market site) |
| Affinity | Community of members who self-identify with a demographic or geographic category, such as women, African Americans, or Arab Americans. Examples: BlackPlanet (African American community and social network site) and iVillage (focusing on women) |
| Sponsored | Network created by commercial, government, and nonprofit organizations for a variety of purposes. Examples: Nike, IBM, Cisco, and political candidates |

health, skiing, and thousands of other topics. Because the audience for interest communities is necessarily much smaller and more targeted, these communities have usually relied on advertising and tenancy/sponsorship deals. Sites such as Spoke.com, Jigsaw.com, Fool.com, Military.com, and Sailing Anarchy all are examples of Web sites that attract people who share a common pursuit. These sites are usually advertising supported.

**Affinity communities** offer members focused discussions and interaction with other people who share the same affinity. Affinity refers to self- and group identification. For instance, people can self-identify themselves on the basis of religion, ethnicity, gender, sexual orientation, political beliefs, geographical location, and hundreds of other categories. For instance, iVillage, Oxygen, and NaturallyCurly are affinity sites designed to attract women. These sites offer women discussion and services that focus on topics such as babies, beauty, books, diet and fitness, entertainment, health, and home and garden. These sites are supported by advertising along with revenues from sales of products.

> **affinity communities**
> offer members focused discussions and interaction with other people who share the same affinity

**Sponsored communities** are online communities created by government, nonprofit, or for-profit organizations for the purpose of pursuing organizational goals. These goals can be diverse, from increasing the information available to citizens; for instance, a local county government site such as Westchestergov.com, the Web site for Westchester County (New York) government; to an online auction site such as eBay; to a product site such as Tide.com, which is sponsored by an offline branded product company (Procter & Gamble). Cisco, IBM, HP, and hundreds of other companies have developed their internal corporate social networks as a way of sharing knowledge.

> **sponsored communities**
> online communities created for the purpose of pursuing organizational (and often commercial) goals

## SOCIAL NETWORK FEATURES AND TECHNOLOGIES

Social networks have developed software applications that allow users to engage in a number of activities. Not all sites have the same features, but there is an emerging feature set among the larger communities. Some of these software tools are built into the site, while others can be added by users to their profile pages as widgets (described in earlier chapters). **Table 11.2** describes several social network functionalities.

## THE FUTURE OF SOCIAL NETWORKS

While today's social network scene is highly concentrated among the top 10 general social network sites, this is unlikely to remain the case. Social networks are springing up all over the Internet based on intensely felt interests of smaller groups of people, draining potential members from the general sites. General social network sites are poor places to meet new people, and most online social networks reflect offline friendships and associations.

Today's social networks are places you visit online, but increasingly browsers, portals, and general Web sites will have social network functionality built in, making it less necessary that you go to a social network site, and more likely that social networks will come to you (see *Insight on Technology: Social Operating Systems: Facebook vs. Google*). The biggest Web e-mail services (who also happen to be the big portals) are adding features that allow users to perform sociable functions like tracking friends, creating profiles, and joining other groups. Network aggregators are also

| TABLE 11.2 | SOCIAL NETWORK FEATURES AND TECHNOLOGIES |
|---|---|
| FEATURE | DESCRIPTION |
| Profiles | Users create Web pages that describe themselves on a variety of dimensions. |
| Friends network | Ability to create a linked group of friends. |
| Network discovery | Ability to find other networks and find new groups and friends. |
| Favorites | Ability to communicate favorite sites, bookmarks, content, and destinations. |
| Games, widgets, and apps | Over 60% of Facebook visitors use one or more of nearly 100,000 apps and games on the site. |
| E-mail | Send e-mail within the social network site to friends. |
| Storage | Storage space for network members, content. |
| Instant messaging | Immediate one-to-one contact with friends through the community facility. |
| Message boards | Posting of messages to groups of friends, and other groups' members. |
| Online polling | Polling of member opinion. |
| Chat | Online immediate group discussion; Internet relay chat (IRC). |
| Discussion groups | Discussion groups and forums organized by topic. |
| Experts online | Certified experts in selected areas respond to queries. |
| Membership management tools | Ability of site managers to edit content, and dialog; remove objectionable material; protect security and privacy. |

emerging: SocialURL, ProfileFly, and ProfileLinker allow people to aggregate feeds from their different social network profiles, making it less necessary to visit the destination site itself.

## 11.2 ONLINE AUCTIONS

Online auction sites are among the most popular consumer-to-consumer (C2C) e-commerce sites on the Internet, although the popularity of auctions and their growth rates have slowed in recent years due to customers' preferences for a "buy now" fixed-price model. Nevertheless, the online auction industry in the United States grew by over 10% in 2008 despite the recession and then settled into a slower growth rate of 2% for 2009. The market leader in C2C auctions is eBay, which has 91 million active users in the United States and over 140 million items listed on any given day within 18,000 categories. In August 2010, eBay had around 70 million unique visitors, placing it 14th in the list of top 50 Web properties, not far below arch rival Amazon which had 79 million visitors, 11th on the top 50 list (comScore, 2010). In 2009, eBay's had $8.7 billion in net revenues from its Marketplaces segment, a 5% decrease from 2008 due to the recession. In addition, customers have moved away from auctions

## INSIGHT ON TECHNOLOGY

# SOCIAL OPERATING SYSTEMS: GOOGLE VS. FACEBOOK

In the ongoing battles between hype and substance on the Internet, fantasy and reality, hubris and humility, Silicon Valley takes no prisoners and has no equals. Google wants to organize the world's information, Amazon wants to be the world's store, and now Facebook wants to be the "social operating system" for the Internet, according to founder and CEO Mark Zuckerberg. Facebook wants to connect the world in one big social network (that it owns). He wants Facebook to "connect everyone" in what he calls "the social graph." Microsoft, owner of the world's desktops with a 95% market share, will just have to move on over while Facebook engineers this feat. Google will have to be satisfied being a search engine where people don't hang around very long. In September 2010, Facebook announced it has over 500 million users worldwide. In the United States, Facebook has about 150 million unique visitors a month, and over 100 million people worldwide now actively using Facebook on their mobile devices—a significant increase from 65 million last year.

What can a social operating system possibly be? When we think of an operating system such as Windows, Mac OS, or Linux, we think of a software tool that controls the resources of the computer and provides the platform on which applications are built, launched, and operate. How can Facebook replace this? The answer is, it can't. But what Facebook can do is build, or encourage others to build, thousands of software applications that run inside the Facebook garden (just like Apple apps run in the Apple garden).

In 2007, Facebook took its two major assets—its membership base and its technology—and made them available to everyone. It adopted a strategy that involved opening up its technology platform to anyone who wanted to create an application and make it available to Facebook users. Developers could develop widgets and other Java applications to perform thousands of different tasks, and even use the apps to display ads and keep all the revenues. As a result, Facebook has become a kind of Web inside the Web—a platform or area where Web pages created by users (called "profiles") are linked together by the users themselves into networks, and where the applications are supplied by outside developers. The applications range from tools such as iLike, which lets you find friends who share your musical tastes, to games like FarmVille, which has 62 million active monthly users. iLike is now making more money on Facebook selling ads and getting commissions from selling songs and concert tickets than it does from its own Web site, iLike.com.

As of September 2010, Facebook's platform engages more than 1 million developers in 180 countries and supports more than 550,000 active applications. Over 250 applications have more than 1 million users, and 70% of Facebook users engage with platform apps every month. In contrast, in 2010, there are about 250,000 Apple iPhone apps.

The only problem? Facebook's applications operate in a closed sandbox where only Facebook users can play. The rest of the world is shut out, and none of the applications play on other social networks, of which there are thousands. As it turns out, Facebook managers want to connect the world as long as everyone plays (and spends time and money) in Facebook's backyard. The same is true of

(continued)

Apple's iPhone apps: they only play on the iPhone operating system.

At some point in the future, these applications will be robust enough to include typical Microsoft Office functionality such as word processing and spreadsheets. But they probably won't, because these applications are already well performed by Microsoft Office and others. Instead, businesses will be turning to Facebook to enhance the productivity of their employees by developing collaboration and meeting tools. Microsoft isn't that worried, because people will still need a Windows or other operating system such as Mac OS to gain access to Facebook. So the social network operating system is not a substitute for a computer operating system. Not yet. Does Microsoft want to play in this new arena? Yes. It invested $250 million in Facebook in October 2007 for a 1.6% stake. This valued Facebook at $15 billion, and was a sign of how desperate Microsoft was to play in this new field. In 2010, analysts estimate that Facebook will earn between $1.2 and $2 billion, more than enough to be profitable. Still, it's quite a distance to the $15 billion value on which Microsoft based payment for for its tiny Facebook share.

Not to be outdone by a mere start-up, Google refuses to give up the top spot in Silicon Valley's pantheon of creative genius. If Facebook promises to connect the world, Google wants to make sure it can play there too. Actually, Google wants to create a social network world that runs on its standards and that would be universal to all social networks now and in the future. There are thousands of smaller, more specialized social networks that are growing at faster rates than Facebook and MySpace. Google has created a set of standard programs that enable three generic social network core functions and that would be usable on all social networks. You can see these programs at Opensocial.org. These core functions are profile information (user data), friends information (social graph), and activities (events like news, schedules, reports of friends movements).

OpenSocial already has many friends who will host these applications, such as MySpace, Orkut, LinkedIn, XING, Bebo, hi5, Hyves.net, Ning, and Socialtext, among others. Developers include Oxylabs, Viadeo, and Oracle, along with thousands of individual small developers. All told, if you add up all the social networks that host OpenSocial applications, as of September 2010, it has reached over 600 million users, big enough to compete with Facebook. The advantage for developers is that they can develop one application and have it run on all social networks. Another advantage is that this functionality can be added to any program, browser, or Office application. For instance, you might be working on a particularly annoying spreadsheet and get help instantly from one of your business pals who's a wiz at spreadsheets. Or be in a Word document and suffer a loss of words. What better time to call in help from your friends? One consequence is that social network functionality can be added to any program, and you will no longer have to go a social network site such as Facebook in order to network. A social network is a functionality, not a URL. As a functionality, it can be available to all, and built into any software application.

■■■■ **SOURCES:** "Facebook Platform Statistics," Facebook.com, September 30, 2010; "comScore: Facebook's May US Traffic Nears Record…for Number of New Users" by Eldon, InsideFacebook.com, June 7, 2010; "Facebook Crosses the 500-Million Threshold, Comscore Says," by Jennifer Valentino-DeVries, *Wall Street Journal*, May 18, 2010; "Facebook Mobile: 100 Million and Growing," Facebook.com, February 10, 2010; "Facebook's Private Surprise," by Taylor Buley, Forbes, September 16, 2009.

towards a fixed-price model such as Amazon and other competitors. provide In the United States alone, there are several hundred auction sites, some specializing in unique collectible products such as stamps and coins, others adopting a more generalist approach in which just about any good can be found for sale. Increasingly, established portals and online retail sites—from Yahoo and MSN to JCPenney and Sam's Club—are adding auctions to their sites. Auctions constitute a significant part of all B2B e-commerce in 2010, and over a third of procurement officers use auctions to procure goods. What explains the extraordinary popularity of auctions? Do consumers always get lower prices at auctions? Why do merchants auction their products if the prices they receive are so low?

## DEFINING AND MEASURING THE GROWTH OF AUCTIONS AND DYNAMIC PRICING

**Auctions** are markets in which prices are variable and based on the competition among participants who are buying or selling products and services. Auctions are one type of **dynamic pricing**, in which the price of the product varies, depending directly on the demand characteristics of the customer and the supply situation of the seller. There is a wide variety of dynamically priced markets, from simple haggling, bartering, and negotiating between one buyer and one seller, to much more sophisticated public auctions in which there may be thousands of sellers and thousands of buyers, as in a single stock market for a bundle of shares.

In dynamic pricing, merchants change their prices based on both their understanding of how much value the customer attaches to the product and their own desire to make a sale. Likewise, customers change their offers to buy based on both their perceptions of the seller's desire to sell and their own need for the product. If you as a customer really want the product right now, you will be charged a higher price in a dynamic pricing regime, and you will willingly pay a higher price than if you placed less value on the product and were willing to wait several days to buy it. For instance, if you want to travel from New York to San Francisco to attend a last-minute business conference, and then return as soon as possible, you will be charged twice as much as a tourist who agrees to stay over the weekend.

In contrast, traditional mass-market merchants generally use **fixed pricing**—one national price, everywhere, for everyone. Fixed pricing first appeared in the nineteenth century with the development of mass national markets and retail stores that could sell to a national audience. Prior to this period, all pricing was dynamic and local, with prices derived through a process of negotiation between the customer and the merchant. Computers and the development of the Internet have contributed to a return of dynamic pricing. The difference is that with the Internet, dynamic pricing can be conducted globally, continuously, and at a very low cost.

There are many other types of dynamic pricing that preceded the Internet. Airlines have used dynamic pricing since the early 1980s to change the price of

**auctions**
markets in which prices are variable and based on the competition among participants who are buying or selling products and services

**dynamic pricing**
the price of the product varies, depending directly on the demand characteristics of the customer and the supply situation of the seller

**fixed pricing**
one national price, everywhere, for everyone

airline tickets depending on available unused capacity and the willingness of business travelers to pay a premium for immediate bookings. Airline yield management software programs seek to ensure that a perishable item (an empty airline seat is useless once the plane takes off) is sold before flight time at some price above zero.

The use of coupons sent to selected customers, and even college scholarships given to selected students to encourage their enrollment, are a form of both price discrimination and dynamic pricing. In these examples, the price of the item is adjusted to demand and available supply, and certain consumers are discriminated against by charging them higher prices while others are advantaged by receiving lower prices for the same products, namely, a reduced price for an item or a college education.

Newer forms of dynamic pricing on the Internet include bundling, trigger pricing, utilization pricing, and personalization pricing. As discussed in Chapter 6, bundling of digital goods is the practice of including low-demand products in a bundle "for free" in order to increase total revenues. **Trigger pricing**, used in m-commerce applications, adjusts prices based on the location of the consumer—for example, walking within 400 yards of a restaurant may trigger an immediate 10% dinner coupon on a portable Web device. **Utilization pricing** adjusts prices based on utilization of the product; for example, Progressive Insurance Company adjusts the annual cost of automobile insurance based on mileage driven. **Personalization pricing** adjusts prices based on the merchant's estimate of how much the customer truly values the product; for instance, Web merchants may charge committed fans of a musician higher prices for the privilege of receiving a new DVD before its official release to retail stores. Higher-cost hardbound books sell primarily to committed fans of writers, while less-committed fans wait for cheaper paperback versions to appear.

Auctions—one form of dynamic pricing mechanism—are used throughout the e-commerce landscape. The most widely known auctions are **consumer-to-consumer (C2C) auctions**, in which the auction house is simply an intermediary market maker, providing a forum where consumers—buyers and sellers—can discover prices and trade. Less well known are **business-to-consumer (B2C) auctions**, where a business owns or controls assets and uses dynamic pricing to establish the price. Established merchants on occasion use B2C auctions to sell excess goods. This form of auction or dynamic pricing will grow along with C2C auctions. Online auctions are expected to grow in the range of around 5% to 10% annually between 2009 and 2013. In 2009, C2C auction sites in the United States generated about $25 billion in gross revenue, and B2C auction sites generated about $19 billion.

Some leading online auction sites are listed in **Table 11.3**. Auctions are not limited to goods and services. They can also be used to allocate resources, and bundles of resources, among any group of bidders. For instance, if you wanted to establish an optimal schedule for assigned tasks in an office among a group of clerical workers, an auction in which workers bid for assignments would come close to producing a nearly optimal solution in a short amount of time (Parkes and Ungar, 2000). In short, auctions—like all markets—are ways of allocating resources among independent agents (bidders).

---

**trigger pricing**

adjusts prices based on the location of the consumer

**utilization pricing**

adjusts prices based on utilization of the product

**personalization pricing**

adjusts prices based on the merchant's estimate of how much the customer truly values the product

**consumer-to-consumer (C2C) auctions**

auction house acts as an intermediary market maker, providing a forum where consumers can discover prices and trade

**business-to-consumer (B2C) auctions**

auction house sells goods it owns, or controls, using various dynamic pricing models

| TABLE 11.3 | LEADING ONLINE AUCTION SITES |
|---|---|
| *GENERAL* | |
| eBay | The world market leader in auctions: 72 million visitors a month and millions of products. |
| uBid | Marketplace for excess inventory from pre-approved merchants. |
| eBid | In business since 1998. Operates in 18 countries, including U.S. Currently, the top competitor to eBay. Offers much lower fees. |
| Bid4Assets | Liquidation of distressed assets from government and the public sector, corporations, restructurings, and bankruptcies. |
| Auctions.samsclub | Sam's Club brand merchandise in a variety of categories. |
| *SPECIALIZED* | |
| BidZ | Live auction format for online jewelry. |
| Racersauction | Specialized site for automobile racing parts. |
| Philatelic Phantasies | Stamp site for professionals, monthly online stamp auction. |
| Teletrade | America's largest fully automated auction company of certified coins including ancient gold, silver, and copper coins. Also offers sports cards. |
| Baseball-cards.com | The Internet's first baseball card store. Offers weekly auctions of baseball, football, basketball, hockey, wire photos, and more. |
| Oldandsold | Online auction service specializing in quality antiques. Dealers pay a 3% commission on merchandise sold. |

## WHY ARE AUCTIONS SO POPULAR? BENEFITS AND COSTS OF AUCTIONS

The Internet is primarily responsible for the resurgence in auctions. Although electronic network-based auctions such as AUCNET in Japan (an electronic automobile auction for used cars) were developed in the late 1980s, these pre-Internet auctions required an expensive telecommunications network to implement. The Internet provides a global environment and very low fixed and operational costs for the aggregation of huge buyer audiences composed of millions of consumers worldwide who can use a universally available technology (Internet browsers) to shop for goods.

### Benefits of Auctions

Aside from the sheer game-like fun of participating in auctions, consumers, merchants, and society as a whole derive a number of economic benefits from participating in Internet auctions. These benefits include:

- **Liquidity:** Sellers can find willing buyers, and buyers can find sellers. The Internet enormously increased the liquidity of traditional auctions that usually required all participants to be present in a single room. Now, sellers and buyers can be located anywhere around the globe. Just as important, buyers and sellers can find a global market for rare items that would not have existed before the Internet.

- **Price discovery:** Buyers and sellers can quickly and efficiently develop prices for items that are difficult to assess, where the price depends on demand and supply, and where the product is rare. For instance, how could a merchant (or buyer) price a Greek oil lamp made in 550 B.C. (to use just one example of the rare items that can be found on eBay)? How could a consumer even find a Greek oil lamp without the Internet? It would be difficult and costly for all parties.

- **Price transparency:** Public Internet auctions allow everyone in the world to see the asking and bidding prices for items. It is difficult for merchants to engage in price discrimination (charging some customers more) when the items are available on auctions. However, because even huge auction sites such as eBay do not include all the world's online auction items (there are other auction sites in the world), there still may be more than one world price for a given item (there are inter-market price differences).

- **Market efficiency:** Auctions can, and often do, lead to reduced prices, and hence reduced profits for merchants, leading to an increase in consumer welfare—one measure of market efficiency. Online auctions provide consumers the chance to find real bargains at potentially give-away prices; they also provide access to a very wide selection of goods that would be impossible for consumers to physically access by visiting stores.

- **Lower transaction costs:** Online auctions can lower the cost of selling and purchasing products, benefiting both merchants and consumers. Like other Internet markets, such as retail markets, Internet auctions have very low (but not zero) transaction costs. A sale at an auction can be consummated quickly and with very low transaction costs when compared to the physical world of markets.

- **Consumer aggregation:** Sellers benefit from large auction sites' ability to aggregate a large number of consumers who are motivated to purchase something in one marketspace. Auction-site search engines that lead consumers directly to the products they are seeking make it very likely that consumers who visit a specific auction really are interested and ready to buy at some price.

- **Network effects:** The larger an auction site becomes in terms of visitors and products for sale, the more valuable it becomes as a marketplace for everyone by providing liquidity and several other benefits listed previously, such as lower transaction costs, higher efficiency, and better price transparency. For instance, because eBay is so large—garnering close to 90% of all C2C auction commerce in the United States—it is quite likely you will find what you want to buy at a good price, and highly probable you will find a buyer for just about anything.

### Risks and Costs of Auctions for Consumers and Businesses

There are a number of risks and costs involved in participating in auctions. In some cases, auction markets can fail—like all markets at times. (We describe auction market failure in more detail later.) Some of the more important risks and costs to keep in mind are:

- **Delayed consumption costs:** Internet auctions can go on for days, and shipping will take additional time. If you ordered from a mail-order catalog, you would likely receive the product much faster, or if you went to a physical store, you would be able to obtain the product immediately.
- **Monitoring costs:** Participation in auctions requires your time to monitor bidding.
- **Equipment costs:** Internet auctions require you to purchase a computer system, pay for Internet access, and learn a complex operating system.
- **Trust risks:** Online auctions are the single largest source of Internet fraud. Using auctions increases the risk of experiencing a loss.
- **Fulfillment costs:** Typically, the buyer pays fulfillment costs of packing, shipping, and insurance, whereas at a physical store these costs are included in the retail price.

Auction sites such as eBay have taken a number of steps to reduce consumer participation costs and trust risk. For instance, auction sites attempt to solve the trust problem by providing a rating system in which previous customers rate sellers based on their overall experience with the merchant. Although helpful, this solution does not always work. Auction fraud is the leading source of e-commerce complaints to federal law enforcement officials. One partial solution to high monitoring costs is, ironically, fixed pricing. At eBay, consumers can reduce the cost of monitoring and waiting for auctions to end by simply clicking on the "Buy It Now!" button and paying a premium price. The difference between the "Buy It Now" price and the auction price is the cost of monitoring. Also, most online auctions reduce monitoring costs by providing both a watch list and proxy bidding. **Watch lists** permit the consumer to monitor specific auctions of interest, requiring the consumer to pay close attention only in the last few minutes of bidding. **Proxy bidding** allows the consumer to enter a maximum price, and the auction software automatically bids for the goods up to that maximum price in small increments.

**watch lists**
permit the consumer to monitor specific auctions of interest

**proxy bidding**
allows the consumer to enter a maximum price, and the auction software automatically bids for the goods up to that maximum price in small increments

Nevertheless, given the costs of participating in online auctions, the generally lower cost of goods on Internet auctions is in part a compensation for the other additional costs consumers experience. On the other hand, consumers experience lower search costs and transaction costs because there usually are no intermediaries (unless, of course, the seller is an online business operating on an auction site, in which case there is a middleman cost), and usually there are no local or state taxes.

Merchants face considerable risks and costs as well. At auctions, merchants may end up selling goods for prices far below what they might have achieved in conventional markets. Merchants also face risks of nonpayment, false bidding, bid rigging, monitoring, transaction fees charged by the auction site, credit card transaction processing fees, and the administration costs of entering price and product information. We explore the benefits and risks for merchants later in this chapter.

## Market-Maker Benefits: Auctions as an E-commerce Business Model

Online auctions have been among the most successful business models in retail and B2B commerce. EBay, the Internet's most lucrative auction site, has been profitable nearly since its inception. The strategy for eBay has been to make money off every stage in the auction cycle. EBay earns revenue in several ways: transaction fees based on the amount of the sale, listing fees for display of goods, financial service fees from payment systems such as PayPal, and advertising or placement fees where sellers pay extra for special services such as particular display or listing services. In addition, eBay purchased Skype, the Internet telephone company, so that buyers and sellers could communicate online with one another during the auction process. In 2006, eBay paid $2.6 billion for Skype, then wrote down its value on its books in 2008. In 2009, eBay determined that Skype was a "bad fit" for the company, and in November 2009, sold 70% of its interest in Skype to a consortium of investors in a deal that valued the business at $2.75 billion.

However, it is on the cost side that online auctions have extraordinary advantages over ordinary retail or catalog sites. Auction sites carry no inventory and do not perform any fulfillment activities—they need no warehouses, shipping, or logistical facilities. Sellers and consumers provide these services and bear these costs. In this sense, online auctions are an ideal digital business because they involve simply the transfer of information.

Even though eBay has been extraordinarily successful, the success of online auctions is qualified by the fact that the marketplace for online auctions is highly concentrated. eBay dominates the online auction market, followed by eBid and uBid. Many of the smaller auction sites are not profitable because they lack sufficient sellers and buyers to achieve liquidity. In auctions, network effects are highly influential, and the tendency is for one or two very large auction sites to dominate, with hundreds of smaller specialty auction sites (sites that sell specialized goods such as stamps) being barely profitable.

## TYPES AND EXAMPLES OF AUCTIONS

Auction theory is a well-established area of research, largely in economics (McAfee and McMillan, 1987; Milogram, 1989; Vickrey, 1961). Much of this research is theoretical, and prior to the emergence of public Internet auctions, there was not a great deal of empirical data on auctions or consumer behavior in auctions. Previous literature has identified a wide range of auction types, some of which are seller-biased, and others of which are more buyer-biased. Internet auctions are very different from traditional auctions. Traditional auctions are relatively short-lived (such as a Sotheby's art auction), and have a fixed number of bidders, usually present in the same room. Online Internet auctions, in contrast, can go on much longer (a week), and have a variable number of bidders who come and go from the auction arena.

### Internet Auction Basics

Before a business turns to auctions as a marketing channel, its managers need to understand some basic facts about online auctions.

**Market Power and Bias in Dynamically Priced Markets** Dynamically priced markets are not always "fair" in the sense of distributing market power to influence prices. **Figure 11.3** illustrates four different market bias situations that occur in dynamic markets.

In situations in which the number of buyers and sellers is few or equal in size, markets tend to be neutral, favoring neither the buyer nor the seller. One-on-one

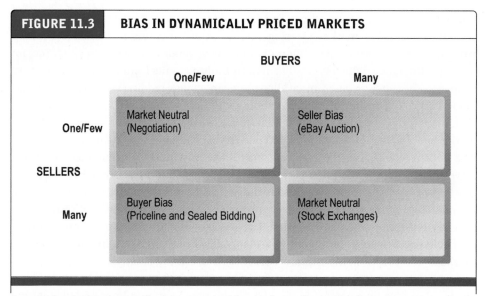

**FIGURE 11.3    BIAS IN DYNAMICALLY PRICED MARKETS**

Dynamically priced markets can be either neutral or biased in favor of buyers or sellers.

negotiations, barter markets, and stock exchanges all have this quality of neutrality, although specialists and market makers exact a commission for matching buy and sell orders. In stock markets, which are sometimes called a "double auction" because bids and offers are made continuously, many sellers and buyers call out prices for bundles of stock (of which there is a very large supply) until a deal is struck. In contrast, auctions such as those run by eBay and reverse auctions offered by companies such as Priceline have built-in biases. Usually on eBay, there is just one seller or a small number of sellers marketing goods that are in limited supply (or even rare goods) to millions of buyers who are competing on price. Priceline offers just the opposite bias and shares many features with a sealed-bid RFQ (request for quote) market. In Priceline's reverse auctions (described in greater detail later in this chapter), buyers post their unique needs for goods and services and a price they are willing to pay, while many sellers compete against one another for the available business. Of course, inherent bias in a marketplace does not mean consumers and merchants cannot find "good deals" and thousands of motivated customers willing to purchase goods at profitable prices.

However, the inherent biases should provide cautions to both merchants and consumers; namely, goods in auctions sometimes sell for far above their fair market value as they get bid too high, and sometimes for far less than their fair market value as merchants become too desperate for business. **Fair market value** could be defined here as the average of prices for that product or service in a variety of dynamic and fixed-price markets around the world. We explore other auction market failures in a later section.

**Price Allocation Rules: Uniform vs. Discriminatory Pricing** There are different rules for establishing the winning bids and prices in auctions where there are multiple units for sale, say, 10 Lenovo laptop PCs. With a **uniform pricing rule**, there are

**fair market value**
the average of prices for a product or service in a variety of dynamic and fixed-price markets around the world

**uniform pricing rule**
there are multiple winners and they all pay the same price

**discriminatory pricing**
winners pay different amounts depending on what they bid

multiple winners and they all pay the same price (usually the lowest winning bid—sometimes called a market clearing price). Other auctions use **discriminatory pricing** in which winners pay different amounts depending on what they bid. See, for instance, Ubid.com, which typically auctions multiple units from manufacturers. Like so many other auction rules, price allocation can change bidding strategy in auctions. For instance, in a uniform pricing auction for 10 Lenovo laptops, you may bid a very high price for a few units, knowing that others will not follow, but you will only pay a price equal to the lowest winning bid needed to clear out the units from the market. The person who bid for the 10th unit may have only bid 75% as high as your offer. Nevertheless, that is the price you will actually pay—the price needed to "clear the market" of all units. However, under a discriminatory pricing rule, you would be forced to pay your high bid. Obviously, from a buyer's point of view, uniform pricing is better, but from a merchant's point of view, discriminatory pricing is much better.

**Public vs. Private Information in Dynamically Priced Markets** In some dynamic markets, the prices being bid are secret, and are known only to one party. For instance, a firm may issue a request for bid to electrical contractors for provision of electrical service on a new building. Bidders are requested to submit sealed bids, and the lowest bidder (subject to qualifications) will be the winner. In this instance, the bidders do not know what others are bidding, and must bid their "best" price. The danger here is **bid rigging**, in which bidders communicate prior to submitting their bids, and rig their bids to ensure that the lowest price is higher than it might otherwise be (which benefits the bidder, who in this instance is receiving the bid price as payment for services to be rendered). This is a common problem in sealed-bid markets. However, in auction markets, bid prices are usually public information, available to all. Here the risks are that bidders agree offline to limit their bids, that sellers use shills to submit false bids, or that sellers use the market itself as a signaling device, driving prices up. Open markets permit large players to signal prices or engage in **price matching**, where sellers agree informally or formally to set floor prices on auction items below which they will not sell. Generally such collusion exists on the sell side, where there are just a few sellers or auction houses in a position to fix prices.

**bid rigging**
bidders communicate prior to submitting their bids, and rig their bids to ensure that the lowest price is higher than it might otherwise be

**price matching**
sellers agree informally or formally to set floor prices on auction items below which they will not sell

### Types of Auctions

Now that you have learned some basic auction market rules and practices, it's time to consider some of the major forms of dynamically priced markets and auctions, both online and offline. **Table 11.4** describes the major types of auctions, how they work, and their biases. As you can see in Table 11.4, aside from the different formats and rules, there are many other differences among auctions. As noted above, there are both discriminatory and uniform pricing rules, although the latter seem to be most common. Also, in some auctions, there are multiple units for sale, whereas in others, there is only a single unit for sale. The major types of Internet auctions are English, Dutch Internet, Name Your Own Price, and Group Buying.

**English auction**
most common form of auction; the highest bidder wins

**English Auctions** The **English auction** is the easiest to understand and the most common form of auction on eBay. Typically, there is a single item up for sale from a single seller. There is a time limit when the auction ends, a reserve price below which

| TABLE 11.4 | TYPES OF AUCTIONS AND DYNAMIC PRICING MECHANISMS | |
|---|---|---|
| AUCTION TYPE | MECHANISM | BIAS |
| Sealed-bid auction (B2B e-procurement— Ariba Sourcing; Elance) | Sealed-bid auction, RFQs. Winner is chosen from lowest bidders at acceptable quality levels. | Buyer bias: Multiple vendors competing against one another |
| Vickrey auction (private auction) | Sealed-bid auction, single unit; highest bidder wins at the second-highest bid price. | Seller bias: Single seller and multiple buyers competing against one another |
| English auction (eBay) | Public ascending price, single unit; highest bidder wins at a price just above the second-highest bid. Buyers can skip bidding at each price, but return at higher prices. | Seller bias: Single seller and multiple buyers competing against one another |
| Traditional Dutch (Dutch flower market) | Public descending-price auction, single unit; seller lowers price until a buyer takes the product. | Seller bias: Single seller and multiple buyers competing against one another |
| Dutch Internet (eBay Dutch auction) | Public ascending price, multiple units. Buyers bid on quantity and price. Final per-unit price is lowest successful bid, which sets a uniform price for all higher bidders as well (uniform price rule). | Seller bias: Small number of sellers and many buyers |
| Japanese auction (private auction) | Public ascending price, single unit; highest bidder wins at a price just above second-highest bid (reservation price) and buyers must bid at each price to stay in auction. | Seller bias: Single seller and many buyers |
| Yankee Internet auction (variation on Dutch Internet auction) | Public ascending price, multiple units. Buyers bid on quantity and price per unit. Bidders ranked on price per unit, units, and time. Winners pay their actual bid prices (discriminatory rule). | Seller bias: Single seller and multiple buyers competing against one another |
| Reverse auction | Public reverse English auction, descending prices, single unit. Sellers bid on price to provide products or services; winning bid is the lowest-price provider. Similar to sealed-bid markets. | Buyer bias: Multiple sellers competing against one another |
| Group buying (Demand aggregators) | Public reverse auction, descending prices, multiple units. Buyers bid on price per unit and units. Groups of sellers bid on price; winning bid is lowest-price provider. | Buyer bias: Multiple sellers competing against one another |
| Name Your Own Price (Priceline) | Similar to a reverse auction except the price the consumer is willing to pay is fixed and the price offered is nonpublic. Requires a commitment to purchase at the first offered price. | Buyer bias: Multiple sellers competing against one another for an individual's business |
| Double auction (Nasdaq and stock markets) | Public bid-ask negotiation; sellers ask, buyers bid. Sale consummated when participants agree on price and quantity. | Neutral: Multiple buyers and sellers competing against one another. Market bias: trading specialists (matchmakers) |

NOTE: "Public" means all participants can observe prices offered.

the seller will not sell (usually secret), and a minimum incremental bid set. Multiple buyers bid against one another until the auction time limit is reached. The highest bidder wins the item (if the reserve price of the seller has been met or exceeded). English auctions are considered to be seller-biased because multiple buyers compete against one another—usually anonymously.

**Traditional Dutch Auctions** In the traditional Dutch auction in Aalsmeer, Holland, 5,000 flower growers—who own the auction facility—sell bundles of graded flowers to 2,000 buyers. The Dutch auction uses a clock visible to all that displays the starting price growers want for their flowers. Every few seconds, the clock ticks to a lower price. When buyers want to buy at the displayed price, they push a button to accept the lot of flowers at that price. If buyers fail to bid in a timely fashion, their competitors will win the flowers. The auction is very efficient: on average, Aalsmeer conducts 50,000 transactions daily for 15 million flowers. Dutch flower auctions are now conducted over the Internet. Buyers no longer have to be present at the market to bid, and sellers no longer have to have their flowers present in adjacent warehouses, but can ship directly from their farms (Kambil and vanHeck, 1996).

**Dutch Internet Auctions** In **Dutch Internet auctions**, such as those on eBay, OnSale, and others, the rules and action are different from the classical Dutch auction. The Dutch Internet auction format is perfect for sellers that have many identical items to sell. Sellers start by listing a minimum price, or a starting bid for one item, and the number of items for sale. Bidders specify both a bid price and the quantity they want to buy. The uniform price reigns. Winning bidders pay the same price per item, which is the lowest successful bid. This market clearing price can be less than some bids. If there are more buyers than items, the earliest successful bids get the goods. In general, high bidders get the quantity they want at the lowest successful price, whereas low successful bidders might not get the quantity they want (but they will get something). The action is usually quite rapid, and proxy bidding is not used. **Table 11.5** shows closing data from a sample Dutch Internet auction for a bundle of laptop computers. In Table 11.5, the bids are arranged by price and then quantity. Under a uniform pricing rule, the lowest winning bid that clears the market of all 10 laptops is $736 and all winners pay this amount. However, the lowest winning bidder, JB505, will only receive three laptops, not four, because higher bidders are given their full allotments.

**Name Your Own Price Auctions** The **Name Your Own Price auction** was pioneered by Priceline, and is the second most-popular auction format on the Web. Although Priceline also acts as an intermediary, buying blocks of airline tickets and vacation packages at a discount and selling them at a reduced retail price or matching its inventory to bidders, it is best known for its Name Your Own Price auctions, where users specify what they are willing to pay for goods or services, and multiple providers bid for their business. Prices do not descend and are fixed: the initial consumer offer is a commitment to purchase at that price. In 2009, Priceline had almost $2 billion in revenues, and in 2010, attracts around 10 million unqiue visitors a month. It is one of the top-ranked travel sites in the United States. Today, it also arranges for the sale of new cars, hotel accommodations, car rentals, long distance telephone service, and home finance.

**Table 11.6** describes the products and services available in Priceline's Name Your Own Price auctions. Clearly, a major attraction of Priceline is that it offers

**Dutch Internet auction**

public ascending price, multiple unit auction. Final price is lowest successful bid, which sets price for all higher bidders

**Name Your Own Price auction**

auction where users specify what they are willing to pay for goods or services

| TABLE 11.5 | A MULTI-UNIT DUTCH INTERNET AUCTION |
|------------|-------------------------------------|

**CLOSING AUCTION DATA**

| | |
|---|---|
| Lot number | 8740240 |
| Total Number of Units | 10 |
| Description | HP Pavilion DV7T Laptop; Win 7; Intel Core i5, 3 GHz, 17" widescreen; 4 GB memory; 500 GB hard drive |
| Reserve Price | None |

| BIDDER | DATE | TIME | BID | QUANTITY |
|--------|------|------|-----|----------|
| JDMTKIS | 10/25/10 | 18:35 | $750 | 4 |
| KTTX | 10/25/10 | 18:55 | $745 | 3 |
| JB505 | 10/25/10 | 19:05 | $736 | 4 |
| VAMP | 10/25/10 | 19:10 | $730 | 2 |
| DPVS | 10/25/10 | 19:20 | $730 | 1 |
| RSF34 | 10/25/10 | 19:24 | $725 | 1 |
| CMCAL | 10/25/10 | 19:25 | $725 | 2 |

consumers a market biased in their favor and very low prices, up to 40% off. Brand-name suppliers compete with one another to supply services to consumers. However, it is unclear at this time if the Priceline business model can extend to other categories of products. Experiments to sell gasoline and groceries through Priceline failed.

| TABLE 11.6 | PRICELINE NAME YOUR OWN PRICE OFFERINGS |
|------------|-----------------------------------------|

| SERVICE/PRODUCT | DESCRIPTION |
|-----------------|-------------|
| Airline seats | Brand-name carriers bid for individual consumer business—perishable items that airlines are motivated to sell at the last minute. |
| Hotel rooms | Brand-name hotels bid for consumer business—perishable services that hotels are motivated to sell on a last-minute basis. |
| Rental cars | Brand-name rental companies bid for consumer business—perishable services that rental companies are motivated to sell on a last-minute basis. |
| Vacation packages | Brand-name hotels and air carriers bid for consumer business—perishable services that providers are motivated to sell on a last-minute basis. |
| Cruises | Cruise ship companies bid for consumer business; especially active in off-season periods. |

But how can Priceline offer discounts up to 40% off prices for services provided by major name brand providers? There are several answers. First, Priceline "shields the brand" by not publicizing the prices at which major brands sell. This reduces conflict with traditional channels, including direct sales. Second, the services being sold are perishable: if a Priceline consumer did not pay something for the empty airline seat, rental car, or hotel room, sellers would not receive any revenue. Hence, sellers are highly motivated to at least cover the costs of their services by selling in a spot market at very low prices.

The strategy for sellers is to sell as much as possible through more profitable channels and then unload excess capacity on spot markets such as Priceline. This works to the advantage of consumers, sellers, and Priceline, which charges a transaction fee to sellers.

**Group Buying Auctions: Demand Aggregators** A **demand aggregator** facilitates group buying of products at dynamically adjusted discount prices based on high-volume purchases. The originator of demand aggregation was Mercata, formed in 1998, and the Web's largest retail demand aggregator until it ceased operations in January 2001, when needed venture capital financing did not materialize. Mercata holds several patents covering online demand aggregation. The largest supplier today of demand aggregation software is Ewinwin, a B2B demand aggregator. In general, demand aggregation did not work well for retail sales, but it has found a home in B2B commerce as a way of organizing group buying. Trade associations and industry-buying groups have traditionally pursued group buying plans in order to reduce costs from large suppliers.

Online demand aggregation is built on two principles. First, sellers are more likely to offer discounts to buyers purchasing in volume, and, second, buyers increase their purchases as prices fall. Prices are expected to dynamically adjust to the volume of the order and the motivations of the vendors.

Although online sites dedicated to retail group buying were not a commercial success, their software and business practices have been integrated into B2B and business-to-government (B2G) sites as one of many dynamic-pricing mechanisms. For instance, the federal government's Department of Homeland Security is building a centralized purchasing portal that will aggregate the demand for IT commodities (such as PCs, routers, and other equipment) from many different constituent agencies in order to reduce costs. In general, demand aggregation is suitable for MRO products (commodity-like products) that are frequently purchased by a large number of organizations in high volume.

**Professional Service Auctions** Perhaps one of the more interesting uses for auctions on the Web is eBay's marketplace for professional services, Elance. This auction is a sealed-bid, dynamic-priced market for freelance professional services from legal and marketing services to graphics design and programming. Firms looking for professional services post a project description and request for bid on Elance. Providers of services bid for the work. The buyer can choose from among bidders on the basis of both cost and perceived quality of the providers that can be gauged from the feedback of clients posted on the site. This type of auction is a reverse Vickrey-like auction where sealed bids are submitted and the winner is usually the low-cost provider of services. Another similar site is SoloGig.

**demand aggregators**

suppliers or market makers who group unrelated buyers into a single purchase in return for offering a lower purchase price. Prices on multiple units fall as the number of buyers increase

Auction Aggregators (Mega Auctions) With thousands of auctions available on the Web, how can you, your customers, or your business find the right auction for products of interest that you want to either buy or sell? **Auction aggregators** (sometimes called mega auctions) offer one solution to this problem of multiple Internet markets and inter-market price differences. Auction aggregators use computer programs to search thousands of Web auction sites, accumulating information on products, bids, auction duration, and bid increments. Consumers search auction aggregator sites for products of interest, and the site returns a list of both fixed-price sales locations and auction locations where the product is for sale. Auction aggregators work by sending Web crawlers to thousands of auction sites every night (and on some sites during the day as well), gathering all information on product listings—just like an ordinary single consumer would. However, the major sites have effectively prevented auction aggregators from searching their sites without a license.

**auction aggregators**
use computer programs to search thousands of Web auction sites, and aggregate information on products, bids, auction duration, and bid increments

## WHEN TO USE AUCTIONS (AND FOR WHAT) IN BUSINESS

There are many different situations in which auctions are an appropriate channel for businesses to consider. For much of this chapter, we have looked at auctions from a consumer point of view. The objective of consumers is to receive the greatest value for the lowest cost. Switch perspectives now to that of a business. Remember that the objective for businesses using auctions is to maximize their revenue (their share of consumer surplus) by finding the true market value of products and services, a market value that hopefully is higher in the auction channel than in fixed-price channels. **Table 11.7** provides an overview of factors to consider.

The factors to consider include:

- **Type of product:** Online auctions are most commonly used for rare and unique products for which prices are difficult to discover, and there may have been no market for the goods. However, Priceline has succeeded in developing auctions

| TABLE 11.7 | FACTORS TO CONSIDER WHEN CHOOSING AUCTIONS |
| --- | --- |
| CONSIDERATIONS | DESCRIPTION |
| Type of product | Rare, unique, commodity, perishable |
| Stage of product life cycle | Early, mature, late |
| Channel-management issues | Conflict with retail distributors; differentiation |
| Type of auction | Seller vs. buyer bias |
| Initial pricing | Low vs. high |
| Bid increment amounts | Low vs. high |
| Auction length | Short vs. long |
| Number of items | Single vs. multiple |
| Price-allocation rule | Uniform vs. discriminatory |
| Information sharing | Closed vs. open bidding |

for perishable commodities (such as airline seats) for which retail prices have already been established, and some B2B auctions involve commodities such as steel (often sold at distress prices). New clothing items, new digital cameras, and new computers are generally not sold at auction because their prices are easy to discover; catalog prices are high, sustainable, and profitable; they are not perishable; and there exists an efficient market channel in the form of retail stores (online and offline).

- **Product life cycle:** For the most part, businesses have traditionally used auctions for goods at the end of their product life cycle and for products where auctions yield a higher price than fixed-price liquidation sales. However, products at the beginning of their life cycle are increasingly being sold at auction. Early releases of music, books, videos, games, and digital appliances can be sold to highly motivated early adopters who want to be the first in their neighborhood with new products. Online sales of event tickets from music concerts to sports events now account for upwards of 25% of all event ticket sales in the United States.

- **Channel management:** Established retailers such as JCPenney and Wal-Mart, and manufacturers in general, must be careful not to allow their auction activity to interfere with their existing profitable channels. For this reason, items found on established retail-site auctions tend to be late in their product life cycle, or have quantity purchase requirements.

- **Type of auction:** Sellers obviously should choose auctions where there are many buyers and only a few, or even one, seller. English ascending-price auctions such as those at eBay are best for sellers because as the number of bidders increases the higher the price tends to move.

- **Initial pricing:** Research suggests that auction items should start out with low initial bid prices in order to encourage more bidders to bid (see "Bid increments" below). The lower the price, the larger the number of bidders will appear. The larger the number of bidders, the higher the prices move.

- **Bid increments:** It is generally safest to keep bid increments low so as to increase the number of bidders and the frequency of their bids. If bidders can be convinced that, for just a few more dollars, they can win the auction, then they will tend to make the higher bid and forget about the total amount they are bidding.

- **Auction length:** In general, the longer auctions are scheduled, the larger the number of bidders and the higher the prices can go. However, once the new bid arrival rate drops off and approaches zero, bid prices stabilize. Most eBay auctions are scheduled for three days.

- **Number of items:** When a business has a number of items to sell, buyers usually expect a "volume discount," and this expectation can cause lower bids in return. Therefore, sellers should consider breaking up very large bundles into smaller bundles auctioned at different times.

- **Price allocation rule:** Most buyers believe it is "fair" that everyone pay the same price in a multi-unit auction, and a uniform pricing rule is recommended. EBay Dutch Internet auctions encourage this expectation. The idea that some buyers should pay more based on their differential need for the product is not widely supported. Therefore, sellers who want to price discriminate should do so by holding auctions for the same goods on different auction markets, or at different times, to prevent direct price comparison.

- **Closed vs. open bidding:** Closed bidding has many advantages for the seller, and sellers should use this approach whenever possible because it permits price discrimination without offending buyers. However, open bidding carries the advantage of "herd effects" and "winning effects" (described later in the chapter) in which consumers' competitive instincts to "win" drive prices higher than even secret bidding would achieve.

## SELLER AND CONSUMER BEHAVIOR AT AUCTIONS

In addition to these structural considerations, you should also consider the behavior of consumers at auction sites. Research on consumer behavior at online auction sites is growing, but is still in its infancy. However, early research has produced some interesting findings.

### Seller Profits: Arrival Rate, Auction Length, and Number of Units

The profit to the seller is a function of the arrival rate, auction length, and the number of units for auction. However, each of these relationships suffers a declining return to scale and rapidly falls off after an optimal point is reached (Vakrat and Seidman, 1998, 1999) (see **Figure 11.4**). For this reason, in real-world auctions on eBay, sellers with a large number of units to sell, say, hundreds of PC laptops, usually have multiple concurrent auctions with about 10 units for sale in each auction, with a duration of three days. The auction is just long enough to attract most of the likely bidders, but not so long as to run up the cost of posting the auction beyond a profitable level. The more popular an auction (the more bidders who arrive), the longer an auction should be, up to the point where the costs of maintaining the auction listing outweigh the additional profit brought by the last bidder. These dynamics suggest a kind of bidding frenzy for popular items, in which the prices bid depend on the number of bidders, length of time, and units offered.

### Auction Prices: Are They the Lowest?

It is widely assumed that auction prices are lower than prices in other fixed-price markets. Empirical evidence is mixed on this assumption. Vakrat and Seidmann (1999) found auction prices were 25% lower on average than prices for the identical goods found in catalogs produced by the same retailers. Brynjolfsson and (2000) also found that auction prices for CDs were lower than online store prices. Lee found, however, that auction prices for used cars in Japan on the AUCNET auction site were actually higher than fixed-price markets, in part because the quality of cars on the auction site was higher than cars found in car lots (Lee et al., 1999–2000).

There are many reasons why auction prices might be higher than those in fixed-price markets for items of identical quality, and why auction prices in one

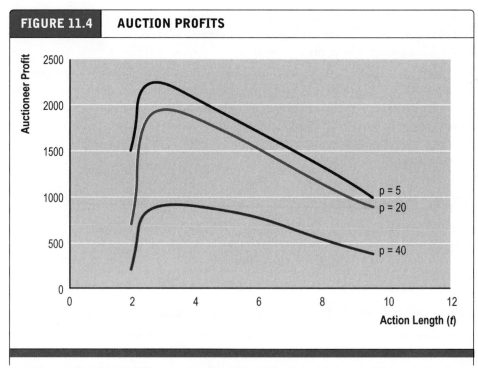

**FIGURE 11.4** | **AUCTION PROFITS**

An auction's profit is determined by the arrival rate at the auction (p), and the length of the auction (t). Profitability rises rapidly at first, but then falls off rapidly as costs rise. Profits also rise with the number of units auctioned up to a maximum point, and then fall off rapidly.

SOURCE: Based on data from Vakrat and Seidmann, 1998.

auction market may be higher than those in other auction markets. A considerable body of research has shown that consumers are not driven solely by value maximization, but instead are influenced by many situational factors, irrelevant and wrong information, and misperceptions when they make market decisions (Simonson and Tversky, 1992). Auctions are social events—shared social environments, where bidders adjust to one another (Hanson and Putler, 1996). Briefly, bidders base their bids on what others previously bid, and this can lead to an upward cascading effect (Arkes and Hutzel, 2000). In a study of hundreds of eBay auctions for Sony PlayStations, CD players, Mexican pottery, and Italian silk ties, Dholakia and Soltysinski (2001) found that bidders exhibited **herd behavior** (the tendency to gravitate toward, and bid for, auction listings with one or more existing bids) by making multiple bids on some auctions (coveted comparables), and making no bids at auctions for comparable items (overlooked comparables). Herd behavior was lower for products where there was more agreement and more objective clues on the value of the products—Sony PlayStations, for instance, compared to Italian silk ties. Herd behavior resulted in consumers paying higher prices than necessary for reasons having no foundation in economic reality.

The behavioral reality of participating in auctions can produce many unintended results. Winners can suffer **winner's regret**, the feeling after winning

**herd behavior**

the tendency to gravitate toward, and bid for, auction listings with one or more existing bids

**winner's regret**

the winner's feeling after an auction that he or she paid too much for an item

an auction that they paid too much for an item, which indicates that their winning bid does not reflect what they thought the item was worth but rather what the second bidder thought the item was worth. Sellers can experience **seller's lament**, reflecting the fact that they sold an item at a price just above the second place bidder, never knowing how much the ultimate winner might have paid or the true value to the final winner. Auction losers can experience **loser's lament**, the feeling of having been too cheap in bidding and failing to win. In summary, auctions can lead to both winners paying too much and sellers receiving too little. Both of these outcomes can be minimized when sellers and buyers have a very clear understanding of the prices for items in a variety of different online and offline markets.

The *Insight on Society* story, *Swoopo: Online Auction or Game of Chance?* discusses an online auction site whose business model is designed to exploit some of the behavioral economics associated with online auctions.

## Consumer Trust in Auctions

Auction sites have the same difficulties creating a sense of consumer trust as all other e-commerce Web sites, although in the case of auction sites, the operators of the marketplace do not directly control the quality of goods being offered and cannot directly vouch for the integrity of customers. This opens the possibility for criminal actors to appear as either sellers or buyers. EBay is the single largest source of consumer fraud on the Internet. Several studies have found that trust and credibility increase as users gain more experience, if trusted third-party seals are present, and if the site has a wide variety of consumer services for tracking purchases (or fraud), thus giving the user a sense of control (Krishnamurthy, 2001; Stanford-Makovsky, 2002; Nikander and Karnonen, 2002; Bailey, et al., 2002; Kollock, 1999). Because of the powerful role that trust plays in online consumer behavior, eBay and most auction sites make considerable efforts to develop automated trust-enhancing mechanisms such as seller and buyer ratings, escrow services, and authenticity guarantees (see the next section).

## WHEN AUCTION MARKETS FAIL: FRAUD AND ABUSE IN AUCTIONS

Markets fail to produce socially desirable outcomes (maximizing consumer welfare) in four situations: information asymmetry, monopoly power, public goods, and externalities.

Online and offline auction markets are particularly prone to fraud, which produces information asymmetries between sellers and buyers and among buyers, which in turn causes auction markets to fail. According to the Internet Crime Complaint Center (IC3), Internet auction fraud was the fourth most reported offense, generating over 10% of all complaints (National White Collar Crime Center/FBI, 2010). The median loss was $610, and the most common fraudulent payment mechanisms were money orders and credit cards. Internet auction fraud was 6th on the Federal Trade Commission (FTC)'s list of top consumer complaints for 2009, with over 57000 complaints (about 4%) (Federal Trade Commission, 2010). However, this data fails to measure the overall extent of auction fraud because many consumers do not

**seller's lament**
concern that one will never know how much the ultimate winner might have paid, or the true value to the final winner

**loser's lament**
the feeling of having been too cheap in bidding and failing to win

# INSIGHT ON SOCIETY

## SWOOPO: ONLINE AUCTION OR GAME OF CHANCE?

When reporters, bloggers, and others write about Swoopo, they use words like "addictive" and "insidious." They compare it to crack cocaine. Some question whether it's really an online auction site, or just a gambling site using the auctions as a ruse. And others wonder if it's even legal in the United States to operate a site with Swoopo's rules. Swoopo, founded in Germany in 2005 and originally called Telebid, bills itself as an online auction Web site that provides "a fun and exciting model for the next generation of online auctions." That sounds good. Except that no matter how much "skill" a bidder has, there is no way to influence the outcome of an individual auction. And it costs money to bid—that sounds like betting.

How does the site work? On Swoopo, registered bidders compete to purchase merchandise, primarily but not exclusively electronics, at greatly discounted prices. Unlike eBay, Swoopo uses a B2C model, offering the merchandise directly to consumers, not acting as a middleman for consumers to sell their products to other consumers. Hundreds of items are auctioned simultaneously. Some are localized or U.S. only, others are open to registered bidders anywhere in the world.

In a Swoopo auction, the item is initially offered at a very low price, which goes up in small increments, typically $.12 per bid, but sometimes as little as $.01. Registered bidders pay $.60 for every bid they make. And here's the kicker—every time a bid is made, the auction clock is reset by adding time, usually 20 seconds. So unlike eBay, no one can come in at the last second, make a big bid, and "swipe" the item.

When bidders register on Swoopo, they purchase BidPacks in increments of 40, 75, 150, 400, or 1,000 at a cost of 60 cents per bid. Then they can start "shopping." Bidders can also use BidButler, an automated tool that allows the bidder to set a minimum bid and a maximum bid and let BidButler take care of the rest. That way the bidder doesn't have to stay on the Swoopo site and follow the live auction.

The Web site's FAQ page offers advice about how to bid and pitfalls to avoid. The language implies that there are "strategies" that will increase the odds of "winning" a particular item. But bidders can do nothing to increase their odds of winning, and at $.60 a bid, the company, like the "house" in Las Vegas or Atlantic City, is the one making the money. In order to further the illusion that users can win many items in a short period of time, Swoopo limits registered users to "winning" a maximum of eight items in a 28-day period.

Here's a concrete example. Recently, a MacBook Pro sold on Swoopo for $35.86. Its suggested retail price is $1,799, so it sounds like a pretty good deal. It's particularly good for Swoopo. In this auction, each bid raised the price by $.01 increments, so there were 3,568 bids made. Before selling the computer, Swoopo took in $2,151 in bid fees. The winner bid more than 750 times, paying $469.80 in fees. So the winner did pretty well, but losers may spend hundreds of dollars in bidding fees before walking away empty-handed. Swoopo does offer bidders the option to "Swoop it Now," or buy the same item offered in an auction for the full price (minus the amount that person has already spent on bids) while the auction is still going on.

Swoopo combines elements of gambling, game theory, behavioral economics, and science to create a site that some consumers will find addictive. By adding 20 seconds to the clock every time a bid is made, Swoopo creates the impression that an auction is about to end, although it may go on for hours more. But poten-

(continued)

tial bidders get the sense that time is running out, so they keep bidding to make sure they don't lose the item at the last minute. And after making multiple bids, people begin to operate on the theory of "sunk cost," feeling like they've already spent a certain amount of money and all they need to do is spend a little more to win the item. However, that is not the case. As long as the auction is still running, the money a bidder has spent in the past has nothing do with winning the item or even improving the chances of winning. Spending more money gets bidders no closer to their goal. Under this fallacy of the sunk cost, Swoopo efficiently gets people to make bad choices.

Further, there's an urge to believe that there are strategies that will beat the system. But there are none. In fact, the bigger and more popular Swoopo gets, the harder it will be to win because more people will bid for each item. It's like the lottery. You can't win if you don't play, but buying more tickets doesn't increase the chance of winning, since you can't control the number of tickets other people buy.

There's also something called the jackpot effect that comes into play on Swoopo. When bidders fixate on the "big prize," they forget the incremental costs of participation. It works like a slot machine, but with Swoopo the other bidders are the random number generators. The home page even looks like a slot machine, with six live auctions counting down all the time. And the site uses all kinds of language to make it sound like users have some control—they do not.

Even the science of how the brain functions comes into play with Swoopo. Research has shown that people don't need to win to get the dopamine boost that comes with winning. They just need to think they're close to winning—that if they keep at it the reward will come. And even when they lose, or have what they perceive as a "near miss" experience, it feels awful, yet it provides the illusion of control. People think a near miss means they are more likely to win the next time, even though the reality is that the odds don't bear this out.

As of 2010, Swoopo had 2.5 million registered users. Its revenue has doubled every year since its founding, despite the fact that CEO Frank Han claims to lose money on 65% of the auctions. The losses are usually on the smaller-ticket items like DVDs, while the company makes money on bigger-ticket items like the MacBook Pro. In the spring of 2009, Swoopo announced that August Capital, a U.S.-based venture capital firm, was investing $10 million to help the company expand worldwide.

Swoopo is not the only e-commerce company in this business. As Swoopo grows in size, many bidders are flocking to smaller sites such as Bid-Cactus, RockyBid, and other Swoopo "clones," which are sites generated by complex scripts featuring the basic functionality of Swoopo auctions. Many of Swoopo's competitors use devious practices such as using bots to increase auction values and failing to send items that its users win. As a result, Swoopo's image and bottom line have suffered, and there has been upheaval at the company: former CEO Gunnar Piening left the company in late 2009, and his successor, Ralph Werner, also departed just 8 months later in 2010.

Finally, in addition to the behavioral questions, there are legal questions regarding the Swoopo's payment-per-bid system. States don't specifically allow this kind of system, but they don't specifically prohibit it either. No lawsuits have been filed yet, so for now, the question of whether bidding on items on Swoopo is really gambling and not participating in an online auction remains an open one.

**SOURCES:** "New Swoopo CEO Campaigns Against Copycats," by Liz Gannes, GigaOm.com, April 8, 2010; "Swoopo Loses Another CEO," by Jochen Krisch, ExcitingCommerce.com, March 2010; "Swoopo! Do Penny Auction Sites Run Afoul of California Gambling Laws?" by David Johnson, Digitalmedi-allawyerblog.com, August 18, 2009; "Sites Ask Users to Spend to Save," by Brad Stone, New York Times, August 16, 2009; "This Company is Inside Your Head," by John Rosevear, Fool.com, August 14, 2009; "At Swoopo, Shopping's Steep Spiral into Addiction," by Mark Gimein, Washingtonpost.com, July 12, 2009; "Swoopo: The Frontal Cortex," by Jonah Lehrer, Scienceblogs.com, July 10, 2009; "August Capital Helps Fund Online Shopping Site Swoopo," Silicon Valley/San Jose Business Journal, April 2, 2009.

report being defrauded to the FTC. **Table 11.8** lists the most common and important frauds.

eBay and many other auction sites have investigation units that receive complaints from consumers and investigate reported abuses. Nevertheless, with millions of visitors per week and hundreds of thousands of auctions to monitor, eBay is highly dependent on the good faith of sellers and consumers to follow the rules.

## 11.3  E-COMMERCE PORTALS

*Port: From the Latin porta, an entrance or gateway to a locality.*

Portals are the most frequently visited sites on the Web if only because they typically are the first page to which many users point their browser on startup. The top portals such as Yahoo, MSN, Facebook, and AOL have hundreds of millions of unique visitors worldwide each month. Web portal sites are gateways to the more than 100 billion Web pages available on the Internet. Perhaps the most important service provided by portals is that of helping people find the information they are looking for on the Web. The original portals in the early days of e-commerce were search engines. Consumers would pass through search engine portals on their way to rich, detailed, in-depth content on the Web. But portals have evolved into much more complex Web sites that provide news, entertainment, maps, images, social networks, in-depth information, and education on a growing variety of topics all contained at the portal site. Portals today seek to be a sticky destination site, not merely a gateway through which visitors pass. In this respect, Web portals are very much like television networks: destination sites for content supported by advertising revenues. Portals today want visitors to stay a long time—the longer the better. For the most part they succeed: portals are places where people linger for a long time.

**enterprise portals**
help employees navigate to the enterprise's human resource and corporate content

Portals also serve important functions within a business or organization. Most corporations, universities, churches, and other formal organizations have **enterprise portals** that help employees or members navigate to important content, such as human resources information, corporate news, or organizational announcements. For instance, your university has a portal through which you can register for courses, find out classroom assignments, and perform a host of other important student activities. Increasingly, these enterprise portals also provide general-purpose news and financial real-time feeds provided by content providers outside the organization, such as MSNBC News and generalized Web search capabilities. Corporate portals and intranets are the subject of other textbooks focused on the corporate uses of Web technology and are beyond the scope of this book (see Laudon and Laudon, 2011). Our focus here will be on e-commerce portals.

## THE GROWTH AND EVOLUTION OF PORTALS

Web portals have changed a great deal from their initial function and role. As noted above, most of today's well-known portals began as search engines. The initial

| TABLE 11.8 | TYPES OF AUCTION FRAUDS |
|---|---|
| **TYPE OF FRAUD** | **DESCRIPTION** |
| **Feedback Offenses** | |
| Shill feedback | Using secondary IDs or other auction site members to inflate seller ratings |
| Feedback abuse | Any abuse of the feedback forum |
| Feedback extortion | Threatening negative feedback in return for a benefit |
| Feedback solicitation | Offering to sell, trade, or buy feedback |
| **Buying Offenses** | |
| Transaction interference | E-mailing buyers to warn them away from a seller |
| Invalid bid retraction | Using the retraction option to make high bids, discovering the maximum bid of current high bidder, then retracting bid |
| Persistent bidding | Persisting in making bids despite a warning that bids are not welcome |
| Unwelcome buyer | Buying in violation of seller's terms |
| Bid shielding | Using secondary user IDs or other members to artificially raise the bidding price of an item |
| Nonpayment after buying | Blocking legitimate buyers by bidding high, then not paying |
| **Selling Offenses** | |
| Shill bidding | Using secondary user IDs or bidders who have no actual intention to buy to artificially raise the price of an item |
| Seller nonperformance | Accepting payment and failing to deliver the promised goods, either at all, or delivering goods not as described in auction (counterfeit or poor quality) |
| Nonselling seller | Refusing payment, failure to deliver after a successful auction |
| Fee avoidance | Any of a variety of mechanisms for avoiding paying listing fees |
| Transaction interception | Pretending you are a seller and accepting payment |
| **Contact Information/Identity Offenses** | |
| Misrepresentation of identity | Claiming to be an employee of the auction site; representing oneself as another auction site member |
| False or missing contact information | Providing false information or leaving information out |
| Dead/invalid e-mail addresses | Providing false contact information |
| Underage user | User under 18 |
| **Miscellaneous Offenses** | |
| Interference with site | Using any software program that would interfere with auction site operations |
| Bid siphoning | E-mailing another seller's bidders and offering the same product for less |
| Sending spam | Sending unsolicited offers to bidders |

function provided by portals such as Yahoo, Lycos, Excite, AltaVista, Ask Jeeves, and later Google was to index Web page content and make this content available to users in a convenient form. Early portals expected visitors to stay only a few minutes at the site. As millions of people signed on to the Internet in the late 1990s, the number of visitors to basic search engine sites exploded commensurately. At first, few people understood how a Web search site could make money by passing customers on to other destinations. But search sites attracted huge audiences, and therein lay the foundation for their success as vehicles for marketing and advertising. Search sites, recognizing the potential for commerce, expanded their offerings from simple navigation to include commerce (the sale of items directly from the Web site as well as advertising for other retail sites), content (in the form of news at first, and later in the form of weather, investments, games, health, and other subject matter), and distribution of others' content. These three characteristics have become the basic definition of portal sites, namely, sites that provide three functions: navigation of the Web, commerce, and content.

Because the value of portals to advertisers and content owners is largely a function of the size of the audience each portal reaches, portals compete with one another on reach and unique visitors. *Reach* is defined as the percentage of the Web audience that visits the site in a month (or some other time period), and *unique visitors* is defined as the number of uniquely identified individuals who visit in a month. Portals are inevitably subject to network effects: The value of the portal to advertisers and consumers increases geometrically as reach increases, which, in turn, attracts still more customers. These effects have resulted in the differentiation of the portal marketspace into three tiers: a few general-purpose mega portal sites that garner 60%–80% of the Web audience, second-tier general-purpose sites that hover around 20%–30% reach, and third-tier specialized vertical market portals that attract 2%–10% of the audience. As described in Chapter 3, the top five portals/search engines (Google, Yahoo, MSN/Bing, AOL, and Ask.com) account for over 95% of online searches. A similar pattern of concentration is observed when considering the audience share of portals/search engines as illustrated in **Figure 11.5** (see page 746). However this picture is changing as large audiences move to social network sites, and millions of users make these sites their opening or home pages.

For more insight into the nature of the competition and change among the top portals, read *Insight on Business: The Transformation of AOL.*

## TYPES OF PORTALS: GENERAL-PURPOSE AND VERTICAL MARKET

**general-purpose portals**

attempt to attract a very large general audience and then retain the audience on-site by providing in-depth vertical content

There are two primary types of portals: general-purpose portals and vertical market portals. **General-purpose portals** attempt to attract a very large general audience and then retain the audience on-site by providing in-depth vertical content channels, such as information on news, finance, autos, movies, and weather.. General-purpose portals typically offer Web search engines, free e-mail, personal home pages, chat rooms, community building software, and bulletin boards. Vertical content channels on general-purpose portal sites offer content such as sports scores, stock tickers, health tips, instant messaging, automobile information, and auctions.

# INSIGHT ON BUSINESS

## THE TRANSFORMATION OF AOL

AOL began its life in the early 1980s as Control Video Corporation, providing an online service called Gameline for the Atari 2600 video game console. For $1 a game, subscribers could temporarily download games, keep track of high scores, and play the downloaded game until they downloaded another one. The company didn't make enough money, and in May 1983, it was reorganized as Quantum Computer Services, providing a dedicated online service for Commodore 64 and 128 computers called Quantum Link. In 1988, the company added online services called Apple Link and PC Link, and in 1989, its name was changed to America Online.

In February 1991, AOL launched an online program for the DOS operating system (the early Microsoft operating system that used text commands) and one for Windows the following year. AOL positioned itself as the online service for people who were not familiar with computers. This was in contrast to CompuServe, which served the technical community. Positioning AOL as the company for those who weren't comfortable with technology was very effective initially, but as broadband connections became widespread, and users more sophisticated, over time AOL suffered because it was perceived as stodgy, slow, and uncool.

AOL provided proprietary software, and enabled communication among users through chat rooms. The company charged users hefty hourly fees, but in 1996, AOL switched over to a subscription-based model, charging $19.99 per month. AOL's user base grew to 10 million people. AOL distributed its program by sending millions of CD-ROMs in the mail to potential adopters. Its popularity was based on its ease of use and brand exposure—AOL was everywhere. Many users got their first exposure to the Web, e-mail, instant messaging, and chat rooms through their AOL memberships. The interface was user-friendly. However, from early on, there were complaints about dropped connections and busy signals, and the company was slow to provide access to the open Internet for its subscribers. But it continued to grow. In 1996, in another boon to its brand, AOL signed a five-year agreement that it would be bundled with Windows on new PCs. The first major Web portal for the general public was on its way.

In 1999, CEO Steve Case said that Windows was in the past, and predicted that AOL would be the next Microsoft. This is not exactly how the story unfolded. While AOL grew to be the number one supplier of dial-up Internet connections for millions of Americans, when the company tried to exploit the tremendous name recognition and prominence of the brand, it failed over and over again. Its biggest failure, though not its only one, was not anticipating the impact that broadband would have on the way that people would choose to access the Internet. But that's getting ahead of the story.

In 2000, before the company's spectacular fall began, Time Warner bought AOL for $165 billion. Despite the media fanfare, there were problems with the merger from the start. It is now known as perhaps the largest single investment error in the history of the Web. On the announcement of the purchase, high-flying AOL stock dropped sharply due to fears that Time Warner's old media assets would drag AOL down. After all, Time Warner was an "old" media company that supposedly had little to offer the Internet and Web, and had no Web assets or experience. In the

(continued)

first year after the purchase, the merged company already had difficulty reaching growth targets, possibly because AOL had improperly inflated its pre-merger revenue. In 2002, advertising revenue declined sharply. The number of AOL ISP subscribers peaked in the fall of that year, at 26.7 million, and has been declining ever since. Today there are 4.4 million ISP subscribers, and they are dropping off steadily at the rate of 200,000 per month.

There are those who believe it didn't have to turn out that way. The merging of one of the foremost providers of "old fashioned" content with one of the largest distributors of "online" content might have made sense if it had been managed differently. But it wasn't.

With very few people involved in the deal, senior staff at both companies didn't feel like they had a stake in the success of the merged entity. Key players at Time Warner resented the merger, and thought it was a waste of time and money. To make matters worse, corporate leadership did little to persuade brand/division heads that it was their responsibility to make the merged company work. Time Warner executives feared the AOL team would try to take over the company and force them out so they refused to collaborate. Remarkably, Time Warner's top content providers, including CNN, HBO, Fortune, and Sports Illustrated, put their content almost anywhere on the Web except AOL.

Then came broadband. For most of its history, AOL users were forced to stay on the AOL platform because there were few higher bandwidth alternatives. The company unfortunately underestimated how attractive broadband would become. By 2004, people were rapidly embracing broadband. At the same time, Google's search engine advertising took off and banner advertising on the site took off with it. Yahoo was successful with banner display ads, and they added content that drew the broadband audience. AOL/Time Warner had plenty of content available, including news, text, magazines, and skilled writers and producers, but they were unable to bring it to the Web. Quickly, AOL began to look like a brand that was not sophisticated and not in tune with the times. Even when AOL made its subscriber-only content freely available, it was too little, too late.

By 2006, AOL abandoned marketing its access services to concentrate on free Web sites. The CEO was fired, and replaced by an NBC executive who didn't have an Internet background, ushering in a tumultuous era with three CEOs and five VPs of marketing in a three-year period.

In 2007, AOL began pursuing a new strategy of creating several different brands. In 2008, Time Warner was in ongoing talks to sell AOL to Microsoft or Google. In 2009, Time Warner decided instead to spin off the company. Before doing that, they bought back Google's 5% stake in the company for $283 million. Google had paid $1 billion for that stake in 2005.

The third CEO in three years, Tim Armstrong, came on board in 2009. He added senior staff members from Google and Yahoo. Armstrong has focused on turning the company into the biggest creator of premium content on the Web and the largest seller of online display ads. He describes AOL as "a small little company that has gone through some challenging times that is trying to find a way to come up with ideas that will connect with an audience."

He had his work cut out for him. In 2009, AOL's revenue was $3.2 billion, down 37% in two years. The company's market value is clearly well below its $20 billion valuation in 2005. Current estimates are closer to $5.7 billion, less than 30% of the 2005 number, and a small fraction of the $165 billion purchase price in 2000. In the short term, Armstrong has announced that AOL

(continued)

will not abandon its ISP subscriber business, which, despite its slow contraction, still provides valuable revenue for the company.

You can see AOL's new strategy in place at AOL's corporate headquarters in New York City, where 300 staff members (there are 7,000 staffers worldwide) work full-time producing content. Many of these are new employees recently laid off by "old" media such as magazines and newspapers. They are joined by freelancers and programmers all over the world, who are cranking out copy and editing photos, and posting all of it to more than 80 AOL-owned Web sites, 10 of them ranked in Technorati's top 100. The shrinking newspaper and magazine industries have helped AOL to hire top talent from publications such as the *New York Times, Washington Post, USA Today, Time* and *Newsweek* to write this content. Finally, AOL is focusing on content and digital distribution platforms like Web sites and blogs. The company is trying to cultivate the feeling of a start-up company, casting its transition as a "start-around."

There is some evidence that the start-around may work. AOL launched the Web site Politics Daily in April 2009, and the site already averages around 3 million unique visitors per month. Politico, a much more established name, averages only 2.85 million. In aggregate, the media properties of AOL, sites such as Engadget, TMZ, and FanHouse, have 107 million unique visitors per month. This audience is monetized through display advertising. Many of these sites are not visibly AOL properties. Armstrong says that's just smart business. Disney, he points out, owns ABC and ESPN, but doesn't make that obvious to TV watchers on a daily basis. If sites are to be seen as authentic, they can't be seen as a product of an unimaginative conglomerate. Another part of the strategy involved focusing on local experiences and content, including providing self-service applications for consumers and advertisers. So AOL will build local networks with local services.

Armstrong says local advertising is a prime area for innovation and that AOL already has a significant audience. He adds that local advertising accounts for 39% of all advertising dollars spent annually in the United States.

In 2010, AOL announced several more purchases that illustrated this strategy, including TechCrunch, 5Min, and Thing Labs. TechCrunch, one of the most popular tech blogs on the Internet, has 3.8 million unique monthly U.S. visitors, and makes $10 million a year in revenue. 5Min features instructional, knowledge, and lifestyle videos, and Thing Labs is a Web-based software company specializing in social media applications. The moves continued a trend of bolstering its in-house content creation with outside acquisitions.

AOL's strategy to focus on content and advertising is risky. The company still makes 40% of its revenue from its dwindling dial-up subscriptions, and it's unclear whether or not they'll be able to recoup that money via content creation. Content is expensive, and the banner ad supply inventory is huge. The price charged for banner ads is exceptionally low because they don't work well compared to search ads, and they are not considered culturally hip. But then again, neither is Yahoo, and millions of people have Yahoo as their home page, use Yahoo e-mail, and read its news and celebrity content.

The vertical blogs AOL is creating and acquiring attract a committed, dedicated audience that will respond to targeted ads at a much higher rate than generic portal content such as Yahoo's. Develop a network of a thousand blogs like this, and you might have a business. How many such vertical markets like that exist? Enough to keep AOL blog creators busy and profitable: as noted, AOL's sites draw more than 100 million U.S. unique visitors per month.

Finally, while the spin-off from Time Warner is important, some believe that the recruitment of top Google and Yahoo executives

(continued)

is more important. They bring more educated analysis of consumer behavior, which can lead to better targeted advertising, more revenue, and a successful company. But as AOL's revenues continue to drop across the board, the pressure is mounting for the company to prove that their new strategy will be a success.

■ **SOURCES:** "AOL Buys TechCrunch, 5Min and Thing Labs," by Jessica E. Vascellaro and Emily Steel, *New York Times*, September 29, 2010; "AOL's New Phase and Phrase: It's a 'Start-Around'," by Brian Stelter, *New York Times*, June 8, 2010; "AOL Blossoms as Print Retreats," by David Carr, *New York Times*, August 17, 2009; "Google Dumps Investment," Venturebeat, *New York Times*, July 27, 2009; "Eleven Years of Ambition and Failure at AOL," by Saul Hansell, *New York Times*, July 24, 2009; "Daring to Dream of a Resurgent AOL," by Saul Hansell, *New York Times*, July 23, 2009; "Before Spin-off, AOL Tries for that Start-up Feeling," New York Times, July 20, 2009; "Advertising Overhaul Among Changes at AOL," by Rachel Metz, Thestreet.com, July 20, 2009.

**vertical market portals**

attempt to attract highly focused, loyal audiences with a deep interest in either community or specialized content

**Vertical market portals** (sometimes also referred to as destination sites or vortals) attempt to attract highly focused, loyal audiences with a deep interest either in community or specialized content—from sports to the weather. In addition to their focused content, vertical market portals have recently begun adding

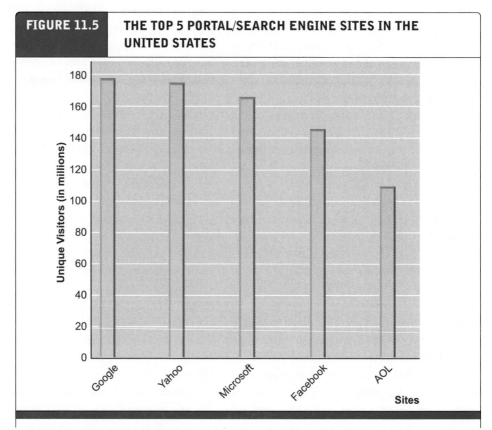

| FIGURE 11.5 | **THE TOP 5 PORTAL/SEARCH ENGINE SITES IN THE UNITED STATES** |

SOURCE: Based on data from comScore, 2010b.

many of the features found in general-purpose portals. For instance, Facebook has recently become a portal—the home page for millions of users, and a gateway to the Internet. Facebook is an affinity group portal because it is based on friendships among people. Facebook offers e-mail, search (Bing), games, and apps. News is limited.

The concentration of audience share in the portal market reflects (in addition to network effects) the limited time budget of consumers. This limited time budget works to the advantage of general-purpose portals. Consumers have a finite amount of time to spend on the Web, and as a result, most consumers visit fewer than 30 unique domains each month. Facing limited time, consumers concentrate their visits at sites that can satisfy a broad range of interests, from weather and travel information, to stocks, sports, and entertainment content.

General-purpose sites such as Yahoo try to be all things to all people, and attract a broad audience with both generalized navigation services and in-depth content and community efforts. For instance, Yahoo has become the Web's largest source of news: more people visit Yahoo News than any other news site including online newspapers. Yet recent changes in consumer behavior on the Web show that consumers are spending less time "surfing the Web" and on general browsing, and more time doing focused searches, research, and participating in social networks. These trends will advantage special-purpose, vertical market sites that can provide focused, in-depth community and content.

As a general matter, the general-purpose portals are very well-known brands, while the vertical content and affinity group portals tend to have less well-known brands. **Figure 11.6** lists examples of general-purpose portals and the two main types of vertical market portals.

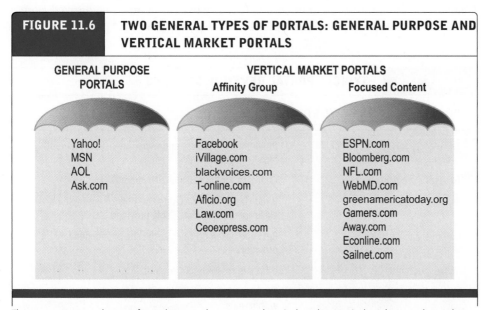

| FIGURE 11.6 | TWO GENERAL TYPES OF PORTALS: GENERAL PURPOSE AND VERTICAL MARKET PORTALS |

| GENERAL PURPOSE PORTALS | VERTICAL MARKET PORTALS | |
| --- | --- | --- |
| | Affinity Group | Focused Content |
| Yahoo! | Facebook | ESPN.com |
| MSN | iVillage.com | Bloomberg.com |
| AOL | blackvoices.com | NFL.com |
| Ask.com | T-online.com | WebMD.com |
| | Aflcio.org | greenamericatoday.org |
| | Law.com | Gamers.com |
| | Ceoexpress.com | Away.com |
| | | Econline.com |
| | | Sailnet.com |

There are two general types of portals: general-purpose and vertical market. Vertical market portals may be based on affinity groups or on focused content.

## PORTAL BUSINESS MODELS

Portals receive income from a number of different sources. The revenue base of portals is changing and dynamic, with some of the largest sources of revenue declining. **Table 11.9** summarizes the major portal revenue sources.

ISP services revenue represents a declining part of the revenue base for portal sites, although for AOL, for instance, it still generates a significant amount of revenue. More and more Americans have switched to broadband connections provided by giant telephone and cable companies. The business strategies of both general-purpose and vertical portals have changed greatly because of the rapid growth in search engine advertising and intelligent ad placement networks such as Google's AdSense, which can place ads on thousands of Web sites based on the content of the Web site. General portal sites such as AOL, MSN, and Yahoo did not have well-developed search engines, and hence have not grown as fast as Google, which has a powerful search engine. Portal sites have invested billions of dollars to catch up with Google. On the other hand, general portals have content, which Google did not originally have, although it added to its content by purchasing YouTube, and adding Google sites devoted to news, financial information, images, and maps. Yahoo and MSN visitors stay on-site a long time reading news, content, and sending e-mail. Facebook users stay on site and linger three times as long as visitors to traditional portals like Yahoo. For this reason social network sites, Facebook in particular, are direct competitors of Yahoo, Google, and the other portals. General portals are attempting to provide more premium content focused on sub-communities of their portal audience. Advertisers on portals are especially interested in focused, revenue-producing premium content available on Web portals because it attracts a more committed audience.

For instance, financial service firms pay premium advertising rates to advertise on portal finance service areas such as Yahoo's Finance pages. As noted in Chapters 6 and 7, there is a direct relationship between the revenue derived from a customer and the focus of the customer segment (see **Figure 11.7**).

| TABLE 11.9 | **TYPICAL PORTAL REVENUE SOURCES** |
|---|---|
| PORTAL REVENUE SOURCE | DESCRIPTION |
| ISP services | Providing Web access and e-mail services for a monthly fee |
| General advertising | Charging for impressions delivered |
| Tenancy deals | Fixed charge for guaranteed number of impressions, exclusive partnerships, "sole providers" |
| Commissions on sales | Revenue based on sales at the site by independent providers |
| Subscription fees | Charging for premium content |
| Applications and games | Games and apps are sold to users; advertising is placed within apps |

| FIGURE 11.7 | **REVENUE PER CUSTOMER AND MARKET FOCUS** |
|---|---|

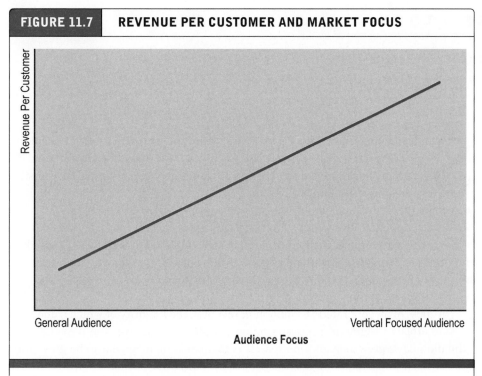

The more focused and targeted the audience, the more revenue that can be derived per customer for an appropriately targeted product or service.

The survival strategy for general-purpose portals in the future is therefore to develop deep, rich, vertical content in order to reach customers at the site. The strategy for much smaller vertical market portals is to put together a collection of vertical portals to form a vertical portal network, a collection of deep, rich content sites. The strategy for search engine sites such as Google is to obtain more content to attract users for a long time and expose them to more ad pages (or screens).

# eBay:
## Is the Party Over?

S ince its inception, eBay has been synonymous with Internet auctions. The company has been the first and by far the most successful Internet auction business, mushrooming into a gigantic electronic marketplace hosting over 25 million sellers all over the world. Founded in 1995 by Pierre Omidyar and originally known as AuctionWeb, eBay has come a long way from its first sale, a broken laser pointer. The company now sells a staggeringly diverse array of goods and is one of the world's most easily recognizable and well-known Web sites. Hundreds of thousands of people support themselves by selling on eBay, and many millions more use eBay to supplement their income. During the holiday season, eBay is often the most visited site on the Web.

In 2009, eBay generated $8.7 billion in revenue, the majority of which came from its Marketplaces segment, representing only a 2% increase over the previous year. Why did eBay's growth stall? One reason is that consumers appear to be gravitating toward fixed-price retailers, such as Amazon, which has sustained steady growth despite the economic downturn. For many buyers, the novelty of online auctions has worn off, and these buyers have returned to the easier and simpler method of buying fixed-price goods. Search engines and comparison-shopping sites have also taken

away some of eBay's auction business by making items easier to find on other Web sites. As it turns out, many do not want to wait for an auction to conclude, and just want to buy the product.

In response, eBay's leadership has begun taking the necessary steps to meet the shift in demand by consumers from auctions to fixed-price goods. The company unveiled a three-year revival plan in which the overall goal was to create a comprehensive array of marketplaces located in one central online location. Bidding on auctions, clicking on ads, scanning classifieds, and making outright purchases will all be possible from the flagship eBay site and its affiliates.

CEO John Donahoe wants to focus eBay's business on the "secondary market," which includes overstock and out-of-season items as well as the used and antique items that eBay has been known for. He wants the eBay buying experience to emulate that of a low-price bulk retailer such as Costco, where "the inventory is somewhat fluid, but everything they've got is a great deal." He's also going after Overstock.com, which has done exceptionally well selling overstocked and discontinued items. To that end, Donahoe is trying to move eBay away from auctions toward fixed-price listings. Although this move has appealed to investors, it angered many of the smaller sellers of unique goods that have in the past come to symbolize the company's success. Some longtime sellers chose to move their business elsewhere.

eBay has traditionally derived the bulk of its revenue from fees and commissions associated with its sales transactions. A portion of eBay's revenue comes from direct advertising on the site, and some comes from end-to-end service providers such as PayPal (also owned by eBay), which increase the ease and speed of eBay transactions. The site imposes several types of fees on sellers, including posting fees for listing items as well as a collection fee on sold items. Traditionally, eBay was seen as a favorable proposition for smaller sellers to find markets for rare goods, or goods that are otherwise difficult to value.

In order to provide more incentive for bulk sellers of fixed-price goods to post their items on the site, eBay significantly adjusted its fee structure as part of its revival plan. The company reduced posting fees for adding an item online and increased the collection fee for sold items. For example, the fee to list a $25 auction item dropped to $1.00 from $1.20, but eBay's sales commission on the same item rose from 5.75% to 8.75%. In August 2008, eBay lowered its listing fees for all sellers offering fixed-priced items under its Buy It Now format. EBay's managers apparently believe that sellers are very sensitive to high listing fees, which are highly visible to sellers, and less sensitive to sales commissions. Lowering the fees on the front end, and raising them on the back end, is one way to maximize eBay revenue.

For bulk sellers, this was a boon. Prior to the change, posting large quantities of items was an expensive undertaking, because only a fraction of those posted items actually sold. Paying these posting fees represented the bulk of their expenditures. But for smaller sellers of unique, expensive items, increasing the percentages of collection fees meant that they would make significantly less per sale.

EBay also adjusted its search ordering system so that highly rated merchants appear first and receive more exposure. Previously, the first items to be displayed were those for which an auction was about to end. EBay's new search system uses a complicated formula that takes into account an item's price and how well that item's seller ranks in customer satisfaction. At first glance, this adjustment doesn't benefit any particular group of sellers more than the rest. But eBay also rolled out a rating system that made acquiring a high rating a much more time-consuming undertaking, favoring larger sellers with the time and energy to build a favorable rating. The company also removed the ability of sellers to assign negative ratings to buyers, a feature which many sellers felt protected them against late or non-payment on the part of buyers. The company's reasoning for this change was to stop sellers from rating buyers poorly as revenge for poor customer satisfaction ratings. Smaller sellers were incensed, claiming that the company was unnecessarily mistreating the group that spurred them to market dominance.

Not long ago, eBay's growth strategy focused on expansion in geography and scope and on continuing innovation to enhance the variety and appeal of products on its sites. eBay has always been active in developing and acquiring new products and services that encompass all the activities people perform on the Internet. Earlier this decade, the company fashioned a diversified portfolio of companies with a hand in each of the Internet's big cash pots: shopping, communicating, search, and entertainment. They are now realizing that some of these acquisitions were not good fits with their core business.

PayPal, whose service enables the exchange of money between individuals over the Internet, brings additional transaction-based fee revenue, and has been a significant bright spot for eBay's future prospects. eBay is banking on PayPal becoming the standard payment method for online transactions. The service already receives much of its business from payment transactions that are not associated with eBay. Management is using PayPal, whose merchant services business is expected to grow 40% in 2010, to help refocus the business and jump-start stagnant growth. In 2010, eBay's payment services (PayPal) will produce 34% of its revenues, 40% of its profits, and is growing at 26% a year. At this rate, in a few years, eBay will become a financial services company as well as a transaction platform.

In 2005, eBay acquired Shopping.com, an online shopping comparison site, and Skype Technologies, which provides a service for free or low-cost voice calls over the Internet. Markets that eBay traditionally had trouble penetrating, such as real estate, travel, new-car sales, and expensive collectibles, require more communication among buyers and sellers than eBay currently offers, and Skype provides voice communication services to help sellers and purchasers reach a price and conclude a transaction.

But in 2009, eBay sold 70% of its interest in Skype, admitting it was a mistake to acquire the company. eBay assumed that buyers and sellers would use Skype to communicate about transactions, but the feature never caught on as expected.

eBay continues to expand through acquisitions. The company acquired the ticket-reselling Web site StubHub, bought a 25% stake in classified ad site Craigslist, and purchased Kurant (now ProStores), whose technology helps users set up online stores. Some analysts report that while many of eBay's individual acquisitions appear to have been successful, they haven't created the synergy that was intended, and diversification has detracted from eBay's core business, auctions.

These analysts seem to have missed the point. eBay mangers are intentionally jettisoning the auction format despite the oppositions of thousands of eBay merchants. Donahoe regularly appears on lists of "disliked CEOs," and sellers have voiced their discontent via online forums and shareholder meetings. But Donahoe and the rest of eBay's management have maintained that hosting fixed-price sales by reliable retailers makes shopping more customer-friendly and predictable. In early 2010, Donahoe responded to the concerns of smaller merchants by eliminating posting fees for lower priced items and making an assortment of other changes to make posting items easier and cheaper in an effort to spur growth.

It's too early to tell whether these changes have paid off. On the bright side, eBay beat analysts' estimates with $2.2 billion in revenues in the second quarter of 2010, and the company is projected to have a strong holiday season this year. However, eBay's site traffic is continuing to slowly erode as consumers gravitate towards Amazon and other similar sites. EBay still has a way to go to recoup its dot-com glory days. Can the Web's most prominent online auction site change course so dramatically from the formula that made it successful?

**SOURCES:** "eBay Inc. Reports Strong Second Quarter Revenue and Earnings Growth," Market-Watch.com, July 21, 2010; "eBay Cuts Auction Fees for Sellers," by Scott Morrison, *Wall Street Journal*, January 27, 2010; "Is John Donahoe Finally Turning eBay Around?" by Kevin Kelleher, www.gigaom.com, June 14, 2009; "EBay Outlines Three-Year Revival Plan," by Peter Burrows, *Business Week*, March 12, 2009; "Auctions Fade in eBay's Bid for Growth," by Geoffrey A. Fowler, *Wall Street Journal*, May 26, 2009; "EBay Retreats in Web Retailing," by Geoffrey A. Fowler, Wall Street Journal, March 12, 2009 "EBay to Unload Skype in IPO, Citing Poor Fit," Geoffrey A. Fowler, *Wall Street Journal*, April 15, 2009.

### Case Study Questions

1. Contrast eBay's original business model with its latest proposed business model.

2. What are the problems that eBay is currently facing? How is eBay trying to solve these problems?

3. Are the solutions eBay is seeking to implement good solutions? Why or why not? Are there any other solutions that eBay should consider?

4. Who are eBay's top three competitors online, and how will eBay's new strategy help it compete? Will eBay be providing a differentiated service to customers?

## 11.5 REVIEW

## KEY CONCEPTS

■ Explain the difference between a traditional social network and an online social network.

Social networks involve:
- A group of people
- Shared social interaction
- Common ties among members
- A shared area for some period of time

By extension, an online social network is an area online where people who share common ties can interact with one another.

■ **Understand how a social network differs from a portal.**

The difference between social networks and portals has become blurred. Originally, portals began as search engines. Then they added content and eventually many community-building features such as chat rooms, bulletin boards, and free Web site design and hosting. Social network sites began as content-specific locations and added more general portal services such as Web searching, general news, weather, and travel information, as well as a wide variety of e-commerce services.

■ **Describe the different types of social networks and online communities and their business models.**

- *General communities:* Members can interact with a general audience segmented into numerous different groups. The purpose is to attract enough members to populate a wide range of topical discussion groups. Most general communities began as non-commercial subscription-based endeavors, but many have been purchased by larger community portal sites.
- *Practice networks:* Members can participate in discussion groups and get help or simply information relating to an area of shared practice, such as art, education, or medicine. These generally have a nonprofit business model in which they simply attempt to collect enough in subscription fees, sales commissions, and limited advertising to cover the cost of operations.
- *Interest-based communities:* Members can participate in focused discussion groups on a shared interest such as boats, horses, skiing, travel, or health. The advertising business model has worked because the targeted audience is attractive to marketers. Tenancy and sponsorship deals provide another similar revenue stream.
- *Affinity communities:* Members can participate in focused discussions with others who share the same affinity or group identification, such as religion, ethnicity, gender, sexual orientation, or political beliefs. The business model is a mixture of subscription revenue from premium content and services, advertising, tenancy/sponsorships, and distribution agreements.
- *Sponsored communities:* Members can participate in online communities created by government, nonprofit, or for-profit organizations for the purpose of pursuing organizational goals. These types of sites vary widely from local government sites to branded product sites. They use community technologies and techniques to distribute information or extend brand influence. The goal of a branded product site is to increase offline product sales. These sites do not seek to make a profit and in fact are often cost centers.

■ **Describe the major types of auctions, their benefits and costs, and how they operate.**

Auctions are markets where prices vary (dynamic pricing) depending on the competition among the participants who are buying or selling products or services. They can be classified broadly as C2C or B2C, although generally the term C2C auction refers to the venue in which the sale takes place, for example, a consumer-oriented Web site such as eBay, which also auctions items from established merchants. A B2C auction refers to an established online merchant that offers its own auctions. There are also numerous B2B online auctions for buyers of industrial parts, raw materials, commodities, and services. Within these three broad categories of auctions are several major auction types classified based upon how the bidding mechanisms work in each system:

- *English auctions:* A single item is up for sale from a single seller. Multiple buyers bid against one another within a specific time frame, with the highest bidder winning the object, as long as the high bid has exceeded the reserve bid set by the seller, below which he or she refuses to sell.
- *Traditional Dutch auctions:* Sellers with many identical items sold in lots list a starting price and time for the opening of bids. As the clock advances, the price for each lot falls until a buyer offers to buy at that price.
- *Dutch Internet auctions:* Sellers with many identical items for sale list a minimum price or starting bid, and buyers indicate both a bid price and a quantity desired. The lowest winning bid that clears the available quantity is paid by all winning bidders. Those with the highest bid are assured of receiving the quantity they desire, but only pay the amount of the lowest successful bid (uniform pricing rule).
- *Name Your Own Price or reverse auctions:* Buyers specify the price they are willing to pay for an item, and multiple sellers bid for their business. This is one example of discriminatory pricing in which winners may pay different amounts for the same product or service depending on how much they have bid.
- *Group buying or demand aggregation auctions:* In the group-buying format, the more users who sign on to buy an item, the lower the price for the item falls. These are generally B2B or B2G sites where small businesses can collectively receive discount prices for items that are purchased in high volumes.

Benefits of auctions include:

- *Liquidity:* Sellers and buyers are connected in a global marketplace.
- *Price discovery:* Even difficult-to-price-items can be competitively priced based on supply and demand.
- *Price transparency:* Everyone in the world can see the asking and bidding prices for items, although prices can vary from auction site to auction site.
- *Market efficiency:* Consumers are offered access to a selection of goods that would be impossible to access physically, and consumer welfare is often increased due to reduced prices.
- *Lower transaction costs:* Merchants and consumers alike are benefited by the reduced costs of selling and purchasing goods compared to the physical marketplace.
- *Consumer aggregation:* A large number of consumers who are motivated to buy are amassed in one marketplace—a great convenience to the seller.
- *Network effects:* The larger an auction site becomes in the numbers of both users and products, the greater the benefits become and therefore the more valuable a marketplace it becomes.
- *Market-maker benefits:* Auction sites have no inventory carrying costs or shipping costs, making them perhaps the ideal online business in that their main function is the transfer of information.

Costs of auctions include:

- *Delayed consumption:* Auctions can go on for days, and the product must then be shipped to the buyer. Buyers will typically want to pay less for an item they cannot immediately obtain.
- *Monitoring costs:* Buyers must spend time monitoring the bidding.
- *Equipment costs:* Buyers must purchase, or have already purchased, computer systems and Internet service, and learned how to operate these systems.
- *Trust risks:* Consumers face an increased risk of experiencing a loss as online auctions are the largest source of Internet fraud.
- *Fulfillment costs:* Buyers must pay for packing, shipping, and insurance, and will factor this cost into their bid price.

Auction sites have sought to reduce these risks through various methods including:

- *Rating systems:* Previous customers rate sellers based on their experience with them and post them on the site for other buyers to see.
- *Watch lists:* These allow buyers to monitor specific auctions as they proceed over a number of days and only pay close attention in the last few minutes of bidding.
- *Proxy bidding:* Buyers can enter a maximum price they are willing to pay, and the auction software will automatically place incremental bids as their original bid is surpassed.

■ Understand when to use auctions in a business.

Auctions can be an appropriate channel for businesses to sell items in a variety of situations. The factors for businesses to consider include:

- *The type of product:* Rare and unique products are well suited to the auction marketplace as are perishable items such as airline tickets, hotel rooms, car rentals, and tickets to plays, concerts, and sporting events.
- *The product life cycle:* Traditionally, auctions have been used by businesses to generate a higher profit on items at the end of their life cycle than they would receive from product liquidation sales. However, they are now more frequently being used at the beginning of a product's life cycle to generate premium prices from highly motivated early adopters.
- *Channel management:* Businesses must be careful when deciding whether to pursue an auction strategy to ensure that products at auction do not compete with products in their existing profitable channels. This is why most established retail firms tend to use auctions for products at the end of their life cycles or to have quantity purchasing requirements.
- *The type of auction:* Businesses should choose seller-biased auctions where there are many buyers and only one or a few sellers, preferably using the English ascending price system to drive the price up as high as possible.
- *Initial pricing:* Auction items should start with a low initial bid in order to attract more bidders, because the more bidders an item has, the higher the final price will be driven.
- *Bid increments:* When increments are kept low, more bidders are attracted and the frequency of their bidding is increased. This can translate into a higher final price as bidders are prodded onward in small steps.
- *Auction length:* In general, the longer an auction runs, the more bidders will enter the auction, and the higher the final price will be. However, if an auction continues for too long, the bid prices will stabilize and the cost of posting the

auction may outweigh the profit from any further price increases.
* *Number of items:* If a business has a large quantity of items to sell, it should break the lot up into smaller bundles and auction them at different times so that buyers do not expect a volume discount.
* *Price allocation rule:* Because most buyers are biased toward the uniform pricing rule, sellers should use different auction markets, or auction the same goods at different times in order to price discriminate.
* *Closed vs. open bidding:* Closed bidding should be used whenever possible because it benefits a seller by allowing price discrimination. However, open bidding can sometimes be beneficial when herd behavior kicks in, causing multiple bids on highly visited auctions, while overlooked and lightly trafficked auctions for the same or comparable items languish. This generally occurs when there are few objective measures of a product's true value in the marketplace.

■ Recognize the potential for auction abuse and fraud.

Auctions are particularly prone to fraud, which produces information asymmetries between buyers and sellers. Some of the possible abuses and frauds include:
* *Bid rigging:* Agreeing offline to limit bids or using shills to submit false bids that drive prices up.
* *Price matching:* Agreeing informally or formally to set floor prices on auction items below which sellers will not sell in open markets.
* *Shill feedback, defensive:* Using secondary IDs or other auction members to inflate seller ratings.
* *Shill feedback, offensive:* Using secondary IDs or other auction members to deflate ratings for another user (feedback bombs).
* *Feedback extortion:* Threatening negative feedback in return for a benefit.
* *Transaction interference:* E-mailing buyers to warn them away from a seller.
* *Bid manipulation:* Using the retraction option to make high bids, discovering the maximum bid of the current high bidder, and then retracting the bid.
* *Non-payment after winning:* Blocking legitimate buyers by bidding high, then not paying.
* *Shill bidding:* Using secondary user IDs or other auction members to artificially raise the price of an item.
* *Transaction non-performance:* Accepting payment and failing to deliver.
* *Non-selling seller:* Refusing payment or failing to deliver after a successful auction.
* *Bid siphoning:* E-mailing another seller's bidders and offering the same product for less.

■ Describe the major types of Internet portals.

Web portals are gateways to the more than 100 billion Web pages available on the Internet. Originally, their primary purpose was to help users find information on the Web, but they evolved into destination sites that provided a myriad of content from news to entertainment. Today, portals serve three main purposes: navigation of the Web, content, and commerce. Among the major portal types are:

- *Enterprise portals:* Corporations, universities, churches, and other organizations create these sites to help employees or members navigate to important content such as corporate news or organizational announcements.
- *General-purpose portals:* Examples are AOL, Yahoo, and MSN, which try to attract a very large general audience by providing many in-depth vertical content channels. Some also offer ISP services on a subscription basis, search engines, e-mail, chat, bulletin boards, and personal home pages.
- *Vertical market portals:* Also called destination sites, they attempt to attract a highly focused, loyal audience with an intense interest in either a community they belong to or an interest they hold. Recent studies have found that users with limited time resources are interested in concentrating their Web site visiting on focused searches in areas that appeal to them. Vertical market portals can be divided into two main classifications, although hybrids that overlap the two classifications also exist.
- *Affinity groups:* Statistical aggregates of people who identify themselves by their attitudes, values, beliefs, and behavior. Affinity portals exist to serve such broad constituencies as women, African Americans, and gays as well as much more focused constituencies such as union members, religious groups, and even home-schooling families.
- *Focused content portals:* These sites contain in-depth information on a particular topic that all members are interested in. They can provide content on such broad topics as sports, news, weather, entertainment, finance, or business, or they can appeal to a much more focused interest group such as boat, horse, or video game enthusiasts.

■ **Understand the business models of portals.**

Portals receive revenue from a number of different sources. The business model is presently changing and adapting to declines in certain revenue streams, particularly advertising revenues. Revenue sources can include:
- *ISP services:* Providing Web access and e-mail services for a monthly fee
- *General advertising:* Charging for impressions delivered
- *Tenancy deals:* Locking in long-term, multiple-year deals so a company is guaranteed a number of impressions with premium placement on home pages and through exclusive marketing deals
- *Subscription fees:* Charging for premium content
- *Commissions on sales:* Earning revenue based on sales at the site by independent merchants.

The survival strategy for general-purpose portals is to develop deep, rich, vertical content in order to attract advertisers to various niche groups that they can target with focused ads. The strategy for the small vertical market portals is to build a collection of vertical portals, thereby creating a network of deep, rich content sites for the same reason.

## QUESTIONS

1. Why did most communities in the early days of e-commerce fail? What factors enable online social networks to prosper today?
2. How does a social network differ from a portal? How are the two similar?

3. What is an affinity community, and what is its business model?
4. What is personalization or personal value pricing, and how can it be used at the beginning of a product's life cycle to increase revenues?
5. List and briefly explain three of the benefits of auction markets.
6. What are the four major costs to consumers of participating in an auction?
7. Under what conditions does a seller bias exist in an auction market? When does a buyer bias exist?
8. What are the two price allocation rules in auction markets? Explain the difference between them.
9. What is an auction aggregator and how does it work?
10. What types of products are well suited for an auction market? At what points in the product life cycle can auction markets prove beneficial for marketers?
11. What three characteristics define a portal site today?
12. What is a vertical market portal, and how might recent trends in consumer behavior prove advantageous to this business model?
13. What are the two main types of vertical market portals, and how are they distinguished from one and other?
14. List and briefly explain the main revenue sources for the portal business model.

## PROJECTS

1. Find two examples of an affinity portal and two examples of a focused-content portal. Prepare a presentation explaining why each of your examples should be categorized as an affinity portal or a focused-content portal. For each example, surf the site and describe the services each site provides. Try to determine what revenue model each of your examples is using and, if possible, how many members or registered visitors the site has attracted.

2. Examine the use of auctions by businesses. Go to any auction site of your choosing and look for outlet auctions or auctions directly from merchants. Research at least three products up for sale. What stage in the product life cycle do these products fall into? Are there quantity purchasing requirements? What was the opening bid price? What are the bid increments? What is the auction duration? Analyze why these firms have used the auction channel to sell these goods and prepare a short report on your findings.

3. Visit one for-profit-sponsored and one nonprofit-sponsored social network. Create a presentation to describe and demonstrate the offering at each site. What organizational objectives is each pursuing? How is the for-profit company using community building technologies as a customer relations management tool?

## CHAPTER 12

# B2B E-commerce: Supply Chain Management and Collaborative Commerce

## LEARNING OBJECTIVES

**After reading this chapter, you will be able to:**

- Define B2B commerce and understand its scope and history.
- Understand the procurement process, the supply chain, and collaborative commerce.
- Identify the main types of B2B e-commerce: Net marketplaces and private industrial networks.
- Understand the four types of Net marketplaces.
- Identify the major trends in the development of Net marketplaces.
- Identify the role of private industrial networks in transforming the supply chain.
- Understand the role of private industrial networks in supporting collaborative commerce.

# Volkswagen
## Builds Its B2B Net Marketplace

Volkswagen AG is the world's largest car manufacturer, producing 6.3 million cars, trucks, and vans in 2010, and generating over $147 billion in revenue. In addition to the Volkswagen brand, the Volkswagen Group also owns luxury carmakers such as Audi, Bentley, Scania Bugatti, and Lamborghini, and family car makers SEAT in Spain and Skoda in the Czech Republic. The company has 370,000 employees and operates plants in Europe, Africa, the Asian/Pacific rim, and the Americas.

The various companies and 61 production plants in the Volkswagen Group annually purchase components, automotive parts, and indirect materials worth about 75.4 billion euros, or about $100 billion (which constitutes about 83% of Volkswagen's annual revenue). Obviously, the procurement process and relationships with suppliers are absolutely critical for Volkswagen's success.

Today, the Volkswagen Group manages almost all of its procurement needs via the Internet. It began building its Internet platform, VWGroupSupply.com, in 2000. The Volkswagen Group was looking for ways to create more efficient relationships with its suppliers and reduce the cost of paper-based procurement processes. However, the company did not want to automate procurement using a public independent exchange or an industry consortium because it would have had to adapt its own business processes to a common framework that could be used by many different organizations. Volkswagen hoped that by building its own B2B network, it could compete more effectively against other automakers. Volkswagen decided, for instance, not to participate in Covisint, the giant automotive industry consortium backed by major car manufacturers such as Ford, General Motors, and DaimlerChrysler, which provided procurement and other supply chain services for these companies, other automotive manufacturers, and their suppliers.

Instead, Volkswagen opted for a private platform that would allow it to integrate its suppliers more tightly with its own business processes, and where it could control more precisely who was invited to participate. VWGroupSupply now handles over 90% of all global purchasing for the Volkswagen Group, including all automotive and parts components. It is one of the most comprehensive e-procurement systems in the global automotive industry. From an initial seven applications, the platform now offers over 60 different online applications, such as requests for quotations (RFQs), contract negotiations, catalog purchases, purchase order management, engineering change management, vehicle program management, and payments, among others. The Volkswagen Group developed the platform using technology from a number of vendors, including Ariba, IBM, and i2 Technologies.

Suppliers of all sizes can access VWGroupSupply with standard Web browser software. The Web site is limited to suppliers who have done business with one or more companies in the Volkswagen Group and potential new suppliers who go through an authorization process. Currently, over 36,000 suppliers are registered, and there are over 110,000 users. The system maintains a common data repository with details on each supplier concerning procurement, logistics, production, quality, technical design, and finance.

VWGroupSupply's online catalog currently contains about 2.5 million items from 590 global suppliers. There are 14,200 internal users of the online catalog who have conducted over 1.5 million transactions with a value totaling 380 million euros ($447 million). The catalog uses the eCl@ss standard for classifying its contents. All suppliers who participate in the catalog ordering process classify their products using this standard.

Online negotiations involve multiple bids by suppliers for various purchasing contracts. VWGroupSupply ensures that all participants meet its technical and commercial qualifications. Before an online solicitation begins, the system informs vendors about the data and precise rules governing the negotiations. In 2010, VWGroupSupply conducted around 3,000 online contract negotiations online, with a value of 11.9 billion euros ($16.6 billion).

Shifts in market demand have a drastic impact on Volkswagen's production activities and affect the ability of suppliers to deliver. Production bottlenecks can result if suppliers are unprepared for a sudden upsurge in demand. If suppliers stock too much inventory, they may incur excess costs from running at overcapacity. VWGroupSupply has an application called electronic Capacity Management (eCAP) to alert both Volkswagen and its suppliers to changes in trends in advance.

eCAP enables suppliers to track Volkswagen's continually updated production plans and materials requirements in real time online. This capability captures information about participating suppliers' planned maximum and minimum capacities. If Volkswagen production requirements go beyond these limits, the system sets off an alarm so both parties can react quickly. eCAP maintains information on over 400 suppliers and 4,000 critical parts.

In March 2009, VWGroupSupply unveiled a new Web site intended to provide better navigation, greater clarity, new content, and a simplified registration process for new suppliers.

**SOURCES:** VWGroupSupply.com, September 2010; "Automotive B2B Developments at Odette25," GXS.com, June 22, 2010; "Best Practices: VW Revs Up its B2B Engine," by Martin Hoffman, *Optimize*, March 2004.

The VWGroupSupply case illustrates the exciting potential for B2B e-commerce to lower production costs, speed up new product delivery, and ultimately revolutionize both the manufacturing process inherited from the early twentieth century and the way we purchase industrial products. VWGroupSupply is an example of just one type of B2B e-commerce, but there are many other equally promising efforts to using the Internet to change the relationships among manufacturers and their suppliers. The success of VWGroupSupply and similar networks operated by the major automobile firms in the world stands in contrast to an earlier industry-sponsored Net marketplace called Covisint. Founded in 1999 by five of the world's largest automakers (General Motors, Ford, Chrysler, Nissan, and Peugeot), Covisint hoped to provide an electronic market connecting thousands of suppliers to a few huge buyers using auctions and procurement services. While initially successful, Covisint was dismantled and sold off in June 2004. Its auction business was sold to FreeMarkets, an early B2B auction company which itself was sold to Ariba later in 2004. In 2010, Ariba survives as a successful software firm focusing on the procurement process. The rest of Covisint's procurement software and operations were sold to CompuWare, a software services company, which maintains the Covisint brand name and provides software services to the automotive industry.

The failure of Covisint and the simultaneous growth in B2B e-commerce efforts such as VWGroupSupply illustrates the difficulties of achieving the broad visions established during the early days of e-commerce. From a high point of 1,500 online B2B exchanges in 2000, the number has dwindled to less than 200 survivors today. Like B2C commerce, the B2B marketplace has consolidated, evolved, and moved on to more attainable visions. In the process, many B2B efforts have experienced extraordinary success. There are many failed efforts to consider as well; these provide important lessons to all managers.

In this chapter, we examine the many different types of Internet-based B2B commerce in detail. In Section 12.1, we define B2B commerce and place it in the context of trends in supply chain management, which, ultimately, is the objective of B2B commerce—to help businesses manage the flow of supplies needed for production. The next two sections describe the two fundamental types of B2B e-commerce: Net marketplaces and private industrial networks. We describe four major types of Net marketplaces, their biases (seller, buyer, and neutral), accessibility (private versus public), and value creation dynamics, and then the emergence of private Internet-based industrial networks that tie a smaller number of organizations into a collaborative commercial system.

**Table 12.1** summarizes the leading trends in B2B e-commerce in the 2010–2011 period. Perhaps the most important theme is the growing comfort level that business firms have with the Internet as a viable method of purchase, payment,

| TABLE 12.1 | MAJOR TRENDS IN B2B E-COMMERCE, 2010–2011 |
|---|---|

- B2B e-commerce continues to grow, although at a somewhat slower pace than in previous years due to the widespread economic recession, as business firms gain experience and knowledge in exploiting the Internet.
- Business firms increase their comfort level with Internet security and payments, helping to expand their use of B2B channels.
- Business firms turn to cloud computing and software-as-a-service (SaaS) to obtain B2B services rather than build their own.
- Growing realization that the most important benefits to B2B commerce are not lower costs of raw materials (although these costs do decline), but rather gains in supply chain efficiency, better spend management, and improved business processes.
- Decline in growth of independent Net marketplace exchanges, but rapid growth in e-procurement firms and private industrial networks.
- Rapid growth in collaborative commerce B2B applications based on private networks.
- Continued consolidation in the B2B Net marketplace and software vendor markets as fewer but stronger firms purchase weaker firms born in early years of B2B e-commerce.
- B2B communities emerge allowing firms in the same industry to collectively work on reducing costs by integrating their enterprise resource planning (ERP) systems.
- B2B systems move to cloud providers like IBM, Oracle, Amazon, Google, and HP as their core technology.
- More B2B software providers switch to a SaaS model, providing inexpensive online access to trading platforms.

and collaboration among partners in the supply chain. A second theme is the emergence of cloud-based computing where firms obtain computing services and capabilities using the Internet rather than buying computers and software.

## 12.1    B2B E-COMMERCE AND SUPPLY CHAIN MANAGEMENT

The trade between business firms represents a huge marketplace. The total amount of B2B trade in the United States in 2010 is about $16 trillion, with B2B e-commerce (online B2B) contributing about $3.6 trillion of that amount (U.S. Census Bureau, 2010; authors' estimates). By 2014, B2B e-commerce should grow to about $5.1 trillion in the United States, assuming an average growth rate of about 9%.

The process of conducting trade among business firms is complex and requires significant human intervention, and therefore, it consumes significant resources. Some firms estimate that each corporate purchase order for support products costs them, on average, at least $100 in administrative overhead. Administrative overhead includes processing paper, approving purchase decisions, spending time using the telephone and fax machines to search for products and arrange for purchases, arranging for shipping, and receiving the goods. Across the economy, this adds up to trillions of dollars annually being spent for procurement processes that could potentially be automated. If even just a portion of inter-firm trade were automated, and parts of the entire procurement process assisted by the Internet, then literally trillions of dollars might be released for more productive uses, consumer prices potentially would fall, productivity would increase, and the economic wealth of the nation would expand. This is the promise of B2B e-commerce. The challenge of B2B e-commerce is changing existing patterns and systems of procurement, and designing and implementing new Internet-based B2B solutions.

## DEFINING AND MEASURING THE GROWTH OF B2B COMMERCE

Before the Internet, business-to-business transactions were referred to simply as *trade* or the *procurement process*. The term **total inter-firm trade** refers to the total flow of value among firms. Today, we use the term **B2B commerce** to describe all types of computer-enabled inter-firm trade, such as the use of the Internet and other networking technologies to exchange value across organizational boundaries. This definition of B2B commerce does not include digital transactions that occur within the boundaries of a single firm—for instance, the transfer of goods and value from one subsidiary to another, or the use of corporate intranets to manage the firm. We use the term **Internet-based B2B commerce** (or **B2B e-commerce**) to describe specifically that portion of B2B commerce that is enabled by the Internet.

## THE EVOLUTION OF B2B COMMERCE

B2B commerce has evolved over a 35-year period through several technology-driven stages (see **Figure 12.1**). The first step in the development of B2B commerce in the mid-1970s was **automated order entry systems** that involved the use of telephone modems

**total inter-firm trade**
the total flow of value among firms

**B2B commerce**
all types of computer-enabled inter-firm trade

**Internet-based B2B commerce (B2B e-commerce)**
that portion of B2B commerce that is enabled by the Internet

**automated order entry systems**
involve the use of telephone modems to send digital orders

---

| FIGURE 12.1 | THE EVOLUTION OF THE USE OF TECHNOLOGY PLATFORMS IN B2B COMMERCE |
| --- | --- |

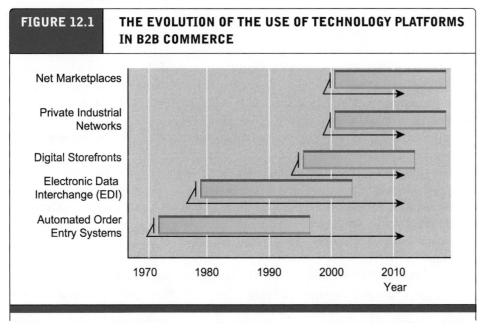

B2B commerce has gone through many stages of development since the 1970s. Each stage reflects a major change in technology platforms from mainframes to private dedicated networks, and finally to the Internet.

**seller-side solutions**
seller-biased markets that are owned by, and show only goods from, a single seller

**electronic data interchange (EDI)**
a communications standard for sharing business documents and settlement information among a small number of firms

**buyer-side solutions**
buyer-biased markets that are owned by buyers and that aim to reduce the procurement costs of supplies for buyers

**hub-and-spoke system**
suppliers connected to a central hub of buyers via private dedicated networks

**vertical market**
one that provides expertise and products for a specific industry

**horizontal markets**
markets that serve many different industries

**B2B electronic storefronts**
online catalogs of products made available to the public marketplace by a single supplier

**Net marketplace**
brings hundreds to thousands of suppliers and buyers into a single Internet-based environment to conduct trade

to send digital orders to health care products companies such as Baxter Healthcare. Baxter, a diversified supplier of hospital supplies, placed telephone modems in its customers' procurement offices to automate re-ordering from Baxter's computerized inventory database (and to discourage re-ordering from competitors). This early technology was replaced by personal computers using private networks in the late 1980s, and by Internet workstations accessing electronic online catalogs in the late 1990s. Automated order entry systems are **seller-side solutions**. They are owned by the suppliers and are seller-biased markets—they show only goods from a single seller. Customers benefited from these systems because they reduced the costs of inventory replenishment and were paid for largely by the suppliers. Automated order entry systems continue to play an important role in B2B commerce.

By the late 1970s, a new form of computer-to-computer communication called **electronic data interchange (EDI)** emerged. We describe EDI in greater detail later in this chapter, but at this point, it is necessary only to know that EDI is a communications standard for sharing business documents such as invoices, purchase orders, shipping bills, product stocking numbers (SKUs), and settlement information among a small number of firms. Virtually all large firms have EDI systems, and most industry groups have industry standards for defining documents in that industry. EDI systems are owned by the buyers, and hence they are **buyer-side solutions** and buyer-biased because they aim to reduce the procurement costs of supplies for the buyer. Of course, by automating the transaction, EDI systems also benefit the sellers by reducing costs of serving their customers. The topology of EDI systems is often referred to as a **hub-and-spoke system**, with the buyers in the center and the suppliers connected to the central hub via private dedicated networks.

EDI systems generally serve vertical markets. A **vertical market** is one that provides expertise and products for a specific industry, such as automobiles. In contrast, **horizontal markets** serve many different industries.

Electronic storefronts emerged in the mid-1990s along with the commercialization of the Internet. **B2B electronic storefronts** are perhaps the simplest and easiest to understand form of B2B e-commerce, because they are just online catalogs of products made available to the public marketplace by a single supplier—similar to Amazon for the B2C retail market. Owned by the suppliers, they are seller-side solutions and seller-biased because they show only the products offered by a single supplier.

Electronic storefronts are a natural descendant of automated order entry systems, but there are two important differences: (1) the far less expensive and more universal Internet becomes the communication media and displaces private networks, and (2) electronic storefronts tend to serve horizontal markets—they carry products that serve a wide variety of industries. Although electronic storefronts emerged prior to Net marketplaces (described next), they are usually considered a type of Net marketplace.

**Net marketplaces** emerged in the late 1990s as a natural extension and scaling-up of the electronic storefronts. There are many different kinds of Net marketplaces , which we describe in detail in Section 12.2, but the essential characteristic of a Net marketplace is that they bring hundreds to thousands of suppliers—each with electronic catalogs and potentially thousands of purchasing firms—into a single Internet-based environment to conduct trade.

Net marketplaces can be organized under a variety of ownership models. Some are owned by independent third parties backed by venture capital, some are owned by established firms who are the main or only market players, and some are a mix of both. Net marketplaces establish the prices of the goods they offer in four primary ways—fixed catalog prices, or more dynamic pricing, such as negotiation, auction, or bid/ask ("exchange" model). Net marketplaces earn revenue in a number of ways, including transaction fees, subscription fees, service fees, software licensing fees, advertising and marketing, and sales of data and information.

Although the primary benefits and biases of Net marketplaces have to be determined on a case-by-case basis depending on ownership and pricing mechanisms, it is often the case that Net marketplaces are biased against suppliers because they can force suppliers to reveal their prices and terms to other suppliers in the marketplace. Net marketplaces can also significantly extend the benefits of simple electronic storefronts by seeking to automate the procurement value chain of both selling and buying firms.

Private industrial networks also emerged in the late 1990s as natural extensions of EDI systems and the existing close relationships that developed between large industrial firms and their suppliers. Described in more detail in Section 12.3, **private industrial networks** (sometimes also referred to as a *private trading exchange*, or *PTX*) are Internet-based communication environments that extend far beyond procurement to encompass truly collaborative commerce. Private industrial networks permit buyer firms and their principal suppliers to share product design and development, marketing, inventory, production scheduling, and unstructured communications. Like EDI, private industrial networks are owned by the buyers and are buyer-side solutions with buyer biases. These systems are directly intended to improve the cost position and flexibility of large industrial firms (Kumaran, 2002).

Naturally, private industrial networks have significant benefits for suppliers as well. Inclusion in the direct supply chain for a major industrial purchasing company can allow a supplier to increase both revenue and margins because the environment is not competitive—only a few suppliers are included in the private industrial network. These networks are the most prevalent form of Internet-based B2B commerce, and this will continue into the foreseeable future.

**private industrial networks (private trading exchange, PTX)**
Internet-based communication environments that extend far beyond procurement to encompass truly collaborative commerce

## THE GROWTH OF B2B E-COMMERCE 2009–2014

In the period 2010–2014, B2B e-commerce is projected to grow from about 30% to 35% of total inter-firm trade in the United States, or from $3.6 trillion in 2010 to $5.1 trillion in 2014 (see **Figure 12.2**).

Several observations are important to note with respect to Figure 12.2. First, it shows that the initial belief that electronic marketplaces would become the dominant form of B2B e-commerce is not supported. Second, private industrial networks play a dominant role in B2B e-commerce, both now and in the future. Third, non-EDI B2B e-commerce is the most rapidly growing type of B2B e-commerce, and EDI is still quite large but will decline over time.

| FIGURE 12.2 | **GROWTH OF B2B COMMERCE 2000–2014 (IN TRILLIONS)** |

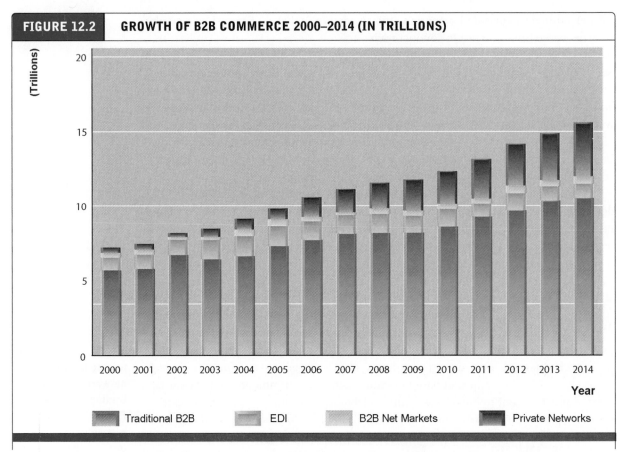

Private industrial networks are the fastest growing form of online B2B e-commerce, which includes EDI, B2B Net marketplaces, and private industrial markets.
SOURCES: Based on data from U.S. Census Bureau, 2010; authors' estimates.

### Industry Forecasts

Not all industries will be similarly affected by B2B e-commerce, and not all industries can similarly benefit from B2B. Several factors influence the speed with which industries migrate to B2B e-commerce and the volume of transactions. Those industries in which there is already significant utilization of EDI (indicating concentration of buyers and suppliers) and large investments in information technology and Internet infrastructure can be expected to move first and fastest to B2B e-commerce utilization. The aerospace and defense, computer, and industrial equipment industries meet these criteria. Where the marketplace is highly concentrated on either the purchasing or selling side, or both, conditions are also ripe for rapid B2B e-commerce growth, as in the energy and chemical industries. In the case of health care, the federal government, health care providers (doctors and hospitals), and major insurance companies are moving rapidly towards a national medical record system and the use of Internet for managing medical payments.

## POTENTIAL BENEFITS OF B2B E-COMMERCE

Regardless of the specific type of B2B e-commerce, as a whole, Internet-based B2B commerce promises many strategic benefits to participating firms—both buyers and sellers—and impressive gains for the economy as a whole. B2B e-commerce can:

- Lower administrative costs
- Lower search costs for buyers
- Reduce inventory costs by increasing competition among suppliers (increasing price transparency) and reducing inventory to the bare minimum
- Lower transaction costs by eliminating paperwork and automating parts of the procurement process
- Increase production flexibility by ensuring delivery of parts "just in time"
- Improve quality of products by increasing cooperation among buyers and sellers and reducing quality issues
- Decrease product cycle time by sharing designs and production schedules with suppliers
- Increase opportunities for collaborating with suppliers and distributors
- Create greater price transparency—the ability to see the actual buy and sell prices in a market

B2B e-commerce offers potential first-mover strategic benefits for individual firms as well. Firms that move their procurement processes online first will experience impressive gains in productivity, cost reduction, and potentially much faster introduction of new, higher-quality products. While these gains may be imitated by other competing firms, it is also clear from the brief history of B2B e-commerce that firms making sustained investments in information technology and Internet-based B2B commerce can adapt much faster to new technologies as they emerge, creating a string of first-mover advantages.

## THE PROCUREMENT PROCESS AND THE SUPPLY CHAIN

The subject of B2B e-commerce can be complex because there are so many ways the Internet can be used to support the exchange of goods and payments among organizations. Ultimately, B2B e-commerce is about changing the **procurement process** (the way business firms purchase the goods they need to produce the goods they will ultimately sell to consumers) of thousands of firms across the United States and the world.

One way to enter this area of Internet-based B2B commerce is to examine the existing procurement process (see **Figure 12.3**). Firms purchase goods from a set of suppliers, and they in turn purchase their inputs from a set of suppliers. This set of firms is linked through a series of transactions referred to as the **supply chain**. The supply chain includes not just the firms themselves, but also the relationships among them and the processes that connect them.

There are seven separate steps in the procurement process. The first three steps involve the decision of who to buy from and what to pay: searching for suppliers of specific products; qualifying both the seller and the products they sell; and

**procurement process**
tthe way firms purchase the goods they need to produce goods for consumers

**supply chain**
firms that purchase goods, their suppliers, and their suppliers' suppliers. Includes not only the firms themselves, but also the relationships among them, and the processes that connect them

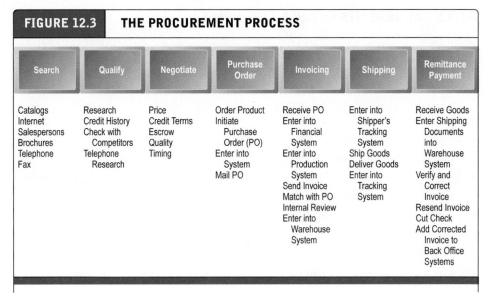

The procurement process is a lengthy and complicated series of steps that involves the seller, buyer, and shipping companies in a series of connected transactions.

**direct goods**

goods directly involved in the production process

**indirect goods**

all other goods not directly involved in the production process

**MRO goods**

products for maintenance, repair, and operations

**contract purchasing**

involves long-term written agreements to purchase specified products, under agreed-upon terms and quality, for an extended period of time

**spot purchasing**

involves the purchase of goods based on immediate needs in larger marketplaces that involve many suppliers

negotiating prices, credit terms, escrow requirements, quality, and scheduling of delivery. Once a supplier is identified, purchase orders are issued, the buyer is sent an invoice, the goods are shipped, and the buyer sends a payment. Each of these steps in the procurement process is composed of many separate sub-activities. Each of these activities must be recorded in the information systems of the seller, buyer, and shipper. Often, this data entry is not automatic and involves some manual labor.

## Types of Procurement

Two distinctions are important for understanding how B2B e-commerce can improve the procurement process. First, firms make purchases of two kinds of goods from suppliers: direct goods and indirect goods. **Direct goods** are goods integrally involved in the production process; for instance, when an automobile manufacturer purchases sheet steel for auto body production. **Indirect goods** are all other goods not directly involved in the production process, such as office supplies and maintenance products. Often these goods are called **MRO goods**—products for maintenance, repair, and operations.

Second, firms use two different methods for purchasing goods: contract purchasing and spot purchasing. **Contract purchasing** involves long-term written agreements to purchase specified products, with agreed-upon terms and quality, for an extended period of time. Generally, firms purchase direct goods using long-term contracts. **Spot purchasing** involves the purchase of goods based on immediate needs in larger marketplaces that involve many suppliers. Generally, firms use spot purchasing for indirect goods, although in some cases, firms also use spot purchasing for direct goods.

According to several estimates, about 80% of inter-firm trade involves contract purchasing of direct goods, and 20% involves spot purchasing of indirect goods (Sodhi,

2001; Kaplan and Sawhney, 2000). This finding is significant for understanding B2B e-commerce, as we see below.

Although the procurement process involves the purchasing of goods, it is extraordinarily information-intense, involving the movement of information among many existing corporate systems. The procurement process today is also very labor-intensive, directly involving over 4.5 million employees in the United States, not including those engaged in transportation, finance, insurance, or general office administration related to the process (U.S. Census Bureau, 2010b).

In the long term, the success or failure of B2B e-commerce depends on changing the day-to-day behavior of these 4.5 million people. The key players in the procurement process are the purchasing managers. They ultimately decide who to buy from, what to buy, and on what terms. Purchasing managers ("procurement managers" in the business press) are also the key decision makers for the adoption of B2B e-commerce solutions.

The Internet could make an important contribution in simplifying the procurement process by bringing buyers and sellers together in a single marketplace and reducing search, research, and negotiating costs. This would appear to be very helpful for spot purchases of indirect goods. Later in the procurement process, the Internet could make an important contribution simply as a powerful communications medium, transferring information among the sellers, buyers, and shippers, and helping managers coordinate the procurement process. This would appear to be very helpful for contract purchases of direct goods. To a large extent, this is the promise of B2B e-commerce. But it is not the whole story.

Although Figure 12.3 captures some of the complexity of the procurement process, it is important to realize that firms purchase thousands of goods from thousands of suppliers. The suppliers, in turn, must purchase their inputs from their suppliers. Large manufacturers such as Ford Motor Company have over 20,000 suppliers of parts, packaging, and technology. The number of secondary and tertiary suppliers is at least as large. Together, this extended **multi-tier supply chain** (the chain of primary, secondary, and tertiary suppliers) constitutes a crucial aspect of the industrial infrastructure of the economy. **Figure 12.4** depicts a firm's multi-tier supply chain.

The supply chain depicted in Figure 12.4 is a three-tier chain simplified for the sake of illustration. In fact, large Fortune 1000 firms have thousands of suppliers, who in turn have thousands of smaller suppliers. The complexity of the supply chain suggests a combinatorial explosion. Assuming a manufacturer has four primary suppliers and each one has three primary suppliers, and each of these has three primary suppliers, then the total number of suppliers in the chain (including the buying firm) rises to 53. This figure does not include the shippers, insurers, and financiers involved in the transactions.

Immediately, you can see from Figure 12.4 that the procurement process involves a very large number of suppliers, each of whom must be coordinated with the production needs of the ultimate purchaser—the buying firm.

**multi-tier supply chain**
the chain of primary, secondary, and tertiary suppliers

## The Role of Existing Legacy Computer Systems

Complicating any efforts to coordinate the many firms in a supply chain is the fact that each firm generally has its own set of legacy computer systems, often home-

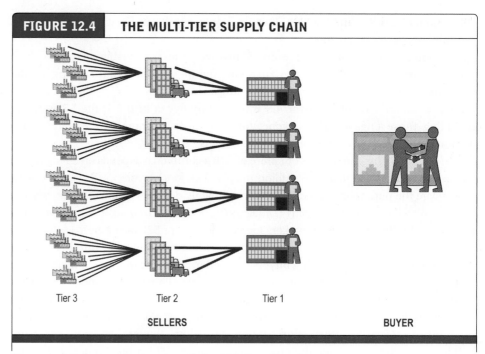

**FIGURE 12.4** | **THE MULTI-TIER SUPPLY CHAIN**

Tier 3          Tier 2          Tier 1

SELLERS                                          BUYER

The supply chain for every firm is composed of multiple tiers of suppliers.

**legacy computer
systems**
generally are older
mainframe and
minicomputer systems used
to manage key business
processes within a firm in a
variety of functional areas

**materials
requirements planning
(MRP) system**
legacy system that enables
companies to predict,
track, and manage all the
constituent parts of
complex manufactured
goods

**enterprise resource
planning (ERP)
system**
a more sophisticated MRP
system that includes
human resource and
financial components

grown or customized, that cannot easily pass information to other systems. **Legacy computer systems** generally are older mainframe systems used to manage key business processes within a firm in a variety of functional areas from manufacturing, logistics, finance, and human resources. Converting these older systems to new Internet and client/server-based systems is very expensive and takes many years.

One typical legacy system is a **materials requirements planning (MRP) system** that enables companies to predict, track, and manage all the constituent parts of complex manufactured goods such as automobiles, machine tools, and industrial equipment. An MRP system stores and generates a bill of material (BOM) that lists all the parts needed to manufacture a product. The MRP system also generates a production schedule that describes the order in which parts are used and the production time for each step in production. The BOM and production schedule are then used to generate purchase orders to suppliers. The MRP system can be run as often as needed, generating a dynamic production environment.

Many larger firms have installed **enterprise resource planning (ERP) systems**, which are more sophisticated MRP systems that include the human resource and financial components of the production process. With an ERP system in place, orders from customers are translated into BOMs, production schedules, and human resource and financial requirements, including notifying the finance department to issue invoices to customers and pay suppliers. ERP systems were not originally designed to coordinate the flow of information among a large set of supplier firms, but most ERP vendors now supply B2B modules that can manage B2B processes.

## TRENDS IN SUPPLY CHAIN MANAGEMENT AND COLLABORATIVE COMMERCE

It is impossible to comprehend the actual and potential contribution of Internet-based B2B commerce, or the successes and failures of B2B e-commerce vendors and markets, without understanding ongoing efforts to improve the procurement process through a variety of supply chain management programs that long preceded the development of e-commerce.

**Supply chain management** (**SCM**) refers to a wide variety of activities that firms and industries use to coordinate the key players in their procurement process. For the most part, today's procurement managers still work with telephones, e-mail, fax machines, face-to-face conversations, and instinct, relying on trusted long-term suppliers for their strategic purchases of goods directly involved in the production process.

There have been four major developments in supply chain management over the two decades that preceded the development of the Internet and set the ground rules for understanding how B2B e-commerce works (or fails to work). These developments are supply chain simplification, electronic data interchange (EDI), supply chain management systems, and collaborative commerce.

### Supply Chain Simplification

Many manufacturing firms have spent the past two decades reducing the size of their supply chains and working more closely with a smaller group of "strategic" supplier firms to reduce both product costs and administrative costs, while improving quality. Following the lead of Japanese industry, for instance, the automobile industry has systematically reduced the number of its suppliers by over 50%. Instead of open bidding for orders, large manufacturers have chosen to work with strategic partner supply firms under long-term contracts that guarantee the supplier business, but also establish quality, cost, and timing goals. These strategic partnership programs are essential for just-in-time production models, and often involve joint product development and design, integration of computer systems, and tight coupling of the production processes of two or more companies. **Tight coupling** is a method for ensuring that suppliers precisely deliver the ordered parts at a specific time and to a particular location, to ensure the production process is not interrupted for lack of parts.

### Electronic Data Interchange (EDI)

As noted in the previous section, B2B e-commerce did not originate with the Internet, but in fact has its roots in technologies such as EDI that were first developed in the mid-1970s and 1980s. EDI is a broadly defined communications protocol for exchanging documents among computers using technical standards developed by the American National Standards Institute (ANSI X12 standards) and international bodies such as the United Nations (EDIFACT standards).

EDI was developed to reduce the cost, delays, and errors inherent in the manual exchanges of documents such as purchase orders, shipping documents, price lists, payments, and customer data. EDI differs from an unstructured message because its messages are organized with distinct fields for each of the important pieces of

**supply chain management (SCM)** refers to a wide variety of activities that firms and industries use to coordinate the key players in their procurement process

**tight coupling** a method for ensuring that suppliers precisely deliver the ordered parts, at a specific time and particular location, to ensure the production process is not interrupted for lack of parts

information in a commercial transaction such as transaction date, product purchased, amount, sender's name, address, and recipient's name.

Each major industry in the United States and throughout much of the industrial world has EDI industry committees that define the structure and information fields of electronic documents for that industry. EDI communications at first relied on private point-to-point circuit-switched communication networks and private value-added networks that connected key participants in the supply chain (Laudon and Laudon, 2011). Estimates indicate that B2B e-commerce EDI transactions will total about $1 trillion in 2010, about 30% of all B2B e-commerce. (U.S. Census Bureau, 2010a, authors' estimates). In this sense, EDI is particularly important in the development of B2B e-commerce.

EDI has evolved significantly since the 1980s (see **Figure 12.5**). Initially, EDI focused on document automation (Stage 1). Procurement agents created purchase orders electronically and sent them to trading partners, who in turn shipped order

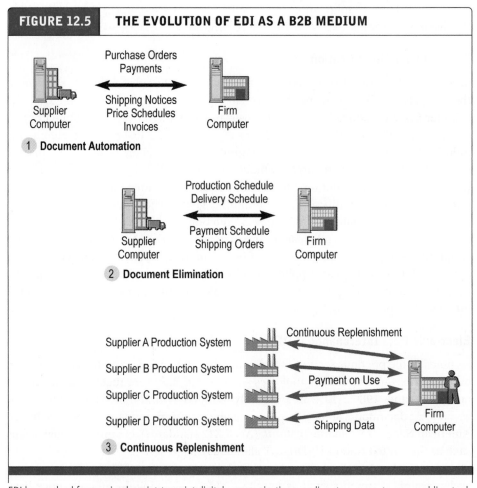

| FIGURE 12.5 | **THE EVOLUTION OF EDI AS A B2B MEDIUM** |

EDI has evolved from a simple point-to-point digital communications medium to a many-to-one enabling tool for continuous inventory replenishment.

fulfillment and shipping notices electronically back to the purchaser. Invoices, payments, and other documents followed. These early implementations replaced the postal system for document transmission, and resulted in same-day shipping of orders (rather than a week's delay caused by the postal system), reduced errors, and lower costs.

The second stage of EDI development began in the early 1990s, driven largely by the automation of internal industrial processes and movement toward just-in-time production and continuous production. The new methods of production called for greater flexibility in scheduling, shipping, and financing of supplies. EDI evolved to become a system for document elimination. To support the new automated production processes used by manufacturers, EDI was used to eliminate purchase orders and other documents entirely, replacing them with production schedules and inventory balances. Supplier firms were sent monthly statements of production requirements and precise scheduled delivery times, and the orders would be fulfilled continuously, with inventory and payments being adjusted at the end of each month.

In the third stage of EDI, beginning in the mid-1990s, suppliers were given online access to selected parts of the purchasing firm's production and delivery schedules, and, under long-term contracts, were required to meet those schedules on their own without intervention by firm purchasing agents. Movement toward this continuous access model of EDI was spurred in the 1990s by large manufacturing and process firms (such as oil and chemical companies) that were implementing ERP systems. These systems required standardization of business processes and resulted in the automation of production, logistics, and many financial processes. These new processes required much closer relationships with suppliers, who were required to be more precise in delivery scheduling and more flexible in inventory management. This level of supplier precision could never be achieved economically by human purchasing agents. This third stage of EDI introduced the era of continuous replenishment. For instance, Wal-Mart and Toys"R"Us provide their suppliers with access to their store inventories, and the suppliers are expected to keep the stock of items on the shelf within pre-specified targets. Similar developments occurred in the grocery industry.

Today, EDI must be viewed as a general enabling technology that provides for the exchange of critical business information between computer applications supporting a wide variety of business processes. EDI is an important industrial network technology, suited to support communications among a small set of strategic partners in direct, long-term trading relationships. The technical platform of EDI has changed from mainframes to personal computers, and the telecommunications environment is changing from private, dedicated networks to the Internet (referred to as Internet-based EDI, or just Internet EDI). Most industry groups are moving toward XML as the language for expressing EDI commercial documents and communications.

The strength of EDI is its ability to support direct commercial transactions among strategically related firms in an industrial network, but this is its weakness as well. EDI is not well suited for the development of electronic marketplaces, where thousands of suppliers and purchasers meet in a digital arena to negotiate prices. EDI supports direct bilateral communications among a small set of firms and does not permit the multilateral, dynamic relationships of a true marketplace. EDI does not provide for price transparency among a large number of suppliers, does not scale easily to include new participants, and is not a real-time communications environment. EDI does not have a rich communications environment that can simultaneously support e-mail messaging, sharing of graphic documents, network meetings, or user-friendly flexible database creation and management. For these features, Internet-based software has emerged that is described below. EDI is also an expensive proposition, and a staff of dedicated programmers is required to implement it in large firms; in some cases, a considerable amount of time is also needed to reprogram existing enterprise systems to work with EDI protocols. Small firms are typically required to adopt EDI in order to supply large firms, and there are less-expensive, small-firm solutions for implementing EDI.

### Supply Chain Management Systems

**supply chain management (SCM) systems**

continuously link the activities of buying, making, and moving products from suppliers to purchasing firms, as well as integrating the demand side of the business equation by including the order entry system in the process

Supply chain simplification, focusing on strategic partners in the production process, ERP systems, and continuous inventory replenishment, are the foundation for contemporary **supply chain management (SCM) systems**. Supply chain management systems continuously link the activities of buying, making, and moving products from suppliers to purchasing firms, as well as integrating the demand side of the business equation by including the order entry system in the process. With an SCM system and continuous replenishment, inventory is eliminated and production begins only when an order is received (see **Figure 12.6**). This is especially important in industries in which the product is perishable or experiences declining market value rapidly after production. Personal computers fit this description.

Hewlett-Packard (HP) has a Web-based order-driven supply chain management system that begins with either a customer placing an order online or the receipt of an order from a dealer. The order is forwarded from the order entry system to HP's production and delivery system. From there, the order is routed to one of several HP contractor supplier firms. One such firm is Synnex in Fremont, California. At Synnex, computers verify the order with HP and validate the ordered configuration to ensure the PC can be manufactured (e.g., will not have missing parts or fail a design specification set by HP). The order is then forwarded to a computer-based production control system that issues a bar-coded production ticket to factory assemblers. Simultaneously, a parts order is forwarded to Synnex's warehouse and inventory management system. A worker assembles the computer, and then the computer is boxed, tagged, and shipped to the customer. The delivery is monitored and tracked by HP's supply chain management system, which links directly to one of several overnight delivery systems operated by Airborne Express, Federal Express, and UPS. The elapsed time from order entry to shipping is 48 hours. With this system, Synnex and HP have eliminated the need to hold PCs in inventory, reduced cycle time from one week to 48 hours, and reduced errors. HP has extended this system to become a global B2B order tracking, reporting, and support system for large HP customers. The site now operates in 10 languages, 43 currencies, and more than 200 countries (Synnex Corporation, 2010; Hewlett-Packard, 2010).

## FIGURE 12.6   SUPPLY CHAIN MANAGEMENT SYTEMS

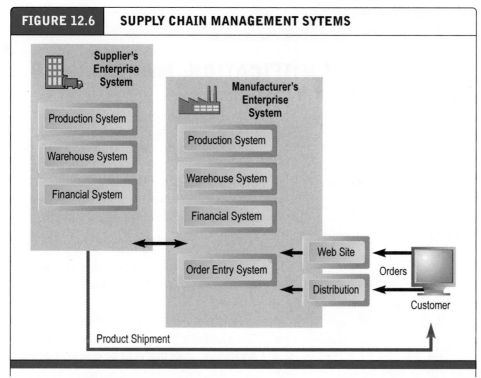

SCM systems coordinate the activities of suppliers, shippers, and order entry systems to automate order entry through production, payment, and shipping business processes.

Implementing an order-driven, Web-based supply chain management system is not always easy, however, as *Insight on Technology: RFID AutoIdentification: Making Your Supply Chain Visible* illustrates.

### Collaborative Commerce

Collaborative commerce is a direct extension of supply chain management systems, as well as supply chain simplification. **Collaborative commerce** is defined as the use of digital technologies to permit organizations to collaboratively design, develop, build, and manage products through their life cycles. This is a much broader mission than EDI or simply managing the flow of information among organizations. Collaborative commerce involves a definitive move from a transaction focus to a relationship focus among the supply chain participants. Rather than having an arm's-length adversarial relationship with suppliers, collaborative commerce fosters sharing of sensitive internal information with suppliers and purchasers. Managing collaborative commerce requires knowing exactly what information to share with whom. Collaborative commerce extends beyond supply chain management activities to include the collaborative development of new products and services by multiple cooperating firms.

A good example of a collaborative commerce system is provided by Group Dekko. Group Dekko produces a variety of components including wire harnesses, molded

**collaborative commerce**
the use of digital technologies to permit organizations to collaboratively design, develop, build, and manage products through their life cycles

# INSIGHT ON TECHNOLOGY

## RFID AUTOIDENTIFICATION: MAKING YOUR SUPPLY CHAIN VISIBLE

It's 10 p.m. Do you know where your containers are? If you're in business anywhere in the world today, and that business involves physical goods, then chances are quite good that your business depends on the movement of goods in containers. In fact, there are more than 200 million sea cargo containers moving every year among the world's seaports, and nearly 50% of the value of all U.S. imports arrive via sea cargo containers each year. The containers are loaded onto ships, and stacked high on the deck. The containers also fit on the back of trucks and on railway carriages. So when the containers are unloaded from the ship, they continue their journey from the port on the back of trucks or trains. It is a fast and efficient way of moving cargo. A standard container is about 20 feet long, 8 feet wide, and 8 feet high, and can hold about 47,900 lbs of cargo.

Prior to the development of containers, all ocean-going cargo was loaded and unloaded onto ships in huge nets by dock workers, one package at a time. While the container revolutionized ocean shipping, vastly increasing productivity and reducing breakage, keeping track of 200 million cargo containers is difficult. While each container has its own permanent ID number painted on the side, as well as a bar code identification tag, this number must be entered manually by dock workers or scanned up close. Identification of containers is slow and prone to errors. If you had to find one container on a dock containing over 1,000 containers, you would have to read each ID number until you found the one you wanted.

Tracking containers is just one part of the larger B2B product identification problem. Retailers such as Wal-Mart, Target, and Amazon find it difficult and expensive to track millions of annual shipments into and out of their warehouses

and sales floors; the automotive industry finds it costly and difficult to synchronize the flow of parts into its factories; the U.S. Department of Defense logistics system finds it difficult to keep track of the movement of troop supplies; and the airline industry often loses bags in transit.

Thirty years ago, the development of the Uniform Product Code (UPC) and the ubiquitous bar code label was an initial first step towards automating the identification of goods. But the bar code technology of the 1970s still required humans or sometimes machines to scan products. The problem with bar codes is that they don't talk—they are passive labels that must be read or scanned.

Today, a new technology to replace bar codes is being deployed among the largest manufacturing and retailing firms. Radio frequency identification (RFID) involves the use of tags attached to products or product containers that transmit a radio signal in the 850 megahertz to 2.5 gigahertz range that continuously identifies themselves to radio receivers in warehouses, factories, retail floors, or on board ships. RFID labels are really tiny computer chips and a battery that are used to transmit each product's electronic product code to receivers nearby.

RFID has several key advantages over the old bar code scanner technology. RFID eliminates the line-of-sight reading requirement of bar codes and greatly increases the distance from which scanning can be done from a few inches up to 90 feet. RFID systems can be used just about anywhere—from clothing tags to missiles to pet tags to food—anywhere that a unique identification system is needed. The tag can carry information as simple as a pet owner's name and address or the cleaning instruction on a sweater to as complex as instructions on how to assemble a car. Best of all, instead of looking at a warehouse filled with thousands of packages that can't talk, you could be

(continued)

listening to these same thousands of packages each chirping a unique code, identifying themselves to you. Finding the single package you are looking for is much simplified. RFID tags produce a steady stream of data that can be entered into Internet- and intranet-based corporate applications such as SCM and ERP systems.

In 2010, the global RFID market is estimated to be $5.5 billion, with a U.S. market of $3 billion. The RFID market is expanding rapidly because of the growing use of RFIDs by governments, as well as private industry.

The tagging of apparel by companies such as Marks & Spencer and American Apparel is now in the rollout phase with 200 million RFID labels being used for apparel (including laundry) globally in 2010. In total, about 2.35 billion tags will be sold in 2010. Major computer firms such as Microsoft, IBM, and Hewlett-Packard are investing over several hundred million dollars each over the next five years to develop RFID software that will link RFID data to firms' SCM systems. Wal-Mart, the world's largest retailer, has made RFID an important part of its supply chain strategy. It began by mandating that its top 100 suppliers place RFID tags on all cases and pallets headed for the firm's Dallas distribution centers. Currently, about 600 of Wal-Mart's U.S. suppliers are tagging cases and pallets of some of the products they ship. About 1,000 Wal-Mart stores are RFID-enabled, with another 400 planned, as well as six of its distribution centers. In 2010, Wal-Mart introduced even more sophisticated electronic ID tags to track individual pairs of jeans and underwear (as opposed to pallets of clothing). Wal-Mart will place so-called removable "smart tags" on each piece of clothing. The smart tags can be read by handheld scanners at the point of sale, or elsewhere in the store. The smart tags will allow Wal-Mart managers to learn, for instance, which size of Wrangler jeans is missing, and which sizes should be reordered. In January 2008, the RFID program at Sam's Club became mandatory, with suppliers charged $2 per pallet for deliveries without RFID tags. Although Wal-Mart remains committed to the technology and estimates that it could increase sales by $287 million by using RFID technology, its implementation to date has had mixed results because suppliers have been reluctant to pay the costs of attaching RFID tags to pallets. Wal-Mart has had to subsidize this cost in order to gain acceptance from suppliers.

As adoption of the technology increases, RFID will have a profound impact on B2B e-commerce by reducing the cost of tracking goods through industry supply chains, reducing errors, and increasing the chances that the right product will be sent to the right customer.

■■■ **SOURCES:** "Walmart Will Track You and Your Undies With RFIDs," by Matthew Zuras, Switched.com, July 26, 2010; "Wal-Mart Radio Tags to Track Clothing," by Miguel Bustillo, *Wall Street Journal*, July 23, 2010; "RFID Market Projected to Grow in 2010," by Ilya Leybovich, Thomasnet.news.com, March 11, 2010; "RFID Printers Adapt to Changing Market Needs," by Brian Albright, *Integrated Solutions*, September 2009; "Bar Code Labelling, RFID, ASNs All Smooth the Flow of Goods," SCDigest.com, September 9, 2009; "Global RFID Market to be Worth USD 5.56 Billion in 2009," Report, ThePaypers.com, August 27, 2009; "IDTechEx Report: Apparel RFID 2008-2018," by Cathryn Hindle, Just-style.com, August 12, 2009; "The Up and Down of Wal-Mart RFID Implementation," by EcoSensa, March 24, 2009; "Apparel RFID 2008-2018" by Cathryn Hindle, *IDTechEx Report*, August 12, 2008; "Wal-Mart RFID Plan Has Mixed Results," *RFID News*, April 28, 2008; "Wal-Mart Gets Tough on RFID," by Mary Hayes Weier, *InformationWeek*, January 19, 2008.

plastic parts, and metal stamping for automobiles, appliances, and office furniture. In order to work with its large customers—automobile and appliance manufacturers—Group Dekko had to implement quality-control procedures conforming with international standard ISO 9000. The Group Dekko Services Department implemented a common, shared database of ISO documents using a software package called Lotus Domino to coordinate the efforts of the partner firms in Group Dekko. Lotus Domino is the Internet-based version of Lotus Notes, a collaborative document management and communications package. In this way, the separate Dekko companies could share standards, documents, graphics, and experiences in implementing the quality standards. This environment is being extended to share engineering drawings, bills of material, pricing, and routing information for new products. The goal is to involve Group Dekko companies, as well as their suppliers and customers, in the complete flow of design and product information.

Although collaborative commerce can involve customers as well as suppliers in the development of products, for the most part, collaborative commerce is concerned with the development of a rich communications environment to enable inter-firm sharing of designs, production plans, inventory levels, delivery schedules, and even the development of shared products (see **Figure 12.7**).

Efforts to develop closer collaboration among suppliers and purchasers originated in the late 1970s at Xerox Parc, Xerox Corporation's research center in Palo Alto. Development of the appropriate software to enable rich communications was furthered by research conducted by Lotus Development Corporation in the early 1990s. The development of the Internet as a rich communications medium has displaced proprietary software tools, and today, collaborative commerce almost always involves the use of Internet technologies to support sharing of graphic designs, documents, messages, and network meetings.

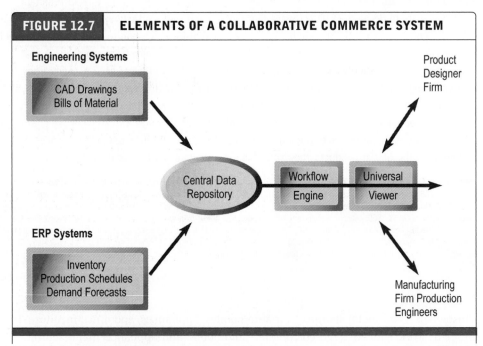

| FIGURE 12.7 | ELEMENTS OF A COLLABORATIVE COMMERCE SYSTEM |

A collaborative commerce application includes a central data repository where employees at several different firms can store engineering drawings and other documents. A workflow engine determines who can see this data and what rules will apply for displaying the data on individual workstations. A viewer can be a browser operating on a workstation.

Collaborative commerce is very different from EDI, which is a technology for structured communications among firms. Collaborative commerce is more like an interactive teleconference among members of the supply chain. EDI and collaborative commerce share one characteristic: they are not open, competitive marketplaces, but instead are, technically, private industrial networks that connect strategic partners in a supply chain.

In Section 12.3, we discuss collaborative commerce in greater depth as a technology that enables private industrial networks.

## MAIN TYPES OF INTERNET-BASED B2B COMMERCE

There are two generic types of Internet-based B2B commerce systems: Net marketplaces and private industrial networks (see **Figure 12.8**). Within each of these general categories are many different subtypes that we discuss in the following sections.

Net marketplaces (also referred to as exchanges) bring together potentially thousands of sellers and buyers into a single digital marketplace operated over the Internet. Net marketplaces are transaction-based, support many-to-many as well as one-to-many relationships, and bear some resemblance to financial markets such as the New York Stock Exchange. There are many different types of Net marketplaces, with different pricing mechanisms, biases, and value propositions that will be explored in Section 12.2 (Kerrigan, et al., 2001). Private industrial networks bring together a small number of strategic business partner firms that collaborate to develop highly efficient supply chains and satisfy customer demand for products. Private industrial networks are relationship-based, support many-to-one or many-to-few relationships, and bear some resemblance to internal collaborative work environments. There are

---

| **FIGURE 12.8** | **TWO MAIN TYPES OF INTERNET-BASED B2B COMMERCE** |

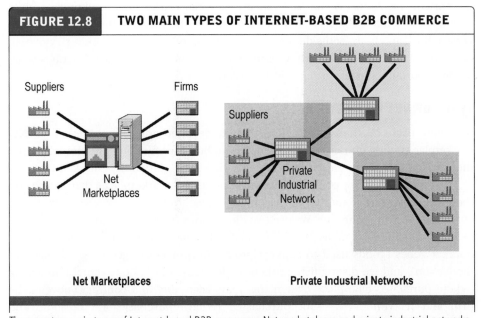

There are two main types of Internet-based B2B commerce: Net marketplaces and private industrial networks.

many different types of private industrial networks, as discussed in Section 12.3. Private industrial networks are by far the largest form of B2B e-commerce, and account for over 10 times as much revenue as Net marketplaces.

## 12.2 NET MARKETPLACES

One of the most compelling visions of B2B e-commerce is that of an electronic marketplace on the Internet that would bring thousands of fragmented suppliers into contact with hundreds of major purchasers of industrial goods for the purpose of conducting "frictionless" commerce. The hope was that these suppliers would compete with one another on price, transactions would be automated and low cost, and as a result, the price of industrial supplies would fall. By extracting fees from buyers and sellers on each transaction, third-party intermediary market makers could earn significant revenues. These Net marketplaces could scale easily as volume increased by simply adding more computers and communications equipment.

In pursuit of this vision, well over 1,500 Net marketplaces sprang up in the early days of e-commerce. Unfortunately, many of them have since disappeared and the population is expected to stabilize at about 200. Still, many survive, and they are joined by other types of Net marketplaces—some private and some public—based on different assumptions that are quite successful

### THE VARIETY AND CHARACTERISTICS OF NET MARKETPLACES

There is a confusing variety of Net marketplaces today, and several different ways to classify them. For instance, some writers classify Net marketplaces on the basis of their pricing mechanisms—auction, bid/ask, negotiated price, and fixed prices—while others classify markets based on characteristics of the markets they serve (vertical versus horizontal, or sell-side versus buy-side), or ownership (industry-owned consortia versus independent third-party intermediaries). **Table 12.2** describes some of the important characteristics of Net marketplaces.

### TYPES OF NET MARKETPLACES

Although each of these distinctions helps describe the phenomenon of Net marketplaces, they do not focus on the central business functionality provided, and they are not capable by themselves of describing the variety of Net marketplaces.

In **Figure 12.9**, we present a classification of Net marketplaces that focuses on their business functionality; that is, what these Net marketplaces provide for businesses seeking solutions. We use two dimensions of Net marketplaces to create a four-cell classification table. We differentiate Net marketplaces as providing either indirect goods (goods used to support production) or direct goods (goods used in production), and we distinguish markets as providing either contractual purchasing (where purchases take place over many years according to a contract between the firm and its vendor) or spot purchasing (where purchases are episodic and anonymous—vendors and buyers do not have an ongoing relationship and may not

| **TABLE 12.2** | **OTHER CHARACTERISTICS OF NET MARKETPLACES: A B2B VOCABULARY** |
|---|---|
| CHARACTERISTIC | MEANING |
| Bias | Sell-side vs. buy-side vs. neutral. Whose interests are advantaged: buyers, sellers, or no bias? |
| Ownership | Industry vs. third party. Who owns the marketplace? |
| Pricing mechanism | Fixed-price catalogs, auctions, bid/ask, and RFPs/RFQs. |
| Scope/Focus | Horizontal vs. vertical markets. |
| Value creation | What benefits do they offer customers or suppliers? |
| Access to market | In public markets, any firm can enter, but in private markets, entry is by invitation only. |

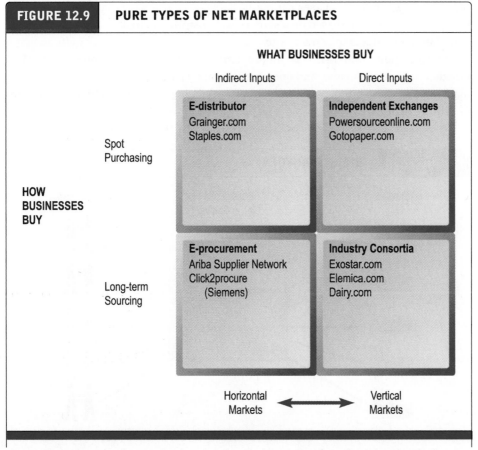

**FIGURE 12.9    PURE TYPES OF NET MARKETPLACES**

There are four main types of Net marketplaces based on the intersection of two dimensions: how businesses buy and what they buy. A third dimension—horizontal versus vertical markets—also distinguishes the different types of Net marketplaces.

know one another). The intersection of these dimensions produces four main types of Net marketplaces that are relatively straightforward: e-distributors, e-procurement networks, exchanges, and industry consortia. Note, however, that in the real world, some Net marketplaces can be found in multiple parts of this figure as business models change and opportunities appear and disappear. Nevertheless, the discussion of "pure types" of Net marketplaces is a useful starting point.

Each of these Net marketplaces seeks to provide value to customers in different ways. We discuss each type of Net marketplace in more detail in the following sections.

### E-distributors

**e-distributor**

provides electronic catalog that represents the products of thousands of direct manufacturers

E-distributors are the most common and most easily understood type of Net marketplace. An **e-distributor** provides an electronic catalog that represents the products of thousands of direct manufacturers (see **Figure 12.10**). An e-distributor is the equivalent of Amazon.com for industry. E-distributors are independently owned intermediaries that offer industrial customers a single source from which to order indirect goods (often referred to as MRO) on a spot, as-needed basis. A significant percentage of corporate purchases cannot be satisfied under a company's existing contracts, and must be purchased on a spot basis. E-distributors make money by charging a markup on products they distribute.

Organizations and firms in all industries require MRO supplies. The MRO function maintains, repairs, and operates commercial buildings and maintains all the machinery of these buildings from heating, ventilating, and air conditioning systems to lighting fixtures.

---

**FIGURE 12.10**   **E-DISTRIBUTORS**

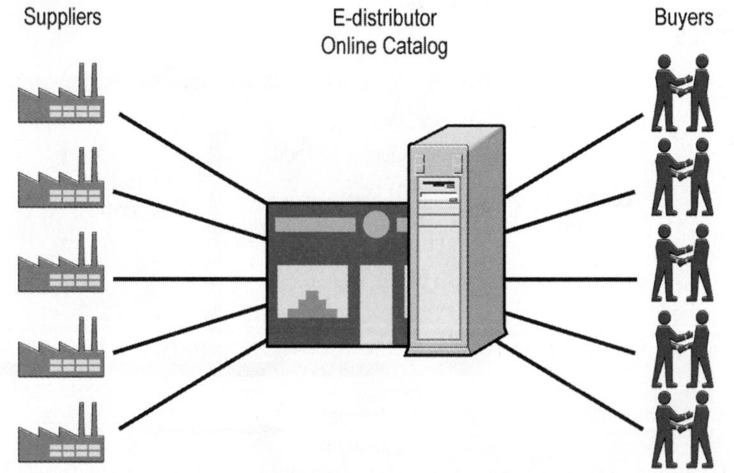

E-distributors are firms that bring the products of thousands of suppliers into a single online electronic catalog for sale to thousands of buyer firms. E-distributors are sometimes referred to as one-to-many markets, one seller serving many firms.

E-distributors operate in horizontal markets because they serve many different industries with products from many different suppliers. E-distributors usually operate "public" markets in the sense that any firm can order from the catalog, as opposed to "private" markets, where membership is restricted to selected firms.

E-distributor prices are usually fixed, but large customers receive discounts and other incentives to purchase, such as credit, reporting on account activity, and limited forms of business purchasing rules (for instance, no purchases greater than $500 for a single item without a purchase order). The primary benefits offered to industrial customers are lower search costs, lower transaction costs, wide selection, rapid delivery, and low prices.

The most frequently cited example of a public e-distribution market is W.W. Grainger. Grainger is involved in both long-term systematic sourcing as well as spot sourcing, but its emphasis is on spot sourcing. Grainger's business model is to become the world's leading source of MRO suppliers, and its revenue model is that of a typical retailer: it owns the products, and takes a markup on the products it sells to customers. At Grainger.com, users get an electronic online version of Grainger's famous seven-pound catalog, plus other parts not available in the catalog (adding up to around 475,000 parts), and complete electronic ordering and payment (W.W. Grainger Inc., 2010).

## E-procurement

An **e-procurement Net marketplace** is an independently owned intermediary that connects hundreds of online suppliers offering millions of maintenance and repair parts to business firms who pay fees to join the market (see **Figure 12.11**). E-procurement Net marketplaces are typically used for long-term contractual purchasing of indirect goods (MRO); they create online horizontal markets, but they also provide for members' spot sourcing of MRO supplies. E-procurement companies make money by charging a percentage of each transaction, licensing consulting services and software, and assessing network use fees (Trkman and McCormack, 2010).

E-procurement companies expand on the business model of simpler e-distributors by including the online catalogs of hundreds of suppliers and offering value chain management services to both buyers and sellers. **Value chain management (VCM) services** provided by e-procurement companies include automation of a firm's entire procurement process on the buyer side and automation of the selling business processes on the seller side. For purchasers, e-procurement companies automate purchase orders, requisitions, sourcing, business rules enforcement, invoicing, and payment. For suppliers, e-procurement companies provide catalog creation and content management, order management, fulfillment, invoicing, shipment, and settlement.

E-procurement Net marketplaces are sometimes referred to as many-to-many markets. They are mediated by an independent third party that purports to represent both buyers and sellers, and hence claim to be neutral. On the other hand, because they may include the catalogs of both competing suppliers and competing e-distributors, they have a likely bias in favor of the buyers. Nevertheless, by aggregating huge buyer firms into their networks, they provide distinct marketing benefits for suppliers and reduce customer acquisition costs.

**e-procurement Net marketplace**
independently owned intermediary that connects hundreds of online suppliers offering millions of maintenance and repair parts to business firms who pay fees to join the market

**value chain management (VCM) services**
include automation of a firm's entire procurement process on the buyer side and automation of the selling business processes on the seller side

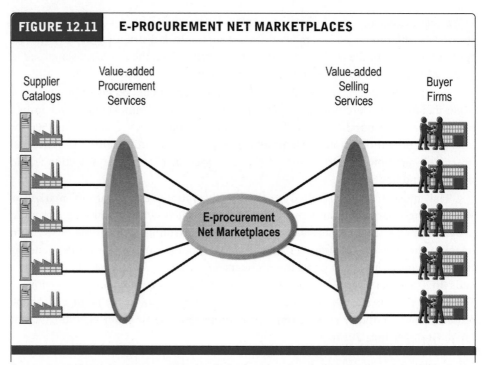

**FIGURE 12.11** | **E-PROCUREMENT NET MARKETPLACES**

E-procurement Net marketplaces aggregate hundreds of catalogs in a single marketplace and make them available to firms, often on a custom basis that reflects only the suppliers desired by the participating firms.

Players in this market segment include Ariba (which purchased its primary competitor, FreeMarkets, in 2004), Perfect Commerce, BravoSolution, A.T. Kearney Procurement & Analytic Solutions, and Emptoris. The very large enterprise software firms—Oracle, SAP, i2, and JDA Software Group (which acquired Manugistics in 2006)—now also offer procurement solutions to their customers and compete directly against the early entrants in this market.

Air Products & Chemicals, Inc., a worldwide supplier of industrial gases, chemicals, and environmental solutions, uses Ariba Sourcing software to manage supplier negotiations and to enable employees to purchase using online catalogs. According to the company, using Ariba Sourcing allowed it to achieve savings of 15%-40%, and decrease sourcing cycle times. "What used to take four weeks now takes only two," according to Air Products' Strategic Sourcing Manager (Ariba, 2010).

### Exchanges

**exchange**
independently owned online marketplace that connects hundreds to potentially thousands of suppliers and buyers in a dynamic, real-time environment

An **exchange** is an independently owned online marketplace that connects hundreds to potentially thousands of suppliers and buyers in a dynamic, real-time environment (see **Figure 12.12**). Exchanges generally create vertical markets that focus on the spot-purchasing requirements of large firms in a single industry, such as computers and telecommunications, electronics, food, and industrial equipment, although there are exceptions to this generalization as described in

| **FIGURE 12.12** | **EXCHANGES** |
| --- | --- |

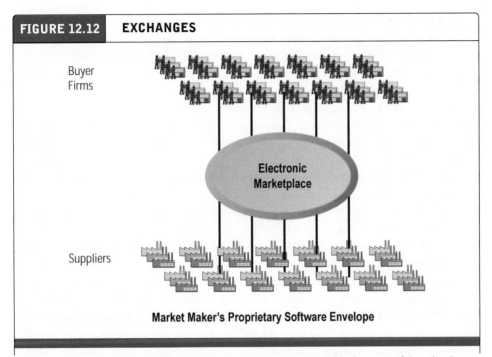

Buyer
Firms

**Electronic
Marketplace**

Suppliers

**Market Maker's Proprietary Software Envelope**

Independent exchanges bring potentially thousands of suppliers to a vertical (industry-specific) marketplace to sell their goods to potentially thousands of buyer firms. Exchanges are sometimes referred to as many-to-many markets because they have many suppliers serving many buyer firms.

this section. Exchanges were the prototype Internet-based marketplace in the early days of e-commerce; as noted above, over 1,500 were created in this period, but most have failed.

Exchanges make money by charging a commission on the transaction. The pricing model can be through an online negotiation, auction, RFQ, or fixed buy-and-sell prices. The benefits offered to customers of exchanges include reduced search cost for parts and spare capacity. Other benefits include lower prices created by a global marketplace driven by competition among suppliers who would, presumably, sell goods at very low profit margins at one world-market price. The benefits offered suppliers are access to a global purchasing environment and the opportunity to unload production overruns (although at very competitive prices and low profit margins). Even though they are private intermediaries, exchanges are public in the sense of permitting any bona fide buyer or seller to participate.

Exchanges tend to be biased toward the buyer even though they are independently owned and presumably neutral. Suppliers are disadvantaged by the fact that exchanges put them in direct price competition with other similar suppliers around the globe, driving profit margins down. Exchanges have failed primarily because suppliers have refused to join them, and hence, the existing markets have very low liquidity, defeating the very purpose and benefits of an exchange. **Liquidity** is typically measured by the number of buyers and sellers in a market, the volume of transactions, and the size of transactions. You know a

**liquidity**
typically measured by the number of buyers and sellers in a market, the volume of transactions, and the size of transactions

market is liquid when you can buy or sell just about any size order at just about any time you want. On all of these measures, many exchanges failed, resulting in a very small number of participants, few trades, and small trade value per transaction. The most common reason for not using exchanges is the absence of traditional, trusted suppliers.

While most exchanges tend to be vertical marketplaces offering direct supplies, some exchanges offer indirect inputs as well, such as electricity and power, transportation services (usually to the transportation industry), and professional services. **Table 12.3** lists a few examples of some current independent exchanges.

The following capsule description of two exchanges provides insight into their origins and current functions.

Global Wine & Spirits (GWS) (Globalwinespirits.com) is somewhat unique among independent exchanges, not only as a start-up that has managed to survive, but also as a latecomer to the B2B e-commerce community. GWS opened in 1999, but did not begin to trade products online until May 2001. Based in Montreal, Quebec, GWS is operated by Mediagrif Interactive Technologies Inc., a Canadian company that operates a number of independent exchanges in a variety of industries. GWS offers a spot marketplace for wines, where wine and spirit producers offer wines for sale; a "call for tenders" market, where members make offers to purchase wines and spirits; a trade database with listings of thousands of industry professionals; and a wine and spirits catalog with over 35,000 products and 6,700 companies (Globalwinespirits.com, 2010).

Inventory Locator Service (ILS) has its roots as an offline intermediary, serving as a listing service for aftermarket parts in the aerospace industry. Upon opening in 1979, ILS initially provided a telephone and fax-based directory of aftermarket parts to airplane owners and mechanics, along with government procurement professionals. As early as 1984, ILS incorporated e-mail capabilities as part of its RFQ services, and by 1998, it had begun to conduct online auctions for hard-to-find parts. In 2010, ILS maintains an Internet-accessible database of over 5 billion aerospace and marine industry parts, and has also developed an eRFQ feature that helps users streamline their sourcing processes. The network's 22,000 subscribers in 93 different countries access the site over 60,000 times a day. (Inventory Locator Service, 2010).

| TABLE 12.3 | EXAMPLES OF INDEPENDENT EXCHANGES |
|---|---|
| EXCHANGE | FOCUS |
| PowerSource Online | Computer parts exchange |
| Converge | Semiconductors and computer peripherals |
| Smarterwork | Spare professional services from Web design to legal advice |
| Active International | Trading in underutilized manufacturing capacity |
| IntercontinentalExchange | International online marketplace for over 600 commodities |

## Industry Consortia

An **industry consortium** is an industry-owned vertical market that enables buyers to purchase direct inputs (both goods and services) from a limited set of invited participants (see **Figure 12.13**). Industry consortia emphasize long-term contractual purchasing, the development of stable relationships (as opposed to merely an anonymous transaction emphasis), and the creation of industry-wide data standards and synchronization efforts. Industry consortia are more focused on optimizing long-term supply relationships than independent exchanges, which tend to focus more on short-term transactions. The ultimate objective of industry consortia is the unification of supply chains within entire industries, across many tiers, through common data definitions, network standards, and computing platforms. In addition, industry consortia, unlike independent exchanges described previously, take their marching orders from the industry and not from venture capitalists or investment bankers. This means any profits from operating industry consortia are returned to industry business firms.

Industry consortia sprang up in 1999 and 2000 in part as a reaction to the earlier development of independently owned exchanges, which were viewed by large

**industry consortium**
industry-owned vertical market that enables buyers to purchase direct inputs (both goods and services) from a limited set of invited participants

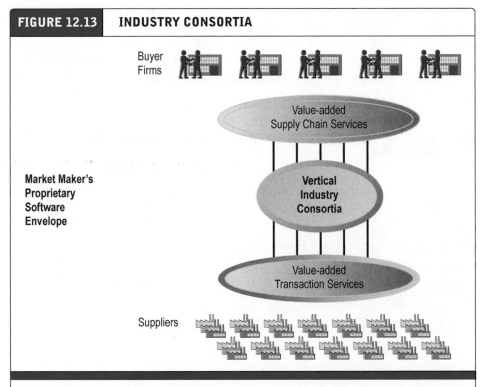

| **FIGURE 12.13** | **INDUSTRY CONSORTIA** |
|---|---|

Buyer Firms

Value-added Supply Chain Services

**Market Maker's Proprietary Software Envelope**

Vertical Industry Consortia

Value-added Transaction Services

Suppliers

Industry consortia bring thousands of suppliers into direct contact with a smaller number of very large buyers. The market makers provide value-added software services for procurement, transaction management, shipping, and payment for both buyers and suppliers. Industry consortia are sometimes referred to as many-to-few markets, where many suppliers (albeit selected by the buyers) serve a few very large buyers, mediated by a variety of value-added services.

industries (such as the automotive and chemical industries) as market interlopers that would not directly serve the interests of large buyers, but would instead line their own pockets and those of their venture capital investors. Rather than "pay-to-play," large firms decided to "pay-to-own" their markets. Another concern of large firms was that Net marketplaces would work only if large suppliers and buyers participated, and only if there was liquidity. Independent exchanges were not attracting enough players to achieve liquidity. In addition, exchanges often failed to provide additional value-added services that would transform the value chain for the entire industry, including linking the new marketplaces to firms' ERP systems. More than 60 industry consortia now exist, with many industries having more than one (see **Table 12.4**).

The industries with the most consortia are food, metals, and chemicals, although these are not necessarily the largest consortia in terms of revenue. Many very large Fortune 500 and private firms are investors in several industry consortia. For instance, Cargill—the world's largest private corporation—invested in six consortia that exist at various points in Cargill's and the food industry's tangled value chain.

Industry consortia make money in a number of ways. Industry members usually pay for the creation of the consortia's capabilities and contribute initial operating capital. Then industry consortia charge buyer and seller firms transaction and subscription fees. Industry members—both buyers and sellers—are expected to reap benefits far greater than their contributions through the rationalization of the procurement process, competition among vendors, and closer relationships with vendors.

Industry consortia offer many different pricing mechanisms, ranging from auctions to fixed prices to RFQs, depending on the products and the situation. Prices

| TABLE 12.4 | INDUSTRY CONSORTIA BY INDUSTRY (SEPTEMBER 2010) |
|---|---|
| INDUSTRY | NAME OF INDUSTRY CONSORTIA |
| Aerospace | Exostar |
| Automotive | SupplyOn |
| Chemical | Elemica |
| Financial | MuniCenter |
| Food | Dairy.com, EFSNetwork |
| Hospitality | Avendra |
| Medical Services, Supplies | GHX (Global Healthcare Exchange) |
| Metals and Mining | Quadrem |
| Paper and Forest Products | PaperFiber |
| Shipping | OceanConnect |
| Textiles | The Seam (Cotton Consortium) |
| Transportation | Transplace |

can also be negotiated, and the environment, while competitive, is nevertheless restricted to a smaller number of buyers—selected, reliable, and long-term suppliers who are often viewed as "strategic industry" partners. The bias of industry consortia is clearly toward the large buyers who control access to this lucrative market channel and can benefit from competitive pricing offered by alternative suppliers. Benefits to suppliers come from access to large buyer firm procurement systems, long-term stable relationships, and large order sizes.

Industry consortia can and often do force suppliers to use the consortia's networks and proprietary software as a condition of selling to the industry's members. Although exchanges failed for a lack of suppliers and liquidity, the market power of consortia members ensures suppliers will participate, so consortia may be able to avoid the fate of voluntary exchanges. Clearly, industry consortia are at an advantage when compared to independent exchanges because, unlike the venture-capital-backed exchanges, they have deep-pocket financial backing from the very start and guaranteed liquidity based on a steady flow of large firm orders. Yet industry consortia are a relatively new phenomenon, and the long-term profitability of these consortia, especially when several consortia exist for a single industry, has yet to be demonstrated.

The following capsule descriptions of two industry consortia illustrate their vitality and growth potential.

Exostar is an aerospace industry consortium. Its founding partners include BAE Systems, Boeing, Lockheed Martin, Raytheon, and Rolls-Royce. Exostar has taken a slow but steady approach to building its technology platform. It has kept its focus on the direct procurement and supply chain needs of its largest members, and taken its time developing a portfolio of technology solutions that meet its needs. Its current products include Supply Pass, an integrated suite of tools that enables suppliers to handle buyer transactions via the Internet; SourcePass, which provides a dynamic bidding environment for buyers and sellers; and ProcurePass, which enables buyers to handle supplier transactions online, among others. As of September 2010, Exostar served a community of more than 70,000 trading partners (Exostar, 2010).

Serving the mining, minerals, and metals industries, Quadrem initially opened in May 2000 with 14 founding members. Its current shareholders include some of the world's largest natural resource companies, such as Alcoa, DeBeers, and Phelps Dodge, and together represent about $90 billion in annual spending. As of 2010, Quadrem's network includes more than 60,000 suppliers and 1,500 buyers, and handles more than $22 billion in annual orders (Quadrem International Ltd., 2010).

## THE LONG-TERM DYNAMICS OF NET MARKETPLACES

Net marketplaces are changing rapidly because of the widespread failures of early exchanges and a growing realization by key participants that real value will derive from B2B e-commerce only when it can change the entire procurement system, the supply chain, and the process of collaboration among firms. Several industry consortia have transformed themselves into industry data standards and synchronization forums. The consolidation of Net marketplaces has resulted in remaining firms that are much stronger and that are beginning to grow rapidly once again. In fact, B2B online transaction volumes are growing worldwide and within the United States at 20%–30% per year.

**Figure 12.14** depicts some of these changes. Pure Net marketplace exchanges are moving away from the simple "electronic marketplace" vision, and toward playing a more central role in changing the procurement process. Independent exchanges are ideal buy-out candidates for industry consortia because they have often developed the technology infrastructure. In any event, consortia and exchanges are beginning to work together in selected markets. Likewise, e-distributors are securing admission to large e-procurement systems and also seeking admission to industry consortia as suppliers of indirect goods.

Other notable trends include the movement from simple transactions involving spot purchasing to longer-term contractual relationships involving both indirect and direct goods (Wise and Morrison, 2000). The complexity and duration of transactions is increasing, and both buyers and suppliers are becoming accustomed to working in a digital environment, and making less use of the fax machine and telephone. To date, Net marketplaces, as well as private industrial networks, have emerged in a political climate friendly to large-scale cooperation among very large firms. However, the possibility exists that Net marketplaces may provide some firms with an ideal platform to collude on pricing, market sharing, and market access, all of which would be anti-competitive and reduce the efficiency of the marketplace.

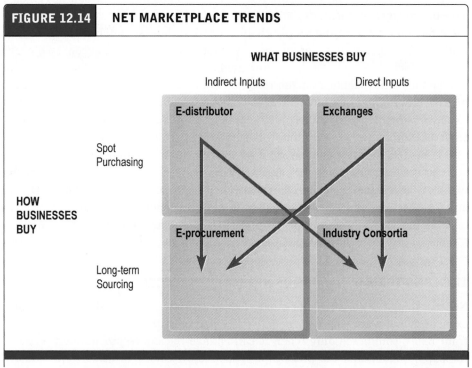

| **FIGURE 12.14** | **NET MARKETPLACE TRENDS** |

E-distributors and exchanges are migrating their business models toward more sustained, higher value-added relationships with buyer firms by providing e-procurement services and participating in industry consortia.

## 12.3 PRIVATE INDUSTRIAL NETWORKS

Private industrial networks today form the largest part of B2B e-commerce, both on and off the Internet. Industry analysts estimate that in 2010, over 50% of B2B expenditures by large firms will be for the development of private industrial networks. Private industrial networks can be considered the foundation of the "extended enterprise," and the notion that firms can extend their boundaries and their business processes to include supply chain and logistics partners.

### WHAT ARE PRIVATE INDUSTRIAL NETWORKS?

As noted at the beginning of this chapter, private industrial networks are direct descendants of existing EDI networks, and they are closely tied to existing ERP systems used by large firms. A private industrial network (sometimes referred to as a private trading exchange, or PTX) is a Web-enabled network for the coordination of trans-organizational business processes (sometimes also called collaborative commerce). A **trans-organizational business process** requires at least two independent firms to perform (Laudon and Laudon, 2010). For the most part, these networks originate in and closely involve the manufacturing and related support industries, and therefore we refer to them as "industrial" networks, although in the future they could just as easily apply to some services. These networks can be industry-wide, but often begin and sometimes focus on the voluntary coordination of a group of supplying firms centered about a single, very large manufacturing firm. Private industrial networks can be viewed as "extended enterprises" in the sense that they often begin as ERP systems in a single firm, and are then expanded to include (often using an extranet) the firm's major suppliers. **Figure 12.15** illustrates a private industrial network originally built by Procter & Gamble (P&G) in the United States to coordinate supply chains among its suppliers, distributors, truckers, and retailers.

**trans-organizational business process**
process that requires at least two independent firms to perform

In P&G's private industrial network shown in Figure 12.15, customer sales are captured at the cash register, which then initiates a flow of information back to distributors, P&G, and its suppliers. This tells P&G and its suppliers the exact level of demand for thousands of products. This information is then used to initiate production, supply, and transportation to replenish products at the distributors and retailers. This process is called an efficient customer response system (a demand-pull production model), and it relies on an equally efficient supply chain management system to coordinate the supply side.

Not surprisingly, there is not a great deal of detailed information about private industrial networks. Most companies that originate and participate in these networks view them as a competitive advantage, and therefore they are reluctant to release information about how much they cost and how they operate.

GE, Dell Computer, Cisco Systems, Microsoft, IBM, Nike, Coca-Cola, Wal-Mart, Nokia, and Hewlett-Packard are among the firms operating successful private industrial networks.

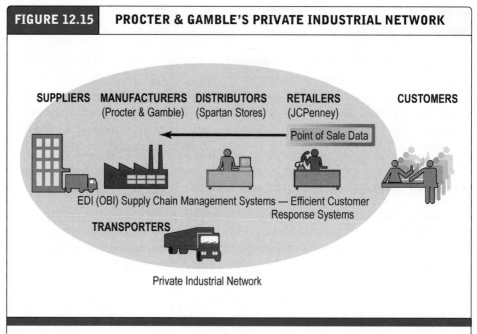

**FIGURE 12.15**   **PROCTER & GAMBLE'S PRIVATE INDUSTRIAL NETWORK**

Procter & Gamble's private industrial network attempts to coordinate the trans-organizational business processes of the many firms it deals with in the consumer products industry.

## CHARACTERISTICS OF PRIVATE INDUSTRIAL NETWORKS

The central focus of private industrial networks is to provide an industry-wide global solution to achieve the highest levels of efficiency. The specific objectives of a private industrial network include:

- Developing efficient purchasing and selling business processes industry-wide
- Developing industry-wide resource planning to supplement enterprise-wide resource planning
- Increasing supply chain visibility—knowing the inventory levels of buyers and suppliers
- Achieving closer buyer-supplier relationships, including demand forecasting, communications, and conflict resolution
- Operating on a global scale—globalization
- Reducing industry risk by preventing imbalances of supply and demand, including developing financial derivatives, insurance, and futures markets

Private industrial networks serve different goals from Net marketplaces. Net marketplaces are primarily transaction-oriented, whereas private industrial networks focus on continuous business process coordination between companies. This can include much more than just supply chain management, such as product design, sourcing, demand forecasting, asset management, sales, and marketing. Private industrial networks do support transactions, but that is not their primary focus.

Private industrial networks usually focus on a single sponsoring company that "owns" the network, sets the rules, establishes governance (a structure of authority, rule enforcement, and control), and invites firms to participate at its sole discretion. Therefore, these networks are "private." This sets them apart from industry consortia, which are usually owned by major firms collectively through equity participation. Whereas Net marketplaces have a strong focus on indirect goods and services, private industrial networks focus on strategic, direct goods and services.

For instance, Ace Hardware, a cooperative of 5,100 retail hardware stores, uses a private industrial network to manage inventory levels and collaborate with suppliers by linking 14 Ace distribution centers and nine key suppliers. In the past, a team of 30 Ace procurement managers used faxes, phones, and an older EDI system to buy products for retail members. It took 7 to 10 days to process an order. Suppliers had no access to inventory levels in retail stores or Ace distribution centers, forcing them to guess their likely production requirements. Manco, one large supplier of Ace, now uses the Internet-based private industrial network to accurately gauge demand for more than 200 products, from duct tape to shelf liners, that it supplies Ace. The more streamlined ordering process allowed Manco to reduce distribution costs by 28% and freight costs by 18% (VICS, 2004; ADX Corporation, 2004; Gleason, 2003).

Perhaps no single firm better illustrates the benefits of developing private industrial networks than Wal-Mart, described in *Insight on Business: Wal-Mart Develops a Private Industrial Network*.

## PRIVATE INDUSTRIAL NETWORKS AND COLLABORATIVE COMMERCE

Private industrial networks can do much more than just serve a supply chain and efficient customer response system. They can also include other activities of a single large manufacturing firm, including design of products and engineering diagrams, as well as marketing plans and demand forecasting. Collaboration among businesses can take many forms and involve a wide range of activities—from simple supply chain management to coordinating market feedback to designers at supply firms (see **Figure 12.16**).

One form of collaboration—and perhaps the most profound—is industry-wide **collaborative resource planning, forecasting, and replenishment** (CPFR), which involves working with network members to forecast demand, develop production plans, and coordinate shipping, warehousing, and stocking activities to ensure retail and wholesale shelf space is replenished with just the right amount of goods. If this goal is achieved, hundreds of millions of dollars of excess inventory and capacity could be wrung out of an industry. This activity alone is likely to produce the largest benefits and justify the cost of developing private industrial networks.

A second area of collaboration is *demand chain visibility*. In the past, it was impossible to know where excess capacity or supplies existed in the supply and distribution chains. For instance, retailers might have significantly overstocked shelves, but suppliers and manufacturers—not knowing this—might be building excess capacity or supplies for even more production. These excess inventories would

**collaborative resource planning, forecasting, and replenishment (CPFR)**

involves working with network members to forecast demand, develop production plans, and coordinate shipping, warehousing, and stocking activities to ensure that retail and wholesale shelf space is replenished with just the right amount of goods

# WAL-MART DEVELOPS A PRIVATE INDUSTRIAL NETWORK

Wal-Mart is a well-known leader in the application of network technology to the coordination of its supply chain. With sales of more than $405 billion for the fiscal year ending January 31, 2010, Wal-Mart has been able to use information technology to achieve a decisive cost advantage over competitors. As you might imagine, the world's largest retailer also has the world's largest supply chain, with more than 60,000 suppliers worldwide. In the next five years, the company plans to expand from around 4,200 retail stores in the United States (including Sam's Clubs) to over 5,000, and increase its selection of goods to include automobiles, pianos, groceries, high-fashion clothing, and personal computers. In other words, Wal-Mart's strategic plan is to be where they are not now. In September 2010, Wal-Mart offered to purchase South African retailer Massmart Holdings Inc., which has 292 stores throughout Africa, for $4.6 billion. All of this will require an even more capable private industrial network than what is now in place.

In the late 1980s, Wal-Mart developed the beginnings of collaborative commerce using an EDI-based SCM system that required its large suppliers to use Wal-Mart's proprietary EDI network to respond to orders from Wal-Mart purchasing managers. In 1991, Wal-Mart expanded the capabilities of its EDI-based network by introducing Retail Link. This system connected Wal-Mart's largest suppliers to Wal-Mart's own inventory management system, and it required large suppliers to track actual sales by stores and to replenish supplies as dictated by demand and following rules imposed by Wal-Mart. Wal-Mart also introduced financial payment systems that ensure that Wal-Mart does not own the goods until they arrive and are shelved.

In 1997, Wal-Mart moved Retail Link to an extranet that allowed suppliers to directly link over the Internet into Wal-Mart's inventory management system. In 2000, Wal-Mart hired an outside firm to upgrade Retail Link from being a supply chain management tool toward a more collaborative forecasting, planning, and rep-lenishment system. Using demand aggregation software provided by Atlas Metaprise Software, Wal-Mart purchasing agents can now aggregate demand from Wal-Mart's 4,200 separate stores in the United States into a single RFQ from suppliers. This gives Wal-Mart tremendous clout with even the largest suppliers. Wal-Mart and Atlas plan to first build a global sourcing network. Previously, Wal-Mart's foreign location buyers relied on a mix of telephones, fax, and e-mail to communicate their spending forecasts. The new system allows them to submit forecasts via the Internet. Wal-Mart headquarters in turn issues worldwide RFQs for all stores. The Atlas software helps Wal-Mart purchasing agents select a winning bid and negotiate final contracts.

In addition, suppliers can now immediately access information on inventories, purchase orders, invoice status, and sales forecasts, based on 104 weeks of online, real-time, item-level data. The system does not require smaller supplier firms to adopt expensive EDI software solutions. Instead, they can use standard browsers and PCs loaded with free software from Wal-Mart. There are now over 20,000 suppliers—small and large—participating in Wal-Mart's network.

In 2002, Wal-Mart switched to an entirely Internet-based private network. Wal-Mart adopted AS2, a software package from iSoft Corporation, a Dallas-based software company. AS2 implements EDI-INT (an Internet-based

(continued)

standard version of EDI), and the result is a radical reduction in communications costs. Wal-Mart uses Sterling Commerce (the largest single provider of EDI communication systems to industry) and IBM to support this EDI initiative. The AS2 initiative lets suppliers connect, deliver, validate, and reply to data securely over the Internet. IBM uses its expertise to assist Wal-Mart suppliers in selecting and implementing the appropriate AS2-certified solutions that best meet their needs. Sterling Commerce provides interoperability services for EDI-INT AS2 connectivity between Wal-Mart and its suppliers. In 2007, Wal-Mart's rapid growth, especially global operations, forced it go outside for its financial services operation systems. Wal-Mart hired SAP, an enterprise software mangement firm, to build a global financial management system for Wal-Mart. Wal-Mart has finally started to outgrow its homegrown systems.

Despite the recession, in 2009–2010, Wal-Mart's sales are growing slowly while other retailers suffer declining revenues of 5%–10%. In the first half of 2010, Wal-Mart's revenues of $202 billion were up 5% from 2009, and its profits were $6.8 billion, up 6% from 2009. Same-store sales in the U.S. increased by 5.6% in the first quarter. Wal-mart continues to innovate its products and services. In 2009, it announced it would develop a Web site where Wal-Mart suppliers could sell their goods directly to consumers (watch out Amazon), and that it would enter into the medical records business by building a package of hardware, software, and support for small doctor's offices at half the price of competitors.

Wal-Mart's success spurred its competitors in the retail industry to develop industry-wide private industrial networks such as Global NetXchange (now Agentrics) in an effort to duplicate the success of Wal-Mart. Wal-Mart executives have said Wal-Mart would not join these networks, or any industry-sponsored consortium or independent exchange, because doing so would only help its competitors achieve what Wal-Mart has already accomplished with Retail Link. To compete with the efficiencies attained by Wal-Mart, other retailers, such as JCPenney, have implemented their own extensive private industrial networks to link suppliers to their stores' inventories directly over the Internet. JCPenney has even given over some of its inventory control and product selection to its largest apparel provider, TAL Apparel Ltd. of Hong Kong.

**SOURCES:** Wal-Mart Stores Inc., Report on Form 10-Q for the fiscal quarter ended June 30, 2010, filed Septemer 1, 2010; Wal-Mart Stores Inc., Report on Form 10-K for the fiscal year ended January 31, 2010, filed March 31, 2010; "Wal-Mart Says Its Market Share Is Rising," by Stephanie Rosenblum, *New York Times*, May 15, 2009; "Wal-Mart Stores Web Site Creates New Program That Lets Outside Retailers Offer Products," Taragana.com, August 31, 2009; "Wal-Mart Plans to Market Digital Health Records System," by Steve Lohr, *New York Times*, March 14, 2009; "Wal-Mart Stores Inc.—Requirements," Walmart.com, September 25, 2008; "How Wal-Mart Lost Its Technology Edge," by Thomas Wailgum, *Network World*, October 5, 2007; "Who Gains, Who Loses, from RFID's Growing Presence in the Marketplace?," Knowledge@Wharton, March 23, 2005.

raise costs for the entire industry and create extraordinary pressures to discount merchandise, reducing profits for everyone.

A third area of collaboration is *marketing coordination and product design*. Manufacturers that use or produce highly engineered parts use private industrial networks to coordinate both their internal design and marketing activities, as well as related activities of their supply and distribution chain partners. By involving their suppliers in product design and marketing initiatives, manufacturing firms can ensure that the parts produced actually fulfill the claims of marketers. On the reverse flow, feedback

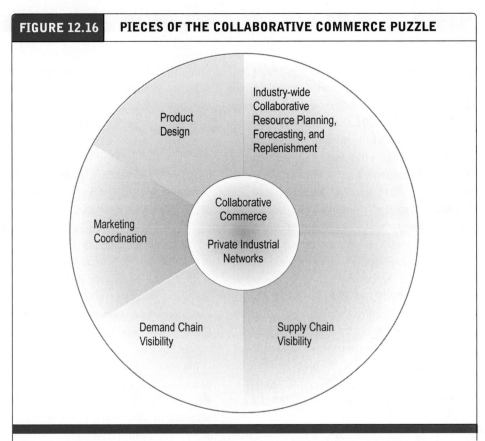

**FIGURE 12.16**  **PIECES OF THE COLLABORATIVE COMMERCE PUZZLE**

Collaborative commerce involves many cooperative activities among supply and sales firms closely interacting with a single large firm through a private industrial network.

from customers can be used by marketers to speak directly to product designers at the firm and its suppliers. For the first time, "closed loop marketing"—customer feedback directly impacting design and production—described in Chapter 6—can become a reality.

Chrysler, for instance, developed a collaborative commerce application called the Supply Partner Information Network (SPIN) for its suppliers. SPIN is an extranet-based supply chain management and support system that permits supplier employees at locations around the world to access Chrysler's real-time procurement, inventory, and demand forecasting systems, as well as longer-term strategy applications. Chrysler's Part Quality Supply System operating within SPIN tracks all production parts from supplier to shipper, factory installation, and after-market replacement. Chrysler estimated it increased productivity of its entire "extended enterprise" family of suppliers by 20%.

## IMPLEMENTATION BARRIERS

Although private industrial networks represent a large part of the future of B2B, there are many barriers to its complete implementation (Watson and Fenner, 2000).

Participating firms are required to share sensitive data with their business partners, up and down the supply chain. What in the past was considered proprietary and secret must now be shared. In a digital environment, it can be difficult to control the limits of information sharing. Information a firm gives gladly to its largest customer may end up being shared with its closest competitor.

Integrating private industrial networks into existing ERP systems and EDI networks poses a significant investment of time and money. Most ERP systems were not designed initially to work as extranets, or even to be very Internet-friendly. Most ERP systems are based on models of business processes that are entirely internal to the firm.

Adopting private industrial networks also requires a change in mindset and behavior for employees. Essentially, employees must shift their loyalties from the firm to the wider trans-organizational enterprise and recognize that their fate is intertwined with the fate of their suppliers and distributors. Suppliers in turn are required to change the way they manage and allocate their resources because their own production is tightly coupled with the demands of their private industrial network partners. All participants in the supply and distribution chains, with the exception of the large network owner, lose some of their independence, and must initiate large behavioral change programs in order to participate (Laudon, 2000).

## INDUSTRY-WIDE PRIVATE INDUSTRIAL NETWORKS

Single-firm networks can be so successful that they become adopted by the entire industry, and they can be used also to coordinate activities among firms in different industries altogether. For instance, the P&G system described previously was so successful that P&G sold the software to IBM, which then re-sold the system to the entire consumer products industry in the United States. P&G believed that only by changing the entire industry of supply, procurement, and distribution could it achieve its goals of efficiency and effectiveness. Other examples of industry-wide private industrial networks include 1SYNC and Agentrics. 1SYNC was formed by the merger of UCCnet and Transora in August 2005. 1SYNC offers a collaborative community of trading partners that includes 4,000 leading manufacturers in the alcohol and beverage, automotive, entertainment, grocery, healthcare, and office supplies industry. 1SYNC offers a range of data synchronization services that enable the elimination of costly data errors, increased supply chain efficiencies, and the advancement of next-generation technologies such as its Electronic Product Code (1SYNC, 2010).

Agentrics was established in 2000 under the name GlobalNetXchange (GNX) by eight of the world's largest retailers: Sears, Carrefour, Coles Myer, KarstadtQuelle, Kroger, MetroAG, Pinault-Printemps-Redoute, and Sainsbury. In 2005, GNX merged with WorldWide Retail Exchange, a retail industry consortium, and changed its name to Agentrics. Agentrics focuses on auctions and other services and standards for the retail industry. Agentrics' customers include 50 of the world's largest retailers and more than 250 suppliers (Agentrics, 2010).

**Figure 12.17** illustrates an industry-wide private industrial network.

In the future, barring intervention by antitrust enforcers, we can expect many private industrial networks to expand into much larger industry-wide networks seeking to coordinate all the thousands of key players in vertical industries.

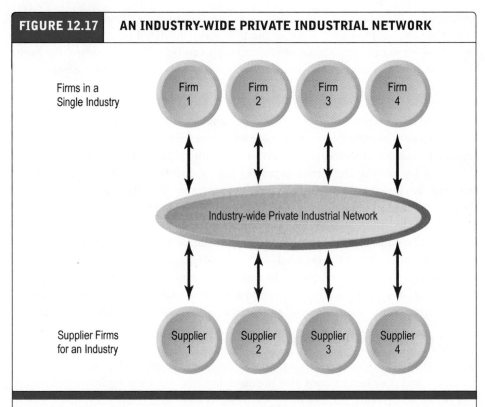

**FIGURE 12.17** | **AN INDUSTRY-WIDE PRIVATE INDUSTRIAL NETWORK**

Some private industrial networks expand to encompass an entire industry, coordinating the business processes for suppliers, transporters, production firms, and ultimately distributors and retailers.

## THE LONG-TERM DYNAMICS OF PRIVATE INDUSTRIAL NETWORKS

It is apparent that as large firms become more accustomed to working closely with both their supply chain partners and their distributors on the demand side, they will seek to push the boundaries of their networks to extend across the industry as a whole, to other industries, and to elaborate new roles for themselves and others. For instance, the computer manufacturer Hewlett-Packard discovered through its private industrial network that resin manufacturers were charging higher prices for resins they shipped to the molding manufacturers who make the plastic cases for HP computers. The molding manufacturers historically are very slow in paying their bills, and as a result, their resin suppliers raised their prices. HP moved in as a market maker and purchased resins from the suppliers at a market price, then re-sold them at the same price to the molders. HP has more clout to collect from the molders than resin manufacturers (Turek and Gilbert, 2001). In the next five years, we may see that individual large firms will be able to intervene in global supply relationships in order to overcome bottlenecks that otherwise would be hidden from manufacturers.

## 12.4 CASE STUDY

# Elemica:
## Cooperation, Collaboration, and Community

I t may seem unusual to refer to an entire industry as a "community," a word reserved typically for collections of people who more or less know one another. Trade associations are one example of an industrial community. Trade associations form in an effort to pursue the interests of all members in the community although usually they do not include customers in the community. Elemica is a B2B industry trading hub aiming to revolutionize the entire supply chain of the chemical, tire and rubber, energy, and selected manufacturing industries worldwide by creating a "community of suppliers, customers, and trade partners" who have mutual interests. Elemica's purpose is not just to foster cooperation on a one-to-one inter-firm basis, or just to foster collaboration on multi-firm projects, but instead to lift all boats on an industry tide by making all firms more efficient. Elemica is one of the few survivors of the early B2B e-commerce years. In 2010, Elemica connects over 2,500 companies to its network and clears over $60 billion in transactions a year.

Elemica is a global e-commerce company founded by 22 leading corporations in the chemical industry (including oil and industrial gases) to provide cloud-based order

management and supply chain applications and services. Elemica enables one-stop shopping through a single platform so companies can buy and sell chemicals to one another through their own ERP systems, or using a Web alternative. It also helps companies automate all of their business processes, creating efficiencies and economies of scale that lead to an improved bottom line.

How does Elemica achieve community among a diverse, global collection of firms where firms are often both customers and vendors to one another? The really unusual aspect of Elemica is that the "social glue" bringing members of the community together is the ability to link together the ERP systems of participating companies, and use this "super platform" to permit the companies to communicate with one another electronically, and to conduct transactions, handle logistics, and keep the books. Elemica is a commerce platform that has effectively standardized industry business transactions for all network members regardless of the type of ERP system they have, and it's leveled the playing field for trade partners who are less technically sophisticated. It's a neutral platform that facilitates millions of transactions for industry suppliers, customers, and third-party providers. In this sense, Elemica is one of the most sophisticated technology platforms in the B2B space.

One of the largest investments for a company is its ERP system. Despite these investments, intercompany relationships—the backbone of their supply chain—are often left to outdated and unreliable processes. These shortcomings cost billions in lost productivity, revenue, and profit. Elemica's eCommerce platform changes that by helping its clients leverage their ERP investment by making it work for transactions to external trade partners. Elemica's ERP-to-ERP connectivity enables companies to link their internal IT systems through a neutral platform so that information is moved into each company's database while maintaining confidentiality and security. The chemical and oil industries were among the first users of ERP systems (referred to in the early years as "manufacturing resource planning systems"). These large-scale systems were developed by single firms in order to rationalize and control the manufacturing process. They achieved this objective by identifying the outputs, inputs, and processes involved in manufacturing and automating key elements including inventory control and planning, process control, warehousing and storage, and shipping/logistics. If a company needed to produce 10 tons of polyethylene plastic, its ERP system could tell it precisely how many tons of petrochemical inputs were required, when they should be delivered to manufacturing, the machinery and labor force required to manufacture the product, how long it would take, where it would be stored, and how it would be shipped. The systems can estimate the cost at any stage.

Elemica is the first e-commerce company in the chemical industry to successfully commercialize ERP-to-ERP connectivity. Elemica facilitates transactions of all types including order processing and billing, and logistics management. However, unlike some other companies in the field, Elemica does not buy, sell, or own raw material products. Instead it acts as an intermediary, or hub, linking companies together to automate confidential transactions. Like eBay or a credit card company, Elemica's revenue comes from charging transaction fees on a per-transaction basis. Elemica's network of clients opens the door for a company that connects to do business with all other connected buyers and sellers.

Elemica offers a variety of e-commerce services for suppliers and customers in the chemical industry, so they can automate their business process and their internal purchasing. Elemica provides a modular, hosted solution to simplify sales, procurement, and financial processes; integrate supply chain partners to diminish communication barriers; and reduce overhead and errors.

Elemica integrates information flow among global trading partners using a Cloud-based business process network (BPN). Each client needs only a single connection to Elemica, and Elemica manages the connections to that company's external trade partners. That means a company needs only maintain one connection to Elemica (important when it's time for ERP maintenance or upgrade) rather than maintain a variable number of connections and infrastructure to all its trade partners. Once a company connects to Elemica, it can have access to thousands of other customers. Clients are charged for the service based on volume of usage. This is much more efficient than older EDI solutions to inter-company transactions. Elemica provides the platform for collaborative e-commerce through a fully automated integrated network of suppliers, customers, and third-party providers.

Elemica offers four modules: Logistics Management, Customer Management, Supplier Management, and Sourcing Management. Using these modules, companies can automate ordering, invoicing, tracking of shipments, and day-to-day business operations. Companies can sign up for one module or multiple modules depending on their needs.

Here's an example of how Elemica works. Let's say you need to order vinyl acetate from one of your suppliers. You put the order into your internal ERP system, the order is automatically routed to Elemica, Elemica routes the order to your supplier's internal ERP system, and you get a confirmed receipt of the order. Elemica's platform ensures the accuracy of the item number and purchase order number and sends an alert if there's an issue. Once an order is confirmed, Elemica's platform can be leveraged to plan and coordinate delivery, and automatically invoice and pay one another. For small or medium firms that may not have an ERP system, Elemica has a Web portal with online software that allows firms to participate in the community with suppliers and customers. The platform offers a closed-loop process, end to end, from the purchase order, to acknowledgments, load tenders and responses, carrier status updates, and dock scheduling. All of this takes place in a few seconds with little or no human intervention. Elemica has even developed a solution that allows a customer to send a purchase order via email or a print driver (alleviating fax processes) that's then routed to Elemica, and Elemica then routes it to the supplier in their preferred format, integrated with their ERP system as though it was a true electronic order. Elemica provides a holistic approach to order management, allowing suppliers to automate the process with both strategic and core customers, without asking their customers to change their processes. It's a win-win situation for suppliers and customers.

Unlike the automobile industry or the airline industry, where a few companies dominate, the $1.3 trillion chemical industry is made up of many companies of all sizes. The top 10 companies generate only 10% of the industry's annual revenue total, and the largest player, Dow Chemical, is responsible for 2%. In addition, unlike many other industries, chemical companies often buy the output of other chemical companies and use it as raw materials for products, so they are often each other's competitors and customers.

By the late 1990s, senior leaders at some of the larger chemical companies were aware of changes in technology that made the adaptation of information technology and the tools of e-commerce more appealing. The question was how to best use these advances to benefit their businesses, and how to establish industry standards for electronic transactions to make it approachable and attainable for all. Leaders from companies like Dow Chemical and DuPont began discussing this subject and determined that a cooperative alliance would be the most efficient way to move forward. They were met with initial skepticism by marketing and sales staff, worried that online procurement would negatively affect relationships. Further, senior corporate leadership wasn't sure that e-commerce would have any use in the chemical industry at all. And companies were cautious about the expense of investing in the infrastructure necessary for e-commerce.

However, there were compelling opportunities that were impossible to dismiss, including lowering costs, creating closer connections with customers and suppliers, and differentiating companies on something other than price. At the same time, new start-ups like e-Chemicals and PlasticsNet were making traditional chemical companies nervous. What would happen if their efforts to use information technology to streamline an inefficient supply chain helped them capture market share? In other words, if the more traditional companies didn't move forward, they might end up losing the revenue race.

When Dow began looking at start-ups that were using e-commerce and talking to their customers, they found that customers were concerned about making an investment to establish online connections with multiple firms. Dow and DuPont decided that the best and most economically efficient option was to offer customers the choice of a neutral one-to-one link. This would remove the obstacle of multiple connections. And they decided to do this through a strong, third-party network so that customers and suppliers could mutually benefit from the community concern about lack of control with a third party, led the two companies to decide that the answer was to create and invest in a neutral e-commerce company, partnering with other companies to create the critical mass to make it viable.

In 1999, the corporate boards of Dow and DuPont agreed that there were major advantages to online transaction processing and additional online connections among buyers and sellers. Clearly, the customer didn't want to make multiple connections due to cost and time involved, so a "hub" concept was the most viable. And a neutral community was the best approach.

All participants shared the common goal of creating a neutral platform to facilitate inter-company transactions and enhance business processes, and all were provided ownership in the new company. Dow and DuPont also reviewed the concept with the relevant regulatory agencies and received up-front approval. Ultimately, 22 global chemical companies were involved in the launch of Elemica.

When Elemica opened its doors in 1999, there were 50 start-up B2B e-commerce companies in the chemical industry. Nearly all of these B2B companies were third-party- owned Net marketplaces suitable at best for short-term sourcing of some direct inputs. By 2009, only a handful of these Net marketplaces for the chemical industry exist. Elemica focuses on building longer-term business relationships by creating committed and contractual supply chains. The company acts only as a facilitator of business transactions, and does not directly buy and sell chemical products.

Companies who sign on with Elemica have the support of Elemica's Professional Services & Implementation Team to work with staff to ensure a successful on-boarding process and acceptance of the business value with key trading partners. Many of Elemica's staff came from the chemical industry and are integral to the success of this training. Once companies witnessed that more orders were being delivered and received on time, and that their bills were going out faster and being paid faster, the up-front on-boarding and training became easier.

Today, Elemica, a privately held company, has 150 employees, more than 2,600 partners in its supply chain network, and processes greater than $60 billion in annual transactions. Its headquarters is in Pennsylvania, and it has overseas offices in Amsterdam, Frankfurt, London, Seoul, Shanghai, Singapore, and Tokyo.

In July 2009, Elemica announced a merger with RubberNetwork LLC, a $10 billion global rubber and tire company. Mike McGuigan, president and CEO of Elemica, continues to run the merged company.

Elemica's business model has been successful primarily because it addresses the e-commerce needs of chemical, tire & rubber, energy and selected manufacturing-companies of all sizes. It does this by offering multiple options for connecting to its hub system, multiple products that can be used alone or in combination, and by ensuring that only one connection integrated with a client's ERP is needed for all transactions. Customers can use Elemica, and take advantage of technology it offers, without purchasing an additional internal system.

With Elemica modules and technology, companies benefit from improved operational efficiency, reduced costs due to elimination of redundant systems and excess inventory, and a much higher percentage of safe and reliable deliveries. The flexibility of Elemica's modules and connections combines simplification, standardization, and efficiency. And clients have increased their profitability and improved cash flow through faster payment.

Several very large chemical companies use Elemica's platform. In Europe, Shell Oil started using Elemica after recognizing that it had ongoing problems with the coordination of paperwork processing and deliveries. Truck drivers would arrive at delivery sites and wait up to two hours while paperwork was filled out. These delays were costing Shell money. Once Shell began using Elemica, things improved. Today, paperwork is processed 24 hours a day, and truck waiting time has been cut from an average of two hours to an average of 15 minutes. Given this success, Shell continues to expand its relationship with Elemica.

Dow Chemical began to transition to full procurement automation with Elemica in 2007. More than 300 of their MRO suppliers are now linked to Elemica's platform. Errors are down 75%, and Dow has achieved economies of scale that have led to meaningful financial savings. Elemica helped Dow unify multiple, disparate business processes, reduced the cost of getting contracted items from suppliers, and increased efficiency in procurement, operations, IT, and accounts payable.

Air Products & Chemicals, Inc. is a global provider of gases and chemicals with 22,000 employees worldwide, and $10 billion in revenue. A major customer asked them for online ordering, but the initial method proposed would have required

**SOURCES:** "Elemica Procurement Case Study: Dow," Elemica Corporation, September 2010; "Elemica Order Management Case Study: BP," Elemica Corporation, September 2010; "Elemica Case Study: LanXess," Elemica Corporation, September 2010; "Elemica and Rubber- Network Merge," SDCExec.com, August 25, 2009; "Case Study: Elemica," http://www.ebusinesswatch. org/studies, August 25, 2009; "Once Elemica Tackled the Hard Part, the Rest Was Easy," SupplyChainBrain.com August 05, 2009; "Elemica Merger with Rubber Network," Philly.com, August 3, 2009; "Elemica Automates B2B Transactions Between Trading Partners—Speeding Up Orders by 78%," Softwareag.com, January 2009; "Top Chemical Company Selects Elemica's Business Process Network to Automate Global Procurement," Redorbit.com, December 18, 2008; "Elemica: Standards and Business," by Mike McGuigan, CEO, November 6, 2007, www.pidx.org/events/upload/Elemica. ppt; "Elemica: Simplification + Efficiency = Increased Profitability," by Fran Keeth, Elemica Business Leadership Forum, Philadelphia, Pennsylvania, wwwstatic. shell.com, September 13, 2005,; "The Journey of Elemica: An e-Commerce Consortium," by Andrew Liveris, Business Group President, Performance Chemicals. Strategic Alliances Conference, www.dow.com/ebusiness/news/ecs peech.htm, April 9, 2002

considerable additional work for both parties. Since both companies were connected to Elemica, there was a better option—the Elemica Supply Chain Hosted Solution.

In April 2010, Elemica introduced what might seem like a no-brainer: two systems designed to eliminate e-mail and faxed paper orders, both of which are poor solutions to order fulfillment. Print-to-Market and Email-to-Market convert what were traditionally faxed or e-mailed orders, and delivers them to suppliers in their preferred electronic format. As a result, sellers receive orders electronically instead of manually, leading to a significant reduction in errors, faster order processing, and improvements in the management of order changes. Both products require no IT resources for suppliers or their customers. The fact that there was a significant market for products that attempt to eliminate faxes and e-mail messages from the order entry stream is an indication that order entry in the United States still has a long way to go before achieving complete automation.

## Case Study Questions

1. Why is Elemica described as an example of an industry consortia Net marketplace? How does it differ from other types of Net marketplaces?

2. If you were a small chemical company, what concerns would you have about joining Elemica?

3. Elemica claims to provide a community for participants where they can transact, coordinate, and cooperate to produce products for less. Yet these firms also compete with one another when they sell chemicals to end-user firms in the automobile, airline, and manufacturing industries. How is this possible?

4. Review the concept of "an industry-wide private industrial network," and describe how Elemica illustrates many of the features of such a network.

## 12.5 REVIEW

### KEY CONCEPTS

■ Define B2B commerce and understand its scope and history.

Before the Internet, business-to-business transactions were referred to simply as *trade* or the *procurement process*. Today, we use the term *B2B commerce* to describe all types of computer-assisted inter-firm trade, and the term *Internet-based B2B commerce* or *B2B e-commerce* to describe specifically that portion of B2B commerce that uses the Internet to assist firms in buying and selling a variety of goods to each other. The process of conducting trade among businesses consumes many business resources, including the time spent by employees processing orders, making and approving purchasing decisions, searching for products, and arranging for their purchase, shipment, receipt, and payment. Across the economy, this amounts to trillions of dollars spent annually on procurement processes. If a significant portion of this inter-firm trade could be automated and parts of the procurement process assisted by the Internet, millions or even trillions of dollars could be freed up for other uses, resulting in increased productivity and increased national economic wealth.

In order to understand the history of B2B commerce, you must understand several key stages including:

- *Automated order entry systems*, developed in the 1970s, used the telephone to send digital orders to companies. Telephone modems were placed in the offices of the customers for a particular business. This enabled procurement managers to directly access the firm's inventory database to automatically reorder products.

- *EDI* or *electronic data interchange*, developed in the late 1970s, is a communications standard for sharing various procurement documents including invoices, purchase orders, shipping bills, product stocking numbers (SKUs), and settlement information for an industry. It was developed to reduce the costs, delays, and errors inherent in the manual exchange of documents.

- *Electronic storefronts* emerged in the 1990s along with the commercialization of the Internet. They are online catalogs containing the products that are made available to the general public by a single vendor.

- *Net marketplaces* emerged in the late 1990s as a natural extension and scaling-up of the electronic storefront. The essential characteristic of all Net marketplaces is that they bring hundreds of suppliers, each with its own electronic catalog, together with potentially thousands of purchasing firms to form a single Internet-based marketplace.

- *Private industrial networks* also emerged in the late 1990s with the commercialization of the Internet as a natural extension of EDI systems and the existing close relationships that developed between large industrial firms and their suppliers.

Before you can understand each of the different types of Net marketplaces, you must be familiar with several other key concepts:

- *Seller-side solutions* are owned by the suppliers of goods and are seller-biased markets that only display goods from a single seller. Customers benefit because these systems reduce the costs of inventory replenishment and are paid for mainly by the suppliers. Automated order entry systems are seller-side solutions.

- *Buyer-side solutions* are owned by the buyers of goods and are buyer-biased markets because they reduce procurement costs for the buyer. Sellers also benefit because the cost of serving a company's customers is reduced. EDI systems are buyer-side solutions.

- *Vertical markets* provide expertise and products targeted to a specific industry. EDI systems usually serve vertical markets.

- *Horizontal markets* serve a myriad of different industries. Electronic storefronts are an example of a horizontal market in that they tend to carry a wide variety of products that are useful to any number of different industries.

■ **Understand the procurement process, the supply chain, and collaborative commerce.**

- The *procurement process* refers to the way business firms purchase the goods they need in order to produce the goods they will ultimately sell to consumers. Firms purchase goods from a set of suppliers who in turn purchase their inputs from a set of suppliers. These firms are linked in a series of connected transactions.
- The *supply chain* is the series of transactions that links sets of firms that do business with each other. It includes not only the firms themselves but also the relationships between them and the processes that connect them.

There are seven steps in the procurement process:
- Searching for suppliers for specific products
- Qualifying the sellers and the products they sell
- Negotiating prices, credit terms, escrow requirements, and quality requirements
- Scheduling delivery
- Issuing purchase orders
- Sending invoices
- Shipping the product

Each step is composed of separate sub-steps that must be recorded in the information systems of the buyer, seller, and shipper. There are two different types of procurements and two different methods of purchasing goods:
- *Purchases of direct goods*—goods that are directly involved in the production process.
- *Purchases of indirect goods*—goods needed to carry out the production process but that are not directly involved in creating the end product.
- *Contract purchases*—long-term agreements to buy a specified amount of a product. There are pre-specified quality requirements and pre-specified terms.
- *Spot purchases*—for acquisition of goods that meet the immediate needs of a firm. Indirect purchases are most often made on a spot-purchase basis in a large marketplace that includes many suppliers.

The term *multi-tier supply chain* is used to describe the complex series of transactions that exists between a single firm with multiple primary suppliers, the secondary suppliers who do business with those primary suppliers, and the tertiary suppliers who do business with the secondary suppliers.

Trends in supply chain management (the activities that firms and industries use to coordinate the key players in their procurement process) include:
- *Supply chain simplification,* which refers to the reduction of the size of a firm's supply chain. Firms today generally prefer to work closely with a strategic group of suppliers in order to reduce both product costs and administrative costs. Long-term contract purchases containing pre-specified product quality requirements and pre-specified timing goals have been shown to improve end-product quality and ensure uninterrupted production.
- *Supply chain management systems,* which coordinate and link the activities of suppliers, shippers, and order entry systems to automate the order entry process from start to finish, including the purchase, production, and moving of a product from a supplier to a purchasing firm.
- *Collaborative commerce,* which is a direct extension of supply chain management systems as well as supply chain simplification. It is the use of digital technologies to permit the supplier and the purchaser to share sensitive

company information in order to collaboratively design, develop, build, and manage products throughout their life cycles.

- ■ **Identify the main types of B2B commerce: Net marketplaces and private industrial networks.**

There are two generic types of B2B commerce and many different subtypes within those two main categories of Internet commerce:
- *Net marketplaces,* which are also referred to as exchanges or hubs, assemble hundreds to thousands of sellers and buyers in a single digital marketplace on the Internet. They can be owned by either the buyer or the seller, or they can operate as independent intermediaries between the buyer and seller.
- *Private industrial networks* bring together a small number of strategic business partners who collaborate with one another to develop highly efficient supply chains and to satisfy customer demand for product. They are by far the largest form of B2B commerce.

- ■ **Understand the four types of Net marketplaces.**

There are four main types of "pure" Net marketplaces:
- *E-distributors* are independently owned intermediaries that offer industrial customers a single source from which to make spot purchases of indirect or MRO goods. E-distributors operate in a horizontal market that serves many different industries with products from many different suppliers.
- *E-procurement Net marketplaces* are independently owned intermediaries connecting hundreds of online suppliers offering millions of MRO goods to business firms who pay a fee to join the market. E-procurement Net marketplaces operate in a horizontal market in which long-term contractual purchasing agreements are used to buy indirect goods.
- *Exchanges* are independently owned online marketplaces that connect hundreds to thousands of suppliers and buyers in a dynamic real-time environment. They are typically vertical markets in which spot purchases can be made for direct inputs (both goods and services). Exchanges make money by charging a commission on each transaction.
- *Industry consortia* are industry-owned vertical markets where long-term contractual purchases of direct inputs can be made from a limited set of invited participants. Consortia serve to reduce supply chain inefficiencies by unifying the supply chain for an industry through a common network and computing platform.

- ■ **Identify the major trends in the development of Net marketplaces.**

- In the early days of e-commerce, independent exchanges were the prototype Internet-based marketplace and over 1,500 of them were created; however, most of them did not succeed. The main reason independent exchanges failed is that they did not attract enough players to achieve liquidity (measured by the number of buyers and sellers in the market, the transaction volume, and the size of the transactions).
- Industry consortia sprang up partly in reaction to the earlier development of independently owned exchanges that were viewed by large industries as interlopers who would not directly serve their needs. Industry consortia are profitable because they charge the large buyer firms transaction and subscription fees, but the rationalization of the procurement process, the competition among the vendors, and the closer relationship with the vendors are benefits that more

than offset the costs of membership to the firms. However, the long-term profitability of consortia has yet to be proven.

- The failure of the early exchanges is one reason Net marketplaces are changing so rapidly. Participants have come to realize that the real value of B2B e-commerce will only be realized when it succeeds in changing the entire procurement system, the supply chain, and the process of collaboration among firms.

■ **Identify the role of private industrial networks in transforming the supply chain.**

- Private industrial networks, which presently dominate B2B commerce, are Web-enabled networks for coordinating trans-organizational business processes (collaborative commerce). These networks range in scope from a single firm to an entire industry.

- Although the central purpose of a private industrial network is to provide industry-wide global solutions to achieve the highest levels of efficiency, they generally start with a single sponsoring company that "owns" the network. This differentiates private industrial networks from industry consortia that are usually owned collectively by major firms through equity participation.

- Private industrial networks are transforming the supply chain by focusing on continuous business process coordination between companies. This coordination includes much more than just transaction support and supply chain management. Product design, demand forecasting, asset management, and sales and marketing plans can all be coordinated among network members.

■ **Understand the role of private industrial networks in supporting collaborative commerce.**

Collaboration among businesses can take many forms and involve a wide range of activities. Some of the forms of collaboration used by private industrial networks include the following:

- *CPFR* or *industry-wide collaborative resource planning, forecasting, and replenishment* involves working with network members to forecast demand, develop production plans, and coordinate shipping, warehousing, and stocking activities. The goal is to ensure that retail and wholesale shelf space is precisely maintained.

- *Supply chain and distribution chain visibility* refers to the fact that, in the past, it was impossible to know where excess capacity existed in a supply or distribution chain. Eliminating excess inventories by halting the production of overstocked goods can raise the profit margins for all network members because products will no longer need to be discounted in order to move them off the shelves.

- *Marketing and product design collaboration* can be used to involve a firm's suppliers in product design and marketing activities as well as in the related activities of their supply and distribution chain partners. This can ensure that the parts used to build a product live up to the claims of the marketers. Collaborative commerce applications used in a private industrial network can also make possible closed loop marketing in which customer feedback will directly impact product design.

## QUESTIONS

1. Explain the differences among total inter-firm trade, B2B commerce, and B2B e-commerce.
2. What are the key attributes of an electronic storefront? What early technology are they descended from?
3. List at least five potential benefits of B2B e-commerce.
4. Name and define the two distinct types of procurements firms make. Explain the difference between the two.
5. Name and define the two methods of purchasing goods.
6. Define the term supply chain and explain what SCM systems attempt to do. What does supply chain simplification entail?
7. Explain the difference between a horizontal market and a vertical market.
8. How do the value chain management services provided by e-procurement companies benefit buyers? What services do they provide to suppliers?
9. What are the three dimensions that characterize an e-procurement market based on its business functionality? Name two other market characteristics of an e-procurement Net marketplace.
10. Identify and briefly explain the anti-competitive possibilities inherent in Net marketplaces.
11. List three of the objectives of a private industrial network.
12. What is the main reason why many of the independent exchanges developed in the early days of e-commerce failed?
13. Explain the difference between an industry consortium and a private industrial network.
14. What is CPFR, and what benefits could it achieve for the members of a private industrial network?
15. What are the barriers to the complete implementation of private industrial networks?

## PROJECTS

1. Choose an industry and a B2B vertical market maker that interests you. Investigate the site and prepare a report that describes the size of the industry served, the type of Net marketplace provided, the benefits promised by the site for both suppliers and purchasers, and the history of the company. You might also investigate the bias (buyer versus seller), ownership (suppliers, buyers, independents), pricing mechanism(s), scope and focus, and access (public versus private) of the Net marketplace.

2. Examine the Web site of one of the e-distributors listed in Figure 12.9, and compare and contrast it to one of the Web sites listed for e-procurement Net marketplaces. If you were a business manager of a medium-sized firm, how would you decide where to purchase your indirect inputs—from an e-distributor or an e-procurement Net marketplace? Write a short report detailing your analysis.

3. Assume you are a procurement officer for an office furniture manufacturer of steel office equipment. You have a single factory located in the Midwest

with 2,000 employees. You sell about 40% of your office furniture to retail-oriented catalog outlets such as Quill in response to specific customer orders, and the remainder of your output is sold to resellers under long-term contracts. You have a choice of purchasing raw steel inputs—mostly cold-rolled sheet steel—from an exchange and/or from an industry consortium. Which alternative would you choose and why? Prepare a presentation for management supporting your position.

4. Find a Net marketplace that has failed (possible candidates include Aerospan.com, Chemdex.com, Petrocosm.com, E-steel.com, or another of your choosing). Investigate the reasons behind its failure. Prepare a short report on your findings and your analysis of the lessons that can be learned from its demise.

# References

## CHAPTER 1

Aguiar, Mark and Erik Hurst. "Life-Cycle Prices and Production." *American Economic Review* 97:5, 1533-1559. (January 1, 2008).

Alessandria, George. "Consumer Search, Price Dispersion, and International Relative Price Fluctuations." *International Economic Review* 50:3, 803-829 (September 1, 2009).

Bailey, Joseph P. *Intermediation and Electronic Markets: Aggregation and Pricing in Internet Commerce*. Ph. D., Technology, Management and Policy, Massachusetts Institute of Technology (1998a).

Bakos, Yannis. "Reducing Buyer Search Costs: Implications for Electronic Marketplaces." *Management Science* (December 1997).

Banerjee, Suman and Chakravarty, Amiya. "Price Setting and Price Discovery Strategies with a Mix of Frequent and Infrequent Internet Users." (April 15, 2005). SSRN: http://ssrn.com/abstract=650706.

Baye, Michael R. "Price Dispersion in the Lab and on the Internet: Theory and Evidence." *Rand Journal of Economics* (2004).

Baye, Michael R., John Morgan, and Patrick Scholten. "Temporal Price Dispersion: Evidence from an Online Consumer Electronics Market." *Journal of Interactive Marketing* (January 2004).

Brynjolfsson, Erik, and Michael Smith. "Frictionless Commerce? A Comparison of Internet and Conventional Retailers." *Management Science* (April 2000).

Compete.com. "Site Profile for Digg.com." September 30, 2010).

comScore. "comScore Releases August 2010 U.S. Online Video Rankings." (September 30, 2010a).

comScore. "comScore Media Metrix Ranks Top 50 U.S. Web Properties for August 2010." (September 23, 2010b).

eBay, Inc. Report on Form 10-K for the fiscal year ending December 31, 2009 filed with the Securities and Exchange Commission (February 17, 2010).

eMarketer, Inc. (Jeffrey Grau) "Retail E-commerce Forecast: Room to Grow. (March 2010a)

eMarketer, Inc. (Lisa E. Phillips). "US Internet Users." (April 2010b).

eMarketer, Inc. "Online Sales of the Top 500 US Retail Websites, by Company Type, 2009 (billions and % share)." (May 1, 2010c).

eMarketer, Inc. "Top 10 Online Retailers, Ranked by Online Sales, 2009 (billions)." (May 1, 2010d)

Evans, Philip, and Thomas S. Wurster. *Blown to Bits: How the New Economics of Information Transforms Strategy*. Cambridge, MA: Harvard Business School Press (2000).

Evans, Philip, and Thomas S. Wurster. "Getting Real About Virtual Commerce." *Harvard Business Review* (November-December 1999).

Evans, Philip, and Thomas S. Wurster. "Strategy and the New Economics of Information." *Harvard Business Review* (September-October 1997).

Fink, Eugene, Josh Johnson, and Jerry Hu. "Exchange Market for Complex Goods: Theory and Experiments." *Communications of the ACM*. (April, 2004).

Forrester Research. "Forrester Research Web Influenced Retail Sales Forecast 12/09," (February 25, 2010).

Google. "More Google Products." Google.com (accessed September 30, 2010).

Internet Retailer. "Top 500 Guide 2010 Edition." (2010).

Internet Systems Consortium, Inc. "ISC Internet Domain Survey." (January 2010).

Internet World Stats. "Internet Usage Statistics : The Internet Big Picture: -World Internet Users and Population Stats (as of June 30, 2010)." (September 2010).

Kalakota, Ravi, and Marcia Robinson. *e-Business 2.0: Roadmap for Success, 2nd edition*. Reading, MA: Addison Wesley (2003).

Kambil, Ajit. "Doing Business in the Wired World." *IEEE Computer* (May 1997).

Kincaid, Jason. "Five Years In, YouTube Is Now Streaming Two Billion Views Per Day." TechCrunch.com, May 16, 2010.

Mesenbourg, Thomas L. "Measuring Electronic Business: Definitions, Underlying Concepts, and Measurement Plans." U. S. Department of Commerce Bureau of the Census (August 2001).

Naone, Erica. "Peer to Peer File Sharing Usurped by Streaming Video." *Technology Review* (October 14, 2009).

Nash-equilibrium.com. "Relative Dispersion as of October 1, 2010." (October 1, 2010).

National Retail Foundation. "NRF Forecasts 2.5% Increase in Retail Sales for 2010." (January 26,

2010).

Pew Internet & American Life Project. "Daily Internet Activities." (September 2010).

Photobucket.com "About Photobucket." (September 30, 2010).

PricewaterhouseCoopers/National Venture Capital Association. MoneyTree Report, Data: Thomson Financial (2010).

Rayport, Jeffrey F., and Bernard J. Jaworski. *Introduction to E-commerce, 2nd edition*. New York: McGraw-Hill (2003).

Reuters. "Retail Industry Sales Seen Up 2.5 Percent for 2010." (April 1, 2010).

Secondlife.com. "Economic Statistics (Raw Data Files), Logged_in_users.xml." (September 30, 2010).

Shapiro, Carl, and Hal R. Varian. *Information Rules. A Strategic Guide to the Network Economy*. Cambridge, MA: Harvard Business School Press (1999).

Sinha, Indajit. "Cost Transparency: The Net's Threat to Prices and Brands." *Harvard Business Review* (March-April 2000).

Smith, Michael; Joseph Bailey; and Erik Brynjolfsson. "Understanding Digital Markets: Review and Assessment." In Erik Brynjolfsson and Brian Kahin (eds.) *Understanding the Digital Economy*. Cambridge MA: MIT Press (2000).

Tversky, A., and D. Kahneman. "The Framing of Decisions and the Psychology of Choice." *Science* (January 1981).

U.S. Census Bureau. "Census Bureau Projects U.S. Population of 308 Million on New Year's Day 2010." (December 29, 2009)

U.S. Census Bureau. *Statistical Abstract of the United States: 2010* (2010a).

U.S. Census Bureau. "E-Stats Report 2008 E-commerce Multi-Sector Report." (May 27, 2010b).

Varian, Hal R. "When Commerce Moves On, Competition Can Work in Strange Ways." *New York Times* (August 24, 2000a).

Varian, Hal R. "5 Habits of Highly Effective Revolution." *Forbes ASAP* (February 21, 2000b).

Wikipedia.org. "Wikipedia: About." (September 30, 2010).

Wikimedia.org. "User:Stu/comScore data on Wikimedia." (September 30, 2010)

WordPress.com. "Stats." (September 2010)

**CHAPTER 2**

Agentrics LLC. "Fact Sheet." Agentrics.com (January 2010).

Arthur, W. Brian. "Increasing Returns and the New World of Business." *Harvard Business Review* (July-August 1996).

Bakos, Yannis. "The Emerging Role of Electronic Marketplaces on the Internet." *Communications of the ACM* (August 1998).

Barney, J. B. "Firm Resources and Sustained Competitive Advantage." *Journal of Management* Vol. 17, No. 1 (1991).

Bellman, Steven; Gerland L. Lohse; and Eric J. Johnson. "Predictors of Online Buying Behavior." *Communications of the ACM* (December 1999).

Day, George S.; Adam J. Fein; and Gregg Ruppersberger. "Shakeouts in Digital Markets." *California Management Review* Vol. 45, No. 3 (Winter 2003).

eBay, Inc. eBay Inc. Reports Strong Second Quarter Revenue and Earnings Growth." (July 21, 2010).

Fisher, William W. III. "The Growth of Intellectual Property: A History of the Ownership of Ideas in the United States." Cyber.law.harvard.edu/people/tfisher/iphistory.pdf (1999).

Gerace, Thomas. "Encyclopedia Britannica." Harvard Business School Case Study 396-051 (1999).

Ghosh, Shikhar. "Making Business Sense of the Internet." Harvard Business Review (March-April 1998).

JiWire.com. "Wi-Fi Finder." (September 30, 2010).

Kambil, Ajit. "Doing Business in the Wired World." *IEEE Computer* (May 1997).

Kambil, Ajit; Ari Ginsberg; and Michael Bloch. "Reinventing Value Propositions." Working Paper, NYU Center for Research on Information Systems (1998).

Kanter, Elizabeth Ross. "The Ten Deadly Mistakes of Wanna-Dots." *Harvard Business Review* (January 2001).

Kaplan, Steven, and Mohanbir Sawhney. "E-Hubs: The New B2B Marketplaces." *Harvard Business Review* (May-June 2000).

Kim, W. Chan, and Renee Mauborgne. "Knowing a Winning Business Idea When You See One." *Harvard Business Review* (September-October 2000).

Magretta, Joan. "Why Business Models Matter." *Harvard Business Review* (May 2002).

Nielsen Company. "Bing Overtakes Yahoo! as the #2 U.S. Search Engine" (September 14, 2010).

Porter, Michael E. "Strategy and the Internet." *Harvard Business Review* (March 2001).

Porter, Michael E. *Competitive Advantage: Creating and Sustaining Superior Performance*. New York: Free Press (1985).

Rigdon, Joan I. "The Second-Mover Advantage." *Red Herring* (September 1, 2000).

Teece, David J. "Profiting from Technological Innovation: Implications for Integration, Collaboration, Licensing and Public Policy." *Research Policy* 15 (1986).

Timmers, Paul. "Business Models for Electronic Markets" *Electronic Markets* Vol. 8, No. 2 (1998).

U.S. Census Bureau Statistical Abstract of the United States: 2010 (2010a).

U.S. Census Bureau. "E-Stats Report 2008 E-commerce Multi-Sector Report." (May 27, 2010b).

## CHAPTER 3

Apple, Inc. "Apple Premieres iTunes 9." (September 9, 2010).

Arstechnica.com. "Capitol Hill, The Internet, and Broadband: An Ars Technica Quarterly Report." (September 2010).

Berners-Lee, Tim; Robert Cailliau; Ari Luotonen; Henrik Frystyk Nielsen; and Arthur Secret. "The World Wide Web." *Communications of the ACM* (August 1994).

Bluetooth.com. "Press & Analysts." (2010).

Brandt, Richard. "Net Assets: How Stanford's Computer Science Department Changed the Way We Get Information." *Stanford Magazine* (November/December 2004).

Bush, Vannevar. "As We May Think." *Atlantic Monthly* (July 1945).

Cerf, V., and R. Kahn, "A Protocol for Packet Network Intercommunication." *IEEE Transactions on Communications*, Vol. COM-22, No. 5, pp 637-648 (May 1974).

Cisco Systems, Inc. "IP Multicast Technical Overview." (August 2007).

Computer Science and Telecommunications Board. National Research Council (NRC). Networking Health: Prescriptions for the Internet." Washington DC: National Academy Press (2000).

comScore. "comScore Releases August 2010 U.S. Search Engine Rankings." (September 16, 2010a).

comScore. "comScore Media Metrix Ranks Top 50 Web Properties for August 2010." (September 23, 2010b).

comScore. "comScore Releases May 2010 U.S. Online Video Rankings" (June 24, 2010c).

eMarketer, Inc. (Paul Verna). "Podcasting: Into the Mainstream." (March 2009)

eMarketer, Inc. (Lisa E. Phillips). "US Internet Users." (April 2010a).

eMarketer, Inc. "Active Mobile Internet Users Worldwide, 2009 & 2010 (millions)." (March 23, 2010b).

eMarketer, Inc. (Paul Verna). "The Blogosphere: Colliding with Social and Mainstream Media." (September 2010c).

Federal Networking Council. "FNC Resolution: Definition of 'Internet.'" (October 24, 1995).

Gartner, Inc. "Gartner Says Worldwide Cloud Services Market to Surpass $68 Billion in 2010." (June 22, 2010).

Gaudin, Sharon. " PC Shipments Set to Grow 22% in 2010, Gartner Says." *Computerworld* (May 26, 2010).

Geni.net. "Global Environment for Network Innovations." (September 2008).

Gross, Grant. "NSF Seeks Ambitious Next-Generation Internet Project." *Computerworld* (August 29, 2005).

Hansell, Saul. "Plugging in $40 Computers." *New York Times* (March 5, 2009).

International Data Corporation (IDC). "Worldwide Quarterly Mobile Phone Tracker." (February 4, 2010).

Internet Corporation for Assigned Names and Numbers (ICANN). "Top-Level Domains (gTLDs)." Icann.org (2010).

Internet Society. "ISOC's Standards Actitivies." Internet Society. (September 2010).

Internet Society. "RFC 2616: Hypertext Transfer Protocol-HTTP/1.1." (June 1999).

Internet Society. "RFC 2821: Simple Mail Transfer Protocol" (April 2001).

Internet Society. "RFC 1939: Post Office Protocol-Version 3." (May 1996).

Internet Society. "RFC 3501: Internet Message Access Protocol-Version 4rev1" (March 2003).

Internet Society. "RFC 0959: File Transfer Protocol." (October, 1985).

Internetworldstats.com "Internet Usage Statistics : The Internet Big Picture-World Internet Users and Population Stats." As of June 30, 2010 (September 2010)

Kleinrock, Leonard. *1964 Communication Nets: Stochastic Message Flow and Delay*. New York: McGraw-Hill (1964).

Leiner, Barry M.; Vinton G. Cerf; David D. Clark; Robert E. Kahn; Leonard Kleinrock; Daniel C. Lynch; Jon Postel; Larry G. Roberts; and Stephen Wolff. "All About the Internet: A Brief History of the Internet." *Internet Society* (ISOC) (August 2000).

Marketshare.hitslink.com. "Top Browser Share Trend." (September 2010).

National Research Council. "The Internet's Coming

of Age." Washington DC: National Academy Press (2000).

Netcraft. "September 2010 Web Server Survey." (September 17, 2010).

NLR.net. "National LambdaRail: About Us." (September 2010).

Pew Internet & American Life Project. "Daily Internet Activities." (September 2010).

Point Topic. "Global Broadband Statistics" (June 22, 2009).

Radicati Group. "The Radicati Group Releases "Email Statistics Report, 2010-2014."" (April 19, 2009).

Shein, Esther. "Netbook Sales to Almost Double by 2013." *Information Week* (July 23, 2010).

Stross, Randall. "The PC Doesn't Have to Be an Anchor." *New York Times* (April 18, 2009).

Technorati, Inc. "State of the Blogoshpere/2009" (2009).

U.S. Department of Commerce. "Letter to ICANN Chairman." http://www.ntia.doc.gov/comments/2008/ICANN_080730.html (July 30, 2008).

Visualware, Inc., "VisualRoute Traceroute Server." Visualroute.visualware.com (September 2007).

Zakon, Robert H. "Hobbes' Internet Timeline v8.1." Zakon.org (2005).

Ziff-Davis Publishing. "Ted Nelson: Hypertext Pioneer." Techtv.com (1998).

Zillman, Marcus. "Deep Web Research." LLRX.com (2005).

## CHAPTER 4

Banker, Rajiv D., and Chris F. Kemerer. "Scale Economies in New Software Development." *IEEE Transactions on Software Engineering*, Vol. 15, No. 10 (1989).

Bluefly, Inc. Report Form 10-K for theYear Ended December 30, 2008 filed with the Securities & Exchange Commission (March 5, 2009).

Doyle, Barry and Cristina Videria Lopes. "Survey of Technologies for Web Application Development." ACM, Vol.2., No. 3. (June 2005).

eMarketer, Inc. (Lisa E. Phillips). "US Internet Users" (April 2010).

Google. "Google Analytics Product Tour." (2009).

Hostway. "Hostway Pet Peeves Survey: Top Line Results." Hostway.com, (2007).

IBM (High Volume Web Sites Team). "Best Practices for High-Volume Web Sites." *IBM Redbooks* (December 2002).

IBM (Nigel Trickett, Tatsuhiko Nakagawa, Ravi Mani, Diana Gfroerer). "Understanding IBM eServer pSeries Performance and Sizing." IBM Redbooks

(January 24, 2003).

Laudon, Kenneth C. and Jane P. Laudon. Management Information Systems: *Managing the Digital Firm*. 12th edition. Upper Saddle River, NJ: Prentice Hall (2011).

Lientz, Bennet P., and E. Burton Swanson. Software *Maintenance Management*. Reading MA: Addison-Wesley (1980).

RealStoryGroup.com. "Research: CMS Vendor Evaluations." (September 2010).

WebTrends, Inc. "WebTrends Analytics 9." (2009).

## CHAPTER 5

Associated Press. "FBI Ditches Carnivore Surveillance System." Foxnews.com (January 18, 2005).

Boncella, Robert J. "Web Security for E-Commerce." *Communications of the Association for Information Systems*, Vol. 4. (November 2000).

Borden, Anne. "Credit Card Theft: An 'Inside Job'." Lawyersandsettlements.com (May 14, 2007).

Butterfield, Ethan. "Agencies Making Little Progress Against Cybervandalism." *Government Computer News* (September 1, 2005).

Channelinsider.com. "Network Solutions Suffers Large Data Breach." (July 24, 2009).

Computer Security Institute. "CSI Computer Crime and Security Survey 2009." (2009).

Cybersource, Inc. "Online Fraud Report-2010 Edition." (2010).

Davies, Shaun. "Japan's Wallet Phone Explosion." News.ninemsn.com.au (March 4, 2009).

Denning, Dorothy E., and William E. Baugh. "Hiding Crimes in Cyberspace." *Information, Communication, and Society* Vol. 2, No. 3 (Autumn 1999).

Electronic Privacy Information Center (EPIC). "Cryptography and Liberty 2000. An International Survey of Encryption Policy." Washington D. C. (2000).

Fiserv, Inc. "2007 Consumer Bills Payment Trends Survey: Volume of Electronic Payments." (2007).

Forrester Research, Inc. (Emmettt Higdon). "US Online Bill Payment Forecast: 2009 To 2014" (October 19, 2009).

Forrester Research. "State of Enterprise IT Security: 2008-2009." (December 24, 2008).

Javelin Strategy & Reseach. "2010 Identity Fraud Survey Report." (February 10, 2010).

Javelin Strategy & Research "Online Retail Payments Forecast 2010-2014 Report." (February 17, 2010).

Kerner, Sean Michael. "Researchers: Conficker Still a Threat." Internetnews.com (July 31, 2009).

MacKie-Mason, K. Jeffrey and Kimberly White. "Evaluating and Selecting Digital Payment Mechansims." Selected Papers from the 1996 Telecommunications Policy Research Conference, Lawrence Erlbaum Associates, Inc, 1996.

Markoff, John. "VeriSign Moves to Address an Internet Security Problem." *New York Times* (February 8, 2007).

Microsoft, Inc. "Microsoft Security Intelligence Report Volume 8 (July through December 2009)" (March 2010).

Mills, Elinor. "Firms Tackle Virus-laden Web sites, Ads." CNET News (May 26, 2010).

National White Collar Crime Center and the Federal Bureau of Investigation. "Internet Crime Complaint Center 2009 Internet Crime Report." (2010).

Peretti, Kimberly. "Data Breaches: What the Underground World of 'Carding' Reveals," *Santa Clara Computer and High Technology Journal*, Vol. 25 (2008).

Ponemon Institute. "Fourth Annual US Cost of Data Breach Study: Benchmark Study of Companies." (January 2009).

Schwartz, John. "Fighting Crime Online: Who is in Harm's Way?" *New York Times* (February 8, 2001).

Stein, Lincoln D. *Web Security: A Step-by-Step Reference Guide*. Reading, MA: Addison-Wesley (1998).

Symantec, Inc. "Internet Security Threat Report Volume XV: April 2010." (April 2010).

US-CERT "Cyber Security Bulletin SB10-270 Vulnerability Summary for the Week of September 20, 2010." (September 27, 2010).

## CHAPTER 6

Adomavicius, Gediminas, and Alexander Tuzhilin. "Expert-Driven Validation of Rule-Based User Models in Personalization Applications." *Data Mining and Knowledge Discovery* (January 2001a).

Adomavicius, Gediminas, and Alexander Tuzhilin. "Using Data Mining Methods to Build Customer Profiles." *IEEE Computer* (February 2001b).

Ailawadi, K.L.; D.R. Lehmann; and S.A. Neslin. "Revenue Premium as an Outcome Measure of Brand Equity." *Journal of Marketing* (October 2003).

Akerlof, G. "The Market for 'Lemons' Quality Under Uncertainty and the Market Mechanism." *Quarterly Journal of Economics* (August 1970).

Awad, Neveen; Michael Smith, and Mayuram Krishnan. "The Consumer Online Purchase Decision: A Model of Consideration Set Formation and Buyer Conversion Rate Across Market Leaders and Market Followers." Working Paper Series, SSRN (September 2007).

Ba, Sulin, and Paul Pavlou. "Evidence on the Effect of Trust Building Technology in Electronic Markets: Price Premiums and Buyer Behavior." *MIS Quarterly* (September 2002).

Bailey, J., and Erik Brynjolfsson. "An Exploratory Study of the Emerging Role of Electronic Intermediaries." *International Journal of Electronic Commerce* (Spring, 1997).

Bakos, J. Y., and Erik Brynjolfsson. "Bundling and Competition on the Internet: Aggregation Strategies for Information Goods." *Marketing Science* (January 2000).

Barry, John and Ed Keller. *The Influentials: One American in Ten Tells the Other Nine How to Vote, Where to Eat, and What to Buy.* Free Press (2003).

Baye, Michael R.; John Morgan; and Patrick Scholten. "Price Dispersion in the Small and in the Large: Evidence from an Internet Price Comparison Site." Nash-equilibrium. com, (August 2002a).

Baye, Michael R.; John Morgan; and Patrick Scholten. "The Value of Information in an Online Consumer Market." *Journal of Public Policy and Marketing* (August 2002b).

Bell, David R. and Sangyoung Song. "Social Contagion and Trial on the Internet: Evidence from Online Grocery Retailing." Unpublished paper. The Wharton School, University of Pennsylvania (May 12, 2004).

Berg, Julie, John Matthews, and Constance O'Hare, "Measuring Brand Health to Improve Top Line Performance." (Fall 2007).

Brynjolfsson, Erik, and M. D. Smith. "Frictionless Commerce? A Comparison of Internet and Conventional Retailer." *Management Science* (April 2000).

Brynjolfsson, Erik; Michael D. Smith; and Yu Hu. "Consumer Surplus in the Digital Economy: Estimating the Value of Increased Product Variety at Online Booksellers." *Working Paper, Information, Operations, and Management Sciences Research Seminar Series*, Stern School of Business (April 17, 2003).

Carpenter, Phil. *eBrands: Building an Internet Business at Breakneck Speed*. Cambridge MA: Harvard Business School Press (2000).

Carr, Nicholas. "Does the Internet Make You

Dumber?" *New York Times* (June 5, 2010).

Catalyst. "Buying Power." (February 25, 2010).

Chan, P. K. "A Non-Invasive Learning Approach to Building Web User Profiles." In *Proceedings of ACM SIGKDD International Conference* (1999).

Channel Advisor, "How Consumers Shop Online." (2009).

Clay, K.; K. Ramayya; and E. Wolff. "Retail Strategies on the Web: Price and Non-Price Competition in the On Line Book Industry." Working Paper, *MIT E-commerce Forum* (1999).

Compaq, Inc. "Compaq White Paper." Compaq.com (November 1998).

comScore. "Smartphone Subscribers Now Comprise Majority of Mobile Browser and Application Users in U.S." (October 1, 2010).

Corritore, C.L., B. Kracher, S. Wiedenbeck, "On-line trust: concepts, evolving themes, a model," *International Journal of Human-Computer Studies* (2006).

Cross, Robert. "Launching the Revenue Rocket: How Revenue Management Can Work For Your Business." *Cornell Hotel and Restaurant Administration Quarterly* (April 1997).

Doolin, Bill; Stuart Dillion, and Fiona Thompson. "Perceived Risk, the Internet Shopping Experience, and Online Purchasing Behvaior." In Annie Becker (editor), Electronic Commerce: Concepts, Methodologies, Tools and Applications. Information Science Reference (2007).

Ellison, Sarah. "Web-Brand Study Says Awareness Isn't Trust." *Wall Street Journal* (June 7, 2000).

eMarketer, Inc. (Lisa E. Phillips). "US Internet Users." (April 2010a).

eMarketer, Inc. (Jeffrey Grau). "Retail E-commerce Forecast: Room to Grow" (March 2010b).

eMarketer, Inc. "US Internet Users Who Have Changed Their Mind About Buying Online due to Privacy/Security Concerns, by Age," (April 14, 2010c).

eMarketer, Inc. (Paul Verna). The Blogosphere: Colliding with Social and Mainstream Media (September 2010d).

eMarketer, Inc. "US Social Network Ad Spending, by Venue, 2009 & 2010." (July 28, 2010e).

eMarketer, Inc. "B2B Spending on Social Media to Explode." (June 1, 2010f)

eMarketer, Inc. (Debra Williamson) "Social Media Marketing by the Numbers." (February 2010g).

eMarketer, Inc. "Sources Used by US Online Buyers," Chart (August 2009a).

eMarketer, Inc. (Noah Elkin). "Mobile Social Networks" (November 2009b.)

eMarketer, Inc. (Paul Verna). "The Blogosphere: A Mass Movement from Grass Roots." (May 2008a).

Evans, P., and T. S. Wurster. "Getting Real About Virtual Commerce." *Harvard Business Review* (November-December 1999).

Fawcett, Tom, and Foster Provost. "Adaptive Fraud Detection." *Data Mining and Knowledge Discovery* (1997).

Fawcett, Tom, and Foster Provost. "Combining Data Mining and Machine Learning for Effective User Profiling." In *Proceedings of the Second International Conference on Knowledge Discovery and Data Mining* (1996).

Federal Communications Commission. "Broadband Adoption and Use in America." (February 23, 2010).

Feldwick, Paul. "What Is Brand Equity Anyway, and How Do You Measure It?" *Journal of the Market Research Society* (April 1996).

Forrester Research, Inc. "Designing Transactive Content." (February 1998).

Forrester Research, Inc. "Transactive Content." (October 1997).

Forrester Research, Inc. (Sucharita Mulpuru and Peter Hult) "US Online Retail Forecast, 2009 To 2014 Online Retail Hangs Tough For 11% Growth In A Challenging Economy." (March 5, 2010a).

Forrester Research, Inc. "Retailers Plan To Expand Online Customer Service Channels In 2010." (March 18, 2010).

Godin, Seth. *Permission Marketing.* New York: Simon & Schuster (1999).

Golder, Peter. "What History Teaches Us About the Endurance of Brands." *Stern Business* (Fall 2000).

Greenfield, Patricia. "Technology and Informal Education: What Is Taught, What Is Learned. *Science Magazine* (January, 2009).

Gulati, Ranjay, and Jason Garino. "Getting the Right Mix of Bricks and Clicks." *Harvard Business Review* (May-June 2000).

Giuliani, John. "Dotomis Riding Personalized Media Beyond Behavioral Targeting." AdExchanger.com (September 15, 2009).

Higgins, Michelle. "Blink and You'll Miss These Deals." *New York Times* (May 17, 2009).

Humphreys, Jeffrey M. "The Multicultural Economy 2008." Terry College of Business, University of Georgia (January 2009).

Interbrand. "Best Global Brands: 2010 Rankings." (September 2010).

Internet Retailer. "Top 500 Guide 2010 Edition."

(2010).

Kim, D. and I. Benbasat. "The Effects of Trust-Assuring Arguments on Consumer Trust in Internet Stores," *Information Systems Research* (2006).

Kim, D. and I. Benbasat. "Designs for Effective Implementation of Trust Assurances in Internet Stores," *Communications of the ACM* (July 2007).

Kotler, Philip, and Gary Armstrong. *Principles of Marketing, 13th Edition*. Upper Saddle River, NJ: Prentice Hall (2009).

Leiter, Daniel B. and Thierry Warin. "An Empirical Study of Price Disperson in Homogeneous Goods Markets." Middlebury College Economics Discussion Paper No. 07-10. 2007

Lohse, L. G., G. Bellman, and E. J. Johnson. "Consumer Buying Behavior on the Internet: Findings from Panel Data." *Journal of Interactive Marketing* (Winter 2000).

Malamud, Ofer and Cristian Pop-Eleches. "Home Computer Use and the Development of Human Capital." University of Chicago and NBER Columbia University (January 2010).

McIntyre, Douglas. "10 Brands That May Disappear in 2010." 24/7Wallstreet.com (July 8, 2010).

Mishra, D. P., J. B. Heide, and S. G. Cort. "Information Asymmetry and Levels of Agency Relationships." *Journal of Marketing Research*. (1998).

Mobasher, Bamshad. "Data Mining for Web Personalization." Center for Web Intelligence, School of Computer Science, Telecommunication, and Information Systems, DePaul University, Chicago, Illinois. (2007).

Nash-equilibrium.com. "Relative Dispersion." (September 9, 2008).

Nie, Norman, and Lutz Erbring. "Internet and Society: A Preliminary Report." *Stanford Institute for the Quantitative Study of Society* (February 17, 2000).

Nielsen Company. "What Americans Do Online: Social Media and Games Dominate Activity." (August 2, 2010).

Opinion Research Corporation. "Online Consumer Product Reviews Have Big Influence." Opinion Research Corporation (April 16, 2009).

Pavlou, Paul. "Institution-Based Trust in Interorganizational Exchange Relationships: The Role of Online B2B Marketplaces on Trust Formation." *Journal of Strategic Information Systems* (2002).

Pavlou, Paul A. and Angelika Dimoka. "The Nature and Role of Feedback Text Comments in Online Marketplaces: Implications for Trust Building, Price Premiums, and Seller Differentiation." *Information Systems Research* (August 2006).

Pavlou, P. A. and M. Fygenson (2005). "Understanding and Predicting Electronic Commerce Adoption: An Extension of the Theory of Planned Behavior." *MIS Quarterly* (2005).

Pew Internet & American Life Project. "May-June 2005 Tracking Survey." (August 9, 2005a).

Pew Internet & American Life Project (Amanda Lenhart, Mary Madden and Paul Hitlin). "Teens and Technology." (July 27, 2005b).

Pew Internet & American Life Project. "Daily Internet Activities." (September 2010a).

Pew Internet & American Life Project. "Demographics of Internet Users." (September 2010b).

Rayport, J. F., and J. J. Sviokla. "Exploiting the Virtual Value Chain." *Harvard Business Review* (November-December 1995).

Reichheld, Frederick F., and Phil Schefter. "ELoyalty: Your Secret Weapon on the Web." *Harvard Business Review* (July-August 2000).

Retail Advertising & Marketing Association (RAMA). "Social Media: An Inside Look at the People Who Use It." (March 3, 2010).

Rodgers, Zachary. "Measuring Blog Marketing." Clickz.com (January 12, 2005).

Saunders, Peter Lee, and Andrea Chester. "Shyness and the Internet: Social Problem or Panacea?" Division of Psychology, School of Health Sciences, RMIT University, City Campus, Melbourne, Victoria, Australia (2008).

Scholten, Patrick, and S. Adam Smith. "Price Dispersion Then and Now: Evidence from Retail and E-tail Markets." Nash-equilibrium.com. (July 2002).

Shapiro, Carl, and Hal Varian. *Information Rules: A Strategic Guide to the Network Economy.* Cambridge, MA: Harvard Business School Press (1999).

Shapiro, Carl, and Hal Varian. "Versioning: The Smart Way to Sell Information." *Harvard Business Review* (November-December 1998).

Shklovski, Irina; Sara Kiesler, and Robert Kraut. "The Internet and Social Interaction: A Meta-analysis and Critique of Studies, 1995-2003." Carnegie Mellon University (2004).

Sinha, Indrajit. "Cost Transparency: The Net's Real Threat to Prices and Brands." *Harvard Business Review* (March-April 2000).

Smith, M. D.; J. Bailey; and E. Brynjolfsson.

"Understanding Digital Markets: Review and Assessment," in E. Brynjolfsson and B. Kahin (eds.), *Understanding the Digital Economy*. Cambridge, MA: MIT Press (1999).

Starbuck, William, and Paul C. Nystrom. "Why Many Firms Run Into Crises, and Why Some Survive." Working Paper. Stern School of Business, Management and Organizational Behavior (1997).

Sterling Commerce and Deloitte Consulting. "What Consumers Want in Their Shopping Experience." (August 2007).

Surowiecki, James. The Wisdom of Crowds: *Why the Many are Smarter than the Few and How Collective Wisdom Shapes Business, Economies, Societies and Nations*. New York: Doubleday, (2004).

Sweeney, Campbell. "One-Touch Shopping, For Members Only." *New York Times* (March 3, 2010).

Takahashi, Dean. "Freemium Summit: Evernote shares the insider secrets of free apps," Mobileventurebeat.com (March 26, 2010).

Trendstream. "The Global Web Index Wave 1." (November 2009).

Teece, David J. "Profiting from Technological Innovation: Implications for Integration, Collaboration, Licensing and Public Policy." *Research Policy*, 15 (1986).

TRUSTe. "2009 Study: Consumer Attitudes About Behavioral Targeting." (March 4, 2009).

USC Annenberg School Center for the Digital Future. "Web Insight 67." (April 12, 2010).

Van den Poel, Dirk and Wouter Buckinx. "Predicting Online Purchasing Behavior." *European Journal of Operations Research*, Vol. 166, Issue 2 (2005).

von Hippel, Eric. *The Sources of Innovation*. New York: Oxford University Press (1994).

von Hippel, Eric. *Democratizing Innovation*. Cambridge : MIT Press, (2005).

Watts, Duncan. *Six Degrees of Freedom*. W.W. Norton (2004).

Wigand, R. T., and R. I. Benjamin. "Electronic Commerce: Effects on Electronic Markets." *Journal of Computer Mediated Communication* (December 1995).

Williamson, O. E. *The Economic Institutions of Capitalism*. New York: Free Press (1985).

Wolfinbarger, Mary, and Mary Gilly. "Shopping Online for Freedom, Control and Fun." *California Management Review* (Winter 2001).

**CHAPTER 7**

Anderson, Eric; Erik Brynjolfsson, Yu Hu, and Duncan Simester, "Understanding the Impact of Marketing Actions in Traditional Channels on the Internet: Evidence From a Large Field Experiment." (January 2005).

Battelle, John. "Search Blog." Battellemedia.com/archives/000063.php (November 13, 2003).

Beval Saddlery Ltd. "Products." Beval.com (2008).

Briggs, Rex. "How Internet Advertising Works." ESO-MAR "Net Effects" Conference, London. (February 22, 1999).

Cable & Telecommunications Association for Marketing."Tracking Entertainment and Technology: Consumer Value in Media." June/July Pulse Report (August 4, 2009).

Cable & Telecommunications Association for Marketing (CTAM). "Social Networking Feeds Americans' Hunger for Television." (June 23, 2010).

Center for Digital Democracy, "In the Matter of Real Time Targeting and Auctioning, Data Profiling Optimization, and Economic Loss to Consumers and Privacy." Before the Federal Trade Commission. Washington D.C. (April 2010.)

Click Forensics. "Click Fraud Rate Rises Slightly in Q2 2010 to 18.6 Percent" (July 21, 2010).

Clifford, Stephanie. "There's An App for That. But a Revenue Stream?" *New York Times* (August 10. 2009).

comScore. "comScore Releases May 2010 U.S. Online Video Rankings." (June 24, 2010a).

comScore. "comScore Media Metrix Ranks Top 50 U.S. Web Properties for August 2010." (September 21, 2010b).

Consumer Reports WebWatch. "Searching for Disclosure: How Search Engines Alert Consumers to the Presence of Advertising in Search Results." Consumerwebwatch.org (November 2004).

Consumer Reports Web Watch. "Still in Search of Disclosure: Re-evaluating How Search Engines Explain the Presence of Advertising in Search Results." (June 9, 2005).

Davern, Michael J.; Dov Te'eni; and Jae Yun Moon. "Information Environments and Human Behavior Over Time: From Initial Preferences to Mature Usage." Department of Information Systems, Stern School of Business, New York University (2001).

Direct Marketing Association (DMA). "DMA Releases 2010 Response Rate Trend Report." (June 15, 2010).

Direct Marketing Association (DMA), "DMA: The Power of Direct Marketing." (October 19, 2009)

Dynamic Logic. "Video Ads Achieve Greater Branding Impact With Fewer Impressions." *Beyond the Click: Insights from Marketing Effectiveness Research* (December 2004).

eGain. "Multichannel Experience Most Dysfunctional Aspect of Customer Service, According to New North America Research Survey." (February 23, 2010).

Ellison, Nicole, Charles Steinfeld, and Cliff Lampe. "Spatially Bounded Online Social Networks and Social Capital: The Role of Facebook." Department of Telecommunications, Information Studies, and Media, Michigan State University. Paper presented at the Annual Conference of the International Communication Association, Dresden, Germany (June 2006).

eMarketer, Inc. (David Hallerman) "US Ad Spending: How Big a Bounce?" (June 2010a).

eMarketer, Inc. (Jeffrey Grau), "The Role of Catalogs in the Multichannel Model." (March 2010b).

eMarketer, Inc. (Jeffrey Grau). "US Retail E-commerce Forecast: Room to Grow." (March 2010c.)

eMarketer, Inc., "Online Advertising Metrics in North America." (June 2010d).

eMarketer, Inc. "E-mail Marketing Performance Metrics in North America." (September 2010e)

eMarketer, Inc. "US Social Network Ad Spending, by Venue, 2009 & 2010." (July 28, 2010e).

eMarketer, Inc. "The Sad Tale of the Abandoned Cart." (June 30, 2009b).

eMarketer, Inc. "How Much Time People Really Spend with Ads." (August 24, 2009c).

eMarketer, Inc. (Paul Verna) "The Blogosphere: Mass Movement From the Grass Roots." (May 2008a).

eMarketer, Inc. (David Hallerman) "Behavioral Targeting: Marketing Trends." (June 2008b).

eMarketer, Inc. (David Hallerman). "US Advertising Spending." (November 2007).

eMarketer, Inc. (David Hallerman). "Ad Spending Trends: The Internet and Other Media." (October 2005).

E-Tailing Group. "9th Annual Merchant Survey." (April 20, 2010).

Eyeblaster. "Trends of Time and Attention in Online Advertising." (July 22, 2009).

Fair Isaac Corporation. "New Fair Isaac Research Indicates Click Fraud is Potentially Large Problem in Parts of Search Engine Advertising." (May 18, 2007).

Flanigan, Andrew, and Miriam J. Metzger. "The Role of Site Features, User Attributes, and Information Verification Behaviors on the Perceived Credibility of Web-based Information." *New Media & Society*, Vol. 9, No. 2 (2007).

Fogg, B.J., Cathey Soohoo, David Danielson, Leslie Marable, Julliane Stanford, and Ellen Tauber. "How Do Users Evaluate the Credibility of Web Sites? A Study with Over 2,500 Participants." Proceedings of DUX2003, Designing for User Experiences. (2003).

Google, Inc.. "Eye-tracking Studies: More than Meets the Eye." googleblog.blogspot.com (February 6, 2009).

Hotchkiss, Gord , Tracy Sherman, Rick Tobin, Cory Bates and Krista Brown. "Search Engine Results 2010." Enquiroresearch.com (September, 2007).

Interactive Advertising Bureau. "IAB Standards and Guidelines." Iab.net (September 2008). Interactive Advertising Bureau (IAB)/PricewaterhouseCoopers. "IAB Internet Advertising Revenue Report 2010 Full Year Results" (March 2010).

Internet Retailer. Top 500 Guide 2010 Edition. (2010a).

Internet Retailer. 2010 Guide to Retail Web Site Design & Usability. (2010b).

Kane, Yukari and Emily Steel. "Apple Fights Rival Google on New Turf." *Wall Street Journal* (April 8, 2010).

LeClaire, Jennifer. "Quattro Wireless to Be Closed as Apple Focuses on iAd." Toptechnews.com (August 20, 2010).

Lohse, L. G.; G. Bellman; and E. J. Johnson. "Consumer Buying Behavior on the Internet: Findings from Panel Data." *Journal of Interactive Marketing* (Winter 2000).

Network Advertising Initiative. "Study Finds Behaviorally Targeted Ads More Than Twice as Valuable, Twice as Effective as Non-targeted Ads." (March 24, 2010).

National Conference of State Legislatures. "State Laws Relating to Unsolicited Commercial of Bulk E-mail (SPAM)." (February 10, 2010).

Nielsen, Jakob. "F-Shaped Pattern For Reading Web Content, Nielsen's Alertbox." (April 17, 2006).

Nielsen Company. "Facebook Users Average 7 hrs a Month in January as Digital Universe Expands." (February 16, 2010).

Novak, T. P.; D. L. Hoffman; and Y. F. Yung. "Measuring the Customer Experience in Online Environments: A Structural Modeling Approach." *Marketing Science* (Winter, 2000).

Pew Internet & American Life Project. "Daily Internet Activities." (September 2010).

Pew Internet & American Life Project (Lee Rainie). "Search Engine Use November 2005." (November 2005).

Shrestha, Sav and Kelsi Lenz. "EyeGaze Patterns while Searching vs. Browsing a Website." Software Usability Research Laboratory, Department of Psychology, Wichita State University, Wichita, KS 67260-0034 (September, 2007).

Story, Louise. "It's an Ad, Ad, Ad World." *New York Times* (August 6, 2007).

Sullivan, Danny. "FTC Recommends Disclosure to Search Engines." Searchenginewatch.com (February 13, 2003).

Symantec Message Labs. "MessageLabs Intelligence: August 2010 Report" (August 2010).

Tsai, Janice; S. Egelman, L. Cranor, and A. Acquisti. "The Effect of Online Privacy Information on Purchasing Behavior: An Experimental Study." Paper presented at the Workshop on the Economics of Information Security, June 7-8, 2007, Pittsburgh, PA. (June 2007).

Turow, Joseph; Jennifer King; Chris Hoofnagle; Amy Bleakley; and Michael Hennessy. "Americans Reject Tailored Advertising and Three Activities that Enable It." Available at SSRN: http://ssrn.com/abstract=1478214 University of California, Berkeley; University of Pennsylvania. (September 29, 2009).

**CHAPTER 8**

*Apple Computer, Inc. v. Microsoft Corp.* 709 F. Supp. 925, 926 (N. D. Cal. 1989); 799 F. Supp. 1006, 1017 (N. D. Cal., 1992); 35 F. 3d 1435 (9th Cir.); cert. denied, 63 U. S. L. W. 3518 (U.S., Feb. 21, 1995) (No. 94-1121).

Associated Press. "Google Settles Final Piece of Geico Case." BizReport.com (September 8, 2005).

*Audi AG and Volkswagen of America, Inc. v. Bob D'Amato* No. 05-2359, 6th Circuit (November 27, 2006).

*Bernina of America, Inc. v. Fashion Fabrics Int'l., Inc.* 2001 U. S. Dist. LEXIS 1211 (N. D. Ill., Feb. 8, 2001).

*Bilski et al. v. Kappos*, 561 U.S. _____(2010).

*Brown Bag vs. Symantec Corp.*, 960 F. 2d 1465 (9th Cir. 1992).

Chiappetta, Vincent. "Defining the Proper Scope of Internet Patents: If We Don't Know Where We Want to Go, We're Unlikely to Get There." *Michigan Telecommunications Technology Law Review* (May 2001).

Clifford, Stephanie. "Web Privacy on the Radar in Congress." *New York Times* (August 10, 2008).

*Diamond v. Chakrabarty*, 447 US 303 (1980).

Dueker, Kenneth Sutherlin. "Trademark Law Lost in Cyberspace: Trademark Protection for Internet Addresses." *Harvard Journal of Law and Technology* (Summer 1996).

*E. & J. Gallo Winery v. Spider Webs Ltd.* 129 F. Supp. 2d 1033 (S.D. Tex., 2001) aff'd 286 F. 3d 270 (5th Cir., 2002).

Elgin, Ben and Bruce Einhorn. "The Great Firewall of China." *BusinessWeek* (January 12, 2006).

eMarketer, Inc. "The Controversy Over Personalized Ads." (June 25, 2009).

eMarketer, Inc. "Some Users Distrust Search Engines." (July 23, 2007a).

eMarketer, Inc. "When Bad Ads Harm Good E-commerce." (July 3, 2007b).

Federal Trade Commission. "FTC Staff Revises Online Behavioral Advertising Principles" (February 12, 2009).

Federal Trade Commission. "Privacy Online: Fair Information Practices in the Electronic Marketplace." (May 2000a).

Federal Trade Commission. "Online Profiling: A Report to Congress." (June 2000b).

Federal Trade Commission. "Privacy Online: A Report to Congress." (June 1998).

Federal Trade Commission. "Individual Reference Services: A Report to Congress." (December 1997).

Field v. Google, Inc. 412 F.Supp. 2nd 1106 (D. Nev., 2006).

Fisher, William W. III. "The Growth of Intellectual Property: A History of the Ownership of Ideas in the United States." Law.harvard.edu/Academic_Affairs/coursepages/tfisher/iphistory.html (1999).

*Ford Motor Co. v. Lapertosa* 2001 U. S. Dist. LEXIS 253 (E. D. Mich. Jan. 3, 2001).

Frackman, Andrew; Claudia Ray, and Rebecca C. Martin. *Internet and Online Privacy: A Legal and Business Guide.* ALM Publishing (2002).

*Google, Inc. v. American Blind & Wallpaper Factory, Inc.* Case No. 03-5340 JF (RS) (N.D. Cal., April 18, 2007).

*Government Employees Insurance Company v. Google, Inc.* Civ. Action No. 1:04cv507 (E.D. VA, December 15, 2004).

Greenhouse, Linda. "20 Year Extension of Existing Copyrights Is Upheld." *New York Times* (January 16, 2003a).

Greenhouse, Linda. "Justices Back Law to Make Libraries Use Internet Filters." *New York Times*

(June 24, 2003b).

Greenhouse, Linda. "Supreme Court Upholds Child Pornography Law." *New York Times* (May 20, 2008).

Gross, Grant. "House Panel Votes to Extend Net Tax Ban." *InfoWorld* (October 11, 2007).

Gruenwald, Juliana. "Poll Finds Public Concern Over Online Privacy." National Journal.com, June 8, 2010.

Hafner, Katie and Matt Richtel. "Google Resists U.S. Subpoena of Search Data." *New York Times* (January 20, 2006).

Harmon, Amy. "Pondering Value of Copyright vs. Innovation." *New York Times* (March 3, 2003).

Helft, Miguel. "Facebook Bows to Pressure of Privacy." *New York Times* (May 26, 2010).

Ho, Victoria. "China Accused of Rerouting Search Traffic to Baidu." CNETNews.com (October 22, 2007).

Hoofnagle, Chris Jay. "Privacy Self-Regulation: A Decade of Disappointment." Electronic Privacy Information Center (Epic.org) (March 4, 2005).

*Kelly v. ArribaSoft.* 336 F3rd 811 (CA 9th, 2003).

Laudon, Kenneth. "Markets and Privacy." *Communications of the ACM* (September 1996).

Leon, Pedro G., and Lorrie F. Cranor, Allecia M. McDonald, and Robert McGuire. "Token Attempt: The Misrepresentation of Website Privacy Policies through the Misuse of P3P Compact Policy Tokens." CMU-CyLab-10-014, Carnegie Mellon University (September 10, 2010).

MarkMonitor. "MarkMonitor Year-in-Review Report Shows How Rising Rates of Online Brand Abuse Are Used to Monetize Web Traffic." (March 15, 2010).

McMillan, Robert. "Porn Typosquatter Fined Again by FTC." *InfoWorld* (October 16, 2007).

Miller, John W. and Christopher Rhoads, "U.S. Fights to Keep Control Of Global Internet Oversight." *Wall Street Journal* (November 16, 2005).

Nakashima, Ellen. "NebuAd Halts Plans for Web Tracking." *Washington Post* (September 4, 2008).

Nash, David B. "Orderly Expansion of the International Top-Level Domains: Concurrent Trademark Users Need a Way Out of the Internet Trademark Quagmire." *The John Marshall Journal of Computer and Information Law* Vol. 15, No. 3 (1997).

Nettis Environment Ltd. v. IWI, Inc. 46 F. Supp. 2d 722 (N. D. Ohio 1999).

Network Advertising Initiative. "IAB and NAI Release Technical Specifications for Enhancing Notice to Consumers for Online Behavioral Advertising." (April 14, 2010).

Network Advertising Initiative. "Participating Networks." (September 2009a).

Network Advertising Initiative. "Highlights from the Federal Trade Commission Staff Report for Online Behavioral Advertising." (February 17, 2009b).

New York Times. "Bailouts Gone Wild. Porn Chiefs Seek $5 Billion." (January 7, 2009).

*Nissan Motor Co., Ltd. v. Nissan Computer Corp.* 289 F. Supp. 2d 1154 (C. D. Cal. ), aff'd, 2000 U. S. App. LEXIS 33937 (9th Cir. Dec. 26, 2000).

*PaineWebber Inc. v. Fortuny,* Civ. A. No. 99-0456-A (E. D. Va. Apr. 9, 1999).

*Perfect 10, Inc. v. Amazon.com, Inc.* 487 F3rd 701 (CA 9th, 2007).

Pew Internet & American Life Project. "Daily Internet Activities." (September 2010).

*Playboy Enterprises, Inc. v. Global Site Designs, Inc.* 1999 WL 311707 (S. D. Fla. May 15, 1999).

*Playboy Enterprises, Inc. v. Netscape Communications, Inc.* 354 F. 3rd 1020 (9th Cir., 2004).

Ram, Vidya. "Google's Luxury Victory." *Forbes* (September 22, 2009).

Schwartz, John. "Justices Take Broad View of Business Methods Patents." *New York Times* (June 28, 2010).

Sharma, Amol, and Don Clark. "Tech Guru Riles the Industry By Seeking Huge Patent Fees." *Wall Street Journal* (September 17, 2008).

*State Street Bank & Trust Co. v. Signature Financial Group,* 149 F. 3d 1368 (1998).

Stone, Brad. "Scaling the Digital Wall in China." *New York Times*, January 15, 2010

Story, Louise. "F.T.C. Member Vows Tighter Controls of Online Ads." New York Times (November 2, 2007).

Takenaka, Toshiko. "International and Comparative Law Perspective on Internet Patents." *Michigan Telecommunications Technology Law Review* (May 15, 2001).

Tam, Pui-Wing and Ben Worthen. "Funds Invest in Privacy Start-Ups." *Wall Street Journal* (June 20, 2010).

Thurm, Scott. "The Ultimate Weapon: It's the Patent." *Wall Street Journal* (April 17, 2000a).

*Ticketmaster v. Tickets.com.* 2000 U.S. Dist. Lexis 4553 (C.D. Cal., August 2000).

United States Copyright Office. "Digital Millennium Copyright Act of 1998: U.S. Copyright Office Summary." (December 1998).

United States Department of Health, Education and

Welfare (US-DHEW). Records, Computers and Rights of Citizens. Cambridge, MA: MIT Press (1973).

United States Patent and Trademark Office. "Class 705 Application Filing and Patents Issued Data." (May 13, 2010).

Van Kirk, Andrew. "Platform for Privacy Preferences (P3P): Privacy Without Teeth." (March 10, 2005).

Varian, Hal, "Forget Taxing Internet Sales. In Fact, Just Forget Sales Taxes Altogether." New York Times (March 8, 2001).

W3C Platform for Privacy Preferences Initiative." P3P 1.0: A New Standard in Online Privacy." Platform for Privacy Preferences Initiative. (June 16, 2003).

Washington Post, The et al. v. TotalNews, Inc., et al., S.D.N.Y., Civil Action Number 97-1190 (February 1997).

Winston, Brian. Media Technology and Society: A History From the Telegraph to the Internet. Routledge (1998).

Wondracek, G. , Thorsen Holz, Christian Platzer, Engin Kirda, and Christopher Kruegel. "Is the Internet for Porn? An Insight into the Online Adult Industry." In Proceedings (online) of the 9th Workshop on Economics of Information Security, Cambridge, MA (June 2010).

Worthen, Ben. "Red Light Sites Give Green Light to IT Innovation." ITBusiness.ca (August 13, 2009).

## CHAPTER 9

Amazon.com, Inc. Amazon.com Inc. Form 10-K for the fiscal year ended December 31, 2009, filed with the Securities and Exchange Commission (January 28, 2010).

Brown, Jeffrey, and Austan Goolsbee. "Does the Internet Make Markets More Competitive? Evidence from the Life Insurance Industry." John F. Kennedy School of Government, Harvard University. Research Working Paper RWP00-007 (2000).

Brynjolfsson, Erik; Astrid Andrea Dick and Michael D. Smith. "Search and Product Differentiation at an Internet Shopbot," Center for eBusiness@MIT (December, 2004).

California Association of Realtors. "2008 Survey of California Home Buyers." (September 11, 2008).

Careerbuilder.com. "More Employers Screening Candidates via Social Networking Sites." (September 2010).

Center for Realtor Technology, National Association of Realtors. "2007 Technology Survey." (2007).

comScore,. "comScore State of Online Banking."

(April 21, 2009a).

comScore,. "The 2010 State of Online Banking Report." (May 11, 2010a).

comScore. "comScore Media Metrix Ranks Top-Growing Properties and Site Categories for January 2010." (February 23, 2010b).

Dell Inc. Form 10-K for the fiscal year ended January 30, 2010, filed with the Securities and Exchange Commission (March 16, 2009).

eMarketer, Inc. (Jeffery Grau). "Retail E-commerce Forecast: Room to Grow." (March 2010a).

eMarketer, Inc. (Noah Elkin) "Mobile Banking ." (May 2010b)

eMarketer, Inc. (Victoria Petrock) "Online Leisure Travel." (April 2010c)

eMarketer, Inc. "Frequency With Which US Internet Users Perform Financial Transactions Online." (April 27, 2009).

eMarketer, Inc. (Jeffrey Grau). "E-commerce in the US: Retail Trends." (May 2005).

Evans, Philip, and Thomas S. Wurster. Blown to Bits:How the New Economics of Information Transforms Strategy. Cambridge, MA: Harvard Business School Press (2000).

Fiserv. "Fiserv Survey Shows Online Banking Growing, Now Used by Four of Five Online Households." (July 14, 2009).

Halkias, Maria. "J.C. Penney to Quit Catalogs But Will Keep Sending 'Look' Books that Refer Shoppers to Stores, Website." Dallasnews.com (September 25, 2010).

Hitwise. "Top 20 Banking Websites." (September 25, 2010).

Internet Retailer. "Top 500 Guide 2010 Edition." (2010).

JC Penney Company, Inc. Report on Form 10-K for the fiscal year ended January 31, 2010 filed with the Securities and Exchange Commission (March 31, 2010).

Lands' End, Inc. "About Lands' End." Landsend.com (2010).

Laudon, Kenneth C., and Jane P. Laudon. Management Information Systems: Managing the Digital Firm, 12th edition. Upper Saddle River, NJ: Prentice Hall (2011).

LinkedIn.com. "LinkedIn Launches New Tools to Boost HR Professionals' Efficiency as Responses to Job Posting Double in Challenging Economy." (February 2, 2009).

MarketingCharts.com. "Top 10 Online Trading Sites - March 2010." (March 2010).

Microsoft. "Automakers Should Turn to Technology to Target Millennials, Reports New Microsoft

Survey." (January 26, 2009).

Mortgage Bankers Association. "MBA Mortgage FInance Forecast." December 8, 2009.

Pew Internet & American Life Project. "Daily Internet Activities." (September 2010).

Pew Internet & American Life Project. "Generations Online in 2009 Charts." (January 28, 2009b).

Reuters. "Number of U.S. Online Banking Customers Continues to Grow Despite Challenging Financial Times." (April 21, 2009).

U. S. Census Bureau. "Census of Service Industries." (2001).

U.S. Census Bureau. *Statistical Abstract of the United States 2010* (2010).

U.S. Department of Labor. Dictionary of Occupational Titles, 4th edition. (1991).

University of Southern California Annenberg School Center for the Digital Future "2009 Digital Future Report." (April 28, 2009).

Weil, Jonathon. "Securities Rules Help to Close the Earning Reports GAAP." *Wall Street Journal* (April 24, 2003).

Yodlee, Inc. "Yodlee Names Jim Frankola Chief Financial Officer." (June 22, 2010).

## CHAPTER 10

American Association of Publishers. "Industry Statistics 2009." (April 7, 2010).

Bivings Group. "The Use of the Internet by America's Largest Newspapers." (December 18, 2008).

Book Industry Study Group. "What We Do: ONIX for Books: Downloads andLists." Bisg.org (2009).

Boxer, Sarah. "Paintings Too Perfect? The Great Optics Debate." New York Times (December 4, 2001).

Brand, Stuart. "The First Hackers conference in 1984." Transcript in The Media Lab: Inventing the Future at MIT, Viking Penguin, (1987).

comScore. "comScore Releases August 2010 U.S. Online Video Rankings." (September 30, 2010a).

comScore. "comScore Releases May 2010 U.S. Online Video Rankings." (June 24, 2010b).

comScore." "The New York Times Ranks as Top Online Newspaper According to May 2010 U.S. comScore Media Metrix Data." (June 16, 2010c).

Editeur.org. "ONIX for Books."(2009).

Efrati, Amir. "Tweet This Milestone: Twitter Passes MySpace." Wall Street Journal (September 28, 2010).

eMarketer, Inc. (Lisa Phillips) "US Internet Users, 2010." (April 2010a)

eMarketer, Inc. (XXX) "Paid Music Content." (January 2010b)

eMarketer, Inc. (Paul Verna) "Video Content and Syndication." (July 2010b)

eMarketer, Inc. (XXX) "US Ad Spending." (June 2010c).

eMarketer, Inc. "Top 10 US Online Newspaper Groups, Ranked by Total Unique Visitors, May 2010." (June 16, 2010d).

eMarketer, Inc. (Paul Verna) "Paid Video Content." (December 2009a)

eMarketer, Inc. (Paul Verna) "User-Generated Content: More Popular than Profitable." (January 2009b).

eMarketer, Inc. Newspapers in Crisis (Carol Krol). (January 2009c).

Emigh, Jacqueline. "Analysts: Consumers Drop TV, Turn to Internet for Entertainment." Betanews.com (November 25, 2009).

Frank N. Magid Associates. "Magid Media Futures 2009." (June 2009).

Google Inc. "AdWords Help: Overview and Value of Advertising on YouTube." (2010).

Liedtke, Michael and Ryan Nakashima. "Netflix to Stream Paramount, Lionsgate, MGM Movies." msnbc.msn.com (August 10, 2010).

Motion Picture Association of America. "Theatrical Market Statistics 2009." (March 20, 2010).

Newspaper Association of America. "Trends and Numbers." (September 2010.)

NPD Group. "Video Games Revenues." (January 2010).

Online Publishers Association. "Internet Activity Index (IAI)" (September 30, 2010).

Pew Internet & American Life Project (Kristen Purcell). "Understanding the Participatory News Consumer."  (March 2010a).

Pew Internet & American Life Project (XXX) "The State of Online Video." (June 3, 2010b)

Pew Internet & American Life Project (John B. Horrigan). "The Internet as a Resource for News and Information About Science." (November 20, 2006).

U.S. Census Bureau. Statistical Abstract of the United States 20109 (2010).

Veronis Suhler Stevenson. "VSS Communications Industry Forecast, 2004-2014." (August 10, 2010).

## CHAPTER 11

Arkes, H. R., and L. Hutzel. "The Role of Probability of Success Estimates in the Sunk Cost Effect." Journal of Behavioral Decisionmaking (2000).

Bailey, Brian P.; Laura J. Gurak; and Joseph Konstan, "Do You Trust Me? An Examination of Trust in

Computer-Mediated Exchange," In Human Factors and Web Development, 2nd Edition. Mahwah, NJ: Lawrence Erlbaum (2002).

Brynjolfsson, Erik, and Michael Smith. "Frictionless Commerce? A Comparison of Internet and Conventional Retailers." Management Science (April 2000).

comScore. "comScore Media Metrix Ranks Top 50 U.S. Web Properties for August 2010." (September 23, 2010a).

comScore. "comScore Releases August 2010 U.S. Search Engine Rankings." (September 16, 2010).

Dholakia, Utpal, and Kerry Soltysinski. "Coveted or Overlooked? The Psychology of Bidding for Comparable Listings in Digital Auctions." Marketing Letters (2001).

eMarketer, Inc. "Top 10 Countries, Ranked by Unique Social Networking Site Users, July 2009 & July 2010 (millions an % change) (August 25, 2010a).

eMarketer, Inc. "Top 10 Social Networking Websites Among US Internet Users, Ranked by Market Share of Visits, August 2010." (September 9, 2010b)

eMarketer, Inc. "US Social Network Ad Spending, by Venue, 2009 & 2010 (millions and % of total)." (July 28, 2010).

Federal Trade Commission. "FTC Releases Report if 2009 Top Consumer Complaints." (February 24, 2010).

Hafner, Katie. "The Epic Saga of The Well: The World's Most Influential Online Community (and It's Not AOL)." Wired (May 1997).

Hagel, John III, and Arthur G. Armstrong. Net Gain: Expanding Markets Through Virtual Communities. Cambridge, MA: Harvard Business School Press (1997).

Hanson, Ward, and D. S. Putler. "Hits and Misses: Herd Behavior and Online Product Popularity." Marketing Letters (1996).

Hillery, George A. "Definitions of Community: Areas of Agreement." Rural Sociology (1955).

Hiltzik, Michael. Dealers of Lightning: Xerox PARC and the Dawn of the Computer Age. New York: Harper Collins (1999).

Hitwise.com "US Data Center. "Top Social Networking Sites."" (August 2010)

Kambil, Ajit, and Eric van Heck. "Competition in the Dutch Flower Market." New York University, Stern School of Business, Center for Information Systems Research (1996).

Kiesler, Sara. "The Hidden Messages in Computer Networks." Harvard Business Review (January-February 1986).

Kiesler, Sara; Jane Siegel; and Timothy W. McGuire. "Social Psychological Aspects of Computer-Mediated Communication." American Psychologist (October 1984).

Kollock, Peter. "The Production of Trust in Online Markets" In Advances in Group Processes (Vol 16) edited by E. J. Lawler, M. Macy, S. Thyne and H. A. Walker. Greenwich, CT: JAI Press (1999).

Krishnamurthy, Sandeep. "An Empirical Study of the Causal Antecedents of Customer Confidence in ETailers." First Monday (January 2001).

Laudon, Kenneth C. and Jane P. Laudon. Management Information Systems: Managing the Digital Firm. 12th edition. Upper Saddle River, NJ, Prentice Hall (2011).

Lee, H. G.; J. C. Westland; and S. Hong. "The Impact of Electronic Marketplaces on Product Prices: An Empirical Study of Aucnet." International Journal of Electronic Commerce (Winter 1999-2000).

McAfee R., and John McMillan. "Auctions and Bidding." Journal of Economic Literature (June 1987).

Milogram, Paul R. "Auctions and Bidding: A Primer." Journal of Economic Perspectives (Summer 1989).

National White Collar Crime Center and the Federal Bureau of Investigation. "Internet Crime Complaint Center 2009 Internet Crime Report." (2010).

Nielsen Company. "Social Networking Usage Surges Globally." (September 2010).

Nikander, Pekka, and Kristina Karvonen. "Users and Trust in Cyberspace." In the Proceedings of Cambridge Security Protocols Workshop 2000, April 3-5, 2000, Cambridge University (2002).

Parkes, David C., and Lyle Ungar. "Iterative Combinatorial Auctions: Theory and Practice." Proceedings of the 17th National Conference on Artificial Intelligence (AAAI-00) (2000).

Rheingold, Howard. Hosting Web Communities. New York: John Wiley and Sons (1998). Also see Rheingold.com for more recent articles by Rheingold.

Rheingold, Howard. The Virtual Community. Cambridge MA: MIT Press (1993).

Stanford Persuasive Technology Lab and Makovsky & Company. "Stanford-Makovsky Web Credibility Study 2002." Stanford Persuasive Technology Lab. (Spring 2002).

Vakrat, Yaniv, and Abraham Seidmann. "Can Online Auctions Beat Online Catalogs?" Proceedings of the 20th Conference on Information Systems (December 1999).

Vakrat, Yaniv, and Abraham Seidmann. "Analysis and Design Models for Online Auctions." Proceedings of the 4th Informs Conference on Information Systems and Technology. (May 1998).

Vickrey, William. "Counterspeculation, Auctions and Competitive Sealed Tenders." Journal of Finance (March 1961).

## CHAPTER 12

ADX Corporation. "Ace Hardware Expands Relationship with ADX for Improved Supply Chain Integration." (January 12, 2004).

Agentrics. "Fact Sheet." (January 2010).

Ariba Inc. "Ariba Case Studies: Air Products." (September 2010)

Exostar LLC. "About Exostar." (September 2010).

Gleason, Karen. "CPFR At Ace Hardware." (2003).

Globalwinespirits.com. "About GWS." Globalwinespirts.com (September 2010).

Hewlett-Packard. "HP.com Business to Business." Hp.com (September 2010).

Inventory Locator Service LLC. ILSmart.com "About Us." (September 2010).

Kaplan, Steven, and Mohanbir Sawhney. "E-Hubs: The New B2B Marketplaces." Harvard Business Review (May-June 2000).

Kerrigan, Ryan; Eric Roegner; Dennis Swinford; and Craig Zawada. "B2B Basics." McKinsey Quarterly (2001).

Kumaran, S. "A Framework-Based Approach to Building Private Trading Exchanges." IBM Systems Journal (July 2002).

Laudon, Kenneth C. and Jane P. Laudon. Management Information Systems: Managing the Digital Firm. 12h edition. Upper Saddle River, NJ: Prentice Hall (2011).

Laudon, Kenneth C. "The Promise and Potential of Enterprise Systems and Industrial Networks." The Concours Group (2000).

1Sync. "About Us" 1Sync.org (September 2010).

Quadrem. "About Us." (September 2010).

Sodhi, Manmohan S. "2001: A Cyberspace Odyssey." OR.MS Today (February 2001).

Synnex Corporation. Form 10-K for the fiscal year ended November 30, 2009, filed with the Securities and Exchange Commission (February 5, 2010).

Turek, Norbert, and Gilbert, Alorie. "Atlas Shoulders The Private Exchange Load." InfoWeek (March 26, 2001).

Trkman, P.; McCormack, K.; "Estimating the Benefits of Implementing E-Procurement," Engineering Management, IEEE Transaction, Volume 57, Issue 2, May 2010

U.S. Census Bureau. "eStats Report 2008 E-commerce Multi-sector Report." Table 7 (May 27, 2010a).

U.S. Census Bureau. Statistical Abstract of the United States: 2010. (2010b).

VICS. (Voluntary Interindustry Commerce Standards). "Collaborative Planning, Forecasting, and Replenishment (CPFR)." (May 2004).

Watson, James K., and Joe Fenner. "So Many Choices, So Little Integration." Informationweek.com (October 16, 2000).

Wise, Richard, and Dave Morrison. "Beyond the Exchange: The Future of B2B." Harvard Business Review (November-December 2000).

W.W. Grainger. Inc. Form 10-K for the fiscal year ended December 31, 2009, filed with the Securities and Exchange Commission (February 25, 2010).

# Index

## A

abandonment rate, 463, 468, 489
Abdulmutallab, Umar Farouk, 272
Abine, 520
About.com, 35, 90
abuse, 9
Acacia Technologies, 538, 539
acceptance testing, 218
access controls, 304
Access Now Inc., 248
accessibility, of Web sites, 247-249
accessibility rules, 246
account segregation, 613
accountability, 500
accumulating balance payment systems, 312-313, 314, 335
Ace Hardware, 795
Ackerman, Jason, 77
Ackley, Matthew, 487
ACPA (Anticybersquatting Consumer Protection Act (1999)), 541, 566
acquisition rate, 463, 468, 489
Actiontuners, 427
Active International, 788
Active Server Pages. *See* ASP
ActiveX, 245, 258
actual product, 364
Acxiom, 511, 526
Acxiom Relevance-X, 526
ad exchange, 458, 486
ad networks, viruses in ads, 273
ad nonsense, 445
ad server, 175, 228, 256
ad targeting, 423
ADA (Americans with Disabilities Act), accessibility of Web sites and, 247-249
AdGabber, 710
Adidas, 401, 452
AdMob, 445
Adobe, 682
Adobe eBook Store, 682
Adobe Flash, 181
Adobe SiteCatalyst, 477-478
AdSense, 85, 396-397, 441, 444, 528, 748
Advanced Encryption Standard. *See* AES
advergames, 453
advertising
to children, 454-457
costs of, 473

mobile advertising, 8, 98, 125, 445-446
online video ads, 427-429, 466-467
privacy and, 526-527
real-time advertising, 9
real time advertising on exchanges, 474-487
on search engines, 438-445, 470
social networks, 8, 452-453
tolerance for, 656
trends in, 430, 431
*See also* banner ads; exchanges; marketing; online advertising
advertising exchanges, 438
advertising networks, 392-394, 505
advertising revenue model, 69, 71, 661, 681, 702
Advertising.com, 438
advocacy groups, privacy and information rights, 520
adware, 276, 278, 332
AdWords, 85, 178, 544
AES (Advanced Encryption Standard), 288, 333
affiliate broker, 395
affiliate marketing, 394-395
affiliate network, 395
affiliate relationship marketing, 446, 488
affiliate revenue model, 70, 71
affinity communities, 717, 754
affinity groups, 384, 758
age, of online consumers, 347
Agentrics, 92, 94-95, 799
aggregator model, 694
aggregator software application, 183
Air Products & Chemicals, 786, 805
airline reservations. *See* online travel services
Akamai, 27, 192-196, 219, 538
Al Qaeda, Internet use by, 271-272
Alcatel-Lucent, 98
Allen, Paul, 539
Allstate, video advertising by, 428
AltaVista, 83, 177, 178, 742
Amazon
about, 8, 27, 39, 66, 73, 81, 88, 97, 104, 233, 386, 390, 391, 668
accessibility of website, 248
affiliate program, 394
Amazon Payments, 328
business model, 69, 71, 80, 589-591
case study, 588-596
cloud computing, 764
comparison shopping, 603
e-book store, 676, 682
financial analysis, 591-592, 593

## H

# R

Racersauction, 723
RackSpace, 397
radio, 649-651, 687
radio frequency identification. *See* RFID
RadioShack, 248, 369
Ramada, accessibility of website, 248
"ramen sites," 36
Random House, 682
RBOCs, 147
RDES, 288
reach, 14, 15, 56, 102, 463, 468, 489, 742
Reader's Digest, 369
real estate services, online, 606, 615-617
Real Media 24/7, 442, 507
Real Networks, 522
real-time advertising, 9
real time advertising on exchanges, 474-487
real-time customer service chat systems, 408
"real time" search, 65
RealEstate.com, 616
RealJukebox, 522
Really Simple Syndication. *See* RSS
RealMedia Player, 181
RealNetworks, 219, 663
RealOne, 666
Realtor.com, 616
recency, 463, 468, 489
recreational drugs, drug sales on the Internet, 555-559, 567
recruitment (jobs). *See* job recruitment
Red Bull, 65
Red Bull Art of the Can, 455
Reddit, 19
redundancy, 144
Reed Elsevier, 412-413, 522
referrals, 446
Register.com, 476
registration forms, 374
regulation, location-based data, 99
regulatory control, 41-42, 45
Rehabilitation Act, Section 508, 247-248
REI, 81, 104, 250-255, 391, 461
relational databases, 382
Relativity Media, 343
Relevance-X, 526
remote sales, taxation of, 550-551, 567
RentACoder.com, 217
rental cars, 619
responsibility, 500
restaurant reservations, online, 35, 629-633
RestorationHardware.com, 450
retail sector, 81, 580
    *see also* e-tailers; online retail
retention rate, 463, 468, 489
revenue model

advertising revenue model, 69, 71, 661, 681, 702
described, 68-69, 71, 116
e-books, 681, 704
free sites, 411, 656, 661
marketing revenue model, 661, 702
mixed revenue model, 702
online content, 660-664, 702
online entertainment, 691
pay-for-download revenue model, 661, 662, 681, 702
pay-per-view (PPV), 343, 661, 662, 702
sales revenue model, 69, 71
subscription revenue model, 69, 71, 645-648, 662, 702
transaction fee revenue model, 69, 71
reverse auction, 729, 755
Revson, Charles, 365
RFID (radio frequency identification), 319, 322, 323, 329, 778-789
    Wal-Mart and, 778
Rhapsody.com, 54, 69, 80, 86, 661
RIAA (Recording Industry Association of America), 546
Rich Internet applications. *See* RIA
rich media ads, 436-437, 470, 471, 488
richness, 14, 15-16, 56, 102, 373, 497
*Riding the Bullet* (King), 676
Right Media, 486
Right to Financial Privacy Act of 1978, 513
risk assessment, 302
risk aversion, 502
RiteAid, 391, 428
Robinson, Patrick, 428
Robozilla, 604
RockShop.com, 573
Rockybid, 739
Roo, 438
root servers, 136
rootkits, 276
Rosetta Stone, 544
router, 132, 295
routing algorithm, 132
Royal Ahold, 76
RSA, 272
RSS (Really Simple Syndication), 180, 183, 199
RubberNetwork, 805
Ruby on Rails, 217
rule-based data mining, 384
Russia
    cyberwar by, 261, 262
    social networks, 712
RustockB, 262

# S

S-HTTP (Secure Hypertext Transfer Protocol), 299, 334

# Credits

## CHAPTER 1

p. 3, graphic, adapted from © Alex Slobodkin, 2010; ©thesuperph, 2010, iStockPhoto LP; Figure 1.2, reprinted by permission of Harvard Business School Press. From *Blown to Bits: How the New Economics of Information Transforms Strategy*, by Evans, Philip, and Thomas S. Wurster. Cambridge, MA, 2000. Copyright © 2000 by the Harvard Business School Publishing Corporation; all rights reserved; Figure 1.3, used with permission of Internet Systems Consortium, Inc. (http://ww.isc.org), 2010; Figure 1.6, based on data from eMarketer, Inc., © 2010, used with permission; Figure 1.7, based on data provided by PricewaterhouseCoopers/National Venture Capital Association MoneyTree Report, Data: Thomson Financial; Figure 1.8, based on data from eMarketer, Inc., © 2010, used with permission.

## CHAPTER 2

Figure 2.1, screenshot of Ancestry.com subscription page, © Ancestry.com, 2009; p. 83, screenshot of Bing.com, Microsoft product screen shot reprinted with permission from Microsoft Corporation; Figure 2.3, reprinted by permission of Harvard Business Review. From "Strategy and the Internet" by Michael E. Porter, March 2001. Copyright © 2001 by the Harvard Business School of Publishing Corporation; all rights reserved; p. 109, screenshot of Pandora.com home page © 2010 Pandora Media, Inc.

## CHAPTER 3

p. 123, screenshot of Wikitude.me © Mobilizy GmbH, 2009; Figure 3.10, © Visualware, Inc., 2007. Used with permission; Figure 3.11, from National Academy Press, © 2000; Figure 3.14, from Internet2.edu, © 2008; Figure 3.17, adapted from Cisco Systems, 2007, Internet2.edu, 2000; p. 192 screenshot of Akamai.com © 2009 Akamai Technologies, Inc.;

## CHAPTER 4

p.203, screenshot of Tommy.com; © 2010, Tommy Hilfiger Licensing, LLC.; p. 216, screenshot of NaturallyCurly.com home page © NaturallyCurly.com, Inc. 2009. Used with permission; Figure 4.10, screenshot of WebTrends Analytics 9, © WebTrends, Inc., 2009. Used with permission; Figure 4.10, screenshot of Google Analytics © Google Inc, 2009; Figure 4.13, from !BM, 2003; Figure 4.16, based on data from Hostway Corporation's survey, Consumers' Pet Peeves about Commercial Web Sites, 2007.

## CHAPTER 5

p. 261, screenshot of VisualDDoS, Sandia National Laboratories: Center for Cyber Defenders Program, 2007; Figure 5.1, based on data from Computer Security Institute, 2009; Table 5.1, based on data from the Symantec Internet Security Threat Report © Symantec Corporation, 2010. Used with permission. Figures 5.3 and 5.4, from Communications of the Association for Information Systems, Vol. 4, Article 11, November 2000; Table 5.6, from MacKie-Mason; K. Jeffrey; and Kimberly White: "Evaluating and Selecting Digital Payment Mechanisms," Selected Papers From the 1996 Telecommunications Policy Research Conference, published by Lawrence Erlbaum Associates, Inc.; p. 326, screenshot of PayPal.com home page: These materials have been reproduced with the permission of PayPal, Inc. © 2010 PAYPAL, INC. ALL RIGHTS RESERVED.

## CHAPTER 6

p. 341, screenshot of Netflix.com home page, reproduced by permission of Netflix, Inc., © 1997-2010 Netflix, Inc. All rights reserved. Photograph on Netflix.com home page "Family on couch" © Remy Haynes Photography; Figures 6.1 and 6.7 adapted from Kotler and Armstrong, *Principles of Marketing*, 13e, 2009. Reprinted by permission of Pearson Education, Inc., Upper Saddle River, NJ; Figure 6.2, From ChannelAdvisor 2009 report "How Consumers Shop Online,", © ChannelAdvisor, 2009; Figure 6.5, based on data from eMarketer, Inc.,© 2010, used with permission; Figure 6.9, from nash-equilibrium.com; © 2008 by Michael R. Baye, John Morgan and Patrick Sholten. All rights reserved; Figure 6.10, from Azimuth Interactive, Inc., © 2010; Figure 6.13, from Adomavicius, Gediminas, and Alexander Tuzhilin, "Using Data Mining Methods to Build Customer Profiles," IEEE Computer (February 2001b) © IEEE 2001. Used with permission; p. 398, screenshot from VML SEER ™, © VML, 2007. Used with permission; Figure 6.19, reprinted by permission, Bakos and Brynjolfsson, "Bundling Information Goods: Pricing, Profits, and Efficiency," Management Science, December, 1999. Copyright 1999, the Institute for

Operations Research and the Management Sciences (INFORMS), 7240 Parkway Drive, Suite 310, Hanover, MD 21076 USA; p. 413, screenshot of ExchangeHunterJumper.com, © 2010 Eohippus, LLC; Table 6.1, from Pew Internet & American Life Project. "Online Actitivies, Daily," (last updated September 2010) http://www.pewinternet.org/Trend-Data/Online-Activities-Daily.aspx, accessed September 30, 2010; Table 6.2, from Pew Internet & American Life Project, "Demographics of Internet Users," (last updated May 2010), http://www.pewinternet.org/Trend-Data/Whos-Online.aspx, accessed September 30, 2010; Table 6.4 based in part on data from eMarketer, Inc. © 2007, used with permission.

## CHAPTER 7

p. 425, screenshot of Actiontuners.com home page © Action Marketing, 2008. Used with permission; Figure 7.1, based on data from eMarketer, Inc. © 2010, used with permission; Table 7.2 based on data from eMarketer, Inc. © 2010, used with permission; Figure 7.2, from Interactive Advertising Bureau, 2008; Figure 7.3, based on data from eMarketer, Inc. © 2010, used with permission;Figure 7.5, screenshot of Google search results, Google Inc., 2010; Figure 7.6, From Symantec's MessageLabs Intelligence Report, August 2010, © 2010; Figure 7.7, screenshot from Beval.com © 2006 Beval Saddlery, Ltd.;Figure 7.9, based in part on data from eMarketer, Inc. © 2010, used with permission; Figure 7.11, from Fogg, B.J., Cathy Soohoo, David Danielson, Leslie Marable, Julianne Stanford, and Ellen Tauber. "How Do Users Evaluate the Creditability of Web Sites? A Study with Over 2,500 Participants." Consumer Reports WebWatch (www.consumerwebwatch.org) and Stanford University Persuasive Technology Lab. Proceedings of DUX2003, Designing for User Experiences (2003);Table 7.5 based in part on data from eMarketer, Inc. © 2010, used with permission

## CHAPTER 8

p. 491, screenshot of Secondlife.com home page, © Linden Lab, 2007; Figure 8.2(A) from www.w3.org/P3P/brochure.html, © 3/16/2003 World Wide Web Consortium (Massachusetts Institute of Technology, European Research Consortium for

Informatics and Mathematics, Keio University). All Rights Reserved; p. 558, screenshot of Google Books © Google Inc, 2009.

## CHAPTER 9

p. 571, screenshot of Bluenile.com home page © Blue Nile, Inc., 2009. Used with permission; Figures 9.4, 9.5, based on data from eMarketer, Inc., © 2010, used with permission.

## CHAPTER 10

p. 649, screenshot of WSJ.com reprinted with permission of Wall Street Journal Online, Copyright © 2010 Dow Jones & Company, Inc. All Rights Reserved Worldwide; Figure 10.7 © 2009 eMarketer, Inc. Used with permission.

## CHAPTER 11

p. 717, screenshot of LinkedIn.com © LinkedIn Corporation, 2010. Used with permission; Figure 11.2, © 2009 eMarketer, Inc. Used with permission; Figure 11.4, reprinted by permission, Vakrat, Yaniv, and Abraham Siedmann, "Analysis and Design Models for Online Auctions." *Proceedings of the 4th Informs Conference on Information Systems and Technology, May 1998*. Copyright 1998, the Institute for Operations Research and the Management Sciences (INFORMS), 7240 Parkway Drive, Suite 310, Hanover, MD 21076 USA; p. 758, Screenshot of eBay.com: "These materials have been reproduced with the permission of eBay Inc." © 2009 EBAY INC. ALL RIGHTS RESERVED.

## CHAPTER 12

p. 769, screenshot of VWGroupSupply.com home page, © Volkswagen Aktiengesellschaft, 2009; p. 811, screenshot of Elemica.com home page © Elemica Inc. 2010.

*continued from front inside cover*

## CHAPTER 7 E-COMMERCE MARKETING COMMUNICATIONS

Opening Case: Video Ads: Shoot, Click, Buy

Insight on Society: Marketing to Children of the Web in the Age of Social Networks

Insight on Business: Are the Very Rich Different from You and Me?

Insight on Technology: It's 10 P.M. Do You Know Who Is On Your Web Site?

Case Study: Instant Ads: Real Time Advertising

## CHAPTER 8 ETHICAL, SOCIAL, AND POLITICAL ISSUES IN E-COMMERCE

Opening Case: Discovering Law and Ethics in a Virtual World

Insight on Business: Chief Privacy Officers

Insight on Technology: The Privacy Tug of War: Advertisers vs. Consumers

Insight on Society: The Internet Drug Bazaar

Case Study: The Google Books Settlement: Is It Fair?

## CHAPTER 9 ONLINE RETAILING AND SERVICES

Opening Case: Blue Nile Sparkles For Your Cleopatra

E-Commerce in Action: Amazon.com

Insight on Technology: Using the Web to Shop 'Till You Drop

Insight on Society: Hotel Tax Battle: The Online Travel Industry vs. Local Government

Insight on Business: Zipcars

Case Study: OpenTable